THE ENCYCLOPEDIA
OF FILM COMPOSERS

"HOLLYWOOD'S FINEST" GATHERED TOGETHER. To find a photograph with two or three Hollywood composers pictured together is rare. A picture of twenty-three such men is a treasure trove. This photograph was taken at the Los Angeles Friar's Club in 1946 when Bramwell Coles, head of the Salvation Army's International Music Department in London, visited Hollywood. Meredith Willson, a longtime admirer of the Salvation Army, organized a luncheon in Coles's honor. *Photofest*

Seated (left to right) are Franz Waxman, Dimitri Tiomkin, Meredith Willson, Bramwell Coles, Earl E. Lawrence, and William Grant Still.

Standing (left to right) are Abe Meyer, Leith Stevens, William Broughton (grandfather of current film composer Bruce Broughton), Anthony Collins, Johnny Green, Miklós Rózsa, Victor Young, Werner Heymann, Leo Shuken, Arthur Bergh, Alex Steinert, Robert Emmett Dolan, Frank Skinner, Wilbur Hatch, Carlos Morales, and Louis Lipstone.

THE ENCYCLOPEDIA OF FILM COMPOSERS

Thomas S. Hischak

ROWMAN & LITTLEFIELD
Lanham • Boulder • New York • London

Published by Rowman & Littlefield
A wholly owned subsidiary of The Rowman & Littlefield Publishing Group, Inc.
4501 Forbes Boulevard, Suite 200, Lanham, Maryland 20706
www.rowman.com

Unit A, Whitacre Mews, 26-34 Stannary Street, London SE11 4AB

British Library Cataloguing in Publication Information Available

Library of Congress Cataloging-in-Publication Data

Hischak, Thomas S.
 The encyclopedia of film composers / Thomas S. Hischak.
    pages cm
 Includes bibliographical references and index.
  ISBN 978-1-4422-4549-5 (hardback : alk. paper) — ISBN 978-1-4422-4550-1 (ebook) 1.
Film composers—Biography—Dictionaries. 2. Motion picture music—Bio-bibliography—
Dictionaries. I. Title.
  ML102.M68H572 2015
  781.5'420922—dc23
  [B]   2014040469

Printed in the United States of America

For Dawn Van Hall,
who loves the movies

CONTENTS

ABBREVIATIONS

AA	Academy Award winner
AAN	Academy Award nominee
aka	also known as
b.	born
BAFTA	British Academy of Film & Television Arts Award
BAFTA-N	BAFTA nomination
GG	Golden Globe Award winner
GGN	Golden Globe nomination
UK	United Kingdom
USA	United States
USSR	former Soviet Union

FORMAT FOR ENTRIES

After the biographical information and a discussion of the composer's work, there follows a list of feature film credits. For each movie the year of release is followed by the title, awards won or nominated for, director, and country or countries that produced the film. For foreign-language movies, the English title under which it was released in the United States is usually used. British and American movies that had a different title when released in the other country have the alternative title listed as aka (also known as). If a film was given a different title for television broadcast or video release, that is also noted as aka. Only feature-length movies (including documentaries) that played in theatres are listed. A film is listed under a composer's credits if he or she is the sole or one of two composers of the score. Movies in which three or more composers contributed to the soundtrack score or films in which a composer's song or theme is interpolated into another artist's soundtrack are not included.

ACKNOWLEDGMENTS

Once again I must thank first and foremost my wife, Cathy, for the hours she devoted to reading, proofing, and providing input on the manuscript. I continue to value her accuracy as much as her knowledge and instincts. Thanks also to movie music expert and devotee Glenn Wooddell, CD producer Marilee Bradford, photo expert Ron Mandelbaum at Photofest, and editor Stephen Ryan at Rowman & Littlefield.

INTRODUCTION

Movie Composers, or Who Wrote Miss Gulch's Theme?

The composers and lyricists of movie musicals are often famous. Their songs sometimes become hits and due recognition follows. Composers for nonmusical movies are rarely famous. Only a handful receive much recognition. Even Oscar-winning composers often fall into obscurity. Yet the music for, say, *Gone with the Wind*, is as essential to that film as the song "White Christmas" is for *Holiday Inn*. Everyone knows Irving Berlin wrote "White Christmas"; how many even recognize the name Max Steiner, the composer of the *Gone with the Wind* score? Both men wrote thousands of pages of sheet music but Berlin wrote songs and Steiner wrote scores. Songs are recorded, replayed, and become a part of our national consciousness. Movie scores (even the best of them) only faintly echo in our heads. The music is rarely heard outside of the context of the movie for which they were written. In fact, when a movie composer has a big hit, it is usually when the theme song of the film is set to words and becomes a song, as with "Goldfinger" or "Born Free." It seems the song will always win out over the score.

Consider the Hollywood classic *The Wizard of Oz*. Harold Arlen wrote the music and E. Y. Harburg penned the lyrics for the delectable songs. Yet it was Herbert Stothart who composed most of the rest of the music heard in the movie. The insistent, menacing music that accompanies Miss Gulch on her bicycle is as memorable, in its own way, as "Over the Rainbow." Yet we are not even sure who wrote it. Several studio composers contributed to *The Wizard of Oz*. It was probably Stothart who wrote this theme, since he composed most of the nonsinging parts of the soundtrack. But the point remains that *The Wizard of Oz* would be less effective without Miss Gulch's theme and all the other unsung music that fills that movie.

This book is about 252 composers who wrote for the movies. A few of them also composed songs, but for the most part they are true film composers: they created scores. A handful of these artists were or are famous enough that the public knows them well: Henry Mancini, John Williams, Danny Elfman, Randy Newman, Marvin Hamlisch, Paul Williams, and a few others. It is not a very long list. Film students and movie enthusiasts will recognize a great many more names, extolling the virtues of Bernard Herrmann, Jerry Goldsmith, John Barrie, Franz Waxman, and others. But as talented and awarded as these composers are, they are not as familiar to audiences in the same way as actors, directors, or even producers are. Like the music they write for the screen, the composers contribute to the effectiveness of the movies but are only noticed subconsciously. That is the nature of movie music. The score supports the movie without (hopefully) overpowering it. Our memories of the most catchy or thrilling movie music are connected to the film itself. One can recall with a delightful shudder Bernard Herrmann's music for the shower scene in *Psycho*. Yet listening to that music out of context or not knowing the scene it was scored for, it intrigues but fails to ignite. The finest film music lives on because it is so closely associated with the visual images on-screen (and in our memory). One cannot listen to the "Pink Panther Theme" without visualizing the cartoon panther. The exotic main theme from *Lawrence of Arabia* immediately conjures up visions of the vast, hot, dry desert. The beguiling theme from *Laura* brings us back to that suspense movie and the way the dead Laura haunted every place she had been. This is the true legacy of movie music. What worked so effectively on the screen continues to work in our minds when we hear the music again.

Movies have always been musical. The early silent film-makers often came from the stage where a piano in the pit was an integral part of the melodrama being performed. (The term "melodrama" actually means "music drama.") Silent films were usually accompanied by live music as well, be it a rickety, out-of-tune upright piano in a neighborhood cinema or a mammoth pipe organ or large orchestra in a movie palace. No one expected the characters to talk, but there was no reason for a film to be completely silent. Some scores for silent movies were written with the film in mind (some themes even became famous) but often a generic collection of music sufficed. The early talkies continued the musical tradition, replacing the piano or organ with a recorded full orchestra. When sound movies became popular, the musical score was given more prominence and composers wrote specific music for specific scenes in specific movies. This introduced the integrated film score, and ever since, filmmakers have understood and appreciated the importance of the movie composer.

The 252 composers covered in this book have been selected because of some significant contribution they made to movie music. Some have many credits and remained active for decades. Others may have had extensive music careers elsewhere and only scored a film on occasion. Included here are world-famous concert composers who also dabbled in films. Some are young with limited credits but promising careers. All deserve recognition. Both Hollywood and foreign film composers are included. The emphasis may be on the American and British film industry because those movies are obviously more familiar to English-speaking audiences. Yet any study of the art of screen scoring must include such accomplished foreign composers as Georges Delerue, Nino Rota, and Mikis Theodorakis. Each composer's entry consists of biographical information, a description of the composer's career and musical style, and a complete list of feature film score credits. "Complete" is a wishful word when it comes to screen scores because hundreds of movies do not credit who wrote the music. Sometimes more than

one composer was hired to work on one film. Other times a composer was paid to arrange or orchestrate music by another writer. So I have only included movie credits in which the composer was either the sole writer or one of two composers who scored that film. In addition to the year and the country that made the movie, I have included the director for each film. I do this not to support the argument that the director is the primary creator of a movie but rather to show the collaborations between the composer and certain directors. The relationship between a director and the composer is a tricky but essential one, and when that collaboration is successful, it is easy to see why certain directors preferred to work with certain composers over and over again. It is hoped that the list of a composer's films and directors will give the reader not only a sense of that artist's career but maybe even capture the temperament of a person's body of work.

In the 1970s, serious attention began to be paid to screen composers and a number of books on the subject were written. Some of these have been updated since and others have joined them over the decades. Yet these books end up talking about the same twenty or thirty composers when there are hundreds who have made noteworthy contributions to the art of film music. It is the intention of this work to fill in that huge gap. This is not a critical study in which superior music is praised and inferior work is berated. Instead the purpose is to describe the musical accomplishments of each composer and try to capture what is significant in each composer's best scores. Researching and writing this book has given me a new and deeper appreciation for the movie composer. Music I strongly or vaguely remembered came flooding back to me as I listened again to their scores and wrote about each composer's career. Music I had not heard before revealed the range and versatility of these composers. They have a talent for conjuring up strong emotions as we view images in the dark. Like that insistent music for Miss Gulch on her bicycle, the work of the movie composer cannot be erased from our consciousness.

ADDINSELL, Richard (Stewart) (1904–1977) A British composer for the stage, concert hall, and screen, he is most remembered today for his popular concert piece *Warsaw Concerto* which came from one of his movie scores.

Richard Addinsell was born in London, the son of a chartered accountant, and attended Oxford University to study law. But his interest in music encouraged him to leave Oxford and study at the Royal College of Music. Before completing his degree, Addinsell left school to write music for the London stage, particularly music halls and comic revues. He also composed incidental music for plays in London and New York, most memorably *Alice in Wonderland* on Broadway in 1932. Addinsell tried his luck in Hollywood in the early 1930s but ended up only doing some incidental music or arrangements for American movies. Discouraged, he returned to England where he was hired as one of the five composers for the movie musical *His Lordship* in 1936. The next year he was sole composer for the historical drama *Fire over England* and his score attracted enough attention to launch his screen career.

Addinsell worked with such noted British directors as Victor Saville, Michael Powell, David Lean, Alfred Hitchcock, and Laurence Olivier throughout his career, and his list of credits is an eclectic mix that includes film adaptations of plays or classic literature, silly comedies, and patriotic melodramas during World War II. His most notable movie in the last category is the melodrama *Dangerous Moonlight* (retitled *Suicide Squadron* in the States) about a shell-shocked composer-pianist (Anton Walbrook) in bomb-ravaged Poland. The producers tried to get Sergei Rachmaninoff to write the concerto for piano and orchestra that is performed in the film, but he declined. Instead Addinsell was instructed to write a Rachmaninoff-like piece, and he came up with his famous *Warsaw Concerto*, a piece that has been performed and recorded many times over the years. Among the other memorable movies that Addinsell wrote for the British and American cinema are *Blithe Spirit*, *The Prince and the Showgirl*, *Under Capricorn*, *Tom Brown's School Days*, *The Black Rose*, *A Tale of Two Cities*, the Alastair Sim *A Christmas Carol* (origi-

nally titled *Scrooge*), and *Goodbye, Mr. Chips*. Addinsell left movies in the mid-1960s and became somewhat of a recluse, his only composing being for performer Joyce Grenfel's West End revues and one-woman shows. He lived quietly with his longtime partner, fashion designer Victor Stiebel, and left the royalties for *Warsaw Concerto* to a neighboring family who was discreet about Addinsell and Stiebel's relationship. Addinsell died at the age of seventy-three. Many of his screen scores are lost, but his one classical piece continues to find favor in the concert hall.

While the dazzling piano and orchestra piece *Warsaw Concerto* is Addinsell's finest composition, it is not typical of his screen music. His talent for scoring movies can be better heard in such films as *Tom Brown's School Days* and *South Riding*, which contain traces of English folk music, or in *The Black Rose* and *Fire over England*, in which he employs a vigorous regal sound reminiscent of Edward Elgar's work. For the *Prince and the Showgirl*, Addinsell wrote a lively waltz for the main theme, some delightful ditties for the music hall, a honky-tonk piece for the street, and some lighthearted pomp for the embassy. The music for the drawing room comedy *Blithe Spirit* is indeed spirited, with violins racing up and down the scale, while the propulsive music for *A Tale of Two Cities* is highlighted by a bold brass section that competes with a flowing string section. Addinsell's music for the drama *Love on the Dole* is pure 1940s melodrama music, lush and full of orchestrated rise and fall of emotions. A similar sound is heard throughout the early David Lean film *The Passionate Friends*. A flowing accordion and string theme in *The Greengage Summer* (retitled *Loss of Innocence* in the States) is very delicate and evocative of simpler times. Perhaps Addinsell's best comic score is the one he wrote for *The Beachcomber*, which is silly even as it uses an exotic South Seas flavor. While there are plenty of holiday carols in the 1951 *A Christmas Carol/Scrooge*, the main theme is a dark and heavy piece of suspense music one might expect in a spy thriller. *Goodbye, Mr. Chips* has an expansive main theme that alternates between reeds and strings but the most memorable part of the score is Addinsell's original boys' school alma mater. For Hitchcock's feverish melodrama *Under Capricorn* set in Australia, Addinsell composed a fluid theme in which a guitar plays against a string orchestra suggesting both romance and dread. Addinsell's last screen project, the dark contemporary drama *Life at the Top*, has a romantic theme played on strings that contrasts effectively with a solo trumpet for the gritty scenes.

Although Addinsell had a scattered and incomplete musical education, he is considered one of the more "classical" of British screen composers. There is a consistent high quality in his thirty-five feature film scores, not to mention versatility. Unfortunately a lot of his early screen sheet music is lost and all that remains are faded prints and some recordings with poor-quality sound. Musicologist Philip Lane has reconstructed some of Addinsell's music from these inferior tracks and had the scores orchestrated and recorded. Fortunately one of the finest British screen composers of the 1940s and 1950s can be better appreciated today.

Credits

(all films UK unless stated otherwise)

Year	Film	Director
1936	The Amateur Gentleman	Thornton Freeland
1937	Fire over England	William K. Howard
1937	Dark Journey	Victor Saville
1937	Troopship (aka Farewell Again)	Tim Whelan
1938	South Riding	Victor Saville
1938	The Beachcomber (aka Vessel of Wrath)	Erich Pommer
1939	Goodbye, Mr. Chips	Sam Wood, Sidney Franklin
1939	The Lion Has Wings	Adrian Brunel, Brian Desmond Hurst, Michael Powell, Alexander Korda
1940	Blackout (aka Contraband)	Michael Powell
1940	Gaslight	Thorold Dickinson
1941	Old Bill and Son	Ian Dalrymple
1941	Suicide Squadron (aka Dangerous Moonlight)	Brian Desmond Hurst (UK/USA)
1941	Love on the Dole	John Baxter
1941	This England	David MacDonald
1942	The Big Blockade	Charles Frend
1942	The Avengers (aka The Day Will Dawn)	Harold French
1945	Blithe Spirit	David Lean
1949	The Passionate Friends	David Lean
1949	Under Capricorn	Alfred Hitchcock
1950	The Black Rose	Henry Hathaway (USA/UK)
1950	Highly Dangerous	Roy Ward Baker
1951	A Christmas Carol (aka Scrooge)	Brian Desmond Hurst (UK/USA)
1951	Tom Brown's Schooldays	Gordon Parry
1951	Encore	Harold French, Pat Jackson, Anthony Pelissier
1953	The Secret Cave	John Durst
1953	Sea Devils	Raoul Walsh (USA/UK)
1954	Beau Brummell	Curtis Bernhardt (USA)
1955	Out of the Clouds	Basil Dearden
1957	Paradise Lagoon (aka The Admirable Crichton)	Lewis Gilbert
1957	The Prince and the Showgirl	Laurence Olivier (UK/USA)
1958	A Tale of Two Cities	Ralph Thomas
1961	Loss of Innocence (aka The Greengage Summer)	Lewis Gilbert
1961	The Roman Spring of Mrs. Stone	José Quintero (USA)
1962	The Waltz of the Toreadors	John Guillermin
1962	The War Lover	Philip Leacock (UK/USA)
1965	Life at the Top	Ted Kotcheff

ADDISON, John (Mervyn) (1920–1998) A British the-atre, television, and film composer who also scored several Hollywood movies late in his career, he is probably most remembered for his eight films directed by Tony Richardson.

John Addison was born in West Chobham, England, the son of an army colonel, and was educated at Wellington College for a military career. When his interests switched to music, Addison enrolled at the Royal College of Music in London to study composition, but his studies were interrupted by the outbreak of World War II. He served as a tank commander in Europe and participated in the unsuccessful Operation Market Garden to invade Germany. (This campaign was the subject of the 1977 movie *A Bridge Too Far*, which Addison scored.) After the armistice, Addison returned to the Royal College, completed his degree, and stayed on as a composition teacher. He was content teaching and composing for the concert stage but the brothers Roy and John Boulting convinced him to get involved in screen music. Addison scored the brothers' 1950 thriller *Seven Days to Noon*, followed by six more of their films over the next decade. He scored many other low-budget movies in Britain during the 1950s but received little recognition.

He first worked with Tony Richardson when he supervised the music in the screen version of *Look Back in Anger* in 1959. Addison composed the score for the small-scale but acclaimed Richardson screen dramas *The Entertainer*, *A Taste of Honey*, and *The Loneliness of the Long Distance Runner* before the two men had an international hit with the raucous period comedy *Tom Jones* in 1963. The movie won wide praise and many awards, including an Oscar for Addison. He went on to score subsequent movies by Richardson and other British directors, but *Tom Jones* had brought him to the attention of Hollywood and many of his post-1965 films were American. Highlights in his later career include such British and American films as *The Loved One*, *All at Sea*, *Torn Curtain*, *The Charge of the Light Brigade*, *Start the Revolution without Me*, *Sleuth*, *The Seven-Per-Cent Solution*, and *A Bridge Too Far*. Addison's TV movies and miniseries include *Hamlet* (1970), *Black Beauty* (1978), *The Bastard* (1978), *Centennial* (1978), *Charles & Diana: A Royal Love Story* (1982), *I Was a Mail Order Bride* (1982), *Dead Man's Folly* (1986), and *The Phantom of the Opera* (1990), as well as such series as *The Eddie Capra Mysteries*, *Nero Wolfe*, *Amaz-ing Stories*, and the long-running *Murder, She Wrote*. His other compositions include the London stage musical comedies *Cranks* (1956) and *Keep Your Hair On* (1958), the ballet *Carte Blanche* (1959), and various instrumental pieces, such as trios and concertos for woodwinds and strings.

Addison's music is characterized by a lively sense of melody and his ability to be playful in his compositions. This is best witnessed in his delectable *Tom Jones* score. A slightly off-kilter harpsichord races through the music, even when it comes to the lovely waltzing love theme. Instruments not yet invented in the movie's eighteenth-century period, such as the saxophone, battle with the classical instruments in a deliciously chaotic manner. A similar frolicsome flavor can be found in the contemporary comedy-thriller *Sleuth*. Using pizzicato strings against the flute and saxophone gives the score a comic and witty air that supports the game playing of the two major characters (Laurence Olivier and Michael Caine). The nautical comedy *All at Sea* has a ridiculous sea chantey theme with giddy hornpipes adding to the movie's offbeat charm. An expected solo violin in the classical vein is used as Sherlock Holmes's theme in the thriller *The Seven-Per-Cent Solution*, but Addison has fun adding a waltzing motif when the famous sleuth (Nicol Williamson) goes to Vienna to meet Dr. Freud (Alan Arkin). Soon the two musical styles are at war, and the score turns rhythmic in a very effective way. Addison's score for *A Bridge Too Far* is more straightforward with engaging march themes and a full orchestra soaring in a patriotic manner. It may not be highly inventive but the score is stirring all the same. Also conventional but very effective is his score for Alfred Hitchcock's *Torn Curtain*. The movie was originally scored by the Hollywood master Bernard Herrmann, but the director and composer quarreled over the music and Herrmann was dismissed. Hitchcock chose Addison to write a new score for the Cold War thriller and critics complained it was not up to Herrmann's high standards. All the same, the music moves in a forceful and driving way that matches the story's suspense and Addison's craftsmanship is not to be overlooked. Neither can one ignore the quieter scores Addison wrote for those small-scale, more intimate Richardson films earlier in his career. In *The Loneliness of the Long Distance Runner*, lonesome violins are set against a pathetic percussion march, giving the score a weary yet desperate force. The music is appropriately tawdry as it tries to be cheerful in *The Entertainer*. Whether in the music hall or at a beauty pageant, the music (used sparingly) is thin and unconvincing, just as the title character (Laurence Olivier) and his jokes are hollow. Addison also wrote the music for two vaudeville songs that Olivier sings in the film and they are expert pastiches of music hall entertainment.

As busy as Addison was writing for the screen, he dedicated a good deal of his time to his other compositions, from background music for British plays to concert works to American television miniseries. He became a resident of the United States in 1977, retired from movies and television in 1990, and died eight years later at the age of seventy-eight.

Credits

(all films UK unless stated otherwise)

Year	Film	Director
1950	Seven Days to Noon	John and Roy Boulting
1951	Pool of London	Basil Dearden
1951	High Treason	Roy Boulting
1952	Brandy for the Parson	John Eldridge
1952	The Hour of 13	Harold French
1953	Paratrooper	Terence Young
1953	The Man Between	Carol Reed
1954	High and Dry (aka The Maggie)	Alexander Mackendrick
1954	The Black Knight	Tay Garnett
1954	Make Me an Offer	Cyril Frankel
1955	One Good Turn	John Paddy Carstairs
1955	That Lady	Terence Young (Spain/UK)
1955	Touch and Go	Michael Truman
1955	Josephine and Men	Roy Boulting
1955	The Cockleshell Heroes	José Ferrer
1956	Private's Progress	John Boulting
1956	Reach for the Sky	Lewis Gilbert
1956	Three Men in a Boat	Ken Annakin
1957	The End of the Road	Wolf Rilla
1957	The Shiralee	Leslie Norman
1957	Lucky Jim	John Boulting
1957	All at Sea (aka Barnacle Bill)	Charles Frend
1958	Hell, Heaven or Hoboken (aka I Was Monty's Double)	John Guillermin
1959	Man in a Cocked Hat	Roy Boulting, Jeffrey Dell
1960	School for Scoundrels	Robert Hamer
1960	The Entertainer	Tony Richardson
1960	A French Mistress	Roy Boulting
1961	His and Hers	Brian Desmond Hurst
1961	A Taste of Honey	Tony Richardson
1962	Go to Blazes	Michael Truman
1962	The Loneliness of the Long Distance Runner	Tony Richardson
1963	Tom Jones (AA)	Tony Richardson
1963	The Model Murder Case	Michael Truman
1964	Girl with Green Eyes	Desmond Davis
1964	Guns at Batasi	John Guillermin
1965	The Uncle	Desmond Davis
1965	The Amorous Adventures of Moll Flanders	Terence Young
1965	The Loved One	Tony Richardson (USA)
1966	A Fine Madness	Irvin Kershner (USA)
1966	Time Lost and Time Remembered	Desmond Davis
1966	Torn Curtain	Alfred Hitchcock (USA)
1967	The Honey Pot	Joseph L. Mankiewicz (USA)
1967	Smashing Time	Desmond Davis

Year	Film	Director
1968	*The Charge of the Light Brigade* (BAFTA-N)	Tony Richardson
1969	*Brotherly Love* (aka *Country Dance*)	J. Lee Thompson (UK/USA)
1970	*Start the Revolution without Me*	Bud Yorkin (USA)
1971	*Cry of the Penguins*	Alfred Viola
1972	*Sleuth* (AAN)	Joseph L. Mankiewicz (USA/UK)
1974	*Luther*	Guy Green (UK/Canada/USA)
1974	*Dead Cert*	Tony Richardson
1975	*Ride a Wild Pony*	Don Chaffey (Australia/USA)
1976	*Swashbuckler*	James Goldstone (USA)
1976	*The Seven-Per-Cent Solution*	Herbert Ross (UK/USA)
1977	*Joseph Andrews*	Tony Richardson
1977	*A Bridge Too Far* (BAFTA)	Richard Attenborough (USA/UK)
1980	*The Pilot*	Cliff Robertson (USA)
1982	*Highpoint*	Peter Carter (Canada)
1983	*Strange Invaders*	Michael Laughlin (USA)
1984	*Grace Quigley*	Anthony Harvey (USA)
1985	*Code Name: Emerald*	Jonathan Sanger (USA)

ADLER, Larry (1914–2001) A harmonica virtuoso on-stage, on the radio, and in the movies, he was also a composer who scored some American and British films during his unfortunately short screen career.

Born Lawrence Cecil Adler in Baltimore, Maryland, to a Jewish Russian family who loved classical music, Adler taught himself to play the harmonica (or the "mouth organ" as he called it) as a boy, and by the time he was fourteen he was performing professionally. While most saw the harmonica as a folk instrument, Adler found recognition playing classical pieces as well as popular songs of the day. In New York City, he soon got the attention of orchestra leaders who hired Adler as a specialty performer. After touring in vaudeville and making records and radio broadcasts, Adler appeared on Broadway in such musicals as *Smiles* (1931), *Flying Colors* (1933), and *Keep Off the Grass* (1940), and starred in the revue *Paul Draper and Larry Adler* (1944). Adler toured with dancer Draper across the country and later overseas to entertain American GIs during World War II.

Adler began working in movies in 1934, performing on the soundtracks of various films. His harmonica pyrotechnics can be heard in such movies as *Operator 13* (1934), *Many Happy Returns* (1934), *The Big Broadcast of 1937* (1936), *The Singing Marine* (1937), *Sidewalks of London* (aka *St. Martin's Lane*) (1938), *Music for Millions* (1944), and *Three Darling Daughters* (1948), and he appeared in six movies, usually as himself playing the harmonica.

Adler was even more popular in Great Britain after he appeared on radio there and was featured in a musical revue on the London stage. The sale of harmonicas in the British Isles increased twenty times and over three hundred thousand Brits were members of Adler's fan club. By the late 1940s he was recognized as the greatest harmonica artist in the world and such distinguished composers as Darius Milhaud, William Walton, and Ralph Vaughan Williams wrote pieces specifically for Adler to perform on his "mouth organ."

Adler's life took a tragic turn in the early 1950s when he and Draper were accused of being Communists by the House Un-American Activities Committee. Adler refused to name names or sign a loyalty oath, and even sued a concert organization for libel when it cancelled an engagement, calling Adler "pro-Communist in sympathy." The trial resulted in a hung jury and in 1952 Adler left the States to live in England, never returning again. It was in Great Britain that his movie composing career began. He wrote the music for the surprise hit comedy *Genevieve* in 1953 and his score was nominated for an Oscar. Because Adler was blacklisted in the States, his name was removed from the credits for American showings of *Genevieve* and the Academy did not acknowledge his contribution in the nomination; thirty-one years later the Academy sent him an official nomination certificate. He went on to score six more British films, most memorably *Jumping for Joy*, *King and Country*, and *A High Wind in Jamaica*. While remaining in Britain, he also scored the Hollywood movies *The Great Chase* and *The Hook*. Although Adler was free to return to his native country by the 1970s, he opted to remain in England where he continued to perform and record up into his eighties.

The two most interesting screen scores by Adler are his first and his last. *Genevieve* is a delightful British comedy about an antique auto rally where two friends (John Gregson and Kenneth More) race their vintage cars from London to Brighton. The main musical theme, written and played by Adler on the harmonica, has a casual air, the piano playing the chords and the harmonica having fun with the gliding melody. The harmonica is also heard playing a radiant waltz which seems to skip with joy, a sparkling passage as the cars struggle through the streets of London, and a triumphantly silly tune when the autos arrive in Brighton. One of the highlights in the comedy is when an inebriated Kay Kendall plays a Dixieland jazz number on the trumpet (dubbed by Kenny Baker).

A High Wind in Jamaica is an exciting adventure about some children trapped on a pirate ship and how they turn dastardly circumstances into a playful lark. The title song (lyric by Christopher Logue) is a narrative ballad sung by Mike LeRoy that opens the movie, then the full orchestra picks up the melody and turns it into a dramatic fanfare that echoes the crashing of waves on the rocks. When the ballad returns at the end of the film, it has the tone of an elegy. There is a pleasing theme for the scenes in which the pirate captain (Anthony Quinn) befriends one of the children (Deborah Baxter) and Adler provides a jaunty sea chantey for a seaside tavern. By this time he had abandoned the use of the harmonica in his screen scores so this soundtrack proves itself without his virtuoso performing. It is unfortunate that Adler left the movies after *A High Wind in Jamaica*. The famous harmonica artist might have become a known and respected screen composer. But then, much of Adler's life was a case of "what might have been." Autobiography: *It Ain't Necessarily So* (1985).

Credits

(all films UK unless stated otherwise)

Year	Film	Director
1953	Genevieve (AAN)	Henry Cornelius
1956	Jumping for Joy	John Paddy Carstairs
1958	A Cry from the Streets	Lewis Gilbert
1961	The Hellions	Irving Allen, Ken Annakin (UK/So. Africa)
1962	The Great Chase	Harvey Cort, etc. (USA)
1963	The Hook	George Seaton (USA)
1964	King and Country	Joseph Losey
1965	A High Wind in Jamaica	Alexander Mackendrick

ALEXANDER, Jeff (1910–1989) A multitalented Hollywood songwriter, arranger, conductor, and composer, he scored many radio and television programs and thirty-two feature films, including light comedies, westerns, and five Elvis Presley musicals.

Born Myer Goodhue Alexander in Seattle, Washington, Jeff Alexander took piano lessons as a boy. By the time he was a teenager, Alexander was performing in vaudeville as a singer and dancer. As an adult he composed and arranged music for Big Bands, ending up in New York City in 1939, where he wrote, arranged, and conducted the music for radio programs, including Benny Goodman's *Camel Caravan*, *Hollywood Star Playhouse*, *The Lucky Strike Show*, and *Amos 'n' Andy*. Alexander moved to Los Angeles in 1947, where he made his movie debut as composer and musical director for the animated short *It's a Grand Old Nag*. When other composing assignments were not offered to him, Alexander became a vocal arranger for movie musicals, supervising the singing in such notable films as *On the Riviera* (1951), *Singin' in the Rain* (1952), *Because You're Mine* (1952), *Jupiter's Darling* (1955), *Hit the Deck* (1955), *It's Always Fair Weather* (1955), and *Kismet* (1955). The first feature film Alexander scored was the western *Westward the Women* in 1951 followed by twenty years of scores for movies of varying quality. He specialized in fluffy romantic comedies, such as *The Tender Trap*, *The Mating Game*, *The High Cost of Loving*, and *Ask Any Girl*, and westerns, as with *Escape from Fort Bravo*, *Gun Glory*, *The Rounders*, and *The Sheepman*, as well as combinations of both genres, such as *Support Your Local Sheriff!* and *Dirty Dingus Magee*. Alexander scored six Glenn Ford movies and such Presley vehicles as *Jailhouse Rock*, *Kid Galahad*, and *Clambake*. Among his other noteworthy films are *Rogue Cop*, *Ransom!*, *All the Fine Young Cannibals*, and *The Wings of Eagles*.

In 1960, he turned to television and wrote music for several series, including *Bachelor Father*, *My Three Sons*, *The Lieutenant*, *Valentine's Day*, *Please Don't Eat the Daisies*, and *Julia*, as well as some 1970s TV movies. Alexander also wrote songs for some of his films and TV shows, such as the hits "Come Wander with Me," "The Wings of Eagles," and "Soothe My Lonely Heart." His works for the concert hall include a symphony, tone poems, and chamber pieces. Alexander retired from show business in 1980 and died nine years later from cancer.

Hollywood used Alexander's considerable talents in a variety of ways. He served as conductor, orchestrator, vocal arranger, music director, and composer as needed but he was rarely given very ambitious or high-quality projects to score. Even the lucrative Presley films had modest budgets and attention was put on the songs rather than the soundtrack scores. All the same, Alexander came up with some commendable music during his two decades in Hollywood.

Perhaps his best score for a western can be found in *Escape from Fort Bravo*. The title theme is a robust anthem sung by a male chorus with some interesting key changes. There is the hint of tribal music in other passages, which gives the score a sense of locale and a touch of dignity. The folkish romantic theme becomes the languid ballad "Soothe My Lonely Heart" (lyric also by Alexander) that

is sung on the soundtrack by Bill Lee. Without slipping into cliché, Alexander came up with a western score that was fresh without moving far from the traditional. The score for *The Wings of Eagles*, a biopic about World War I flying ace "Spig" Wead (John Wayne), includes passages from "Anchors Aweigh" to "Aloha Oe" but Alexander provides some stirring music for the air scenes. There is also a twinkling domestic theme for remembering the family back home and a melancholy passage to score the troubled marriage of Spig and his wife (Maureen O'Hara). Another biopic, *All the Fine Young Cannibals*, is the thinly disguised story of jazz trumpeter and singer Chet Baker (Robert Wagner). Some blues and jazz standards are heard in the film but Alexander provides some expert original music as well. The main theme is a flowing blues that has an urgency and restlessness about it. Uan Rasey does the trumpet playing for Wagner on the soundtrack and Alexander gives him some rich, mellow music to perform. The movie may be a cliché-ridden travesty but it certainly sounds right.

Alexander's romantic contemporary comedies are pretty much interchangeable and often the music of one starts to echo another. Such pert and "modern" film comedies like *The Mating Game*, *It Started with a Kiss*, and *The Tender Trap* are more remembered for their title songs, which were written by others. Alexander fills in with chipper passages for the farce and generic merry themes for the romance. More satisfying are the scores for two comic westerns that Alexander did at the end of his Hollywood career. *Dirty Dingus Magee* starts in the middle of a chase and the music wastes no time in pulling out all the stops. The rousing main theme has Jew's harp, player piano, and banjo, with a kazoo making sour comments as furious strings race along. There is a lazy cowpoke theme heard on a trombone that seems to laugh at itself, the saloon music is deliciously honky-tonk, and even the drumming of the local tribe seems to slip into a bit of jazz. *Support Your Local Sheriff!* has a rapid western theme with strumming banjos and lively harmonicas but crazy flutes to give it some sass. There are also fun player-piano passages and a wry cowboy ballad that refuses to take itself seriously. Parodying the conventional western score seems to agree with Alexander because his work sparkles in these two final efforts.

Credits

(all films USA)

Year	Film	Director
1951	Westward the Women (aka Pioneer Women)	William A. Wellman
1953	Remains to Be Seen	Don Weis
1953	The Affairs of Dobie Gillis	Don Weis
1953	Escape from Fort Bravo	John Sturges
1954	Prisoner of War	Andrew Marton
1954	Rogue Cop (aka Kelvaney)	Roy Rowland
1955	The Tender Trap	Charles Walters
1956	Ransom!	Alex Segal
1956	These Wilder Years	Roy Rowland
1956	The Great American Pastime	Herman Hoffman
1957	Slander (aka A Public Figure)	Roy Rowland
1957	The Wings of Eagles	John Ford
1957	Gun Glory	Roy Rowland
1957	Jailhouse Rock	Richard Thorpe
1958	The Sheepman	George Marshall
1958	The High Cost of Loving	José Ferrer
1958	Party Girl	Nicholas Ray
1959	The Mating Game	George Marshall
1959	Ask Any Girl	Charles Walters
1959	It Started with a Kiss	George Marshall
1959	The Gazebo	George Marshall
1960	All the Fine Young Cannibals	Michael Anderson
1961	The George Raft Story (aka Spin of a Coin)	Joseph M. Newman
1961	The Murder Men	John Peyser
1962	Kid Galahad	Phil Karlson
1965	The Rounders	Burt Kennedy
1967	Double Trouble	Norman Taurog
1967	Clambake	Arthur H. Nadel
1968	Day of the Evil Gun	Jerry Thorpe
1968	Speedway	Norman Taurog
1969	Support Your Local Sheriff!	Burt Kennedy
1970	Dirty Dingus Magee	Burt Kennedy

ALEXANDER, Van (b. 1915) A highly respected songwriter, bandleader, arranger, and composer for film and television, he scored seventeen mostly forgettable movies during his dozen years in Hollywood.

Van Alexander was born Alexander Feldman in New York City and as early as his high school years was arranging music and conducting his own band. Alexander studied composition and music theory at Columbia University then began his professional career when he sold two orchestra arrangements to bandleader Chic Webb. The vocalist for the band was a young Ella Fitzgerald. Alexander wrote a jazzy version of the nursery rhyme ditty "A-Tisket, A-Tasket" for Fitzgerald and Webb and it became a resounding hit for the band, on records, and as one of Fitzgerald's signature song for decades. He was soon in great demand, writing arrangements for famous singing stars and Big Bands. Alexander formed his own band in the 1940s and toured the country with success but by the end of that decade the Big Band rage was waning. Alexander accepted bandleader Bob Crosby's invitation to try Hollywood, so in the early 1950s he freelanced as an arranger for various studios. In 1954 he wrote and arranged an original score for the Mickey Rooney vehicle *The Atomic Kid* and that same year repeated both jobs on the TV series *The Mickey Rooney Show*. (It seems Alexander was the unofficial composer/arranger for Rooney in the 1950s, going on to score eight movies that the star appeared in and/or produced-directed.) Before retiring from movies in 1968, Alexander scored gangster films, silly comedies, and horror thrillers, few of them first-class projects. Yet there were also some noteworthy efforts, such as *When Gangland Strikes*, *Andy Hardy Comes Home*, *Baby Face Nelson*, *The Big Operator*, and *The Last Mile*. Alexander found more substantial work in television, composing and arranging music for such series as *The Donna Reed Show*, *The Farmer's Daughter*, *Hazel*, *Bewitched*, and *I Dream of Jeannie*. Throughout his career, Alexander (sometimes under the name Al Feldman) made arrangements and cowrote many songs that were recorded, among the most popular being "I'll Close My Eyes," "Got a Pebble in My Shoe," "There's a Ship Comin' In," and another nursery rhyme hit "Where, O Where Has My Little Dog Gone?" He served as mentor to several younger composers and arrangers and even wrote a textbook about arranging music in 1950 titled *First Arrangement*.

There is no question that Alexander's musical strengths lie in his expert arrangements rather than in his screen compositions, but then he never got to score a first-rate or outstanding film. In most cases it is safe to say that the music was better than the movie. Two William Castle schlock thrillers, *Strait-Jacket* and *I Saw What You Did*, both starred an over-the-hill and overwrought Joan Crawford. Obviously patterned after the previous *Whatever Happened to Baby Jane?* (1962), the two movies make that Gothic thriller look rather subdued. *Strait-Jacket* opens with a scream, an axe murderess (Crawford) is pictured on the front page of a newspaper, and the jazzy-pop score begins. Crawford's character has her own theme, a sexy piece of hot jazz, and the gory scenes are scored with frantic strings and police sirens. *I Saw What You Did (And*

I Know Who You Are) has a better premise: two teenage girls (Sara Lane and Andi Garrett) randomly dial a phone number and announce the title phrase to the man (John Ireland) who answers. The fact that he has just committed a murder jumpstarts the plot. The score is less frantic, with some lyrical clarinet passages and a slow jazz theme for Crawford who plays the murderer's mistress. The rest is standard suspense music with teasing repetition and blaring brass at the crucial moments. Both of these movies are considered campy cult favorites today, but at the time they did little to distinguish Alexander's screen career.

In the 1950s Mickey Rooney was trying to break away from his wholesome teenage image of the 1940s and looked for challenging projects. Playing the title role in the gangster film *Baby Face Nelson* was one of these, and Alexander scored it with a strident jazz soundtrack. With the look of a film noir and the temperament of a documentary, the movie has a stark appearance. The music is also fairly blunt, although some of the jazz is rather smooth and cool in some passages. The chase scenes are scored with bullet-like chords and screaming trumpets. It may all sound more 1950s than the plot's 1930s setting, but it is a commendable score all the same. Perhaps the closest Alexander came to scoring a top-tier film is the prison drama *The Last Mile*. The main theme is a zesty jazz piece without a touch of the morose or melodramatic that would be expected for a story about the inmates on death row. The sound throughout is Big Band jazz, but there are enough dissonant and blue notes to make it clear we are not at the Savoy Ballroom. Such a strong score in a very watchable movie makes one realize how Hollywood never made good use of Alexander's talents.

Credits

(all films USA unless stated otherwise)

Year	Film	Director
1954	*The Atomic Kid*	Leslie H. Martinson
1955	*The Twinkle in God's Eye*	George Blair
1956	*Jaguar*	George Blair
1956	*When Gangland Strikes*	R. G. Springsteen
1957	*Baby Face Nelson*	Don Siegel
1958	*Andy Hardy Comes Home*	Howard W. Koch
1958	*Senior Prom*	David Lowell Rich
1959	*The Last Mile*	Howard W. Koch
1959	*The Big Operator* (aka *Anatomy of the Syndicate*)	Charles F. Haas

Year	Film	Director
1959	*Girls Town* (aka *The Innocent and the Damned*)	Charles F. Haas
1960	*The Private Lives of Adam and Eve*	Mickey Rooney, Albert Zugsmith
1960	*Platinum High School* (aka *Trouble at Sixteen*)	Charles F. Haas
1962	*Safe at Home!*	Walter Doniger
1963	*13 Frightened Girls!*	William Castle
1964	*Strait-Jacket*	William Castle
1965	*I Saw What You Did*	William Castle
1966	*Tarzan and the Valley of Gold*	Robert Day (USA/Switzerland)

ALWYN, William (Smith) (1905–1985) A British composer, conductor, and renowned flautist who taught at the Royal Academy of Music for thirty years, he scored some of Great Britain's finest films of the 1940s and 1950s.

Born in Northampton, England, William Alwyn studied piccolo and flute as a boy. He was only fifteen years old when he was accepted at the Royal Academy, studying the flute and composition. After graduation, he played flute for the London Symphony Orchestra and then in 1925 returned to the Academy where he taught composition until 1955. Alwyn was first associated with movies when he was hired to play flute for a small orchestra that performed for silent films. He did not return to movies until World War II, when he was asked by the Ministry of Information to score a series of documentaries and propaganda features to boost British morale. After scoring twenty short films, Alwyn wrote his first feature score in 1942, the historical drama *Courageous Mr. Penn*. Although he wrote music for many other short and feature-length movies during the war, his best screen work came after the end of hostilities. Alwyn's music for the American-British documentary *The True Glory* in 1945 brought him attention and his moody, entrancing score for director Carol Reed's classic *Odd Man Out* two years later secured his screen reputation. He collaborated again with Reed on *The Fallen Idol* and *The Ballad of the Running Man*, and with other top British directors he scored such memorable films as *The Winslow Boy*, *The Rocking Horse Winner*, *The Mudlark*, *Green for Danger*, *The Magic Box*, and *A Night to Remember*. Alwyn also wrote scores for some Hollywood movies, including the swashbuckler *The Crimson Pirate* and the Disney adventures *Swiss Family Robinson* and *In Search of the Castaways*. Although he scored over seventy movies during his career, Alwyn spent most of his life teaching and composing noncinema music. His output for the concert stage is impressive: five symphonies, eight concertos, four operas, and dozens of piano pieces, art songs, and chamber works. He was a founder of the Composers' Guild of Great Britain, frequently conducted his own work and others, and often wrote about music. The William Alwyn Archive at Cambridge University contains much of his work, and some of Alwyn's music that was lost has been reconstructed and recorded by Philip Lang and Christopher Palmer.

Alwyn's concert music often employed dissonance, and he experimented with twelve-tone serialism by creating his own tonal system, but his screen music is in a more traditional vein, particularly in his Hollywood films. *The Crimson Pirate* is filled with robust symphonic music that suggests exotic locales as well as tuneful marches and playful sea chanteys. The music in *Swiss Family Robinson* is also in the grand manner, a full orchestra exploding in the style of Erich Wolfgang Korngold and Miklós Rózsa. The same can be said for *In Search of the Castaways*, although there are more pleasing lyrical moments in that adventure movie. But such music is not what Alwyn is all about. It is the way he scores smaller and quieter movies that gives him distinction. The tender character drama *The Fallen Idol* about lost ideals has a minimalist score that creates suspense by breaking long periods of silence with ominous chords. On the other hand, there is plenty of music in the fantastical tragedy *The Rocking Horse Winner* about a British youth (John Howard Davies) who can predict racetrack winners when he rides his new rocking horse. There are sections of chaotic suspense as the boy discovers his strange powers and some frenzied sequences in which music echoes the demonic hold the rocking horse has over him. The boy (Andrew Ray) in *The Mudlark* is given lighter, more romantic music for his adventure with Queen Victoria (Irene Dunne), some passages even recalling Arthur Sullivan's merry tunes. Alwyn wrote a delightful calypso sequence for the comedy *The Rake's Progress* (released in the States as *Notorious Gentleman*) and the music throughout is light and witty, just as it is in the Alec Guinness comedy *The Card* (*The Promoter* in the United States). Alwyn was given too few comic films to score, probably because he was considered a serious concert composer.

He was expert in creating tension in his scores. The suspense in the medical mystery thriller *Green for Danger* is musicalized in a subtle way, the chords rising and falling to the tempo of a heartbeat. The tension in *The Ballad of the Running Man* is achieved through a percussion and brass score with a propulsive beat that might serve for a James Bond film. There is a majestic quality in the music for *A Night to Remember* as befitting its subject, the sinking of the *Titanic*. Yet the music has enough touches of dissonance to suggest the tragic fate of the ship and its passengers. Alwyn scored a handful of "Irish troubles"

movies, and they have their own kind of lyrical tension. A persistent kettle drum pervades the music in *Shake Hands with the Devil*. Furious violins underscore the action scenes in *Captain Boycott* and a solo female voice sings an Irish folk tune to set the locale in the quieter scenes. Alwyn's finest Irish movie, one of the high points of the genre, is *Odd Man Out*, and his score for the melodrama is arguably his best. The film is an extended chase in which a wounded Irish nationalist (James Mason) moves through the streets of Belfast trying to evade the police. The score's main theme is forceful but flowing with a touch of folk hidden amid the full orchestrations. The action scenes are rarely musicalized in the movie, the most-noticed music saved for the antihero's visions of the past and the final sequence with him dying in the snow. It is a superior score and one that shows as much restraint as it does talent. Biographies: *William Alwyn: The Art of Film Music*, Ian Johnson (2005); *The Innumerable Dance: The Life and Work of William Alwyn*, Adrian Wright (2008).

Credits

(all films UK unless stated otherwise)

Year	Film	Director
1942	*Courageous Mr. Penn* (aka *Penn of Pennsylvania*)	Lance Comfort
1942	*Wings and the Woman*	Herbert Wilcox
1943	*Squadron Leader X*	Lance Comfort
1943	*Fires Were Started*	Humphrey Jennings
1943	*Escape to Danger*	Lance Comfort, Victor Hanbury
1944	*Soldier, Sailor*	Alexander Shaw
1944	*Our Country*	John Eldridge
1944	*Tunisian Victory*	Frank Capra, Hugh Stewart, John Huston (USA/UK)
1944	*On Approval*	Clive Brook
1944	*The Way Ahead*	Carol Reed
1944	*The Gay Intruders*	Maurice Elvey
1945	*Great Day*	Lance Comfort
1945	*The True Glory*	Garson Kanin (UK/USA)
1945	*Notorious Gentleman* (aka *The Rake's Progress*)	Sidney Gilliat
1946	*Land of Promise*	Paul Rotha
1946	*I See a Dark Stranger* (aka *The Adventuress*)	Frank Launder
1946	*Green for Danger*	Sidney Gilliat
1947	*A City Speaks*	Paul Rotha
1947	*Odd Man Out*	Carol Reed
1947	*Captain Boycott*	Frank Launder
1947	*The October Man*	Roy Ward Baker
1947	*Take My Life*	Ronald Neame
1948	*Three Dawns to Sydney*	John Eldridge
1948	*So Evil My Love*	Lewis Allen (USA/UK)
1948	*Escape*	Joseph L. Mankiewicz (UK/USA)
1948	*The Winslow Boy*	Anthony Asquith

Year	Film	Director
1948	The Fallen Idol	Carol Reed
1949	The History of Mr. Polly	Anthony Pelissier
1949	The Rocking Horse Winner	Anthony Pelissier
1949	The Cure for Love	Robert Donat
1950	Daybreak in Udi	Terry Bishop
1950	Golden Salamander	Ronald Neame
1950	Madeleine	David Lean
1950	The Great Manhunt	Sidney Gilliat
1950	The Mudlark	Jean Negulesco (UK/USA)
1950	The Magnet	Charles Frend
1951	Night without Stars	Anthony Pelissier
1951	No Resting Place	Paul Rotha
1951	Bikini Baby (aka Lady Godiva Rides Again)	Frank Launder
1951	I'll Never Forget You (aka The House in the Square)	Roy Ward Baker
1951	The Magic Box	John Boulting
1952	The Promoter (aka The Card)	Ronald Neame
1952	Island of Desire (aka Saturday Island)	Stuart Heisler
1952	Crash of Silence (aka Mandy)	Alexander Mackendrick
1952	The Crimson Pirate	Robert Siodmak (USA)
1953	The Long Memory	Robert Hamer
1953	Malta Story	Brian Desmond Hurst
1953	The Master of Ballantrae	William Keighley
1953	Personal Affair	Anthony Pelissier
1954	Man with a Million	Ronald Neame
1954	The Rainbow Jacket	Basil Dearden
1954	Savage World	Terry Bishop
1954	Land of Fury (aka The Seekers)	Ken Annakin
1954	Svengali	Noel Langley
1955	PT Raiders (aka The Ship That Died of Shame)	Basil Dearden
1955	Bedevilled	Mitchell Leisen (USA)
1955	Wee Geordie (aka Geordie)	Frank Launder
1956	The Black Tent	Brian Desmond Hurst
1956	Safari	Terence Young
1956	Smiley	Anthony Kimmins
1956	Zarak	Terence Young
1957	She Played with Fire	Sidney Gilliat
1957	Big Time Operators (aka The Smallest Show on Earth)	Basil Dearden
1957	Stowaway Girl (aka Manuela)	Guy Hamilton
1958	Carve Her Name with Pride	Lewis Gilbert
1958	The Silent Enemy	William Fairchild
1958	I Accuse	José Ferrer
1958	A Night to Remember	Roy Ward Baker
1959	Shake Hands with the Devil	Michael Anderson (Ireland/USA)
1959	Killers of Kilimanjaro	Richard Thorpe
1959	Third Man on the Mountain	Ken Annakin (USA)
1959	Devil's Bait	Peter Graham Scott
1960	The Professionals	Don Sharp
1960	Swiss Family Robinson	Ken Annakin (USA)
1961	The Naked Edge	Michael Anderson (UK/USA)
1962	Burn, Witch, Burn (aka Night of the Eagle)	Sidney Hayers
1962	Walk in the Shadow (aka Life for Ruth)	Basil Dearden
1962	In Search of the Castaways	Robert Stevenson (USA)
1963	The Ballad of the Running Man (aka The Running Man)	Carol Reed

AMFITHEATROF, Daniele (1901–1983) A Russian-born Italian composer and conductor with a promising but unfulfilled concert career, he worked in Hollywood for twenty-seven years and contributed music to over one hundred feature films.

He was born in St. Petersburg, Russia, the son of noted writer Aleksander Amfitheatrof and Illaria Amfitheatrof, a classically trained pianist and singer. When Amfitheatrof was only three months old, the family was sent to Siberia because of Aleksander's anti-czarist writings. Two years later the family was released and allowed to return to St. Petersburg, but instead they immigrated to Italy. The young Amfitheatrof studied music privately with his mother and Ottorino Respighi in Rome before the family returned to Russia in 1914. Despite the upheaval of the revolution of 1917, the teenager received a strong musical education from private tutors and at the Petrograd Conservatory. The family escaped from Communist Russia in 1922 and returned to Italy where Amfitheatrof studied at the Royal Conservatory of Santa Cecilia in Rome. He became an Italian citizen and remained in Rome, where he was hired as choral conductor of the Augusteo Symphony, then as artistic director of Italian Radio. Amfitheatrof was soon an in-demand conductor who led opera companies, orchestras, and choral ensembles across Europe. His concert hall compositions also gained renown, one of them, *American Panorama* in 1933, leading to an offer to conduct in the United States. He worked with the Minneapolis Symphony Orchestra and the Boston Symphony then, with the war beginning in Europe, elected to stay in America.

Although Amfitheatrof had scored three films in Italy, including Max Ophüls's highly praised *Everybody's Woman*, he did not return to the movies until 1938, when he was hired as a music director at Paramount. The next year he began scoring Hollywood movies, usually in collaboration with others. A frequent co-composer during this time was David Snell. By the early 1940s he was usually the sole composer as he scored a wide variety of films. For the next twenty years Amfitheatrof was very busy in Hollywood. Among his many notable movies are *Comrade X*, *Mr. and Mrs. North*, *DuBarry Was a Lady*, *Lassie Come Home*, *Bataan*, *Trial*, *I'll Be Seeing You*, *The Virginian*, *Letter from an Unknown Woman*, *Smash-Up*, *The Desert Fox*, *The Desperate Hours*, *The Mountain*, and *Major Dundee*, receiving Oscar nominations for

Guest Wife and *Song of the South*. He also scored many documentary shorts, his stock music was used in over one hundred other movies, and he frequently conducted his own scores. Amfitheatrof's connection with Hollywood hurt his concert career, and he was no longer hired to conduct symphonies or commissioned to compose new works. Somewhat bitter and disillusioned, he retired from movies in 1965 and returned to Italy where he lived as a recluse until his death eighteen years later at the age of eighty-one.

Amfitheatrof's mastery of many kinds of music is evident in his first film, Ophüls's *Everybody's Woman*, about a singing star (Isa Miranda) who attempts suicide but ends up reliving her life in flashbacks. As always, Ophüls moves his camera like few directors have and Amfitheatrof follows suit with a varied score that moves from one theme to another as quickly as the visuals change. Among the many musical selections is a jazzy theme for the heroine heard on a record but at the same time used to illustrate the crass world of show business. A beautifully filmed opera scene has passionate and insistent music that continues to play in succeeding scenes. There is also a tripping waltz that sounds contemporary rather than Viennese, a sublime passage played on a high-pitched violin, and some frenzied, symphonic music for the dramatic scenes. Few screen composers have made such an auspicious debut. Unfortunately, *Everybody's Woman* would not find international acceptance until decades later.

In Hollywood, Amfitheatrof was given all kinds of movies to score and he matched them with musical variety. *Lassie Come Home* is a heartwarming film intended to soothe wartime audiences. Amfitheatrof wrote a lilting and resplendent main theme that captures a domestic quality without turning sentimental. There is also a jolly passage for a dog act that sounds like a giddy circus theme. Contrast this score with that for the sobering melodrama *The Beginning or the End* about developing the atomic bomb. The music throughout is odd and disconcerting. The main theme is a strident jazz piece in which the beat and the melody are both harsh and threatening. The use of organ, theremin, and raspy brass is unique and disarming. *The Mountain*, about two brothers (Spencer Tracy and Robert Wagner) trying to reach a wrecked plane in the Alps, has a brisk and vigorous main theme with brass boldly announcing itself while strings and choral voices echo a beckoning call. There is also a flowing passage played on reeds and plucked strings that is enticing. The terse melodrama *Trial* has strikingly unique music, something suggesting modern dance or experimental jazz. The use of various kinds of percussion is particularly original—piano keys becoming drums and organ notes piercing through the other instruments. Occasionally a melody surfaces but it is soon overcome by the chaotic accompaniment. One can scarcely believe that one composer wrote three such different scores.

The fervent percussion that opens the biopic *The Desert Fox: The Story of Rommel* is oppressive and gains in menace as the brass instruments join in. The music throughout, like the movie itself, finds a way to convey the hypnotic power of Rommel (James Mason) without sanctifying him. The documentary tone of the *The Desert Fox* is aided by Amfitheatrof's no-nonsense score. The less military moments in the story have a tender theme, but it too has a sour, dissonant quality. The Civil War drama *Major Dundee* has a memorable march that is whistled and sung, then played by boastful horns and drums. There is a haunting theme that is used for the film's few moments of pathos, a rhythmic selection heard on fifes that recalls a merry folk dance, and some stirring music for the many action scenes. *Major Dundee*

was Amfitheatrof's last movie score and it is clear he was at the peak of his powers when he retired.

Yet arguably his best score is *Letter from an Unknown Woman*, another Ophüls movie but this time in America. The romantic melodrama concerns the love of a young girl (Joan Fontaine) for a pianist (Louis Jourdan) so music plays a major role in the plot. Amfitheatrof based his main theme on Franz Liszt's piano etude "Un Sospiro," using variations of the piece to represent the pianist who plays it in a concert at one point. The theme is a series of gentle yet glowing crescendos with strings, brass, and flutes intertwining in a captivating manner. The felicitous waltz heard when the couple dine in a restaurant is original and thoroughly intoxicating. Amfitheatrof created variations of this as well and used it later in the movie. *Letter from an Unknown Woman* has a bittersweet finale and the music is heartbreaking even as it remains smart and knowing. To say that Amfitheatrof was underrated by Hollywood is a gross understatement. Few composers brought so much musical knowledge and talent to the movies and got so little back in return. Today he is better appreciated and highly admired. Much of his screen music is too good to remain unnoticed.

Credits

(all films USA unless stated otherwise)

Year	Film	Director
1934	Everybody's Woman	Max Ophüls (Italy)
1936	Dimmed Lights	Adelqui Migliar (Italy)
1936	L'esclave blanc	Jean-Paul Paulin (Italy/France)
1939	Bridal Suite	Wilhelm Thiele
1939	Fast and Furious	Busby Berkeley
1939	Nick Carter, Master Detective	Jacques Tourneur
1940	The Man from Dakota	Leslie Fenton
1940	And One Was Beautiful	Robert B. Sinclair
1940	Phantom Raiders (aka Nick Carter in Panama)	Jacques Tourneur
1940	We Who Are Young	Harold S. Bucquet
1940	Third Finger, Left Hand	Robert Z. Leonard
1940	Comrade X	King Vidor
1940	Keeping Company	S. Sylvan Simon
1941	Free and Easy	George Sidney, Edward Buzzell
1941	The Getaway (aka Enemy Within)	Edward Buzzell, Richard Rosson
1941	H. M. Pulham, Esq.	King Vidor
1942	The Bugle Sounds	S. Sylvan Simon
1942	Mr. and Mrs. North	Robert B. Sinclair
1942	The Vanishing Virginian	Frank Borzage
1942	A Yank on the Burma Road	George B. Seitz

Year	Film	Director
1942	*Joe Smith, American*	Richard Thorpe
1942	*Sunday Punch*	David Miller
1942	*Jackass Mail*	Norman Z. Leonard
1942	*Calling Dr. Gillespie*	Harold S. Bouquet
1942	*Tish*	S. Sylvan Simon
1942	*Eyes in the Night*	Fred Zinnemann
1942	*Northwest Rangers*	Joseph M. Newman
1942	*Dr. Gillespie's New Assistant*	Willis Goldbeck
1942	*White Cargo*	Richard Thorpe
1942	*Andy Hardy's Double Life*	George B. Seitz
1942	*Aerial Gunner*	William H. Pine
1943	*High Explosive*	Frank McDonald
1943	*Harrigan's Kid*	Charles Reisner
1943	*A Stranger in Town*	Roy Rowland
1943	*Dr. Gillespie's Criminal Case*	Willis Goldbeck
1943	*DuBarry Was a Lady*	Roy Del Ruth
1943	*Bataan*	Tay Garnett
1943	*Lassie Come Home*	Fred M. Wilcox
1943	*Cry "Havoc"*	Richard Thorpe
1943	*Lost Angel*	Roy Rowland
1944	*Days of Glory*	Jacques Tourneur
1944	*Bathing Beauty*	George Sidney
1944	*I'll Be Seeing You* (aka *Double Furlough*)	William Dieterle, George Cukor
1945	*I Was a Criminal* (aka *Captain of Koepenick*)	Richard Oswald
1945	*Guest Wife* (AAN)	Sam Wood
1945	*Miss Susie Slagle's*	John Berry
1946	*The Virginian*	Stuart Gilmore
1946	*O.S.S.*	Irving Pichel
1946	*Suspense*	Frank Tuttle
1946	*Song of the South* (AAN)	Wilfred Jackson, Harve Foster
1946	*Temptation*	Irving Pichel
1947	*The Beginning or the End*	Norman Taurog
1947	*Smash-Up: The Story of a Woman*	Stuart Heisler
1947	*Ivy*	Sam Wood
1947	*Singapore*	John Brahm
1947	*The Lost Moment*	Martin Gabel
1947	*The Senator Was Indiscreet*	George S. Kaufman
1948	*Letter from an Unknown Woman*	Max Ophüls
1948	*Another Part of the Forest*	Michael Gordon
1948	*Rogues' Regiment*	Robert Florey
1948	*You Gotta Stay Happy*	H. C. Potter
1948	*An Act of Murder* (aka *I Stand Accused*)	Michael Gordon
1949	*The Fan*	Otto Preminger
1949	*House of Strangers* (aka *East Side Story*)	Joseph L. Mankiewicz
1949	*Sand*	Louis King
1950	*Backfire* (aka *Somewhere in the City*)	Vincent Sherman
1950	*Under My Skin*	Jean Negulesco
1950	*The Capture* (aka *Daybreak*)	John Sturges
1950	*The Damned Don't Cry*	Vincent Sherman
1950	*Devil's Doorway*	Anthony Mann
1950	*Copper Canyon*	John Farrow
1951	*Storm Warning*	Stuart Heisler
1951	*Bird of Paradise*	Delmer Daves
1951	*The Painted Hills* (aka *Lassie's Adventures in the Goldrush*)	Harold F. Kress
1951	*Tomorrow Is Another Day*	Felix E. Feist
1951	*Angels in the Outfield*	Clarence Brown

Year	Film	Director
1951	The Desert Fox: The Story of Rommel	Henry Hathaway
1953	Scandal at Scourie (aka My Mother and Mr. McChesney)	Jean Negulesco
1953	Devil's Canyon	Alfred L. Werker
1954	The Naked Jungle (aka Bushmaster)	Byron Haskin
1954	Human Desire(aka The Human Beast)	Fritz Lang
1954	Day of Triumph	John T. Coyle, Irving Pichel
1955	The Desperate Hours	William Wyler
1955	Trial	Mark Robson
1956	The Last Hunt	Richard Brooks
1956	The Mountain	Edward Dmytryk
1957	The Unholy Wife (aka The Lady and the Prowler)	John Farrow
1957	Spanish Affair	Luis Marquina, Don Siegel (USA/Spain)
1958	From Hell to Texas (aka The Hell-Bent Kid)	Henry Hathaway
1958	Fräulein	Henry Koster
1959	That Kind of Woman	Sidney Lumet
1959	Edge of Eternity (aka The Dancing Bucket)	Don Siegel
1960	Heller in Pink Tights	George Cukor
1965	Major Dundee	Sam Peckinpah

ANTHEIL, George (1900–1959) A renowned pianist and experimental composer of opera, ballets, and concert music, he occasionally wrote film scores, usually for dark dramas presented by independent producer-directors. Labeled the "Bad Boy of Music" for his revolutionary approaches to composition, he fell into obscurity after his premature death but has recently been rediscovered.

Born Georg Carl Johann Antheil in Trenton, New Jersey, the son of German immigrants, he began playing the piano at the age of six. As a teenager he studied composition with distinguished teachers in Philadelphia and New York and associated with avant-garde composers, artists, and writers. While pursuing further study at the Philadelphia Settlement Music School, Antheil wrote the first of his *mechane* music, pieces that went beyond traditional musical instruments and utilized anvils, car horns, electric bells, airplane propellers, and other unconventional items. At the age of twenty-two, Antheil went to Europe where he was soon the toast of Paris and Berlin for his unorthodox symphonies, sonatas, operas, and ballets. In Europe he befriended some of the finest artists of the era, from Jean Cocteau to Igor Stravinsky. He continued to experiment with music, writing a piece for a collective of player pianos, and scoring some short art films. The most famous of these is *Ballet Méchanique*, which is not a ballet at all but a nineteen-minute Dadaist film by Fer-

nand Léger and Dudley Murphy with cinematography by Man Ray. Antheil's music from the film was performed as a concert piece in Paris in 1926 and the next year at Carnegie Hall. He lived and worked in Germany in the late 1920s but his dissident music did not find favor with the rising Nazi Party, so Antheil returned to the States and settled in New York City. By this time his work had grown a bit more conventional and Hollywood became interested in him.

Antheil's eccentric personality did not go well with the studio system, so most of his screen work was for independent producers and directors. Cecil B. DeMille, for example, had created his own producing organization by the 1930s and hired Antheil to score two action movies, *The Plainsman* and *The Buccaneer*. Writer-directors Ben Hecht, John Huston, Nicholas Ray, and Stanley Kramer also used Antheil during a Hollywood career that lasted from 1935 to 1957. Most memorable of the four Humphrey Bogart movies he scored are *In a Lonely Place* and *Knock on Any Door*, but many of Antheil's movies are little known today. He rarely scored more than one movie a year, spending most of his time and energies on his operas, ballets, and concert pieces. Unlike most composers, Antheil had wide interests outside of music. He studied and wrote about medicine and politics, arranged exhibits of abstract art, authored a nationally syndicated advice column, and gained some renown as an inventor. (During World War II, he and actress Hedy Lamarr patented a device that could mislead torpedoes by altering the frequency using an early form of computer code.) Antheil died of a heart attack at the age of fifty-eight, leaving a legacy of six symphonies, six operas, many sonatas, quartets, and chamber pieces, and thirty short and feature films.

Because Antheil had somewhat mellowed in his composition works by the time he went to Hollywood, his most avant-garde music is not heard in his feature films. Yet one can recognize a refreshingly novel approach in some of his scores. His music for the two Cecil B. DeMille epics sounds more modern than one expects from such genre movies. *The Plainsman* is on a large scale but centers on the relationship between Wild Bill Hickok (Gary Cooper) and Calamity Jane (Jean Arthur). Antheil provides a rough-and-tumble theme for the two unlikely lovers, as well as effective underscoring for the action sequences. *The Buccaneer* score is more romantic and melodic, as expected in a swashbuckler. Fredric March plays the pirate Jean Lafitte who has plenty of adventures during the War of 1812. The score is exciting when it needs be, sentimental when required. Listening to it one would never suspect an avant-gardist wrote the music. Near the end of his career, Antheil returned to the action movie for *The Pride and the Passion*, a somewhat overwrought film about Spanish peasants hoping to stop Napoleon's army with their giant cannon. The adventure piece is miscast and the dialogue is sometimes embarrassing but it is visually and musically a vibrant cinema experience. Antheil's main theme is a zesty Spanish bolero that also serves as a march when needed. A lilting love theme for the triangle involving a Spanish revolutionary (Frank Sinatra), a British naval officer (Cary Grant), and a fiery senorita (Sophia Loren) is Hollywood romantic with just a touch of the Spanish. There is a vivacious flamenco for Loren to dance to and plenty of Spanish guitars for the peasants cutting loose. In one of the movie's most tense scenes, the cannon is pulled up by ropes from a ravine where it has fallen. The sequence becomes a nail-biter with Antheil's bass notes that seem ready to explode if the ropes snap.

Two film noir movies directed by Nicholas Ray afforded Antheil the opportunity to write two expert dra-

matic scores. In *Knock on Any Door*, Bogart plays a weary lawyer who defends a juvenile (John Derek) from the slums on a murder charge. The score often resembles a jazz opera as certain instruments each have an aria of their own. In one masterful sequence, the youth is hiding from the police and from a rooftop watches the funeral of his girlfriend who has committed suicide. The music has such bitterness and sadness in it that one feels as if the character has delivered a soliloquy. Bogart plays a washed-up screenwriter suspected of murder in the noir classic *In a Lonely Place*. Because the writer has an uncontrolled temper at times, the music is often harsh and explosive. Yet the love theme for the writer and his neighbor (Gloria Grahame) is enticing as it wavers and repeats its key phrases without completely resolving itself. These two dramas may not boast innovative scores, but they show that Antheil was an accomplished screen composer who thoroughly understood the medium.

The Specter of the Rose is a thriller set in the world of ballet and Antheil's score includes music for modern dance, a waltz, and a macabre ballet. The waltz has a sweeping motion that sometimes turns a bit sour. The modern dance piece, titled "Lights of the City," is a Stravinsky-like spoof with a pretentious look and a dissonant piano score. The final ballet, in which the dancer-villain (Ivan Kirov) dances himself to death, is also very modern, moving from a bizarre waltz to a pounding fugue to an expressionistic frenzy. This is surely a score written by an avant-gardist. The same thing can be said for the horror film *Dementia*, which has some narration but no dialogue and relies greatly on its musical score. The movie takes the point of view of a mentally unbalanced woman (Adrienne Barrett) during one night as she encounters various nightmarish characters. A moaning female voice (Marni Nixon), repetitive descending chords, sour trumpets, chaotic piano passages, strident violin glides, and some surreal jazz riffs are among the delightful oddities in this remarkable score. Here at last is the Bad Boy of Music using the movie medium in an exciting, unconventional way. What kind of work would Antheil have done if he could have scored movies in the 1960s and 1970s? Autobiography: *Bad Boy of Music* (1945). Official website: www.antheil.org.

Credits

(all films USA)

Year	Film	Director
1935	*Once in a Blue Moon*	Ben Hecht, Charles MacArthur
1936	*The Plainsman*	Cecil B. DeMille
1937	*Make Way for Tomorrow*	Leo McCarey
1938	*The Buccaneer*	Cecil B. DeMille
1940	*Angels Over Broadway*	Ben Hecht, Lee Garmes
1946	*Specter of the Rose*	Ben Hecht
1946	*Plainsman and the Lady*	Joseph Kane
1946	*That Brennan Girl*	Alfred Santell
1947	*Repeat Performance*	Alfred L. Werker
1949	*Knock on Any Door*	Nicholas Ray
1949	*We Were Strangers*	John Huston
1949	*The Fighting Kentuckian*	George Waggner
1949	*Tokyo Joe*	Stuart Heisler
1950	*House by the River*	Fritz Lang
1950	*In a Lonely Place*	Nicholas Ray
1951	*Sirocco*	Curtis Bernhardt
1952	*The Sniper*	Edward Dmytryk
1952	*Actor's and Sin*	Lee Garmes, Ben Hecht
1953	*The Juggler*	Edward Dmytryk
1954	*Hunters of the Deep*	Ben Chapman
1955	*Not as a Stranger*	Stanley Kramer
1955	*Dementia (aka Daughter of Horror)*	John Parker
1957	*The Pride and the Passion*	Stanley Kramer
1957	*The Young Don't Cry*	Alfred L. Werker

ARMSTRONG, Craig (b. 1959) A Scottish composer and performer of popular, classical, and experimental music, he is becoming one of the most in-demand artists for scoring movies both in Great Britain and in the States.

Craig Armstrong was born and raised in Glasgow, Scotland, and studied composition, piano, and violin at the Royal Academy of Music in London. After graduation, Armstrong returned to Glasgow to serve as house composer for the Tron Theatre Company. He then went on to write music for the Royal Shakespeare Company and other theatre groups, as well as for experimental art-theatre works and performance art. In 1989 Armstrong first wrote for television, scoring the Scottish Television (STV) miniseries *Winners and Losers*. He made his movie debut when he scored a short film directed by Peter Mullen, whom he had worked with in the theatre. He contributed some music to the Baz Luhrmann version of *Romeo + Juliet* in 1996 (the co-composers were Nellee Hooper and Marius de Vries), then Mullan hired him to score his solo feature debut, the comedy-drama *Orphans* in 1998. Armstrong's second score, for the crime adventure *Plunkett & Macleane*, included a track titled "Escape," which caught on with the public and was later used in film trailers, sporting events, and television programs. International recognition did not come until Armstrong scored the popular Luhrmann musical *Moulin Rouge!* in 2001. His first Hollywood movie, the biopic *Ray* in 2004, was a critical and popular success as well. Moving back and forth between Europe and the States, Armstrong has scored such memorable films as *The Bone Collector*, *Love Actually*, *The Magdalene Sisters*, *World Trade Center*, *Elizabeth: The Golden Age*, *The Incredible Hulk*, *Wall Street: Money Never Sleeps*, and the 2013 remake of *The Great Gatsby*. He often arranges, orchestrates, and conducts his screen scores. Only a portion of Armstrong's career has been in the movies. His concert compositions and operas have been premiered by renowned English and Scottish companies, including the Scottish Opera, BBC Symphony Orchestra, London Sinfonietta, and the Royal Scottish National Orchestra. Armstrong has written for and performed with various bands, worked with pop and rock stars on concerts and recordings, and has recorded many of his own albums of popular music, innovative electronic music, and his concert works. He was honored with the Order of the British Empire in 2010 for his contribution to music.

Armstrong's screen music has been called New Age, techno, and other vaguely modern styles. It certainly sounds modern, even in period films, yet it has a wonderfully universal feel to it that is usually compelling. The main theme for the contemporary urban drama *Orphans* is played on piano and is cautious yet has a sense of purpose. It is not in the classical mode yet has a timeless quality that works for the film and as an independent piece. The playful eighteenth-century adventure *Plunkett & Macleane* has a modern sensibility, so Armstrong's New Age sound works very well. The famous "Escape" theme is indeed catchy with its wavering strings, reverent choir, and majestic sound. The piece slowly but firmly builds to a crescendo, then changes tempo and pounds its way to another height. The score also includes a propulsive theme that moves at a Latin beat but is closer to rock or reggae, a wordless hymn that also builds beautifully, some ominous passages that quietly spell out the presence of lurking menace, and the lyrical "Ruby" theme that is both romantic and melancholy. Some critics did not like the use of modern songs in the La Belle Epoque period musical *Moulin Rouge!* but audiences were not bothered and enjoyed the anachronistic movie. Armstrong's original music blended into the contemporary songs but, unlike them, seemed to understand the tale's tragicomic nature. The love theme for the writer Christian (Ewan McGregor) and the Parisian courtesan-singer Satine (Nicole Kidman) is passionate but full of dread and foreboding. There is also an energized bolero, an enticingly slow lament played on piano and strings, and a flowing theme for Satine's death that almost seems too deep for the cartoonish characters that fill the movie. Ironically, a dozen years later when director Luhrmann used rock and pop songs by Jay-Z, Amy Winehouse, U2, and others for the period movie *The Great Gatsby*, audiences were not so enamored of the anachronism. But again Armstrong's soundtrack score seems to understand F. Scott Fitzgerald's characters. The theme for the wealthy Buchanans is lush and regal with a sense of entitlement. The musical motif for the spoiled but delectable Daisy (Carey Mulligan) is mellifluous and delicate even as it pushes forward in a determined way.

The movie opens with the unusual "Infinite Hope" theme, a drunken blues with a quivering clarinet set to the tempo of a death march. *The Great Gatsby* did not repeat the success of *Moulin Rouge!* but in both cases Armstrong's music deserved a better movie.

The serial killer thriller *The Bone Collector* has a score that often undercuts the gruesome tale and actually soothes on occasion. One passage is dreamy and gliding without a trace of menace. The chilling music for the killer's deeds is powerfully determined as echoing chords, a pounding bass line, and confused strings and keyboard seem to attack one's ears. The main theme is not so oppressive yet it flows steadily and has enough dissonance to set the tone for this unrelenting movie. *World Trade Center* is as disturbing in its own way and the tragic outcome overshadows the whole movie. Armstrong's main theme is graceful as both the orchestration and the percussive accents gently build in purpose. *World Trade Center* is not a defeatist film and offers hope; the music at the resolution does likewise. There is a warm and victorious feel to the musical finale without becoming blindly optimistic. On the other hand, there is little or no hope in the searing drama *The Magdalene Sisters* about Irish girls tormented for their sins by fanatical nuns. A story like this needs little musical embellishment so Armstrong offers a reflective piano theme that has disturbing sustained notes slowly overpowering the simple melody. As is his usual method, this sometimes moves into soft rock with electronic instruments once it reaches a crescendo. The *Wall Street* sequel *Wall Street: Money Never Sleeps* is scored like a thriller with a restless piano theme, a pulsating rhythmic passage that comes perilously close to disco, and a riff on electric guitar that seems to laugh with scorn. The Ray Charles biopic *Ray* is filled with so many wonderful Charles recordings (lip-synced and acted with skill by Jamie Foxx) that few can recall the soundtrack music by Armstrong. The vintage recordings do not illustrate Charles's troubled life but Armstrong suggests it in the main theme, a free-flowing piano piece with quixotic tempo changes and a haunting orchestral accompaniment. There is also a dulcet theme for the wife Della (Kerry Washington) that overflows with warmth and intimacy. The blind singer-musician's determination is musicalized with a rocking theme that sounds like a jazzy boxing match. The more poetic aspect of the character is scored with a New Age passage with a determined electric guitar and accented with sound effects. Once again, none of this seems appropriate for the period of the movie's setting but is successful in conveying mood and character.

Oddly, Armstrong's score for the futuristic *In Time* is more romantic and classic jazz than techno. The main theme does suggest a future world, but the strings are in a sonorous symphonic mode and it is the electronic sound effects that give the music a sci-fi temperament. There is a death scene scored with such sorrow that the descending phrases and sustained notes seem to mourn to the tempo of a pulse. Finally, one has to acknowledge Armstrong's lighter side. He has not scored many comedies but *Love Actually* has achieved cult status since 2003, and it has a deliciously fun and romantic score. The movie is a series of interconnected vignettes that take place in contemporary London during Christmastime and the soundtrack has many popular songs heard at different points. There are also many different levels of comedy and romance, all of it reflected in Armstrong's score. Some passages are unrestrained romanticism with gliding strings and piano music that seem to float through space. Others are bittersweet with a cautious subtext, all the more enticing because of the tentative nature of the music. There is a wildly passionate theme that borders on the absurd, a folk selection heard on classical guitar, a jaunty passage that glows with confidence, and a rhapsodic theme for the prime minister (Hugh Grant) that has a pompous flavor but is still engaging. It is hoped that Armstrong will get to score more romantic comedies in future, for they reveal another aspect of his estimable talent. Websites: www.craigarmstrong.com and www.craigarmstrongonline.com.

Credits

Year	Film	Director
1998	*Orphans*	Peter Mullan (UK)
1999	*Plunkett & Macleane*	Jake Scott (UK)
1999	*Best Laid Plans*	Mike Barker (UK)
1999	*The Bone Collector*	Phillip Noyce (USA/Canada)
2001	*Moulin Rouge!* (GG; BAFTA)	Baz Luhrmann (USA/Australia)
2001	*Kiss of the Dragon*	Chris Nahon (France/USA)
2002	*The Magdalene Sisters*	Peter Mullan (Ireland/UK)
2002	*The Quiet American*	Phillip Noyce (Germany/USA/UK/Australia/France)
2003	*Love Actually*	Richard Curtis (UK/USA/France)
2004	*The Clearing*	Pieter Jan Brugge (USA/Germany)
2004	*Ray* (aka *Unchain My Heart*) (BAFTA-N)	Taylor Hackford (USA)
2005	*Fever Pitch*	Bobby and Peter Farrelly (USA/Germany)
2005	*Must Love Dogs*	Gary David Goldberg (USA)
2006	*World Trade Center*	Oliver Stone (USA)
2007	*Elizabeth: The Golden Age*	Shekhar Kapur (UK/France/USA/Germany)
2008	*The Day After Peace*	Jeremy Gilley (UK)
2008	*The Incredible Hulk*	Louis Leterrier (USA)
2010	*Wall Street: Money Never Sleeps*	Oliver Stone (USA)
2010	*Neds*	Peter Mullan (UK/France/Italy)
2011	*In Time*	Andrew Niccol (USA)
2013	*The Great Gatsby*	Baz Luhrmann (Australia/USA)

ARNOLD, David (b. 1962) A British record producer and composer of television and movies who has been active since the early 1990s, he is most known for his action films, including five James Bond thrillers.

Born in Luton, England, the son of a professional boxer, David Arnold began writing music at the age of ten when his parents gave him a guitar. Arnold played in rock bands in high school and then professionally on tour. A friend from school, Danny Cannon, first got Arnold involved in movies when he asked him to score some film shorts. When Cannon made his first feature in 1993, the low-budget thriller *The Young Americans*, Arnold wrote some of the score, including the song "Play Dead" which was recorded by singer Björk and climbed the charts in Great Britain. The next year Arnold scored the sci-fi favorite *Stargate* for director Roland Emmerich. The two men later collaborated again on the 1996 giant hit *Independence Day* and the infamous 1998 flop *Godzilla*. Arnold's score for the adventure *Last of the Dogmen* has such a strong score that it is continually raided for stock music for film trailers. Since childhood, Arnold has been an avid fan of the James Bond movies and the music John Barry wrote for them. In 1997 he produced an album titled *Shaken and Stirred* in which he reinterpreted the famous Bond themes by various composers. Barry was so impressed with Arnold's treatment of the music that he recommended that the young composer score the next Bond movie, *Tomorrow Never Dies*. Arnold went on to also write the music for the Bond installments *The World Is Not Enough, Die Another Day, Casino Royale*, and *Quantum of Solace*.

Although Arnold has established himself as a composer of action movies, including such streetwise John Singleton films as *Shaft, 2 Fast 2 Furious, Bad Boy*, and *Four Brothers*, he also has found success scoring such offbeat comedies as *The Stepford Wives, Zoolander, Morning Glory, Hot Fuzz*, and *Paul*, and character dramas like *Stoned, Enough, Amazing Grace*, and *Made in Dagenham*. He has scored four films by director Michael Apted, including the *Chronicles of Narnia* fantasy titled *The Voyage of the Dawn Treader*. Arnold has been writing music for British television since 1997, scoring many documentaries, TV movies, and series, the last category including *Little Britain, Little Britain USA, Free Agents*, and *Sherlock*. As a record producer and artist, he has worked with many rock, pop, and folk bands and singers. Arnold has also written music for many special occasions, most memorably as musical director for the 2012 Olympic Games in London. He is not to be confused with the British concert conductor David Arnold (b. 1951).

Arnold did not receive a formal music education and often relies on conductor and orchestrator Nicholas Dodd. Yet he often embraces a classical sound in his scores, usually favoring a symphonic sound rather than electronic one. For example, the imaginative if somewhat incoherent sci-fi film *Stargate* has a very symphonic score that tends to be more romanticized than modern. The choral sections are celestial, the instruments are mostly traditional, and the music itself is sweeping and grand rather than high tech or experimental. There is a rousing theme that has a Middle Eastern flavor (the plot begins in Egypt), the menacing music for the evil emperor (Jaye Davidson) is sinister in an old-fashioned way, a vivacious march packs a wallop, and the movie's many special effects are scored with unpretentious panache. The very popular aliens-attack-Earth film *Independence Day* borrows liberally from many previous (and better) sci-fi movies, although the scale here is bigger and the storytelling is noisier. Arnold's score is also on an epic scale and, while it may not have the poetic quality of *Stargate*, it sure has the robust temperament of Emmerich's movie. Again Arnold relies on a conventional orchestra and a grand symphonic approach to the music. The choral voices this time are darker, suggesting the sound of hell rather than a celestial tone. The aliens' arrival is scored with such ominous passages that it is a wonder the earthlings trust them for a minute. The many scenes of destruction begin with a serene prelude, then the music explodes along with all the familiar monuments crashing to the ground. The final victory march is jubilant with fortissimo glee as the different sections of the orchestra compete to see who can jump higher and faster. Audiences noticed the music in *Independence Day* because they had no choice. The film secured Arnold's Hollywood status but better music was yet to come.

It is not surprising that Arnold's Bond film scores are often an homage to composer Barry. He was the first to give Agent 007 his sound and Arnold acknowledges this in his music. Of course, all the Bond thrillers over the years have quoted Barry's music but Arnold seems to understand those old themes best. The score for *Tomorrow Never Dies* sometimes sounds like the 1960s with its slick and casual temperament. Other sections are more 1990s with some quietly disturbing passages that hint at disillusion and regret. Some of the chase music employs jazz and reggae, other passages come close to hip-hop and rap. The title song by Sheryl Crow and Mitchell Froom is a lazy rock-pop piece that Crows sing over the opening credits. But more in the style of Barry is Arnold's music that became the song "Surrender" (lyric by Don Black), which was sung on the soundtrack by k. d. lang at the end of the movie. It is a sultry piece with a slow jazz feeling even as it builds in intensity. This is indeed the Bond sound. *The World Is Not Enough* and Arnold's other Bond scores have some marvelous passages, but there is something so Barry-like in the soundtrack for *Tomorrow Never Dies* that it seems to stand out. Just about everything stands out in Arnold's exhilarating score for the quasi-western *Last of the Dogmen*. The rousing music that celebrates nature, the tender passages for the character scenes, the hint of mysticism in the music dealing with the Native Americans, and the pulsating theme for the action scenes are all handled traditionally but with a refreshing vitality. Because the plot is a modern one about searching for a tribe hidden away from time, the score rarely recalls a western soundtrack yet at times it captures the majesty of that genre. The movie may not be for all tastes but the music is very accessible and highly commendable.

Of the handful of comedies scored by Arnold, perhaps the most interesting musically is the sci-fi farce *Paul* about two British nerds (Simon Pegg and Nick Frost) who take a road trip to visit UFO sites and end up helping the title alien return home. The opening theme is a high-tech ballad heard on a high-pitched pipe that attempts to be suspenseful but is too playful to be taken seriously. Another passage is a western pastiche complete with harmonica that tries to compete with the more ominous music surrounding it. There is plenty of folksy travel music, an eerie and clichéd sci-fi theme, and some silly chase music. The ending spoofs the finale of *E.T.*, and the music gets as grandiose as John Williams's score does at the conclusion of that film. Also satirical is the remake of *The Stepford Wives* with its chorus of female scat singers, giddy xylophone passages, and its pseudowitch ritual chants. The main theme is a sprightly waltz that is very Old World but seems to capture the superficiality of American suburbia. Another spoof, the spy comedy *Zoolander*, has a mock Bond score as it might have been done in the swinging 1960s. Yet Arnold uses rock, disco, hip-hop, and other more recent styles for this contemporary ribbing of the fashion world and a model (Ben Stiller) who becomes a secret agent. This is gleeful scoring on a mighty silly level. The 1960s are recalled in a different light in the realistic drama *Made in Dagenham*. Based on the 1968 strike by women workers in a British car factory, the film is about ordinary people becoming leaders. The main theme is an "easy listening" piece that sounds like the era, lively enough to have a beat but shying from a rocking sound. Much of the rest of the score is composed of 1960s pop songs but Arnold's soundtrack is a fine and subtle work that quietly reinforces the characters and their transitions from cogs in a factory to empowered women.

Among Arnold's most recent projects is the score for the third of *The Chronicles of Narnia* films. The music in *The Voyage of the Dawn Treader* has been cited as the composer's finest screen work. It is certainly one of his most classical works. The main theme is a delicate hymn with a sense of awe and majesty yet is still restrained and even cautious. Even the choir is practically subliminal. Arnold uses the piano as the featured instrument and when the full orchestra is utilized it seems to be kept under tight control. Like the other Narnia installments, this one has its religious parallels, which the music supports without getting too ponderous. The action scenes are scored with vigor, the choir coming on strong as in a Carl Orff piece. There is also a theme that is so passionate it moves from being an anthem to a driving battle cry. Of late Arnold has concentrated on work away from the movies, particularly television and his music duties for the Olympics. It is hoped he will return to screen music soon and continue to provide provocative scores for a variety of films. Official website: www.davidarnold.com.

Credits

Year	Film	Director
1993	*The Young Americans*	Danny Cannon (UK)
1994	*Stargate*	Roland Emmerich (France/USA)
1995	*Last of the Dogmen*	Tab Murphy (USA)
1996	*Independence Day*	Roland Emmerich (USA)
1997	*A Life Less Ordinary*	Danny Boyle (USA/UK)
1997	*Tomorrow Never Dies*	Roger Spottiswoode (UK/USA)
1998	*Godzilla*	Roland Emmerich (USA/Japan)
1999	*The World Is Not Enough* (aka *Bond 19*)	Michael Apted (UK/USA)
2000	*Shaft*	John Singleton (Germany/USA)
2001	*Baby Boy*	John Singleton (USA)
2001	*The Musketeer*	Peter Hyams (Germany/Luxembourg/UK/USA)

Year	Film	Director
2001	*Zoolander*	Ben Stiller (USA/Australia/Germany)
2002	*Changing Lanes*	Roger Michell (USA)
2002	*Enough*	Michael Apted (USA)
2002	*Die Another Day*	Le Tamahori (UK/USA)
2003	*2 Fast 2 Furious (aka The Fast and the Furious 2)*	John Singleton (USA/Germany)
2004	*The Stepford Wives*	Frank Oz (USA)
2005	*Four Brothers*	John Singleton (USA)
2005	*Stoned*	Stephen Woolley (UK)
2006	*Amazing Grace*	Michael Apted (UK/USA)
2006	*Casino Royale (aka Bond Begins)* (BAFTA-N)	Martin Campbell (UK/Czech Rep/USA/Germany/ Bahamas)
2007	*Hot Fuzz*	Edgar Wright (UK/France/USA)
2008	*How to Lose Friends and Alienate People*	Robert B. Welde (UK)
2008	*Quantum of Solace*	Marc Forster (UK/USA)
2008	*Agent Crush*	Sean Robinson (UK/USA)
2010	*Made in Dagenham*	Nigel Cole (UK)
2010	*Morning Glory*	Roger Michell (USA)
2010	*The Chronicles of Narnia: The Voyage of the Dawn Treader*	Michael Apted (USA)
2011	*Paul*	Greg Mottola (USA/UK)

ARNOLD, Malcolm (Henry) (1921–2006) A distinguished British composer for ballet, theatre, and the concert hall, he was very active in movies in the 1950s and 1960s, scoring sixty-five feature films for David Lean, Carol Reed, and other top British directors.

Malcolm Arnold was born in Northampton, England, the youngest of five children in a wealthy family in the shoe business. Both parents were musical and as a youngster Arnold was given lessons in violin, piano, and trumpet. Despite a rigid classical training, as a teenager he became fascinated with jazz after seeing Louis Armstrong in concert. Arnold studied composition and the trumpet at the Royal College of Music, but he never graduated, leaving school in 1941 when he began his professional career as second trumpet in the London Philharmonic. By the end of the decade the famous orchestra was premiering his musical compositions. His prodigious output as a concert composer includes nine symphonies, twenty concertos, choral music, song cycles, string quartets, and chamber music, as well as five ballets and two operas. From the beginning, Arnold received awards and citations for his music and was already an internationally acclaimed composer before he started working in films. He began writing music for documentary shorts for the Rank Organization in 1946 and four years later scored his first feature, the comedy *Badger's Green*. Other features, shorts, and documentaries followed, but it was the popularity of the aerial drama *No Highway in the Sky* in 1951 that brought Arnold wide recognition. The next year he worked with director Lean for the first time. *Breaking the Sound Barrier* was a modest success but the two men would find worldwide acclaim for their collaborations *Hobson's Choice* and *The Bridge on the River Kwai*, the second winning seven Oscars including Best Score. Among the other outstanding British movies that Arnold scored are *The Captain's Paradise*, *I Am a Camera*, *The Deep Blue Sea*, *The Key*, *Whistle Down the Wind*, *The Heroes of Telemark*, and *The Chalk Garden*. Although he remained in England during most of his career, Arnold also scored several Hollywood films, including such notable works as *Trapeze*, *The Inn of the Sixth Happiness*, *Solomon and Sheba*, *The Lion*, *The Thin Red Line*, and *Suddenly, Last Summer*. In the 1960s and 1970s, Arnold worked occasionally in television, scoring series and miniseries, most memorably *David Copperfield* (1969) and *Hard Times* (1977). He often orchestrated and conducted his movie scores, as well as some written by others. One of his last screen projects was not heard by the public. Arnold agreed to orchestrate the music that his friend William Walton wrote for the war film *Battle of Britain* (1969). Walton was old and ailing at the time and had difficulty meeting the deadlines for the extensive score so Arnold composed several passages himself. The studio was not pleased with the finished soundtrack and rejected it in favor of a new one by Ron Goodwin. Only music from the climactic air battle was retained. Not until decades later was the Walton-Arnold soundtrack recorded and it became clear how accomplished the score was and how much of it was written by Arnold. By 1980 he retired from the movies and concentrated on concert projects for the next twenty-five years, still active when he died at the age of eighty-four. During his lifetime Arnold received more honorary degrees and titles than perhaps any other British composer, including a knighthood in 1993.

Among the qualities of Arnold's music, both for the concert hall and the screen, is his lively sense of melody. His music may sometimes be very complex or subtle yet it is often tuneful as well. This means it can be enjoyed on many levels and, in terms of cinema, can serve all genres of film. Arnold scored some of the silliest comedies and the most piercing dramas of his era. One of his specialties was writing exotic or ethnic music for different locations, such as Scotland (*Tunes of Glory*), China (*The Inn of the Sixth Happiness*), Norway (*The Heroes of Telemark*), India (*Nine Hours to Rama*), the biblical Middle East (*Solomon and Sheba*), 1920s Berlin (*I Am a Camera*), and Africa (*The Roots of Heaven* and *The Lion*). His most famous movie, *The Bridge on the River Kwai*, is set in World War II Burma, but the characters are British, American, and Japanese. The most remembered music from the film, the whistling military "Colonel Bogey March," was written by Kenneth Alford back in 1914. Arnold's orchestration and variations of the catchy tune is expert, used in different ways throughout the movie. At one point it is heard in counterpoint to an original march theme by Arnold, the two marches together making a thrilling impact. The rest of the score is symphonic with various themes ranging from the exotic to the harsh. This being an antiwar film, the heroic theme is engaging without being blindly patriotic. The brass section is dissonant and unsettling even as the percussion instruments pound away with a victorious air. This same theme becomes poetic as it becomes the music that celebrates the bridge. Filmed in present-day Sri Lanka under terrible conditions, *The Bridge on the River Kwai* took much longer to film than anticipated. When the production team finished location shooting and editing, it was realized how outstanding the movie was and the studio wanted to open it before the approaching deadline for the Oscars. Producer Sam Spiegel approached several

Hollywood composers asking for a full score in two weeks. All of them balked but when director Lean suggested Arnold, the British composer agreed and legend has it that he wrote the score in ten days. It remains one of Arnold's most exciting pieces of music.

Another Lean film, the character comedy *Hobson's Choice*, also has a march for the main theme but this time it is zany and fun with laughing brass and a lively melody played on strings. There is also a flowing waltz theme that is more folk than Viennese and some playfully bizarre music for Hobson (Charles Laughton) when he is drunk and starts to hallucinate. A lesser known comedy, *The Belles of St. Trinian's*, was popular in Great Britain and spawned four sequels. This farce set in a girls' boarding school has a delightful score by Arnold. The school song is a delicious parody of a school alma mater, there is a scampering march with a dissonant air that sounds chaotic, a passage with sarcastic reeds, a cockeyed romantic track, and a giddy honky-tonk theme. The rural drama *Whistle Down the Wind* has a magical main theme that twinkles and flows as it conveys the countryside setting and the mystical aspects of this movie about some children who mistake a fugitive (Alan Bates) for Jesus Christ. There is a jaunty waltz passage that captures the innocence of the children and an interesting version of the Christmas carol "We Three Kings" that bounces along with optimism. There is also a touch of mysticism in the drama *The Chalk Garden* about a troubled teenager (Hayley Mills) being raised by her grandmother (Edith Evans). The theme for the girl is a six-note phrase that repeats in an insistent manner. The theme for her tutor, the mysterious Miss Madrigal (Deborah Kerr), is a lovely but disconcerting melody that floats up the scale as played on the harp, strings, and French horn. These two motifs reappear and crisscross just as pupil and teacher do in the story. Arnold's *The Chalk Garden* score is pure romanticism complete with an eye on the supernatural and the dangerous.

If moviegoers left *The Bridge on the River Kwai* humming the "Colonel Bogey March," the ditty running through their heads after seeing *The Inn of the Sixth Happiness* was the children's song "This Old Man" also known as "Nick Nack Paddy Whack." This is unfortunate because the score is one of Arnold's best. An English woman (Ingrid Bergman) becomes a missionary in China and her teaching the village children to sing the familiar march is one of the movie's highlights. Yet how much richer is the opening theme with its bold Asian flavor, its grand symphonic sound, and the surging crescendos and brass fanfares that convey the spirit of the tale. The majesty of the Chinese landscape is captured in certain passages that use Western instruments to create the ethnic sounds of the people. Other selections remain very Western and dramatize the action through the missionary's point of view. *The Inn of the Sixth Happiness* is on a grand scale yet remains very human; the music can be said to do likewise. It is Arnold at his most dramatic, a potent reminder of his screen music legacy. Biographies: *Philharmonic Concerto: The Life and Music of Sir Malcolm Arnold*, Piers Burton-Page (1994); *Malcolm Arnold: Rogue Genius*, Anthony Meredith and Paul Harris (2004); *Malcolm Arnold: A Composer of Real Music*, Raphael D. Thöne. Official website: www.malcolmarnold.co.uk.

Credits

(all films UK unless stated otherwise)

Year	Film	Director
1949	*Badger's Green*	John Irwin
1949	*The Forbidden Street* (aka *Britannia Mews*)	Jean Negulesco
1950	*Eye Witness* (aka *Your Witness*)	Robert Montgomery
1950	*Up for the Cup*	Jack Raymond
1951	*No Highway in the Sky*	Henry Koster
1951	*Home to Danger*	Terence Fisher
1952	*Murder on Monday* (aka *Home at Seven*)	Ralph Richardson
1952	*Dead on Course* (aka *Wings of Danger*)	Terence Fisher
1952	*Curtain Up*	Ralph Smart
1952	*Stolen Face*	Terence Fisher
1952	*Breaking the Sound Barrier*	David Lean
1952	*It Started in Paradise*	Compton Bennett
1952	*The Ringer*	Guy Hamilton
1952	*The Holly and the Ivy*	George More O'Ferrall
1953	*Four Sided Triangle*	Terence Fisher
1953	*The Captain's Paradise*	Anthony Kimmins
1953	*Break to Freedom* (aka *Albert R.N.*)	Lewis Gilbert
1954	*You Know What Sailors Are*	Ken Annakin
1954	*Devil on Horseback*	Cyril Frankel
1954	*Hobson's Choice*	David Lean
1954	*The Sleeping Tiger*	Joseph Losey
1954	*Twist of Fate* (aka *Beautiful Stranger*)	David Miller
1954	*The Belles of St. Trinian's*	Frank Launder
1954	*The Sea Shall Not Have Them*	Lewis Gilbert
1955	*A Prize of Gold*	Mark Robson
1955	*The Night My Number Came Up*	Leslie Norman
1955	*Marriage a la Mode* (aka *The Constant Husband*)	Sidney Gilliat
1955	*I Am a Camera*	Henry Cornelius
1955	*Value for Money*	Ken Annalin
1955	*The Deep Blue Sea*	Anatole Litvak
1955	*The Woman for Joe*	George More O'Ferrall
1956	*1984*	Michael Anderson
1956	*Wicked as They Come*	Ken Hughes
1956	*Trapeze*	Carol Reed (USA)
1956	*Port Afrique*	Rudolph Maté
1956	*Hell in Korea* (aka *A Hill in Korea*)	Julian Amyes
1956	*Tiger in the Smoke*	Roy Ward Baker
1956	*Man of Africa*	Cyril Frankel
1957	*Island in the Sun*	Robert Rossen
1957	*The Bridge on the River Kwai* (AA)	David Lean (UK/USA)
1957	*Blue Murder at St. Trinian's*	Frank Launder
1958	*Dunkirk*	Leslie Norman

Year	Film	Director
1958	The Key (aka Stella)	Carol Reed
1958	The Roots of Heaven	John Huston (USA)
1958	The Inn of the Sixth Happiness	Mark Robson (USA)
1959	The Boy and the Bridge	Kevin McClory
1959	Solomon and Sheba	King Vidor (USA)
1959	Suddenly, Last Summer	Joseph L. Mankiewicz (USA)
1960	The Angry Silence	Guy Green
1960	Tunes of Glory	Ronald Neame
1960	The Pure Hell of St. Trinian's	Frank Launder
1961	No Love for Johnnie	Ralph Thomas
1961	Whistle Down the Wind	Bryan Forbes
1961	Operation Snafu (aka On the Fiddle)	Cyril Frankel
1962	Lisa (aka The Inspector)	Philip Dunne (UK/USA)
1962	The Lion	Jack Cardiff (USA)
1963	Nine Hours to Rama (aka Nine Hours to Live)	Mark Robson (UK/USA)
1963	Tamahine	Philip Leacock
1964	The Chalk Garden	Ronald Neame (UK/USA)
1964	The Thin Red Line	Andrew Marton (USA)
1965	Gypsy Girl (aka Sky West and Crooked)	John Mills
1965	The Heroes of Telemark	Anthony Mann
1966	The Great St. Trinian's Train Robbery	Sidney Gilliat, Frank Launder
1967	Africa: Texas Style	Andrew Marton (UK/USA)
1969	The Reckoning	Jack Gold

AURIC, Georges (1899–1983) An experimental French composer for the theatre, opera, and ballet, he scored over one hundred feature films ranging from classic British comedies and French surreal masterpieces to some beloved Hollywood favorites.

Georges Abel Louis Auric was born in Lodeve, France, and studied piano as a boy, making his professional concert debut at the age of fourteen. Auric also started composing at a young age and some of his early works were performed by the National Society of Music when he was still a teenager. Auric later studied music at the Montpellier Conservatory, the Paris Conservatory, and the Schola Cantorum de Paris and became a protégé of composer Erik Satie and poet-dramatist Jean Cocteau. From the beginning, Auric's music was unconventional and by the 1920s he had a reputation as a composer of the avant-garde movement. He was classified as one of Les Six by the critics, a half dozen composers who were dazzling Paris with their original and innovative works. The six (Francis Poulenc, Darius Milhaud, Arthur Honegger, Louis Durey, Germaine Tailleferre, and Auric) rebelled against classical rules and introduced circus, music hall, and other forms of populist music into their compositions. Most of them later worked in films, though not to the extent that Auric did.

In 1921 Auric worked with Cocteau on a ballet; the two would later collaborate on a handful of notable movies. At this time Auric also wrote ballets for impresario Sergei Diaghilev, as well as operas, music for theatre productions, and orchestral pieces.

He made an auspicious film debut in 1931 when he scored René Clair's left-wing comedy *À nous la liberté*. The next year he wrote the music for Cocteau's surreal fantasy *The Blood of a Poet*. Both movies were controversial, much discussed, and brought attention to Auric as a screen composer. Over the next fifteen years he scored thirty French films, then in 1945 was asked to write the music for Gabriel Pascal's high-budget screen adaptation of George Bernard Shaw's *Caesar and Cleopatra*. The success of that film opened the doors to the British cinema and Auric went on to score some of the most beloved English movies of the postwar era, including *Hue and Cry*, *The Lavender Hill Mob*, *The Queen of Spades*, *Dead of Night*, *Passport to Pimlico*, *The Spider and the Fly*, *The Good Die Young*, and *Moulin Rouge*, the last introducing the haunting ballad "Where Is Your Heart" (English lyric by Bill Engvick). Auric's first movie for Hollywood was his most famous, the romantic comedy *Roman Holiday* in 1953, followed by such works as *Bonjour tristesse*, *The*

Innocents, and *Heaven Knows, Mr. Allison*. Yet most of Auric's screen career was in Europe, where he scored such memorable movies as Cocteau's *Beauty and the Beast, Les parents terribles, Orpheus*, and *The Eagle Has Two Heads*; Jules Dassin's *Rififi* and *He Who Must Die*; Max Ophüls's *Lola Montes*; Henri-Georges Clouzot's *The Spies* and *The Wages of Fear*; and many others. In the 1960s he scored some French television series but fewer and fewer movies as he concentrated on concert and ballet works, political causes, writing music criticism, and his duties as director of the Opera National de Paris and the Opera Comique. Auric continued to compose until his death at the age of eighty-three.

While most of Auric's screen music is not as experimental as what he wrote for the stage and concert hall, one hears traces of the avant-garde in some of his movie scores. His very first film assignment, the deliciously satirical *À nous la liberté*, hints at the rebel side of Auric. Although the movie is an early French talkie, there is little dialogue and the zany story is told through visuals and music. Characters break out in song, flowers sing, factory assembly lines move in time to circus tunes, pedestrians walk to the pace of ballet music, a windstorm sounds like a frenzied carousel, and slapstick scenes are scored like a parade. The score also includes silly marches, comic dance music, a lazy tango, and a merry foxtrot. *À nous la liberté* runs ninety-seven minutes which means there is nearly that much delightful music by Auric. The Cocteau films are far more serious and poetic and Auric's music is often entrancing. The surreal *Beauty and the Beast* is a period piece and the score is often symphonic in the French classical tradition. Horns and percussion announce the sweeping main theme, then strings and woodwinds add a magical quality to the piece. The beast's mystical castle with its famous human wall sconces has its own enchanting theme with sweet voices just as the beast's music features low brass that suggest both royalty and dread. Some events inside the castle utilize dissonant, experimental music that recalls a modern dance piece while other passages are more impressionistic. This is a groundbreaking movie and the score meets the challenge of supporting the dazzling images with equally beguiling music.

For the more conventional movie *Roman Holiday*, Auric came up with a pleasing Hollywood score. The main theme is a sparkling piece with wavering strings and boastful brass. The Italianate setting is established by a lively tarantella and the princess (Audrey Hepburn) is introduced with regal court music that could come from anywhere in Europe. Another American film, *Bonjour tristesse*, is less conventional and it has a more unorthodox score. The symphonic sound is tempered by some modern touches, as befits this comedy-drama about a complex father-daughter-mistress triangle. A rhythmic theme played by muted trumpet, bongos, and castanets is cheerful but a little off-kilter with a wry subtext. Even a violin and piano waltz seems to suggest a less-than-happy outcome. For the ghost tale *The Innocents*, Auric provides some very atmospheric music in a minor key. He avoids many of the suspense genre clichés and uses a chamber ensemble rather than a symphonic sound. Also, music is used sparingly throughout this tale of two children (Martin Stephens and Pamela Franklin) possessed by the spirits of two dead lovers. Sometimes a ticking clock or the sound of the wind suffices. But when the music does start, it is harsh and abrasive with echoing voices and strident strings. There is also a children's ditty titled "O Willow Waly" (lyric by Paul Dehn) sung by a solo voice that has the format of a rural folk song but is actually quite creepy. For the less subtle horror anthology film *Dead of Night*, Auric seems to be seduced by the genre and romanticizes the nervous strings and the sinister brass. It is a British movie, but there is more than a touch of Grand Guignol in the music.

Three European films scored by Auric deserve a closer look. The French-German biopic *Lola Montes* is a surreal look at the famous femme fatale (Martine Carol) as presented by director Ophüls as a circus attraction. Auric's music encompasses waltzes, polkas, marches, regal fanfares, and an enticing main theme that is as cozy as a sidewalk cafe tune. Ophüls's famous ever-moving camera is matched by a score that rarely stops. *Caesar and Cleopatra*, Shaw's very modern approach to history, was less lively on the screen than on the stage but Pascal's 1945 British film was visually and musically vibrant. The opening theme is romantic and mysterious in a European way with no hint of Egyptian music. The Romans march to a very English kind of music, the court is scored with British pomp and circumstance, and the natives dance to tunes not unlike a village green frolic. There is some Middle Eastern chanting, but for the most part this is a very Shavian piece in temperament and music. Arguably Auric's finest score is the resplendent one he wrote for *Moulin Rouge*, a British film directed by an American (John Huston) about a French artist, Henri de Toulouse-Lautrec (José Ferrer). While the simple but indelible "Song from Moulin Rouge" or "Where Is Your Heart" is most remembered, the whole score is a Parisian frolic with vigorous cancan music, melancholy laments, passionate love themes, rowdy music

hall tunes, a delicate minuet, and fiery dramatic passages for the scenes illustrating Lautrec's unhappy life. Here is a score that truly dances its way through a film, and one realizes that Auric, with his extensive background in modern ballet, was the ideal composer for the job. Biography: *Georges Auric*, Golea Antoine (1958).

Credits

(all films France unless stated otherwise)

Year	Film	Director
1931	À nous la liberté	René Clair
1932	The Blood of a Poet	Jean Cocteau
1934	Ladies Lake	Marc Allégret
1935	Mysteries of Paris	Félix Gandéra
1936	Under Western Eyes	Marc Allégret
1937	La danseuse rouge	Jean-Paul Paulin
1937	The Messenger	Raymond Rouleau
1937	The Meddler	Marc Allégret
1937	A Picnic on the Grass	Marcel Cravenne
1937	The Alibi	Pierre Chenal
1938	Storm	Marc Allégret
1938	Tamara la complaisante	Jean Delannoy, Félix Gandéra
1938	The Lafarge Case	Pierre Chenal
1938	Street without Joy	André Hugon
1938	The Curtain Rises	Marc Allégret
1938	Trois minutes—les saisons	unknown
1938	Les oranges de Jaffa	Alexander Alexeieff, Claire Parker
1939	Son oncle de Normandie	Jean Dréville
1939	Le corsaire	Marc Allégret
1940	De la ferraille a l'acier victorieux	unknown
1942	Opéra-musette	René Lefevre, Claude Renoir
1942	Gambling Hell	Jean Delannoy
1942	L'assassin a peur la nuit	Jean Delannoy
1942	Midnight in Paris	Georges Lacombe
1942	Little Nothings	Raymond Leboursier
1942	La belle aventure	Marc Allégret
1943	Love Eternal	Jean Delannoy
1944	Le bossu	Jean Delannoy
1945	Farandole	André Zwoboda
1945	François Villon	André Zwoboda
1945	Dead of Night	Alberto Cavalcanti, etc. (UK)
1945	La part de l'ombre	Jean Delannoy
1945	Caesar and Cleopatra	Gabriel Pascal (UK)
1946	Beauty and the Beast	Jean Cocteau, René Clement
1946	Pastoral Symphony	Jean Delannoy
1947	Hue and Cry	Charles Crichton (UK)
1947	Torrents	Serge de Poligny
1947	Les jeux sont faits	Jean Delannoy
1947	It Always Rains on Sunday	Robert Hamer (UK)
1948	La septieme porte	André Zwoboda
1948	Ruy Blas	Pierre Billon (France/Italy)
1948	Corridor of Mirrors	Terence Young (UK)
1948	The Eagle Has Two Heads	Jean Cocteau
1948	Aux yeux du souvenir	Jean Delannoy

Year	Film	Director
1948	*Another Shore*	Charles Crichton (UK)
1948	*Les parents terribles*	Jean Cocteau
1949	*Silent Dust*	Lance Comfort (UK)
1949	*The Queen of Spades*	Thorold Dickinson (UK)
1949	*Passport to Pimlico*	Henry Cornelius (UK)
1949	*Daughter of the Sands*	André Zwoboda (France/Morocco)
1949	*The Spider and the Fly*	Robert Hamer (UK)
1949	*Maya*	Raymond Bernard
1950	*Orpheus*	Jean Cocteau
1950	*Cage of Gold*	Basil Dearden (UK)
1951	*Dear Caroline*	Richard Potter
1951	*The Galloping Major*	Henry Cornelius (UK)
1951	*The Lovers of Bras-Mort*	Marcello Pagliero
1951	*The Lavender Hill Mob*	Charles Crichton (UK)
1952	*Leathernose*	Yves Allégret (France/Italy)
1952	*La P . . . respectueuse*	Charles Brabant, Marcello Pagliero
1952	*Moulin Rouge*	John Huston (UK)
1953	*The Titfield Thunderbolt*	Charles Crichton (UK)
1953	*The Wages of Fear*	Henri-Georges Clouzot (France/Italy)
1953	*Roman Holiday*	William Wyler (USA)
1953	*The Slave*	Yves Ciampi (Italy/France)
1954	*The Good Die Young*	Lewis Gilbert (UK)
1954	*The Detective*	Robert Hamer (UK)
1954	*Flesh and Desire*	Jean Josipovici (France/Italy)
1954	*The Divided Heart*	Charles Crichton (UK)
1955	*Abdullah's Harem* (aka *Abdulla the Great*)	Gregory Ratoff (UK/Egypt)
1955	*Rififi*	Jules Dassin
1955	*Chéri-Bibi*	Marcello Pagliero (Italy/France)
1955	*Nagana*	Hervé Bromberger
1955	*Cavalrymen*	Alex Joffé (Spain/France)
1955	*Lola Montes*	Max Ophüls (France/W. Germany)
1956	*Walk into Hell* (aka *Walk into Paradise*)	Lee Robinson, Marcello Pagliero (Australia)
1956	*Gervaise*	René Clément
1956	*Bold Adventure*	Gérard Philipe, Joris Ivens (France/E. Germany)
1956	*The Hunchback of Notre Dame*	Jean Delannoy (France/Italy)
1957	*Heaven Knows, Mr. Allison*	John Huston (USA)
1957	*The Crucible*	Raymond Rouleau (France/E. Germany)
1957	*He Who Must Die*	Jules Dassin (Italy/France)
1957	*The Story of Esther Costello*	David Miller (UK)
1957	*The Spies*	Henri-Georges Clouzot (Italy/France)
1958	*Bonjour tristesse*	Otto Preminger (USA)
1958	*The Night Heaven Fell*	Roger Vadim (France/Italy)
1958	*Dangerous Exile*	Brian Desmond Hurst (UK)
1958	*Next to No Time*	Henry Cornelius (UK)
1958	*Christine*	Pierre Gaspard-Huit (France/Italy)
1959	*The Journey*	Anatole Litvak (USA)
1959	*SOS Pacific*	Guy Green (UK)
1960	*Sergeant X of the Foreign Legion*	Bernard Borderie
1960	*Festival*	Wolfgang Liebeneiner (Italy/France/W. Germany)
1961	*Princess of Cleves*	Jean Delannoy (France/Italy)
1961	*Goodbye Again*	Anatole Litvak (France/USA)
1961	*Bridge to the Sun*	Etienne Périer (France/USA)
1961	*The Innocents* (aka *The Turn of the Screw*)	Jack Clayton (USA/UK)
1961	*Les croulants se portent bien*	Jean Boyer
1961	*Midnight Meeting*	Roger Leenhardt
1962	*The Burning Court*	Julien Duvivier (France/Italy/W. Germany)
1962	*Bells without Joy*	Charles Brabant (France/Italy)
1963	*The Mind Benders*	Basil Dearden (UK)

Year	Film	Director
1965	*Thomas the Impostor*	Georges Franju
1965	*La communale*	Jean L'Hôte
1966	*The Sleeping Sentinel*	Jean Dréville (Italy/France)
1966	*Danger Grows Wild* (aka *Poppies Are Also Flowers*)	Terence Young (France/Austria/USA)
1966	*La grande vadrouille*	Gérard Oury (France/UK)
1968	*Therese and Isabelle*	Radley Metzger (France/USA/Netherlands)
1969	*The Christmas Tree* (aka *When Wolves Cry*)	Terence Young (France/Italy)

AXT, William (1888–1959) A prolific but overlooked Hollywood composer who was active in silents as well as talkies, he scored nearly two hundred feature films during his two-decade career.

Born in New York City, Axt received a public school education in the Bronx before going on to study music at the National Conservatory of Music of America and privately in Berlin. He earned a doctor of musical arts from the University of Chicago, graduating in 1922. (He remains one of the very few screen composers to receive such a high degree and he often insisted that he be credited as Dr. William Axt in film credits. In Hollywood he was nicknamed "Dr. Billy.") Before getting involved in movies, Axt got experience as assistant conductor of the Hammerstein Grand Opera Company and as musical director for the house orchestra at the Capitol Theatre. He began working for MGM in 1919 scoring silent films, usually in collaboration with other studio composers. After contributing music to such popular silents as *The Mark of Zorro*, *The Prisoner of Zenda*, *Greed*, *He Who Gets Slapped*, *The Big Parade*, *The Navigator*, and *Ben-Hur*, Axt teamed with David Mendoza on Warner's *Don Juan*, the first feature movie to have a music and sound effects soundtrack synchronized to the film stock. The 1926 swashbuckler had no recorded dialogue, but in the Vitaphone process the sound was put on discs that matched each reel of the movie. *Don Juan* was successful enough that Warner Brothers continued to experiment with sound, and the next year they offered *The Jazz Singer*.

Axt went on to score (again usually with others) other notable silents, including *Faust*, *Annie Laurie*, *The Student Prince in Old Heidelberg*, *The Pagan*, *Marianne*, and the Greta Garbo version of *Camille* titled *Love*. (Axt soon became sole composer for just about all of Garbo's silent and talking films.) With the advent of all-talking pictures,

Axt was assigned to write music for more and more movies on his own. Because he was a fast and talented artist, he was given everything to score, from star vehicles to large-scale projects to B pictures. Between 1929 and 1939, he worked on over one hundred sound features, including such notable works as *Anna Christie*, *The Rogue Song*, *Romance*, *Susan Lenox*, *Private Lives*, *Mata Hari*, *When Ladies Meet*, *Dinner at Eight*, *The Thin Man*, *Bombshell*, *Manhattan Melodrama*, *David Copperfield*, *Forsaking All Others*, *Suzy*, *Libeled Lady*, *Thoroughbreds Don't Cry*, and *The Last of Mrs. Cheyney* (which he had scored years earlier as a silent). Axt was never nominated for an Oscar and was little known outside of Hollywood circles, but "Dr. Billy" was highly respected by fellow composers and was considered by the studios as one of the most dependable of artists. Axt retired from the movies in 1939 and bought a ranch where he raised horses and cattle for twenty years before he died at the age of seventy. MGM often used some of Axt's stock music in later films, a common studio practice at the time, and some of his music can even be heard in *Gone with the Wind* (1939).

While it is best to concentrate on Axt's solo credits to best appreciate his music, one cannot ignore the importance and the impact of *Don Juan* which he scored with Mendoza. Since Axt was the senior member of the team and the most musically astute, one might assume that much of the score is his. What need not be assumed is the effect this movie had at the time. The score was lavishly symphonic and, as recorded by the New York Philharmonic, it was impressive on many levels. Not only was the sound quality quite good but also the way the action and the music/sound effects were coordinated was thrilling to audiences. The score itself has many different themes, all of them original for the film, which was also unique for the time. The main theme is expectedly Spanish and very tuneful while an engaging habanera passage is used as the leitmotif for the Castilian hero (John Barrymore). A sultry dance passage featuring lively flutes is used a few times throughout the movie when Juan mixes with high society. The most memorable part of both the movie and the score is the climactic duel between Juan and the evil Count Donati (Montague Love). The synchronized sword fighting sounds were a thrillingly new experience and the vigorous musical accompaniment matched the visuals with rowdy glee.

Of Axt's many silent film scores, the only one he composed totally on his own was *He Who Gets Slapped*, a daring Lon Chaney vehicle based on an allegorical Russian play. This bizarre tale, about an inventor (Chaney) who becomes an abused clown in the circus, was given a surreal look by the MGM artists and Axt's score is often modern and experimental. The circus themes are garish and dissonant, while the dramatic scenes are scored with a sympathetic but eerie subtext. The score for the 1936 version of *David Copperfield* has as many moods and temperaments as the Dickens tale itself. Several of the major characters have their own themes, ranging from the sentimental to the comic. The squawking music for the philosophical Mr. Micawber (W. C. Fields) captures the comedy and tragedy of the character and seems to come right from Fields's screen persona. *Mata Hari* has one of

Axt's most interesting scores for a Garbo movie. The exotic music that accompanies her sultry dance seems to drip with lust, the violins gliding down the scale in a seductive manner. There is also brusk military music, romantic airs for the love scenes, and dark dramatic passages for the tragic ending.

Perhaps *The Thin Man* has the best score Axt wrote for a comedy. The main theme is frivolous yet still elegant, much like the married detectives (Myrna Loy and William Powell). The suspense takes a backseat to the comedy in the film and the music seems to realize this, even the dramatic moments scored wryly. *Libeled Lady*, another stylish comedy with Powell, has a swing score but with some quietly droll passages. On the other hand, there is little humor in the Powell drama *Manhattan Melodrama*. Axt is remarkably restrained in his scoring for this character study about two friends (Powell and Clark Gable) on opposite sides of the law. The movie begins with sprightly charm but the gravity of the situation creeps up on the audience and the final scene is quite disturbing. The score also moves from light fare to a subdued but deadly serious finale. None of these scores received much recognition then or even now because Axt's music is taken for granted. It serves its purpose and doesn't draw attention to itself. Yet the many popular movies he scored certainly benefited from the unnoticed Dr. Billy.

Credits

(all films USA unless stated otherwise)

Year	Film	Director
1920	The Mark of Zorro	Fred Niblo
1922	The Prisoner of Zenda	Rex Ingram
1923	Richard the Lion-Hearted	Chester Whithey
1924	The Sea Hawk	Frank Lloyd
1924	The Navigator	Donald Crisp, Buster Keaton
1924	He Who Gets Slapped	Victor Sjöström
1924	Greed	Erich von Stroheim
1925	The Big Parade	King Vidor, George W. Hill
1925	Ben-Hur	Fred Niblo, etc.
1926	Mare Nostrum	Rex Ingram
1926	La Boheme	King Vidor
1926	Don Juan	Alan Crosland
1926	Bardelys the Magnificent	King Vidor
1926	Faust	F. W. Murnau (Germany)
1926	The Fire Brigade	William Nigh
1927	Slide, Kelly, Slide	Edward Sedgwick
1927	The Student Prince in Old Heidelberg	Ernst Lubitsch, John M. Stahl
1927	Love	Edmund Goulding, John Gilbert

Year	Film	Director
1927	The Trail of '98	Clarence Brown
1928	The Cossacks	George W. Hill, Clarence Brown
1928	White Shadows in the South Seas	W. S. Van Dyke, Robert J. Flaherty
1928	The Mysterious Lady	Fred Niblo
1928	Our Dancing Daughters	Harry Beaumont
1928	Excess Baggage	James Cruze
1928	While the City Sleeps	Jack Conway
1928	The Wind	Victor Sjöström
1928	The Viking	Roy William Neill
1928	Show People	King Vidor
1928	Alias Jimmy Valentine	Jack Conway
1928	The Masks of the Devil	Victor Sjöström
1928	West of Zanzibar	Tod Browning
1928	A Lady of Chance	Robert Z. Leonard
1928	A Woman of Affairs	Clarence Brown
1929	Bellamy Trial	Monta Bell
1929	Wild Orchids	Sidney Franklin
1929	Desert Nights	William Nigh
1929	The Duke Steps Out	James Cruze
1929	Tide of Empire	Allan Dwan
1929	The Pagan	W. S. Van Dyke
1929	Where East Is East	Tod Browning
1929	The Last of Mrs. Cheyney	Sidney Franklin
1929	Thunder	William Nigh
1929	The Single Standard	John S. Robertson
1929	Madame X	Lionel Barrymore
1929	Marianne	Robert Z. Leonard
1929	Our Modern Maidens	Jack Conway
1929	Speedway	Harry Beaumont
1929	The Unholy Night	Lionel Barrymore
1929	The Kiss	Jacques Feyder
1929	Untamed	Jack Conway
1929	It's a Great Life	Sam Wood
1929	Navy Blues	Clarence Brown
1929	Devil-May-Care	Sidney Franklin
1929	Their Own Desire	E. Mason Hopper
1930	The Bishop Murder Case	David Burton, Nick Grinde
1930	Chasing Rainbows	Charles Reisner
1930	Anna Christie	Clarence Brown
1930	The Woman Racket	Albert H. Kelley, etc.
1930	The Ship from Shanghai	Charles Brabin
1930	Free and Easy	Edward Sedgwick
1930	Redemption	Fred Niblo, Lionel Barrymore
1930	The Rogue Song	Lionel Barrymore, Hal Roach
1930	The Unholy Three	Jack Conway
1930	Call of the Flesh	Charles Brabin
1930	Romance	Clarence Brown
1930	Doughboys	Edward Sedgwick
1930	Madam Satan	Cecil B. DeMille
1930	A Lady's Morals	Sidney Franklin
1931	Inspiration	Clarence Brown
1931	Susan Lenox	Robert Z. Leonard
1931	Private Lives	Sidney Franklin
1931	Mata Hari	George Fitzmaurice
1932	Polly of the Circus	Alfred Small
1932	The Wet Parade	Victor Fleming
1932	Are You Listening?	Harry Beaumont

Year	Film	Director
1932	*As You Desire Me*	George Fitzmaurice
1932	*The Washington Masquerade*	Charles Brabin
1932	*Blondie of the Follies*	Edmund Goulding
1932	*The Mask of Fu Manchu*	Charles Brabin, Charles Vidor
1932	*Payment Deferred*	Lothar Mendes
1932	*Prosperity*	Sam Wood
1932	*Whistling in the Dark*	Elliott Nugent, Charles Resiner
1933	*The Secret of Madame Blanche*	Charles Brabin
1933	*Clear All Wires*	George W. Hill
1933	*Gabriel Over the White House*	Gregory La Cava
1933	*Hell Below*	Jack Conway
1933	*Looking Forward*	Clarence Brown
1933	*Reunion in Vienna*	Sidney Franklin
1933	*Nuisance*	Jack Conway
1933	*When Ladies Meet*	Harry Beaumont, Robert Z. Leonard
1933	*Midnight Mary*	William A. Wellman
1933	*Storm at Daybreak*	Richard Boleslawski
1933	*Dinner at Eight*	George Cukor
1933	*Beauty for Sale*	Richard Boleslawski
1933	*Broadway to Hollywood*	Willard Mack, Jules White
1933	*Penthouse*	W. S. Van Dyke
1933	*Bombshell*	Victor Fleming
1933	*Eskimo*	W. S. Van Dyke
1933	*Should Ladies Behave*	Harry Beaumont
1934	*Fugitive Lovers*	Richard Boleslawski
1934	*You Can't Buy Everything*	Charles Reisner
1934	*This Side of Heaven*	William K. Howard
1934	*The Mystery of Mr. X*	Edgar Selwyn, Richard Boleslawski
1934	*Lazy River*	George B. Seitz
1934	*Men in White*	Richard Boleslawski
1934	*Manhattan Melodrama*	W. S. Van Dyke, George Cukor
1934	*Sadie McKee*	Clarence Brown
1934	*Hollywood Party*	Charles Reisner, etc.
1934	*The Thin Man*	W. S. Van Dyke
1934	*Operator 13*	Richard Boleslawski
1934	*Stamboul Quest*	Sam Wood
1934	*Paris Interlude*	Edwin L. Marin
1934	*The Girl from Missouri*	Jack Conway, Sam Wood
1934	*A Straight Is the Way*	Paul Sloane
1934	*Hide-Out*	W. S. Van Dyke
1934	*Death on the Diamond*	Edward Sedgwick
1934	*A Wicked Woman*	Charles Brabin
1934	*Forsaking All Others*	W. S. Van Dyke
1935	*David Copperfield*	George Cukor
1935	*The Murder Man*	Tim Whelan
1935	*Woman Wanted*	George B. Seitz
1935	*Pursuit*	Edwin L. Marin
1935	*O'Shaughnessy's Boy*	Richard Boleslawski
1935	*It's in the Air*	Charles Reisner
1935	*Rendezvous*	William K. Howard, Sam Wood
1935	*The Perfect Gentleman*	Tim Whelan
1935	*Whipsaw*	Sam Wood
1935	*Last of the Pagans*	Richard Thorpe
1936	*The Garden Murder Case*	Edwin L. Marin
1936	*Three Live Ghosts*	H. Bruce Humberstone
1936	*Tough Guy*	Chester M. Franklin
1936	*Three Godfathers*	Richard Boleslawski

Year	Film	Director
1936	*Petticoat Fever*	George Fitzmaurice
1936	*The Unguarded Hour*	Sam Wood
1936	*The 3 Wise Guys*	George B. Seitz
1936	*We Went to College*	Joseph Santley
1936	*Suzy*	George Fitzmaurice
1936	*Piccadilly Jim*	Robert Z. Leonard
1936	*Old Hutch*	J. Walter Ruben
1936	*Libeled Lady*	Jack Conway
1936	*All American Chump*	Edwin L. Marin
1936	*Tarzan Escapes*	Richard Thorpe, etc.
1936	*Mad Holiday*	George B. Seitz
1937	*Under Cover of Night*	George B. Seitz
1937	*The Last of Mrs. Cheyney*	Richard Boleslawski, Dorothy Arzner
1937	*Espionage*	Kurt Neumann
1937	*Song of the City*	Errol Taggart
1937	*Parnell*	John M. Stahl
1937	*Between Two Women*	George B. Seitz
1937	*London By Night*	Wilhelm Thiele
1937	*Big City*	Frank Borzage, George B. Seitz
1937	*Thoroughbreds Don't Cry*	Alfred E. Green
1937	*Beg, Borrow or Steal*	Wilhelm Thiele
1937	*Bad Man of Brimstone*	J. Walter Ruben
1938	*Everybody Sing*	Edwin L. Marin
1938	*The First Hundred Years*	Richard Thorpe
1938	*Yellow Jack*	George B. Seitz
1938	*Woman against Woman*	Robert B. Sinclair
1938	*Fast Company*	Edward Buzzell
1938	*Rich Man, Poor Girl*	Reinhold Schünzel
1938	*Three Loves Has Nancy*	Richard Thorpe
1938	*Listen, Darling*	Edwin L. Marin
1938	*Spring Madness*	S. Sylvan Simon
1938	*The Girl Downstairs*	Norman Taurog
1939	*Stand Up and Fight*	W. S. Van Dyke
1939	*Within the Law*	Gustav Machaty
1939	*Sergeant Madden*	Josef von Sternberg
1939	*The Kid from Texas*	S. Sylvan Simon
1939	*Tell No Tales*	Leslie Fenton
1939	*Miracles for Sale*	Tod Browning
1940	*Untamed*	George Archibald

B

BACALOV, Luis (b. 1933) A busy screen composer for the Italian cinema for over fifty years, he has scored 120 feature films in various genres but was most often hired for westerns and crime thrillers.

Luis Bacalov was born in Buenos Aires, Argentina, a descendant of Bulgarians who immigrated to South America at the turn of the twentieth century. He took piano lessons as a boy and made his professional concert debut while he was still young. When he started composing his own pieces, Bacalov incorporated the music of Latin American countries into his work even as he utilized his training in classical music. After working as a conductor and composer for radio and television in Colombia, Bacalov went to Italy, where he got involved in the movies. Although he continued to write chamber pieces and solo music for violin, piano, and other instruments, Bacalov started to concentrate on film scores in the early 1960s. His first movie to receive international acclaim was Pier Paolo Pasolini's *The Gospel according to St. Matthew* in 1964, for which he received an Oscar nomination. Soon he was scoring French, German, and other European films. Bacalov began writing music for "spaghetti westerns" in 1966 with *Django* and got a reputation for scoring crime dramas and action movies as well. He moved into English-language films with *The Man Called Noon* in 1973 and first worked for Hollywood with *Polish Wedding* in 1998. Among his other American or British works are *The Love Letter*, *It Had to Be You*, *Assassination Tango*, *The Dust Factory*, *Sea of Dreams*, *Secret of the Andes*, and *Quiet Flows the Dawn*. Yet most of Bacalov's many films are from continental Europe and include such notable titles as *A Bullet for the General*, *Seduction*, *The Grand Duel*, *In the Name of the Father*, *City of Women*, *Entre Nous*, *The Border*, *His Name Was King*, and *Il postino* (*The Postman*), winning an Oscar for the last. He has scored two dozen Italian TV movies and miniseries as well as many short films. Since the arrival of the new century, Bacalov has composed less for the screen and more for the concert hall, writing many acclaimed choral and orchestral works. He also maintains an active conducting career and has recently served as artistic director for the Orchestra della Magna Grecia in Taranto, Italy.

As one might expect, the Latin American influence can sometimes be found in Bacalov's screen scores, particularly the tango. *The Love Letter* has a delectable tango theme played on harp, mandolin, and accordion. Although the romantic comedy is set in a New England town, the gentle tango feels more than appropriate for this low-key romance. The music in *Assassination Tango*, a thriller partially set in Argentina, is more ethnic and includes a sultry tango theme that is rapid and passionate. One can also hear a Latin flavor in Bacalov's music for the western *Django*. An electric guitar is used but it sometimes sounds more like a classical guitar with its intricate finger work. The main theme is rhythmic and percussive, sung on the soundtrack by Rocky Roberts and an echoing chorus as if it were a wailing ballad from the 1950s. Other passages include a lovely Spanish serenade, slow honky-tonk piano and violin saloon music, an atmospheric suspense theme featuring a bass guitar, and a melancholy waltz. *Django* spawned many sequels with little in common except the character name. Bacalov scored some of them and his original music was used in others. Director Quentin Tarantino's 2012 version, titled *Django Unchained*, used the theme from the original as well as two songs Bacalov wrote for *Summertime Killer* (1972). Tarantino must be a fan of Bacalov's music, for he used some of it in the bloody action movie *Kill Bill Vol. 1* (2003). The theme came from the spaghetti western *The Grand Duel* thirty years earlier. With its howling wind, lonesome harmonica, and rhythmic guitar, the main theme for *The Grand Duel* is mesmerizing. The music manages to be romantic and sinister at the same time. Other passages are just as engaging. There is a flute section in which the notes turn harsh, an energetic hootenanny theme played on fiddle and drums, and a majestic passage with wordless voices howling happily. Another western, *His Name Was King*, has a more rocking score. The title song comes close to the Motown sound. This music too was picked up by Tarantino for *Django Unchained*.

Bacalov only got to work once with two of Italy's top directors, Federico Fellini and Pasolini. For the latter's *The Gospel according to St. Matthew*, he wrote a rhythmic "Gloria," chanted much like an African tribal or Caribbean work with call-and-response, zesty humming, and vibrant drumming. The unusual biblical movie also has some dissonant passages played on rumbling brass, stirring choral hymns, and delicate solos on the flute and other piercing instruments. Fellini's fantasy *City of Women* also uses call and response in its very intriguing score. Gregorian chant mixes with New Wave, choral sections sound like a drug trip, the percussion and electric instruments have a space age sound, and some passages employ cool jazz. It is perhaps Bacalov's most bizarre score, but then Fellini had that kind of impact on his composers. In a more conventional mode is the very popular *Il postino* (*The Postman*). This tender character drama is scored with warm and nostalgic music. There is basically only one theme but so many variations are used throughout the movie that it remains fresh. As played on an accordion, the theme is romantic; heard later on reeds, it captures the Italian locale gently and firmly. The tempo also varies, the theme sometimes tearfully delicate, other times moving ahead in a chipper manner. The score for *Il postino* is Bacalov's most well

known, partially because it is so accessible but also because it is so captivating.

A little more edgy, but still accessible, is the score for *Seduction*, an Italian film by Bacalov's most frequent director-collaborator, Fernando Di Leo. (The two men worked on ten movies together.) There is a good deal of jazz in the score, but the music is also very romantic at times, played either by a large ensemble or as a piano and string duet. As the title suggests, this movie is about passion, and the musical variety used to express that emotion is very impressive. One of Bacalov's most recent screen works, the Mexican-American idyllic fantasy *Sea of Dreams*, has one of his best scores. A sterling example of "magical realism," the movie is about an island village and how the sea around it shapes its destiny. There is an otherworldly quality to the music, which is sometimes played on a primitive flute that rises above a full orchestra. The main theme is a flowing and reflective four-note phrase in which different instruments have solo sections. There is also a spirited polka heard on an accordion, a sparkling theme played on carefree guitars, a cheerful bolero performed by a dance band, and a brooding passage with grumbling strings and a wailing voice to convey the cruel aspects of the sea. Listening to this music, which is so far removed from the westerns Bacalov scored, one is taken with the eclectic nature of his work. Unfortunately Bacalov has only rarely gotten the opportunity to score outstanding movies and could not break away enough from his thriller-western niche, so his film career, though prolific, is not a true testament to his musical talent.

Credits

(all films Italy unless stated otherwise)

Year	Film	Director
1954	These Phantoms	Eduardo De Filippo
1960	La banda del buco	Mario Amendola
1962	Those Two in the Legion	Lucio Fuici
1963	The Empty Canvas	Damiano Damiani (Italy/France)
1963	Wine, Whiskey and Salt Water	Mario Amendola
1964	Donde tú estés	Germán Lorente (Spain/Italy/France)
1964	The Gospel according to St. Matthew (AAN)	Pier Paolo Pasolini (Italy/France)
1964	Hard Time for Princes	Ettore Scola (Italy/France)
1965	Let's Talk about Men	Lina Wertmüller

Year	Film	Director
1965	*OSS 77—Operazione fior di loto*	Bruno Paolinelli (France/Italy)
1965	*Kiss the Other Sheik*	Luciano Salce, etc. (Italy/France)
1966	*A Maiden for a Prince*	Pasquale Festa Campanile (Italy/France)
1966	*Django* (aka *Jango*)	Sergio Cobucci (Italy/Spain)
1966	*A Question of Honour*	Luigi Zampa (Italy/France)
1966	*La strega in amore* (aka *The Witch*)	Damiano Damiani
1966	*A Bullet for the General*	Damiano Damiani
1967	*A Rose for Everyone*	Franco Rossi
1967	*We Still Kill the Old Way*	Elio Petri
1967	*How to Win a Billion . . . and Get Away with It*	Gianni Puccini
1967	*For Love . . . For Magic*	Duccio Tessari
1967	*Sugar Colt*	Franco Giraldi (Spain/Italy)
1967	*Hallelujah for Django*	Maurizio Lucidi
1967	*Ghosts, Italian Style*	Renato Castellani
1968	*Catch as Catch Can*	Franco Indovina
1968	*All Out*	Umberto Lenzi (Italy/Spain)
1968	*The Vatican Affair*	Emilio Miraglia (Italy/W. Germany)
1968	*The Black Sheep*	Luciani Salce
1968	*Big Baby Doll*	Franco Giraldi
1968	*The Protagonists*	Marcello Fondato
1969	*Appointment in Beirut*	Nino Zanchin (Italy/Spain/W. Germany/Argentina)
1969	*Death on High Mountain*	Fernando Cerchio (Spain/Italy)
1969	*In the Name of the Father*	Ruggero Deodato
1969	*The Price of Power* (aka *The Price of Honor*)	Tonino Valerii (Italy/Spain)
1969	*L'amica*	Alberto Lattuada
1970	*Lonely Hearts*	Franco Giraldi
1970	*Chapaqua's Gold*	Giancarlo Romitelli (Italy/France)
1971	*La supertestimone*	Franco Giraldi
1971	*La grande scrofa nera*	Filippo Ottoni
1971	*The Designated Victim*	Maurizio Lucidi
1971	*His Name Was King*	Giancarlo Romitelli
1971	*Roma bene*	Carlo Lizzani (Italy/France/W. Germany)
1972	*Great Treasure Hunt*	Tonino Ricci (Italy/Spain)
1972	*Caliber 9*	Fernando Di Leo
1972	*Beati i ricchi*	Salvatore Samperi
1972	*The Grand Duel*	Giancarlo Santi (Italy/W. Germany/France)
1973	*The Police Serve the Citizens?*	Romolo Guerrieri (France/Italy)
1973	*The Boss*	Fernando Di Leo
1973	*Halleluja to Vera Cruz*	Stelvio Massi
1973	*In Love with Sex* (aka *The Models*)	Claude Pierson (France/Canada/Italy)
1973	*The Man Called Noon*	Peter Collinson (Spain/Italy/UK)
1973	*Stateline Motel*	Maurizio Lucidi
1973	*Seduction*	Fernando Di Leo
1973	*The Red Rose*	Franco Giraldi
1974	*I Fix America and Return*	Nanni Loy
1974	*Shoot First, Die Later*	Fernando Di Leo (Italy/France)
1974	*Loaded Gun* (aka *Stick 'Em Up, Darlings*)	Fernando Di Leo
1975	*My Mother's Friend*	Mauro Ivaldi
1975	*Kidnap Syndicate*	Fernando Di Leo
1975	*One Man against the Organization*	Sergio Grieco (Italy/France/Spain)
1976	*Copita da improvviso benessere*	Franco Giraldi
1976	*Street People*	Maurizio Lucidi, Guglielmo Garroni
1976	*I prosseneti*	Brunello Rondi
1976	*Nick the Sting*	Fernando Di Leo
1976	*Rulers of the City* (aka *Mr. Scarface*)	Fernando Di Leo (Italy/W. Germany)
1976	*The Last Round*	Stelvio Massi

Year	Film	Director
1977	Grazie tante—Arrivederci	Mauro Ivaldi
1977	Blood and Diamonds	Fernando Di Leo
1979	Improvviso	Edith Bruck
1980	Madness	Fernando Di Leo
1980	City of Women	Federico Fellini (Italy/France)
1980	The Girl from Millelire Street	Gianni Serra
1981	Habibi, amor mío	Luis Gómez Valdivieso (Spain/Italy)
1981	The Game Is Over	Pier Giuseppe Murgia
1981	Os saltimbancos trapalhoes	J. B. Tanko (Brazil)
1983	Entre nous	Diane Kurys (France)
1983	Le jeune marié	Bernard Stora (France)
1983	The Art of Love	Walerian Borowczyk (France/Italy)
1984	The Judge	Philippe Lefebvre (France)
1984	A Strange Passion	Jean-Pierre Dougnac (Canada/Italy/France)
1985	Le transfuge	Philippe Lefebvre (Belgium/France)
1985	Inganni	Luigi Faccini
1987	Maniac Killer	Andrea Bianchi (France)
1988	The Mask	Fiorella Infascelli
1988	Donna d'ombra	Luigi Faccini
1988	The Legendary Life of Ernest Hemingway	José María Sánchez
1989	Esmeralda Bay	Jesús Franco (Spain/France)
1989	Burro	José María Sánchez (Italy/Spain)
1991	Cruel Fable	Roberto Leoni
1991	Starry Night	Luigi Faccini
1991	A Simple Story	Emidio Greco
1994	Il postino: The Postman (AA; BAFTA)	Michael Radford (Italy/France/Belgium)
1996	The Border	Franco Giraldi
1996	Ilona Arrives with the Rain	Sergio Cabrera (Colombia/Italy/Spain)
1996	Laura: The Rebel Years	Rosalia Polizzi (Italy/Argentina)
1996	Stella's Favor	Giancarlo Scarchilli
1997	The Truce	Francesco Rosi (Italy/France/Germany)
1997	The Debt	Nicolás Buenaventura, Manuel José Álvarez (France/Colombia/Cuba)
1998	Polish Wedding	Theresa Connelly (USA)
1998	Frontera sur	Gerardo Herrero (Spain/Argentina/France/Germany)
1998	B. Monkey	Michael Radford (UK/USA)
1999	Dirty Linen	Mario Monicelli
1999	Milonga	Emidio Greco
1999	The Love Letter	Peter Chan (USA)
1999	Secret of the Andes	Alejandro Azzano (USA/Argentina)
1999	Deceit	Claudia Florio
1999	The Children of the Century	Diane Kurys (France)
2000	It Had to Be You	Steven Feder (USA)
2000	Woman on Top	Fina Torres (USA)
2000	The Sky Is Falling	Andrea and Antonio Frazzi
2001	Check and Mate	Claudia Florio
2002	The Council of Egypt	Emidio Greco (Italy/France/Hungary)
2002	Assassination Tango	Robert Duvall (USA/Argentina)
2004	The Dust Factory	Eric Small (USA)
2006	Sea of Dreams (aka The Bride of the Sea)	José Pepe Bojórquez (Mexico/USA)
2006	Quiet Flows the Don	Sergey Bondarchuk (UK)
2007	Hotel Meina	Carlo Lizzani (Italy/France/Serbia)
2007	L'uomo privato	Emidio Greco
2008	La rabbia	Louis Nero
2010	News from the Excavations	Emidio Greco
2011	Karol	Orlando Corradi
2012	Hidden Moon	José Pepe Bojórquez (Mexico/USA)

BACHARACH, Burt (b. 1928) A very popular song-writer with dozens of Top 40 hit songs, the esteemed conductor-arranger has also composed some memorable soundtracks for the screen.

Burt Freeman Bacharach was born in Kansas City, Missouri, the son of a journalist who had a nationally syndicated column, and moved with his family to New York City when he was four. Bacharach studied piano and cello but was more interested in a football career. As a teenager, he discovered jazz, visiting jazz clubs in Manhattan and starting his own student band with himself as conductor and pianist. Bacharach studied music at McGill University in Montreal, at Manhattan's Mannes School of Music and the New School for Social Research, and at the Music Academy of the West in Santa Barbara, California. During this time he also started writing and arranging his own music. While serving in the army as a musician, he met singer Vic Damone and worked as his arranger and accompanist after he was discharged. Soon Bacharach was in great demand, working with such artists as Steve Lawrence, Polly Bergen, Joel Grey, Perry Como, Marlene Dietrich, the Drifters, and the Ames Brothers. In 1957 he teamed up with lyricist Hal David and they had their first of many hit songs together, "The Story of My Life." With David and others, Bacharach wrote such popular songs as "Make It Easy on Yourself," "Walk On By," "I Say a Little Prayer," "Do You Know the Way to San Jose," "This Girl's in Love with You," "One Less Bell to Answer," "What the World Needs Now," "Wives and Lovers," "A House Is Not a Home," and "(There's) Always Something There to Remind Me." Of all the artists who had hit records with his songs, perhaps Dionne Warwick is the one most identified with Bacharach.

He first got involved in the movies when he composed the main theme for the sci-fi film *The Blob* in 1958, but he received little recognition until he and David wrote the title theme song for *The Man Who Shot Liberty Valance* (1962). It was the first in a line of many hits songs written for movies scored by others, among them "Alfie," "Send Me No Flowers," "The April Fools," "Close to You," "Love in a Goldfish Bowl," "Promise Her Anything," and "Made in Paris." Bacharach's first soundtrack credit was when he wrote the score for the Austrian film *Forever My Love* as well as the title song with David. He went on to score the comedies *What's New Pussycat* (which also had a hit title song), *Casino Royale* (with the popular

"The Look of Love"), *Butch Cassidy and the Sundance Kid* (with the song hit "Raindrops Keep Fallin' on My Head"), *Arthur* (with the popular theme song "Best That You Can Do"), *Night Shift* (with several songs including "The Love Too Good to Last"), *Arthur 2: On the Rocks*, *Love Hurts*, and *Isn't She Great*. For the misguided movie musical *Lost Horizon*, Bacharach and David wrote a full musical score but only "The World Is a Circle" enjoyed any success. It is estimated that a Bacharach song can be heard in over one hundred movies and even more television shows. Bacharach is also a very successful record producer, often utilizes his conducting and piano skills in concert, and has long been active in television scoring and conducting variety shows and special events such as the Academy Awards. With David he wrote the score for the long-running Broadway musical *Promises Promises* (1968) and there have been a handful of theatre revues featuring Bacharach's songs.

Although Bacharach is considered primarily a song-writer, his soundtrack scores are very accomplished. As with his songs, the Bacharach style is distinguished by his clever use of jazz harmonies, the way his chord progressions surprise and delight, the unusual manner in which he changes meter midway through a song, his numerous occasions for modulation, and his syncopated rhythms. He favors brass instruments, even in love songs, and sometimes will choose an unlikely instrument, such as the flugelhorn. The title theme for *What's New Pussycat* is pure 1960s pop, coming early in that decade and helping define the new sound. Embracing jazz while avoiding rock, the theme is as sarcastic in its tone as in its music. One passage in the score is played on kazoos and harpsichord, another mixes various brass instruments in a cockeyed manner, while one jazzy theme uses a frenzied electric organ. The lovely "Here I Am" theme played by piano and strings repeats a three-note phrase splendidly and there is some seductive music that even in 1965 was a pop spoof. The Bacharach trademark trumpets open the popular title theme for spy spoof *Casino Royale*. This rhythmic delight has plenty of Latin touches yet feels more jazzy than south of the border. The way the strings glide in as if to comment on the main melody is masterful and playful. "The Look of Love," as sung and as an instrumental, provides the romantic theme for a comedy that has no tender moments. The rest of the score is mostly a mock–James Bond soundtrack, musically ribbing the new genre. The score is more romantic in

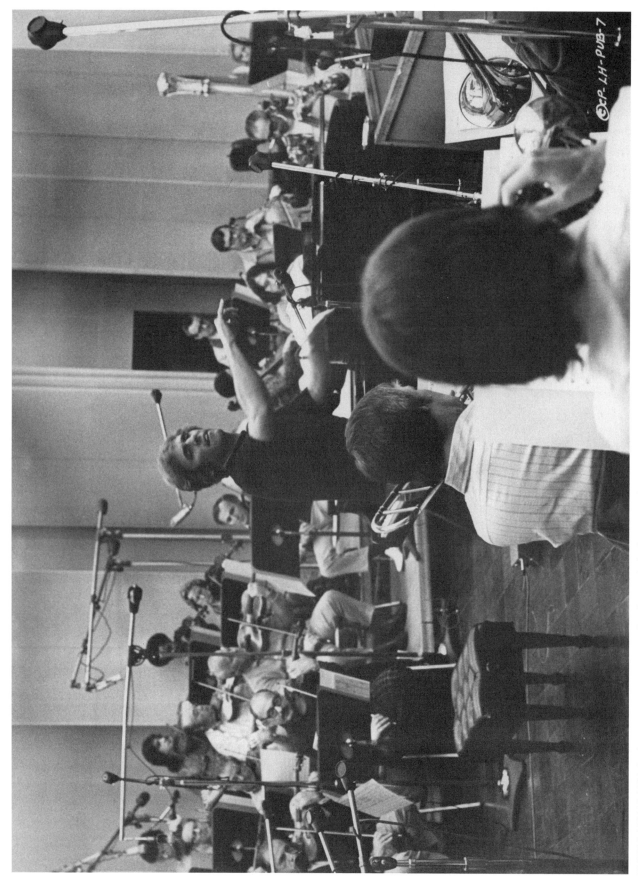

BURT BACHARACH. In the 1960s, everyone was familiar with the brassy Bacharach sound for pop songs and movie soundtracks. Here he is in 1973 conducting the soundtrack recording for *Lost Horizon*, one of the few times the Bacharach sound was not right for the subject matter. *Columbia Pictures / Photofest © Columbia Pictures*

Arthur, a comedy that is not a spoof. Aside from the engaging song "The Best That You Can Do" (better known as "Caught between the Moon and New York City"), the score is filled with a variety of pop themes, the piano usually in the forefront. Flutes play against the keyboard in one bubbly theme and some beautifully restrained trumpets and strings are heard in the romantic theme. The "Money" theme has a rock beat but the instruments are used in a jazz manner. For the sequel *Arthur 2: On the Rocks*, Bacharach came up with a smooth theme, "The Best of Time," which is cool jazz with a pop sensibility.

The comic antiwestern *Butch Cassidy and the Sundance Kid* gave Bacharach the opportunity to break away from contemporary comedies but his score is still very much in the pop style. A scat-singing chorus performs the jazzy theme "South American Getaway" as if we were again in Manhattan. The popular "Raindrops Keep Fallin' on My Head" pastiches a rustic, carefree cowboy song but the rhythms are too hip. Yet all this anachronistic music works in the movie because the tone of the story and characters is glib. Such an incongruous combination does not work in *Lost Horizon*, a large-scale musical that seems to misfire at every turn. If the mystical tale of Shangri-La needs music, it certainly isn't pop. The musical numbers are not only inappropriate, they seem to ambush every scene and character. When some of the music is heard instrumentally between the songs, the effect is little better. This score might suffice for a spoof of the James Hilton novel but in any other format if fails to satisfy. Perhaps the Bacharach sound is so distinctive and so late twentieth century that it refuses to travel anywhere else. Yet music does not have to be of all time to be top notch and Bacharach's music is certainly that. Autobiography: *Anyone Who Had a Heart: My Life and Music* (2013); biography: *Bacharach: Maestro! The Life of a Pop Genius*, Michael Brocken (2003). Unofficial website: bacharachonline.com.

Credits

(all films USA unless stated otherwise; * for Best Song)

Year	Film	Director
1962	*Forever My Love*	Ernst Marischka (Austria)
1965	*What's New Pussycat* (AAN*)	Clive Donner, Richard Talmadge (France/USA)
1967	*Casino Royale* (AAN*)	Val Guest, Ken Hughes, etc. (UK/USA)
1969	*Butch Cassidy and the Sundance Kid* (AA; AA*; GG; GGN*; BAFTA)	George Roy Hill
1973	*Lost Horizon*	Charles Jarrott
1979	*I Love You, I Love You Not*	Armenia Balducci (Italy)
1981	*Arthur* (AA*; GG*; BAFTA-N)	Steve Gordon
1982	*Night Shift*	Ron Howard
1988	*Arthur 2: On the Rocks*	Bud Yorkin
1990	*Love Hurts*	Bud Yorkin
2000	*Isn't She Great*	Andrew Bergman (USA/UK/Germany/Japan)

BAKALEINIKOFF, Mischa (1890–1960) A prodigious Russian-born music director in Hollywood who supervised and/or conducted the music for over 250 films, he also wrote scores for sixty features, most of them B movies at Columbia Pictures.

Born in Moscow, Russia, Mikhail Romanovich Bakaleinikoff came from a large musical family that included brothers active in the concert world, the flautist-composer-conductor Nikolai and violinist-composer-conductor Vladimir. The three brothers were studying at the Moscow Conservatory when the Russian Revolution broke out; they immigrated to America in 1926. All three found work in Hollywood performing in movie palace orchestras, Mischa playing both cello and double bass viol. With the arrival of sound, Bakaleinikoff worked as a musician in the Columbia orchestra, eventually conducting and supervising the music as well. During the 1930s, he contributed original music to a dozen talkies, but it was usually in collaboration with others and he was rarely credited. By the 1940s Bakaleinikoff was busy as a conductor and musical director at Columbia, working on dozens of features every year. Not until the 1950s did he score a significant number of films solo, but these were almost all B pictures: westerns, sci-fi flicks, crime dramas, and comic series such as Blondie and the Three Stooges. Neither the studio nor Hollywood considered Bakaleinikoff a viable composer and relied on his conducting and musical direction skills. Yet his composition credits include some memorable movies, including a few camp classics. Among his notable scores are those for *Apache Territory, Hellcats of the Navy, It Came from Beneath the Sea, Battle of Rogue River, Earth vs. the Flying Saucers, Comanche Station, 20 Million Miles to Earth, The Hard Man, Screaming Mimi, The Tijuana Story, Domino Kid*, and *The Lineup*. As was customary at Columbia, Bakaleinikoff's music was reused in other films made by the studio. It is estimated that themes from his scores can be heard in over one hundred Columbia movies that Bakaleinikoff did not score. He was still working and as busy as ever when he died at the age of sixty-nine.

It is thought by some that Bakaleinikoff was on the brink of moving into first-class projects as a composer when he died; others feel that Columbia was more than satisfied with his conducting and musical direction and would never have given him anything but B movies. Yet the studio used and reused his stock music so often that maybe it was just a matter of time before his composition skills would be recognized. Listening to Bakaleinikoff's work today, one finds much to admire. His westerns, for example, often have commendable scores. *Apache Territory* opens with a quiet guitar tune played under Rory Calhoun's opening narration, then the main theme heard over the credits is a rambunctious march with tribal drums and lively brass and strings. Later there is a pleasing harmonica solo, a homespun domestic theme played on strings, and a rousing passage for the climactic battle heard on kettle drums and brass fanfares. *Comanche Station* also uses a good deal of tribal music and there is an effective suspense passage in which percussion and brass alternate in an effective manner. The domestic theme here is simple but evocative, the lyrical beckoning of the trumpets and the strings flowing easily. *The Phantom Stagecoach* has a catchy title song sung by Vaughn Monroe; it clips and clops along with a touch of the exotic to convey a bit of mystery. There is an exciting and varied score for *The Stranger Wore a Gun*, including robust marches, spirited

chase music, merry saloon tunes, and some atmospheric scoring for the natural grandeur of the Arizona territory. *The Stranger Wore a Gun*, with its all-star cast and classier production values, was a step above a B movie, an opportunity Bakaleinikoff was given too infrequently.

Most 1950s sci-fi flicks are fodder for camp viewing today and Bakaleinikoff's efforts during that decade are no exception. A giant octopus attacks ships and San Francisco in *It Came from Beneath the Sea* and the harsh horns and furious strings add to the fun. The invasion in *Earth vs. the Flying Saucers* is symphonic with a whirling sound effect for the alien spacecraft. The military rebuttal is scored with trumpeting fanfares and explosive chords. An egg from Venus hatches on our planet in *20 Million Miles to Earth* and the Venetian monster that is released has much in common with the misunderstood King Kong. Bakaleinikoff gives the creature a musical theme that is less strident than that for most movie monsters. Just as stop-action animator Ray Harryhausen gives the Venetian human emotions, Bakaleinikoff's music is not so otherworldly and actually romantic at times. Of course the mistreated creature ends up attacking everyone, but again the music is dramatic without getting too weird. In fact, the scoring for the American spaceship that brings the egg from Venus sounds more alien with its sustained electronic chords and whizzing sound effects. While the special effects in these 1950s sci-fi movies are often clumsy by today's standards, the scoring of the creatures becomes all the more important. It may not be subtle music but it knows what it has to do.

Perhaps the best scripts and productions Bakaleinikoff got to score were the police dramas, some in the film noir mode. *Miami Exposé* is a mobster tale with some startling scenes, including a bomb exploding on a plane in flight and a murder at a country club pool. The music is filled with shouting brass and keeps its energy as the plot keeps racing forward. Lee J. Cobb is the tough police detective and he seems to bark right along with the music. The plot of the grim *Cell 2455 Death Row* is told by a juvenile delinquent murderer (William Campbell) and his narration pulls no punches. The score is similarly forthright, far from subtle with its blunt chords and squealing trumpets. *The Crooked Web*, an engrossing tale about trying to recover gold that was buried in Germany during World War II, is less violent but just as gripping. The opening theme is a bold anthem that borders on the patriotic. The music then restrains itself for much of the thriller, even during the twist ending, which is scored quietly. Arguably the best of these noirish movies is the taut melodrama *The Lineup* about the police investigation of a San Francisco mobster with drug connections. The movie starts with a murder and a chase, the music jumping into full throttle. Then the music for the credits is a grand march, modern and full of consequence. Music is used sparingly throughout the film, often restrained brass and jazzy riffs. The final car chase is exceptionally potent and the music moves into high gear with rapidly descending scales, ominous bass chords, and restless trumpets. Had Bakaleinikoff been handed more projects like this, his rank as a screen composer might have risen. Instead he was a reliable and expert musical director in a factory churning out music for movies for the public demand.

Credits

(all films USA)

Year	Film	Director
1930	Men without Law	Louis King
1932	McKenna of the Mounted	D. Ross Lederman
1932	White Eagle	Lambert Hillyer
1932	Forbidden Trail	Lambert Hillyer
1933	Thrill Hunter	George B. Seitz
1935	The New Adventures of Tarzan	Edward A. Kull, Wilbur McGaugh
1943	Crime Doctor	Michael Gordon
1944	Sergeant Mike	Henry Levin
1946	Throw a Saddle on a Star	Ray Nazarro
1947	Blondie's Big Moment	Abby Berlin
1947	The Lone Wolf in Mexico	D. Ross Lederman
1947	Sport of Kings	Robert Gordon
1947	Smoky River Serenade	Derwin Abrahams
1947	Blondie in the Dough	Abby Berlin
1948	The Strawberry Roan	John English
1949	The Big Sombrero	Frank McDonald
1949	Manhattan Angel	Arthur Dreifuss
1950	The Palomino	Ray Nazarro
1950	Beware of Blondie	Edward Bernds
1950	Hoedown	Ray Nazarro
1953	Serpent of the Nile	William Castle
1953	Valley of Head Hunters	William Berke
1953	The Stranger Wore a Gun	André De Toth
1953	Mission Over Korea	Fred F. Sears
1953	Gun Fury	Raoul Walsh
1953	Prisoners of the Casbah	Richard L. Bare
1954	Battle of Rogue River	William Castle
1955	New Orleans Uncensored	William Castle
1955	Cell 2455 Death Row	Fred F. Sears
1955	It Came from Beneath the Sea	Robert Gordon
1955	The Crooked Web	Nathan Juran
1956	Over-Exposed	Lewis Seiler
1956	Earth vs. the Flying Saucers	Fred F. Sears
1956	Miami Exposé	Fred F. Sears
1956	The White Squaw	Ray Nazarro
1956	Reprisal!	George Sherman
1956	7th Cavalry	Joseph H. Lewis
1956	Rumble on the Docks	Fred F. Sears
1957	Zombies of Mora Tau	Edward L. Cahn
1957	The Phantom Stagecoach	Ray Nazarro
1957	The Guns of Fort Petticoat	George Marshall

Year	Film	Director
1957	*Hellcats of the Navy*	Nathan Juran
1957	*20 Million Miles to Earth*	Nathan Juran
1957	*The Giant Claw*	Fred F. Sears
1957	*The 27th Day*	William Asher
1957	*No Time to Be Young*	David Lowell Rich
1957	*Domino Kid*	Ray Nazarro
1957	*The Tijuana Story*	László Kardos
1957	*The Hard Man*	George Sherman
1958	*Return to Warbow*	Ray Nazarro
1958	*The World Was His Jury*	Fred F. Sears
1958	*Going Steady*	Fred F. Sears
1958	*The Lineup*	Don Siegel
1958	*Screaming Mimi*	Gerd Oswald
1958	*The Case against Brooklyn*	Paul Wendkos
1958	*Apache Territory*	Ray Nazarro
1959	*Have Rocket—Will Travel*	David Lowell Rich
1959	*The Flying Fontaines*	George Sherman
1960	*Comanche Station*	Budd Boetticher
1960	*The Enemy General*	George Sherman

BAKER, Buddy (1918–2002) A staff composer and musical director for Disney movies, television, and theme parks for twenty-six years, he scored two dozen feature films for the studio, most of them live-action features, and several animated shorts.

Norman Dale Baker was born in Springfield, Missouri, and took trumpet and piano lessons as a boy. In high school and in Boy Scouts he organized and led his own band. Baker studied music at his home state's Southwest Baptist College, then in 1938 went to Los Angeles where he found work as a trumpet player and an arranger for radio programs, eventually becoming the musical director for Bob Hope's radio show. Baker also wrote arrangements for Big Bands such as those led by Jack Teagarden, Harry James, and Bob Crosby, coming up with a major hit with Stan Kenton's recording of "And Her Tears Flowed Like Wine." When the big orchestras started to wane in the 1950s, Baker taught music at Los Angeles City College. His first movie work was scoring the film noir melodrama *Wicked Woman* for United Artists in 1953. Baker joined the Disney Company in 1955 when he assisted composer George Bruns on the music for television's *Davy Crockett*. By 1960 he was co-composer for the adventure feature *Toby Tyler, or Ten Weeks with a Circus*. His first solo Disney score was for the musical *Summer Magic* three years later. Baker was eventually named a staff composer though not for animated features. Instead he scored live-action comedies, such as *The Misadventures of Merlin Jones, The Gnome-Mobile, The Monkey's Uncle, Charley and the Angel, The Apple Dumpling Gang, The Devil and Max Devlin,* and *The Shaggy D.A.*, and heartwarming animal dramas, as with *Rascal, A Tiger Walks, The Bears and I, King of the Grizzlies,* and *Napoleon and Samantha,* winning an Oscar nomination for the last. The only animated features Baker scored for Disney were *The Fox and the Hound* and the anthology film *The Many Adventures of Winnie the Pooh*.

Baker also wrote the music for such memorable animated Disney shorts as *I'm No Fool as a Pedestrian* (1956), *I'm No Fool in Water* (1957), *Donald in Mathmagic Land* (1959), *The Litterbug* (1961), *Aquamania* (1961), and several Winnie the Pooh cartoons. For Disney television, he wrote music for *The Mickey Mouse Club, Disneyland, Zorro,* and *Walt Disney's Wonderful World of Color*. Baker contributed music to Disney attractions at the 1964–1965 New York World's Fair, Disneyland, Walt Disney World, and Tokyo Disneyland; in 1968 he was named the musical director for EPCOT. Among the attractions he scored at the various parks are the World of Motion, American Adventure, If You Had Wings, Haunted Mansion, Carousel of Progress, Wonders of China, Kitchen Kaberet, Universe of Energy, Impressions de France, Journey to the Center of the Earth, and Listen to the Land. One of his most recognized pieces of music is the loud fanfare that accompanies the Walt Disney Home Video logo at the start of the company's videos and later DVDs. When Baker left Disney in 1983, he was the last staff composer left in Hollywood. In 1987 he scored the animated feature *The Puppetoon Movie* for Image International and the war film *Forgotten Heroes* before retiring in 1990, although he returned to Disney one last time in 1999 to conduct the music for *The Many Adventures of Winnie the Pooh* heard at various theme parks. Baker returned to education in the 1980s, teaching at the USC Thornton School of Music until his death two decades later at the age of eighty-four.

Baker's music is characterized by its tuneful quality, sense of fun, and its ability to stick in the ear without assaulting it. One has to hear the Haunted Mansion's "Grim Grinning Ghosts" only once and it stays in your memory. The repetitive rousing theme for *The Swamp Fox* was heard for only eight episodes on *Disneyland* in 1959 yet it is remarkable how many viewers still remember it. The great irony of Baker's screen career is that, while the studio was putting out some first-class animated features, he scored second- and third-rate live-action movies. Many of them were popular in their day and a few are still favorites on video but, in truth, most of these family movies have dated badly and are samples of the Disney Company at its lowest point. It is all the more ironic that the music in them is usually estimable. *The Misadventures of Merlin Jones* and its sequel *The Monkey's Uncle* both have bubblegum, pop title songs by Disney's favorite 1960s songwriters, Richard M. and Robert B. Sherman. The lyrics are painfully dated but the music is delightfully retro today. Less period and more durable is the soundtrack music by Baker. Each of the wacky inventions created by student scientist Merlin (Tommy Kirk) is scored with cockeyed comic tunes, his mental communications with a cat is a pseudoexotic Middle Eastern passage, and the antics of his pet monkey is pure silent screen farcical music. This is the pattern for most of the 1960s and 1970s Disney comedies: a bouncy, insipid title song followed by a skillfully clever score by Baker. *The Apple Dumpling Gang* and its sequel have delicious mock-western music, satirizing musical clichés with rapid banjo music, risible harmonica tracks, and

slapstick saloon tunes. The fantasy *The Gnome-Mobile*, about human encounters with gnomes in California's redwood forests, has a lush orchestrated sound that is sometimes symphonic but always lightweight. There is also some vivacious dance music for the little Irish creatures that is quite catchy.

The live-action animal movies tend to be less fun musically but sometimes richer and more engaging. A pleasing folk theme played on a harmonica and guitar is used to introduce the nostalgic *Rascal* about a boy (Bill Mumy) and his pet raccoon. The entire score is warm and nostalgic, capturing rural life in Wisconsin during a summer long ago. *The Bears and I* has an atmospheric woodwind theme that conveys the rustic but demanding terrain of the Northwest wilderness. *King of Grizzlies* has a more varied score, the music moving from a lazy harmonica passage to a wry theme featuring bassoons and flutes for the bears themselves. The title characters in *Napoleon and Samantha* are a young boy (Johnny Whitaker) and girl (Jodie Foster) who bring an aging circus lion called Major into the Oregon mountains to be safe from humans. It is easy to see why the Academy singled out this Disney adventure movie for its score. The lyrical passages are lilting and flowing, the action scenes are scored with exciting symphonic music, and the tender moments in the score are melodic as well as emotional. Baker's last score for Disney is perhaps his finest. He finally got to score a first-class animated feature with *The Fox and Hound*, and he came up with a backwoods sound that could be comic, romantic, or fierce. The movie's opening credits begin without music, only the wind and other sounds of nature setting the mood. Then these forest sounds turn into sustained chords with a mysterious air, eventually breaking into vivacious chase music. The friendship of the title animals is scored with potent sincerity, sometimes with a simple theme played by piano and woodwinds, other times with the playfulness of a circus march on merry strings. The harmonica passage in which the domesticated fox is set loose in the wilderness is superb character scoring. There are only five songs (by various songwriters) in *The Fox and the Hound*, all but one very brief. It is Baker's soundtrack that carries the film, and this score ranks high in the Disney animated canon. What Baker might have written were he given more animated features is a pleasing thought. As it was, he provided some splendid music for movies that rarely deserved it.

Credits

(all films USA)

Year	Film	Director
1953	*Wicked Woman*	Russell Rouse
1960	*Toby Tyler, or Ten Weeks with a Circus*	Charles Barton
1960	*The Hound That Thought He Was a Raccoon*	Tom McGowan
1963	*Summer Magic*	James Neilson
1964	*The Misadventures of Merlin Jones*	Robert Stevenson
1964	*A Tiger Walks*	Norman Tokar
1965	*The Monkey's Uncle*	Robert Stevenson
1967	*The Gnome-Mobile*	Robert Stevenson
1969	*Rascal*	Norman Tokar
1969	*Guns in the Heather* (aka *Spy-Busters*)	Robert Butler
1970	*King of the Grizzlies*	Ron Kelly
1971	*The Million Dollar Duck*	Vincent McEveety
1972	*Napoleon and Samantha* (AAN)	Bernard McEveety
1972	*Run, Cougar, Run* (aka *Seeta, the Mountain Lion*)	Jerome Courtland
1973	*Charley and the Angel*	Vincent McEveety
1973	*Superdad*	Vincent McEveety
1974	*The Bears and I*	Bernard McEveety
1975	*The Apple Dumpling Gang*	Norman Tokar
1976	*No Deposit, No Return*	Norman Tokar
1976	*Treasure of Matecumbe*	Vincent McEveety
1976	*The Shaggy D.A.*	Robert Stevenson
1975	*The Best of Walt Disney's True-Life Adventures*	James Algar
1977	*The Many Adventures of Winnie the Pooh*	John Lounsbery, Wolfgang Reitherman
1978	*Hot Lead and Cold Feet*	Robert Butler
1979	*The Apple Dumpling Gang Rides Again* (aka *Trail's End*)	Vincent McEveety
1981	*The Devil and Max Devlin*	Steven Hilliard Stern
1981	*The Fox and the Hound*	Ted Berman, etc.
1987	*The Puppetoon Movie*	Arnold Leibovit
1990	*Forgotten Heroes*	Jack Marino

BAND, Richard (Howard) (b. 1953) A skillful movie composer from a family of independent filmmakers, he is most known for his horror and sci-fi scores from mostly low-budget schlock favorites.

Richard Band was born in Los Angeles, the son of independent film producer-director Albert Band, and grew up living in Sweden, France, and Italy where his father worked on movies. Band taught himself to play the guitar and as a teenager worked professionally in Rome. He formed his own band and toured Italy before returning to the States in 1970 at the age of seventeen. After studying music privately and at Immaculate Heart College, he worked as an assistant director on independent films directed by his elder brother, Charles Band, eventually producing a dozen movies himself. Band began writing music for films when he and composer Joel Goldsmith (son of Hollywood composer Jerry Goldsmith) cowrote the score for the sci-fi movie *Laserblast* in 1978. He scored by himself a dozen sci-fi and horror movies before finding recognition with his music for the cult horror classic *Re-Animator* in 1985. Band was busy scoring independent feature films in the 1980s and 1990s, including several directed by his brother Charles and produced by his father. Among the more notable titles are *The Day Time Ended*, *The Caller*, *Bride of Re-Animator*, *Prehysteria*, *The Pit and the Pendulum*, *From Beyond*, and *Shatterbrain*, as well as many direct-to-video movies, such as *Puppet Master* (1989) and *Josh Kirby: Time Warrior* (1995) and their many sequels. Since the turn of the new century, he has concentrated more on television, scoring series, including *Stargate SG–1*, *Masters of Horror*, and *Walker, Texas Ranger*, and some TV movies. Band has also composed music for film shorts, documentaries, and many video games. He is the cofounder of the Big Score and Gratis Music Library, which collects and preserves screen music from around the world.

While there is little variety in the type of movies Band scores, he often finds unique ways to score these often-laughable schlock films that usually mix comic and grotesque horror with preposterous science fiction elements. The score for *Re-Animator* is a clever mixture of classical forms and a very modern beat. Strings and brass echo each other in the main theme, a rhythmic piece with some avant-garde violin work and fluttering flutes. There is an arresting theme that soothes like a lullaby even as it foreshadows doom. The suspense music is sometimes an homage to Bernard Herrmann's *Psycho* score, yet so much is fresh and original that it is little wonder that *Re-Animator* made Band famous. *From Beyond* did not find the same kind of success until years after it was released, but the score is equally accomplished. The main theme is a stately processional that wavers and floats as it slowly moves forward. Radiant chimes, descending strings, and rumbling brass all merge as sound effects punctuate the piece. The score also includes some haunting vocal airs, a sweeping waltz with a Celtic flavor, and a delicate passage played on piano with electronic chords and strings surrounding it. The highlight of Band's score for *The Pit and the Pendulum* is a Gregorian chant that changes into a sorrowful dirge featuring a lonesome trumpet. The score is filled with vigorous religious music (to convey the presence of the Spanish Inquisition in the plot), including a passage of Carl Orff–like vocal counterpoint that is thrilling.

The theme for *Puppet Master*, first in a series of television movies and then on-screen, is a melodic and oddly comic piece of carnival music. It has a classical flavor yet is filled with electronic embellishments and variations on its waltz tempo, so it feels new rather than pastiche. African tribal music is spoofed in the music for *Shrunken Heads*. There is a cartoonish march theme with growling vocals and sound effects that is delightfully droll. The main theme for *The Day Time Ended* lampoons both Richard Strauss and John Williams with snippets of *Thus Spoke Zarathustra*, *Jaws*, and *Star Wars* worked into the music. The score also has some lush romantic music, especially a passage in which a repetitive piano provides the bass line and strings carry the melody. There is a lot of classy scoring in the cheesy *Shatterbrain* (known widely also as *The Resurrected*) but the fine symphonic passages are overwhelmed by the sound effects. More satisfying is the score for *The Alchemist* with its elegant main theme that waltzes along, gaining a fuller sound and some menace as it develops its simple melody. A fantasy movie that is not like all of these gory horror films is the family-friendly *Dragonworld* about a Scottish lad (Courtland Mead) who raises money for his poor family by using his pet dragon as a tourist attraction. It is a modest, unpretentious film with an outstanding score. The main theme is a lilting Celtic air played on pipes and strings that makes you feel like you are flying over the Scottish landscape on the back of a dragon. There is also zestful dance music, a sorrowful dirge played on bagpipes, and an amusing theme for the friendly dragon itself. *Dragonworld* is no classic, but it feels like one when compared to the usual fare Band has scored. Has ever a superior composer scored so many inferior movies? And done it with such relish? Official website: www.richardbandmusic.com.

Credits

(all films USA unless stated otherwise)

Year	Film	Director
1978	*Laserblast*	Michael Rae
1979	*The Day Time Ended* (aka *Earth's Final Fury*)	John "Bud" Cardos
1980	*Dr. Heckyl and Mr. Hype*	Charles B. Griffith
1981	*Lunch Wagon*	Ernest Pintoff
1981	*The Best of Sex and Violence* (aka *Screams of Flesh and Blood*)	Ken Dixon
1982	*Parasite*	Charles Band
1982	*Time Walker*	Tom Kennedy
1983	*The House on Sorority Row*	Mark Rosman

Year	Film	Director
1983	Metalstorm: The Destruction of Jared-Syn	Charles Band
1983	The Alchemist	Charles Band
1984	Night Shadows (aka Mutant)	John "Bud" Cardos, Mark Rosman
1984	Ragewar (aka The Dungeonmaster)	David Allen, etc.
1985	Ghost Warrior	J. Larry Carroll
1985	Ghoulies (aka Beasties)	Luca Bercovici
1985	Zone Troopers	Danny Bilson
1985	Re-Animator	Stuart Gordon
1986	Troll	John Carl Buechler (USA/Italy)
1986	TerrorVision	Ted Nicolaou
1986	From Beyond	Stuart Gordon
1987	The Caller	Arthur Allan Seidelman
1988	Prison	Renny Harlin
1989	Arena	Peter Manoogian (Italy/USA)
1989	Bride of Re-Animator	Brian Yuzna
1990	Shadowzone	J. S. Cardone
1991	The Pit and the Pendulum (aka The Inquisitor)	Stuart Gordon
1991	The Arrival (aka The Unwelcomed)	David Schmoeller
1991	Shatterbrain (aka The Resurrected)	Dan O'Bannon (USA/Canada)
1992	Doctor Mordrid	Albert and Charles Band
1993	Prehysteria!	Albert and Charles Band
1994	Shrunken Heads	Richard Elfman
1994	Dragonworld	Ted Nicolaou
1996	Zarkorr! The Invader	Michael Deak, Aaron Osborne
1996	Robo Warriors (aka Robot Jox 3)	Ian Barry
1996	Head of the Family	Charles Band
1997	Hideous!	Charles Band
2007	Nympha	Ivan Zuccon (Italy)
2011	Evil Bong 3-D: The Wrath of Bong	Charles Band
2011	Eyes Only	John C. Todd
2012	Shiver	Julian Richards
2012	Puppet Master X: Axis Rising	Charles Band
2013	Ooga Booga	Charles Band
2013	Unlucky Charms	Charles Band
2013	Throwback	Travis Bain (Australia)

BARRY, John (1933–2011) A versatile and prolific British film composer, arranger, and conductor who found wide success on both sides of the Atlantic, Barry was one of the most admired film artists in movies during a career of nearly fifty years. His ninety-five feature films range from action movies to lush historical pieces to contemporary dramas. Although Barry is most remembered for his eleven James Bond movies, his body of work is very eclectic and served as inspiration for a group of young screen composers in the 1980s and 1990s.

He was born John Barry Pendergast in the city of York, England, the son of a classical pianist mother and an Irish immigrant father from Cork who worked as a movie projectionist during the silent era. The young Barry grew up with the movies, his father running a chain of cinemas in northern England before World War II. He taught himself to play the trumpet through a correspondence course, then, after serving in the army, started his own jazz band, the John Barry Seven. For the group he wrote and arranged original music, and some of their songs found favor, recorded by Johnny Smith, the Ventures, and others. In 1959, the BBC commissioned Barry to write a theme song for its series *Juke Box Jury*, and the number "Hit and Miss" climbed the charts. This led to his first film, *Beat Girl* (1960), for which he composed, arranged, and conducted a pop-sounding score. (The movie was retitled *Wild for Kicks* in America.)

Barry's prodigious screen career took flight in 1962 when Eon Productions hired him for the first James Bond film, *Dr. No*. Monty Norman wrote the main musical

JOHN BARRY. This rather gloomy but artistic pose suggests Barry's determined and dedicated approach to film music. The prolific composer scored eleven James Bond movies and his themes are heard in all of the other installments. Barry stated that *Goldfinger* (1964) was his favorite Bond score. *PBS / Photofest © PBS*

theme for the action movie but the producers were not happy with it. Barry rearranged the theme and composed the rest of the music in the film, giving the score a distinctive jazz sound that was as refreshing as it was catchy. The "James Bond Theme" would be heard in all the subsequent Bond films, becoming one of the most recognized musical signatures in the history of the movies. Perhaps Barry's most accomplished Bond score was for *Goldfinger* in 1964, both the title song and the soundtrack becoming best sellers. Barry was quickly in demand for his new sound, but soon he started branching out into other types of music for very different kinds of movies. *Zulu* in 1964 was his first epic-scale movie and the first time his more expansive, even bombastic, sound was heard. This was the sound that attracted Hollywood, and from 1965 on Barry was busy composing for both American and British movies. In addition to the James Bond films, Barry's outstanding screen hits include *Born Free*, *The Lion in Winter*, *Midnight Cowboy*, *Body Heat*, *Out of Africa*, *A View to a Kill*, and *Dances with Wolves*. Yet some of his best work was heard in such modest or unsuccessful movies as *The Knack*, *The Chase*, *King Rat*, *The Wrong Box*, *Walkabout*, *The Black Hole*, *King Kong*, *The Cotton Club*, *The Day of the Locust*, *Raise the Titanic*, *They Might Be Giants*, *The Deep*, *Somewhere in Time*, *Chaplin*, *Enigma*, *The Scarlet Letter*, and *Mary, Queen of Scots*.

It is difficult to pinpoint the Barry musical style. He favors a rich string sound in some scores, emphasizes a bold brass quality in others, and often experiments with unique sounds. He was among the earliest to utilize a synthesizer in a movie score with *On Her Majesty's Secret Service*. For *The Lion in Winter*, he mixed Gregorian chant with a harsh Stravinsky-like sound. The music in *Born Free* and *Somewhere in Time* is warm and sentimental, while the scores for *Midnight Cowboy* and *The Black Hole* are quirky and chilly. The music in *Mary, Queen of Scots* is a faithful homage to the Renaissance sound, while *The Cotton Club* nicely pastiches the Harlem jazz flavor. The lush orchestrations in *Dances with Wolves* and *Out of Africa* are contrasted by the simpler scores, such as the sultry saxophone in *Body Heat* or the silly bassoon in *The Knack*. For *King Rat*, a solo oboe and French horn are featured in a melancholy wartime score that includes hymns, a rumbling march, and a recurring theme played on a cimbalom. Barry usually arranged and conducted his screen scores and later in his career was kept busy performing concert versions

of his most popular soundtrack music. He also composed theme songs for such British television series as *Drumbeat*, *Vendetta*, *The Newcomers*, and *The Persuaders!*, as well as such acclaimed TV movies as *The Glass Menagerie* (1973), *Love Among the Ruins* (1975), *Eleanor and Franklin* (1977), and *The War Between the Tates* (1977). He was less successful with his stage musicals. *Billy* was a West End hit in 1974, but his two other London musicals, *Passion Flower Hotel* (1965) and *Brighton Rock* (2004), failed to run, and his two American musicals, *Lolita, My Love* (1971) and *The Little Prince and the Aviator* (1981), both closed before reaching Broadway.

After having heard the "James Bond Theme" in so many movies over the decades, one tends to forget how unique and refreshing Barry's 007 sound was when it debuted in 1962 with *Dr. No*. Two years later the *Goldfinger* soundtrack recording was a surprise success, staying on the charts for over a year; this is in addition to the very popular single in which Shirley Bassey sang the title song (lyric by Anthony Newley and Leslie Bricusse), as she did on the soundtrack. The instrumental version of the song is just as thrilling with its shouting brass competing with kettle drums and low woodwinds. When slowed down the same music is romantic and seductive, when given a jazz treatment it is mysterious and dangerous, and later played on electric guitar it is pure 1960 pop-rock. Another prominent theme in *Goldfinger* is an up-tempo jazz piece in which a saxophone leads the way then horns and strings follow. Strings glide back and forth during the suspense scenes and a rhythmic, jazzy march is heard during the assault on Fort Knox. Barry's other outstanding jazz score is the one he wrote for the modern film noir drama *Body Heat*. Kathleen Turner and William Hurt play a pair of strangers who connect sexually then get involved in a tapestry of lies and deceit. The famous main theme, a cool jazz piece played on synthesized keyboard and alto saxophone, is so sultry that it fairly drips with passion. A melancholy passage with repetitive musical phrases is less carnal and more reflective as strings sway around a simple melody. Strings dominate a lovely flowing theme that is graceful and elegant but still has a sinister subtext. By the end of the movie the passion is spent and the music is romantic but regretful as the opening theme becomes a minor-key lament played on strings and a mournful saxophone.

The popular family film *Born Free*, about British game wardens in Kenya who adopt a lion cub, was the first to bring Barry acclaim outside of the Bond thrillers. The expansive and stirring title song (lyric by Don Black) was an international hit, and Barry's Oscar-winning score is pretty much different variations of that same theme. Because he comes up with so many variations of the melody and adds many textures by using African instruments, the score feels like many different themes. There are other musical passages in the film, including a felicitous piece in which strings and drums seem to float over the landscape, a brisk up-tempo theme with lively African percussion and Western horns, and a boastful march with proud brass and rhythmic drums and other percussive sounds. Barry's other Oscar-winning Africa score is similar yet richer. *Out of Africa* follows the life of Danish writer Isak Dinesen (Meryl Streep) as she tries to run a plantation in Kenya. She gets help from a British farmer (Robert Redford) who provides the love interest. There is no catchy song to build the score on this time, and Barry goes for the lyrical rather than the tuneful. The main theme is a graceful piece with long extended musical notes and phrases that takes its time before resolving into a full-fledged melody. The theme for the heroine is a lilting flute and clarinet passage that is interrupted by a growling percussive interlude to suggest Dinesen's fierce determination to succeed in Kenya. The score also features some African tribal singing by children that is both haunting and moving, a tense theme with rumbling percussion and tribal flutes that conveys the dangers of the landscape, and a mellow clarinet passage that is so delicate it seems ready to dissolve at any moment. Just as Barry does not strive for authentic tribal music in *Out of Africa*, so too does he avoid pure Native American music in the epic *Dances with Wolves* about a white Union army soldier (Kevin Costner) who becomes a member of the Sioux tribe. The music is always from the white soldier's point of view, although his perspective grows more like the tribesmen as the movie progresses. The score is one of the longest and most complicated of Barry's career. The movie encompasses many ideas and a wide array of diverse characters, all of which is scored with fifteen different themes. *Dances with Wolves* is also one of Barry's most symphonic scores, with a big orchestral sound for most passages, making the musically quieter and more intimate sections stand out. In the opening theme a solo trumpet slowly wails its way through a simple melody, which is picked up by a full orchestra and becomes rhapsodic at first then eventually stirring. This theme is identified with the hero and is

heard throughout the epic in various versions and played by different instruments, including harmonica, strings, and high-pitched bagpipes. The love theme for the hero and the tribeswoman (Mary McDonnell) he woos and marries is a heartfelt piece featuring a solo flute and a tentative melody that is as fragile as it is poignant. A robust traveling theme with low brass and high strings is contagious as it builds in intensity and tempo. Also memorable is a moving passage that celebrates the dignity of the land and the Native Americans who understand how to live peacefully with it. French horns are featured in this passionate theme that musicalizes the central idea behind the whole movie.

Two very different historical films reveal much about the versatility of Barry's scores. *Mary, Queen of Scots* tells the familiar tale of the rivalry between the Scottish Mary (Vanessa Redgrave) and English Queen Elizabeth I (Glenda Jackson). A beautiful costume film with questionable historical accuracy, its score makes attempts to sound Tudor without being slavish to the sound. Barry's main theme is a smooth and romanticized piece played by a modern orchestra. It moves along trippingly, like a stream, picking up a solo flute along the way to herald its lilting melody. This also becomes the theme for Mary when played on strings with harp accents, but a doleful strain enters the piece when slowed down and Mary's tragic future is foreshadowed in the minor-key chords. More in the Renaissance vein is a vigorous march on crumhorns and other period instruments that conveys the majesty and power of Elizabeth, a dreamy ballad played on lute and horn and sung in French, a harpsichord and flute passage with ominous tones, and a chanted hymn featuring horn and strings instead of an organ. Both the movie and the score take history at face value and are pretty solemn about it. That cannot be said about *The Lion in Winter*, which uses history and conjecture to create a sparkling comedy-drama with a very modern sensibility. King Henry II (Peter O'Toole) gathers his three sons (Anthony Hopkins, John Castle, and Nigel Terry), along with his mistress (Jane Merrow) and his imprisoned wife Eleanor of Aquitaine (Katharine Hepburn), for an 1183 Christmas family reunion filled with intrigue, backbiting, and both political and romantic maneuvering. The dazzling anachronistic dialogue is heard against realistic settings and details, making the movie unique and offbeat. Barry's score, considered his best by many, is a clever fusion of medieval and modern. The opening theme is an expressionistic

Gregorian chant with rhythmic trumpets and strings and an ardent choir singing a Latin text. Carl Orff had experimented with this sort of mix in his famous cantata *Carmina Burana* thirty years earlier, but Barry's version is closer to Stravinsky with its unconventional tempos and brazen sense of pride. The other unforgettable passage in *The Lion in Winter* is the luminous chorale heard when the queen comes down the river on the royal barge to be reunited with her tempestuous husband. Female voices sing (again in Latin) a glowing refrain that is so beautiful and ethereal that it might be an angels' chorus yet is not at all religious or solemn. The rest of the score is equally successful in juxtaposing the old and the new, as with a grim passage with stern male voices singing a wordless dirge, the deep vibrating brass instruments growling during certain scenes, and a series of descending musical phrases played by harsh trumpets when family matters turn deadly.

While *The Lion in Winter* may be Barry's slyest score, *Somewhere in Time* is perhaps his most romantic. A contemporary playwright (Christopher Reeve) is so fascinated by a famous early twentieth-century actress (Jane Seymour) that he wills himself back through time to 1912 where he meets her and they have a profound but tragic romance. The 1980 movie was a box office disappointment and Barry's score was pretty much ignored at the time. Not until the film showed up on cable and videotape years later did it gather a following and the soundtrack recording make the charts. The piece of music that figures importantly in the story and the score is not by Barry, but is Sergei Rachmaninoff's "Rhapsody on a Theme of Paga-

nini." Yet Barry holds his own against the Russian master with his ravishing soundtrack score. The main theme is a glittering serenade that flows so smoothly it doesn't seem to ever stop for breath. The piano plays the simple but captivating melody with a full orchestra giving support; then the orchestra picks up the tune and the piano adds effervescent embellishments. Another entrancing passage, played on sustained strings and pizzicato strings, has a restless undercurrent that is dangerous yet seductive. The music turns mystical for the time travel section. Ominous brass and worrisome strings slowly build in power, a piano offers a few unresolved glissandos, and the tone becomes menacing. The relationship between the two lovers is best musicalized by a melancholy piece on a solo violin that manages to be romantic yet full of foreboding. One might say that the music in *Somewhere in Time* is the antithesis of the James Bond scores. Taken together they can only begin to illustrate the diversity of Barry's work.

In addition to five Oscars and many other awards, Barry was appointed Officer of the Order of the British Empire in 1999. For health reasons, he retired from composing soon after. Barry died of a heart attack at the age of seventy-seven in Oyster Bay, Long Island, his home in the States since 1980. Many rank Barry as the most important British screen composer of his era. He was certainly one of the most popular and admired, and he left us a lot of terrific music. Biographies: *John Barry: The Man with the Midas Touch*, Geoff Leonard, Pete Walker, and Gareth Bramley (2008); *John Barry: A Sixties Theme*, Eddi Fiegel (2001).

Credits

(* for Best Song)

Year	Film	Director
1960	*Beat Girl* (aka *Wild for Kicks*)	Edmond T. Gréville (UK)
1962	*The L Shaped Room*	Bryan Fobes (UK)
1962	*Dr. No*	Terence Young (UK)
1962	*Mix Me a Person*	Leslie Norman (UK)
1962	*The Amorous Mr. Prawn*	Anthony Kimmins (UK)
1963	*From Russia with Love* (GGN)	Terence Young (UK)
1963	*The Winston Affair* (aka *Man in the Middle*)	Guy Hamilton (UK)
1964	*They All Died Laughing*	Don Chaffey (UK)
1964	*Zulu*	Cy Endfield (UK)
1964	*Séance on a Wet Afternoon*	Bryan Forbes (UK)
1964	*Goldfinger*	Guy Hamilton (UK)
1965	*The Ipcress File*	Sidney J. Furie (UK)

Year	Film	Director
1965	The Party's Over	Guy Hamilton (UK)
1965	Mister Moses	Ronald Neame (USA)
1965	The Knack . . . and How to Get It	Richard Lester (UK)
1965	Four in the Morning	Anthony Simmons (UK)
1965	King Rat	Bryan Forbes (USA)
1965	Thunderball	Terence Young (UK)
1966	The Chase	Arthur Penn (USA)
1966	Born Free (AA*; GG*)	James Hill (USA)
1966	The Wrong Box	Bryan Forbes (UK)
1966	The Quiller Memorandum	Michael Anderson (UK/USA)
1967	You Only Live Twice	Lewis Gilbert (UK)
1967	Dutchman	Anthony Harvey (UK)
1967	The Whisperers	Bryan Forbes (UK)
1968	Boom!	Joseph Losey (UK)
1968	Petulia	Richard Lester (USA)
1968	Deadfall	Bryan Forbes (UK)
1968	The Lion in Winter (AA; BAFTA; GGN)	Anthony Harvey (USA)
1969	The Appointment	Sidney Lumet (USA)
1969	Midnight Cowboy	John Schlesinger (USA)
1969	On Her Majesty's Secret Service	Peter R. Hunt (UK)
1970	Monte Walsh	William A. Fraker (USA)
1971	Murphy's War	Peter Yates (UK)
1971	The Last Valley	James Clavell (UK/USA)
1971	Walkabout	Nicolas Roeg (UK)
1971	They Might Be Giants	Anthony Harvey (USA)
1971	Diamonds Are Forever	Guy Hamilton (UK)
1971	Mary, Queen of Scots (AAN; GGN)	Charles Jarrot (UK)
1972	The Public Eye	Carol Reed (UK)
1972	Alice's Adventures in Wonderland	William Sterling (UK)
1973	A Doll's House	Patrick Garland (UK)
1974	The Tamarind Seed	Blake Edwards (UK/USA)
1974	The Dove (GGN*)	Charles Jarrott (USA)
1974	The Man with the Golden Gun	Guy Hamilton (UK)
1975	The Day of the Locust	John Schlesinger (USA)
1976	Robin and Marian	Richard Lester (USA)
1976	King Kong	John Guillermin (USA)
1977	The White Buffalo	J. Lee Thompson (USA)
1977	The Deep (GGN*)	Peter Yates (USA)
1977	First Love	Joan Darling (USA)
1978	St. Joan	Stephen Rumbelow (UK)
1978	The Betsy	Daniel Petrie (USA)
1978	The Game of Death	Robert Clouse (Hong Kong/USA)
1978	Starcrash	Luigi Cozzi (USA/Italy)
1979	Hanover Street	Peter Hyams (UK)
1979	The Black Hole	Gary Nelson (USA)
1979	Moonraker	Lewis Gilbert (UK/France)
1980	Raise the Titanic	Jerry Jameson (UK/USA)
1980	Somewhere in Time (GGN)	Jeannot Szwarc (USA)
1980	Touched by Love	Gus Trikonis (USA/Canada)
1980	Inside Moves	Richard Donner (USA)
1980	Night Games	Roger Vadim (France/USA)
1981	The Legend of the Lone Ranger	William A. Fraker (USA/UK)
1981	Body Heat	Lawrence Kasdan (USA)
1982	Hammett	Wim Wenders (USA)
1982	Frances	Graeme Clifford (USA)
1982	Murder by Phone	Michael Anderson (Canada/USA)
1983	High Road to China	Brian G. Hutton (USA)

Year	Film	Director
1983	Octopussy	John Glen (UK/USA)
1984	Mike's Murder	James Bridges (USA)
1984	Until September	Richard Marquand (USA)
1984	The Cotton Club	Francis Ford Coppola (USA)
1985	A View to a Kill (GGN*)	John Glen (UK/USA)
1985	Jagged Edge	Richard Marquand (USA)
1985	Out of Africa (AA; BAFTA-N; GG)	Sydney Pollack (USA)
1986	A Killing Affair	David Saperstein (USA)
1986	Howard the Duck	Willard Huyck (USA)
1986	Peggy Sue Got Married	Francis Ford Coppola (USA)
1987	The Living Daylights	John Glen (UK)
1987	Hearts of Fire	Richard Marquand (USA)
1988	Masquerade	Bob Swaim (USA)
1990	Dances with Wolves (AA; BAFTA-N; GGN)	Kevin Costner (USA/UK)
1992	Chaplin (AAN; GGN)	Richard Attenborough (USA)
1993	Indecent Proposal	Adrian Lyne (USA)
1993	My Life	Bruce Joel Rubin (USA)
1993	Ruby Cairo	Graeme Clifford (USA/Japan)
1994	The Specialist	Luis Llosa (Peru/USA)
1995	Cry, the Beloved Country	Darrell Roodt (South Africa/USA)
1995	Across the Sea of Time	Stephen Low (USA)
1995	The Scarlet Letter	Roland Joffé (USA)
1997	Swept from the Sea (aka Amy Foster)	Beeban Kidron (UK/USA)
1998	Mercury Rising	Harold Becker (USA)
1998	Playing by Heart	Willard Carroll (UK/USA)
2001	Enigma	Michael Apted (UK/USA)

BASSMAN, George (1914–1997) A popular Big Band orchestrator, composer, and vocal arranger, he contributed original music to thirty feature films in the 1950s and 1960s.

Born in New York City to Ukrainian Lithuanian parents, George Bassman grew up in Boston, where as a boy he took piano lessons and studied music at the Boston Conservatory. As a teenager, Bassman left his lessons and his home to tour as a pianist with a jazz band, also writing arrangements and some original music for the group. Eventually he wrote arrangements for name bands such as those led by Fletcher Henderson, Andre Kostelanetz, and Tommy Dorsey, composing the popular "I'm Getting Sentimental over You" (lyric by Ned Washington), which became Dorsey's theme song. Bassman went to Hollywood in 1935 and quickly found work doing arrangements and orchestrations for RKO and then MGM. Among the many famous films he worked on are *Suzy* (1936), *A Day at the Races* (1937), *Damsel in Distress*

(1937), *Love Finds Andy Hardy* (1938), *The Wizard of Oz* (1939), *Gone with the Wind* (1939), *Strike Up the Band* (1940), *For Me and My Gal* (1942), *Girl Crazy* (1943), and *Best Foot Forward* (1943). Bassman's screen composing career began in 1938 when he scored the cartoon short *Poultry Pirates* for MGM. That same year he contributed some of the music for the live-action feature *Little Orphan Annie*, followed by such musicals as *Babes in Arms*, *Go West*, *Broadway Melody of 1940*, *Lady Be Good*, and *Cabin in the Sky*, all cowritten with other composers. Bassman's first solo score was for *Hullabaloo* in 1940. That year he also worked on Broadway, doing orchestrations for the musical revue *Meet the People*. By the mid-1940s Bassman was usually the sole composer on his screen projects, often orchestrating them as well. His notable composer credits during the 1940s include *The Canterville Ghost*, *The Clock*, *Whistling in Brooklyn*, *Abbott and Costello in Hollywood*, *A Letter for Evie*, and *The Postman Always Rings Twice*.

Bassman's screen career came to a crashing halt in 1950 when he was called before the House Un-American Activities Committee and he admitted that his whole family had been members of the Communist Party. The studios would not use him, but fortunately some independent producers hired Bassman for a few films, most memorably his score for *The Joe Louis Story* and his arrangements for *Marty* (1955). With doors closed to him in movies and television, Bassman returned to New York and did the orchestrations for two 1950 Broadway musicals, *Alive and Kicking* and *Guys and Dolls*. By the end of the 1950s he was able to return to movies, writing two of his best scores for *Middle of the Night* and *Ride the High Country*. Bassman did some television work in the 1960s; then, after scoring and conducting the movie *Mail Order Bride* in 1964, he left Hollywood after fights with directors and producers kept him from working. He fell into obscurity and was not heard about again until his death in 1997 at the age of eighty-three. In addition to his many movies, Bassman's legacy includes a handful of successful songs, including "You've Got Something," "The Bicycle Song," "I Didn't Have the Heart to Tell You," and "Again and Again," and his orchestration of George Gershwin's one-act jazz opera *Blue Monday*, a 1922 piece that Bassman worked on again late in his career.

Based on the eighteen movies he scored by himself, there is a good deal of variety in Bassman's work, though often his early interest in jazz, swing, and the Big Band sound comes to the surface. In the 1944 screen version of Oscar Wilde's tale *The Canterville Ghost*, the setting remains an English castle but set during World War II with plenty of American GIs in the plot. The medieval ghost (Charles Laughton) is given some pseudo period music at first but once he starts interacting with the humans the score gets more romantic, even sentimental in the mawkish scenes with Margaret O'Brien. The musical highlight of the movie is a scene in which the locals and the GIs mix at a dance. A scratchy waltz played on piano and fiddle is turned into spirited boogie-woogie music as the GIs take over the dance floor. Also set during wartime, the tearful romance *The Clock* has a score that centers on the sweethearts (Judy Garland and Robert Walker) rather than on the popular music of the era. The main theme is a lush rhapsody that is a series of crescendos that never fully

resolve. Some passages convey the hustle and bustle of 1940s Manhattan; there is some bluesy nightclub music, a sprightly theme for the couple's all-night milk run, and no-holds-barred passionate music with a heavenly choir for the love scenes. The score for the biopic *The Joe Louis Story* is tougher with touches of jazz and swing throughout. This unsentimental film about the heavyweight champ (Coley Wallace) boasts a bold, Big Band main theme that has a fervent air about it. The music was later used for a popular recording by Harry James's orchestra with Art Van Damme on accordion. The soundtrack score has warm domestic passages for the hero's early years in Alabama, some blues for the years in Detroit, and some forceful music to convey Joe's determination to make something of himself. Oddly, the boxing scenes, which use some documentary footage, are without music, making them more real and unromanticized.

Perhaps Bassman's most known score is that for the western *Ride the High Country*. The familiar main theme is a stirring western ballad that is stately and slow but builds carefully into an engaging piece of Americana. There is also a delicate passage played on strings and flute for scenes involving the female characters, a merry clodhopping theme with a light touch, some harsh and chaotic music for an attempted rape, and a love theme that is a soft and wavering piece for guitar, violin, and woodwinds. Bassman's most famous movie is the 1946 film noir classic *The Postman Always Rings Twice*. Over the years much has been written about the seething lust in this movie that shows no skin or overt lovemaking. The performances by Lana Turner and John Garfield and the skillful direction by Tay Garnett have been justly praised, but much of the sensuality of the movie comes from Bassman's music. The opening titles are scored like a furious storm, the recurring romantic phrases filled with danger and lust. Later in the film this same music is slowed down and rearranged to become the sultry theme for Turner's character, eventually becoming the music for the murderous couple. Even a simple Latin tune played on a guitar becomes a sexy rumba once Turner and Garfield start to dance to it. This is superior screen music by a masterful movie composer. Bassman's time in Hollywood was relatively brief but nonetheless very productive and potent.

Credits

(all films USA)

Year	Film	Director
1938	*Little Orphan Annie*	Ben Holmes
1939	*Babes in Arms*	Busby Berkeley
1940	*Broadway Melody of 1940*	Norman Taurog
1940	*Hullabaloo*	Edwin L. Marin
1940	*Go West*	Edward Buzzell
1941	*Lady Be Good*	Norman Z. McLeod, Busby Berkeley
1942	*Ship Ahoy*	Edward Buzzell
1943	*Cabin in the Sky*	Vincente Minnelli, Busby Berkeley
1943	*Young Ideas* (aka *Faculty Row*)	Jules Dassin
1943	*Whistling in Brooklyn*	S. Sylvan Simon
1944	*The Canterville Ghost*	Jules Dassin, Norman Z. McLeod
1945	*Main Street after Dark*	Edward L. Cahn
1945	*The Clock*	Vincente Minnelli, Fred Zinnemann
1945	*Abbott and Costello in Hollywood*	S. Sylvan Simon
1946	*A Letter for Evie*	Jules Dassin
1946	*The Postman Always Rings Twice*	Tay Garnett
1946	*Two Smart People*	Jules Dassin
1947	*The Arnelo Affair*	Arch Oboler
1947	*Little Mister Jim*	Fred Zinnemann
1947	*The Romance of Rosy Ridge* (aka *The Night Raiders*)	Roy Rowland
1953	*The Joe Louis Story*	Robert Gordon
1953	*Louisiana Territory*	Harry W. Smith
1956	*Canyon Crossroads*	Alfred L. Werker
1959	*Middle of the Night*	Delbert Mann
1962	*Ride the High Country*	Sam Peckinpah
1964	*Mail Order Bride* (aka *The Wranglers*)	Burt Kennedy

BATES, Tyler (b. 1966?) A busy performer, record producer, and composer for movies, television, and video games, he has scored over sixty feature films since 1993, mostly in the horror and sci-fi genres.

Tyler Bates was born in Los Angeles and grew up in Chicago where he learned to play the alto saxophone and electric guitar. As a teenager, Bates started composing original music and experimenting with ways to mix tracks and change recording speeds while making his own recordings. Despite this early proficiency with music, he was educated at the Chicago Board of Option Exchange and began a career in a trading firm in the stock exchange even as he performed in Chicago-area rock bands. In 1993 Bates decided to make music his career and moved back to Los Angeles, where he began contributing to the scores of B horror movies. His first solo score was for the thriller *Deep Down* in 1994. That same year he cofounded the band Pet and started performing in the Los Angeles area.

By 1996 Pet had a best-selling album and was touring with other bands, but the next year Bates left the group in order to concentrate on screen music. His first film to receive wide recognition was the Sylvester Stallone crime drama *Get Carter* in 2000, and four years later Bates had his first box office hit with the remake of the George Romero cult favorite *Dawn of the Dead*. Because the movie was so successful, Bates was in demand for other horror and sci-fi remakes. He went on to write new music for several remakes of old favorites, including *Halloween*, *Day of the Dead*, *The Day the Earth Stood Still*, and *Conan the Barbarian*. Bates has also scored many original horror and sc-fi movies, including *Slither*, *The Devil's Rejects*, *Doomsday*, *See No Evil*, *Watchmen*, and *Guardians of the Galaxy*. Among his movie credits outside of the sci-fi and horror genres are *Killer Joe*, *Super*, *You Got Served*, *The Way*, and *300*. Bates has scored seven TV movies, most memorably *Alien Avengers* (1997) and its 1998 sequel, and some television series, including *Military Diaries*, *Black Sash*, *PG Porn*, *Low Winter Sun*, *Sym-Bionic Titan*, and *Californication*. He has also written music for many popular video games.

Bates's fascination with mixing various sounds in the recording studio is central to his music. Not only are different instruments enhanced or distorted, music and sound effects coexist in just about all of his scores. In his first important movie, *Get Carter*, Bates takes an up-tempo blues theme and adds an electric guitar riff and special effects. The result is both casual and menacing as the piece slowly develops its main musical phrase. Much of the *Get Carter* score, like the action, is propulsive and unrelenting, but there is a quiet passage played by a solo violin and electric keyboard that is delicate and entrancing. This kind of fusion of music and sound effects is ideal for both the horror and sci-fi scores Bates has written. In remaking past favorites in these genres, Bates is able to make the music sound very different from the original scores. In *Dawn of the Dead*, some passages are a series of overlapping sustained notes that are broken up by some hints of a melody. There is an eerie theme played on the high notes of an electric keyboard that is surprisingly gentle, and one explosive attack theme is a weird march with chaotic tempo changes. This kind of music was not heard in Romero's 1978 low-budget original. There is less variety in the score for another remake, *Halloween*, but again Bates's talent for mixing music and sound is ideal for this slasher favorite. The main theme has deadly chanting, shattering sound effects, and a rapid pounding on keyboard and percussion. Yet underneath it all is the classic horror music cliché of a progression of chords punctuating the action. Much of the rest of the *Halloween* score is similar, a slow building of seething noise and chords to an echoing climax. There is one quieter passage that stands out, a simple theme heard on a piano that teases with a melody then fades away rather than resolve itself.

Among the challenges in remaking the sci-fi classic *The Day the Earth Stood Still* is not only living up to the 1951 original but erasing the memory of Bernard Herrmann's dazzlingly unique score. Whereas the Herrmann music is stately, restrained, and otherworldly, Bates's score for the remake has a rock beat and an electronic format. Much of the music is busy with choral chanting, chaotic sound effects, and lots of reverberation. Yet there are some poetic moments in the music, passages with a sense of awe and grandeur, and even a fragile section that uses the electronics to produce a delicate hymn of sorts. It is quite clear in all of

Bates's scores for these big-budget remakes that he makes a bold effort to rethink the music, and often he succeeds very effectively. As for the original horror and sci-fi movies Bates has scored, they too utilize the advantages of mixing music and created sound without worrying about any comparisons to earlier films. In the futuristic comic-strip nightmare *Watchmen*, the score opens with rousing choral work and a powerful symphonic passage even though it is all done to a vigorous rock beat. There is also a beguiling serenade played on various strings that cautiously reaches for a full melodic phrase, a theme in which high-frequency sound effects and lots of reverb are used to create suspense in a classic manner, an echoing ballad played on electric guitar, and a lullaby also heard on electric guitar but this time simple and unembellished. The zombie movie *Slither* has a racing theme in which various instruments try to outrun each other even as the bass line remains steady and unperturbed. For the action scenes in the film the music gets even more frantic, cutting through all the sound effects like a tank. For the darkly comic action film *Killer Joe*, a heavy metal theme competes with plenty of mixing of sound effects into the music. Much of the score is jaunty and rhythmic but also heavy and unremitting. One might say the *Killer Joe* score is as abrasive as the movie is intense.

A different kind of tension fills the score for *300*, a retelling of the ancient battle of Thermopylae, which pitted three hundred Spartans against the superior Persian forces. This period piece has a very modern temperament, not to mention a comic-book fascination with blood and gore. Bates's score also sounds very modern at times as pounding electronic music takes on the majesty of a conventional symphonic treatment. There is plenty of chanting that has the flavor of vivid Greek folk music, but there is also the echoing male chorus that suggests the sounds of a Greek orthodox hymn. This is an aggressive and rambunctious score to say the least, but there are some commendable softer moments, such as a love theme that is a lament with moaning brass instruments and long sustained chords that support the melancholy female vocal. Quite in contrast to *300* is the reflective film *The Way*, about a journey of resolution and renewal on El Camino de Santiago in France and Spain. Bates would seem to be a very unlikely candidate to score such a movie, but it turns out his method of using electronics in creating music is also ideal for this film. Much of the music is ethnic but it is usually arranged and mixed with a touch of the mystical. The main theme is a poignant piano piece with accompanying chimes and sustained strings, all helping to create a reverent but far from stuffy tone. When a folk tune is played by both ethnic and electronic instruments, the effect is both folksy and exotic. In one passage, a solo Spanish guitar is echoed by electronic notes, then both are heard in counterpoint to a lovely violin passage. The choral chanting in another section is sublime, the sustained voices and wavering orchestra doing a felicitous pas de deux with each other. The score for *The Way* might strike one as a whole new direction for Bates but in truth it is just another facet of his continual experimenting with music and sound. Official website: www.tylerbates.com.

Credits

(all films USA unless stated otherwise)

Year	Film	Director
1993	Blue Flame	Cassian Elwes
1994	Deep Down (aka Conversations in Public Places)	John Travers
1995	Ballistic (aka Fists of Justice)	Kim Bass
1995	Not Like Us	Dave Payne
1995	Criminal Hearts (aka High Desert Run)	Dave Payne
1997	The Last Time I Committed Suicide	Stephen Kay
1998	Denial (aka Something about Sex)	Adam Rifkin
1998	Suicide, the Comedy (aka The Intervention)	Glen Freyer
1999	Born Bad	Jeff Yonis
1999	Thicker Than Water	Richard Cummings Jr.
2000	Get Carter	Stephen Kay
2001	Kingdom Come	Doug McHenry
2001	What's the Worst That Could Happen?	Sam Weisman
2001	Night at the Golden Eagle	Adam Rifkin
2002	Lone Star State of Mind (aka Cowboys and Idiots)	David Semel
2002	Love and a Bullet	Kantz, Ben Ramsey
2002	City of Ghosts (aka Beneath the Banyan Trees)	Matt Dillon
2002	Half Past Dead	Don Michael Paul (Germany/USA)
2003	Baadasssss! (aka How to Get the Man's Foot Outta Your Ass)	Mario Van Peebles
2004	You Got Served	Chris Stokes
2004	Dawn of the Dead	Zack Snyder (USA/Canada/Japan/France)
2005	The Devil's Rejects (aka House of 1000 Corpses)	Rob Zombie (USA/Germany)
2006	Slither	James Gunn (Canada/USA)
2006	See No Evil (aka Eye Scream Man)	Gregory Dark
2006	300	Zack Snyder
2007	Halloween (aka Halloween: Retribution)	Rob Zombie
2008	Doomsday	Neil Marshall (UK/USA/S. Africa/Germany)
2008	Day of the Dead (aka The Need to Feed)	Steve Miner
2008	The Day the Earth Stood Still	Scott Derrickson (USA/Canada)
2009	Watchmen	Zack Snyder
2009	Halloween II	Rob Zombie
2009	The Haunted World of El Superbeasto	Rob Zombie
2010	The Way	Emilio Estevez (USA/Spain)
2010	Super	James Gunn
2011	Sucker Punch	Zack Snyder (USA/Canada)
2011	Conan the Barbarian	Marcus Nispel
2011	Killer Joe	William Friedkin
2011	The Darkest Hour	Chris Gorak
2013	The Sacrament	Ti West
2014	Not Safe for Work	Joe Johnston
2014	7500	Takashi Shimizu (Japan/USA)
2014	Guardians of the Galaxy (aka Full Tilt)	James Gunn

BAXTER, Les (1922–1996) A prolific and multitalented musician, singer, conductor, arranger, bandleader, songwriter, and composer who is credited with creating exotica music in the early 1950s, he scored over one hundred feature films between 1953 and 1993, mostly B pictures or movies by secondary studios.

Born in the little town of Mexia, Texas, Les Baxter took piano lessons as a young child, and with his eye on a career as a concert pianist, went on to study at the Detroit Conservatory and Pepperdine College, but after graduation he pursued a singing career instead. In 1945 Baxter was hired as one of the singing "Meltones" who accompanied Mel Tormé in concert and on records. Soon he tired of singing and got interested in arranging and conducting music. He found work doing so in radio, eventually becoming the musical director for Bob Hope's radio program. Baxter found greater success at Capitol Records, where he arranged and conducted many hit songs for Nat King Cole, Margaret Whiting, and others. He also had success with instrumental recordings, forming his own orchestra and hitting the charts many times. His 1948 album *Music out of the Moon* was one of the first records to experiment with space-age sound effects, in particular the use of the musical instrument called the theremin. In 1952 he developed another new sound in his *Ritual of the Savage* album: exotica music. This pseudo-Polynesian music embraced the flavor of the Orient, conjuring up pagan ceremonials and the lure of tropical islands. The result was both adventurous and soothing and quickly became popular, Baxter's albums going on to be nationwide hits. Denny Martin, Arthur Lyman, and other arrangers-composers also made exotica records and the sound retained its popularity on the Easy Listening charts into the 1990s. In the 1960s Baxter founded the folk group the Balladeers, who had a single hit with "River Is Wide," which utilized Phil Spector's "wall of sound" technique. By the 1980s he turned to writing music for special events and theme parks.

Baxter first got involved with film music in 1953 when he was asked to write a new score for the American release of Ingmar Bergman's *Summer with Monika*. That same year he wrote exotica music for the melodrama *Tanga-Tika*, which was set on the island of Tahiti. In 1954 United Artists offered Baxter $5,000 if he would quickly compose, arrange, and conduct a score for their low-budget western *The Yellow Tomahawk*. Hollywood legend has it that he did all three tasks in one day. Baxter's screen composing career was launched, but unfortunately it was a career in minor movies and minor studios. He was very busy scoring B pictures in the 1950s, in 1956 alone writing music for fifteen feature films. In the 1960s Baxter worked mostly for American International Pictures writing scores for Roger Corman horror films, Annette Funicello beach movies, and trashy sexploitation flicks, as well as the American scores for many foreign horror or adventure movies. Although he remained very active in the 1970s, the movies did not get better. By the 1980s Baxter was passed over for younger talent, though he continued to score the occasional film until 1993. His television career was sporadic but noteworthy. He first wrote music for a series in 1957 and over the years scored some TV movies and other series, most memorably *The Tycoon* and the original whistling *Lassie* theme, which was used for decades. A controversy arose in the 1980s when some composers who worked with Baxter claimed that he did not write or arrange most of his music but had ghost composers do it for him. Other composers, arrangers, and musicians came to Baxter's defense, saying that he occasionally hired out parts of the job but that he did indeed write and arrange his scores.

There are no movie classics among Baxter's many screen credits, but there are several popular films and some that are cult favorites today. *Beach Blanket Bingo* and the half dozen beach movies still have a following and some of the Corman horror films, in particular *House of Usher*, *Pit and the Pendulum*, *Tales of Terror*, and *The Raven*, certainly have their legions of fans. Some other notable movies Baxter scored include *The Lone Ranger and the Lost City of Gold*, *Pharaoh's Curse*, *Fort Bowie*, *An Evening of Edgar Allan Poe*, *Lost Battalion*, *Wild in the Streets*, *The Dunwich Horror*, *Frogs*, *Lightning in a Bottle*, and *A Boy Ten Feet Tall*. Baxter himself confessed he could never turn down any film project, and he was loyal to various directors even though they rarely came up with a decent product. Yet Baxter was a very skillful and multitalented artist, and he approached *Goliath and the Vampires* and *How to Stuff a Wild Bikini* with the same enthusiasm as if he were handed *Citizen Kane*. To say the music is usually better than the movie is an understatement. Regardless of one's opinion of the Corman films, most agree that the scores are quite good. *Pit in the Pendulum*, for example, has a main theme that combines high-pitched strings with deep bass drums and ominous horns. This creates the hint of Spanish music (the story is set in Spain) yet comes across almost like jazz. *House of Usher*, on the other hand, has a fanfare main theme that is robust and triumphant yet still has a sense of menace. Just as boastful is the theme for *Tales of Terror* with a whole symphony sliding down the scales as creepy, high-pitch chanting floats above. In a comic vein is the horror spoof *The Raven*. The score likewise has a slapstick tone, making fun of horror music clichés. What could sound creepy becomes ridiculous in *The Raven*, from squawking brass that seems to laugh to fluttering woodwinds that sound like they are giggling. An interesting thing about the Corman movies: although they often have cheesy production values, the scores sound full bodied and expensive.

The beach movies are filled with pop songs written by various songwriters, so Baxter was left to fill in with appropriate "hip" music ranging from soft rock to limbo tunes. Most of the songs are mindlessly simple, but often the soundtrack scores are complicated and clever. A little bit of Baxter's signature exotica music pops up occasionally, though the atmosphere is less soothing and more tribal. The main theme for *Muscle Beach Party*, for example, is a risible mix of chaotic jazz, Oriental percussion sounds, and lighthearted rock and roll. It should be a mess of a mash-up but is actually quite fun. *Beach Blanket Bingo* uses everything from feverous calypso to silent movie piano tunes. The score for *Bikini Beach* overflows with 1960s pop music, from jazzy saxophone riffs to bubblegum twist tunes. These silly surfing musicals were so popular a series of "bikini" comedies followed. Perhaps the funniest of them was the *Goldfinger* spoof *Dr. Goldfoot and the Bikini Machine*, which was scored with some delightful pastiche James Bond music. Baxter also mixes in 1950s sci-fi music and some sexy hot jazz. It is hard to take this music any more seriously than the films themselves but there

is a kind of cockeyed efficiency to the scores. The same can be said for the schlock thriller *Frogs* about the frisky reptiles taking revenge on the humans who are destroying their swamp. The opening credits have no music, just the natural sounds of the wetlands, but once the green critters start to attack, the vibrating electric notes start to echo and increase in volume until they are screaming. In some passages the music sounds like it is underwater; other times musical gurgling takes over. One wonders how Baxter could retain his enthusiasm through years of such movies.

What about Baxter's not-so-awful films? *The Lone Ranger and the Lost City of Gold* was a glorified television episode using the TV stars Clayton Moore (Ranger) and Jay Silverheels (Tonto). Baxter provided an earnest but routine western score. The chase music is vigorous and the domestic theme warm and sentimental. Maybe such a straightforward, high-class movie could not inspire Baxter to anything out of the ordinary. Even classier is the juvenile adventure *A Boy Ten Feet Tall* about the orphaned youth Sammy (Fergus McClelland) who journeys across Africa to get to his only surviving relative. The British movie was titled *Sammy Going South* and was scored by Tristram Cary, but the movie was cut and retitled for the States and Baxter wrote a new score. This is not the South Seas, but Baxter uses his exotica talents to write a very ethnic-sounding score filled with tribal rhythms and lush traditional music to convey the majesty of the landscape. The main theme is a British march (Sammy is a Brit), which is also used as a catchy children's ditty. In this case a better movie prompted Baxter to write better music. Yet *A Boy Ten Feet Tall* still lacks the vitality of the scores for those schlock Corman movies. Perhaps that is the irony in Baxter's screen career. Was he only able to match the musical chemistry of his record albums when the films were crass and obvious? Official website: www.lesbaxter.com.

Credits

(all films USA unless stated otherwise)

Year	Film	Director
1953	*Summer with Monika*	Ingmar Bergman (Sweden)
1953	*Tanga-Tika*	Dwight Long
1954	*The Yellow Tomahawk*	Lesley Selander
1954	*No Time for Shame*	Arne Ragneborn (Sweden)
1954	*A Life at Stake*	Paul Guilfoyle
1956	*Hot Blood* (aka *Bad Blood*)	Nicholas Ray

Year	Film	Director
1956	Quincannon, Frontier Scout	Lesley Selander
1956	Wetbacks	Hank McCune
1956	The Black Sleep (aka Dr. Cadman's Secret)	Reginald Le Borg
1956	Rebel in Town	Alfred L. Werker
1956	Hot Cars	Don McDougall
1956	A Woman's Devotion (aka Battle Shock)	Paul Henreid
1957	Voodoo Island (aka Silent Death)	Reginald Le Borg
1957	Tomahawk Trail	Lesley Selander
1957	Pharaoh's Curse	Lee Sholem
1957	The Storm Rider (aka Long Rider Jones)	Edward Bernds
1957	Revolt at Fort Laramie	Lesley Selander
1957	War Drums	Reginald Le Borg
1957	Untamed Youth	Howard W. Koch
1957	Outlaw's Son (aka Gambling Man)	Lesley Selander
1957	Bop Girl Goes Calypso	Howard W. Koch
1957	Jungle Heat	Howard W. Koch
1957	The Girl in Black Stockings	Howard W. Koch
1957	The Invisible Boy	Herman Hoffman
1957	Hell Bound	William J. Hole Jr.
1957	The Dalton Girls	Reginald Le Borg
1957	Escape from Red Rock	Edward Bernds
1958	Fort Bowie	Howard W. Koch
1958	The Bride and the Beast	Adrian Weiss
1958	The Lone Ranger and the Lost City of Gold	Lesley Selander
1958	The Fiend Who Walked the West	Gordon Douglas
1958	Macabre	William Castle
1959	Goliath and the Barbarians	Carlo Campogalliani (Italy)
1959	La ciudad sagrada	Ismael Rodríguez (Mexico)
1960	House of Usher	Roger Corman
1960	Black Sunday	Mario Bava (Italy)
1960	Goliath and the Dragon	Vittorio Cottafavi (Italy/France)
1960	Alakazam the Great!	Daisaku Shirakawa, etc. (Japan)
1961	Reptilicus	Sidney W. Pink (Denmark/USA)
1961	Guns of the Black Witch	Domenico Paolella (Italy/France)
1961	Master of the World	William Witney
1961	The Pit and the Pendulum	Roger Corman
1961	Goliath and the Vampires	Sergio Corbucci, Giacomo Gentilomo (Italy)
1961	Maciste at the Court of the Great Kahn (aka Samson and the 7 Miracles of the World)	Riccardo Freda (Italy/France)
1961	White Slave Ship	Silvio Amadio (Italy/France)
1961	Erik the Conqueror	Mario Bava (Italy/France)
1961	Fall Girl (aka A Crowd for Lisette)	R. John Hugh
1962	Marco Polo	Piero Pierotti, etc. (Italy/France)
1962	Lost Battalion	Eddie Romero (USA/Philippines)
1962	Tales of Terror	Roger Corman
1962	Panic in the Year Zero!	Ray Milland
1962	La guerra continua	Leopoldo Savona (Italy/France/Yugoslavia)
1962	Daughter of the Sun God	Kenneth Hartford
1963	The Young Racers	Roger Corman
1963	The Raven	Roger Corman
1963	The Evil Eye	Mario Bava (Italy)
1963	A Boy Ten Feet Tall (aka Sammy Going South)	Alexander Mackendrick (UK)
1963	Operation Bikini	Anthony Carras
1963	X: The Man with the X-Ray Eyes	Roger Corman
1963	Beach Party	William Asher
1963	Black Sabbath	Mario Bava (Italy/UK/France)
1963	Samson and the Slave Queen	Umberto Lenzi (Italy/Spain)
1963	The Comedy of Terrors	Jacques Tourneur

Year	Film	Director
1964	*Muscle Beach Party*	William Asher
1964	*Bikini Beach*	William Asher
1964	*Pajama Party*	Don Weis
1965	*Beach Blanket Bingo*	William Asher
1965	*How to Stuff a Wild Bikini*	William Asher
1965	*Sergeant Dead Head*	Norman Taurog
1965	*Dr. Goldfoot and the Bikini Machine*	Norman Taurog
1966	*The Ghost in the Invisible Bikini (aka Beach Party in a Haunted House)*	Don Weis
1966	*Fireball 500*	William Asher
1966	*Dr. Goldfoot and the Girl Bombs*	Mario Bava (Italy/USA)
1967	*The Glass Sphinx*	Luigi Scattini (Italy/Egypt/Spain)
1967	*Young Rebel (aka Cervantes)*	Vincent Sherman (Spain/France/Italy)
1968	*The Mini-Skirt Mob*	Maury Dexter
1968	*Wild in the Streets*	Barry Shear
1968	*The Young Animals (aka Born Wild)*	Maury Dexter
1968	*Terror in the Jungle*	Tom DeSimone
1968	*Bora Bora*	Ugo Liberatore (Italy/France)
1968	*Annabelle Lee (aka Diabolic Wedding)*	Harold Daniels, Gene Nash (Peru/USA)
1969	*All the Loving Couples (aka All the Swinging Couples)*	Mack Bing
1969	*Hell's Belles*	Maury Dexter
1969	*Target: Harry (aka What's in It for Harry?)*	Roger Corman
1969	*Flareup*	James Neilson
1970	*An Evening of Edgar Allan Poe*	Kenneth Johnson
1970	*The Dunwich Horror*	Daniel Haller
1970	*Cry of the Banshee*	Gordon Hessler (UK)
1970	*Trampa para una niña*	Ismael Rodríguez (Mexico)
1971	*El orgo*	Ismael Rodríguez (Mexico/Guatemala)
1971	*Dagmar's Hot Pants, Inc. (aka Dagmar & Co.)*	Vernon P. Becker (Denmark/Sweden/USA)
1972	*Baron Blood*	Mario Bava (W. Germany/Italy)
1972	*Frogs*	George McCowan
1972	*One Minute before Death*	Rogelio A. González (USA/Mexico)
1972	*Blood Sabbath (aka Yyalah)*	Brianne Murphy
1973	*I Escaped from Devil's Island*	William Witney (Mexico/USA)
1973	*The Devil and Leroy Bassett*	Robert E. Pearson
1974	*Savage Sisters (aka Ebony Tower and Jade)*	Eddie Romero (USA/Philippines)
1975	*Switchblade Sisters (aka The Jezebels)*	Jack Hill
1978	*Born Again*	Irving Rapper
1982	*The Beast Within*	Philippe Mora
1989	*Reflection of Evil*	Todd Hughes
1991	*Yma Sumac—Hollywood's Inkaprinzessin*	Gunther Czernetsky (Germany)
1993	*Lightning in a Bottle*	Jeff Kwitny

BECK, Christophe (b. 1972) A more recent but prolific television and film composer from Canada, he has scored over one hundred movies since 1996, most of them contemporary comedies and some of them very popular.

He was born Jean-Christophe Beck in Montreal, Canada, and began piano lessons when he was five years old. Before he was a teenager Beck formed his own band and in high school continued his music studies by learning to play drums and saxophone. Beck studied music at Yale University, where he wrote musicals and an opera as well as serving as musical director for the Spizzwinks and the Whiffenpoofs. He then studied film scoring at the Thornton School of Music at the University of Southern California. Beck began his career in 1993 scoring television series such as *White Fang, Two, Spy Game, FX: The Series, Angel,* and *The Practice*, but it was his music for

Buffy the Vampire Slayer in 1997 that launched his career. Although Beck began scoring feature films the year before, most of his screen projects were overlooked until he found success with his music for the cheerleading comedy *Bring It On* in 2000. He has since scored such notable titles as *Under the Tuscan Sun, Cheaper by the Dozen, Garfield, The Pink Panther, The Sentinel, We Are Marshall, Phoebe in Wonderland, What Happens in Vegas, The Hangover* and its two sequels, *Death at a Funeral, Year of the Dog, The Muppets, Pitch Perfect, The Guilt Trip, Frozen, Muppets Most Wanted,* and *Crazy, Stupid, Love.* Beck has returned to television on occasion to score TV movies and he has also written music for direct-to-video films and documentary shorts.

Much of Beck's screen career has been scoring comedies of widely varying quality yet his most pleasing music is that which he wrote for his atypical films such as *Under the Tuscan Sun, We Are Marshall, The Sentinel, Frozen,* and *Phoebe in Wonderland.* Still, there is something to be said about his music for the comedies, successful or otherwise. The rhythmic rock music for *Bring It On* often turns into symphonic fanfares, mockingly giving weight to something as inconsequential as stealing cheerleading moves. For a film that doesn't quite know what it's satirizing, the music is confident and sincere as it pounds away merrily. *Date Night* has some cool jazz passages that seem to grin, as well as heavy metal music that sounds comic, its accents silly and crass. The main theme is percussion and electric keyboard chase music with a sense of James Bond adventure, as befits the ordinary married couple (Tina Fey and Steve Carell) who get caught up in a suspense movie. The two new *Pink Panther* films use Mancini's famous theme song, then Beck provides mock mystery music set to a pulsating beat. While he never matches Mancini's genius for writing truly funny music, Beck writes some delightful passages using a comic oboe, swirling strings, and clodhopping brass. There is also a gliding lament played on piano, strings, and woodwinds that goes deeper than these slapstick films. *The Hangover*, the raunchiest and (consequently) the most popular of Beck's comedies, has a rambunctious score that suggests the drunken road trip that is the centerpiece of the movie. There is a jazz theme that oozes with "cool," a rhythmic traveling theme with some steady and smooth guitar and organ playing, a lazy and reflective guitar solo, and some propulsive rock music that seems to celebrate just being alive.

The more serious Beck movies offer more engaging music, as might be expected, yet one can still pick out Beck's characteristic sense of rhythm. Perhaps the most heart wrenching of these melodramas is *We Are Marshall*, the true tale of a college trying to reestablish its football team after a tragic plane crash in which team members and fans died. The main theme is a slow fanfare heard on brass and strings, a solemn lament that avoids being mawkish. It is not a melodic piece but rather a series of climbing phrases that sobers and inspires. Other memorable passages in the score include a piano and violin section that seems to weep but moves ahead boldly, a rousing percussion theme that sparkles with confidence, and a pounding march of sorts that feels like a race. The Secret Service thriller *The Sentinel* is a slick action film with a captivating score. The opening theme is a series of electronic sounds and sustained chords that transitions into a melancholy but rhythmic piece of jazz. The whole score has such a sense of menace that it retains its energy and verve long after the movie loses steam. The psychological drama *Phoebe in Wonderland*, about a withdrawn girl (Elle Fanning) who comes out of her secret world when she acts in a school production of *Alice in Wonderland*, has a superb score that is as magical as it is resplendent. The main theme is a simple but elegant tune played by a chamber ensemble, each instrument doing a variation of the central musical phrase. Throughout the score strings and piano are used either contrapuntally or in unison, just as in another passage a xylophone dances with strings in a sprightly fashion. This is Beck in a classical mode and it is as delectable as it is unexpected.

The popular romance *Under the Tuscan Sun* is filled with Italianate music, particularly in the mandolin passages, yet it never slips into cliché. Some sections are exuberant as the music seems to glory in the lovely landscape; other passages glide along like a mystical serenade with a bittersweet flavor. Yet the music is always propelled forward, never languishing in sentiment even when the movie does. While the generic pop songs in the Disney animated movie *Frozen* get all the attention, it is Beck's soundtrack score that was responsible for creating much of the atmosphere and local color. Set in a mythical Scandinavian land, *Frozen* has a very distinctive wintery look. So too, the music is full of a sense of the foreign and exotic. The opening music is a zesty a cappella chant, with male and female choirs in counterpoint. The theme for the two sister princesses is a vivacious folk dance heard on busy strings. The trolls have their own howling, mysterious music, and there is a radiant waltz that is as glittering and wintry as the visuals it accompanies. The score also includes a lilting choral hymn, some marvelously eerie music for the sorcery aspect of the plot, and a grandi- ose theme for the dazzling ice castle. Perhaps Beck's career is moving away from so many adolescent comedies and toward more substantial film projects. If *Frozen* and its like are the result, then these scores are exciting to contemplate. Official website: www.christophebeck.com.

Credits

(all films USA unless stated otherwise)

Year	Film	Director
1996	*Past Perfect*	Jonathan Heap (USA/Canada)
1997	*Hostile Intent*	Jonathan Heap (Canada)
1997	*The Alarmist* (aka *Life During Wartime*)	Evan Dunsky
1998	*Starstruck* (aka *Dust and Stardust*)	John Enbom
1998	*Bone Daddy* (aka *Palmer's Bones*)	Mario Azzopardi (Canada/USA)
1998	*Airborne*	Julian Grant (Canada)
1998	*Dog Park*	Bruce McCulloch (Canada/USA)
1999	*Let the Devil Wear Black*	Stacy Title
1999	*Guinevere*	Audrey Wells
1999	*Thick as Thieves*	Scott Sanders
1999	*Coming Soon*	Colette Burson
2000	*The Broken Hearts Club: A Romantic Comedy*	Greg Berlanti
2000	*Bring It On* (aka *Cheer Fever*)	Peyton Reed
2000	*Big Time*	Douglas Petrie
2002	*Slap Her, She's French!* (aka *She Gets What She Wants*)	Melanie Mayron (Germany/UK/USA)
2002	*Big Fat Liar* (aka *Lost and Found*)	Shawn Levy (USA/Germany)
2002	*Interstate 60: Episodes of the Road*	Bob Gale (Canada/USA)
2002	*Stealing Harvard* (aka *Say Uncle*)	Bruce McCulloch
2002	*The Tuxedo* (aka *T.U.X.*)	Kevin Donovan
2003	*Just Married*	Shawn Levy (USA/Germany)
2003	*The Event*	Thom Fitzgerald (Canada/USA)
2003	*Confidence*	James Foley (USA/Canada/Germany)
2003	*American Wedding* (aka *American Pie 3*)	Jesse Dylan (USA/Germany)
2003	*Dickie Roberts: Former Child Star*	Sam Weisman
2003	*Under the Tuscan Sun*	Audrey Wells (USA/Italy)
2003	*Cheaper by the Dozen*	Shawn Levy
2004	*Saved!*	Brian Dannelly (USA/Canada)
2004	*Garfield: The Movie*	Peter Hewitt
2004	*A Cinderella Story*	Mark Rosman (USA/Canada)
2004	*Little Black Book*	Nick Hurran
2004	*Without a Paddle*	Steven Brill
2004	*Taxi*	Tim Story (USA/France)
2005	*Elektra*	Rob Bowman (Canada/USA)
2005	*Ice Princess*	Tim Fywell (USA/Canada)
2005	*The Perfect Man*	Mark Rosman
2005	*3 Needles*	Thom Fitzgerald (Canada)
2005	*Two for the Money* (aka *For the Money*)	D. J. Caruso
2005	*Yours, Mine & Ours*	Raja Gosnell
2006	*The Pink Panther* (aka *The Birth of the Pink Panther*)	Shawn Levy (USA/Czech Republic)
2006	*The Sentinel*	Clark Johnson
2006	*Garfield 2* (aka *A Tail of Two Kitties*)	Tim Hill (UK/USA)
2006	*Zoom* (aka *The Return of Zoom*)	Peter Hewitt
2006	*School for Scoundrels* (aka *The Better Man*)	Todd Phillips
2006	*We Are Marshall*	McG
2007	*Year of the Dog*	Mike White

Year	Film	Director
2007	Charlie Bartlett	Jon Poll
2007	License to Wed	Ken Kwapis (USA/Australia)
2007	The Seeker: The Dark Is Rising	David L. Cunningham
2007	Fred Claus (aka Joe Claus)	David Dobkin
2008	Phoebe in Wonderland	Daniel Barnz
2008	Drillbit Taylor	Steven Brill
2008	What Happens in Vegas	Tom Vaughan
2009	The Greatest	Shana Feste
2009	The Pink Panther 2 (aka The Next Pink Panther)	Harald Zwart
2009	The Hangover	Todd Phillips (USA/Germany)
2009	I Love You, Bess Cooper	Chris Columbus (Canada/USA)
2009	Post Grad (aka The Post Grad Survival Guide)	Vicky Jenson
2009	The Marc Pease Experience	Todd Louiso
2009	All About Steve	Phil Traill
2010	Percy Jackson & the Olympians: The Lightning Thief	Chris Columbus (Canada/USA)
2010	Hot Tub Time Machine	Steve Pink
2010	Date Night	Shawn Levy
2010	Death at a Funeral	Neil LaBute
2010	Red	Robert Schwentke
2010	Due Date	Todd Phillips
2010	Burlesque	Steve Antin
2011	Cedar Rapids	Miguel Arteta
2011	The Hangover Part II	Todd Phillips
2011	Crazy, Stupid, Love	Glenn Ficarra, John Requa
2011	Tower Heist (aka Trump Heist)	Brett Ratner
2011	The Muppets (aka Being Green)	James Bobin
2012	This Means War	McG
2012	The Watch (aka Neighborhood Watch)	Akiva Schaffer
2012	Pitch Perfect	Jason Moore
2012	The Guilt Trip (aka My Mother's Curse)	Anne Fletcher
2013	Charlie Countryman (aka The Necessary Death of Charlie Countryman)	Fredrik Bond (Romania/USA)
2013	The Hangover Part III	Todd Phillips
2013	The Internship	Shawn Levy
2013	R.I.P.D.	Robert Schwentke
2013	Runner Runner	Brad Furman
2013	Frozen (aka The Snow Queen)	Chris Buck, Jennifer Lee
2014	Endless Love	Shana Feste
2014	Muppets Most Wanted	James Bobin
2014	Edge of Tomorrow	Doug Liman

BELTRAMI, Marco (b. 1966) A much-in-demand movie and television composer who has scored over eighty feature films within a twenty-year period, he is most known for his horror and action movie scores.

Marco Beltrami was born in New York City, the son of Italian and Greek immigrants, and grew up on Long Island where he began piano lessons at the age of six. Beltrami played keyboard in rock bands when he was in high school then got interested in synthesized music when he was educated at Brown University, privately in Italy, at the Yale School of Music, and by Jerry Goldsmith at the USC Thornton School of Music. He did not abandon his classical music studies, hoping to combine traditional and electronic music in his concert pieces, which were premiered by the Chicago Civic Orchestra, Oakland East Bay Symphony, Sao Paulo State Orchestra, and others. Beltrami first wrote scores for television in 1994, the same year he wrote the music for the feature film *Death Match* about kickboxing. He received more acclaim the next year for his music for the series *Land's End* and the short *The Bicyclist* before director Wes Craven asked him to score his shocker *Scream*. Beltrami confessed he had never even seen a horror movie before but quickly got interested in the genre, resulting in a hit for Craven and wide recognition for the young composer. Beltrami has gone on to score the three *Scream* sequels and three other Craven films. He has written the music for many other directors, mostly in the horror, sci-fi, or action genres. Among his more notable credits are *Mimic, Dracula 2000, Resident Evil, Terminator 3, The Hurt Locker, Repo Men, The Woman in Black, World War Z, The Wolverine, Don't Be Afraid of the Dark, Soul Surfer, Live Free or Die Hard, The Faculty*, and *I, Robot*. He is also in demand for scoring movie remakes, such as *The Omen, Flight of the Phoenix, The Thing, 3:10 to Yuma*, and *Carrie*. Beltrami has returned to television on occasion, writing music for such series as *Glory Days, The Practice, V*, and *1854*, as well as a half dozen TV movies, including *Inhumanoid* (1996), *David and Lisa* (1998), and *Tuesdays with Morrie* (1999).

Despite his lack of experience with horror movie music, Beltrami's fascination with the synthesizer and his interest in electronic music served him well in scoring *Scream* and the many other scary movies in his career. His music for the genre is unabashedly propulsive and as unsubtle as the visuals on the screen. Yet Beltrami quickly learned the power of pulling back at times so that the shock moments were all the more bombastic. The main theme for *Scream* is highly electronic with heavy metal percussion, enhanced choral passages, and special sound effects. Some sections of the score sound like the instruments are chomping and chewing all the notes then spitting them out with a vengeance. Yet even *Scream* has quieter sections, such as a piano passage with wavering electronic strings that moves forward shyly, or a child's vocal passage that reeks of innocence and dread. *The Omen* has some choir hymns (with a demonic flavor, of course) that consist of repetitive musical phrases that seem to be flagellating the ear. One section has ominous chords that turn into rambunctious percussion riffs while in another violins are used effectively as they reach such a high register that they reverberate. There is also a lilting flute passage that is so fragile it dissolves once the weighty accompaniment decides to overpower it. Although *World War Z* is one of his later compositions, it has the ardent fervor of these earlier works. The score starts with an explosion and pulsating chords and rarely lets up for the rest of the film. There are plenty of nervous violins playing over harsh brass shouting, and a deceptive theme in which serene strings are drowned out by busy

trumpets. Even the poignant domestic theme has a sense of danger lurking around the corner.

Beltrami seems to have learned quickly because his horror and sci-fi scores have gotten richer and have more variety. The main theme for *The Wolverine* is a slow and graceful symphonic piece that is mournful yet soothing; then the tempo picks up, the percussion competes with the strings, and it all sounds like a surreal race in slow motion. There is an echoing passage with sustained electronic notes that is also very majestic in temperament. The many action scenes in *The Wolverine* are often scored with percussion passages that seem tribal and yet are very techno, a collage of sound effects all on the run. *Carrie* has a title theme that is expectedly eerie, yet lyrical with its twinkling chimes and descending strings. It is all remarkably restrained, especially for a movie as full throttle as *Carrie*. The music for the prom massacre is explosive with swirling sounds and screeching violins, but there is also a slower movement that is so tentative that it barely seems to be breathing until the rhythmic heartbeat turns into a lovely lullaby or sorts. Beltrami's scores for action films also use a lot of synthesized music and effects. The music in *Terminator 3* often moves from low, sustained notes to high choral voices, the effect being rather a regal one. Much of the score is driving and pounding, with plenty of echoing sound effects. There is an insistent theme in which a repeated phrase makes interesting variations as it increases in power, and there are some symphonic passages, such as the ending of the movie, that are sublime and memorable. Beltrami scored two of the many *Die Hard* sequels, and his music for *Live Free or Die Hard* has some interesting passages. It is pretty much a hard rock score with pop songs, but the soundtrack includes a theme in which violins are furiously chomping at the bit, trying to break out but stuck in a repetitive pattern. In one sequence, the strings alternate with the brass in a series of jabs and punches. There are not many opportunities for subdued moments or reflective music in the *Die Hard* movies.

Beltrami's handful of movies outside the horror and action genres provide opportunities to use his classical music training. For the odd but engaging melodrama *The Sessions*, about a polio victim (John Hawkes) trying to lose his virginity, the score relies on conventional instruments. There is a rhythmic yet loose theme played by a solo clarinet with orchestra that has an expansive feeling without actually being very rangy. There is also a jaunty passage for violin with accompanying strings that is so graceful it seems to float. For the more terse scenes there is some disturbing music in which sustained notes are in counterpoint to a piano carelessly playing a tuneful ditty. Another victim melodrama based on a true story, *Soul Surfer* centers on a teen surfer (AnnaSophia Robb) who is determined to compete even after a shark encounter has taken away her right arm. Set in Hawaii, the score is overflowing with atmospheric music, including a rhythmic tribal passage that is mostly percussion and chanting, and a lackadaisical theme heard on piano, ukulele, and electric guitar that suggests a mellow kind of freedom. The main theme for *Soul Surfer* is a delicate hymn played on piano and strings with vocal Polynesian chanting. Like *The Sessions*, this is a far cry from Beltrami's usual fare, to say the least.

While most might choose the Oscar-nominated score for *The Hurt Locker* as Beltrami's best, the fact is that music was co-composed with Buck Sanders and it is impossible to separate each man's contribution. But Beltrami's other Oscar nod was for the remake of *3:10 to Yuma* and that was a solo effort. Although it is a period western, the film has a very modern sensibility. Beltrami provides music that quietly creates tension and adds to the suspenseful story. The main theme is a slow, seething passage heard on high strings with rumbling accompaniment. There is a memorable guitar passage with a nervous tempo that carefully climbs the scale with a bit of apprehension. Low echoing chords and a tribal beat are used for the Native American aspect of the film, and there is a lovely ballad played by solo guitar with orchestra that starts simply with a few musical phrases then develops the idea musically and emotionally. All of it is quite impressive for a composer with no experience scoring westerns. Some point to *The Hurt Locker*, *3:10 to Yuma*, and other recent non-horror-action films and say Beltrami has matured as a screen composer. Possibly, but it is more likely these movies allow him to do what he has been capable of from the beginning. Official website: www.marco-beltrami.com.

Credits

(all films USA unless stated otherwise)

Year	Film	Director
1994	Death Match	Joe Coppoletta
1995	The Whispering	Gregory Gieras
1996	Scream (aka Scary Movie)	Wes Craven
1997	Mimic (aka Judas)	Guillermo del Toro
1997	Scream 2 (aka Scream Again)	Wes Craven
1998	54 (aka Studio 54)	Mark Christopher
1998	The Faculty (aka Feelers)	Robert Rodriguez
1999	The Minus Man	Hampton Fancher
1999	The Florentine	Nick Stagliano
1999	Walking across Egypt (aka Leading with Her Heart)	Arthur Allan Seidelman
2000	The Crow: Salvation (aka The Crow 3)	Bharat Nalluri (Germany/USA)
2000	Scream 3 (aka Ghostface)	Wes Craven
2000	The Incorporated	Kenneth Guertin
2000	The Watcher (aka Driven)	Joe Charbanic
2000	Highway 395	Fred Dryer
2000	Dracula 2000	Patrick Lussier
2000	Goodbye, Casanova	Mauro Borrelli
2001	Angel Eyes (aka Heart of Town)	Luis Mandoki
2001	Joy Ride (aka Candy Cane)	John Dahl
2002	The Dangerous Lives of Altar Boys	Peter Care
2002	I Am Dina	Ole Bornedal (Norway/Sweden/France/Germany/ Denmark)
2002	Resident Evil	Paul W. S. Anderson (UK/Germany/ France/ USA)
2002	Blade 2: Bloodhunt	Guillermo del Toro (USA/Germany)
2002	The First $20 Million Is the Hardest	Mick Jackson
2003	Terminator 3: Rise of the Machines	Jonathan Mostow (USA/Germany/UK)

Year	Film	Director
2004	Hellboy	Guillermo del Toro
2004	I, Robot (aka Hardwired)	Alex Proyas (USA/Germany)
2004	Flight of the Phoenix	John Moore
2005	Cursed	Wes Craven (USA/Germany)
2005	xXx: State of the Union	Lee Tamahori
2005	The Three Burials of Melquiades Estrada	Tommy Lee Jones (USA/France)
2005	Red Eye	Wes Craven
2006	Underworld: Evolution (aka Underworld 2)	Len Wiseman
2006	The Omen	John Moore
2007	Captivity	Roland Joffé (USA/Russia)
2007	The Substitute	Ole Bornedal (Denmark)
2007	The Invisible	David S. Goyer (USA/Canada)
2007	Live Free or Die Hard (aka Die Hard 4)	Len Wiseman (USA/UK)
2007	3:10 to Yuma (AAN)	James Mangold
2008	The Eye	David Moreau, Xavier Palud (USA/Canada)
2008	The Hurt Locker (AAN)	Kathryn Bigelow
2008	Mesrine: Killer Instinct	Jean-François Richet (France/Canada/Italy)
2008	Amusement	John Simpson
2008	Max Payne	John Moore (Canada/USA)
2008	Mesrine: Public Enemy #1	Jean-François Richet (France/Canada)
2009	In the Electric Mist	Bertrand Tavernier (USA/France)
2009	Knowing	Alex Proyas (USA/UK/Australia)
2010	Repo Men (aka Repossession Mambo)	Miguel Sapochnik (USA/Canada)
2010	Jonah Hex	Jimmy Hayward
2010	My Soul to Take	Wes Craven
2010	Don't Be Afraid of the Dark	Troy Nixey (USA/Australia/Mexico)
2011	Soul Surfer	Sean McNamera
2011	Scream 4	Wes Craven
2011	The Thing	Matthijs van Heijningen Jr. (USA/Canada)
2012	The Sessions (aka Six Sessions)	Ben Lewin
2012	The Woman in Black	James Watkins (UK/Canada/Sweden)
2012	Deadfall (aka Blackbird)	Stefan Ruzowitzky (USA/France)
2012	Trouble with the Curve	Robert Lorenz
2012	Stab 6: Ghostface Returns	Joshua Patrick Dudley
2013	Warm Bodies	Jonathan Levine
2013	A Good Day to Die Hard (aka Die Hard 5)	John Moore
2013	World War Z	Marc Forster (USA/Malta)
2013	The Wolverine (aka Wolverine 2)	James Mangold (USA/UK)
2013	Snowpiercer	Joon-ho Bong (S. Korea/USA/France/Czech Republic)
2013	Carrie	Kimberly Peirce
2014	November Man	Roger Donaldson
2015	Seventh Son	Sergey Bodrov (UK/USA/Canada)
2015	The Homesman	Tommy Lee Jones

BENJAMIN, Arthur (Leslie) (1893–1960) A renowned Australian pianist, teacher, conductor, and composer for the concert hall and the opera, he worked sporadically in the British cinema between 1934 and 1958, scoring some major feature films.

Born in Sydney, Australia, Arthur Benjamin grew up in Brisbane, and was a child prodigy, making his piano concert debut when he was six years old. Three years later Benjamin began private lessons, later studying piano and composition at the Royal College of Music in London. While serving in the Royal Flying Corps during World War I, he was shot down over Germany and remained in a prison camp for the rest of the war. Benjamin returned to Australia in 1919 and taught piano at the New South Wales State Conservatory of Music in Sydney but two years later went to England again and for thirteen years taught at the Royal College of Music, gaining recognition as an outstanding piano teacher. Although he had begun writing chamber music while in prison, Benjamin's career as a composer did not flourish until the 1920s when his string quartets and other instrumental works found favor. In the 1930s he also wrote symphonic works and operas. During World War II he conducted the Canadian Broadcasting Corporation Symphony Orchestra and, through radio and live concerts, became a major figure in Canadian music. In the years after the war, Benjamin taught and conducted on three continents, premiering his own works and those by others in Australia, Great Britain, Canada, and the States.

Benjamin first became involved in movies in 1934 when director Alfred Hitchcock needed a dramatic symphonic piece of music for a climactic scene in his spy thriller *The Man Who Knew Too Much*. Benjamin scored the whole film, composing "Storm Cloud Cantata" for the concert scene at the Albert Hall in which an assassin attempts to shoot the prime minister during a section when the crashing cymbals will drown out his gunshot. That same year Benjamin wrote a fanciful score for the period adventure movie *The Scarlet Pimpernel*. Over the next three years he scored six other British movies then did not return to screen music until after the war. Benjamin wrote music for another six features, as well as long and short documentaries and two TV movies, before his death from cancer in 1960 at the age of sixty-six. Among his other notable screen scores are those for *The Guv'nor* (known in the States as *Mister Hobo*), *The Clairvoyant*, *Under the Red Robe*, *Return of the Scarlet Pimpernel*, *An Ideal Husband*, and *Above Us the Waves*, as well as two esteemed documentaries, *Under the Caribbean* and *The Conquest of Everest*. His classical musical output was prodigious, including five operas, symphonies, concertos, chamber music, choral works, and sacred music. His most performed and recorded work is the vibrant *Jamaican Rumba* from the orchestral suite *Two Jamaican Pieces* (1938). While all of Benjamin's concert work has been published and recorded, the sheet music for some of his film scores is lost, the music existing only in the surviving prints of the movies.

Although the number of movies Benjamin scored is limited, he was fortunate to be connected with some reputable films. Hitchcock's first film version of *The Man Who Knew Too Much* is not as well known as his 1956 remake, but there is much to recommend in the original, including the score. The "Storm Cloud Cantata" is filled with triumphant brass and, as the plot dictates, explosive percussion, yet there are some quieter, lyrical passages as well. An adagio section for chorus, strings, and reeds is a felicitous piece that soothes yet, in the context of the scene, builds suspense by its ignorance of the assassination attempt. (When Hitchcock remade this story in 1956, he retained Benjamin's music for the concert sequence.) The rest of the score for *The Man Who Knew Too Much* is also symphonic. The opening theme is a regal march with proud fanfares, and the chase music is in the grand manner, almost like a cavalry charge. The comic adventure classic *The Scarlet Pimpernel* opens with frenzied flutes swirling around "The Marseillaise," then there is a nod to the British with an original military march that has a wry flavor. There is also an elegant court processional and nimble ballroom dance music. Few costume pieces are as witty as *The Scarlet Pimpernel*, and Benjamin's spirited music adds to the fun. Another stylish period piece is Oscar Wilde's social comedy *An Ideal Husband*, which producer-director Alexander Korda gave a lavish and colorful production that dripped with Victoriana. The Arthur Sullivan–like score has a dizzying string polka, a melodious march that rings of empire, and fanciful salon music that injects some zest into the very talky movie. The historical costume drama *Under the Red Robe*, about the French cardinal Richelieu (Raymond Massey) and his battle with the Huguenots, opens with a vigorous series of fanfares that lead into a resplendent march that has a Gallic flavor. Much of the rest of the score is more than a little brusk and sensible, but the love theme is a bit feisty and bubbly.

The contemporary movies Benjamin scored have less grandiose but still symphonic music. The delightful comedy *Mister Hobo/The Guv'nor*, about a tramp (George Arliss) who is mistaken for a Rothschild, has a felicitous score with a catchy main theme that is homey and honest. There is busy music for the hustle and bustle of Paris and a majestic but amusing theme for the tramp and his sense of freedom and the open road. The intelligent psychic thriller *The Clairvoyant*, about a phony mind reader (Claude Rains) who acquires real powers, has some intriguing music. The opening theme is tempestuously stormy with symphonic rising and falling like a whirlwind. When the clairvoyant has a real foreshadowing, there is a simple but mesmerizing theme of distorted strings that also wavers up and down. Also of interest is the music for a horse race, a propulsive flurry of notes played by trumpets. *Above Us the Waves*, an action film set during the World War II battle for the Atlantic, has some stirring music. One theme captures the ebb and flow of the sea with a series of horn and string crescendos, while another, played by a harmonica and orchestra, is a sea chantey with a melancholy air. There is a rousing flamenco passage in the romantic melodrama *Wings of the Morning*, as well as a triumphant march with a Spanish flavor and a frenzied fandango with furious violins and woodwinds. The first Technicolor film made in Great Britain, *Wings of the Morning*, has impressive decor and atmospheric scenes in England and Spain. Benjamin's score does justice to both locales. The same can be said for his music for *Turn of the Tide*, set in an English fishing village. The main theme, with its echoing trumpet calls and wavering strings, captures the town's brutal connection to the sea.

Of Benjamin's handful of short and feature-length documentaries, *The Conquest of Everest* is considered a classic in the genre. Surely his music for the movie is a cinematic highlight. There is a bold main theme that uses brass and strings in an exhilarating manner, the music climbing the scale with bravado parallel to the determination of Edmund Hillary and his crew. Another passage featuring tense strings repeats a musical phrase at different octaves, also giving the feeling of ascent. The triumphal victory music at the end of the documentary is far from subtle yet seems justified in the context of the visuals. *The Conquest of Everest* is filled with pride and the music is celebratory on a grand scale. Like William Walton, Howard Blake, William Alwyn, and other masterful British composers from the concert world who worked occasionally in films, Benjamin left his mark on the British cinema by providing superb scores for some fine movies. Fourteen feature films is not an impressive number, but moviegoers are lucky to have them and to be able to enjoy Benjamin's enthralling music.

Credits

(all films UK unless stated otherwise)

Year	Film	Director
1934	*The Man Who Knew Too Much*	Alfred Hitchcock
1934	*The Scarlet Pimpernel*	Harold Young
1935	*Turn of the Tide*	Norman Walker
1935	*Mister Hobo* (aka *The Guv'nor*)	Milton Rosmer
1935	*The Clairvoyant* (aka *The Evil Mind*)	Maurice Elvey
1937	*Wings of the Morning*	Harold D. Schuster, Glenn Tryon
1937	*Under the Red Robe*	Victor Sjöström (UK/USA)
1937	*Return of the Scarlet Pimpernel*	Hanns Schwarz
1947	*Master of Bankdam*	Walter Forde
1947	*An Ideal Husband*	Alexander Korda
1953	*The Conquest of Everest*	George Lowe
1954	*Under the Caribbean*	Hans Hass (Switzerland)
1955	*Above Us the Waves*	Ralph Thomas
1958	*The Naked Earth*	Vincent Sherman

BENNETT, Richard Rodney (1936–2012) An acclaimed British composer for the concert hall, he scored thirty-six feature films with music as eclectic as that found in his many orchestral pieces.

Richard Rodney Bennett was born in Broadstairs, Kent, England, the son of poet and children's books author Rodney Bennett and pianist-singer Joan Esther. The family moved to the county of Devon where Ben-

nett grew up with an early interest in music. He later studied at the Royal Academy of Music and in Paris with composer-conductor Pierre Boulez. Bennett was greatly influenced by this avant-garde artist and Boulez's ideas about modern music show up in Bennett's work. His first published piece, a sonata for piano, came out in 1954, followed by a prodigious output that includes symphonies, operas, choral works, sonatas, concertos, and many small ensemble compositions; in all, over 150 musical works. Bennett scored his first film in 1957 and would return to the medium on and off over the next forty years. Most of his credits are British movies, but he also wrote for Hollywood on occasion. The variety in his movies is notable, ranging from sophisticated comedies, such as *Indiscreet* and *Four Weddings and a Funeral*, to mystery-thrillers, as with *Blind Date* (titled *Chance Meeting* in the States) and *Murder on the Orient Express*, to historical epics, such as *Lady Caroline Lamb* and *Nicholas and Alexandra*, to disturbing dramas, as with *Equus* and *Secret Ceremony*, to literary classics, for example *The Devil's Disciple* and *Far from the Madding Crowd*. Bennett's other noteworthy films include *Enchanted April*, *Yanks*, *Billy Liar*, *The Brink's Job*, *Billion Dollar Brain*, and *The Nanny*. He also worked in television throughout his career. Among his TV movies and miniseries are *Sherlock Holmes in New York* (1976), *The Ebony Tower* (1984), *Murder with Mirrors* (1985), *Tender Is the Night* (1985), *Poor Little Rich Girl: The Barbara Hutton Story* (1987), *The Charmer* (1987), *The Attic: The Hiding of Anne Frank* (1988), *Strange Interlude* (1988), *The Tale of Sweeney Todd* (1997), and *Gormenghast* (2000). Bennett returned to the Royal Academy as a teacher in the 1960s and also taught briefly at the Peabody Institute in Baltimore. He was appointed Commander of the Order of the British Empire in 1977, was named the chair of composition at the Academy in the 1990s, and was knighted in 1998.

Bennett's music has been described as modernist, yet he wrote in so many different styles that no one label fits. His interest in the avant-garde is matched by a love of jazz. He was very interested in the innovative musical movement called "serialism" early in his career, while in his last decades he experimented a good deal with musical collage. While little of the truly avant-garde can be found in his film scores, there is remarkable musical variety in his screen work. For the movie version of Thomas Hardy's *Far from the Madding Crowd*, Bennett wrote a simple but haunting theme made up of five notes that climb the scale then retreat back down. Sometimes played on a solo flute and other times by an oboe, the music suggests the loneliness of the rural life that drives the characters. The different themes for the different relationship are just as captivating, ranging from very primitive folk to fanciful to military. It is a quiet yet piercing score for a low-key, leisurely paced movie. The fussy and unintentionally silly period movie

Lady Caroline Lamb is beautiful to look at, and the music is totally engaging. The title character (Sarah Miles) is annoyingly fickle and impulsive, so Bennett wrote an unpredictable theme played by a solo viola that seems to go in different directions without resolving itself. The main theme is a lovely, flowing piece in which a lone violin is backed by a full contingent of strings. Bennett matches the lush decor in the movie with some busy rococo music, but it is the character themes that are the most pleasing. For the big-budget history film *Nicholas and Alexandra*, Bennett's music often focuses on the intimacy of the tale. There are fervent Russian folk songs and plenty of pomp and majesty, but the score is most proficient in conveying character. The doomed title couple (Michael Jayston and Janet Suzman) is musicalized with a seven-note motif that descends gracefully as it is repeated. The royal daughters are captured in a simple folk melody in which a five-note pattern is used effectively. The main theme for this long and turbulent movie is a march that is heard with gusto in some sections of the film, as a morose march of death in others. The World War II melodrama *Yanks* boasts an enticing love theme that avoids sentimentality and reflects the self-aware romances in the story. There is a bittersweet quality to the piece, just as the clouds of war shadow the movie. A different kind of cloud hangs over the comedy *Four Weddings and a Funeral* and this too is reflected in Bennett's gentle main theme, a surprisingly lyrical and restrained piece for a film that is often raucous and farcical.

The more experimental side of Bennett's music can be heard in two of his scores for mystery-thrillers. The spy movie *Billion Dollar Brain* has a splendid main theme with chaotic trumpets, furious piano scales, and a restless melody that propels itself through waves of percussion. As busy as it all is, there is still a romantic streak in the music. For the seductive "Anya" theme, woodwinds languidly tumble up and down. The action scenes in the film are scored with fervent fanfares and a touch of the tango, and there is a tentative military theme that has all the chill of the Cold War. More romanticized is the score for *Murder on the Orient Express*, a stylish Agatha Christie mystery that has a lot of talk, but with the all-star cast it is high-class entertainment. The main theme is a fashionable orchestral piece that might be heard at a 1930s upper-class restaurant. A piano sometimes takes on the foxtrot melody but as the theme recurs throughout the film it takes on different moods. There is a superb theme for the train itself, a sweeping waltz with a percussive beat that speeds up as the Orient Express does. A French horn is heard against strings, giving the famous train a regal character all its own. But the most unusual and fascinating part of the score is the music heard under the montage of a past crime that occurs right after the credits. This wordless sequence uses newspaper headlines and photos to provide the exposition necessary to the plot. This might have been a clumsy way to give the audience information, but with Bennett's mu-

sic it is a tour de force of movie storytelling. The sinister melody and series of foreboding chords are mesmerizing and chilling, especially as the high-pitched strings are filtered through a slight echo chamber. Rarely has a movie mystery started off so potently. Yet just about all of Bennett's scores are noteworthy, making it clear that his too-little time spent in movies must be treasured. Biography: *Richard Rodney Bennett: The Complete Musician*, Anthony Meredith, Paul Harris (2010).

Credits

(all films UK unless stated otherwise)

Year	Film	Director
1957	Pickup Alley (aka Interpol)	John Gilling
1957	Menace in the Night (aka Face in the Night)	Lance Comfort
1958	The Safecracker	Ray Milland
1958	Indiscreet	Stanley Donen (UK/USA)
1958	The Man Inside	John Gilling
1959	The Man Who Cheated Death	Terence Fisher
1959	The Angry Hills	Robert Aldrich
1959	Chance Meeting (aka Blind Date)	Joseph Losey
1959	The Devil's Disciple	Guy Hamilton, Alexander Mackendrick (UK/USA)
1961	The Mark	Guy Green
1962	Only Two Can Play	Sidney Gilliat
1962	Satan Never Sleeps	Leo McCarey (USA)
1963	The Wrong Arm of the Law	Cliff Owen
1963	Heavens Above!	John and Roy Boulting
1963	Billy Liar	John Schlesinger
1964	One Way Pendulum	Peter Yates
1965	The Nanny	Seth Holt
1966	The Witches	Cyril Frankel
1967	Far from the Madding Crowd (AAN)	John Schlesinger
1967	Billion Dollar Brain	Ken Russell
1968	Secret Ceremony (BAFTA-N)	Joseph Losey
1970	The Buttercup Chain	Robert Ellis Miller
1970	Figures in a Landscape (BAFTA-N)	Joseph Losey
1971	Nicholas and Alexandra (AAN)	Franklin J. Schaffner (USA)
1973	Lady Caroline Lamb (BAFTA-N)	Robert Bolt (UK/Italy)
1973	Voices	Kevin Billington
1974	Murder on the Orient Express (AAN; BAFTA)	Sidney Lumet
1975	The Executioner (aka Permission to Kill)	Cyril Frankel (UK/Austria/USA)
1977	The Accuser	Jean-Louis Bertuccelli (France)
1977	Equus (BAFTA-N)	Sidney Lumet (USA/UK)
1978	The Brink's Job	William Friedkin (USA)
1979	Yanks (BAFTA-N)	John Schlesinger (USA/W. Germany/UK)
1982	The Return of the Soldier	Alan Bridges
1991	Enchanted April	Mike Newell
1994	Four Weddings and a Funeral (BAFTA-N)	Mike Newell
1996	Swann	Anna Benson Gyles (Canada/UK)

BENNETT, Robert Russell (1894–1981) The most influential and renowned orchestrator in the history of the American musical theatre, he was also an accomplished conductor and composer who worked briefly in Hollywood in the 1930s.

Born in Kansas City, Missouri, to a musical family—his father a trumpet player and violinist, his mother a pianist—Robert Russell Bennett knew how to play a variety of instruments by the time he was in his teens. He then studied composition and began working as a copyist for a music publisher. During World War I he conducted army bands, then returned to New York City as a music arranger. His first Broadway assignment was orchestrating the score for *Daffy Dill* in 1922. By the time he orchestrated the hit operetta *Rose-Marie* two years later, Bennett was the most sought-after talent in his field. He was also the busiest orchestrator in the American theatre, his musical arrangements heard in over three hundred stage musicals. More importantly, Bennett was instrumental in creating the Broadway orchestra sound that is so familiar to generations of theatergoers. A list of Bennett's Broadway credits is practically a record of the musical theatre in the 1920s through the 1960s. He worked on just about all the musicals by Richard Rodgers and Lorenz Hart, Jerome Kern, Irving Berlin, George Gershwin, Cole Porter, Rodgers and Oscar Hammerstein, and many others. Because orchestrators were often not listed in playbill programs or movie credits, there were many shows that Bennett worked on that are uncredited. He was also very busy arranging music for television, concerts, ballets, and special events. All in all, it is estimated that Bennett orchestrated more music than any other American. Bennett composed incidental music for plays and television programs and wrote many concert works, including symphonies, operas, choral pieces, chamber music, tone poems, and band selections. Some of these are so accomplished that many wondered why he was content to arrange other composers' works rather than concentrate on his own compositions. Bennett spent only three years in Hollywood and contributed to some twenty films. He was usually hired as an orchestrator or arranger of the dance music for musicals, but he composed some incidental music when it was needed. His music can be heard in the Kern musicals *Swing Time*, *Joy of Living*, and *High, Wide and Handsome*, Berlin's *Carefree*, and Gershwin's *Damsel in Distress*. On a few occasions he wrote (or cowrote) the entire score for a nonmusical movie. Bennett rarely received screen credit, and often several composers worked on the same film, so his contribution is difficult to identify. Frustrated and missing New York, he returned east in 1940 to pick up his prolific Broadway career.

Bennett's genius as an orchestrator can be heard in some sixty movies, some that he worked on directly and others based on Broadway musicals that used his arrangements for the screen. But there is one film in which his composition talents are evident: *Intermezzo: A Love Story*. Being a melodrama about a concert violinist (Leslie Howard) who falls in love with his daughter's piano teacher (Ingrid Bergman), there are classical selections played and heard throughout the film, but in between is a score that is quite laudable. The major love theme for the two ill-fated lovers is based on Heinz Provost's "Intermezzo," a piece they perform together. Bennett's soundtrack score has a lovely domestic theme for the violinist's family life, a dainty and playful theme for their young daughter, and sprightly music for the lovers' travels across Europe. The bittersweet ending, when the violinist returns to his wife, is scored with just the right sense of pathos and resigned happiness. Max Steiner contributed some music to *Intermezzo*, and many orchestrators (including Bennett) worked on the different passages, but one senses that this is Bennett's movie. It was, sadly, his last. Autobiography: *The Broadway Sound: The Autobiography and Selected Essays of Robert Russell Bennett*, George Ferencz (ed.) (1999).

Credits

(all films USA)

Year	Film	Director
1936	*Swing Time*	George Stevens
1937	*High, Wide and Handsome*	Rouben Mamoulian
1937	*Damsel in Distress*	George Stevens

Year	Film	Director
1938	*Lawless Valley*	David Howard
1938	*Radio City Revels*	Benjamin Stoloff
1938	*Joy of Living*	Tay Garnett
1938	*Carefree*	Mark Sandrich
1938	*Annabel Takes a Tour*	Lew Landers
1939	*Pacific Liner*	Lew Landers
1939	*Twelve Crowded Hours*	Lew Landers
1939	*The Story of Vernon and Irene Castle*	H. C. Potter
1939	*Career*	Leigh Jason
1939	*5th Avenue Girl*	Gregory La Cava
1939	*Intermezzo: A Love Story*	Gregory Ratoff

BERNARD, James (1925–2001) A reputable British composer and orchestrator who brought a new sound to horror movies in the 1950s and 1960s, he is most known for his many scores for Hammer Films.

James Bernard was born in Nathia Gali, India, the son of a British army officer stationed there, but because of his poor health the boy was sent with his elder brother to live with their grandparents in England. Bernard showed an early aptitude on the piano and was given lessons while he was still very young. He later studied music at Wellington College, where he befriended fellow student Christopher Lee, who would later star in many of Bernard's movies at Hammer. Renowned composer Benjamin Britten encouraged Bernard by critiquing and even contributing to Bernard's early compositions. After serving in the Royal Air Force during World War II, he continued his music studies at the Royal College of Music. In 1950 he and his longtime partner, author Peter Dehn, wrote the screenplay for the British thriller *Seven Days to Noon* and won an Oscar for their efforts. But Bernard never wrote scripts again and concentrated on composing, beginning his career scoring programs for BBC Radio. While assisting Britten on the preparation for the opera *Billy Budd*, Bernard impressed producer-director Val Guest from Hammer Films and was hired to score the sci-fi thriller *The Quatermass Experiment* in 1955. Although he was restricted to a small number of musicians, Bernard composed and orchestrated a skillful horror score that avoided many of the Hollywood clichés and introduced a new and sparer soundtrack sound to the genre. Over the next two decades, Bernard scored twenty-four movies for Hammer, including such popular favorites as *The Horror of Dracula*, *The Curse of Frankenstein*, *Kiss of the Vampire*, *The Hound of the Baskervilles*, *She*, *The Devil Rides Out*, *The Plague of the Zombies*, and *The Scars of Dracula*. For other studios he wrote music for a variety of genres, including the scores for *Pacific Destiny*, *Across the Bridge*, *X: The Unknown*, and *Elephant Gun*. Bernard also scored short films, most memorably the award-winning *Door in the Wall* (1956), and documentaries, as with *The Immortal Land* (1958) and *A Place for Gold* (1960). Although he retired from movies in the late 1970s, Bernard returned to work to write music for the thriller *Murder Elite* in 1985 and scored some television documentaries about past horror films, such as *Flesh and Blood: The Hammer Heritage of Horror* (1994) and *Universal Horror* (1998). He also wrote a new score for the 1922 silent horror classic *Nosferatu*, which was broadcast on television in 1997.

Just as the Hammer films have a strong following today, so too do Bernard's scores. Out of necessity, he limited his orchestrations to modest-size but creative ensembles, such as using a combination of just strings and percussion. He is famous for his clashing harmonies and for repeating musical motifs that go higher and higher at dramatic moments. Perhaps his quintessential score is the one he wrote for *Horror of Dracula*, in which the name of the vampire was turned into a long, howling musical phrase. Bernard uses tympani and other percussion instruments to create a harsh sound, and the strings sometimes have sustained notes that resemble high woodwinds. One memorable effect is the way high strings descend and are replaced by deeper stringed instruments as the music tumbles down the scale. *Kiss of the Vampire* has a theme played on electric guitar and percussion that stops just shy of rock music. There is also a Rachmaninoff-like piano concerto that is disarmingly engaging because it is so unexpected. The recurring motif in *The Curse of Frankenstein* fluctuates like a series of waves, the cymbals providing the crashing of the water. The main theme in *She* is a seductive lullaby played on various strings. It repeats a simple musical phrase in a teasing manner then moves up the scale to do it again in another key. *Scars of Dracula* has a more symphonic sound, as a full string section plays in counterpoint to a simple percussive musical line. This is a more romantic score than most of Bernard's Hammer works, yet it too utilizes some of his best characteristics, such as that mesmerizing way of climbing the scale and toying with melody rather than succumbing to it. A more intellectual kind of suspense can be found in the Sherlock Holmes adventure *The Hound of the Baskervilles*, but in the Hammer version the atmosphere is still Gothic horror. Bernard's music follows suit, as with the passage in which brass and strings bombard their way up the scale and in one section in which drunken strings seem to dance a macabre kind of gavotte.

It is interesting to compare Bernard's few non-Hammer scores and hear how different, yet the same, they are. The best of these is the expert crime thriller *Across the Bridge*. Bernard gave the Hitchcock-like movie a Hitchcock-like score. It has a propulsive main theme in which a full orchestra races as if pursued by the demanding percussion. It is an exciting piece of music, not so much for the suspense aspect but because it is so urgent. Throughout the score Bernard returns to this theme in a more subdued manner, yet still it is tantalizing. This music makes a clear distinction between horror and thrills and, as much as many love the Hammer movies, one wishes Bernard did more films like *Across the Bridge*. Another interesting comparison is between Bernard's Hammer horror music and his new score for the old classic *Nosferatu*, the original Dracula film. Echoing electronic music is used throughout the score, and there is a lot of reverberation and distorted sound, sometimes punctuated by an unembellished solo piano. One passage is a repetitive series of motifs played on electric guitar, allowing for different variations as it speeds up. Another section is a rapid piece on electric keyboard that sounds more like a dizzying drug trip than a horror movie. This is perhaps Bernard's most modern-sounding score (it was written in 1997, four years before his death) and is not in the style that his fans might expect. The *Nosferatu* music comes across as new and unique, particularly in an age when music in horror movies has grown grandiose and bombastic. Biography: *James Bernard: Composer to Count Dracula*, David Huckvale (2006).

Credits

(all films UK unless stated otherwise)

Year	Film	Director
1955	*The Quatermass Experiment* (aka *The Creeping Unknown*)	Val Guest
1956	*Pacific Destiny*	Wolf Rilla
1956	*X: The Unknown*	Joseph Losey, Leslie Norman
1957	*The Curse of Frankenstein*	Terence Fisher
1957	*Quatermass II: Enemy from Space*	Val Guest
1957	*Across the Bridge*	Ken Annakin
1957	*Windom's Way*	Ronald Neame
1958	*Horror of Dracula*	Terence Fisher
1958	*Elephant Gun* (aka *Nor the Moon by Night*)	Ken Annakin
1959	*The Hound of the Baskervilles*	Terence Fisher
1959	*The Stranglers of Bombay*	Terence Fisher
1961	*The Terror of the Tongs* (aka *Terror of the Hatchet Men*)	Anthony Bushell
1963	*These Are the Damned* (aka *The Damned*)	Joseph Losey
1963	*The Kiss of the Vampire*	Don Sharp
1964	*The Gorgon*	Terence Fisher
1964	*The Secret of Blood Island*	Quentin Lawrence
1965	*She*	Robert Day
1966	*The Plague of the Zombies*	John Gilling

Year	Film	Director
1966	*Dracula: Prince of Darkness*	Terence Fisher
1967	*Frankenstein Created Woman*	Terence Fisher
1967	*Torture Garden*	Freddie Francis
1968	*The Devil Rides Out*	Terence Fisher
1968	*Dracula Has Risen from the Grave*	Freddie Francis
1969	*Frankenstein Must Be Destroyed*	Terence Fisher
1970	*Taste the Blood of Dracula*	Peter Sasdy
1970	*Scars of Dracula*	Roy Ward Baker
1973	*Frankenstein and the Monster from Hell*	Terence Fisher
1974	*The Legend of the 7 Golden Vampires* (aka *The 7 Brothers Meet Dracula*)	Roy Ward Baker, Cheh Chang (UK/Hong Kong)
1985	*Murder Elite*	Claude Whatham
1997	*Nosferatu* (1922)	F. W. Murnau (Germany)

BERNSTEIN, Elmer (1922–2004) Perhaps the Hollywood composer with the most eclectic credits, his 150-plus films include low-budget sci-fi flicks, multimillion-dollar epics, lowbrow sex comedies, highbrow historical pieces, urban film noir, rural melodramas, musical comedies, documentaries, spy thrillers, war adventures, sensitive character studies, and a lot of westerns.

Elmer Bernstein was born in New York City to parents who emigrated from the Ukraine and Austria-Hungary and as a child studied dance and acting with hopes for a stage career. At the same time he pursued painting and music, receiving awards for both his art and compositions. A prodigy on the piano, Bernstein studied with Juilliard teacher Henriette Michelson, who introduced him to composer Aaron Copland. Encouraged by such mentors, Bernstein concentrated on music. He achieved some recognition as a concert pianist, eventually doing a solo program at Manhattan's Town Hall in 1950. After serving in the army during World War II, Bernstein was asked to write music for radio broadcasts by the United Nations. These led to television assignments and his first feature film, the football drama *Saturday's Hero* in 1951. Just as his career was gathering steam, Bernstein was called before the House Un-American Activities Committee because he had written some music reviews for a Communist journal. Bernstein declared he had never attended a party meeting and refused to name names. Hollywood offers dried up, and he was forced to score such low-budget B movies as *Robot Monster*, *Cat Woman of the Moon*, and *Miss Robin Crusoe*.

Bernstein's career was jump-started again in 1955 with his chilling score for *The Man with the Golden Arm*, receiving his first of fourteen Oscar nominations. Very different but also noticed was his dramatic score the next year for the Cecil B. DeMille epic *The Ten Commandments*. Soon Bernstein was in demand, and he accepted all kinds of jobs, scoring a wide variety of movies genres with many different directors. His robust score for *The Magnificent Seven* in 1960 seemed to point the way for a career in westerns, and he did dozens more during his fifty-year career (including seven John Wayne movies). But Bernstein was equally triumphant with quieter and more intimate movies as well, such as *Summer and Smoke*, *To Kill a Mockingbird*, and *Birdman of Alcatraz*. Hollywood continued to hire him for big period pictures, such as *Hawaii*, *Thoroughly Modern Millie*, and *Gold*, then in the 1970s he found himself scoring a string of very popular contemporary comedies, such as *Animal House*, *Airplane!*, *Meatballs*, *Trading Places*, *Stripes*, and *Ghostbusters*. Yet Bernstein's career never followed a predictable pattern. Instead it would be punctuated with delightful surprises, as with his superior scores for such different movies as *Sweet Smell of Success*, *My Left Foot*, *Walk on the Wild Side*, *The Age of Innocence*, *The Grifters*, *The Great Escape*, *Rambling Rose*, *The Chosen*, and *Far from Heaven*. His television career began in 1953 scoring documentary shorts, but by the 1960s he was writing music for such series as *Johnny Staccato*, *Riverboat*, *Hollywood and the Stars*, and *The Big Valley*. Subsequent credits include *Owen Marshall: Counselor at Law*, *The Rookies*, and *Ellery Queen*. Bernstein's TV movies and miniseries include *Men of the Dragon* (1974), *Captains and the Kings* (1976), *The Chisholms* (1979), *Guyana Tragedy: The Story of Jim Jones* (1980), *Gulag* (1985), and *Introducing Doro-*

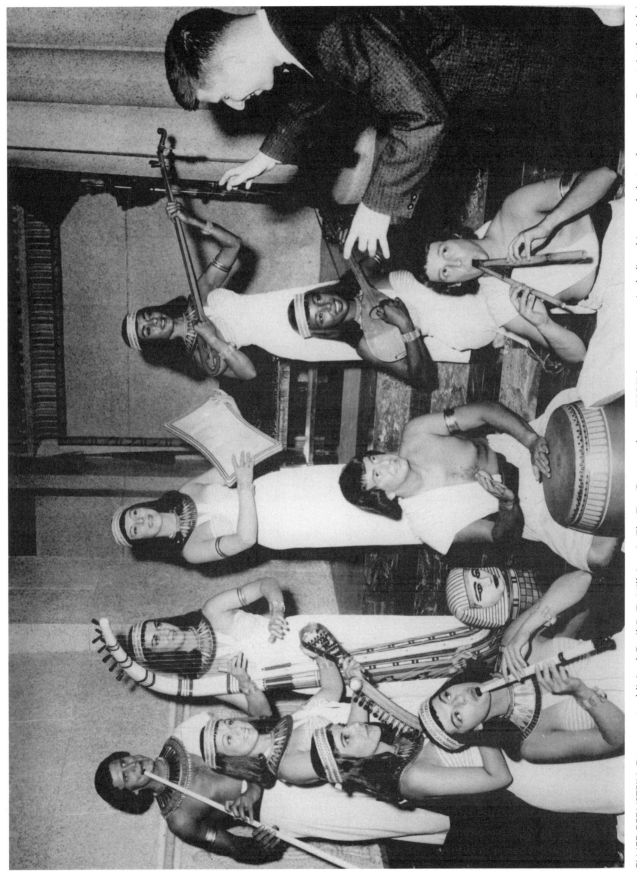

ELMER BERNSTEIN. Paramount publicized Cecil B. DeMille's epic *The Ten Commandments* (1956) in many ways, including this posed photo of composer Bernstein (far right) conducting some of the ancient Egyptian musicians and their instruments. The musicians are actors but some of the instruments are authentic. *Paramount Pictures / Photofest ©
Paramount Pictures*

thy Dandridge (1999), as well as several feature-length documentaries. He also scored two Broadway musicals, How Now, Dow Jones (1967) and Merlin (1983), but both failed to run. Bernstein conducted the recording of his screen scores and sometimes supervised the music for other composers' music. He also conducted on the concert stage with success and made several recordings of his own work as well as music by others. Among Bernstein's many classical compositions are orchestral suites, string quartets, song cycles, and works for violin and piano. For a time he taught at the University of Southern California's Thornton School of Music. Bernstein received many awards and honors during his lifetime and he returned the favor by mentoring struggling musicians and composers. His estate helps fund the Young Musicians Foundation. Several of his film scores have been recorded by others over the years. In fact, his scores for the movies The Journey of Natty Gann (1985), The Scarlet Letter (1995), Last Man Standing (1996), and Gangs of New York (2002) were not used in the final cuts but were later released on CD all the same. In the film world, he was referred to as "Bernstein West" to distinguish him from "Bernstein East," composer-conductor Leonard Bernstein. The two men were not related but were friends and even shared a physical resemblance to each other.

It is next to impossible to pinpoint Bernstein's musical style since his movie scores are so eclectic. Some of his screen work, such as a few of the westerns, is reminiscent of Copland's music, a tribute to the man who encouraged him as a youth. One can also detect aspects of Copland in such nonwesterns as God's Little Acre, Amazing Grace and Chuck, and To Kill a Mockingbird. Other times Bernstein has a grandiose style in the true Tinseltown tradition. For example, the music in The Ten Commandments is more about Hollywood than the Bible. Bernstein was adept at period music without being slavish to the era. The delightful score surrounding the songs (by various writers) in Thoroughly Modern Millie is Roaring Twenties but with a touch of 1960s sensibility. The entrancing salon music throughout The Age of Innocence transports the listener to an era (Old New York) that is not widely known to modern audiences. Yet there is much to be said for Bernstein's contemporary scores as well. The jaunty, jazzy themes in Sweet Smell of Success suggest a careless but dangerous lifestyle. The lively yet chaotic saxophone in The Man with the Golden Arm is a confused form of jazz.

In a lighter vein, the music for Ghostbusters is a cartoonish kind of vaudeville ditty while the mock suspense music in Airplane! seems like a Hitchcock parody.

Perhaps it is Bernstein's music for westerns that most comes to mind when considering his prolific career. The main theme from The Magnificent Seven has become a cliché now because of its use in Marlboro cigarette commercials for so many years. Yet imagine the impact of hearing such bold and masculine music coming from the screen for the first time. The Magnificent Seven, an expert American adaptation of the Japanese classic Seven Samurai (1954) into a Wild West adventure, works on many levels. Yet it was Bernstein's score that was so innovative. One might say it changed the sound of the Hollywood western. The famous main theme, with its charging brass and rushing strings, is so full of energy and grandeur that it seems to gallop along at a swift and cocky speed. Sections of the music have a strong Spanish flavor, other parts a classical format. The andante part of the theme becomes more poetic the slower it moves. This opening musical sequence alone is a fully developed little symphony and its impact cannot be underestimated; every subsequent western score was somehow affected by it. The villain of the film (Eli Wallach) has his own theme, a brass and drums motif that pounds away relentlessly as if the music is shooting bullets. Also memorable is a gentle passage heard on oboe that is augmented by a vigorous trumpet and guitar, a festive tarantella played on horns and marimba, and a romantic folk song for flute and guitar that is dreamy and languid. Like everyone else, Bernstein had a tough act to follow every time he scored a western. The main theme in The Sons of Katie Elder is similarly robust, but just not as catchy. Trumpets announce themselves with a forceful series of propulsive fanfares then break into a traveling melody with a Spanish flourish. Another up-tempo theme played on guitar and horns is marching music with a touch of the exotic as it tries to be seductive and boastful at the same time. There is also some fluid Spanish dance music that is slow and romantic without dragging out the musical lines. Bernstein's score for The Hallelujah Trail is more satisfying because this comic western, about a wagon full of liquor being driven through the desert, is slaphappy, unpretentious fun, and the music makes no effort to sound like The Magnificent Seven. The main theme is a rambunctious march with a gleeful sense of adventure as fife, brass, and drum scurry along happily. At one point a gospel-like chorus of singers do a syncopated version of the tune with lusty abandon. There is also a merry song in which a male chorus sings a mockingly patriotic number about the militia, a delicious theme played on a player piano and various instruments that reminds one of the soundtrack for a silent comedy, and a blatantly sentimental passage featuring a solo violin and weeping strings. The more subtle, perhaps more youthful, sounds in *True Grit* suggest an adventure that is more internal. This story, about a girl (Kim Darby) who hires an over-the-hill, drunken gunfighter (John Wayne) to hunt down her father's killer, calls for more than a bombastic score. The main theme is again a sparkling assault of brass and drums but there is a more poetic tone when the melody is slowed down and reveals a simple kind of sincerity. The title song (lyric by Don Black), which was sung by Glen Campbell on the soundtrack, was one of four of Bernstein's songs to be nominated for an Oscar.

After his westerns, Bernstein's scores for large-scale epics are the most known. Few movies were larger than Cecil B. DeMille's 1956 remake of his silent epic *The Ten Commandments* and Bernstein's score is one of his longest and most old fashioned, fulfilling DeMille's wish for music reminiscent of Hollywood's glory days. The opening titles are scored with sparkling horns, vigorous strings, and a symphonic sound that builds from one fanfare to another. This same music is later tamed and used as the theme for Moses (Charlton Heston). Among the many other themes heard throughout the nearly four-hour movie are a Hebrew-sounding passage that delicately descends the scale with grace and sorrow, grandiose triumphal music for imperial Egypt, an exotic love theme for the romance between Moses and the aristocratic beauty Nefretiri (Anne Baxter), chaotic symphonic chords and phrases for the destruction of the Egyptian army in the Red Sea, and the zesty, stirring march heard during the mass exodus out of Egypt. Bernstein originally scored this powerful scene with solemn, plodding music, which DeMille rejected, insisting on an up-tempo theme. A very different kind of epic, *Hawaii*, has a very different kind of score. The tale of American missionaries' attempt to bring Christianity to the natives of the Hawaiian Island in the nineteenth century was about the clash of two cultures. This is reflected in Bernstein's score, which mixes the reverent church music of New England with the tribal sounds of Polynesia. Bernstein discovered that the primary instruments of the latter are simple flutes and drums, so he built some of the themes around those sounds. The main theme is a five-note musical motif played on passionate strings that seem to be tossed upon a violent sea. There is also a Western march that uses the same five notes. The more exotic themes on flute and drum are sometimes very serene and lilting but often with an urgent, even dangerous, subtext to underline the inner and social turmoil in the epic. The Oscar-nominated song from *Hawaii* was "My Wishing Doll" (lyric by Mack David). Also in the epic vein is the rousing adventure *The Buccaneer* about the pirate Jean Lafitte (Yul Brynner) and the War of 1812. Much of the music is more a series of fanfares than fully developed melodies, creating excitement without resolution. The gushing love theme, on the other hand, is fervently melodic, as is a rowdy march and the vivacious music for the action scenes. Similarly, the contagious march in *The Great Escape* is so effective it is not surprising to learn that it became a favorite at sporting events.

Although Bernstein firmly established himself as a master of exciting screen music, many rate his "quieter" scores as superior. *To Kill a Mockingbird* is perhaps the best argument. This child's view of life in an Alabama town during the Depression remains one of Hollywood's finest dramas. It has outstanding writing, direction, and acting, but the delicate yet significant Bernstein score contributes a great deal to the movie. The fragile main theme is heard first on a piano and then on a Copland-like solo flute that seems to be tossed back and forth through the air, then the theme slowly grows into a full orchestral sound that is just short of overpowering. Some of the score has a childlike sense of awe, other passages are more lighthearted and even frolicsome. Bernstein scores the mysterious Radley house with odd and unsettling chords and minor-key music that pauses in the most uncomfortable way. Another quietly affecting drama, *My Left Foot*, can be thought of as an Irish variation on the *To Kill a Mockingbird* score. This poignant yet unsentimental film, about an Irish writer-painter (young Hugh O'Conor then adult Daniel Day-Lewis) stricken with cerebral palsy but determined to succeed against all odds, does not have very much music but what is there is subtly penetrating. The main theme, played by a small ensemble of woodwinds, strings, harp, and piano, is haunting and disturbing, yet one is drawn in rather than repulsed, just as the movie manages to do. Some spirited Irish airs are used throughout the movie, but none are there just for local color. Restraint seems to be the goal of the filmmakers and Bernstein's music echoes this. A different kind of restraint is found in *Far from Heaven*, the story of a 1950s suburban housewife (Julianne Moore) who finds herself drawn to the African American gardener (Dennis Haysburt) while her husband (Dennis Quaid) struggles with his closet homosexuality. What could have been a torrid melodrama is instead honest and very moving. Bernstein's main theme complements this restraint as strings, flute, and harp carefully climb the scale with a sense of yearning that is almost painful. Woodwinds and then a full orchestra fill out the theme but even when the music gains in strength there is still a feeling of foreboding. The seemingly happy home in Connecticut is conveyed by a domestic theme on piano and strings but the discontent under the surface is conveyed with a bit of jazz and some mournful passages filled with dissonance.

For a Bernstein score that is both intimate and epic, there is his music for *The Age of Innocence*. Martin Scorsese's radiant version of Edith Wharton's novel of 1870s New York City is an elegant period piece rendered with accuracy and style. Yet the film manages to retain a slightly contemporary point of view, heard in Joanne Woodward's sterling narration and in Bernstein's music, which mixes classical forms with synthesized touches. The story of a high-society gentleman (Daniel Day-Lewis) torn between his love for his conventional fiancée (Winona Ryder) and a supposedly scandalous countess (Michelle Pfeiffer) is a sad one, but there are no melodramatics and Scorsese asked Bernstein to avoid sentimentality in the score. Instead the music is formal, usually in waltz time, and aching with regret. The main theme is a minor-key waltz in which a six-note phrase sways back and forth with purpose. The themes for the three major characters are variations of this phrase, such as the music for the countess, which reverses the pattern and comes across as a bit exotic. Old New York society is scored with a stuffy waltz while the unconventional matriarch of the family (Miriam Margolyes) is musicalized by a major-key waltz that celebrates itself with glee. Bernstein's use of the synthesizer throughout the score is so subtle that the effect is never jarring or anachronistic. In fact, most viewers assumed that the music used for the underscoring in *The Age of Innocence* was as authentic as the operas and Viennese waltzes heard in the story. Over the decades Bernstein had demonstrated that he could write any kind of music for any kind of film. Yet to bridge the 1870s and the 1990s with music and not strike one wrong chord was quite an achievement indeed. Official website: www.elmerbernstein.com.

Credits

(all films USA unless stated otherwise; * for Best Song)

Year	Film	Director
1951	Saturday's Hero	David Miller
1952	Boots Malone	William Dieterle
1952	Sudden Fear	David Miller
1952	Battles of Chief Pontiac	Felix E. Feist
1953	Never Wave at a WAC	Norman Z. McLeod
1953	Robot Monster	Phil Tucker
1953	Cat Woman of the Moon	Arthur Hilton
1954	Miss Robin Crusoe	Eugene Frenke
1954	Make Haste to Live	William A. Seiter
1954	Silent Raiders	Richard Bartlett
1955	The Eternal Sea	John H. Auer
1955	The View from Pompey's Head	Philip Dunne
1955	The Man with the Golden Arm (AAN)	Otto Preminger
1955	Storm Fear	Cornel Wilde
1955	It's a Dog's Life	Herman Hoffman
1956	The Naked Eye	Louis Clyde Stoumen
1956	The Ten Commandments	Cecil B. DeMille
1957	Drango	Hall Bartlett, Jules Bricken
1957	Men in War	Anthony Mann

Year	Film	Director
1957	*Fear Strikes Out*	Robert Mulligan
1957	*Sweet Smell of Success*	Alexander Mackendrick
1957	*The Tin Star*	Anthony Mann
1958	*Desire under the Elms*	Delbert Mann
1958	*Saddle the Wind*	Robert Parrish
1958	*Kings Go Forth*	Delmer Daves
1958	*God's Little Acre*	Anthony Mann
1958	*Anna Lucasta*	Arnold Laven
1958	*The Buccaneer*	Anthony Quinn
1958	*Some Came Running*	Vincente Minnelli
1959	*The Race for Space*	David L. Wolper
1959	*The Miracle*	Irving Rapper
1959	*The Story on Page One*	Clifford Odets
1960	*The Fabulous Fifties*	Charles and Ray Eames
1960	*The Rat Race*	Robert Mulligan
1960	*From the Terrace*	Mark Robson
1960	*The Magnificent Seven* (AAN)	John Sturges
1961	*By Love Possessed*	John Sturges
1961	*The Young Doctors*	Phil Karlson
1961	*The Comancheros*	Michael Curtiz
1961	*Summer and Smoke* (AAN; GGN)	Peter Glenville
1962	*Walk on the Wild Side* (AAN*)	Edward Dmytryk
1962	*Birdman of Alcatraz*	John Frankenheimer
1962	*To Kill a Mockingbird* (AAN; GG)	Robert Mulligan
1962	*A Girl Named Tamiko*	John Sturges
1962	*How the West Was Won* (AAN)	John Ford, etc.
1963	*Hud*	Martin Ritt
1963	*The Great Escape*	John Sturges
1963	*The Caretakers*	Hall Bartlett
1963	*Rampage*	Phil Karlson
1963	*Kings of the Sun*	J. Lee Thompson
1963	*Love with the Proper Stranger*	Robert Mulligan
1963	*The Making of the President 1960*	Mel Stuart
1964	*The World of Henry Orient*	George Roy Hill
1964	*The Carpetbaggers*	Edward Dmytryk
1964	*Four Days in November*	Mel Stuart
1965	*Baby the Rain Must Fall*	Robert Mulligan
1965	*The Hallelujah Trail*	John Sturges
1965	*The Sons of Katie Elder*	Henry Hathaway
1965	*The Reward*	Serge Bourguignon
1966	*7 Women*	John Ford
1966	*The Silencers*	Phil Karlson
1966	*Cast a Giant Shadow*	Melville Shavelson
1966	*Hawaii* (AAN*; GG)	George Roy Hill
1966	*Return of the Seven* (AAN)	Burt Kennedy (USA/Spain)
1967	*Thoroughly Modern Millie* (AA; GGN)	George Roy Hill
1968	*The Scalphunters*	Sydney Pollack
1968	*I Love You, Alice B. Toklas!*	Hy Averback
1969	*Where's Jack?*	James Clavell (UK)
1969	*Midas Run*	Alf Kjellin
1969	*True Grit* (AAN*; GGN*)	Henry Hathaway
1969	*The Bridge at Remagen*	John Guillermin
1969	*Guns of the Magnificent Seven*	Paul Wendkos
1969	*The Gypsy Moths*	John Frankenheimer
1970	*Kifaru . . . The Black Rhino*	Irwin Rosten
1970	*The Liberation of L. B. Jones*	William Wyler
1970	*A Walk in the Spring Rain*	Guy Green

Year	Film	Director
1970	Cannon for Cordoba	Paul Wendkos
1971	Doctors' Wives	George Schaefer
1971	Big Jake	George Sherman
1971	See No Evil	Richard Fleischer (UK)
1972	SX-70	Charles and Ray Eames
1972	The Magnificent Seven Ride!	George McCowan
1972	The Amazing Mr. Blunden	Lionel Jeffries (UK)
1973	Cahill U.S. Marshal	Andrew V. McLaglen
1974	McQ	John Sturges
1974	Gold (AAN*)	Peter R. Hunt (UK)
1974	Nightmare Honeymoon	Elliot Silverstein
1974	The Trial of Billy Jack	Tom Laughlin
1975	Report to the Commissioner	Milton Katselas
1975	Mr. Quilp (aka The Old Curiosity Shop)	Michael Tuchner (UK)
1976	The Shootist	Don Siegel
1976	From Noon Till Three (GGN)	Frank D. Gilroy
1976	The Incredible Sarah	Richard Fleischer (UK)
1977	Daumier: Paris and the Spectator	Charles and Ray Eames
1977	Billy Jack Goes to Washington	Tom Laughlin
1977	The Look of America	Charles and Ray Eames
1978	Animal House	John Landis
1978	Bloodbrothers	Robert Mulligan
1979	Zulu Dawn	Douglas Hickox (USA, So. Africa)
1979	Meatballs	Ivan Reitman (Canada)
1979	The Great Santini	Lewis John Carlino
1980	Saturn 3	Stanley Donen (UK)
1980	Airplane!	Jim Abrahams, Jerry/David Zucker
1981	Going Ape!	Jeremy Joe Kronsberg (USA/UK)
1981	Stripes	Ivan Reitman
1981	Heavy Metal	Gerald Potterton (Canada)
1981	An American Werewolf in London	John Landis (UK/USA)
1981	Honky Tonk Freeway	John Schlesinger (USA/UK)
1981	The Chosen	Jeremy Kagan
1982	Genocide	Arnold Schwartzman
1982	Five Days One Summer	Fred Zinnemann
1982	Airplane II: The Sequel	Ken Finkleman
1983	Spacehunter: Adventures in the Forbidden Zone	Lamont Johnson (Canada/USA)
1983	Trading Places (AAN)	John Landis
1983	Class	Lewis John Carlino
1984	Ghostbusters	Ivan Reitman
1985	Marie Ward—Zwischen Galgen und Glorie	Angelika Weber (W. Germany)
1985	The Black Cauldron	Ted Berman, Richard Rich
1985	Spies Like Us	John Landis
1985	Prince Jack	Bert Lovitt
1986	Legal Eagles	Ivan Reitman
1986	Three Amigos!	John Landis
1987	Amazing Grace and Chuck	Mike Newell
1987	Leonard Part 6	Paul Weiland
1988	Da	Matt Clark
1988	Funny Farm	George Roy Hill
1988	The Good Mother	Leonard Nimoy
1989	Slipstream	Steven Lisberger (UK)
1989	My Left Foot	Jim Sheridan (Ireland/UK)
1990	One Day in Dallas	Gregory Bernstein
1990	The Field	Jim Sheridan (Ireland/UK)
1990	The Grifters	Stephen Frears
1991	Oscar	John Landis

Year	Film	Director
1991	*A Rage in Harlem*	Bill Duke (UK/USA)
1991	*Rambling Rose*	Martha Coolidge
1992	*The Babe*	Arthur Hiller
1993	*The Cemetery Club*	Bill Duke
1993	*Mad Dog and Glory*	John McNaughton
1993	*Lost in Yonkers*	Martha Coolidge
1993	*The Age of Innocence* (AAN)	Martin Scorsese
1993	*The Good Son*	Joseph Ruben
1995	*Roommates*	Peter Yates
1995	*Search and Destroy*	David Salle
1995	*Canadian Bacon*	Michael Moore
1995	*Devil in a Blue Dress*	Carl Franklin
1995	*Frankie Starlight*	Michael Lindsay-Hogg (France/UK)
1996	*Bulletproof*	Ernest R. Dickerson
1997	*Buddy*	Caroline Thompson
1997	*Hoodlum*	Bill Duke
1997	*The Rainmaker*	Francis Ford Coppola
1998	*Twilight*	Robert Benton
1999	*The Deep End of the Ocean*	Ulu Grosbard
1999	*Wild Wild West*	Barry Sonnenfeld
1999	*Bringing Out the Dead*	Martin Scorsese
2000	*Keeping the Faith*	Edward Norton
2000	*Chinese Coffee*	Al Pacino
2002	*Far from Heaven* (AAN; GGN)	Todd Haynes

BERNSTEIN, Leonard (1918–1990) One of the most renowned American conductors of the twentieth century, he was also a prolific composer of ballet, opera, musical theatre, and one film score important enough for him to be included in this book.

He was born Louis Bernstein in Lawrence, Massachusetts, the son of Ukrainian Jewish parents who were not musical but appreciated classical music. Bernstein began piano lessons as a boy then was later educated at Harvard and the Curtis Institute of Music before becoming assistant conductor at the Berkshire Music Center and eventually the conductor of the New York Philharmonic. He became famous overnight when in 1943 he replaced the ill conductor Bruno Walter at the last minute and, without any rehearsal, conducted the Philharmonic in a dazzling concert. Soon Bernstein was conducting distinguished orchestras around the world. Many of his performances were recorded, heard on the radio, and televised. In the 1950s he became a familiar face to Americans for his acclaimed *Young People's Concerts* on CBS-TV. Bernstein wrote his first symphony in 1942 and for the rest of his career composed for every medium, from the concert stage to television. His musical legacy includes three symphonies,

three ballets, two short operas, three choral works, several sonatas, chamber works, symphonic suites, piano pieces, incidental music for theatre and television, and five Broadway musicals: *On the Town* (1944), *Wonderful Town* (1953), *Candide* (1956), *West Side Story* (1957), and *1600 Pennsylvania Avenue* (1976). Although *On the Waterfront* is his only score for a feature film, his music can be heard in over one hundred movies. Some of his Broadway songs and ballet music were retained in the screen versions of *On the Town* (1949) and *West Side Story* (1961) but he did not compose any original music for those movies. His only original television score was for *The Lark* (1957) but so many of his concerts, musicals, ballets, and songs were televised over the decades that Bernstein's music flooded the American consciousness.

His music uses a wide variety of forms, from jazz to Latin to classical, and can be explosive and thrilling as well as tender and reflective. Much of this can be found in his celebrated score for *On the Waterfront*. Although Bernstein was very famous by 1954, he had not yet been approached to score a nonmusical movie by one of the big studios. Producer Sam Spiegel was impressed by Bernstein's musical comedy scores (this was three years before

West Side Story) and offered *On the Waterfront* to the composer who looked on the project as a new challenge and accepted. Bernstein had no experience scoring a film and approached the piece as a ballet or an opera, coming up with various themes and trying to musicalize the action on-screen. Some sections of the final film, in which the music tries too hard or is too obvious, point out Bernstein's inexperience, but for the most part it is a superior score. The main theme is a mournful French horn solo that captures the desolate loneliness and quiet even in an urban setting. This serenity is overwhelmed by the pulsating percussion of the city and a jazz saxophone competes with kettle drums until the music explodes in a thrilling Bernstein manner. The love theme, when played by a flute and harp, is enticing in its simplicity. When the same theme is given a full orchestration it loses something, as it overpowers the dialogue between the two lovers (Marlon Brando and Eva Marie Saint). Another memorable theme is the subdued string movement under two death scenes, in both cases starting quietly but building into a painful release of emotions. There is much in the *On the Waterfront* score that is like ballet and opera, and one can imagine the music being used onstage for either. How disappointing (and surprising) to think that Bernstein never scored another film. Autobiography: *Findings*, 1982; biographies: *Leonard Bernstein*, Meryle Secrest (1996); *Leonard Bernstein*, Humphrey Burton (1995). Official website: www. leonardbernstein.com.

Credits

Year	Film	Director
1954	On the Waterfront (AAN)	Elia Kazan (USA)

BLACK, Stanley (1913–2002) A prolific British pianist, bandleader, musical director, arranger, conductor, and composer, he was one of the busiest screen composers for the British cinema during the postwar years.

Born Solomon Schwartz in London, the son of a Jewish boot maker, Stanley Black began taking piano lessons at the age of seven. It was soon clear that he was a child prodigy, writing his own music and having his compositions performed on BBC Radio when he was only twelve and three years later winning a national contest for musical arranging. Black studied at the Matthay School of Music and then began his career as pianist, arranger, and composer for various bands. In the 1930s he also played with many famous jazz artists and made some memorable recordings with the American saxophonist Coleman Hawkins. After serving in the Royal Air Force during World War II, he became the house arranger for Decca Records and conducted the BBC Dance Orchestra in hundreds of radio broadcasts. Black was responsible for introducing new kinds of Latin music to British listeners through his records, radio, and later television programs. He also composed themes for radio shows and later had two of his own television programs, *Black Magic*, and *The Marvelous World of Stanley Black*. He first became involved with films when he did some music arrangements for a few British movies in the late 1930s and early 1940s. Black scored the government-made documentary short *The Ten Year Plan* (1945) and contributed some music to the crime drama *It Always Rains on Sunday* (1947) before scoring his first feature, the historical drama *Mrs. Fitzherbert* in 1947. His arrangements and score for the horror movie *The Monkey's Claw* the next year brought him wide recognition and Black's busy screen career was launched.

Over the next two decades he scored eighty British movies in all genres, from comedies and musicals to thrillers and melodramas. Among the most notable are *Laughter in Paradise*, *The Naked Truth*, *Too Many Crooks*, *The Crawling Eye*, *Behind the Headlines*, *Dual Alibi*, *Make Mine a Million*, *Jungle Fighters*, *Hand in Hand*, *The Rattle of a Simple Man*, and the Cliff Richard musicals *The Young Ones* and *Summer Holiday*. Black also served as conductor and/or arranger on many of his movies as well as dozens of films scored by others. In the 1960s and 1970s, Black returned to his classical music training and started conducting concerts for the London Philharmonic, the Royal Philharmonic, and the London Symphony. He also went to Asia and the Americas and conducted the finest orchestras there. Black made many recordings of classical music and the Stanley Black Orchestra made numerous records of ethnic music, jazz, and symphonic suites from

Broadway shows. After scoring a series of television documentaries titled *Discovering Britain with John Betjeman* in 1964, Black worked less and less in movies. His last feature film score was the biopic *Valentino* in 1977 although he continued to arrange and conduct the occasional movie until 1984. Black received many awards and honors during his later years, including the OBE in 1986. He was still conducting until a few years before he died in 2002 at the age of eighty-nine.

Black was so involved in all aspects of music during his busy life that in many ways his screen compositions take a backseat to his many recordings, broadcasts, and concerts. Also, very few of his films were popular outside of Great Britain, so his screen scores are not as well known as his other recordings. Yet one can hear Black's versatile musical talents in these scores. Nearly half of his 1950s movies are comedies, among them many British favorites. There are some delightful scores using jazz, classical, and pop music. The diplomatic satire *Top Secret* (retitled *Mr. Potts Goes to Moscow* in the States) opens with a mock Russian rhapsody in which heavy chords are offset by giddy brass instruments playing a zesty tune. The score for *Laughter in Paradise*, about an incognito maid (Fay Compton) with an impossible employer, has playful strings that flutter carelessly, speeding up when things get tense and winding down when the maid tires out. There is another clever theme with laughing brass and reeds. The opening music for *One Wild Oat* is a sprightly piece with a repeated three-note phrase that is both a fanfare and a laugh. The comedy also has an amusing march on strings and woodwinds that is catchy and a gliding waltz theme featuring woodwinds for the awkward love scenes. For the boarding school comedy *Bottoms Up*, Black wrote a farcical school song (lyric by Sid Colin), which is a jaunty march, later in the film speeded up for some of the slapstick scenes. The comic

crime movie *Too Many Crooks* has a jazzy main theme with snide brass and vivacious xylophone all punctuated by silly bongo drums. This too is later reprised at a faster tempo until it becomes a wacky march.

The music for the more serious movies Black scored is equally masterful. The crime drama *The Man in the Back Seat* has a superb jazz score. The main theme consists of variations on a musical phrase played by different jazz instruments with each variation. The opening music for *Dual Alibi*, a British film noir, has violins racing up and down the scale before breaking into a tortured waltz. The rest of the score alternates between romantic themes and harsh dramatic ones. Black scored a handful of horror movies, the most preposterous being *The Crawling Eye* about a giant eyeball that attacks a mountain village. The use of music in this schlock thriller is unusual. Before the opening credits there is silence while the first attack is made with no musical embellishment. The main theme follows, a blast of trumpets and tympani in a series of chords all suggesting a deadly race. Later attacks are also silent, though the suspense music leading up to them consists of wavering brass that somehow manages to move up the scale without one noticing it. In contrast is the gentle character drama *Hand in Hand* about a young Roman Catholic boy (Denis Gilmore) who befriends a young Jewish girl (Loretta Parry). Black uses warm romantic music featuring harp and piccolo throughout the film. In a lighter vein is a merry march with fluttering woodwinds in counterpoint to repeated phrases on strings, and there is a flowing waltz theme for a scene when the two kids float down a stream on a raft. Just as Black was proficient in many kinds of music, he was also expert at scoring different kinds of movies. In his day, Black was one of the most famous names in both popular and classical music in Great Britain. Today his records thrive but his movies are mostly forgotten, particularly outside his homeland.

Credits

(all films UK unless stated otherwise)

Year	Film	Director
1947	*Mrs. Fitzherbert*	Montgomery Tully
1948	*The Fatal Night*	Mario Zampi
1948	*The Monkey's Paw*	Norman Lee
1948	*The Hideout* (aka *The Small Voice*)	Fergus McDonell

Year	Film	Director
1948	*Dual Alibi*	Alfred Travers
1949	*Third Time Lucky*	Gordon Parry
1949	*The Interrupted Journey*	Daniel Birt
1950	*Paul Temple's Triumph*	Maclean Rogers
1950	*Come Dance with Me*	Mario Zampi
1950	*Shadow of the Past*	Mario Zampi
1951	*One Wild Oat*	Charles Saunders
1951	*Laughter in Paradise*	Mario Zampi
1951	*Lilli Marlene*	Arthur Crabtree
1952	*Mr. Potts Goes to Moscow* (aka *Top Secret*)	Mario Zampi
1952	*Holiday Week*	Arthur Crabtree
1953	*Recoil*	John Gilling
1953	*White Fire* (aka *Three Steps to the Gallows*)	John Gilling
1953	*Escape by Night*	John Gilling
1954	*Impulse*	Charles de Lautour, Cy Enfield
1954	*Tonight's the Night* (aka *Happily Ever After*)	Mario Zampi
1954	*Orders Are Orders*	David Paltenghi
1955	*The Gilded Cage*	John Gilling
1955	*As Long as They're Happy*	J. Lee Thompson
1955	*Cross-Up* (aka *Tiger by the Tail*)	John Gilling
1955	*An Alligator Named Daisy*	J. Lee Thompson
1955	*Breakaway*	Henry Cass
1955	*A Yank in Ermine*	Gordon Parry
1956	*Now and Forever*	Mario Zampi
1956	*Bond of Fear*	Henry Cass
1956	*Passport to Treason*	Robert S. Baker
1956	*Teenage Bad Girl* (aka *My Teenage Daughter*)	Herbert Wilcox
1956	*Behind the Headlines*	Charles Saunders
1956	*High Terrace*	Henry Cass
1957	*Stranger in Town*	George Pollock
1957	*City after Midnight* (aka *That Woman Opposite*)	Compton Bennett
1957	*Dangerous Youth* (aka *These Dangerous Years*)	Herbert Wilcox
1957	*Time Lock*	Gerald Thomas
1957	*The Circle* (aka *The Vicious Circle*)	Gerald Thomas
1957	*The Mailbag Robbery* (aka *The Flying Scot*)	Compton Bennett
1957	*Your Past Is Showing* (aka *The Naked Truth*)	Mario Zampi
1957	*Professor Tim*	Henry Cass (Ireland)
1958	*The Man Who Wouldn't Talk*	Herbert Wilcox
1958	*Wonderful Things!*	Herbert Wilcox
1958	*Black Tide* (aka *Stormy Crossing*)	C. M. Pennington-Richards
1958	*Blood of the Vampire*	Henry Cass
1958	*The Crawling Eye* (aka *The Trollenberg Terror*)	Quentin Lawrence
1958	*Further Up the Creek*	Val Guest
1959	*Broth of a Boy*	George Pollock (Ireland)
1959	*Make Mine a Million*	Lance Comfort
1959	*Rebound* (aka *Violent Moment*)	Sidney Hayers
1959	*Too Many Crooks*	Mario Zampi
1959	*Jack the Ripper*	Robert S. Baker, Monty Berman
1959	*The Battle of the Sexes*	Charles Crichton
1959	*Tommy the Toreador*	John Paddy Carstairs
1960	*The Flesh and the Fiends* (aka *Mania*)	John Gilling
1960	*Bottoms Up*	Mario Zampi
1960	*Hell Is a City*	Val Guest
1960	*Follow That Horse!*	Alan Bromly
1960	*Sands of the Desert*	John Paddy Carstairs
1960	*Stop Me Before I Kill!* (aka *The Full Treatment*)	Val Guest
1960	*The Siege of Sidney Street*	Robert S. Baker, Monty Berman
1960	*Boyd's Shop*	Henry Cass (Ireland)

Year	Film	Director
1961	*Five Golden Hours*	Mario Zampi (Italy/UK)
1961	*Hand in Hand*	Philip Leacock
1961	*Jungle Fighters* (aka *The Long and the Short and the Tall*)	Leslie Norman
1961	*House of Mystery*	Vernon Sewell
1961	*Double Bunk*	C. M. Pennington-Richards
1961	*The Man in the Back Seat*	Vernon Sewell
1961	*The Day the Earth Caught Fire*	Val Guest
1961	*Wonderful to Be Young!* (aka *The Young Ones*)	Sidney J. Furie
1962	*The Pot Carriers*	Peter Graham Scott
1963	*Summer Holiday*	Peter Yates
1963	*Maniac*	Michael Carreras
1963	*What a Crazy World*	Michael Carreras
1963	*80,000 Suspects*	Val Guest
1963	*West 11*	Michael Winner
1964	*Swingers' Paradise* (aka *Wonderful Life*)	Sidney J. Furie
1964	*The Girl-Getters* (aka *The System*)	Michael Winner
1964	*Rattle of a Simple Man*	Muriel Box
1965	*City in the Sea* (aka *The City under the Sea*)	Jacques Tourneur
1969	*Crossplot*	Alvin Rakoff
1974	*Mission: Monte Carlo*	Roy Ward Baker, Basil Dearden
1977	*Valentino*	Ken Russell (UK/USA)

BLAKE, Howard (David) (b. 1938) A highly respected British pianist, conductor, and composer for the concert hall, ballet, opera, and a dozen feature movies, he is most known to the general public for his radiant score for the animated short *The Snowman*.

Born in London to a family that loved music—his mother a violinist and pianist and his father a tenor in the church choir—Howard Blake grew up in Brighton. Blake sang in operettas, gave piano recitals, and soon began composing original pieces. He won a scholarship to the Royal Academy of Music where he studied piano, but he lost interest in composing because he had no interest in the avant-garde music that was so prevalent at the time. After graduation Blake performed in pubs and nightclubs, then got work as an arranger and pianist for EMI Records. His interest in film began when he got a job as an assistant projectionist at the National Film Theatre in London and became fascinated with movie music. Blake's first film score was for the Peter Brook short *Ride of the Valkyrie* (1967) and the next year he wrote music for the popular television series *The Avengers*. His first feature film assignment was the comedy *Some Will, Some Won't* in 1970, but wide recognition did not come until seven years later

when he scored Ridley Scott's first film, *The Duelists*. When Raymond Briggs's children's book *The Snowman* was made into an animated short in 1982, Blake was hired to write the score. Both the film and Blake's music became internationally famous, the song "Walking in the Air" (lyric also by Blake) becoming a chart record as well. He also scored other film shorts and TV movies in England as well as such American and British feature films as *Flash Gordon*, *The Lords of Discipline*, *A Month in the Country*, *A Midsummer Night's Dream*, and *My Life So Far*. Movies have been only a relatively small part of Blake's prolific music career. In the 1980s he was very productive writing ballets, concertos, chamber pieces, oratorios, song cycles, operas, and various kinds of orchestral works. Blake has had a very eclectic career, winning honors from the British government and famed institutions; scoring movies; writing commissioned work for festivals and special occasions; and even turning out TV commercial jingles. In 1983 he founded Highbridge Music Ltd. to publish and handle the performance rights to his over six hundred musical works. For years he was the executive director of the Performance Rights Society, and he was cofounder of the Association of Professional Composers in 1979.

Blake's music for the screen is as eclectic as his career. The period drama *The Duelists* is set during the Napoleonic Wars and is beautifully filmed; Blake created a sparkling classical-sounding score that supports the stunning visuals. A string orchestra plays the main theme, a restless and passionate piece in which rising crescendos add to the drama. As the title suggests, the movie includes a series of rapier duels and most of these are presented without music, quite against the Hollywood tradition. Only in the final and climactic duel on horseback does Blake introduce rumbling percussion and worried strings that climb up the scale as in the main theme. Male rivalry takes a different form in *The Lords of Discipline* set in a Southern military school in the 1960s. The haunting main theme poses flutes against a distorted bass line as forbidding percussion creates tension. There is also a touch of jazz in the music that keeps it modern. Blake wrote an extensive score for the campy sci-fi adventure *Flash Gordon* but only a portion of it was used. Instead there are rock songs by Queen and others that are used extensively and Blake's playful music is secondary. Recordings of the unused score have been released and there is some marvelous music in them, including a witty theme for Emperor Ming (Max von Sydow) that is regal and silly at the same time. The music for the unintentionally funny *Amityville 3-D* is in the expected horror film mode with wordless voices and a pounding tempo. Yet Blake adds some nice touches, such as hesitating strings, piano, and oboe that ignore the percussion and merge in a lilting passage. The pre–World War I spy thriller *The Riddle of the Sands* has a stately score that conveys suspense in quiet and subtle ways. The main theme is graceful and rhythmic, conveying the sweeping motion of water. (Much of the movie is set on a yacht at sea.) One musical passage rises and falls with the waves in an enticing manner.

All of Blake's many musical works, both for the screen and elsewhere, is somewhat eclipsed by his score for *The Snowman*. The contagious six-note phrase in the "Walking in the Air" theme (and song) is one of those rare pieces of music that needs to be heard only once and it is never forgotten. The hymnlike theme is both reverent and spirited, gleeful and bittersweet. The brief prologue for *The Snowman* has the only spoken words in the film and no music; the rest of the twenty-six minutes is a glorious blend of visuals and music. Snow falling is heralded with brass and excited piano chords, the creation of the snowman is a flute-piano piece that captures the boy's glee, a ride on a motorcycle is scored with a vigorous series of rising and falling strings, and the dance of the snowmen at the North Pole is a sparkling Scottish air. Blake is not embarrassed that of his hundreds of works his most beloved music is that for an animated short. How can one not be proud of this twenty-six minutes of pure musical joy? Official website: www.howardblake.com.

Credits

(all films UK unless stated otherwise)

Year	Film	Director
1970	*Some Will, Some Won't*	Duncan Wood
1970	*All the Way Up*	James MacTaggart
1973	*The Rainbow Boys* (aka *The Rainbow Gang*)	Gerald Potterton (Canada)
1977	*The Duellists*	Ridley Scott
1978	*The Odd Job*	Peter Madak
1979	*The Riddle of the Sands*	Tony Maylam (USA/UK)
1980	*Flash Gordon* (BAFTA-N)	Mike Hodges
1983	*The Lords of Discipline*	Franc Roddam (USA)
1983	*Amityville 3-D*	Richard Fleischer (USA)
1987	*A Month in the Country*	Pat O'Connor
1996	*A Midsummer Night's Dream*	Adrian Noble
1999	*My Life So Far*	Hugh Hudson (UK/USA)

BLANCHARD, Terence (b. 1962) An acclaimed African American jazz trumpeter, bandleader, and composer, he has scored thirty-two feature films since 1991, including eleven movies with director Spike Lee.

Born Terence Oliver Blanchard in New Orleans, Louisiana, the only son of an insurance company manager and an opera singer, he began piano lessons at the age of five. Three years later he also took up the trumpet but showed little proficiency at first. As a teenager, Blanchard took classes at the New Orleans Center for Creative Arts, then returned to the trumpet when he studied with jazz saxophonist Paul Jeffrey at Rutgers University. His first professional experience was playing in Lionel Hampton's Orchestra, then he replaced trumpeter Wynton Marsalis in Art Blakely's Jazz Messengers, for which he did arrangements as well. In the 1980s, Blanchard teamed with pianist Mulgrew Miller and saxophonist Donald Harrison and became one of the foremost artists in the resurgence of jazz in that decade. After many concerts and five albums, Blanchard went solo in 1990, performing in clubs and recording some solo albums that climbed the jazz charts. He first got involved in films when he played trumpet on the soundtrack for *School Daze* (1988) then performed on the soundtracks of two Spike Lee films, *Do the Right Thing* (1989) and *Mo' Better Blues* (1990). Lee hired him to score his next movie, *Jungle Fever*, in 1991, and the two artists worked so well together that Blanchard has written the music for every Lee film since then. Among their notable collaborations are *Malcolm X*, *Get On the Bus*, *Crooklyn*, *Summer of Sam*, *Clockers*, *25th Hour*, *Miracle at St. Anna*, *Inside Man*, and the documentary *Four Little Girls*. For other directors, Blanchard has written music for a variety of movies, including *Barbershop*, *Eve's Bayou*, *Next Friday*, *Original Sin*, *Dark Blue*, *Cadillac Records*, and *Red Tails*. Blanchard often conducts and performs on his soundtracks and his trumpet playing can be heard in dozens of movies scored by others.

He has also worked frequently in television, scoring twenty documentaries, miniseries, and TV movies, including *Assault at West Point* (1994), *The Promised Land* (1995), *The Color of Courage* (1998), *Having Our Say: The Delany Sisters' First 100 Years* (1999), *Bojangles* (2001), *Jim Brown: All American* (2002), *Their Eyes Were Watching God* (2005), *When the Levee Broke* (2006), and *Gun Hill* (2011). As busy as Blanchard has been in movies and television, he has remained very active in composing, performing, and recording jazz. In addition to many award-winning albums, he has written a requiem for Katrina victims titled *A Tale of God's Will*, incidental music for Broadway plays, and an opera, *Champion*, about gay prizefighter Emile Griffith, which premiered in 2013. A frequent guest and judge at jazz festivals, he is also the artistic director of the Thelonius Monk Institute of Jazz at the University of Southern California.

Blanchard's music has been described as in the "funky hard bop" style, a later version of the bebop of the 1950s. Hard bop tends to be more urban and aggressive than the cool jazz style. Many of Blanchard's scores are for very urban movies yet one finds all kinds of jazz and even nonjazz music in his screen work. Like the best movie composers, he senses the rhythm of the film then chooses the kind of music that works best. For the stylish biopic *Malcolm X*, which takes place in the 1940s through 1965, the music shifts as time passes. The main theme is a jazz funeral dirge with a ponderous beat and a forlorn trumpet solo. The mourning, wordless vocals in the theme are sustained but the percussion bursts in at times creating a very edgy piece of music.

The score also has a hesitant jazz piece played on a bass string without accompaniment before a trumpet solo breaks through with a heartfelt blues lament, the piano playing a nervous countermelody. There is a passage with a simple tune that is engaging in the way it develops, moving from solo trumpet to a full jazz combo. Another memorable passage is a restless blues with a chaotic melody and an anxious bass line. Like many of the contemporary films Blanchard has scored, *Clockers* and *Crooklyn* both use lots of rock or rap songs by others. But his score for the bank heist movie *Inside Man* is pretty much all his and is filled with fine music. There is an echoing chant with rock and Latin flourishes, a flowing symphonic theme that ripples with waves of music repeating a simple motif with different instruments, and a rambunctious passage that switches keys and tempos as the music seems to fall into a bottomless pit and get swallowed up by the harsh chords. Another passage moves slowly like a funeral march but cries out with energy as opposed to one sprightly jazz passage that moves from carefree abandon to a desperate chase. The cop melodrama *Dark Blue* has a brooding score. There is a superb theme with trumpet solo and piano that seems weary but is still full of life, even its sustained notes breathing fire. Another moody passage uses high-pitched pipes and howling sound effects to add to the tentative piano and the jittery bass.

Two World War II movies scored by Blanchard are of more than passing interest. *Red Tails*, about the African American flyers known as the Tuskegee Airmen, has a vigorous symphonic main theme with a series of fanfares that often break into flight. There is also a rhythmic passage in which a rocking bass line competes with a flowing orchestral march. Military percussion and gliding trumpets compete with an inspiring choral passage in one of the film's most moving sections. African American soldiers known as Buffalo Soldiers fight in Italy during the same war as in *Miracle at St. Anna* but this time the score is more lyrical. The main theme is a delicate lullaby heard on piano in which a four-note phrase is repeated without resolving itself yet is still entrancing. The music for the climactic battle is a bolder version of this same musical idea but this time it resolves with explosive musical chords and trumpet fanfares. The theme returns yet again in a passage that mourns for the victims of the war, this time with a funeral

march beat. A convicted drug dealer (Ed Norton) and his last day of freedom before beginning a seven-year prison sentence are the subject of *25th Hour*, the only Blanchard score to be nominated for major awards and possibly his best screen work. This is a character piece rather than an action movie, and the music throughout is restrained but emotive. The opening music is a melancholy lullaby heard on strings with echoing voices. The tone is solemn and stately as it transitions into a forceful and flowing orchestrated anthem. There is also a sad blues passage in which the piano plays a nimble melody against sorrowful brass accompaniment. Also quite compelling is a delicate motif heard on clarinet and other reeds with an insistent beat and a self-confident temperament. There is little or no jazz in these last mentioned films. Blanchard, who has been involved in more American movies than any other jazz artist, is able to forsake his favorite sound when the movie demands it. Biography: *Contemporary Cat: Terence Blanchard with Special Guests*, Anthony Magro (2002). Official website: www.terenceblanchard.com.

Credits

(all films USA unless stated otherwise)

Year	Film	Director
1991	Jungle Fever	Spike Lee
1992	Malcolm X	Spike Lee (USA/Japan)
1993	Sugar Hill	Leon Ichaso
1994	The Inkwell (aka Drew's Inkwell)	Matty Rich
1994	Crooklyn	Spike Lee
1994	Trial By Jury	Heywood Gould
1995	Clockers	Spike Lee
1996	Get On the Bus	Spike Lee
1997	'Til There Was You	Scott Winant
1997	Four Little Girls	Spike Lee
1997	Eve's Bayou	Kasi Lemmons
1999	Summer of Sam (aka The Son of Sam)	Spike Lee
2000	Next Friday (aka Friday 2)	Steve Carr
2000	Love & Basketball	Gina Prince-Bythewood
2000	Bamboozled	Spike Lee
2001	The Caveman's Valentine	Kasi Lemmons
2001	Original Sin (aka Dancing in the Dark)	Michael Cristofer (France/USA)
2001	Glitter (aka All That Glitters)	Vondie Curtis-Hall
2002	Barbershop	Tim Story
2002	People I Know	Daniel Algrant (USA/Germany)
2002	Dark Blue	Ron Shelton (USA/UK/Germany)
2002	25th Hour (GGN)	Spike Lee
2004	Negroes with Guns: Rob Williams and the Black Power	Sandra Dickson, Churchill Roberts
2004	She Hate Me	Spike Lee
2006	Inside Man	Spike Lee

Year	Film	Director
2006	*Waist Deep*	Vondie Curtis-Hall
2006	*Who the #$&% Is Jackson Pollock?* (aka *Finding Jackson Pollock*)	Harry Moses
2007	*Talk to Me* (aka *Petey Greene's Washington*)	Kasi Lemmons
2008	*Miracle at St. Anna*	Spike Lee (UK/Italy)
2008	*Cadillac Records*	Darnell Martin
2010	*Bunraku*	Guy Moshe
2012	*Red Tails*	Anthony Hemingway

BLISS, Arthur (1891–1975) A distinguished British conductor and composer of many ballets, operas, and orchestral pieces, he was involved with only a handful of movies but wrote some noteworthy soundtrack scores.

He was born Arthur Edward Drummond Bliss in the London suburb of Barnes, the eldest of three sons of a businessman. His mother died when Bliss was only four years old so he was raised by his father who had a great appreciation of the arts. He received a first-class education at Rugby, Cambridge (where he studied the literary classics), and the Royal College of Music, yet most of his musical training came from contact with such composers as Edward Elgar, Gustav Holst, and Ralph Vaughan Williams. After serving in World War I, Bliss pursued a conducting and composition career, quickly finding success in both. His music was considered innovative and refreshing in the 1920s as his symphonic and chamber works found favor and he was asked to conduct prestigious orchestras and music festivals across Britain. By the end of the decade Bliss's compositions turned to more traditional forms but he was still in demand in Europe and the States. By the 1930s Bliss was considered old fashioned by the advocates of a new generation of British composers such as Benjamin Britten and William Walton. Bliss was in the States for the premiere of a piano concerto at the 1939 New York World's Fair when World War II broke out in Europe. He remained in the States and taught at the University of California, Berkeley, for two years before returning to England to help the war effort by serving as director of the BBC Symphony Orchestra. After the war, Bliss returned to composing and wrote some of his finest works, including the opera *The Olympians* (1949).

He became involved with movies in 1936 when director William Cameron Menzies consulted with Bliss and conductor Muir Mathieson in the preparation of the screen version of H. G. Wells's futuristic novel *Things to Come*. In a unique arrangement, the two artists worked on the score before and during the filming rather than the conventional method of being brought in after production was completed. That same year Bliss scored the acclaimed documentary *Conquest of the Air* and in 1937 did some work on the score for *I, Claudius*, an expensive and doomed film project that was never completed. After the war, Bliss returned to the British cinema to score the dramas *Christopher Columbus*, *Men of Two Worlds*, *Abandon Ship*, and the musical *The Beggar's Opera*. He also wrote a complete score for the film version of George Bernard Shaw's *Caesar and Cleopatra* (1945) but all of the music was discarded by the studio and replaced by a new score by Georges Auric. During the 1950s, Bliss was not only busy writing for the concert hall, he also served as Master of the Queen's Music and composed music for state ceremonies and special events. Although Bliss did not score any other movies after 1957, he did write music for some popular television documentaries, most memorably *War in the Air* (1954) and *An Age of Kings* (1960). He remained active as a composer until a year before his death at the age of eighty-three. Bliss received numerous awards, citations, and honors during his lifetime, including the Order of the British Empire in 1950. His legacy includes ten ballets, two operas, and many orchestra, choral, chamber, piano, hymn, fanfare, and vocal works.

While Bliss's contribution to British cinema is limited to a handful of films, his screen music is significant. The way music is used in the intelligent sci-fi movie *Things to Come* is often remarkable. Parts of the score are stirring in a traditional way even as there is something otherworldly about the music. The opening music is a grand procession of sorts yet has some gentle sections that are very lyrical before it becomes very foreboding. There is a complex military march in which different instruments take on contrasting harsh and soft sections. While the march is tuneful and rousing, one senses that there is some terrible Fascist power behind it. The big attack scene is scored with pounding symphonics and percussive explosions. The hopeful finale is conveyed beautifully with an expansive, hymnlike passage in which a solo flute seems to break through the clouds and offer solace. *Things to Come* is a very talky film that has dated somewhat but visually and musically it is still a wonder. *Conquest of the Air*, a documentary about the human quest for flight, has many marvelous musical passages. The opening music is a proud march that might lead one to think this is a patriotic propaganda film. Then the score grows more poetic. In one section, trilling piccolos and flutes seem giddy with excitement as they soar across the upper register of the scale. In another, the brass instruments seem to be in competition over which can glide upward in the most elaborate manner. Leonardo da Vinci's attempts to fly are scored with a lovely rhapsody in which strings float above a series of peaceful brass and woodwind repeated phrases. Legend has it that much of Bliss's music for *Conquest of the Air* was left on the cutting room floor. Yet what remains is a masterwork of its own.

The film version of John Gay's 1728 "ballad opera" *The Beggar's Opera* uses the uncredited eighteenth-century music, so Bliss mostly filled in with background scoring

between arias, duets, and choral numbers. The historical adventure *Christopher Columbus* has a main theme that is grandiose with a Renaissance flavor but also suggests the tumult of the open sea. There is also a Spanish tone to much of the score, including some religious hymns and even exotic Moorish sections. The lifeboat drama *Seven Waves Away* (retitled *Abandon Ship* in the States) opens with a simple sailor chantey played on a harmonica with no accompaniment. This quiet beginning foreshadows the documentary-like tale about survival that needs little music. When Bliss does bring in the orchestra, the effect is startling, as with a chaotic passage used during a storm at sea. The melodrama *Men of Two Worlds* is set in Africa where a tribesman (Robert Adams) returns to his village after being educated in music in England. Since the African is a skilled musician, Bliss uses the piano and Western music rather than the expected jungle music. Yet he does not ignore the locale, mixing in native tones in his music. In one section, a piano alternates with brass in a tribal-like bolero then a chorus brings a heavy and menacing temperament to the music. Another piano passage sounds Rachmaninoff-like as it wavers between furious chords and lilting musical phrases. There is also an ominous section in which strings and a male choir waltz away in counterpoint. This is expert cinema scoring. How fortunate that such a gifted composer left at least a few film scores for us to appreciate. Autobiography: *As I Remember* (1970). Official website: www.arthurbliss.org.

Credits

(all films UK unless stated otherwise)

Year	Film	Director
1936	*Things to Come*	William Cameron Menzies
1936	*Conquest of the Air*	Alexander Esway, Zoltan Korda, etc.
1946	*Men of Two Worlds* (aka *Witch Doctor*)	Thorold Dickinson
1949	*Christopher Columbus*	David MacDonald
1953	*The Beggar's Opera*	Peter Brook
1957	*Abandon Ship* (aka *Seven Waves Away*)	Richard Sale (USA/UK)

BREIL, Joseph Carl (1870–1926) Arguably the first true movie composer, this pioneering American singer, composer, conductor, and arranger wrote the music for the first silent movie to use an original score rather than generic musical motifs.

Joseph Carl Breil was born in Pittsburgh, the son of a lawyer who had emigrated from Prussia. After being educated at Duquesne University and other Pittsburgh-area schools, Breil was sent to the University of Leipzig in Germany to study law, but instead he learned music composition and singing. As a tenor, he performed opera in Europe before returning to the States where he taught music and later served as choir director for St. Paul's Cathedral in Pittsburgh. By the turn of the century, Breil was in New York conducting operas, writing incidental music for plays, and composing art songs and popular ditties for singers. As the musical editor for the famous music publishing firm of Chappell, he had many contacts in show business and was often called on to provide music for different occasions and places. When the 1912 French movie *Queen Elizabeth*, featuring Sarah Bernhardt, was to be shown in the States, Breil was asked to score the forty-four-minute period piece. Instead of employing stock musical themes, he wrote original music for most of the score. This is the first record of this being done in America. The legendary filmmaker D. W. Griffith was impressed with the music and hired Breil to score his long (165 minutes) silent epic feature *The Birth of a Nation*. Breil used passages from Wagner, Tchaikovsky, Liszt, and others in his score, but much of it was original, ranging from sweeping marches to tender lullabies. The love theme for the movie was published by Chappell as "The Perfect Song" and it enjoyed some popularity. (Many years later the tune was used for the radio program *Amos and Andy*.) Breil's score for *The Birth of a Nation* consisted of 226 separate music

cues for the conductor who led a seventy-piece orchestra in the premiere showing. In many ways the history of movie music starts in 1915 with Breil and *The Birth of a Nation*.

During the next decade, Breil wrote scores for seven more features and arranged and/or conducted a handful of others. For Griffith's moral epic *Intolerance*, Breil wrote music in an exotic style for the Babylon sequences, religious music for the Bible section, pseudo-Renaissance themes for the French Huguenot scenes, and tense suspense music for the modern tale. When the silent horror classic *The Phantom of the Opera* opened in 1925, different music scores were used in different cities; Breil composed the music for the world premiere in San Francisco. During his film career he returned to classical music on occasion and composed some notable operas, including *The Seventh Chord* (1913) and *The Legend* (1919). When his last opera, *Der Asra*, was not well received at the Met, Breil suffered a nervous breakdown that led to a fatal heart attack. Although he died before the birth of sound films and the first music soundtracks to be recorded on celluloid, Breil gave movie music an identity and a prominence that led to a whole new genre of music. His screen scores were lush, sentimental, and effective, introducing the power of movie music.

Credits

(all films USA)

Year	Film	Director
1915	The Birth of a Nation	D. W. Griffith
1915	Double Trouble	Christy Caganne
1916	Intolerance	D. W. Griffith
1918	The Birth of a Race	John W. Noble
1923	The White Rose	D. W. Griffith
1923	The White Sister	Henry King
1924	The Dramatic Life of Abraham Lincoln	Phil Rosen
1924	America	D. W. Griffith
1925	The Phantom of the Opera	Rupert Julian

BROUGHTON, Bruce (b. 1945) A very busy composer for television, he has also scored forty feature films, mostly in the comedy genre.

Born Bruce Harold Broughton in Los Angeles, he grew up in several different cities because his parents were Sal-

vation Army officers who went where they were assigned. As a youth, Broughton took piano lessons and learned how to play the various brass instruments in the Salvation Army band. He studied composition under screen composer David Raksin at the University of Southern

California then served in the U. S. Army playing French horn in a military band. After Broughton was discharged, he went to CBS where he scored television series such as *Gunsmoke*, *Barnaby Jones*, and *Logan's Run*. When his scores for *Hawaii Five-O* and *Dallas* won Emmy Awards, Broughton was in great demand. Over the decades he has written music for such TV series as *Quincy M.E.*, *Dallas*, *Amazing Stories*, *Tiny Toon Adventures*, and *JAG*, as well as over thirty TV movies and miniseries, including *How the West Was Won* (1979), *The Blue and the Gray* (1982), *The Master of Ballantrae* (1984), *Sorry, Wrong Number* (1989), *The Old Man and the Sea* (1990), *O Pioneers!* (1992), *Honor and Glory* (1998), *Jeremiah* (1998), *The Ballad of Lucy Whipple* (2001), *Eloise at the Plaza* (2003), *Warm Springs* (2005), and *Safe Harbor* (2009). Because he was labeled a television composer, no offers from Hollywood came until 1983, and it was two years later that he was hired for a first-class project, the all-star-cast western *Silverado*. Broughton's score was nominated for an Oscar and he was finally accepted into the film business.

Although Broughton has scored a wide variety of genres, from family dramas to thrillers, most of his movies are comedies. Such films rarely get much attention for their music, but often Broughton's scores were noticed and applauded. The comedies themselves may vary in quality but there is top-notch scoring in such films as *Sweet Liberty*, *Harry and the Hendersons*, *Betsy's Wedding*, *For Love or Money*, *Honey I Blew Up the Kid*, *House Arrest*, and *Stay Tuned*. Among his scores for other genres are such notable titles as *Young Sherlock Holmes*, *Tombstone*, *The Rescuers Down Under*, *Infinity*, *Doughboy*, *Narrow Margin*, *The Presidio*, *Lost in Space*, the 1994 remake of *The Miracle on 34th Street*, and *Homeward Bound* and its sequel. Broughton was always better treated in television, where he was given challenging movies and often was awarded by the television community. Late in his career he also scored video games. He has also written and conducted music for the concert stage, has been active in the Academy of Motion Picture Arts and Sciences, Society of Composers and Lyricists, and the Academy of Television Arts and Sciences, and has taught at the University of Southern California and UCLA.

Some might argue that Broughton's two finest screen scores are the ones he wrote for two westerns, *Silverado* and *Tombstone*. Both films were made when the genre was not particularly popular in Hollywood. The plot of *Silverado* contains most of the clichés associated with westerns, as four very different men join forces against evil. The main theme has a five-note phrase that climbs the scale boldly, French horns and violins supporting it in a heroic manner. There is also a quieter and more graceful theme that suggests the wholesome integrity of the people hoping to live in such brutal territory. A solo clarinet carries this lilting passage which contrasts nicely with the vigorous music throughout the score. Broughton avoids the expected western musical clichés in *Tombstone*, a film about Wyatt Earp (Kurt Russell) trying to leave his gunfighting life behind him. Concentrating on the characters rather than action or locale, Broughton came up with a very unusual (and in the opinion of many, brilliant) western score. There is no vivacious opening theme, but instead the movie begins quietly with tranquil music for the arrival of the Earp family. When the villains enter town, their theme is a brooding series of chords played by metal percussion, low violins, and a threatening bass line. Other parts of the score re-create the squalid feel of the local bar, the comic shenanigans of eccentric Doc Holliday (Val Kilmer), the violence of the famous O.K. Corral shoot-out, and the romance of Earp and his love interest (Dana Delany). Also unusual, the movie ends not with triumphant fanfares but rather a delicate waltz. If *Tombstone* does not sound like other westerns, it is not accidental. Avoiding the expected guitar and harmonica, Broughton uses an international array of unlikely instruments: a French contrabass sarrusophone, Irish tin whistle, Hungarian cimbalom, and an odd variety of different types of trombone. Had he written nothing else for Hollywood, these two contrasting western scores alone would place Broughton among Tinseltown's most accomplished composers.

Perhaps as masterful as these two scores is the one he wrote for the juvenile adventure *Young Sherlock Holmes*. From the first notes of the main theme the listener is drawn in by the fervent and rushing bass line, which is broken up by a melody played on a piccolo. As schoolboys Holmes (Nicholas Rowe) and Watson (Alex Cord) get involved in a dastardly plot, the music provides suspense with a youthful imagination. Sometimes the music recalls Bernard Herrmann's *Psycho* score as filtered through a Victorian sentiment. For a creepy human sacrifice scene, Broughton takes his cue from Carl Orff's *Carmina Burana*, complete with fortissimo chorus and a seven-beat tribal pattern that is oppressive. All this is very different from the warm music Broughton wrote for family movies. The two *Homeward Bound* scores are lyrical and endearing without being sentimental. As three domestic pets journey though the wilderness to get home, various themes are used, often relating to the animals or the danger the trio encounters. Sometimes the rural passages are quaint as they suggest a hoedown; other themes are more classical in spirit, the fiddling turning into sweeping violins. The dreamy and engaging score for the melodrama *The Boy Who Could Fly* is perhaps Broughton at his most delicate. The main theme conveys flight, although, as in the story, flying is a state of mind. There is a sensational flying scene in the animated *The Rescuers Down Under* when an Australian boy rides on the back of an eagle. If music ever soared, this passage certainly does. The brass and strings climb then break loose in a majestic passage that is as expansive as it is fun. This score is filled with wonderful touches. The opening is a propulsive tribal theme that introduces the moviegoer to the vast outback. Again different animals have their own theme, many of them comic. Even the theme for the poacher-villain and his lizard sidekick has a family-friendly tone, playing off their incompatibility rather than their evil. When it comes to family films, few stories beat *The Miracle on 34th Street*. Broughton's score for the remake cannot avoid the sentimental, particularly when Christmas bells and a heavenly chorus play heavily in the main theme. Yet the music is brisk and unfussy and one quickly finds that one is thoroughly engaged. The love theme is a cool jazz delight and a magical North Pole theme is quirky enough that the tone is playful rather than reverent.

As for all those comedies that Broughton scored, few are very good. It is safe to say that the music is often more fun than what is going on on the screen. One of the more satisfying efforts is the domestic comedy *Betsy's Wedding*, which has a slapstick wedding polka theme that mixes klezmer and Neapolitan in a giddy manner. *Baby's Day Out* has a raucous waltz theme that is as cockeyed as it is merry, *Honey I Blew Up the Kid* has a silly and jazzy march, while *Stay Tuned* has a vigorous march that is deflated by frequency waves. *For Love or Money* opts for a more romantic sound with a dreamy saxophone playing its seductive main theme. Perhaps the best of these comic scores is that for *Harry and the Hendersons*. Even though the tale is a contemporary one about a family who befriends Bigfoot, the main theme is a pseudoclassical piece with period instruments furiously rushing about. There is also a felicitous farewell theme that turns out to be more sincere than one expects. Broughton does not seem to be deterred by scoring unpromising material. Perhaps that is why he has been so successful in television. But the small screen often gave him some excellent projects to score. If only Hollywood had done so. Official website: www.brucebroughton.com.

Credits

(all films USA unless stated otherwise)

Year	Film	Director
1983	*The Prodigal*	James F. Collier
1984	*The Ice Pirates*	Stewart Raffill
1985	*Silverado* (AAN)	Lawrence Kasdan
1985	*Young Sherlock Holmes*	Barry Levinson
1986	*Sweet Liberty*	Alan Alda
1986	*The Boy Who Could Fly*	Nick Castle
1987	*Square Dance*	Daniel Petrie
1987	*Harry and the Hendersons*	William Dear
1987	*The Monster Squad*	Fred Dekker
1987	*Big Shots*	Robert Mandel
1987	*Cross My Heart*	Armyan Bernstein
1988	*The Presidio*	Peter Hyams
1988	*The Rescue*	Ferdinand Fairfax
1988	*Last Rites*	Donald P. Bellisario
1989	*Jacknife*	David Hugh Jones (USA/Canada)
1990	*Betsy's Wedding*	Alan Alda

Year	Film	Director
1990	*Narrow Margin*	Peter Hyams
1990	*The Rescuers Down Under*	Hendel Butoy, Mike Gabriel
1991	*All I Want for Christmas*	Robert Lieberman
1992	*Honey I Blew Up the Kid*	Ranald Kleiser
1992	*Stay Tuned*	Peter Hyams
1993	*Homeward Bound: The Incredible Journey*	Duwayne Dunham
1993	*So I Married an Axe Murderer*	Thomas Schlamme
1993	*For Love or Money*	Barry Sonnenfeld
1993	*Tombstone*	George P. Cosmatos, Kevin Jarre
1994	*Holy Matrimony*	Leonard Nimoy
1994	*Baby's Day Out*	Patrick Read Johnson
1994	*Miracle on 34th Street*	Les Mayfield
1996	*Carried Away*	Bruno Barreto
1996	*Homeward Bound 2: Lost in San Francisco*	David R. Ellis
1996	*House Arrest*	Harry Winer
1996	*Infinity*	Matthew Broderick
1997	*Shadow Conspiracy*	George P. Cosmatos
1997	*A Simple Wish*	Michael Ritchie
1998	*Krippendorf's Tribe*	Todd Holland
1998	*Lost in Space*	Stephen Hopkins
1998	*One Tough Cop*	Bruno Barreto
2004	*Last Flight Out*	Jerry Jameson
2006	*Bambi II*	Brian Pimental
2011	*The Pledge*	J. W. Myers
2013	*A Christmas Tree Miracle*	J. W. Myers

BRUNS, George (1914–1983) A prolific songwriter and composer whose feature film scores are only one aspect of his varied career, he was the most important music arranger, conductor, musician, and composer at the Disney studios in the 1950s and 1960s.

George Edward Bruns was born in Sandy, Oregon, the son of a sawmill worker, and studied piano as a child. Bruns enrolled at Oregon State University to pursue an engineering career, but while there he played piano, trombone, string bass, and other instruments in a college band. He left school to play with various bands in Portland before he was hired as music director at both KOIN and KEX radio stations. In the 1940s he was the trombonist for Portland's Castle Jazz Band and other groups before relocating in 1949 to Los Angeles, where he joined Turk Murphy's Jazz Band. A recording by the band was used in the cartoon short *Little Guy with a Big Horn*, and this led to other movie jobs. Walt Disney hired Bruns in 1953 as a music arranger and conductor, with Bruns eventually becoming the studio's musical director for twenty years. While at Disney, Bruns not only arranged and conducted the soundtracks for such movies as *Sleeping Beauty* and *Babes in Toyland* (getting Oscar nominations for each), he

also wrote songs for the studio's films, television shows, and later theme parks. Bruns composed the music for some of Disney's most famous songs of the period, including "The Ballad of Davy Crockett" and the "Zorro" theme for television and the catchy "Yo Ho (A Pirate's Life for Me)" for Disneyland's Pirates of the Caribbean attraction.

After Bruns wrote soundtrack scores for two Davy Crockett films in the 1950s, he moved more into film composing. He wrote songs and the soundtrack scores for *Westward Ho, the Wagons* and *Johnny Tremain* before composing the sparkling music for the animated *101 Dalmatians*. This contemporary Disney movie had a new and original sound that matched its very modern graphics. Bruns went on to write the soundtrack scores for the Disney animated favorites *The Sword in the Stone*, *The Jungle Book*, *The Aristocats*, and *Robin Hood*, sometimes writing a song or two as well. He was also kept busy scoring a series of Disney live-action comedies, such as the very popular *The Absent-Minded Professor* and *The Love Bug*. Among his other Disney credits are some adventure features, such as *The Fighting Prince of Donegal*, many animated shorts, and songs for such TV shows as *Calvin and the Colonel*, *Beetle Bailey*, *Cowboy in Africa*, and *Walt Disney's Won-*

derful World of Color. Bruns continued to perform as well, playing in his own Wonderland Dixieland Jazz Band in concert and recordings and joining the Disney band Firehouse Five Plus Two onstage and in the recording studio. He retired in 1976 and returned to Oregon where he died seven years later of a heart attack at the age of sixty-eight.

Because the songs in Disney movies get so much attention, Bruns's soundtrack scores are often overlooked. Usually these songs were written by others and Bruns had to incorporate the tunes into his score. Yet there is so much music between the songs in these movies that often the tone of the feature is determined more by Bruns's score than the individual songs. In *101 Dalmatians*, for example, there are only three songs (two of them very short) yet the movie is filled with wonderful music. The opening sequence set in the songwriter Roger's London flat is scored in a lazy, casual way with Roger's fingering at the piano blending with Bruns's charming piano score. Later in the movie, the music moves from suspense sections to comic ones with ease. The score is contemporary without being trendy, which is why it holds up so well over time. The songs in *The Aristo-*

cats (by various songwriters) range from childlike ditties to jazz, but it is Bruns's soundtrack score that creates the Parisian atmosphere. Similarly, the contemporary-sounding songs in *The Jungle Book* are delightful, but it is Bruns's pseudoexotic score that gives one a sense of the Indian jungle. Both *The Sword in the Stone* and *Robin Hood* have scores that suggest medieval England without being slavish to the sound. Bruns is less successful writing for Disney's live-action features. The music in the comedies is catchy without being memorable. The adventures are better, particularly the Revolutionary War movie *Johnny Tremain*, with its patriotic main theme, rustic colonial passages, and military marches. The score also includes two songs (lyrics by Tom Blackburn). "Johnny Tremain of Old Boston Town" is a catchy folk ballad that moves into a hoedown section while "The Liberty Tree" is a tuneful march with the lustiness of a sea chantey and the confidence of an anthem. Many feel that Bruns's music for animated shorts and television is superior to his feature scores. Yet one thing is clear: there is so much more to Bruns than the composer of "The Ballad of Davy Crockett."

Credits

(all films USA; * for Best Song)

Year	Film	Director
1955	*Davy Crockett: King of the Wild Frontier*	Norman Foster
1956	*Davy Crockett and the River Pirates*	Norman Foster
1956	*Westward Ho, the Wagons*	William Beaudine
1957	*Johnny Tremain*	Robert Stevenson
1961	*101 Dalmatians*	Clyde Geronimi, Hamilton Luske, Wolfgang Reitherman
1961	*The Absent-Minded Professor*	Robert Stevenson
1963	*Son of Flubber*	Robert Stevenson
1963	*The Sword in the Stone* (AAN)	Wolfgang Reitherman
1966	*The Ugly Dachshund*	Norman Tokar
1966	*Follow Me, Boys!*	Norman Tokar
1966	*The Fighting Prince of Donegal*	Michael O'Herlihy
1967	*Island of the Lost*	John Florea
1967	*The Adventures of Bullwhip Griffin*	James Neilson
1967	*The Jungle Book*	Wolfgang Reitherman
1968	*Daring Game*	Laslo Benedek
1968	*The Horse in the Gray Flannel Suit*	Norman Tokar
1968	*The Love Bug*	Robert Stevenson
1970	*The Aristocats*	Wolfgang Reitherman
1973	*Robin Hood* (AAN*)	Wolfgang Reitherman
1974	*Herbie Rides Again*	Robert Stevenson

BURNS, Ralph (1922–2001) A much respected music director, orchestrator, and conductor in the music business and on Broadway for many years, he was also a songwriter and composer who worked sporadically in the movies in the 1970s and 1980s, particularly with director-choreographer Bob Fosse.

Ralph Jose P. Burns was born in Newton, Massachusetts, and took piano lessons as a child. While studying at the New England Conservatory of Music, he became interested in jazz and began his career playing jazz piano in clubs and hanging out with the top bandleaders and singers of the 1940s. After graduation, Burns was hired as a member of Woody Herman's band, where he performed, arranged, and composed music, coming up with such hits as "Bijou," "Northwest Passage," "Apple Honey," and "Early Autumn." He worked with other name bands and did the music arrangements for many recordings, most memorably Ray Charles's hits "Come Rain or Come Shine" and "Georgia on My Mind." Burns made his Broadway debut with his musical supervision of the revue *Phoenix '55* in 1955. He went on to orchestrate and/or arrange the music for two dozen subsequent shows, including such successes as *Little Me* (1962), *Funny Girl* (1964), *Golden Boy* (1964), *Sweet Charity* (1966), *No, No, Nanette* (1971), *Pippin* (1972), *Chicago* (1975), *They're Playing Our Song* (1979), *Peter Pan* (1979), and *Thoroughly Modern Millie* (2002). Having worked with Fosse on eight Broadway musicals, Burns was the director's first choice to arrange the music when he made his film directorial debut with *Sweet Charity* in 1969, affording Burns his movie debut as well. After orchestrating the scores of the comedies *Move* (1970) and *Bananas* (1971), Burns got to write original musical scoring for Fosse's *Cabaret*, also adapting the John Kander and Fred Ebb Broadway songs for the screen and winning an Oscar for his efforts. Burns went on to write incidental music for the movie musicals *All That Jazz*, *Pennies from Heaven*, *The Muppets Take Manhattan*, and *Movie, Movie*, as well as original soundtrack scores for such notable films as *Lenny*, *Urban Cowboy*, *My Favorite Year*, *National Lampoon's Vacation*, and the animated *All Dogs Go to Heaven*. His television credits include scores for the TV movies *Make Me an Offer* (1980), *Golden Gate* (1981), *The Phantom of the Opera* (1983), *Ernie Kovacs: Between the Laughter* (1984), *After the Promise* (1987) and *Sweet Bird of Youth* (1989). Burns

also conducted and/or arranged the music for other films that he did not compose, such as *Mame* (1974), *New York, New York* (1977), *High Anxiety* (1977), *A Chorus Line* (1985), and *The Addams Family* (1991), and won an Oscar for *Annie* (1982). He was considered one of the most versatile and accomplished talents in show business and was still working and in great demand when he died at the age of seventy-nine.

Burns's talent for composing is somewhat overshadowed by his more recognized achievements in arranging music for jazz bands, singers, Broadway, and the movies. Since much of his work in film musicals involved using and adapting songs by others, his true mark as a composer is best found in his nonmusical movies. Burns's jazz background served him well in scoring *Lenny*, Fosse's biographical drama about renegade comic Lenny Bruce (Dustin Hoffman). Three standard pieces by Miles Davis are used in the movie but the rest is Burns. The documentary style of the film does not allow for traditional scoring. In fact, Fosse uses the voice track of some of Lenny's comic routines as background for scenes that usually have music. But when Burns's music comes in, it is the sound of urban angst. There is a livelier form of jazz in Fosse's *Star 80*, an even bleaker look at celebrity than *Lenny*. Burns uses some Hispanic music as well, particularly for the character of the pimp-hustler (Eric Roberts), and some chilling electronic music leading up to the murder of a pinup girl (Mariel Hemingway). Among Burns's lighter scores is the comedy *My Favorite Year*, for which he got to write swashbuckling music for the scenes involving an action movie star (Peter O'Toole). Set in the 1950s, the score also includes some romantic period themes, a tender passage played on a guitar and horn, and a main theme that is very nostalgic. The sound of the Roaring Twenties is featured in Burns's score for *Lucky Lady*, a failed comedy with great decor and music. Hot jazz, Charleston numbers, honky-tonk, and ragtime all blend together in this vivacious score. The opening theme is so sparkling that only a superior comedy could hope to measure up to the excitement. There are some enticing Latin-flavored passages as well as delightful squawking brass in some gangster music but it is all for naught when what's on the screen is not working. For the animated feature *All Dogs Go to Heaven*, there is a flavorful score by Burns that includes light jazz, bossa nova, Big Band, zippy waltzes, some touching romantic passages, spirited marches for the action scenes, and a heaven theme with celestial voices. Even with its seven songs written by others, *All Dogs Go to Heaven* has more Burns music than perhaps any of his films. Yet it is still not enough to give the famous arranger-conductor a notable reputation as a Hollywood composer. Instead he was the music man who made everybody else sound good.

Credits

(all film USA unless stated otherwise)

Year	Film	Director
1972	*Cabaret* (AA)	Bob Fosse
1974	*Piaf: The Early Years*	Guy Casaril (France)
1974	*Lenny*	Bob Fosse
1975	*Lucky Lady*	Stanley Donen
1978	*Movie Movie*	Stanley Donen
1979	*All That Jazz* (AA)	Bob Fosse
1980	*Urban Cowboy*	James Bridges
1981	*Pennies from Heaven*	Herbert Ross
1982	*My Favorite Year*	Richard Benjamin
1982	*Kiss Me Goodbye*	Robert Mulligan
1983	*Star 80*	Bob Fosse
1983	*National Lampoon's Vacation*	Harold Ramis
1984	*The Muppets Take Manhattan*	Frank Oz
1985	*Moving Violations*	Neal Israel
1985	*Perfect*	James Bridges
1987	*In the Mood* (aka *The Woo Woo Kid*)	Phil Alden Robinson
1989	*Bert Rigby, You're a Fool*	Carl Reiner
1989	*All Dogs Go to Heaven*	Don Bluth, etc. (Ireland/UK/USA)

BURWELL, Carter (b. 1955) A busy conductor, orchestrator, and composer of over seventy movies, he has long been associated with the filmmaking Coen brothers, though younger viewers know him more for his *Twilight* films.

Born in New York City, the son of a math teacher and a fabrics designer, Carter Burwell took piano lessons as a child but did not become interested in music until he discovered blues and improvisational performing in high school. Burwell attended Harvard, where he studied electronic music and animation but also got interested in computer science. After graduation he created his own animated film short, which won some awards, and pursued a computer career as an image processor at Cold Spring Harbor Laboratory. Burwell combined his love for animation and computers working on television and movie projects utilizing both fields of expertise. He also continued his music interests playing in various bands and sometimes composing pieces as well. When one of his compositions was performed at the Avignon Festival in France in 1984, it attracted the attention of brothers Joel and Ethan Coen, who were embarking on their first movie, *Blood Simple*. Burwell wrote the score and that of just about every other Coen brothers film since then. Among their most notable collaborations are *Miller's Crossing, Raising Arizona, Barton Fink, The Hudsucker Proxy, Fargo, The Ladykillers, No Country for Old Men,* and *True Grit*. With avant-garde director Spike Jonze he has scored such movies as *Being John Malkovich, Adaptation,* and *Where the Wild Things Are*. Burwell's composing credits for other directors include such diverse movies as *A Knight's Tale, Doc Hollywood, Buffy the Vampire Slayer, A Goofy Movie, The Spanish Prisoner, The Jackal, Rob Roy, Gods and Monsters, Hamlet, The Alamo,* and three of the *Twilight* films. For television he has scored the miniseries *Mildred Pierce* (2011) and he has also written a chamber opera, music-theatre pieces, and music for experimental theatre productions. Burwell often orchestrates and conducts his own work and has taught screen scoring at various schools and festivals.

Because the Coen brothers' films are often weird and nihilistic, it is wrongly thought that Burwell's music is also offbeat and out of left field. Some scores match this description, but most of his music, for the Coens and other directors, is written to fit the particular style of the individual movie, and the diversity of his screen projects has allowed him a great deal of freedom. Consider the variety of music to be found just within the Coen movies. Their first collaboration, *Blood Simple*, has little music. The one returning motif, a progression of piano chords supported by electronic manipulation and a haunting melody played on the high notes, is used sparingly yet very effectively. Burwell insists that less music is better than too much music and one notices throughout his work that the scores are sometimes subtle to the point of subliminal. This can be heard in the dark comedy *Fargo* about incompetent crooks and murderers. The snowy silence of the North Dakota location is broken by a solo violin playing a folk melody with gentle support from plucked and bowed strings. One passage heard on the oboe is filled with sorrow while brassy chords and sustaining strings play under some of the more violent scenes. The harp is used throughout this score to convey the gentle falling of snow but also for restrained suspense. There is even less music in *No Country for Old Men*, a bloodbath of a film about a Texas hunter (Josh Brolin) pursued by police and killers for a bundle of drug money. An odd but effective mix of shaker, metal and drum percussion, guitar chords, and electronics are used for the main theme, which is heard fully only at the end of the film. For the rest of the time only snatches are played, giving this sad chase movie a melancholy tone. The quirky comedy *Raising Arizona*, on the other hand, has plenty of music, and it is as wacky as the story of a misfit couple (Nicolas Cage and Holly Hunter) and their botched kidnapping caper. The main theme is a silly country tune with scat vocalizing and whistling, the effect being comic and crazed. Some fanciful guitar work accompanies a choir and more whistling is used as the music races in time to the visuals on the screen. A dreamy theme heard near the end of the film is optimistic and even reverent as a choir joins various percussive sounds that bounce along happily. The western remake *True Grit* is rather conventional for the Coen brothers, and Burwell's score is equally traditional without falling into cliché. The hymn "Leaning on the Everlasting Arms" by Elisha A. Hoffman and Anthony J. Showalter is given a gentle interpretation on the piano and

is used at the beginning and end of the movie with a firm restraint. In between, the music is darker and more dramatic, sometimes using marching drums and occasionally restless strings and brass, and other times creepy sustained chords (as in the snake scene). Just as the Coens do not make the same kind of movie over and over again, so too, Burwell avoids repeating himself in scoring them.

There is a lilting score for *Before the Devil Knows You're Dead*, a Sidney Lumet movie much in the style of a Coen film. Lovely harp arpeggios and French horns provide a calming tone that contrasts with the chaotic feelings of two brothers (Ethan Hawke and Philip Seymour Hoffman) before and after a crime. Even more lyrical is the score for the Scottish period piece *Rob Roy*. Burwell composed some authentic-sounding Celtic folk tunes that contrast nicely with the more modern passages using electronic instrumentation. "Morag's Lament" is a haunting piece sung in Gaelic and accompanied by ethnic pipes while a traditional orchestra plays the dramatic music for the battle scenes. Similarly, Burwell incorporates some Mexican folk music into his score for the 2004 version of *The Alamo*. Throughout the film he uses wood flutes and mandolins with conventional instruments so it doesn't sound like just another action movie. The extended battle scene late in the film is particularly rousing as it uses several variations of a five-note motif. Spike Jonze is even more experimental than the Coen brothers, and Burwell has written some of his most ambitious music for this unique director. Perhaps Jonze's best film, *Being John Malkovich* has many levels of reality and Burwell's music also moves from conventional passages to truly strange ones. There is a sublime theme in which a delicate chord progression soothes and delights as subdued strings, muffled tambourine, and chimes play out the near melody. *Adaptation* also works on two levels, real people and book characters. For a surreal sequence about evolution, Burwell's music is mystical and foreboding. On the other hand, a solo oboe is featured in a cockeyed waltz that is nonetheless very pleasing.

Burwell has collaborated with director Bill Condon on a handful of films, none more popular than the *Twilight* series. These romantic vampire films call for sci-fi themes as well as teenage pop music. The first installment (directed by Catherine Hardwicke) effectively provides both sounds. There is the expected distorted instrumentation for the supernatural scenes and some pulsating and rocking sections for the high school scenes, but the score also has some intricate guitar playing, a romantic theme heard on piano and oboe, and some mesmerizing passages with choral voices. Perhaps most memorable is "Bella's Lullaby," which is far from comforting but rather haunting and dissonant. The two sequels, using *Breaking Dawn* in the titles, were directed by Condon and are scored with more music but still show restraint on Burwell's part. The romantic themes are more lush perhaps, the guitar passages more lively, and the dramatic music bordering on grandiose, but it is clear that Burwell's music helps these rather superficial movies sound like a class act. A more accomplished collaboration between Condon and Burwell is

the character study *Gods and Monsters* about the final days of gay Hollywood director James Whale (Ian McKellen). With few characters and little physical action, this drama requires little scoring, but what is there is superb. Whale dwells on his past making horror films and sometimes the music suggests that kind of music. But mostly the score returns to a very poignant theme in which a piano and strings play variations on a four-note motif, switching keys as easily as it develops from nostalgia to lamenting. *Gods and Monsters* is perhaps Burwell at his purest, using music only when it most counts. Official website: www. carterburwell.com.

Credits

(all films USA unless stated otherwise)

Year	Film	Director
1984	*Blood Simple*	Joel and Ethan Coen
1986	*Psycho III*	Anthony Perkins
1987	*Raising Arizona*	Joel and Ethan Coen
1988	*Pass the Ammo*	David Beaird
1988	*The Beat*	Paul Mones
1988	*It Takes Two*	David Beaird
1989	*Checking Out*	David Leland (UK)
1990	*Miller's Crossing*	Joel and Ethan Coen
1991	*Barton Fink*	Joel and Ethan Coen (USA/UK)
1991	*Doc Hollywood*	Michael Caton-Jones
1991	*Scorchers*	David Beaird (UK/USA)
1992	*Buffy the Vampire Slayer*	Fran Rubel Kuzui
1992	*Waterland*	Stephen Gyllenhaal (UK)
1992	*Storyville*	Mark Frost
1993	*This Boy's Life*	Michael Caton-Jones
1993	*Kalifornia*	Dominic Sena
1993	*A Dangerous Woman*	Stephen Gyllenhaal
1993	*Wayne's World 2*	Stephen Surjik
1994	*The Hudsucker Proxy*	Joel and Ethan Coen (UK/USA/Germany)
1994	*It Could Happen to You*	Andrew Bergman
1994	*Airheads*	Michael Lehmann
1995	*Bad Company*	Damian Harris
1995	*Rob Roy*	Michael Caton-Jones (USA/UK)
1995	*A Goofy Movie*	Kevin Lima
1995	*The Celluloid Closet*	Rob Epstein, Jeffrey Friedman (France/UK/Germany/ USA)
1995	*Two Bits*	James Foley
1996	*Fargo*	Joel and Ethan Coen (USA/UK)
1996	*Fear*	James Foley
1996	*Joe's Apartment*	John Payson
1996	*The Chamber*	James Foley
1997	*Picture Perfect*	Glenn Gordon Caron
1997	*Assassin(s)*	Mathieu Kassovitz (France)
1997	*Conspiracy Theory*	Richard Donner
1997	*The Locusts*	John Patrick Kelley
1997	*The Spanish Prisoner*	David Mamet
1997	*The Jackal*	Michael Caton-Jones (USA/UK/France)

Year	Film	Director
1998	Gods and Monsters	Bill Condon (USA/UK)
1998	The Big Lebowski	Joel and Ethan Coen (USA/UK)
1998	Velvet Goldmine	Todd Haynes (UK/USA)
1998	The Hi-Lo Country	Stephen Frears (USA/UK/Germany)
1999	The Corruptor	James Foley
1999	The General's Daughter	Simon West (Germany/USA)
1999	Being John Malkovich	Spike Jonze
1999	Three Kings	David O. Russell (USA/Australia)
1999	Mystery, Alaska	Jay Roach (Canada/USA)
2000	Hamlet	Michael Almereyda
2000	What Planet Are You From?	Mike Nichols
2000	Before Night Falls	Julian Schnabel
2000	Book of Shadows: Blair Witch 2	Joe Berlinger
2001	A Knight's Tale	Brian Helgeland
2001	The Man Who Wasn't There	Joel and Ethan Coen (USA/UK)
2002	The Rookie	John Lee Hancock
2002	Searching for Paradise	Myra Paci
2002	S1m0ne	Andrew Niccol
2002	Adaptation	Spike Jonze
2003	Intolerable Cruelty	Joel and Ethan Coen
2004	The Ladykillers	Ethan and Joel Coen
2004	The Alamo	John Lee Hancock
2004	Kinsey	Bill Condon (USA/Germany)
2006	Fur: An Imaginary Portrait of Diane Arbus	Steven Shainberg
2006	The Hoax	Lasse Hallström
2007	No Country for Old Men	Ethan and Joel Coen
2007	Before the Devil Knows You're Dead	Sidney Lumet
2008	In Bruges	Martin McDonagh (UK/USA)
2008	Burn after Reading	Ethan and Joel Coen (USA/UK/France)
2008	Twilight	Catherine Hardwicke
2009	A Serious Man	Ethan and Joel Coen (USA/UK/France)
2009	Where the Wild Things Are (GGN)	Spike Jonze (USA/Australia/Germany)
2009	The Blind Side	John Lee Hancock
2010	Howl	Rob Epstein, Jeffrey Friedman
2010	The Kids Are All Right	Lisa Cholodenko
2010	True Grit	Ethan and Joel Coen
2011	The Twilight Saga: Breaking Dawn - Part 1	Bill Condon
2011	Moving Gracefully Toward the Exit	Jean-Bernard Andro, Patrice M. Regnier
2012	Seven Psychopaths	Martin McDonagh (UK)
2012	The Twilight Saga: Breaking Dawn - Part 2	Bill Condon
2013	The Fifth Estate	Bill Condon (USA/Belgium)

BUTTOLPH, David (1902–1983) A prolific Hollywood composer, arranger, and conductor, he contributed music to over 250 feature movies between 1933 and 1963.

He was born James David Buttolph Jr., in New York City, and showed promise as a pianist at a young age. Buttolph later studied at the Juilliard School of Music then began his career as an accompanist and songwriter. Loving opera and wanting to learn more about classical music, he went to Europe in 1923 for four years, during which time he studied with opera maestros at the Akademie für Musik in Vienna, coached opera singers, and played jazz in nightclubs. When Buttolph returned to the States, he was hired as conductor of the National Concert Orchestra on radio and served as arranger and director of the singing group the National Cavaliers. While still in New York, Buttolph made some arrangements for Twentieth Century-Fox, then in 1933 he moved to Hollywood where he became a studio composer under Alfred Newman. Many of the Fox movies used more than one composer and Buttolph contributed music to many films in collaboration with others. His first solo effort was the western *Smoky* in 1933, but most of his scores in the 1930s and 1940s were group efforts. He wrote music for all genres, including musicals, horror films, westerns, crime dramas, and star vehicles for Shirley Temple, Laurel and Hardy, Sonia Henie, Betty Grable, and others. Among his many notable movies before World War II are *David Harum, Baby Take a Bow, Pigskin Parade, Seventh Heaven, The Return of Frank James, Western Union, Tobacco Road, Blood and Sand,* and *Sun Valley Serenade.* During and after the war he was given more and more solo assignments, such as *My Favorite Blonde, This Gun for Hire, Wake Island, Junior Miss, Guadalcanal Diary, Shock, 13 Rue Madeleine, Till We Meet Again, Rope, Kiss of Death, Boomerang, Colorado Territory, The Enforcer, House of Wax, Beast from 20,000 Fathoms, The Bounty Hunter, The Horse Soldiers,* and *PT 109.* In the 1960s, Buttolph moved into television, writing music for such series as *Laramie, Maverick, Wagon Train, Frontier Circus, The Virginian,* and *The Travels of Jamie McPheeters.* He often arranged and conducted his own scores and those by others and his stock music was later used by Fox in over fifty other movies. Buttolph retired from Hollywood in 1964 and spent much of the next twenty years traveling the world before his death at the age of eighty.

Buttolph was a team player at Fox, often arranging and contributing extra music to movies scored by Alfred Newman and others. Of his hundreds of film projects, it has been determined that he was sole composer on 133 of them. Since these movies include every genre, big- and low-budget productions, and famous and obscure directors, it is difficult to come to a consensus about them and their scores. Buttolph had extensive musical training and experience with all kinds of music from classical to jazz; he used it all in his screen music. One may not be able to easily define his style, but it is clear there are some first-rate scores in his body of work. The large-scale adventure *Western Union,* about running telegraph wires across the West despite some renegades, is one of the best of Buttolph's many westerns. It has a robust western score in the classic mold. There is a rugged march theme that reeks of masculine pride, a flowing nature theme that is breezy and optimistic, and the expected tribal music for the Native Americans. This is Hollywood Americana in splendid form. The oddball comedy-drama *Tobacco Road* can best be described as anti-Americana as a family of

Georgia sharecroppers represent the derelict side of rural life. Buttolph's score is wry and lightly satirical. The main theme is a silly hoedown featuring a lively harmonica and some spirited fiddles. There is also a domestic theme that is a pseudo–folk song with a Southern flavor, some comic tunes plucked on a banjo, and even some sentimental passages on strings that are pure "mellerdrammer." John Ford's Civil War adventure *The Horse Soldiers* has a splendid score but most of the music is based on traditional period songs which Buttolph adapted and arranged beautifully. For example, the ballad "I Left My Love" is turned into a cocky march accompanied by percussion and, surprisingly, strings. This score is a tribute to Buttolph's expert arranging and conducting rather than composing skills.

Some of Buttolph's most known scores are for horror and sci-fi films. The cult favorite *The Beast from 20,000 Fathoms* has a memorable main theme in which low, vibrating brass are in counterpoint with woodwinds tumbling down the scale. Some passages have ominous low notes that seem to breathe in and out deeply like a monster and others use short squawks from various instruments to convey a shock effect. The early 3-D thriller *House of Wax* also has a startling theme: a sort of macabre fanfare with threatening deep chords from the brass section, nervous high notes by the reeds, and strings that seem to linger. One section of this exciting score uses fluttering flutes and pizzicato strings in a restless combination, while a quieter theme has quivering strings and rumbling brass that drip with dread. Buttolph also uses ascending and descending scales throughout *House of Wax* to add to the suspense. A more psychological thriller, *Shock,* has opening music that matches the thunder and lightning on-screen, then the strings painfully descend the scale like a dying animal. There is a nightmare scene that moves from a restful lullaby into expressionistic music with waves of crashing chords. Other passages are more subtle, such as the groaning notes that ascend the scale like a breathless squeezebox. *Rope,* Alfred Hitchcock's experiment in moviemaking without cutting, is also a psychological piece. There is little music in this talky but interesting film set in real time in one Manhattan apartment. Buttolph opens the movies with serene and elegant music, suggesting upper-class luxury with its sweeping strings and nimble woodwinds. Then the music turns sinister and dissonant as the camera closes in on the murder.

Two film noir scores by Buttolph deserve mention because they draw on his past experience with arranging and playing jazz. The thriller *Kiss of Death* opens with a fanfare stuck in a repetitive pattern, then the music breaks out and races forward furiously. The score also includes a lazy, bluesy passage that is weary yet enticing and a poignant theme for the plot's romance. The most famous scene in *Kiss of Death*, in which a hoodlum (Richard Widmark) pushes a wheelchair-ridden woman down a staircase, is still shocking. No music is used or is necessary for this startling sequence. *This Gun for Hire*, a classic film noir about revenge, has a superb blues and jazz score. There is a haunting blues theme that is tentative yet casual, capturing the nihilistic nature of the antihero (Alan Ladd). Also notable is a smooth jazz passage with a bossa nova beat that is very romantic and very catchy. Trying to find a musical thread through Buttolph's scores is futile. He was an estimable arranger and composer who made many Hollywood movies better because of his music.

Credits

(all films USA)

Year	Film	Director
1933	*Smoky*	Eugene Forde
1934	*David Harum*	James Cruze
1934	*George White's Scandals*	Thornton Freeland, etc.
1934	*Hold That Girl*	Hamilton MacFadden
1934	*Sleepers East*	Kenneth MacKenna
1934	*Murder in Trinidad*	Louis King
1934	*Wild Gold*	George Marshall
1934	*She Learned about Sailors*	George Marshall
1934	*Baby Take a Bow*	Harry Lachman
1934	*Handy Andy*	David Butler
1934	*365 Nights in Hollywood*	George Marshall
1934	*Bright Eyes*	David Butler
1935	*One More Spring*	Henry King
1935	*Navy Wife*	Allan Dwan
1935	*This Is the Life*	Marshall Neilan
1936	*Everybody's Old Man*	James Flood
1936	*Pigskin Parade*	David Butler
1936	*Reunion*	Norman Taurog
1936	*One in a Million*	Sidney Lanfield
1937	*Nancy Steele Is Missing!*	George Marshall
1937	*Seventh Heaven*	Henry King
1937	*Cafe Metropole*	Edward H. Griffith
1939	*The Gorilla*	Allan Dwan
1939	*Hotel for Women*	Gregory Ratoff
1939	*Here I Am a Stranger*	Roy Del Ruth
1939	*Barricade*	Gregory Ratoff
1939	*Everything Happens at Night*	Irving Cummings
1940	*Star Dust*	Walter Lang
1940	*I Was an Adventuress*	Gregory Ratoff
1940	*Girl in 313*	Ricardo Cortez
1940	*Four Sons*	Archie Mayo
1940	*The Man I Married*	Irving Pichel
1940	*The Return of Frank James*	Fritz Lang
1940	*Public Deb No. 1*	Gregory Ratoff
1940	*The Bride Wore Crutches*	Shepard Traube
1940	*Street of Memories*	Shepard Traube
1941	*Western Union*	Fritz Lang
1941	*Tobacco Road*	John Ford
1941	*Murder among Friends*	Ray McCarey

Year	Film	Director
1941	*Scotland Yard*	Norman Foster
1941	*Blood and Sand*	Rouben Mamoulian
1941	*For Beauty's Sake*	Shepard Traube
1941	*Man Hunt*	Fritz Lang
1941	*A Very Young Lady*	Harold D. Schuster
1941	*Sun Valley Serenade*	H. Bruce Humberstone
1941	*Man at Large*	Eugene Forde
1941	*Last of the Duanes*	James Tinling
1941	*Great Guns*	Monty Banks
1941	*Swamp Water*	Jean Renoir, Irving Pichel
1941	*Confirm or Deny*	Archie Mayo, Fritz Lang
1941	*Cadet Girl*	Ray McCarey
1941	*Bahama Passage*	Edward H. Griffith
1942	*Lady for a Night*	Leigh Jason
1942	*Castle in the Desert*	Harry Lachman
1942	*Song of the Islands*	Walter Lang
1942	*My Favorite Blonde*	Sidney Lanfield
1942	*Moontide*	Archie Mayo, Fritz Lang
1942	*This Gun for Hire*	Frank Tuttle
1942	*The Mad Martindales*	Alfred L. Werker
1942	*It Happened in Flatbush*	Ray McCarey
1942	*In Old California*	William C. McGann
1942	*A-Haunting We Will Go*	Alfred L. Werker
1942	*Wake Island*	John Farrow
1942	*Berlin Correspondent*	Eugene Forde
1942	*Street of Chance*	Jack Hively
1942	*Thunder Birds* (aka *Soldiers of the Air*)	William A. Wellman
1942	*American Empire*	William C. McGann
1943	*Immortal Sergeant*	John M. Stahl
1943	*Hello Frisco, Hello*	H. Bruce Humberstone
1943	*Crash Dive*	Archie Mayo
1943	*Bomber's Moon*	Edward Ludwig, etc.
1943	*Corvette K-225*	Richard Rosen, Howard Hawks
1943	*Guadalcanal Diary*	Lewis Seiler
1944	*Buffalo Bill*	William A. Wellman
1944	*The Hitler Gang*	John Farrow
1944	*Till We Meet Again*	Frank Borzage
1944	*The Big Noise*	Malcolm St. Clair
1944	*The Fighting Lady*	Edward Steichen, William Wyler
1945	*Circumstantial Evidence*	John Larkin
1945	*The Bullfighters*	Malcolm St. Clair, Stan Laurel
1945	*Where Do We Go from Here?*	Gregory Ratoff, George Seaton
1945	*The Caribbean Mystery*	Robert D. Webb
1945	*Nob Hill*	Henry Hathaway
1945	*Junior Miss*	George Seaton
1945	*Within These Walls*	H. Bruce Humberstone
1945	*The House on 92nd Street*	Henry Hathaway
1945	*The Spider*	Robert D. Webb
1945	*Doll Face*	Lewis Seiler
1946	*Shock*	Alfred L. Werker
1946	*Claudia and David*	Walter Lang
1946	*Johnny Comes Flying Home*	Benjamin Stoloff
1946	*Strange Triangle*	Ray McCarey
1946	*Do You Love Me*	Gregory Ratoff
1946	*Somewhere in the Night*	Joseph L. Mankiewcz
1946	*It Shouldn't Happen to a Dog*	Herbert I. Leeds
1946	*If I'm Lucky*	Lewis Seiler
1946	*Three Little Girls in Blue*	H. Bruce Humberstone, John Brahm

Year	Film	Director
1946	*Home, Sweet Homicide*	Lloyd Bacon
1946	*13 Rue Madeleine*	Henry Hathaway
1947	*The Brasher Doubloon*	John Brahm
1947	*Boomerang!*	Elia Kazan
1947	*Moss Rose*	Gregory Ratoff
1947	*I Wonder Who's Kissing Her Now*	Lloyd Bacon
1947	*Kiss of Death*	Henry Hathaway
1947	*Mother Wore Tights*	Walter Lang
1947	*The Foxes of Harrow*	John M. Stahl
1948	*Bill and Coo*	Dean Riesner
1948	*To the Victor*	Delmer Daves
1948	*Rope*	Alfred Hitchcock
1948	*Smart Girls Don't Talk*	Richard L. Bare
1948	*June Bride*	Bretaigne Windust
1948	*John Loves Mary*	David Butler
1948	*Colorado Territory*	Raoul Walsh
1949	*Look for the Silver Lining*	David Butler
1949	*One Last Fling*	Peter Godfrey
1949	*The Girl from Jones Beach*	Peter Godfrey
1949	*Roseanna McCoy*	Irving Reis, Nicholas Ray
1949	*The Story of Seabiscuit*	David Butler
1950	*Montana*	Ray Enright, Raoul Walsh
1950	*Chain Lightning*	Stuart Heisler
1950	*Return of the Frontiersman*	Richard L. Bare
1950	*Pretty Baby*	Bretaigne Windust
1950	*Three Secrets*	Robert Wise
1951	*The Enforcer*	Bretaigne Windust, Raoul Walsh
1951	*The Redhead and the Cowboy*	Leslie Fenton
1951	*Along the Great Divide*	Raoul Walsh
1951	*Fighting Coast Guard*	Joseph Kane
1951	*Fort Worth*	Edwin L. Marin
1951	*Ten Tall Men*	Willis Goldbeck
1951	*Submarine Command*	John Farrow
1952	*Lone Star*	Vincent Sherman
1952	*This Woman Is Dangerous*	Felix E. Feist
1952	*Talk about a Stranger*	David Bradley
1952	*The Sellout*	Gerald Mayer
1952	*Carson City*	André De Toth
1952	*The Winning Team*	Lewis Seiler
1952	*My Man and I*	William A. Wellman
1953	*The Man Behind the Gun*	Felix E. Feist
1953	*She's Back on Broadway*	Gordon Douglas
1953	*House of Wax*	André De Toth
1953	*The System*	Lewis Seiler
1953	*South Sea Woman*	Arthur Lubin
1953	*The Beast from 20,000 Fathoms*	Eugene Lourié
1953	*Thunder over the Plains*	André De Toth
1953	*Calamity Jane*	David Butler
1953	*The Eddie Cantor Story*	Alfred E. Green
1953	*Crime Wave*	André De Toth
1954	*Phantom of the Rue Morgue*	Roy del Ruth
1954	*Riding Shotgun*	André De Toth
1954	*Secret of the Incas*	Jerry Hopper
1954	*The Bounty Hunter*	André De Toth
1954	*Long John Silver*	Byron Haskin
1955	*Pete Kelly's Blues*	Jack Webb
1955	*Jump into Hell*	David Butler
1955	*I Died a Thousand Times*	Stuart Heisler

Year	Film	Director
1955	*Target Zero*	Harmon Jones
1956	*The Lone Ranger*	Stuart Heisler
1956	*The Steel Jungle*	Walter Doniger
1956	*Santiago*	Gordon Douglas
1956	*A Cry in the Night*	Frank Tuttle
1956	*The Burning Hills*	Stuart Heisler
1957	*The Big Land*	Gordon Douglas
1957	*The D.I.*	Jack Webb
1958	*The Deep Six*	Rudolph Maté
1959	*Westbound*	Budd Boetticher
1959	*The Horse Soldiers*	John Ford
1960	*Guns of the Timberland*	Robert D. Webb
1963	*PT 109*	Leslie H. Martinson
1963	*The Raiders*	Herschel Daugherty
1963	*The Man from Galveston*	William Conrad

BUTTS, R. Dale (1910–1990) A successful arranger and composer who spent his twelve-year Hollywood career at Republic Pictures, he is most remembered for his many Roy Rogers musical westerns.

Robert Dale Butts was born in Lamasco, Kentucky, and studied at a music conservatory in Louisville. Butts began his professional career in Louisville where he played piano on the local radio, marrying singer Dale Evans. In 1928 he was hired as pianist and arranger for NBC Radio in Chicago, remaining there until 1941 when he and his wife went to Hollywood. Three years later Butts and Evans were hired by Republic; she as a singer-actress and he as one of the staff composers, writing and arranging music for over one hundred movies during the next dozen years. Butts and Evans were divorced in 1945 when she fell in love with costar Roy Rogers, yet Butts went on to work with the couple on several westerns at Republic. As a staff composer, Butts often worked with two or more other artists on the scores for the westerns, comedies, and crime dramas the studio turned out quickly. His first solo score was for the romantic comedy *Three Little Sisters* in 1944 but most of his other 1940s projects were team efforts. Among the many noteworthy Republic movies he contributed music to during that decade are *Don't Fence Me In*, *Flame of Barbary Coast*, *Home on the Range*, *The Crimson Key*, *Rainbow Over Texas*, *The Invisible Wall*, *My Pal Trigger*, *Eyes of Texas*, and *Too Late for Tears*. In the 1950s Butts scored more and more films by himself. Most were westerns for Rogers, Gene Autry, and Rex Allen, but there were also some interesting nonwesterns, such as *The City That Never Sleeps*, *The WAC from Walla Walla*, *Sea of Lost Ships*, *The Shanghai Story*,

No Man's Woman, *Stranger at My Door*, and *Terror at Midnight*. Butts orchestrated many of his scores and those by others, and Republic reused parts of his scores in over eighty other movies. He left Republic in 1957 and wrote music for a few television series in the early 1960s, including *Riverboat*, *Whispering Smith*, and *Laramie*. Butts disappeared from film and television records in 1962 and next to nothing is known about him until his death twenty-eight years later at the age of seventy-nine.

Because Butts's entire Hollywood career was spent at a second-class studio, he is not given a great deal of attention by movie music fans. The Rogers musicals were very popular but most had songs by other composers, so Butts usually was left with scoring some chase music and turning the cowboy tunes into background music. Listening to the nonwesterns Butts scored solo gives one a much better idea of what this prolific composer and arranger was up to. *Flame of Barbary Coast*, which he coscored with Mort Glickman, was the only Butts movie to get an Oscar nomination for music. It is about a romantic triangle (John Wayne, Joseph Schildkraut, and Ann Dvorak) set in San Francisco conveniently in time for the big earthquake. The score consists of lots of celebratory marches, dance hall music, and saloon tunes, as well as song standards from the period. There is a sweetly sentimental romantic theme heard on strings that is routine, to say the least. It is a wonder why the Academy chose this score to nominate in 1946. (They also gave an Oscar nod to the sound recording, which is more impressive.)

Republic was famous for its serials, and two of them afforded fun scores by Butts. *Trader Tom of the China Seas* was a twelve-part adventure with lots of action and some fine music. The main theme is heavily flavored with Oriental music that is as exotic as it is inauthentic. Action scenes at sea are scored with crashing brass chords like a storm even when skies are clear, and the fight scenes on land use blaring horns that ascend the scale with panache. Another serial, *Panther Girl of the Kongo*, is about a white woman (Phyllis Coates) doing good deeds in the jungle. Its main theme is a catchy bolero-like piece of music in which horns and percussion pound with the weight of the elephant that Coates rides. Both serials are more than a little silly, but the music is engaging. Butts takes a different tack with his film noir movies. The opening music for *Double Jeopardy* is brash and restless with nervous strings and trumpet fan-

fares that dwindle into a world-weary blues theme. There is also a sexy, bluesy passage played on a saxophone and some snappy jazz music heard throughout the melodrama. Another noir sample, *Too Late for Tears*, opens with brass fanfares, then howling trumpets and a bluesy string section take over. The movie has lots of moody string passages that play variations on a simple musical phrase. There is also an effective motif in which wavering horns repeat themselves in a dizzying manner. Aside from a few of the Roy Rogers musicals, Butts rarely got to score a first-rate movie at Republic. Instead he wrote a lot of music for a lot of mediocre films for a dozen years then gave it up and sank into obscurity.

Credits

(all films USA)

Year	Film	Director
1944	The Yellow Rose of Texas	Joseph Kane
1944	Three Little Sisters	Joseph Santley
1944	Sing, Neighbor, Sing	Frank McDonald
1944	My Buddy	Steve Sekely
1944	The Big Bonanza	George Archainbaud
1945	Flame of Barbary Coast (AAN)	Joseph Kane
1945	Swingin' on a Rainbow	William Beaudine
1945	Sunset in El Dorado	Frank McDonald
1945	Don't Fence Me In	John English
1946	Gay Blades	George Blair
1946	Home on the Range	R. G. Springsteen
1946	The Catman of Paris	Lesley Selander
1946	Rainbow Over Texas	Frank McDonald
1946	My Pal Trigger	Frank McDonald, Yakima Canutt
1946	Roll on Texas Moon	William Witney
1946	Sioux City Sue	Frank McDonald
1946	Heldorado	William Witney
1947	The Crimson Key	Eugene Forde
1947	Second Chance	James Tining
1947	The Invisible Wall	Eugene Forde
1948	Eyes of Texas	William Witney
1948	Night Time in Nevada	William Witney
1948	Son of God's Country	R. G. Springsteen
1948	The Denver Kid	Philip Ford
1948	The Plunderers	Joseph Kane
1948	Homicide for Three	George Blair
1948	The Far Frontier	William Witney
1949	The Last Bandit	Joseph Kane
1949	Hellfire	R. G. Springsteen
1949	Too Late for Tears	Byron Haskin
1949	Down Dakota Way	William Witney
1950	Bells of Coronado	William Witney
1950	Rock Island Trail	Joseph Kane
1950	Women from Headquarters	George Blair
1950	The Savage Horde	Joseph Kane

Year	Film	Director
1950	*Trigger Jr.*	William Witney
1950	*Sunset in the West*	William Witney
1950	*Hit Parade of 1951*	John H. Auer
1950	*North of the Great Divide*	William Witney
1951	*Spoilers of the Plains*	William Witney
1951	*Oh! Susanna*	Joseph Kane
1951	*Heart of the Rockies*	William Witney
1951	*In Old Amarillo*	William Witney
1951	*Lost Planet Airmen*	Fred C. Brannon
1951	*South of Caliente*	William Witney
1951	*The Sea Hornet*	Joseph Kane
1952	*Colorado Sundown*	William Witney
1952	*The Last Musketeer*	William Witney
1952	*Bal Tabarin*	Philip Ford
1952	*Woman of the North Country*	Joseph Kane
1952	*Toughest Man in Arizona*	R. G. Springsteen
1952	*The WAC from Walla Walla*	William Witney
1953	*San Antone*	Joseph Kane
1953	*Old Overland Trail*	William Witney
1953	*City That Never Sleeps*	John H. Auer
1953	*Champ for a Day*	William A. Seiter
1953	*Shadows of Tombstone*	William Witney
1953	*Sea of Lost Ships*	Joseph Kane
1953	*Red River Shore*	Harry Keller
1953	*Geraldine*	R. G. Springsteen
1954	*Trader Tom of the China Seas*	Franklin Adreon
1954	*Phantom Stallion*	Harry Keller
1954	*Hell's Half Acre*	John H. Auer
1954	*The Shanghai Story*	Frank Lloyd
1954	*Man with the Steel Whip*	Franklin Adreon
1954	*The Outcast*	William Witney
1954	*Hell's Outpost*	Joseph Kane
1955	*Panther Girl of the Kongo*	Franklin Adreon
1955	*Carolina Cannonball*	Charles Lamont
1955	*Santa Fe Passage*	William Witney
1955	*I Cover the Underworld*	R. G. Springsteen
1955	*City of Shadows*	William Witney
1955	*The Road to Denver*	Joseph Kane
1955	*Double Jeopardy*	R. G. Springsteen
1955	*King of the Carnival*	Franklin Adreon
1955	*Lay That Rifle Down*	Charles Lamont
1955	*Headline Hunters*	William Witney
1955	*No Man's Woman*	Franklin Adreon
1955	*The Vanishing American*	Joseph Kane
1956	*Stranger at My Door*	William Witney
1956	*Terror at Midnight*	Franklin Adreon
1956	*Dakota Incident*	Lewis R. Foster
1956	*Thunder over Arizona*	Joseph Kane
1956	*A Strange Adventure*	William Witney
1956	*The Man Is Armed*	Franklin Adreon

BYRNE, David (b. 1952) A multihyphenate artist involved in many forms of music but still most remembered as a founder of the New Wave group Talking Heads, he has included movie directing, producing, and composing in his eclectic career.

David Byrne was born in Dunbarton, Scotland, the son of an electronics engineer, and grew up in America, first in Hamilton, Ontario, Canada, and then in Arbutus, Maryland. Before he reached his teens, Byrne was playing harmonica, guitar, accordion, and violin. Although he performed in a band in high school, after graduation Byrne pursued an art career at the Rhode Island School of Design and the Maryland Institute College of Art. He left school when he formed his first professional band, the Artistics, which only lasted a year. In 1975 he founded Talking Heads, one of the most influential musical groups of its era. It defined the New Wave sound and experimented with funk, pop, world music, punk and other alternative rock music. Talking Heads made eight studio albums and performed in concert until 1988, reuniting in 1991 to introduce one final song together. In Byrne's solo albums and concerts he utilized ethnic and international music, experimented with orchestral and operatic music, and mixed a brass ensemble with rock music in unique ways. He has also composed for modern dance, theatre, and opera. Byrne founded the world music record company Luaka Bop in 1990 and in 2005 created his own Internet radio station, Radio David Byrne. In addition to all his musical interests, Byrne has written nine nonfiction books. He has also returned to his art background and produced public art installations, and his photographs, sketches, and other artworks have been shown in galleries and museums. Byrne's first direct experience with film was writing some of the music and performing in Jonathan Demme's 1984 concert film *Stop Making Sense* featuring the Talking Heads. Two years later Byrne composed, cowrote, directed, and appeared in the comic musical movie *True Stories*, which featured several songs by the Talking Heads. In 1987 Italian director Bernardo Bertolucci hired Byrne to write some of the music for his historical epic *The Last Emperor*, the score winning an Oscar for Byrne and co-composers Ryûichi Sakamoto and Cong Su. He has since scored two American films, the comedy *Married to the Mob* and the documentary *Between the Teeth* (which he codirected), as well as the international movies *In Spite of Wishing and Wanting*, *Young Adam*, and *This Must Be the*

Place (the last co-composed with Will Oldham). Byrne has written music for some film shorts and the television series *Alive from Off Center* and *Big Love*. Music composed and performed by Byrne and fellow artists can be heard in over one hundred television programs and movies ranging from *Risky Business* (1983) to *Skid Row* (2013).

While Byrne's involvement with movies has been sporadic, he has nonetheless written some superior music for the screen. His main theme for *The Last Emperor* is justly famous. It is a slow and mesmerizing piece played by a solo violin and accompanied by drums and xylophone. While it has an exotic Asian flavor, it is also very modern with subtle electronic embellishments. The theme is also memorable for the way it skillfully increases in texture and tempo as it evolves. Byrne's interest and devotion to world music can be experienced in this one piece. *True Stories* is a hilarious mockumentary of sorts about a Texas town celebrating its anniversary with a talent show. The characters (including narrator Byrne) are wacky and delightful, and so is the score. Much of the music is songs by Talking Heads and others but Byrne's soundtrack is a sly commentary in itself. There is a recurring theme in which reeds waver back and forth dizzily in a cockeyed manner, a breezy piece of country music that is just off center, a weird calliope tune played out of tune, and a woodwind canon with repeated phrases that all sound like the instruments are laughing. Various singers and groups ranging from New Order to Rosemary Clooney are heard on the soundtrack for the comedy *Married to the Mob*. In between Byrne provides some ethnic, rock, and pop musical themes, most memorably a romantic passage with a sexy and rhythmic bounce. On a much more dour note, the British-French melodrama *Young Adam* has some haunting music. This uncomfortable tale is about a drifter (Ewan McGregor) who gets a job on a river barge in Scotland and keeps secret his knowledge about the corpse of a young woman found in the water. The opening theme is a chilly lament heard on a violin and soft organ chords backed with twinkling sound effects. There is a cool jazz piece played on an electric keyboard and percussion that is casual until the strings enter and cast a sorrowful shadow. Even the love scenes are scored with restrained strings that seesaw rather than blossom. Byrne plays himself in concert in the drama *This Must Be the Place* which takes its title from a Talking Heads hit. A burnt-out, retired rock star (Sean Penn) seeks revenge on the ex-Nazi who tortured his father. It is a grim movie, but Byrne's score is a welcome relief, in particular a jazz theme for strings and percussion. A vibrant rhythmic piece for trumpet, percussion, electric keyboard, and ethnic instruments is a highlight of *In Spite of Wishing and Wanting*, a Belgian film of a dance performance. There is also a punk rock theme that uses recorded sounds and choral accents effectively. This is dance music rather than screen scoring but it is still first rate. Even with only seven feature films to his credit, Byrne is always worth exploring and wishing for more. Biographies: *David Byrne*, John Howell (1992); *Song and Circumstance: The Work of David Byrne from Talking Heads to the Present*, Sytze Steenstra (2010). Official website: www.davidbyrne.com.

Credits

Year	Film	Director
1986	*True Stories*	David Byrne (USA)
1987	*The Last Emperor* (AA; GG; BAFTA-N)	Bernardo Bertolucci (China/Italy/UK/France)
1988	*Married to the Mob*	Jonathan Demme (USA)
1994	*Between the Teeth*	David Byrne, David Wild (USA)
2002	*In Spite of Wishing and Wanting*	Wim Vanderkeybus (Belgium)
2003	*Young Adam*	David Mackenzie (UK/France)
2011	*This Must Be the Place*	Paolo Sorrentino (Italy/France/Ireland)

CALKER, Darrell (1905–1964) A classical and popular music conductor-bandleader, arranger, and composer who worked in ballet, radio, and film, he is most remembered for his music for dozens of animated shorts, especially Woody Woodpecker cartoons, and for independent B movies, in particular several Hopalong Cassidy westerns.

Darrell W. Calker was born in Washington, D.C., and as a child had a good ear for music, becoming a virtuoso on the classical guitar. Calker attended the Episcopal Cathedral School in the District of Columbia and as a teen sang in the cathedral choir. After graduating from the Curtis Institute of Music in Philadelphia, Calker composed scores for symphony orchestras and for two of Europe's most distinguished dance troupes, the Ballets Russes de Monte Carlo and Saddler Wells Royal Ballet. In the late 1930s, Calker settled in Los Angeles, where he played guitar in Hollywood soundtrack orchestras and performed with his own jazz band on the radio. At the same time he continued to compose works for orchestra, swing bands, and jazz combos. In 1941, animation producer-director Walter Lantz hired Calker to score cartoons featuring Andy Panda, Homer Pigeon, Oswald the Lucky Rabbit, and Woody Woodpecker. For eight years he worked for Lantz, providing music for over eighty cartoons. On occasion Calker was able to convince celebrated artists, such as Jack Teagarden, Nat King Cole, and Meade Lux Lewis, to lend their performing talents to his soundtracks. *The Poet and Peasant* (1946) and *Musical Moments from Chopin* (1947), two of his animated shorts utilizing classical music (which he arranged and conducted), received Oscar nominations. The Lantz animation department temporarily closed in 1949 so Calker scored some shorts for Columbia Pictures for a few years. When Lantz began making cartoons again in 1961, Calker returned to the studio and scored twelve shorts before his death in 1964.

Calker's career in feature films was less successful. In 1941 he began contributing music for B movies made by Allied Artists, Eagle-Lion Studios, American Inter-national, and other minor or independent companies, often working with two or more other composers on each movie. The first feature film that he scored on his own was the western *Rolling Home* in 1946, followed by fifty movies over the next fourteen years. These included comedies, crime dramas, sci-fi and horror films, adventure movies, and westerns, in particular such Hopalong Cassidy favorites as *The Dead Don't Dream, Silent Conflict,* and *Sinister Journey*. While none of these independent features were big-budget, high-profile projects, some were commendable, such as *Dangerous Millions, I Cover Big Town, Jungle Flight, Manhandled, Fighting Back, The Fighting Redhead, Dynamite, Outlaw Treasure, Five Bold Women,* and *Son of the Renegade*. As he had been with his cartoons, Calker was conductor, arranger, and/or musical director on many of these films. Near the end of his career, he also worked in television, scoring such animated series as *Mr. Magoo, The Ruff & Reddy Show,* and *The New Three Stooges*.

It seems odd that a man who composed highly praised music for the concert stage and ballet would thrive scoring so many cartoons. Yet the scores for these animated shorts are filled with classical music, jazz, swing, opera, Latin, boogie-woogie, and other musical forms. In fact, the Calker cartoons are a musical education in themselves: Andy Panda conducts Chopin, Homer Pigeon dances to swing, and Woody Woodpecker sings *The Barber of Seville*. Calker seems to be at his loosest and most creative in these vivacious cartoons. The live-action features, on the other hand, are more conventional and routine. Also, while the music budget for cartoons was limited, it was even slimmer for these low-budget features. Calker's western scores use a full orchestra, but they are far from symphonic, relying instead on select brass and string instruments. *Son of the Renegade*, for example, has an old-fashioned horse opera score. The main theme is a sprightly march with boastful horns and folksy fiddle-playing. There is a nature theme that sounds expansive as the orchestra goes tipping up and down the scale while the action scenes rely on low brass phrases. For the fictional biopic *I Killed Wild Bill Hickok*, the music is more romanticized than folk or country, as the whole story is told in a first-person flashback, the music suggesting a memory piece rather than a western. Even the action scenes are symphonic, although far from grandiose, such as the use of muted brass and restrained strings during the climactic shoot-out. The Hopalong Cassidy western *The Dead Don't Dream* has a brief but spirited theme song, then the rest of the score is rather somber, some passages sounding more like film noir music rather than western. In one section wavering strings play a duet with a solo oboe while in another the combination is a high-reaching flute and muted trumpets.

Calker scored several melodramas that aped the film noir genre. One of the better ones is *Manhandled*, an urban drama about a fake psychiatrist (Harold Vermilyea), his suspicious secretary (Dorothy Lamour), and a series of murders. It has a romantic score, smooth and flowing rather than the expected harsh tones the situation might suggest. In the main theme, low brass chords and gliding violins move from soothing to sinister then back again in a skillful manner. At other times, seesawing music avoids monotony by making subtle variations in pitch. A melodrama with more action is *Dynamite* about personal conflicts within a demolition squad. The opening music is lyrical and casual until the first explosion, then furious strings and growling bass notes take over. A chase scene is scored with shouting trumpets and a glissando of strings. Calker scored four movies in the *Big Town* series inspired by a popular radio program. *Big Town after Dark*, about newspaper reporters uncovering a gambling ring, is perhaps the best; it certainly has the finest score. The main theme is a vigorous rhapsody for piano and strings that has a Gershwinesque flavor. The romantic theme is a facile string piece that effortlessly moves from a soft adagio to a fandango tempo, and there is a melancholy passage with descending brass and reeds that sets the urban tone very well.

As competent as all these scores are, they lack the excitement of Calker's cartoon music. Only in his horror and sci-fi scores does he seem to be having as much fun as in his animated projects. Granted, these second-rate, low-budget thrillers are laughable, but sometimes the music is admirable. In *The Amazing Transparent Man*, a safe-cracker (Douglas Kennedy) turns invisible when exposed to radioactivity. The main theme consists of ominous brass notes stuck in repeated scales with muted trumpets high above. This same idea is used throughout the movie, sometimes with a string component added for variety. Suspense is created by alternating strings and brass phrases, a device Calker resorts to frequently in these horror and sci-fi films. *Voodoo Woman* is a contrived Frankenstein story set in a jungle with a playful score that revels in cliché. A leitmotif in the movie consists of tribal drums and high-pitched chanting. Drums continue throughout much of the film, varying in tempo, but more noticeable is a flute solo with woodwind accompaniment that is used for the suspense scenes. The most interesting thing about *Beyond the Time Barrier* is the opening credits. This prophetic futuristic thriller, about a military jet pilot (Robert Clarke) who goes through a time warp and ends up in the very nightmarish year 2024, opens with a catchy military march heard over credits that roll into the distance exactly as in the opening of the *Star Wars* films decades later. Perhaps the silliest of the bunch is *From Hell It Came* about a giant walking tree that attacks a Polynesian village. Calker opens the movie with crashing chords and rumbling drums which transition to a rumba-like theme featuring horns with a mariachi-flavored accompaniment. The killer tree itself is scored with a swirling, high-pitched theme played on a theremin, a laughable cliché itself by 1957. Finally, of more than passing interest is *Superman and the Mole-Men* six years earlier. The sci-fi adventure movie was made as a pilot for a proposed *Superman* television series and was shown in theatres first to offset its cost. George Reeves played the title hero for the first time but the rest of the cast did not appear in the TV series. The film itself, about mole-like creatures that come to the surface through an oil well, is uneven but the music is promising. It opens with a series of trumpet fanfares with robust percussion then turns into a march for strings and drums. Lighter moments in the film are scored with giddy piccolos while the flying special effects (such as they are) have trumpets competing with a loud wind sound. The TV series *Adventures of Superman*, which began in 1952, used a similar march as its theme and also adopted a wind sound for the flying. But it was Leon Klatzkin who scored the series and Calker missed out on having one big hit in his career. Instead he is most remembered for his creative cartoon scores, and rightfully so.

Credits

(all films USA)

Year	Film	Director
1946	*Rolling Home*	William Berke
1946	*Dangerous Millions*	James Tining
1946	*Renegade Girl*	William Berke
1947	*I Cover Big Town* (aka *I Cover the Underworld*)	William C. Thomas
1947	*Backlash*	Eugene Forde
1947	*Shoot to Kill* (aka *Police Reporter*)	William Berke
1947	*Seven Were Saved* (aka *S.O.S. Rescue*)	William H. Pine
1947	*Jewels of Brandenburg*	Eugene Forde
1947	*Big Town* (aka *Guilty Assignment*)	William C. Thomas
1947	*Danger Street*	Lew Landers
1947	*Adventure Island*	Sam Newfield
1947	*Jungle Flight*	Sam Newfield
1947	*Big Town after Dark* (aka *Underworld after Dark*)	William C. Thomas
1948	*Albuquerque*	Ray Enright
1948	*Half Past Midnight*	William F. Claxton
1948	*Silent Conflict*	George Archainbaud
1948	*Arthur Takes Over*	Malcolm St. Clair
1948	*The Dead Don't Dream*	George Archainbaud
1948	*Speed to Spare*	William Berke
1948	*Big Town Scandal* (aka *Underworld Scandal*)	William C. Thomas
1948	*Sinister Journey* (aka *Two Gun Territory*)	George Archainbaud
1948	*Borrowed Trouble*	George Archainbaud
1948	*Fighting Back*	Malcolm St. Clair
1949	*Dynamite*	William H. Pine
1949	*Ride, Ryder, Ride!*	Lewis D. Collins
1949	*Tucson*	William F. Claxton
1949	*Manhandled* (aka *A Man Who Stole a Dream*)	Lewis R. Foster
1949	*The Fighting Redhead*	Lewis D. Collins
1950	*The Flying Saucer*	Mikel Conrad
1950	*Forbidden Jungle*	Robert Emmett Tansey
1950	*Federal Man* (aka *Narcotics Agent*)	Robert Emmett Tansey
1950	*I Killed Geronimo*	John Hoffman
1950	*Border Outlaws* (aka *Border Raiders*)	Richard Talmadge
1951	*Badman's Gold*	Robert Emmett Tansey
1951	*Savage Drums*	William Berke
1951	*The Hoodlum*	Max Nosseck
1951	*Joe Palooka in Triple Cross*	Reginald Le Borg
1951	*FBI Girl*	William Berke
1951	*Cattle Queen* (aka *Queen of the West*)	Robert Emmett Tansey
1951	*Superman and the Mole-Men*	Lee Sholem
1953	*Son of the Renegade*	Reg Browne
1953	*The Marshal's Daughter*	William Berke
1955	*Outlaw Treasure*	Oliver Drake
1956	*I Killed Wild Bill Hickok*	Richard Talmadge
1957	*Voodoo Woman*	Edward L. Cahn
1957	*From Hell It Came*	Dan Milner
1958	*My World Dies Screaming* (aka *Terror in the Haunted House*)	Harold Daniels
1959	*Date with Death* (aka *Blood of the Man Devil*)	Harold Daniels
1960	*The Amazing Transparent Man*	Edgar G. Ulmer
1960	*Beyond the Time Barrier*	Edgar G. Ulmer
1960	*Five Bold Women*	Jorge López Portillo
1960	*Chartroose Caboose*	William "Red" Reynolds

CAMERON, John (b. 1944) A versatile British composer, arranger, songwriter, and conductor for records, theatre, television, and movies, he has scored thirty-two feature films since 1969.

Born in Woodford, England, as a youth John Cameron was interested in all kinds of music, from classical to jazz. Cameron studied music and history at Cambridge University where he provided the music for the famous Footlights theatre group. His first professional job was arranging the music for pop singer Donovan, creating such chart-topping albums as *Sunshine Superman* and *Mellow Yellow*. Cameron not only arranged the music for other top singers but had hit songs of his own composition, as with "If I Thought You'd Ever Change Your Mind" and "Sweet Inspiration." In 1972 he formed the jazz-funk band Collective Consciousness Society, which also had chart hits. Cameron has also worked in the theatre, most memorably as the orchestrator for the original *Les Misérables* in London; those arrangements were later used on Broadway, for international tours, and in the 2012 film version. His television and film career both started in 1967. Cameron arranged the music for the popular British TV series *Once More with Felix* then arranged and conducted the Donovan songs for the movie *Poor Cow*. Two years later he made an auspicious screen composing debut with his score for the drama *Kes*. Cameron was very active in films in the 1970s, scoring such notable movies as *The Rise and Rise of Michael Rimmer*, *The Ruling Class*, *Psychomania* (also known as *The Death Wheelers*), *A Touch of Class*, *Nasty Habits*, *Out of Season*, *The Great Scout & Cathouse Thursday*, and *The London Connection*. Since 1982, he has only returned to screen scoring sporadically, although he has written memorable scores for such movies as *The Young Visitors*, *Hawks*, and *To End All Wars*. Cameron has written music for both British and American television series, such as *The Protectors*, *1990*, *The Optimist*, and *Little House on the Prairie*, and a dozen TV movies, including *Spectre* (1977), *The Thief of Baghdad* (1978), *Witness for the Prosecution* (1982), *Philip Marlowe, Private Eye* (1983), *The Secret Garden* (1987), *Jekyll & Hyde* (1990), *Frankenstein* (1992), and *The Path to 9/11* (2006). He has arranged and conducted many of his scores and those composed by others and continues to work with pop singers and notable bands ranging from Cilla Black and Hot Chocolate to José Carreras and the Choir of New College Oxford.

Most of the movies Cameron has scored were made in the 1970s and often the music in them reflects the period, utilizing pop, disco, rock, and jazz. The comedy *The Rise and Rise of Michael Rimmer*, for example, is set in swinging London and has a freewheeling rock theme with a driving beat and expansive riffs on electric guitar. *The Death Wheelers/Psychomania*, a horror movie about devil worship, has a punk rock score. One theme is a series of descending notes heard on bass guitar, while the main theme is a throbbing and echoing lament punctuated with electric guitar riffs. The dark melodrama *Out of Season* uses for its title sequence a catchy pop waltz played on solo oboe and electric guitar. Even *Nasty Habits*, a delicious Watergate spoof set in a Philadelphia convent, has a pop-jazz score with lots of mock-religious hymns added for satiric effect. The cult classic *The Ruling Class*, about a merrily demented British lord (Peter O'Toole) who thinks he is Jesus Christ, has jazz and rock in the soundtrack score though most of the music heard in the eccentric comedy consists of British anthems and marches, minstrel ditties, and jazzy song standards.

On several occasions Cameron has written some timeless and memorable music for the screen. His Oscar-nominated score for the sophisticated comedy *A Touch of Class* is very modern yet has an old-fashioned sense of romance. The love theme is a delicate flute and harp passage that is tentative but still passionate. Each of the lovers has an individual theme. She (Glenda Jackson) is scored with a flowing waltz featuring strings and a solo trumpet; he (George Segal) has a rhythmic jazz theme with pop accents. George Barrie and Sammy Cahn wrote the movie's song "All That Love Went to Waste," a bouncy pop tune with merry scat voices and a Latin beat, and it blends right into Cameron's felicitous score. Also a great deal of fun is the score for the offbeat comic western *The Great Scout & Cathouse Thursday*, which features the banjo throughout. The main theme is a vivacious march with a solo banjo accompanied by happy whistling and a breezy jazz combo. The score also has some cheerful saloon tunes, wacky traveling music, silly chase music, and a surprisingly tender ballad.

Perhaps Cameron's finest scores are his first, *Kes*, and one of his most recent, *To End All Wars*. The former is an engaging film about an abused and neglected boy (David Bradley) and his pet falcon, or kestral. Cameron uses the rarely heard descant recorder for the score. In the haunting main theme, this recorder is heard with string accompaniment, resulting in a radiant sound of high notes that seem to float and soar. The recorder is also used effectively in a sprightly folk tune in which different instruments in the orchestra pick up the recorder's tune and do variations on it. The setting is Yorkshire, and much of the music in the *Kes* score has a folklike quality that conjures up the majesty and mystery of the landscape. To date, Cameron has scored only two movies in the new century. The 2001 wartime drama *To End All Wars* is about British POWs forced by the Japanese to build a railway line though the Burma jungle. Cameron avoids pseudo-Asian music and instead concentrates on the music of the Scottish prisoners. The score is filled with Gaelic chanting that is both eerie and enticing. Dramatic scenes are scored with restrained pipes and strings and the movie ends with an intoxicating Scottish hymn (vocal by Moya Brennan) that is a very stirring lament. Such strong and indelible music makes one hope that Cameron returns to screen scoring again. Official website: www.johncameronmusic.com.

Credits

(all films UK unless stated otherwise)

Year	Film	Director
1969	Kes	Ken Loach
1970	Every Home Should Have One	Jim Clark
1970	The Rise and Rise of Michael Rimmer	Kevin Billington
1972	The Ruling Class	Peter Medak
1972	The Strange Vengeance of Rosalie	Jack Starrett
1972	Made	John Mackenzie
1973	The Death Wheelers (aka Psychomania)	Don Sharp
1973	Charley-One-Eye	Don Chaffey (UK/USA)
1973	A Touch of Class (AAN)	Melvin Frank
1973	Night Watch	Brian G. Hutton
1973	Scalawag (aka Jamie's Treasure Hunt)	Kirk Douglas, Zoran Calic (Italy/Yugoslavia/USA)
1973	Who? (aka Robo Man)	Jack Gold
1974	The Bunny Caper (aka Sex Play)	Jack Arnold
1974	Moments	Peter Crane
1975	Out of Season (aka Winter Rates)	Alan Bridges
1975	Whiffs	Ted Post (USA)
1975	The Man from Nowhere	James Hill
1976	I Will . . . I Will . . . For Now	Norman Panama (USA)
1976	Pure as a Lily	Franco Rossi (Italy/UK)
1976	The Great Scout & Cathouse Thursday	Don Taylor (USA)
1977	Nasty Habits	Michael Lindsay-Hogg (UK/USA)
1979	The Bermuda Triangle	Richard Friedenberg (USA)
1979	The London Connection (aka The Omega Connection)	Robert Clouse (USA)
1979	Lost and Found	Melvin Frank
1979	Sunburn	Richard C. Sarafian (UK/USA)
1980	The Mirror Crack'd	Guy Hamilton
1982	Jimmy the Kid	Gary Nelson (USA)
1984	The Young Visitors	James Hill
1984	The Jigsaw Man	Terence Young
1988	Hawks	Robert Ellis Miller
1997	Driftwood	Ronan O'Leary (UK/Ireland)
2001	To End All Wars	David L. Cunningham (USA)
2006	After . . .	David L. Cunningham (USA)

CANTELON, Paul (b. 1965) A respected musician and composer for the concert hall, he has since 2005 written the music for fifteen feature films, most of them highly praised dramas with notable scores.

Paul Cantelon was born in Glendale, California, and studied violin as a child, making his concert debut at UCLA at the age of thirteen. Cantelon then became interested in the piano and studied privately and at the Paris Conservatory of Music with his eye on a career as a concert pianist. This dream was delayed by a bicycle accident at the age of seventeen which put him in a coma and, when he awoke, left him with a severe case of amnesia. Cantelon eventually recovered and had to learn music all over again. In 1978, he recorded a piano album of Celtic hymns before returning to school to study piano and composition at the Geneva Conservatory of Music, the Juilliard School in New York, and Trinity College at Cambridge University. He went on to record his first album of original piano music and in the 1990s formed the alternative band Wild Colonials which toured and made albums as well. In 1995 Cantelon wrote a new score to celebrate the eighty-fifth anniversary of the Russian movie classic *Battleship Potemkin* then concentrated on composing and performing for the concert hall. Although some of Cantelon's music was heard in a few short and feature movies as far back as 1994, he did not write a complete film score until *Everything Is Illuminated*, the 2005 oddball comedy-drama set in the Ukraine. Since then he has returned to the movies and scored such commendable dramas as *The Diving Bell and the Butterfly*, *Superheroes*, *The Other Boleyn Girl*, *W.*, *Conviction*, *The Music Never Stopped*, and *Wish You Well*, as well as the documentaries *Diana Vreeland: The Eye Has to Travel* and *Kiss the Water*. Cantelon has also written music for television documentaries and the TV movie *Firelight* (2012).

Cantelon's first feature film, *Everything Is Illuminated*, is not typical of the kind of projects he usually scores. While most are very serious movies on very sober subjects, *Everything Is Illuminated* is downright wacky. A neurotic Jewish American collector (Elijah Wood) travels to the Ukraine, the homeland of his grandfather, and embarks on an unorthodox tour with the casual Alex (Eugene Hutz) and his eccentric grandfather (Boris Leskin). The soundtrack has lots of ethnic songs performed by various groups, but the heart of the movie is in Cantelon's vibrant original music. The main theme is an Eastern European folk tune heard on various strings that bounces along merrily with a cockeyed grin. There is a daffy balalaika passage that increases in tempo and silliness then pulls back for some softer moments. A warm folk waltz, played on guitar, accordion, and balalaika, is cautious even when it speeds up and another waltz on piano is more classical but still has a Russian flavor. The film turns rather serious in the final reel and Cantelon provides some quiet reflective music on plucked and sustained strings that is very poignant. Cantelon has not yet had the opportunity again to score such an unconventional movie.

The French-American melodrama *The Diving Bell and the Butterfly* is the heartbreaking true story of a magazine editor (Mathieu Amalric) who is nearly totally paralyzed and must learn to communicate all over again. The main theme is a simple minor-key piano piece that is tentative and reticent at first but it slowly gets more complex and richer in harmony and melody. Similarly sobering is *The Music Never Stopped* about a father (J. K. Simmons) and his efforts to connect with his brain-damaged son (Lou Taylor Pucci) through music. Cantelon wrote a quiet guitar score with few embellishments, giving the movie a sincere and unadorned sound. The main theme is hesitant and sad at times, free flowing and expansive at other points in the film, the solo guitar moving from lonely plucked strings to fanciful fingering. For the nostalgic coming-of-age tale *Wish You Well*, Cantelon limits himself to piano and strings. The central theme is a fragile, repetitive piece with slight variations that is used throughout the movie but in so many forms that it is barely recognized. Sometimes rapid and restless, other times slow, delicate, and heartfelt, the theme conjures up memories as well as the 1940s rural Virginia setting.

The piano is also featured in *W.*, Oliver Stone's biopic about George W. Bush from his college days to his White House years. Cantelon wisely avoids the banjo or guitar or other instruments that come to mind when scoring the life of a Texan. Instead the main theme is a rural folk tune played on piano and strings that develops as it moves along but never loses its simplicity. There are the expected country-western passages, yet they come in the form of a waltz played on electric and traditional guitars that never slips into cliché and an accordion and woodwind passage that is carefree and spirited. The darker side of the story is scored with a somber piano piece with low, brooding strings that conveys a sense of doom and regret. The historical drama *The Other Boleyn Girl* afforded Cantelon the opportunity to write a period score. Yet the main theme, a mysterious and fluid piece with a touch of Renaissance in the horns, is mostly contemporary, featuring a modern piano with strings. Even the music for a Tudor banquet suggests the period rather than pasticing it. A solo horn is featured in the music for the coronation of Anne Boleyn (Natalie Portman) which also has a stirring

chorus and some vibrant strings. The love theme for Mary Boleyn (Scarlett Johansson) and Henry Tudor (Eric Bana) is graceful and stately yet passionate with a melancholy subtext. Because Catelon is so involved with concert composing and performing, his cinema repertoire is limited. Yet when he does embark on a screen project, it is usually above-average fare and the music is always commendable. Official website: www.paulcantelon.com.

Credits

(all films USA unless stated otherwise)

Year	Film	Director
2005	*Everything Is Illuminated* (aka *The Collector*)	Liev Schreiber
2007	*Suffering Man's Charity* (aka *Ghost Writer*)	Alan Cummings
2007	*The Diving Bell and the Butterfly*	Julian Schnabel (France/USA)
2007	*Superheroes*	Alan Brown
2007	*Year of the Fish*	David Kaplan
2008	*The Other Boleyn Girl*	Justin Chadwick (UK/USA)
2008	*W.* (aka *Bush*)	Oliver Stone (USA/Switzerland/Australia/Hong Kong/ China)
2010	*Conviction* (aka *Betty Anne Waters*)	Tony Goldwyn
2011	*The Music Never Stopped* (aka *Mr. Tambourine Man*)	Jim Kolhberg
2011	*Violet & Daisy*	Geoffrey Fletcher
2011	*Diana Vreeland: The Eye Has to Travel*	Lisa Immordino Vreeland, etc.
2013	*Kiss the Water*	Eric Steel (USA/UK)
2013	*Wish You Well*	Darnell Martin
2013	*Immigrant*	Barry Shurchin
2014	*Effie Gray*	Richard Laxton (UK)

CARBONARA, Gerard (1886–1959) An esteemed violinist, composer, and conductor for the concert hall, in the 1930s and 1940s he scored over seventy Hollywood films, mostly westerns.

Gerard Carbonara was born in New York City and studied at the National Conservatory of Music in his hometown and at the Naples Conservatory in Italy. While in Europe, Carbonara worked as a vocal coach for opera singers, played violin for various symphony orchestras, and conducted operas in several countries. He returned to the States in the late 1920s and got involved in movies just as sound was coming in. Carbonara scored the first talkie made by Paramount Studios, the baseball comedy *Warming Up* in 1928. The soundtrack consisted of music and sound effects, not spoken dialogue. Such was the case with several of his early Paramount movies, most of them

scored with other composers. Carbonara's first solo score for a talking movie was the mystery drama *The Hole in the Wall* in 1929. Over the next twenty years he contributed music to dozens of feature films, including such memorable works as *The Trail of the Lonesome Pine*, *Too Many Parents*, *Big Brown Eyes*, *The Texas Rangers*, *The Moon's Our Home*, *The Arkansas Traveler*, *Stagecoach*, *The Shepherd of the Hills*, *The Night of January 16th*, *Pacific Blackout*, *Among the Living*, *The Town Went Wild*, and *The Kansan*, earning an Oscar nomination for the last. About thirty of his screen scores were solo efforts and most of those were uncredited. Carbonara also wrote new scores for the silent classics *The Gold Rush* (1925) and *The Son of the Sheik* (1926), as well as music for several cartoon shorts. His movie music was later reused by different studios in other films and it is estimated that stock music by Carbonara can be heard in over 150 films. He left Hollywood in 1950 to concentrate on conducting and composing for the concert hall. By the time he died nine years later, Carbonara left a legacy of three symphonies, an opera, many solo piano works, and some commendable duets for violin and piano.

Because Carbonara and other studio composers were rarely credited in 1930s movies, Carbonara's contribution is not always clear. A case in point is the 1939 western classic *Stagecoach*. Because Carbonara was under contract to Paramount, the United Artists release was not allowed to credit him. In fact, no composer was listed in the credits or promotional materials. When *Stagecoach* won the Oscar for best musical scoring, four composers were listed by the studio, none of them Carbonara. So how much of the music heard in that famous film is actually by him? To avoid any misrepresentation, it is best to look at the movies that Carbonara scored alone. His specialty was westerns. Nearly half of his solo scores are for that genre and several are very accomplished. *The Mysterious Rider* has a sentimental main theme that flows more like the music for a romantic melodrama than a horse opera. There is a lush nature theme with a repeated three-note phrase heard on strings and brass with accents on a harp. The fight and chase scenes are scored with trumpets and strings that boldly parade up the scale, and there is a soft nocturne that features a lonesome trumpet solo. *The Kansan*, the western that brought Carbonara his only official Oscar nomination, has fiery opening music with abrupt trumpet fanfares heard against gliding strings. The score also has vigorous orchestral passages that seem to swirl out of control during the action scenes. For contrast, there is a sonorous theme in which an oboe plays over the string section. Not quite a western but a rural melodrama with an Old West sensibility is *The Shepherd of the Hills* set in the Ozark Mountains. The main theme is warm and domestic, a lilting melody with a catchy six-note musical phrase. This is repeated in different formats throughout the film. There is also an expansive nature passage with rising and falling strings that supports the beautiful on-location scenery. Oddly, Carbonara uses Brahms's "Lullaby" as the romantic theme and includes Sam Coslow's hymnlike folk song "There's a Happy Hunting Ground" for one scene. Two comedies that Carbonara scored deserve some attention because they reveal a very different sound. *The Gracie Allen Murder Case*, a comic mystery

movie from 1939, has an effervescent swing theme given a Big Band presentation. The music has some delightful comic touches, such as sour trombones and muted trumpets. There is also a rhythmic foxtrot tune in the score that keeps the film moving along. *The Town Went Wild*, a farce about two feuding families in a small town who find out their teenage sons were switched at birth, also uses comic accents in its music. The main theme is romantic and melodic but it soon turns into a mocking march. Later in the comedy there are musical passages with giddy fiddles and squawking brass. Carbonara was able to successfully move out of the western genre on occasion but not quite often enough.

Having listened to several Carbonara scores, one can return to *Stagecoach* and attempt to determine which part of that famous score he wrote. Six composers are known to have been contracted for the project, though not all of their music ended up in the film. Also, *Stagecoach* uses thirteen traditional American songs in its music, arranged and orchestrated by the six composers. The theme for the stagecoach itself is "Rio Grande" which is heard every time the passengers continue their journey. The alcoholic doctor (Thomas Mitchell) has his own theme, the folk ditty "At the Rover," while the young lady Lucy (Louise Platt) is scored with Stephen Foster's ballad "I Dream of Jeanie (with the Light Brown Hair)." As for the original music, researchers have examined the original handwritten scores and have determined that John Leipold wrote the rousing passage for the attack by the tribesmen, a series of trumpet fanfares contrasted with pseudowarpath music. Leo Shuken wrote the romantic theme, and Richard Hageman is believed to have written the vigorous march for the cavalry. That doesn't leave much music for Carbonara except for the arrangement of "Rio Grande" into a pliable theme song for the whole movie. The song's five-note phrase is turned into an exciting canon by Carbonara, different instruments repeating and overlapping each other in a confident and robust manner. He later uses variations of the song every time the stagecoach is off and running, giving the western a musical as well as metaphoric leitmotif. This is not unlike the scoring of Carbonara's other westerns. So maybe Carbonara is the musical force behind this iconic movie; maybe not. Like too much of his career in Hollywood, Carbonara's music is overlooked, misplaced, or just forgotten.

Credits

(all films USA; * unofficial)

Year	Film	Director
1928	*Warming Up*	Fred C. Newmeyer
1928	*The Patriot*	Ernst Lubitsch
1928	*Sawdust Paradise*	Luther Reed
1928	*Naughty Baby*	Mervyn LeRoy
1929	*The Wolf Song*	Victor Fleming
1929	*The Hole in the Wall*	Robert Florey
1930	*Burning Up*	A. Edward Sutherland
1936	*The Trail of the Lonesome Pine*	Henry Hathaway
1936	*Too Many Parents*	Robert F. McGowan
1936	*Big Brown Eyes*	Raoul Walsh
1936	*The Moon's Our Home*	William A. Seiter
1936	*Sky Parade*	Otho Lovering
1936	*The Case against Mrs. Ames*	William A. Seiter
1936	*Girl of the Ozarks*	William Shea
1936	*Spendthrift*	Raoul Walsh
1936	*The Texas Rangers*	King Vidor
1937	*Racketeers in Exile*	Erie C. Kenton
1937	*The Barrier*	Lesley Selander
1938	*Men with Wings*	William A. Wellman
1938	*The Texans*	James P. Hogan
1938	*The Mysterious Rider (aka Mark of the Avenger)*	Lesley Selander
1938	*The Arkansas Traveler*	Alfred Santell
1938	*The Frontiersman*	Lesley Selander
1938	*Artists and Models Abroad*	Mitchell Leisen
1938	*Tom Sawyer, Detective*	Louis King
1939	*Disbarred*	Robert Florey
1939	*Arrest Bulldog Drummond*	James P. Hogan
1939	*Ambush*	Kurt Neuman
1939	*Stagecoach (AA*)*	John Ford
1939	*Sunset Trail*	Lesley Selander
1939	*King of Chinatown*	Nick Grinde
1939	*The Gracie Allen Murder Case*	Alfred E. Green
1939	*Renegade Trail*	Lesley Selander
1939	*Our Leading Citizen*	Alfred Santell
1939	*Geronimo*	Paul Sloane
1940	*Women without Names (aka Strange Money)*	Robert Florey
1940	*Island of Doomed Men (aka Dead Man's Isle)*	Charles Barton
1940	*I Married Adventure*	Osa Johnson
1940	*The Monster and the Girl*	Stuart Heisler
1941	*The Shepherd of the Hills*	Henry Hathaway
1941	*The Night of January 16th (aka Private Secretary)*	William Clemens
1941	*Among the Living*	Stuart Heisler
1941	*Pacific Blackout (aka Midnight Angel)*	Ralph Murphy
1942	*Tombstone: The Town Too Tough to Die*	William C. McGann
1942	*American Empire*	William C. McGann
1942	*Night Plane from Chungking*	Ralph Murphy
1943	*The Kansan (aka Wagon Wheels) (AAN)*	George Archainbaud
1943	*Henry Aldrich Haunts a House*	Hugh Bennett
1944	*The Town Went Wild*	Ralph Murphy

CARLOS, Wendy (b. 1939) An innovative musician, arranger, and composer who is considered a pioneer in the use of synthesized and electronic music, she has limited but significant film credits.

Wendy Carlos was born Walter Carlos in Pawtucket, Rhode Island, and as a child not only excelled at the piano but also in science and graphic art. Carlos wrote original music and built her own computer at the age of fourteen, winning a Westinghouse scholarship. She got degrees in both music and physics at Brown University then studied music at Columbia University, where she encountered some of the earliest forms of electronic music. After graduation, Carlos worked as a recording engineer and befriended inventor Robert Moog, purchasing one of his synthesizers and experimenting with instrumental and vocal techniques using the new invention. With producer and collaborator Rachel Elkind, Carlos arranged and played the music for the 1968 album *Switched-On Bach*, the first fusion of classical music and synthesized musical performance. The record won awards and was very popular, putting Carlos in the forefront of new and innovative musicians-arrangers. Other synthesized albums followed, including the hit *Well-Tempered Synthesizer*; the first recording of synthesized environmental sounds, titled *Sonic Seasonings*; and *Beauty and the Beast*, which experimented with alternative tunings on an electronic guitar. Further recognition came with Stanley Kubrick's controversial film *A Clockwork Orange* (1971). Carlos not only arranged classical pieces for the synthesizer but introduced synthesized vocals on the soundtrack. "Timesteps," the only section of the score that was original, became famous in its own right and encouraged Carlos to pursue more composing. In 1972, Carlos had a sex change operation and changed her name from Walter to Wendy. Not until 1979, in an extensive interview in *Playboy* magazine, did she give details about her transgender feelings and on her decision to become a woman. Her earlier work was relabeled "W. Carlos" in some publications and music organizations.

After writing music for two film shorts, Carlos wrote her first full movie score for Kubrick's horror thriller *The Shining* in 1980. But Kubrick ended up discarding all of Carlos's score and using preexisting music by various classical and avant-garde composers. (Kubrick had done the same thing to composer Alex North on *2001: A Space Odyssey* in 1968.) Not until 2005 would Carlos's score for *The Shining* be released. For the 1982 Disney sci-fi adventure *TRON*, she wrote a full score using traditional orchestra, pipe organ, and both analog and digital synthesizers. The studio made only a few changes in the score (such as the ending music) and Carlos later added the unused music to her album *Digital Moonscapes* (1984). While the music for *TRON* was praised, the movie was not a box office success on its first release. Carlos did not return to feature films until sixteen years later with *Woundings*, a British futuristic movie about women in combat. The sci-fi war film was not well received and the soundtrack not released until 2005. Carlos has gone on to arrange, compose, and perform on many albums in which she continues to experiment with different kinds of electronic music, even developing new kinds of scales and exploring new ways of counting note values. She has also written an opera, music arrangements for children's records, and scored the video game of *TRON*.

Although *A Clockwork Orange* brought a great deal of attention to Carlos's work, the cinema has not been very gracious to her, and it is understandable why she has not returned to film very often. Yet her contribution to screen music is considerable. Carlos opened the door to synthesized music for the movies and today electronic music is used in all genres of film scoring. Where would the composers of horror and sci-fi films be today without Carlos's early work? But her scores are as accomplished as they are influential. The clumsy but groundbreaking *TRON*, about a computer whiz (Jeff Bridges) who gets trapped inside a dangerous video game contest, had the newest technology in computerized filmmaking and Carlos matched it with a compelling soundtrack. The main theme is a stately, slow-motion march heard on electric piano then by a full synthesized orchestra. It is not a new arrangement of a classical composition (as in the previous *A Clockwork Orange*) but an original piece that has a classical sensibility. The movie's end credits are scored with an elegant waltz played on synthesized woodwinds with choral voices that transitions into a pipe organ processional with a fervent hymnlike quality. In between these regal pieces, *TRON* is filled with some thrilling electronic chase music, reverberating chords that echo the sound of the racing machines, and cybermarch passages with grandiose fanfares. Because the story line was so thin and the issues so clouded, *TRON* failed with the public and only years later developed such a cult following that the sequel *Tron Legacy* was made in 2010.

The antiwar film *Woundings* also failed at the box office. It is a confused and pretentious futuristic melodrama, but again the score was highly commendable. Two memorable passages stand out: a reverberating theme in which the musical sounds ape the whirling sounds of a helicopter, and a rock theme with muted electric guitar riffs that is heard under certain scenes to convey a restless future world. When Carlos herself released parts of her original score for *The Shining* decades after it had been discarded, it was clear that some outstanding music had been rejected. The main theme is indeed haunting but not in the blunt, sensational way Kubrick wanted. Carlos's main theme features vibrato organ chords that slowly but chillingly march forward in defiance to high-pitched sound effects and swirling electronic screams. The melody is so primitive that it seems almost tribal, suggesting a supernatural power of seething evil. Movies may not be a major part of Carlos's remarkable career but her music has meant more to screen scoring than most realize. Official website: www.wendycarlos.com.

Credits

Year	Film	Director
1980	*The Shining*	Stanley Kubrick (UK/USA)
1982	*TRON*	Steven Lisberger (USA)
1998	*Woundings* (aka *Brand New World*)	Roberta Hanley (UK)

CARPENTER, John (b. 1948) A widely known writer, director, and producer of popular horror and sci-fi movies, he has also acted on-screen on occasion and has composed the scores for sixteen of his feature films.

Born in Carthage, New York, John Carpenter grew up in a musical family as the son of a college professor of music. They moved to Bowling Green, Kentucky, when his father was hired by Western Kentucky University. Carpenter was fascinated by the movies as a youth and made his own 8 mm films before he reached his teen years. He was educated at his father's university then went to California where he started studying film at USC's School of Cinematic Arts. Carpenter made some student films then left school to work professionally. He collaborated with John Longenecker on the script for the short *The Resurrection of Broncho Billy*, also editing the movie and composing the score. The low-budget film won the Oscar for Best Live Action Short, and Carpenter's career was launched at the age of twenty-two. Another low-budget effort, the sci-fi feature *Dark Star*, was not only cowritten by Carpenter but he also produced and directed it and wrote the soundtrack score. He repeated all these jobs on *Assault on Precinct 13* in 1976, but wide recognition did not come until two years later with *Halloween*, a horror classic and one of the first "slasher" movies. Made on a limited budget (Carpenter again saved money by cowriting the script and composing the score himself), *Halloween* was a box office hit, became a cult favorite, and inspired not only sequels but a whole new genre of horror movie. Carpenter also became a bona fide screen composer with *Halloween*, the main theme becoming a familiar and popular piece of music. Although he has directed different kinds of movies, Carpenter is still best known for his horror and sci-fi works, such as *The Thing* (1982) and *Starman* (1984). Among the films in this genre, which he scored as well as directed are *The Fog, Escape from New York, Christine, Prince of Darkness, They Live, Village of the Damned,* and *Vampires.* Carpenter has also written and directed for television, as with his TV movie *Elvis* (1991) starring Kurt Russell, who was featured in five of his movies. With the new century, Carpenter went into semiretirement, although he returned to movies when he directed *The Ward* in 2010.

Carpenter's formal music training may be limited, but he grew up in a household in which music was very important. He had no ambitions to become a movie composer, but out of necessity he scored his early films himself to save money and time. After 1981 most of his scores were cowritten with Alan Howarth, Shirley Walker, and others, his only solo effort being *Vampires* in 1998. So it is most accurate to look at his early scores to discover Carpenter the composer. His first feature, the sci-fi comedy *Dark Star*, has for its main theme a country-western number "Benson Arizona" (lyric by Bill Taylor) that the astronauts listen to as the credits appear. The rustic song heard over images of space travel recalls Stanley Kubrick's incongruous use of classical music in space in *2001: A*

Space Odyssey, but here the effect is gently comic rather than pretentious. This satirical ballad is reprised at the end of the movie when an astronaut surfboards through space on a piece of debris. In between is some pseudo-spooky music played on a synthesizer and other electric instruments, complete with the traditional theremin used for the alien's theme. The synthesizer is prominent in Carpenter's most famous score, that for the original *Halloween*. The main theme has an ominous tone as two different beats, a series of chords and a faster, higher tempo, combine to thrilling effect. The five-note motif and the sustained lower register create an urgency and restlessness that sets up the movie's obsession with jarring suspense and ghastly surprises. A four-note pattern with a hesitant tempo serves effectively as the theme for teenager Laurie (Jamie Lee Curtis) who is pursued by an escaped mental patient (Tony Moran). This is bold and obvious screen scoring, but there is nothing subtle about *Halloween* or Carpenter's approach to filmmaking.

The Fog is filled with horror music clichés and has more variety than *Halloween*. Dark chords and a high-pitched theme are played on a pipe organ. Carpenter used non-electric piano for some passages, as in an evocative theme that is reluctant to break into melody but still has a lyrical quality. The synthesizer returns for some of the movie's ghastlier moments and there are special sound effects created electronically that also work well. One of the best synthesizer scores of the 1980s is Carpenter's splendid music for the futuristic *Escape from New York*. Working with composer–computer programmer Alan Howarth, he found a sound for a nightmarish future. The main theme is a rhythmic piece with various electronic sounds heard at different tempos and pitches. The effect is something akin to futuristic jazz. This score is not about horror effects but it has its own sense of suspense as sustained notes, plucky repetition, and playful sliding up and down the scale all work together beautifully. At one point in the score, Carpenter offers a cockeyed, electronic version of Claude Debussy's piano work "The Sunken Cathedral," which is heard over a scene in which a plane approaches the Manhattan of 1997, now one giant prison. *Vampires* has a lot of the expected suspense music as vampire hunters comb the American Southwest for a new breed of the creatures. Yet much of the score is in the rock genre, a sound that seems to fit this odd mix of western and horror film. Because Carpenter has worn so many hats in his films, it seems that one talent may overshadow another. His script writing and directing seem to get the most attention, but something must be said for these scores that work so well on-screen. Carpenter may have become a composer by necessity, but in some cases the results are laudable. Biography: *John Carpenter: The Prince of Darkness*, Gilles Boulenger (2003). Official website: www.theofficialjohncarpenter. com.

Credits

(all films USA and directed by Carpenter unless stated otherwise)

Year	Film	Director
1974	*Dark Star*	
1976	*Assault on Precinct 13*	
1978	*Halloween*	
1980	*The Fog*	
1981	*Escape from New York* (UK/USA)	
1981	*Halloween II*	Rick Rosenthal
1982	*Halloween III: Season of the Witch*	Tommy Lee Wallace
1983	*Christine*	
1986	*Big Trouble in Little China*	
1987	*Prince of Darkness*	
1988	*They Live*	
1994	*In the Mouth of Madness*	
1995	*Village of the Damned*	
1996	*Escape from L.A.*	
1998	*Vampires* (USA/Japan)	
2001	*Ghosts of Mars*	

CASTELNUOVO-TEDESCO, Mario (1895–1968) A renowned Italian composer for the classical guitar, opera house, and concert hall, he spent only a dozen years in Hollywood but during that time contributed music to over two hundred movies.

Born in Florence, Italy, the descendant of an historic banking family, Mario Castelnuovo-Tedesco began taking piano lessons as a child. By the time he was nine, he had already written original pieces for the piano. Although his father wanted him to go into banking, he studied piano and composition privately and at the Cherubini Royal Institute of Music. He began his professional career writing music for the celebrated pianist-composer Alfredo Casella, and soon he was known throughout Europe from having his work performed in concerts and at musical festivals. Castelnuovo-Tedesco's first opera premiered in 1926, followed by other operas, chamber works, orchestral pieces, and music for guitar, violin, voice, and chorus. In 1932 he met the Spanish guitar virtuoso Andrés Segovia and was inspired to write many works for him, the two becoming the most renowned classical guitarist and guitar composer in the world. By the late 1930s, Castelnuovo-Tedesco was denounced by the Italian Fascist government, his music banned from the radio and his concerts cancelled. Concert maestro Arturo Toscanini in New York City sponsored Castelnuovo-Tedesco as a legal immigrant and the composer came to the States in 1939. Although his work was performed in New York, Castelnuovo-Tedesco ended up in Hollywood where he wrote music for MGM and gave private lessons for many young screen composers, including Henry Mancini, Nelson Riddle, André Previn, John Williams, and Jerry Goldsmith. Most of Castelnuovo-Tedesco's screen projects were collaborative efforts, often working with two or more composers on the same film. It is confirmed that he was also a very busy ghostwriter, writing sections of different scores for studio composers who were overworked and unable to make production deadlines. (Miklós Rózsa states in his autobiography that Castelnuovo-Tedesco ghostwrote most of the score for the 1945 film *The Picture of Dorian Gray*.) The first Hollywood movie he officially contributed to was the thriller *Rage in Heaven* in 1941, followed by such notable films as *Address Unknown*, *The Mark of the Whistler*, *Voice of the Whistler*, *I Love a Mystery*, *And Then There Were None*, *Night Editor*, *Mask of the Avenger*, *The Brave Bulls*, *Prison Ship*, *The Long Wait*, and *The Loves of Carmen*, the last at the request of star and producer Rita Hayworth. Castelnuovo-Tedesco became an American citizen in 1946 and spent the rest of his life in the States but often returned to Italy after the war. He left Hollywood in 1954 to concentrate on opera and concert music for the next fourteen years. Before his death in 1968 at the age of seventy-two, he completed his autobiography but it was not published in English until thirty-seven years later.

Of his over two hundred movies, only nineteen were scored by Castelnuovo-Tedesco alone. Among these, there is only one outstanding film, René Clair's mystery *And Then There Were None*. Yet some of the nineteen have splendid scores.

Two film noir movies stand out. *Night Editor*, based on a popular radio series of the same name, showed the dark side of investigative reporting. Castelnuovo-Tedesco's score is filled with swirling woodwinds and strings that suggest mental chaos, some passionate music with an uncomfortable urgency, and passages with violent strings that screech and condemn. This is offset by a domestic theme played on strings and reeds that flows like a lullaby. *The Long Wait*, about an amnesiac (Anthony Quinn) who may or may not be a murderer, was Castelnuovo-Tedesco's last Hollywood score and a fine example of noir music. Worried strings seem to be going in circles as the hero grasps at snatches of memory. Other times screaming violins and squawking brass torment him and assault the audience's ear, much as Bernard Herrmann did six years later in *Psycho*.

The Agatha Christie thriller *And Then There Were None* also has a powerful score. The movie opens with an ominous series of brass fanfares that turn into a childlike ditty with a heavy subtext. This is a reference to *Ten Little Indians*, the title of the play that the film is based on and the ten statuettes in the plot that are used to count off the murders. Woozy woodwinds suggesting seasickness are featured in a restless passage that rises and falls with the waves as the guests take a small boat to the fatal island mansion. Once the guests start getting bumped off, Castelnuovo-Tedesco adds to the suspense through woodwinds and brass alternating as they slowly descend the scale.

When Rita Hayworth needed Spanish and gypsy music for her vehicle *The Loves of Carmen*, it is no surprise she thought of Castelnuovo-Tedesco. Scoring the familiar opera story without using or copying Georges Bizet's music was indeed a challenge, but the result is perhaps

Castelnuovo-Tedesco's finest movie work. The opening passage is a lush gypsy dance played at a moderate tempo by a full orchestra with trumpeting accents. The theme for the wanton Carmen is a waltzing piece with a sultry tone, not quite a vamp's music but far from wholesome all the same. There is a spirited march on restrained brass and zesty strings for the military and another march for the matadors that is filled with trills and fanfares. A merry wedding procession with some vigorous fiddling is heard on one occasion, as well as a skipping waltz that is quite catchy. The Spanish guitar is featured in several passages, such as the carefree folk tune that cavorts up and down the scale or the fiery flamenco theme with castanets heard during the movie's most-remembered scene, Hayworth's vivacious dance for a festival crowd. *The Loves of Carmen* has so much music that it feels like an opera without singing. Of course this is all Castelnuovo-Tedesco's area of expertise and a reminder of how Hollywood rarely used his talents effectively. The short time he spent in films yielded a great deal of music but little of it could match his work away from Hollywood. Autobiography: *A Life in Music: A Book of Memories* (2005).

Credits

(all films USA)

Year	Film	Director
1942	Tortilla Flat	Victor Fleming
1944	The Return of the Vampire	Lew Landers
1944	Two-Man Submarine	Lew Landers
1944	Address Unknown	William Cameron Menzies
1944	The Black Parachute (aka Mission Thirty-Six)	Lew Landers
1944	She's a Soldier Too	William Castle
1944	The Mark of the Whistler (aka Dormant Account)	William Castle
1944	Sergeant Mike	Henry Levin
1944	Dancing in Manhattan	Henry Levin
1945	I Love a Mystery	Henry Levin
1945	The Crime Doctor's Courage	George Sherman
1945	Voice of the Whistler	William Castle
1945	And Then There Were None	René Clair
1945	Prison Ship	Arthur Dreifuss
1946	Night Editor	Henry Levin
1946	Dangerous Business	D. Ross Lederman
1946	Shadowed (aka The Gloved Hand)	John Sturges
1948	The Loves of Carmen	Charles Vidor
1951	The Brave Bulls	Robert Rossen
1951	Mask of the Avenger	Phil Karlson
1952	The Brigand	Phil Karlson
1954	The Long Wait	Victor Saville

CHAPLIN, Charles (1889–1977) One of the cinema's greatest multihyphenates, the British actor, director, screenwriter, and producer also composed scores for his twelve feature films, sometimes decades after they were released as silent movies. Known throughout the world for his screen character of the Little Tramp, Chaplin was an untrained but accomplished composer who found some success as a songwriter as well.

He was born Charles Spencer Chaplin in South London, England, the son of music hall entertainers, and endured a childhood of poverty, a broken home, and a mentally afflicted mother. Chaplin was sent to a workhouse at the age of seven but soon found some freedom as a child performer in regional music halls and variety theatre. He inherited a love of music from his parents and taught himself to play the piano, violin, and cello. At the age of nineteen Chaplin signed up with a vaudeville company which toured America and brought him to Hollywood, where he started performing in comedy shorts in 1914. In four years Chaplin was known around the world for his

Little Tramp comedies, most of which he also wrote and directed. He was a cofounder of United Artists Studios in 1919 and two years later made his first feature-length silent, *The Kid*. He continued making shorts even as he filmed such features as *A Woman of Paris*, *The Gold Rush*, and *The Circus*. Chaplin did not embrace the arrival of talking pictures and refused to use dialogue in his feature *City Lights* in 1931, but he did like having control over the music heard in his movies. So he composed a full score for the bittersweet comedy even though he had no experience or training in musical composition. Using skilled arrangers and orchestrators, he went on to score all his subsequent features, including *The Great Dictator*, his first movie with dialogue. Chaplin's popularity plummeted in the 1940s because of his scandalous private life (a paternity suit and his marriage to eighteen-year-old Oona O'Neill) and the accusation that he had Communist sympathies. He continued to make films, but *Monsieur Verdoux* was not a success and the very-British movie *Limelight*, inspired by his days in the music hall, premiered in London and never found popularity in the States until decades later. When Chaplin left the country in 1952 to attend *Limelight*'s opening, the FBI made it clear that he would not be allowed to return. He completed two more features in England, *A King in New York* and *A Countess from Hong Kong*, and remained in Europe for the rest of his life, returning to Hollywood once in 1972 to receive a special Academy Award. As his health deteriorated and he suffered a series of strokes, Chaplin abandoned any plans to make more films but instead concentrated on composing. As far back as 1942 he had completed a score for *The Gold Rush*; in 1957 he scored his 1918 featurette *Shoulder Arms*, then later went on to score his silent classics *The Circus*, *The Kid*, and *A Woman of Paris*, as well as some of his silent shorts. In 1971 *Limelight* was officially screened in Hollywood and won the Academy Award for its score, his only competitive Oscar. Chaplin was knighted in 1975 and died two years later in Switzerland where he had lived for many years.

As much as Chaplin loved music and was a proficient musician, he could not read music and depended on the help of such Hollywood composer-arrangers as Raymond Rasch, Eric James, Eddie Powell, Larry Russell, Meredith Willson, and David Raksin. Some attributed Chaplin's highly crafted and very effective scores to these men, but interviews and research over the years have revealed that the music was truly Chaplin's and he worked closely with others to get the sound he heard in his head. His first score, for *City Lights*, is very romantic yet avoids becoming maudlin. A waltz played by a solo violin backed by other strings starts hesitatingly then picks up speed, only to halt and reluctantly begin again. A solo clarinet introduces a vigorous Latin theme used for some of the movie's more farcical moments. To get the urban flavor, Chaplin even quotes a brief passage from George Gershwin's *Rhapsody in Blue*. The score for *Modern Times* boasts Chaplin's most famous song, "Smile" (lyric by John Turner and Geoffrey Parsons). Yet the lyric was not added until 1954 and then the song became a hit. The music is used in the 1936 movie as the love theme for the Tramp and the waif (Paulette Goddard) and, as played on fluttering strings, is completely entrancing without the benefit of words. Like all of Chaplin's features, there is almost continuous music in *Modern Times*. For the grinding of the machines, the music is a pulsating race with squawking brass or quacking woodwinds that is oppressive yet still comic. There is a sparkling theme for the assembly line in which the music climbs the scale then descends quickly as the tempo increases to a crazy crescendo. *The Great Dictator* has little original music but Chaplin's brilliant use of classical music for comic effect is noteworthy. When the Dictator (Chaplin) bounces an inflated globe with his feet, a dreamy passage from Richard Wagner's *Lohengrin* is quoted and when Johannes Brahms's "Hungarian Dance" is playing on the radio, the Jewish barber (also Chaplin) furiously shaves a customer in time to the rapid music. These two sequences are musically ingenious and illustrate Chaplin's complete understanding of cinema music.

The main theme for *The Kid* is a flowing waltz that repeats a four-note phrase in a glowing manner. This is perhaps Chaplin's most sentimental film, yet the music (written fifty years after the original release) is elegant and controlled and never descends to bathos. The score also has a tripping waltz and some heartbreaking passages filled with yearning. *The Gold Rush* is arguably Chaplin's least sentimental feature, yet much of the score is still in the romantic vein, as with the main theme, which is a gliding hesitation waltz. Even the Tramp's eating a shoe as if it were a steak dinner is scored with a classical-sounding violin piece as one might hear in a classy Viennese restaurant. *The Circus* is filled with comic scoring that adds to the fun. When the Tramp is accidentally locked in a cage with a sleeping lion, various instruments contribute to his frustration. Chaplin wrote both music and lyric for the song "Swing Little Girl" which never found wide popularity yet is a superb example of a music hall ballad. Chaplin sings the ditty over the opening credits and its music is used effectively throughout *The Circus*. A song that did enjoy some fame is "This Is My Song" (lyric by Chaplin) from *A Countess from Hong Kong*. The Italianate music is totally captivating as it seems to call out with a melancholy passion. This is probably Chaplin's least satisfying movie, but the score is delightful. The opening theme plucks out a pseudo-Chinese tune, a lilting waltz conjures up a European setting, and that lovely song returns to charm us in a way the characters and plot cannot. Finally, there is the glowing score for *Limelight*, which includes three music hall songs written and performed by Chaplin as the down-at-heels comic Calvero. This is perhaps Chaplin's darkest and most autobiographical film, and the music has a very somber subtext, even the comic stage songs coming across as more pathetic than funny. The main theme is a sorrowful lament played by a violin and then a clarinet that conveys Calvero's loneliness and neglect. After he rescues the suicidal dancer Teresa (Claire Bloom), the music grows more hopeful. "Terry's Theme," an expansive piece of music that has moments of gushing optimism, was later turned into the hit song "Eternally" (lyric by Geoffrey Parsons). *Limelight* is filled with music, including ballet music for Teresa, background music behind the acts in the music hall, and a cockeyed duet for Calvero on the violin and his partner (Buster Keaton) on piano. This score deserved the Oscar even if the sentiments behind the award were more apologetic than artistic. How fortunate that Chaplin lived long enough to score all this silent features, making them even more valuable. Of all the superlatives heaped on Chaplin in his last years, his music should be included among them. Autobiography: *My Autobiography* (1964/2003); memoir: *My Father, Charlie Chaplin*, Charles Chaplin Jr. (1960); biographies: *Chaplin: His Life and Art*, David Robinson (1985); *Sir Charlie: Chaplin, the Funniest Man in the World*, Sid Fleischman (2010). Official website: charliechaplin.com.

Credits

(all films USA unless stated otherwise; all directed by Chaplin)

Year	Film
1931	*City Lights*
1936	*Modern Times*
1940	*The Great Dictator*
1942	*The Gold Rush* (1925)
1947	*Monsieur Verdoux*
1952	*Limelight* (AA in 1971)
1957	*A King in New York* (UK)
1957	*Shoulder Arms* (1918)
1967	*A Countess from Hong Kong* (UK/USA)
1969	*The Circus* (1928)
1971	*The Kid* (1921)
1976	*A Woman of Paris* (1976)

CHAPLIN, Saul (1912–1997) One of Hollywood's busiest and most respected musical arrangers and conductors for over forty years, he was also a successful songwriter and scored five feature films.

Saul Chaplin was born Saul Elias Kaplan in the New York City borough of Brooklyn. From a young age he liked to write music. Although he attended New York University's School of Commerce to prepare for a business career, Chaplin took up songwriting after graduation, turning out tunes for vaudeville acts and Tin Pan Alley publishers. With lyricist Sammy Cahn, the two wrote songs and scored early short films made by Warner Brothers in a Brooklyn studio. Nicknamed "Cahn and Chaplin," they went to Hollywood where they contributed songs to a few movies. The two men parted ways when Chaplin became more in demand for arranging and conducting the music for movies, mostly musicals. For the biopic *The Jolsen Story* (1946), he adapted an old Romanian tune that had served as the French waltz ditty "Waves of the Danube" and turned it into "The Anniversary Song," collaborating on a lyric with Jolson. Sometimes titled "The Anniversary Waltz," it became a best seller of sheet music; there were many hit recordings, and the waltz was played at weddings and wedding anniversaries for decades. Chaplin's other runaway song success was an adaptation of the Yiddish tune "Bei Mir Bistu Shein" for which Cahn wrote an English lyric, though the title remained in Yiddish. The novelty number was a major early hit record for the Andrews Sisters. Other notable Chaplin songs include "Please Be Kind," "Until the Real Thing Comes Along," "Shoeshine Boy," "If It's the Last Thing I Do," and "You Wonderful You."

By the late 1950s, Chaplin was not only supervising movie musicals but was producing or coproducing them as well. In such a way he was responsible for the total sound and the singers for such screen musicals as *Can-Can* (1960), *I Could Go on Singing* (1963), *The Sound of Music* (1965), *Star!* (1968), and *Man of La Mancha* (1972). Chaplin was nominated for Academy Awards for his supervision of the music in *Kiss Me Kate* (1953) and *High Society* (1956) and won Oscars for his musical

direction of *An American in Paris* (1951), *Seven Brides for Seven Brothers* (1954), and *West Side Story* (1961). He worked with virtually all of the major singing stars, songwriters, directors of musicals, and choreographers in Hollywood between the mid-1930s and the mid-1970s. Chaplin's music can be heard on the soundtrack of over one hundred films, but he penned a full screen score on only five occasions. He wrote the songs and soundtrack score for the musicals *Time Out for Rhythm* (lyrics by Cahn) and *Merry Andrew* (lyrics by Johnny Mercer), the incidental and background music for *Louisiana Hayride* and *Les Girls*, which had scores by other songwriters, and the soundtrack score for the nonmusical comedy *The Teahouse of the August Moon*. Chaplin's original music in this quartet of movies is not central to the storytelling or the characters. There is appropriate Parisian sidewalk cafe music in *Les Girls*, rural folk in *Louisiana Hayride*, swing numbers in *Time Out for Rhythm*, circus themes in *Merry Andrew*, and Asian-flavored passages in *The Teahouse of the August Moon*. All of it is functional without being very memorable. Chaplin's gift for melody in song was not captured in his screen music, so one has to instead appreciate his expert musical direction, which was a significant contribution to Hollywood. Autobiography: *The Golden Age of Movie Musicals and Me* (1994).

Credits

(all films USA)

Year	Film	Director
1941	Time Out for Rhythm	Sidney Salkow
1944	Louisiana Hayride	Charles Barton
1956	The Teahouse of the August Moon	Daniel Mann
1957	Les Girls	George Cukor
1958	Merry Andrew	Michael Kidd

CHURCHILL, Frank (1901–1942) An accomplished composer and songwriter who, during his tragically short life, wrote a handful of song favorites that are still popular, he worked for the Disney studio for a dozen years and scored some of their earliest hits.

Born in Rumford, Maine, Frank E. Churchill and his family moved to Los Angeles when he was four years old. Churchill took piano lessons as a boy and by the time he was fifteen he was earning money playing the piano for si-

lent films in local cinemas. He began studies at UCLA with the intention of becoming a doctor but dropped out of college to pursue a music career. Churchill got experience playing in clubs in Tijuana, Mexico, and Tucson, Arizona, before returning to California in 1924. After performing and doing musical arrangements for Los Angeles radio station KNX and contributing some background music for RKO Radio Pictures, he was brought to the attention of the Disney studio, which was just embarking on making sound shorts. He was hired by the studio in 1930 to compose background music and songs for the new series of *Silly Symphonies* and other cartoons. Churchill gave the studio its first hit song with "Who's Afraid of the Big Bad Wolf?" (lyric by Ann Ronell), written for the cartoon *The Three Little Pigs* (1933). The catchy ditty was used in other shorts about the pigs, thousands of copies of sheet music were sold, and soon everyone was singing it, the song becoming a Depression-era favorite. Churchill contributed music to twenty-nine Disney cartoons before he was asked to write the songs for the studio's first feature, *Snow White and the Seven Dwarfs* (1937). He co-composed the soundtrack score for the animated classic with Leigh Harline and Paul J. Smith, and he and lyricist Larry Morey wrote eight songs, including such familiar favorites as "I'm Wishing," "Someday My Prince Will Come," "Whistle While You Work," and "Heigh-Ho." Churchill returned to scoring shorts until he was assigned to compose the soundtrack score (rather than the songs) for the animated featurette *The Reluctant Dragon*. For the studio's 1940 feature *Dumbo*, Churchill cowrote the soundtrack with Oliver Wallace as well as four songs (lyrics by Ned Washington), including "Casey Junior," "Look Out for Mr. Stork," and the Oscar-nominated "Baby Mine." With Edward H. Plumb he scored *Bambi* the next year, also writing four songs (lyrics by Morey), including

"Little April Shower" and the Oscar-nominated "Love Is a Song." Soon after completing *Bambi*, Churchill's ongoing depression increased and in 1942 he died from a self-inflicted rifle shot. He was only forty years old.

Two songs by Churchill surfaced years later. "Merrily on Our Way (to Nowhere in Particular)," with lyricist Morey, was altered and used in *The Adventures of Ichabod and Mr. Toad* (1949) and the unused "Never Smile at a Crocodile" (lyric by Churchill) was later added to *Peter Pan* (1953). But Churchill's true legacy is the dozen or so unforgettable songs that help put the Disney studio in the forefront of movie musicals. While appreciating the songs is easy, evaluating his screen soundtracks is more problematic. Churchill's scores for *Snow White and the Seven Dwarfs*, *Dumbo*, and *Bambi* were done in collaboration with others, but many of the forty-nine cartoon shorts were solo efforts and his musical versatility and imagination are quite evident here. All of these cartoons have continuous music that ranges from mock-opera and cowboy songs to classical ballet and urban jazz. Although Churchill did not have formal musical training, his experience playing piano for silent films and later scoring so many shorts made him something of a musical wizard who was much respected by other composers and musicians in Hollywood. It is staggering to consider what Churchill might have accomplished had he enjoyed a longer and happier life.

Credits

(all films USA; * for Best Song)

Year	Film	Director
1937	*Snow White and the Seven Dwarfs* (AAN)	William Cottrell, David Hand, etc.
1941	*The Reluctant Dragon*	Alfred L. Walker, Hamilton Luske, etc.
1941	*Dumbo* (AA; AAN*)	Samuel Armstrong, Norman Ferguson, etc.
1942	*Bambi* (AAN; AAN*)	James Algar, Samuel Armstrong, etc.

CICOGNINI, Alessandro (1906–1995) An internationally renowned Italian film composer very active between 1938 and 1958, he is most remembered for his neorealist postwar movies, in particular his eight collaborations with director Vittorio De Sica, although he wrote some outstanding scores for other European directors as well.

Allesandro Cicognini was born in Pescara, Italy, and received a classical education at the Milan Conservatory

of Music with the intention of a concert career. Cicognini turned to jazz and traditional Italian music in the 1930s and decided that movies were replacing opera and concerts as the source of popular music. He made his screen debut cowriting the score for the historical melodrama *The Two Sergeants* (1936) set during the Napoleonic Wars. Two years later he wrote his first solo score for the pirate adventure *The Black Corsair* for director Amleto Palermi, with whom he worked eight times before and during World War II. Among Cicognini's notable movies during this period are *Department Store, Cavalleria rusticana, The Iron Crown, Four Steps in the Clouds,* and *Two Anonymous Letters.* Although popular actor De Sica appeared in a handful of movies Cicognini scored, the two did not work together as director and composer until the neorealist classic *Shoeshine* in 1946. The film was not only an international success but it introduced the musical sound of neorealism, a haunting fusion of popular and classical traditions with a very modern accent. Over the next fifteen years, the two men collaborated on such memorable films as *Bicycle Thieves, Miracle in Milan, Umberto D., The Gold of Naples,* and *The Last Judgment.*

For Italian directors Mario Camerini, Alessandro Blasetti, Giorgio Bianchi, Riccardo Freda, and others, he scored many notable movies, including *Life of Donizetti, Les Misérables, Tomorrow Is Too Late, Father's Dilemma, Time Gone By, Ulysses, The Iron Swordsman, The Band of Honest Men,* and *Bread, Love and Dreams.* Because of his international reputation, Cicognini was approached by non-Italian filmmakers. His first Hollywood movie was *The Thief in Venice* in 1950, followed by such popular French, British, and American films as *Summertime, It Started in Naples, The Black Orchid, A Breath of Scandal, The Pigeon That Took Rome,* and *The Little World of Don Camillo* and its many sequels. Cicognini retired from screen composing in 1965 to teach composition. Before his death thirty years later, it is believed that he destroyed much of his sheet music and tapes, and most of Cicognini's music today exists only on the film stock. Since the 1990s, various music scholars have worked at re-creating, notating, and recording the music from the 115 movies to which he contributed.

Among the innovations that Cicognini brought to Italian cinema is his use of small ensembles rather than a full orchestra. Some of this was from necessity, but even in his later Hollywood scores he preferred a more intimate orchestration. He also was expert in mixing musical genres. The boogie-woogie sound Cicognini learned from American GIs during the war would later show up right beside Italian folk or classical music in his movies. This inventive use of music can be heard in his first score for De Sica, the powerful *Shoeshine* about delinquent teens in poverty-stricken postwar Rome. There are some melancholy string passages juxtaposed against popular tunes

of the time. Rhapsodic music dissolves into an ominous march theme in one section, a silly dance tune turns into a heartbreaking woodwind passage in another. Similarly, *Bicycle Thieves* (more often translated as *The Bicycle Thief*) has a poignant main theme in which strings and brass intersect in the lyrical way one might find in Italian opera. Hearing such Puccini-like music over the visuals of this neorealist view of life is disconcerting to say the least. Yet even this classical-oriented score is punctuated by lively dance music and zesty folk tunes. A delicate waltz is used throughout the Cicognini–De Sica masterwork *Umberto D.,* the tragic tale of an old man (Carlo Battisti) abandoned by society who sinks to such despair that he nearly destroys his only companion, his pet dog. Sometimes this waltz takes on a heavy, ponderous tone; other times it is as desolate and fragile as the central character. The subplot about a pregnant, unmarried girl (Maria Pia Casilio) is scored with a solo violin and solo flute, the emotive music never stooping to sentimentality. The scores for two other De Sica films deserve mention. Their last movie together, *The Last Judgment* in 1961, has very inventive music. Cicognini places sparkling waltzes amid lyrical passages and bombastic music. It's all very odd and fascinating, and more than appropriate for this offbeat comedy about how various Neapolitans react to the voice of God. Arguably the team's masterpiece, *Miracle in Milan* has an outstanding score. The music in this fantasy, about displaced yet hopeful Milanese living in abject poverty, is sometimes joyous, other times filled with despair. There is a march that is an anthem of freedom for the homeless, a frivolous carnival theme for a balloon man, a surreal musical passage in which the instruments swirl and dance to a folk tune, and an unforgettable finale in which a rowdy circus theme is heard as hundreds of citizens fly over Milan on broomsticks.

Of Cicognini's many movies without De Sica, the most popular is David Lean's Venice romance *Summertime.* The love theme for an American spinster (Katharine Hepburn) and an Italian glass merchant (Rossano Brazzi) is passionate, lyrical, and hopelessly memorable. It is used often throughout the movie yet manages to avoid getting stale. There are some other delightful Italianate passages, ranging from a lively tarantella to a swooning barcarolle, but it is the love theme that lingers. The French-Italian *The Little World of Don Camillo* spawned a series of comedies about the small-town rivalry between a Catholic priest (Fernandel) and a Communist mayor (Gino Cervi). The music in the original is splendid. There is a scintillating waltz featuring solos by various instruments, a slaphappy folk theme that practically dances by itself, and an arresting minor-key passage that is elegantly classical in tone. *It Started in Naples*, a Hollywood romance for Clark Gable and Sophia Loren, is filled with animated Italian folk themes and sweeping romantic music in a lighter vein. (Carlo Savina cowrote the score with Cicognini.) There is also a tarantella theme that is particularly catchy. Sophia Loren finds love in another, more serious, romance from Hollywood titled *The Black Orchid*. Anthony Quinn is the widower who woos her this time. There is a dark subtext

to this story and Cicognini's music seems even richer than usual. Symphonic flourishes are broken up by haunting music, jazz passages, and restlessly fervent splashes of drama. One most remembers a graceful passage in which a flute and accordion perform a lovely pas de deux, and there is a bubbly waltz for the finale. These later movies may seem to be a far cry from De Sica's neorealism but the scores are often just as impressive. Cicognini is the first in a long line of Italian screen composers to find acclaim internationally. Nino Rota and Ennio Morricone have followed in his footsteps and have possibly eclipsed him, but that does not diminish Cicognini's estimable talents and significant scores.

Credits

(all films Italy unless stated otherwise)

Year	Film	Director
1936	The Two Sergeants	Enrico Guazzoni
1937	The Two Misanthropists	Amleto Palermi
1938	The Black Corsair	Amleto Palermi
1938	Departure	Alessandro Blasetti
1938	Ettore Fieramosca	Amleto Palermi
1938	Naples of Former Days	Amleto Palermi
1939	Naples That Never Dies	Augusto Genina
1939	Castles in the Air	Max Neufeld
1939	A Wife in Danger	Mario Camerini
1939	Department Store	Amleto Palermi
1939	Cavalleria rusticana	Alessandro Blasetti
1939	Retroscena	Mario Camerini
1939	Il documento	Alessandro Blasetti
1939	An Adventure of Salvator Rosa	Mario Camerini
1940	Centomila dollari	Amleto Palermi
1940	The Two Mothers	Jean Choux (Italy/Spain)
1940	La nascita di Salome	Carmine Gallone
1940	Passione	Amleto Plaermi
1940	The Sinner	Mario Camerini
1940	A Romantic Adventure	Camillo Mastrocinque
1940	Don Pasquale	Alfredo Guarini
1940	Senza cielo	Ladislao Vajda
1941	The Conspiracy of the Crazy	Camillo Mastrocinque
1941	Ridi pagliaccio!	Alessandro Blasetti
1941	The Iron Crown	Carmine Gallone
1941	First Love	Giorgio Bianchi
1942	La maestrina	Nicola Manzari
1942	3/4 of a Page	Alessandro Blasetti
1942	Four Steps in the Clouds	Gherardo Gherardi, Aldo Rossi
1943	Il nostro prossimo	Camillo Mastrocinque
1943	Scorned Flesh	Carmine Gallone
1943	The Sad Loves	Alessandro Blasetti
1945	Responsibility Comes Back	Giorgio Bianchi
1945	Merry Chase	Mario Camerini
1945	Two Anonymous Letters	

Year	Film	Director
1946	*La sua strada*	Mario Costa
1946	*Shoeshine*	Vittorio De Sica
1947	*Cronaca nera*	Giorgio Bianchi
1947	*Ultimo amore*	Luigi Chiarini
1947	*Life of Donizetti*	Camillo Mastrocinque
1947	*The Adventures of Pinocchio*	Gianetto Guardone
1947	*Fiamme sul mare*	Michal Waszynski
1948	*Unknown Men of San Marino*	Michal Waszynski
1948	*Les Misérables*	Riccardo Freda
1948	*Tempesta su Parigi*	Riccardo Freda
1948	*The Mysterious Rider*	Riccardo Freda
1948	*Bicycle Thieves* (aka *The Bicycle Thief*)	Vittorio De Sica
1949	*The Earth Cries Out*	Duillo Coletti
1949	*Fiamma che non si spegne*	Vittorio Cottafavi
1949	*Vento d'Africa*	Anton Giulio Majano
1949	*The Iron Swordsman*	Riccardo Freda
1949	*Flying Squadron*	Luigi Capuano
1950	*Streets of Sorrow*	Giorgio Pastina
1950	*Paolo e Francesca* (aka *Legend of Love*)	Raffaello Matarazzo
1950	*Ring around the Clock*	Paolo William Tamburella
1950	*Hawk of the Nile*	Giacomo Gentilomo
1950	*Tomorrow Is Too Late*	Léonide Moguy
1950	*Father's Dilemma*	Alessandro Blasetti (Italy/France)
1950	*The Thief of Venice*	John Brahm (USA/Italy)
1951	*Miracle in Milan*	Vittorio De Sica
1951	*Position Wanted*	Giorgio Pastina
1951	*The Seven Dwarfs to the Rescue*	Paolo William Tamburella
1951	*Cops and Robbers*	Mario Monicelli, Steno
1951	*Stormbound*	Luigi Capuano
1952	*Umberto D.*	Vittorio De Sica
1952	*Hello Elephant*	Gianni Franciolini
1952	*The Little World of Don Camillo*	Julien Duvivier (Italy/France)
1952	*Two Cents Worth of Hope*	Renato Castellani
1952	*Wife for a Night*	Mario Camerini
1952	*Wanda the Sinner* (aka *The Shameless Sex*)	Duillio Coletti (Italy/France)
1952	*Times Gone By*	Alessandro Blasetti
1952	*The Flame*	Alessandro Blasetti
1952	*Sunday Heroes*	Mario Camerini
1952	*Carne inquieta*	Silvestro Prestifilippo
1953	*Indiscretion of an American Wife*	Vittorio De Sica (Italy/USA)
1953	*The Return of Don Camillo*	Julien Duvivier (France/Italy)
1953	*Of Life and Love*	Gianni Franciolini, etc.
1953	*Bread, Love and Dreams*	Luigi Comencini
1954	*Secret of Three Points*	Carlo Ludovico Bragaglia
1954	*Crossed Swords*	Milton Krims, Vittorio Vassarotti (Italy/USA)
1954	*Ulysses*	Mario Camerini
1954	*Frisky*	Luigi Comencini
1954	*The Gold of Naples*	Vittorio De Sica
1954	*The Art of Getting Along*	Luigi Zampa
1954	*I Cavalieri dell'illusione*	Marc Allégret (Italy/France)
1955	*Too Bad She's Bad*	Alessandro Blasetti
1955	*Graziella*	Giorgio Bianchi
1955	*It Happens in Roma*	Giuseppe Amato (Italy/France)
1955	*Summertime*	David Lean (UK/USA)
1955	*Are We Men or Corporals?*	Camillo Mastrocinque
1955	*Don Camillo e l'on. Peppone*	Carmine Gallone (France/Italy)
1955	*Scandal in Sorrento*	Dino Risi
1956	*The Band of Honest Men*	Camillo Mastrocinque

Year	Film	Director
1956	*What a Woman!*	Alessandro Blasetti (France/Italy)
1956	*The Bigamist*	Luciano Emmer (Italy/France)
1956	*Loser Takes All*	Ken Annakin (UK)
1956	*The Roof*	Vittorio De Sica (Italy/France)
1956	*Time of Vacation*	Antonio Racioppi
1957	*A Tailor's Maid*	Mario Monicelli (Italy/France)
1957	*The Window to Luna Park*	Luigi Comencini (Italy/France)
1957	*Holiday Island*	Mario Camerini (Italy/France/Monaco/W. Germany)
1958	*Fast and Sexy*	Carlo Lastricati (Italy/France)
1958	*E arrivata la parigina*	Camillo Mastrocinque (Italy/France)
1958	*The Black Orchid*	Martin Ritt (USA)
1958	*Bread, Love and Andalucia*	Javier Setó (Spain/Italy)
1960	*A Breath of Scandal*	Michael Curtiz (Italy/USA)
1960	*It Started in Naples*	Melville Shavelson (USA)
1961	*Don Camillo Monsignore . . . ma non troppo*	Carmine Gallone
1961	*The Last Judgment*	Vittorio De Sica (Italy/France)
1962	*The Pigeon That Took Rome*	Melville Shavelson (USA)
1965	*Don Camillo in Moscow*	Luigi Comencini (Italy/France/W. Germany)

COLOMBIER, Michel (1939–2004) A highly reputable French composer, arranger, and conductor for ballet, television, and film, he spent the last two decades of his life in Hollywood where he scored many movies but, unfortunately, most of them were of inferior quality.

Michel Colombier was born in Lyon, France, the son of an opera orchestra musician who taught the six-year-old boy the piano, violin, composition, and conducting. Colombier began writing original music when he was eleven and a few years later discovered jazz and started improvising with small ensembles. While his classical education continued with studying Gregorian chant and church organ music with his father and classical forms at the Paris Conservatoire, Colombier embraced all forms of music, writing everything from chamber pieces to advertising jingles. He studied with avant-garde composer Michel Magne then became music director for Barclay Records, where he arranged music for Charles Aznavour and others. By the 1960s Colombier was widely acclaimed for his work with distinguished dance companies, such as Les Ballets de L'Opéra de Paris and the American Ballet Theatre, and with dancer-choreographers, including Twyla Tharp, Mikhail Baryshnikov, and Roland Petit. He moved into pop music in the late 1960s and was dubbed "the Funky Frenchman," writing and arranging music for such artists as Petula Clark, the Beach Boys, Barbra Streisand, Roberta Flack, Johnny Mathis, Joni Mitchell, and Herb Alpert, the last collaboration resulting in the pioneering "rock oratorio" *Wings*. During his career Colombier also wrote many ballets, chamber works, symphonies, operas, and concertos. Few internationally known composers had such a diverse career, working with acclaimed symphonies as well as pop icons like Madonna, legendary jazz artists such as Herbie Hancock, and R&B groups like Earth, Wind & Fire.

Colombier's prolific screen career began when he collaborated with Eddie Barclay on the score for the French-language spy film *FX 18* in 1964. His first solo effort was *La famille Hernandez* the following year, followed by several European movies in the 1960s and 1970s. Colombier first worked for Hollywood in 1970 when he scored the sci-fi thriller *Colossus: The Forbin Project*. By 1984 he was working almost exclusively in the States where he scored such movies as *Against All Odds*, *The Money Pit*, *Ruthless People*, *The Golden Child*, *Strictly Business*, *Major League II*, *How Stella Got Her Groove Back*, *Deep Cover*, *The Program*, *Cop*, *New Jack City*, *Purple Rain*, and *White Nights*. Colombier returned to the European cinema with his scores for such films as *Une chambre en ville*, *Hunter Will Get You*, *Asterix and the Big Fight*, and *Élisa*. He also scored over thirty TV movies, most in the States and few of them memorable. Colombier was more successful writing music for television series and miniseries, most notably *The Rhinemann Exchange* (1977), *Messiah* (2001), and *Messiah 2: Vengeance Is Mine* (2002). In all, he scored over one hundred movies and TV programs, even as he maintained a very busy career in pop and classical music.

To say that Colombier's music was usually better than the vehicle it was written for is understatement. Although many of his films were first-class projects by major studios and utilized top directors and actors, very few were any good. The European movies fared better than the Hollywood ones, but even there Colombier was never handed a classic to score. Some of the American films were popular, which kept him in demand in Hollywood, but one quickly realizes that his music is best appreciated on its own. For example, consider the score for *The Golden Child*, a misguided Eddie Murphy comedy that was a box office hit. This convoluted tale of a private eye (Murphy) and a kidnapped Buddhist child (J. L. Reate) with superpowers has a provocative score that encompasses East and West. Tribal chanting is set to electronic beat, Asian-sounding passages are filtered through synthesized instruments, some sections pulsate with rock music, there is a flute theme that is mystical and engaging, and at times a distorted electric organ goes berserk. This is the score for a superior movie, not one of the most castigated films of the 1980s. Much better is the cop thriller *Deep Cover* about urban drug wars. Colombier provides a propulsive main theme played on percussion and electric guitar with vocal and sound effects. Another impressive section is a repetitive percussive passage with a confident beat and accents on electric organ and piano. This thrilling kind of "funk" music is what labeled Colombier the Funky Frenchman.

The Phil Collins title song for the action thriller *Against All Odds* got a lot of attention but Colombier's soundtrack score is also memorable. The main theme's predominant beat is an electric guitar riff with some higher-pitched chords and musical phrases played on electric strings. The love theme is a tentative piece in which piano phrases are in counterpoint to a bluesy and reflective melody. There is an arresting melancholy passage in which an electric guitar carefully plucks out a theme as percussion and reverberating sound effects flow over it. The movie's suspense scenes are scored with descending electronic glissandos and sustained chords, while the action scenes feature chaotic drum solos. Funky is definitely the word also for the score for the crime thriller *New Jack City*. Throughout the movie the music is as restless as it is cocky; a true rap song without singing. The suspense scenes are scored with wavering suspended chords that refuse to resolve or end. For the comedy *Ruthless People*, there is a playful disco theme that is accented with drum and sound effects giving the music a chaotic yet silly flavor. Colombier scored several American comedies, but they rarely caught fire. He was

handed only a few horror films in Hollywood and none of them were a critical or commercial success, although the confused *Midnight Cabaret* has a lovely piano rhapsody that is as free flowing and casual as it is classical in its tone. *Purple Rain*, *White Nights*, and *How Stella Got Her Groove Back*, Colombier's Hollywood movies that had the most success at the box office, have very little of his music on the soundtracks. *Purple Rain*'s star Prince wrote most of his songs for the movie, *How Stella Got Her Groove Back* was mostly composed of songs by others, and *White Nights* used all kinds of preexisting dance music, though there is the beguiling song "People on a String" by Colombier and Kathy Wakefield that is sung by Roberta Flack on the soundtrack.

Of the many European movies Colombier scored, a few stand out. A trio of crime thrillers not only have excellent scores but the films themselves are laudable. Philippe Labro's *L'alpagueur*, known in the States as *Hunter Will Get You*, has a percussive score led by a rock theme with an electric orchestra behind it. The music surges forward throughout the film but takes interesting diversions along the way. There is also one section that foreshadows rap (the movie was made in 1976) with its drums and synthesized sound effects playing off repetition as it bounces about. Labro's *The Inheritor*, about a playboy (Jean-Paul Belmondo) who runs into a deadly business when he inherits his father's fortune, has a lazy jazz theme with electronic accompaniment and restless rock riffs that capture the central character so well. Jean-Pierre Melville's bank robbery movie *A Cop*, better known as *Dirty Money* today, opens without music, just the sound of wind blowing as the credits appear. It is quite late in the film when music does come in and it is a romantic jazz theme that hesitates, transitions into descending piano chords, then returns. There are some atmospheric saxophone solos in the movie, a love theme which becomes a French song (lyric by Charles Aznavour) which is languid and world weary, and a scene in a nightclub in which the jazz music for the showgirls is drowned out by a melancholy passage that is very bluesy. These three 1970s scores seem so much richer than the "funky" sound of Colombier's later work in the States.

Atypical of Colombier's screen scores is the modern opera *Une Chambre en Ville* by writer-director Jacques Demy, who had previously made the sung-though movie musicals *The Umbrellas of Cherbourg* (1964) and *The*

Young Girls of Rochefort (1967) with composer Michel Legrand. Once again all the dialogue is sung, but the plot of *Une Chambre en Ville* is more tragic and the musical numbers move along more like an opera than a musical. The affair between a metalworker (Richard Berry) and a married woman (Dominique Sanda) is set against strikes and police riots in the city of Nantes and ends with an operatic death scene in which the hero dies in his lover's arms. Colombier avoided classical-sounding music and wrote a true modern opera utilizing jazz, blues, pop, and even a little rock. The opening theme is a delicate and sad piece played on piano with a full string orchestra filling in and eventually taking over. The duets are the highlights of the movie, whether they are casual and conversational or passionate and rhapsodic. There is also stirring choral work as hymns, anthems, and marches are sung by various groups. The score for *Une Chambre en Ville* cannot be easily compared to Colombier's other screen work but it hints at the wide range of the composer's musical ideas. Interestingly, Colombier's last score, for the American-Italian-made romance *Swept Away*, returns to his classical roots. The central theme is an eerie adagio nocturne for piano and violin that is intoxicating as it slowly captivates the listener through its repetition that echoes the waves on the Mediterranean shore. Unfortunately this incompetent remake of Lina Wertmüller's 1974 comedy-drama was such a box office and critical disaster that few heard the music. And so Colombier's screen career ended as too much of it had been: wonderful music wasted on inferior films. Official website: www.michelcolombier.com.

Credits

Year	Film	Director
1964	FX 18 (aka Agent Secret FX 18)	Maurice Cloche (France/Italy/Spain)
1964	A Mouse with the Men	Jacques Poitrenaud (France)
1965	La Famille Hernandez	Genevieve Baïlac (France)
1965	The Director's Guns	Claude Sautet (France/Italy/Spain)
1965	L'ur du duc	Jacques Baratier (Italy/France)
1966	A New World	Vittorio De Sica (France/Italy)
1966	The Gardener of Argenteuil	Jean-Paul Le Chanois (France/W. Germany)
1967	If I Were a Spy	Bertrand Blier (France)
1968	Every Bastard a King	Uri Zohar (Israel/Denmark)
1968	To Be Free	Paul Bertault (France)
1969	Mr. Freedom	William Klein (France)
1969	The Bitch Wants Blood	Jean Valere (France/Italy)
1970	Colossus: The Forbin Project	Joseph Sargent (USA)
1971	Law Breakers	Marcel Carné (France/Italy)
1972	A Cop (aka Dirty Money)	Jean-Pierre Melville (France/Italy)
1973	The Magician (aka Autopsy)	José Maria Forqué (Spain/France)
1973	The Inheritor (aka The Exterminator)	Philippe Labro (France/Italy)
1974	Paul and Michelle	Lewis Gilbert (France/UK)
1974	Chance and Violence	Philippe Labro (Italy/France)
1975	Bisexual	Eric Lipmann (France)
1976	Hunter Will Get You	Philippe Labro (France)
1976	Face of Darkness	Ian F. H. Lloyd (UK)
1977	The Model Couple	William Klein (France/Switzerland)
1979	Steel	Steve Carver (USA)
1982	Une Chambre en Ville	Jacques Demy (Italy/France)
1984	Against All Odds	Taylor Hackford (USA)
1984	Purple Rain	Albert Magnoli (USA)
1985	White Nights (GGN)	Taylor Hackford (USA)
1986	The Money Pit	Richard Benjamin (USA)
1986	Ruthless People	Jim Abrahams, David and Jerry Zucker (USA)
1986	The Golden Child	Michael Ritchie (USA)
1987	Surrender	Jerry Belson (USA)
1987	The Wild Pair (aka Hollow Point)	Beau Bridges (USA)
1988	The Couch Trip	Michael Pitchie (USA)
1988	Cop (aka Blood on the Moon)	James B. Harris (USA)
1988	Satisfaction	Joan Freeman (USA)

Year	Film	Director
1988	*In Extremis*	Olivier Lorsac (France)
1989	*Who's Harry Crumb?*	Paul Flaherty (USA/Canada)
1989	*Out Cold*	Malcolm Mowbray (USA)
1989	*Loverboy*	Joan Micklin Silver (USA)
1989	*Asterix and the Big Fight*	Philippe Grimond (France/W. Germany)
1990	*Catchfire* (aka *Backtrack*)	Dennis Hopper (USA)
1990	*Impulse*	Sondra Locke (USA)
1990	*Midnight Cabaret*	Pece Dingo (USA)
1991	*New Jack City*	Mario Van Peebles (USA)
1991	*Diary of a Hitman* (aka *Hit Man*)	Roy London (USA)
1991	*The Dark Wind*	Errol Morris (USA)
1991	*Strictly Business* (aka *Go Natalie!*)	Kevin Hooks, Rolando Hudson (USA)
1992	*Deep Cover*	Bill Duke (USA)
1992	*Folks!*	Ted Kotcheff (USA)
1993	*Posse*	Mario Van Peebles (UK/USA)
1993	*The Program*	David S. Ward (USA)
1994	*Major League II*	David S. Ward (USA)
1995	*Élisa*	Jean Becker (France)
1996	*Barb Wire*	David Hogan (USA)
1996	*Foxfire*	Annette Haywood-Carter (USA)
1997	*Meet Wally Sparks*	Peter Baldwin (USA)
1998	*Claudine's Return* (aka *Kiss of Fire*)	Antonio Tibaldi (USA)
1998	*Woo*	Daisy von Scherier Mayer (USA)
1998	*How Stella Got Her Groove Back*	Kevin Rodney Sullivan (USA)
1999	*Pros and Cons*	Boris Damast (USA)
2000	*Innocents* (aka *Dark Summer*)	Gregory Marquette (USA/Germany/Canada)
2000	*Screwed* (aka *Bailbusted*)	Scott Alexander, Larry Karaszewski (USA)
2002	*Swept Away* (aka *Love, Sex, Drugs & Money*)	Guy Ritchie (UK/Italy)

CONTI, Bill (b. 1942) A popular composer and conductor who has found success both in movies and television, he has scored nearly one hundred feature films but is mostly known for his music for the boxing classic *Rocky* and its sequels.

Born in Providence, Rhode Island, into an Italian American family, Bill Conti was taught how to play the piano by his father. When Conti moved with his family to Miami, Florida, he studied the bassoon and played in the high school band. He studied composition at Louisiana State University, playing in the campus orchestra and marching band, and performing in jazz clubs to pay for his tuition. He then attended Juilliard in New York City, where he received two music degrees before relocating to Italy in 1967 to perform and compose jazz. It was during his seven-year stay in Europe that Conti first worked in films, writing music arrangements and composing the score for some Spanish, Italian, and Swedish movies. After providing some music for Paul Mazursky's comedy *Blume in Love* (which was being filmed in Venice at the time), he returned to the States in 1974 and settled in California

with his concentration now on a cinema career. Conti scored two other comedies for Mazursky, the modest hits *Next Stop, Greenwich Village* and *Harry and Tonto*, then rocketed to fame in 1976 with the low-budget, surprise hit *Rocky* written by and featuring unknown actor Sylvester Stallone. The theme song "Gonna Fly Now" (lyric by Carol Connors and Ayn Robbins) not only became a hit single but over the decades the movie's main theme has been played countless times at sporting events. Conti also scored four of the *Rocky* sequels and throughout his career was often called on to write music for movies involving sports. In addition to boxing, his music can be heard in films about football, basketball, wrestling, baseball, karate, horse racing, golf, running, soccer, and even bull riding.

Conti reunited with Mazursky for the lauded film drama *An Unmarried Woman* and worked again with Stallone as actor and/or director on a half dozen other projects. But his most frequent collaborator is director John G. Avildsen. They first worked together on *Rocky* and reteamed for twelve other movies, including *Slow Dancing in the Big City*, *The Karate Kid* and its sequels, *Lean on Me*, and some of the *Rocky* sequels. Other notable movies that Conti scored with various directors include *The Right Stuff, Masters of the Universe, The Seduction of Joe Tynan, Private Benjamin, Gloria, Handle with Care, Broadcast News, The Adventures of Huck Finn, That Championship Season, Mass Appeal, For Your Eyes Only*, and the 1999 remake of *The Thomas Crown Affair*. Conti has been equally successful in television, writing music for such series as *Dynasty, Murder Ink, Cagney & Lacey, Falcon Crest, The Master*, and *American Gladiators*, as well as many TV movies and miniseries, such as *Smash-Up on Interstate 5* (1976), *The Displaced Person* (1977), *Kill Me If You Can* (1977), *In the Matter of Karen Ann Quinlan* (1977), *The Fantastic Seven* (1979), *Farrell for the People* (1982), *The Terry Fox Story* (1983), *North and South* (1985), *Murderers among Us: The Simon Wiesenthal Story* (1989), *Under Cover* (1991), *Winchell* (1998), *American Tragedy* (2000), and *Judas* (2004). He not only conducts the recording sessions of his film scores but is a popular conductor in many other venues, most memorably for several Academy Awards ceremonies.

Because *Rocky* was a sleeper hit, Conti's score was an impressive surprise. The rousing trumpet fanfare that accompanied the opening credits was like a shot of adrenaline. The theme is that unusual thing, a jazzy march. The vocals as it becomes the song "Gonna Fly Now" are also stirring in a refreshing way. There are sections of the score that are bluesy and reflective, sometimes a solo piano being supported by deep chords, other times a cool jazz arrangement of bass and drums. Pulsating trumpets and vigorous strings are used effectively in the optimistic "Going the Distance" theme, while the love theme for Rocky and Adrian (Talia Shire) is a gentle and tentative version of "Gonna Fly Now." This is a superb score that raises a rather familiar story to new heights. Perhaps the most ambitious movie Conti was ever asked to score was the epic *The Right Stuff*. This semidocumentary history of the American space program has the same kind of fervor to win that *Rocky* had, and the music is just as invigorating. The main theme is a march that begins casually then builds as it takes flight, only to recede at times for a lovely oboe solo. This passage returned for some of the airborne sequences but was just as effective when accompanying the seven chosen astronauts as they appear together for the first time in their space suits. The music when Chuck Yeager (Sam Shepard) breaks the sound barrier is surprisingly restrained, the speed on-screen contrasted by music

that is proud and confident. When John Glenn (Ed Harris) orbits the earth, passages from Gustav Holst's *The Planets* are used, but Conti's score is so much in the same spirit that the effect is not jarring.

The scores for *Rocky* and *The Right Stuff* are Conti at his most exciting, but another and equally masterful sound can be found in his smaller films. *An Unmarried Woman* has a breezy main theme in which jazz is used in a rhythmic manner, the piano seeming to improvise while the brass propels the melody forward. This is a bittersweet movie about a woman (Jill Clayburgh) finding herself after her husband leaves her. The score gets reflective in passages but always maintains a driving, urban tempo. A solo sax sometimes moves into chaotic riffs to indicate her confusion. Another bittersweet film, *Harry and Tonto*, has a flowing theme played on a synthesizer that is both modern and romanticized. As the senior citizen Harry (Art Carney) travels across the country with his cat Tonto, the music also moves in a casual but steady manner. The title theme for *Slow Dancing in the Big City* is a lovely, lyrical piece with a classical flavor, as befitting a romantic movie about a dying ballerina (Anne Ditchburn). The entire score is very melodic without ever sounding like a song, especially when the woodwinds seem to float in the air or a solo piano delicately repeats an entrancing musical phrase. A proud piccolo and other patriotic instruments play the main theme for the political comedy-drama *The Seduction of Joe Tynan*. While not quite a march, there is a sense of political optimism in the theme but also a satirical vein as well. *For Your Eyes Only*, Conti's only James Bond film, has a sexy yet melancholy title song (lyric by Michael Leeson) sung by Sheena Easton in a pop style on the soundtrack. The rest of the score is a playful mixture of jazz, rock, disco, and Latin music. There is also a slow jazz passage titled "Take Me Home" that is quite splendid. Finally, there is the sparkling score for *The Karate Kid*. The way a youth (Ralph Macchio) is given a new perspective on life from an aging karate instructor (Pat Morita) is hinted at with some Asian instruments that are heard within the very Western music. Classical strings and flutes race in a Vivaldi manner, then a Japanese recorder replaces the traditional woodwinds. There are also some fervent and inspirational sections that musicalize karate in the same way Conti brought to other sports. *The Karate Kid* may be only a teenage version of *Rocky*, but again Conti raises the film to something more with his glorious music.

Credits

(all films USA unless stated otherwise; * for Best Song)

Year	Film	Director
1969	*A Candidate for a Killing*	José María Elorrietta (Spain/Italy)
1969	*Juliette de Sade*	Warren Kiefer (Italy/Sweden)
1970	*Microscopic Liquid Subway to Oblivion*	Roberto Loyola (Italy)
1973	*Blume in Love*	Paul Mazursky
1974	*Harry and Tonto*	Paul Mazursky
1976	*Next Stop, Greenwich Village*	Paul Mazursky
1976	*Rocky* (AAN*; GGN)	John G. Avildsen
1977	*Handle with Care* (aka *Citizens Band*)	Jonathan Demme
1978	*An Unmarried Woman* (GGN)	Paul Mazursky
1978	*F.I.S.T.*	Norman Jewison
1978	*Paradise Alley*	Sylvester Stallone
1978	*The Big Fix*	Jeremy Kagan
1978	*Slow Dancing in the Big City*	John G. Avildsen
1978	*Uncle Joe Shannon*	Joseph C. Hanwright
1979	*Five Days from Home*	George Peppard
1979	*Dreamer*	Noel Nosseck
1979	*Rocky II*	Sylvester Stallone
1979	*Goldengirl*	Joseph Sargent
1979	*The Seduction of Joe Tynan*	Jerry Schatzberg
1979	*A Man, a Woman and a Bank*	Noel Black (Canada)
1980	*Gloria*	John Cassavetes
1980	*Private Benjamin*	Howard Zieff
1980	*The Formula*	John G. Avildsen (USA/W. Germany)
1981	*For Your Eyes Only* (AAN*; GGN*)	John Glen (UK)
1981	*Victory*	John Huston
1981	*Carbon Copy*	Michael Schultz (USA/UK)
1981	*Neighbors*	John G. Avildsen
1982	*I, the Jury*	Richard T. Heffron
1982	*Rocky III*	Sylvester Stallone
1982	*Split Image*	Ted Kotcheff (Canada/USA)
1982	*That Championship Season*	Jason Miller
1982	*And They're Off*	Theodore H. Kuhns III
1983	*Bad Boys*	Rick Rosenthal
1983	*The Right Stuff* (AA)	Philip Kaufman
1984	*Unfaithfully Yours*	Howard Zieff
1984	*The Karate Kid*	John G. Avildsen
1984	*The Bear*	Richard C. Sarafian
1984	*The Gold and the Glory* (aka *The Coolangatta Gold*)	Igor Auzins (Australia)
1984	*Mass Appeal*	Glenn Jordan
1985	*Gotcha!*	Jeff Kanew
1985	*Beer*	Patrick Kelly
1986	*Nomads*	John McTiernan
1986	*F/X*	Robert Mandel
1986	*Big Trouble*	John Cassavetes
1986	*The Karate Kid, Part II*	John G. Avildsen
1986	*The Boss' Wife*	Ziggy Steinberg
1987	*I Love N.Y.*	Alan Smithee (aka Gianni Bozzacchi)
1987	*A Prayer for the Dying*	Mike Hodges (UK)
1987	*Masters of the Universe*	Gary Goddard
1987	*Happy New Year*	John G. Avildsen
1987	*Baby Boom*	Charles Shyer
1987	*Broadcast News*	James L. Brooks
1988	*For Keeps?*	John G. Avildsen
1988	*A Night in the Life of Jimmy Reardon*	William Richert

Year	Film	Director
1988	The Big Blue	Luc Besson (France/USA/Italy)
1988	Betrayed	Costa-Gavras (USA/Japan)
1988	Cohen and Tate	Eric Red
1989	Lean on Me	John G. Avildsen
1989	The Karate Kid, Part III	John G. Avildsen
1989	Lock Up	John Flynn
1990	The Fourth War	John Frankenheimer (USA/Canada)
1990	Backstreet Dreams	Rupert Hitzig, Jason O'Malley
1990	Rocky V	John G. Avildsen
1991	Year of the Gun	John Frankenheimer
1991	Necessary Roughness	Stan Dragoti
1991	By the Sword	Jeremy Kagan
1993	A Captive in the Land	John Berry (USSR/USA)
1993	Blood In, Blood Out (aka Bound by Honor)	Taylor Hackford
1993	The Adventures of Huck Finn	Stephen Sommers
1993	Rookie of the Year	Daniel Stern
1994	8 Seconds	John G. Avildsen
1994	The Next Karate Kid	Christopher Cain
1994	The Scout	Michael Ritchie
1995	Napoleon	Mario Andreacchio (Australia/Japan)
1995	Bushwhacked	Greg Beerman
1996	Spy Hard	Rick Friedberg
1996	Entertaining Angels: The Dorothy Day Story	Michael Ray Rhodes
1998	Wrongfully Accused	Pat Proft (Germany/USA)
1998	The Real Macaw	Mario Andreacchio (Australia)
1999	The Thomas Crown Affair	John McTiernan
1999	Desert Heat (aka Inferno)	John G. Avildsen
2001	Tortilla Soup	Maria Ripoll
2002	G	Christopher Scott Cherot
2002	Avenging Angelo	Martyn Burke (USA/France/Switzerland)
2002	2 Birds with 1 Stallone (aka The Gospel of Lou)	Bret Carr
2003	Boys on the Run	Pol Cruchten
2006	Rocky Balboa	Sylvester Stallone
2008	Hold-Up	Michael Mandell
2009	Moonlight Blade	Arthur J. Mangano
2009	The Perfect Game	William Dear
2010	Small Town Hero	Lawrence Kopelman
2011	Two Knives	Michael Mandell

CONVERTINO, Michael (b. 1953?) A talented and more than a little mysterious composer for rock bands and movies, he has managed to remain unseen and little known even though he has scored over two dozen films since 1986.

Only a few facts about the elusive Michael Convertino are available, and even those are unconfirmed. He was born Michael Hurt in New York City and was educated at Yale University, where he played in a jazz band. Convertino later studied music at the Paris Conservatoire then returned to the States, where he composed for and performed in various bands, finding success in the 1980s with the New Wave band the Innocents. His first film proj-

ect was cowriting with David Newman the score for Tim Burton's 1984 live-action short *Frankenweenie* (not to be confused with Burton's 2012 animated feature of the same name, which was scored by Danny Elfman). Convertino collaborated with Keith Levene on the comic thriller *Hollywood Vice Squad* in 1986 before finding success for his solo score for the acclaimed drama *Children of a Lesser God* later that same year. Over the next twenty-four years, Convertino scored a variety of films ranging from silly comedies to disturbing dramas. Among his notable movies are *The Hidden, Bull Durham, The Doctor, A Home of Our Own, Wrestling Ernest Hemingway, Guarding Tess, The Santa Clause, Things to Do in Denver When You're*

Dead, Mother Night, Jungle 2 Jungle, Straight into Darkness, and *Wake Wood.* Convertino has also written music for the television series *Tales from the Crypt* and *Faerie Tale Theatre,* as well as a handful of TV movies, including *Christmas Snow* (1986) and *Shattered Dreams* (1990). Just as there are gaps in his screen career, Convertino himself has been very reclusive. He has no website, has given no interviews, only one known photo of him has ever been released to the press, and even his birth date is questionable. The various directors who have worked with Convertino have been very closemouthed about the mysterious composer except to praise his work.

What is not so hidden about Convertino is the splendid music he has written for movies over the years. His love for jazz is evident in several scores, but more often than not he utilizes classical music techniques in his scores for very modern stories. The drama *Children of a Lesser God,* about the difficult romance between a teacher (William Hurt) and a deaf woman (Marlee Matlin), has a main theme that is a graceful string piece with hesitant accents that make it slightly apprehensive. The result sounds very classical yet the music builds like a pop song. Using such music for a mature love story like *Children of a Lesser God* makes sense, but Convertino also uses classical forms in the farcical *The Santa Clause.* There is a merry main theme that mocks Beethoven as its forceful thrust is undercut by a Mozart-like gavotte. The score also includes a heartfelt melancholy passage featuring the oboe that is very nostalgic and warm, and a vivacious piano and orchestra piece that races ahead happily to a very classical finale. This is very skillful musical pastiching and, whether used for drama or comedy, is enthralling. The comedy-drama *Guarding Tess,* about the offbeat friendship between a former First Lady (Shirley MacLaine) and her Secret Service bodyguard (Nicolas Cage), also uses classical pastiche. The main theme is a playful march with dancing woodwinds and a giddy xylophone joining in. Yet there is also a poignant theme with a flowing melody that keeps reaching up and out as in flight, and a vibrant pseudobaroque piece with energetic strings and laughing reeds. Even the dark, bloody gangster movie *Things to Do in Denver When You're Dead* uses a violin solo that is flowing and casual even as it is played over some violent scenes, creating a very disconcerting feeling.

Jazz figures in the score for the irreverent baseball comedy-romance *Bull Durham.* A jazzy organ piece that is a pseudo gospel hymn is heard under the opening credits and narration and the love theme is a jazz saxophone solo accompanied by swirling chords on an electronic keyboard. The character drama *Wrestling Ernest Hemingway* has a touch of the Irish ballad in the score which is classical in its sensibility but folk in its rendering. This tale of two elderly men, a Cuban barber (Robert Duvall) and an Irish seaman (Richard Harris), who form an unlikely friendship, has a fragile musical theme with halting moments as it cautiously moves forward. There is also a magical passage featuring the harp that flutters up and down the scale effectively. Another character drama, *We Don't Live Here Anymore,* has a haunting minor-key main theme heard on strings and piano that seems a little lost and even meandering as it circles back on itself. The gushing love story *Bed of Roses* has a very romantic score. A gliding orchestral theme featuring strings seems to float up and down the scale in time to the passion on the screen. The score also includes a dreamy piano, woodwind, and string passage with echoing percussion instruments to propel it forward, and a lively percussive theme that is both tribal and funky. (Interestingly, this score was recorded by two different orchestras in different studios and edited together for the final print.)

Convertino sometimes surprises one with his versatility. The action movie *Aspen Extreme,* about a ski competition, has some stirring brass fanfares that are punctuated with confident percussion, ideal for scoring the ski slope climax. The main theme is less robust, a gentle piece with twinkling percussion and a warm brass and string melody. *Mother Night,* based on a Kurt Vonnegut novel about World War II spies, has a memorable mystical theme with descending strings and chime accents that has a surreal quality about it. Such sensitive music heard over scenes of intrigue and betrayal supports Vonnegut's offbeat style of storytelling. There are some surprises also in Convertino's score for the sci-fi thriller *The Hidden.* The main theme features distorted brass and electronic sound effects that play a wavering tune with a foreboding tone. One section in the score is a delicate passage on harp with ominous chords beneath it. A solo trumpet is featured in another passage in which the electric orchestra is dizzy and delirious in their playing. Convertino's most recent screen project, the creepy horror film *Wake Wood,* has such an inventive score that one looks forward to future surprises. A rhythmic theme played by various percussion, including bells, chimes, drums, triangle, and wood block, results in a lively but equally creepy mood. Other highlights in the score include echoing electronic chords set against a repetitive tune as rapping sticks set the tempo, a felicitous theme that uses dripping water and a heartbeat for its tempo, and

reverberating musical phrases heard under some of the movie's most suspenseful scenes. Convertino may remain out of sight if he wishes, as long as such estimable music continues to surface on occasion.

Credits

(all films USA unless stated otherwise)

Year	Film	Director
1986	*Hollywood Vice Squad*	Penelope Spheeris
1986	*Children of a Lesser God*	Randa Haines
1987	*The Hidden*	Jack Sholder
1988	*Bull Durham*	Ron Shelton
1989	*Queen of Hearts*	Jon Amiel (UK/USA)
1990	*The End of Innocence*	Dyan Cannon
1991	*The Doctor*	Randa Haines
1992	*The Waterdance*	Neal Jimenez, Michael Steinberg
1993	*Bodies, Rest & Motion*	Michael Steinberg
1993	*Aspen Extreme*	Patrick Hasburgh
1993	*A Home of Our Own*	Tony Bill
1993	*Wrestling Ernest Hemingway*	Randa Haines
1994	*Guarding Tess*	Hugh Wilson
1994	*Milk Money*	Richard Benjamin
1994	*The Santa Clause*	John Pasquin
1995	*Things to Do in Denver When You're Dead*	Gary Fleder
1996	*Bed of Roses* (aka *Amelia and the King of Plants*)	Michael Goldenberg
1996	*Pie in the Sky*	Bryan Gordon
1996	*Mother Night*	Keith Gordon
1996	*The Last of the High Kings* (aka *Summer Fling*)	David Keating (Denmark/Ireland/UK)
1997	*Jungle 2 Jungle*	John Pasquin (USA/France)
1998	*Dance with Me* (aka *Shut Up and Dance*)	Randa Haines
1998	*Where's Marlowe?*	Daniel Pyne
2002	*Liberty Stands Still*	Kari Skogland (Germany/Canada)
2003	*Milwaukee, Minnesota*	Allan Mindel
2004	*We Don't Live Here Anymore* (aka *Adultery*)	John Curran (USA/Canada)
2004	*Straight into Darkness*	Jeff Burr
2010	*Wake Wood*	David Keating (Ireland/UK)

COODER, Ry (b. 1947) A widely renowned slide guitarist who has embraced many kinds of music during his eclectic career, he has also scored sixteen movies, mostly with director Walter Hill.

Ryland Peter Cooder was born in Los Angeles and grew up in Santa Monica, playing the guitar when he was only three years old. When Cooder was four, an accident left him blind in one eye, causing him to become a withdrawn child who retreated into music. As a teenager he played with various amateur and then professional groups, eventually working with Taj Mahal, Ed Cassidy, Van Dyke Parks, Gordon Lightfoot, Mick Jagger, and the Rolling

Stones. Cooder was a studio musician on several rock albums during the 1960s and by the 1970s found recognition for his own albums. In addition to his mastery of the slide guitar, in which one slides along the strings rather than jumping from one fret to another, Cooder became famous for his versatile way of playing in different musical styles, including traditional folk, gospel, jazz, rock, blues, calypso, salsa, Hawaiian, and Tex-Mex. By the late 1980s, he had incorporated into his albums world music as well, particularly African and Hispanic forms. Cooder has made musical arrangements in which diverse styles have been combined and he has composed original music that draws from his wide interest in different kinds of music. He has made many solo albums as well as collaborative records with such artists as Van Morrison, Eric Clapton, Randy Newman, Ali Farka Touré, Neil Young, and the Doobie Brothers.

Cooder's first experience with movies was in 1970 when he played slide guitar on the soundtrack for the Mick Jagger film *Performance*. Songs by Cooder and his guitar playing have both been heard in two dozen movies since then. In 1980, director Walter Hill approached him about scoring his Jesse James western *The Long Riders* because of Cooder's knowledge of authentic folk music of the period. The resulting soundtrack was a mixture of traditional and new music that was roundly applauded, which encouraged Cooder to score eight more films for Hill, including *Southern Comfort, Brewster's Millions, Crossroads,* and *Geronimo: An American Legend*. Cooder was soon requested by other directors, but the busy musician has made only seven other movies. For British director Tony Richardson he scored the crime drama *The Border*, for French director Louis Malle the Texas melodrama *Alamo Bay*, for American director Mike Nichols the political film *Primary Colors*, and for German director Wim Wenders the character drama *Paris, Texas* and the thriller *The End of Violence*. In 1999 Wenders made an award-winning documentary titled *Buena Vista Social Club* about a group of Cuban folk musicians brought together by Cooder to make a record of traditional music from the island. After a decade away from the movies, Cooder scored the romantic Asian drama *My Blueberry Nights* in 2007. He has also written music for the television series *Tall Tales & Legends* and *Tales from the Crypt*, as well as some documentary shorts.

As versatile as Cooder's music is on his many albums, most of his screen music is in the folk and blues tradition. He earned a reputation for arranging and/or composing music in the American idiom, and Hollywood interpreted this as a western or at least rural sound. Cooder's first score, for the period western *The Long Riders*, utilized some traditional folk songs as well as new compositions in the folk manner. Yet the score, like the film itself, has a very modern sensibility, a sort of hip western in which the James, Miller, and Ford brothers are not so much historical figures as contemporary antiheroes. The score is a celebration of American instruments, including guitar, harmonium, fiddle, and dulcimer. There are some

sparkling guitar and dulcimer duets that bounce along with cocky glee, an evocative string serenade that is lazy yet heartfelt, bubbly square dance music played on fiddle and guitar that sounds authentic, and a languid acoustic waltz that seems to move in slow motion and is far from authentic. This wonderful mixture of the old sound and new techniques can be found in most of Cooder's scores, but rarely does it have such exuberance as in *The Long Riders*. Cooder uses fewer existing folk tunes and writes more original music for another period western, *Geronimo: An American Legend*. Again he employs a variety of American instruments, but they are all filtered to create a Native American sound. The main theme includes tribal chanting that transitions into a howling lament backed by wavering strings, high-pitched Navajo flutes, and electronic bass echoes. Like the rest of the score, it is mystical and evocative. There is a trumpet solo that is regal yet lonely until synthesized chords and chanting take over. A dulcimer plays a sad dance as despondent chords rumble underneath, and in one passage a morose violin plays on the lower register while a solo pipe plays a countermelody high above. These are not your usual Hollywood western scores.

The Border, a disturbing contemporary drama about illegal immigrants and black market children, has a vibrant score that Cooder wrote with Domingo Samudio. Most memorable is a poignant theme played on harmonica and guitar that is soothing yet has a touch of despair at the same time. *Alamo Bay* is about Vietnamese immigrants in Texas and Cooder introduced some Asian instruments and sounds to the soundtrack. The main theme is a marvelous piece in which reverberating guitar and sustained woodwind chords surround a melody that is suspended dangerously in the air before blossoming into a lovely waltz as piano and other instruments join in. *Paris, Texas*, about a drifter (Harry Dean Stanton) who tries to reconnect with his brother, son, and wife, has a blues score in which the slide guitar sound is featured. One guitar passage is full of twangy blue notes that create a cockeyed mood. There is a restless duet in which two guitars seem to dance individually without noticing the other, as contrasted by a bluesy lament that is hesitant and full of pain. The main theme is an eerie and surreal piece of music in which the sliding guitar seems to weep as it repeats a four-note phrase with subtle variations. There is an awkward chill in the story and characters of *Paris, Texas* (minimalist playwright Sam

Shepard wrote the screenplay), and Cooder's offbeat score supports this beautifully.

A movie that must have been very close to Cooder's heart is *Crossroads*, about a young classical guitarist (Ralph Macchio) who learns to play blues guitar from a veteran musician (Joe Seneca). The film is filled with opportunities for some guitar wizardry and Cooder, as composer and musician, surpasses himself. *Crossroads* has many songs as well as unsung passages. Of the latter, highlights include a blues theme on banjo and brass that is quirky and sly, a subdued blues passage in which the slide guitar is used

effectively, and a zesty harmonica theme that moves from folk into rock. A male quartet called the Wonders sings the traditional "Hush (Somebody's Calling My Name)," a drowsy gospel hymn that echoes with weariness. A less likely use of existing material can be found in a scene of dueling guitars in which Cooder takes Niccolo Paganini's violin solo "Caprice No. 5" and turns it into an enthralling guitar duet. Moments like this make one hope that Cooder will return to the movies and return often. Critical study: *The Unbroken Circle: Tradition and Innovation in the Music of Ry Cooder and Taj Mahal*, Fred Metting (2000).

Credits

(all films USA unless stated otherwise)

Year	Film	Director
1980	The Long Riders	Walter Hill
1981	Southern Comfort	Walter Hill (USA/UK)
1982	The Border	Tony Richardson
1984	Paris, Texas (BAFTA-N)	Wim Wenders (W. Germany/UK/France/USA)
1984	Streets of Fire	Walter Hill
1985	Alamo Bay	Louis Malle
1985	Brewster's Millions	Walter Hill
1986	Crossroads	Walter Hill
1986	Blue City	Michelle Manning
1989	Johnny Handsome	Walter Hill
1992	Trespass (aka The Looters)	Walter Hill
1993	Geronimo: An American Legend	Walter Hill
1996	Last Man Standing (aka Gundown)	Walter Hill
1997	The End of Violence	Wim Wenders (France/Germany/USA)
1998	Primary Colors	Mike Nichols (France/USA/Germany/UK/Japan)
2007	My Blueberry Nights	Kar Wai Wong (Hong Kong/China/France)

COPELAND, Stewart (b. 1952) An acclaimed rock drummer who also has composed ballets and operas, he has scored forty-five international feature films ranging from potent political dramas to juvenile comedies.

Stewart Armstrong Copeland was born in Alexandria, Virginia, the son of a Big Band trumpeter who became a CIA agent, and an archeologist with a love for classical music. When Copeland was only a few months old, his family moved to Cairo, Egypt, because of his father's job, and the boy lived much of his youth in Egypt, Syria, and Lebanon where Arabic became his second language. While the family was stationed in Beirut, Copeland attended the American school there, then later was educated at a British private school, the United States International

University in California, and the University of California at Berkeley. He began playing drums at the age of twelve and later also became proficient on guitar and keyboard. Copeland began his professional music career in 1970 in England, where he was road manager for the progressive rock band Curved Air, eventually becoming the group's drummer as well. He found more recognition in 1977 as the cofounder, drummer, vocalist, and composer for the celebrated rock band the Police, for which he wrote many popular songs and recorded several top-selling albums. The Police remained an influential and highly popular group into the mid-1980s, during which time Copeland also recorded solo work under the pseudonym Klark Kent. Also in the 1980s, Copeland became involved with world music, in particular African forms, and after the Police disbanded in 1986, he collaborated with dozens of celebrated artists in the fields of jazz, reggae, pop, New Wave, and classical music. He returned to his classical training in the 1990s and has written music for the concert hall, ballet, and opera.

Director Francis Ford Coppola consulted with Copeland about rock rhythm when he was preparing the film *Rumble Fish* in 1983. Copeland ended up scoring the movie and received laudatory notices for his first screen music. Two years later he scored the documentary *The Rhythmatist* about the roots of rock and roll in Africa. Over the next two decades Copeland frequently returned to movie scoring, working with a wide variety of directors and genres. Among his many notable films are *Wall Street, Talk Radio, Hidden Agenda, Riff-Raff, Wide Sargasso Sea, Rapa Nui, Raining Stones, She's Having a Baby, Fresh, West Beirut, On the Line, Four Days in September, I Am David,* and the documentary *The Leopard Son.* He has written music for such television series as *The Equalizer, Insiders, Dead Like Me, Brutally Normal,* and *The Life and Times of Juniper Lee,* as well as ten TV movies, including *Afterburn* (1992), *Babylon 5: The Gathering* (1993), *Tyson* (1995), *The Assassination File* (1996), *The Taking of Pelham One Two Three* (1998), *Futuresport* (1998), and *Evel Knievel* (2004). Copeland's eclectic career also includes scoring video games, website music channels, and a live arena production of *Ben-Hur* in London in 2009. Yet for many his true claim to fame is as one of the greatest drummers of his era.

If one expects plenty of percussion in Copeland's movie scores, one will not be disappointed. Yet his screen music consists of much more than drums and rhythm. Coming from a rock background, he uses synthesized music even when the score is far from rock. Copeland also frequently utilizes world music, as specified by the subject matter of some of his movies. For his first score, *Rumble Fish,* the subject of American youth gangs is realized in a restless theme on electric keyboard with synthesized horns and strings, the result being jazzy and urban with a freedom that is slightly dangerous. The soundtrack also includes a passage on acoustic piano with a rock beat that is more propulsive than heavy metal, and one section features distorted guitar chords and sound effects to create a chaotic and nightmarish tone. A similar kind of angst can be found in *Talk Radio* about a hate-filled, self-destructive radio talk

show host (Eric Bogosian). The score features a frantic theme on drums, piano, and pizzicato strings that conveys the high pressure and even desperate nature of the central character. The fascinating world of greed in *Wall Street* is scored with a rhythmic theme with synthesized chimes and percussion that is very urban yet has a dreamy quality as well. At various points in the score, dog barks punctuate the music and the dog-eat-dog milieu becomes literal. A different kind of urban nightmare is found in *Fresh* about a twelve-year-old drug pusher (Sean Nelson) living and working in a housing project. The score has some funky blues passages with some intricate electric guitar fingering. The film's main theme is a lazy orchestral piece with electric guitar riffs that makes despair almost sound casual. Belfast is the urban setting for the political thriller *Hidden Agenda.* The movie opens with a simple and serene Irish folk air heard on a flute, but this calm does not last and much of the rest of the score is tense and nervous.

In some ways Copeland's screen music grows richer and more diverse as he leaves the urban environment. Consider his ambitious score for *Rapa Nui* about rival tribes on Easter Island and the legend behind the mysterious stone carvings later discovered there. The main theme is an enthralling fusion of tribal drums, birdlike pipes, and oppressive strings with primitive chanting rising and falling throughout the film. The action scenes are scored with rapid drumming and swirling voices, and there is majesty in the music connected to the creation of the massive stone faces. The nature documentary *The Leopard Son,* filmed on the African savanna, has an entrancing theme with an expansive feeling as strings, reeds, and percussion seem to dance a tribal bolero together. The setting is nineteenth-century Jamaica in *Wide Sargasso Sea,* an imaginative prequel to the novel *Jane Eyre.* The young Englishman Edward Rochester (Nathaniel Parker) marries the local landowner Antoinette (Karina Lombard) then discovers the streak of insanity that runs through her family. Copeland wrote a feverish score filled with synthesized music and sound effects. Electric keyboard and drums battle against ethnic flutes, a haunting woodwind theme wavers like the sea and is both romantic and threatening, there is some tribal chanting with high-pitched pipes, and the ear is teased with a lonely flute solo heard only in brief snatches throughout the movie. All of these scores set in exotic places are far removed from rock yet are still very modern and high tech.

Copeland must have had more than a passing interest in scoring *West Beirut*, set in 1975 in the land he knew well from his youth. A high schooler (Rami Doueiri) sees the civil war around him as an opportunity to exercise his ambitions to become a filmmaker until the horrors of war overshadow any artistic dreams he holds. Copeland's score encompasses much of his eclectic sense of music. There is a simple melody on strings with sustained notes underneath to convey an urgency as well as a sense of wonder. A rock theme on electric piano with percussive accents is heard, as is a classical allegro piano piece with nervous, echoing chords surrounding the carefree melody. Also memorable is a guitar solo with an exotic flavor suggesting the mysterious and nonsensical world the boy lives in. Copeland stopped writing for film and television in 2007, the same year the Police reunited for a concert tour. Since then he has been involved in a variety of projects, unfortunately none involving film. Memoir: *Strange Things Happen: A Life with the Police, Polo, and Pygmies* (2009). Official website: www.stewartcopeland.net.

Credits

(all films USA unless stated otherwise)

Year	Film	Director
1983	*Rumble Fish* (GGN)	Francis Ford Coppola
1985	*The Rhythmatist*	J. P. and Jean-Pierre Dutilleux
1986	*Out of Bounds*	Richard Tuggle
1987	*Wall Street*	Oliver Stone
1988	*She's Having a Baby*	John Hughes
1988	*Talk Radio*	Oliver Stone
1988	*The Jogger*	Robert Resnikoff
1989	*See No Evil, Hear No Evil*	Arthur Hiller
1990	*The First Power*	Robert Resnikoff
1990	*Hidden Agenda*	Ken Loach (UK)
1990	*Taking Care of Business*	Arthur Hiller
1990	*Men at Work*	Emilio Estevez
1991	*Highlander II: The Quickening*	Russell Mulcahy (UK/France)
1991	*Riff-Raff*	Ken Loach (UK)
1993	*Wide Sargasso Sea*	John Duigan (Australia)
1993	*Bank Robber*	Nick Mead
1993	*Raining Stones*	Ken Loach (UK)
1993	*Airborne*	Rob Bowman
1994	*Fresh*	Boaz Yakin (USA/France)
1994	*Decadence*	Steven Berkoff, David Tickner (UK/Germany)
1994	*Rapa Nui*	Kevin Reynolds
1994	*Surviving the Game*	Ernest R. Dickerson
1994	*Silent Fall*	Bruce Beresford
1996	*The Pallbearer*	Matt Reeves
1996	*Boys* (aka *The Girl You Want*)	Stacy Cochran
1996	*The Leopard Son*	Hugo Van Lawick (USA/Netherlands)
1997	*Gridlock'd*	Vondie Curtis-Hall
1997	*Four Days in September*	Bruno Barreto (Brazil/USA)
1997	*Little Boy Blue*	Antonio Tibaldi
1997	*Good Burger*	Brian Robbins
1998	*West Beirut*	Ziad Doueiri (France/Lebanon/Norway)
1998	*Very Bad Things*	Peter Berg
1998	*Pecker*	John Waters
1999	*She's All That*	Robert Iscove
1999	*Made Men*	Louis Morneau
1999	*Simpatico*	Matthew Warchus (UK/France/USA)
2000	*Skipped Parts*	Tamra Davis
2000	*Boys and Girls*	Robert Iscove
2000	*More Dogs Than Bones*	Michael Browning

Year	Film	Director
2000	*Sunset Strip*	Adam Collis
2001	*On the Line* (aka *On the L*)	Eric Bross
2002	*Deuces Wild*	Scott Kalvert (USA/Germany)
2003	*I Am David*	Paul Feig
2004	*Amazon Forever*	Jean-Pierre Dutilleux (France/Brazil)
2005	*Love Wrecked*	Randal Kleiser

COPLAND, Aaron (1900–1990) Generally considered the dean of American composers, this creator of celebrated concert and ballet music also scored a handful of feature films.

Aaron Copland was born in Brooklyn into a family of Lithuanian Jewish immigrants. Although his mother played the piano, Copland showed little interest in music until he was in his teens. Immediately he was as attracted to composing as much as to performing. He took composition lessons first by correspondence course then with private teachers, who encouraged the youth. He later studied at the School of Music for Americans in France then received further education under the renowned French teacher Nadia Boulanger in Paris. Returning to America in 1924, Copland's career was launched with his *Symphony for Organ and Orchestra*. By the 1930s he was widely known for his modernist style, dubbed the "Brooklyn Stravinsky." Yet Copland's music was not popular with the masses and this bothered him. He made a conscious effort to simplify his music, avoid the harsh dissonant forms, and write music that was still in the classical form but more accessible. He was successful in his efforts, writing some of the most beloved pieces of American music in the twentieth century, including such favorites as *El Salón Mexico*, *Fanfare for the Common Man*, *A Lincoln Portrait*, and his famous Third Symphony, probably the most performed American symphony of the century. The music from his ballets *Rodeo*, *Billy the Kid*, and *Appalachian Spring* also became popular and was heard everywhere. Copland also had distinguished careers as a conductor, teacher, and author. His two books, *What to Listen For in Music* and *Music and Imagination*, are as inspiring as they are instructive.

Copland's first composition for film was the short documentary *The City* which was written for the 1939 New York World's Fair. Hollywood director Lewis Milestone admired Copland's talent for musical Americana and convinced him to score the 1939 screen version of the play *Of Mice and Men*. His film debut was praised and nominated for an Academy Award, as was Copland's two subsequent features, *Our Town* and *The North Star*. But Copland's busy career in the concert and ballet world kept his screen work to a minimum. During the war he scored the short documentary *The Cunningham Story* for the U.S. Office of Information. In 1949 he scored two features, *The Red Pony* and *The Heiress*, winning an Oscar for the latter. A dozen years later he returned to film to score the forgettable *Something Wild*. It was another twenty years before original Copland music was heard on-screen again, this time for the Mexican feature *Crimen a fondo*. His concert and ballet music has shown up in many movies and television programs over the years but the output of original compositions for the screen is limited. All the same, these few scores are deemed superior examples of movie scoring.

The music in *Of Mice and Men*, a rural tragedy by John Steinbeck about two itinerant ranch workers (Burgess Meredith and Lon Chaney Jr.), is subtle and sparse. Consequently, when music is used it is very effective, such as the discordant chords during a confrontation scene between two ranch hands or the descending chords after the giant Lenny (Chaney) accidentally strangles the foreman's wife (Betty Field). The opening theme, heard against thunder, has various reeds competing with brass and percussion in a restless and agitated manner. A Jew's harp and other American instruments are featured throughout the score but never in an obvious way. The heartbreaking ending is scored with peaceful and hopeful music as George (Meredith) is forced to kill Lenny before the mob gets to him. Steinbeck's novella *The Red Pony* was filmed a decade later and both the story and the score are less grim and more poetic. A young boy (Peter Miles) growing up on a California ranch gets a lesson in life when he is given a pony by the foreman (Robert Mitchum) whom he worships. This youthful look at the world is musicalized with a fuller sound and a more encompassing range

AARON COPLAND and LEONARD BERNSTEIN. These two music giants from the concert hall, ballet, and theatre had very limited careers in the movies but they each left us some magnificent scores. Here they are in 1980 as Bernstein (left) goes over the music to be performed for Copland's eightieth birthday celebration. *Photofest*

of emotions. The main theme is simple and even child-like, as suggested by the boy hero of the story. The most memorable passage in the score is the stirring "Morning on the Ranch," a catchy walking theme with an expansive feeling as strings and horns repeat an ascending musical phrase until they break out in a full and captivating melodic line with whistling flutes and chimes. There is also a sparkling march, heard while the boy dreams of fantastic images, in which the music is so happy as it climbs the scale that the feeling is contagious. Even more fun is a waltzing circus theme with laughing brass, giddy reeds, and bells providing some succinct punctuation. In contrast, the screen version of Thornton Wilder's allegorical play *Our Town* has an understated score. This gentle yet compelling look at life, love, and death in a small New Hampshire village has a languid and quiet theme, using a five-note phrase that Copland varies in different ways throughout the movie. A solo flute is often featured, its simple and unadorned sound a metaphor for the town itself. One warm passage gracefully wavers as it moves forward without pretension. A modest fanfare is heard in another theme that announces itself with humble pride. It is a nostalgic yet sincere score and one that would inspire many other screen composers.

The North Star, a wartime drama set in Russia, called for a much more aggressive score and one that could not rely on an Americana flavor. The main theme is not overtly Russian but in a wistful European vein. Some sections have a rural flavor; others are darkly dramatic. There is even a catchy folk song ditty sung by the younger char-acters that is achingly optimistic. This is contrasted by a vigorous Russian military march that is filled with fore-boding. The mood is also somber in *The Heiress*, a period drama about thwarted love based on the Henry James novel *Washington Square*. A wispy waltz is used as the theme for the spinster heroine (Olivia de Havilland), and when her hopes are roused, the music reaches painfully for a happy tone. But when the heroine's world collapses, the waltz goes sour and dwindles into discordant melancholy. Copland's score was tinkered with before the premiere of *The Heiress* (his opening music was cut and replaced with a plodding version of the waltz) and the experience was so painful that he withdrew from Hollywood and never fully embraced it again. Yet Copland was proud of his film music and did not consider it inferior to concert composition. In fact, he took themes from *The City*, *Of Mice and Men*, and *Our Town* to create the five-movement concert suite *Music for Movies*.

The influence Copland had on movie music cannot be limited to these few superior scores. His concert and ballet music has been cited by many film composers as the work that inspired them. Whether the result is a quiet score like *To Kill a Mockingbird* or a majestic one such as *The Magnificent Seven*, the Copland sound is prevalent. Autobiographies: *Copland: 1900 through 1942*, with Vivian Perlis (1999); *Copland: Since 1943*, with Vivian Perlis (1999); biography: *Music for the Common Man: Aaron Copland during the Depression and War*, Elizabeth Bergman Crist (2009); *Aaron Copland: The Life and Work of an Uncommon Man*, Howard Pollack (2000).

Credits

(all films USA unless stated otherwise)

Year	Film	Director
1939	*Of Mice and Men* (AAN)	Lewis Milestone
1940	*Our Town* (AAN)	Sam Wood
1943	*The North Star* (AAN)	Lewis Milestone
1949	*The Red Pony*	Lewis Milestone
1949	*The Heiress* (AA)	William Wyler
1961	*Something Wild*	Jack Garfein
1981	*Crimen a fondo*	Jorge Gallardo (Mexico)

COPPOLA, Carmine (1910–1991) A respected classical flautist who also composed and conducted music on occasion, he became a notable screen composer in his sixties when he scored movies directed by his son Francis Ford Coppola.

Born in New York City, Carmine Coppola took flute lessons as a youth and studied music at Juilliard and the Manhattan School of Music before beginning his career as a musician. He played flute for the Radio City Music Hall orchestra and the Detroit Symphony in the 1930s, then during the 1940s he was flautist for Arturo Toscanini's NBC Symphony Orchestra. He left radio in 1951 to pursue a composing career. Coppola conducted some Broadway shows and did music arrangements for others and for Radio City Music Hall in the 1950s and 1960s. He also returned to performing, playing the flute on the soundtrack of many TV and movie cartoons. When the Russian sci-fi movie *Battle Beyond the Sun* was released in the States in 1959, Coppola was hired to write a new soundtrack score. Three years later he worked with his son Francis on their first film together, the low-budget comedy *Tonight for Sure*. When he was slated to direct *The Godfather*, Francis Ford Coppola hired the Italian composer Nino Rota to write the score, but the elder Coppola contributed music to two scenes in the classic gangster movie. He also scored some sections of *The Godfather: Part II* and won an Oscar with Rota. By the time *The Godfather: Part III* was made, Rota had died and Coppola wrote the score alone. Father and son also worked together on *Apocalypse Now, The Outsiders, Gardens of Stone*, and *New York Stories*, as well as *The Black Stallion*, which Francis produced. Among his concert compositions are woodwind quintets, an oboe *fantasie*, and some orchestral works. Perhaps Coppola's most ambitious music project was composing a new score for the 1927 silent epic *Napoleon* when it was restored and rereleased in 1981. He died in 1991 at the age of eighty, a few months after completing the score for *The Godfather: Part III*.

That third installment in the *Godfather* saga is a good place to begin a look at Coppola the composer. His contribution of songs, wedding music, and other bits of music in the first two films is not substantial enough to illustrate Coppola's sense of screen scoring. As expected, Rota's main themes from the first two movies return in the third movie but soon Coppola's original music presides. There is a lyrical *Preludio* with operatic crescendos, a Latin hymn

with strong Italianate flourishes, a flowing love theme that has an Old World flavor, and a restless and menacing passage titled "Altobello." Coppola conducted the score, including the extended scene from Pietro Mascagni's opera *Cavalleria Rusticana*. *The Godfather: Part III*, like its predecessors, overflows with superb music, and even if the movie itself cannot match the first two installments, it is still a musical feast. Coppola's other highly lyrical score is that for the beautifully filmed adventure movie *The Black Stallion*. The main theme, played by a solo guitar with oboe and other instruments rising and falling, is bucolic and expansive yet has minor-key sections and a solemn subtext. Since the title character is a wild Arabian horse, it has a recurring theme played on primitive horns to suggest a nomadic and desolate heritage. The extensive sequence on the deserted island, one of the longest dialogue-free pieces of filmmaking in modern movies, uses music sparingly at first. A high-pitched fife with little accompaniment suffices as the boy (Reno Kelly) and horse tentatively meet and start to trust each other. As their friendship blossoms, so does the score as percussion explodes then the main theme is heard on the harp, a truly marvelous merging of visual and images. The music for the preparation and the running of the climactic race is rich in a way that is very different from the island themes. Fanfares, marches, and anthems provide the excitement but even these are interrupted by musical and visual flashbacks to the island, tying together the whole movie in a thrilling way.

Coppola's least lyrical score is found in *Apocalypse Now* which his son is credited as co-composing. What one most remembers about music in this very dark, expressionistic movie is the use of Richard Wagner's "Ride of the Valkyries" for a stunning helicopter attack. The score also has bits and pieces of existing rock songs and 1960s music but most of the film is set to pulsating drums, muffled electronic sounds, and a scarcity of melody. This oppressive music is more than appropriate for a movie that looks at the Vietnam War with a surreal, nightmarish eye. Once the expedition arrives at the domain of the crazed Colonel Kurtz (Marlon Brando) deep in the Cambodian jungle, the music takes on tribal sounds that are so distorted that we are in the realm of science fiction. Not as oppressive but still powerful is Coppola's score for the drama *The Outsiders* about members of a gang in 1960s Oklahoma. The opening theme is actually rather lilting but has a ponderous bass line that forebodes trouble. Because the harsh tale is seen through the eyes of an imaginative youth (C. Thomas Howell), the music often echoes his thoughts rather than the rivalry and violence all around him. For the daunting task of scoring the nearly four-hour silent classic *Napoleon*, Coppola drew on everything from patriotic anthems to traditional silent screen organ music. This giant epic has some wonderfully intimate scenes among all the marches, revolutions, and battles, giving Coppola the opportunity to flex his musical muscles. There is a rousing theme for the boy Napoleon and his rambunctious classmates in an energetic snowball fight, a felicitous love theme for the young adult Napoleon, frantic passages for the Reign of Terror, and vigorous music for the military pomp and the spectacular battle scenes. For a former flute player who dreamed of one day composing music, *Napoleon* must have been doubly satisfying.

Coppola was the senior member of a movie dynasty that includes his Broadway conductor brother Anton, his children Francis and actress Talia Shire, and his grandchildren, actors Nicolas Cage and Jason Schwartzman and director Sofia Coppola. He made cameo appearances in several of his son's movies, usually playing a musician, and contributed songs to a dozen films. Coppola waited most of his life to become a recognized composer, but he achieved it in the end and left the world some superior screen music. Biography: *The Coppolas: A Family Business*, Vincent Anthony LoBrutto, Harriet R. Morrison (2012).

Credits

(all films USA and directed by Francis Ford Coppola unless stated otherwise; * for Best Song)

Year	Film	Director
1959	Battle Beyond the Sun	Mikhail Karzhukov, etc. (USSR)
1962	Tonight for Sure	
1972	The Godfather	
1975	The Godfather: Part II (AA)	
1978	Mustang: The House That Joe Built	Robert Guralnick
1979	Apocalypse Now (GG; BAFTA-N)	
1979	The Black Stallion (GGN)	Carroll Ballard
1981	Napoleon (1927)	Abel Gance (France)
1983	The Outsiders	
1987	Gardens of Stone	
1989	New York Stories	Francis Ford Coppola, etc.
1989	Blood Red	Peter Masterson (UK/USA)
1990	The Godfather: Part III (AAN*; GGN)	

CORDELL, Frank (1918–1980) A celebrated British musician, conductor, arranger, and composer, he wrote scores for radio, television, and sixteen feature films.

Frank Cordell was born in Kingston upon Thames, England, the son of an army doctor, and by the time he was fourteen he was an accomplished pianist. Three years later he won a *Melody Maker* magazine poll as the most promising jazz pianist in London. Cordell began his professional career working in the music department at Warner Brothers Studios near London until World War II broke out in Europe. He served as a radio navigator in the Royal Air Force during the war, also acting as a bandleader entertaining the troops. He made many Forces Radio broadcasts in Egypt and Palestine, where he met his first wife Magda, a Hungarian refugee who became a noted artist and educator. After the war, Cordell was hired by the BBC as composer, arranger, and conductor for the studio's orchestra. In the mid-1950s he also had his own band, which had some hit records—in particular "The Black Bear," "The Shining Sea," and several mood music albums. With his wife Magda, Cordell founded the Independent Group of the Institute of Contemporary Arts, a salon in London where all kinds of artists congregated and worked. After serving as musical director for HMV (later EMI) Records, he concentrated on film and television but also wrote choral music and orchestral pieces that were performed in concert halls. Cordell made his feature film debut in 1952 writing the score for the mystery drama *The Voice of Merrill*, better known as *Murder Will Out* in the United States. Over the next twenty-five years he worked in the movies sporadically but managed to score some memorable films, including *The Captain's Table, Call Me Genius, Flight from Ashiya, The Bargee, Khartoum, Ring of Bright Water, Cromwell,* and *God Told Me To* (also known as *Demon*). Cordell also wrote music for short and feature-length documentaries, film shorts, and the British TV series *Court Martial*. He retired in the mid-1970s to a sheep farm, which became a place for artists and thinkers ranging from Buckminster Fuller to the Beatles to gather just as Cordell had encouraged in the 1950s. He died in England in 1980 at the age of sixty-two.

Because Cordell's limited number of films are so diverse, it is difficult to say what he excelled at. His orchestra recordings favored romantic music, but his concert works were rather modern. His movie scores are somewhere in between. Cordell's music for the comedies he scored has a classical tone. The nautical farce *The Captain's Table* boasts a deliciously cockeyed march theme in which slaphappy strings and piccolos gleefully compete with one another. The film's few romantic scenes are set to a foxtrot tempo. Another aquatic comedy, *The Bargee*, has a merry theme with a 1960s pop flavor including some playful organ keyboard work. The main theme is a jaunty jig heard on accordion and saxophone. For contrast are the grand symphonic scores he wrote for two historical epics. *Khartoum*, about the governmental and military exploits of General Gordon (Charlton Heston) in 1880s Sudan, has a splashy Hollywood score. There is a proud military march filled with fanfares juxtaposed with exotic desert tribal music, a very British promenade passage, a rousing theme for the imperialist troops, some vigorously dramatic music for the battle scenes, and a quiet, mystical theme that conveys the mystery and danger of the desert.

Musically more ambitious is Cordell's Oscar-nominated score for *Cromwell* about Charles I (Alec Guinness), his rival Oliver Cromwell (Richard Harris), and the English Civil War. The seventeenth-century setting is evoked musically, but Cordell is not limited by it. Stirring brass fanfares mix with a choral version of a hyped-up Gregorian chant, a gentle folk theme featuring flutes is undercut by lamenting voices, and there is a regal march that sounds like it is played on period instruments but in fact is quite modern in its orchestration. This splendid score also has a solemn dirge with rumbling brass and somber male voices, and a sparkling battle theme with furious strings combating trumpet fanfares.

Cordell wrote two very different scores for two mystery thrillers. *Murder Will Out* is an intelligent whodunnit about the murder of a woman blackmailer. The score has a passionate and symphonic main theme featuring an insistent oboe and gushing strings, the effect being more romantic than suspenseful. Cordell's last movie, *God Told Me To*, is closer to sci-fi and horror as a New York City detective (Tony Lo Bianco) investigates a series of random (and gruesome) killings that a demonic force instructs the murderers to commit. The riveting score includes creepy Gregorian chant with swaying strings, distorted sound effects, descending organ glissandos, and the requisite pipe organ chords that reverberate threateningly. There is also a quieter theme with dizzy woodwinds and echoing percussion that is just as disturbing. Quite the opposite is the felicitous score Cordell wrote for *Ring of Bright Water*, a heartwarming tale about a writer (Bill Travers) who develops a deep bond with a pet otter and with a local doctor (Virginia Mckenna) in a small town on the west coast of Scotland. The recurring theme is a sweeping Gaelic folk air that is serene and yet expansive, filled with warmth without turning saccharine. Like all those popular mood music albums Cordell and his orchestra made, this is easy listening with class.

Credits

(all films UK unless stated otherwise)

Year	Film	Director
1952	*Murder Will Out* (aka *The Voice of Merrill*)	John Gilling
1953	*The Steel Key*	Robert S. Baker
1956	*Chocolate Odyssey*	Leonard Reeve
1959	*The Captain's Table*	Jack Lee

Year	Film	Director
1961	Call Me Genius (aka The Rebel)	Robert Day
1964	Flight from Ashiya	Michael Anderson (Japan/USA)
1964	The Bargee	Duncan Wood
1964	Never Put It in Writing	Andrew L. Stone
1966	Khartoum	Basil Dearden, Eliot Elisofon
1969	Mosquito Squadron	Boris Sagal
1969	Ring of Bright Water	Jack Couffer
1970	Hell Boats	Paul Wendkos (USA)
1970	Cromwell (AAN; GGN)	Ken Hughes
1975	The Year of the Wildebeest	Alan Root
1976	A Dirty Knight's Work (aka Trial By Combat)	Kevin Connor
1976	God Told Me To (aka Demon)	Larry Cohen (USA)

CORIGLIANO, John (b. 1938) A highly acclaimed American composer of opera and orchestral works, he has scored only three feature films but made striking innovations in his music for the screen.

He was born in New York City, the son of the concertmaster for the New York Philharmonic between 1943 and 1966, John Corigliano Sr. His mother, Rose Buzen, taught and played piano. Corigliano studied composition at Columbia University and the Manhattan School of Music before getting work as an assistant for Leonard Bernstein's *Young People's Concerts* in the early 1960s. His 1963 Sonata for Violin and Piano won awards at the Spoleto Festival in Italy and brought Corigliano his first recognition. Commissions and grants followed and soon he was a major force in the world of contemporary classical music. Among his dozens of notable works are a praised Clarinet Concerto, his first symphony in 1988, the opera *The Ghosts of Versailles*, an applauded String Quartet, and his Symphony No. 2, which won the Pulitzer Prize for Music in 2001. Corigliano's works have been premiered, performed, or recorded by some of the finest musicians and orchestras in the world. The Corigliano Quartet was founded by others in 1996 to perform his music. He is also an acclaimed teacher and, as Distinguished Professor of Music at Lehman College in the City University of New York, he has mentored many noteworthy composers.

Corigliano was never much interested in the movies or film music until British director Ken Russell approached him in 1979 about scoring his movie *Altered States*. The movie is a deconstruction of the science fiction thriller genre and much of the film takes the form of a hallucinogenic nightmare. Russell requested music that was over the top and experimental and Corigliano obliged with a breakthrough score that has inspired a generation of composers. The music sounds electronic but in fact it is a traditional orchestra with the instruments being distorted, played in odd manners, and mixed in such a way that they do not make their usual sounds. For example, the woodwind musicians play the flutes not by blowing over the embouchure hole but by blowing into it directly, giving the flute a harsh trumpetlike sound. Other times the musicians are instructed to play between the notes given as well as those written down, creating a rapid form of legato. The main character in *Altered States* is a scientist (William Hurt) who experiments with hallucinatory drugs and is reduced to apelike primitivism, and the score is filled with sounds that can only be described as prehistorical. This is not to say that the score is all frantic noise, for there are lovely waltzing sections and some lyrical dance themes. Despite some of the best reviews director Russell ever received from the press, the movie was not a runaway success at the box office, but the score was noticed and opened up new possibilities for screen music.

Although Corigliano was pleased with his first feature film experience, he has only written two other movie scores. *Revolution* was another box office failure and this time even the critics disfavored the period piece. Yet Corigliano's score has some superior sections, in particular an adagio written for one of the battle scenes between the colonists and the British. There is also a lovely "Children's Theme" that sounds period and yet is very modern. With *The Red Violin*, Corigliano's score was met with wide acclaim (and an Academy Award). Music is central to this movie about the various owners of a violin over three centuries, the red-stained violin becoming the focal character. Corigliano made the bold choice of scoring the film with only strings. This might sound like an obvious choice for a solo instrument soundtrack but the music for *The Red Violin* is scored for multiple instruments and the absence of percussion and other sections of the orchestra is very tricky. French director François Girard trusted Corigliano's decision and the resulting score is so rich and full bodied that the listener does not notice the unconventional approach. There is a haunting musical theme for the red violin itself and various other themes for the different characters in various time periods. Sometimes the music is a bit discordant, the different string instruments working against each other.

Then there are other sections using a solo violin (played by Joshua Bell) or vocal chants that make this score so special. Corigliano's music for *The Red Violin* has been heard in the concert hall and ranks with his other classical accomplishments. (Parts of the *Altered States* score were later performed in concert halls as "Three Hallucinations for Orchestra" and themes from *Revolution* have reappeared in some of Corigliano's symphonies.) Few composers for the movies have managed to make such an impact as Corigliano has with only three movies. Biography: *John Corigliano*, Mary Lou Humphrey (1994). Official website: www.johncorigliano.com

Credits

Year	Film	Director
1980	*Altered States* (AAN)	Ken Russell (USA)
1985	*Revolution* (BAFTA)	Hugh Hudson (UK/Norway)
1998	*The Red Violin* (AA)	François Girard (Canada/Italy/USA)

DANNA, Mychael (b. 1958) A Canadian-born composer and orchestrator known for his use of non-Western and electronic minimalist music in his compositions, he has scored nearly one hundred movies, which are usually off-beat and/or unique.

Mychael Danna was born in Winnipeg, Manitoba, Canada, but was still an infant when his family moved to Burlington, Ontario. Danna studied composition at the University of Toronto on a music scholarship and while in that city was for five years the composer-in-residence for the famous McLaughlin Planetarium, writing music for the many star shows. He also pursued writing for the ballet, later composing major works for the Royal Winnipeg Ballet. Although he scored some short films and one feature in the late 1970s, Danna's movie career did not take off until a decade later when he wrote the music for *Family Viewing* by innovative Canadian director Atom Egoyan. Danna's unconventional music was well paired with Egoyan's experimental approach to theatre and filmmaking and the two men have gone on to collaborate on eleven subsequent films, most memorably *Exotica, The Sweet Hereafter, Ararat*, and *Chloe*. Another director Danna has had a fruitful relationship with is Chinese American Ang Lee, working together on *The Ice Storm, Ride with the Devil*, and *Life of Pi*. This last is among the popular movies Danna has scored outside of Canada; others include *Monsoon Wedding, Vanity Fair, Being Julia, Capote, Little Miss Sunshine, Tideland, (500) Days of Summer, The Imaginarium of Doctor Parnassus, The Time Traveler's Wife, Moneyball*, and *Girl, Interrupted*. He has also scored such TV movies as *Gross Misconduct: The Life of Brian Spencer* (1993), *Hush Little Baby* (1994), *Dangerous Offender: The Marlene Moore Story* (1996), *At the End of the Day: The Sue Rodriguez Story* (1998), *Stranger Inside* (2001), and *The Matthew Shepard Story* (2002), as well as such popular series and miniseries as *Camelot, Road to Avonlea, New Amsterdam, Dollhouse*, and *World without End*. Danna sometimes cowrites with his brother, composer Jeff Danna, and, because his wife, Aparna, is from India, he has scored several films with Hindu themes, characters, or locations.

The main theme for the Canadian film *Exotica* has all the characteristics of Danna's musical style: pulsating electronic bass, chanting voices filtered through a synthesizer, ethnic instruments ranging from a sitar to primitive flutes, and minimalist musical lines that avoid melody at all costs. Other passages in the score have a definite Indian sound, there is a space-age theme with a solo clarinet playing against echoing vibrations, and tribal drums meet with electric bass guitar in a "pagan" theme. As strange as it all sounds, the score does not strike one as all that avant-garde when heard with the piercing images on the screen. It is quite clear Egoyan and Danna are soul mates in this kind of filmmaking. For a very different kind of movie, *The Sweet Hereafter*, both men shift gears radically and are still in sync. This disturbing drama is about a small town shattered by the effects of a school bus accident. While Danna's electronic and ethnic instruments and use of repetitive musical phrases are still present, the score is very accessible. The sound of a surreal funeral march with moaning electronics seems to be the only way to express the tumultuous grief of these people. Much lighter in tone, but still with a haunting subtext, is *Monsoon Wedding*. Set in contemporary India, the events surrounding a lavish wedding are scored with an effective mashup of the traditional and the modern. The music is often exotic yet there is a romantic theme played on piano and strings that is very Western. *Girl, Interrupted*, a psychological drama about a mental institution, is set in the late 1960s but Danna's score makes little reference to the outside world. Considering the subject matter, the music is surprisingly soothing at times, as a solo guitar is enhanced by soft electronic sounds in the background or a flute wavers as chimes overpower the near melody. The Palestinian film *The Nativity Story* tells a familiar biblical story and Danna even quotes some traditional Christmas hymns, but much of the score is a subdued version of what he does best. There are ethereal female voices that are accompanied by simple flutes, drumming that competes with vibrating electronics, harsh military drums and percussion for the Romans, and lyrical passages with plucked strings that almost sound medieval.

Danna's Hollywood movies may be less experimental than his Canadian and foreign ones but he does not abandon his style. The biographical *Capote*, which is as much about a famous murder as it is about the famous author (played by Philip Seymour Hoffman), has a chilling score that seems to haunt the listener on different levels. The low horns and restless strings are not so suspenseful as they are ominous. Again Danna eschews overt melody and relies on chords, electronic sounds, or deep strings moaning with long musical lines that do not resolve. Throughout the soundtrack a lone piano returns to attempt a soothing melody but only adds another chill to this very subtle and disconcerting score. For the cockeyed comedy *Little Miss Sunshine*, Danna uses the piano and a repetitive series of guitar chords and plucked strings to convey the frantic nature of these hopelessly clueless characters. The travel music throughout is breezy with thumping percussion, strumming guitars, and a solo whistler. With its Latin beat, the music resembles a crazy western galloping theme. This is a silly and giddy score and perhaps unique for Danna. *Life of Pi* is perhaps the most unconventional Hollywood movie that Danna has scored; it is also one of the most popular of his screen credits. An unusual tale told in retrospect, the film offered Danna some exciting opportunities for music. He opens the movie with a traditional-sounding Hindu lullaby sung in Hindi by a solo female backed by traditional instruments of the culture. Once the plot goes to sea, these Indian sounds get more mystical and even surreal. A variety of non-Asian instruments are added, the voices heard are less real, and the tone is more mythic. Some of the animals that Pi (Suraj Sharma) encounters while adrift on a lifeboat have their own theme, such as an echoing passage punctuated with muted chimes for the whale that symphonically grows as the giant emerges. The flying fish are scored with frenzied strings and exuberant flutes. As for the tiger that is central to the story and theme, Danna creates a theme that is menacing, majestic, and magical. While the score for *Life of Pi* is not quite avant-garde, it is a fascinating example of an innovative composer working within the confines of a mainstream movie hit and staying true to his vision concerning screen music. Official website: www.mychaeldanna.com.

Credits

(all films Canada unless stated otherwise)

Year	Film	Director
1978	*Metal Messiah*	Tibor Takács
1987	*Caribe*	Michael Kennedy
1988	*Family Viewing*	Atom Egoyan
1988	*Blood Relations*	Graeme Campbell (Canada/USA)
1988	*Murder One*	Graeme Campbell (USA/Canada)
1989	*Termini Station*	Allan King
1989	*Cold Comfort*	Vic Sarin
1989	*Speaking Parts*	Atom Egoyan
1989	*One Man Out*	Michael Kennedy (USA/Canada/Mexico)
1990	*Still Life: The Fine Art of Murder*	Graeme Campbell
1991	*The Big Slice*	John Bradshaw (USA/Canada)
1991	*The Adjuster*	Atom Egoyan
1993	*Ordinary Magic*	Giles Walker
1994	*Exotica*	Atom Egoyan
1994	*The Darling Family*	Alan Zweig
1994	*Dance Me Outside*	Bruce McDonald
1994	*Narmada: A Valley Rises*	Ali Kazimi
1995	*Johnny Mnemonic*	Robert Longo (Canada/USA)
1996	*Lilies*	John Greyson
1996	*Kama Sutra: A Tale of Love*	Mira Nair (UK/India/USA)
1997	*The Ice Storm*	Ang Lee (USA)
1997	*The Sweet Hereafter*	Atom Egoyan
1997	*Between the Lines* (aka *Regeneration*)	Gillies MacKinnon (UK/Canada)
1999	*The Confession*	David Hugh Jones (USA)

Year	Film	Director
1999	8MM	Joel Schumacher (USA/Germany)
1999	Felicia's Journey	Atom Egoyan (Canada/UK)
1999	Ride with the Devil	Ang Lee (USA)
1999	Girl, Interrupted	James Mangold (USA/Germany)
2000	Bounce	Don Roos (USA)
2001	Green Dragon	Timothy Linh Bui (USA)
2001	Monsoon Wedding	Mira Nair (India/USA/Italy)
2001	Hearts in Atlantis	Scott Hicks (USA/Australia)
2002	Ararat	Atom Egoyan (Canada/France)
2002	The Guys	Jim Simpson (USA)
2002	Antwone Fisher	Denzel Washington (USA)
2003	Shattered Glass	Billy Ray (USA/Canada)
2003	The Snow Walker	Charles Martin Smith
2004	Vanity Fair	Mira Nair (USA/UK/India)
2004	Being Julia	István Szabó (Canada/USA/Hungary/UK)
2005	Aurora Borealis	James C. E. Burke (USA/Canada)
2005	Where the Truth Lies	Atom Egoyan (Canada/UK)
2005	Capote	Bennett Miller (USA/Canada)
2005	Water	Deepa Mehta (Canada/India)
2005	Tideland	Terry Gilliam (UK/Canada)
2005	Eve and the Fire Horse	Julia Kwan
2006	Little Miss Sunshine	Jonathan Dayton, Valerie Faris (USA)
2006	Lonely Hearts	Todd Robinson (Germany/USA)
2006	The Nativity Story	Catherine Hardwicke (USA)
2007	Breach	Billy Ray (USA)
2007	Fracture	Gregory Hoblit (USA/Germany)
2007	Surf's Up	Ash Brannon, Chris Buck (USA)
2008	Trucker	James Mottern (USA)
2008	Adoration	Atom Egoyan
2008	Stone of Destiny	Charles Martin Smith (Canada/UK)
2008	Heaven on Earth	Deepa Mehta
2008	Management	Stephen Belber (USA)
2008	Lakeview Terrace	Neil LaBute (USA)
2008	Pomegranates and Myrrh	Najwa Najjar (Palestine)
2009	(500) Days of Summer	Marc Webb (USA)
2009	The Imaginarium of Doctor Parnassus	Terry Gilliam (UK/Canada/France)
2009	The Time Traveler's Wife	Robert Schwentke (USA)
2009	Chloe	Atom Egoyan (USA/Canada/France)
2009	Cooking with Stella	Dilip Mehta (Canada/India)
2010	Going the Distance	Nanette Burstein (USA)
2010	The Whistleblower	Larysa Kondracki (Germany/Canada/USA)
2011	Moneyball	Bennett Miller (USA)
2012	Life of Pi (AA;AAN*; GG; BAFTA-N)	Ang Lee (USA/Taiwan/UK)
2013	Devil's Knot	Atom Egoyan (USA)
2014	Foxcatcher	Bennett Miller (USA)
2014	The Captive	Atom Egoyan

DARING, Mason (b. 1949) A rock musician and movie and television composer known for the diverse nature of his music, he has written over seventy TV and film scores, including seventeen movies directed by John Sayles.

Kevin Mason Daring was born in Philadelphia and grew up in various cities in the Northeast because of his father's job with General Electric. Daring began playing trumpet in fourth grade, guitar in the seventh grade, and then played in a rock band in high school and college. After studying music at Amherst College, he earned a law degree from Suffolk Law School and began his legal career in 1977. Daring continued to compose and play music while he was acting as legal counsel for the independent movie production *Return of the Secaucus 7* in 1979. Director John Sayles heard some of Daring's music and incorporated it into the soundtrack. Later that same year, Daring wrote the full score for Sayles's *Lianna*. The two men have collaborated often since then, resulting in such memorable movies as *The Brother from Another Planet, Matewan, Eight Men Out, City of Hope, The Secret of Roan Inish, Passion Fish, Lone Star, Limbo, Men with Guns, Honeydripper*, and *Sunshine State*. By 1984, Daring gave up law and became a full-time composer for films and television. His notable movies without Sayles include *Dogfight, The Opposite of Sex, Music of the Heart, Where the Heart Is, Wild Hearts Can't Be Broken*, and *Walker Payne*. He has written music for such television series as *Adventure, Nova, State of Mind, The American Experience*, and *Frontline*, as well as over twenty TV movies and miniseries, including *Jenny's Song* (1988), *Murder in Mississippi* (1990), *Getting Out* (1994), *The Old Curiosity Shop* (1995), *Hidden in America* (1996), *Evidence of Blood* (1998), *From the Earth to the Moon* (1998), *Bailey's Mistake* (2001), and *A Separate Peace* (2004). Daring has also scored several film shorts and documentaries, and has his own record label, Daring Records, through which he releases some of his music. He has taught college music courses and continues to perform, often with singer Jeanie Stahl.

Just as Sayles is remarkable for the eclectic nature of his movies, so too is Daring's screen music almost chameleon in nature. He has a talent for creating locale through music and those locales are diverse, ranging from Ireland for *The Secret of Roan Inish* and the Texas-Mexico border country for *Lone Star* to the Louisiana bayou for *Passion Fish* and Central America for *Men with Guns*. Daring uses everything from a full orchestra to a solo piano to capture the spirit of each film. Consequently it is difficult to make any generalization about his music except for its high quality. *Eight Men Out*, about the 1919 White Sox baseball scandal, has a Roaring Twenties score filled with Charleston tunes and Dixieland jazz, all in contrast with the sad tale being told. Set in the same time period but in the hills of West Virginia, *Matewan* is filled with cheerful hillbilly music that is often at odds with the grim story of a miners' strike. The exuberant fiddles play with a forced liveliness and there are some rhythmic passages with harmonica, scrub boards, mouth harp, and other backwoods instruments that reveal the spirit behind these troubled people. Daring also composed an original anthem for the miners that sounds authentic and is stirring in its simplicity. *Lone Star*, about a forty-year-old murder that is unearthed in a Texas border town, has a country music score yet the featured instrument in many of

the passages is a lone piano. *Passion Fish*, a character drama set in contemporary rural Louisiana, has a sparkling Mississippi delta blues score played on bayou instruments as well as some delightful guitar solos with fancy fingering.

Daring moves away from folk to a more classically flavored score for *Wild Hearts Can't Be Broken*. Set during the Depression, a rebellious teenager (Gabrielle Anwar) finds herself when she performs a horse diving act for a carnival show. There is a strings and reeds theme that is weighty yet optimistic as it moves from tentative chords to a full-bodied melody. The score also includes a melancholy violin passage that intermittently comes alive in unexpected places and a guitar and clarinet passage that is restless yet determined and confident. Also far from folk is the offbeat sci-fi comedy-drama *The Brother from Another Planet*, in which a mute alien (Joe Morton) is pursued through Harlem by intergalactic bounty hunters. Daring's score (written with Martin Brody) is a vivacious mix of contemporary urban sounds. A funky blues theme heard on trumpets with electronic backup is the recurring theme but there is also a swirling synthesized motif with vibrant percussion and insistent sound effects, some hot salsa music, and a chaotic sci-fi piece of music with electric organ playing frantically.

For many, Daring's finest score is the Irish-flavored one he wrote for the fantasy *The Secret of Roan Inish*. When ten-year-old Fiona (Jeni Courtney) is sent to live with her grandparents in a fishing village on the Irish coast, she delves into legend and the past and searches for a boy raised by a human-seal creature. The score's main theme, first heard on a solo Irish flute, is both haunting and evocative, the sound being very primitive and raw. When other instruments join in, the piece becomes more romantic but remains just as earthy. Another passage is a meandering piece played on various solo Hibernian instruments (whistles, uilleann pipes, Celtic harp, bodhran drums, etc.), which is propelled forward by its confident air. There is also a zesty fiddle theme with orchestral string accompaniment, a chilling lament with chanting voices and moaning strings and pipes, and a soaring lullaby with slides and vibrato that is closer to a dirge than a soothing piece. Although Daring based some of this music on traditional Irish tunes, he gives them such a mystical arrangement that the score often has a very modern tone. Comparing the music in *The Secret of Roan Inish* to other Daring scores is really a matter of apples and oranges; each is a life form of its own. Official website: www.masondaring.com.

Credits

(all films USA unless stated otherwise)

Year	Film	Director
1979	*Lianna*	John Sayles
1984	*The Brother from Another Planet*	John Sayles
1985	*Key Exchange*	Barnet Kellman
1986	*Osa*	Oleg Egorov
1987	*Matewan*	John Sayles
1987	*Shallow Grave*	Richard Styles
1988	*Eight Men Out*	John Sayles
1990	*Little Vegas*	Perry Lang
1991	*Wild Hearts Can't Be Broken*	Steve Miner
1991	*Dogfight*	Nancy Savoca
1991	*City of Hope*	John Sayles
1992	*Fathers & Sons*	Paul Mones
1992	*Passion Fish*	John Sayles
1993	*Ed and His Dead Mother*	Jonathan Wacks
1994	*The Secret of Roan Inish*	John Sayles (USA/Ireland)
1995	*She Lives to Ride*	Alice Stone
1996	*Lone Star*	John Sayles
1997	*Prefontaine*	Steve James
1997	*Men with Guns*	John Sayles
1997	*Cold Around the Heart*	John Ridley
1998	*The Opposite of Sex*	Don Roos
1999	*A Walk on the Moon* (aka *Blouse Man*)	Tony Goldwyn (USA/Australia)
1999	*Limbo*	John Sayles
1999	*Music of the Heart* (aka *50 Violins*)	Wes Craven
2000	*George Wallace: Settin' the Woods on Fire*	Daniel McCabe, Paul Stekler
2000	*Where the Heart Is*	Matt Williams
2001	*Say It Isn't So*	J. B. Rogers
2002	*Sunshine State*	John Sayles
2003	*Casa de Los Babys*	John Sayles (USA/Mexico)
2004	*Silver City*	John Sayles
2006	*Walker Payne* (aka *Walker*)	Matt Williams
2007	*Honeydripper*	John Sayles
2010	*Amigo* (aka *Baryo*)	John Sayles
2013	*Go for Sisters*	John Sayles

DAVIS, Carl (b. 1936) A renowned conductor of the concert hall and a prolific composer for British television, he is also known for his new scores for classic silent movies.

Carl Davis was born in the New York City's borough of Brooklyn and began piano lessons at the age of seven. Davis devoured classical music, ballet, opera, and popular music as a teenager and studied music privately in the States and in Europe. Davis began conducting in Manhattan, eventually working his way up to the New York City Opera and the Robert Shaw Chorale. He started composing music at the age of eighteen and became involved in scoring musical revues. In 1959 he wrote the music for a topical Off-Broadway revue called *Diversions*, which won some awards. The show traveled to the Edinburgh Festival in 1961 and Davis went with it, remaining in Britain ever since. *Diversions* caught the attention of producer-writer Ned Sherrin, who hired Davis to write the theme song for a new TV program, *That Was the Week That Was*. The show was a long-running success and Davis was hired to score series, TV movies, and miniseries. By the 1970s he was considered the top television composer in Britain, with many popular works to his credit, including *The Snow Goose* (1971), *War & Peace* (1972), *Our Mutual Friend* (1976), *The Snow Queen* (1976), *Treasure*

Island (1977), *The Mayor of Casterbridge* (1978), *Wuthering Heights* (1978), *Oppenheimer* (1980), *Private Schulz* (1981), *The Far Pavilions* (1984), *Murrow* (1986), *The Yellow Wallpaper* (1989), *The Crucifer of Blood* (1991), *Covington Cross* (1992), *Oliver's Travels* (1995), *Pride and Prejudice* (1995), *The Great Gatsby* (2000), *Cranford* (2007), and *Upstairs Downstairs* (2012). With over one hundred productions to his credit, Davis is considered the dean of British television music. He has also composed ballets, stage musicals, concert pieces, and music for special events, as with the *Liverpool Oratorio* with Paul McCartney and the music for BBC coverage of the 2006 FIFA World Cup.

Although Davis started scoring feature films in 1969, most of his credits were forgettable British comedies and he concentrated on television where he was usually given high-quality projects to work on. In 1980 he was asked to write a new score for a restored version of *Napoleon*, Abel Gance's 1927 French epic. The mostly forgotten silent film was rediscovered and embraced by the public and Davis's massive score was roundly acclaimed. Davis himself conducted the orchestra in the recording studio and in the live premiere performance. Over the next twenty years, Davis wrote new scores for twenty-two silent movies, including beloved comedies featuring Harold Lloyd and Buster Keaton and such notable works as *The Phantom of the Opera*, *Intolerance*, *Flesh and the Devil*, *The Crowd*, *It*, *The Big Parade*, and *Ben-Hur*. Davis has scored only a limited number of new feature films, but the list includes some outstanding documentaries, as with *Anne Frank Remembered*, *Liberation*, *Fragments of Isabella*, *Champions*, and *Garbo*, and memorable dramas, such as *The Rainbow*, *The French Lieutenant's Woman*, and *Widows' Peak*.

Writing new music for silent films has its challenges and Davis must be applauded for the way he has successfully composed music that is appropriate for the period of the action, for the time of the movie's creation, and for modern audiences. The six-hour *Napoleon* encompasses the Corsican general's youth, early military career, the French Revolution, and his later conquests, all done on a giant scale yet never losing sight of the central character (played as an adult by Albert Dieudonné). The score is similarly diverse and grandiose yet has some tender moments as well. The main theme is slow and stately as it is led by an oboe rather than a military trumpet. The huge battles are matched by a big symphonic sound, yet some

of the more intriguing selections are on a more human scale. A snowball fight among schoolboys is scored with frivolous glee, while Napoleon's dream of grandeur is a fervent and chaotic rhapsody. "The Marseillaise" turns up as expected, but there are some interesting variations on the familiar anthem. (The following year Carmine Coppola composed another score for *Napoleon*, and it was premiered in New York City.) Another ambitious epic, D. W. Griffith's *Intolerance*, has four stories to tell, and Davis offers four scores. The Babylon story is the most visually impressive sequence and the music is splendid. One can hear in the music the marching of the elephants, the exotic blasts of horns, and the frenzied dancing of the slave girls. The modern story uses jazz, the Christ tale has its hymn-like passages, and the St. Bartholomew's Day Massacre is vigorously classical. It is all held together by a lyrical theme that is heard as a mother (Lillian Gish) rocks a cradle through time. Davis mostly avoids organ music clichés in *The Phantom of the Opera*, but that instrument is central to the plot. There are some grand passages that sound like modern sci-fi music, others that are 1920s avant-garde. The Phantom (Lon Chaney) has two contrasting themes, each reflecting the opposing forces within him; as the plot climaxes, the two themes begin to fuse. Perhaps Davis's finest reinterpreting of the silent epic can be found in *Ben-Hur*. The score has a majesty reminiscent of Richard Strauss and a lightness as delicate as Camille Saint-Saëns. The Roman marches are weighty, the fanfares are exultant, the scenes of pathos are filled with sweeping passion, and the mystical moments are scored with music that seems to float. The silent *Ben-Hur* is a magnificent film regardless of which score one hears, but Davis's version adds to the epic's greatness.

The silent comedies offer different scoring challenges. Because the scale is smaller, the orchestrations tend to be less symphonic. Buster Keaton's *The General* has a merry main theme that suggests a frolic, then the rhythm of the famous train sets the cue for the engine's own musical theme. The Civil War era is suggested lightly rather than obviously. The bittersweet aspect of Keaton's screen persona is portrayed by some minor-key passages that never get mawkish. The inventive train chase has some surprisingly subtle sections amid the thrilling action music. Harold Lloyd's *Safety Last* has a delicate piano theme that flutters casually, never coming on too strong; it is an accurate way of describing Lloyd's screen persona. The piano remains the featured instrument throughout, although the strings are used effectively to fill out the sound when more weight is required. It might be pointed out at this point that all of the silents that Davis has scored are superb examples of filmmaking and, as any composer might state, it is much easier to score a great movie than a mediocre one. Yet Davis has found a way to bring new music to accompany old riches, and that is not such an easy task.

Among the thirty new films that Davis has scored, a handful are exceptional. Perhaps the two that stand out the most are *Champions* and *The French Lieutenant's Woman*. The former is a biopic about the jockey Bob Champion (John Hurt), who battled cancer to make a comeback at the Grand National. The score is poetic and inspiring but not in an insipid way. Piano and strings fly though the air as trumpets bravely push the theme forward. The movie itself often slips into easy melodrama and surefire emotional scenes, but the score strikes one as self-aware

and so doggedly determined that it rises above the easy heartstrings. Some of the music for the horse racing is so vibrant and electric that it seems like a folk dance played at a frenzied pace. Quite different is the quieter score for *The French Lieutenant's Woman*, a movie about making a movie of the enigmatic best seller by John Fowles. The Victorian period is conveyed through the choice of various string instruments, but it is the sorrowful violin solo that captures the modern tone of the movie. The story is about unfulfilled or lost love and the romantic score follows suit by not resolving itself, often leaving melodies unfinished and sustained notes fading away. One doesn't hear this kind of scoring in Davis's silent film treatments because movies then were rarely as dark and chilly as *The French Lieutenant's Woman*. As he did with all those wonderful scores for period television movies, Davis knows where a story's temperament lies and sets that to music. Official website: www.carldaviscollection.com.

Credits

(all films USA unless stated otherwise)

Year	Film	Director
1968	The Bofors Gun	Jack Gold (UK)
1970	Praise Marx and Pass the Ammunition	Maurice Hatton (UK)
1970	The Only Way	Bent Christensen (Denmark/USA/UK)
1971	Up Pompeii	Bob Kellett (UK)
1971	I, Monster	Stephen Weeks (UK)
1971	The Chastity Belt	Bob Kellett (UK)
1972	What Became of Jack and Jill?	Bill Bain (UK)
1972	Rentadick	Jim Clark (UK)
1973	The Lovers!	Herbert Wise (UK)
1973	Conflict	Jack Gold
1975	Man Friday	Jack Gold (UK/USA)
1978	The Sailor's Return	Jack Gold (UK)
1979	Birth of the Beatles	Richard Marquand
1980	Napoleon (1927)	Abel Gance (France)
1981	The French Lieutenant's Woman (BAFTA)	Karel Reisz (UK)
1981	The Crowd (1928)	King Vidor
1982	Show People (1928)	King Vidor
1983	A Woman of Affairs (1928)	Clarence Brown
1983	The Wind (1928)	Victor Sjöström
1984	Champions	John Irvin (UK)
1984	Our Hospitality (1923)	John G. Blystone, Buster Keaton
1984	George Stevens: A Filmmaker's Journey	George Stevens Jr.
1985	The Strong Man (1926)	Frank Capra
1985	The Eagle (1925)	Clarence Brown
1985	King David	Bruce Beresford (UK/USA)
1986	Greed (1924)	Erich von Stroheim
1986	The Student Prince in Old Heidelberg (1927)	Ernst Lubitsch, John M. Stahl
1987	The General (1926)	Clyde Bruckman, Buster Keaton
1987	Ben-Hur (1925)	Fred Niblo, etc.

Year	Film	Director
1988	Flesh and the Devil (1926)	Clarence Brown
1988	The Girl in a Swing	Gordon Hessler (USA/UK)
1988	The Big Parade (1925)	King Vidor, George W. Hill
1989	Scandal	Michael Caton-Jones (UK)
1989	Intolerance (1916)	D. W. Griffith
1989	The Rainbow	Ken Russell (UK/USA)
1989	Fragments of Isabella	Ronan O'Leary (Ireland)
1990	Safety Last (1923)	Fred C. Newmeyer, Sam Taylor
1990	Frankenstein Unbound	Roger Corman
1990	The Kid Brother (1927)	Ted Wilde, etc.
1991	Echoes That Remain	Arnold Schwartzman
1992	It (1927)	Clarence G. Badger, Josef von Sternberg
1992	Speedy (1928)	Ted Wilde
1993	The Four Horsemen of the Apocalypse (1921)	Rex Ingram
1993	The Trial	David Hugh Jones (UK)
1994	Widows' Peak	John Irvin (UK/Ireland)
1994	Liberation	Arnold Schwartzman
1995	Anne Frank Remembered	Jon Blair (USA/UK/Netherlands)
1996	The Phantom of the Opera (1925)	Rupert Julian, Lon Chaney
1998	The Raft of Medusa	Iradj Azimi (France)
1999	The Iron Mask (1929)	Allan Dwan
2002	The Book of Eve	Claude Fournier (Canada)
2004	Mothers and Daughters	David Conolly, Hannah Davis (UK)
2005	Garbo	Christopher Bird, Kevin Brownlow
2005	I'm King Kong! The Exploits of Merian C. Cooper	Christopher Bird, Kevin Brownlow
2008	The Understudy	David Conolly, Hannah Davis (UK)

DAVIS, Don (b. 1957) A notable conductor and arranger who was a busy television composer in the 1990s, he has also scored twenty-one feature films, mostly in the horror, action, and sci-fi genres.

Donald Romain Davis was born in Anaheim, California, and began taking trumpet and piano lessons when he was nine. A few years later Davis was writing original music and in high school he arranged, composed, and led a jazz ensemble. He studied music theory, composition, and orchestration privately and at UCLA, moving from jazz and rock into avant-garde music even as he composed chamber orchestra pieces. Television-film composer Joe Harnell was impressed with Davis's music, acted as a mentor for the young composer, and in 1978 hired him as an orchestrator for Harnell's music for the popular TV series *The Incredible Hulk*.

After orchestrating some music for the series *Hart to Hart*, Davis was asked in 1983 to score four episodes of the show, beginning his prolific television composing career. His music for the series *Beauty and the Beast* won him further recognition and awards. His first feature film score was for the sci-fi comedy *Hyperspace* in 1984, but

it was not until he wrote the music for the Wachowskis' oddball thriller *Bound* twelve years later that Davis was established as a movie as well as TV composer. His most popular films were made with Andy and Lana Wachowski: the blockbuster sci-fi action movie *The Matrix* and its two sequels, *The Matrix Reloaded* and *The Matrix Revolutions*. With other directors Davis scored such movies as *The Lesser Evil, House on Haunted Hill, Antitrust, Ballistic: Ecks vs. Sever, The Unsaid, The Good Life,* and *Ten Inch Hero*. His thirty-five TV movies include *A Stoning in Fulham County* (1988), *Home Fires Burning* (1989), *A Little Piece of Heaven* (1991), *Lies Before Kisses* (1991), *Leave of Absence* (1984), *The Beast* (1996), *House of Frankenstein* (1997), *Route 9* (1998), *Murder in Greenwich* (2002), and *Augusta, Gone* (2006). Among the other television series he has scored are *My Life and Times, Tiny Toon Adventures, Capitol Critters, SeaQuest 2032, Taz-Mania,* and *Star Trek: The Next Generation*. Davis has worked as conductor and/or orchestrator on several other movies and television shows, and he has written an opera, *Rio de Sangre*, which has been produced in Milwaukee, Los Angeles, and New York City.

The Matrix scores combine many of Davis's musical interests (pop, synthesized music, avant-garde forms) and were orchestrated for full orchestra and two traditional grand pianos and one "prepared" piano. Among the modern techniques Davis uses is having different sections of the orchestra echo each other at varying speeds, creating a mesmerizing and surreal effect. The main theme for *The Matrix* is an urgent piece with frantic violins, blaring brass, and racing pianos. As through much of the score, the music surges forward, pulls back for quiet but seething passages, then explodes again. Some themes are more electronic sound effects than music yet there are moments of pure music as some instruments sustain chords while others flirt with melody without ever resolving. Since *The Matrix* is about a computer programmer (Keanu Reeves) who also has another identity as a hacker with ties to a nightmarish future, this musical kind of duplicity is highly effective. The scores for *The Matrix Reloaded* and *The Matrix Revolutions* provide variations on Davis's original concept. The main theme for the former is a frantic jazz piece in which keyboard and strings seem to whiz by chaotically. *The Matrix Revolutions* uses robust choral sections and tribal chanting in between manic pounding of percussion and brass that slide up and down the scale.

Unlike *The Matrix* films, the action thriller *Ballistic: Ecks vs. Sever* bombed at the box office, but its music is commendable. It has a rock score with Asian musical touches, mournful chanting, various kinds of strings at play, and propulsive percussion of different types, and it features an electric guitar with synthesized accents. The caper thriller *Bound*, on the other hand, has a fairly conventional suspense score with menacing chords and tingling musical phrases on the piano. The main theme is seductive but chilly with sustained synthesized chords and glissandos, but the tone is very traditional even if the Wachowskis' movie is not. A different kind of thriller is *Antitrust*, about a computer software company with a sinister agenda. Davis wrote a gripping main theme in which synthesized instruments and sounds are heard over a lively dance theme played on guitar and primitive pipes. Later in the film a romantic version of the same theme is surprisingly gentle. The score also has a bold anthem that is a series of little fanfares until it ultimately climaxes like a victory march. The melodrama *The Lesser Evil*, about four adults who are forced to confront a crime they committed together as teenagers, has one of Davis's most subtle scores. The main theme features a piano that casually repeats a musical phrase as muted brass instruments provide a restless countermelody. This results in a pleasing combination but one with a sense of foreboding and grief as well.

Davis's classical side is evident in his score for the psychological drama *The Unsaid*. A troubled psychotherapist (Andy Garcia) gets obsessed with a teenage patient who reminds him of his son who committed suicide. The main theme is a graceful piano and string piece that floats through the air, lightweight yet substantial enough to support an oboe solo that moves in and out of the serenade. There is also an intoxicating passage in which a delicate piano and wavering strings tentatively move into a melancholy crescendo then lighten up again, a poignant theme in which a solo flute and other woodwinds serenely dance above a solo piano, and a dreamlike theme with echoing sustained strings that is disturbing without ever getting harsh or too fast. This is all a far cry from the avant-garde bombast of *The Matrix* and a testament to Davis's versatility. Official website: www.dondavis.net.

Credits

(all films USA unless stated otherwise)

Year	Film	Director
1984	Hyperspace	Todd Durham
1988	Blackout (aka The Attic)	Doug Adams
1996	Bound (aka The Business)	Andy and Lana Wachowski
1997	Warriors of Virtue	Ronny Yu (USA/China)
1998	The Lesser Evil	David Mackay
1998	A League of Old Men	Allan Rich
1999	The Matrix	Andy and Lana Wachowski (USA/Australia)
1999	Universal Soldier: The Return	Mic Rodgers
1999	Turbulence 2: Fear of Flying	David Mackay

Year	Film	Director
1999	*House on Haunted Hill*	William Malone
2001	*Antitrust*	Peter Howitt
2001	*Valentine* (aka *Love Hurts*)	Jamie Blanks
2001	*The Unsaid* (aka *Sins of the Father*)	Tom McLoughlin (Canada/USA)
2001	*Behind Enemy Lines*	John Moore
2002	*Long Time Dead*	Marcus Adams (UK/France)
2002	*Ballistic: Ecks vs. Sever*	Wych Kaosayananda (USA/Germany)
2003	*The Matrix Reloaded* (aka *The Burly Man*)	Andy and Lana Wachowski (USA/Australia)
2003	*The Matrix Revolutions*	Andy and Lana Wachowski (USA/Australia)
2006	*The Marine*	John Bonito
2007	*The Good Life*	Stephen Berra (Canada/USA)
2007	*Ten Inch Hero*	David Mackay

DEBNEY, John (b. 1956) A prolific television and movie composer, he has scored over ninety feature films on diverse subjects, many of them popular animated and/or family movies.

He was born in Glendale, California, the son of Disney Studio producer Louis Debney, and began guitar lessons when he was six years old. While studying music composition at the California Institute of the Arts, Debney played in rock bands and started composing original music. Veteran TV composers Mike Post and Hoyt Curtin were his mentors after he graduated from college and helped Debney get his first jobs writing music for the small screen. His first movie credit was the score for the 1980 short *Deer in the Works* based on a Kurt Vonnegut Jr. story. Two years later Debney wrote music for an episode of *Walt Disney's Wonderful World of Color*, his first of many projects with that studio. Other television assignments followed, such as the series *The Disney Family Album*, *Fame*, *Police Academy*, *The Young Riders*, *A Pup Named Scooby-Doo*, *The Cape*, *SeaQuest 2032*, *Welcome to Pooh Corner*, and *Star Trek: The Next Generation*. Debney's first of over two dozen TV movies and miniseries was *Trenchcoat in Paradise* in 1989, followed by such titles as *The Face of Fear* (1990), *Into the Badlands* (1991), *Still Not Quite Human* (1992), *Johnny's Golden Quest* (1993), *Class of '61* (1993), *Praying Mantis* (1993), *The Halloween Tree* (1993), *In Pursuit of Honor* (1995), *Kansas* (1995), *Doctor Who* (1996), *Justice League of America* (1997), *Running Mates* (2000), *Gundam Savior* (2000), and *Hatfields & McCoys* (2012). He was nominated and won several Emmy Awards and in the 1980s and 1990s was one of the most in-demand composers in television.

Although Debney scored his first feature film in 1987 with the crime drama *The Wild Pair*, he was not widely recognized in Hollywood until his music for the Disney comic fantasy *Hocus Pocus* six years later. By the end of the 1990s, Debney was doing less television and more movies, soon becoming highly sought after for a variety of film projects. Among his many notable movies are *Not Since Casanova*, *Cutthroat Island*, *Liar Liar*, *I Know What You Did Last Summer*, *Paulie*, *My Favorite Martian*, *Inspector Gadget*, *Relative Values*, *The Relic*, *The Replacements*, *The Princess Diaries*, *Bruce Almighty*, *Elf*, *The Passion of the Christ*, *Duma*, *Dreamer: Inspired by a True Story*, *Idlewild*, *The Stoning of Soraya M.*, *Iron Man 2*, *Predators*, *No Strings Attached*, *The Change-Up*, and *The Call*, as well as such popular animated films as *Jetsons: The Movie*, *The Emperor's New Groove*, *Jimmy Neutron: Boy Genius*, *Chicken Little*, *Yogi Bear*, and *The Ant Bully*. Debney has also scored many live-action, documentary, and animated shorts, including two Disney cartoon favorites, *Sport Goofy in Soccermania* (1987) and *Runaway Brain* (1995).

While most screen composers first get recognized for their work on a grand fantasy or powerful drama, Debney established himself in Hollywood with his scores for lightweight projects. The Disney comic adventure *Hocus Pocus*, about three Salem witches (Bette Midler, Sarah Jessica Parker, and Kathy Najimy) returning in modern times to cause havoc, is funny rather than spooky and Debney's main theme, filled with eerie voices, fluttering flutes, and rushing brass, creates excitement rather than thrills. There is also a merry passage on strings that bounces and glides around an oboe solo, a lively waltz that musically twinkles and sparkles, an oddball march played on giddy woodwinds and pizzicato strings, and a swirling passage that seems to confidently race through the air along with the daffy trio of witches. It is a score bound to be noticed and it was. The very popular *Elf*, about a full-sized human (Will Ferrell) raised as one of Santa's elves, has music that is risible in a different way. The main theme is a jaunty polka that suggests a holiday carol but moves at a pop tempo. The score also includes a cockeyed whistling march with a goofy sense of freedom, a mock minuet played on reeds, a flowing passage that seems to climb a mountain and reach a magical crescendo, and a playful accordion and woodwind passage that sounds like a slaphappy walk through the park. The much-less-popular *Inspector Gadget*, a live-action cartoonish spoof of superpowered heroes, has a wacky main theme that is a silly march with a jazzy flavor and vocal accents, all punctuated by a police siren. On the other hand, the romantic comedy *Valentine's Day* has a lovely theme featuring guitar and clarinet that is tentative and shy at times, then breaks out in gliding melodic lines. Another romantic comedy, *The Princess Diaries*, has a score with a classical touch, as expected for a contemporary tale about a commoner (Anne Hathaway) who finds out she is really a princess. The main theme is a felicitous waltz with a magical, glowing quality; this is Cinderella music for a modern fable. Also memorable in the score is a regal string minuet that is far from stuffy and a violin lullaby that has a somber tone but moves forward all the same. *Bruce Almighty*, a comic fantasy about a TV reporter (Jim Carrey) who has to take over God's job for a while, has a surprisingly subdued and touching score. There is a delicate and mystical serenade featuring woodwinds and strings that aches with yearning, as well as a floating passage for piano, celestial voices, and orchestra that is solemn but free flowing.

Of Debney's many animated features, two stand out for their clever scores. The sarcastic *The Emperor's New Groove*, about an Incan emperor (David Spade) who is turned into a llama, has delightful music. The rock star Sting wrote and performed two satirical songs for the movie and Debney provided a soundtrack score that is very eclectic. There is a Big Band theme that swings with glee, a salsa tune that jumps with energy, charming traveling music in which various instruments make musical comments, and an emotive passage featuring harp and oboe that overflows with warmth. The broad action scenes are scored with rapid descending notes and pounding

tuba and percussion, yet it all always remains very playful. Although less successful, *Chicken Little* also has a satiric score. This spoof of the "sky is falling" tale has some deliciously slapstick music, such as a rousing western-like theme that mocks Elmer Bernstein's *The Magnificent Seven* score. There is some pseudo-Stravinsky music with a severe chorus and explosive orchestra, a funny passage played on a bluesy guitar and lazy clarinet, and a more serious theme, heard on a gentle piano, clarinet, and strings, that is heartfelt and just short of mushy.

In its own way, *Iron Man 2* is a form of animation and Debney wrote an action comic score that is often thrilling. The main propulsive theme has roaring brass, violent strings, passionate choral accents, and a sense of dominance that keeps up with the striking visuals. One passage has an electronic bass line with special sound effects and growling brass, while a quieter section has mourning brass and melancholy music that hesitates to move forward but at times dangles on sustained strings. Similar in content and sound is the action-packed *Predators*. There is an electronic main theme in which various kinds of percussion are overwhelmed by brass fanfares and forceful strings. In contrast are the two "dream" movies Debney scored. The horror-thriller *Dream House*, in which a family's perfect home is discovered to have a murderous past, has a driving main theme that moves from restless urgency to some graceful string sections, yet there is always a sense of doom hanging over every note. A later passage is more mellifluous as flute and clarinet rise up over the rest of the subdued orchestra, and there is an affecting theme that is soft and tentative as it strives to climb the scale. *Dreamer: Inspired by a True Story* is a family film about a young girl (Dakota Fanning) and her efforts to save an injured racehorse. The emotive main theme is first heard on solo piano, then slowly the music builds into a tripping piece featuring a solo violin with full orchestra playing its catchy five-note musical phrase. There is expansive music for the horse in full gallop that includes some rural instruments to add a rustic flavor, and the big race is scored with straining strings and brass that is truly exciting. More serious than any of the above is *The Stoning of Soraya M.*, a harrowing drama about a tragic incident in an Iranian town. Debney's main theme for the film includes Muslim chanting, a sorrowful bass violin, and insistent percussion, all creating a sense of ritual but also oppression as the tempo picks up and the anguish builds.

Debney's two most popular scores could not be more different. The pirate adventure *Cutthroat Island* is filled with grandiose music and high-flying panache. The main theme is a vigorous march with trumpet fanfares, rowdy percussion, stirring choral work, and bold orchestral glissandos. Also heard is a tender romantic theme played on harpsichord with a sad subtext, some fiery chase music and an energetic battle passage, and fervent music when the ship sets sail that conjures up a contagious sense of adventure. All this bombastic musical derring-do is a tribute to Erich Wolfgang Korngold and the other great composers of swashbuckling scores, and it is so well done that the music is more an homage than a pastiche. *Cutthroat Island* was a critical and box office dud, but the soundtrack found favor. So too did the score for Mel Gibson's controversial, gritty *The Passion of the Christ*. Debney uses electronic sound effects and synthesized instruments throughout the score to create a sense of mystery and awe. This might be far from authentic and in conflict with the movie's realistic portrayal of the last days in the life of Jesus (Jim Caviezel), yet it works. Among the many highlights in the score is an echoing choral chant that is chilling and even threatening, distorted ethnic instruments that give some authenticity even as they sound modern, sections that rely on various forms of percussion, and a passage that features a primitive flute playing an emotional lament. The crucifixion is scored with violent voices and screaming orchestra with moments of near silence in between, whereas the music for the resurrection has a mounting majesty as drums and choral voices join in a climactic hymn. The Oscar-nominated score was later turned into *The Passion of the Christ Symphony*, utilizing a large choir and orchestra as well as vocal and instrumental soloists, which was first presented in Rome with success. The music in *The Passion of the Christ* may be atypical of Debney's work, but is not surprising given the diversity of projects he had previously scored. Official website: www.johndebney.com.

Credits

(all films USA unless stated otherwise)

Year	Film	Director
1987	*The Wild Pair* (aka *Hollow Point*)	Beau Bridges
1988	*The Further Adventures of Tennessee Buck*	David Keith (Sri Lanka/USA)
1988	*Seven Hours to Judgement*	Beau Bridges
1988	*Not Since Casanova*	Brett Thompson
1990	*Jetsons: The Movie*	Joseph Barbera, William Hanna
1993	*Gunmen*	Deran Sarafian
1993	*Hocus Pocus*	Kenny Ortega
1994	*White Fang 2: Myth of the White Wolf*	Ken Olin
1994	*Little Giants* (aka *A Perfect Season*)	Duwayne Dungam
1995	*Chameleon*	Michael Pavone
1995	*Houseguest*	Randall Miller
1995	*Sudden Death*	Peter Hyams
1995	*Cutthroat Island*	Renny Harlin (USA/France/Italy/Germany)
1996	*Getting Away with Murder*	Harvey Miller (UK/USA)
1996	*Carpool*	Arthur Hiller
1997	*The Relic*	Peter Hyams (UK/Germany/Japan/USA/New Zealand)
1997	*Liar Liar*	Tom Shadyac
1997	*I Know What You Did Last Summer*	Jim Gillespie
1998	*Paulie* (aka *Polly, A Parrot's Tale*)	John Roberts
1998	*I'll Be Home for Christmas*	Arlene Sanford (USA/Canada)
1999	*My Favorite Martian*	Donald Petrie
1999	*Lost & Found*	Jeff Pollack
1999	*Inspector Gadget*	David Kellogg
1999	*Dick*	Andrew Fleming (France/Canada/USA)
1999	*Komodo*	Michael Lantieri (Australia/USA)
1999	*The Adventures of Elmo in Grouchland*	Gary Halvorson

Year	Film	Director
1999	End of Days	Peter Hyams
2000	Relative Values	Eric Styles (UK)
2000	The Replacements	Howard Deutch
2000	The Emperor's New Groove	Mark Dindal
2001	See Spot Run	John Whitesell (USA/Australia)
2001	Heartbreakers (aka Breakers)	David Mirkin
2001	Cats & Dogs	Lawrence Guterman (USA/Australia)
2001	The Princess Diaries	Garry Marshall
2001	Jimmy Neutron: Boy Genius	John A. Davis
2002	Snow Dogs (aka Winterdance)	Brian Levant (Canada/USA)
2002	Dragonfly	Tom Shadyac (USA/Germany)
2002	The Scorpion King	Chuck Russell (USA/Germany/Belgium)
2002	Spy Kids 2: Island of Lost Dreams	Robert Rodriguez
2002	The Tuxedo (aka T.U.X.)	Kevin Donovan
2002	The Hot Chick	Tom Brady
2003	Bruce Almighty	Tom Shadyac
2003	Elf	Jon Favreau (USA/Germany)
2004	Welcome to Mooseport (aka Mooseport)	Donald Petrie (USA/Germany)
2004	The Passion of the Christ (AAN)	Mel Gibson
2004	The Whole Ten Yards (aka The Whole Nine Yards 2)	Howard Deutch
2004	Raising Helen	Garry Marshall
2004	The Princess Diaries 2: Royal Engagement	Garry Marshall
2004	Christmas with the Kranks	Joe Roth
2005	The Pacifier	Adam Shankman (Canada/USA)
2005	Duma (aka How It Was with Dooms)	Carroll Ballard
2005	Dreamer: Inspired by a True Story	John Gatins
2005	Chicken Little	Mark Dindal
2005	Zathura: A Space Adventure (aka Jumanji 2)	John Favreau
2005	Cheaper by the Dozen 2	Adam Shankman (USA/Canada)
2006	Keeping Up with the Steins (aka Lucky 13)	Scott Marshall
2006	The Ant Bully	John A. Davis
2006	Barnyard	Steve Oedekerk (Germany/USA)
2006	Idlewild (aka My Life in Idlewild)	Bryan Barber
2006	Everyone's Hero	Colin Brady, etc. (Canada/USA)
2007	Georgia Rule	Garry Marshall
2007	Evan Almighty (aka Bruce Almighty 2)	Tom Shadyac
2008	Swing Vote	Joshua Michael Stern
2008	Meet Dave (aka Starship Dave)	Brian Robbins
2008	The Stoning of Soraya M.	Cyrus Nowrasteh
2008	My Best Friend's Girl (aka Bachelor No. 2)	Howard Deutch
2009	Hotel for Dogs	Thor Freudenthal (USA/Germany)
2009	Hannah Montana: The Movie	Peter Chelsom
2009	Aliens in the Attic (aka They Came from Upstairs)	John Schultz (USA/Canada)
2009	Old Dogs	Walt Becker
2010	Valentine's Day	Garry Marshall
2010	Iron Man 2	Jon Favreau, Kenneth Branagh
2010	Predators (aka Predator 3)	Nimród Antal
2010	Yogi Bear	Eric Brevig (USA/New Zealand)
2011	No Strings Attached (aka Friends with Benefits)	Ivan Reitman
2011	The Change-Up	David Dobkin
2011	Dream House	Jim Sheridan (USA/Canada)
2011	The Double	Michael Brandt
2011	New Year's Eve	Garry Marshall
2012	A Thousand Words	Brian Robbins
2012	The Three Stooges	Bobby and Peter Farrelly
2012	Alex Cross (aka Cross)	Rob Cohen
2013	Jobs	Joshua Michael Stern
2013	The Call (aka The Hive)	Brad Anderson

Year	Film	Director
2014	*Draft Day*	Ivan Reitman
2014	*Eliza Graves*	Brad Anderson
2014	*Walk of Shame*	Steven Brill
2014	*Broken Horses*	Vidhu Vinod Chopra
2015	*Christ the Lord: Out of Egypt*	Cyrus Nowrasteh

DELERUE, Georges (1925–1992) The very busy French composer who scored a wide variety of movies in Hollywood and Europe, he is perhaps best known for his nine films with director François Truffaut. Over a period of forty-two years, Delerue scored over 350 movies and television programs, as well as operas, ballets, chamber music, and theatre music, making him one of the most prolific composers of the twentieth century.

Georges Delerue was born in Roubaix, France, a sickly child who studied clarinet and then piano but had to drop out of the local music conservatory, Turgot Institute, in order to work at a factory and support his family. At the age of twenty he was able to enroll at the Conservatoire de Paris, paying for tuition by playing jazz piano in bars as well as for weddings and other social events. In the 1940s Delerue composed music for the theatre and ballet as he pursued conducting, winning some competitions in Italy and France. He began composing for television and served as the conductor of orchestras on French National Radio and Television even as he scored low-budget films throughout the 1950s. Delerue was first noticed as a screen composer with the 1957 fantasy *Amour de poche* (released in America as *Girl in His Pocket*) then found international recognition for the French New Wave classic *Hiroshima mon amour*, in which he shared composer credit with Giovanni Fisco. In 1960 he began to work with director Philippe de Broca, the two going on to collaborate on sixteen movies over the next three decades, including such international favorites as *That Man from Rio, Male Companion, Up to His Ears, King of Hearts, Devil by the Tail, Louise,* and *Chouans!* Delerue also worked with such renowned European directors as Jean-Luc Godard, Alain Renais, Ken Russell, Louis Malle, Jack Clayton, Claude Berri, Jules Dassin, Costa-Gavras, and Bernardo Bertolucci, but he is best remembered for his scores for Truffaut, including such notable movies as *Shoot the Piano Player, Jules and Jim, Love at Twenty, Day for Night, Love on the Run, The Woman Next Door,* and *The Last Metro.*

Because so many of the European films that Delerue scored were popular in the United States, Hollywood considered him a top composer and he often worked in the States. His first experience with American films was *Rapture* in 1965. Working with such diverse directors as Mike Nichols, George Roy Hill, Bruce Beresford, Norman Jewison, Fred Zinnemann, George Cukor, Peter Yates, and Oliver Stone, he scored such notable Hollywood movies as *A Little Romance, Platoon, Julia, Day of the Dolphin, Maxie, Steel Magnolias, Beaches, Rich and Famous, Crimes of the Heart, Biloxi Blues, The Black Stallion Returns, Agnes of God,* and *Silkwood.* Delerue continued his association with television over the decades, scoring many European series and miniseries, and he often worked in American television, composing the scores for such TV movies and miniseries as *The Borgias* (1981), *Love Thy Neighbor* (1984), *Silence of the Heart* (1984), *Deadly Intentions* (1985), *Women of Valor* (1986), *Sword of Gideon* (1986), *The Josephine Baker Story* (1991), and *Without Warning: The James Brady Story* (1991). He also never abandoned the stage and concert hall. Between 1948 and 1983, he composed music for the Comedie Français, Theatre du Marais, Theatre Fontaine, Festival de Nimes, Festival d'Avignon, and other renowned stage companies. Also among his credit are ten ballets, four operas, and a dozen light and sound spectaculars. Although Delerue won only one Oscar (for *A Little Romance*), he was much awarded in Europe and was named a Commander of Arts and Letters, a very distinguished French honor, before he died of a heart attack at the age of sixty-seven.

The French journal *Le Figaro* once described Delerue as the "Mozart of cinema," yet his music might be better described as eclectic, melodic, and dramatic, always with a classical touch. His screen scores are pure cinema, capturing the flavor of the subject matter with a bold and even fearless bravado. Few of his movie scores are in the grand Hollywood symphonic tradition because he rarely had a Tinseltown music budget to work with. Instead

GEORGES DELERUE. One of France's most respected screen composers, Delerue (right) collaborated with director François Truffaut on nine films. Their mutual admiration for each other can be seen in this photograph taken on the set of one of their last projects together, *The Last Metro* (1980). *Photofest*

he excelled in small movies that were filled with life and energy on-screen and on the soundtrack. For example, the simple but delightful noir comedy *Shoot the Piano Player* has a bouncy, honky-tonk score that is wryly satirical. The main character (Charles Aznavour) is a classically trained pianist but is reduced to playing lighthearted pieces in third-rate clubs. Delerue's music suggests melancholy even as it breezily pretends to look at life carelessly. *Shoot the Piano Player* was his first score for Truffaut, and the ambivalent sensibility of the director seemed to come alive in Delerue's music. For *Jules and Jim*, another ambivalent masterwork (this time by a beguiling ménage à trois consisting of Jeanne Moreau, Oskar Werner, and Henri Serre), the music manages to suggest a romantic frolic at times, a doomed and mysterious thriller at other times. But during the fatalistic climax of the movie, the music surprisingly gets less harsh and concludes on a winsome note, which makes *Jules and Jim* so bewitching. The Truffaut farce *Such a Gorgeous Kid Like Me* is far from ambivalent, and Delerue's score is frantic and funny, using the banjo at times because the cockeyed heroine (Bernadette Lafont) thinks she is a virtuoso on the American instrument. Another one of Truffaut's lighter movies, *Day for Night*, looks at moviemaking with an affectionate but self-deprecating tone. Delerue composed a very pseudo-Bach score that uses straining horns and furious violins, a baroque piece minus the pomp. There is also a classical flavor in his other scores for Truffaut. *The Last Metro* has a tripping theme that echoes Camille Saint-Saëns and other French masters while *Two English Girls* evokes the more melancholy work of those composers. *The Woman Next Door* has a more contemporary sound and the music has an urgency that leaves little doubt that this romance is headed to a fatal conclusion. If the music in *Jules and Jim* left the audience somewhat puzzled at the end, the score for *The Woman Next Door* closes with a sense of dramatic relief.

Yet there is so much more to Delerue's European scores than the Truffaut films, as delectable as they are. His music for de Broca's comedies is often sublimely charming. For the spy spoof *That Man from Rio*, he mixes Latin rhythms into the waltzing theme, the result being one long musical chase. A very different waltz is used in *King of Hearts*, de Broca's most internationally acclaimed film. A disarming farce about insanity, the movie is scored with gentle, gliding music that suggests a peaceful (if cockeyed) haven

safe from the insanity of World War I. For pure romanticism, there is Delerue's score for de Broca's *Louise* (*Chere Louise*), which avoids sentimentality even as a solo violin moves felicitously along. Other directors and other genres inspired Delerue to write equally arresting scores. The political classic *The Conformist* has a score that builds on a felicitous main theme. What starts out serene picks up tempo as it explores Fascist Italy, moving into a rhythmic waltz and eventually collapsing into a weary resolution. The theme for *Femmes de personne* is a jaunty cool jazz that suggests the 1960s more than the year 1984 when it was made. Yet Godard's *Contempt*, made in 1963, has a lush romantic theme that might have been written in the 1940s. Often a Delerue score is timeless, usually because it is filtered through a classical point of view. This is what might have made him so appealing to Hollywood.

Delerue usually had a bigger budget for his British and American films so the sound is sometimes more lush and symphonic. For the Tudor dramas *Anne of the Thousand Days* and *A Man for All Seasons*, period instruments are used for the fanfares and dances but there is nothing puny about the sound, which might be described as Hollywood Renaissance. Delerue used some Vivaldi music for the modern comedy *A Little Romance* and surrounded it with his own pseudobaroque themes that created much of the movie's charm. The two teenagers (Diane Lane and Thelonious Bernard) on the run are very contemporary but the exotic places they visit, such as Verona and Venice, are viewed romantically and the score manages to mix the modern with the classical in a very appealing way. In contrast, Delerue uses Samuel Barber's *Adagio for Strings* in his *Platoon* score and builds a very slow and reflective theme around it, something that is quite the opposite of the gritty Vietnam War scenes on the screen. There is more of an edge in the music for *Salvador*, another film about the horrors of war. The modern melodrama *Agnes of God* uses somber religious music with a wordless choir. The dissonant quality of the score keeps it from becoming Gregorian, especially the lonesome oboe that mourns throughout. For the comedy *Steel Magnolias*, which turns unabashedly sentimental in the last reel, Delerue found a way to unify the score with a harmonica theme that could be frolicsome or morose. The comedy *Maxie* is both contemporary and Roaring Twenties and the score is bouncy and carefree, satisfying both requirements. The silly, one-joke comedy *Twins* has a surprisingly gentle and melodic score, just as the feverish *Women in Love* has a very casual and meandering main theme. The Southern Gothic comedy *Crimes of the Heart* has a piano score that suggests sophisticated elegance and the hard-hitting social drama *Silkwood* has a flowing string adagio when it doesn't use the more obvious banjo theme. The urban comedy *Rich and Famous* is a rather brash character movie, yet Delerue's score is delicate and graceful. Were all these movies hoping for a bit of class by hiring Delerue to provide such classy music? At least in the case of the splendid drama *Julia*, the classical touches seem right. The scenes in 1930s Germany are scored with a mellow violin theme that is contrasted by an oompah-pah waltz. There is also a lovely main theme with a feel for rhapsodic romanticism in the contemporary film *Day of the Dolphin*, the music matching the mystery and majesty of the sea mammals. One of his most entranc-

ing themes can be found in the sequel *The Black Stallion Returns*. With its simple instrumentation, its sense of the exotic desert, and its lyrical passages, the score sounds like one of Delerue's European films even though it is obvious that a full studio orchestra was available.

Are Delerue's European scores superior to his Hollywood ones? While that is not an easy question to answer, it is safe to say that they are different. America (and often Great Britain) provided the means for a bigger and fuller sound, and Delerue was often hired because they wanted romantic, classically flavored scores. Yet working on a shoestring music budget in Europe did not seem to hamper him and, in fact, enabled him to be more adventurous and inventive. Just as the European movies have their own look and feel, so too the scores have their uniquely vibrant qualities. Official website: www.georges-delerue.com.

Credits

(all films France unless stated otherwise; * winner of France's César Award for music; ** nominated for a César Award)

Year	Film	Director
1950	Le mystere du quai de Conti	Henri Lacoste, Henri Monnier
1951	Ingénieurs de la mer	Jean Reynaud
1952	Les techniciens en pompons rouges	Louis-Emile Galey
1952	L'aventure et ses terras-nuevas	Jean Reynaud
1953	Le largage à six heures du matin	Louis-Emile Galey
1953	Berre, cité du pétrole	Louis-Emile Galey
1954	Regards sur l'Indochine	René Rouy
1954	Premiere croisiere	Jean Reynaud
1954	Madagascar	René Rouy
1954	La grande cité d'Angkor	René Rouy
1954	Au rythme de siècle	Henri Charpentier
1954	Au pays de Guillaume le Conquérant	Daniel Wronecki
1955	Âmes d'argile	Bernard Toublanc-Michel
1956	Tu enfanteras sans douleur	Henri Fabiani
1956	Sur l'Arroyo	Guy Loriquet
1956	Marche française	Henri Fabiani
1956	La rue chinoise	Guy Loriquet
1957	Girl in His Pocket	Pierre Kast
1959	Images pour Baudelaire	Pierre Kast
1959	Fleuve invisible	Carlos Vilardebó
1959	Hiroshima mon amour	Alain Renais (France/Japan)
1960	Une question d'assurance	Pierre Kast
1960	Le bel âge	Pierre Kast
1960	A Mistress for the Summer	Edouard Molinaro
1960	Classe tous risques	Claude Sautet (France/Italy)
1960	Marche ou créve	Georges Lautner (France/Belgium)
1960	The Lovers	Philippe de Broca
1960	The Joker	Philippe de Broca
1960	Love and the Frenchwoman	Jean-Paul Le Chanois (Italy/France)
1960	Shoot the Piano Player	François Truffaut

Year	Film	Director
1961	Sahara Year Four	Max Gérard
1961	Women and War	Georges Lautner
1961	La récréation	Fabien Collin, François Moreuil
1961	Five Day Lover	Philippe de Broca (France/Italy)
1961	The End of Belle	Edouard Molinaro
1961	Le bonheur est pour demain	Henru Fabiani
1961	The Long Absence	Henru Colpi (France/Italy)
1961	The Nina B. Affair	Robert Siodmak (France/W. Germany)
1961	La morte-saison des amours	Pierre Kast
1961	Par-dessus le mur	Jean-Paul Le Chanois
1961	Un coeur gros comme ça	François Reichenbach
1962	Jules and Jim	François Truffaut
1962	Swords of Blood	Philippe de Broca (France/Italy)
1962	Operation Gold Ingot	Georges Lautner (France/Italy)
1962	Le petit garçon de l'ascenseur	Pierre Granier-Deferre
1962	Le monte-charge	Marcel Bluwal (Italy/France)
1962	Love at Twenty	François Truffaut, etc. (France, etc.)
1962	Crime Does Not Pay	Gérard Oury (France/Italy)
1962	La dénonciation	Jacques Doniol-Valcroze
1963	Thank You, Natercia	Pierre Kast
1963	Nunca pasa nada	Juan Antonio Bardem (Spain/France)
1963	Till the End of the World	François Villiers (France/Italy)
1963	The Man from Chicago	Marc Allégret
1963	l'immortelle	Alain Robbe-Grillet (Turkey/Italy/France)
1963	Rififi in Tokyo	Jacques Deray (France/Italy)
1963	The Reluctant Spy	Jean-Charles Dudrumet (France/Italy)
1963	Magnet of Doom	Jean-Pierre Melville (France/Italy)
1963	Portuguese Vacation	Pierre Kast (France/Portugal)
1963	Contempt	Jean-Luc Godard (France/Italy)
1963	Le journal d'un fou	Roger Coggio
1963	Chair de poule	Julien Duvivier (France/Italy)
1964	That Man from Rio	Philippe de Broca (Italy/France)
1964	French Dressing	Ken Russell (UK)
1964	Trouble among Widows	Jacques Poitrenaud (France/Italy)
1964	Greed in the Sun	Henri Verneuil (France/Italy)
1964	The Soft Skin	François Truffaut
1964	Laissez tirer les tireurs	Guy Lefranc (France/Italy)
1964	Des pissenlits par la racine	Georges Lautner (France/Italy)
1964	The Pumpkin Eater	Jack Clayton (UK)
1964	Le Gros Coup	Jean Valére (Italy/France)
1964	The Other Woman	François Villiers (France/Italy/Spain)
1964	The Unvanquished	Alain Cavalier (France/Italy)
1964	Male Companion	Philippe de Broca (Italy/France)
1964	Lucky Jo	Michel Deville
1964	That Tender Age	Gilles Grangier
1964	Mata Hari, Agent H21	Jean-Louis Richard (France/Italy)
1965	The Sucker	Gérard Oury (France/Italy)
1965	The Uninhibited	Juan Antonio Bardem (Spain/France/Italy)
1965	L'amour a la chaîne	Claude de Givray
1965	Rapture	John Guillermin (France/USA)
1965	Killer Spy (aka Pleins feux sur Stanislas)	Jean-Charles Dudrumet
1965	The Lair of Love	Gérald Calderon
1965	Up to His Ears	Philippe de Broca (France/Italy)
1965	Viva Maria!	Louis Malle (France/Italy)
1966	A Man for All Seasons	Fred Zinnemann (UK)
1966	King of Hearts	Philippe de Broca (France/Italy)
1967	The Sunday of Life	Jean Herman (France/Italy/W. Germany)
1967	The 25th Hour	Henri Verneuil (France/Italy)

Year	Film	Director
1967	The Two of Us	Claude Berri
1967	Thursday We Shall Sing Like Sunday	Luc de Heusch (France/Belgium)
1967	Our Mother's House	Jack Clayton (UK)
1967	Oscar	Edouard Molinaro
1968	A Little Virtuous	Serge Korber
1968	The Hotshots	Alex Joffé (France/Italy)
1968	Interlude	Kevin Billington (UK)
1969	The Erasers	Lucien Deroisy, René Micha (Belgium/France)
1969	The Devil by the Tail	Philippe de Broca (France/Italy)
1969	The Brain	Gérard Oury (France/Italy)
1969	Women in Love (BAFTA-N)	Ken Russell (UK)
1969	Hibernatus	Edouard Molinaro (France/Italy)
1969	A Walk with Love and Death	John Huston (USA)
1969	Anne of the Thousand Days (AAN; GGN)	Charles Jarrott (UK)
1969	Mona, l'étoile sans nom	Henri Colpi (France/Romania)
1970	Happy He Who Like Ulysses	Henri Colpi
1970	Give Her the Moon (Les caprices de Marie)	Philippe de Broca (Italy/France)
1970	The Conformist	Bernando Bertolucci (Italy/France/W. Germany)
1970	Promise at Dawn	Jules Dassin (USA/France)
1971	Malpertuis	Harry Kümel (Belgium/France/W. Germany)
1971	Countdown	Roger Piguat (France/Italy)
1971	Mira	Fons Rademakers (Belgium/Netherlands)
1971	The Most Gentle Confessions	Edouard Molinaro (France/Italy/Algeria)
1971	The Horsemen	John Frankenheimer (USA)
1971	Anne and Muriel (aka Two English Girls)	François Truffaut
1972	The Artless One (aka L'Ingénu)	Norbert Carbonnaux
1972	Louise (aka Chere Louise)	Philippe de Broca (France/Italy)
1972	Such a Gorgeous Kid Like Me	François Truffaut
1972	Somewhere, Someone	Yannick Bellon (France/W. Germany)
1973	Day for Night (aka La nuit américaine)	François Truffaut (France/Italy)
1973	The Day of the Jackal	Fred Zinnemann (UK/France)
1973	Love Comes Quietly	Nikolai van der Heyde (Belgium/Netherlands)
1973	The Day of the Dolphin (AAN; GGN)	Mike Nichols (USA)
1974	Alien Thunder	Claude Fournier (Canada)
1974	La femme de Jean	Yannick Bellon
1975	La gifle (aka The Slap)	Claude Pinoteau (France/Italy)
1975	That Most Important Thing: Love	Andrej Zulawski (France/Italy/W. Germany)
1975	Incorrigible	Philippe de Broca
1976	Calmos	Bertrand Blier
1976	Forget Me, Mandoline	Michel Wyn
1976	Nevermore, Forever	Yannick Bellon
1976	Police Python 357 **	Alain Corneau (France/W. Germany)
1976	Boomerang	José Giovanni (France/Italy)
1976	The Game of Solitaire	Jean-François Adam
1976	The Big Operator **	Claude Pinoteau (France/Italy)
1977	Julie Gluepot	Philippe de Broca
1977	Julia (AAN; BAFTA-N)	Fred Zinnemann (USA)
1977	Focal Point	Jean-Claude Tramont
1978	Get Out Your Handkerchiefs *	Bertrand Blier (France/Belgium)
1978	Dear Inspector	Philippe de Broca
1978	Va voir Maman, Papa travaille (aka Your Turn, My Turn)	François Leterrier
1978	Little Girl in Blue Velvet	Alan Bridges
1979	Simon de Beauvoir	Josée Dayan, Malka Ribowska (Belgium/France)
1979	Le cavaleur	Philippe de Broca
1979	Love on the Run *	François Truffaut
1979	Mijn vriend	Fons Rademakers (Belgium/Netherlands)
1979	An Almost Perfect Affair	Michael Ritchie (USA)

Year	Film	Director
1979	A Little Romance (AA; GGN)	George Roy Hill (France/USA)
1979	The Black Sheep	Jean-Pierre Moscardo
1980	First Voyage	Nadine Trintignant
1980	Willie & Phil	Paul Mazursky (USA)
1980	Richard's Things	Anthony Harvey (UK)
1980	The Last Metro *	François Truffaut
1981	Broken English	Michie Gleason (USA)
1981	Documenteur	Agnés Varda (USA/France)
1981	Rich and Famous	George Cukor (USA)
1981	La vie continue	Moshé Mizrahi
1981	Garde a vue	Claude Miller
1981	True Confessions	Ulu Grosbard (USA)
1981	The Woman Next Door	François Truffaut
1982	Josepha	Christopher Frank
1982	A Little Sex	Bruce Paltrow (USA)
1982	La passante du sans-souci **	Jacques Rouffio (France/W. Germany)
1982	Guy de Maupassant	Michel Drach
1982	Partners	James Burrows (USA)
1982	The Escape Artist	Caleb Deschanel (USA)
1983	L'Africain	Philippe de Broca
1983	The Black Stallion Returns	Robert Dalva (USA)
1983	Man, Woman and Child	Dick Richards (USA)
1983	Exposed	James Toback (USA)
1983	One Deadly Summer **	Jean Becker
1983	Confidentially Yours	François Truffaut
1983	Liberty Belle	Pascal Kané
1983	Silkwood	Mike Nichols (USA)
1984	Le bon plaisir	Francis Girod
1984	Femmes de personne	Christopher Frank
1984	Les morfalous	Henri Verneuil
1985	Agnes of God (AAN)	Norman Jewison (USA)
1985	Carné, l'homme a la caméra	Christian-Jaque
1985	Maxie	Paul Aaron (USA)
1986	Salvador	Oliver Stone (UK/USA)
1986	My Letter to George (aka Mesmerized)	Michael Laughlin (Australia/New Zealand/UK)
1986	Family Council	Costa-Gavras
1986	Touch and Go	Robert Mandel (USA)
1986	Descent into Hell	Francis Girod
1986	Crimes of the Heart	Bruce Beresford (USA)
1986	Platoon	Oliver Stone (UK/USA)
1987	A Man in Love	Diane Kurys (France/Italy)
1987	Maid to Order	Amy Holden Jones (USA)
1987	The Pick-Up Artist	James Toback (USA)
1987	The Lonely Passion of Judith Hearne	Jack Clayton (UK)
1988	The House on Carroll Street	Peter Yates (USA)
1988	Chouans!	Philippe de Broca
1988	Biloxi Blues	Mike Nichols (USA)
1988	A Summer Story	Piers Haggard (UK)
1988	To Kill a Priest	Agnieszka Holland (France/USA)
1988	Memories of Me	Henry Winkler (USA)
1988	Heartbreak Hotel	Chris Columbus (USA)
1988	Paris by Night	David Hare (UK)
1988	Twins	Ivan Reitman (USA)
1988	Beaches	Garry Marshall (USA)
1989	Her Alibi	Bruce Beresford (USA)
1989	La révolution française	Robert Enrico, Richard Heffron (France/Italy/W. Germany/UK)
1989	The Spirit	Niklaus Schilling (W. Germany)

Year	Film	Director
1989	Seven Minutes	Klaus Maria Brandauer (W. Germany/Austria)
1989	Steel Magnolias	Herbert Ross (USA)
1990	Joe versus the Volcano	John Patrick Shanley (USA)
1990	A Show of Force	Bruno Barreto (USA)
1990	Cadence	Martin Sheen (USA)
1990	Mister Johnson	Bruce Beresford (USA)
1991	American Friends	Tristram Powell (UK)
1991	La riene blanche	Jean-Loup Hubert
1991	Black Robe	Bruce Beresford (Canada/Australia/USA)
1991	Curly Sue	John Hughes (USA)
1992	Diên Biên Phú**	Pierre Schoendoerffer
1992	Céline	Jean-Claude Brisseau
1992	Man Trouble	Bob Rafelson (USA/Italy)
1992	Rich in Love	Bruce Beresford (USA)

DESPLAT, Alexandre (b. 1961) A very successful French conductor and composer with many international credits, since 2010 he has become arguably the most in-demand composer for English-language films.

Born Alexandre Michel Gerard Desplat in Paris, the son of a French father and Greek mother, he began taking piano lessons at the age of five, later studying trumpet and flute as well. Desplat grew up listening to classical music as well as jazz, and trained privately with French and American composers with the hope of writing for the cinema. When he was twenty-four years old, he scored his first movie, the French romance *Ki lo sa?* in 1985. Six years later Desplat wrote music for French television for the first time and in the 1990s he scored sixteen TV movies. His first feature film to bring him recognition for his music was the 1996 character drama *Un héros trés discret* which was released in English-speaking countries as *A Self-Made Hero*. It was followed by such noteworthy European films as *Love, etc.*, *Empty Days*, *The Luzhin Defence*, *Read My Lips*, *The Nest*, and *A Hell of a Day*. The international success of the 2003 British-Luxembourg film *Girl with a Pearl Earring* brought Desplat to the attention of Hollywood and the next year he scored his first American movie, the mystery-drama *Birth*. With his Oscar-nominated score for *The Queen* in 2006, Desplat's visibility in Hollywood skyrocketed. He has also been nominated for *The Curious Case of Benjamin Button*, *Fantastic Mr. Fox*, *The King's Speech*, *Argo*, and *Philomena*, but to date has not won an Oscar. His many other noteworthy movies since 2006 include *The Painted Veil*, *The Golden Compass*, *Coco before Chanel*, *Julie & Julia*, *The Twilight Saga: New Moon*, both parts of *Harry Potter and the Deathly Hallows*,

Rise of the Guardians, *Tree of Life*, *Carnage*, *Moonrise Kingdom*, *The Ides of March*, *Zero Dark Thirty*, and *The Grand Budapest Hotel*. Desplat has also written for the Paris theatre, the concert hall, and songs for individual artists. He has taught master classes in composition in London and Paris and has conducted his music in venues on both sides of the Atlantic.

Desplat's musical influences range from the French masters, such as Maurice Ravel and Claude Debussy, and American jazz to African tribal music and Latin American sounds. Surely his classical side dominates in *Girl with the Pearl Earring* about the Dutch painter Vermeer (Colin Firth) and the teenage girl (Scarlett Johannson) who is the subject of his famous painting. One of Desplat's favorite instruments in this and other scores is the early keyboard celesta. It provides twinkling chime-like notes for the movie's main theme, a flowing but frantic piece that seems nervous and restless with its swaying strings and lonely flute. The adagio passages in the score feature a solo violin and piano that ache with longing, and there is a repetitive theme with plucked piano notes and sustained strings that is suspenseful even as it is elegant. Another period film with a classical air is *The Painted Veil*, which is set in China where a British couple (Edward Norton and Naomi Watts) try to patch up their failed marriage as they tend to cholera victims. The main theme has felicitous strings with rapid piano and flute interruptions. Desplat creates an Eastern flavor not through Asian instruments but with an electric cello. Also in the score is a graceful and restrained waltz played on piano and strings that is heard under the film's London flashbacks, and the wife Kitty's theme features a trio of flutes performing a serene dance together as if in slow motion.

A British form of classical music can be found in Desplat's two royal entries, *The Queen* and *The King's Speech*. For the latter, about George VI (Colin Firth) and his battle to overcome his tormenting stammer, Desplat subtly echoes the king's impediment with a main theme heard on piano with some string accompaniment. It is a simple melody that keeps a brisk tempo even as it hesitates, doubles back, repeats itself, then continues on. Elizabeth II (Helen Mirren) and her strained loss of popularity after the death of Princess Diana is the subject of *The Queen*. The score's recurring theme is a slow and stately piece that builds in intensity as kettle drums join in then recede and the music slips back into a contemplative mood. Desplat provides a theme for each of the central characters in *The Queen*. Prime Minister Tony Blair (Michael Sheen) has a four-note march, played on strings, piano, and horns, that is very aggressive and confident, yet a piano solo section adds a human touch. The Queen's theme, heard when she is alone and less regal in Scotland, uses English horns and bassoons for a quietly stirring piece that seems to embrace nature as flutes provide birdlike accents. Princess Diana, who does not appear in the film but seems to haunt all the proceedings, has a minor-key theme played on a rapid, rhythmic mandolin with piano and flutes providing a fluid countermelody.

Some of Desplat's most memorable scores have come from interesting but unsatisfying movies. *Birth*, a controversial film about a widow (Nicole Kidman) who suspects that the ten-year-old youth Sean (Cameron Bright) might be the reincarnation of her late husband, has a mesmerizing score. The recurring theme is a delicately bouncy piece played by two flutes, a celesta, French horns, and strings. This music is not only mystifying in itself but is used effectively in the movie to link the dead husband and the boy. There is also a ravishing waltz that is animated and modern, but when later played on a piano it takes on a melancholy tone. Similarly odd is *The Curious Case of Benjamin Button*, a fantasy about a man (Brad Pitt) who lives in reverse, starting life as an old man and growing younger each day. The movie re-creates the different eras that Button lives through by using existing music, such as some Scott Joplin rags and a few jazz standards, but it is Desplat's original music that most intrigues. Button's theme, played on alto saxophone, celesta, and piano, attempts to musically go backward. A melody built around a four-note motif descends step by step within a minor-

key framework. The score also includes a waltz for piano and strings that feels like it is in a daze, a passage featuring muted trumpets, and a harp and string theme heard under a sunrise scene in which the music seems to slowly blossom as a solo violin reaches up and soars.

Three fantasy films of Desplat's have noteworthy scores. *Harry Potter and the Deathly Hollows*, the two-part film that concludes the popular saga, has a restless march theme in which horns and percussion gain speed, explode into chaotic sections with swirling strings, then climax only to dwindle into calm and start all over again. There is a lovely passage in which a solo chanting voice and full orchestra take flight, and for a flashback a passage called "Lily's Theme" is a morose piece with a mourning Celtic-like voice that seems to echo through time and haunt the present. Less popular but musically thrilling is the dark fantasy *The Golden Compass*. Desplat uses many different kinds of music for the different elements in this complicated story about two parallel universes but a few passages stand out. The leitmotif for the title artifact is an eerie yet romantic piece with heavy chords, fluttering flute accents, and some flowing sections that are truly magical. There is also an agitato passage with frantic flutes, expressive piano, and blaring horns, and an airship scene is scored with a vigorous orchestral section that alluringly rises in volume and intensity. The much-maligned but widely seen vampire romance *The Twilight Saga: New Moon* has an entrancing love theme in a minor key for strings, piano, and flute in which a repeated four-note phrase is both creepy and romantic.

It seems that recently Desplat has been given more first-rate movies to score than anyone else in the business. Two films based on actual events in the Middle East, *Argo* and *Zero Dark Thirty*, have powerful scores. *Argo*, about a fake movie crew rescuing American hostages in Tehran in 1980, has some exotic Middle Eastern music heard on an ethnic flute with electronic sustained chords that provide a sense of menace. Other passages in the film flirt with jazz and rock but usually end up going for a more orchestrated sound that stops short of melodrama. *Zero Dark Thirty*, about the long and sustained efforts to hunt down and destroy terrorist leader Osama bin Laden, has a pounding main theme in which drums and low brass replicate a heartbeat with restless variations. The character drama *Philomena*, in which an Irish widow (Judi Dench) looks for the son she gave up as a baby decades ago, has a curious score. The main theme is a spirited waltz heard on pipes and fiddle that suggests an Irish dance in half time. Yet the film is often very sobering and much of the rest of the score avoids such lightheartedness and often reverts to a solo guitar or a woodwind dirge to capture the unrelenting grief that overshadows the tale. The double-plotted *Julie and Julia* has a charming score, in particular the festive accordion theme that conjures up Paris without slipping into gross cliché. And the animated *Fantastic Mr. Fox* has a slapstick banjo and guitar theme in which various instruments, ranging from an ocarina to a Jew's harp, join in the fun. It may have taken Desplat twenty years and over forty movies before he found fame, but he seems to have secured his reputation with more and more fine scores. Official website: www.alexandredesplat.net.

Credits

(all films France unless stated otherwise; * winner of France's César Award for music; ** nominated for a César Award)

Year	Film	Director
1985	Ki lo sa?	Robert Guédiguian
1991	Family Express	Georges Nicolas Hayek (Switzerland/France/Italy)
1992	Lapse of Memory	Patrick Dewolf (Canada/France)
1992	In the Name of the Father and the Son	Patrice Noïa
1992	The Weaker Sexes!	Serge Meynard
1993	Le tronc	Bernard Faroix, Karl Zéro
1993	The Advocate (aka The Hour of the Pig)	Leslie Megahey (France/UK)
1995	Innocent Lies	Patrick Dewolf (UK/France)
1995	Les milles	Sébastien Grall (France/Germany/Poland)
1995	Le plus bel âge . . .	Didier Haudepin
1996	A Self-Made Hero**	Jacques Audiard
1996	Lucky Punch	Dominique Ladoge
1996	The Scream of the Silk*	Yvon Marciano (France/Belgium)
1996	Passage à l'acte	Francis Girod
1996	Love, etc.	Marion Vernoux
1997	Sous les pieds de femmes	Rachida Krim
1998	La femme du cosmonaute	Jacques Monnet
1998	Half a Chance	Patrice Leconte
1998	The Revengers' Comedies (aka Sweet Revenge)	Malcolm Mowbray (UK/France)
1998	Restons groupés	Jean-Paul Salomé
1998	Une minute de silence	Florent-Emilio Siri
1998	Atilano for President	Santiago Aguilar, Luis Guridi (Spain)
1999	Toni	Philoméne Esposito (France/Italy)
1999	It's Not My Fault!	Jacques Monnet
1999	A Monkey's Tale	Jean-François Laguionie (France/UK/Germany/Hungary)
1999	Monsieur Naphtali	Olivier Schatzky
1999	Empty Days	Marion Vernoux
2000	Vive nous!	Camille de Casabianca
2000	Amazon	Philippe de Broca (France/Spain)
2000	The Luzhin Defence	Marleen Gorris (UK/France)
2001	Barnie's Minor Annoyances	Bruno Chiche
2001	Home Sweet Home	Heidi Draper, Michael Raeburn (Zimbabwe/France)
2001	Doors of Glory	Christian Merret-Palmair
2001	Transfixed	Grancis Girod (France/Belgium)
2001	Read My Lips**	Jacques Audiard
2001	A Hell of a Day	Marion Vernoux
2002	The Nest	Florent-Emilio Siri
2003	Laughter and Punishment	Isabelle Doval
2003	Pact of Silence	Graham Guit
2003	Eager Bodies	Xavier Giannoli
2003	Tristan	Philippe Harel

Year	Film	Director
2003	Stormy Weather	Sólveig Anspach (Belgium/Iceland/France)
2003	Girl with a Pearl Earring (GGN; BAFTA-N)	Peter Webber (UK/Luxembourg)
2003	A Sight for Sore Eyes	Gilles Bourdos
2004	Birth	Jonathan Glazer (USA/UK/Germany)
2004	The Corsican File	Alain Berbérbian
2005	Tu vas rire, mais je te quitte	Philippe Harel
2005	The Upside of Anger	Mike Binder (USA/Germany/UK)
2005	The Beat That My Heart Skipped*	Jacques Audiard
2005	Hostage	Florent-Emilio Siri (USA/Germany)
2005	Une aventure	Xavier Giannoli (France/Belgium)
2005	Casanova	Lasse Hallström (USA)
2005	Syriana (GGN)	Stephen Gaghan (USA)
2006	Lies & Alibis	Matt Checkowski, Kurt Mattila (Netherlands/USA)
2006	Firewall (aka The Wrong Element)	Richard Loncraine (USA/Australia)
2006	The Valet	Francis Veber (France/Italy/Belgium)
2006	Quand j'étais chanteur	Xavier Giannoli
2006	The Queen (AAN; BAFTA-N)	Stephen Frears (UK/USA/France/Italy)
2006	The Painted Veil (GG)	John Curran (China/USA/Canada)
2007	Michou d'Auber	Thomas Gilou
2007	Lust, Caution	Ang Lee (USA/China/Taiwan)
2007	Intimate Enemies**	Florent-Emilio Siri (France/Morocco)
2007	Mr. Magorium's Wonder Emporium	Zach Helm (USA/Canada)
2007	The Golden Compass	Chris Wetz (USA/UK)
2008	Afterwards	Gilles Bourdos (Germany/France/Canada)
2008	The Heir Apparent: Largo Winch	Jérôme Salle (France/Belgium)
2008	The Curious Case of Benjamin Button (AAN; GGN; BAFTA-N)	David Fincher (USA)
2009	Chéri	Stephen Frears (UK/France/Germany)
2009	Coco before Chanel	Anne Fontaine (France/Belgium)
2009	A Prophet**	Jacques Audiard (France/Italy)
2009	Army of Crime	Robert Guédiguian
2009	Julie & Julia	Nora Ephron (USA)
2009	Fantastic Mr. Fox (AAN; BAFTA-N)	Wes Anderson (USA)
2009	The Twilight Saga: New Moon	Chris Weitz (USA)
2010	The Ghost* (aka The Ghost Writer)	Roman Polanski (France/Germany/UK)
2010	Tamara Drew	Stephen Frears (UK)
2010	The King's Speech (AAN; GGN; BAFTA)	Tom Hooper (UK/USA/Australia)
2010	Harry Potter and the Deathly Hallows: Part 2	David Yates (UK/USA)
2011	The Burma Conspiracy (aka Largo Winch 2)	Jérôme Salle (France/Belgium/Germany)
2011	The Well-Digger's Daughter	Daniel Auteuil
2011	The Tree of Life	Terrence Malick (USA)
2011	A Better Life	Chris Weitz (USA)
2011	Harry Potter and the Deathly Hallows: Part 1	David Yates (UK/USA)
2011	The Ides of March (aka Farragut North)	George Clooney (USA)
2011	Carnage (aka God of Carnage)	Roman Polanski (France/Germany/Poland/Spain)
2011	Extremely Loud & Incredibly Close	Stephen Daldry (USA)
2012	My Way	Florent-Emilio Siri (France/Belgium)
2012	Moonrise Kingdom	Wes Anderson (USA)
2012	Rust and Bone*	Jacques Audiard (France/Belgium)
2012	Reality	Matteo Garrone (Italy France)
2012	Renoir	Gilles Bourdos
2012	Argo (aka Escape from Tehran) (AAN; GGN; BAFTA-N)	Ben Affleck (USA)
2012	Rise of the Guardians	Peter Ramsey (USA)
2012	Zero Dark Thirty (aka Kill Bin Laden)	Kathryn Bigelow (USA)
2013	Venus in Fur*	Roman Polanski (France/Poland)
2013	Zulu	Jérôme Salle (France/So. Africa)
2013	Marius	Daniel Auteuil

Year	Film	Director
2013	Fanny	Daniel Auteuil
2013	Philomena (AAN)	Stephen Frears (UK/USA/France)
2014	The Monuments Men	George Clooney (USA/Germany)
2014	The Grand Budapest Hotel (AA)	Wes Anderson (USA/Germany)
2014	Godzilla	Gareth Edwards (USA/Japan)
2014	Unbroken	Angelina Jolie (USA)
2014	The Tale of Tales	Matteo Garrone (Italy/France)
2014	The Imitation Game	Morten Tyldum (UK/USA)

DEUTSCH, Adolph (1897–1980) A British-born Hollywood arranger, conductor, songwriter, and composer, he scored over eighty feature films between 1937 and 1961, including some film noir and comedy classics.

Adolph Deutsch was born in London and showed talent for playing piano and composing at a young age. Deutsch was not yet a teenager when he was admitted to the Royal College of Music in London to study piano and composition. At the age of thirteen his uncle brought Deutsch to the States and they settled in Buffalo, where within a year he got a job accompanying silent films in a local movie house. He became a U.S. citizen in 1920 and worked for the Ford Motor Company after finishing high school. Deutsch moved to New York City in the late 1920s where he found work arranging and conducting music for Broadway musicals, including the Gershwins' *Pardon My English* (1933) and Irving Berlin's *As Thousands Cheer* (1933). He also worked in radio for a three-year period doing arrangements for *Paul Whiteman's Music Hall* and other shows, and conducted and arranged music for bands and movie palaces in Chicago and New York. Deutsch's first movie work came in 1930 when he was hired to cowrite with Vernon Duke soundtrack scores for the silent films *The Wedding March* (1928) and *The Dance of Life* (1929). By the late 1930s he was in Hollywood arranging and conducting music for various studios. Director Mervyn LeRoy hired Deutsch to score his film noir mystery *They Won't Forget* in 1937, putting him under contract at Warner Brothers. During the next nine years he scored a variety of movies for the studio, including such memorable titles as *Mr. Dodd Takes the Air*, *Cowboy from Brooklyn*, *The Kid from Kokomo*, *The Fighting 69th*, *Castle on the Hudson*, *Three Cheers for the Irish*, *Saturday's Children*, *High Sierra*, *The Maltese Falcon*, *All Through the Night*, *Larceny, Inc.*, *Across the Pacific*, *George Washington Slept Here*, and *The Mask of Dimitrios*. Moving to MGM in 1948, Deutsch scored many notable movies,

including *Little Women*, *Nobody Lives Forever*, *Stars in My Crown*, *Intruder in the Dust*, *Father of the Bride*, *Million Dollar Mermaid*, *Deep in My Heart*, *Interrupted Melody*, and *Tea and Sympathy*. At MGM, he contributed music and/or arrangements to several musicals, winning Oscars for *Annie Get Your Gun* (1950), *Seven Brides for Seven Brothers* (1954), and *Oklahoma!* (1955), and was nominated for *Show Boat* (1951) and *The Band Wagon* (1953). During his Hollywood career, Deutsch also worked on many films uncredited, either composing, arranging, and/or conducting. (He spent three months in 1938 assisting Max Steiner in writing the massive score for *Gone with the Wind*.) He ended his career scoring such popular movies as *The Matchmaker*, *Some Like It Hot*, and *The Apartment*. Deutsch was the composer of a number of concert pieces, most memorably his *Scottish Suite*, and in 1943 he was co-founder of the Screen Composers Association and served as its first president. He retired from movies in 1960 and died twenty years later at the age of eighty-two.

At Warner Brothers, Deutsch gained a reputation for scoring dark dramas and film noir movies, many of them starring Humphrey Bogart. *The Maltese Falcon*, perhaps the quintessential private eye noir, has an unusually robust score that avoids minor-key mood music and opts instead for a more vigorous approach. The main theme has energetic brass fanfares that come on strong then dwindle into bluesy reeds and muted horns that descend the scale as strings weave in and out. Sections of the score emphasize spooky and fidgety strings, a horn phrase that repeats itself insistently, and some classic suspense music surrounding mention of the "black bird" and during its revelation as a fake. Two other Bogart noir movies have different but equally impressive scores. *High Sierra* includes a series of brass declarations that climb the scale, trying to top themselves. The romantic theme is played on strings that seem suspended in time and there is a melancholy passage with descending strings and mellow horns that is poignant without slipping into the melodramatic. *All Through the Night* has a more rambunctious score with some lighter passages for the comic sidekicks Frank McHugh and William Demarest. There is a lot of ponderous climbing the scale with bold brassy steps and blaring trumpets are used to announce the Nazi villains in the story. In contrast to these dark classics are Deutsch's lighter scores for such comedies as *George Washington Slept Here*. This broad domestic farce has a silly ghostly theme with laughing brass, giggling fifes, and frivolous strings, with snatches of "Yankee Doodle" and "Three Blind Mice" tossed in on occasion to laugh at the colonial connections the run-down house supposedly has to the Founding Father. The comedy is far from subtle and the music enjoys announcing itself, as if scoring a slapstick cartoon. Of Deutsch's period pieces, perhaps the finest score is the one he wrote for the 1950 remake of *Little Women*. It may not be everyone's favorite version of the classic tale but the music is masterful throughout. There is an elegant domestic theme, played on woodwinds and punctuated by the tinkling of a music box, that echoes the period in its tuneful simplicity. Also memorable is a gentle hymnlike passage that is delicate yet full of life.

Near the end of Deutsch's career, he scored two outstanding Billy Wilder films, *Some Like It Hot* and *The Apartment*. The former is filled with period songs to establish the Roaring Twenties milieu and there is some clever use of old music in some scenes, such as a hilarious tango featuring Jack Lemmon (in drag) and Joe E. Brown. Deutsch provided the soundtrack music between all the familiar tunes, including a jazzy theme for the opening credits which features a freewheeling saxophone and a jaunty piano. Actually, it sounds more like 1950s jazz with a Big Band slant than the 1920s but the comic-romantic tone is spot on for the movie. *The Apartment* has a much different tone. The contemporary comedy-drama has a melancholy temperament as the characters find themselves more anguished over love than comforted by it. The recurring theme throughout the movie is a symphonic piece featuring piano and violin that moves at a steady tempo but is filled with melancholy and world-weary pathos. This music was written as the song "Jealous Lover" ten years earlier by British composer Charles Williams. Deutsch retains the classical format of the original but arranges the music with a blues sentiment that manages to be romantic but fatalistic. Known as the "Theme from *The Apartment*," the piece became a very popular instrumental hit, but it remains more Williams than Deutsch. Written for the film and just as memorable is a Deutsch composition titled "Lonely Room." This very bluesy and languid jazz work features a piano that keeps time unemotionally as the brass lazily reach for crescendos without really caring. It is surprisingly melodic for a jazz piece and very affecting in a chilly manner. Deutsch may not be ranked among the top Hollywood composers of his era, but sometimes his music argues that he was underrated.

Credits

(all films USA)

Year	Film	Director
1930	*The Wedding March* (1928)	Erich von Stroheim
1930	*The Dance of Life* (1929)	John Cromwell, A. Edward Sutherland
1937	*They Won't Forget* (aka *Death in the Deep South*)	Mervyn LeRoy
1937	*Mr. Dodd Takes the Air*	Alfred E. Green
1937	*The Great Garrick* (aka *Ladies and Gentlemen*)	James Whale
1938	*Swing Your Lady*	Ray Enright
1938	*Cowboy from Brooklyn*	Lloyd Bacon
1938	*Racket Busters*	Lloyd Bacon
1938	*Valley of the Giants*	William Krighley
1938	*Heart of the North*	Lewis Seiler
1939	*Off the Record*	James Flood
1939	*The Man Who Dared* (aka *City in Terror*)	Crane Wilbur
1939	*The Kid from Kokomo*	Lewis Seiler
1939	*Indianapolis Speedway* (aka *The Roaring Road*)	Lloyd Bacon
1939	*The Angels Wash Their Faces*	Ray Enright

Year	Film	Director
1939	*Espionage Agent*	Lloyd Bacon
1940	*The Fighting 69th* (aka *Father Duffy of the Fighting 69th*)	William Keighley
1940	*Castle on the Hudson*	Anatole Litvak
1940	*Three Cheers for the Irish*	Lloyd Bacon
1940	*Saturday's Children*	Vincent Sherman
1940	*Torrid Zone*	William Keighley
1940	*They Drive by Night*	Raoul Walsh
1940	*Flowing Gold*	Alfred E. Green
1940	*Tugboat Annie Sails Again*	Lewis Seiler
1940	*East of the River*	Alfred E. Green
1941	*High Sierra*	Raoul Walsh
1941	*The Great Mr. Nobody*	Benjamin Stoloff
1941	*Singapore Woman*	Jean Negulesco
1941	*Underground*	Vincent Sherman
194	*Kisses for Breakfast* (aka *She Stayed Kissed*)	Lewis Seiler
1941	*Manpower*	Raoul Walsh
1941	*The Maltese Falcon*	John Huston
1941	*All Through the Night*	Vincent Sherman
1942	*Larceny, Inc.*	Lloyd Bacon
1942	*Juke Girl*	Curtis Bernhardt
1942	*The Big Shot*	Lewis Seiler
1942	*Across the Pacific* (aka *Aloha Means Goodbye*)	John Huston, Vincent Sherman
1942	*You Can't Escape Forever*	Jo Graham
1942	*George Washington Slept Here*	William Keighley
1942	*Lucky Jordan*	Frank Tuttle
1943	*Action in the North Atlantic* (aka *Heroes without Uniforms*)	Lloyd Bacon, Byron Haskin, Raoul Walsh
1943	*Northern Pursuit*	Raoul Walsh
1944	*Uncertain Glory*	Raoul Walsh
1944	*The Mask of Dimitrios*	Jean Negulesco
1944	*The Doughgirls*	James V. Kern
1945	*Escape in the Desert*	Edward A. Blatt
1945	*Danger Signal*	Robert Florey
1946	*Three Strangers*	Jean Negulesco
1946	*Shadow of a Woman*	Joseph Santley
1946	*Nobody Lives Forever*	Jean Negulesco
1947	*Ramrod*	André De Toth
1947	*Blaze of Noon*	John Farrow
1948	*Julia Misbehaves*	Jack Conway
1948	*Luxury Liner*	Richard Whorf
1948	*Whispering Smith*	Leslie Fenton
1949	*Little Women*	Mervyn LeRoy
1949	*The Stratton Story* (aka *The Life of Monte Stratton*)	Sam Wood
1949	*Intruder in the Dust*	Clarence Brown
1950	*Stars in My Crown*	Jacques Tourneur
1950	*The Big Hangover*	Norman Krasna
1950	*Father of the Bride*	Vincente Minnelli
1950	*Mrs. O'Malley and Mr. Malone*	Norman Taurog
1951	*Soldiers Three*	Tay Garnett
1951	*Show Boat* (AAN)	George Sidney
1952	*Million Dollar Mermaid*	Mervyn LeRoy
1953	*Torch Song*	Charles Walters
1953	*The Long, Long Trailer*	Vincente Minnelli
1954	*Deep in My Heart*	Stanley Donen
1955	*Interrupted Melody*	Curtis Bernhardt
1956	*Tea and Sympathy*	Vincente Minnelli
1956	*The Rack*	Arnold Laven

Year	Film	Director
1958	The Matchmaker	Joseph Anthony
1959	Some Like It Hot	Billy Wilder
1960	The Apartment	Billy Wilder
1961	Go Naked in the World	Ranald MacDougall, Charles Walters

DeVOL, Frank (1911–1999) A popular radio, Big Band, movie, and television conductor, arranger, songwriter, performer, and composer, he scored forty-two feature films between 1954 and 1981, including sixteen for director Robert Aldrich.

Born in Moundsville, West Virginia, Frank DeVol grew up in Canton, Ohio, where his father conducted a small orchestra for silent movies. DeVol (sometimes De Vol) learned to play the violin and performed in his father's band, then taught himself to play the saxophone. By the time he was fourteen years old, he was a professional musician and playing in local bands. His family wanted him to be a lawyer, so DeVol attended Miami University in Ohio, but after only six weeks he left college and the law behind. In the 1930s he worked as a saxophone player and arranger for the Horace Heidt Orchestra. He also toured with Alvino Rey's orchestra before finding a career arranging the music for radio shows and studio recordings by such artists as Nat King Cole, Doris Day, Ella Fitzgerald, Vic Damone, Jaye P. Morgan, Dinah Shore, and Sarah Vaughn. He formed his own orchestra in the 1950s and made many recordings of mood music. Although DeVol had made some musical arrangements for films in the 1940s, he did not score his first movie until the 1954 film noir drama *World for Ransom* directed by Robert Aldrich. The two men worked well together and over the next twenty-five years they collaborated on such memorable films as *Kiss Me Deadly, Attack, Whatever Happened to Baby Jane?, The Big Knife, The Flight of the Phoenix, The Dirty Dozen, Ulzana's Raid, Emperor of the North, The Longest Yard,* and *Hush . . . Hush, Sweet Charlotte.* With other directors DeVol scored several noteworthy movies, including comic vehicles for Doris Day, cutting-edge westerns, popular melodramas, and two *Love Bug* sequels. Among his many noteworthy films are *Murder, Inc., Pillow Talk, McLintock!, The Thrill of It All, The Ride Back, Cat Ballou, Send Me No Flowers, Good Neighbor Sam, Lover Come Back, Herbie Goes to Monte Carlo, Texas across the River,* and *Guess Who's Coming to Dinner.*

DeVol began his television career in 1952 as an actor, playing comic supporting roles in sitcoms and appearing as himself on quiz shows and panel programs. He soon gained a reputation for his dry sense of humor playing himself and for his talent for creating oddball characters in TV shows and a few films. After arranging and scoring Edgar Bergman's game show *Do You Trust Your Wife?* in 1956, DeVol occasionally scored TV programs. But in the 1960s he got more involved in television, composing the scores for a dozen TV movies and writing the theme and/or music for such series as *Dr. Kildare, The Virginian, My Three Sons, Family Affair, Dusty's Trail, McCloud, Walt Disney's Wonderful World of Color, The Love Boat, The Brady Bunch,* and *Herbie, the Love Bug.* DeVol wrote and conducted the music for the satirical series *Fernwood Tonight* and played the sad-faced restaurateur-bandleader Happy Kyne who entertained with his musical group the Mirthmakers. In addition to his catchy TV theme songs, DeVol collaborated on many songs, some of which became very popular, such as "Lover Come Back," "Friendly Tavern Polka," "I've Written a Letter to Daddy," and "Hush Hush, Sweet Charlotte." He retired from movies and television in 1983 and became active in the Big Band Academy of America. He died of congestive heart failure sixteen years later at the age of eighty-eight.

DeVol was an already established bandleader when he started scoring movies in 1954, so it is surprising that he rarely used the Big Band sound in his screen music. His first movies were in the film noir genre and he used a full orchestra but turned it into a dramatic ensemble with little of the sweet band sound that had been popular in the 1940s. The dark and gritty *Kiss Me Deadly* was based on a Mickey Spillane pulp novel and effectively captured the author's harsh writing style. DeVol's music is similarly harsh as trumpets seem to scream and strings go berserk at times. The most interesting part of the score is at the end of the film when the frantic music is mixed with oppressive sound effects during the climactic fire sequence. As in several of his movies, DeVol provides the music for a song. In this case he also wrote music and lyric for the low-key blues number "Rather Have the Blues," heard on the soundtrack sung by Nat King Cole in an early scene and by Kitty White later in the film. *The Big Knife*, an unpleasant exposé about the underside of Hollywood, has a brash and threatening opening theme even after it moves into a more lyrical jazz section with a mournful clarinet solo. Also in the score there are languid jazz passages, some bluesy themes with a nervous edge, and a romantic section with a less-morose clarinet. Even the hymnlike choral ending has a bitter sense of loss.

There is no Big Band sound in DeVol's music for two cult classics with deranged characters played by Bette Davis: *Whatever Happened to Baby Jane?* and *Hush . . . Hush, Sweet Charlotte*. Both movies have traditional horror film scores complete with brass explosions, high-pitched strings, and plenty of unsubtle shocks. When Davis serves her invalid sister (Joan Crawford) her dead pet parakeet for lunch in *Whatever Happened to Baby Jane?*, a subtle music cue is not wanted. One of the bizarre highlights in the film is the use of DeVol's children's ditty "I've Written a Letter to Daddy" (lyric by Bob Merrill). It is a morbidly sentimental song that is odd enough when sung by the young Baby Jane (Julie Allred dubbed by Debbie Burton) but when performed by the aging, decrepit Jane (Davis), the effect is truly macabre. The title song (lyric by Mack David) for *Hush . . . Hush, Sweet Charlotte* is not sentimental or macabre but rather a catchy ballad sung on the soundtrack by Al Martino and it became a big hit for Patti Page. Such a warm, romantic number is in contrast to what happens in the movie and quite unlike the rest of DeVol's score.

The title songs for DeVol's comedies were usually written by others and often his scores were based on the title tune. In the case of the Doris Day comedies, she usually sang the title song over the opening credits and was often given another number or two to perform later in the movie. This left DeVol writing variations of these songs for the soundtrack score. (DeVol did get to cowrite with Alan Spilton the snazzy title song for the Day vehicle *Lover Come Back*.) But in the case of the comic western *Cat Ballou*, DeVol got to write both songs and soundtrack score. This spoof of Old West revenge tales is narrated in song by banjo-playing Nat King Cole and Stubby Kaye. They open the film singing "The Ballad of Cat Ballou" then return at different points in the movie to continue narrating through

the breezy cowboy ballad. In between, DeVol provides some lively western music clichés and helps keep the comic tone of the movie alive through some of the soggier portions of the tale. The John Wayne western *McLintock!* is also comic and even romantic. There are a few songs by songwriter "By" Dunham, but much of the score is by DeVol and it is one of his best. The main theme is a raucous western rhapsody with brisk brass, scampering strings, and a wild xylophone. Also memorable is a guitar, horn, and string passage that feels like a classic folk song given the orchestral treatment, its simple melody embellished by the smooth and romantic arrangement.

Two of DeVol's best scores do use a fully orchestrated sound that recalls his band recordings of the 1940s and 1950s. *The Dirty Dozen*, a war movie about a gang of convicted criminals turned into an unusual fighting unit, had its lighter moments and DeVol's score reflects this. The main theme is a bold march with trumpets blaring and drums pounding that turns schizophrenic when furious strings and blustering horns interrupt. Another theme races forward with staccato piano, agitated strings, and horn glissandos all set to a tempo that gains speed as it goes along. During the Dozen's more offbeat adventures, the music turns comic. Also, DeVol made a risible arrangement of "You're in the Army Now" and worked it into the score at appropriate moments. More serious and more symphonic is the score for *The Flight of the Phoenix*, a fascinating character drama about a group of passengers who survive their plane crash in the Sahara and work together to build a new plane out of the wreckage. A brisk opening theme with abrupt stops suggests musically the plane's failure to keep aloft. Then a flowing passage with rapid trumpets is heard during the flying sequence and the crash landing. The vast open desert is conveyed by a fanciful but lonely passage on strings and woodwinds. As the heat overcomes the stranded passengers, the music weaves and glides in a dizzying manner. An Italian song "Senza fine" by Gino Paoli is sung by Connie Francis on the soundtrack, the tune becoming a leitmotif for remembering those far away. The movie ends with a triumphant theme for the final lift off as they escape the desert. DeVol was able to score such inspiring stories as confidently as he musicalized Doris Day, Herbie the Love Bug, and *My Three Sons*. His fame may have rested on his masterful arrangement abilities, but often his screen music was first rate.

Credits

(all films USA; * for Best Song)

Year	Film	Director
1954	*World for Ransom*	Robert Aldrich
1955	*Kiss Me Deadly*	Robert Aldrich
1955	*The Big Knife*	Robert Aldrich
1956	*Pardners*	Norman Taurog
1956	*Attack*	Robert Aldrich
1957	*The Ride Back*	Allen H. Miner, Oscar Rudolph
1957	*Johnny Trouble*	John H. Auer
1959	*Pillow Talk* (AAN)	Michael Gordon
1960	*Murder, Inc.*	Burt Balaban, Stuart Rosenberg
1961	*Lover Come Back*	Delbert Mann
1962	*Boys' Night Out*	Michael Gordon
1962	*Whatever Happened to Baby Jane?*	Robert Aldrich
1963	*The Thrill of It All*	Norman Jewison
1963	*For Love or Money*	Michael Gordon
1963	*Under the Yum Yum Tree*	David Swift
1963	*McLintock!*	Andrew V. McLaglen
1963	*The Wheeler Dealers*	Arthur Hiller
1964	*Good Neighbor Sam*	David Swift
1964	*Send Me No Flowers*	Norman Jewison
1964	*Hush . . . Hush, Sweet Charlotte* (AAN; AAN*)	Robert Aldrich
1965	*Cat Ballou* (AAN)	Elliot Silverstein
1965	*The Flight of the Phoenix*	Robert Aldrich
1966	*The Glass Bottom Boat*	Frank Tashlin
1966	*Texas across the River*	Michael Gordon
1967	*The Ballad of Josie* (aka *Meanwhile, Back at the Ranch*)	Andrew V. McLaglen
1967	*The Happening*	Elliot Silverstein
1967	*Caprice*	Frank Tashlin
1967	*The Dirty Dozen*	Robert Aldrich
1967	*Guess Who's Coming to Dinner* (AAN)	Stanley Kramer
1968	*What's So Bad about Feeling Good?*	George Seaton
1968	*The Legend of Lylah Clare*	Robert Aldrich
1969	*Krakatoa: East of Java* (aka *Volcano*)	Bernard L. Kowalski
1972	*Ulzana's Raid*	Robert Aldrich
1973	*Emperor of the North*	Robert Aldrich
1974	*The Longest Yard*	Robert Aldrich
1975	*Doc Savage: The Man of Bronze*	Michael Anderson
1975	*Hustle* (aka *All the Other Angels*)	Robert Aldrich
1977	*Herbie Goes to Monte Carlo*	Vincent McEveety
1977	*The Choirboys*	Robert Aldrich
1979	*The Frisco Kid* (aka *No Knife*)	Robert Aldrich
1980	*Herbie Goes Bananas*	Vincent McEveety
1981	*. . . All the Marbles* (aka *. . . And All the Marbles*)	Robert Aldrich

DOLAN, Robert Emmett (1906–1972) A highly esteemed conductor, composer, songwriter, producer, and music arranger for Broadway, radio, and Hollywood, he scored forty-five movies in the 1940s and 1950s, mostly comedies and musicals.

Born in Hartford, Connecticut, and taught piano by his mother, Robert Emmett "Bobby" Dolan later studied music at Loyola College (now Concordia University) in Montreal before beginning his career as a pianist for dance bands, nightclubs, and later Broadway shows. As the pianist for the Broadway musical *East Wind* in 1931, Dolan got the attention of Oscar Hammerstein and other songwriters who hired him as musical director and conductor for such shows as *May Wine* (1934), *Forbidden*

Melody (1936), *Hooray for What!* (1937), *Leave It to Me!* (1938), *Very Warm for May* (1939), and *Louisiana Purchase* (1940). In the 1930s he was also very active in radio, where he conducted and, on occasion, composed music for various programs. Dolan also collaborated with various lyricists and wrote songs for radio, records, and later movies and Broadway. Among his hit songs are "Big Movie Show in the Sky," "And So to Bed," "Little by Little," "Your Heart Will Tell You So," "Song of the Highwayman," and "Talk to Me, Baby."

Dolan's movie career began in 1929 when he wrote five songs with lyricist Walter O'Keefe for the early musical *Red Hot Rhythm*. The two also collaborated on songs for *Dancing Sweeties* (1930) and *Sweet Kitty Bellairs* (1930). Dolan did not return to movies until 1941 when he was made a musical director at MGM. His first assignment was to supervise the music in *Birth of the Blues*, arranging the classic blues songs in the film and composing the soundtrack score. He received an Academy Award nomination for this first effort. Dolan was also nominated for his scores for the musicals *Holiday Inn, Star Spangled Rhythm, Incendiary Blonde, Lady in the Dark, Bells of St. Mary's, Blue Skies,* and *Road to Rio*, all of which had songs written by others. Among the other films he scored (and usually supervised the music for) are *The Major and the Minor, Happy Go Lucky, Henry Aldrich Gets Glamour, Dixie, Standing Room Only, Going My Way, Here Come the Waves, Salty O'Rourke, Duffy's Tavern, The Stork Club, Monsieur Beaucaire, Sorrowful Jones, Dear Ruth, The Perils of Pauline, The Great Gatsby, The Three Faces of Eve,* and *Murder, He Says*. For a time in the 1950s, Dolan was also a successful movie producer, presenting the popular musicals *White Christmas* (1954), *The Girl Rush* (1955), and *Anything Goes* (1956). In 1959 he left Hollywood and returned to Broadway where he was musical director for *Juno* (1959) and *Coco* (1969). He also wrote the songs for the Broadway musicals *Texas, Li'l Darlin'* (1949) and *Foxy* (1964), both with lyricist Johnny Mercer, but neither show ran. In the 1960s he wrote scores and/or conducted music for some television programs and taught music at Columbia University, also writing the film score textbook *Music in Modern Media*. Dolan died in 1972 at the age of sixty-six.

With eight Oscar nominations for his musical scores, one would think Dolan was a favorite Hollywood composer. Yet he was most appreciated as an expert arranger and conductor and that octet of honored movies has very little original soundtrack music. Whether he was reorchestrating old standards by Irving Berlin or introducing sparkling new songs by Johnny Burke and Jimmy Van Heusen, Dolan was a master of turning tunes into scintillating movie scores. More than half of his feature films are musicals, including some of the finest of his era. Most of the rest of Dolan's movies are comedies. Many of these have merry scores that were little noticed and rarely appreciated. Two Fred MacMurray romantic comedies serve as good examples. *Standing Room Only* is about a midwestern toy manufacturer (MacMurray) who goes to Washington with his secretary (Paulette Goddard) to secure a government contract and complications ensue because of the housing shortage in the capital. It has a very playful score that takes its cue from the toy business background. There is a jaunty Big Band main theme that marches along with rat-a-tat trumpets setting the beat, a childlike ditty for the toy factory's assembly line, and a romantic theme with swaying strings that doesn't take itself too seriously. Dolan's hillbilly-flavored score for *Murder, He Says* is also delightful. This mystery-farce has a pollster (MacMurray) getting involved with a backwoods family searching for some hidden money. A highlight of the score is Dolan's singsong ditty titled "Honor Flysis" with a nonsense lyric that becomes an important clue in the silly plot. The catchy melody later became the theme for NPR Radio show *All Things Considered*. Dolan scored a handful of Bob Hope comedies, one of the best being *My Favorite Brunette* about a baby photographer who is mistaken for a private eye and gets caught up in sinister doings. The main theme is a swinging number with a string orchestra playing with a slightly tango-like temperament. The film is filled with suspense music but often it has a giddy quality, making it clear this is primarily a comedy and a mystery only to keep the plot going.

On those rare occasions when Dolan was handed a serious drama to score, he did not disappoint but received little recognition for his work. The 1949 version of *The Great Gatsby* is probably the best of the many screen treatments of F. Scott Fitzgerald's iconic "Jazz Age" novel. Dolan sometimes quotes popular twenties tunes in his score but much of the soundtrack is original music utilizing jazz for the partying, a lush string orchestra for the romance, and heavy dramatic music for the bootlegging scenes. Alan Ladd's Jay Gatsby is darker and more aggressive than the other screen portrayals and this is reflected in Dolan's fine score. His penultimate Hollywood project was the psychological drama *The Three Faces of Eve* about a woman (Joanne Woodward) suffering from multiple personality disorder. The main theme is a slightly manic orchestral piece with a lonely oboe and restless strings that is romantic but unsettling. Dolan created a musical theme for each of Eve's three personalities: a flowing, domestic passage for the wife and mother, an eerie and confused theme for the serious Jane,

and a sexy jazz piece for the hedonistic Eve Black. Sometimes it is Dolan's music that cues the audience that Eve is slipping away from one personality and becoming another person. This is masterful screen scoring. Other demanding scores for dramas should have followed, but Dolan left Hollywood two years later for the theatre. He found no success there as a composer and so his reputation rests on his distinguished career as an arranger and conductor of several of the best movie musicals of the postwar years.

Credits

(all films USA)

Year	Film	Director
1941	*Birth of the Blues* (AAN)	Victor Schertzinger
1941	*Louisiana Purchase*	Irving Cummings
1942	*True to the Army*	Albert S. Rogell
1942	*Dr. Broadway*	Anthony Mann
1942	*Are Husbands Necessary?*	Norman Taurog
1942	*Holiday Inn* (AAN)	Mark Sandrich
1942	*The Major and the Minor*	Billy Wilder
1942	*Once Upon a Honeymoon*	Leo McCarey
1942	*Star Spangled Rhythm* (AAN)	George Marshall, A. Edward Sutherland
1943	*Happy Go Lucky*	Curtis Bernhardt
1943	*Henry Aldrich Gets Glamour*	Hugh Bennett
1943	*Dixie*	A. Edward Sutherland
1943	*Let's Face It*	Sidney Lanfield
1944	*Standing Room Only*	Sidney Lanfield
1944	*Lady in the Dark* (AAN)	Mitchell Leisen
1944	*Going My Way*	Leo McCarey
1944	*I Love a Soldier* (aka *When I Come Back*)	Mark Sandrich
1944	*Here Come the Waves*	Mark Sandrich
1945	*Bring on the Girls*	Sidney Lanfield
1945	*Salty O'Rourke*	Raoul Walsh
1945	*Murder, He Says*	George Marshall
1945	*Incendiary Blonde* (AAN)	George Marshall
1945	*Duffy's Tavern*	Hal Walker
1945	*The Bells of St. Mary's* (AAN)	Leo McCarey
1945	*The Stork Club*	Hal Walker
1946	*Monsieur Beaucaire*	George Marshall
1946	*Blue Skies* (AAN)	Stuart Heisler, Mark Sandrich
1946	*Cross My Heart*	John Berry
1947	*My Favorite Brunette* (aka *The Private Eye*)	Elliott Nugent
1947	*Dear Ruth*	William D. Russell
1947	*Welcome Stranger*	Elliott Nugent
1947	*The Trouble with Women*	Sidney Lanfield
1947	*The Perils of Pauline*	George Marshall
1947	*Road to Rio* (AAN)	Norman Z. McLeod
1948	*Saigon*	Leslie Fenton
1948	*Mr. Peabody and the Mermaid*	Irving Pichel
1948	*Good Sam*	Leo McCarey
1949	*My Own True Love*	Compton Bennett
1949	*Sorrowful Jones*	Sidney Lanfield
1949	*The Great Gatsby*	Elliott Nugent
1949	*Top o' the Morning*	David Miller

Year	Film	Director
1950	*Let's Dance*	Norman Z. McLeod
1952	*My Son John*	Leo McCarey
1957	*The Three Faces of Eve*	Nunnally Johnson
1959	*The Man Who Understood Women*	Nunnally Johnson

DONAGGIO, Pino (b. 1941) An Italian singer, songwriter, and composer for television and films, he has scored over 175 movies in Italy and America, including several popular horror thrillers for director Brian De Palma.

Born Giuseppe Donaggio on the island of Burano in Venice, Italy, he grew up in a family in which most played musical instruments. Donaggio began studying violin at the age of ten at the local Benedetto Marcello Conservatory, then at the Giuseppe Verdi Conservatory in Milan. He was something of a child prodigy, making his solo debut as violinist for a Vivaldi radio concert when he was only fourteen. In the late 1950s, Donaggio left classical music and began his career in rock and pop music as a singer and then a songwriter. By 1965 he was not only a popular singer-songwriter throughout Italy but his hit song "Io che non vivo" became an international success under the title "You Don't Have to Say You Love Me." Donaggio made a memorable screen debut scoring the stylish thriller *Don't Look Now* in 1973. Three years later he wrote music for his first American film, Brian De Palma's horror favorite *Carrie*. Donaggio and De Palma have since worked on six other films together: *Home Movies*, *Dressed to Kill*, *Blow Out*, *Raising Cain*, *Body Double*, and *Passion*. By the 1980s, he was scoring movies for several European countries but he remained in Venice and never abandoned the Italian film industry. All the same Donaggio has still managed to score over thirty American movies, including *Haunts*, *Tourist Trap*, *The Howling*, *Piranha*, *The Fan*, *Tex*, *Over the Brooklyn Bridge*, *Gor* and *Gor II*, *Dancers*, *Zelly and Me*, *Kansas*, *Oblivion* and *Oblivion II*, and *Night Game*. Among his notable European movies are *A Whisper in the Dark*, *The Black Cat*, *Nothing Left to Do But Cry*, *The Morro Affair*, *Jenatsch*, *High Frequency*, *Ritual of Love*, *Giovanni Falcone*, *Ordinary Hero*, *State Secret*, *Marching in Darkness*, *Arcane Sorcerer*, *Our Land*, *Winter in Wartime*, *Prima del tramonto*, and *Soul Mate*. Donaggio has also scored many Italian television series, miniseries, and TV movies.

Coming from the world of pop songs, Donaggio has a strong melodic line in much of his screen music. A majority of his films are horror movies or thrillers in which the mood and atmosphere dominate the music. Yet Donaggio scores such films with a melodic air, utilizing strings for the most part and often avoiding the jarring music of most thrillers. His first score, for the dazzling *Don't Look Now*, is a good example. A British couple (Julie Christie and Donald Sutherland) keep seeing images of their deceased daughter in the alleyways of Venice. Rarely has that city had such a sinister look and feel on-screen. Yet the music is often lilting and euphonic. There is a gentle piano passage, childlike in its simplicity, that is used for flashbacks and memories of the drowned child. The score also has a mournful motif that is a hesitant waltz for piano and strings; there is a flute, piano, and mandolin passage that moves at a lively pace but has a sorrowful subtext; and a church organ theme that manages to sound religious and menacing at the same time. For the most suspenseful scenes, there is a strident string passage with grumbling vibrations and a howling electronic wail, and the recurring theme for the murders is scored with high-pitched strings and a low bass violas. *Don't Look Now* has a first-rate score and afforded Donaggio a laudable screen debut.

His scores for director Brian De Palma are all very elegant and rich, surprising for films with obvious shocks and overt thrills. The teen horror flick *Carrie* has a lovely opening title theme with graceful and serene piano, flute, and strings without a hint of danger. A dream sequence features a piccolo dancing through a flowing string movement. The famous scene in which a bucket of blood is poured on Carrie (Sissy Spacek) at a dance is scored in the way Bernard Herrmann would in a Hitchcock film with slowly mounting suspense as various strings climb the scale in different ways. When Carrie's house collapses, the music is a symphonic piece with electronic sound effects playing against a violin solo. Carrie's crazy mother (Piper Laurie) is scored with wavering strings and subdued brass with a religious flavor. The soundtrack also includes two pop ballads, "Born to Have It All" and "I Never Dreamed Someone Like You Could Love Someone Like Me," written by Donaggio and Merrit Malloy and sung on the soundtrack by Katie Irving. De Palma's mystery thriller *Dressed to Kill* has a gliding main theme played on strings that moves in a stately manner, the same music heard later in the shower scene with a solo voice added. There is also a spiraling string theme that conveys confusion without the music getting out of control, suspense music that rises in intensity yet maintains the same rhythmic pattern, and a minor-key romantic theme on piano and strings that seems to float on air. The thriller *Blow Out*, De Palma's homage to Michelangelo Antonioni's iconic *Blow Up* (1966), concerns a sound effects designer (John Travolta) who discovers a murder when replaying a tape he has made. Donaggio's score is quite varied, including a flute, string, and piano theme that has a classical temperament with a sense of urgency, a chaotic piano passage with restless string interruptions, a jazzy section on electronic instruments with some vibrant guitar riffs, and even a disco passage that might be a nod to star Travolta's earlier *Saturday Night Fever* (1977). De Palma's voyeur mystery *Body Double* has a reflective piano main theme that hesitates before giving way to a flowing melody played by a full orchestra. There is a rhythmic theme for the voyeur scenes that has a nervous bass line with sustained organ chords and vocal embellishments. Also in the score is a passage on piano and synthesized keyboard that moves cautiously but consistently forward, and a theme for a low-budget vampire movie being filmed that has screaming descending strings and explosive brass and percussion.

Perhaps Donaggio's best horror film without De Palma is Joe Dante's *The Howling*, which created a new interest in werewolf movies in the 1980s. This film has a more percussive score with plenty of shock value. Sustained high-pitched violins contrast with low bass viola phrases in one passage, while chanting, dizzy strings, and blaring horns compete in another. At one point a pop melody is played on electric instruments that is campy and carnival-like. There are also creepy chimes over wailing strings in one section while a different theme has bold trumpets over raspy lower brass with jittery percussion joining in. Dante offered another terrifying animal in *Piranha*, and Donaggio came up with a pulsating theme in which low- and high-pitched strings compete in a predatory way, the harsh sounds simultaneous with a stabbing motion. The

Italian thriller *The Black Cat* has an oboe and strings main theme in a minor key that suggests something sinister even though the melody is breezy and carefree. *Seed of Chucky* sets classic strings against moaning vocals, *Crawlspace* has a strident female vocal that is off pitch and drips with desperate longing, and in *Tourist Trap* a nervous piano theme is heard against sustained strings and oppressive chimes. It is easy to see why Donaggio was the composer of choice on two continents for such movies.

One cannot overlook Donaggio's scores outside of the horror genre. The cult action epic *Hercules* has a bold trumpet and percussion march that has a quirky tempo, some tripping romantic passages, and an inspiring anthem theme, all of this set against a rapid rock beat that gives the score its energy. Similarly, the campy *The Barbarians* has a jittery fanfare on electronic and traditional instruments set at a furious pace and with a pounding bass. The result is a curious mix of old-time Hollywood adventure score and a vibrating musical chase with more than a touch of disco. The moody character film *The Berlin Affair* has a ponderous main theme played by a full orchestra but punctuated by a steady timpani beat that is almost tribal. The score is filled with classical romanticism yet there is a disquieting aspect to the music, just as the lesbian affair of the title seems more gloomy than romantic. *Zelly and Me* is another character piece but this time about an orphan girl (Alexandra Johnes) living with her grandmother (Glynis Johns) and her nanny Zelly (Isabella Rossellini) in rural Virginia. A piano and woodwind theme uses synthesized accents to bring it to life. There is also some vivid traveling music with a nimble piano playing against strings, as well as a facile flute, strings, and piano section that moves along in an enticing manner. Arguably Donaggio's finest non-horror movie score is for *Winter in Wartime*, a coming-of-age tale about a teenager (Martijn Lakemeier) in wartime Holland who joins the Resistance movement against the Nazis. The score takes the teenager's point of view, as with the youthful voices and delicate piano and string theme that haunt the movie. One passage is achingly beautiful as a piano solo intertwines with a fluid orchestral theme, the piece building in emotion thrillingly. There is also a harp and chanting section of the score in which an oboe intrudes to fill out the melody. A full choir and orchestra are used effectively for the stirring climax of the score, a superb passage that causes one to wonder if too much of Donaggio's talent has been wasted in the horror genre.

Credits

(all films Italy unless stated otherwise)

Year	Film	Director
1973	*Don't Look Now*	Nicolas Roeg (UK/Italy)
1975	*Smiling Maniacs*	Marcello Aliprandi
1976	*A Whisper in the Dark*	Marcello Aliprandi
1976	*Carrie*	Brian De Palma (USA)
1977	*Haunts*	Herb Freed (USA)
1978	*Damned in Venice*	Ugo Liberatore
1978	*Piranha*	Joe Dante (USA)
1978	*China 9, Liberty 37*	Monte Hellman, Tony Brandt (Italy/Spain)
1979	*Tourist Trap*	David Schmoeller (USA)
1979	*Skin Deep*	Marcello Aliprandi
1980	*Home Movies* (aka *The Maestro*)	Brian De Palma (USA)
1980	*Beyond Evil*	Herb Freed (USA)
1980	*Dressed to Kill*	Brian De Palma (USA)
1980	*Desire, the Interior Life*	Gianni Barcelloni (Italy/W. Germany)
1980	*Augh! Augh!*	Marco Toniato
1981	*The Howling*	Joe Dante (USA)
1981	*The Black Cat*	Lucio Fulci
1981	*The Fan* (aka *Trance*)	Ed Bianchi (USA)
1981	*Blow Out* (aka *Personal Effects*)	Brian De Palma (USA)
1982	*Venezia, Carnevale—un amore*	Mario Lanfranchi (Italy)
1982	*Tex*	Tim Hunter (USA)
1982	*Beyond the Door* (aka *Beyond Obsession*)	Liliana Cavani
1982	*Vatican Conspiracy* (aka *Death in the Vatican*)	Marcello Aliprandi (Italy/Spain/Mexico)
1983	*Via Degli Specchi*	Giovanna Gagliardo
1983	*Hercules*	Luigi Cozzi (USA/Italy)
1984	*Over the Brooklyn Bridge*	Menahem Golan (USA)
1984	*The World of Don Camillo*	Terence Hill (Italy)
1984	*Body Double*	Brian De Palma (USA)
1984	*Nothing Left to Do but Cry*	Roberto Benigni, Massimo Troisi (Italy)
1985	*The Lie*	Giovanni Soldati
1985	*Déja Vu*	Anthony B. Richmond (UK)
1985	*The Adventures of Hercules II*	Luigi Cozzi (Italy/USA)
1985	*The Berlin Affair*	Liliana Cavani (Italy/W. Germany)
1985	*Nothing Underneath*	Carlo Vanzina
1985	*Savage Dawn*	Simon Nuchtern (USA)
1986	*Crawlspace*	David Schmoeller (USA)
1986	*The Moro Affair*	Giuseppe Ferrera
1986	*7 Chili in 7 Giorni*	Luca Verdone
1987	*Hotel Colonial*	Cinzia Th. Torrini (Italy/USA)
1987	*The Barbarians*	Ruggero Deodato (USA/Italy)
1987	*Jenatsch*	Daniel Schmid (Switzerland/France/W. Germany)
1987	*Gor*	Fritz Kiersch (USA)
1987	*Devils of Monza*	Luciano Odorisio
1987	*Going Bananas* (aka *My African Adventure*)	Boaz Davidson (USA)
1987	*Sahara Heat*	Aldo Lado (Italy/France)
1987	*Dancers*	Herbert Ross (USA)
1988	*Phantom of Death*	Ruggero Deodato
1988	*Zelly and Me*	Tina Rathborne (USA)
1988	*Appointment with Death*	Michael Winner (USA)
1988	*The Gamble*	Carlo Vanzina
1988	*Kansas*	David Stevens (USA)
1988	*Catacombs* (aka *Curse IV: The Ultimate Sacrifice*)	David Schmoeller (Italy/USA)
1988	*High Frequency*	Faliero Rosati
1988	*Gor II* (aka *Outlaw of Gor*)	John "Bud" Cardos (USA)

Year	Film	Director
1989	*Indio*	Antonio Margheriti
1989	*Night Game*	Peter Masterson (USA)
1989	*Jiboa*	Mario Bianchi
1990	*Two Evil Eyes*	Dario Argento, George A. Romero (Italy/USA)
1990	*Ritual of Love*	Aldo Lado (Italy/France/Germany)
1991	*La setta* (aka *The Devil's Daughter*)	Michele Soavi
1991	*Indio 2—La rivolta*	Antonio Margheriti
1991	*A Demon in My View*	Petra Haffter (Germany)
1992	*All Ladies Do It*	Tinto Brass
1992	*Raising Cain*	Brian De Palma (USA)
1992	*A Fine Romance*	Gene Saks
1993	*Trauma* (aka *Aura's Enigma*)	Dario Argento (Italy/USA)
1993	*Where Are You? I'm Here*	Liliana Cavani
1993	*Giovanni Falcone*	Giuseppe Ferrera
1994	*Oblivion* (aka *Welcome to Oblivion*)	Sam Irvin (USA)
1994	*The Night before Christmas* (aka *The Fight Before Christmas*)	Terence Hill (Italy/Germany/USA)
1994	*Power and Lovers*	Aldo Lado
1995	*Ordinary Hero*	Michele Placido
1995	*State Secret*	Giuseppe Ferrera
1995	*Mollo tutto*	José Maria Sánchez
1995	*Palermo—Milan One Way*	Claudio Fragasso
1995	*Never Talk to Strangers*	Peter Hall (USA/Canada/Germany)
1995	*Unknown Soldier*	Marcello Aliprandi
1995	*Mr. Dog*	Gianpaolo Tescari
1996	*Oblivion 2: Backlash*	Sam Irvin (USA)
1996	*Marching in Darkness*	Massimo Spano
1996	*Festival*	Pupi Avati
1996	*Squillo*	Carlo Vanzina
1996	*Arcane Sorcerer*	Pupi Avati
1997	*The Game Bag*	Maurizio Zaccaro
1997	*La terza luna*	Matteo Bellinelli (Switzerland/Italy/France)
1998	*Coppia omicida*	Claudio Fragasso
1998	*Frivolous Lola*	Tinto Brass
1998	*Il Mio West* (aka *Gunslinger's Revenge*)	Giovanni Veronesi
1999	*Prima del tramonto*	Stefano Incerti
1999	*Un uoma perbene*	Maurizio Zaccaro
1999	*Terra bruiara*	Fabio Segatori
2000	*Trasgredire* (aka *Cheeky*)	Tinto Brass
2000	*Up at the Villa*	Philip Haas (UK/USA)
2000	*On the Beach Beyond the Pier*	Giovanni Fago
2001	*Once Upon a Time in Sicily*	Fabio Conversi (Italy/France)
2001	*The Order*	Sheldon Lettich (Aruba/USA)
2002	*The Bankers of God: The Calvi Affair*	Giuseppe Ferrera
2002	*Soul Mate*	Sergio Rubini
2004	*Concorso di colpa*	Claudio Fragasso
2004	*Pontormo: A Heretical Love*	Giovanni Fago
2004	*Seed of Chucky* (aka *Bride of Chucky 2*)	Don Mancini (Romania/USA/UK)
2006	*Our Land*	Sergio Rubini
2006	*Anthony, Warrior of God*	Antonello Belluco
2007	*Guido che sfidò le Brigate Rosse*	Giuseppe Ferrera
2007	*Milano Palermo—Il ritorno*	Claudio Gragasso
2008	*Colpo d'occhio*	Sergio Rubini
2008	*Winter in Wartime*	Martin Koolhoven (Netherlands/Belgium)
2010	*Le Ultime 56 Ore*	Claudio Fragasso
2011	*Sotto il vestito niente—L'ultima sfilata*	Carlo Vanzina
2012	*Passion*	Brian De Palma (Germany/France)
2013	*Patrick*	Mark Hartley (Australia)

DOYLE, Patrick (b. 1953) Best known for his ten films with director-actor Kenneth Branagh, the Scottish-born composer is also a respected stage actor, appearing in several movies including six that he scored.

Patrick Doyle was born in Uddingston near Glasgow, Scotland, into a musical family and received a classical musical education at the Royal Scottish Academy of Music and Drama, where he studied voice and piano. Doyle was also drawn to acting and had his first success on British television as a performer in children's shows. In 1987 he was hired by Kenneth Branagh as an actor in his Renaissance Theatre Company where many of the company members did double duty, both acting and working on the productions. Doyle scored some Shakespeare works for the company and got more interested in composing. The Renaissance production of *Twelfth Night* was broadcast on British television in 1988, giving his score a wide hearing. When Branagh made his first film, *Henry V*, he asked Doyle to write the music even though the actor-composer had never scored a movie before. The resulting score, with its chilling hymn "Non nobis, Domine," brought the young composer international recognition and launched his screen music career.

Although Doyle performed a supporting role in *Henry V* and he continued to occasionally act in movies, his concentration soon turned to composing. He went on to score such memorable Branagh movies as *Dead Again*, *Much Ado about Nothing*, and *Hamlet*, but was equally successful composing for other directors and scoring such hits as *Carlito's Way*, *A Little Princess*, *Sense and Sensibility*, *Bridget Jones's Diary*, *Gosford Park*, *Nanny McPhee*, *Harry Potter and the Goblet of Fire*, and *Brave*. Doyle has collaborated with French director Régis Wagnier on seven movies and has also worked with such diverse talents as Brian De Palma, Robert Altman, Richard Benjamin, Mike Newell, Garry Marshall, and Ang Lee. His movie credits are truly international, from Hollywood to Hungary. Doyle's career and life suffered a setback in the late 1990s when he was diagnosed with leukemia, but soon in the new century he was cured and he returned to movies. Doyle has also composed some notable concert pieces, such as the orchestral-choral work *The Thistle and the Rose* (commissioned for the Queen Mother's ninetieth birthday), the violin concerto *Corasik*, the Scottish orchestral work *Tam O'Shanter*, and *Impressions of America: A Suite for Orchestra*.

Because of his classical music training, Doyle often references the great composers in his work. His music can be as rousing as a Wagner anthem, as in *Henry V* and *Thor*, or as subtle as a Chopin sonata, as in *Sense and Sensibility* and *Secondhand Lion*s. He mixes African sounds with electronic embellishments in *The Rise of the Planet of the Apes*, uses a sitar and other Indian instruments in *A Little Princess*, employs Irish instruments cunningly in *Into the West*, and uses an unlikely tango in *Indochine*. For the modern-dress version of *Great Expectations*, Doyle utilizes electronic instruments yet still suggests a Victorian Gothic sensibility. Some of his scores are sweepingly symphonic, as in the fluid music for parts of *Eragon* and *Frankenstein*; others highlight solo instruments, as with the jazzy saxophone and piano in *Une femme française* or the jaunty piano in *Gosford Park*. He returned to his Scottish roots in the animated movies *Quest for Camelot* and *Brave*, as well as in the documentary *Jig*. Two scores that stand out for their ability to alternate between soft, romantic themes and urgent, menacing ones are those Doyle wrote for *Dead Again* and *Harry Potter and the Goblet of Fire*. The fourth part of the Harry Potter saga has important scenes that require specific music. Doyle provides a series of marches and processionals for the Tri-Wizard Tournament and a lovely, sprightly waltz heard on a record player when the students practice dancing for the Yule Ball; a fuller version of the waltz is played at the actual ball. The celebratory music for the Quidditch World Cup is a rhythmic folk dance with a Celtic flavor. Such lyrical passages are contrasted with the Voldemort theme in which screaming and descending brass are surrounded by furious strings and rumbling percussion. The music that accompanies the death of Cedric (Robert Pattinson) is a heartfelt lament in which strings seem to weep as they play a floating, angelic melody. This is certainly one of the most diverse scores in the Harry Potter series. For the complicated and clever Hitchcockian thriller *Dead Again*, the sadistic and the sublime are again side by side. Director Branagh plays a Los Angeles detective investigating a long-past murder; he also plays the actual murderer. Low grumbling bass and explosive string attacks are comingled in the main theme, which sometimes is hurried and frantic, other times leisurely and classical. The romance, both past and present, is scored with a fluid and serene love theme in which reeds seem to dance around the strings in a celestial pas de deux. If Branagh's *Dead Again* is a sort of homage to Hitchcock, Doyle's score is a nod to composer Bernard Herrmann and the sound of his Hitchcock music.

Doyle's lighter side is well represented by his score for the family fantasy film *Nanny McPhee*. The magical title nanny (Emma Thompson) uses her special powers to take charge of seven mischievous children and the tricks she conjures up are scored with unabashed delight by Doyle. The main theme is a silly ditty played on a furious harpsichord and a disapproving bassoon. One magical passage with fluttering strings and double-time woodwinds takes so many twists and turns that it seems to keep surprising itself. There is a zesty and rapid dance in which brass fanfares and cymbal crashes compete with a frivolous mouth organ, and in another track a vivacious fiddle and piccolo play a merry gavotte. One of the few quiet moments comes with a simple lullaby that moves from a solo voice to a string piece that glows with warmth and affection. *A Little Princess*, based on another popular children's book, has no magic but there is still a sense of astonishment in Doyle's music. The story of an orphaned British girl (Liesel Matthews) reduced to servitude in a New York boardinghouse is much darker than Nanny McPhee's world. Yet the score remains upbeat and hopeful most of the time. A fragile waltz in slow motion is played on a harp with such delicacy that each note seems afraid of itself. When woodwinds are added, the little tune takes on a mystical quality. There is a busy and energetic harp passage in which other strings provide accompaniment without paying attention to each other's tempo. Similarly, a frantic violin and viola piece seems so worried that each ignores the other and races ahead at its own pace. A flowing theme filled with sitar accents is played when the orphan tells the other children exotic stories about India. Perhaps Doyle's most classically influenced score is the one he wrote for *Sense and Sensibility*, one of the best Jane Austen movie adaptations. The difficulties that two sisters (Emma Thompson and Kate Winslet) endure before they end up with the right husbands are sometimes handled with humor, but this story has some of Austen's most heartbreaking scenes. Doyle's score encompasses both lighthearted and sorrowful emotions. There is some slaphappy traveling music heard on strings and horns that speeds up and changes keys in a giddy and contagious fashion. Also quite effervescent is a graceful yet spry passage that maintains a sparkling quality as various instruments take turns doing variations on the same musical phrase. On the other hand, there is a reflec-

tive, even morose, theme filled with woe as strings stumble down the scale and a piano can barely continue playing the simple melody.

Many might agree that Doyle's most stirring music can be found in the score he wrote for three of Branagh's Shakespeare movies. The powerful scores for *Henry V* and *Hamlet* pay homage to the music of regal British movies of the past just as Branagh pays tribute to the two earlier Laurence Olivier film versions of the plays. A different but equally proficient sound can be heard in the witty comedy *Much Ado about Nothing*. This trio of Bard scores is Doyle at his best. *Henry V* was the first film for Branagh and Doyle, yet there is no trace of the beginner in the direction or the music. Once again, the score is filled with contrasts. Regal and processional music is matched by somber or harsh passages. The famous St. Crispin's Day speech is underscored with a reverent string and horn movement that seems to be aching to break out and attack. As the king's speech builds, the musical instruments get more and more restless. The extensive battle at Agincourt sequence also builds musically. Low strings and horns are tentative at first then accelerate as other instruments are added and the various percussion pieces predominate, eventually exploding in a tumult of chaotic noises that sound like modern atonal music. The musical (and thematic) highlight of the movie is the "Non nobis, Domine" scene. After the battle is over and dead bodies are scattered about in the mud, a lone soldier (Doyle) starts to sing a cappella the rhythmic hymn "Non nobis, Domine." He is gradually joined by other soldiers, creating a strong male chorus as the orchestra carefully joins them, eventually developing into a complex chorale with many parts and a piercing climax. Doyle's score for *Hamlet* is more solemn, as befits the tragic tale, yet there are moments of vigorous music as well. The score's tone is set by Plácido Domingo's singing of the doleful Latin hymn "In pace" on the soundtrack. The ghost scene opens with a rambunctious and angry march rather than the expected gloomy music. A solo oboe and rumbling drums are heard during part of the scene, a solo violin joining later to fill out the complexity of the situation. A vibrant, multihorn fanfare for the court is fiery and majestic. This is in contrast to Hamlet's theme, a heavyhearted passage heard on strings and reeds that avoids sentimentality because it seems so self-aware and knowing. Ophelia's funeral is scored with sustained strings and a simple melody that is more reflective than morose; a variation of the theme is used for Hamlet's death. The movie ends not with a whimper but with a flurry of drums, trumpets, and a male choir climbing the scale with gusto.

Three musical pieces in *Much Ado about Nothing* are so important to the storytelling that Branagh asked Doyle to write them before filming began so that the cast could know them and how they would be used. Two of the pieces are songs using Shakespeare's lyrics. "Sigh No More" is a wistful ballad about the plight of women who are forced to face the inconstancy of men. "Pardon, Goddess of the Night" is a melancholy love song sung at a funeral. Ironically, both of these woeful songs are reprised at the end of the film as a celebratory canon. The third piece written and orchestrated early is the piquant dance music for the masked ball. Doyle wrote the rest of the score after a rough cut was prepared, providing flippant, satirical music for the verbal sparring between Beatrice (Emma Thompson) and Benedick (Branagh) and a sweeping romantic

theme for the younger lovers Claudio (Robert Sean Leonard) and Hero (Kate Beckinsale). The most invigorating music in *Much Ado about Nothing* is the overture, which conjures up memories of the rousing music Hollywood provided for swashbucklers in the Golden Age. This radiant passage begins with confused flutes rushing about in circles then transitions into a sparkling march overflowing with sportive trumpets, frivolous strings, and vivid brass fanfares that do not take themselves too seriously. Finally the main theme surfaces, a rousing processional that glitters with cockeyed fervor.

Doyle's film music has been performed in concert, including a very popular 2007 benefit performance to raise money for the Leukemia Research Fund. The hymn "Non nobis, Domine" from *Henry V* and some of the pseudo-Ivor Novello songs he wrote for *Gosford Park* have found a life outside of the movies. Doyle continues to perform on occasion, most recently providing the voice for one of the animated characters in *Brave*.

Credits

Year	Film	Director
1989	Henry V	Kenneth Branagh (UK)
1990	Shipwrecked	Nils Gaup (Norway/Sweden/USA)
1991	Dead Again (GGN)	Kenneth Branagh (USA)
1992	Indochine	Régis Wargnier (France)
1992	Into the West	Mike Newell (Ireland/UK)
1993	Much Ado about Nothing	Kenneth Branagh (UK/USA)
1993	Needful Things	Fraser Clarke Heston (USA)
1993	Carlito's Way	Brian De Palma (USA)
1994	Exit to Eden	Garry Marshall (USA)
1994	Frankenstein	Kenneth Branagh (USA/Japan)
1995	Une femme française	Régus Wagnier (UK/France/Germany)
1995	A Little Princess	Alfonso Cuarón (USA)
1995	Sense and Sensibility (AAN; GGN; BAFTA-N)	Ang Lee (USA/UK)
1996	Mrs. Winterbourne	Richard Benjamin (USA)
1996	Hamlet (AAN)	Kenneth Branagh (UK/USA)
1997	Donnie Brasco	Mike Newell (USA)
1998	Great Expectations	Alfonso Cuarón (USA)
1998	Quest for Camelot	Frederik Du Chau (USA)
1999	Est—Ouest	Régis Wahnier (France/Russia)
2000	Love's Labour's Lost	Kenneth Branagh (UK/France/USA)
2001	Blow Dry	Paddy Breathnach (USA/UK/Germany)
2001	Bridget Jones's Diary	Sharon Maguire (USA/UK/Ireland)
2001	Gosford Park	Robert Altman (UK/USA/Italy)
2002	Killing Me Softly	Kaihe Chen (USA/UK)
2003	Calendar Girls	Nigel Cole (UK/USA)
2003	Secondhand Lions	Tim McCanlies (USA)
2003	The Galíndez File	Gerardo Herrero (Spain/UK/Italy)
2004	Battle of the Brave	Jean Beaudin (Canada/France/UK)
2005	Man to Man	Régis Wagnier (France/S. Africa/UK)
2005	Wah-Wah	Richard E. Grant (UK/France/S. Africa)
2005	Nanny McPhee	Kirk Jones (USA/UK/France)

Year	Film	Director
2005	Harry Potter and the Goblet of Fire	Mike Newell (UK/USA)
2006	Sir Billi the Vet	Michael Cawood (UK)
2006	Jekyll + Hyde	Nick Stillwell (USA/Canada)
2006	As You Like It	Kenneth Branagh (USA/UK)
2006	Eragon	Stefen Fangmeier (USA/UK/Hungary)
2007	Have Mercy on Us All	Régis Wagnier (France)
2007	The Last Legion	Doug Lefler (UK/Italy/France)
2007	Sleuth	Kenneth Branagh (USA/UK)
2008	Nim's Island	Jennifer Flackett, Mark Levin (USA)
2008	Igor	Anthony Leondis (USA/France)
2010	Main Street	John Doyle (USA)
2011	La ligne droite	Régis Wagnier (France)
2011	Thor	Kenneth Branagh (USA)
2011	Jig	Sue Bourne (UK)
2011	Rise of the Planet of the Apes	Rupert Wyatt (USA)
2012	Brave	Mark Andrews, Brenda Chapman, Steve Purcell (USA)
2013	Jack Ryan	Kenneth Branagh (USA)

DUDLEY, Anne (b. 1956) A British pop and classical musician, a music producer and arranger, and a film and television composer, she has scored over thirty American and European movies over the past three decades.

Anne Dudley was born Anne Jennifer Beckingham in Chatham, England, and took piano lessons as a child. Dudley later studied at the Royal College of Music and King's College, then worked as a musician on classical and pop recordings. In the early 1980s she began arranging music and playing keyboard for record producer Trevor Horn. In 1983 she was a founding member of the innovative and influential group Art of Noise which featured the synthesizer in their avant-garde music. Labeled a "synth-pop" band, Art of Noise made several recordings and was active into the 1990s, returning in the new millennium with a redefined sound. Dudley also arranged concerts of classical and New Wave music, composed her own albums and wrote music for chorales and special events, and produced a variety of recordings, several of them climbing high on the charts. (She changed her name from Beckingham to Dudley when she married music producer and engineer Robert Dudley, with whom she has worked on many occasions.)

Dudley's screen career began in 1985 when she contributed some music to the British crime comedy *Restless Natives*. Two years later she cowrote with Jonathan Jeczalik the score for the American farce *Disorderlies*, followed by mostly forgettable Hollywood and British movies until

she worked with director Neil Jordan on the Irish-English drama *The Miracle* in 1991. The next year the two artists collaborated on the international success *The Crying Game*, which led to composing assignments all over Europe and in the States. Dudley's memorable American movies include *Say Anything . . .* , *Knight Moves*, *The Mighty Quinn*, *American History X*, and the documentary *Lake of Fire*. Her most recognized European film is the comedy-drama *The Full Monty*, for which she won an Oscar, and also noteworthy are *Silence Like Glass*, *Buster*, *Hollow Reed*, *The Miracle Maker*, *Bright Young Things*, *Black Book*, and *Tristan + Isolde*. Dudley also scored such British television series as *Jeeves and Wooster*, *Kavanaugh QC*, *Crime Traveller*, *The 10th Kingdom*, *Trial & Retribution*, and *Breathless*. She has conducted, arranged, and performed keyboard for several of her movies and those by others, most notably her orchestrations and piano playing for *Les Misérables* (2012).

While not all of Dudley's screen scores utilize synthesized music, most have a modern New Wave sensibility, which makes them sound fresh and intriguing. *Knight Moves*, a thriller that revolves around the game of chess, has a highly synthesized theme with sound effects and plenty of reverb that races forward with a nervous energy. The movie also has a suspense-filled passage with echoing chimes, distant explosions, and strings that climb the scale with determination. On the other hand, Dudley's score for *The Crying Game* uses conventional orchestration yet comes across as very modern. There is a gloomy main theme with a military flavor because of its trumpet call and marching percussion. It then moves into a lyrical lament that is delicate and heartfelt. The score also includes a pounding march with threatening strings and propulsive drums, as well as a restless passage for piano, trumpet, and orchestra that forebodes tragedy. Although there were a handful of pop songs by others heard on the soundtrack, it was Dudley's atmospheric score that supplied much of the drama in *The Crying Game*.

The thriller *Black Book*, set during the Resistance movement in Holland during World War II, has a menacing theme in which strings seem to run around in circles as waves of oppressive music sweeps over them. Even the lyrical passages have a chaotic temperament with their unrelenting way of pushing forward. The music is sometimes just as menacing in the crime drama *American History X*, about a former neo-Nazi (Edward Norton) who tries to keep his brother (Edward Furlong) from making the same mistakes he did. There is a disturbing "Benedictus" in which gliding strings and a fragile piano solo seem to mourn even as the piece builds and vocal chanting is added. Much of the score is very symphonic, such as a poignant lament that slowly moves across the scale with a wavering motion, and a sublime theme for a flashback as two young brothers play on a beach and shorebirds take flight in time to the music. The comedy *Buster*, about the crook Buster Edwards (Phil Collins) who participated in the Great British Train Robbery of 1963, has a lively score with both synthesized and traditional orchestration. There is a jaunty theme in which an electric guitar climbs the scale carefully as violins add some classical embellishment. Also memorable is some vivacious music for the train robbery in which strings attack in a Stravinsky-like manner and brass and percussion march forward in fearless confidence.

Dudley's most popular movie, *The Full Monty*, brought her the most recognition but moviegoers tend to remember the many songs by others, which were used throughout the film. This comic melodrama, about unemployed steelworkers in Britain who take to striptease work to earn some money, has a delightful contemporary-sounding score that captures the bittersweet tone of the story. There is a delicious jazz theme featuring laughing saxophones and a carefree harmonica, a cool jazz section that is smooth and self-satisfied, a gliding theme with elegant strings and harmonica accents, and a disco-like passage in which a saxophone behaves like a trumpet. *The Full Monty* may not be Dudley's most typical score, for it uses no synthesized orchestrations, but it is masterful all the same. For a composer-musician coming from the world of pop music, Dudley excels in many kinds of music and seems to have as much endless energy and freshness in her screen scores as she does in her innovative albums. Official website: www.annedudley.co.uk.

Credits

Year	Film	Director
1987	Disorderlies	Michael Schultz (USA)
1987	Hiding Out (aka Adult Education)	Bob Giraldi (USA)
1988	Buster	David Green (UK)
1989	The Mighty Quinn (aka Finding Maubee)	Carl Schenkel (USA)
1989	Say Anything . . .	Cameron Crowe (USA)
1989	Silence Like Glass	Carl Schenkel (W. Germany/USA)
1990	The Misadventures of Mr. Wilt	Michael Tuchner (UK)
1991	The Miracle	Neil Jordan (UK/Ireland)
1991	The Pope Must Diet (aka The Pope Must Die)	Peter Richardson (UK)
1992	Knight Moves	Carl Schenkel (Germany/USA/Canada)
1992	The Crying Game	Neil Jordan (UK/Japan)
1994	Felidae	Michael Schaack (Germany)
1995	Gentlemen Don't Eat Poets (aka The Grotesque)	John-Paul Davidson (UK)
1996	When Saturday Comes	Maria Giese (UK)
1996	Hollow Reed (aka Believe Me)	Angela Pope (UK/Germany/Spain)
1997	The Full Monty (AA; BAFTA-N)	Peter Cattaneo (UK/USA)
1998	American History X	Tony Kaye (USA)
2000	The Miracle Maker	Derek W. Hayes, Stanislav Sokolov (UK/Russia)
2001	Monkeybone	Henry Selick (USA)
2001	Lucky Break (aka Our Lucky Break)	Peter Cattaneo (UK/Germany)

Year	Film	Director
2003	*The Gathering*	Brian Gilbert (UK)
2003	*A Man Apart* (aka *El Diablo*)	F. Gary Gray (USA/Germany)
2003	*Bright Young Things*	Stephen Fry (UK)
2004	*Tabloid*	David Blair (UK)
2006	*Tristan + Isolde*	Kevin Reynolds (USA/UK/Germany/Czech Republic)
2006	*Perfect Creature*	Glenn Standring (N. Zealand/UK)
2006	*Black Book*	Paul Verhoeven (Netherlands/Germany/UK/Belgium)
2006	*Lake of Fire*	Tony Kaye (USA)
2007	*The Walker*	Paul Schrader (USA/UK)
2014	*Walking on Sunshine*	Max Giwa, Dania Pasquini (UK)
2015	*Nadia's Promise*	Stephen Bridgewater (USA)

DUN, Tan (b. 1957) An internationally acclaimed Chinese conductor and composer of opera, concert works, and movies, he has scored feature documentaries and fictional films for various countries in the East and the West.

Tan Dun was born in the village of Si Mao in the Hunan Province of China, where he was fascinated by the music played during various rituals. Dun was not allowed to study music and as a teenager was sent to work on a rice plantation. He taught himself to play different kinds of Chinese string instruments and was later hired to arrange and play music for a touring Peking Opera company. This brought him to Beijing, where he studied violin at the Central Conservatory of Music and met some of the leading composers and musicians in China. In 1986 Dun went to New York City to study music at Columbia University where he was exposed to avant-garde Western music and wrote concert works and his first opera, *Nine Songs* (1989). Using both Eastern and Western music techniques and drawing inspiration from the visual arts, Tan composed a series of operas that were performed in famous venues around the world. Works such as *Marco Polo* (1996), *The Peony Pavilion* (1996), *Tea: A Mirror of the Soul* (2002), and *The First Emperor* (2006) used a diversity of musical instruments, languages, sources, and artists, making Dun an international innovator. He also wrote symphonies, chamber pieces, and organic music that utilized water, paper, stone, and other objects in the performance. He has composed music for art installations, multimedia presentations, and special events, such as the 2008 Beijing Olympics.

Dun first worked in film in 1983 when, as a student in Beijing, he composed the score for the Mandarin drama *Hou Bu Dui Yan*, which was released in the West as *The Candidate*. Six years later he wrote the music for the American documentary *China in Revolution: 1911–1949* and its sequel *The Mao Years: 1949–1976*. He also wrote music for such powerful European documentaries as *Operation K*, *Nan Jing 1937*, and *In the Name of the Emperor*, and he is the subject of two praised documentaries: *Broken Silence*, about his creating the opera *Tea*, and *Taoism in a Bowl of Water*, about his life and work. Dun's first American fiction movie was the crime thriller *Fallen* in 1998, but he is better known for his highly praised scores for the Chinese films *Hero*, *The Banquet*, and *Crouching Tiger, Hidden Dragon*, winning the Oscar for the last. His most recent cinema project is the 2013 American documentary *Heaven's Gate*. Dun's music can also be heard in American television series and documentaries. In such an eclectic and busy career, the cinema is only a small part of his accomplishments, but Dun's screen music is distinguished all the same.

Just as in his operas and concert works, Dun employs both Western and Asian music in his screen scores. For the popular martial arts movie *Crouching Tiger, Hidden Dragon*, there is a solo cello lament (played by Yo-Yo Ma) that is joined by an Asian pipe with a Western orchestra in the background. This decision to move beyond authentic Asian instruments makes the music more accessible around the world but, more importantly, demonstrates how avant-garde Western music blends so beautifully with the ethnic sound. *Crouching Tiger, Hidden Dragon* is filled with marvelous music, including a mystical theme with female vocals that echo the high-pitched pipes and strings and the Oscar-nominated song "A Love before Time" (by Dun and Jorge Calandrelli; lyric by James Schamus and Elaine Chow), a pop ballad that is sung on the soundtrack in English and Mandarin by Coco Lee. The movie is famous for its poetic fight sequences that defy gravity, and Dun scores them with rhythmic percussion passages that have wood block and other Asian embellishments. Also popular internationally was *Hero*, an action-packed tale set in ancient China before emperors ruled the land. Dun not only wrote the masterful score but performed the violin passages with Itzhak Perlman on the soundtrack. The two musicians can be heard in a fluid violin piece backed by a Western orchestra with a stately but free-flowing tone. There is a stirring battle theme in which male bassos pierce through the drums and strings motif and, similarly, the palace scenes are scored with a strident march made up of a men's chorus with brass and strings accompaniment. The score also has a delicate passage played on Asian strings and drums as a high female vocal floats above and a melancholy lament played on various Asian and Western strings.

The Banquet is a loose retelling of the Hamlet story set in the Chinese emperor's household. Again Dun does not strictly adhere to Asian music, as in a lazy but graceful theme with piano playing against Asian strings. A furious piano and percussion passage races forward with a menacing subtext in one section of the film, while another has male vocalizing that punctuates a restless theme filled with Asian percussion and a repeating piano motif. Most thrilling is a minor-key piano and string piece with female chanting that builds from a dirge to a triumphant anthem. Dun's only American feature, *Fallen*, has a very avant-garde score. A crime thriller with some fantastical elements in the telling, the movie is scored with strings and electronic sounds that seem to be played out of tempo, giving a weary and dazed feeling. Other sections have electronic reverberations, distorted musical chords, and instrumental chaos. While there is nothing particularly Asian about the music, neither is there anything American about it. Instead, Dun creates a nightmarish world where sounds and musical instruments create their own landscape. Official website: www.tandunonline.com.

Credits

(* for Best Song)

Year	Film	Director
1983	The Candidate	Lu Chen, Ziniu Wu (China)
1989	China in Revolution: 1911–1949	Kathryn Pierce Dietz, Sue Williams (UK/USA)
1994	The Mao Years: 1949–1976	Sue Williams (UK/USA)
1994	Operation K	Bernhard Bamberger (Austria)
1995	Broken Silence	Eline Flipse (Netherlands)
1995	Nan Jing 1937	Ziniu Wu (Taiwan/Hong Kong)
1998	Fallen	Gregory Hoblit (USA)
1998	In the Name of the Emperor	Christine Choy, Nancy Tong (Canada)
2000	Crouching Tiger, Hidden Dragon (AA; AA*; GGN; BAFTA)	Ang Lee (Taiwan/Hong Kong/USA/China)
2002	Hero	Yimou Zhang (China/Hong Kong)
2003	Taoism in a Bowl of Water	Andreas Morell (Germany)
2006	The Banquet (aka Legend of the Black Scorpion)	Xiaogang Feng (China)
2013	Heaven's Gate	Nic Good (USA)

DUNING, George (1908–2000) The primary composer at Columbia Pictures for twenty years, the musician, arranger, conductor, and composer Duning never became well known outside of the movie business but the variety and proficiency of his one hundred films is noteworthy.

Born in Richmond, Indiana, George Duning was educated at the Cincinnati Conservatory of Music, where he studied the trumpet. After graduation he played with various jazz and dance bands, soon arranging the music as well. Duning was the musical director on the popular radio program *Kay Kyser's Kollege of Musical Knowledge* for eight years and first worked in Hollywood when Kyser's band was featured in some 1940s movies. During World War II, Duning was an arranger and conductor for the Armed Forces Radio Service. He contributed music as well as arrangements for many B musicals at Columbia after the war and on occasion he was hired to score a nonmusical, although they also were B pictures. When Duning arranged the music and provided the background soundtrack for two 1949 hits, *The Jolson Story* and *All the King's Men*, he received more recognition for his compositions and was sometimes given some first-class projects. As Columbia's house arranger-composer, he worked on everything from westerns and melodramas to musicals and comedies, working fast and efficiently while he stayed out of the limelight. (He was nominated for the Oscar five times but never won.) Duning's most known films include *The Devil at Four O'Clock*, *Picnic*, *3:10 to Yuma*, *From Here to Eternity*, *Cowboy*, *The World of Suzie Wong*, *My Sister Eileen*, *Toys in the Attic*, *Critic's Choice*, and *Bell, Book and Candle*. In the 1960s and early 1970s, Duning also worked in television, composing music for such series as *Dennis the Menace*, *The Big Valley*, *Star Trek*, *The Farmer's Daughter*, *Then Came Bronson*, and *The Partridge Family*, as well as several early TV movies. Although he retired in 1980, Duning remained active, serving on the boards of the American Society of Composers, Authors and Publishers (ASCAP), the Academy of Motion Picture Arts and Sciences, the Society for the Preservation of Film Music, and other organizations. By the time he died at the age of ninety-two he was all but forgotten by the public but still revered in the business for the consistently high quality of his work.

With such an eclectic collection of films to his credit, Duning seems to have no particular style or musical individuality. What one notices is the integrity of his scores, whether they be for a disturbing drama like *Picnic* or *Toys in the Attic*, or a silly comedy, such as *Any Wednesday* or *That Touch of Mink*. Of his many westerns, two deserve special attention. The character-driven *3:10 to Yuma*, about an average Joe (Van Heflin) who escorts an outlaw (Glenn Ford) to prison, has touches of the Old West in its music, including the title folk song, but much of the score concentrates on the restless nature of the two men. The myth of the Wild West is deflated somewhat in *Cowboy* in which a Chicago hotel clerk (Ford again) joins a cattle drive and finds out that life on the prairie is more than he bargained for. Duning's score celebrates the West, even quoting familiar western folk tunes. The original music is lively and invigorating, depicting the West with an almost childlike glee. The two westerns, though both directed by Delmer Daves, are as different as night and day; the same can be said about the two scores.

Duning rarely got first-rate dramas to score but when he did he did not disappoint. The rural drama *Picnic* involves the passionate and dangerous romance of a drifter (William Holden) and a small-town girl (Kim Novak). Some of the score is bucolic, creating the atmosphere of the midwestern setting, but Duning adds dissonance to the music behind the feverish lovers. The love theme is lyrical but with enough minor chords to hint that this tempestuous romance is more than likely to burn itself out. In the most musically interesting scene in *Picnic*, the locals are listening to the band play the old favorite "Moonglow." As Holden and Novak start to dance, their own musical theme enters, the two contrasting ballads playing off each other effectively. (Not only was the love song "Theme from *Picnic*" a hit record but a recording combining "Moonglow" and the theme was also on the charts.) Another dangerously passionate romance can be found in *From Here to Eternity*, Duning's most famous film. Ironically, much of the soundtrack uses songs composed by others. Fred Karger and Robert Wells's "Reenlistment Blues" is sung by some of the soldiers and the melody (arranged by Duning) is used as the main theme for the movie. Duning also quotes some Hawaiian favorites in the soundtrack, as befitting a story set at Pearl Harbor right before America entered World War II. But it is the scene of Burt Lancaster and Deborah Kerr embracing on the beach that most remember in *From Here to Eternity* and that passionate music was composed by Duning, as was much of the bluesy music that was the theme for the moody trumpet player (Montgomery Clift). Another superb drama, *Toys in the Attic*, concerns a very dysfunctional trio of siblings in New Orleans. The relationship is complicated, ranging from the vitriolic to the incestuous, and Duning's jazz and blues score is frequently chaotic, confused, and seething.

Another side to Duning's talent can be glimpsed in the many "exotic" movies he was given to score. These usually involved the Orient in some way, as with the romance *The World of Suzie Wong* set in modern-day Hong Kong. Duning uses the Chinese pentatonic scale in the theme for the title barmaid (Nancy Kwan) and Western composition for the American artist (William Holden) who loves her. The way the violins play against the Asian percussion is thematically and musically skillful. The romantic comedy *Cry for Happy*, set in postwar Japan, is also about an East-West romance but the tale is lighter than that of Suzie Wong. Again the music uses both European and Oriental instruments, but the way the score moves from East to West is playful, sarcastic even. For the biblical *Salome*, Duning doesn't worry about the score sounding like the Middle East but uses a series of trumpet bursts, wavering violins, a wandering flute, and plenty of regal pomp to capture the sensual palace atmosphere. With the animated feature *1001 Arabian Nights*, the "exotic" music is also regal, but jazz and blues enter anachronistically. The cartoon nature of the music is so much fun that one can almost hear Duning giggling.

Duning (like many composers) did not relish having to score so many comedies, but on occasion one of them inspired him to turn out first-rate work. A piece of coy fluff, *That Touch of Mink* has a sparkling score that adds class to a rather foolish tale. The main theme bounces freely back and forth between a flowing long musical line and a short peppy one. One wonders if most of the sparks between Cary Grant and Doris Day were not musically controlled. *Houseboat*, this time with Grant and Sophia Loren, has a more romantic score but still a comic one. The domestic

comedy has a lot of heart tugging, but the music is never too sentimental, giving some sincerity to the story and the right tone for characters. A more sarcastic comedy, *Any Wednesday* has a score that flows with urban sophistication. The supposedly naughty triangle involving an executive (Jason Robards), his mistress (Jane Fonda), and his young associate (Dean Jones) is routine, but the whimsical main theme again gives the movie some panache. More adventurous is the clever score for *Bell, Book and Candle*, a comedy about contemporary witchcraft. Duning uses bongos with violins for the bouncy main theme, musicalizes the various witches with pseudomystical passages, and even has a cockeyed humming theme for the cat Pyewacket. For some sections of the soundtrack, Duning recorded sounds on tape and played them at high speed in order to get an otherworldly effect behind the music. This kind of dedication for scoring a light comedy is rare. But then Duning was the kind of movie composer and arranger who never wanted to let his studio down, not to mention those listening to his music. Website: www.georgeduning.com.

Credits

(all films USA unless stated otherwise)

Year	Film	Director
1944	*Kansas City Kitty*	Del Lord
1944	*She's a Sweetheart*	Del Lord
1944	*Carolina Blues*	Leigh Jason
1944	*Meet Miss Bobby Socks*	Glenn Tryon
1944	*Tahiti Nights*	Will Jason
1945	*Let's Go Steady*	Del Lord
1945	*Tonight and Every Night*	Victor Saville
1945	*Youth on Trial*	Budd Boetticher
1945	*Eadie Was a Lady*	Arthur Dreifuss
1945	*Sing Me a Song of Texas*	Vernon Keays
1945	*Eve Knew Her Apples*	Will Jason
1946	*Meet Me on Broadway*	Leigh Jason
1946	*Mysterious Intruder*	William Castle
1946	*The Devil's Mask*	Henry Levin
1946	*The Man Who Dared*	John Sturges
1946	*The Return of Rusty*	William Castle
1946	*Sing While You Dance*	D. Ross Lederman
1946	*It's Great to Be Young*	Del Lord
1947	*Johnny O'Clock*	Robert Rossen
1947	*The Guilt of Jane Ames*	Henry Levin
1947	*The Corpse Came C.O.D.*	Henry Levin
1947	*Two Blondes and a Redhead*	Arthur Dreifuss
1947	*Her Husband's Affairs*	S. Sylvan Simon
1948	*I Love Trouble*	S. Sylvan Simon
1948	*To the Ends of the Earth*	Robert Stevenson

Year	Film	Director
1948	Adventures in Silverado	Phil Karlson
1948	The Man from Colorado	Henry Levin
1948	The Gallant Blade	Henry Levin
1948	The Untamed Breed	Charles Lamont
1948	The Return of October	Joseph H. Lewis
1948	The Dark Past	Rudolph Maté
1948	Ladies of the Chorus	Phil Karlson
1949	Shockproof	Douglas Sirk
1949	Slightly French	Douglas Sirk
1949	The Undercover Man	Joseph H. Lewis
1949	Johnny Allegro	Ted Tetzlaff
1949	The Doolins of Oklahoma	Gordon Douglas
1949	Lust for Gold	S. Sylvan Simon, George Marshall
1949	Jolson Sings Again (AAN)	Henry Levin
1949	All the King's Men (AAN)	Robert Rossen
1949	And Baby Makes Three	Henry Levin
1950	Cargo to Capetown	Earl McEvoy
1950	No Sad Songs for Me (AAN)	Rudolph Maté
1950	Convicted	Henry Levin
1950	The Petty Girl	Henry Levin
1950	When You're Smiling	Joseph Santley
1950	Between Midnight and Dawn	Gordon Douglas
1950	Harriet Craig	Vincent Sherman
1950	The Flying Missile	Henry Levin
1951	Her First Romance	Seymour Friedman
1951	Lorna Doone	Phil Karlson
1951	Two of a Kind	Henry Levin
1951	The Lady and the Bandit	Ralph Murphy
1951	Sunny Side of the Street	Richard Quine
1951	The Mob	Robert Parrish
1951	The Family Secret	Henry Levin
1951	The Barefoot Mailman	Earl McEvoy
1951	Purple Heart Diary	Richard Quine
1951	Man in the Saddle	André De Toth
1952	Scandal Sheet	Phil Karlson
1952	Paula	Rudolph Maté
1952	Affair in Trinidad	Vincent Sherman
1952	Captain Pirate	Ralph Murphy
1952	Rainbow Round My Shoulder	Richard Quine
1952	Assignment: Paris	Robert Parrish, Phil Karlson
1953	The Last of the Comanches	André De Toth
1953	Salome	William Dieterle
1953	Let's Do It Again	Alexander Hall
1953	Cruisin' Down the River	Richard Quine
1953	From Here to Eternity (AAN)	Fred Zinnemann
1954	Battle of Rogue River	William Castle
1954	Drive a Crooked Road	Richard Quine
1955	The Long Gray Line	John Ford
1955	Three for the Show	H. C. Potter
1955	Tight Spot	Phil Karlson
1955	5 Against the House	Phil Karlson
1955	Bring Your Smile Along	Blake Edwards
1955	The Man from Laramie	Anthony Mann
1955	My Sister Eileen	Richard Quine
1955	Count Three and Pray	George Sherman
1955	Picnic (AAN)	Joshua Logan
1955	Queen Bee	Ranald MacDougall
1955	Three Stripes in the Sun	Richard Murphy

Year	Film	Director
1956	*The Eddy Duchin Story* (AAN)	George Sidney
1956	*Storm Center*	Daniel Taradash
1956	*The Solid Gold Cadillac*	Richard Quine
1956	*You Can't Run Away from It*	Dick Powell
1956	*Full of Life*	Richard Quine
1957	*Nightfall*	Jacques Tourneur
1957	*Utah Blaine*	Fred F. Sears
1957	*The Shadow on the Window*	William Asher
1957	*3:10 to Yuma*	Delmer Daves
1957	*Jeanne Eagels*	George Sidney
1957	*Operation Mad Ball*	Richard Quine
1957	*The Brothers Rico*	Phil Karlson
1958	*Cowboy*	Delmer Daves
1958	*Gunman's Walk*	Phil Karlson
1958	*Me and the Colonel*	Peter Glenville
1958	*Houseboat*	Melville Shavelson
1958	*Bell, Book and Candle*	Richard Quine
1959	*It Happened to Jane*	Richard Quine
1959	*The Last Angry Man*	Daniel Mann
1959	*The Wreck of the Mary Deare*	Michael Anderson (UK/USA)
1959	*1001 Arabian Nights*	Jack Kinney
1960	*Man on a String*	André De Toth
1960	*Strangers When We Meet*	Richard Quine
1960	*Stop! Look! and Laugh!*	Don Appell, Louis Brandt
1960	*All the Young Men*	Hall Bartlett
1960	*Let No Man Write My Epitaph*	Philip Leacock
1960	*The World of Suzie Wong* (GGN)	Richard Quine (UK/USA)
1960	*The Wackiest Ship in the Army*	Richard Murphy
1961	*Cry for Happy*	George Marshall
1961	*Two Rode Together*	John Ford
1961	*Gidget Goes Hawaiian*	Paul Wendkos
1961	*The Devil at 4 O'Clock*	Mervyn LeRoy
1961	*Sail a Crooked Ship*	Irving Brecher
1962	*The Notorious Landlady*	Richard Quine
1962	*13 West Street*	Philip Leacock
1962	*That Touch of Mink*	Delbert Mann
1962	*Who's Got the Action?*	Daniel Mann
1963	*Critic's Choice*	Don Weis
1963	*Island of Love*	Morton DaCosta
1963	*Toys in the Attic*	George Roy Hill
1963	*Who's Been Sleeping in My Bed?*	Daniel Mann
1964	*Ensign Pulver*	Joshua Logan
1965	*Dear Brigitte*	Henry Koster
1965	*My Blood Runs Cold*	William Conrad
1965	*Brainstorm*	William Conrad
1966	*Any Wednesday*	Robert Ellis Miller
1973	*Terror in the Wax Museum*	Georg Fenady
1973	*Arnold*	Georg Fenady
1980	*The Man with Bogart's Face*	Robert Day

DUNLAP, Paul (1919–2010) A busy conductor, music director, and composer for movies and television who also wrote for the concert hall, he was most active in Hollywood in the 1950s when he usually scored five feature films each year.

Born William Paul Dunlap in Springfield, Ohio, he received an excellent music education privately with such renowned composer-teachers as Arnold Schoenberg, Nadia Boulanger, and Ernst Toch. Dunlap aspired to a career as a composer for the concert hall and opera but could not support his family writing such serious music, so at the age of thirty-one he went to Hollywood. His first assignment, Samuel Fuller's historical western *The Baron of Arizona*, was a low-budget independent movie but one of quality with a strong performance by Vincent Price as the power-hungry James Addison Reavis. Unfortunately, very few of Dunlap's subsequent movies would have as talented a director or much quality to speak of. He did get to reunite with Fuller for the laudable films *The Steel Helmet*, *Park Row*, *The Naked Kiss*, and *Shock Corridor*, but most of Dunlap's 125 movies were B-level westerns, sci-fi films, cop melodramas, and lowbrow comedies (including five for the Three Stooges). Among all these are some commendable films, such as *Cry Danger*, *Little Big Horn*, *Hellgate*, *Loophole*, *Return from the Sea*, *Black Tuesday*, *Stranger on Horseback*, *The Cruel Tower*, *Lone Texan*, *Decision at Midnight*, *Young Fury*, and *Walk Like a Dragon*, as well as such campy cult favorites as *Lost Continent*, *I Was a Teenage Werewolf*, *Frankenstein—1970*, *The Angry Red Planet*, *I Was a Teenage Frankenstein*, *Target Earth*, *Cyborg 2087*, and *The Three Stooges Meet Hercules*. Dunlap was a tireless and efficient worker, often composing, arranging, and conducting the music within a two-week period. He also found time to score such 1950s television series as *This Is the Life*, *The Man Behind the Badge*, *The Millionaire*, *Studio 57*, *Schlitz Playhouse Tales of Wells Fargo*, *The Restless Gun*, *Cimarron City*, *Gunsmoke*, and *Have Gun—Will Travel*. Dunlap never totally abandoned classical music, writing piano concertos, choral music, and an opera after he retired from Hollywood in 1968. Yet he returned to the movies twelve years later to score the feeble comedy *Gorp* and again in 1984 to write music for the documentary *Bruce Lee, the Legend*.

Dunlap held his screen compositions in low regard, late in life denouncing the movies and wondering why there was renewed interest in some of his films in the 1990s. Yet he made efforts to make his screen scores "interesting" and today he is regarded as an A composer of B movies. Often his better music can be found in his better movies, particularly those with Fuller. The newspaper melodrama *Park Row*, set in 1880s New York City, has some period background music that is heard in taverns and on the streets but the movie is framed by a theme with a four-note phrase that can sound merry or threatening as Dunlap arranges it. This is a symphonic score with the harp featured in some sequences, as well as triumphant trumpets in

others. The score also boasts a romantic waltz that gushes and sways with unabashed passion. The crime melodrama *The Naked Kiss* has a fluid, bluesy theme for the central character, the prostitute Kelly (Constance Towers), that rises and falls gently as it seduces. There is also a hot jazz passage with a crazed saxophone, and a domestic string theme with chime accents that suggests warmth and tranquility. Dunlap uses the traditional French children's song "Little Child (Mon enfant)" effectively in the film. It is sung by Towers and some disabled kids in one scene then returns later for a murder sequence for ironic effect. The Korean War drama *The Steel Helmet* has a bold opening theme with exploding brass and percussion that quickly transitions to a somber but defiant piece of restless anxiety. Also memorable is a reverent hymnlike theme heard in a Buddhist temple that lightly suggests Asian music in its reflective majesty rather than in its instrumentation. Perhaps Dunlap's most impressive score for a Fuller movie is the one he composed for *Shock Corridor*, a stark melodrama about a newspaper reporter (Peter Breck) who has himself committed to a lunatic asylum in order to solve a murder. The opening theme is a string and horn piece that crashes on the ears like waves, creating both a romantic and nervous feeling. Throughout the movie is heard a gently oppressive theme that rises and falls in a disconcerting manner, conveying how the hero's sanity is affected by his surroundings. Sometimes in the score just a series of chords and some sound effects suffice, other times a full orchestra repeats a musical motif. For the hallucination scenes, Dunlap's music seems to attack with a fury.

The scores for Dunlap's cult favorites are less sophisticated than those for the Fuller movies but they are often exciting in a silly or clever way. One has to admire the energy and effort Dunlap put into a movie like *The Three Stooges Meet Hercules*. The laughing trombones, clodhopping percussion, fluttering flutes, and woodwinds squawking like geese combine to make an admirable score that understands the kind of comedy at hand. Most of the campy classics Dunlap scored are low-budget science fiction films with laughable special effects and questionable acting. Yet the music for these sci-fi follies is usually highly proficient. Dunlap's first venture into the sci-fi genre was *Lost Continent*, a half-baked version of the familiar "mysterious island populated by dinosaurs" story. Dunlap approaches the feeble film with vigor, his opening theme filled with shouting brass, furious woodwinds, and bold percussion that seem to announce the arrival of a king rather than some cheap special effects. Robots from Venus attack Chicago in *Target Earth* as eerie woodwinds and splashing percussion climb up the scale quickly and pounding drums suggest doomsday for all. A similarly threatening fate awaits Earth in *The Angry Red Planet* when Mars gets restless. Dunlap's score suggests that none of this is very likely. There is a cool jazz march theme that moves in a cocky manner, repeating a catchy musical phrase that is more comic than menacing; a sort of flippant "*Peter Gunn* Theme." For suspense, he provides quick, sharp brass notes echoed on the xylophone and a march played on low, grumbling brass that sounds like a nasty metronome. Two "teenage" thrillers each have noteworthy scores. *I Was a Teenage Frankenstein* has fiery piano chords punctuating the surging orchestral waves that sweep ahead in a manic manner,

giving this tale of a young monster (made from college students' body parts) more weight than the incongruous happenings on-screen. Even more popular, *I Was a Teenage Werewolf* is a cult icon of sorts. The restless teenager Tony (Michael Landon) wants psychiatric help but instead gets an injection with lupine side effects. The score has a jazzy theme that comes on like a fanfare but soon resolves into a bluesy melody that keeps rising at the end of each musical phrase as if asking a musical question. When Tony is running through the woods, there is restless chase music that is propulsive and crazed. The score also has a quieter theme with muted brass and nervous strings that convey confusion. Tony's transformation into a werewolf is scored with rumbling brass and rapidly repeating chords and the score (and movie) ends with an odd waltz. This is all very enjoyable screen music. It is sad that Dunlap was not proud of it.

Credits

(all films USA unless stated otherwise)

Year	Film	Director
1950	The Baron of Arizona	Samuel Fuller
1950	Hi-Jacked	Sam Newfield
1951	The Steel Helmet	Samuel Fuller
1951	Cry Danger	Robert Parrish
1951	Little Big Horn	Charles Marquis Warren
1951	Lost Continent	Sam Newfield
1951	Journey into Light	Stuart Heisler
1952	The San Francisco Story	Robert Parrish
1952	Breakdown	Edmond Angelo
1952	Park Row	Samuel Fuller
1952	Hellgate	Charles Marquis Warren
1953	Fort Vengeance	Lesles Selander
1953	Hannah Lee: An American Primitive (aka Outlaw Territory)	Lee Garmes, John Ireland
1953	The Royal African Rifles	Lesley Selander
1953	Combat Squad	Cy Roth
1953	Jack Slade	Harold D. Schuster
1954	Duffy of San Quentin	Walter Doniger
1954	Dragonfly Squadron	Lesley Selander
1954	Loophole	Harold D. Schuster
1954	Fangs of the Wild	William F. Claxton
1954	Return from the Sea	Lesley Selander
1954	Shield for Murder	Howard W. Koch, Edmond O'Brien
1954	Target Earth	Sherman A. Rose
1954	Cry Vengeance	Mark Stevens
1954	Black Tuesday	Hugo Fregonese
1955	Big House, U.S.A.	Howard W. Koch
1955	Stranger on Horseback	Jacques Tourneur
1955	Robbers' Roost	Sidney Salkow

Year	Film	Director
1955	*Finger Man*	Harold D. Schuster
1955	*Fort Yuma*	Lesley Selander
1955	*The Return of Jack Slade* (aka *Son of Slade*)	Harold D. Schuster
1955	*Last of the Desperados*	Sam Newfield
1955	*Desert Sands*	Lesley Selander
1955	*Shack Out on 101*	Edward Dein
1956	*Three Bad Sisters*	Gilbert Kay
1956	*The Wild Dakotas*	Sigmund Neufeld, Sam Newfield
1956	*Ghost Town*	Allen H. Miner
1956	*Crime against Joe*	Lee Sholem
1956	*Walk the Dark Street*	Wyott Ordung
1956	*The Broken Star*	Lesley Selander
1956	*The Come On*	Russell Birdwell
1956	*The Three Outlaws*	Sam Newfield
1956	*Frontier Gambler*	Sam Newfield
1956	*Magnificent Roughnecks*	Sherman A. Rose
1956	*Strange Intruder*	Irving Rapper
1956	*The Cruel Tower*	Lew Landers
1956	*Emergency Hospital*	Lee Sholem
1956	*The Women of Pitcairn Island*	Jean Yarbrough
1956	*The Brass Legend*	Gerd Oswald
1956	*Stagecoach to Fury*	William F. Claxton
1956	*Dance with Me, Henry*	Charles Barton
1957	*The Quiet Gun* (aka *Fury at Rock River*)	William F. Claxton
1957	*Crime of Passion*	Gerd Oswald
1957	*Curfew Breakers* (aka *Hooked*)	Alexander J. Wells
1957	*Dragoon Wells Massacre*	Harold D. Schuster
1957	*Lure of the Swamp*	Hubert Cornfield
1957	*I Was a Teenage Werewolf*	Gene Fowler Jr.
1957	*God Is My Partner*	William F. Claxton
1957	*Apache Warrior*	Elmo Williams
1957	*Portland Exposé*	Harold D. Schuster
1957	*Under Fire*	James B. Clark
1957	*Young and Dangerous*	William F. Claxton
1957	*Blood of Dracula*	Herbert L. Strock
1957	*I Was a Teenage Frankenstein*	Herbert L. Strock
1957	*Oregon Passage*	Paul Landres
1957	*Guns Don't Argue*	Richard C. Kahn, Bill Karn
1958	*The Power of the Resurrection* (aka *The Passion and the Power of the Christ*)	Harold D. Schuster
1958	*Gun Fever*	Mark Stevens
1958	*The Toughest Gun in Tombstone*	Earl Bellamy
1958	*How to Make a Monster*	Herbert L. Strock
1958	*Gang War*	Gene Fowler Jr.
1958	*Frankenstein—1970*	Howard W. Koch
1958	*Wolf Larsen* (aka *The Far Wanderer*)	Harmon Jones
1958	*Frontier Gun*	Paul Landres
1959	*Lone Texan*	Paul Landres
1959	*Invisible Invaders*	Edward L. Cahn
1959	*Here Come the Jets*	Gene Fowler Jr.
1959	*The Rebel Set*	Gene Fowler Jr.
1959	*The Oregon Trail*	Gene Fowler Jr.
1959	*Five Gates to Hell*	James Clavell
1959	*The Four Skulls of Jonathan Drake*	Edward L. Cahn
1959	*The Angry Red Planet* (aka *Invasion of Mars*)	Ib Melchior
1959	*The Rookie*	George O'Hanlon
1959	*The Purple Gang*	Frank McDonald
1959	*Stump Run*	Eddie Dew

Year	Film	Director
1960	*Gunfighters of Abilene*	Edward L. Cahn
1960	*Twelve Hours to Kill*	Edward L. Cahn
1960	*Walk Like a Dragon*	James Clavell
1960	*Desire in the Dust*	William F. Claxton
1960	*The Crowning Experience*	Marion Clayton Anderson, Richard Tegström
1961	*Seven Women from Hell* (aka *Womanhunt*)	Robert D. Webb
1962	*The Three Stooges Meet Hercules*	Edward Bernds
1962	*The Three Stooges in Orbit*	Edward Bernds
1963	*Black Zoo*	Robert Gordon
1963	*The Three Stooges Go Around the World in a Daze*	Norman Maurer
1963	*Shock Corridor*	Samuel Fuller
1963	*Decision at Midnight*	Lewis Allen (USA/UK)
1964	*Law of the Lawless*	William F. Claxton
1964	*Stage to Thunder Rock*	William F. Claxton
1964	*The Naked Kiss*	Samuel Fuller
1965	*The Outlaws Is Coming*	Norman Maurer
1965	*Young Fury*	Christian Nyby
1965	*Operation C.I.A.*	Christian Nyby
1966	*Destination Inner Space*	Francis D. Lyon
1966	*Dimension 5*	Franklin Adreon
1966	*Cyborg 2087*	Franklin Adreon
1966	*Castle of Evil*	Francis D. Lyon
1967	*Savage Justice* (aka *The Sweet and the Bitter*)	James Clavell
1967	*The Money Jungle* (aka *The Billion Dollar Caper*)	Francis D. Lyon
1968	*The Destructors*	Francis D. Lyon
1968	*Panic in the City*	Eddie Davis
1980	*Gorp*	Joseph Ruben
1984	*Bruce Lee, the Legend*	Leonard Ho (Hong Kong)

E

EASDALE, Brian (1909–1995) A highly respected British composer for the concert hall and the opera house, he scored only fourteen feature films but among them are the masterworks *Black Narcissus* and *The Red Shoes*.

Born in Manchester, England, Brian Easdale began improvising original piano pieces at the age of five. Five years later he was hired as an organist at Temple Church in London. Easdale studied music at the Westminster Abbey Choir School and later the Royal College of Music. A precocious youth, Easdale wrote his first opera before he was eighteen years old and several concert pieces by the time he was thirty. Composer Benjamin Britten recognized Easdale's talents and acted as his mentor during the prewar years. After having served in the Royal Artillery during World War II, Easdale returned to composing and wrote more operas, choral works, and orchestral and vocal pieces, including *Missa Coventriensis* for the consecration of Coventry Cathedral in 1962. He first worked in cinema when he wrote music for some documentary shorts in the 1930s and government training films during the war. Director Carol Reed suggested Easdale to codirectors Michael Powell and Emeric Pressburger, who hired him to score their groundbreaking movie *Black Narcissus* in 1947. Both the film and the score were lauded around the world. When house composer Allan Gray dropped out of the production of Powell and Pressburger's *The Red Shoes*, Easdale was commissioned to compose the massive score in a very short period of time. The result was one of the finest scores in all British cinema and the first one to win an Academy Award. *The Red Shoes* required a great deal of underscoring and dance music, including the famous fifteen-minute title ballet. Easdale's music for the movie has since been heard in concert halls and performed by ballet companies. He worked again with Powell and Pressburger on *Hour of Glory*, *Gone to Earth*, *The Fighting Pimpernel*, and *Pursuit of the Graf Spee*, and with Powell alone on *Peeping Tom* and *The Queen's Guards*. Easdale also scored a few other non-Powell movies, most memorably Reed's *Outcast of the Islands*. In the 1960s Easdale left the cinema and concentrated on operas and orchestral pieces. For twenty years he battled alcoholism but finally conquered his addiction and lived to the age of eighty-six.

The Red Shoes has a score that pleases in many ways. More than just ballet music, Easdale captures the many moods of the story away from the ballet stage. When the dancer Vicki (Moira Shearer) first meets the impresario Lermontov (Anton Walbrook) at a party, a moody piece is being played on the piano that foreshadows their difficult relationship. When Vicki listens to a broadcast of the new opera *Cupid and Psyche* on the radio, the music echoes her indecision about love versus a dance career. The music for the famous *The Red Shoes Ballet* is particularly dramatic, telling a story that parallels the Hans Christian Andersen tale with that of Vicki. Portions of the score are heard throughout the movie as Julian (Marius Goring) composes it. When heard in its entirety, the music overwhelms one and holds its place next to the selections of *Swan Lake*, *Les Sylphides*, and *Giselle* presented earlier. Easdale writes mostly in the romantic style, yet much of the music comes across as modern because of its dissonance and expressionistic harmonies. Had he not written anything else for the screen, Easdale's reputation as a movie composer would be secured by this one score.

Nearly as accomplished is the film *Black Narcissus* in which the Technicolor process was used in ingenious ways. It is difficult to believe that this drama about establishing a convent high in the Himalayas was filmed completely in the studio using projections, photographs, images painted on glass, and miniatures. The way cinematographer Jack Cardiff lit and filmed the movie suggested the style of Dutch artist Vermeer, going so far as to put pastel-colored chalk on the backdrops to make them more painterly. Easdale's mix of religious and sensual music in the score underlines the movie's principal idea even as it supports the impressionistic visuals. There is a lovely mystical theme that suggests Asian music but remains in the romantic tradition; atmospheric chanting heard during some delicate passages on flute and harp; and suspense music that uses threatening vocals and restless, wavering strings and brass. It is also interesting how the insistent sound of the wind in these mountains and the giant convent bell accompany the music at times. The World War II action drama *Pursuit of the Graf Spee*, perhaps better known as *The Battle of the River Plate*, has an aggressive main theme with trumpet fanfares, propulsive timpani, and bold strings building up to explosive crescendos. The score also includes a stirring passage with a harp and brass chords punctuating the flowing music, and a symphonic anthem that confidently builds to an ardent climax. *Outcast of the Islands*, an intriguing tale based on a Joseph Conrad story, concerns a British fugitive from justice (Trevor Howard) in the islands off the Malay coast. Easdale provides a powerful, rumbling theme in which the music surges forward like waves, the brass announcing the strength of nature and the strings tossing up and down the scale like flotsam and jetsam. There is also a very British, very majestic passage heard on horns that has a triumphal temperament.

The passionate romance *Gone to Earth* has a curious history. British directors Powell and Pressburger were hired by Hollywood to make a movie of Mary Webb's rural tale of a gypsy girl (Jennifer Jones) who befriends foxes and seduces a British fox hunting squire (David Farrar).

(The title is a hunting expression called out when the fox has fled to its underground den.) Producer David Selznick did not like the 1950 finished product and tried to reedit it, but Powell and Pressburger brought him to court. The directors lost the case, Selznick made major changes in the movie and rereleased it two years later under the title *The Wild Heart*. Most agree the Selznick version is inferior but luckily Easdale's score was not greatly altered. The main theme is a romantic piece with gliding piano and grasping strings, a harp providing a magical touch that is important to the story. There is a delicate nature theme heard on harp, bells, and strings with horn accents, and the hunting sequences are scored with furious chase music with oppressive vocals and chaotic crescendos, even the dogs' howling becoming part of the music. At one point in the movie the church choir that is heard is a bit rustic and ragged because director Powell liked the sound of the actual choir at the Shropshire parish where they filmed. For the tragic finale, a hunting horn and the human cry "gone to earth" conclude the tale and the score. Easdale spent a small portion of his long career in movies yet, ironically, it is his screen music that is most remembered and praised today.

Credits

(all films UK unless stated otherwise)

Year	Film	Director
1947	Black Narcissus	Michael Powell, Emeric Pressburger
1948	The Red Shoes (AA)	Michael Powell, Emeric Pressburger
1949	Hour of Glory (aka The Small Back Room)	Michael Powell, Emeric Pressburger
1950	Gone to Earth (aka The Wild Heart)	Michael Powell, Emeric Pressburger
1950	The Fighting Pimpernel (aka The Elusive Pimpernel)	Michael Powell, Emeric Pressburger
1951	Outcast of the Islands	Carol Reed
1952	The Wild Heart (aka Gone to Earth)	Michael Powell, Emeric Pressburger, Rouben Mamoulian (UK/USA)
1954	The Green Scarf	George More O'Ferrall
1956	Adventure On	Thomas Stobart
1956	Pursuit of the Graf Spee (aka The Battle of the River Plate)	Michael Powell, Emeric Pressburger
1957	Miracle in Soho	Julian Amyes
1960	Peeping Tom (aka Face of Fear)	Michael Powell
1961	The Queen's Guards	Michael Powell
1968	Happy Deathday	Henry Cass

EASTWOOD, Clint (b. 1930) The popular screen actor and director who has become a Hollywood icon because of his antihero characters and films, he has also composed scores for seven feature films.

Clinton Eastwood Jr. was born in San Francisco, the son of a steelworker and a factory employee, and grew up in various cities along the West Coast as his father worked for different companies. Eastwood attended a technical high school and showed little interest in acting, movies, or music as a teenager. After graduation he worked at a variety of jobs, from lifeguard and grocery clerk to golf caddy and forest firefighter, before he was drafted into the army. Although Eastwood saw no action during the Korean War, he was involved in a plane crash in which he and the pilot had to swim three miles to survive. An employee at Universal thought the six-foot, four-inch-high Eastwood might make an impressive actor and arranged for a screen test. The young Eastwood was criticized for his amateurish acting technique and stiff delivery of lines but he photographed well, and bit parts in low-budget movies followed. First recognition came on television where Eastwood was featured in the western series *Rawhide* in 1958. International notoriety came when he starred in a series of "spaghetti westerns" by Italian director Sergio Leone. *A Fistful of Dollars* in 1964 was a resounding success, as were its many sequels and spin-offs and Eastwood was soon in demand for Hollywood westerns as well. By the 1970s he found a new facet to his career playing the tough cop Harry Callahan in a series of *Dirty Harry* action movies. Whether he appeared in war films, thrillers, or even comedies, Eastwood was thought of as the hard antihero who spoke little and displayed little emotion.

His directing career began with the suspense drama *Play Misty for Me* in 1971, followed by over thirty features, many of them with Eastwood in the cast. In the new century, Eastwood moved into deeper characterizations and more challenging vehicles. He has long been interested in music in film and has made movies about music, as with the features *Honkytonk Man* (1982) and *Bird* (1988), and the documentaries *Thelonious Monk: Straight No Chaser* (1988) and *Dave Brubeck: In His Own Sweet Way* (2010). Eastwood contributed some theme music to the films *The Unforgiven* (1992), *A Perfect World* (1993), and *Absolute Power* (1996) before writing his own full score for the crime mystery *Mystic River* in 2003, a film he directed but did not star in. He has returned to scoring on six other occasions

to date, including the well-received *Million Dollar Baby*, *Flags of Our Fathers*, *Grace Is Gone* (directed by James C. Strouse), *Changeling*, and *J. Edgar*. Eastwood is also a successful film producer with his own production company.

It is somewhat surprising that with Eastwood's obvious affection for jazz that his first film score, *Mystic River*, is in the classical mode. This dark and somber tale, about three Bostonians (Sean Penn, Kevin Bacon, and Tim Robbins) tied together by the memory of a long-past murder, is well served by Eastwood's haunting yet nostalgic music. The delicate main theme is built on a four-note phrase that returns throughout the movie just as the past quietly but firmly reappears. The score also has some electronic music that is eerie and jarring and there are choral passages sung by the Tanglewood Festival Chorus that add to the weighty tone of the movie. Eastwood's music for *Million Dollar Baby* is also delicate even though the tale is set in the world of boxing. The theme for Maggie (Hilary Swank), a nobody who wants to be a professional boxer, is very engaging, with piano and strings descending the scale in a dreamy manner. There are also some intricate guitar sections that convey the loneliness and distance that lies between these characters. The war film about Iwo Jima, *Flags of Our Fathers*, has appropriately robust music for the battle scenes but the main theme is again a gentle passage first heard on a piano and then later played on guitar and trumpet. Electronic music competes with a piano in the restless main theme for the biopic *J. Edgar* about FBI chief Hoover. It is a very avant-garde sound for a period piece, yet Eastwood's music is intriguing and effective. Finally, the 1920s thriller *Changeling* has a score that alternates between the lyrically sublime and frantic tension. This upsetting tale of a mother (Angelina Jolie) who has to take on the police to get her kidnapped son back has a melancholy theme played on a lonely trumpet that is a slow jazz that compares favorably to the kind of music Eastwood celebrated in *Bird* and *Honkytonk Man*. How unlikely that the monosyllabic actor of the 1960s and 1970s would develop into a consummate filmmaker who lists screen music among his accomplishments. His son Kyle Eastwood is a jazz musician who has composed music for such films as *Letters from Iwo Jima* (2006), *Gran Torino* (2008), and *Invictus* (2009). Biographies: *Clint Eastwood: Master Filmmaker at Work*, Michael Goldman (2012); *Clint: A Retrospective*, Richard Schickel (2010). Official website: wwwclinteastwood.net.

Credits

(all films USA and directed by Clint Eastwood unless stated otherwise)

Year	Film	Director
2003	*Mystic River* (USA/Australia)	
2004	*Million Dollar Baby*	
2006	*Flags of Our Fathers*	
2007	*Grace Is Gone* (GGN)	James C. Strouse
2008	*Changeling* (GGN)	
2010	*Hereafter*	
2011	*J. Edgar*	

EDELMAN, Randy (b. 1947) A busy songwriter, composer, arranger, and conductor of pop records, television, and movies, he has scored over sixty feature films since 1972, most of them light comedies, yet his best-known screen music comes from his dramas.

The son of a teacher and an accountant, Randy Edelman was born in Paterson, New Jersey, and grew up in Teaneck. As a boy he learned to play the piano and as a teenager began writing his own songs. While a student at the University of Cincinnati, Edelman wrote music for regional theatre and freelanced as a music arranger for James Brown's recordings at King Records. His first jobs after graduation were playing piano in the pit orchestras of Broadway musicals, arranging music for CBS Records, and composing and arranging music for various entertainers. Edelman performed his original songs as the opening act for popular singers, many of whom later recorded his work, in concert venues in America, Europe, Australia, and Asia. His solo albums found favor in the late 1960s, and his songs, such as "Weekend in New England," "If Love Is Real," "Piano Picker," "Concrete and Clay," "Everybody Wants to Find a Bluebird," "Uptown, Uptempo Woman," and "I Can't Make Music," were sung by such diverse artists as the Carpenters, Blood Sweat and Tears, Petula Clark, Kool and the Gang, Barry Manilow, the Fifth Dimension, Dionne Warwick, and Bing Crosby.

Edelman made his screen score debut writing the music for the character drama *Outside In* in 1972 but got more recognition the next year for scoring the JFK assassination thriller *Executive Action*. Yet most of Edelman's Hollywood career has been writing music for contemporary comedies ranging from Disney family movies to offbeat farces to romantic films. Among his many notable comedies are *Ghostbusters II*, *Kindergarten Cop*, *While You Were Sleeping*, *The Mask*, *Twins*, *My Cousin Vinny*, *Leap Year*, *27 Dresses*, *Angels in the Outfield*, and *Beethoven*. Edelman has also scored melodramas, such as *Come See the Paradise*, *Dragon: The Bruce Lee Story*, and *The Indian in the Cupboard*; fantasies like *DragonHeart* and *The Mummy: Tomb of the Dragon Emperor*; and historical films, as with *Gettysburg*, *Gods and Generals*, and *The Last of the Mohicans*. He began his television career scoring the TV movie *Snatched* in 1973, followed by a dozen other small-screen features, including *Blood Sport* (1973), *A Doctor's Story* (1984), *Scandal Sheet* (1985), *Dennis the Menace* (1987), *Citizen X* (1995), *The Hunley* (1999), *A Season on the Brink* (2002), and *The Ten Commandments* (2006). Among the television series he has written music for are *MacGyver*, *Maximum Security*, and *The Adventures of Brisco County Jr.* Music from Edelman's movie and TV scores has been heard at many sporting events and as the theme song for NBC-TV sports programming, including coverage of different Olympics. He has conducted concert versions of his film music with leading symphony orchestras across America and supervised recordings of his work for various record labels.

One of Edelman's talents for screen music is his strong melodic line. Coming from a pop music background and having a classical music education, he is not afraid to let melody predominate in his scores. Yet there is more to his screen work than extended tunes. He often changes key, tone, and tempo within one theme, making his scores very dramatic and striking. Having scored so many comedies, Edelman still manages to find variety in featherlight love themes, farcical background scoring, and animated action music. His comedies always sound contemporary yet he rarely uses rock, preferring a pop sound with touches of jazz and even Big Band. Also, not far below the surface there is a classical temperament that can be detected in more than the love themes. In the family comedy *Beethoven*, for example, Edelman has fun with both pop and classical music. The title dog is a slobbering St. Bernard, and the score often has a lumbering, oafish quality. But the music also pays tribute to the dog's namesake. The main theme is a delightful mix of both sentiments. It begins as a moody symphonic piece one might expect in a horror film but a solo piano soon enters and gleefully takes over with a classical sonata pastiche with funny percussive accents and sound effects; Beethoven on a whoopee cushion. The frantic fantasy *The Mask*, in which a bank clerk (Jim Carrey) morphs into a superhero when he dons a special mask, has a schizophrenic score. The main theme is a jazzy 1940s piece with some tender sections that are bluesy and even heartfelt. The character's transformations are scored with pastiched Gothic horror music but with some modern touches. There is a carnival theme that is silly and contagious, recalling something freakish out of a Fellini movie, and the score has its quiet passages played on flute and strings that are smooth and romantic.

Edelman has scored so many romantic comedies, both estimable and feeble, that one is amazed at his ability to find freshness in each movie. The popular *While You Were Sleeping* has for its main theme a jaunty jazz piece played on piano and percussion that sounds carefree and loose. The recurring love theme, played on piano and strings, is soft and cautious until the melody slowly emerges into an oboe solo. The main theme for the perennial bridesmaid's comedy *27 Dresses* is a breezy passage on piano, guitar, and plucked strings that seems to stroll along with a nonchalant tone. There is also a provocative passage on electric guitar and keyboard that propels itself forward without hesitation, sounding hip without slipping into rock. *Leap Year*, a romantic comedy set in Ireland, has its Celtic flourishes, as when Irish fiddles play a rhythmic dance that moves from the vigorous to the romantic and back again without embarrassment. The score also includes a piano and guitar theme that sparkles with joy as it moves forward in a confident manner, and a delicate passage on piano and strings that is very graceful as it carefully flows up and down the scale. It is little wonder why Edelman is the composer of choice for these very modern, slightly daffy kinds of romance films.

While his so-called "serious" films are in the great minority of his career, Edelman's most praised and most remembered scores are from such movies. Few melodramas are as heartwrenching as *Come See the Paradise*, a too-true tale of a Caucasian American (Dennis Quaid) whose Japanese American wife (Tamlyn Tomita) is taken from him and put in an internment camp during World War II. Edelman's recurring love theme is a far cry from those for his comedies. Instead, a hesitant piano solo is so cautious it always seems on the brink of stopping until it finds the strength to burst forth and roll forward with passion. The score also has some Japanese songs, sections of electronic instrumentation, and a propulsive theme that pushes forward with a pounding beat. This last passage later became a favorite in film trailers for action movies. The biopic *Dragon: The Bruce Lee Story* has an Asian-flavored score yet the predominant instrument in most passages is the piano. The slow and stately main theme, played on piano and strings, begins with a reverential tone then builds to a full-bodied symphonic piece with a series of majestic crescendos. Asian flutes and strings are featured in a rhapsodic theme, and there is a frantic passage on various percussion instruments that seems to race against itself as it climbs the scale.

A different ethnic sound is heard in the family movie *The Indian in the Cupboard*, which has a score filled with wonder without getting bombastic. A small toy figure of a Native American warrior (Litefoot) comes alive for a nine-year-old boy (Hal Scardino) resulting in some sobering realizations about tribal culture. The main theme is a slow march with tribal drums and sustained strings yet the melody is played on piano and echoed by brass instruments. There is also a beautiful passage in which a violin solo seems filled with awe as tribal percussion provides the tempo and native flutes pick up the melodic line. There is much to be in awe of in the adventure fantasy *DragonHeart*, a multilayered action film with a somber look at medieval chivalry. The main theme is a stirring symphonic piece punctuated with muted drums. In one invigorating passage, the orchestra soars up the scale with a sense of lightheaded grandeur, and in another section solemn horns, sustained strings, and choral chanting combine in a lilting fashion. Some sections of the score include electronic instruments and these also have reappeared in many movie trailers. *DragonHeart* is not only one of Edelman's finest scores, it is a movie in which the music matches the stunning visuals without overpowering them.

Edelman's three most famous scores are for the historical pieces *Gettysburg*, *Gods and Generals*, and *The Last of the Mohicans*. This last was mostly composed by Trevor Jones with Edelman coming in later and providing musical underscoring for certain scenes. Edelman was contracted to score the Civil War epic *Gods and Generals*, but production was delayed for two years and he had to depart from the project after composing only the main theme; the rest of the score is by John Frizzell. But the *Gettysburg* music is the sole work of Edelman and it is perhaps his best score. The main title is a stately march in formal but heartfelt tempo. The percussion remains steady as the orchestra builds in intensity and climbs the scale, and there are some synthesized embellishments that provide a unique sound for the period music. *Gettysburg* runs nearly four hours (the director's cut is four and a half hours) and much of that time is scored, so there are many different themes and leitmotifs. Among them is a rambunctious theme on guitars and fifes that has a folk flavor as it moves in a sprightly manner; a poignant, hymnlike passage featuring a solo guitar over sustained strings, muted brass, and percussive crescendos; and a fragile arrangement of "Dixie" played on a steel-string guitar and strings. The many battle scenes use sustained strings, low brass chords, and ominous echoing drums. So much of the *Gettysburg* score is thrilling that it is not surprising to learn that it has become a staple at Fourth of July concerts. Edelman has not been very active in movies since 2008, but when he has returned to screen scoring the quality of his music is worth the wait. Official website: www.randyedelman.com.

Credits

(all films USA unless stated otherwise)

Year	Film	Director
1972	*Outside In* (aka *Red, White and Busted*)	Allen Baron, G. D. Spradlin
1973	*Executive Action*	David Miller
1987	*The Chipmunk Adventure*	Janice Karman
1988	*Feds*	Daniel Goldberg
1988	*Twins* (aka *The Experiment*)	Ivan Reitman
1989	*Troop Beverly Hills*	Jeff Kanew
1989	*Ghostbusters II*	Ivan Reitman
1990	*Quick Change*	Howard Franklin, Bill Murray
1990	*Come See the Paradise*	Alan Parker
1990	*Kindergarten Cop*	Ivan Reitman
1991	*Drop Dead Fred*	Ate de Jong (USA/UK)
1991	*Eyes of an Angel* (aka *The Tender*)	Robert Harmon
1991	*V. I. Warshawski*	Jeff Kanew
1991	*Shout*	Jeffrey Hornaday
1992	*My Cousin Vinny*	Jonathan Lynn
1992	*Beethoven*	Brian Levant
1992	*The Last of the Mohicans* (GGN; BAFTA-N)	Michael Mann
1992	*The Distinguished Gentleman*	Jonathan Lynn
1993	*Dragon: The Bruce Lee Story*	Rob Cohen
1993	*Gettysburg* (aka *The Killer Angels*)	Ronald F. Maxwell
1993	*Beethoven's 2nd*	Rod Daniel
1994	*Greedy*	Jonathan Lynn
1994	*Angels in the Outfield*	William Dear
1994	*The Mask*	Chuck Russell
1994	*Pontiac Moon*	Peter Medak
1995	*Billy Madison*	Tamra Davis
1995	*Tall Tale*	Jeremiah S. Chechik
1995	*While You Were Sleeping*	Jon Turteltaub
1995	*The Indian in the Cupboard*	Frank Oz
1995	*The Big Green*	Holly Goldberg Sloan
1996	*Down Periscope*	David S. Ward
1996	*Diabolique*	Jeremiah S. Chechik
1996	*The Quest*	Jean-Claude Van Damme (USA/Canada)

Year	Film	Director
1996	DragonHeart	Rob Cohen
1996	Daylight	Rob Cohen
1997	Anaconda	Luis Llosa (USA/Brazil/Peru)
1997	Gone Fishin'	Christopher Cain
1997	Leave It to Beaver	Andu Cadiff
1997	For Richer or Poorer	Bryan Spicer
1998	Six Days Seven Nights	Ivan Reitman
1999	Edtv	Ron Howard
2000	Passion of Mind	Alain Berliner
2000	The Whole Nine Yards	Jonathan Lynn
2000	The Skulls	Rob Cohen (USA/Canada)
2000	Shanghai Noon	Tom Dey (USA/Hong Kong)
2001	Head over Heels	Mark Waters
2001	China: The Panda Adventure	Robert M. Young
2001	Osmosis Jones	Bobby and Peter Farrelly
2001	Who Is Cletis Tout?	Chris Ver Wiel (USA/Canada)
2001	Corky Romano	Rob Pritts
2001	Black Knight	Gil Junger
2002	Frank McKlusky, C.I.	Arlene Sanford
2002	xXx (aka Triple X)	Rob Cohen
2003	National Security	Dennis Dugan
2003	Shanghai Knights (aka Shanghai Noon 2)	David Dobkin (USA/Hong Kong)
2003	Gods and Generals	Ronald F. Maxwell
2004	Connie and Carla	Michael Lembeck
2004	Surviving Christmas	Mike Mitchell
2005	Son of the Mask (aka Baby Formula)	Lawrence Guterman (USA/Germany)
2006	The Last Time	Michael Caleo
2007	Underdog	Frederik Du Chau
2007	Balls of Fury	Robert Ben Garant
2008	27 Dresses	Anne Fletcher
2008	The Mummy: Tomb of the Dragon Emperor (aka The Mummy 3)	Rob Cohen (USA/China/Germany/Canada)
2010	Leap Year	Anand Tucker (USA/Ireland)
2011	The Greening of Whitney Brown (aka Destination Home)	Peter Skillman Odiorne
2015	The Boy Next Door	Rob Cohen

EIDELMAN, Cliff (b. 1964) A more recent songwriter, conductor, and composer for the concert hall, ballet, and movies, he has scored a variety of films in his relatively young career.

Cliff Eidelman was born in Los Angeles and began violin lessons when he was eight years old, then moved on to learn several other instruments, guitar eventually becoming his favorite means of expression. As a teenager, Eidelman was fascinated with jazz and in high school formed his own band and worked in clubs in the Los Angeles area. He briefly studied jazz at the Guitar Institute of Technology; then, as a music student at Santa Monica College, Eidelman was commissioned to write and conduct a ballet and an overture. While he was studying composition and orchestration at the University of Southern California,

his work attracted the attention of film director Monica Teuber who hired him while he was still a student to write and conduct the score for the German drama *Magdalene*. Before that movie was released in 1989, Eidelman had written three other movie scores, most memorably one for the Holocaust drama *Triumph of the Spirit*. This score was so well received that it later was given several concert performances. *Star Trek VI: The Undiscovered Country* in 1991 was Eidelman's first box office hit and the admired score by the twenty-seven-year-old composer placed him in the ranks of the in-demand artists in Hollywood. The next year he scored the epic *Christopher Columbus: The Discovery* but many of his subsequent scores have been for youth-oriented movies such as *Free Willy 3: The Rescue, Montana, The Lizzie McGuire Movie, The Sisterhood of the*

Traveling Pants, and *He's Just Not That Into You*. Yet Eidelman has also scored more mature films, including *Leap of Faith, One True Thing, An American Rhapsody, Untamed Heart, Open Window, Big Miracle*, and the documentary *Ocean Men: Extreme Dive*. He occasionally writes music for television, including the TV movies *Judgment* (1990), *Backfield in Motion* (1991), and *Witness Protection* (1999). Eidelman has conducted the recording of all his film scores and has been guest conductor with many symphony orchestras in Europe and the States, sometimes performing his *Symphony for Orchestra and Two Pianos* and other pieces. In 2006 he released *My Muse*, an album of original songs for which he wrote both music and lyrics.

From his first screen scores, Eidelman has the sound of a pro. There is a richness even in his music for so-called chick flicks that reveals a firm grasp of classic, jazz, and pop techniques. The German drama *Magdalene*, about the difficult romance between an Austrian priest (Steve Bond) and a Salzburg prostitute (Nastassja Kinski), has a thrilling score by beginner Eidelman. There is a tender piano and horn theme that has the sensibility of a lament yet finds more and more strength as it goes along. This is a common characteristic in Eidelman's music; it changes and develops within each theme rather than just repeating or getting louder. For example, the *Magdalene* score also has a slow and stately string and chorus theme with an oboe solo that moves like a solemn processional until it climaxes with voices of desperation. Suspense is created by an abrasive revolution theme in which brass and percussion explode and the chorus sings a vigorous anthem of defiance. This is contrasted with a warm and flowing passage with soothing strings and woodwinds. Perhaps Eidelman's most sobering screen project is *Triumph of the Spirit* about a Greek Olympic boxer (Willem Dafoe) committed to a concentration camp and forced to entertain the Nazi officers. The main theme is a pulsating string and horn piece with a touch of klezmer music as it seems to rise above mourning and sparkles with life. This is offset by vocal chanting against a furious countermelody. The train bringing prisoners to Auschwitz is scored with a Hebrew chant (the lyric is in the Sephardic Jewish dialect) with a restless rhythm and racing strings and brass. In another passage, a male chorus sings a hymn with a female soloist rising above, all set to balalaika accents. These two scores were written by Eidelman when he was only in his twenties, yet they have the assurance and skill of a veteran.

Eidelman's most famous score is the one he wrote for *Star Trek VI: The Undiscovered Country*, one of the best movies in the series and boasting some of the finest music. There is a resplendent horn solo backed by strings that has a classical temperament, a fluid symphonic passage that builds to stirring crescendos, and a menacing theme with wavering brass and jittery percussion topped by a foreboding choir. Another threatening passage has harsh sound effects over pounding bass and percussion. This self-described "operatic score" climaxes in a bombastic yet compelling passage in which the orchestra climbs in scale and intensity for a bold finish. Also grandiose is Eidelman's score for the historic adventure movie *Christopher Columbus: The Discovery*. Although the film is far from dazzling, the score is first class in the way it incorporates a Spanish flavor without slipping into cliché. A flowing, seagoing theme gently rises and falls like rhythmic ocean waves and there is a regal horn passage in which strings seem to dance around the surging brass. Also memorable is a hesitant theme that glides along for a few notes then halts indecisively, as opposed to a racing passage that is full of confidence and vigor. Eidelman has scored more than his fair share of oceanic movies. In addition to the documentary *Ocean Men: Extreme Dive*, he wrote the music for two films in which people battle to save sea mammals. *Free Willy 3: The Rescue* has a main theme in which horns conjure up the sound of the title killer whale and drums convey the Native American connection to the creature. There is an elaborate piano and string passage that is classical in its sensibility yet has a relaxing freedom that sets its own pace. Also very potent is a gracefully sublime theme that is quite robust as dancelike fiddles and whales call out together in a tribal celebration. *Big Miracle*, about some Alaskans' efforts to save a family of gray whales from getting trapped in an ice field, has a driving theme with steady percussion, nervous strings, and the sound of whales crying out. There is also a restless passage with edgy strings and lilting piano music which parallels the tension on-screen.

As sometimes happens in Hollywood, Eidelman's score for the offbeat romance *Untamed Heart* was mostly cut and replaced by song standards. What survives on-screen is a theme in which woodwinds and piano carefully and tentatively surround a violin solo that is melancholy yet keeps moving forward. Also briefly heard is a felicitous waltz on piano and strings that slowly builds in intensity in the

Eidelman manner. Three of his scores for "chick flicks" deserve mention. The coming-of-age comedy-drama *Now and Then*, in which a quartet of preteens spend an eventful summer in 1970, has a nostalgic main theme in which piano and clarinet are featured against strings as the music pushes forward with a traveling tempo and chimes provide some pungent accents. An oboe and piano are central in a delicate theme that shyly approaches a melody until other woodwinds come in and fill out the sound. There is also a reflective and somewhat eerie piece in which high-pitched strings are contrasted with sustained notes on the viola, then various percussion instruments pick up the tempo and the music bounces along with mild glee. Another

quartet of female friends is the subject of *The Sisterhood of the Traveling Pants*. A theme played on piano, cello, and clarinet cautiously repeats the same musical phrase. Also effective is a lazy piano and string passage that glides along peacefully. The popular romantic movie *He's Just Not That Into You* has a happy harp and clarinet theme that is carefree and bouncy, and there is also a rhythmic guitar passage that starts simply but gets more complex as it changes key and grows in stature and resolution. One might say that each of Eidelman's musical sequences can be looked at as a miniature symphony, developing and pleasing the ear as it blossoms. Official website: wwwcliff eidelman.com.

Credits

(all films USA unless stated otherwise)

Year	Film	Director
1988	To Die For	Deran Sarafian
1989	Animal Behavior	Kjehl Rasmussen, H. Anne Riley
1989	Triumph of the Spirit	Robert M. Young
1989	Magdalene	Monica Teuber (W. Germany)
1990	Crazy People	Tony Bill, Barry L. Young
1991	Delirious	Tom Mankiewicz
1991	Star Trek VI: The Undiscovered Country	Nicholas Meyer
1992	Christopher Columbus: The Discovery	John Glen (UK/USA/Spain)
1992	Leap of Faith	Richard Pearce
1993	Untamed Heart (aka The Baboon Heart)	Tony Bill
1993	The Meteor Man	Robert Townsend
1994	My Girl 2	Howard Zieff
1994	A Simple Twist of Fate	Gillies MacKinnon
1995	Now and Then (aka The Gaslight Addition)	Lesli Linka Glatter
1997	The Beautician and the Beast	Ken Kwapis
1997	Free Willy 3: The Rescue	Sam Pillsbury
1998	Montana	Jennifer Leitzes
1998	One True Thing	Carl Franklin (USA/Brazil)
2000	Harrison's Flowers	Élie Chouraqui (France)
2001	An American Rhapsody	Éva Gárdos (USA/Hungary)
2001	Ocean Men: Extreme Dive	Bob Talbot (Germany)
2003	The Lizzie McGuire Movie (aka Ciao Lizzie!)	Jim Fall
2005	Sexual Life	Ken Kwapis
2005	The Sisterhood of the Traveling Pants	Ken Kwapis (USA/Greece/Mexico)
2006	Open Window (aka Fever)	Mia Goldman
2009	He's Just Not That Into You	Ken Kwapis (USA/Germany/Netherlands)
2012	Big Miracle	Ken Kwapis (USA/UK)

ELFMAN, Danny (b. 1953) A very busy songwriter, performer, and composer for television and movies, he is perhaps best known for his many fantasy films for director Tim Burton.

He was born Daniel Robert Elfman in Los Angeles, his father a teacher and his mother an author of children's books. Elfman was not a good student and dropped out of high school to travel across Europe with his elder brother

Richard who founded an experimental music-theatre group called Le Grand Magic Circus. Acting, singing, and playing the violin, Elfman toured with the group in Africa where he learned about various kinds of ethnic music. He was out of commission for nearly a year when he contracted malaria, but he eventually recovered and returned to California where he studied music privately. In 1972, Richard Elfman founded the New Wave band Oingo Boingo, which the younger Elfman performed in as well as wrote songs for. When Richard left to pursue a film career, Danny took over the group, which remained active performing and recording until 1995. The brothers made their film debut together in 1982 with *Forbidden Zone*, a wacky musical sci-fi spoof in which Oingo Boingo (including Danny) appeared; Richard produced and directed and the score was written by the younger Elfman. Over the years the low-budget black-and-white movie has been colorized and has become a cult favorite. Elfman's screen career was solidified in 1985 when director Tim Burton hired him to score the adult-children's comedy *Pee-wee's Big Adventure*. The following year Elfman also composed the music for the popular television series version of Pee-wee. Elfman and Burton have gone on to collaborate on fourteen more films to date. Elfman wrote songs as well as the soundtrack score for a handful of these, sometimes singing on the soundtrack as well, as in *The Nightmare before Christmas* and *Corpse Bride*. Among the other notable Burton films he has scored are *Beetlejuice*, *Batman* and two of its sequels, *Edward Scissorhands*, *Big Fish*, *Charlie and the Chocolate Factory*, *Alice in Wonderland*, and *Frankenweenie*. For such acclaimed directors as Gus Van Sant, Sam Raimi, Warren Beatty, Ang Lee, Barry Sonnenfeld, and others, he has written scores for such noteworthy movies as *Spider-Man* and its first sequel, *Dick Tracy*, *Good Will Hunting*, *Milk*, *Black Beauty*, *Mission: Impossible*, *Men in Black* and its two sequels, *Flubber*, *Dolores Claiborne*, *Chicago*, *Charlotte's Web*, *Meet the Robinsons*, *Hitchcock*, and *Oz the Great and Powerful*. For television, Elfman has written theme songs for several series, including *The Simpsons*, *Dilbert*, *Desperate Housewives*, *Point Pleasant*, *Tales from the Crypt*, *The Flash*, and *Batman: The Animated Series*. He has also composed music for video games, the Cirque du Soleil, and the concert hall, most memorably "The Overeager Overture" and "Serenada Schizophrana" which premiered at Carnegie Hall in 2005.

Elfman grew up watching old movies and cites Bernard Herrmann, Erich Wolfgang Korngold, and Max Steiner as the screen composers who most influenced him. From the classical world of music, he has been impressed with the work of Carl Orff, Maurice Ravel, Igor Stravinsky, Erik Satie, and Sergei Prokofiev. Modernists Philip Glass and Lou Harrison have also made their mark on Elfman, particularly in some of his sci-fi movies. Yet for all these diverse influences, Elfman has managed to come up with a sound that is distinctly his own. One of the few movie composers who is self-taught, he sees screen scoring as a theatrical art rather than an aesthetic one. His music is often weird because his movies are usually weird. He has some very conventional scores, but what most sticks in the mind is the music that accompanies dazzling images. The animated *The Nightmare before Christmas* is perhaps the quintessential Elfman project. He not only wrote the soundtrack score but also the music and lyrics to eleven songs and did the singing vocals for the central character, the Halloween King, Jack Skellington. The songs, which are often short, blend into the soundtrack score so smoothly that the film plays like a cockeyed operetta. Like the Tim Burton story (the director was Henry Selick, not Burton), the music is creepy and funny at the same time. There are also some very lyrical passages, such as "Sally's Song," in which the grotesque becomes poetic. "This Is Halloween" is a pounding, minor-key march, while the exuberant "What's This?" has the merry frenzy of a Rossini overture. The Kurt Weill–like "Making Christmas" theme is that rare thing: an oppressive Christmas carol. The similarly dark stop-motion feature *Corpse Bride* also has score, song, and vocals by Elfman, but the story is not as strong and the film was not nearly as successful. Yet the music in *Corpse Bride* is equally accomplished. The main title is in the romantic mode with a touch of the macabre with its swirling strings and female chorus. The sound of the harpsichord throughout the score is as enchanting as are the plucked strings that are used for everything from the ticking of a clock to a heartbeat. Some songs pastiche Gilbert and Sullivan, as in a patter number and a vigorous choral passage, and there is a honky-tonk piano spoof. This film has less overt humor and more quiet moments, which Elfman fills with lilting music, as with a delectable piano duet played by the hero and heroine.

Some of the live-action Burton-Elfman movies retain the sensibility of an animated film, as with *Beetlejuice* and

Edward Scissorhands. The theme song for the former is a bizarre mashup of calypso ("Day-O" is quoted), circus music, and horror movie music clichés. With its rapid clarinet sections, its oompah band, and frantic strings, this is scoring that beautifully sets up the furious comedy to follow. The rest of the score is just as clever, as it utilizes the tango, waltzing melodies, the minuet, pompous marches, and other dance ideas. Elfman has similar fun in *Edward Scissorhands*, where a habanera theme surfaces throughout the movie for a sexy and comic effect. The main theme is a swirling waltz backed by a boys' choir, also used later in the movie for a dance on the ice. Also memorable is a sequence in which Edward (Johnny Depp) speedily trims bushes, dogs, and a woman's hair as furious gypsy music plays. The comedy *Flubber* is also a kind of live-action cartoon, and Elfman's score is endlessly creative, not only in its composition but in the instrumentation. The celesta, theremin, vibraphone, synthesizer, and bells are used throughout, keeping the sci-fi aspects of the movie funny. All of the farce and magic is scored, climaxing in a wild mambo in which the glob of flubber splits apart to form an incongruous chorus line. The Batman and Spider-Man movies are pretty much cartoons even though they are live action. Elfman scores these action pieces with a dark grandeur that is as intriguing as it is unexpected. The theme for the first *Batman* in the series has a justly famous main theme. It moves from a brooding, mysterious opening into a driving march in a minor key with brass instruments chasing and soaring. A similar but distinctive idea is used in the main theme for *Batman Returns*. A chorus is added to the pulsating music, giving it a spiritual flavor. For the first *Spider-Man* in 2002, Elfman wrote a catchy theme in which pounding chords rise in tone and intensity. This is sometimes played on violins, other times on bongo drums, by a full brass section, or sung by a choir. In this same live-action cartoon category is the wry comedic adventure series *Men in Black*. The opening of the first installment, in which the camera takes a horsefly's point of view as it soars over a highway, is scored ingeniously. Satirizing Rimsky-Korsakov's "Flight of the Bumble-Bee," the rapid four-note motif is accompanied by roaring brass, rhythmic bass, and horns that replicate the sounds of traffic. The rest of the movie has little extended music but rather brief passages to highlight either a comic or violent punch line.

Elfman's scores for nonfantasy movies are not as well known but deserve some attention. The main theme for the melodrama *Good Will Hunting* is slow and reflective, as played by oboe, strings, and a wooden flute. The theme returns, sometimes played by steel-string guitar, and a chorus adds warmth without overwhelming the tender music. The period drama *Sommersby*, a romantic film set right after the Civil War, has a somber and graceful theme in which a lone trumpet seems to wail with loneliness. The love theme is very tentative as it shyly moves away from a two-note phrase to try and resolve itself. The music in *Hitchcock*, about the making of *Psycho*, has an unsettling three-note motif that is more about the growing chasm between Hitchcock (Anthony Hopkins) and his wife (Helen Mirren) than murder or even suspense. It is played on high-pitched strings and low woodwinds and is disarmingly memorable. One might go far as to say it is a slowed-down, more melancholy version of Bernard Herrmann's famous piercing violins in *Psycho*'s infamous shower scene. Conversely, the live-action version of the popular children's tale *Charlotte's Web* has a sweetly optimistic score. A flowing theme played by strings and a racing piano conveys innocent optimism. Another passage is giddy with glee, making the score very atypical of Elfman. Another popular children's story, *Black Beauty*, was beautifully filmed in 1994 and Elfman's score is rich and satisfying without a note of satire or sci-fi. He uses a simple but evocative folk theme throughout, sometimes played on the harp but usually with strings and horns. There is a majesty in the music, giving nature and the horses in the tale an almost mythic quality. The vibrant music that accompanies the running and prancing of these animals is a far cry from the pulsating movement music in those comic book films. The biographical *Milk*, about the gay activist Harvey Milk, has a strong dramatic score that does not outshine its story and characters. The main theme is a slightly urgent piece in which wavering strings and a solo oboe move rhythmically until they resolve with a piano solo.

It is those films that border on reality and fantasy that provide the most interesting opportunity for music. In Elfman's case, *Big Fish* is that opportunity. This extended tall tale has bits of the bizarre and, as filmed by Burton, is clearly a stylized view of the world. The music is similarly surreal yet accessible. The movie opens with an enchanting theme that suggests magic, warmth, and a dream state. A chorus is heard intermittently, more welcoming than spooky, and the use of traditional folk instruments adds a domestic flavor. "Sandra's Theme" is more restless, the melody fighting against some strings set in a stubborn pattern. This cockeyed epic is filled with heartfelt music, making it one of his finest scores outside of the horror-fantasy genre. Elfman has scored comedies, delicate character pieces, and even documentaries, but he is so much associated with the offbeat Burton films and the comic book adaptations that those are the projects he is most often offered. Yet this is not as limiting as it sounds, because he seems to keep coming up with new ways to score these kinds of movies and remains one of the best in that field.

Credits

(all films USA unless stated otherwise)

Year	Film	Director
1982	Forbidden Zone	Richard Elfman
1985	Pee-wee's Big Adventure	Tim Burton
1986	Back to School	Alan Metter
1986	Wisdom	Emilio Estevez
1987	Summer School	Carl Reiner
1988	Beetlejuice	Tim Burton
1988	Midnight Run	Martin Brest
1988	Big Top Pee-wee	Randal Kleiser
1988	Hot to Trot	Michael Dinner
1988	Scrooged	Richard Donner
1989	Batman	Tim Burton (USA/UK)
1990	Nightbreed	Clive Barker
1990	Dick Tracy	Warren Beatty
1990	Darkman	Sam Raimi
1990	Edward Scissorhands	Tim Burton
1992	Article 99	Howard Deutch
1992	Batman Returns	Tim Burton (USA/UK)
1993	Sommersby	Jon Amiel (France/USA)
1993	The Nightmare before Christmas (GGN)	Henry Selick
1994	Black Beauty	Caroline Thompson (USA/UK)
1995	Dolores Claiborne	Taylor Hackford
1995	To Die For	Gus Van Sant (USA/UK)
1995	Dead Presidents	Albert and Allen Hughes
1996	Freeway	Matthew Bright
1996	Mission: Impossible	Brian De Palma
1996	The Frighteners	Peter Jackson (N. Zealand/USA)
1996	Extreme Measures	Michael Apted
1996	Mars Attacks!	Tim Burton
1997	Men in Black	Barry Sonnenfeld
1997	Flubber	Les Mayfield
1997	Good Will Hunting (AAN)	Gus Van Sant
1998	A Simple Plan	Sam Raimi (UK/Germany/France/USA)
1998	A Civil Action	Steven Zaillian
1999	Instinct	Jon Turteltaub
1999	Anywhere But Here	Wayne Wang
1999	Sleepy Hollow	Tim Burton (USA/Germany)
2000	Proof of Life	Taylor Hackford
2000	The Family Man	Brett Ratner
2001	Spy Kids	Robert Rodriguez
2001	Planet of the Apes	Tim Burton
2002	Spider-Man	Sam Raimi
2002	Men in Black II	Barry Sonnenfeld
2002	Red Dragon	Brett Ratner (USA/Germany)
2002	Chicago (BAFTA-N)	Rob Marshall (USA/Germany)
2003	Hulk	Ang Lee

Year	Film	Director
2003	Big Fish (AAN; GGN)	Tim Burton
2004	Spider-Man 2	Sam Raimi
2005	Charlie and the Chocolate Factory	Tim Burton (USA/UK)
2005	Corpse Bride	Tim Burton, Mike Johnson (UK/USA)
2006	Nacho Libre	Jared Hess (Germany/USA)
2006	Charlotte's Web	Gary Winick (USA/Germany)
2007	Meet the Robinsons	Stephen J. Anderson
2007	The Kingdom	Peter Berg (USA/Germany)
2008	Standard Operating Procedure	Errol Morris
2008	Wanted	Timur Bekmambetov (USA/Germany)
2008	Hellboy II: The Golden Army	Guillermo del Toro (USA/Germany)
2008	Milk (AAN)	Gus Van Sant
2009	Notorious	George Tillman Jr.
2009	Terminator Salvation	McG (USA/Germany/UK/Italy)
2009	Taking Woodstock	Ang Lee
2010	The Wolfman	Joe Johnston
2010	Alice in Wonderland (GGN; BAFTA-N)	Tim Burton
2010	The Next Three Days	Paul Haggis (USA/France)
2010	Do Not Disturb	Eric Balfour, etc.
2011	Restless	Gus Van Sant
2011	Real Steel	Shawn Levy (USA/India)
2012	Dark Shadows	Tim Burton (USA/Australia)
2012	Men in Black 3	Barry Sonnenfeld (USA/United Arab Emirates)
2012	Silver Linings Playbook	David O. Russell
2012	Frankenweenie	Tim Burton
2012	Hitchcock	Sacha Gervasi
2012	Promised Land	Gus Van Sant (USA/United Arab Emirates)
2013	Oz the Great and Powerful	Sam Raimi
2013	Epic	Chris Wedge
2013	The Unknown Known	Errol Morris
2013	American Hustle	David O. Russell
2014	Mr. Peabody & Sherman	Rob Minkoff
2014	Big Eyes	Tim Burton

ELLINGTON, Duke (1899–1974) The renowned African American bandleader, songwriter, pianist, and composer who is one of the giants in the history of American jazz, he scored only four feature films but his music has been heard in over 250 movies and television shows.

Born Edward Kennedy Ellington in Washington, D.C., to music-loving parents, he began piano lessons at the age of seven. Taught by his piano teacher to maintain a dignified poise at all times, the boy soon got the nickname "Duke" and he used it for the rest of his life. When he was fifteen and working as a soda jerk, Ellington wrote his first song, "Soda Fountain Rag." A gifted graphic artist as well, he turned down a scholarship to study art at the Pratt Institute in Brooklyn and instead began playing ragtime professionally. In the 1920s he formed his own band and played early jazz at the Cotton Club and other New York nightspots. Ellington and his band became famous, appearing on radio, in movies, and in concert, also making dozens of records. In the 1940s he concentrated on writing songs in the jazz idiom and went on to compose over one thousand pieces during his lifetime, including such classics as "Satin Doll," "It Don't Mean a Thing If It Ain't Got That Swing," "Solitude," "Prelude to a Kiss," "Sophisticated Lady," "Do Nothin' Till You Hear from Me," "In a Sentimental Mood," and "Mood Indigo." Ellington was involved with all aspects of show business, from honky-tonks to television. He wrote original music for the Broadway musicals *Blue Holiday* (1945), *Beggar's Holiday* (1946), and *Pousse-Café* (1966), and his songs were later heard in the Broadway shows *Bubbling Brown Sugar* (1976), *Sophisticated Ladies* (1981), *Uptown . . . It's Hot!* (1986), *Play On!* (1997) and *Swing!* (1999). In addition to songs and jazz instrumental pieces, Ellington also wrote symphonic suites, such as *Harlem* and *Black*,

Brown, and Beige, and with composer-lyricist-arranger Billy Strayhorn, musical suites based on John Steinbeck's *Sweet Thursday* and Henrik Ibsen and Edvard Grieg's *Peer Gynt*.

Ellington was involved in the movies as far back as 1929 when he and his band appeared in the musical short *Black and Tan*. He usually played himself in such features as *Belle of the Nineties* (1934), *The Hit Parade* (1937), *Birth of the Blues* (1941), and *Reveille with Beverly* (1943). His songs were heard in many other 1930s and 1940s movies, but he did not write original music for a feature film until 1959 when he scored the courtroom drama *Anatomy of a Murder*. (Ellington also appeared in the movie as the pianist Pie Eye.) The jazz score, considered a landmark in screen music, was praised and Ellington was prompted to write music for three subsequent films: the romance *Paris Blues*, the crime adventure *Assault on a Queen*, and the sci-fi racial drama *Change of Mind*. His final years were occupied with a series of "sacred concerts," more recordings, and personal appearances. When Ellington died from lung cancer at the age of seventy-five, his son Mercer took over leadership of the famous band and conducted it until his death in 1996. Few American composers were so honored, beloved, and memorialized as Ellington was during and after his lifetime. In the opinion of many, he is America's greatest composer.

The score for *Anatomy of a Murder* is not only superb jazz but was innovative in the way it was used. Previously, when jazz music was heard in a movie, the musicians and singers were present in the scene, visually telling moviegoers where the music was coming from. Consequently, most jazz in movies was found in nightclubs and other performance venues. *Anatomy of a Murder*, about a soldier (Ben Gazarra) who is on trial for murdering the bartender who may or may not have raped his wife (Lee Remick), takes place mostly in the courtroom. Except for a brief scene in a roadhouse, jazz is heard but not seen. For the first time the sound of jazz was used to create mood and tension outside of a musical setting. Like much of Ellington's music, the jazz in the film is sometimes mixed with a Big Band sound. There is a driving theme in which the brass shout while the main motif is played on muted instruments. Sometimes a solo trumpet cries out in a wailing manner, other times piano and clarinet provide sharp and abrasive squawks. Parts of the score are cool jazz played by a small ensemble; other sections feature a moody piano with subdued percussion. There is also a free and easy passage featuring saxophone that is very smooth and bluesy, and a Dixieland jazz section that really hops. Ellington and Strayhorn pushed the jazz idiom in new directions in *Anatomy of a Murder* and opened up new possibilities for screen scoring.

Paris Blues is about two ex-patriot Americans, a white trombonist (Paul Newman) and an African American saxophonist (Sidney Poitier), who are drawn to the Parisian love of jazz but are tempted to return to the States when they fall in love with two visiting American women. Ellington's Oscar-nominated score includes Strayhorn's "Take the 'A' Train" and Louis Armstrong bringing down the house playing Ellington's "Wild Man Moore," but it is the jazz soundtrack score that is most compelling. The main theme is a mesmerizing piece featuring a solo flute moving in and out of the cool jazz arrangement, which is rich and evocative. There is a graceful blues passage that is so smooth it seems to float and a Big Band romantic theme that is casual yet sultry when a muted trumpet is featured. *Assault on a Queen*, about an attempt to rob the ocean liner *Queen Mary* while at sea, is a second-rate thriller, but there is much to recommend in Ellington's score. The title theme is a brisk jazz piece played by full orchestra and is more like dance music than that for a heist movie. The jazz on the soundtrack sometimes conveys suspense though it is rarely supported by the events on-screen. Neither does Ellington's slick jazz music work effectively in an even weaker movie, *Change of Mind*. This interesting but ineffective movie, about the social and racial implications that arise when a white man's brain is transplanted into an African America's skull, cannot be saved by music. Sadly, it was Ellington's last screen project. On the bright side, there are hours of Ellington music heard in such diverse movies as *Check and Double Check* (1930), *Air Force* (1943), *A Hatful of Rain* (1957), *The Turning Point* (1977), *The Cotton Club* (1984), *When Harry Met Sally* (1989), *The Addams Family* (1991), *A League of Their Own* (1992), *Saving Private Ryan* (1998), *The Green Mile* (1999), *The Notebook* (2004), and *American Hustle* (2013). Autobiography: *Music Is My Mistress* (1973); biographies: *Duke: A Life of Duke Ellington*, Terry Teachout (2013); *Beyond Category: The Life and Genius of Duke Ellington*, John Edward Hasse (1995). Official website: wwwdukeellington.com.

Credits

(all films USA)

Year	Film	Director
1959	Anatomy of a Murder	Otto Preminger
1961	Paris Blues (AAN)	Martin Ritt
1966	Assault on a Queen	Jack Donohue
1969	Change of Mind	Robert Stevens

ELLIS, Don (1934–1978) An acclaimed jazz trumpeter, arranger, and bandleader whose progressive style was lauded by jazz enthusiasts, he scored eight feature films before his untimely death.

Donald Johnson Ellis was born in Los Angeles, the son of a preacher and church organist, and was raised in Minneapolis, where he became interested in jazz at an early age. As a preteen, Ellis formed his own jazz ensemble at school then later studied composition and trumpet at Boston University and the Berklee School of Music. In 1956 he was hired as trumpeter for the Glenn Miller Orchestra but soon was drafted and stationed in Germany. While in the army, Ellis played with the Seventh Army Soldiers Show Band and the Army Jazz Orchestra, touring and writing jazz arrangements and original music, which the bands performed. He was discharged in 1958 and took up his career as trumpeter for swing and dance bands, most memorably for bandleaders Woody Herman and Maynard Ferguson, making some classic recording with the latter. By the late 1950s Ellis was getting attention for his avant-garde jazz arrangements and compositions. He toured the States and Europe then in New York founded the Improvisational Workshop Orchestra, a jazz ensemble that utilized elements of rock and Asian music. The ever-restless Ellis returned to music studies at the University of California and the State University of New York at Buffalo then did another career shift by playing trumpet for the New York Philharmonic under Leonard Bernstein. Returning to Los Angeles, he formed another ensemble, the Hindustani Jazz Sextet, and continued to experiment with the trumpet, adding a fourth valve and an electric mouthpiece. His most famous group, the Don Ellis Orchestra, found wide success at jazz festivals in the 1960s and 1970s and through their innovative recordings that featured guest jazz artists.

Ellis first worked in film in 1968 when he was the featured trumpet player on the soundtrack for Lalo Schifrin's score for *Bullet*. The next year he wrote his own score for the British sci-fi movie *Moon Zero Two* but it was Ellis's music for the iconoclastic cop thriller *The French Connection* in 1971 that brought him recognition as a screen composer. He also scored the 1975 sequel and another Manhattan police drama *The Seven-Ups*, both of which have first-rate scores. Ellis's other films were less satisfying but boasted expert scores. He also wrote music for the television series *Mission: Impossible*, *Movin' On*, and *Doctor's Hospital*, as well as the score for the TV movie *The Deadly Tower* (1975). Ellis would probably have continued writing for movies and television had he not died prematurely at the age of forty-four. He had suffered from heart disease his whole adult life and died of a heart attack in 1978, a year before his last movie project, *Natural Enemies*, was released.

The score for *The French Connection* might be described as jazz fusion, for Ellis uses Big Band, Latin, and even rock alongside the jazz music. There is a riveting theme in which brass and a solo viola pound furiously away as drums and castanets provide accents and an electric keyboard adds a funky flavor. It sounds like all of Manhattan compressed into a single piece of music. Another passage has romantic strings juxtaposed against jazz piano and guitar. A solo trumpet calls out as a chaotic jazz ensemble tries to overwhelm it but ends up joining in. For the movie's most famous scene, a nail-biting chase on the subway, Ellis uses a harsh lower string motif and contrasts it with high-pitched pizzicato violins and furious piano glides. Then a solo trumpet joins in and seems to comment on all the commotion. The music for *French Connection II* is equally thrilling. Although set in Marseille rather than New York City, the movie is still an urban crime melodrama packed with action. The schizophrenic main theme alternates between frantic jazz and an eerie electronic waltz heard on a solo trumpet and backed by sustained sour notes on a synthesizer. Suspense is conveyed by a halting passage in which squawking brass grumble in a menacing manner. This film also has a memorable chase scene and exciting music to add to it. Blaring brass have contrasting long and short notes while the rest of the instruments race ahead. *The Seven-Ups* may not be as stimulating as the two *French Connection* films, but it still pleases. Ellis's score is less jazz and more Hollywood action music but is nonetheless penetrating. In one passage a string orchestra makes passionate leaps over the growling bass line. In an-

other section, strained off-key strings play sustained notes at such a high register that they turn into sound effects. There is also an effective theme in which pizzicato violins dominate over low rumbling from the deeper strings. Oddly, the nine-minute car chase through Manhattan has no music at all. A generation earlier, Duke Ellington opened up the world of jazz to the movies. The fruition of that can be heard in the scores by Ellis, Quincy Jones, and a handful of others. Biography: *Don Ellis: A Man for Our Time*, Anthony Agostinelli (1986).

Credits

(all films USA unless stated otherwise)

Year	Film	Director
1969	Moon Zero Two	Roy Ward Baker (UK)
1971	The French Connection	William Friedkin
1972	Kansas City Bomber	Jerrold Freedman
1973	The Seven-Ups	Philip D'Antoni
1975	French Connection II	John Frankenheimer
1977	Ruby (aka Blood Ruby)	Curtis Harrington
1977	The Ransom (aka Maniac!)	Richard Compton
1979	Natural Enemies	Jeff Kanew

ESHKERI, Ilan (b. 1977?) A versatile British songwriter, musician, and composer with a very eclectic career in television, movies, and the concert hall, since 2000 he has been scoring feature films that are also very diverse.

Ilan Eshkeri was born in London to a musical family and took guitar and violin lessons as a child, then as a teenager played in a rock band. Eshkeri studied music and English literature at Leeds University, where he met and worked with film composers and a music producer who helped launch his professional career. His first screen score was for the 2000 low-budget comedy *The Quarry Men* followed by the sci-fi movie *Trinity*. Recognition did not come until 2003 when he scored the popular British TV movie *Colosseum: Rome's Arena of Death*. The next year Eshkeri collaborated with composer Lisa Gerrard on the score for the gangster film *Layer Cake*, which was an international success. The director, Matthew Vaughn, worked again with Eshkeri on two other box office hits, *Stardust* and *Kick-Ass*, though the latter required three other composers. He has since scored everything from action films to history pieces, including such notable

movies as *Telstar: The Joe Meek Story*, *The Young Victoria*, *Ninja Assassin*, *From Time to Time*, *Centurion*, *Coriolanus*, *Johnny English Reborn*, *Spike Island*, *The Invisible Woman*, *Austenland*, and *47 Ronin*. Eshkeri has written music for such British television series as *Trial & Retribution*, *Waking the Dead*, *Strike Back*, and *Fleming*. He has scored documentaries, most memorably *David Attenborough's Natural History Museum Alive* (2014), and short films, including the popular *The Snowman and the Snowdog* (2012). Eshkeri has performed his music in concert and his songs have been recorded by various pop and classical music artists.

Eshkeri's first significant solo score is found in *Stardust*, a fanciful adventure set in a fantasy kingdom. The music is mostly in a classical mode and is filled with a magical kind of awe that fits so well with the fairy-tale-like story and characters. There is a recurring mystical theme with low rumbling drums, gliding strings, and celestial voices that sets the tone for the movie. Another effective passage has flowing strings with plucked strings providing a bubbly accent. There is also a radiant theme in which sustained notes contrast against sharp notes that dance up and down the scale, as opposed to a vigorous passage in which various instruments race ahead in different ways yet seem all in sync. Also in a classical vein is Eshkeri's music for the historical drama *The Young Victoria*. Like the portrayal of the youthful Queen Victoria (Emily Blunt), the music is far from stodgy or demure. The main theme is a zesty piano piece played against sustained orchestral chords. While there is a slow and stately passage for orchestra with piano and harp accents, there is also more than a bit of pomp in a grandiose theme for full orchestra and chorus. The lyrical love theme is ardent and passionate but in a restrained way. Eshkeri quotes from Franz Schubert and Johann Strauss Jr. in the score, although his arrangement of two waltzes by the latter are so resplendent that they sound new. The romantic comedy *Austenland* also has a classical score, this time happily pastiching early nineteenth-century music rather than paying homage to it. A contemporary American named Jane (Keri Russell) is so obsessed with Jane Austen and her characters that she travels to a British resort catering to such fans and soon finds herself running amuck in Regency England. The movie may run out of original ideas early on but Eshkeri's score is endlessly fresh and appealing as it never takes itself too seriously. There is a minuet featuring oboe and violins that undulates across the scale in a fluid manner, and a sparkling waltz that never lags as it goes through various variations. Best of all is a sonata for a string and woodwind ensemble that is playful and vivacious, suggesting a romp through a garden.

A period piece of quite a different temperament is the action drama *Centurion* about some soldiers in ancient Rome caught in guerrilla warfare. Eshkeri avoids any attempt at period authenticity and provides a high-tech score that uses synthesized and traditional music, sound effects, and vocals to tell this rather modern tale. Growling sound effects are echoed by drums and electronic waves of music, a delicate and melancholy theme is played by various and diverse strings, and there is a funeral dirge with a solo voice rising above a jittery bass line and the sound of the wind. The battle scenes are scored with a lot of electronic effects, sometimes with sustained notes that border on high-frequency sounds. Similarly, the 2011 screen version of Shakespeare's *Coriolanus*, directed by and starring Ralph Fiennes, has a score that might best be described as hard rock fusion. There are primitive sounds that echo, tribal drums, electric guitar riffs, and harsh violin chords, all presented in a nightmarish tone. One percussion theme seethes with frustration as various noises and pounding notes contribute to the propulsive forward motion of the piece. Such a modern sound is also found in medieval Japan in Eshkeri's score for *47 Ronin*, an action adventure with some fantastical elements. The main theme features a lonely cello and Asian flute lament surrounded by vibrations that turns into a powerful chase in which Western instruments mix with Asian ones. The theme for the Shogun (Cary-Hiroyuki Tagawa) is a pounding march with primitive drums and high-tech echoes and vibrations. In some passages electronic wails and a morose viola solo are heard over sustained Western strings. Even the love theme, played on piano and cello with synthesized background instruments and sounds, manages to feel modern and, at the same time, traditionally Japanese.

Two contrasting movies to further illustrate Eshkeri's versatility are the horror film *Hannibal Rising* and the spy spoof *Johnny English Reborn*. The childhood of the serial killer Hannibal Lecter (Aaran Thomas and then Gaspard Ulliel) is the subject of *Hannibal Rising*. The score is more subtle than most horror films but it is nonetheless very potent. The opening theme is a creepy piece featuring piano and oboe with menacing vocals. A passage with nervous strings and a rising and falling motif played by the rest of the orchestra is not only foreboding but quite disarming. There is also a chilling passage in which a lonesome piano is surrounded by sweeping musical phrases. Eshkeri includes a Requiem and an Agnus Dei in the score but they are turned into eerie and threatening Gregorian chants that are less about mourning or celebrating than they are about revenge. Just as moviegoers were already familiar with Hannibal Lecter from a previous film, so too did audiences (especially British ones) already know Johnny English (Rowan Atkinson) from a 2003 comedy. The antics of this accidental secret agent are scored with glee by Eshkeri in *Johnny English Reborn*. The comic spy tale has a mocking jazz score that pastiches James Bond music with trumpets shouting and a pounding beat that comes close to disco. The action scenes have grandiose music with a full symphony jumping all over the scale. The very physical comic Atkinson does not need words but his shenanigans require the right kind of music and he certain gets it in Eshkeri's score. Here is a composer who is difficult to label. Each score speaks for itself. Official website: ilaneshkeri.com.

Credits

(all films UK unless stated otherwise)

Year	Film	Director
2000	*The Quarry Men*	Toby White
2003	*Trinity*	Gary Boulton-Brown
2004	*Layer Cake*	Matthew Vaughn
2007	*Hannibal Rising* (aka *Hannibal 4*)	Peter Webber (UK/Czech Republic/France/Italy)
2007	*Closure* (aka *Straightheads*)	Dan Reed
2007	*Stardust*	Matthew Vaughn (UK/USA/Iceland)
2007	*Strength and Honour*	Mark Mahon (Ireland)
2007	*Virgin Territory* (aka *Angels and Virgins*)	David Leland (Italy/UK/France)
2008	*The Disappeared*	Johnny Kevorkian
2008	*Telstar: The Joe Meek Story*	Nick Moran
2009	*The Young Victoria*	Jean-Marc Vallée (UK/USA)
2009	*Ninja Assassin*	James McTeigue (USA/Germany)
2009	*From Time to Time*	Julian Fellowes
2010	*Centurion*	Neil Marshall (UK/France)
2010	*The Kid*	Nick Moran
2011	*Knuckle*	Ian Palmer (UK/Ireland)
2011	*Coriolanus*	Ralph Fiennes
2011	*Blooded*	Edward Boase
2011	*Blitz*	Elliott Lester (UK/France/USA)
2011	*Retreat*	Carl Tibbetts
2011	*Johnny English Reborn*	Oliver Parker (USA/France/UK)
2012	*Tough Talk*	Callum Rees
2012	*Spike Island*	Mat Whitecross
2012	*Ashes*	Mat Whitecross
2013	*I Give It a Year*	Dan Mazer
2013	*Austenland*	Jerusha Hess (UK/USA)
2013	*The Invisible Woman*	Ralph Fiennes
2012	*Justin and the Knights of Valour*	Manuel Sicilia (Spain)
2013	*47 Ronin*	Carl Rinsch (USA)

FALTERMEYER, Harold (b. 1952) An influential German composer, arranger, and record producer, he brought the "synthpop" sound to American movies.

Born Harald Faltermeier in Munich, Germany, into a musical family, his grandparents included a violinist and classical alto soprano and his father was a civil engineer who was also a pianist. Faltermeyer began piano lessons at the age of six and by the time he was eleven he was studying at Munich's Academy of Music. As a teenager he volunteered as a technician at the Deutsche Grammophon studios, where he learned about synthesized and electric music, mixing and editing records, and even doing some conducting and arranging. Composer-producer Giorgio Moroder was impressed with Faltermeyer and in 1977 brought him to Los Angeles, where he arranged music for some of the top recording artists. Wide recognition came in 1979 when Faltermeyer wrote songs for and arranged the music on the Donna Summer disco album *Bad Girls*, which was an international success. Through his connection with Moroder, he got to arrange the music for the films *Midnight Express* (1978) and *American Gigolo* (1980). He contributed original music to the score of the German comedy *Didi—Der Doppelgänger* in 1984 before scoring his first Hollywood movie, the thriller *Thief of Hearts*. Later that same year, Faltermeyer's music for the box office hit comedy *Beverly Hills Cop* was also a success, particularly the "Axel F" theme, which was recorded by many artists and became an international phenomenon. In 1986 Faltermeyer had similar success with his score for the romantic action drama *Top Gun*, this time the theme "Top Gun Anthem" becoming famous. Faltermeyer received an Oscar nomination for his song "Shakedown" (written with Keith Forsey and Bob Seger) in the sequel *Beverly Hills Cop II*. Among Faltermeyer's other notable movies are *Fletch* and its sequel *Fletch Lives*, *The Running Man*, *Fatal Beauty*, *Tango & Cash*, and *Cop Out*. Faltermeyer left Hollywood in 1989 and moved back to Germany to raise a family. He scored some European

movies and opened his own recording studio in Munich. From there he has composed and produced many records for popular artists. Among the singers he has worked with over the years in Germany and the States are Patti LaBelle, Blondie, the Pet Shop Boys, Barbra Streisand, Bob Seger, Bonnie Tyler, Glenn Frey, Billy Idol, and La Toya Jackson. Faltermeyer has also written music for German television series, TV movies, the theatre, and video games. With his children grown, Faltermeyer returned to Los Angeles in 2009 and has resumed his movie and record-producing career in the States.

The synthesizer is the main instrument in the kind of music labeled "synthpop" in the 1980s, a sound Faltermeyer embraced, enhanced, and brought to film scoring. His background and years of experience as a studio technician arranging and mixing music helped Faltermeyer bring the sound to his early screen scores. *Beverly Hills Cop* was only his second solo assignment yet the intriguing fusion of disco, hard rock, jazz, and other styles sounds so confident and accomplished in the score that it dazzles. *Beverly Hills Cop* is a sarcastic vehicle for comic Eddie Murphy and, as such, does not require strong musical accompaniment. But Faltermeyer's masterful synthesized score seems to grow out of Murphy's smart-aleck humor. The famous "Axel F" is a slaphappy disco theme played on electric keyboard with crackling percussion accents. It is so contagious that one can understand its widespread popularity. There is also a rhythmic passage in the score with electronic notes that vibrate and waver as the pulsating percussion holds the fiery piece together. Also first rate is a dancing theme with sparkling synthesized riffs and vivacious keyboard fingering. A racetrack robbery is scored with a propulsive hard rock sound, a series of electronic chords that explode then shift a third of a step and explode again. *Fletch*, another comic cop caper, has a weaker script and a lesser star (Chevy Chase) but again the score is a synthesized delight, particularly a fun disco theme with whimsical electronic sounds that repeat the simple musical line with a variety of wacky "voices."

A third cop film, *Tango & Cash*, is more serious but still has some comic swagger as two cops (Sylvester Stallone and Kurt Russell) are framed and they set out to clear their names. Faltermeyer sets banging metal percussion against a zesty Latin melody played on trumpets and then on electric keyboard. There is less disco and more rock in this fervent score. An energetic tango is played on an electronic harmonica; an oppressive theme uses a deep, gloomy bass line and high-pitched whistles; and even the love theme is pulsating as it lyrically glides through all the echoes and pounding. An action cop movie with a sci-fi twist is *The Running Man*, an Arnold Schwarzenegger vehicle about a deadly game show used to execute convicts. The score, written with assist by Vassal Benford, has a frantic main theme played on electric keyboard with traditional strings with long sustained notes giving the piece solidity. As the title suggests, there is some piercing chase music with explosive climaxes as it climbs the scale but never seems to resolve. There is a creepy passage with echoing electronics, grumbling bass line, and a synthesized heartbeat, and another theme has a grinding pattern broken by some fanciful keyboard fingering and high-pitched sounds that come close to human chanting.

Perhaps the screen score that conveys the richness of the "synthpop" sound best is the one Faltermeyer wrote for *Top Gun*. A Tom Cruise vehicle about navy cadet flyers, the movie mixes action, romance, and a strong sense of determination into a highly appealing commercial package. It is Faltermeyer's music that gives the film class and poetry. The acclaimed "Top Gun Anthem" is a good example. The piece has a slightly disco-beat percussion but the melodic line has slow and stately music that begins like a hymn with chimes then carefully but confidently builds into a thrilling declaration of victory. The love theme has a slow disco tempo with bursts of percussion throughout but its sultry melody is played on synthesized strings and finds a softness not far below the surface. Another splendid passage is a delicate lament with a lonesome electric keyboard playing above long and low sustained organ chords. The *Top Gun* score includes pop songs by others ("Take My Breath Away" by Giorgio Moroder and lyricist Tom Whitlock was nominated for an Oscar) and Moroder provided some of the music for the flying sequences, but the heart of the movie is in Faltermeyer's soundtrack score. Just as these hit movies were quickly cloned and copied, Faltermeyer's unique "synthpop" music has influenced many later scores by others. Official website: www.haroldfaltermeyer.net.

Credits

(all films USA unless stated otherwise; * for Best Song)

Year	Film	Director
1984	*Didi—Der Doppelgänger*	Reinhard Schwabenitzky (W. Germany)
1984	*Thief of Hearts*	Douglas Day Stewart
1984	*Beverly Hills Cop*	Martin Brest
1985	*Fletch*	Michael Ritchie
1986	*Fire and Ice*	Willy Bogner (W. Germany)
1986	*Top Gun* (GGN)	Tony Scott
1987	*Beverly Hills Cop II* (AAN*; GGN; BAFTA-N)	Tony Scott
1987	*Fatal Beauty*	Tom Holland (USA/Japan)
1987	*The Running Man*	Paul Michael Glaser
1989	*Fletch Lives* (aka *Fletch Saved*)	Michael Ritchie
1989	*Tango & Cash* (aka *The Set Up*)	Andrey Konchalovskiy, Albert Magnoli
1990	*Fire, Ice & Dynamite*	Willy Bogner (Germany)
1992	*Kuffs*	Bruce A. Evans
1994	*Asterix Conquers America*	Gerhard Hahn (Germany/France)
1994	*White Magic*	Willy Bogner (Germany/USA)
2010	*Cop Out* (aka *A Couple of Cops*)	Kevin Smith

FARNON, Robert (Joseph) (1917–2005) A very popular and influential Canadian composer, arranger, musician, and conductor for radio, movies, television, and the concert hall, he scored a variety of British films in the postwar years.

Robert Farnon was born in Toronto, Canada, and studied the trumpet as a youth, becoming adept as a jazz trumpet player. While still in his teens, Farnon was hired as lead trumpet player for the Canadian Broadcasting Company's studio orchestra and was also arranging and writing jazz music when war broke out in Europe. Farnon served in the Canadian armed forces overseas where he was made conductor and arranger of the Canadian Army Band. At the end of World War II he settled in England where his reputation as an expert arranger and composer of light classical music spread and soon he was working with the top bands and artists in both Great Britain and the States. Farnon composed and conducted a number of popular records, most memorably "Jumping Bean," "Portrait of a Flirt," "Destiny Waltz," "A Star Is Born," and "Westminster Waltz." His arrangements were often cited as the best in the business, particularly his orchestration of strings, and artists ranging from André Previn to Quincy Jones have acknowledged the great influence Farnon had on their work.

His work in movies began in 1945 when he wrote and arranged some music for the British romance *A Yank in London*. After doing arrangements for other movies, Farnon got to write the full score for the comedy *Just William's Luck* directed by Val Guest. The two men also collaborated on the sequel *William Comes to Town*, *It's a Wonderful World*, and *Expresso Bongo*. Farnon's other notable British movies include *Spring in Park Lane, Elizabeth of Ladymead, Maytime in Mayfair, Captain Horatio Hornblower R.N., Circle of Danger, The Little Hut, The Truth about Spring, Shalako, Friend or Foe*, and *The Road to Hong Kong*, the last being the final Bing Crosby–Bob Hope "road" movie. Although Farnon worked frequently with Decca and other American record companies, he scored only a few Hollywood films, most notably *His Majesty O'Keefe* and *Gentlemen Marry Brunettes*. He also wrote music for British documentaries, TV movies, and television series, such as *Armchair Theatre, Colditz, Secret Army*, and *Kessler*. By the 1970s Farnon wrote less for the movies and concentrated on writing for the concert hall. He completed three symphonies and a handful of concer-

tos before his death at the age of eighty-seven. His music is preserved and perpetuated by the Robert Farnon Society.

While much of Farnon's musical output might be described as "easy listening," his screen scores are often quite dramatic and integrated with each film's tone and temperament. His most famous score is that for the historical epic *Captain Horatio Hornblower R.N.* This is a grand adventure score in the Hollywood tradition with its sweeping symphonic theme punctuated with euphonic brass fanfares. There is a reflective string passage in which woodwinds tentatively search out a melody, a love theme that is lush and passionate with little restraint, and a vigorous track that has the robust excitement of a ship at full sail. For a very American sound, one should consider Farnon's western score for *Shalako*. The rousing main theme with strings, harmonica, and brass playing a zesty folk tune is turned into a boisterous title song (lyric by Jim Dale) for the opening and closing credits. The score has an expansive nature theme in which fluttering reeds provide a counterpoint to the masculine drums. There is also a harmonica theme that is rustic without being cliché ridden. For contrast there is the lighthearted score Farnon wrote for *The Road to Hong Kong*. Crosby and Hope sing five delightful songs by Jimmy Van Heusen (music) and Sammy Cahn (lyric) but just as playful is Farnon's soundtrack score. Pseudo-Chinese musical phrases are mixed in with jazz and even vaudeville soft-shoe music. The main theme, based on the Van Heusen–Cahn ditty "Teamwork," is a silly mix of Asian and Western music that echoes the spoofing sense of humor of the movie.

It's a Wonderful World is a comedy about music and afforded Farnon the opportunity to use Big Band, blues, jazz, and even his "light orchestra" sound. This satire on avant-garde music concerns two London songwriters (Terence Morgan and George Cole) who create a sensation by playing their music backward. Farnon wrote one of the songs, "A Few Kisses Ago" (lyric by director Val Guest), and the eclectic soundtrack score. There are zippy Big Band passages, some cool and hot jazz, and even a blues theme with strings that seem to weep. The music for the comedy *Spring in Park Lane* might also be labeled "easy listening" but it more resembles a lightweight Hollywood romantic score. The familiar plot is about an aristocrat (Michael Wilding) who disguises himself as a footman and falls in love with the young lady (Anna Neagle) of the house. There is a waltzing theme that is so chipper that the piccolos sound like birds, a gliding foxtrot passage that has some fanciful embellishments, and a love theme that is a tripping waltz played on strings as only Farnon could make strings sound. While Farnon's legacy lies in his nonmovie music, these scores remind one of his valuable contribution to the art of light orchestra composition and orchestration. Robert Farnon Society website: www. rfsoc.org.uk.

Credits

(all films UK unless stated otherwise)

Year	Film	Director
1947	Just William's Luck	Val Guest
1948	Spring in Park Lane	Herbert Wilcox
1948	Elizabeth of Ladymead	Herbert Wilcox
1948	William Comes to Town	Val Guest
1949	Paper Orchid	Roy Ward Baker
1949	Maytime in Mayfair	Herbert Wilcox
1951	Captain Horatio Hornblower R.N.	Raoul Walsh
1951	Circle of Danger	Jacques Tourneur
1955	His Majesty O'Keefe	Byron Haskin, Burt Lancaster (USA)
1954	Let's Make Up (aka Lilacs in the Spring)	Herbert Wilcox
1955	Gentlemen Marry Brunettes	Richard Sale (USA)
1955	All for Mary	Wendy Toye
1956	It's a Wonderful World	Val Guest
1957	True as a Turtle (aka Plain Sailing)	Wendy Toye
1957	The Little Hut	Mark Robson
1958	The Sheriff of Fractured Jaw	Raoul Walsh (UK/USA)
1959	Expresso Bongo	Val Guest
1962	The Road to Hong Kong	Norman Panama
1965	The Truth about Spring	Richard Thorpe (UK/USA)
1968	Shalako	Edward Dmytryk (UK/W. Germany)
1977	The Disappearance	Stuart Cooper (UK/Canada)
1979	Bear Island	Don Sharp (Canada/UK)
1982	Friend or Foe	John Kirsh

FENTON, George (b. 1950) A busy British theatre, television, and movie composer who works on both sides of the Atlantic, his seventy-three feature films are extremely diverse, ranging from contemporary comedies and elegant period pieces to social dramas and surreal projects.

He was born George Richard Ian Howe in London and educated at St. Edward's School in Oxford, an institution he credits for his love for music and one for which he later served as a governor. Fenton began his career as an actor, appearing in London plays and on British television, often playing a musical instrument in the productions. He first worked with director Stephen Frears as an actor on the television play *A Day Out* in 1972; the two would later collaborate as director and composer on five movies. Fenton managed a band, wrote some arrangements and composi-

tions for recording studios, and had a chart hit with his version of the Beatles' "Maxwell's Silver Hammer." In 1974 he wrote the musical score for a Royal Shakespeare Company production of *Twelfth Night* which opened the door for a composing career in the theatre. Over the years he has written scores for many plays by such distinguished companies as the Royal National Theatre, The Riverside Studios, The Royal Court, and the Royal Theatre Exchange. Fenton began his television career in 1976 and soon was one of the most successful and awarded composers on British TV, scoring such celebrated miniseries as *The Jewel in the Crown* (1984) and *Talking Heads* (1988). He also wrote music for such popular series as *Out, Objects of Desire*, and *Bergerac*, as well as many TV movies, including *Doris and Doreen* (1978), *One Fine Day* (1979), *Parole* (1982), *Walter and June* (1983), *An Englishman Abroad* (1983), *Saigon: The Year of the Cat* (1983), and *Pride* (2004). Fenton's music can also be heard on British television as the theme songs for several news programs and talk shows.

Fenton's film career began inauspiciously in 1971 when he contributed some music to the low-budget *Private Road* in which he also appeared. His scores for *Bloody Kids* and *Hussy* eight years later did little to promote his composing talents but in 1982 he provided enough music to Ravi Shankar's score for the hit *Gandhi* that he shared the Oscar for Best Score. By the late 1980s, Fenton was scoring movies regularly. He was never labeled as a composer of a particular genre and was in demand in both Hollywood and Europe, so Fenton got to write music for a wider variety of movies than most artists. Among his popular period films are *Dangerous Liaisons*, *Anna and the King*, *Mrs. Henderson Presents*, *A Handful of Dust*, *Memphis Belle*, and *Stage Beauty*. His many comedies include *High Spirits*, *We're No Angels*, *The Object of My Affection*, *You've Got Mail*, *Sweet Home Alabama*, *Born Yesterday*, and *Last Holiday*, while he also scored such potent dramas as *The Crucible*, *Cry Freedom*, *The History Boys*, *Shadowlands*, and *In Love and War*. Fenton's credits also include unique, difficult-to-label projects such as *The Fisher King*, *Groundhog Day*, and *The Zero Theorem*. He has many documentaries to his credit, including the television works *The Trials of Life* (1990), *Life in the Freezer* (1993), *China: Beyond the Clouds* (1994), *A French Affair* (2003), *Planet Earth* (2006), and *Life and Death in Shanghai* (2007), and such feature film documentaries as *Earth*, *Deep Blue*, *One Life*, *The Spirit of '45*, and *Baka: A Cry from the Rain Forest*. Fenton has worked closely with several major movie directors, often collaborating with Frears, Richard Attenborough, Andy Tennant, Neil Jordan, and Ken Losch. He has won many American and British awards and is active in many film organizations, including the Association of Professional Composers, which he founded. (The organization later became the British Academy of Songwriters, Composers and Authors.)

Fenton's music is almost as eclectic as the subject matter of his movies. He cites the Beatles and Henry Mancini as two of his strongest musical influences. With such diverse inspiration, it makes sense that his music is so chameleonlike. The urgent, pulsating theme for the diabolical French drama *Dangerous Liaisons* is contrasted by the stately Edward Elgar–like music for the English

biographical drama *Shadowlands*. The thriller *Mary Reilly* has an Irish flavor with a sorrowful violin and chorus, the World War I drama *In Love and War* has a gentle, romantic sweep, *Anna and the King* combines Asian instruments in a percussive theme, and there is dreamy music heard on oboe in the fairy tale *Ever After: A Cinderella Story*. While a snazzy 1940s foxtrot introduces the seriocomic *Mrs. Henderson Presents*, a silly march is used for the military spoof *Valiant* and a simple but foreboding dance on drum and pipes sets the tone for the Puritan drama *The Crucible*. One can search for a musical thread or a recurring composition characteristic in these and other Fenton scores but it is fruitless. From his first important score, *Gandhi*, one notices a strong musical sensibility for what works on-screen. Much of *Gandhi* has marvelously evocative Indian themes by Ravi Shankar, but in between are eloquent passages in the European tradition that Fenton wrote. A solo oboe weeps as strings tentatively play a melody in one section. British music, from military marches to playful carnival ditties, contrast with the native sounds of India throughout the epic film. Fenton managed a similar counterpoint five years later when he scored the powerful *Cry Freedom*, about South African activist Steve Biko (Denzel Washington), for *Gandhi* director Attenborough. There is a lovely mixture of tribal South African music, solo and choral chanting, and European orchestration in this biographical drama. There is also a splendid title song (lyric by Jonas Gwangwa) which was nominated for an Oscar.

A particularly English sound can be heard in a handful of Fenton scores. The drama *A Handful of Dust*, set mostly in Britain in the 1930s, has a sublime theme that is highly romantic yet ominous, the European sound interrupted by primitive instruments to foreshadow the story's ironic ending in a jungle. The academic tale *The History Boys* has a punk rock score appropriate for its 1980s setting yet there are moments of very classical British music (and old song standards) to remind one of the long tradition of education behind it all. The score for *84 Charing Cross Road*, about the correspondence between a London bookseller (Anthony Hopkins) and a New York writer (Anne Bancroft), has American jazz and blues for the Manhattan scenes and quaint English tea dance melodies for the London sequences. Even the romantic melodrama *White Mischief*, about Brits in Africa during World War II, is filled with very British themes ranging from melancholy violin solos to sentimental foxtrots.

Fenton is equally successful in capturing American sounds in his Hollywood scores. The contemporary comedy *You've Got Mail* is filled with recognized songs because the earlier Tom Hanks–Meg Ryan hit *Sleepless in Seattle* did likewise and ended up with a best-selling soundtrack album. Fenton ties *You've Got Mail* together with a breezy jazz piece that is light and comic, yet very much on the edge emotionally. There is also a flowing romantic theme performed by piano and orchestra that is very much in the Hollywood tradition, not unexpected in a film based on a 1940 comedy, *The Shop around the Corner*. There is some first-rate blues and jazz in the score for *The Long Walk Home*, set in the segregated South of the mid-1950s. Some of the passages are lazy and breezy, others tense and restless. Yet this is a restrained score for a movie that avoids sentimentality as it explores early civil rights and feminism. A quirky sense of Americana can be found in Fenton's score for *Groundhog Day*, the cult classic about a TV reporter (Bill Murray) forced to relive one day over and over again. The main motif is nostalgic and appealing as a solo flute floats through the air. The title theme is an intimate ensemble of brass, piano, and clarinet that performs a waggish piece which suggests a cockeyed local band. Another section of the score has a funky jazz style while there is also a bluesy passage with gliding strings. Part of the charm of this surreal comedy is how so much remains normal as the reporter is stuck in time, a concept supported by the score which never stoops to science fiction or supernatural music. Equally odd but much darker is director Terry Gilliam's *The Fisher King*, a fable set among people trying to live outside the real world. There is eerie sci-fi music this time, used effectively during some of the fantasy sequences. The film has a magical theme with a solo clarinet rising above quivering strings and one passage is a lovely cool jazz. Yet in many ways the real score for *The Fisher King* is the noise of New York City, from police sirens to blasts of pop music on the radio.

Perhaps Fenton's most masterful music is that which he has written for television and film documentaries, particularly those dealing with nature. *Deep Blue* has an expansive nature fanfare that is bold and powerful with the orchestra rising and falling in an ocean-like surging. There is also a kind of hesitation waltz with woodwinds climbing the scale as if breaking the surface. *One Life* is more percussive with tribal rhythms, choral voices, and a series of crescendos exploding all over the place. *Earth* uses a solo horn to herald the beginning of life and a solo female chanting to bring the movie to a sunset closing. In between is a variety of captivating music. Some themes are delicate and mystical, others are violent and majestic. The music from these nature documentaries is quite compelling on its own but it is the way Fenton composes his themes to accentuate the visuals on the screen that is truly superior. A flock of thousands of migrating birds taking flight over water is a stunning image, and the score matches it in intensity. A line of elephants is scored with a regal passage, while a pod of whales is given felicitous music worthy of their seemingly weightless strength. Fenton's documentaries about people provide a very different sound. *The Spirit of '45*, about postwar socialism in Great Britain, has a subtle but steady trumpet playing a quiet and melancholy theme. Period songs are used throughout for nostalgic purposes, but it is Fenton's score that conveys the tone of the movie.

Fenton composed Asian music to use throughout *China: Beyond the Clouds*, but he adds Western instruments and even American-European pop music at times to make a dramatic statement. The main theme is a cunning mix of Chinese flute and a violin, then both Asian and Western instruments fill out the melody. The scores from these documentaries bring us back to Fenton's chameleon-like musical talents. He is an international composer in a real sense, his music not confined to any one nation or culture.

Credits

(* for Best Song)

Year	Film	Director
1979	*Bloody Kids*	Stephen Frears (UK)
1980	*Hussy*	Matthew Chapman (UK)
1982	*Ghandi* (AAN; BAFTA-N)	Richard Attenborough (UK/India)
1983	*Runners*	Charles Sturridge (UK)

Year	Film	Director
1984	The Company of Wolves	Neil Jordan (UK)
1986	Clockwise	Christopher Morahan (UK)
1987	White Mischief	Michael Radford (UK/USA)
1987	84 Charing Cross Road	David Hugh Jones (UK/USA)
1987	Billy the Kid and the Green Baize Vampire	Alan Clarke (UK)
1987	Cry Freedom (AAN*; GGN; BAFTA-N)	Richard Attenborough (UK)
1988	A Handful of Dust	Charles Sturridge (UK)
1988	High Spirits	Neil Jordan (UK/USA)
1988	The Dressmaker	Jim O'Brien (UK)
1988	Dangerous Liaisons (AAN; BAFTA-N)	Stephen Frears (USA/UK)
1989	We're No Angels	Neil Jordan (USA)
1990	Memphis Belle (BAFTA-N)	Michael Caton-Jones (UK/Japan/USA)
1990	The Long Walk Home	Richard Pearce (USA)
1990	White Palace	Luis Kandoki (USA)
1991	The Fisher King (AAN)	Terry Gilliam (USA)
1992	Final Analysis	Phil Joanou (USA)
1992	Hero (aka Accidental Hero)	Stephen Frears (USA)
1993	Groundhog Day	Harold Ramis (USA)
1993	Born Yesterday	Luis Mandoki (USA)
1993	Shadowlands	Richard Attenborough (UK)
1994	China Moon	John Bailey (USA)
1994	Ladybird Ladybird	Ken Loach (UK)
1994	Mixed Nuts	Nora Ephron (USA)
1995	Land and Freedom	Ken Loach (UK/Spain/Germany/Italy)
1996	Mary Reilly	Stephen Frears (USA)
1996	Heaven's Prisoners	Phil Joanou (USA/UK)
1996	Multiplicity	Harold Ramis (USA)
1996	Carla's Song	Ken Loach (UK/Spain/Germany)
1996	The Crucible	Nicholas Hytner (USA)
1996	In Love and War	Richard Attenborough (USA)
1997	The Woodlanders	Phil Agland (UK)
1998	Dangerous Beauty	Marshall Herskovitz (USA)
1998	The Object of My Affection	Nicholas Hytner (USA)
1998	My Name Is Joe	Ken Loach (Spain/Italy/UK/France)
1998	Ever After: A Cinderella Story	Andy Tennant (USA)
1998	Living Out Loud	Richard LaGravenese (USA)
1998	You've Got Mail	Nora Ephron (USA)
1999	Entropy	Phil Joanou (USA)
1999	Grey Owl	Richard Attenborough (UK/Canada)
1999	Anna and the King (GGN; GGN*)	Andy Tennant (USA)
2000	Bread and Roses	Ken Loach (UK/France/Germany)
2000	Center Stage	Nicholas Hytner (USA)
2000	Lucky Numbers	Nora Ephron (France/USA)
2001	Summer Catch	Michael Tollin (USA)
2001	The Navigators	Ken Loach (UK/Germany/Spain)
2002	Sweet Sixteen	Ken Loach (UK/Germany/Spain)
2002	Sweet Home Alabama	Andy Tennant (USA)
2003	Imagining Argentina	Chistopher Hampton (Spain/UK/USA)
2003	Deep Blue	Andy Byatt, Alastair Fothergill (UK)
2004	Ae Fond Kiss	Ken Loach (UK/Belgium/Italy/Spain)
2004	Stage Beauty	Richard Eyre (UK/USA/Germany)
2005	Hitch	Andy Tennant (USA)
2005	Tickets	Abbas Kiarostami, etc. (Italy/UK)
2005	Valiant	Gary Chapman (UK/USA)
2005	Bewitched	Nora Ephron (USA)
2005	Mrs. Henderson Presents (BAFTA-N)	Stephen Frears (UK/USA)
2006	Last Holiday	Wayne Wang (USA)
2006	The Wind That Shakes the Barley	Ken Loach (Ireland/UK)

Year	Film	Director
2006	The History Boys	Nicholas Hytner (UK)
2007	Earth	Alastair Fothergill, Mark Linfield (UK/USA)
2007	It's a Free World . . .	Len Loach (UK/Italy/Germany/Spain/Poland)
2008	Fool's Gold	Andy Tennant (USA)
2009	Looking for Eric	Ken Loach (UK/France/Italy/Belgium/Spain)
2010	The Bounty Hunter	Andy Tennant (USA)
2011	One Life	Michael Gunton, Martha Holmes (UK)
2012	Baka: A Cry from the Rainforest	Phil Agland (UK)
2012	The Angels' Share	Ken Loach (UK/France/Belgium)
2013	The Spirit of '45	Ken Loach (UK)
2013	The Zero Theorem	Terry Gilliam (USA/Romania)

FEUER, Cy (1911–2006) A very successful show business multihyphenate—music director, composer, musician, director, producer, and all-around impresario—in theatre and movies, between 1938 and 1942 he contributed music to over seventy feature films.

Born Seymour Arnold Feuer in the New York City borough of Brooklyn, he was the son of Yiddish theatre manager Herman Feuer, who died when the boy was thirteen. The young Feuer was an excellent trumpet player, so he dropped out of school and supported his mother and younger brother by playing in movie palace orchestras in New York. He later toured with Leon Belasco and His Society Orchestra and when the band played in California in 1936, he quit his trumpet playing and went to Hollywood, where he found work arranging music for the movies. Over the next ten years Feuer was musical director for over two hundred movies. By the end of the 1930s, he was heading the music department at Republic Pictures. It is estimated that he contributed original music to eighty films, most of them B-level westerns and over half of them with two or more collaborators. Feuer worked with composer William Lava for the first time on the western *Heroes of the Hills* in 1938, and the twosome went on to score twenty subsequent films, most memorably *I Stand Accused, Orphans of the Streets, The Mysterious Miss X, Mountain Rhythm, She Married a Cop*, and *Sabotage.* Feuer's first of twenty-two movies that he scored alone was *Federal Man-Hunt* in 1938, followed by such solo efforts as *Rocky Mountain Rangers, The Trail Blazers, Prairie Pioneers, Saddlemates, King of the Texas Rangers, West of Cimarron, Westward Ho, Jesse James Jr.*, and *Sons of the Pioneers.* He received Oscar nominations for his scores for *Storm over Bengal, She Married a Cop, Hit Parade of 1941*, and *Mercy Island*, all composed with others.

Feuer's screen career was interrupted by World War II, during which he was a captain in the army air force. After the armistice, he did not return to Hollywood but settled in New York, where he teamed up with Broadway producer Ernest H. Martin. Their first effort was the hit musical *Where's Charley?* in 1948, which introduced movie songwriter Frank Loesser to Broadway. Among the other shows Feuer produced (often with Martin) were *Guys and Dolls* (1950), *Can-Can* (1953), *How to Succeed in Business without Really Trying* (1961), *The Act* (1977), and *I Remember Mama* (1979). He both produced and directed *The Boy Friend* (1954), *Silk Stockings* (1955), *Whoop-Up* (1958), *Little Me* (1962), *Skyscraper* (1965), and *Walking Happy* (1966). Feuer returned to Hollywood on occasion to produce the screen musicals *Where's Charley?* (1952), *Cabaret* (1972), *Piaf: The Early Years* (1974), and *A Chorus Line* (1985), getting an Oscar nomination for *Cabaret*. Feuer was one of Broadway's most colorful producers, discovering talent and always keeping in the public eye. Three years after he finished his autobiography, Feuer died of bladder cancer at the age of ninety-five.

While it is easy to assess Feuer's abilities as musical director, his composition talents are less obvious. Most of his scores were written with others, so one has to look at the two dozen movies he worked on alone. Almost all of them are westerns and pretty routines ones at that. Of the few still available to view, *Jesse James Jr.* serves as a good example. Despite its title, the oater is not a biopic of the outlaw's offspring but a mildly entertaining tale about bringing the telegraph to the town of Sundown. (The later title *Sundown Fury* is somewhat more accurate.) There is a spirited string and trumpet theme that suggests open spaces and the restlessness of the wilderness. The orchestrations are impressive considering the limited resources and low budget for this and other Republic films. Suspense is conveyed with a series of busy strings and blaring brass, the chase music consists of rapid, short trumpet calls, and the comic theme for the bicycle-riding sidekick Pop Sawyer (Al St. John) is done with laughing woodwinds. This is competent, practical scoring and

commendable especially when one considers Feuer and his colleagues turned out dozens of these each year. Supervising so many scores at once must have taken its toll and it is understandable why Feuer abandoned films for the bright lights of Broadway. Autobiography: *I Got the Show Right Here*, with Ken Gross (2003).

Credits

(all films USA)

Year	Film	Director
1938	Heroes of the Hills	George Sherman
1938	A Desperate Adventure	John H. Auer
1938	Come On, Leathernecks!	James Cruze
1938	The Night Hawk	Sidney Salkow
1938	I Stand Accused	John H. Auer
1938	Storm over Bengal (AAN)	Sidney Salkow
1938	Orphans of the Street	John H. Auer
1938	Federal Man-Hunt	Nick Grinde
1939	Fighting Thoroughbreds	Sidney Salkow
1939	The Mysterious Miss X	Gus Meins
1939	Pride of the Navy	Charles Lamont
1939	Street of Missing Men	Sidney Salkow
1939	My Wife's Relatives	Gus Meins
1939	Mountain Rhythm	B. Reeves Eason
1939	Mickey the Kid	Arthur Lubin
1939	She Married a Cop (AAN)	Sidney Salkow
1939	Should Husbands Work?	Gus Meins
1939	Flight at Midnight	Sidney Salkow
1939	Sabotage	Harold Young
1939	Main Street Lawyer	Dudley Murphy
1939	The Covered Trailer	Gus Meins
1939	Thou Shalt Not Kill	John H. Auer
1939	Money to Burn	Gus Meins
1940	Pioneers of the West	Lester Orlebeck
1940	Forgotten Girls	Phil Rosen
1940	Covered Wagon Days	George Sherman
1940	Rocky Mountain Rangers	George Sherman
1940	Women in War	John H. Auer
1940	Hit Parade of 1941 (AAN)	John H. Auer
1940	The Trail Blazers	George Sherman
1941	Wyoming Wildcat	George Sherman
1941	Ice-Capades (AAN)	Joseph Santley
1941	Prairie Pioneers	Lester Orlebeck
1941	Saddlemates	Lester Orlebeck
1941	Desert Bandit	George Sherman
1941	Gangs of Sonora	John English
1941	Outlaws of Cherokee Trail	Lester Orlebeck
1941	The Apache Kid	George Sherman
1941	King of the Texas Rangers	John English, William Witney
1941	Mercy Island (AAN)	William Morgan
1941	West of Cimarron	Lester Orlebeck
1942	Arizona Terrors	George Sherman
1942	Code of the Outlaw	John English
1942	Stagecoach Express	George Sherman
1942	Raiders of the Range	John English

Year	Film	Director
1942	Jesse James Jr.(aka Sundown Fury)	George Sherman
1942	Westward Ho	John English
1942	The Cyclone Kid	George Sherman
1942	Sons of the Pioneers	Joseph Kane

FIEDEL, Brad (Ira) (b. 1951) A prolific composer for television and movies between 1975 and 1996 who is best known for his creative use of electronic music and the synthesizer, he scored thirty-three feature films, many in the action-sci-fi genres.

Brad Fiedel was born in New York City, the son of a composer-musician father and a dancer mother, and was raised on Long Island where he started piano lessons when he was six years old. Fiedel soon began composing his own songs and performed them as a teenager. He was resident composer at City University of New York before he began his show business career as a keyboard player for the popular duo Hall and Oates. Fiedel got interested in independent moviemaking in the 1970s and started scoring low-budget films in 1975. While some of these were interesting projects, such as the *Jaws* spoof titled *Gums* and the comedy-drama *Looking Up*, Fiedel was getting little money and no recognition, so he turned to the small screen. He first worked in television when he wrote the score for the TV movie *Mayflower: The Pilgrims' Adventure* in 1979. He has since scored forty-nine other TV movies, including *Playing for Time* (1980), *The People vs. Jean Harris* (1981), *Mae West* (1982), *Dreams Don't Die* (1982), *Calendar Girl Murders* (1984), *Under Siege* (1986), *Popeye Doyle* (1986), *Right to Die* (1987), *Cold Sassy Tree* (1989), *Blood Ties* (1991), *Rasputin* (1996), *Purgatory* (1999), and *Y2K* (1999), as well as some series and miniseries. It was director James Cameron who recharged Fiedel's career in 1984 when he hired him to score the modest-budgeted sci-fi thriller *The Terminator*. Both the movie and the high-tech score were instant hits, and the two men collaborated again on two other box office successes, *Terminator 2: Judgment Day* and *True Lies*. Fiedel was soon in demand for first-class film projects, and for the next decade he was busy scoring such notable movies as *Fright Night, Desert Bloom, The Big Easy, The Serpent and the Rainbow, The Accused, True Believer,* and *Johnny Mnemonic*. Fiedel left the movies in 1995 to concentrate on writing songs and creating theatre-music pieces in which he performs his own music.

While Fiedel was not the first screen composer to write totally synthesized scores, his use of electronic sounds and music was so bold and uncompromising that he startled audiences. Cameron's visuals can take some of the credit, but *The Terminator* and the other Cameron thrillers have soundtracks that take the viewer deeper into the intriguing stories and nightmarish worlds. Fiedel's most famous piece of music is the theme for *The Terminator*. This tale, about a cyborg in human form (Arnold Schwarzenegger) sent from the future to assassinate a woman (Linda Hamilton) before she gives birth to a future threat, is a high-powered action film, so it is disarming to find out the main theme is rather subdued. The six-note musical phrase on an echoing electric keyboard comes across as emotionless, much like the cyborg himself. Then heavy metal sounds enter and provide a piercing pattern but the main musical line remains unchanged. The result is a very heroic theme but with a somber subtext. (Fiedel reuses this theme in his *Terminator 2: Judgment Day* score and composer Marco Beltrami quotes from it in his music for the 2003 *Terminator 3: Rise of the Machines*.) Other highlights in *The Terminator* score include a percussive theme with deep, bass electronic echoes and high-pitched sounds like knives as they scrape on metal, and a synthesized keyboard pattern that is repeated at one tempo while a counterpattern moves at a slower pace. There is even less melody and more electronic effects in Fiedel's score for *Terminator 2: Judgment Day*. Most memorable is a percussion theme in which synthesized drums compete with manufactured clanking sounds. There is also a high-frequency passage with a rat-a-tat pattern that sounds like a futuristic typewriter, some electronically enhanced voices, and a rapid pounding track that is heard over sustained hissing and string sounds. In contrast to all this is a quieter and lyrical theme on electric keyboard with electronic grumbling in the distance.

For Cameron's *True Lies*, Fiedel came up with a score that is less electronic and has more conventional orchestrations, although the propulsive temperament is the same. This story of a secret agent (Schwarzenegger again) battling terrorists is more an action movie than a sci-fi nightmare, and the music seems more grounded. The main theme is frantic chase music with rowdy percussion, blaring brass, and furious strings that transitions into a bouncy andante with electric flute accents. One of the most exciting passages has competing strings and percussion that gain in speed as they steadily change pitch and race each other up the scale. Robert Longo's sci-fi thriller *Johnny Mnemonic*, about a future in which the Internet controls everything, was not as successful as the Cameron thrillers, but the music is just as accomplished. The score is filled with sci-fi music clichés—vibrating electronic chords, eerie echoes, and spiraling scales—with a wry sense of humor that is missing in the film itself. There is an outstanding pinball theme in which furious keyboard notes fight through the chaos of various percussion and synthesized trumpets, all the instruments climbing the scale only to slide down to the bottom and start all over again.

Even when Fiedel scores more realistic dramas, he uses synthesized music but in a much more restrained manner. The crime melodrama *True Believer*, about two civil liberties attorneys (James Woods and Robert Downey Jr.) who dig up an eight-year-old murder case, has a subtle score that is quite the opposite of those for the Cameron movies. Suspense is conveyed by seething but subdued electronic music, and there is a gentle but unsettling synthesized piano theme that is quite emotive. Even more penetrating is the drama *The Accused* about a gang rape and the prosecutor (Jodie Foster) who tries to untangle the complex legal barriers between her client (Kelly McGillis) and justice. Fiedel's score features a restless and surging theme on strings, piano, and synthesized percussion and horns that is compelling without being overwhelming. He also uses vivid sustained notes that are pierced by a climbing motif on electronic keyboard. This other side of Fiedel's musical talent cannot be ignored and makes one hope he will again return to screen composing. Official website: www.bradfiedel.net.

Credits

(all films USA unless stated otherwise)

Year	Film	Director
1975	*The Astrologer* (aka *Suicide Cult*)	James Glickenhaus
1975	*Deadly Hero* (aka *Troubled Times*)	Ivan Nagy
1976	*Gums*	Robert J. Kaplan
1976	*Damian's Island*	Don Murray
1976	*Apple Pie*	Howard Goldberg
1977	*Looking Up*	Linda Yellen
1981	*Night School*	Ken Hughes
1981	*Just Before Dawn*	Jeff Lieberman
1983	*Hit and Run* (aka *Trust Me*)	Charles Braverman
1983	*Eyes of Fire*	Avery Crounse
1984	*The Terminator*	James Cameron (UK/USA)
1985	*Fraternity Vacation*	James Frawley
1985	*Fright Night*	Tom Holland
1985	*Compromising Positions*	Frank Perry
1986	*Desert Bloom*	Eugene Corr
1986	*Let's Get Harry*	Stuart Rosenberg
1986	*The Big Easy*	Jim McBride
1987	*Nowhere to Hide*	Mario Azzopardi (USA/Canada)
1988	*The Serpent and the Rainbow*	Wes Craven
1988	*Fright Night Part 2*	Tommy Lee Wallace
1988	*The Accused* (aka *Reckless Endangerment*)	Jonathan Kaplan (USA/Canada)
1989	*True Believer*	Joseph Ruben
1989	*Blue Steel*	Kathryn Bigelow
1989	*Immediate Family*	Jonathan Kaplan (USA/Canada)
1991	*Terminator 2: Judgment Day*	James Cameron (USA/France)
1992	*Gladiator*	Rowdy Herrington
1992	*Straight Talk*	Barnet Kellman

Year	Film	Director
1993	*The Real McCoy*	Russell Mulcahy
1993	*Striking Distance* (aka *Three Rivers*)	Rowdy Herrington
1994	*Blink*	Michael Apted
1994	*True Lies*	James Cameron
1995	*Johnny Mnemonic*	Robert Longo (Canada/USA)
1996	*Eden*	Howard Goldberg

FIELDING, Jerry (1922–1980) A distinctive composer, conductor, and arranger for radio, television, and movies, he is perhaps best known for his scores for violent action movies featuring Steve McQueen, Charles Bronson, and Clint Eastwood.

Jerry Fielding was born Joshua Itzhak Feldman in Pittsburgh, Pennsylvania, the son of impoverished Russian immigrants who loved music. Fielding studied trombone and clarinet as a youth and as a teenager played in his high school band. Although he won a scholarship to study at the Carnegie Institute for Instrumentalists, Fielding was only able to attend a short time because of ill health that plagued him for years. Bedridden for long periods of time, he took comfort in listening to the radio and was drawn to different kinds of music, in particular the new Big Band sound and Bernard Herrmann's dramatic music for Orson Welles's broadcasts. When Fielding was well enough to continue his education, he studied composition and musical arrangement with the pit conductor of the local Stanley Theatre. This led to his first jobs arranging music for Alvino Rey and other swing bands on tour. One of his arrangements, for "Picnic in Purgatory," was a hit for Rey and Fielding. Among the other famous orchestras for which Fielding wrote arrangements were Les Brown, Tommy Dorsey, Claude Thornhill, Jimmie Lunceford, Charlie Barnet, and Kay Kyser. He worked on the radio with Kyser and was also bandleader for such popular programs as *The Life of Riley*, *The Hardy Family*, and the comic quiz show *You Bet Your Life* with Groucho Marx. Fielding was also active in early television and even had his own music program in 1952, *The Jerry Fielding Show*. The next year his career fell apart when he was called before the House Un-American Activities Committee and refused to name friends as Communists. He was blacklisted from television and films and spent much of the 1950s performing in nightclubs and making records as the Jerry Fielding Orchestra.

Fielding's career was resurrected in the 1960s, writing the theme song and/or music soundtracks for television series such as *Star Trek*, *McHale's Navy*, *Hogan's Heroes*, *Mission: Impossible*, *Shane*, *Tarzan*, *He & She*, *The Bionic Woman*, *McMillan & Wife*, *Kolchak: The Night Stalker*, *The Snoop Sisters*, and *On the Rocks*. He made his screen debut writing the score for the low-budget war drama *The Nun and the Sergeant* in 1962 and later that year received cinematic recognition when director Otto Preminger hired him to score the all-star political drama *Advise & Consent*. Fielding's career took a new turn in 1969 when he scored Sam Peckinpah's western *The Wild Bunch*. It was such a success that Fielding worked with Peckinpah again on three similar movies and was soon in great demand for violent melodramas, several of them with director Michael Winner and some of them with director-actor Clint Eastwood. Among Fielding's many notable movies are *Johnny Got His Gun*, *Straw Dogs*, *Junior Bonner*, *Scorpio*, *Demon Seed*, *The Mechanic*, *The Killer Elite*, *The Bad News Bears*, *The Outlaw Josey Wales*, *The Gauntlet*, *Semi-Tough*, and *Escape from Alcatraz*. In the 1970s he also scored over two dozen TV movies, including *Shepherd's Flock* (1971), *A War of Children* (1972), *Class of '55* (1972), *Shirts/Skins* (1973), *Honky Tonk* (1974), *Hustling* (1975), *Grandpa Max* (1975), *Little Ladies of the Night* (1977), and *Mr. Horn* (1979). In all, Fielding completed thirty-four feature films before his premature death from a heart attack at the age of fifty-seven.

Fielding was an exacting composer with strong opinions about how music should be used in films. This made him few friends in Hollywood, but directors such as Winner, Peckinpah, and Eastwood rehired him with no hesitation. Some of Fielding's scores, such as *The Getaway* (1972), were rejected by the studio when he refused to rewrite or modify his music, and he dropped out of other projects, such as *Pat Garrett and Billy the Kid* (1973), because he disagreed with director Peckinpah. He aimed to create atmosphere and character in his scores rather than the expected dramatic accompaniment. The western *The Wild Bunch*, for example, does not have much subtlety as its gritty story enfolds in the Mexican-American desert, yet Fielding's score is far from obvious or melodramatic. The main theme is a haunting mix of percussive phrases and brass instruments that spiral downward, creating a jazzy tone rather than the expected prairie sound. The score does embrace folk music at times, and some intricate guitar work can be heard in the action scenes. The violence may dictate the action but the music conveys the utter loneliness of the characters. More jazz and touches of swing are used in *Advise & Consent*. The main theme is bouncy and carefree with a Big Band arrangement, but as the film delves behind the scenes of Washington politics the score gets more somber and disturbing. Fielding's personal favorite among his scores is the one he wrote for the futuristic thriller *Demon Seed* about a computer that becomes dangerously powerful. It is a unique score, utilizing sound effects, vibrations, squeaking high notes, and rhythmic percussion motifs. Electronic music often gives way to a romantic theme played on conventional strings. The score also briefly includes the entrancing ballad "Heart of Mine" (lyric by Ned Washington). A Frank Sinatra recording of the song was originally intended for *Advise & Consent*, but when Sinatra found out it was to be heard as background in a gay bar, he refused to give permission to use it.

Perhaps Fielding's two finest scores are those for Peckinpah's *Straw Dogs* and Eastwood's *The Outlaw Josey Wales*, both nominated for Oscars (as was *The Wild Bunch*). The disturbing thriller *Straw Dogs* is about an American couple (Dustin Hoffman and Susan George) who move to Britain to escape urban violence but encounter it in new forms in an English community. The score has a classically flavored theme in which strings and horns alternate in a melancholy manner. This balanced, flowing motif is contrasted by eerie and upsetting sequences with repetitive musical phrases in a jazz mode. While this score relies on Fielding's swing background, it turns that loose genre into something upsetting and tense. *The Outlaw Josey Wales*, a dark western set against the last days of the Civil War, was directed by and starred Eastwood and has some of Peckinpah's nihilism. The movie has a percussive march for its main theme complete with merry fifes that build in intensity like a parade gone sour. The many action scenes are scored with restless strings and trumpeting fanfares, but it is when the score turns quiet and vengeful that the music is most effective. Finally, one must consider Fielding's score for *Johnny Got His Gun*, one of the most powerful of all antiwar movies. Set after World War I, the film opens with a vigorous drum march heard over archival footage. What follows is a lyrical score with several different themes, many of them prompted by memories of the quadruple amputee (Timothy Bottoms). These flashbacks range from pastoral pieces of prewar romance to jarringly chaotic music for the war itself. Other sequences are Stravinsky-like in their furious string work and unusual time signature. A violin solo is morbidly solemn, while another theme plucked out on a harp is practically celestial. Fielding later turned this score into an orchestral suite, and in many ways it is the hallmark of his work, both musically and thematically. A renegade working within a tightly controlled system, Fielding managed to write some vibrant music that expressed his ideas about cinema scoring and the cruel world depicted in his films.

Credits

(all films USA unless stated otherwise)

Year	Film	Director
1962	*The Nun and the Sergeant*	Franklin Adreon
1962	*Advise & Consent*	Otto Preminger
1964	*McHale's Navy*	Edward Montagne
1964	*For Those Who Think Young*	Leslie H. Martinson
1965	*McHale's Navy Joins the Air Force*	Edward Montagne
1969	*The Wild Bunch* (AAN)	Sam Peckinpah
1970	*Suppose They Gave a War and Nobody Came?*	Hy Averback
1971	*Lawman*	Michael Winner

Year	Film	Director
1971	*Johnny Got His Gun*	Dalton Trumbo
1971	*The Nightcomers*	Michael Winner (UK)
1971	*Straw Dogs* (AAN)	Sam Peckinpah (USA/UK)
1972	*Chato's Land* (aka *Chato*)	Michael Winner (UK)
1972	*Junior Bonner*	Sam Peckinpah
1972	*The Mechanic*	Michael Winner
1973	*Scorpio* (aka *The Scorpio File*)	Michael Winner
1973	*The Outfit*	John Flynn
1973	*The Deadly Trackers*	Barry Shear, Samuel Fuller
1974	*The Super Cops*	Gordon Parks
1974	*Bring Me the Head of Alfredo Garcia*	Sam Peckinpah (USA/Mexico)
1974	*The Gambler*	Karel Reisz
1975	*The Killer Elite*	Sam Peckinpah
1975	*The Black Bird*	David Giler
1976	*The Bad News Bears*	Michael Ritchie
1976	*The Outlaw Josey Wales* (AAN)	Clint Eastwood
1976	*The Enforcer*	James Fargo
1977	*Demon Seed*	Donald Cammell
1977	*Semi-Tough*	Michael Ritchie
1977	*The Gauntlet*	Clint Eastwood
1978	*Gray Lady Down*	David Greene
1978	*The Big Sleep*	Michael Winner (UK)
1979	*Beyond the Poseidon Adventure*	Irwin Allen
1979	*Escape from Alcatraz*	Don Siegel
1980	*Funeral Home* (aka *Cries in the Night*)	William Fruet (Canada)
1980	*Below the Belt*	Robert Fowler

FOX, Charles (b. 1940) A popular songwriter and prolific composer for television and Hollywood, he scored thirty-seven feature films between 1967 and 1996, most of them comedies.

Born in New York City, the son of Jewish immigrants from Poland, Charles Fox began piano lessons when he was seven years old, and at fifteen played in a Catskill resort band. Fox attended the High School of Music and Art before studying music with Nadia Boulanger in Paris, jazz with Lenny Tristano, and electronic music with Vladimir Ussachevsky at Columbia University. He began his professional career writing and arranging salsa music for top Hispanic artists, as well as orchestrations for *The Tonight Show* orchestra under the direction of Skitch Henderson. Soon he was scoring commercials, film shorts, and pop songs. With various artists, Fox had many song hits, none bigger than "Killing Me Softly with His Song" with Norman Gimbel. Among his other popular songs are "I Got a Name," "Ready to Take a Chance Again," "Making Our Dreams Come True," "Richard's Window," "The First Years," "Different Worlds," "Together Through the Years," "My Fair Share," and "90210 Beverly Hills,"

now the official theme song for the California city. His first film assignment was cowriting with Terry Knight the score for the crime drama *The Incident* in 1967. The next year he wrote the music for the international phenomenon *Barbarella*, Roger Vadim's camp fantasy that made Jane Fonda a star. Fox's first Hollywood hit was the romantic comedy–drama *Goodbye, Columbus* in 1969. Fox was soon in demand to score comedies, although he was also hired to write music for dramas on occasion. Among his notable movies are *Pufnstuf*, *The Last American Hero*, *The Laughing Policeman*, *A Separate Peace*, *One on One*, *Nine to Five*, *Two-Minute Warning*, *Little Darlings*, *Why Would I Lie?*, *The Adventures of Bob & Doug McKenzie: Strange Brew*, *The Gods Must Be Angry II*, *It Had to Be You*, *European Vacation*, *Foul Play*, and *The Other Side of the Mountain*, getting Oscar nominations for Best Song for the last two.

The first of Fox's memorable television theme songs was that for *ABC Wide World of Sports* in 1961. He then went on to write the theme songs and/or music for such programs as *The Match Game*, *What's My Line?*, *Happy Days*, *The Love Boat*, *Angie*, *To Tell the Truth*, *Laverne & Shirley*, *Monday Night Football*, *Valerie*, *Wonder Woman*,

The Bugaloos, A Family for Joe, The Paper Chase, The Hogan Family, Conan, and *Love, American Style.* Fox has scored forty-four TV movies, including *Johnny Belinda* (1967), *The Stranger Within* (1974), *The Legend of Valentino* (1975), *The Love Boat* (1976), *Victory at Entebbe* (1976), *Betrayed by Innocence* (1986), *The Parent Trap II* (1986), *Christmas Comes to Willow Creek* (1987), *Baby M* (1988), *Absolute Strangers* (1991), *Christmas in Connecticut* (1992), *The Great O'Grady* (1993), *A Death in the Family* (2002), and *The Monday Night Miracle* (2007). By the new century Fox left movies and television and wrote for the ballet, theatre, and concert hall, as well as for special events, such as the oratorio *Lament and Prayer* set to the words of Pope John Paul II for a Polish tribute in 2010.

While most of Fox's hit songs and television themes can be described as chipper, catchy, pleasing, and upbeat, his screen scores often reveal a richer and more penetrating sound. Many of his film credits are lightweight comedies, so often the music is not noticed as in more serious fare. Also, many of the movies in the 1970s and 1980s opted for memorable pop songs and title songs (several of which Fox composed) so the soundtrack music is even more forgotten. In the comic-romantic mystery *Foul Play,* the hit song was "Ready to Take a Chance Again" (lyric by Norman Gimbel) sung by Barry Manilow on the soundtrack. Fox uses the same music in different ways throughout the film, becoming a reflective piece as well as a romantic one. The score also has a disco theme that is slick and sassy as it skips along in a carefree manner. For an opera sequence, Fox devises a classical spoof played on harmonica and orchestra that freely quotes from Arthur Sullivan's *The Mikado* overture. The romance *Goodbye, Columbus* has a pop title song by Jerry Yester sung by the Association, but Fox provides a jaunty jazz theme with a rock flavor that is neither too heavy nor high tech. The nimble saxophones playing cool jazz give the movie a deeper resonance than the bubblegum music in the hit song. One of Fox's most playful scores is his early one for *Barbarella.* He cowrote four pop songs with Bob Crewe for this wacko sci-fi sex comedy but it is the soundtrack score that most impresses. The breezy main theme swings like the American 1960s and has a European pop sound as well. There is a risible jazz passage with saxophone squawks and trumpet giggles with a rock bass line. Often this mock sci-fi score uses electronic echoes and rowdy sound effects set against a pop theme that bounces along in an idiotic way.

Two of Fox's more serious movies provide commendable music. The thriller *Two-Minute Warning,* about a crazed sniper who plans to open fire on the crowd at a championship football game, has an electric (literally) score with a pulsating beat and high-frequency sounds on a keyboard with a siren-like quality. Throughout the movie sustained notes and sounds build suspense through an insistent, repetitious riff heard on different instruments. Sometimes the manufactured musical sounds waver, echo, vibrate, and even explode, making for a nail-biting score that matches the tension on the screen. Much quieter and more romanticized is the heart-tugging score for the heart-tugging melodrama *The Other Side of the Mountain.* Interestingly, Fox's screen career has been filled with sports movies: basketball in *One on One,* race car driving in *Six Pack* and *The Last American Hero,* and track and field in *Our Winning Season. The Other Side of the Mountain* centers on skiing, and the score's main theme is fluid and loose, ideal for the free-flowing downhill racing on the screen. The true story, about a championship skier (Marilyn Hassett) paralyzed in a ski accident and the death of her fiancé (Beau Bridges), is scored with lush and poignant music. With such lilting passages, it is not difficult to understand how one of Fox's tunes became the popular ballad "Richard's Window" when sung by Olivia Newton-John on the soundtrack. But then much of Fox's dazzling career has been about hit songs and his screen scores are no exception. Autobiography: *Killing Me Softly: My Life in Music* (2010). Official website: www.charlesfoxmusic.com.

Credits

(all films USA unless stated otherwise; * for Best Song)

Year	Film	Director
1967	*The Incident*	Larry Peerce
1968	*Barbarella*	Roger Vadim (France/Italy)

Year	Film	Director
1968	*The Green Slime*	Kinji Fukasaku (USA/Japan)
1969	*Goodbye, Columbus*	Larry Peerce
1970	*Pufnstuf*	Hollingsworth Morse
1971	*Making It*	John Erman
1971	*Star Spangled Girl*	Jerry Paris
1972	*A Separate Peace*	Larry Peerce
1973	*The Last American Hero* (aka *Hard Driver*)	Lamont Johnson
1973	*The Laughing Policeman*	Stuart Rosenberg
1975	*Bug* (aka *The Hephaestus Plague*)	Jeannot Szwarc
1975	*The Other Side of the Mountain* (AAN*; GGN; GGN*)	Larry Peerce
1976	*The Duchess and the Dirtwater Fox*	Melvin Frank
1976	*Two-Minute Warning*	Larry Peerce
1977	*One on One* (aka *Catch a Falling Star*)	Lamont Johnson
1978	*Our Winning Season*	Joseph Ruben
1978	*Foul Play* (aka *Killing Lydia*) (AAN*; GGN*)	Colin Higgins
1980	*The Last Married Couple in America*	Gilbert Cates
1980	*Little Darlings*	Ronald F. Maxwell
1980	*Why Would I Lie?*	Larry Peerce
1980	*Oh, God! Book II* (aka *Tracy and Friend*)	Gilbert Cates
1980	*Nine to Five* (aka *From 9 to 5*)	Colin Higgins
1982	*Six Pack*	Daniel Petrie
1982	*Zapped!* (aka *The Wiz Kid*)	Robert J. Rosenthal
1982	*Love Child*	Larry Peerce
1983	*Trenchcoat*	Michael Tuchner
1983	*The Adventures of Bob & Doug McKenzie: Strange Brew*	Rick Moranis, Dave Thomas (Canada/USA)
1985	*Doin' Time*	George Mendeluk
1985	*European Vacation* (aka *National Lampoon's European Vacation*)	Amy Heckerling
1986	*The Longshot*	Paul Bartel
1987	*Love at Stake*	John Moffitt
1988	*Short Circuit 2* (aka *More Imput*)	Kenneth Johnson
1988	*Going to the Chapel*	Paul Lynch
1989	*The Gods Must Be Crazy II*	Jamie Uys (S. Africa/Botswana/USA)
1989	*It Had to Be You*	Joseph Bologna, Renée Taylor
1990	*Repossessed*	Bob Logan
1996	*Gordy*	Mark Lewis

FRANKEL, Benjamin (1906–1973) A prominent British composer for the concert hall, he was very active in movies in the postwar years, scoring sixty feature films between 1945 and 1965.

Born in London into a Polish Jewish family, Benjamin Frankel was proficient on the violin and piano at a young age. Frankel won a scholarship to study at the Worshipful Company of Musicians when he was only fourteen and was soon writing and arranging jazz music, some of which was recorded by Fred Elizalde's band. In the 1930s Frankel was busy arranging music for dance bands, record companies, and the theatre. After World War II, he turned to composing classical music and found renown

for his violin concerto in memory of the Jews murdered during the Holocaust. Among his other works for the concert hall are eight symphonies, many chamber works, concertos, vocal pieces, and overtures, as well as an opera. Frankel first got involved with movies in 1934 when he composed a song and the soundtrack score for the British musical *Radio Parade of 1935*. He scored and conducted two other movies in the 1930s then did not return to the British cinema until the war years when he wrote music for film shorts. Frankel's first notable screen score was for the psychological melodrama *The Seventh Veil* in 1945. It was directed by Compton Bennett who collaborated again with Frankel on the praised *The Years Between* and *Day-*

break. Among the other lauded directors Frankel worked with was Anthony Asquith, the two men collaborating on five films, including *The Importance of Being Earnest, The Final Test,* and *Libel.* With other directors Frankel scored such accomplished movies as *Dear Murderer, A Girl in a Million, Mine Own Executioner, Sleeping Car to Trieste, The End of the Affair, The Prisoner, Night and the City, So Long at the Fair, The Curse of the Werewolf, Hotel Sahara,* and *The Man in the White Suit.* At the end of his screen career, Frankel wrote music for a handful of Hollywood films, most memorably *The Night of the Iguana* and *Battle of the Bulge.* It is widely believed that during the 1950s Frankel was the highest-paid film composer in Britain. After scoring some British television series in the 1960s, Frankel returned to writing exclusively for the concert and opera stage. He served as chairman of the International Society for Contemporary Music and taught composition at the Guildhall School of Music for ten years. Frankel died in 1973 at the age of sixty-seven and soon his name and work fell into obscurity. Not until a series of German recordings of his music was released in 1996 was there a renewed interest in Frankel. Today his music is preserved and perpetuated by the Benjamin Frankel Society.

While Frankel's screen music often uses a full symphonic sound, it doesn't sound like a Hollywood orchestra. The music is not as refined and polished but instead has a more strident and raw quality, some of which can be attributed to his conducting. This makes for some dramatically harsh music for the serious films and a sharper and more tingling sound for the comedies. In the drama *The Seventh Veil,* a psychiatrist (Herbert Lom) tries to discover the secret to understanding a suicidal pianist (Ann Todd) by delving into her past. Frankel provides an oppressive and menacing score that includes nervous brass and reeds in a series of musical explosions as jittery strings race up and down in a frantic manner. The suspense scenes are scored with frantic violins and repetitive phrases played by the brass. There is even an odd Big Band foxtrot on accordion, flutes, and other woodwinds that sometimes slips into a waltz and then into a jitterbug, all of it echoing the patient's mental confusion. For the spy caper *Sleeping Car to Trieste,* which is set on the Orient Express, Frankle takes his musical cue from the famous train. Confused brass instruments play a musical phrase that sounds like transport horns while strings saw away in a frenzy, the result echoing the racing wheels of the train.

There is also an unsettling passage in which distant horns and foreboding strings clash causing musical confusion as the plot thickens. Jules Dassin's film noir classic *Night and the City,* about a London hustler (Richard Widmark) trying to get into the prizefighting racket, has a menacing theme with descending violin scales interrupted by harsh brass chords. In one passage woodwinds play a sad lament while strings swirl around it in an accelerating fury. This is Frankel's unique and dynamic screen sound: a symphony of conflict and drama.

The Years Between, a drama about postwar England and the strain long separation plays on marriages, has a very clever main theme. The sound of Big Ben chiming is heard, then various brass and strings echo the sound musically while woodwinds play against it at a slower tempo. In another section of the score, wild violins and growling trumpets seem to race forward out of control, and there is a symphonic passage in which the music alternates between a fiery tempest-like quality and lilting tranquility. One of the most powerful movies Frankel got to score was *The Prisoner* about an imprisoned cardinal (Alec Guinness), who is declared an enemy of a totalitarian state, and his interrogator (Jack Hawkins). This is a dramatic score with full orchestra at full throttle. There is a weighty theme with a slow progression forward by the orchestra as strings swirl around in circles. In one section a fanfare is drowned out by ponderous brass and percussion and there is also a restless march with halting drums and sustained strings that conveys a sense of impotent power. *So Long at the Fair* is an intriguing mystery in which an Englishman (David Tomlinson) disappears in his hotel during the 1896 Paris Exposition. The score has a famous piece of music, heard as the central characters ride in a carriage to the fair. The music is a sprightly piece that bounces along with glee as brass fanfares complement the clopping tempo of the music. This often played and recorded carriage music is perhaps Frankel's most popular slice of film music.

It is interesting that Frankel's most innovative screen score comes not from a drama but from a horror film. *The Curse of the Werewolf* is Hammer Films' garish and hammy version of the familiar tale, this time set in seventeenth-century Spain with a long, involved story of how the werewolf (Oliver Reed) came to be. Frankel's music has been cited as the first screen score to use Arnold Schoenberg's twelve-tone (or serial) principles. This meant little to moviegoers but even the most tone deaf probably recognized that there is something different and exciting about the music. Shouting trumpets announce themselves like a fanfare yet they also seem to threaten as well. The strings sweep up the scale as the brass descend it, creating a kind of controlled musical chaos. There is a pounding passage in which the percussion hammers away and the rest of the orchestra screams as it slides up and down, as if being driven crazy by the musical assault. Because so much "serialism" has been used in film scores over the years, the soundtrack for *The Curse of the Werewolf* may not strike listeners today as anything more than fun horror music, as indeed it is.

The full Hollywood orchestral sound can be heard in Frankel's American movie scores. Yet there is still a vibrant kind of harshness that is very much his own. John Huston's film version of Tennessee Williams's play *The Night of the Iguana* has a strident and disturbing main theme with swirling strings, blaring horns, and restless woodwinds that conveys the feeling of speeding toward disaster. The drama, about a group of social outcasts at a second-rate seaside hotel, is set on the Mexican coast and one of the quieter themes in the score features a Spanish guitar and woodwinds dancing together up and down the

scale. There is also a foreboding, twinkling theme with descending chimes and strings, and a chaotic passage with metal clanging, frantic strings, and shouting horns. A different kind of drama is musicalized in *Battle of the Bulge*, Ken Annakin's World War II action film that took liberties with history but captured the complexity of the battlefield by showing characters on both sides of the conflict. Frankel's score avoids patriotic flag-waving yet still has a sense of pride. Military drums are contrasted with vivid and rapid strings, pounding tympani, and plodding brass in a cockeyed march that suggests chaos rather than order. There is also a fanfare section that is boastful and confident with a vivacious melody propelled by light-footed percussion. At one point Frankel even quotes from the German "Panzer Song" march. As he had for his British films, Frankel conducted the *Battle of the Bulge* recording so the result is a Frankel score played by a Hollywood orchestra. This was his last film, and one might say he went out with a bang. How fortunate that when Frankel's concert works were rediscovered in the 1990s, his screen scores were also given some much-deserved attention. Benjamin Frankel Society website: www.musicweb-international.com/frankel/.

Credits

(all films UK unless stated otherwise)

Year	Film	Director
1934	Radio Parade of 1935	Arthur B. Woods
1935	No Monkey Business	Marcel Varnel
1936	Love in Exile	Alfred L. Werker
1943	They Met in the Dark	Carl Lemac
1945	Flight from Folly	Herbert Mason
1945	The Seventh Veil	Compton Bennett
1946	The Years Between	Compton Bennett
1946	A Girl in a Million	Francis Searle
1947	Dear Murderer	Arthur Crabtree
1947	Dancing with Crime	John Paddy Carstairs
1947	Mine Own Executioner	Anthony Kimmins
1947	Night Beat	Harold Huth
1948	Bond Street	Gordon Parry
1948	Daybreak	Compton Bennett
1948	Dulcimer Street (aka London Belongs to Me)	Sidney Gilliat
1948	Sleeping Car to Trieste	John Paddy Carstairs
1948	Lost Daughter (aka Portrait from Life)	Terence Fisher
1949	The Gay Lady (aka Trottie True)	Brian Desmond Hurst
1949	The Amazing Mr. Beecham (aka The Chiltern Hundreds)	John Paddy Carstairs
1949	Give Us This Day (aka Christ in Concrete)	Edward Dmytryk
1950	Night and the City	Jules Dassin

Year	Film	Director
1950	Double Confession	Ken Annakin
1950	So Long at the Fair (aka The Black Curse)	Antony Darnborough, Terence Fisher
1950	The Clouded Yellow	Ralph Thomas
1951	The Long Dark Hall	Reginald Beck, Anthony Bushell
1951	Hotel Sahara	Ken Annakin
1951	The Man in the White Suit	Alexander Mackendrick
1951	Island Rescue	Ralph Thomas
1952	Mr. Denning Drives North	Anthony Kimmins
1952	The Importance of Being Earnest	Anthony Asquith
1952	The Paris Express (aka The Man Who Watched Trains Go By)	Harold French (UK/USA)
1953	Project M7 (aka The Net)	Anthony Asquith
1953	Always a Bride	Ralph Smart
1954	The Love Lottery	Charles Crichton
1954	The Final Test	Anthony Asquith
1954	Malaga (aka Fire over Africa)	Richard Sale (USA)
1954	Chance Meeting (aka The Young Lovers)	Anthony Asquith
1954	Mad about Men	Ralph Thomas
1954	Aunt Clara	Anthony Kimmins
1955	The Man Who Loved Redheads	Harold French
1955	Up to His Neck	John Paddy Carstairs
1955	The End of the Affair	Edward Dmytryk
1955	The Prisoner	Peter Glenville
1955	A Kid for Two Farthings	Carol Reed
1955	Footsteps in the Fog	Arthur Lubin
1955	Simon and Laura	Muriel Box
1955	Storm over the Nile	Zoltan Korda, Terence Young
1956	Tears for Simon (aka Lost)	Guy Green
1956	The Iron Petticoat	Ralph Thomas
1957	Brothers in Law	Roy Boulting
1958	Happy Is the Bride	Roy Boulting
1958	Orders to Kill	Anthony Asquith
1958	I Only Arsked!	Montgomery Tully
1959	Libel	Anthony Asquith
1959	Season of Passion (aka Summer of the Seventeenth Doll)	Leslie Norman (Australia/UK/USA)
1960	Surprise Package	Stanley Donen (USA)
1961	The Curse of the Werewolf	Terence Fisher
1962	Guns of Darkness	Anthony Asquith
1963	The Old Dark House	William Castle (UK/USA)
1964	The Night of the Iguana	John Huston (USA)
1965	Battle of the Bulge	Ken Annakin (USA)

FRIED, Gerald (b. 1928) A successful composer of over 250 movies and television programs, he scored many feature films between 1953 and 1979 but few of them are as memorable as his TV credits which include *Roots* and *Star Trek*.

Gerald Fried was born and raised in the Bronx borough of New York City, taking oboe lessons as a boy and attending high school with future film director Stanley Kubrick. Fried studied at the Juilliard School of Music then began his professional music career in 1948 as oboist for the Dal-

las Symphony and then the New York Little Orchestra. Dissatisfied with being a musician, he relocated to Los Angeles hoping to write music for the movies. When Kubrick turned from photography to filmmaking, he enlisted his school friend to write the music for his documentary short *Day of the Fight* in 1951. Two years later Fried scored Kubrick's first feature film, the low-budget war drama *Fear and Desire*, followed by the crime movie *Killer's Kiss*. The first Kubrick feature to find recognition was the stylish 1957 film noir classic *The Killing*, for which Fried wrote a thrilling score. But Fried wrote music for only one more Kubrick project, the antiwar drama *Paths of Glory* later that same year; Kubrick relocated to England and the two never collaborated again. Instead Fried began scoring a series of low-budget movies, mostly horror and gangster films, although on occasion he was handed an above-average project, such as *Dino, Terror in a Texas Town, A Cold Wind in August, Twenty Plus Two, Deathwatch, The Killing of Sister George, Too Late the Hero, The Grissom Gang, What Ever Happened to Aunt Alice?, The Bell Jar,* and *One Potato, Two Potato.* Fried received an Academy Award nomination for the nature documentary *Birds Do It, Bees Do It* in 1974. Five years later he retired from Hollywood.

If Fried's cinema career was something of a disappointment, his television career was anything but. He made his small-screen debut writing the music for three episodes of *M Squad* in 1958 and from then on was kept busy scoring series, TV movies, documentaries, and special televised events. Among the series he wrote music for are *Shotgun Slade, Riverboat, The Man Who Never Was, Gilligan's Island, The Man from U.N.C.L.E., Iron Horse, It's About Time, Mission: Impossible, Flamingo Road, Dynasty,* and *Star Trek.* For this last series Fried wrote the cult favorite "*Star Trek* Fight Music" for the episode "Amok Time"; the music was later performed and recorded by various artists, was heard in other movies, and was used for the wake-up call for the astronauts on the Space Shuttle *Discovery.* Fried's many TV movies and miniseries include *Danger Has Two Faces* (1968), *Francis Gary Powers: The True Story of the U-2 Spy Incident* (1976), *The Spell* (1977), *Cruise into Terror* (1978), *The Immigrants* (1978), *The Rebels* (1979), *The Ordeal of Dr. Mudd* (1980), *The Silent Lovers* (1980), *The Mystic Warrior* (1984), and *Napoleon and Josephine: A Love Story* (1987). But his most notable credit was scoring one episode of the groundbreaking miniseries *Roots* in 1977 (Quincy Jones composed the music for the other parts) and all of the episodes for *Roots: The Next Generations* two years later. Fried left television in the 1980s and retired, though he has occasionally returned to playing the oboe in concert.

Although Fried worked on few successful films, his scores are often praiseworthy. When given a superior movie to score, he often soars. The music for *The Killing* is terse and defiant in a noir way. Fried scores this stark, black-and-white thriller about a racetrack heist with a jazz score that moves from seething underscoring to chaotic

passages with wild piano and xylophone. One theme has restless strings as jittery brass and punchy percussion join in the confusion, while another section features anxious brass fanfares that seem to announce doom. The robbery itself is scored with pounding brass and military-like drums that sometimes explode; other times they create a grumbling background. Military drums are central to Fried's score for *Paths of Glory,* a brutally eloquent World War I drama in which there are no heroes. The musical variations played by military drums are oppressive and demanding rather than patriotic or victorious. One attack sequence is made all the more haunting by the quiet but disturbing music in which various percussion instruments cautiously move forward with muted cymbals and kettle drums provide unsettling accents. Fried's score for *Too Late the Hero,* a 1970 World War II drama with striking parallels to the then-current conflict in Vietnam, has a very different military sound. There are a handful of march themes heard in the film and they are very different. The main theme is a series of brass and percussion riffs that tease rather than resolve, then they transition into a military march with a jazz temperament. There is also a driving, earnest march theme played on horns and percussion that gets more and more confident as it goes along. There is even a slaphappy march on piccolo, strings, and muted trumpets that sounds like the circus coming into town.

Jazz predominates in two films that focus on the female sex. *A Cold Wind in August* is an engrossing movie about an ex-stripper and prostitute (Lola Albright) who slips into a passionate affair with a teenage boy (Scott Marlowe). Fried scores the love scenes with edgy and disturbing jazz rather than romantic music. One passage features jittery saxophone and trumpet riffs that are very sultry and oddly unromantic. There is also a cool jazz theme featuring a solo saxophone that casually rises and falls like a stripper's dance, as opposed to the hot jazz passages that are played on a sneering trumpet. The dark comedy *The Killing of Sister George* has the distinction of being the first Hollywood film in which the main characters are lesbians. A British soap opera actress (Beryl Reid) is "killed off" of a series and loses her much-younger lover (Susannah York) to a female television producer (Coral Browne). Composer Frank De Vol, who usually scored director Robert Aldrich's films, was so disgusted by the lesbian lovemaking scenes in the movie that he refused to score it. Fried was called in at the last moment and wrote a very tense jazz score with a comic twist. The main theme is a jarring piece with strings that furiously glide across the scale, percussion and bass that pulsate nervously, and an electric guitar that casually plucks out the melody oblivious to all the other sounds. Just as the tone of the movie is funny in an unsettling way, so too is the music melodic and harsh at the same time. Fried will always be known more as a successful television composer than one for the movies but his screen scores should not be underestimated.

Credits

(all films USA unless stated otherwise)

Year	Film	Director
1953	Fear and Desire (aka Shape of Fear)	Stanley Kubrick
1955	Killer's Kiss (aka Kiss Me, Kill Me)	Stanley Kubrick
1956	The Killing (aka Bed of Fear)	Stanley Kubrick
1957	The Vampire	Paul Landres
1957	Bayou (aka Poor White Trash)	Harold Daniels
1957	Trooper Hook	Charles Marquis Warren
1957	Dino	Thomas Carr
1957	Paths of Glory	Stanley Kubrick
1958	The Return of Dracula (aka Curse of Dracula)	Paul Landres
1958	The Flame Barrier	Paul Landres
1958	Machine-Gun Kelly	Roger Corman
1958	I Bury the Living (aka Killer on the Wall)	Albert Band
1958	Curse of the Faceless Man	Edward L. Cahn
1958	The Cry Baby Killer	Jus Addiss
1958	Terror in a Texas Town	Joseph H. Lewis
1958	The Lost Missile	Lester and William Berke
1958	I Mobster	Roger Corman
1959	Timbuktu	Jacques Tourneur
1959	High School Big Shot	Joel Rapp
1959	Cast a Long Shadow	Thomas Carr
1961	A Cold Wind in August	Alexander Singer
1961	Twenty Plus Two	Joseph M. Newman
1961	The Second Time Around	Vincent Sherman
1962	The Cabinet of Caligari	Roger Kay
1964	One Potato, Two Potato	Larry Peerce
1966	One Spy Too Many	Joseph Sargent
1966	Deathwatch	Vic Morrow
1966	One of Our Spies Is Missing	E. Darrell Hallenbeck
1967	The Karate Killers (aka The Five Daughters Affair)	Barry Shear
1968	The Killing of Sister George	Robert Aldrich
1969	What Ever Happened to Aunt Alice?	Lee H. Katzin, Bernard Girard
1970	Too Late the Hero (aka Suicide Run)	Robert Aldrich
1971	The Enchanted Years	Nicolas Noxon
1971	The Grissom Gang	Robert Aldrich
1973	The Baby	Ted Post
1974	Birds Do It, Bees Do It (AAN)	Nicolas Noxon, Irwin Rosten
1976	Survive!	René Cardona (Mexico)
1976	Vigilante Force	George Armitage
1979	The Bell Jar	Larry Peerce

FRIEDHOFER, Hugo (1901–1981) A workhorse of an orchestrator, composer, arranger, and conductor, he contributed to over 250 Hollywood movies, often with little acknowledgment. In fact, Friedhofer wrote scores alone or with others for fifty-seven feature films before he received his first screen credit. Yet everyone in Hollywood knew he was one of the top composers and orchestrators of his era.

He was born Hugo Wilhelm Friedhofer in San Francisco, the son of a German immigrant who had studied music in Dresden. Friedhofer played cello as a youth and, after studying music at the University of California, Berkeley, he played cello in the People's Symphony Orchestra. He arranged and orchestrated music for silent film palaces, then went to Hollywood in 1929, where his first job was arranging the music for the early musical *Sunny Side Up*. After a few years at Fox, he moved to Warner Brothers, where he stayed for fifty years. Although he contributed to the scores of many feature films there, Friedhofer was better known as an orchestrator. He orchestrated many of the scores by fellow German composers Max Steiner and Erich Wolfgang Korngold and was soon considered one of the top orchestrators in Hollywood. But orchestrators get very little attention and even after he started scoring movies on his own Friedhofer was always in the shadows of others. Some attention finally came his way when his score for *The Best Years of Our Lives* won an Academy Award. He wrote music for many genres, including gangster dramas, musicals, westerns, domestic melodramas, swashbucklers, screwball comedies, and even Spanish-language movies Hollywood made for export. His most notable credits include *The Bishop's Wife, An Affair to Remember, Boy on a Dolphin, Joan of Arc, The Young Lions, Above and Beyond, The Woman in the Window,* and *Between Heaven and Hell,* all of which were nominated for Best Score Oscars. Among the other films that he scored are *The Adventures of Marco Polo, Daddy Long Legs, The Trail of the Lonesome Pine, Broken Arrow, Lifeboat, Gilda, Hondo, Ace in the Hole,* and *One-Eyed Jacks.* Friedhofer scored some television series in the 1960s and 1970s, including *I Spy, Voyage to the Bottom of the Sea,* and *Barnaby Jones,* then ended his career writing music for some third-rate features in the late 1960s and early 1970s. He retired from movies in 1973 and died eight years later at the age of eighty.

Friedhofer's music was generally more subtle than most Tinseltown composers. Perhaps orchestrating so many loud and lush scores had wearied him of what he considered the overwrought Hollywood sound. His score for Samuel Goldwyn's postwar drama *The Best Years of Our Lives* is perhaps his finest. There are six distinct musical motifs in the film, none of which is loud or obvious. The main theme is a flowing piece with muted brass doing variations on a three-note phrase. The music that accompanies each of the GIs' homecoming is somber and revealing without being maudlin. There is also an uplifting theme that is used when the men fly over their hometown before landing. The music under some of the most heartbreaking scenes, such as those dealing with the young sailor Homer (Harold Russell) who has had both hands amputated, is masterfully restrained. The entire score is a marvel of understatement and *The Best Years of Our Lives* is all the more potent because of it. Both producer Goldwyn and director William Wyler were not pleased with the score, wanting a more dramatic and passionate sound. It looked like Friedhofer's composing career was over until the score won the Oscar and he was in demand, particularly for dramas. Another heart tugger that Friedhofer scored with taste is *An Affair to Remember*. The memorable title song (sometimes listed as "Our Love Affair") was written by Harry Warren (music), Leo McCarey, and Harold Adamson (lyric) and Friedhofer used it throughout the movie with emotional power. Less subtle than the music for *The Best Years of Our Lives*, the score is nevertheless effective without being overdone.

In a much lighter vein is Friedhofer's charming score for the comedy-romance *The Bishop's Wife* about an angel (Cary Grant) who comes down to earth to aid a troubled married couple (David Niven and Loretta Young). The opening theme sets the tone perfectly: a sprightly concerto with celestial undertones that is more playful than religious. The angel has a musical motif that sounds heavenly yet is spiced up with a very worldly saxophone. Also romantic but with a restless subtext is the music for *The Sun Also Rises* based on Ernest Hemingway's novel about American expatriates in Paris after World War I. The love theme is superb, lyrical and European in its flavor, but the main theme is more unsettling as the disillusioned hero (Tyrone Power) searches for happiness in various ways. The optimistic ending is accompanied by a soaring, hopeful theme. Another kind of searching can be found in the early Friedhofer movie *The Adventures of Marco Polo*. The main theme makes no attempt to re-create either Italy or the exotic Orient but instead has romantic, driving music that suggests a mythic quest. Later in the score there are touches of the East, although the instruments remain Western. *Boy on a Dolphin* is set on a Greek island and the score suggests Aegean folk songs without being slavish to the sound. The Greek instruments provide the appropriate flavor, but the music is basically romantic with exotic touches. The character drama *The Young Lions*, about three very different soldiers (Montgomery Clift, Marlon Brando, and Dean Martin) in World War II, uses a brassy military march theme that is undercut by violins, which adds a touch of romance. There is also an enticing love theme in the movie that could stand on its own as a ballad. Of Friedhofer's many westerns, perhaps the finest score was heard in *Broken Arrow*, a movie that was sympathetic to the Native Americans. Friedhofer's music has a tribal tone that blends with a vigorous theme that suggests conquering the West. Some of the music is ambiguous. The Native Americans are accompanied at times by warlike rhythms, other times by melancholy and domestic tones. For *Ace in the Hole*, a very cynical film about exploitive journalism, Friedhofer eschews melody and offers a disturbing, unresolved kind of music. For his last notable score, that for the unsuccessful revenge western *One-Eyed Jacks*, Friedhofer wrote a flowing main theme that did not sound like a western at all. Throughout the score he plays trumpets against strings and when a melody surfaces it is more European than American folk. It is a splendid score, but one questions if it helped the problematic movie at all.

Because Hollywood had more talented composers than orchestrators, Friedhofer was often passed over for composing jobs because he was more needed as an orchestrator. This made him bitter at times and he was very cynical about his contribution to the movies. Yet other composers have stated that Friedhofer knew more about music than almost anyone else in Hollywood and he has served as inspiration for later composers and orchestrators. Today his scores are studied and performed in concert, something that the acerbic Friedhofer would find ironic. Biography: *Hugo Friedhofer, The Best Years of His Life: A Hollywood Master of Music for the Movies*, Linda Danly (2002).

Credits

(all films USA unless stated otherwise)

Year	Film	Director
1930	The Dancers	Chandler Sprague
1930	Just Imagine	David Butler
1931	Daddy Long Legs	Alfred Santell
1931	Goldie	Benjamin Stoloff
1931	La ley del harem	Lewis Seiler
1931	Heartbreak	Alfred L. Werker
1932	After Tomorrow	Frank Borzage
1932	Careless Lady	Kenneth MacKenna
1932	Amateur Daddy	John G. Blystone
1932	The Trial of Vivienne Ware	William K. Howard
1932	Mystery Ranch	David Howard
1932	Rebecca of Sunnybrook Farm	Alfred Santell
1932	The First Year	William K. Howard
1932	Sherlock Holmes	William K. Howard
1933	Second Hand Wife	Hamilton MacFadden
1933	El último varón sobre la Tierra	James Tinling
1933	Broadway Bad	Sidney Lanfield
1933	It's Great to Be Alive	Alfred L. Werker
1933	Melodía prohibida	Frant R. Strayer
1934	My Lips Betray	John G. Blystone
1934	As Husbands Go	Hamilton MacFadden
1934	Coming-Out Party	John G. Blystone
1934	George White's Scandals	Thornton Freeland, Harry Lachman, George White
1934	Now I'll Tell	Edwin J. Burke

Year	Film	Director
1935	*The Little Colonel*	David Butler
1935	*Here's to Romance*	Alfred E. Green
1935	*Navy Wife*	Allan Dwan
1936	*The Prisoner of Shark Island*	John Ford
1936	*The Trail of the Lonesome Pine*	Henry Hathaway
1936	*White Fang*	David Butler
1938	*The Adventures of Marco Polo*	Archie Mayo, John Cromwell
1938	*Topper Takes a Trip*	Norman Z. McLeod
1942	*China Girl*	Henry Hathaway
1943	*The Fighting Guerrillas*	Louis King
1943	*Paris after Dark*	Léonide Moguy
1943	*The Gang's All Here*	Busby Berkeley
1944	*Lifeboat*	Alfred Hitchcock
1944	*The Lodger*	John Brahm
1944	*Roger Touhy, Gangster*	Robert Flory
1944	*Home in Indiana*	Henry Hathaway
1944	*Wing and a Prayer*	Henry Hathaway
1944	*The Woman in the Window* (AAN)	Fritz Lang
1945	*Brewster's Millions*	Allan Dwan
1945	*Getting Gertie's Garter*	Allan Dwan
1946	*Gilda*	Charles Vidor
1946	*The Bandit of Sherwood Forest*	Henry Levin, George Sherman
1946	*So Dark the Night*	Joseph H. Lewis
1946	*The Best Years of Our Lives* (AA)	William Wyler
1947	*Body and Soul*	Robert Rossen
1947	*Wild Harvest*	Tay Garnett
1947	*The Bishop's Wife* (AAN)	Henry Koster
1948	*The Swordsman*	Joseph H. Lewis
1948	*Adventures of Casanova*	Roberto Gavaldón (USA/Mexico)
1948	*Black Bart*	George Sherman
1948	*A Song Is Born*	Howard Hawks
1948	*Sealed Verdict*	Lewis Allen
1948	*Joan of Arc* (AAN)	Victor Fleming
1948	*Enchantment*	Irving Reis (UK/USA)
1949	*Bride of Vengeance*	Mitchell Leisen
1950	*Guilty of Treason*	Felix E. Feist
1950	*Three Came Home*	Jean Negulesco
1950	*No Man of Her Own*	Mitchell Leisen
1950	*Captain Carey, U.S.A.*	Mitchell Leisen
1950	*Broken Arrow*	Delmer Daves
1950	*Edge of Doom*	Mark Robson
1950	*Two Flags West*	Robert Wise
1950	*The Sound of Fury*	Cy Endfield
1951	*Cry Danger*	Robert Parrish
1951	*Ace in the Hole*	Billy Wilder
1951	*Queen for a Day*	Arthur Lubin
1951	*Journey into Light*	Stuart Heisler
1952	*The Marrying Kind*	George Cukor
1952	*Rancho Notorious*	Fritz Lang
1952	*The Outcasts of Poker Flat*	Joseph M. Newman
1952	*The San Francisco Story*	Robert Parrish
1952	*Lydia Bailey*	Jean Nugulesco
1952	*Big Jim McLain*	Edward Ludwig
1952	*Just for You*	Elliott Nugent
1952	*Face to Face*	John Brahm, Bretaigne Windust
1952	*Thunder in the East*	Charles Vidor
1952	*Above and Beyond* (AAN)	Melvin Frank, Norman Panama
1953	*Plunder of the Sun*	John Farrow

Year	Film	Director
1953	Island in the Sky	William A. Wellman
1953	Hondo	John Farrow
1953	Man in the Attic	Hugo Fregonese
1954	Vera Cruz	Robert Aldrich
1955	White Feather	Robert D. Webb
1955	Violent Saturday	Richard Fleischer
1955	Soldier of Fortune	Edward Dmytryk
1955	Seven Cities of Gold	Robert D. Webb
1955	The Girl in the Red Velvet Swing	Richard Fleischer
1955	The Rains of Ranchipur	Jean Negulesco
1956	The Harder They Fall	Mark Robson
1956	The Revolt of Mamie Stover	Raoul Walsh
1956	Between Heaven and Hell (AAN)	Richard Fleischer
1957	Oh, Men! Oh, Women!	Nunnally Johnson
1957	Boy on a Dolphin (AAN)	Jean Negulesco
1957	An Affair to Remember (AAN)	Leo McCarey
1957	The Sun Also Rises	Henry King
1958	The Young Lions (AAN)	Edward Dmytryk
1958	The Bravados	Henry King
1958	The Barbarian and the Geisha	John Huston
1958	In Love and War	Philip Dunne
1959	Woman Obsessed	Henry Hathaway
1959	This Earth Is Mine	Henry King
1959	The Blue Angel	Edward Dmytryk
1959	Never So Few	John Sturges
1961	One-Eyed Jacks	Marlon Brando
1961	Homicidal	William Castle
1962	Geronimo	Arnold Laven
1962	Beauty and the Beast	Edward L. Cahn
1964	The Secret Invasion	Roger Corman
1971	Von Richthofen and Brown	Roger Corman
1972	Die Sister, Die!	Randall Hood
1972	Private Parts	Paul Bartel

FRONTIERE, Dominic (b. 1931) An esteemed jazz accordion musician, arranger, and composer for television and movies, he scored twenty-eight feature films of widely diverse genres in the 1960s and 1970s.

Dominic Frontiere was born in New Haven, Connecticut, into a musical family who encouraged the boy to study different instruments. Frontiere was proficient on several by the time he was seven and later concentrated on the accordion, making his Carnegie Hall debut on it when he was twelve. He began his professional career playing in Big Bands after World War II and then enrolled at UCLA to study composition and orchestration. Frontiere then returned to the accordion and made jazz recordings, which brought him national recognition. He first became involved with movies when he played the accordion on the soundtrack of the western *Many Rivers to Cross* in 1955, followed by performances in other scores, most memorably his solo sections in *Around the World in Eighty Days* (1959) and *Days of Wine and Roses* (1962). By the mid-1950s, Frontiere began arranging music for the movies, eventually becoming the head of the music department at Twentieth Century-Fox and then Paramount. He first contributed original music for the screen in 1959 when he wrote the song "Xenobia" (lyric by Milton Raskin) for the American dubbed version of the Italian film *Sheba and the Gladiator*. His first full score was for the crime drama *Seven Thieves* the next year. For the next two decades Frontiere was busy scoring everything from John Wayne westerns and Bob Hope comedies to horror movies and offbeat cult films. Among his notable credits are *Hang 'Em High*, *Incubus*, *Massacre Harbor*, *Popi*, *Chisum*, *The Marriage-Go-Round*, *Billie*, *Hammersmith Is Out*, *Barquero*, *Freebie and the Bean*, *Cancel My Reservation*, *Cleopatra Jones and the Casino of Gold*, *The Stunt Man*, and the popular documentary *On Any Sunday*. Frontiere's career and life suffered a setback in 1986 when he was convicted of a large-scale scalping scheme of thousands of Super Bowl tickets. After serving nine months in a federal prison, he occasionally returned to writing music and scored the romantic mystery *Color of Night*. Frontiere's television career was even more successful. It began when he scored an episode of *Rawhide* in 1961 then took off two years later when he wrote the theme and soundtrack score for the sci-fi anthology series *The Outer Limits*. Frontiere's mix of jazz and sound effects was a musical breakthrough for television and the theme remains his most famous piece of music. Among the other TV series he scored are *Branded*, *12 O'Clock High*, *The Flying Nun*, *The Rat Patrol*, *Iron Horse*, *That Girl*, *The Name of the Game*, *The Immortal*, *Vega$*, and *Matt Houston*. Frontiere also wrote music for twenty-three TV movies and miniseries, including *Fanfare for a Death Scene* (1964), *Swing Out, Sweet Land* (1970), *Movin' On* (1972), *Yesterday's Child* (1977), *Washington: Behind Closed Doors* (1977), *Shooting Stars* (1983), *Velvet* (1984), *Brutal Glory* (1989), and *Palomino* (1991). He retired from movies and television in the 1990s and has occasionally returned to performing and recording.

For the most part, Frontiere's music for movies and television is the pop-jazz sound of the 1960s and 1970s. Yet there is much that is still appealing about this high-spirited, funky kind of music. Listening to the bouncy theme for the teenage movie *Billie*, one might laugh at its gyrating dance music played on electric keyboard and saxophone. The music is just shy of true rock but it rocks all the same. The campy action film *Cleopatra Jones and the Casino of Gold* has a pulsating theme filled with energetic brass, strings, and percussion suggesting a chase as various instruments try to keep up with the beat. It is pure 1970s, even in its jazz passage that is casual yet rhythmic as various percussive instruments punctuate the brass and its repeated musical motif. Dated but still of interest is the music for the dark Faustian comedy *Hammersmith Is Out* with its echoing electronic theme on an electric harpsichord and synthesized horns with scat voices, all of it just short of comic. On the other hand, there are several Frontiere scores that do not date and can be enjoyed today on their own terms. Perhaps the best of them is that written for the Clint Eastwood western *Hang 'Em High*, an obvious attempt by Hollywood to make a "spaghetti western" using the same star from the popular Italian movies. The music is an homage to Ennio Morricone's scores for those films yet Frontiere's music is very accomplished in its own right. The main theme, played on harmonica, electric guitar, brass, and various percussion, has a moderate tempo with a steady progressive movement even when it slows down for some intricate finger work on the strings. This catchy theme became a Top-Ten hit for Booker T. & the M.G.s and listening to it today one can understand why. The score also has a flowing romantic passage on various strings and muted horns, and a melancholy theme featuring a solo violin that lingers on each phrase before moving on. A similar western with a similar, if less compelling, score is *Barquero*. The main theme here is a snappy brass, woodwind, and percussion piece that has the tempo of a Spanish flamenco as a solo trumpet is featured almost like a solo dancer. The score also has some vigorous music played on blasting brass and rhythmic guitar strings. One hears a very different kind of music in the John Wayne western *Chisum*. Eastwood and Lee Van Cleef (the star of *Barquero*) are antihero actors but Wayne is clearly the good guy, so the score for *Chisum* is majestic and symphonic rather than edgy and modern. The main theme is a rousing folk tune with a catchy melody and ardent tone. This music is used in the title song (lyric by Andrew J. Fenady) which is sung by Merle Haggard and a spirited male chorus. Yet the same music recurs throughout the movie, sometimes in a romantic and reflective manner, other times as a grandiose anthem. The score also has exciting chase music with horn fanfares and vivid strings, and some quiet passages on strings and harmonica that are very warm and evocative.

Although it was written in 1994, *Color of Night* has some lingering music from the 1970s. This convoluted thriller, about a psychiatrist (Bruce Willis) being stalked by an unknown killer, has a haunting main theme on xylophone and chimes with a lullaby-like flavor, but it gets menacing when agitated strings, gliding woodwinds, and creepy choral chanting enter. Frontiere also composed the music for the film's song "The Color of the Night" (with Jud Friedman and Lauren Christy), a pulsating ballad with a disco beat sung by Christy on the soundtrack. One of the few popular feature documentaries of the 1970s to become a hit, *On Any Sunday* is a fascinating movie about Steve McQueen (who financed it) and others who are devoted to motorcycle racing. Frontiere captures the excitement of the sport with a jazz score that sizzles with energy. There is a rapid jazz passage in which the brass, electric guitar, and keyboard music is given accents by various percussion including a recurring snare drum riff. Another funky theme seems to be improvised and loose as it keeps returning to its main musical motif. For contrast, there is a cool jazz passage heard on synthesized guitar and supported by female voices that is romantic in a hip 1960s pop way. Perhaps Frontiere's most unusual score is for his most unusual movie, the cult classic *The Stunt Man*. This unconventional tale, about a fugitive (Steve Railsback) from the law who gets involved with an eccentric movie director (Peter O'Toole) who is making a film about World War I, is filled with wonderful cockeyed music. The main theme is an oddball march played in a minor key on brass and reeds that has the quality of European circus music. There is also a synthesized theme on strings, woodwinds, and keyboard in which notes seems to slide instead of being sustained, and a vigorous passage with a tango beat as strings, brass, and percussion dance away with fervor. This same music was also used in the film as the song "Bits and Pieces" (lyric by Norman Gimbel) and sung on the soundtrack by Dusty Springfield. *The Stunt Man* is the kind of movie that inspires composers to try daring things. Unfortunately Frontiere was rarely handed such projects. All the same, he has made his mark writing splendid music even when his movies were less than stellar.

Credits

(all films USA unless stated otherwise; * for Best Song)

Year	Film	Director
1960	Seven Thieves	Henry Hathaway
1960	One Foot in Hell	James B. Clark
1961	The Marriage-Go-Round	Walter Lang
1962	Hero's Island	Leslie Stevens
1964	A Global Affair	Jack Arnold
1965	Billie (aka Ginger)	Don Weis
1966	Incubus	Leslie Stevens
1968	Hang 'Em High	Ted Post
1968	Massacre Harbor	John Peyser
1969	Popi	Arthur Hiller
1969	Number One (aka Pro)	Tom Gries
1970	Chisum	Andrew V. McLaglen
1970	Barquero	Gordon Douglas
1971	On Any Sunday	Bruce Brown
1972	Hammersmith Is Out	Peter Ustinov
1972	Cancel My Reservation	Paul Bogart
1973	The Train Robbers	Burt Kennedy
1973	A Name for Evil	Bernard Girard
1974	Freebie and the Bean	Richard Rush
1975	Brannigan	Douglas Hickox (UK)
1975	Cleopatra Jones and the Casino of Gold	Charles Bail (Hong Kong/USA)
1976	The Gumball Rally	Charles Bail
1976	Pipe Dreams	Stephen Verona
1980	Defiance	John Flynn
1980	The Stunt Man (GG)	Richard Rush
1981	Modern Problems	Ken Shapiro
1985	The Aviator	George Miller
1994	Color of Night (GGN*)	Richard Rush

FUSCO, Giovanni (1906–1968) An Italian musician, composer, arranger, and conductor of the concert hall and the movies, he scored over ninety European feature films, most memorably innovative works directed by Alain Renais and Michelangelo Antonioni.

Born in Sant'Agata de Goti, Italy, into a large family of musicians, conductors, singers, and composers, Giovanni Fusco began piano lessons at an early age. By the time Fusco was nine, he was playing piano in silent movie houses. He studied at the School of Music of St. Cecilia in Rome, then later at the Academy of St. Cecilia, where he took organ lessons, and the Music Conservatory at Pesaro, where he learned composition. In the 1930s Fusco wrote operas, ballets, oratorios, choral pieces, music for the theatre, sonatas, and instrumental works. He also gained a reputation as an expert conductor. Yet he was always drawn to the movies and the improvised piano music he had played as a youth. Fusco's first direct experience with filmmaking was in 1936 when he contributed music to the comedy *Joe il rosso*. His first solo score came three years later with the historical drama *Doctor Antonio* but throughout his career Fusco often collaborated with one or more composers on his scores. Moviemaking during the war was problematic, but in the late 1940s Fusco was very active in screen scoring and remained so through the 1960s. A turning point in his career came in 1950 when he worked with young director Michelangelo Antonioni on his first feature, the intense romance *Story of a Love Affair*. The two men collaborated again on *The Lady without Camilias*, *L'avventura*, *Le amiche*, *Il grido*, *L'eclisse*, *I vinti*, and *Red Desert*. As Antonioni became an internationally acclaimed artist, so was Fusco's music applauded throughout Europe and America. He got to work with many of the top directors in Europe, in particular Alain Renais for whom he scored the modern classics *Hiroshima mon amour* and *La guerre est finie* (known equally well as *The War Is Over*). Among Fusco's other noteworthy movies are *The Pirate's Dream*, *Mad about Opera*, *Traviata '53*, *Abandoned*, *Lipstick*, *Climates of Love*, *Girl from La Mancha*, *La corruzione*, *A Nun at the Crossroads*, *Time of Difference*, *The Sea*, and *Milano nera*. Fusco was also very committed to short and feature-length documentary films and scored ten of them. He was composing for the screen up until his death in 1968 at the age of sixty-one. Two years later his last score was heard in Costa-Gavras's lauded political thriller *The Confession*.

Fusco was forty-five years old and an established composer of the concert hall and movies when he first worked with the young Antonioni yet he must have recognized that this new kind of filmmaking required new approaches to scoring. The two became close friends and kindred spirits, their eight movies together exploring and experimenting with both filmmaking and music. *L'avventura* is a puzzling movie about a boat trip in which a wealthy Italian woman (Lea Massari) goes missing and she is searched for by her lover (Gabriele Ferzetti) and best friend (Monica Vitti). As the adventure progresses, the missing woman is forgotten and the two searchers become lovers. Such a beguiling mystery and romance needed a sound that echoed Antonioni's detached, mystical tone. Fusco's main theme is a propelling piece with various strings racing forward yet seeming to be going nowhere. An alto saxophone is featured in a rhythmic passage with male voices and an electric keyboard adding variations to the repetitive musical motif. There is even a bolero played on strings, reeds, and percussion that is classical in form but very modern in its sensibility. *L'avventura* is the movie that infuriated and delighted critics and moviegoers and put Antonioni on the cinema map. Fusco's unorthodox score deserves some of the credit. *L'eclisse* (*The Eclipse*) has another odd yet fascinating love match, this time between a troubled translator (Monica Vitti) and a materialistic stockbroker (Alain Delon). Fusco provides a jaunty but dissonant jazz theme with a saxophone featured over a rambunctious rhythm section. The score also includes a slow cool-jazz piece with a muted saxophone playing a simple but heartfelt melody. Perhaps this rather impersonal romance is best conveyed in a jazz piano passage that is hip and loose as it bounces along in a carefree manner. Jazz is also central in the character drama *La corruzione* (*Corruption*) directed by Mauro Bolognini. There is a smooth jazz theme featuring a solo sax that moves at a steady beat even as it seems lazy and irresponsible. For the suspense scenes, Fusco writes repetitive percussion music with electric sound effects punctuated by brass chords.

The most famous movie Fusco scored is the French New Wave classic *Hiroshima mon amour* directed by Alain Renais, but a good portion of the music is by Georges Delerue and it is difficult to accurately discuss Fusco's contribution. Yet Renais's *La guerre est finie/The War Is Over* is scored solely by Fusco, and its pseudoclassical music is radiant. It is also quite daring because this tale, about a Communist chief (Yves Montand) searching for comrades in Rome, is very stark and minimalist and one expects dark and gloomy underscoring. Instead Fusco undercuts the blunt storytelling (which includes many flashbacks) with fanciful music that seems to comment on the hero, who has fought too many battles and has lost his enthusiasm for life. This can be heard in a synthesized harpsichord theme that sounds classical except for the harsh notes that denote a certain weariness. The movie's main theme is a delicate classical piece heard on harp, harpsichord, and strings with a discomforting subtext as it climbs the scale and takes on a menacing tone. The softer moments in the film are scored with a romantic, mystical theme with celestial voices, chimes, and violins adding a painfully nostalgic sentiment. Such music might not work in an Antonioni movie, but Fusco worked with so many directors during his career that he knew every film has its own directorial (and musical) voice. Official website: www.giovannifusco.com.

Credits

(all films Italy unless stated otherwise)

Year	Film	Director
1936	Joe il rosso	Raffaello Matarazzo
1938	The Duchess of Parma	Alessandro Blasetti
1939	Doctor Antonio	Enrico Guazzoni
1940	Il peccato di Rogelia Sanchez	Carlo Borghesio, Roberto de Ríbon
1940	Pazza di gioia	Carlo Ludovico Bragaglia
1940	The Pirate's Dream	Mario Mattoli
1940	Miseria e nobiltà	Corrado D'Errico
1940	Non me lo dire!	Mario Mattoli
1941	Due cuori sotto sequestro	Carlo Ludovico Bragaglia
1942	Man of the Sea	Belisario L. Randone, Roberto de Ríbon
1943	Measure for Measure	Marco Elter
1943	Due cuori	Carlo Borghesio
1945	Fear No Evil	Giuseppe Maria Scotese
1946	Le modelle di via Margutta	Giuseppe Maria Scotese
1946	The Room Upstairs	Georges Lacombe (France)
1946	One Between the Crowd	Ennio Cerlesi
1946	Humanity	Jack Salvatori
1948	Mad about Opera	Mario Costa
1949	Lieutenant Craig: Missing	Giacomo Gentilomo
1949	Man of Death	Carlo Campogalliani
1950	Mistress of the Mountains	Fernando Cerchio
1950	Story of a Love Affair (aka Paula)	Michelangelo Antonioni
1951	Ha fatto tredici	Carlo Manzoni
1952	Mistress of Treves	Arthur Maria Rabenalt (France/Italy/W. Germany)
1952	There Were 300	Gian Paolo Callegari
1953	Le marchand de Venise	Pierre Billon (France/Italy)
1953	The Lady without Camelias	Michelangelo Antonioni (Italy/France)
1953	I vinti	Michelangelo Antonioni (Italy/France)
1953	Traviata '53	Vittorio Cottafavi (Italy/ France)
1953	Canzoni a due voci	Gianni Vernuccio
1954	Killers of the East (aka Black Devils of Kali)	Gian Paolo Callegari, Ralph Murphy (Italy/USA)
1954	Jailbirds	Vittorio Cottafavi (Italy/France)
1954	Orphan of the Ghetto	Carlo Campogalliani
1955	Abandoned	Francesco Maselli
1955	Le amiche	Michelangelo Antonioni
1955	Yalis, la vergine del roncador	Francesco De Robertis, Leonardo Salmieri
1955	I quattro del getto tonante	Fernando Cerchio
1956	Retaggio di sangue	Max Calandri
1956	La trovatella di Milano	Giorgio Capitani

Year	Film	Director
1957	Il grido	Michelangelo Antonioni (Italy/USA)
1957	I misteri di Parigi	Fernando Cerchio (Italy/France)
1957	Vecchio cinema . . . che passione!	Aldo Crudo
1957	L'angelo delle Alpi	Carlo Campogalliani
1958	Aphrodite, Goddess of Love	Mario Bonnard
1958	Avventura nell'arcipelago	Dino B. Partesano
1959	Hiroshima mon amour	Alain Renais (France/Japan)
1960	The Cossacks	Viktor Tourjansky, Giorgio Venturini (Italy/France)
1960	Lipstick	Damiano Damiani (Italy/France)
1960	L'avventura	Michelangelo Antonioni (Italy/France)
1960	Silver Spoon Set	Francesco Maselli (Italy/France)
1960	Cleopatra's Daughter	Fernando Cerchio (Italy/France)
1960	The Pharaoh's Woman	Viktor Tourjansky
1960	Un eroe del nostro tempo	Sergio Capogna
1961	Man nennt es amore	Rolf Thiele (W. Germany)
1961	The Trojan Horse	Giorgio Ferroni (Italy/France/Yugoslavia)
1961	L'oro di Roma	Carlo Lizzani (Italy/France)
1961	Milano nera	Gian Rocco, Pino Serpi
1962	Climates of Love	Stellio Lorenzi (France)
1962	L'eclisse	Michelangelo Antonioni (Italy/France)
1962	La monaca di Monza	Carmine Gallone (France/Italy)
1962	Invasion 1700 (aka Daggers of Blood)	Fernando Cerchio (Italy/France/Yugoslavia)
1962	The Avenger	Giorgio Venturini (Italy/France/Yugoslavia)
1963	Secret Violence	Girorgio Moser
1963	Lo sceicco rosso	Fernando Cerchio (Italy/France)
1963	Rocambole	Bernard Borderie (Italy/France)
1963	Girl from La Mancha	Vicente Escrivá (Spain/Italy/W. Germany)
1963	Stories in the Sand	Riccardo Fellini
1963	The Sea	Giuseppe Patroni Griffi
1963	La corruzione	Mauro Bolognini (Italy/France)
1963	Outlaws of Love	Valentino Orsini, etc.
1963	Sandokan the Great	Umberto Lenzi (Italy/Spain/France)
1964	Pariahs of Glory	Henri Decoin (France/Italy/Spain)
1964	Red Desert	Michelangelo Antonioni (Italy/France)
1964	Time of Difference	Drancesco Maselli (Italy/France)
1964	Tre notti d'amore	Renato Castellani, etc.
1964	I pirati della Malesia	Unberto Lenzi (Italy/Spain/W. Germany/France)
1964	Three Sergeants of Bengal	Umberto Lenzi (Spain/Italy)
1965	Temple of a Thousand Lights	Umberto Lenzi
1966	The War Is Over	Alain Renais (France/Sweden)
1966	The Killer Lacks a Name	Tulio Demicheli (Spain/Italy)
1967	A Nun at the Crossroads	Julio Buchs (Spain/Italy)
1967	The Subversives	Paolo and Vittorio Taviani
1967	Domani non siamo più qui	Brunello Rondi
1968	Mafia	Damiano Damiani (Italy/France)
1968	The Sex of Angels	Ugo Liberatore (Italy/W. Germany)
1968	Garter Colt	Gian Rocco
1968	A Black Veil for Lisa	Massimo Dallamano (Italy/W. Germany)
1968	Run, Psycho, Run	Brunello Rondi
1969	Love and Anger	Bernardo Bertolucci, etc. (Italy/France)
1969	Five Days in Sinai	Maurizio Lucidi (Italy/Israel)
1970	The Confession	Costa-Gavras (France/Italy)

GIACCHINO, Michael (b. 1967) A highly successful composer for television, movies, theme parks, and video games, many of his thirty feature films are action movies, both animated and live action.

Michael Giacchino was born in Riverside, New Jersey, the son of Sicilian immigrants, and raised in nearby Edgewater Park, where he started making his own animated movies and scoring them when he was only ten years old. Giacchino studied film production at the School of Visual Arts in Manhattan and music at Juilliard, working for Universal Pictures and Disney as an intern while still a student. In the early 1990s Giacchino relocated to Los Angeles where he worked in the publicity department at Disney and took music classes at UCLA. His professional music career began with scoring video games produced by Disney Interactive and DreamWorks, some of them becoming very popular, such as *The Lost World: Jurassic Park*, the *Medal of Honor* series, *Small Soldiers*, *Alias*, *Call of Duty*, and different versions of *The Lion King*. Although Giacchino began scoring feature films in 1997 with the thriller *Legal Deceit*, he found more recognition in television, where he wrote the music for such series as *Alias*, *Six Degrees*, *Lost*, *Alcatraz*, and *Fringe*, as well as several TV movies. His film career took a major turn in 2004 when he scored the popular Pixar movie *The Incredibles*, followed by such Pixar favorites as *Ratatouille* (which brought him his first Oscar nomination), *Up* (winning many awards including the Academy Award), and *Cars 2*. Giacchino has also found wide recognition for his scores for *Star Trek* and its sequel *Star Trek Into Darkness*, *Mission: Impossible III* and its sequel *Mission: Impossible—Ghost Protocol*, *Let Me In*, *Speed Racer*, *Cloverfield*, *Super 8*, *50/50*, and the documentary *Earth Days*. He usually orchestrates and conducts his screen scores, as he does for his film shorts, video game music, and television work. Giacchino has also scored music for attractions at the Disney theme parks worldwide, most memorably for the revamped Space Mountain and Star Tours rides, and music for special events, such as the Academy Awards and the millennium celebration *Camden 2000*.

Giacchino brought a new sound to video games in the 1990s, eschewing computerized, robotic music in favor of symphonic scores that were not always racing ahead and had quieter, calmer sections. His scores for action movies likewise find variety as they provide adrenaline-inducing themes as well as gentler moments. The animated *The Incredibles* is a spoof of comic superheroes yet also includes nostalgia for the genre it is satirizing. Bob Parr (voiced by Craig T. Nelson) and his superpowered family try to live normal lives but soon bust out of their humdrum existence to save their town from a new menace. The main theme has jazzy action music with frantic brass and woodwinds, racing strings, a flipped-out xylophone, and a bluesy saxophone solo. The Parrs' dreary normal life is scored with a silly minor-key theme on woodwinds that is giddy yet downhearted. The chase music, with its blaring trumpets, a vivid bass line, and pounding drums, is exciting but doesn't take itself too seriously. This is contrasted by dreamy sections in the score that capture Bob's desire to quit his dead-end job with an insurance firm and return to his action-packed life. Less satirical than *The Incredibles* are the Pixar movies *Ratatouille* and *Up* and their scores are even richer. The former film is about a Parisian rat (voiced by Patton Oswalt) who dreams of being a gourmet cook. The French-flavored score uses the expected accordion a lot, but even for an animated comedy the music avoids Gallic cliché. A flowing Parisian cafe theme features the accordion but is supported by piano, celesta, mandolin, and even harmonica to fill out the sound. There is a sweeping romantic theme for the city of Paris, some lively jazz music that the rats play on such improvised instruments as a paper clip and a saltshaker, and a contagiously happy piece played while a ratatouille dish is prepared. The piano is the featured instrument in Giacchino's wonderful score for *Up*, an offbeat but highly involving "road" movie involving grumpy old Frederickson (voiced by Ed Asner), a chipper Boy Scout (voiced by Jordan Nagai), and an air balloon journey to a South American jungle. The movie opens with an extended montage about the younger Frederickson and his beloved wife Ellie. It is a heartbreaking sequence with few words but emotive music, a lilting waltz that takes on a jazz tone at times but ends with a sorrowful blues when Ellie dies. This same theme takes on a more expansive, symphonic sound when Frederickson's house is lifted into the air by hundreds of balloons and floats over the landscape. Also memorable is a comic theme played on a bassoon and plucked violins for the slaphappy dog Dug (voiced by Bob Peterson) and a swinging passage with a Big Band sound. *Up* is perhaps Giacchino's most classic Hollywood score with its tender lyrical moments as well as vigorous orchestral sections that lift one's spirits.

Outside of the Pixar movies, Giacchino's most famous score is for the 2009 space adventure *Star Trek*. Arguably the best of all the movies in the franchise, this look at the early years of the spaceship *Enterprise* and its crew is given a superb score by Giacchino that does not ape the previous *Star Trek* films but does quote from the original TV series' theme by Alexander Courage. The score is held together by a simple but effective motif in which a five-note melody in a minor key is played by a solo French horn in the prologue and by various instruments in different tempos throughout

the movie. There is a sensitive passage heard on strings that is used for the young Spock (Zachary Quinto), a rousing brass passage heard during an attack scene, and a descending theme played on violins and horns that is very delicate and engaging. Giacchino uses everything from celestial voices to electronic sounds to grandiose fanfares in the *Star Trek* score, giving the film a majesty that is truly epic in scope and sentiment. Director Matt Reeves did not want a soundtrack score for his unique sci-fi movie *Cloverfield* in which an alien attack is viewed through an amateur's camcorder. The only music heard throughout the film is diegetic snatches on the radio or some other on-screen source, but Reeves did want music for the final credits that summed up the events just witnessed. Giacchino obliged with the "*Cloverfield* Overture" (also titled "Roar!"), an explosive piece with wordless vocals, pounding brass, and tribal drums. The piece has a five-note motif that is first heard on piano but then builds in intensity and orchestration until it is truly roaring. While it does not constitute a full score, "Roar!" is a thrilling piece of screen music and one of Giacchino's finest works. Official website: www.michaelgiacchinomusic.com.

Credits

(all films USA unless stated otherwise)

Year	Film	Director
1997	Legal Deceit	Monika Harris
1998	No Salida	Bill Birrell
1999	My Brother the Pig	Erik Fleming
2001	The Trouble with Lou	Gregor Joackim
2002	Redemption of the Ghost	Richard Friedman
2003	Sin	Michael Stevens
2004	The Incredibles	Brad Bird
2005	Sky High	Mike Mitchell
2005	The Family Stone (aka Hating Her)	Thomas Bezucha
2005	Looking for Comedy in the Muslim World	Albert Brooks
2006	Mission: Impossible III	J. J. Abrams (USA/Germany/China)
2007	Ratatouille (AAN)	Brad Bird, Jan Pinkava
2008	Cloverfield	Matt Reeves
2008	Speed Racer (aka Race Chasers)	Andy and Lana Wachowski (USA/Australia/Germany)
2009	Earth Days	Robert Stone
2009	Star Trek (aka Corporate HQ)	J. J. Abrams (USA/Germany)
2009	Up (AA; GG; BAFTA)	Pete Docter, Bob Peterson
2009	Land of the Lost	Brad Silberling
2009	Checkmate	Pierce Gardner
2010	Let Me In (aka Fish Head)	Matt Reeves (UK/USA)
2011	Super 8	J. J. Abrams
2011	Cars 2	John Lasseter, Brad Lewis

Year	Film	Director
2011	*Monte Carlo*	Thomas Bezucha (USA/Hungary)
2011	*50/50 (aka I'm with Cancer)*	Jonathan Levine
2011	*Mission: Impossible—Ghost Protocol*	Brad Bird (USA/United Arab Emirates/Czech Republic)
2012	*John Carter (aka A Princess of Mars)*	Andrew Stanton
2013	*Star Trek Into Darkness*	J. J. Abrams
2014	*This Is Where I Leave You*	Shawn Levy
2014	*Dawn of the Planet of the Apes*	Matt Reeves
2014	*Jupiter Ascending*	Andy and Lana Wachowski
2015	*Tomorrowland*	Brad Bird

GLASS, Philip (b. 1937) Arguably the leading avant-garde composer of the past forty years, he is internationally acclaimed for his operas, ballets, and concert pieces, but he has also written music for over sixty feature films. Many of these are documentaries on a wide range of subjects, others are commercial features, and some defy description, just as his music often does.

Philip Morris Glass was born in Baltimore, the son of Jewish immigrants from Lithuania, and grew up listening to a wide variety of music in his father's record store. Glass studied the flute as a child at the Peabody Conservatory of Music and entered the University of Chicago at the age of fifteen. Although he studied mathematics and physics, Glass became interested in the musical forms that arose after World War II. He studied music in Paris and then at Juilliard where he pursued work on composition. By the early 1960s his instrumental works won contests and scholarships, including a Fulbright grant to study with the renowned music teacher Nadia Boulanger in Paris. While in Europe and later back in New York, Glass devoted himself to avant-garde theatre, film, and music. He was particularly influenced by the Indian composer and sitar musician Ravi Shankar, who led Glass to study Buddhism and Asian culture. All of these ideas and media became part of his music, using ethnic instruments and writing music that went far beyond the Western tradition. He has received wide recognition for his theatre-music pieces, which he calls "operas" though they rarely resemble conventional opera. *Einstein on the Beach* (1976) is the most famous of these, but there were many other music-theatre works and concert pieces that either thrilled or irritated audiences and critics. Yet by the end of the century, Glass was considered a living legend and the foremost composer of the avant-garde around the world.

Glass first wrote music for the screen in 1968 when he scored the low-budget documentary *Inquiring Nuns*

by Gordon Quinn. For experimental filmmaker Godfrey Reggio, he wrote the music for the feature *Koyaanisqatsi*, which was a combination of travelogue, documentary, and tone poem. The film's startling techniques, such as the use of time-lapse photography and vivid montage, were heightened by the inventive Glass score. The two men also collaborated on the cult favorites *Powaqqatsi* and *Naqoyqatsi*, which were similarly unusual and mystifying. Throughout his screen career, Glass has worked with documentary directors from around the world, providing provocative music for movie projects about physics, war, religion, crime, nature, medicine, and other subjects. His list of commercial feature films is not long but is impressive. Although his music might be considered too offbeat and cerebral for mainstream audiences, some of his movie scores have been very accessible and appreciated by audiences and critics. Films such as *Bent, Kundun, The Truman Show, The Hours, Cassandra's Dream, Elena*, and *Notes on a Scandal* are far from experimental yet the music Glass wrote for each is bold and unconventional. The fact that these scores are so effective in supporting the movies comes as a surprise to many who consider Glass too avant-garde for popularity.

While Glass's music is often described as minimalist, he denies the label and argues that he is more interested in repetition of musical ideas than deconstructing traditional music as minimalists do. Although his work is greatly influenced by world music, there is much in a Glass composition that adheres to classical Western tradition. He received a classical music education, and his symphonies, concertos, and chamber music are often structured like pieces by Schubert and Mozart. Usually it is his use of unfamiliar instruments and un-Western scales and rhythms that make his music sound so different to Americans. Also, his use of dissonance and repetition often is interpreted as unmelodic and therefore not traditionally lyrical. Yet

Glass's music is not all that difficult to decipher and as the decades have passed his work has become easier to appreciate. The fact that many of Glass's film projects are experimental and far from mainstream allows his nontraditional music to work very effectively. A traditional musical score for movies as offbeat as *Candyman* or *The Illusionist* would not only be inappropriate but impotent.

Glass has always been drawn to the unusual and the foreign so naturally his film music would be inspired rather than intimidated by such movies. *Koyaanisqatsi*, for example, is about the destruction of the environment by the encroachment of industry and it is filled with dynamic visuals: rush-hour traffic speeded up in a surreal manner, clouds billowing like explosions, demolition of buildings slowed down into a poetic dance of debris, third-world tribal rituals presented expressionistically, and so on. Glass filled his score with broken ethnic instruments, cathedral pipe organ sections, choral chants by Hopi natives, and trumpet fanfares. For *Kundun*, Martin Scorsese's movie bio about the early life of the Dalai Lama, Glass used instruments native to Tibet and incorporated enough Asian musical forms to create atmosphere without losing the Western moviegoer. The three different time periods in *The Hours* are united musically by a classical-sounding theme in which strings repeat and resound in a foreboding way. Similarly, the tension in the contemporary drama *Notes on a Scandal* is echoed in the persistent orchestral theme punctuated by pizzicato strings and death-march percussion. The string quartet used in *Bent* suggests the German concentration camp routine by repeating the same rising and falling themes, a sort of Viennese waltz gone sour. For Woody Allen's dark drama *Cassandra's Dream*, the Glass orchestral score evokes the tossing and turning of a rough sea. Very little of the movie is set on water, but the central image of the title boat is there in the music throughout. A very unique Glass movie score is the one he composed in 1999 to go with Tod Browning's 1931 classic horror film *Dracula*. The early talkie is primitive in many ways and the original soundtrack was rushed and incomplete. Glass's new score avoids clichéd horror movie themes and instead opts for a very classical string composition that feels both modern and period. The Glass repetition is there, but it builds so carefully that the moviegoer does not feel manipulated.

Glass is actively involved in the operas, theatre pieces, concerts, and movies that he scores. In 1967 he founded the Philip Glass Ensemble that performed his works because most musicians could not or would not understand his music. Today his music is performed around the world and the offbeat composer of the avant-garde is practically an institution rather than a radical cry for new music. Autobiography: *Music by Philip Glass* (1988); biography: *Glass: A Portrait*, Robert Maycock (2003). Official website: www.philipglass.com.

Credits

(all films USA unless stated otherwise)

Year	Film	Director
1968	*Inquiring Nuns*	Gordon Quinn
1970	*Marco*	Gordon Quinn, Gerald Temaner
1978	*North Star: Mark di Suvero*	François De Menil (France/USA)
1982	*Koyaanisqatsi*	Godfrey Reggio
1985	*Empire City*	Michael Blackwood
1985	*Mishima: A Life in Four Chapters*	Paul Schrader (USA/Japan)
1986	*The Kitchen Presents Two Moon July*	Tom Bowes
1986	*Dead End Kids*	JoAnne Akalaitis
1987	*Hamburger Hill*	John Irvin
1988	*Powaqqatsi*	Godfrey Reggio
1988	*The Thin Blue Line*	Errol Morris
1989	*The Church* (aka *La chiesa*)	Michele Soavi (Italy)
1990	*Mindwalk*	Bernt Amadeus Capra
1991	*A Brief History of Time*	Errol Morris (UK/Japan/USA)
1992	*Mirror of the Past*	Jytte Rex (Denmark)
1992	*Candyman*	Bernard Rose

Year	Film	Director
1993	Compassion in Exile: The Life of the 14th Dalai Lama	Mickey Lemie
1995	Candyman: Farewell to the Flesh	Bill Condon
1995	The Interview	Monique Gardenberg (Brazil/USA)
1996	The Secret Agent	Christopher Hampton (UK)
1997	Bent	Sean Mathais (UK/Japan)
1997	Kundun (AAN; GGN)	Martin Scorsese
1998	The Truman Show (GG)	Peter Weir
1999	The Eden Myth	Mark Edlitz
1999	Dracula (1931)	Tod Browning
2000	Armonie dell'estasi	Gianpaolo Tescari (Italy)
2002	Naqoyqatsi	Godfrey Reggio
2002	The Baroness and the Pig	Michael MacKenzie (Canada)
2002	The Hours (AAN; GGN; BAFTA)	Stephen Daldry (USA/UK)
2003	Fog of War: Eleven Lessons from the Life of Robert S. McNamara	Errol Morris
2004	Secret Window	David Koepp
2004	Taking Lives	D. J. Caruso (USA/Australia)
2004	The Origins of AIDS	Peter Chappell, Catherine Rex Eyrolle (Canada/Belgium/France)
2004	Undertow	David Gordon Green
2004	Going Upriver: The Long War of John Kerry	George Butler
2005	La moustache	Emmanuel Carrere (France)
2005	Faith's Corner	Darrell Roodt (So. Africa)
2005	Neverwas	Joshua Michael Stern (USA/Canada)
2005	The Giant Buddhas	Christian Frei (Switzerland)
2006	Tiger	P. Kocambasi, P. M. Starost (Germany)
2006	The Illusionist	Neil Burger (USA/Czech Republic)
2006	Abused	Charles Braverman
2006	Imaginary Friend	Marcello Daciano
2006	A Broken Sole	Antony Marsellis
2006	Notes on a Scandal (AAN)	Richard Eyre (UK)
2007	Hard-Hearted (aka Kremen)	Aleksei Mizgiryov (Russia)
2007	Cassandra's Dream	Woody Allen (USA/UK/France)
2007	No Reservations	Scott Hicks (USA/Australia)
2007	Glass: A Portrait of Philip Glass in Twelve Parts	Scott Hicks (Australia/USA)
2007	Animals in Love	Laurent Charbonnier (France)
2008	Objects and Memory	Brian Danitz, Jonathan Fein
2009	Les regrets	Cédric Kahn (France)
2009	Transcendent Man	Robert Barry Ptolemy
2010	Mr. Nice	Bernard Rose (UK/Spain)
2010	Astral City: A Spiritual Journey	Wagner de Assis (Brazil)
2011	Rebirth	James Whitaker
2011	Elena	Andrey Zvyagintsev (Russia)
2012	The Apostle	Fernando Cortizo (Spain)
2013	Visitors	Godfrey Reggio

GLASSER, Albert (1916–1998) A busy composer for radio, television, and over 150 B movies during the postwar years, he is particularly known for his sci-fi film scores and his many westerns, especially those featuring the legendary Cisco Kid.

Born in Chicago, Albert Glasser attended the University of Southern California on scholarship. After graduation he began his movie career in 1935 copying music for Warner Brothers, and got an informal education on screen scoring as he worked under some of the top composers of the 1930s and 1940s. He moved up to orchestrator when World War II broke out and arranged the music for short films and radio broadcasts put out by the U.S. War Department and the Office of War Information. In 1941 Glasser contributed original music to the scores of the Roy Rogers western *Bad Man of Deadwood* and the

Gene Autry vehicle *Under Fiesta Stars*. The next year he was sole composer for the Alaskan adventure *Klondike Kate* and in 1944 he scored his first of many sci-fi and horror movies, *The Monster Maker*. Because he was a fast worker who composed, orchestrated, and conducted screen music with little turnaround time, Glasser was in great demand by the smaller movie companies on Poverty Row. He was also hired by the major studios on occasion, but it was usually for low-budget westerns, crime dramas, or horror films. Many of the features Glasser scored were westerns, the most popular being a series of movies about the Robin Hood–like bandit the Cisco Kid (usually played by Duncan Renaldo) and his sidekick Pancho (often Martin Garraiaga). While he never got to score a movie classic, some of his films are noteworthy, including *The Cisco Kid Returns*, *Law of the Lash*, *In This Corner*, *The Valiant Hombre*, *I Shot Jesse James*, *The Daring Caballero*, *The Amazing Colossal Man*, *Huk!*, *Please Murder Me*, *The Boss*, *The Big Caper*, *Bailout at 43,000*, *The Cyclops*, *When Hell Broke Loose*, and *Confessions of an Opium Eater*. Glasser also scored many radio programs, including *Hopalong Cassidy* and *Tarzan*, and wrote music for dozens of early television shows, most memorably the small-screen version of *The Cisco Kid*. He retired from movies in 1962 but briefly returned later in the decade to score the Mexican movie *El tesoro de Atahualpa* and the schlock sci-fi thriller *The Cremators*. Glasser died in Los Angeles in 1998 at the age of eighty-two. Although little known to the public during his three-decade career, some of Glasser's best screen music was collected in 1978 and put on an LP titled *The Fantastic Film Music of Albert Glasser*, bringing him some recognition while he was still alive.

Listening to Glasser's screen music, one does not suspect that the films are low-budget B movies because the sound is often fully orchestrated and performed with confident relish. Perhaps Glasser was as clever and practical with his music budget as he was inventive with his composition and arrangements. His first horror effort, *The Monster Maker*, is unusually polished and full of surprises. He uses for his opening theme a merry march played on strings with brass fanfares and echoing motifs that have an ominous tone. Later there is a violin theme that is both morose and disconcerting, and sustained notes on an organ and mournful woodwind phrases are used to create suspense in this modern take on the Frankenstein idea. *The Amazing Colossal Man*, about a lieutenant (Glenn

Langan) exposed to plutonium who grows into a giant and terrorizes Las Vegas, is actually a better movie than it sounds and Glasser's score is often masterful. There is a percussive march theme with blaring brass that keeps returning to a six-note motif but is interrupted by a melancholy string passage that seems to weep in the higher register. An eerie motif with distorted strings and angry trumpets is used effectively throughout, and there is a bombastic section with squawking brass and horn fanfares that climb the scale with a destructive attitude. Another giant, this time with only one eye, causes havoc in Mexico in *The Cyclops*. Most memorable in this score is a grandiose processional that keeps trying to top itself with louder and higher notes. A variation of this can be heard in *Huk!*, one of Glasser's few dramas with no supernatural elements. Set in the Philippines, it is a romance-action movie about an uprising of guerrilla fighters called the Huk. Glasser's main theme is a frantic piece with brass and percussion racing each other in a furious manner as strings sweep up and down the scale.

Glasser's music for westerns is more conventional and offers few surprises. For the Cisco Kid films, he returns to a favorite theme, a Mexican habanera with a rapid pace and a spirited sense of glee. Often there is a sentimental theme that recalls a Spanish folk ballad and somewhere in the score is usually a proud march that quietly but firmly proclaims itself with gusto. One of his better non–Cisco Kid westerns is *Law of the Lash* with cowboy favorite Lash La Rue as a U.S. Marshal hunting down a gang of stagecoach bandits. The score opens with a domestic theme that conveys warmth, stability, and protection. There is a pokey traveling theme that mimics the plodding of a horse and a comic motif with bouncy reeds and strings. The fight scenes are scored with triumphant horns quickly reaching crescendos and a chase sequence with a Native American drumbeat and vigorous strings that seem to be running in place. It is all quite competent and better than grade B but, all the same, mostly expected.

What is full of the unexpected is Glasser's eclectic score for one of his last projects, *Confessions of an Opium Eater*. This 1962 Vincent Price film is not a horror tale but is filled with horrific scenes and sounds. The dapper adventurer Gilbert de Quincey (Price) rescues Caucasian and Asian females from the nineteenth-century San Francisco slave markets and encounters bizarre and dangerous characters along the way. Glasser's ambitious score uses jazz, classical forms, Asian pastiches, and even a touch of rock and roll. There is distorted electronic music, synthesized sound effects, echoing wavelength frequencies, and reverberating gongs, turning a period piece into a very modern opium dream. High-pitched Chinese strings are plucked in a delicate yet disturbing way, a passage for percussion and theremin glides up and down the scale with dizzying confusion, and a gentle Oriental theme played on Asian instruments transitions into a chaotic symphony of human screams and shouting trumpets. In various sections Glasser even uses the caterwauling of cats, the piercing squawks of parrots, the sound of water running, and the creaking of wooden ships. *Confessions of an Opium Eater* may or may not cross the line from B to A movie, but the score is definitely first class and a highlight in his long career.

Credits

(all films USA unless stated otherwise)

Year	Film	Director
1943	Klondike Kate	William Castle
1944	The Monster Maker (aka The Devil's Apprentice)	Sam Newfield
1944	The Contender	Sam Newfield
1944	Call of the Jungle	Phil Rosen
1945	The Kid Sister (aka All in the Family)	Sam Newfield
1945	The Cisco Kid Returns	John P. McCarthy
1945	The Cisco Kid in Old Mexico	Phil Rosen
1947	Law of the Lash	Ray Taylor
1947	Philo Vance Returns (aka Infamous Crimes)	William Beaudine
1947	Border Feud	Ray Taylor
1947	Killer at Large (aka Gangway for Murder)	William Beaudine
1947	The Gas House Kids in Hollywood	Edward L. Cahn
1947	Trail of the Mounties	Howard Bretherton
1948	The Cobra Strikes (aka Crime without Clues)	Charles Reisner
1948	Assigned to Danger	Budd Boetticher
1948	The Return of Wildfire	Ray Taylor, Paul Landres
1948	In This Corner	Charles Reisner
1948	Urubu: The Vulture People	George P. Breakston
1948	The Valiant Hombre	Wallace Fox
1948	Last of the Wild Horses	Robert L. Lippert, Paul Landres
1949	I Shot Jesse James	Samuel Fuller
1949	The Gay Amigo (aka The Daring Rogue)	Wallace Fox
1949	Grand Canyon	Paul Landres
1949	Omoo-Omoo the Shark God	Leon Lenard
1949	The Daring Caballero (aka Guns of Fury)	Wallace Fox
1949	Treasure of Monte Cristo	William Berke
1949	Satan's Cradle (aka The Devil's Den)	Ford Beebe
1949	Apache Chief	Frank McDonald
1949	Tough Assignment	William Beaudine
1950	Hollywood Varieties	Paul Landres
1950	The Girl from San Lorenzo	Derwin Abrahams
1950	Everybody's Dancin'	Will Jason
1950	I Shot Billy the Kid	William Berke
1950	Border Rangers	William Berke
1950	The Bandit Queen	William Berke
1951	Three Desperate Men (aka The Daltons Last Raid)	Sam Newfield
1951	Tokyo File 212	Dorrell and Stuart E. McGowan (USA/Japan)
1951	Oriental Evil	George P. Breakston, C. Ray Stahl
1951	Secrets of Beauty (aka Why Men Leave Home)	Erie C. Kenton
1951	The Bushwhackers (aka The Rebel)	Rod Amateau
1952	Geisha Girl	C. Ray Stahl

Year	Film	Director
1952	*Invasion U.S.A.*	Alfred E. Green
1953	*Problem Girls* (aka *The Velvet Cage*)	Ewald André Dupont
1953	*Port Sinister*	Harold Daniels
1953	*The Neanderthal Man*	Ewald André Dupont
1953	*Man of Conflict* (aka *My Dad*)	Hal R. Makelim
1953	*Paris Model* (aka *Nude at Midnight*)	Alfred E. Green
1953	*Captain John Smith and Pocahontas*	Lew Landers
1954	*Dragon's Gold*	Jack Pollexfen, Aubrey Wisberg
1955	*Murder Is My Beat* (aka *The Long Chance*)	Edgar G. Ulmer
1955	*Top of the World*	Lewis R. Foster
1956	*Please Murder Me*	Peter Godfrey
1956	*The Indestructible Man*	Jack Pollexfen
1956	*Huk!*	John Barnwell
1956	*The Boss*	Byron Haskin
1956	*Flight to Hong Kong*	Joseph M. Newman
1957	*Four Boys and a Gun*	William Berke
1957	*The Big Caper*	Robert Stevens
1957	*Bailout at 43,000*	Francis D. Lyon
1957	*Destination 60,000*	George Waggner
1957	*Monster from Green Hell*	Kenneth G. Crane
1957	*Beginning of the End*	Bert I. Gordon
1957	*The Buckskin Lady*	Carl K. Hittleman
1957	*The Cyclops*	Bert I. Gordon
1957	*Valerie*	Gerd Oswald
1957	*Street of Sinners*	William Berke
1957	*The Hired Gun*	Ray Nazarro
1957	*Motorcycle Gang*	Edward L. Cahn
1957	*The Amazing Colossal Man*	Bert I. Gordon
1957	*The Saga of the Viking Women and Their Voyage to the Waters of the Great Sea Serpent*	Roger Corman
1958	*Giant from the Unknown*	Richard E. Cunha
1958	*The Attack of the Puppet People* (aka *I Was a Teenage Doll*)	Bert I. Gordon
1958	*Snowfire*	Dorrell and Stuart E. McGowan
1958	*High School Confidential!* (aka *Young Hellions*)	Jack Arnold
1958	*War of the Colossal Beast*	Bert I. Gordon
1958	*Girl in the Woods*	Tom Gris
1958	*Teenage Cave Man*	Roger Corman
1958	*Earth vs. the Spider*	Bert I. Gordon
1958	*Cop Hater*	William Berke
1958	*When Hell Broke Loose*	Kenneth G. Crane
1958	*The Mugger*	William Berke
1959	*Night of the Quarter Moon* (aka *Flesh and Flame*)	Hugo Haas
1959	*The Beat Generation* (aka *This Rebel Age*)	Charles F. Haas
1959	*Inside the Mafia*	Edward L. Cahn
1960	*Oklahoma Territory*	Edward L. Cahn
1960	*The Boy and the Pirates*	Bert I. Gordon
1960	*The High Powered Rifle* (aka *Dark City*)	Maury Dexter
1960	*Tormented* (aka *Eye of the Dead*)	Bert I. Gordon
1961	*Kipling's Women*	Fred Hudson, Larry Smith
1961	*20,000 Eyes*	Jack Leewood
1962	*Confessions of an Opium Eater* (aka *Souls for Sale*)	Albert Zugsmith
1962	*Air Patrol*	Maury Dexter
1968	*El tesoro de Atahualpa*	Vincente Oroná (Mexico/Peru)
1972	*The Cremators*	Harry Essex

GLENNIE-SMITH, Nick (b. 1951) A British musician, conductor, choral arranger, and composer, he has also written or cowritten the scores for fifteen very different movies.

Nick Glennie-Smith was born in London and began an education in classical music as a boy of eight. But Glennie-Smith fell in love with rock and roll, so as a teenager he abandoned his studies to play keyboard and other instruments in rock bands. He eventually became an in-demand musician, working with such artists as Phil Collins, Paul McCartney, Tina Turner, and Cliff Richard. Glennie-Smith became involved with movies when he was hired as a soundtrack musician for the 1986 British film *When the Wind Blows*. Later he assisted Hans Zimmer on some scores, both as a composer and as a conductor. For *The Lion King* (1994), for example, he arranged and conducted the stirring choral sections of the film. Glennie-Smith was credited as co-composer with Zimmer for the scores for *Children of Glory*, *Point of No Return*, and *The Rock*. Among the films he has scored alone are *Home Alone 3*, *We Were Soldiers*, *Fire Down Below*, *The Man in the Iron Mask*, and *Secretariat*. He has also scored some TV movies and theme park attractions. Glennie-Smith remains a much-sought-after conductor in Britain and Hollywood, conducting everything from *The Simpsons Movie* (2007) to Academy Awards ceremonies.

Glennie-Smith's choral work on *The Lion King* cannot be overestimated. It is one of that score's triumphs, and Zimmer himself has credited the younger composer for his important contribution to the popular movie. It is difficult to discuss Glennie-Smith's contribution to the scores he cowrote with Zimmer and others. For the impressive score for the action film *The Rock*, Zimmer got a majority of the attention but it has been stated by people involved in the movie that most of the soundtrack music is by Glennie-Smith. So it is probably most efficient to look at the scores he worked on alone. Of these, perhaps the most accomplished is the music he wrote for *Secretariat*, a film about the famous racehorse. The main theme is a reverent, even awestruck, piece with low strings and regal percussion all slowly building into a rousing, propulsive passage heralded by a trumpet that suggests victory and

glory. Later sections of the score are elegant and restrained in a classical mode, the melody played by strings and a solo oboe with backup by French horn. For the race scenes, Glennie-Smith uses a piano with orchestra to get a more strident sound. If *Secretariat* has been accused of sugarcoating the true story of this racehorse, one might blame this gorgeous score. For the period adventure movie *The Man in the Iron Mask*, Glennie-Smith left restraint behind and came up with a passionate and sparkling score. The theme "Heart of a King" is heard on a solo flute at one point, a lush romantic surge at other times. For the action scenes, of which there are plenty, the percussive accents in the music come across as magnified sounds of swords in battle. For a masked ball, the sweeping music is as vigorous as it is regal. Although the composer uses a full-bodied choir at times, a trademark of his mentor Zimmer, Glennie-Smith's score for this swashbuckler has its own distinctive quality.

A weeping piccolo is the arresting feature of the main theme for *We Were Soldiers*, a movie about the early years of the Vietnam War. This is indeed a somber score but an entrancing one. While the action is often violent, the music is highly controlled and even remote, as if viewing the war from a distance. By contrast, the sprightly score for the comedy *Home Alone 3* is intimate and warm, surprising for such a broad farce. Some themes are delightfully frivolous, using everything from high-pitched chimes and low-pitched woodwinds. Others are mocking hard rock with a devilish tone. But it is the domestic theme that glows and helps turn the characters into more than plot pawns. For the misguided sci-fi movie *A Sound of Thunder*, Glennie-Smith provided the only real excitement on-screen with his propulsive score. The music is driven and even oppressive at times, allowing the unconvincing dinosaurs to create a little suspense. The more lyrical passages in the score are very satisfying with long musical lines and a touch of majesty. The movie sat on the shelf for three years before it was distributed and the soundtrack was never released. No wonder Glennie-Smith has worked less and less since 2006. Looking at his modest repertoire, one cannot help but be impressed. It is an eclectic collection of music and as laudable as it is varied. Official website: www.nickglennie-smith.com.

Credits

(all films USA unless stated otherwise)

Year	Film	Director
1996	Two If By Sea	Bill Bennett
1996	The Rock	Michael Bay
1997	Fire Down Below	Félix Enríquez Alcalá
1997	Home Alone 3	Raja Gosnell
1997	Cyclops, Baby	D. J. Caruso (USA/Canada)
1998	The Man in the Iron Mask	Randall Wallace (USA/France)
2000	Highlander: Endgame	Douglas Aarniokoski
2002	We Were Soldiers	Randall Wallace (USA/Germany)
2004	Ella Enchanted	Tommy O'Haver (USA/Ireland/UK)
2005	A Sound of Thunder	Peter Hyams (UK/USA/Germany/Czech Rep.)
2005	The Little Polar Bear 2: The Mysterious Island	Piet De Rycker, Thilo Rothkirch (Germany)
2006	Children of Glory	Krisztina Goda (Hungary)
2010	Secretariat	Randall Wallace
2013	A Belfast Story	Nathan Todd (Ireland)
2014	Heaven Is for Real	Randall Wallace

GLICKMAN, Mort (1898–1953) A prolific composer for B movies at Republic Pictures, he provided music for nearly two hundred films within a period of only twenty years.

Born in Chicago, according to local legend, Mort Glickman was the son of a producer of Yiddish theatre. Little is known about Glickman's life or career until 1939, when he showed up in Los Angeles and began working for Republic. He contributed music to a handful of movies that had several composers listed, but within a year he was the sole composer for most of the studio's low-budget output. Glickman was musical director for many films, and his music was often used by Republic in subsequent features. Since Glickman (and most of the other composers) rarely got screen credit, it is difficult to account for every movie for which he composed music; it is estimated that the number is well over 175. Many of these were musical westerns starring Roy Rogers, Gene Autry, or "Wild Bill" Elliott, and there were also many comedies featuring Judy Canova, Republic's top female star. On occasion Glickman got to score a mystery, gangster, war, or science fiction movie, but he never got to work on a big-budget project until *Invaders from Mars* in 1953. The famous Hollywood designer William Cameron Menzies made this creative sci-fi movie at Republic and technically the listed composer was Raoul Kraushaar with whom Glickman worked many times. It is now widely believed that Kraushaar wrote very little of the *Invaders from Mars* score and

that it is the work of Glickman. The success of this early and imaginative science fiction film might have opened up a whole new career for Glickman, but sadly he died from heart failure that same year; he was fifty-four years old.

The music for Glickman's musical westerns is very genial, tuneful, and atmospheric without being too dramatic. His 1940s and 1950s westerns are not the dark or brooding kind that would surface in the 1960s. The villains are given minor chords but most of the music is uncluttered and melodic. Sometimes a Spanish flavor seeps in and the occasional guitar, banjo, or harmonica can be heard, but most of the music is played by a full orchestra as in any other movie musical. Of course such a musical tone in the score made it easy for Rogers or Autry to break into a cowboy song without the transition being too jarring. The songs were not written by Glickman, although sometimes he used the melody in the opening credits or elsewhere in the movie. *Grand Canyon Trail*, a 1948 Rogers western about a ghost town and a silver mine, can serve as a good example of what Glickman did so many times for Republic. The opening is a fully orchestrated version of a folk song with horns behaving like harmonicas and the melody moving along at a brisk pace. The villain's theme is oddly tribal, suggesting an attack from the natives although there are none in the movie. A fistfight is scored with rousing brass, the romantic scenes with violins, and an ambush with squawking trombones. It is all very efficient if rather uninspired.

Glickman seems to have been more inspired by some of his nonwestern films. The caveman (or cavewoman) movie *Prehistoric Women* has a sci-fi-like theme with flutes racing up and down the scale as horns announce themselves proudly. The tribal drumming for the all-woman community is routine, but when a man is captured the score gets more interesting, even the drumming taking on more character. It is a pretty silly movie, but how Glickman must have relished getting away from all that sagebrush. *The Sword of Monte Cristo* is one of the few swashbucklers Glickman (or Republic) ever made. The score is often raucous and bombastic, then gently romantic at times. The score for the war adventure *Minesweeper* relies on "Anchors Aweigh" too much, but the suspenseful scenes involving the hazardous job of locating mines is scored effectively, the music descending as the men go below and the danger forecast with quivering strings. The cops and gamblers melodrama *Gambler's Choice* uses "Sidewalks of New York" a bit too often to remind viewers that the setting is 1900 Manhattan, but once the action and tension take over the music is sometimes very exciting. All these examples of Glickman's efforts to write exceptional music

were no preparation for what he achieved in *Invaders from Mars*. The 1953 sci-fi thriller is not only one of the first of its kind, it remains unique because the invasion, a quiet infiltration rather than a full frontal attack, is viewed through the point of view of a young boy (Jimmy Hunt). Glickman did not settle for anything routine this time around and the score is filled with wonderful touches. The movie opens with a brash call of trumpets with a wavering bass line that speeds up then slows down ominously. In some passages, violins sound almost like high-frequency waves as they restlessly struggle to break away from a repeating musical phrase. For scenes at the sandpit where the flying saucer lands and humans are swallowed up, an echoing choir is heard, an effect Glickman achieved in postproduction. This haunting use of ethereal voices becomes the theme for the Martians themselves. Such an effect was quite original in 1953 but would later become a sci-fi cliché. In fact, the entire score for *Invaders from Mars* would serve as the blueprint for sci-fi films in the 1950s and beyond. Glickman, a composer faced with mediocre movies throughout his whole career, finally had a chance to soar and he did not waste it.

Credits

(all films USA)

Year	Film	Director
1940	*Behind the News*	Joseph Santley
1940	*Bowery Boy*	William Morgan
1941	*Robin Hood of the Pecos*	Joseph Kane
1941	*Ridin' on a Rainbow*	Lew Landers
1941	*Arkansas Judge*	Frank McDonald
1941	*Petticoat Politics*	Erie C. Kenton
1941	*A Man Betrayed*	John H. Auer
1941	*Mr. District Attorney*	William Morgan
1941	*Sis Hopkins*	Joseph Santley
1941	*Rookies on Parade*	Joseph Santley
1941	*Lady from Louisiana*	Bernard Vorhaus
1941	*County Fair*	Frank McDonald
1941	*The Gay Vagabond*	William Morgan
1941	*Angels with Broken Wings*	Bernard Vorhaus
1941	*Puddin' Head*	Joseph Santley
1941	*Mountain Moonlight*	Nick Grinde
1941	*Hurricane Smith*	Bernard Vorhaus
1941	*Citadel of Crime*	George Sherman
1941	*Rags to Riches*	Joseph Kane
1941	*Bad Man of Deadwood*	Joseph Kane
1941	*Doctors Don't Tell*	Jacques Tourneur
1941	*Sailors on Leave*	Albert S. Rogell
1941	*Down Mexico Way*	Joseph Santley

Year	Film	Director
1941	*Public Enemies*	Albert S. Rogell
1941	*The Devil Pays Off*	John H. Auer
1941	*Tuxedo Junction*	Frank McDonald
1941	*Mr. District Attorney in the Carter Case*	Bernard Vorhaus
1942	*Pardon My Stripes*	John H. Auer
1942	*Cowboy Serenade*	William Morgan
1942	*A Tragedy at Midnight*	Joseph Santley
1942	*Sleepytime Gal*	Albert S. Rogell
1942	*Yokel Boy*	Joseph Santley
1942	*Shepherd of the Ozarks*	Frank McDonald
1942	*The Affairs of Jimmy Valentine*	Bernard Vorhaus
1942	*Spy Smasher*	William Witney
1942	*The Girl from Alaska*	Nick Grinde, William Witney
1942	*Moonlight Masquerade*	Jogn H. Auer
1942	*Perils of Nyoka*	William Witney
1942	*Joan of Ozark*	Joseph Santley
1942	*Hi, Neighbor*	Charles Lamont
1942	*The Sombrero Kid*	George Sherman
1942	*The Old Homestead*	Frank McDonald
1942	*Shadows on the Sage*	Lester Orlebeck
1942	*Bells of Capistrano*	William Morgan
1942	*King of the Mounties*	William Witney
1942	*Outlaws of Pine Ridge*	William Witney
1942	*Valley of Hunted Men*	John English
1942	*Hearty of the Golden West*	Joseph Kane
1942	*The Traitor Within*	Frank McDonald
1942	*Secrets of the Underground*	William Morgan
1942	*The Sundown Kid*	Elmer Clifton
1943	*Mountain Rhythm*	Frank McDonald
1943	*London Blackout Murders*	George Sherman
1943	*G-Men vs. the Black Dragon*	Spencer Bennet, William Witney
1943	*Thundering Trails*	John English
1943	*Dead Man's Gulch*	John English
1943	*Carson City Cyclone*	Howard Bretherton
1943	*The Purple V*	George Sherman
1943	*The Blocked Trail*	Elmer Clifton
1943	*King of the Cowboys*	Joseph Kane
1943	*The Mantrap*	George Sherman
1943	*Santa Fe Scouts*	Howard Bretherton
1943	*Calling Wild Bill Elliott*	Spencer Bennet
1943	*Daredevils of the West*	John English
1943	*Days of Old Cheyenne*	Elmer Clifton
1943	*Swing Your Partner*	Frank McDonald
1943	*Riders of the Rio Grande*	Howard Bretherton, Albert DeMond
1943	*False Faces*	George Sherman
1943	*The Man from Thunder River*	John English
1943	*Song of Texas*	Joseph Kane
1943	*Bordertown Gun Fighters*	Howard Bretherton
1943	*Fugitive from Sonora*	Howard Bretherton
1943	*Secret Service in Darkest Africa*	Spencer Bennet
1943	*Silver Spurs*	Joseph Kane
1943	*Black Hills Express*	John English
1943	*Beyond the Last Frontier*	Howard Bretherton
1943	*Wagon Tracks West*	Howard Bretherton
1943	*West Side Kid*	George Sherman
1943	*Headin' for God's Country*	William Morgan
1943	*Hoosier Holiday*	Frank McDonald
1943	*A Scream in the Dark*	George Sherman

Year	Film	Director
1943	The Man from the Rio Grande	Howard Bretherton
1943	The Masked Marvel	Spencer Bennet
1943	Minesweeper	William Berke
1943	Overland Mail Robbery	John English
1943	Mystery Broadcast	George Sherman
1943	Death Valley Manhunt	John English
1943	Canyon City	Spencer Bennet
1943	California Joe	Spencer Bennet
1943	Whispering Footsteps	Howard Bretherton
1943	Raiders of Sunset Pass	John English
1944	Pride of the Plains	Wallace Fox
1944	Hands Across the Border	Joseph Kane
1944	Captain America	Elmer Clifton, John English
1944	Beneath Western Skies	Spencer Bennet
1944	Mojave Firebrand	Spencer Bennet
1944	Hidden Valley Outlaws	Howard Bretherton
1944	The Laramie Trail	John English
1944	Outlaws of Santa Fe	Howard Bretherton
1944	Gambler's Choice	Frank McDonald
1944	Forty Thieves	Lesley Selander
1944	Song of Nevada	Joseph Kane
1944	Machine Gun Mama	Harold Young
1944	San Fernando Valley	John English
1944	Tahiti Night	Will Jason
1944	The Big Bonanza	George Archainbaud
1945	Manhunt of Mystery Island	Spencer Bennet, etc.
1945	Lone Texas Ranger	Spencer Bennet
1945	Flame of Barbary Coast	Joseph Kane
1945	Man from Oklahoma	Frank McDonald
1945	Gangs of the Waterfront	George Blair
1945	The Purple Monster Strikes	Spencer Bennet, Fred C. Brannon
1945	Along the Navajo Trail	Frank McDonald
1945	Sunset in El Dorado	Frank McDonald
1945	Don't Fence Me In	John English
1946	The Phantom Rider	Spencer Bennet, Fred C. Brannon
1946	Home on the Range	R. G. Springsteen
1946	King of the Forest Rangers	Spencer Bennet, Fred C. Brannon
1946	Passkey to Danger	Lesley Selander
1946	Man from Rainbow Valley	R. G. Springsteen
1946	Traffic in Crime	Lesley Selander
1946	Red River Renegades	Thomas Carr
1946	Daughter of Don Q	Spencer Bennet, Fred C. Brannon
1946	The Inner Circle	Philip Ford
1946	The Invisible Informer	Philip Ford
1946	The Mysterious Mr. Valentine	Philip Ford
1946	The Crimson Ghost	Fred C. Brannon, William Witney
1946	The Magnificent Rogue	Albert S. Rogell
1946	Santa Fe Uprising	R. G. Springsteen
1946	Lone Star Moonlight	Ray Nazarro
1946	Stagecoach to Denver	R. G. Springsteen
1947	Son of Zorro	Spencer Bennet, Fred C. Brannon
1947	Last Frontier Uprising	Lesley Selander
1947	Vigilantes of Boomtown	R. G. Springsteen
1947	Homesteaders of Paradise Valley	R. G. Springsteen
1947	Spoilers of the North	Richard Sale
1947	Oregon Trail Scouts	R. G. Springsteen
1947	Web of Danger	Philip Ford
1947	Rustlers of Devil's Canyon	R. G. Springsteen

Year	Film	Director
1947	*Blackmail*	Lesley Selander
1947	*Jesse James Rides Again*	Fred C. Brannon, Thomas Carr
1947	*Marshal of Cripple Creek*	R. G. Springsteen
1947	*Along the Oregon Trail*	R. G. Springsteen
1947	*Under Colorado Skies*	R. G. Springsteen
1947	*Bandits of Dark Canyon*	Philip Ford
1948	*Slippy McGee*	Albert H. Kelley
1948	*G-Men Never Forget*	Fred C. Brannon, Yakima Canutt
1948	*Oklahoma Badlands*	Yakima Canutt
1948	*Madonna of the Desert*	George Blair
1948	*Lightnin' in the Forest*	George Blair
1948	*California Firebrand*	Philip Ford
1948	*The Bold Frontiersman*	Philip Ford
1948	*Dangers of the Canadian Mounted*	Fred C. Brannon, Yakima Canutt
1948	*King of the Gamblers*	George Blair
1948	*The Timber Trail*	Philip Ford
1950	*Prehistoric Women*	Gregg C. Tallas
1950	*The Sword of Monte Cristo*	Maurice Geraghty
1951	*Bride of the Gorilla*	Curt Siodmak
1951	*Elephant Stampede*	Ford Beebe
1951	*The Longhorn*	Lewis D. Collins
1952	*Waco*	Lewis D. Collins
1952	*Fargo*	Lewis D. Collins
1952	*Untamed Women*	W. Merle Connell
1952	*Bomba and the Jungle Girl*	Ford Beebe
1952	*The Maverick*	Thomas Carr
1953	*Invaders from Mars*	William Cameron Menzies

GOLD, Ernest (1921–1999) An Austrian-born composer who scored many B pictures in the 1940s and 1950s, he found fame in the 1960s in television and with a series of popular movies, many for director-producer Stanley Kramer.

Born Ernst Siegmund Golder in Vienna, his father was a violinist, his mother a singer, and his grandfather president of the revered Viennese Society of Friends of Music. Gold started taking piano lessons at the age of six and soon after was composing his own music. As a teenager he loved going to the movies just to listen to the music and professed an interest in writing soundtrack scores someday. Gold began his studies at the State Academy of Music but in 1938, when Austria united with Nazi Germany, the Jewish Golder family fled from Europe and settled in New York City. It was there that his compositions were performed at Carnegie Hall and on NBC Radio, but critics found his music too romantic for the new trends in modern music. So Gold moved to California in 1945 and found work as an orchestrator, arranger, and occasionally composer for B movies. For a dozen years Gold struggled,

working on mediocre films with little satisfaction or recognition. He did get to score some popular western musicals for Roy Rogers, Dale Evans, and Gene Autry, but all the attention was on the cowboy songs written by others. His first quality project was the 1958 racial drama *The Defiant Ones* directed by Stanley Kramer. The two worked together on six subsequent movies: *On the Beach*, *Inherit the Wind*, *Judgment at Nuremberg*, *The Secret of Santa Vittoria*, *Ship of Fools*, and *It's a Mad, Mad, Mad, Mad World*. Of Gold's films with other directors, the most notable is the epic *Exodus*. This last went on to become his most celebrated screen score, with many best-selling recordings in different formats. His other noteworthy movies include *The Young Philadelphians*, *The Runner Stumbles*, *Fun with Dick and Jane*, and *Too Much, Too Soon*. Gold also arranged and conducted the scores of several movies scored by others. He began his television career in the late 1950s, writing music for such series as *M Squad*, *Wagon Train*, *Hawaii Five-O*, and *Alfred Hitchcock Presents*. Gold also scored a half dozen TV movies and the popular miniseries based on Gore Vidal's *Lincoln* (1988). His con-

(Iw-521)-149

ERNEST GOLD. Because he scored everything from intimate dramas to giant spectacles, Gold was never labeled by Hollywood as the composer for only certain kinds of movies. His score for the potent drama *Inherit the Wind* (1960) included some traditional hymns and spirituals, two of them sung on the soundtrack by a young Leslie Uggams (pictured with Gold). *United Artists / Photofest © United Artists* cert music includes a piano concerto, a string quartet, and a piano sonata. After *Lincoln*, Gold retired from movies and television but continued to conduct orchestras in the Los Angeles area until he suffered a stroke and died at the age of seventy-seven. Although he worked in Hollywood for forty years, Gold's most productive period lasted only ten years, roughly from 1958 to 1968. During that time he wrote some superb scores, mostly for very demanding dramas. He is considered the last of a generation of European romantic composers who fled the Nazis and provided superior music for Hollywood. His legacy was continued in his son with singer Marni Nixon, Andrew Gold (1951–2011), an accomplished musician, singer, and songwriter who had some hit songs and worked with the top performers of the 1980s and 1990s.

Arguably Gold's finest work is the evocative and stirring score for *Exodus*. While many were displeased with Otto Preminger's screen version of Leon Uris's enthralling novel about the early years of Israel, the music was far from disappointing. The blaring trumpets suggest the Old Testament, but then the main theme has enough modern touches that the post–World War II era is well represented. The *Exodus* theme is so fervent that one can easily understand how it became a powerful anthem for Israel and later, with a lyric by Pat Boone, a popular song. But there is much more to the score than the famous main title and the way it reenters throughout the movie. The action scenes are helped by some dramatic scoring featuring furious drums, restless trumpets, and screaming violins. The love theme is exotic and ravishing, while, to add to the topicality, the Israeli national anthem "Hatikvah" appears in some passages. *Exodus* looks ahead optimistically to a new nation; *Ship of Fools* forecasts the Holocaust. The passengers on a ship traveling from Vera Cruz to Germany is a somewhat forced microcosm of pre–World War II ideas and beliefs. The opening theme is a Latin frolic that has some dissonance and hard chords to suggest this is not a holiday cruise. Viennese musical pastiche is heard later in the score, not only to reflect the German destination but the film's ironic statement about how such a civilized nation can create so much destruction. The love theme for the doomed ship's doctor (Oskar Werner) and a political exile (Simone Signoret) is lyrical

in a European way, just shy of operetta schmaltz. There is also some fiery Spanish music, associated with the Latin dance troop on board, that has some masterful alternations in rhythm. *Judgment at Nuremberg* is Kramer's postwar drama about the trial of four Nazi officers for crimes against humanity, a sort of companion piece to *Ship of Fools*. Gold opens the movie with an oppressive roll of drums that sounds like explosions then launches into a robust German march song. This ironic main theme is soon replaced by somber, minor-key music that takes its cue from the bombed-out city of Nuremberg. For a scene in a cafe, there is a lighthearted waltz that seems to refute that any evil ever occurred.

To examine Gold's other side, two comedies are worth looking at. *The Secret of Santa Vittoria* is a merry piece about a small Italian town whose residents hide their huge inventory of wine from the German army. The main theme is a sprightly Italianate folk tune that ignores its World War II setting. In the movie's most memorable scene, hundreds of townspeople pass thousands of bottles of wine along a human conveyor belt. The main theme is reprised for this scene but now with just a touch of the military to it, suggesting the defiant spirit of locals. As time is running out, the bottles move faster, the music increases in tension, punctuated by the crash of a fallen bottle or two. *It's a Mad, Mad, Mad, Mad World* is Kramer's comedy on an epic scale. The score boasts an overture, an intermission, an entr'acte, and exit music. It also has a delightful title theme with a circus flavor. All the orchestra's instruments seem to be laughing as they flutter and waltz up and down the scale. Gold's music also conveys the idea that this is going to be a big comedy, something akin to the comic equivalent of *Exodus*. With a lyric by Mack David, the main theme was turned into an Oscar-nominated song, but the words are not as funny as the music itself. This theme is reprised throughout the long score, but there is also a sparkling Spanish passage as the huge cast romps across Southern California as if they were at a frantic festival. Maybe this comedy and *Exodus* have something else in common besides their size. Gold scores each with bold and vigorous strokes of panache. How unfortunate that he was given so few opportunities to do so.

Credits

(all films USA unless stated otherwise; * for Best Song)

Year	Film	Director
1945	*The Girl of the Limberlost*	Mel Ferrer
1946	*Smooth as Silk*	Charles Barton
1946	*The Falcon's Alibi*	Ray McCarey
1946	*G.I. War Brides*	George Blair
1947	*Lighthouse*	Frank Wisbar
1947	*Bells of San Angelo*	William Witney
1947	*Saddle Pals*	Lesley Selander
1947	*The Trespasser*	George Blair
1947	*Springtime in the Sierras*	William Witney
1947	*Robin Hood of Texas*	Lesley Selander
1947	*Wyoming*	Joseph Kane
1947	*Philo Vance's Secret Mission*	Reginald Le Borg
1947	*Exposed*	George Blair
1948	*The Main Street Kid*	R. G. Springsteen
1948	*The Gay Ranchero*	William Witney
1948	*G-Men Never Forget*	Fred C. Brannon, Yakima Canutt
1948	*Old Los Angeles*	Joseph Kane
1948	*Under California Stars*	William Witney
1948	*The Gallant Legion*	Joseph Kane
1951	*Unknown World*	Terry O. Morse
1953	*Jennifer*	Joel Newton
1953	*Man Crazy*	Irving Lerner
1954	*The Other Woman*	Hugo Haas
1955	*The Naked Street*	Maxwell Shane
1956	*Unidentified Flying Objects: The True Story of Flying Saucers*	Winston Jones
1956	*Edge of Hell*	Hugo Haas
1956	*Running Target*	Marvin R. Weinstein
1957	*The Iron Sheriff*	Sidney Salkow
1957	*Affair in Havana*	Laslo Benedek
1957	*Man on the Prowl*	Art Napoleon
1958	*The Screaming Skull*	Alex Nicol
1958	*Too Much, Too Soon*	Art Napoleon
1958	*Wink of an Eye*	Winston Jones
1958	*The Defiant Ones*	Stanley Kramer
1958	*Tarzan's Fight for Life*	H. Bruce Humberstone
1959	*The Young Philadelphians*	Vincent Sherman
1959	*Battle of the Coral Sea*	Paul Wendkos
1959	*On the Beach* (AAN; GG)	Stanley Kramer
1960	*Inherit the Wind*	Stanley Kramer
1960	*Exodus* (AA; GGN)	Otto Preminger
1961	*A Fever in the Blood*	Vincent Sherman
1961	*The Last Sunset*	Robert Aldrich
1961	*Judgment at Nuremberg*	Stanley Kramer
1962	*Pressure Point*	Hubert Cornfield, Stanley Kramer
1963	*A Child Is Waiting*	John Cassavetes
1963	*It's a Mad, Mad, Mad, Mad World* (AAN; AAN*)	Stanley Kramer
1965	*Ship of Fools*	Stanley Kramer
1969	*The Secret of Santa Vittoria* (AAN; GGN; GGN*)	Stanley Kramer
1975	*The Wild McCullochs*	Max Baer Jr.
1977	*Cross of Iron*	Sam Peckinpah (UK/W. Germany)
1977	*Fun with Dick and Jane*	Ted Kotcheff
1979	*Good Luck, Miss Wyckoff*	Marvin J. Chomsky
1979	*The Runner Stumbles*	Stanley Kramer
1980	*Tom Horn*	William Wiard
1982	*Safari 3000*	Harry Hurwitz

GOLDENTHAL, Elliot (b. 1954) An innovative composer for the concert hall and the theatre, he has scored two dozen films, several of them stylized pieces directed by Julie Taymor or Joel Schumacher, as well as five movies for Neil Jordan.

Elliot Goldenthal was born in Brooklyn, New York, the son of a housepainter and a seamstress, and began performing and writing music at an early age. By the time he was in high school, Goldenthal was playing in rock bands and composing serious music, including a ballet that was produced when he was only fourteen. Goldenthal studied composition at the Manhattan School of Music then began his career composing music in a unique style that mixed various music forms together in an imaginative way. Over the years he has found acclaim for his oratorio *Fire Water Paper*, two brass quintets, a scherzo, his ballet *Othello*, and his opera *Grendel*. Goldenthal has also written scores for various theatre pieces, including *The King Stag, The Green Bird, Juan Darien: A Carnival Mass*, and *The Transposed Heads*, the last three staged by Taymor. He first worked in movies when he scored the low-budget drama *Cocaine Cowboys* in 1979. A decade later he found more recognition for his score for *Drugstore Cowboy*. Although Goldenthal's work in movies has been sporadic, he has managed to score many unusual films as well as conventional Hollywood dramas. For the Irish director Jordan, he wrote music for the stylized *Interview with the Vampire* and *In Dreams* as well as scores for the realistic dramas *Michael Collins, The Butcher Boy*, and *The Good Thief*. With Schumacher he scored such popular films as *A Time to Kill* and *Batman Forever*. Perhaps his most experimental scores have been in Taymor's *Across the Universe, Frida, Titus*, and *The Tempest*. Goldenthal's other notable movies include *S.W.A.T., Cobb, Pet Sematary, Sphere, Alien 3*, and *Public Enemies*. He has also scored some TV movies, most memorably *Fool's Fire* (1992) and *Roswell* (1994).

Although Goldenthal might be labeled an avant-gardist, his music is often very accessible, both in the concert hall and on-screen. His blending of various styles and using instruments in offbeat ways might make his music cerebral but never alienating. His use of jazz with classical forms, the way his harmonies might suddenly become atonal, and the manner in which his instruments seem to whine are all very effective and exciting, particularly when matched with equally exciting visuals on the screen. Goldenthal's first score to fully explore his taste for the experimental was *Interview with the Vampire*, a Gothic horror film set in contemporary San Francisco. While the movie met with mixed reviews, Goldenthal's score was roundly praised. The theme for Lestat (Tom Cruise) is a minor-key tarantella played on strings and harpsichord, the mood being frivolous and menacing. In another passage, a boys choir sings a creepy baroque chant with dissonant accompaniment on organ and strings, and there is a hesitant waltz in which a violin seems to be weeping. Perhaps most bewitching is the theme titled "Madeleine's Lament," a sorrowful series of descending notes played on shrill strings. Violent and suspenseful in another way is *Alien 3*, which Goldenthal opens with an echoing Agnus Dei sung by a solo boy's voice. As expected in this sci-fi series, a lot of electronic instrumentation is used but often the music has a classical foundation. The film even ends with a symphonic adagio that seems to drift off into space. Goldenthal finds fresh ways to musicalize *Batman Forever*, using mechanical noise against a sweeping orchestra filled with dark crescendos. For one chase scene the jazz music is filtered through a synthesizer so that the notes appear to melt. A passage titled "Fledermausmarschmusik" scurries about like a bat while another track is so mournful that even the electric instruments sound like they are too weary to go on. The psychological thriller *In Dreams* is filled with dissonant music yet much of this disturbing score is fascinating. There is an entrancing nocturne on a piano that plays variations of a phrase without resolving itself. A passage aptly titled "Agitato Dolorosa" is played by strings that struggle to break away from the same musical phrase. Even the elegy at the end of the film is restless; the nightmare never seems to end.

Goldenthal has scored only a few conventionally plotted and realistically portrayed movies. Perhaps the best of them is *Michael Collins*, a biopic about the founder of the Irish Republican Army. Director Jordan and Goldenthal wanted to avoid a traditionally Irish score in order to emphasize the tragic nature of the story. Although some Celtic folk songs are quoted, the music does not have the familiar sound of the Emerald Isle. For the dramatic opening of the film showing the Easter Uprising of 1916, Goldenthal opts for a mixture of Gaelic voices, a wooden flute, and a full orchestra performing in a minor key. The waltz theme for Kitty Kiernan (Julia Roberts) is unbridled in its romanticism, while the funeral of Collins (Liam Neeson) is very traditional, its deep descending chords finding power and strength rather than defeat. Another period biopic, *Cobb*, is a very unsentimental look at the life of baseballer Ty Cobb (Tommy Lee Jones) and Goldenthal keeps sentiment out of his music. The main theme consists of jittery strings against a solo trumpet in a minor key. A full orchestra is used for other themes, but the dissonance keeps everything from being too symphonic. At one point the instruments are so distorted that when a melody emerges it is cockeyed. A more contemporary drama, the racially charged *A Time to Kill*, has a score that avoids the conventional with squealing violins and squawking horns that intrude on the long, flowing musical lines. There is a restlessness in the music that matches the tension in the small town where a rape has led to a murder. There are blues sections in which a solo trumpet seems to weep and other passages where the brass sound like they are shouting in protest.

Many would agree that Goldenthal's most interesting scores are those he wrote for the Taymor movies. Because her approach to moviemaking, whether it is Shakespeare or the Beatles, is very visual with startling images on the screen, the music cannot be timid. The most praised Taymor-Goldenthal collaboration is the biopic *Frida* about the Mexican artist Frida Kahlo (Salma Hayek) and her tempestuous relationship with artist Diego Rivera (Alfred Molina). Taymor used Frida's colorful palate for the look of the movie and Goldenthal's score is equally vibrant. He avoids clichéd Spanish atmospheric music and instead writes lusty folk music, vigorous Spanish guitar solos, a sensual tango danced by two women,

and a beautiful love theme that seems so cautious about love that it pulls back whenever you expect it to resolve. The two Shakespeare films that Taymor and Goldenthal collaborated on are uniquely different. The *Titus* score opens with a male choir in a rousing Carl Orff style, the Latin chanting and the busy instrumentals at war with each other. A Roman procession becomes a montage of clanking machinery and synthesized echoes. Battle scenes bring out trumpet fanfares against repetitive strings while a religious rite is scored with a solo boy's voice that is picked up by a morose string section. For a Roman orgy, the music swings in a Big Band manner but a pastoral piece on fluttering flutes sounds primitive and simple. *Titus* is a disturbing and controversial film that turns Shakespeare upside down; the score is similarly provocative. *The Tempest*, on the other hand, is fairly conventional once one gets used to the magician-patriarch played by Helen Mirren as Prospera. Yet Goldenthal's score is far from conventional, opening with New Wave electronic sounds and a groggy rendition of "O Mistress Mine" sung by Reeve Carney. There is plenty of rock and roll in the score, along with tribal drumming, magical synthesized vibrations, electric organ with the vibrato at full throttle, some hot jazz, and a touch of reggae. *The Tempest* has often inspired artists to search for new ways to present this Elizabethan sci-fi piece. The Taymor-Goldenthal version is no exception. But such experimentation can be found in all of Goldenthal's music. Aside from Philip Glass, has anyone else brought such strange and unorthodox music to the screen?

Credits

(all films USA unless stated otherwise)

Year	Film	Director
1979	*Cocaine Cowboys*	Ulli Lommel
1980	*Blank Generation*	Ulli Lommel
1989	*Pet Sematary*	Mary Lambert
1989	*Drugstore Cowboy*	Gus Van Sant
1991	*Grand Isle*	Mary Lambert
1992	*Alien 3*	David Fincher
1993	*Demolition Man*	Marco Brambilla
1994	*Golden Gate*	John Madden
1994	*Interview with the Vampire: The Vampire Chronicles* (AAN; GGN)	Neil Jordan
1994	*Cobb*	Ron Shelton
1995	*Batman Forever*	Joel Schumacher (USA/UK)

Year	Film	Director
1995	Voices (aka Voices from a Locked Room)	Malcolm Clarke (UK/USA/Canada)
1995	Heat	Michael Mann
1996	A Time to Kill	Joel Schumacher
1996	Michael Collins (AAN; GGN)	Neil Jordan (UK/Ireland/USA)
1997	Batman & Robin	Joel Schumacher (USA/UK)
1997	The Butcher Boy	Neil Jordan
1998	Sphere	Barry Levinson
1999	In Dreams	Neil Jordan
1999	Titus	Julie Taymor (Italy/USA/UK)
2001	Final Fantasy: The Spirits Within	Hironobu Sakaguchi, Motonori Sakakibara (USA/Japan)
2002	Frida (AA; AAN*; GG)	Julie Taymor (USA/Canada/Mexico)
2002	The Good Thief	Neil Jordan (France/UK/Ireland)
2003	S.W.A.T.	Clark Johnson
2007	Across the Universe	Julie Taymor (USA/UK)
2009	Public Enemies	Michael Mann
2010	The Tempest	Julie Taymor

GOLDSMITH, Jerry (1929–2004) A prolific American composer for radio, television, and Hollywood with 167 feature films to his credit, he was also one of the most versatile composers in postwar America, scoring everything from westerns and horror flicks to historical epics and science fiction favorites.

Jerrald King Goldsmith was born in Pasadena, California, the son of an engineer and a schoolteacher. As a child, Goldsmith studied piano with notable teachers and was headed for a career as a concert pianist. But at the age of sixteen he was so impressed with Miklós Rózsa's score for the thriller *Spellbound* that he later enrolled at the University of Southern California to study under Rózsa and later at Los Angeles City College. Goldsmith worked as a singing coach, accompanist, choral director, and assistant conductor before he was hired to score radio series at CBS. By 1955 he scored his first television program, the live series *Climax!*, and in 1957 he wrote his first screen score for the low-budget western *Black Patch*. Goldsmith's first notable film music was heard in the 1962 western *Lonely Are the Brave* and later that same year he was nominated for an Oscar for his score for the biopic *Freud*. Once he was on the A-list of Hollywood composers, Goldsmith was offered many movies to score, and he took on a tremendous amount of them, even as he continued to compose for television. Although his music was consistently accomplished, many of the movies he scored were inferior. For each outstanding Goldsmith project there were a half dozen that were critical and box office failures.

In the 1960s he scored such memorable movies as *Lilies of the Field*, *The List of Adrian Messenger*, *Seven Days in May*, *The Flim-Flam Man*, *A Patch of Blue*, *The Detective*, *The Sand Pebbles*, and *Planet of the Apes*. This last film was a collaboration with director Franklin J. Schaffner; the two men worked together on six other films, and many feel that Goldsmith's finest work was with Schaffner, as with *Patton*, *Papillon*, *Islands in the Stream*, and *The Boys from Brazil*. Notable Goldsmith scores from the 1970s and 1980s include *Chinatown*, *The Wind and the Lion*, *The Omen*, *Lionheart*, *Logan's Run*, *Alien*, *MacArthur*, *Poltergeist*, *Star Trek: The Motion Picture*, *Star Trek V: The Final Frontier*, and *Gremlins*. Although he remained busy in the 1990s and the early years of the new century, Goldsmith scored mostly mediocre movies. The exceptions include *Total Recall*, *Basic Instinct*, *L.A. Confidential*, *First Knight*, *Six Degrees of Separation*, and *The Mummy*. Throughout his career Goldsmith was fortunate to score films that launched a series of sequels which he would score as well. *Star Trek: The Motion Picture*, the first installment on the big screen, was followed by other *Star Trek* movies, *First Blood* led to the Rambo series, *Planet of the Apes* had a handful of sequels, *Our Man Flint* introduced a series of dapper spy movies, and *The Omen* returned in different forms over the decades. Goldsmith never totally abandoned television. His small-screen credits include the series *Perry Mason*, *Playhouse 90*, *Twilight Zone*, *Thriller*, *Gunsmoke*, *The Man from U.N.C.L.E.*, *The Waltons*, and *Police Story*, as well as such

JERRY GOLDSMITH. With an impressive Hollywood career lasting nearly fifty years, Goldsmith and his music always seemed to be in fashion. More importantly, his music is still thrilling. Here he is conducting the soundtrack recording for the action movie *The River Wild* (1994). *Universal Pictures / Photofest © Universal Pictures*

significant TV movies and miniseries as *The Expendables* (1962), *Crosscurrent* (1971), *The Homecoming: A Christmas Story* (1971), *The Red Pony* (1973), *A Tree Grows in Brooklyn* (1974), *QB VII* (1974), *Contact on Cherry Street* (1977), *Masada* (1981), and *The Bogie Man* (1992). Like many screen composers, Goldsmith also wrote for the concert stage and some of his symphonies and chamber pieces were performed by renowned orchestras across the country. He also wrote fireworks music, the musical theme for Universal Pictures' logo, and the soundtrack for the Disney theme park attraction Soarin'.

Because Goldsmith wrote so many kinds of music for so many movies, it is difficult to categorize his style. He tends to be more influenced by modern music than romanticism, yet there are scores that embrace a classical sound. Goldsmith cited Igor Stravinsky, Aaron Copland, Béla Bartók, and other twentieth-century composers as his inspiration, yet he stated that he is equally influenced by movie composers, Rózsa and Bernard Herrmann in particular. Just as important, Goldsmith was a relentless experimenter. He not only utilized all kinds of music and instruments, he made some notable innovations along the way and created totally original sounds for motion picture scores. For the sci-fi classic *Planet of the Apes*, Goldsmith had the orchestra re-create the grunting sounds of apes, instructed the horns to play without mouthpieces, used steel mixing bowls for the percussion section, and employed an echoplex to delay the sounds and give the illusion of an echo. The main theme for the movie is neither melodic nor harmonic, but a three-note motif played first on a flute then picked up by violins while a piano and percussion instruments add all kinds of sharp noises. Without actually imitating apes, the piece captures a primitive kind of animal frenzy. When the astronauts first discover the land of the apes, the sound of triumphal brass chords is stirring as they gaze upon a waterfall and the music seems to cascade with the tumbling water. An attack by the ape army is scored with rigorous brass so out of control that the result is a kind of frantic chaos. Looking back at this score decades later, it is even more impressive when one realizes that Goldsmith created all these unique sounds without the use of a synthesizer or computer. *Planet of the Apes* made such an impact on screen music that sci-fi films would never be scored the same. The high-tech, avant-garde sci-fi score was born.

A similar echo technique was also used effectively in the biopic *Patton*, the World War II epic about the famous general. The main theme is a three-note trumpet motif in march time with an organ and drum underscoring. A piccolo then plays the melody with orchestral accompaniment. This is a rather striking if expected piece of music for a war film. What makes the theme distinctive is the way the three notes echo, giving the military sound a repeating effect, something that parallels the belief George Patton (George C. Scott) has in reincarnation. Variations of the main theme are heard throughout the movie, the echoing trumpets reentering at crucial points in the narrative. Another World War II epic, *MacArthur*, is less satisfying, perhaps because General Douglas MacArthur (Gregory Peck) was not as interesting a character as Patton. All the same, Goldsmith's score is commendable. The main march theme is played on trumpets with a fervent sense of pride. What is unusual is the way the string accents are plucked on the bass strings inside a piano rather than played pizzicato on string instruments. Such musical "tricks" in these and other Goldsmith scores are far from gimmicky. Whatever style or techniques he used grew out of the film itself. This is the essence of Goldsmith's versatility.

Chinatown, a modern attempt at a 1930s film noir, is set in the past and Goldsmith's score remains true to that prewar sound in spirit if not in practice. One theme has sustained electronic strings, a bell that sounds like a busy signal, brushes and other odd percussion, and a bluesy trumpet. Another track is mostly eerie sound effects that reverberate as low strings break in unexpected points. The love theme is a slow jazz piece with a mellow trumpet, languid strings, and piano embellishments. Another passage features a lonesome trumpet with harp and violin phrases that seem tentative if not downright frightened. The orchestration for *Chinatown* is also unique. Goldsmith does not use a full orchestra but instead an odd ensemble that includes four pianos, four harps, and a solo trumpet. This is noir music with a modern slant. Two other period movies, set in the Middle Ages no less, also have a modern sensibility in their music. *Lionheart* is about a young knight (Eric Stoltz) who gathers up a regiment of homeless children to follow King Richard to the Crusades. Horns and strings quietly proclaim the main theme, which has a solemn but heartfelt tone. As a traditional orchestra is added and the piece turns into a stirring march, synthesized instruments and electronic percussion are added, giving the music a very contemporary sound. A circus-like passage is played on electronic keyboard while conventional strings swirl around it, and the love theme is a graceful piece that mixes electronic and traditional strings. *First Knight*, a retelling of the legend of King Arthur (Sean Connery), Guinevere (Julia Ormond), and Sir Lancelot (Richard Gere), has a ravishing score that avoids any period instruments or attempts to sound authentic. The theme for Camelot is a slow and majestic serenade with restrained horns and sustained strings that takes a while before it builds up enough passion to become a full-fledged anthem. There is a captivating march that flows more like a romantic ballad than a military piece, particularly when a solo oboe is featured. There are some choral passages in the score, none more striking than the track titled "Arthur's Farewell" in which a vibrant mixed chorus sings an up-tempo hymn in Latin and some electronic and conventional chords and phrases follow their own restless tempo.

For a composer who scored several films each year, Goldsmith was still able to come up with surprises on occasion. *Papillon* has no music under the opening credits nor during much of the first third of the film. Not until the two prisoners (Dustin Hoffman and Steve McQueen) escape from Devil's Island does the music come in, a simple waltz heard on an accordion that is embellished more and more as they return to civilization. A solo flute is featured in a lovely passage which aches with loneliness until an oboe and piano introduce a more confident section and the strings take the cue and move into a sweeping rhapsody. There is also a French sidewalk cafe ditty on synthesized accordion that keeps a steady pace but has a mournful subtext. A short but exhilarating passage takes the flight of a butterfly as its inspiration; various instruments take turns fluttering up and down the scale in a rapid and giddy manner. The medical thriller *Coma*, about a young doctor (Genevieve Bujold) who discovers that her hospital is purposely putting patients into comas in order to sell their body parts, also has no music for much of the first half. Not until the doctor realizes that she is being watched do the strings and timpani come in and the suspense builds. Goldsmith used four pianos (some played on the keys, other plucked directly on the strings) in the recording of the *Coma* score, so it often has a strident tone. There is a memorable theme in which the strings move from a romantic mood to a sinister one as various unconventional

percussion and synthesized sounds are heard, in particular creepy glissandos on electric strings and piano. A more psychological suspense is heard in Goldsmith's score for *Freud*, John Huston's skillful biopic in which Montgomery Clift plays the famous Viennese doctor. The main theme is a curious mix of propulsive high notes on plucked strings and low, moody horns that suggest mystery and even danger. Even more arresting is the music for a dream sequence in which synthesized instruments echo and linger as they play a sorrowful gavotte in slow motion. The music for *Freud* is often dissonant, the brass battling the strings to convey the tortured conscience. A similarly offbeat sound is created in the psychodrama *Seconds* about a middle-aged businessman (John Randolph) who undergoes an unusual surgery that transforms him into a younger man (Rock Hudson) with a different personality. The results are unpleasant, to say the least, and the film is very tense and uncomfortable. Goldsmith's score is also uncomfortable. The opening theme is a jarring piece in which a pipe organ's minor chords are contrasted by a violin solo, creating an unconventional funeral march. Other parts of the score rely on electronic echoes, high-frequency sounds, and strings that could be shrill or growling.

Much less neurotic are the lyrical scores Goldsmith wrote for *Islands in the Stream* and *Lilies of the Field*. The latter movie is a heartwarming tale about an itinerant handyman (Sidney Poitier) who is badgered into building a chapel for some German nuns who have settled in the Arizona desert. Goldsmith uses the familiar hymn "Amen" in various forms throughout the movie, sometimes performed as solos on the harmonica, banjo, or other appropriate instruments. The original music in the score is bluesy, such as a soulful harmonica solo, or bucolic, as in a very peaceful nature theme featuring a solo trumpet that is very Copland-like. *Islands in the Stream*, in which a reclusive artist (George C. Scott) on a Caribbean island is reunited with his three estranged sons (Hart Bochner, Brad Savage, and Michael-James Wixted), has one of Goldsmith's most felicitous scores. (He stated on several occasions that this was his favorite score.) In the opening music vivacious woodwinds compete with lilting strings to suggest a swirling sea that can be harmonious or disruptive. A quieter variation of this music is quite haunting as it is slowed down and a muted trumpet is featured in a Spanish-flavored interpretation. There is also an up-tempo theme on guitar, strings, and castanets that sounds like a festive Caribbean dance, a solo flute track that is very reflective, and a driving passage with various instruments repeating the same uphill musical phrase. Interestingly, Goldsmith's score for the thriller *Boys from Brazil* is also filled with flowing and sublime music. This disturbing story, about a former Nazi doctor (Gregory Peck) cloning future Hitlers, uses the waltz form throughout the score because of the doctor's Viennese background. The opening theme is a sprightly European waltz that sweeps and accelerates without any hint of evil. Then Goldsmith works wonders, turning the waltz form into something sinister when reorchestrated with oppressive sounds, something mysterious when slowed down and given unexpected accents, and something powerful and destructive when given a full orchestral assault. There is even a Latin variation of the waltz (the doctor is hiding away in South America) which is surprisingly catchy.

With Goldsmith's strong sense of melody, it is surprising that more songs have not come out of his scores. An exception is the best-selling ballad "And We Were Lovers" (lyric by Leslie Bricusse), which was fashioned out of a theme from the action-romance film *The Sand Pebbles*. Set in China in 1926, the love affair between an American sailor (Steve McQueen) and a missionary teacher (Candace Bergen) enfolds against political and military turmoil that has parallels to the Vietnam War. The score has a lovely yet brooding theme that leaps up a full octave as plucked strings and wood block percussion provide the sound of the story's exotic locale. The song version of this melody, a big hit for Shirley Bassey, Jack Jones, and others, loses the Oriental flavor but is still exotic. Other sections of *The Sand Pebbles* score use swaying Asian dance music and fully orchestrated dramatic passages in the grand manner. Bergen found herself caught up in another foreign locale in *The Wind and the Lion*, in which she was captured by a Berber chieftain (Sean Connery) in Morocco, greatly irritating President Teddy Roosevelt (Brian Keith). Again Goldsmith provides an invigorating score with touches of the exotic. Restless trumpets and African percussion compete in a sparkling fanfare that leads into the luscious main theme. Another passage uses various forms of expressive percussion to serve as the theme for the chieftain. Vivacious strings with chiming accents and Asian horns convey the exciting power of the Berbers while a serene passage on high-pitched flutes conjures up the mystery and seductive quality of the Moroccan desert.

The love theme is one of Goldsmith's most entrancing with its wavering strings and solo oboe that moves slowly but with a seething passion.

The first big-screen version of *Star Trek*, the 1979 adventure *Star Trek: The Motion Picture*, is not considered one of the better efforts in the franchise, but Goldsmith's outstanding score laid the foundation for later installments composed by him and others. The modestly interesting tale of the *Enterprise* crew searching for a powerful force in the universe is given an epic sweep because Goldsmith scored the movie like one of his earthbound epics. The theme for the spacecraft itself is a heroic tour de force in which trumpets and percussion overlap each other as they push ahead with gusto. This famous melody was quoted in later films and was used in the television series *Star Trek: The Next Generation*, so it is probably Goldsmith's most well-known piece of music. The other themes in the film are just as splendid. The battle with the Klingons is scored with a rhythmic theme that is paced like a tireless machine, the electronic effects helping to give the piece a mechanized tone. At different points in the attack music, harps, plucked violins, and piccolos join the fracas, the traditional once again fused with high tech. The theme for the lovely advisor Ilia (Persis Khambatta) on board the *Enterprise* is a magical lullaby played on strings with twinkling harp and piano embellishments. This score, and John Williams's for *Star Wars* two years earlier, have been cited as establishing the palate for the modern sci-fi score. In some ways Goldsmith's score for the horror film *The Omen* also established a new sound for that genre: the use of religious music for sinister effect. He was not the first to use Gregorian chant and Latin hymns in a horror context but the score for *The Omen* was so overpowering that it inspired many other such uses of religious music. The unforgettable hymn "Ave Satani" seems to be reverent but is dissonant enough to eventually turn into a satanic chant. The piece was so catchy that it was nominated for a Best Song Oscar. Throughout the score are haunting chorale pieces that are also menacing, often accompanied by vigorous brass. The more piercing ones seem to be an homage to Carl Orff; a sort of *Carmina Burana* that has gone to the dark side. A variation on this is the wordless children's chorus that is used so effectively in Goldsmith's score for *Poltergeist*.

Because he scored so many movies during his forty-five-year career, Goldsmith is considered one of Hollywood's premier composers. But more important is the manner in which he approached each film. A Goldsmith score grows out of the individual movie so much that it is difficult to find a pattern or arc to his work. He saw each film as a unique challenge and rarely relied on what had worked for him in the past. Goldsmith was very selective about when he used music. Because the scores are so provocative, the moviegoer doesn't notice that there is often very little musical underscoring. He understood the power of screen music but was never seduced into overdoing it. Although Goldsmith received only two Oscars (out of nineteen nominations), he was respected by the film community as one of the best. As his colleague Henry Mancini once stated, "he scares the hell out of us!" Biographies: *Jerry Goldsmith: Music Scoring for American Movies*, Mauricio Dupuis (2013); *Jerry Goldsmith*, Karlin Tilford (1995).

Credits

(all films USA unless stated otherwise; * for Best Song)

Year	Film	Director
1957	Black Patch	Allen H. Miner
1959	City of Fear	Irving Lerner
1959	Face of a Fugitive	Paul Wendkos
1960	Studs Lonigan	Irving Lerner
1962	The Crimebusters	Boris Sagal
1962	Lonely Are the Brave	David Miller
1962	The Spiral Road	Robert Mulligan
1962	Freud (AAN)	John Huston
1963	The List of Adrian Messenger	John Huston
1963	The Stripper	Franklin J. Schaffner
1963	A Gathering of Eagles	Delbert Mann
1963	Lilies of the Field	Ralph Nelson
1963	Take Her, She's Mine	Henry Koster
1963	The Prize	Mark Robson
1964	The General with the Cockeyed Id	John Sutherland
1964	To Trap a Spy	Don Medford
1964	Seven Days in May (GGN)	John Frankenheimer
1964	Shock Treatment	Denis Sanders
1964	Fate Is the Hunter	Ralph Nelson
1964	Rio Conchos	Gordon Douglas
1965	The Satan Bug	John Sturges
1965	In Harm's Way	Otto Preminger
1965	Von Ryan's Express	Mark Robson
1965	Morituri	Bernhard Wicki
1965	A Patch of Blue (AAN)	Guy Green
1966	Our Man Flint	Daniel Mann
1966	The Trouble with Angels	Ida Lupino
1966	Stagecoach	Gordon Douglas
1966	The Blue Max	John Guillermin (UK)
1966	Seconds	John Frankenheimer
1966	The Sand Pebbles (AAN; GGN)	Robert Wise
1967	In Like Flint	Gordon Douglas
1967	The Flim-Flam Man	Irvin Kershner
1967	Hour of the Gun	John Sturges
1968	Sebastian	David Greene (UK)
1968	Planet of the Apes (AAN)	Franklin J. Schaffner
1968	The Detective	Gordon Douglas
1968	Bandolero!	Andrew V. McLaglen
1969	100 Rifles	Tom Gries
1969	The Illustrated Man	Jack Smight
1969	The Chairman	J. Lee Thompson (UK/USA)

Year	Film	Director
1969	*Justine*	George Cukor
1970	*Patton* (AAN)	Franklin J. Schaffner
1970	*The Ballad of Cable Hogue*	Sam Peckinpah
1970	*Tora! Tora! Tora!*	Richard Fleischer, Kinji Fukasaku, Toshio Masuda (USA/Japan)
1970	*The Traveling Executioner*	Jack Smight
1970	*Rio Lobo*	Howard Hawks
1971	*The Mephisto Waltz*	Paul Wendkos
1971	*Escape from the Planet of the Apes*	Don Taylor
1971	*Wild Rovers*	Blake Edwards
1971	*The Last Run*	Richard Fleischer
1972	*The Culpepper Cattle Co.*	Dick Richards
1972	*The Other*	Robert Mulligan
1972	*The Man*	Joseph Sargent
1973	*Shamus*	Buzz Kulik
1973	*Ace Eli and Rodger of the Skies*	John Erman
1973	*One Little Indian*	Bernard McEveety
1973	*The Don Is Dead*	Richard Fleischer
1973	*Papillon* (AAN)	Franklin J. Schaffner (USA/France)
1974	*The Terrorists*	Caspar Wrede (UK)
1974	*Chinatown* (AAN; GGN; BAFTA-N)	Roman Polanski
1974	*S*P*Y*S*	Irvin Kershner
1975	*Breakout*	Tom Gries
1975	*The Reincarnation of Peter Proud*	J. Lee Thompson
1975	*The Wind and the Lion* (AAN; BAFTA-N)	John Milius
1975	*Take a Hard Ride*	Antonio Margheriti (Spain/USA)
1975	*Breakheart Pass*	Tom Gries
1976	*The Last Hard Men*	Andrew V. McLaglen
1976	*Logan's Run*	Michael Anderson
1976	*The Omen* (AA; AAN*)	Richard Donner (USA/UK)
1976	*High Velocity*	Remi Kramer
1976	*The Cassandra Crossing*	George P. Cosmatos (W. Germany/Italy/USA)
1977	*Twilight's Last Gleaming*	Robert Aldrich (USA/W. Germany)
1977	*Islands in the Stream*	Franklin J. Schaffner
1977	*MacArthur*	Joseph Sargent
1977	*Damnation Alley*	Jack Smight
1977	*Capricorn One*	Peter Hyams (USA/UK)
1978	*Coma*	Michael Crichton
1978	*Damien: Omen II*	Don Taylor
1978	*The Swarm*	Irwin Allen
1978	*The Boys from Brazil* (AAN)	Franklin J. Schaffner (UK/USA)
1978	*Magic*	Richard Attenborough
1978	*The Great Train Robbery*	Michael Crichton (UK)
1979	*Alien* (GGN; BAFTA-N)	Ridley Scott (USA/UK)
1979	*Players*	Anthony Harvey
1979	*Star Trek: The Motion Picture* (AAN; GGN)	Robert Wise
1980	*Cabo Blanco*	J. Lee Thompson (Mexico/USA)
1981	*The Salamander*	Peter Zinner (USA/UK/Italy)
1981	*Omen III: The Final Conflict*	Graham Baker (UK/USA)
1981	*Inchon*	Terence Young (So. Korea/USA)
1981	*Outland*	Peter Hyams (UK)
1981	*Raggedy Man*	Jack Fisk
1982	*Night Crossing*	Delbert Mann (UK)
1982	*Poltergeist* (AAN)	Tobe Hooper
1982	*The Secret of NIMH*	Don Bluth
1982	*The Challenge*	John Frankenheimer (USA/Japan)
1982	*First Blood*	Ted Kotcheff
1983	*Dusty*	John Richardson (Australia)

Year	Film	Director
1983	*Psycho II*	Richard Franklin
1983	*Twilight Zone: The Movie*	Joe Dante, John Landis, George Miller, Steven Spielberg
1983	*Under Fire* (AAN; GGN)	Roger Spottiswoode
1984	*The Lonely Guy*	Arthur Hiller
1984	*Gremlins*	Joe Dante
1984	*Supergirl*	Jeannot Szwarc (UK/USA)
1984	*Runaway*	Michael Crichton
1985	*Baby: Secret of the Lost Legend*	Bill L. Norton
1985	*Rambo: First Blood Part II*	George P. Cosmatos
1985	*Explorers*	Joe Dante
1985	*Legend*	Ridley Scott (USA/UK)
1985	*King Solomon's Mines*	J. Lee Thompson
1986	*Link*	Richard Franklin (UK)
1986	*Poltergeist II: The Other Side*	Brian Gibson
1986	*Hoosiers* (AAN)	David Anspaugh (UK/USA)
1987	*Extreme Prejudice*	Walter Hill
1987	*Innerspace*	Joe Dante
1987	*Lionheart*	Franklin J. Schaffner (Hungary/USA)
1987	*Rent-a-Cop*	Jerry London
1988	*Rambo III*	Peter MacDonald
1988	*Criminal Law*	Martin Campbell
1989	*The 'Burbs*	Joe Dante
1989	*Leviathan*	George P. Cosmatos (USA/Italy)
1989	*Warlock*	Steve Miner
1989	*Star Trek V: The Final Frontier*	William Shatner
1990	*Total Recall*	Paul Verhoeven
1990	*Gremlins 2: The New Batch*	Joe Dante
1990	*The Russia House*	Fred Schepisi
1991	*Not without My Daughter*	Brian Gilbert
1991	*Sleeping with the Enemy*	Joseph Ruben
1992	*Medicine Man*	John McTiernan
1992	*Basic Instinct* (AAN; GGN)	Paul Verhoeven (USA/France)
1992	*Mom and Dad Save the World*	Greg Beeman
1992	*Mr. Baseball*	Fred Schepisi (USA/Japan)
1992	*Forever Young*	Steve Miner
1992	*Love Field*	Jonathan Kaplan
1993	*Matinee*	Joe Dante
1993	*The Vanishing*	George Sluizer
1993	*Dennis the Menace*	Nick Castle
1993	*Rudy*	David Anspaugh
1993	*Malice*	Harold Becker (Canada/USA)
1993	*Six Degrees of Separation*	Fred Schepisi
1994	*Angie*	Martha Coolidge
1994	*Bad Girls*	Jonathan Kaplan
1994	*The Shadow*	Russell Mulcahy
1994	*The River Wild*	Curtis Hanson
1994	*I.Q.*	Fred Schepisi
1995	*Congo*	Frank Marshall
1995	*First Knight*	Jerry Zucker
1995	*Powder*	Victor Salva
1996	*City Hall*	Harold Becker
1996	*Executive Decision*	Stuart Baird
1996	*Chain Reaction*	Andrew Davis
1996	*The Ghost and the Darkness*	Stephen Hopkins
1996	*Star Trek: First Contact*	Jonathan Frakes
1997	*Fierce Creatures*	Fred Schepisi, Robert Young (UK/USA)
1997	*L.A. Confidential* (AAN; GGN; BAFTA-N)	Curtis Hanson

Year	Film	Director
1997	*Air Force One*	Wolfgang Petersen (USA/Germany)
1997	*The Edge*	Lee Tamahori
1998	*Deep Rising*	Stephen Sommers (USA/Canada)
1998	*U.S. Marshals*	Stuart Baird
1998	*Mulan (AAN; GGN)*	Tony Bancroft, Barry Cook
1998	*Small Soldiers*	Joe Dante
1998	*Star Trek: Insurrection*	Jonathan Frakes
1999	*The Mummy*	Stephen Sommers
1999	*The 13th Warrior*	John McTiernan
1999	*The Haunting*	Jan de Bont
2000	*Hollow Man*	Paul Verhoeven (USA/Germany)
2001	*Along Came a Spider*	Lee Tamahori (USA/Germany/Canada)
2001	*The Last Castle*	Rod Lurie
2002	*The Sum of All Fears*	Phil Alden Robinson (USA/Germany)
2002	*Star Trek: Nemesis*	Stuart Baird

GOODWIN, Ron (1925–2003) A popular British conductor, bandleader, and composer for records, the concert hall, television, and movies, he is most remembered for his scores for a series of war movies in the 1960s and 1970s.

He was born Ronald Alfred Goodwin in Plymouth, England, the son of a policeman, and began piano lessons when he was five years old. Four years later his family moved to London where he took up the trumpet and played in the school band, later forming his own band in high school. After graduation, Goodwin worked briefly as a clerk for an insurance company then was hired as a copyist and music arranger for a music publisher. Soon he was playing trumpet in Big Bands and arranging the music for orchestras and singers, including Petula Clark and Jimmy Young. Goodwin conducted and did arrangements for hundreds of records in the 1950s, including those by his own band Ron Goodwin and His Concert Orchestra. His particular style of swing and jazz in a classical format made many of his records hits and in the concert hall he found fame for his programs that mixed classical and film music. Goodwin first worked in movies when he was asked to write some dance music for the wartime thriller *The Night My Number Came Up* in 1955. After scoring a few documentaries, he got to write the music for his first feature in 1958, the low-budget melodrama *Man with a Gun*. Wide recognition did not come until 1960 when he scored the horror/sci-fi movie *Village of the Damned*, which quickly became a cult favorite. Further fame came with the popular comedy-mystery *Murder She Said*, in which Margaret Rutherford played the sleuth Miss Marple. Goodwin also scored the three successful sequels, *Murder at the Gallop*, *Murder Most Foul*, and *Murder Ahoy*. Throughout the 1960s and 1970s he scored a variety of British movies but was most praised for his war films, including *633 Squadron*, *Operation Crossbow*, *Where Eagles Dare*, *Battle of Britain*, and *Force 10 from Navarone*. Among his many other noteworthy movies are *The Trials of Oscar Wilde*, *The Day of the Triffids*, *Johnny Nobody*, *Ladies Will Do*, *A Home of Your Own*, *Children of the Damned*, *Of Human Bondage*, *Those Magnificent Men in Their Flying Machines*, *The Early Bird*, *The Trap*, *Frenzy*, *Deadly Strangers*, *The Littlest Horse Thieves*, and *Candleshoe*. Goodwin left the movies in 1979 to concentrate on conducting, leading notable symphonies across Europe, Australia, and Asia. He also wrote music for the concert hall, most memorably his *Drake 400 Suite* (1980), *New Zealand Suite* (1983), and *Armada Suite* (1988) which were commissioned by renowned orchestras. A longtime sufferer of asthma, Goodwin died in 2003 at the age of seventy-seven.

Goodwin's screen music is very eclectic, ranging from classical to pop, but he seems to favor marches, most obviously in his war films. His first score in that genre, *633 Squadron*, has a rapid march on drums and horns that races ahead like an attack and doubles back only to repeat the main motif in a different key. When the RAF squadron escapes out of Nazi-occupied Norway, screaming brass and grumbling woodwinds with descending strings all merge to convey a sense of determined action. There is also a notable love theme in the action movie, a graceful nocturne on strings and woodwinds that is passionate yet restrained. Also set during World War II, *Where Eagles Dare* concerns an attack on a castle to rescue an American general. The main theme is a simple drum march that builds in intensity as growling brass and eager strings enter with a foreboding tone even as the music gets majestic. This exciting score also has a complex string passage with interesting counterpoint that suggests confusion, a percussive march with horn and string support that continues to build without reaching a resolution, and chase music that is propulsive and exciting as it climbs the scale, pulls back, then climbs again. On the softer side is a quiet passage on harp and woodwinds that still manages to be suspenseful. Sir William Walton was hired to write the score for the epic *Battle of Britain* but, being old and sickly, was not able to complete it. The studio was not pleased with what Walton had done and asked Goodwin to write a replacement score. He balked, not wishing to usurp the revered Walton. In the end, some of Walton's music was retained but much of this extensive score was by Goodwin and it is among his finest works. The main theme is a propulsive march that has a processional feel at times, a robust victory temperament at other times. Among the many other outstanding sections of the score are a sweeping theme on strings that seems to soar and glide across the musical scale, a lyrical march in half time that takes its time to accelerate into a full-fledged musical assault, and a gentle passage at the end that is a hymnlike anthem on strings and brass that builds to a patriotic climax.

Marches figure in many of Goodwin's comedy scores as well. The large-scale, all-star-cast comedy *Those Magnificent Men in Their Flying Machines* has a score as extensive as that for *Battle of Britain*. This daffy farce, about flyers from different nations competing in an air race, has a catchy main theme: a merry march in which the music rises and falls like a faltering plane. The same melody is used for the title song with the music echoing the words about going up and down. The score also has a delightful theme that is a zany march with a Big Band sound featuring breezy woodwinds and cockeyed percussion. Goodwin wrote pastiche anthems for the different competing countries, including a French cancan, a German oompah-pah march, a British processional, and a patriotic American ditty. For the flying race there is sparkling music in which furious strings and brass fanfares compete with each other. The far-from-frightening Miss Marple mysteries are comedies and for *Murder She Said* and its sequels there is a delicious Miss Marple theme, a vigorous string and electric keyboard piece that mixes classical and rock-and-roll music in a silly and contagious manner. This is comic scoring at its best, just one of Goodwin's remarkable talents.

Goodwin scored a handful of horror and sci-fi movies, two of which are genre favorites and both have interesting scores. *Village of the Damned* is about a peaceful English hamlet in which the blond-haired children gain supernatural powers. The opening theme is a serene harp and flute piece with a bucolic temperament to establish the idealistic British town. Soon the music turns sinister and even chaotic as the demon-like children start to reveal their true nature.

Space aliens take the form of strangling plants in the silly but effective *The Day of the Triffids*. Goodwin's main theme is a pounding series of menacing fanfares that attack, diminish into harp glissandos, then pounce again. A decade later, Goodwin returned to the thriller genre with success. Alfred Hitchcock's *Frenzy*, one of the director's grizzlier movies, has no supernatural powers in it but it is quite frightening all the same. Hollywood veteran Henry Mancini was hired to score this tale about a serial killer who rapes his victims then strangles them with his necktie. According to Hollywood legend, Hitchcock greatly disliked Mancini's score, complaining that he was trying to copy the sound of Hitchcock's former composer Bernard Herrmann. Mancini scored the opening aerial shots of London with delicate but creepy music played on pipe organ and strings that sounded like a classic horror film score. Goodwin was brought in to write a whole new score and he opened the film with a flowing main theme with a British anthem feeling that sounds like innocuous travelogue music. Just as in *Village of the Damned*, this idealistic music turns into a dissonant and disturbing theme once the murders begin. Horns seem to gallop forward and the suspense builds with this music, though Goodwin and Hitchcock use it sparingly; some of the most disturbing scenes are left silent. Although he was still at the peak of his powers in the late 1970s, Goodwin left the movies with little regret. He had scored fifty films and left behind a wide array of memorable scores. Official website: www.rongoodwin.co.uk.

Credits

(all films UK unless stated otherwise)

Year	Film	Director
1958	*Man with a Gun*	Montgomery Tully
1959	*Whirlpool*	Lewis Allen
1959	*The Witness*	Geoffrey Muller
1960	*The Trials of Oscar Wilde*	Ken Hughes
1960	*In the Nick*	Ken Hughes
1960	*Village of the Damned*	Wolf Rilla
1961	*The Man at the Carlton Tower*	Robert Tronson
1961	*Partners in Crime*	Peter Duffell
1961	*Clue of the New Pin*	Allan Davis
1961	*Invasion Quartet*	Jay Lewis
1961	*Johnny Nobody*	Nigel Patrick
1961	*Murder She Said*	George Pollock
1962	*Postman's Knock*	Robert Lynn
1962	*Village of Daughters*	George Pollock
1962	*Kill or Cure*	George Pollock
1962	*I Thank a Fool*	Robert Stevens
1963	*Follow the Boys*	Richard Thorpe (UK/USA)
1963	*The Day of the Triffids* (aka *Invasion of the Triffids*)	Steve Sekely, Freddie Francis
1963	*Sword of Lancelot* (aka *Lancelot and Guinevere*)	Cornel Wilde
1963	*Murder at the Gallop*	George Pollock
1963	*The Cracksman*	Peter Graham Scott
1963	*Ladies Will Do*	C. M. Pennington-Richards
1964	*A Home of Your Own*	Jay Lewis
1964	*Children of the Damned*	Anton Leader
1964	*Murder Most Foul*	George Pollock
1964	*633 Squadron*	Walter Grauman (UK/USA)
1964	*Of Human Bondage*	Ken Hughes, etc.
1964	*Murder Ahoy*	George Pollock
1964	*Go Kart Go*	Jan Darnley-Smith
1965	*Operation Crossbow* (aka *The Great Spy Mission*)	Michael Anderson
1965	*Those Magnificent Men in Their Flying Machines*	Ken Annakin
1965	*The Alphabet Murders*	Frank Tashlin
1965	*The Early Bird*	Robert Asher
1966	*That Riviera Touch*	Cliff Owen
1966	*The Trap*	Sidney Hayers (Canada/UK)
1967	*Mister Ten Per Cent*	Peter Graham Scott
1967	*The Magnificent Two*	Cliff Owen
1968	*Decline and Fall . . . of a Birdwatcher*	John Krish
1968	*Where Eagles Dare*	Brian G. Hutton (USA/UK)
1969	*Those Daring Young Men in Their Jaunty Jalopies* (aka *Monte Carlo or Bust!*)	Ken Annakin, Sam Itzkovitch (UK/France/Italy)
1969	*Submarine X-1*	William A. Graham
1969	*Battle of Britain*	Guy Hamilton
1970	*The Executioner*	Sam Wanamaker
1972	*Frenzy* (GGN)	Alfred Hitchcock
1973	*Gawain and the Green Knight*	Stephen Weeks
1975	*Deadly Strangers*	Sidney Hayers
1975	*One of Our Dinosaurs Is Missing*	Robert Stevenson (UK/USA)
1976	*Spanish Fly*	Bob Kellett (UK/Spain/Canada)
1976	*The Littlest Horse Thieves* (aka *Escape from the Dark*)	Charles Jarrott (UK/USA)
1977	*Candleshoe*	Norman Tokar (UK/USA)
1978	*Force 10 from Navarone*	Guy Hamilton (UK/USA)
1979	*Unidentified Flying Oddball* (aka *A Spaceman in King Arthur's Court*)	Russ Mayberry (USA)
1983	*Al-mas' Ala Al-Kubra*	Mohamed Shukri Jameel (Iraq/UK)

GREEN, Johnny (1908–1989) A much-respected musical director, composer, conductor, arranger, and songwriter, he wrote the background score for only thirty feature films but worked on fifty others, and his songs can be heard on over 140 soundtracks.

Born John Waldo Green in New York City, he was the son of a wealthy and influential banker who loved music but discouraged his son from going into the arts. Green was only fifteen when he was accepted at Harvard to study economics. While there he worked on student theatricals and did arrangements for the campus Gold Coast Orchestra. Before graduation, Green was already working with Guy Lombardo arranging music and writing songs, his first hit "Coquette" (with Carmen Lombardo and Gus Kahn) on the charts while Green was still a student. To please his father, Green worked on Wall Street, but after a year quit to arrange and conduct music for early talkies being made in the Astoria Studios in New York City. At the same time he arranged music for dance bands on radio and records and contributed songs to Broadway revues. In 1930 his most famous song, the torchy ballad "Body and Soul" (lyric by Edward Heyman, Robert Sour, and Frank Eyton) was a hit in America and Europe, went on to be recorded dozens of times, and would be often interpolated into Broadway shows and films. Yet Green was usually thought of as an arranger and conductor and too rarely was hired to write music. Many popular singers, from Fred Astaire to Ethel Merman, made records with Johnny Green's Orchestra in the 1930s, and he continued to have song hits, including "Out of Nowhere," "I'm Yours," "Easy Come, Easy Go," "I Cover the Waterfront," " I Wanna Be Loved (By You)," and "You're Mine You."

Green was hired by Paramount to write the scores for nonmusicals between 1930 and 1933 but none of the movies found favor with the critics or the public and Green was once again thought of only as an arranger and conductor. He did get to write an orchestra piece entitled *Nightclub* which premiered at Carnegie Hall in 1933, and some of his music was heard onstage in London and New York, but it was Johnny Green's Orchestra that was famous, heard on records and radio. By 1941 he was back in Hollywood, writing the background music for some successful musicals, most of them long forgotten now. Green was still in great demand as a musical director and in 1949 he was made head of the music department at MGM. With orchestrator Conrad Salinger, he changed the structure of

the studio orchestra and created a new and more vibrant sound, the one now associated with MGM in the 1950s. He sometimes composed background music for musicals with songs by others but his true claim to fame during this period is his musical direction of such beloved musicals as *Easter Parade*, *An American in Paris*, *High Society*, *Singin' in the Rain*, *Brigadoon*, *Royal Wedding*, *Summer Stock*, *Bye Bye Birdie*, *West Side Story*, and *Oliver!* For such efforts he was nominated for an Oscar thirteen times, winning on five occasions, but rarely for his composing. (Green also conducted the orchestra for seventeen Academy Award telecasts.) As a conductor, Green worked with some of the finest symphony orchestras in the United States, and he frequently worked in television, composing and conducting the music for series and specials. His last screen credit was the marathon dance drama *They Shoot Horses, Don't They?* in 1969. Green adapted his song "Easy Come, Easy Go" into the main theme and arranged the music for several 1930s standards heard in the film, including three of his own song hits. It was a fitting summation of his remarkable career.

Writing the background music for a movie musical with songs by others is a thankless job in many ways but Green did it beautifully. For *High Society*, for example, he wrote elegant jazz-flavored music that linked the Cole Porter songs. The various opera sequences in *The Great Caruso* were united by his original musical theme, a minor-key symphonic piece. The vibrant songs by Jule Styne and Sammy Cahn in *It Happened in Brooklyn* are boosted by Green's atmospheric background music. For *Oliver!* he took musical sections from Lionel Bart's popular songs to score the dialogue scenes, composing some original themes for the dramatic sequences such as the murder of Nancy and the climactic chase on the rooftops of London. Green wrote rather silly pseudo-Russian music for the Danny Kaye vehicle *The Inspector General* which had some very un-Russian songs by Sylvia Fine. Similarly, his Latin-flavored score for the misguided musical *Pepe* is perhaps the only satisfying aspect of that oddball movie. The only major nonmusical film that Green got to score was the epic *Raintree County* and it hints at what Hollywood lost by not letting him compose more often. The main theme in the Civil War–era drama is a sonorous folk song, "The Ballad of Raintree County" (lyric by Paul Francis Webster), which is sung by Nat King Cole over the opening credits and returns in different variations throughout the

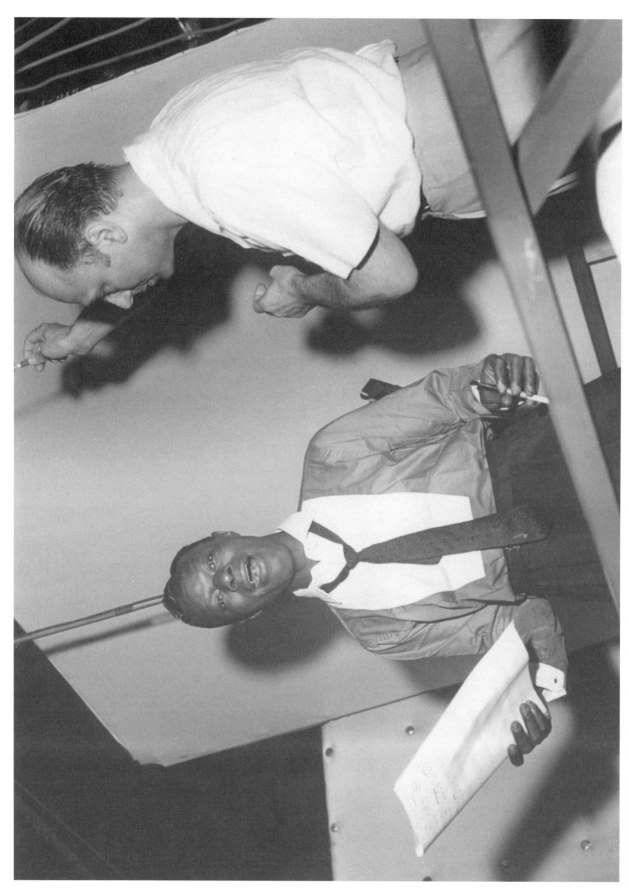

JOHNNY GREEN. Generally thought of as Hollywood's top music arranger for many years, Green was too little known for his original scores, such as the sparkling one he wrote for *Raintree County* (1957). Green (right) conducts the recording session with Nat "King" Cole singing the title song. *MGM / Photofest © MGM*

long film. It is a warm yet lonely melody that has a bucolic flavor, but the theme takes on different moods effectively as Green returns to it later in the score. The *Raintree County* score also has some bustling music for a country race, a sublime love theme, military music for the glory and horror of war, and disturbingly dissonant music for the dramatic scenes involving the mental illness of the heroine

(Elizabeth Taylor). Because *Raintree County* was not the box office follow-up to *Gone with the Wind* that MGM was hoping for, Green's score was not fully appreciated (although it was nominated for an Oscar). Had the movie been a hit, Green's career might have taken a different turn. Instead he remained one of Hollywood's top musical directors.

Credits

(all films USA unless stated otherwise)

Year	Film	Director
1930	The Sap from Syracuse	A. Edward Sutherland
1931	Honor among Lovers	Dorothy Arzner
1931	The Girl Habit	Edward F. Cline
1931	Secrets of a Secretary	George Abbott
1931	My Sin	George Abbott
1931	La pura verdad	Florián Rey, Manuel Romero
1932	Wayward	Edward Sloman
1932	The Wiser Sex	Berthold and Victor Viertel
1932	Misleading Lady	Stuart Walker
1943	Pilot #5	George Sidney
1944	Broadway Rhythm	Roy Del Ruth
1944	Bathing Beauty	George Sidney
1945	The Sailor Takes a Wife	Richard Whorf
1946	Easy to Wed	Edward Buzzell
1947	It Happened in Brooklyn	Richard Whorf
1947	Fiesta (AAN)	Richard Thorpe
1947	Something in the Wind	Irving Pichel
1949	The Inspector General (GG)	Henry Koster
1951	The Great Caruso (AAN)	Richard Thorpe
1952	Because You're Mine	Alexander Hall
1956	High Society (AAN)	Charles Walters
1957	Raintree County (AAN)	Edward Dmytryk
1960	Pepe (AAN; GGN)	George Sidney (Mexico/USA)
1963	Twilight of Honor	Boris Sagal
1966	Johnny Tiger	Paul Wendkos
1966	Alvarez Kelly	Edward Dmytryk
1968	Oliver! (AA)	Carol Reed (UK)
1969	They Shoot Horses, Don't They? (AAN)	Sydney Pollack

GRUSIN, Dave (b. 1934) A highly successful composer, arranger, musician, songwriter, and record producer, he has scored many television series and TV movies and over sixty feature films, eight of them directed by Sydney Pollack.

Dave Grusin was born in Littleton, Colorado, the son of a Latvian immigrant who played the violin and a pianist mother. Grusin took up the piano and the clarinet as a youth, played in the school band, and while still a

high school student performed in professional bands in the Denver area. He studied music at the University of Colorado at Boulder with the intention of going into music education. After graduation, Grusin went to New York City where he played in various jazz bands and nightclubs, often making arrangements as well as playing piano. He started to pursue a graduate degree at the Manhattan School of Music but quit in 1963 when he was hired by singer Andy Williams to become musical director for the star's popular television variety show. Grusin was also an in-demand arranger and accompanist for other singers. He soon was arranging and composing music for other television programs and writing the theme music for such shows as *The Ghost & Mrs. Muir, It Takes a Thief, The Name of the Game, Dan August, Maude, Baretta, Good Times*, and *St. Elsewhere*. His first experience with movies was in 1967 when he was asked to provide some music for *The Graduate*. With its vibrant collection of songs by Paul Simon and Art Garfunkle, *The Graduate* changed the direction of screen music, the studios for many years after opting for a series of pop songs rather than a soundtrack score. Grusin provided some incidental or background music for the famous film but all the attention was on the very popular songs.

Grusin's first full screen score was for the 1967 comedy *Divorce American Style*, followed by a variety of other comedies, dramas, cop films, and westerns. In 1974 he scored the drama *The Yakuza*, about the Japanese Mafia, and worked with director Sydney Pollack for the first time. The two men found the collaboration so fulfilling that Grusin later scored such noteworthy Pollack movies as *Three Days of the Condor, Absence of Malice, Tootsie, Havana*, and *The Firm*, winning Oscar nominations for his scores for the last two. Grusin was also nominated for *Heaven Can Wait, The Champ, On Golden Pond*, and *The Fabulous Baker Boys*, and won for *The Milagro Beanfield War*. Among his other significant films are *The Heart Is a Lonely Hunter, Tell Them Willie Boy Is Here, The Great Northfield Raid, The Friends of Eddie Coyle, Murder by Death, The Goodbye Girl, The Midnight Man, The Front, . . . And Justice for All, The Goonies, My Bodyguard, The Pope of Greenwich Village*, and *Selena*. Grusin has scored many TV movies since 1968, including *Prescription: Murder* (1968), *The Forgotten Man* (1971), *A Howling in the Woods* (1971), *The Family Rico* (1972), *The Trial of Chaplain Jensen* (1975), *Eric* (1975), *On the Edge* (1987), *Dinner with Friends* (2001), and *Harmony* (2010). He is also an acclaimed jazz musician and record producer. Grusin cofounded GRP Records with Larry Rosen in 1978 and has since presented many highly praised and award-winning records with music by himself and others. Since 2000, he has done few movies and concentrates on recording, producing, touring, and performing.

Although Grusin's screen music is characterized by his strong melodic sense and vivid rhythms, he has also writ-

ten some very delicate and atmospheric music on occasion. Jazz is an important aspect of his music and some scores make splendid use of jazz forms. *The Fabulous Baker Boys*, about two brother musicians (Jeff and Beau Bridges) who play in small clubs, is filled with song standards, so Grusin's marvelous underscoring is not as noticeable. The main theme is a cool jazz piece featuring saxophone that is detached, breezy, and surprisingly seductive. There is also a moody, reflective jazz track that seems aimless yet slowly builds and captivates on the listener. The main theme for the very popular comedy *Tootsie* is a lighthearted jazz piece that rolls along with a happy and confident air. This cross-dressing comedy classic, about an actor (Dustin Hoffman) who finds fame as a female character actress on television, also has a more subdued jazz theme heard on electric keyboard that is also expert. Grusin wrote a funky jazz piece for a montage showing the growing popularity of the actor/actress. It has the tempo of a march but the sensibility of an improvised musical gavotte. The *Tootsie* score also has the Oscar-nominated song "It Might as Well Be You" (lyric by Alan and Marilyn Bergman), a pop love song that is very engaging. Perhaps the most potent use of jazz in a Grusin score can be found in *The Firm*, a taut thriller about a Mafia-like law firm. Director Pollack asked Grusin for the entire score to be performed on piano only and the composer obliged with a superb piano jazz score. The main theme is a piece played on two pianos that is bluesy and casual yet has a restless quality that is almost menacing. For the climactic chase sequence, Grusin used a prepared piano to get a very avant-garde sound, going so far as knocking on the wooden frame of the instrument. (As in *The Fabulous Baker Boys* and some of his other films, Grusin was the pianist on the soundtrack.) *The Firm* also has a gentle love theme that is so hesitant at first that it aches with feeling then finds the resolve to transition into a sort of jazzy serenade.

The character comedy *On Golden Pond* is a good example of Grusin's talent for atmospheric music. This tale, about an aging couple (Henry Fonda and Katharine Hepburn) and the domestic events that occur one summer at their lakeside cottage, calls for a very sensitive score, and Grusin wrote some of his most tender music. The call of the loon and other wildlife sounds blend into the music for the captivating main theme played on piano with a tentative delicacy that then breaks out into a full melodic line with the help of woodwinds. Later passages are less melodic and more modern with dissonant phrases repeated in an almost avant-garde manner. One theme is a rhythmic pop passage on electric keyboard with a buoyant melody that is youthful and full of glee. The soundtrack album of *On Golden Pond* was a surprise hit, remaining on the charts for weeks. *Heaven Can Wait*, another comedy with touching moments, is about a pro football player (Warren Beatty) who returns from his premature death to set things right. The recurring theme throughout the movie is based on a four-note phrase. It is first heard as a carnival ditty that bounces along with a careless spirit as it plays variations of that simple musical phrase. Later it is heard on a saxophone and can be very sexy or melancholy. There is also a lyrical love theme in the score that is gentle and unassuming yet full of emotion. In contrast, the broad farce *Murder by Death* has a deliciously comic score. This pastiche of several movie detectives all gathered in one place for a murder is very cartoonish, and so is Grusin's music. There is a daffy theme on oboe and strings that seems to mock itself as it tries to be mysterious and only ends up being funny. The suspense music is in the conventional vein with descending low strings and high string glissandos, but the tone is flippant. This kind of playfulness can also be heard in the adolescent adventure film *The Goonies* about a group of kids looking for pirate treasure. The percussive main theme has vibrant strings, blaring brass, and an urgency that is catching. There is also a slaphappy march heard on trumpets and drums that bounces along merrily. The suspense music, with its descending chimes, piercing strings, and plodding bass line, is effective without being gruesome.

In the opinion of some, Grusin's finest screen music is that written about Spanish settings and people. The drama *Havana*, about the complicated romance between an American gambler (Robert Redford) and the Cuban wife (Lena Olin) of a revolutionary in 1958 Havana, has an entrancing love theme. It is a smooth jazz passage with muted trumpet and keyboard that has a melancholy feel even when the tempo increases and it becomes occasionally rhythmic. There is also a symphonic theme that glides along as it moves from one subtle crescendo to another and conveys a sense of power slowly coming to the surface. But it is the main theme in *Havana* that is most thrilling. A Cuban band with soaring trumpet, clicking castanets, strumming guitars, and effervescent flutes plays a passionate habanera that seethes with passion and excitement. *Selena*, the biopic about Latin singer Selena Quintanilla-Perez (Jennifer Lopez), uses many of the actual singer's recordings for the soundtrack score but Grusin provides some first-rate background music that subtly hints at Spanish musical forms. There is a dreamy theme that builds in intensity as it resolves its long musical lines, and a piano passage that is heartfelt and emotive without being sentimental. Even richer is the score for *The Milagro Beanfield War*, a fantastical comedy-drama about the residents of a small New Mexico town who try to stop the development of their land into a country club. Grusin uses waltz time in much of the score but the music rarely sounds like that European dance form. In one festive number, hand clapping and an electric keyboard set the pace as a Mexican band plays a vivacious flamenco. Another passage is a mystical yet joyous piece played on harp, concertina, and celesta that has the flavor of a Spanish folk dance. There is also a lovely flowing theme for solo guitar and violins that changes tempo and mood as it sweeps along with fiery passion. Perhaps that is the key word to describe Grusin's screen music. Be it cool jazz or tuneful dance music or romantic serenade, there is always a sense of passion. Official website: www.grusin.net.

Credits

(all films USA unless stated otherwise; * for Best Song)

Year	Film	Director
1967	Divorce American Style	Bud Yorkin
1967	Waterhole #3	William A. Graham
1968	A Man Called Gannon	James Goldstone
1968	Where Were You When the Lights Went Out?	Hy Averback
1968	The Heart Is a Lonely Hunter	Robert Ellis Miller
1968	Candy	Christian Marquand (France/Italy/USA)

Year	Film	Director
1969	*The Mad Room*	Bernard Girard
1969	*Winning*	James Goldstone
1969	*Tell Them Willie Boy Is Here*	Abraham Polonsky
1969	*Generation*	George Schaefer
1970	*Halls of Anger*	Paul Bogart
1970	*Adam at Six A.M.*	Robert Scheerer
1971	*The Pursuit of Happiness*	Robert Mulligan
1971	*Shoot Out*	Henry Hathaway
1971	*The Gang That Couldn't Shoot Straight*	James Goldstone
1972	*The Great Northfield Minnesota Raid*	Philip Kaufman
1972	*Fuzz*	Richard A. Colla
1973	*The Friends of Eddie Coyle*	Peter Yates
1974	*The Midnight Man*	Roland Kibbee, Burt Lancaster
1974	*The Nickel Ride*	Robert Mulligan
1974	*The Yakuza*	Sydney Pollack (USA/Japan)
1975	*W.W. and the Dixie Dancekings*	John G. Avildsen
1975	*Three Days of the Condor*	Sydney Pollack
1976	*Murder by Death*	Robert Moore
1976	*The Front*	Martin Ritt
1977	*Mr. Billion*	Jonathan Kaplan
1977	*Fire Sale*	Alan Arkin
1977	*Bobby Deerfield*	Sydney Pollack
1977	*The Goodbye Girl*	Herbert Ross
1978	*Heaven Can Wait* (AAN)	Warren Beatty, Buck Henry
1979	*The Champ* (AAN)	Franco Zeffirelli
1979	*. . . And Justice for All*	Norman Jewison
1979	*The Electric Horseman*	Sydney Pollack
1980	*My Bodyguard*	Tony Bill
1981	*Absence of Malice*	Sydney Pollack
1981	*On Golden Pond* (AAN)	Mark Rydell (UK/USA)
1982	*Author! Author!*	Arthur Hiller
1982	*Tootsie* (AAN*; BAFTA-N*)	Sydney Pollack
1984	*Scandalous*	Rob Cohen (UK/USA)
1984	*Racing with the Moon*	Richard Benjamin
1984	*The Pope of Greenwich Village*	Stuart Rosenberg
1984	*The Little Drummer Girl*	George Roy Hill
1984	*Falling in Love*	Ulu Grosbard
1985	*The Goonies*	Richard Donner
1986	*Lucas*	David Seltzer
1987	*Ishtar*	Elaine May
1988	*The Milagro Beanfield War* (AA; GGN)	Robert Redford
1988	*Clara's Heart*	Robert Mulligan
1988	*Tequila Sunrise*	Robert Towne
1989	*A Dry White Season*	Euzhan Palcy
1989	*The Fabulous Baker Boys* (AAN; GGN; BAFTA-N)	Steve Kloves
1990	*Havana* (AAN; GGN)	Sydney Pollack
1990	*The Bonfire of the Vanities*	Brian De Palma
1991	*For the Boys* (GGN)	Mark Rydell
1993	*The Firm* (AAN)	Sydney Pollack
1995	*The Cure*	Peter Horton
1996	*Mulholland Falls*	Lee Tamahori
1997	*Selena*	Gregory Nava
1998	*Hope Floats*	Forest Whitaker
1999	*Random Hearts*	Sydney Pollack
2006	*Even Money* (aka *Jump Shot*)	Mark Rydell (USA/Germany)
2013	*Skating to New York*	Charles Minsky

HADJIDAKIS, Manos (aka Manos Hatzidakis) (1925–1994) A Greek musician and composer of songs, concert works, and over seventy film scores, he and composer Mikis Theodorakis are responsible for popularizing Greek music around the world in the 1960s.

Manos Hadjidakis was born in Xanthi, Greece, and studied violin, piano, and accordion as a child. When his parents divorced, seven-year-old Manos moved with his mother to Athens, where they endured poverty and the occupation of Germans during World War II. He worked at various jobs as a teenager and attended the University of Athens for a time, studying philosophy and music. In the late 1940s, Hadjidakis began composing songs and background music for the theatre, in particular the Art Theatre of Athens. He also scored his first film in 1946 but did not become active in movies until the 1950s. His interest in Greek folk music prompted him to write articles about music and compose his own songs, often set to lyrics by experimental poet Nikos Gatsos. He also wrote for the concert hall but found wider recognition for the popular recordings made of his songs by notable Greek singers such as Nana Mouskouri and Melina Mercouri. By 1952 Hadjidakis was heavily involved in screen composition and for over ten years was busy scoring Greek films for such directors as Yorgos Javellas and Alekos Sakellarios. But it was the American-Greek movie *Never on Sunday*, directed by and starring Jules Dassin and featuring Mercouri, that was an international sensation, and Hadjidakis's score introduced modern Greek folk music to the outside world.

The subject of many of Hadjidakis's songs and films was political, and his music-theatre piece *Street of Dreams* in 1962 was very controversial. As he continued to experiment with new forms of folk music, he also was labeled a radical by the rising junta party in Greece. Pressure was exerted on him, so when he was asked to go to New York City in 1966 to score a stage musical version of *Never on Sunday*, Hadjidakis left Greece and did not return for eight years. The musical, retitled *Illya Darling* and starring Mercouri, opened on Broadway in 1967 but was not a success. All the same, Hadjidakis remained in the States

and continued to compose songs and concert pieces but few movies. When the junta dictatorship fell in 1972, Hadjidakis returned to Greece, where he continued his movie career and became involved in many musical organizations, such as the State Orchestra, the National Opera, the Orchestra of Colours, and various music and theatre festivals. He also founded his own record company, called Sirius, and a cultural magazine in which he continued to write about music theory. Although he scored only a few movies in the 1970s and 1980s, Hadjidakis remained an international screen composer thanks to such popular films as *Topkapi*, *The River*, *300 Spartans*, *Nine Miles to Noon*, *Blue*, and *America, America*. He completed the score for *Love Knot* before his death from heart failure in 1994 at the age of sixty-eight. In 2008 he was the subject of the Greek documentary *Manos Hadjidakis: Reflection in the Mirror*.

The impact the *Never on Sunday* score had on audiences around the world was considerable. While some moviegoers might have been familiar with the sound and instrumentation of Greek folk music, Hadjidakis's score made that sound accessible, modern, and even sexy. The famous main theme is a simple, steady melody with plenty of repetition and a pleasing release section. It is in a song format and as a song it became an international best seller. (The English lyric is by Billy Towne.) The story of an exuberant, unconventional prostitute (Mercouri) and the American scholar (Dassin) who tries to educate her called for a musical theme that expressed her free spirit. In the film the variations of this theme keep it lively and never overdone. Because it is a simple and catchy piece of music, audiences liked it and remembered it. And if they should forget, there were dozens of recordings just in English by various singers. When Mikis Theodorakis's score for *Zorba the Greek* came out four years later, the popularity of Greek music was solidified. Yet *Never on Sunday* is Hadjidakis before he began to experiment with the folk form in movies. For the comic thriller *Topkapi* his music is more complex and even finer, though this admired score was not nearly as popular. The plot concerns an internationally diverse bunch of crooks in Turkey and their elaborate plans to steal a priceless artifact from the Topkapi Palace in Istanbul. The opening theme is faster, more complicated, and funnier than the *Never on Sunday* theme. If Mercouri was a free spirit in that movie, here she is a mysterious lady of crime and the music notices the change. *Topkapi* has some vibrant Turkish belly dancing music, a silly theme played by fluttering flutes and frantic bouzouki strings, frenzied chase music, ethnic tunes for a mud wrestling sequence, and wry, festive end music with the culprits all in prison and marching in time to the daffy beat.

Hadjidakis uses a completely different sound for the Hollywood action movie *The 300 Spartans*. A traditional orchestra plays the robust, military march theme heard over the credits. There is also a lovely romantic theme with strings, and a lively regal passage that celebrates the majesty of the Spartan forces with sincere patriotism. For the American western *Blue*, the music is also without satire. The Spanish-influenced main theme involves intricate guitar work backed by a full orchestra. *The Invincible Six* has a catchy main theme played on chimes and drums while *The Pedestrian* has a melancholy theme played on woodwinds and an enticing slow dance performed on bou-

zoukis. A very heartfelt score can be found in Elia Kazan's *America, America* about his Greek ancestor who emigrated from Turkey to the States early in the twentieth century. The score begins with Muslim chanting, then glides into a Greek folk song that is weary yet hopeful. As sung in Greek by a male trio, it is both haunting and reverent. There is a lilting harmonica passage as well as a graceful waltz for the world that the young hero (Stathis Giallelis) sees from the outside. The youth's many difficulties in getting to America are scored with some striking music that stops shy of the melodramatic. By the end of the movie, the sounds of the city infiltrate the European tunes. As the hero works diligently as a shoe shine boy in Manhattan, the music seems to pick up on his optimism. *America, America* is one of Hadjidakis's richest scores and a key to his international appeal. He brought Greek music to moviegoers around the globe then showed how it could fit many moods and stories. With Theodorakis, he brought a new dimension to screen music that has since inspired many other movie composers to utilize European and Asian folk music in their scores. Biography: *Mikis and Manos: A Tale of Two Composers*, Nick Papandreou, Poppy Alexiou (2012). Official website: www.hadjidakis.gr.

Credits

(all films Greece unless stated otherwise; * for Best Song)

Year	Film	Director
1946	Unsubdued Slaves	Vion Papamihalis, Mario Ploritis
1949	Red Cliff	Grigoris Grigoriou
1949	Two Worlds	Yannis Filippou, Iasson Novak
1952	Dead City	Frixos Iliadis
1952	The Grouch	Yorgos Javellas
1952	Lily of the Harbor	Yorgos Javellas
1953	Heaven Is Ours	Dinos Dimopoulos
1954	The Magic City	Nikos Koundouros
1954	Nyhterini peripeteia	Angelos Terzakis
1955	Stella	Mihalis Kakogiannis
1955	Dva zrna grozdja	Mladomir Djordjevic (Yugoslavia/Greece)
1955	The Counterfeit Coin	Yorgos Javellas
1955	The Hurdy-Gurdy	Alekos Sakellarios
1956	The Road with the Acacias	Dimitris Ioannopoulos
1956	The Ogre of Athens	Nikos Koundouros
1956	The Lovers Arrive	Yorgos Javellas
1956	The Fortune Teller	Alekos Sakellarios
1956	Dollars and Dreams	Ion Daifas
1957	Bed of Grass	Gregg C. Tallas
1957	Tis tyhis ta grammena	Filippos Fylaktos
1957	I dipsa	A. T. Dimitriev

Year	Film	Director
1958	Trouble for Fathers	Alekos Sakellarios
1958	A Matter of Dignity (aka The Final Lie)	Mihalis Kakogiannis
1958	Horse and Carriage	Dinos Dimopoulos
1958	The Outlaws	Nikos Koundouros
1958	We Have Only One Life	Yorgos Javellas
1958	Laterna, ftoheia kai garyfallo	Alekso Sakellarios
1958	One Street Organ, One Life	Sokrates Kapsaskis
1958	Ola gia to paidi tis	Kostas Strantzalis
1958	I limni ton pothon	Giorgo Zervos
1958	A Hero in His Sleepers	Alekos Sakellarios
1959	Zalongo, the Fort of Freedom	Stelios Tatasopoulos
1959	The Brave's Island	Dimis Dadiras
1959	Maiden's Cheek	Alekso Sakellarios
1959	Love Stories	Sokrates Kapsaskis
1960	Never on Sunday (AA*)	Jules Dassin (Greece/USA)
1960	Loves of a Greek in Paris	Hristos Kyriakopoulos
1960	Madalena	Dinos Dimopoulos
1960	Moment of Passion	Maria Plyta
1960	The Young Lady's Fool	Giannis Dalianides
1960	The Underdog	Dinos Dimopoulos
1960	The River	Nikos Koundouros (Greece/USA)
1960	Randevou stin Kerkyra	Dimis Dadiras
1960	I kyria dimarhos	Roviros Manthoulis
1961	Alice in the Navy	Alekos Sakellarios
1961	Lisa, Tosca of Athens	Sokrates Kapsaskis
1961	Alloimono stous neous	Alekos Sakellarios
1961	Love and Tempest	Sokrates Kapsaskis
1961	I Liza kai i alli	Dinos Dimopoulos
1961	Hamena Oneira	Alekos Sakellarios
1962	Aliki My Love	Rudolph Maté (UK/Greece)
1962	It Happened in Athens	Andrew Marton (USA)
1962	The 300 Spartans	Rudolph Maté (USA)
1963	Siralardaki heyecanlar	Alekos Sakellarios (Greece/Turkey)
1963	America, America	Elia Kazan (USA)
1963	Nine Miles to Noon	Herbert J. Leder (USA)
1963	Htypokardia sto thranio	Alekos Sakellarios (Turkey/Greece)
1964	Dry Summer	Metin Erksan, David E. Durston (Turkey)
1964	Topkapi	Jules Dassin (USA)
1966	The Steps	Leonard Hirschfield (Greece/USA)
1968	Blue	Silvio Marizzano (USA)
1968	Assignment Skybolt	Gregg C. Tallas
1970	The Invincible Six (aka The Heroes)	Jean Negulesco (USA/Iran)
1973	The Pedestrian	Maximillian Schell (Switzerland/W. Germany/Israel)
1974	Sweet Movie	Dusan Makavejev (Canada/France/W. Germany)
1975	C.I.A. Secret Story	Giuseppe Ferrara (Italy)
1979	Honeymoon	Giorgos Panousopoulos
1984	Memed My Hawk	Peter Ustinov (Yugoslavia/UK)
1988	A Heron for Germany	Stavros Tornes
1991	Quiet Days in August	Pantelis Voulgaris
1995	Love Knot	Giorgos Panousopoulos

HAGEMAN, Richard (1882–1966) An internationally acclaimed composer and conductor for the concert hall, opera, and movies, the Dutch-born Hageman worked in Hollywood for only thirteen years and scored only eighteen feature films but several of them are outstanding, including seven with director John Ford.

Born in Leeuwarde, Netherlands (several sources claim he was born in 1881), Richard Hageman was a child prodigy on the piano, giving concerts of classical music at the age of six. Hageman received scholarships to study music at the Brussels Conservatory and the Royal Conservatory of Amsterdam before beginning his career as an accompanist for the Amsterdam Royal Opera House. By the time he was eighteen, Hageman was conducting the opera orchestra and accompanying famous artists. It was as chanteuse Yvette Guilbert's accompanist that he came to America to tour the States; he decided to stay and eventually became an American citizen. Hageman was conductor for the Metropolitan Opera for eighteen years, coached opera singers at the Curtis Institute, and was music director for the Chicago Civic Opera. He also conducted concerts across America, from the Philadelphia Orchestra to the Hollywood Bowl. Hageman first got involved with movies in 1938 when he contributed some music to the score for the aerial drama *Men with Wings*. That same year he wrote his first full score, for the historical adventure *If I Were King*, and received an Academy Award nomination. The next year he was one of four composers and arrangers to work on John Ford's western classic *Stagecoach* and shared the Oscar with his co-artists. Hageman was the sole composer for Ford's *The Long Voyage Home*, *The Fugitive*, *Fort Apache*, *3 Godfathers*, *Wagon Master*, and *She Wore a Yellow Ribbon*. For other directors he wrote music for such noteworthy movies as *Hotel Imperial*, *Rulers of the Sea*, *The Shanghai Gesture*, *Mourning Becomes Electra*, *Angel and the Badman*, *The Howards of Virginia*, and *This Woman Is Mine*, receiving Oscar nominations for the last two. Hageman was also a respected composer for the opera house and wrote art songs (most memorably "The Night Has a Thousand Eyes" and "Do Not Go, My Love") and over fifty chamber pieces. Throughout his life he occasionally returned to the concert stage as a pianist and even acted in eleven movies, playing himself or musician characters. Hagemen left Hollywood in 1953 to concentrate on conducting and died thirteen years later at the age of eighty-three.

Hageman was forty-eight years old and a widely lauded conductor and composer before he worked on his first film. Even so, his score for *If I Were King* sounds like the work of a Hollywood veteran. This rousing romantic adventure about the poet-rebel François Villon (Ronald Colman) in fifteenth-century Paris is a high-energy romp, and Hageman's score is equally spirited. The main theme is a brisk march with parading drums, shouting trumpets, zesty woodwinds, and swirling strings. There is a rapid string and horn theme that sounds like a parade on double time, some vivacious dance music for a tavern celebration, a flowing minuet on period flutes and horns, and a waltzing love theme on harp and violins that manages to keep pace with the rest of the movie. The action scenes are scored with vigorous symphonic music with plenty of crescendos and fanfares in the true Hollywood tradition. Hageman's first effort quickly put him on the A-list of screen composers. Intriguing scores, like the one for *The Shanghai Gesture*, kept him on the list. This oddball movie about gambling, booze, and drugs in the Chinese city might be described as an exotic film noir movie. The score certainly is a mix of East and West. The main theme is a ponderous and threatening noir passage with a touch of the East in some string accompaniment. There is a very Western march that seems to cut through the exotic themes and overrun them, very appropriate since most of the characters in the movie are non-Asian. There is an eerie theme with plucked strings, and rhythmic dance music featuring a low clarinet and a high flute. For the suspense scenes, Hageman uses Western noir music rather than Eastern, although the menacing brass is punctuated with Asian gongs.

In the Ford westerns that Hageman contributed to, little of the soundtrack score is totally original. *Stagecoach*, *She Wore a Yellow Ribbon*, *Fort Apache*, and others all utilize folk tunes and traditional songs, often adapted and arranged in a skillful manner. The title song in *She Wore a Yellow Ribbon*, for example, is used throughout the western yet in such different ways that it never gets monotonous. The Ford movie that gave Hageman an opportunity to compose a lot of original music is *The Long Voyage Home*, a quiet, subtle, and unromantic look at the lonely lives of men at sea. The opening music is a masterful adaptation of various seas chanteys, then the tone changes as the film begins on a Pacific port and a chorus softly sings an exotic South Seas chant that has a seductive and dangerous subtext. There is a warm and soothing theme that suggests waving palms and rolling seas but even that is tinged with loneliness. A sailing theme, in which strings and horns waver precariously, is also very melancholy in its way. This poetic yet realistic depiction of international sailors was adapted from four Eugene O'Neill one-act plays and, with its sterling cinematography by Gregg Toland and estimable ensemble cast, *The Long Voyage Home* is arguably Ford's most quietly captivating movie.

Much of the credit goes to Hageman, who brought years of musical experience to this splendid score. Also based on an O'Neill stage work, *Mourning Becomes Electra* transports the ancient Greek Orestia legend to New England after the Civil War. The opening music is the folk song "Shenandoah" sung by a male chorus and the tune returns throughout the film as a leitmotif. Hageman provided the restless, dramatic music that underscores the domestic conflict within the cursed Mannon family. Since the emotions in the tale are oversized, the music is often a bit over-blown by today's standards. A better description of the music is operatic, a sound with which Hageman was very familiar. Each of the main characters has a distinct theme and many of the verbal confrontations are underscored with agitated music. Perhaps the best way to enjoy the *Mourning Becomes Electra* score is to accept it as an opera without singing. And the best way to appreciate Hageman is to understand that he was an exceptional musical talent who dallied with movies for a short time and then moved on, leaving behind some superb scores.

Credits

(all films USA unless stated otherwise)

Year	Film	Director
1938	*If I Were King* (AAN)	Frank Lloyd
1939	*Hotel Imperial*	Robert Florey
1939	*Rulers of the Sea*	Frank Lloyd
1939	*Stagecoach* (AA)	John Ford
1940	*The Howards of Virginia* (AAN)	Frank Lloyd
1940	*The Long Voyage Home* (AAN)	John Ford
1941	*This Woman Is Mine* (aka *Fury at Sea*) (AAN)	Frank Lloyd
1941	*Paris Calling* (aka *Paris Bombshell*)	Edwin L. Marin
1941	*The Shanghai Gesture*	Josef von Sternberg
1947	*Angel and the Badman*	James Edward Grant
1947	*The Fugitive*	John Ford, Emilio Fernández (USA/Mexico)
1947	*Mourning Becomes Electra*	Dudley Nichols
1948	*Fort Apache*	John Ford
1948	*3 Godfathers*	John Ford
1949	*She Wore a Yellow Ribbon*	John Ford
1950	*Wagon Master*	John Ford
1952	*Adventures in Vienna*	Emil E. Reinert (Austria/USA)
1953	*Stolen Identity*	Gunther von Fritsch (Austria/USA)

HAJOS, Karl (1889–1950) A Hungarian-born songwriter, music director, and composer for the theatre and movies, he was very active in Hollywood during the first two decades of the talkies.

He was born in Budapest, Hungary, and studied piano privately and composition at the University of Budapest and the local Academy of Music. Hajos composed the music for a handful of operettas in his native country then immigrated to the States in 1924, settling in New York City, where he wrote the music for the Broadway operettas *Natja* (1925) and *White Lilacs* (1928). With the advent of sound, he relocated to Hollywood, where he started contributing music to silent films that used a sound effects and music soundtrack only. The Pola Negri romance *Loves of an Actress* in 1928 is believed to be his first solo assignment but most of Hajos's work in Hollywood is uncredited and records are unreliable. He is thought to be the sole composer for over fifty movies, and co-composer for over 150 others. Hajos's first notable score was for William A. Wellman's melodrama *Beggars of Life*, followed by such significant movies as *The Wolf of Wall Street*, *The Canary Murder Case*, *Illusion*, *The Greene Murder Case*, *The Virginian*, *Manslaughter*, *Morocco*, *Dishonored*, *City Streets*, *Werewolf of London*, *Two Wise Maids*, *Charlie Chan in the Secret Service*, *The Story of Temple Drake*, *The Caravan Trail*, *Search for Danger*, *It's a Small World*, *Summer*

Storm, and *The Man Who Walked Alone*, the last two receiving Academy Award nominations for Best Score. Although Hajos worked for Paramount for a time, most of his career was as a freelance composer who wrote for several studios and a wide range of directors including Josef von Sternberg, Victor Fleming, Dorothy Arzner, Henry Hathaway, John Cromwell, Douglas Sirk, and Rouben Mamoulian. He was still active in Hollywood when he died in 1950 at the age of sixty-one.

Like his fellow Hungarian Miklós Rózsa, Hajos wrote screen music in the classical tradition and utilized aspects of opera and operetta in his scoring. He used distinct musical motifs and was expert at varying and repeating musical themes with such expertise that one is not readily aware of the repetition. Hajos favored waltz time and often includes European-style songs in his scores even though most of his movies are set in contemporary America. *Beggars of Life*, Paramount's first feature with spoken dialogue, is a good example. This powerful drama, about a girl (Louise Brooks) on the run and the hobo (Wallace Beery) she teams up with, has a rhythmic waltz theme that takes slight pauses, giving it a distinctive coyness. As with many of the early nonmusical talkies, there is little underscoring in the movie, but this melody returns and is also used for the title song (lyric by J. Keim Brennan). Two other early sound films, both starring a young William Powell as sleuth Philo Vance, also have limited but interesting music. *The Canary Murder Case* opens and closes with a haunting waltz featuring strings and piccolo. Because the victim (Louise Brooks again) is a singing stage star, there is a scene in a theatre and a song by Hajos much in the style of his European operettas. The opening music in *The Greene Murder Case* is dramatically mysterious with long sustained phrases on the brass instruments and a melodic theme on gentle violins. By 1933 and the release of the disturbing drama *The Story of Temple Drake*, Paramount was using more underscoring and Hajos wrote his first noteworthy full score. Based on William Faulkner's novel *Sanctuary*, the movie is famous for pushing the boundaries of what could be shown in an American film. Temple Drake (Miriam Hopkins) is a high-society flirt who uses her sexuality to lead men on. But when she ends up in a farmhouse that serves as a hideout for some crooks, she is raped by the vicious Trigger (Jack La Rue). More than any other single film, *The Story of Temple Drake* was responsible for instituting the Hollywood Production Code.

Hajos's score is brash, dissonant, and as upsetting as the story. The sinister opening theme consists of harsh brass and cymbal crashes as the strings try to play a romantic waltz. There is creepy, drunken music for the farmhouse, and the lead-up to the rape itself is scored with menacing descending chords that increase in intensity. This is operetta music on the edge.

Like all of the movies discussed above, *Charlie Chan in the Secret Service* is set in the United States but because the title sleuth (Sidney Toler) is Chinese, Hajos suggests some Asian musical forms in his score. The opening music is somewhat Eastern with its gongs and other Asian percussion but the brass fanfares that enter to create excitement are definitely Western. In one passage restless strings and horn blasts speed up as they ascend the scale, and the movie is filled with conventional suspense music with some Asian string phrases to lend an Eastern flavor. Not set in America and even more foreign in sound are *Morocco* and *Summer Storm*. The former, about a cabaret singer (Marlene Dietrich) who falls for a legionnaire (Gary Cooper), has the suggestive song "What Am I Bid for My Apple?" (lyric by Leo Robin) sung by Dietrich. There is also a lot of underscoring. *Morocco* opens with exotic desert music heard on strings and horns with a gong for punctuation. There is festive music for the marketplace and plenty of background tunes for the many scenes in the cabaret. *Summer Storm* is even more foreign, being based on an Anton Chekhov story and set in rural Russia. Reset during the time of the Russian Revolution, the tale of a predatory peasant (Linda Darnell) and the aristocrat (George Sanders) she seduces is not far from the stage operetta milieu Hajos had scored in the past. The film is rich with music: a lyrical Russian song right out of a Romany operetta, a gypsy lament sung in tavern, a sprightly march for the French Foreign Legion troops, and a lively but heavy waltz with a Teutonic flavor.

Two very different movies illustrate Hajos's talent for leitmotif. *It's a Small World* is an odd but captivating film by William Castle about an adult man (Paul Dale) with the body of a preteen. Combination freak show and tender melodrama, the movie moves through many diverse emotions and Hajos's score captures these in a simple but flexible theme. It is a bouncy ditty that climbs the scale with a dapper confidence, a kind of children's tune to echo the hero's dilemma. This motif is used throughout the film, sometimes in a chipper manner, other times with sincere delicacy. It is also the melody for the title song (lyric by Charles Newman), which Dale sings with heartbreaking cheerfulness. *Werewolf of London* also has a pliable main theme. Three notes are heard on brass and then are echoed by alternate notes. This seven-note minor-key melody descends the scale in a manner that suggests something very supernatural. Hajos returns to this theme with different variations throughout the movie, sometimes as a graceful string passage, other times as a morose dirge. Although he did not get to score as many first-class films as Rózsa did, Hajos also brought the European sound to Hollywood and made it work effectively for the screen.

Credits

(all films USA unless stated otherwise)

Year	Film	Director
1928	Loves of an Actress	Rowland V. Lee
1928	Homecoming	Joe May (Germany)
1928	Beggars of Life	William A. Wellman
1928	The Woman from Moscow	Ludwig Berger
1928	Scarlet Seas	John Francis Dillon
1929	The Love Doctor	Melville W. Brown
1929	The Wolf of Wall Street	Rowland V. Lee
1929	The Canary Murder Case	Malcolm St. Clair, Frank Tuttle
1929	A Dangerous Woman	Gerald Grove, Rowland V. Lee
1929	The Studio Murder Mystery	Frank Tuttle
1929	River of Romance	Richard Wallace
1929	The Greene Murder Case	Frank Tuttle
1929	Charming Sinners	Robert Milton
1929	Illusion	Lothar Mendes
1929	Woman Trap	William A. Wellman
1929	The Virginian	Victor Fleming
1929	Darkened Rooms	Louis J. Gasnier
1930	Slightly Scarlet	Louis J. Gasnier, Edwin H. Knopf
1930	A Man from Wyoming	Rowland V. Lee
1930	Manslaughter	George Abbott
1930	Grumpy	George Cukor, Cyril Gardner
1930	Anybody's Woman	Dorothy Arzner
1930	The Sea God	George Abbott
1930	The Spoilers	Edwin Carewe
1930	Morocco (aka Amy Jolly)	Josef von Sternberg
1930	The Right to Love	Richard Wallace
1931	Scandal Sheet	John Cromwell
1931	Dishonored	Josef von Sternberg
1931	Unfaithful	John Cromwell
1931	City Streets	Rouben Mamoulian
1932	McKenna of the Mounted	D. Ross Lederman
1933	Tonight Is Ours	Stuart Walker
1933	The Thundering Herd (aka Buffalo Stampede)	Henry Hathaway
1933	The Story of Temple Drake (aka Sanctuary)	Stephen Roberts
1933	White Woman	Stuart Walker
1933	Girl without a Room	Ralph Murphy
1934	All of Me (aka Chrysalis)	James Flood
1935	Werewolf of London	Stuart Walker
1935	Manhattan Moon (aka Sing Me a Love Song)	Stuart Walker
1935	She Gets Her Man	William Nigh
1936	The Bold Caballero	Wells Root
1936	Happy Go Lucky	Aubrey Scotto
1937	Two Wise Maids	Phil Rosen
1937	Circus Girl (aka Without a Net)	John H. Auer

Year	Film	Director
1937	*The Painted Stallion*	Alan James, etc.
1944	*Charlie Chan in the Secret Service*	Phil Rosen
1944	*Summer Storm* (AAN)	Douglas Sirk
1945	*Fog Island*	Terry O. Morse
1945	*The Man Who Walked Alone* (AAN)	Christy Cabanne
1945	*The Phantom of 42nd Street*	Albert Herman
1945	*The Missing Corpse* (aka *Stranger in the Family*)	Albert Herman
1945	*Dangerous Intruder*	Vernon Keays
1946	*The Mask of Diijon*	Lew Landers
1946	*The Caravan Trail*	Robert Emmett Tansey
1946	*Driftin' River*	Robert Emmett Tansey
1946	*Wild West* (aka *Prairie Outlaws*)	Robert Emmett Tansey
1947	*Wild Country*	Ray Taylor
1947	*Range Beyond the Blue*	Ray Taylor
1947	*West to Glory*	Ray Taylor
1948	*Appointment with Murder* (aka *A Date with Murder*)	Jack Bernhard
1949	*Search for Danger*	Jack Bernhard
1949	*The Lovable Cheat*	Richard Oswald
1949	*Call of the Forest*	John F. Link Sr.
1950	*It's a Small World*	William Castle
1952	*Kill or Be Killed*	Max Nosseck

HAMLISCH, Marvin (1944–2012) A very popular songwriter, composer, conductor, pianist, and arranger who found wide success in every branch of show business, he wrote the soundtrack scores for thirty-two movies. Because of his concerts and television appearances, Hamlisch was one of the few American composers of his era who was well known to the general public.

Marvin Frederick Hamlisch was born in New York City, the son of an accordion player and bandleader who was born in Vienna. Hamlisch played the piano by ear as a child and could immediately repeat a tune he heard on the radio. At the age of seven he was admitted into Juilliard's Pre-College Division, the youngest student that program had ever accepted. Hamlisch continued his studies at Queens College and while still a student got jobs as a rehearsal pianist and dance music arranger for Broadway shows. He wrote his first hit song, "Sunshine, Lollipops, and Rainbows" (lyric by Howard Liebling) in 1965 and two years later had another hit with "California Nights" (lyric by Liebling), both songs recorded by Lesley Gore. While playing piano for a party, Hamlisch impressed film producer Sam Spiegel who hired him to score the movie *The Swimmer* in 1968. After writing soundtrack scores and songs for ten other movies, the twenty-nine-year-old Hamlisch won three Oscars in one night: for the score for *The Way We Were*, for its title song (lyric by Alan and Mar-ilyn Bergman), and for his musical arrangements of Scott Joplin rags for the soundtrack of *The Sting*. He scored another triumph two years later when he won the Pulitzer and other prizes for the long-running Broadway musical *A Chorus Line*. With various collaborators Hamlisch also composed the scores for the stage musicals *They're Playing Our Song* (1978), *Jean Seberg* (1983), *Smile* (1986), *The Goodbye Girl* (1993), *Sweet Smell of Success* (2002), and *The Nutty Professor* (2012).

By the 1980s Hamlisch became a familiar face across America as pianist and conductor on television and in concerts, often performing his own music. He continued to write movie scores, which often included a hit song. He also composed songs that were interpolated into others' films. Hamlisch was usually hired to score movie comedies, such as the Woody Allen films *Take the Money and Run* and *Bananas* and the Neil Simon comedies *I Ought to Be in Pictures*, *Chapter Two*, and *The Prisoner of Second Avenue*, as well as such comic successes as *Kotch*, *Seems Like Old Times*, *Three Men and a Baby*, and *Same Time, Next Year*. But he also wrote expert scores for such dramas and thrillers as *Paper Tiger*, *The Spy Who Loved Me*, *Sophie's Choice*, *Frankie and Johnny*, and *The Mirror Has Two Faces*. Hamlisch composed music for a handful of television series, including *Doc Elliot*, *Hot L Baltimore*, *Beacon Hill*, and *Omnibus*, as well as several TV mov-

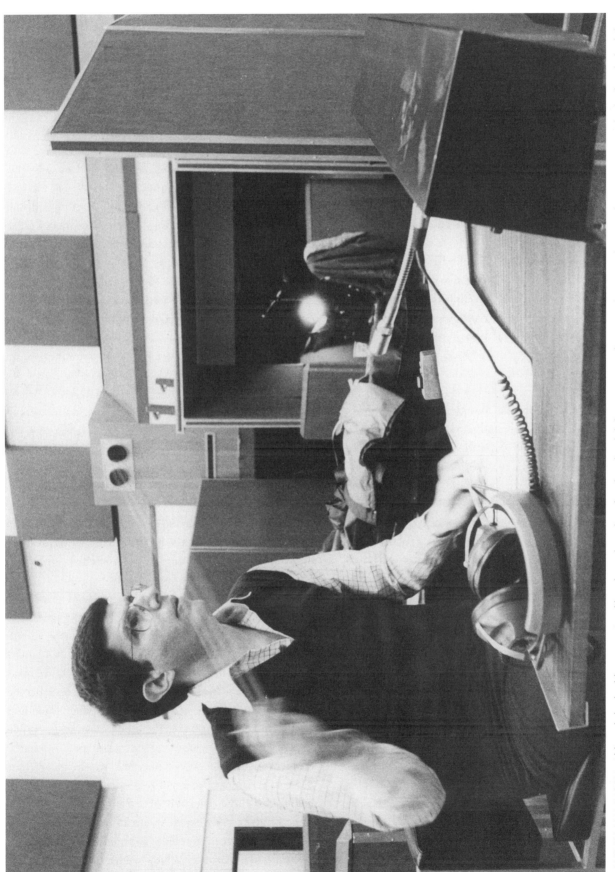

MARVIN HAMLISCH. Although he had been scoring films for only a decade when he did the James Bond movie *The Spy Who Loved Me* (1977), Hamlisch already had three Oscars to his credit. He not only composed the soundtrack score for this Bond movie but also wrote the music for its hit song "Nobody Does It Better." *United Artists / Photofest*
© *United Artists*

ies, including *Love from A to Z* (1974), *The Entertainer* (1976), *A Streetcar Named Desire* (1984), *The Two Mrs. Glenvilles* (1987), *When the Time Comes* (1987), *David* (1988), *Switched at Birth* (1991), *Seasons of the Heart* (1994), *Candles on Bay Street* (2006), and *Behind the Candelabra* (2013). Hamlisch loved popular music and took it very seriously, bringing it to concert halls across the country. He wrote one symphonic piece, *Anatomy of Peace* in 1991, which has been performed in the United States and Europe. One of the few artists to win Oscar, Grammy, Tony, and Emmy Awards and the Pulitzer Prize, he also received many other honors before his death at the age of sixty-eight.

While some may describe Hamlisch's music as pop, his musical training was so strong that his popular music is well crafted, surprisingly complex, yet effortless to appreciate. He drew on the traditions of jazz, ragtime, Latin music, swing, and sometimes even rock and disco. It is understandable why Hamlisch was asked to score so many film comedies because he is one of the few movie composers who could write funny music. Consider the hilarious opening credits for Woody Allen's Caribbean farce *Bananas*. A mariachi band plays and sings "Quiero La Noche" (lyric by Hamlisch) with silly guitar strumming and rapid drumming that sounds like bullets. The same melody is used as the love theme and, given an English lyric (by Liebling) is sung as "Cause I Believe in Loving" during the end credits. In between is a daffy Herb Alpert spoof with a solo trumpet squawking away, a robust matador march, a farcical passage played on kazoos and brass, and chaotic chase music that mocks itself with hand clapping. Perhaps it was the zany Allen humor or the Latin setting, but Hamlisch seems to have had more fun with the *Bananas* score than any other. Of the deeply serious films he scored, *The Swimmer* shows remarkable mastery, especially considering it is his first movie. This dark look at empty lives in suburbia has a flowing but unsettling main theme led by a harp then echoed on electric keyboard then violins. It is elegantly classical and dissonantly modern at the same time. Hamlisch introduces two other distinct themes in the film, a driving jazz piece and a modern cha-cha, all three converging for the devastating finale. This is the dramatic scoring of a seasoned pro, not a beginner. Perhaps the most sobering film in the Hamlisch catalog is *Sophie's Choice*, a disturbing tale about a Polish refugee (Meryl Streep) and her haunted past. The theme for the

title heroine is a lovely seven-note motif played on strings and oboe. It has a touch of European classicism to it yet is also bluesy befitting the postwar Manhattan setting. The story is told through the eyes of a young Southern writer (Peter MacNichol) who is scored with a rustic plantation folk theme, the banjos avoiding cliché by their waltzing tempo.

Hamlisch's most popular songs and scores have been those from romantic movies, best typified by *The Way We Were*. The main theme (which also serves as the melody for the hit title song with a lyric by Marilyn and Alan Bergman) is an expert example of musical restraint, its engaging music cautiously going up and down the scale, which gives it a melancholy feel. Hamlisch was asked to write a minor-key piece as the central theme but he argued that such a tone would broadcast the bittersweet ending of the movie. So "The Way We Were" is written in a major key but suggests that bittersweet quality all the same. Hamlisch got to score only one action movie, the James Bond installment titled *The Spy Who Loved Me*. The hit song from the film, "Nobody Does It Better" (lyric by Carol Bayer Sager), is sung over the credits by Carly Simon and became a pop favorite. It is a cool jazz number that is sexy even as it is aloof, much like the Bond character himself. For a spy adventure, the score is very melodic with some wonderful passages using electronically altered keyboard, an exotic theme played on Asian instruments, some fiery suspense music performed by low strings and high brass, and a romantic interpretation of "Nobody Does It Better" played delicately on electric guitar and then a saxophone.

Finally, some mention should be made of Hamlisch's most popular soundtrack, *The Sting*. Using a half dozen Scott Joplin rags, adding some original scoring for the dramatic scenes, and relying on arrangements by Gunther Schuller and himself, Hamlisch created one of the most delectable soundtracks of the era. Instead of using the most familiar Joplin piece, "Maple Leaf Rag," Hamlisch selected for the main theme the little-known-to-the-public "The Entertainer," a slow rag with many possibilities for mood changes. The rag not only held the movie together, "The Entertainer" became the most beloved Joplin song, Hamlisch's piano recording of it climbing the charts. *The Sting* brought a neglected American musical genius back into the American public's consciousness, something rarely accomplished by a movie. Hamlisch played "The

Entertainer" on television and in concerts for decades and it became his signature song. How strange to be most recognized by a number he did not compose. Luckily, Hamlisch was so popular that he was never a one-song artist. He gave popular music class and his movie scores are a testament to his ability to write mainstream hits without sacrificing craftsmanship and ingenuity. Autobiographies: *The Way I Was*, with Gerald C. Gardner (1994); *Marvin Makes Music* (2012). Official website: www.marvinhamlisch.us.

Credits

(all films USA unless stated otherwise; * for Best Song)

Year	Film	Director
1968	The Swimmer	Frank Perry, Sydney Pollack
1969	The April Fools	Stuart Rosenberg
1969	Take the Money and Run	Woody Allen
1970	Move	Stuart Rosenberg
1970	Flap	Carol Reed
1971	Bananas	Woody Allen
1971	Kotch (AAN*; GG*)	Jack Lemmon
1971	Something Big	Andrew V. McLaglen
1972	The War Between Men and Women	Melville Shavelson
1973	The World's Greatest Athlete	Robert Scheerer
1973	Save the Tiger	John G. Avildsen
1973	The Way We Were (AA, AA*; GG*)	Sydney Pollack
1975	The Prisoner of Second Avenue	Melvin Frank
1977	The Spy Who Loved Me (AAN, AAN*; GGN, GGN*; BAFTA-N)	Lewis Gilbert (UK)
1978	Same Time, Next Year (AAN*; GGN*)	Robert Mulligan
1978	Ice Castles (AAN*; GGN*)	Donald Wrye
1979	Starting Over (GGN*)	Alan J. Pakula
1979	Chapter Two	Robert Moore
1980	Seems Like Old Times	Jay Sandrich
1982	I Ought to Be in Pictures	Herbert Ross
1982	Sophie's Choice (AAN)	Alan J. Pakula (UK/USA)
1983	Romantic Comedy	Arthur Hiller
1985	D.A.R.Y.L.	Simon Wincer (UK/USA)
1987	Three Men and a Baby	Leonard Nimoy
1988	Little Nikita	Richard Benjamin
1989	The January Man	Pat O'Connor
1989	The Experts	Dave Thomas (Canada/USA)
1991	Frankie and Johnny	Garry Marshall
1992	Missing Pieces	Leonard Stern (UK/USA)
1995	Open Season	Robert Wuhl (USA/Canada)
1996	The Mirror Has Two Faces (AAN*; GGN*)	Barbra Streisand
2009	The Informant! (GGN)	Steven Soderbergh

HANCOCK, Herbie (b. 1940) A celebrated jazz and rhythm and blues pianist, bandleader, and composer with a special interest in electronic music, he scored ten Hollywood movies and three feature-length documentaries. The African American artist has concentrated on film dramas and comedies about the black experience in America using electronic music in innovative ways.

He was born Herbert Jeffrey Hancock in Chicago and was a child prodigy at the piano, performing a Mozart piano concerto with the Chicago Symphony when he was only eleven years old. As a high school student, he became interested in jazz when he discovered the music of Oscar Peterson and Bill Evans. Hancock was also interested in science, so he did a double major of electrical engineering and music at Grinnell College. After graduation, Hancock worked with trumpeter Donald Byrd and other artists at Blue Note Records. His debut album, *Takin' Off*, came out in 1963 and produced the hit "Watermelon Man." That same year he became a member of Miles Davis's famed quintet and for five years recorded many albums with Davis, including *Bitches Brew*, which introduced jazz fusion. As a solo artist and with his own group, the Head-hunters, Hancock went on to make many award-winning albums, some of which crossed over to climb both the jazz and R&B charts. He introduced and produced recordings by trumpeter Wynton Marsalis, teamed with other jazz and R&B artists in concert and on record, and was active in world music organizations, including the International Committee of Artists for Peace, which he cofounded. In the first decade of the twenty-first century, Hancock was featured in five concert films and composed some original music for the documentary *Herbie Hancock: Possibilities*.

Hancock made an auspicious movie debut when he was asked to score the 1966 landmark film *Blow-Up* directed by Michelangelo Antonioni. While some rock songs were heard in the movie, it was Hancock's jazz score that at-tracted so much attention. Music from Hancock's albums would be heard in dozens of subsequent movies and tele-vision shows but he did not write another original score for the screen until 1973 with the ironic crime thriller *The Spook Who Sat by the Door*. The next year Hancock scored the most popular movie of his career, the powerful *Death Wish*, which spawned two sequels. He returned to the movies only sporadically over the next four decades but his screen projects are often unique or controversial. For *'Round Midnight*, about a tenor sax jazz musician (Dexter Gordon) battling alcoholism, Hancock won an Oscar and other awards. His other films range from the comedies *Harlem Nights* and *Livin' Large!* to the disturbing dramas *A Soldier's Story* and *Jo Jo Dancer, Your Life Is Calling*. Hancock contributed some music to the documentaries *On the Shoulders of Giants*, about the basketball team the Harlem Rens, and *Occupy Los Angeles*. His handful of tele-vision credits range from the animated feature *Hey, Hey, Hey, It's Fat Albert* (1969) to the TV movie *The George McKenna Story* (1986).

One of the first jazz musicians to utilize the synthesizer in his music, Hancock incorporates the syncopated drums of funk and touches of soul as well. With his classical music education, he is adept at using classical forms even while maintaining the improvisation techniques of jazz. Hancock's interest in blues as well has made his music far reaching and easily enjoyed by listeners of various musi-cal genres. This is demonstrated in the main theme for *Blow-Up*, an up-tempo piece that has the trumpets playing jazz against the electric guitars of R&B. Other parts of the score use cool jazz, rhythmic saxophone improvisation, a bluesy love theme, and a fast jazz passage with bongos and brass. The soundtrack for *'Round Midnight* is considered one of the all-time great jazz movie albums, not only for Hancock's music but for the celebrated jazz musicians assembled to record it. Jazz legend Dexter Gordon plays the ill-fated hero and does the sax playing as well. Han-cock appears on-screen as a secondary character and he is joined on the soundtrack by other renowned musicians. Much of the score consists of jazz favorites such as the title song which is given a soulful rendition by Gordon on saxophone, Hancock on piano, and Bobby McFerrin doing the haunting scat singing. Hancock wrote a quirky passage titled "Berangere's Nightmare" which has such a loose improvisational feel that the musicians seem to enter and exit the piece at random. "Still Time" is a lovely piano and saxophone duet which is dreamy and engaging. Even better is "Chan's Song" for bass and piano which is slow jazz with the classical flavor of Claude Debussy. (Much of the film takes place in Paris in 1959.)

The comedies also have some delectable jazz music. The opening theme of *Harlem Nights* is slow and sensual for a comic crime spree set in the 1930s yet it certainly sets up the locale and the ambiance of the place. *Livin' Large!* is a contemporary tale and the score has a funk flavor and even utilizes early rap. The drama *A Soldier's Story*, about prejudice within a unit of African American soldiers in a Louisiana army camp in the 1940s, has a lazy, Southern tone in the score and Hancock uses the harmonica at times and moves into swing in other sec-tions. A similar approach can be found in *Jo Jo Dancer, Your Life Is Calling*, set in Peoria, Illinois, in the same era. *Death Wish* is one of the few movies Hancock scored that doesn't have an African American sensibility but the urban setting and the driving plot are well served by his restless jazz score. The main theme is a rhythmic jazz piece yet violins are used effectively in the background. Strings are also prominent in the revenge theme in which piano and electric percussion drive the music in an uncer-tain but feverish way. Another section of the score uses echoing piano chords, low woodwinds, and a runaway saxophone for a chase scene. "Joanna's Theme" is an exhilarating cool jazz that is warm with affection. Hancock's piano performance is particularly fluid as it builds to a series of minor crescendos. The *Death Wish* score is a good example of Hancock using his considerable improvisation talents in a very cinematic manner. That is what makes his screen scores so unique and timeless. Biographies: *Herbie Hancock: Blue Chip Keyboardist*, Ken Trethewey (2010); *You'll Know When You Get There: Herbie Hancock and the Mwandishi Band*, Bob Gluck (2012). Official website: www.herbiehancock.com.

Credits

(all films USA unless stated otherwise)

Year	Film	Director
1966	*Blow-Up*	Michelangelo Antonioni (UK/USA)
1973	*The Spook Who Sat by the Door*	Ivan Dixon
1974	*Death Wish*	Michael Winner
1984	*A Soldier's Story*	Norman Jewison
1986	*Jo Jo Dancer, Your Life Is Calling*	Richard Pryor
1986	*'Round Midnight* (AA; GGN; BAFTA-N)	Bernard Tavernier (USA/France)
1988	*Action Jackson*	Craig R. Baxley
1988	*Colors*	Dennis Hopper
1989	*Harlem Nights*	Eddie Murphy
1991	*Livin' Large!*	Michael Schultz
2006	*Herbie Hancock: Possibilities*	Doug Brio, Jon Fine
2011	*On the Shoulders of Giants*	Deborah Morales
2012	*Occupy Los Angeles*	Joseph Garcia Quinn

HARLINE, Leigh (1907–1969) A prolific songwriter and composer who scored many Disney cartoon shorts and over one hundred feature films, he is most remembered for his music in the animated classics *Snow White and the Seven Dwarfs* and *Pinocchio*.

Born Leigh Adrian Harline in Salt Lake City, Utah, the youngest of the thirteen children of Swedish immigrants, he was raised in the Mormon Church, studying piano and organ as a teenager and continuing at the University of Utah. After graduation, Harline moved to California where he got jobs as conductor, composer, arranger, pianist, and singer for various radio stations in Los Angeles and San Francisco. In 1933 he was hired by Walt Disney to work on animated shorts, including the famous *Silly Symphonies* cartoons. Harline wrote songs for some, soundtrack music for others, and arranged classical music for a handful as well. In a four-year period, he scored twenty-eight shorts for Disney. When the studio embarked on its first feature-length movie, *Snow White and the Seven Dwarfs*, Harline and Paul J. Smith were assigned to write the music score, but the songs were by Frank Churchill and Larry Morey.

The film was a runaway hit, and all four men were nominated for an Oscar. Harline continued to score shorts for Disney, and in 1940 he was assigned both the soundtrack score and the songs for the second Disney feature, *Pinocchio*. With lyricist Ned Washington, he wrote five songs for the movie, including "When You Wish Upon a Star," arguably the most famous Disney song and later the theme song for the entire Disney empire. Both the song and Harline and Smith's soundtrack for *Pinocchio* score won Oscars, and it seemed like the very successful collaboration with Disney would continue. But after a handful of more shorts, Harline parted ways with the studio and never returned.

In 1938 Harline scored the popular comedy *Blondie* for Columbia Pictures and returned to write music for the many *Blondie* sequels and other movies. Harline was kept busy at various studios over the next three decades scoring all kinds of films, from comedies and musicals to westerns and melodramas. He rarely got to write the songs but was assigned the soundtrack music for over a dozen movie musicals, including *My Gal Sal, You Were*

Never Lovelier, The Best Things in Life Are Free, Orchestra Wives, Step Lively, Road to Utopia, and *Call Me Mister.* Harline scored several Jerry Lewis–Dean Martin comedies for Paramount in the 1950s but did not stay with any one studio. Among the popular films he scored for different companies are *The Pride of the Yankees, The More the Merrier, Johnny Angel, Mr. Blandings Builds His Dream House, The Farmer's Daughter, It Happens Every Spring, The Bachelor and the Bobby-Soxer, The Miracle of the Bells, Monkey Business, River of No Return,* and *The Enemy Below.* By the 1960s Harline was not getting very many quality projects, though he received plaudits and an Oscar nod for the children's adventure movie *The Wonderful World of the Brothers Grimm.* He began writing music for television in 1958 and scored such series as *The Travels with Jaimie McPheeters, Daniel Boone,* and *Shirley Temple's Storybook* before his death at the age of sixty-two from throat cancer.

Animated features are generally shorter than live-action ones but they usually have more music. The soundtrack scores for *Snow White and the Seven Dwarfs* and *Pinocchio* are pioneers in the field, yet today they seem as polished and engaging as the best screen music. Harline was very experienced with "cartoon music," but for *Snow White and the Seven Dwarfs,* he and Smith wrote a dramatic soundtrack score as one would with a live-action adventure. As memorable as the songs are, one also recalls the sinister music for the evil Queen, the mysterious theme for the Magic Mirror, the scoring behind Snow White's flight into a dark forest, and the climactic encounter between the witch and the dwarfs. There is even more variety in *Pinocchio.* Stromboli's puppet show is scored with robust international music, the Blue Fairy has her own enchanting theme, the nightmarish carnival music on Pleasure Island forebodes evil doings, and the music as Pinocchio and Geppetto try to escape from Monstro the whale is as exciting as any heard in a swashbuckler. As accomplished as many of Harline's later scores are, they rarely can compare to the splendid music he wrote for these two animated classics.

Harline cowrote the music for so many movies and made uncredited contributions to dozens of others that one needs to concentrate on his solo efforts when exploring his work. For the comedy *The More the Merrier,* about the housing shortage in Washington, D.C., during World War II, Harline wrote a fun march for the opening credits and followed it up with some sarcastic versions of patriotic music, complete with military trumpet calls in a minor key. For the *Blondie* series, the main theme is a silly waltz that changes tempo as quickly as it changes instruments. Harline's music for the Cary Grant comedy *Mr. Blandings Builds His Dream House* is a sprightly Big Band theme with playful crescendos and plenty of jumping up and down the scale. The comedy-drama *The Farmer's Daughter* has an up-tempo romantic waltz theme that is quite engaging. It is turned into a comic theme for some of the movie's lightest moments and slowed down to become an arresting love theme. On the more serious side, Harline wrote pulsating film noir soundtracks for the psychological thriller *Crack-Up* and the George Raft suspense melodrama *Nocturne,* the latter also boasting a lush main theme which also served for the title song (lyric by Mort Greene). Another Raft film, *Johnny Angel,* has a haunting main theme that suggests mystery as much as suspense. Low woodwinds compete with high sustained strings to set a mood in which either murder or romance can occur. The war film *The Desert Rats* has a vigorous military march theme by Harline who then incorporates various British, Scottish, and Australian folk songs into his music. One of his last movies, *The Wonderful World of the Brothers Grimm,* brought him back to the kind of projects he started with at Disney. The main theme is a catchy frolic that slides up and down the scale and has a European carnival flavor. As it is whistled over the opening credits it is as instantly memorable as it is delightful.

Another theme is a sparkling waltz with percussive highlights that make it magical. The love theme is a flowing piece with flutes imitating birds and other woodwinds fluttering as well. Here is a movie overflowing with music, be it the songs by Bob Merrill or Harline's melodic soundtrack score. Perhaps Harline should have stayed at Disney, where such music was needed and appreciated.

Credits

(all films USA; * for Best Song)

Year	Film	Director
1937	*Snow White and the Seven Dwarfs* (AAN)	William Cottrell, etc.
1938	*Blondie*	Frank R. Strayer
1939	*There's That Woman Again*	Alexander Hall
1939	*Blondie Meets the Boss*	Frank R. Strayer
1939	*The Lady and the Mob*	Benjamin Stoloff
1939	*Blondie Brings Up Baby*	Frank R. Strayer
1940	*Pinocchio* (AA; AA*)	Norman Ferguson, etc.
1940	*Blondie on a Budget*	Frank R. Strayer
1940	*Blondie Has Servant Trouble*	Frank R. Strayer
1940	*So You Won't Talk*	Edward Sedgwick
1940	*Blondie Plays Cupid*	Frank R. Strayer
1941	*Mr. Bug Goes to Town* (aka *Hoppity Goes to Town*)	Dave Fleischer, Shamus Culhane
1942	*The Lady Has Plans*	Sidney Lanfield
1942	*Right to the Heart*	Eugene Forde
1942	*The Night before the Divorce*	Robert Siodmak
1942	*Rings on Her Fingers*	Rouben Mamoulian
1942	*True to the Army*	Albert S. Rogell
1942	*My Gal Sal*	Irving Cummings
1942	*Henry and Dizzy*	Hugh Bennett
1942	*The Postman Didn't Ring*	Harold D. Schuster
1942	*The Pride of the Yankees* (AAN)	Sam Wood
1942	*Careful, Soft Shoulder*	Oliver H. P. Garrett
1942	*Orchestra Wives*	Archie Mayo
1942	*You Were Never Lovelier* (AAN)	William A. Seiter
1943	*Margin for Error*	Otto Preminger
1943	*They Got Me Covered*	David Butler
1943	*The More the Merrier*	George Stevens
1943	*Jitterbugs*	Malcolm St. Clair
1943	*The Sky's the Limit* (AAN)	Edward H. Griffith
1943	*Johnny Come Lately* (AAN)	William K. Howard
1943	*Government Girl*	Dudley Nichols
1943	*Tender Comrade*	Edward Dmytryk
1944	*Show Business*	Edwin L. Marin
1944	*A Night of Adventure*	Gordon Douglas
1944	*Step Lively*	Tim Whelan
1944	*The Falcon in Mexico*	William Berke
1944	*Music in Manhattan*	John H. Auer
1944	*Heavenly Days*	Howard Estabrook
1944	*Girl Rush*	Gordon Douglas
1944	*Something for the Boys*	Lewis Seiler
1945	*What a Blonde*	Leslie Goodwins
1945	*Pan-Americana*	John H. Auer
1945	*Having Wonderful Crime*	A. Edward Sutherland
1945	*China Sky*	Ray Enright
1945	*The Brighton Strangler*	Max Nosseck
1945	*Mama Loves Papa*	Frank R. Strayer
1945	*Isle of the Dead*	Mark Robson
1945	*First Yank into Tokyo*	Gordon Douglas
1945	*Johnny Angel*	Edwin L. Marin
1945	*Man Alive*	Ray Enright
1946	*Road to Utopia*	Hal Walker
1946	*From This Day Forward*	John Berry
1946	*The Truth about Murder*	Lew Landers
1946	*Ding Dong Williams*	William Berke

Year	Film	Director
1946	*Till the End of Time*	Edward Dmytryk
1946	*Crack-Up*	Irving Reis
1946	*Child of Divorce*	Richard Fleischer
1946	*Lady Luck*	Edwin L. Marin
1946	*Nocturne*	Edwin L. Marin
1947	*Beat the Band*	John H. Auer
1947	*The Farmer's Daughter*	H. C. Potter
1947	*A Likely Story* (aka *Due South*)	H. C. Potter
1947	*Honeymoon*	William Keighley
1947	*The Bachelor and the Bobby-Soxer*	Irving Reis
1947	*Tycoon*	Richard Wallace
1948	*The Miracle of the Bells*	Irving Pichel
1948	*Mr. Blandings Builds His Dream House*	H. C. Potter
1948	*The Velvet Touch*	Jack Gage
1948	*They Live by Night*	Nicholas Ray
1948	*The Boy with Green Hair*	Joseph Losey
1948	*Every Girl Should Be Married*	Don Hartman
1949	*The Judge Steps Out*	Boris Ingster
1949	*It Happens Every Spring*	Lloyd Bacon
1949	*The Big Steal*	Don Siegel
1949	*The Woman on Pier 13*	Robert Stevenson
1950	*Perfect Strangers*	Bretaigne Windust
1950	*My Friend Irma Goes West*	Hal Walker
1950	*The Happy Years*	William A. Wellman
1951	*The Company She Keeps*	John Cromwell
1951	*Call Me Mister*	Lloyd Bacon
1951	*That's My Boy*	Hal Walker
1951	*The Guy Who Came Back*	Joseph M. Newman
1951	*His Kind of Woman*	John Farrow, Richard Fleischer
1951	*Behave Yourself!*	George Beck
1951	*On the Loose*	Charles Lederer
1951	*I Want You*	Mark Robson
1951	*Double Dynamite*	Irving Cummings
1952	*The Las Vegas Story*	Robert Stevenson
1952	*Sailor Beware*	Hal Walker
1952	*Monkey Business*	Howard Hawks
1952	*My Wife's Best Friend*	Richard Sale
1952	*My Pal Gus*	Robert Parrish
1953	*Taxi*	Gregory Ratoff
1953	*Down among the Sheltering Palms*	Edmund Goulding
1953	*The Desert Rats*	Robert Wise
1953	*Pickup on South Street*	Samuel Fuller
1953	*A Blueprint for Murder*	Andrew L. Stone
1953	*Vicki*	Harry Horner
1953	*Money from Home*	George Marshall
1954	*River of No Return*	Otto Preminger, Jean Negulesco
1954	*Susan Slept Here*	Frank Tashlin
1954	*Broken Lance*	Edward Dmytryk
1954	*Black Widow*	Nunnally Johnson
1955	*House of Bamboo*	Samuel Fuller
1955	*The Girl in the Red Velvet Swing*	Richard Fleischer
1955	*Good Morning, Miss Dove*	Henry Koster
1955	*The Last Frontier*	Anthony Mann
1956	*The Bottom of the Bottle*	Henry Hathaway
1956	*23 Paces to Baker Street*	Henry Hathaway
1956	*The Best Things in Life Are Free*	Michael Curtiz
1956	*Teenage Rebel*	Edmund Goulding
1956	*The Girl Can't Help It*	Frank Tashlin

Year	Film	Director
1957	*The True Story of Jesse James*	Nicholas Ray
1957	*The Wayward Bus*	Victor Vicas
1957	*No Down Payment*	Martin Ritt
1957	*The Enemy Below*	Dick Powell
1958	*Ten North Frederick*	Philip Dunne
1958	*Man of the West*	Anthony Mann
1959	*The Remarkable Mr. Pennypacker*	Henry Levin
1959	*Warlock*	Edward Dmytryk
1959	*These Thousand Hills*	Richard Fleischer
1959	*Holiday for Lovers*	Henry Levin
1960	*Visit to a Small Planet*	Norman Taurog
1960	*The Facts of Life*	Melvin Frank
1961	*The Honeymoon Machine*	Richard Thorpe
1962	*The Wonderful World of the Brothers Grimm* (AAN)	Henry Levin, George Pal
1964	*7 Faces of Dr. Lao*	George Pal
1965	*Strange Bedfellows*	Melvin Frank

HARLING, W. Franke (1887–1958) A British-born organist, songwriter, arranger, and composer, he spent less than twenty years in Hollywood but contributed to the scores of over fifty feature films.

He was born William Franke Harling in London, England, and was educated at the Grace Church Choir School in Manhattan and the Royal Academy of Music in London. Harling was organist and choir director at the Church of the Resurrection in Brussels before returning to the States where he was music director at the U.S. Military Academy at West Point. While there he composed the Academy's hymn, "The Corps," and its official march song, "West Point Forever."

He wrote original music for the Broadway play *Pan and the Young Shepherd* (1918), returning to the New York stage with his opera *Deep River* (1926) and musical comedy *Say When* (1928). Harling arrived in Hollywood just as sound was coming in and contributed music to some silents that were being retooled as talkies. He scored Paramount's early talking picture, *Interference*, then went on to contribute music for many others, often in collaboration with several other composers and always uncredited. He won an Oscar with three other composers for their adaptation of American folk songs used in *Stagecoach* (1939). Among the notable movies Harling scored solo or with only one collaborator are *Scandal Sheet, Broken Lullaby, Shanghai Express, Trouble in Paradise, One Hour with You, The Bitter Tea of General Yen, Destination Unknown, Penny Serenade, Souls at Sea,* and *Three Russian Girls,* winning Oscar nominations for the last two. Harling was also a very accomplished songwriter and two of his most famous songs were written for films scored by others: "Beyond the Blue Horizon" (with Richard A. Whiting and Leo Robin) from *Monte Carlo* (1930) and "Sing, You Sinners" (lyric by Sam Coslow) from *Honey* (1930). His concert works include tone poems, art songs, pieces for cello and orchestra, and the jazz-opera *A Light from St. Agnes.* Harling, who had become an American citizen, retired from the movies in 1945 and lived in California until his death thirteen years later.

Like so many studio composers in the 1930s, Harling was often assigned to a movie with others, sometimes five composers contributing to one soundtrack. About one dozen of his credits were co-composed with one collaborator, leaving roughly thirty screen scores that he did solo. Among these are some classic films by celebrated directors with noteworthy scores. For Ernst Lubitsch's melodrama *Broken Lullaby* about a former soldier (Phillips Holmes) and his guilt after World War I, Harling wrote a dramatic, operatic score with weighty passages for the powerful scenes and sentimental laments for the mournful ones. The title lullaby is indeed a melancholy one, one that welcomes death rather than sleep. The Paramount drama feels very much like a European film and Harling's score adds to its Old World feel. Harling also scored Lubitsch's *Trouble in Paradise*, perhaps the most stylish and memorable of his comedies. If the score for *Broken Lullaby* recalls a Teutonic opera, the music in *Trouble in Paradise* can only be described as an Austrian operetta. The romantic triangle of con man (Herbert Marshall), con gal (Miriam

Hopkins), and their easy mark (Kay Francis) is scored with frivolous and sardonic waltzes, serenades, and tangos, the music adding to the famous "Lubitsch touch." In one droll scene at the opera, the singers are heard declaring how much they love each other, the pages of the conductor's score flip to the next act, and the same singers vocalize their hatred for one another. If Lubitsch were a composer, this is the kind of music he would have written.

Harling seems to have been given more than his fair share of movies with Asian settings. For Frank Capra's *The Bitter Tea of General Yen*, Harling sets up the Chinese locale with gongs, chimes, fluttering percussion, and trumpet fanfares. It is all the stuff of cliché today, but in 1933 this romance between an American woman (Barbara Stanwyck) and an Asian warlord (Nils Asther) was quite unique and Harling's pseudo-Asian music was considered very exotic. The mix of Chinese musical forms and Western ones is best heard in the famous dream scene in which Stanwyck's tormented feelings about East and West are realized. For the screen adaptation of the play (not the opera) *Madame Butterfly* in 1932, selections from the Puccini opera are quoted and Harling fills in with pseudo-Japanese music. Western instruments are used (as in the opera), particularly flutes and strings, and the effect is a very accessible version of Asian music. A very different Occidental tone is set in Josef von Sternberg's *Shanghai Express*, one of Marlene Dietrich's best vehicles. She plays the femme fatale Shanghai Lilly who pretends to live only for herself but ends up being the one who saves a group of Westerners traveling by train through civil war–torn China. Harling takes his musical cue from the train rather than the culture and the score is brisk and restless except for the steamy love scenes. The scenes with the Chinese troops are scored with Asian touches but much of the music is more dramatic than authentic.

The tearjerker *Penny Serenade*, about parents (Irene Dunne and Cary Grant) whose unborn baby dies and their attempt to deal with their grief by adopting a child, was directed so intelligently by George Stevens that he disguises the soap opera elements. The score is not as successful in holding back the emotions. The graceful main theme is sprightly and optimistic, but once an earthquake hits (which causes her to miscarry) and matters get heavy, the music has a grim subtext. More than a little sentimental as well is the tribute to early military aviation, William A. Wellman's *Men with Wings*. The score boasts a vigorous march for its main theme then moves into nostalgic passages as the characters are established. When they take up the challenge of creating an American air force, the music becomes proud and teary eyed in the process. Harling scored three movies for director James Whale, none of them in the horror genre. The diabolical melodrama *A Kiss Before the Mirror* has a flowing score that does not give away the intentions of a jealous husband (Frank Morgan) to murder his wife. The drawing room melodrama *One More River* has a symphonic score with waltzing passages and romantic airs that are far from upsetting. Whale's light touch in the European comedy *By Candlelight* is matched by Harling's frothy music. This convoluted but delicious tale of a prince's butler (Paul Lukas) being mistaken as the prince (Nils Asther) is scored with Continental waltzes and elegant chamber music. There was so much more to the director of *Frankenstein*, just as Harling was a much finer composer than Hollywood gave him credit for.

Credits

(all films USA)

Year	Film	Director
1928	*The Whip*	Charles Brabin
1928	*Interference*	Lothar Mendes, Roy Pomeroy
1929	*Dangerous Curves*	Lothar Mendes
1929	*Charming Sinners*	Robert Milton
1929	*The Marriage Playground*	Lothar Mendes
1930	*The Kibitzer*	Edward Sloman
1930	*Behind the Make-Up*	Robert Milton
1930	*Only the Brave*	Frank Tuttle
1930	*The Right to Love*	Richard Wallace
1931	*Scandal Sheet*	John Cromwell

Year	Film	Director
1931	The False Madonna	Stuart Walker
1932	Broken Lullaby	Ernst Lubitsch
1932	Shanghai Express	Josef von Sternberg
1932	One Hour with You	Ernst Lubitsch, George Cukor
1932	Two Seconds	Mervyn LeRoy
1932	The Crash	William Dieterle
1932	Trouble in Paradise	Ernst Lubitsch
1932	Men Are Such Fools	William Nigh
1932	Madame Butterfly	Marion Gering
1933	The Bitter Tea of General Yen	Frank Capra
1933	Destination Unknown	Tay Garnett
1933	The Kiss Before the Mirror	James Whale
1933	Man's Castle	Frank Borzage
1933	Cradle Song	Mitchell Leisen
1933	By Candlelight	James Whale
1934	One More River	James Whale
1935	So Red the Rose	King Vidor
1937	Souls at Sea (AAN)	Henry Hathaway
1938	Men with Wings	William A. Wellman
1941	Adam Had Four Sons	Gregory Ratoff
1941	Penny Serenade	George Stevens
1941	Adventure in Washington	Alfred E. Green
1942	The Lady Is Willing	Mitchell Leisen
1943	I Escaped from the Gestapo	Harold Young
1943	Three Russian Girls (AAN)	Henry S. Kesler, Fyodor Otsep
1944	Johnny Doesn't Live Here Any More	Joe May
1944	When the Lights Go On Again	William K. Howard

HAYASAKA, Fumio (1914–1955) A celebrated Japanese composer and teacher, he managed in his short life to score forty-seven feature films and groomed a whole generation of Japanese screen composers. Arguably the finest Japanese movie composer of his time, he is most known around the world for his films with director Akira Kurosawa.

Fumio Hayasaka was born in Sendai on the Japanese island of Honshu but grew up on the island of Hokkaido where he received no formal musical training but studied music theory and composition on his own. His boyhood friend Ifukube Akira was also a self-taught composer and at the age of nineteen Hayasaka and Akira founded the New Music League and presented concerts of original work. Some of Hayasaka's concert compositions won national awards and he was encouraged to move to Tokyo in 1939 to break into movie music. That year he scored his first film, *The Lady Ties a Ribbon*, followed by a variety of other movies during World War II. Both the Japanese film industry and Hayasaka's career blossomed after the war. He first worked with director Kurosawa on *Drunken Angel* in 1948, the two men becoming friends and soul mates. Kurosawa taught the young composer about film technique and Hayasaka broadened the director's ideas of music. The two collaborated on six more films over the next six years. *Rashomon* in 1950 became the first Japanese movie to be shown and applauded around the world. The other notable Kurosawa-Hayasaka movies include *Stray Dog*, *The Idiot*, *Ikiru*, and *Seven Samurai*. Hayasaka worked with all the top Japanese directors of his day, including eight movies with Kenji Mizoguchi, most memorably *Sansho the Bailiff* and *Ugetsu*. As busy as Hayasaka was scoring twenty-eight feature films between 1950 and 1956, he found time to compose many concert pieces, teach screen music techniques to up-and-coming composers, and founded Japan's Association of Film Music. While working on a new score for Kurosawa, Hayasaka died of tuberculosis at the age of forty-one. Kurosawa was devastated and fell into a deep depression that served as the background for his 1955 movie *Record of a Living Being* (aka *I Live in Fear*).

Hayasaka's musical style, both for his screen scores and his concert pieces, is a delicate mixture of Western romanticism and traditional Japanese music. Having taught himself about Western music, Hayasaka took an Asian approach to understanding the conventional methods of the romantic composers, particularly those late in the period. He was just beginning to experiment with modern music and atonal ideas in his concert pieces when he died. The film scores use predominately Western instruments and echo Western opera and ballet. This was encouraged by Japanese movie producers who hoped that their films would find an international market if the music was more accessible to Westerners. Yet the traditional sound of Japan can be found in all of Hayasaka's movie scores. *Rashomon*, the film classic that looks at a rape and murder with different points of view, has a score that opens with a teasing melody that is played on both traditional Japanese instruments and Western strings. The music forebodes danger and the rape-murder to follow. Later passages are fully Western with a Japanese drum or pipe to flavor the sound with Asian accents. When the crime is related by the various witnesses, the music alters with each point of view. By the end of the movie a flowing Western melody is performed on Asian instruments. This kind of scoring did not happen by accident. Kurosawa and Hayasaka discussed how music was to be used during the actual filming rather than after production as is usually the case. Scenes were shot with Hayasaka on the set giving suggestions to both actors and director on how the music would sound at certain points. This was not only innovative but downright radical.

The music for Kurosawa's character drama *Ikiru* is much more Western even though the story about a fatally ill businessman (Takashi Shimura) is a contemporary Japanese one. The Western orchestra plays the main theme in which competing brass convey a restlessness and sense of confusion. There is also a lovely passage that has a reflective quality not unlike gentle Japanese garden music, a harp substituting for an Asian string instrument. The score for Mizoguchi's *Ugetsu*, about various inhabit-ants in a small village during the age of the samurai, is very Asian. It opens with a Japanese chant and single drum then reeds and strings are added for a full traditional sound. Yet there is also something modern about the music, with its sustained notes and eerie chords. The different domestic scenes in the movie are scored with warm, tranquil themes while the action sequences have dissonant and even surreal music. For the Kurosawa masterwork *Seven Samurai*, Hayasaka utilizes all kinds of music. This exciting tale about a band of samurai who defend a poor village from bandits was even more popular around the world than *Rashomon*. The score has a chanting male choir that sounds almost Russian, as does a brooding passage played on low Western strings. The fanfare that accompanies the samurai team recalls both an American western and a German march. A Japanese reed instrument and traditional percussion are joined by Western brass for some of the grander passages. The music for the climactic battle between the bandits and the samurai is very Hollywood in sound yet has the tempo of an Asian dance. *Seven Samurai* is one of the cinema's finest action epics but the music is always on a very personal and intimate level.

Perhaps Hayasaka's greatest contribution to screen scoring is his idea of music as counterpoint to the action. Rather than have the score accompany or heighten the visual images, the music can sometimes move in a different direction or follow a different pattern. This may be used for obvious ironic effect but can also be very subtle and even unconscious. Today we are used to film music avoiding the expected path and going for contrast; a horse race scored with a lullaby or a hymn heard over a battle scene. Hayasaka and Kurosawa began experimenting with this idea in 1948 and it reached maturity in their movie masterpieces of the 1950s. Westerners were dazzled when they discovered the new Japanese cinema in that decade. Subconsciously they were also hearing something just as revealing.

Credits

(all films Japan)

Year	Film	Director
1939	*The Lady Ties a Ribbon*	Satsuo Yamamoto
1940	*Kaigun bakugekitai*	Sotoji Kimura
1940	*Traveling Actors*	Mikio Naruse

Year	Film	Director
1941	Gubijisô	Nobuo Nakagawa
1941	Shidô monogatari	Hisatora Kumagai
1941	Shirasagi	Yasujirô Shimazu
1942	Wakai sensei	Takeshi Sato
1942	Bouquet in the Southern Seas	Yutaka Abe
1942	Map for Mother	Yasujirô Shimazu
1946	An Enemy of the People	Tadashi Imai
1947	Four Love Stories	Kajirô Yamamoto, etc.
1947	24 Hours of a Secret Life	Tadashi Imai, etc.
1947	Actress	Teinosuke Kinugasa
1948	A Flower Blooms	Kon Ichikawa
1948	Drunken Angel	Akira Kurosawa
1948	Ikiteiru gazô	Yasuki Chiba
1948	Girl with a Rainbow	Kiyoshi Saeki
1949	Spring Flirtation	Kajirô Yamamoto
1949	Stray Dog	Akira Kurosawa
1950	Desertion at Dawn	Senkichi Taniguchi
1950	Mado kara tobidase	Koji Shima
1950	Scandal	Akira Kurosawa
1950	Light Snowfall	Yutaka Abe
1950	Rashomon	Akira Kurosawa
1950	Portrait of Madame Yuki	Kenji Mizoguchi
1950	Yoru no hibotan	Yasuki Chiba
1951	The Idiot	Akira Kurosawa
1951	Miss Oyu	Kenji Mizoguchi
1951	The Lady from Musashino	Kenji Mizoguchi
1951	A Married Life	Mikio Naruse
1951	The Life of a Horsetrader	Keigo Kimura
1952	Nagasaki no Uta wa Wasureji	Tomotaka Tasaka
1952	Ikiru (aka To Live)	Akira Kurosawa
1953	Ugetsu (aka Tales of Ugetsu)	Kenji Mizoguchi
1953	Hiroba no kodoku	Shin Saburi
1954	Sansho the Bailiff	Kenji Mizoguchi
1954	Seven Samurai	Akira Kurosawa
1954	Kimi shinitamo koto nakare	Seiji Maruyama
1954	The Princess Sen	Keigo Kimura
1954	The Crucified Lovers (aka A Story from Chikamatsu)	Kenji Mizoguchi
1954	Smuggling Ship	Toshio Sugie
1954	Hanran: Ni-ni-roku jiken	Yutaka Abe
1955	Princess Yang Kwei-Fei	Kenji Mizoguchi
1955	The Taira Clan	Kenji Mizoguchi
1955	Asunaro monogatari	Hiromichi Horikawa
1955	Samurai of the Great Earth	Kiyoshi Saeki
1956	Happiness Is Under That Star	Toshio Sugie

HAYES, Isaac (1942–2008) One of the giants in American soul music, the African American composer, singer, songwriter, actor, and producer had a limited career in movies but is still remembered for his acclaimed soundtrack for *Shaft*.

Born Isaac Lee Hayes Jr. in Covington, Kentucky, into a poor sharecropper family, he began singing in church when he was five years old. Hayes taught himself to play the piano, organ, and flute and was offered scholarships to study music at a handful of colleges, but instead he supported his family working in a meatpacking facility in Memphis and performing in clubs. By the 1960s he was writing songs with David Porter, finding early success with such hits as "Soul Man" and "When Something Is Wrong with My Baby." Hayes's album *Hot Buttered Soul* in 1969 was an immediate hit and remains a landmark in soul music. Other popular albums followed, and Hayes became an important record producer, presenting work by himself and many other artists. As a songwriter and performer, he embraced all aspects of show business from concerts to television and he became a symbol of the art of soul music in America. Hayes first got involved with movies when he collaborated with Wes Montgomery on the score for the Norman Mailer drama *Maidstone* in 1970. The next year he wrote a dynamic score for the action movie *Shaft*, the song "Theme from *Shaft*" winning the Oscar, the score roundly applauded and awarded, and the song and soundtrack album going to the top of the charts. In 1974 Hayes scored and acted in two crime thrillers, *Tough Guys* and *Truck Turner*. He went on to act in thirty-two more feature films as well as several television series, TV movies, and made-for-video features. His most remembered roles are the Duke in *Escape from New York* and the voice of "Chef" in the animated *South Park* TV series, videos, movie, and video game. After a twenty-five-year absence from screen composing, Hayes wrote the music for the dramas *Ninth Street* and *Bui Doi*. In 2008 he died of a stroke at the age of sixty-five. Hayes received many awards and honors during his lifetime and left a legacy of dozens of albums and songs that are the essence of soul music. His music can be heard in over one hundred movies and television programs ranging from *The Blues Brothers* (1980) to *Behind the Candelabra* (2013).

The ironic thing about Hayes's screen music is that it utilizes jazz and blues more than soul. The popular "Theme from *Shaft*," for example, is a pulsating jazz piece on electric guitar, brass, flute, percussion, and synthesizer that does variations on a rising and falling riff. More an instrumental work than a song, the spoken lyric is a series of questions to which a female chant answers with the title name. John Shaft (Richard Roundtree) is a hip African American private eye, a screen novelty when the movie came out in 1971. Gordon Parks directed in a taut yet breezy manner and the movie was a landmark of sorts, a classic blaxploitation thriller. Hayes's *Shaft* score captures Gordon's stimulating style not only in the title theme but in the dozen other tracks he wrote for the film. There is a breezy traveling theme on woodwinds and brass with high squeaking notes that form the pulse of the piece, a smooth jazz passage that seems lazy and sexy at the same time, a blues section that is quite entrancing, a vibrant jazz theme on electric organ and saxophone that jumps across the scale, and a frenzied piece on electric guitar that races forward even as the bass line remains steady. It is not difficult to see why this score became a best-selling album.

Hayes's music for two other crime movies is almost as accomplished as that in *Shaft*. Hayes himself played the title bounty hunter in *Truck Turner* and again the music is thrilling. The title theme is a vivacious, even frantic, piece with synthesized sound effects heard against the brass instruments. Again the lyric is simple, punctuated by the name of Turner chanted in rhythm. The score also has a jaunty traveling theme with a happy beat and a playful electric guitar heard over ascending strings. Even better is the music in *Tough Guys*, sometimes listed as *Three Tough Guys* even though the title song refers to "two tough guys." Hayes stars as an ex-cop who pursues bank robbers across Chicago. The percussive main theme has rapid electronic instruments and blaring brass as the lyric pronounces "two tough guys." This rich score also includes a flowing cool jazz theme featuring nimble fingering on the saxophone, a busy rhythmic passage on electric saxophone and conventional brass that bounces along at propelling pace, and a percussion theme that plays like a funky march. After 1974, Hayes's movie career concentrated on acting rather than composing, but in addition to his handful of scores his music has returned to the screen in many other features. Official website: www.isaachayes.com.

Credits

(all films USA unless stated otherwise; * for Best Song; ** also acted in the movie)

Year	Film	Director
1970	*Maidstone*	Norman Mailer
1971	*Shaft* (AAN; AA*; GG; GGN*; BAFTA-N)	Gordon Parks
1974	*Tough Guys* (aka *Three Tough Guys*)**	Duccio Tessari (Italy/France/USA)
1974	*Truck Turner***	Jonathan Kaplan
1999	*Ninth Street***	Tim Rebman, Kevin Willmott
2001	*Bui Doi*	Roger Dick French

HAYTON, Lennie (1908–1971) A top Hollywood music arranger who also conducted, composed, and played piano in famous orchestras, he contributed music to over fifty feature films, including some classic MGM musicals.

Leonard George Hayton was born in New York City and took piano lessons as a child. Hayton began his career as a jazz pianist, working with such famous bands as those led by Paul Whiteman, Frankie Trumbauer, Eddie Lang, Red Nichols, Joe Venuti, Jimmy Dorsey, and Bix Beiderbecke, as well as his own Lennie Hayton Orchestra. He also composed and did arrangements for these bands. Among his popular compositions are "Mood Hollywood" (with Dorsey), "Flying Fingers," and "Midnight Mood." His most famous arrangement is the one he did with Hoagy Carmichael for Artie Shaw's version of "Stardust." Hayton went to Hollywood in 1940 and became a musical director for MGM during a golden age of movie musicals. During his thirteen years at the studio he arranged, conducted, and wrote music for dramas, comedies, and musicals. Most of the films Hayton scored were in collaboration with other composers and his most famous movies were musicals in which others wrote the songs while he provided the arrangements and incidental music between numbers. For his expert handling of the music in musicals, he received Oscar nominations for *The Harvey Girls*, *The Pirate*, *Singin' in the Rain*, and *Star!*, winning the Academy Award for *On the Town* (with Roger Edens) and *Hello, Dolly!* (with Lionel Newman). Hayton's other musicals include *The Barkleys of Broadway*, *Best Foot Forward*, *Yolanda and the Thief*, and *Words and Music*. Among his significant nonmusicals are *Barnacle Bill*, *Any Number Can Play*, *Battleground*, *Living in a Big Way*, *The Hucksters*, *Salute to the Marines*, *Side Street*, and *See Here, Private Hargrove*. Hayton was married to singer Lena Horne, one of the first biracial marriages in Hollywood. As tempestuous as the relationship was, he always served as her musical director and the couple remained married for twenty-five years, ter-

minated by his death from heart failure at the age of sixty-three. Unlike most conductor-arrangers in show business, Hayton was well known to the public because of his work with top singers, particularly Frank Sinatra, Bing Crosby, and Horne. He was easily recognized by his trademark captain's hat worn at an angle when he conducted. When he left MGM in 1953, Hayton concentrated on concerts and recordings. He returned to movies for the 1960s musicals *Star!* and *Hello, Dolly!* A likable but difficult man, Hayton indulged in heavy drinking and smoking, which led to his premature death in 1971.

Although he wrote some original music for the famous musicals he scored, much of Hayton's contribution was arranging the songs by the various songwriters and providing incidental music to bridge scenes and songs. Of the many nonmusicals he scored, only eighteen were solo efforts, most of them written for forgettable movies that MGM lavished little attention or money on. The best of them, the World War II classic *Battleground*, has little music. In fact, the only memorable part of the score is a military cadence count chanted by the soldiers that slowly builds and is taken over by the brass to become a full-fledged march. There are similar but less effective marches in the other war movies Hayton scored, such as *Stand By for Action*, *Salute to the Marines*, and *Battle Circus*. Such intriguing dramas as *The Hucksters*, about the cutthroat advertising business, and *Dr. Kildare's Victory*, part of a series of hospital movies starring Lew Ayres, have surprisingly little underscoring. It seems that MGM entrusted its expensive musicals to Hayton the arranger but were not very confident of his composing skills and gave all of the prestige nonmusicals to other composers. This does not diminish Hayton's contribution to the Hollywood musical during the war and postwar years. He was instrumental in creating the sound of those classic song-and-dance movies just as he was in making Big Bands and singers sound their best.

Credits

(all films USA)

Year	Film	Director
1941	*Barnacle Bill*	Richard Thorpe
1941	*Love Crazy*	Jack Conway
1942	*The Bugle Sounds* (aka *Steel Cavalry*)	S. Sylvan Simon, Richard Thorpe
1942	*A Yank on the Burma Road*	George B. Seitz

Year	Film	Director
1942	*Dr. Kildare's Victory*	W. S. Van Dyke
1942	*Born to Sing*	Edward Ludwig
1942	*This Time for Keeps* (aka *Over the Waves*)	Charles Reisner
1942	*Mokey*	Wells Root
1942	*Grand Central Murder*	S. Sylvan Simon
1942	*Maisie Gets Her Man*	Roy Del Ruth
1942	*Pierre of the Plains*	George B. Seitz
1942	*Eyes in the Night*	Fred Zinnemann
1942	*Whistling in Dixie*	S. Sylvan Simon
1942	*Stand By for Action* (aka *This Man's Navy*)	Robert Z. Leonard
1943	*Assignment in Brittany*	Jack Conway
1943	*Pilot #5*	George Sidney
1943	*Best Foot Forward*	Edward Buzzell
1943	*Salute to the Marines*	S. Sylvan Simon
1943	*Swing Shift Maisie*	Norman Z. McLeod
1944	*See Here, Private Hargrove*	Wesley Ruggles
1944	*Meet the People*	Charles Reisner
1945	*Yolanda and the Thief*	Vincente Minnelli
1946	*The Harvey Girls* (AAN)	George Sidney
1947	*Living in a Big Way*	Gregory La Cava
1947	*The Hucksters*	Jack Conway
1948	*The Pirate* (AAN)	Vincente Minnelli
1948	*Words and Music*	Norman Taurog
1949	*The Barkleys of Broadway*	Charles Walters
1949	*Any Number Can Play*	Mervyn LeRoy
1949	*Battleground*	William A. Wellman
1949	*On the Town* (AA)	Stanley Donen, Gene Kelly
1949	*Side Street*	Anthony Mann
1951	*Inside Straight*	Gerald Mayer
1951	*Strictly Dishonorable*	Melvin Frank, Norman Panama
1952	*Love Is Better Than Ever*	Stanley Donen
1952	*Singin' in the Rain* (AAN)	Stanley Donen, Gene Kelly
1953	*Battle Circus* (aka *MASH 66*)	Richard Brooks
1968	*Star!* (aka *Loves of a Star*) (AAN)	Robert Wise
1969	*Hello, Dolly!* (AA)	Gene Kelly

HEFTI, Neal (1922–2008) A popular composer, arranger, musician, and conductor of Big Bands, radio shows, movies, and television sitcoms, he is most known for his catchy theme songs for light comedies.

Born Neal Paul Hefti in Hastings, Nebraska, to a poor family that often depended on charity groups to survive, Hefti started studying the trumpet when he was eleven. When he was in high school he earned money for his family playing in area bands. Because Count Basie, Dizzy Gillespie, Cab Calloway, and other jazz bands played on tour at nearby Omaha, the young Hefti saw them and was heavily influenced by them. While still in high school,

Hefti started writing music arrangements for small-time bands and after graduation he toured with various groups before working for name orchestras such as Charlie Barnet, Horace Heidt, Charlie Spivak, and Woody Herman. For the last Hefti made arrangements for such popular songs as "Woodchopper's Ball" and "Caldonia," and with various lyricists wrote many Big Band swing hits, including "Wild Root," "The Good Earth," "You Are," "Li'l Darlin'," "Cute," "Coral Reef," and "Flight of the Foo Foo Birds." During the 1950s Hefti moved away from swing and got more involved with his old love jazz, and got to work with some of the idols from his youth, in particular

Count Basie. He formed his own band for a while, made recordings with celebrated singers such as Frank Sinatra, and was musical director and conductor for television's *Arthur Godfrey Show* and *The Kate Smith Show*.

Hefti's film career dates back to 1944 when he appeared as a member of Charlie Spivak's Orchestra in the movie *Pin Up Girl*. He did not return to Hollywood until 1957 when he composed the incidental music between all the star turns in the musical *Jamboree!* Director Richard Quine hired Hefti in 1964 to write and conduct the soundtrack score and title song (lyric by Quine) for the comedy *Sex and the Single Girl*, opening doors in Hollywood for the veteran composer. After a handful of dramas and comedies, Hefti found wide recognition for his charming score for the Neil Simon comedy *Barefoot in the Park*. Both the film and the main theme were a success, soon eclipsed by his music for another Simon comedy, *The Odd Couple*. Both themes were used again when the movies were turned into television sitcoms. Perhaps Hefti's most recognized piece of music is his theme song for the popular TV series *Batman* which ran from 1966 to 1968. The jazzy piece has since been heard in many movies and television programs, the audience always recognizing the famous theme. After a few more films and some TV movies in the 1970s, Hefti left Hollywood to concentrate on concerts and records. He retired in the late 1980s and died of throat cancer two decades later at the age of eighty-five.

Because of his many record albums with jazz and Big Band greats, Hefti is most admired as a trumpeter, arranger, and conductor in the genres of jazz and swing. For Hollywood, he excelled at a breezy, catchy kind of music with a 1960s sensibility. Although Henry Mancini may have dominated the field for this kind of music, Hefti has his own distinctive sound in the era's comedies. The theme for the silly *Sex and the Single Girl* is in the Big Band style with smooth brass and electric keyboard. It feels very hip even as the orchestrated technique is rather old fashioned. The lightheaded *How to Murder Your Wife* has a cool jazz score played on the soundtrack by an expert combo with wonderful solo sections for flute and piano. The farcical *Boeing Boeing* uses a merry march played on

electric organ with sassy chorals to add to the silliness. The main title for the dark comedy *Oh Dad, Poor Dad, Mamma's Hung You in the Closet and I'm Feeling So Sad* is a bizarre children's ditty sung by a chipper children's chorus. The offbeat film also has a pleasing love theme with a bossa nova flavor. Also very romantic in a more fluid manner is the main theme for *Barefoot in the Park*, a pure early 1960s sound with its combination of the modern and the sentimental. The best comedy Hefti got to score, *The Odd Couple*, inspired his finest theme, a light jazz classic with a simple melody embellished by a series of rhythmic chords. There are other jazz delights in the movie, some in the furious mode, others cooler and more sophisticated. Few movie scores capture an era and attitude like *The Odd Couple* does.

On the few occasions when Hefti was hired to score a noncomedy, he usually returned to his affection for jazz and Big Band. The biopic *Harlow* is set in the 1930s so Hefti uses an early swing style in telling the tragic story of sex symbol Jean Harlow (Carroll Baker). The main theme lent itself to the song "Girl Talk" (lyric by Bobby Troup) which enjoyed some popularity. The jazzy theme song for the private eye yarn *P.J.* uses electric keyboard against a conventional brass section, the effect being casual and even blasé. The western *Duel at Diablo* has a rhythmic score with a Spanish vein running through it. The use of different brass instruments in counterpoint to each other is quite expert and engaging. There is a delicate passage titled "Ellen's Theme" which is a weary carousel tune. The melodrama *Synanon*, about dope addiction, has a melancholy score in which muted instruments and minor keys abound. The main theme repeats a musical phrase on an electric keyboard almost to the point of monotony then slowly builds on the phrase, resulting in music that chills with loneliness. Another passage is livelier as a five-note motif bounces and grows but there is a false sense of joy in the music. With only three "serious" movies to his credit, Hefti displays a noteworthy talent for scoring many different kinds of moods outside of the comic. His Hollywood career lasted only a dozen years, but in that time he delighted movie audiences as he did jazz enthusiasts. Website: www.nealhefti.com.

Credits

(all films USA)

Year	Film	Director
1957	Jamboree!	Roy Lockwood
1964	Sex and the Single Girl	Richard Quine
1965	How to Murder Your Wife	Richard Quine
1965	Synanon	Richard Quine
1965	Harlow	Gordon Douglas
1965	Boeing Boeing (aka Boeing [707] Boeing [707])	John Rich
1966	Lord Love a Duck	George Axelrod
1966	Duel at Diablo	Ralph Nelson
1967	Oh Dad, Poor Dad, Mamma's Hung You in the Closet and I'm Feeling So Sad	Richard Quine, Alexander Mackendrick
1967	Barefoot in the Park	Gene Saks
1968	P.J.	John Guillermin
1968	The Odd Couple	Gene Saks
1971	A New Leaf	Elaine May
1972	The Last of the Red Hot Lovers	Gene Saks
1976	Won Ton Ton: The Dog Who Saved Hollywood	Michael Winner

HEINDORF, Ray (1908–1980) A prolific composer, conductor, songwriter, and arranger who supervised the music in over 175 Warner Brothers movies, he wrote the soundtrack scores for some thirty feature films between 1932 and 1972.

He was born Raymond John Heindorf in Haverstraw, New York, the son of a Railroad Express agent, and studied piano as a youth. In high school Heindorf earned money playing piano at the local silent movie house then after graduation headed to New York City where he worked as a music arranger. With the advent of sound movies, Heindorf went to Hollywood and found work as an arranger for MGM's *The Hollywood Revue of 1929* before switching to Warner Brothers where he worked as conductor, orchestrator, and sometime composer for the next forty years. Heindorf became music director at Warners in 1948 and was considered one of the most astute and versatile music supervisors in Hollywood. He directed the music in many of Warner's top dramas and comedies, including *Street Scene* (1931), *Captain Blood* (1935), *Four Daughters* (1938), *The Sea Hawk* (1940), *The Male Animal* (1942), *King's Row* (1942), *Fighter Squadron* (1948), *Flamingo Road* (1949), *Strangers on a Train* (1951), *A Streetcar Named Desire* (1951), *I Confess* (1953), *Them!* (1954), *The Spirit of St. Louis* (1957), *Auntie Mame* (1958), and *The Miracle* (1959). But most of Heindorf's movies were musicals. He received Oscar nominations for the musical scoring of *Up in Arms* (1944), *Hollywood Canteen* (1944), *Rhapsody in Blue* (1945), *Night and Day* (1946), *My Wild Irish Rose* (1947), *Look for the Silver Lining* (1949), *West Point Story* (1950), *Calamity Jane* (1954), and *Damn Yankees* (1958) and won for *This Is the Army* (1943). Among the many other notable musicals he orchestrated, arranged, and/or conducted are *Whoopee!* (1930), *Hallelujah, I'm a Bum* (1933), *42nd Street* (1933), *Dames* (1934), *Gold Diggers of 1935*, *Blues in the Night* (1941), *Young Man with a Horn* (1950), and *The Desert Song* (1953).

His composing career was considered secondary by the studios. Heindorf wrote incidental music for many musicals but much of the score consisted of adapting music written by the songwriters. For this task he won Academy Awards for *Yankee Doodle Dandy* and *The Music Man* and was nominated for his scoring in *Wonder Man*, *Romance on the High Seas*, the 1952 remake of *The Jazz Singer*, the 1954 version of *A Star Is Born*, and *Finian's Rainbow*. His original music can also be heard in the musicals *The Singing Kid*, *Gold Diggers of Paris*, *On Your Toes*, *April Showers*, *I'll See You in My Dreams*, *The Pajama Game*, *Pete Kelly's Blues*, and *The Helen Morgan Story*, many of these cowritten with Heinz Roemheld and other Warner composers. Heindorf was not often given nonmusicals to score, but he did get to compose music for such films as *The Roaring Twenties*, *Young at Heart*, *No Time for Sergeants*, and the documentary feature *Survival of Spaceship*

Earth. On occasion Heindorf wrote songs for Hollywood, such as "Hold Me in Your Arms" from *Young at Heart*, "Melancholy Rhapsody" from *Young Man with a Horn*, the title song from *Pete Kelly's Blues*, and the Oscar-nominated "Some Sunday Morning" from *San Antonio* (1945). This last song was later heard in over twenty movie shorts and features. He also wrote music for television, as with the series *Sugarfoot* and *Adam-12*, and made several jazz recordings with pianist Art Tatum in the 1950s. Heindorf retired from Hollywood in 1968 but returned to score *Survival of Spaceship Earth* and to supervise the music for Warner's *1776* (1972).

As influential as Heindorf was in creating the musical sound at Warner Brothers, there is very little of his original music by which to judge his composing skills. The most efficient way to examine Heindorf the composer is to look at the nonmusical films he scored by himself. For the comedy *No Time for Sergeants*, about a lovable country hick (Andy Griffith) befuddling the U.S. Army, Heindorf wrote a merry military march, a warm but wry folk passage, and some sexy jazz music for the few females in the film. The melodrama *Young at Heart* features Doris Day and Frank Sinatra singing a few songs, but most of the soundtrack score is a dramatic one that does not depend on the music from the songs. There is a lovely domestic theme that is soothingly engaging and a dramatic one that avoids too much sentimentality. *Pete Kelly's Blues* is a gritty drama that has many standout songs sung by Ella Fitzgerald and Peggy Lee. Surrounding these is a dark and bluesy

soundtrack score. The heavy chords of gangster melodramas runs throughout and in the big shoot-out scene this kind of music is heard in counterpoint to a dizzy carousel tune. Of course Heindorf knew the gangster genre well, having supervised the music for several Warner crime movies in the 1930s. He got to compose as well as orchestrate and conduct the score for *The Roaring Twenties* in 1939. Some old song standards are here in the various speakeasies but the action scenes are pure 1930s scoring, the Charleston mixed with ominous minor-key musical phrases. Perhaps the best opportunity to study Heindorf the composer is in the 1972 documentary *Survival of Spaceship Earth*, a powerful warning about the future of the planet that was sponsored by the United Nations. The opening theme is a rousing passage in the classical vein played by orchestra and piano, a swirling melody that floats yet has a ponderous bass line. The sounds of thunder and water are added to the drama, setting up the movie's tone of informing and disturbing the audience. Some passages are reflective and soothing, others dissonant and harsh. Jazz is employed when urban life and its effect on the biosphere is illustrated. There is mysterious and eerie music as bacteria invades and destroys living creatures and more than a touch of sci-fi music when the documentary forecasts the future. It is not difficult to understand why Heindorf came out of retirement to score this feature because never before had he been given such an important movie and the chance to write pure music free from songs, period tunes, and preexisting melodies.

Credits

(all films USA)

Year	Film	Director
1932	*Crooner*	Lloyd Bacon
1934	*A Lost Lady*	Alfred E. Green, Phil Rosen
1935	*Broadway Hostess*	Frank McDonald
1936	*The Singing Kid*	William Keighley, Busby Berkeley
1937	*Varsity Show*	William Keighley
1937	*Hollywood Hotel*	Busby Berkeley
1938	*Gold Diggers of Paris*	Ray Enright
1939	*Naughty But Nice*	Ray Enright
1939	*On Your Toes*	Ray Enright
1939	*The Roaring Twenties*	Raoul Walsh
1942	*Yankee Doodle Dandy* (AA)	Michael Curtiz
1945	*Wonder Man* (AAN)	H. Bruce Humberstone
1948	*April Showers*	James V. Kern
1948	*Romance on the High Seas* (AAN)	Michael Curtiz

Year	Film	Director
1951	*Come Fill the Cup*	Gordon Douglas
1951	*I'll See You in My Dreams*	Michael Curtiz
1952	*Where's Charley?*	David Butler
1952	*April in Paris*	David Butler
1952	*The Jazz Singer* (AAN)	Michael Curtiz
1954	*Lucky Me*	Jack Donohue
1954	*A Star Is Born* (AAN)	George Cukor
1954	*Young at Heart*	Gordon Douglas
1955	*Pete Kelly's Blues*	Jack Webb
1955	*Sincerely Yours*	Gordon Douglas
1955	*Serenade*	Anthony Mann
1957	*The Pajama Game*	George Abbott, Stanley Donen
1957	*The Helen Morgan Story*	Michael Curtiz
1958	*No Time for Sergeants*	Mervyn LeRoy
1959	*-30-*	Jack Webb
1962	*The Music Man* (AA)	Morton DaCosta
1968	*Finian's Rainbow* (AAN)	Francis Ford Coppola
1972	*Survival of Spaceship Earth*	Dirk Wayne Summers

HERRMANN, Bernard (1911–1975) A distinctive and highly acclaimed composer of opera and instrumental works, he is most remembered for his dynamic film scores, particularly those for Alfred Hitchcock. Greatly admired by other movie composers, Herrmann's screen work served as an inspiration for generations of promising composers.

Born Max Herman in New York City, his Russian Jewish parents exposed him to opera at a young age and provided violin lessons. When he was only thirteen, Herrmann won a violin competition, which encouraged him to make music his career. After studying at New York University and Juilliard, he formed the New Chamber Orchestra of New York when he was only twenty years old. Herrmann first gained success as a conductor on the radio, joining CBS in 1934 and eventually becoming the conductor of the CBS Symphony Orchestra. In its highly praised broadcasts, such as *Invitation to Music* and *Exploring Music*, the radio orchestra introduced many new or overlooked composers to the American public. Herrmann's original compositions were premiered by such famous conductors as Leopold Stokowski, Eugene Ormandy, and Thomas Beecham. His cantata *Moby Dick* premiered in 1938 and his opera *Wuthering Heights* was first presented in 1951.

Yet it was in radio, television, and movies that Herrmann found wider recognition and more lucrative work. While at CBS he wrote original music for radio dramas, including the suspense classic *The Hitch-Hiker*, written by his then wife Lucille Fletcher. He was also the composer for Orson Welles's radio shows, including the famous *War of the Worlds* broadcast in 1938. Although he had never scored a film before, Herrmann was hired by Welles to write the music for *Citizen Kane*, resulting in a rich and memorable score that ranged from eerie themes to selections from a fictitious opera. Herrmann also scored Welles's second film, *The Magnificent Ambersons*, but the movie and its score were so altered by the studio that the composer asked that his name be removed from the credits. But it was not these two masterpieces that brought Herrmann his first and only Academy Award; instead he won for his soundtrack music for *The Devil and Daniel Webster* in 1941. Hollywood soon labeled Herrmann as a composer of brooding or suspenseful music, so during his thirty-five-year career he was rarely given comedies or romances to score. His music for *Jane Eyre, Anna and the King of Siam, Prince of Players*, and other period pieces was well received, as was his more sinister scores such as those for *The Day the Earth Stood Still* and *Cape Fear*. Herrmann was also adept at writing scores for fantasy movies, creating memorable music for *The 7th Voyage of Sinbad, Journey to the Center of the Earth*, and *Jason and the Argonauts*.

Herrmann's greatest recognition came with his association with Hitchcock. They first worked together on the dark comedy *The Trouble with Harry*, followed by such movie classics as *The Man Who Knew Too Much, Vertigo, North by Northwest*, and *Psycho*. For these unique films

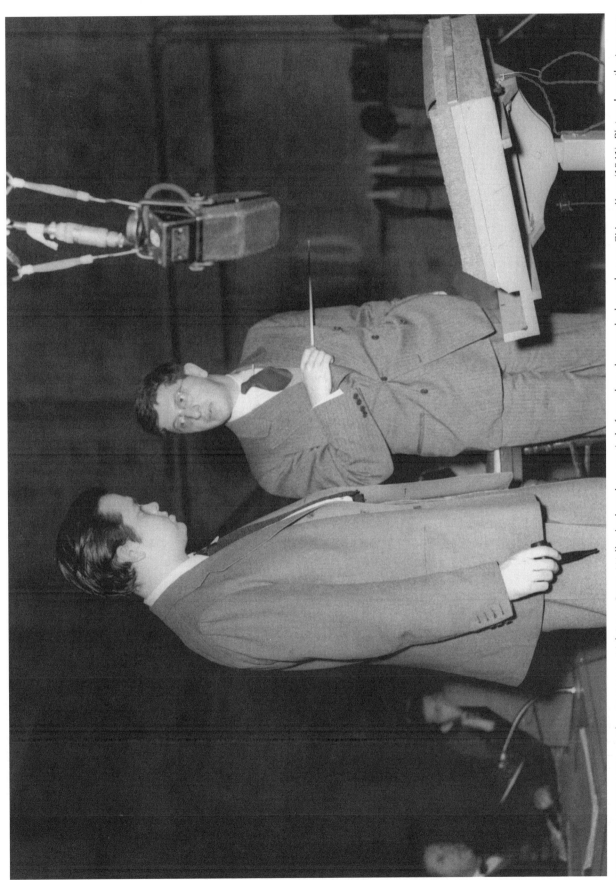

BERNARD HERRMANN. Neither Herrmann (right) nor Orson Welles had made a movie before when they worked together on *Citizen Kane* (1941). Pictured are the two men conferring during a recording session for that film classic. Herrmann had earlier scored Welles's radio program *War of the Worlds* and perhaps the novice director preferred a familiar radio colleague rather than a seasoned Hollywood composer. *RKO Radio Pictures / Photofest © RKO Radio Pictures*

Herrmann created innovative and effective music that matched Hitchcock's macabre style beautifully. He also scored two movies for the distinguished French director François Truffaut and the up-and-coming suspense director Brian De Palma. His last movie credit was the dark melodrama *Taxi Driver* directed by Martin Scorsese. Herrmann arranged and/or conducted the music for most of his feature films and supervised the music for many other films by other composers. He also wrote the theme songs for several television shows, including Hitchcock's 1960s series. (Herrmann wrote the original theme song for *The Twilight Zone* but after the first season it was replaced by the more famous one by Marius Constant.) An avid Anglophile, Herrmann moved to England in 1967 but was back in the States when he died of a heart attack at the age of sixty-four.

More serious study has been made of Herrmann's work than possibly any other movie composer. There is even a Bernard Herrmann Society to study, record, and write about his opera, concert, and movie music. One cannot make generalizations about his work. He favors the violin but often uses the instrument in original ways. The screeching violins during the famous shower scene in *Psycho* seem to go beyond music into sound effects. (Hitchcock originally wanted no music during the scene but Herrmann persuaded him to do otherwise.) The *Psycho* score is also unusual because it is all strings and only strings. The opening music is a hurried series of repetitive chords which tease the listener until a melody surfaces, but it has to compete with the returning chords. The music behind the romancing of Marion (Janet Leigh) and Sam (John Gavin) is a slow string passage with a more lamentable rather than romantic air. The Bates Motel has a hesitant theme in which the string chords and sustained notes seem tentative and suspicious. The strident, stabbing strings heard in the shower are repeated when Norman (Anthony Perkins) murders the investigator (Martin Balsam). The score (and movie) ends with a serene passage on sustained strings that is unsettling and unresolved. The haunting theme in Hitchcock's *Vertigo* is a lush Wagner-like passage that actually feels bluesy at times. It consists of two falling notes that also suggest the sound of the San Francisco foghorn heard throughout the movie. This is one of Hitchcock's most stylized thrillers with romance, murder, and fear of heights all intertwined in an elaborate package. The opening music actually feels like falling, its repetitive musical phrases descending then exploding, only to rise and fall again. The

love theme is graceful and mysterious with strings descending again but this time it is a peaceful and seductive falling. When the hero (James Stewart) relives his past bouts of vertigo, the music is a furious piece of chaos with shouting brass, rapid harp glissandos, and furious percussion.

While Hitchcock's movies might usually share the same sense of thrills and suspense, Herrmann's scores for them vary greatly. For *The Trouble with Harry*, the music is quirky, almost silly. This dark comedy, about a dead body that seems to pop up in different locations around a New England town, has a decidedly eccentric score, starting with the opening music: a laughing four-note motif played on staccato brass and reeds that turns a bit menacing when a French horn is added with a cautionary melodic line. This daffy theme is repeated every time a different person discovers Harry's body. The bucolic fall landscape is scored with a sublime passage in which oboe and English horn take turns in singing the praise of autumn. This is music to be noticed and enjoyed. By contrast, the subdued music in the documentary-like *The Wrong Man* practically disappears. This somber, thrill-free look at a man (Henry Fonda) mistaken for a criminal has one of Herrmann's most subtle scores. The opening music heard at the Stork Club in Manhattan is a lively rumba with celebratory brass and joyous percussion. What follows is a slow jazz theme featuring a solo clarinet that seems to wail as it repeats a descending phrase without any resolution. The music haunts one without relying on suspense or surprise. Two Hitchcock films that travel about quite a bit have exciting but different scores. *The Man Who Knew Too Much* begins in Marrakesh where an American couple (James Stewart and Doris Day) accidentally learn about a planned assassination. When their son (Christopher Olson) is kidnapped, the story moves to London for a famous scene in the Albert Hall in which an assassin tries to shoot a dignitary during the loudest part of a concert. The concert piece, *Storm Clouds Cantata* by Arthur Benjamin, comes from Hitchcock's 1934 version of the tale. Also in the score is the popular and Oscar-winning song "Que Sera Sera (Whatever Will Be Will Be)" by Jerry Livingston and Ray Evans that ends up being an integral part of the plot. Herrmann provided the rest of the music, including the rousing opening music in which mighty brass and demanding drums move forward like a fearful procession. There is some exotic music for the Moroccan scenes and disturbing suspense passages during moments of intrigue in a London church and at an embassy mansion. The plot of *North by Northwest* stays in the States but it quickly covers a lot of distance, from Manhattan to Mount Rushmore to be exact. More of an adventure than a moody suspense movie, this Hitchcock classic often has a tongue-in-cheek tone as once again an innocent man (Cary Grant) runs from the police and the criminals. The score is similarly playful at times, sacrificing mood and atmosphere for excitement and thrills. The opening theme is vigorous traveling music with racing flutes, reeds, brass, and percussion each jumping ahead of each other in a cocky and happy manner. Every time Grant is off and running, there are variations of this racing theme. One passage has pizzicato strings and rumbling brass and percussion on the run, and the chase across the stone faces of Mount Rushmore has kettle drums competing with snare drums as the original theme is more frantic than ever. Even the love theme, a lovely descending clarinet played against rhythmic strings, has a steady beat that seems to hurry things along. As for the movie's most famous scene, in which a crop-dusting plane tries to run Grant down in a cornfield, there is no music during the sequence until the end when the plane collides with a tanker trunk and Herrmann provides dissonant chords to match the explosion on-screen.

There is, of course, much more to Herrmann's film music than the Hitchcock movies. His first effort, *Citizen Kane*, demonstrates that he understood and mastered the art of screen scoring from the beginning. Orson Welles's first film as well, *Citizen Kane* remains one of the masterworks of American cinema and Herrmann's score is no small part of that achievement. Even before filming began, Welles requested Herrmann to write an original opera sequence in which a soprano aria opens the first act. While the resulting music is a wry pastiche of grand opera, the passage is surprisingly commendable. The fact that Susan (Dorothy Comingore) cannot sing makes for an unpleasant musical experience, but it is not the notes that offend. *Citizen Kane* opens with chilling woodwinds that play a low and haunting theme with a film noir flavor. This matches Welles's gloomy opening images so well that one believes the sequence was shot to fit the music. There are several leitmotifs in the film, including a sprightly four-note phrase played on a vibraphone and strings and first heard when the youth Charlie (Buddy Swan) is playing in the snow. The "Rosebud" theme, a slow march with sorrowful strings and a woeful bass line, returns and

seems to haunt Kane (Welles) all his life. There is a bluesy lament featuring a lonely clarinet that serves as the theme for the unlucky Susan. Among the many other significant musical passages in this complex score is a rapid, giddy gallop played on merry woodwinds and brass, a dainty but waggish hornpipe polka played on reeds, a vivacious scherzo in which the instruments seem to bounce up and down, a rowdy cancan for a chorus line of showgirls, and a fluid waltz for Kane's romancing of the aristocratic Emily (Ruth Warrick). What a remarkable debut for director-actor and composer! Welles the actor but not the director was featured in *Jane Eyre* for which Herrmann wrote one of his most engaging period scores. The main theme is romantic and passionate with a dark subtext heard in the way the strings descend and the low brass seems agitated. There is a somewhat hopeful love theme in which strings and reeds glide across the scale, but much of the rest of the score hints as the dangerous secrets that Mr. Rochester (Welles) is keeping from Jane (Joan Fontaine). Squawking reeds and nervous strings create mystery in one passage, a frolicsome dance heard on woodwinds and brass is a bit too strident to be fully comfortable, and low and sustained notes are used as a motif for the west wing of the mansion and Rochester's tortured past.

One of the many impressive aspects of Herrmann's scores is his farsighted use of electronic instruments. His score for the cerebral sci-fi classic *The Day the Earth Stood Still* is perhaps the most glowing example of technology used for artistic expression. The story of an alien (Michael Rennie) who comes to Earth to promote peace among its citizens has no exploding lasers or intergalactic attacks. So Herrmann avoided a traditionally melodramatic sci-fi score for more restrained yet still otherworldly music. He utilized the electronic theremin and electric strings alongside brass, guitar, harps, and prepared piano to create a unique (and quite unforgettable) sound. The opening theme is a series of sustained notes that descend the scale gracefully then rise to make little crescendos. There is a frantic yet low-key passage in which piano and reeds seem to be having an argument with each other. The theme for the giant, silent robot Gort is a series of harsh chords heard under quivering electronic waves; it is both a frightening yet mesmerizing piece of music. This is contrasted with the lyrical passages in the score, such as a lovely nocturne in which synthesized notes seem to twinkle and dream in time to distant bells and chimes. For *Fahrenheit 451*, a very different sci-fi movie,

Herrmann used such traditional instruments as harps, strings, xylophone, and glockenspiel with a vibraphone, yet the effect is just as otherworldly. In a future world where all books are banned and burned and the citizens seem drained of curiosity or emotion, a fireman (Oskar Werner) and a radical (Julie Christie) fight the system, only to find peace in a land where books are kept alive through memorization. The main theme is a deceptively serene piece with wavering strings that imitate the sound of a theremin. When the firemen set out to find banned books, Herrmann provides rhythmic travel music with eager strings and rat-a-tat xylophone notes. Oddly, the burning of the books is scored with a tripping waltz in which overlapping violins are joined by a celesta, harp, and various bells. The movie ends in a forest where book lovers set their favorite works to memory. The glittering music heard on various strings and percussion is so lilting that it seems like a breath of fresh air after so much emotional confinement.

Two of the grittier, harshly realistic films that Herrmann scored late in his career reveal how his talent never waned or faltered. A lawyer (Gregory Peck) and his family are stalked and tormented by an ex-con (Robert Mitchum) in the nail-biting thriller *Cape Fear*. Herrmann's score is reminiscent of the kind of music heard in his Hitchcock movies yet there is a cruelty here that goes beyond suspense and the abrasive score captures it in music. The main theme consists of brass notes that descend the scale as other instruments follow suit with an awful dread. This motif returns throughout the movie without losing its menacing quality. For the final confrontation, the motif is reversed, the brass and other instruments ascending the scale with furious purpose. *Taxi Driver* is a bleak yet fascinating look at a loner (Robert De Niro) who observes the sordid side of urban life as he works the night shift as a cab driver. The movie boasts Herrmann's only jazz score. He had never been enamored of the jazz sound and avoided it throughout his long career. But when director Martin Scorsese convinced him that jazz

was the appropriate sound for *Taxi Driver*, Herrmann worked with assistant Christopher Palmer to rework one of his old stage melodies into the jazz idiom. The main theme is a bluesy lament featuring an alto saxophone that keeps reaching up but doesn't seem to escape from its melancholia. A muted trumpet and then an open trumpet join in, then strings as well, but all keep falling back into despair. A sultry jazz passage on saxophone is used for the squalid sexual activities that the antihero encounters. As the taxi driver moves closer to the edge, the music gets more disruptive. Repetitions on the harp and timpani going berserk convey this emotional disintegration with a violent temper. After he is involved in a bloody shoot-out, the cabbie is somewhat mollified and the movie ends with sad but resolved music.

Herrmann was a meticulous and stubborn artist who insisted on total control of his music. He publicly stated that most directors had no understanding of music and that the score should be the composer's purview. Even though Hitchcock trusted him and gave him free rein on his soundtracks, the two men quarreled vehemently over the score for *Torn Curtain*. Herrmann's score was rejected by the director and the studio; Herrmann never worked with Hitchcock again. Yet as difficult as Herrmann might have been, he was greatly respected by other composers during his lifetime, and contemporary artists rank him near the top of all movie composers. He is one of the few film composers whose work has frequently been performed in concert and recorded by world-class symphony orchestras. There have also been television and radio documentaries about Herrmann and his music. Perhaps more than anyone else, Herrmann brought a classical respectability to screen scoring. Biographies: *A Heart at Fire's Center*, Steven C. Smith (1991); *Bernard Herrmann: Film, Music and Narrative*, Donald Bruce (1988); *Bernard Herrmann: Hollywood's Music-Dramatist*, Edward Johnson (1977). Bernard Herrmann Society website: www.bernardherrmann.org.

Credits

(all films USA unless stated otherwise)

Year	Film	Director
1941	*Citizen Kane* (AAN)	Orson Welles
1941	*The Devil and Daniel Webster* (AA)	William Dieterle
1942	*The Magnificent Ambersons*	Orson Welles

Year	Film	Director
1944	*Jane Eyre*	Robert Stevenson
1945	*Hangover Square*	John Brahm
1946	*Anna and the King of Siam* (AAN)	John Cromwell
1947	*The Ghost and Mrs. Muir*	Joseph L. Mankiewicz
1951	*The Day the Earth Stood Still* (GGN)	Robert Wise
1952	*On Dangerous Ground*	Nicholas Ray
1952	*Five Fingers*	Joseph L. Mankiewicz
1952	*The Snows of Kilimanjaro*	Henry King
1953	*White Witch Doctor*	Henry Hathaway
1953	*Beneath the 12-Mile Reef*	Robert D. Webb
1953	*King of the Khyber Rifles*	Henry King
1954	*Garden of Evil*	Henry Hathaway
1954	*The Egyptian*	Michael Curtiz
1955	*Prince of Players*	Philip Dunne
1955	*The Kentuckian*	Burt Lancaster
1955	*The Trouble with Harry*	Alfred Hitchcock
1956	*The Man in the Gray Flannel Suit*	Nunnally Johnson
1956	*The Man Who Knew Too Much*	Alfred Hitchcock
1956	*The Wrong Man*	Alfred Hitchcock
1957	*A Hatful of Rain*	Fred Zinnemann
1958	*Vertigo*	Alfred Hitchcock
1958	*The Naked and the Dead*	Raoul Walsh
1958	*The 7th Voyage of Sinbad*	Nathan Juran
1959	*North by Northwest*	Alfred Hitchcock
1959	*Blue Denim*	Philip Dunne
1959	*Journey to the Center of the Earth*	Henry Levin
1960	*Psycho*	Alfred Hitchcock
1960	*The Three Worlds of Gulliver*	Jack Sher
1961	*Mysterious Island*	Cy Endfield (UK/USA)
1962	*Tender Is the Night*	Henry King
1962	*Cape Fear*	J. Lee Thompson
1963	*Jason and the Argonauts*	Don Chaffey (UK/USA)
1964	*Marnie*	Alfred Hitchcock
1965	*Joy in the Morning*	Alex Segal
1966	*Fahrenheit 451*	François Truffaut (UK)
1968	*The Bride Wore Black*	François Truffaut (France/Italy)
1968	*Twisted Nerve*	Roy Boulting (UK)
1969	*Bezeten—het gat in de mur*	Pim de la Parra (W. Germany/Netherlands)
1969	*The Battle of Neretva*	Veljko Bulajic (Italy/W. Germany/Croatia)
1971	*The Night Digger*	Alastair Reid (UK)
1972	*Endless Night*	Sidney Gilliat (UK)
1973	*Sisters*	Brian De Palma
1974	*It's Alive*	Larry Cohen
1976	*Taxi Driver* (AAN; BAFTA)	Martin Scorsese
1976	*Obsession* (AAN)	Brian De Palma

HESS, Nigel (b. 1953) A busy composer for theatre and British TV movies, series, and miniseries, his three feature films are noteworthy and, like most of his work, quite accomplished.

Nigel Hess was born in the county of Somerset, England, and educated at the Weston-super-Mare Grammar School for Boys and Cambridge University where he studied music and got involved with the campus theatrical troupe Footlights Revue Company. Hess continued his interest in writing music for plays, eventually becoming the principal composer for the Royal Shakespeare Company for many years. He made his television scoring debut in 1981 with the TV documentary series *The Shattered Dream: Employment in the Eighties* and that same year composed music for his first series, *Kinvig*. Hess's subsequent series include *Rocky Hollow*, *Vanity Fair*, *Hot Metal*,

Maigret, Us Girls, Wycliffe, Hetty Wainthropp Investigates, Ballykissangel, New Tricks, Last of the Summer Wine and *Mystery! Campion.* Among his many TV movies and mini-series are *A Woman of Substance* (1985), *Anna of the Five Towns* (1985), *Reunion at Fairborough* (1985), *Cyrano de Bergerac* (1985), *The Browning Version* (1985), *London Embassy* (1987), *The Dog It Was That Died* (1989), *Summer's Lease* (1989), *Titmuss Regained* (1991), *Every Woman Knows a Secret* (1999), and *Love or Money* (2001). Hess did not make his feature film debut until 2000 with *An Ideal Husband,* a comedy-drama based on an Oscar Wilde play. Four years later he received wide acclaim for his score for the period drama *Ladies in Lavender.* Hess wrote music for a handful of productions at London's Globe Theatre. One of them, *The Merry Wives of Windsor,* was turned into a film in 2011 with an expanded score by Hess. Although television composing takes up much of his time, Hess has also written for the concert hall and the ballet. He has a vocal group called Chameleon, which has made recordings, and his own music publishing company, Myra Music, named in honor of his great-aunt, pianist Myra Hess.

Hess has received many awards for his television music, and he is considered one of the composers of choice in the British TV industry. Because he has only three feature films, Hess has no screen awards and much less recognition than he deserves. There are six movie and TV versions of Wilde's quixotic comedy-drama *An Ideal Husband,* and the 2000 film directed by William P. Cartlidge is far from the best. The Victorian drawing room piece was awkwardly updated to the 1990s, not only making several plot points ridiculous but turning Wilde's brittle dialogue into quotations. The score has a classical flavor but does not intrude

onto the contemporary setting. The main theme is light and rhythmic, suggesting old-time romance with a new point of view. A quiet character drama set in an English seaside village in the 1930s, *Ladies in Lavender* is totally engrossing and boasts a superior score. The Polish concert violinist Andrea (Daniel Brühl) is washed up on the shore half-drowned and is cared for by two elderly sisters (Maggie Smith and Judi Dench) who not only nurse him back to health but arrange for him to return to the concert world. Andrea plays classic pieces by Claude Debussy, Jules Massenet, and others and Hess's original music in the score complements the masters beautifully. The main theme is a graceful violin passage that wavers with lyrical fluttering, an old-fashioned romantic piece but highly accessible and satisfying. There is a cautious and beguiling passage for piano and violin that is both mysterious and melancholy. The theme for the two sisters is a delicate piano piece that conveys their emotionally fragile temperaments. The *Ladies in Lavender* score is filled with wonderful old and new music and, as played by violinist Joshua Bell on the soundtrack, enhances the movie's idea that music touches those who may lack any other kind of romance in their lives. The Globe Theatre, a reconstructed Elizabethan theatre on the banks of the Thames, strives for authenticity in all its elements and Hess's score for the screen adaptation of the Globe's *The Merry Wives of Windsor* uses period instruments, some of which lend to the comedy with their squawking and nasal sounds. Hess has scored dozens of Shakespeare productions for the stage and it is fortunate that one of them is now preserved on film. One can only hope other Hess music makes its way to the movies. Official website: www.myramusic.co.uk.

Credits

(all films UK)

Year	Film	Director
2000	*An Ideal Husband*	William P. Cartlidge
2004	*Ladies in Lavender*	Charles Dance
2011	*The Merry Wives of Windsor*	Christopher Luscombe

HEYMANN, Werner Richard (1896–1961) A German composer who was very popular in Europe before World War II, he scored over one hundred movies in his native country and Hollywood.

Born in Königsberg, Germany (present-day Kaliningrad, Russia), Werner Richard Heymann was the son of a Jewish merchant and a mother who played the piano. Heymann was a musical prodigy, playing the piano by ear at the age of three, taking up the violin a few years later, and writing full compositions by the time he was eight. Before he was a teenager, Heymann was a member of the local philharmonic and studying composition. In 1918 his symphonic tribute to his deceased brother was performed by the Vienna Philharmonic Orchestra then later in Berlin. Heymann settled in the German capital where he got involved with the Dada art movement, the pacifist political movement, and writing music for the theatre and cabarets. Throughout the 1920s his music (particularly his operetta songs) was heard in nightclubs, concert halls, on records, and in cabarets and theatres. Heymann got involved with movies in 1926 when he collaborated with Ernö Rapee on the orchestral soundtrack for the silent film *Two Brothers*. He went on to score two dozen other silent features, his most famous works being F. W. Murnau's classic *Faust* (with Rapee) and Fritz Lang's *Spies*. Heymann was in even greater demand when talking movies were introduced in Europe, scoring over twenty dramas, musicals, and comedies, and becoming one of the most important composers in German cinema. Among his early European talkies are *Melody of the Heart*, *Three Good Friends*, *The Road to Paradise*, *Le bal*, *Congress Dances*, *Liebe ist Liebe*, and *I By Day, You By Night*.

With the rise of the Nazi Party, the Jewish radical Heymann left Germany in 1933 and settled briefly in Paris, where he wrote an operetta and scored some French films. Heymann was soon in Hollywood where his reputation preceded him and he was immediately hired to score features, mostly comedies. He first worked with director Ernst Lubitsch on the Marlene Dietrich vehicle *Angel* in 1937, the two later collaborating on such beloved comedies as *Bluebeard's Eighth Wife*, *Ninotchka*, *The Shop around the Corner*, *That Uncertain Feeling*, and *To Be or Not to Be*, the last two bringing Heymann Oscar nominations. His other noteworthy Hollywood movies include *Escape to Glory*, *He Stayed for Breakfast*, *This Thing Called Love*, *Topper Returns*, *Bedtime Story*, *A Night to Remember*, *Hail the Conquering Hero*, *Our Hearts Were Young and Gay*, *Together Again*, *It's in the Bag!*, *Kiss and Tell*, *Hold That Blonde!*, *The Sin of Harold Diddlebock*, *One Million B.C.*, and *Knickerbocker Holiday*, the last two getting Academy Award nominations for Best Score. After scoring the 1950 comedy *Emergency Wedding*, Heymann moved back to Germany and continued composing for the theatre and concert hall. He also wrote music for nine German movies before he died in Munich at the age of sixty-five.

While many composers came to Hollywood in the late 1930s to escape Nazism, Heymann is one of the few to eventually return to his homeland. Possibly his love of operetta drew him back to Germany because in America that genre was dead and buried by the war. Ironically, it was mostly deceased in Germany as well and his attempts to return to the operetta form onstage and in movies mostly failed. But that does not diminish the effect he had on early German talkies and on Hollywood comedies. Although Heymann never scored a full-scale operetta in Hollywood, his music for a handful of comedy classics overflows with an Old World operatic flavor. The Lubitsch comedies are a good example. There is not a great deal of music in these wry, romantic, silly films. Part of the famous "Lubitsch touch" is his ability to know when music is not necessary. The delightful romantic comedy *Ninotchka*, about a stolid Russian (Greta Garbo) who is seduced by Paris, has the expected Parisian music for atmosphere and the growling Russian music for comic contrast. Yet most of the film has no music, sometimes allowing silence to carry the scene, as in the extended comic bit in which champagne, cigars, and finally pretty women are delivered to a hotel bedroom. The beloved romantic comedy *The Shop around the Corner*, set in Budapest, is also mostly scoreless. The opening music, a flowing foxtrot with strings, woodwinds, and brass dancing together in a romantic but up-tempo manner, sets the tone. Yet little music follows except the musical cigarette box that keeps playing the Russian folk song "Ochi Tchornya." The audacious 1942 satire *To Be or Not to Be*, which satirizes Nazism and is still a bit uncomfortable to watch today, used Chopin and Haydn when music is called for. All Heymann provided was filler, including a minor-key march on woodwinds that is comic but unsettling. Only in Lubitsch's *That Uncertain Feeling* was there enough music that Heymann was noticed and Oscar nominated. Not as well received as Lubitsch's other comedies of the period, it is still a marvelous example of the magical Lubitsch touch. *That Uncertain Feeling* concerns a wealthy woman (Merle Oberon) who has to choose between her husband (Melvyn Douglas) and a crazy pianist (Burgess Meredith), a radical artiste she met in her psychiatrist's office. The score opens with a waltzing main theme with crescendos and fanfares that suggest both romance and turbulence. Whenever Meredith plays the piano, the music is pretentious, chaotic, and mockingly modern. The wife thinks it is art but eventually she is as annoyed with the music as the audience is.

Heymann's two comedies with writer-director Preston Sturges are more American in spirit than Lubitsch's movies but even they have the operetta flavor. *The Sin of Harold Diddlebock* is about a timid clerk (Harold Lloyd) who becomes a bold romancer with the power of alcohol. The silent comic Lloyd came out of retirement to appear in this wacky talkie, which was tailor made for him. The score has a rather serious opening theme in which a symphony climbs the scales then a violin solo takes over with a sentimental air. During a flashback to Harold's college days (using footage from Lloyd's classic *The Freshman*), Heymann provides a brisk and farcical march for a football sequence. The movie allows Lloyd to do some extended sequences without dialogue; these are scored with muted brass and squawking trombones playing a comic tune quite in the spirit of the old silents. Sturges's satire on patriotism, *Hail the Conquering Hero*, has a lot of music, mostly song standards and two original songs written by Sturges himself. Heymann's opening theme is a bustling military march with patriotic strings and bugles, yet the tone is comic if not a little mocking. Discharged from the Marines because of his hay fever, the "hero" (Eddie Bracken) of the title is turned into a local Medal of Honor winner by some friendly Marines, all against the fellow's wishes. Sturges's pace is sometimes frantic and Heymann's underscoring is often high strung and madcap, turning patriotic airs into comic ones.

The war years, Heymann's most fertile time in Hollywood, called for escapist humor in many forms, one of them being the plight of naive young females who unintentionally cause havoc. Heymann scored a handful of these slight but popular comedies. In *Kiss and Tell*, two teenagers (Shirley Temple and Virginia Welles) mistakenly set the whole town talking about an unwed pregnancy. It is all pretty slight, but the music is lively. The opening theme is a sunny swing theme played on a string and horn orchestra, more sweet than hot. The romantic theme is upbeat and optimistic even when it slows down and gets sentimental. The movie was so popular that Temple and Welles returned in the sequel *A Kiss for Corliss* and Heymann again provided a cheerfully innocuous score. A bit more substantial is the comedy *Our Hearts Were Young and Gay*. This time two teenage females (Gail Russell

and Diana Lynn) set off on an ocean liner to tour Europe and cause complications just by being so naive. The main theme is a sweeping waltz with some odd pauses to give it a frivolous tone. Once the girls arrive in Paris, there is a playful cancan theme that sounds like the operettas that Heymann so loved. The poor, put-upon Cosmo Topper (Roland Young) is the naive one in *Topper Returns*. This time Joan Blondell plays the lovely ghost only he can see or hear and a haunted house is the setting. The opening theme is mysterious music with a smirk as low strings and horn fanfares turn into a jaunty piece that bounces along carelessly. The haunted house theme, with its descending notes and prickly accents, is more cartoonish than chilling. There is frivolous, romantic music with waltzing strings and lush harmony that is used for the ghost and a comic walking theme with a silly oboe and echoing organ chords that captures the incongruous tone of the whole movie.

Was Heymann adept at scoring anything but comedies and spoofs? Hollywood gave him little opportunity to try. Yet among his silent movies in Germany are some very serious works, none more so than *Faust*. Murnau's visually stunning version of the Goethe play is both romantic and expressionistic. Heymann and Rapee wrote a symphonic score in the German classical tradition with lyrical passages for the romance, a rousing death march for the four horsemen of the apocalypse, a sultry waltz for the orgiastic scenes, harp and woodwind hymns for the religious sections, frenzied music for the most bizarre scenes, and a driving funeral dirge for the final damnation. Not much operetta here. Heymann scored Lang's thriller *Spies* on his own and one notices some light opera in the music. A criminal mastermind (Rudolf Klein-Rogge) is always one step ahead of his rivals but is thrown when his lady spy (Gerda Maurus) falls in love with a government agent (Willy Fritsch) disguised as a vagrant. *Spies* opens with a rhythmic suspense theme played on piano and strings with two distinct tempos in counterpoint, both growing in intensity and passion. There is a menacing passage with muted brass fanfares and sinister percussion, and a silly waltz on strident horns and quivering strings that is merrily dissonant. Perhaps most memorable is a clown sequence with a goofy comic theme on piano, horns, and percussion that varies its tempo as it plods along like an out-of-whack circus parade. So Heymann could indeed be more serious. But even then he never totally left the sound of European operetta behind.

Credits

Part One (all films Germany unless stated otherwise)

Year	Film	Director
1926	*Two Brothers* (aka *The Brothers Schellenberg*)	Karl Grune
1926	*The Wooing of Eve*	Max Mack
1926	*Michel Strogoff*	Viktor Tourjansky (France/Germany)
1926	*Vienna—Berlin*	Hans Steinhoff (Austria)
1926	*Wie einst im Mai*	Willi Wolff
1926	*The White Horse Inn*	Richard Oswald
1926	*Der Mann in Feuer*	Erich Waschneck
1926	*Sein grosser Fall*	Fritz Wendhausen
1926	*Das Mädel auf der Schaukel*	Felix Basch
1926	*Faust*	F. W. Murnau
1926	*Der Sohn des Hannibal*	Felix Basch
1926	*A Sister of Six*	Ragnar Hyltén-Cavallius (Sweden/Germany)
1926	*It's Easy to Become a Father*	Erich Schönfelder
1927	*Aftermath*	Erich Waschneck
1927	*A Modern Du Barry*	Alexander Korda
1927	*Meine Tante—deine Tante*	Carl Froelich
1927	*Durchlaucht Radieschen*	Richard Eichberg
1927	*Die Bräutigame der Babette Bomberling*	Victor Janson
1927	*Valencia*	Jaap Speyer
1927	*Jugendrausch*	Georg Asagaroff, Wladyslaw Starewicz
1927	*Regine, die Tragödie einer Frau*	Erich Waschneck
1927	*The Last Waltz*	Arthur Robison
1927	*Die heilige Lüge*	Holger-Madsen
1927	*Der grosse Sprung*	Arnold Fanck
1928	*Spies*	Fritz Lang
1929	*Melody of the Heart*	Hanns Schwarz
1930	*Liebeswalzer*	Wilhelm Thiele
1930	*The Love Waltz*	Carl Winston
1930	*Three Good Friends*	Wilhelm Thiele
1930	*The Road to Paradise*	Wilhelm Thiele, Max de Vaucorbeil
1931	*Her Grace Commands*	Hanns Schwarz
1931	*Princesse, á vos ordres!*	Wilhelm Thiele, Max de Vaucorbeil
1931	*Bombs over Monte Carlo*	Hanns Schwarz
1931	*Le bal*	Wilhelm Thiele
1931	*Der Kongress tanzt*	Erik Charell
1931	*Le congrés s'amuse*	Jean Boyer, Erik Charell
1931	*Le Capitaine Craddock*	Hanns Schwarz, Max de Vaucorbeil
1932	*Liebe ist Liebe*	Hans Hinrich, Paul Martin
1932	*Le vainqueur*	Hans Hinrich, Paul Martin
1932	*Congress Dances*	Erik Charell
1931	*Monte Carlo Madness*	Hanns Schwarz
1932	*A Blonde Dream*	Paul Martin
1932	*I By Day, You By Night*	Ludwig Berger
1933	*Adorable* (aka *Princess at Your Orders*)	William Dieterle (USA)
1933	*Idylle au Caire*	Claude Heymann, Reinhold Schünzel
1933	*Early to Bed*	Ludwig Berger
1934	*Caravane*	Erik Charell (France/Austria/USA)
1936	*Symphonie d'amour*	Yves Mirande, Rober Siodmak (France)

Part Two (all films USA unless stated otherwise)

Year	Film	Director
1937	*The King and the Chorus Girl* (aka *Grand Passion*)	Mervyn LeRoy
1937	*Angel*	Ernst Lubitsch
1938	*Bluebeard's Eighth Wife*	Ernst Lubitsch
1939	*Ninotchka*	Ernst Lubitsch
1940	*The Earl of Chicago*	Richard Thorpe, Victor Saville
1940	*The Shop around the Corner*	Ernst Lubitsch
1940	*Primrose Path*	Gregory La Cava
1940	*One Million B.C.* (aka *Battle of the Giants*) (AAN)	Hal Roach Jr., Hal Roach
1940	*Escape to Glory* (aka *Passage West*)	John Brahm
1940	*He Stayed for Breakfast*	Alexander Hall
1940	*This Thing Called Love*	Alexander Hall
1941	*Topper Returns*	Roy Del Ruth
1941	*That Uncertain Feeling* (AAN)	Ernst Lubitsch
1941	*She Knew All the Answers*	Richard Wallace
1941	*My Life with Caroline*	Lewis Milestone
1941	*Bedtime Story*	Alexander Hall
1942	*To Be or Not to Be* (AAN)	Ernst Lubitsch
1942	*The Wife Takes a Flyer* (aka *Highly Irregular*)	Richard Wallace
1942	*They All Kissed the Bride* (aka *He Kissed the Bride*)	Alexander Hall
1942	*Flight Lieutenant*	Sidney Salkow
1942	*A Night to Remember*	Richard Wallace
1943	*Appointment in Berlin*	Alfred E. Green
1944	*Henry Aldrich, Boy Scout*	Hugh Bennett
1944	*You Can't Ration Love*	Lester Fuller
1944	*Knickerbocker Holiday* (AAN)	Harry Joe Brown
1944	*Henry Aldrich Plays Cupid*	Hugh Bennett
1944	*Hail the Conquering Hero*	Preston Sturges
1944	*Our Hearts Were Young and Gay*	Lewis Allen
1944	*My Pal Wolf*	Alfred L. Werker
1944	*Three Is a Family*	Edward Ludwig
1944	*Together Again*	Charles Vidor
1944	*Mademoiselle Fifi*	Robert Wise
1945	*It's in the Bag!*	Richard Wallace
1945	*Kiss and Tell*	Richard Wallace
1945	*Hold That Blonde!*	George Marshall
1947	*The Sin of Harold Diddlebock* (aka *Mad Wednesday*)	Preston Sturges
1947	*Lost Honeymoon*	Leigh Jason
1947	*Always Together*	Frederick De Cordova
1948	*The Mating of Millie*	Henry Levin
1948	*Let's Live a Little* (aka *Hell Breaks Loose*)	Richard Wallace
1949	*Tell It to the Judge*	Norman Foster
1949	*A Kiss for Corliss* (aka *Almost a Bride*)	Richard Wallace
1950	*A Woman of Distinction*	Edward Buzzell
1950	*The Petty Girl*	Henry Levin
1950	*Emergency Wedding*	Edward Buzzell
1951	*Durch Dick und Dünn*	Theo Lingen (W. Germany)
1951	*Heidelberger Romanze*	Paul Verhoeven (W. Germany)
1952	*Unnatural*	Arthur Maria Rabenalt (W. Germany)
1954	*Ein Haus voll Liebe*	Hans Schweikart (W. Germany)
1954	*Geliebtes Fräulein Doktor*	Hans H. König (W. Germany)
1955	*The Congress Dances*	Franz Antel (Austria)
1955	*Die Drei von der Tankstelle*	Hans Wolff (W. Germany)
1956	*Le chemin du Paradis*	Willi Forst, Hans Wolff (France/W. Germany)
1960	*Bombs on Monte Carlo*	Georg Jacoby (W. Germany/France)

HIRSCHFELDER, David (b. 1960) An internationally recognized Australian musician, performer, and composer who started out as a keyboardist in pop-rock groups, he has scored fifty films and TV movies on three continents.

Born and raised in Ballarat, in the Australian province of Victoria, David Hirschfelder began composing tunes as a child after his father gave him a toy electric organ. As a teenager he wrote and performed jazz and rock songs then studied classical music at Melbourne University. Hirschfelder began his professional music career as keyboard player for the jazz fusion band Pyramid, then went on as a musician in such groups as Peter Cupples Band, Little River Band, Blowout Dragon, and singer John Farnham's backup band. He sometimes wrote pieces for these groups and composed advertising jingles for Australian radio and television. Some of Hirschfelder's pop songs found popularity both at home and in Britain, which led to his scoring the TV movie *Shadows of the Heart* in 1990. That same year he wrote the theme music for the popular television series *Skirts* and the next year made an auspicious feature film debut with his score for *Strictly Ballroom*. The low-budget Australian movie became an international success, putting both director Baz Luhrmann and Hirschfelder on the map. By 1998 he was also scoring films in England and America and received Oscar nominations for the biopics *Shine* and *Elizabeth*. Other notable movies scored by Hirschfelder include *Sliding Doors*, *The Weight of Water*, *Criminal Ways*, *Shake Hands with the Devil*, *The Railway Man*, *Australia*, *Aquamarine*, and the animated *Legend of the Guardians*. He has also scored several miniseries and TV movies, including *Bootleg* (2002), *The Five People You Meet in Heaven* (2004), *Kidnapped* (2005), and six *Blackjack* detective movies.

The music throughout *Strictly Ballroom* is exhilarating and, although Hirschfelder composed only sections of it, he arranged just about all of its many songs and instrumental selections, turning a somewhat archaic dance style into something thrilling. Orchestrating rhythmic Spanish music with electric instruments, for example, is done with such panache that the old sound is reborn. It helps that Luhrmann directed the movie with cockeyed frenzy and that the choreography by John O'Connell is so sparkling, but the unique sound of *Strictly Ballroom* is the work of Hirschfelder. Another movie filled with music, *Shine*, posed a very different challenge for Hirschfelder.

This is the true story of Australian pianist David Helfgott (Geoffrey Rush), a child prodigy who found fame as an adult but was driven into a mental institution by all the pressure. Years later he attempts a comeback and finds renewed life with Gillian (Lynn Redgrave). The movie is filled with classic piano pieces by Chopin, Schumann, Liszt, and so forth, which Hirschfelder does not rearrange. For the soundtrack score, he wrote original music based on themes from the classics, in particular a Sergei Rachmaninoff piano concerto. The music Helfgott performs throughout the movie only hints at the torment going on inside; it is Hirschfelder's soundtrack score that captures both the sublime joy and the dark corners of the character. The main theme does not feature the piano at first, but relies on woodwinds and violins with harp and piano as background. It is a sorrowful piece until the frustration builds and the piano is central. Rarely has a piece of music summed up a movie character so fully.

Sixteen years after working with Luhrmann on *Strictly Ballroom*, Hirschfelder collaborated with him again on the epic movie *Australia* which was decidedly old fashioned and a long way from the director's usual fare. The film is an obvious tribute to the spirit of the nation as a British widow (Nicole Kidman) adopts her new land and battles nature, government, and World War II to survive. Hirschfelder's rich and passionate score is also old fashioned but never clichéd or soppy. Much of the action is rural, so Hirschfelder adds harmonica, Jew's harp, and other rustic instruments to the symphonic and choral selections. A cattle drive is scored with vigorous brass and strings, while a stampede uses furious guitar strings. The love theme for the widow and her cattleman (Hugh Jackson) is indeed romantic yet restrained and very tentative. Like the epics of old, the *Australia* score quotes from classical music (Bach and Elgar) and popular song ("Somewhere Over the Rainbow"). The action film *Sanctum* reveals another aspect of Hirschfelder's music. A group of explorers are trapped underground and underwater so suspense and tension is high. The score is often poetic although never less than gripping. Confused violins ramble up and down the scale and low brass rumble discontentedly. There are some gentle sequences, such as the chanting of a Maori hymn, and moments of symphonic triumph, but mostly one remembers the restless energy and overwhelming tension in the score. In contrast, the music for the comic fantasy *Aquamarine* is magical and soothing. The sound of whales and other sea life is added to vocals, playful electronic effects, and an enticing guitar melody. For a silly tale about two teenage girls (Emma Roberts and Joanna "JoJo" Levesque) who befriend a runaway mermaid (Sara Paxton), the music has quite a bit of earnest charm and sincerity. The movie is jam-packed with existing pop songs, but the real magic comes through Hirschfelder's soundtrack score, which encompasses lyrical serenades, lush waltzes, and warm melodies.

The score for *Elizabeth* is quite a mixed bag. Although the Elizabethan period is captured beautifully, there is a modern sensibility in Cate Blanchett's young Elizabeth struggling to survive and triumph. Hirschfelder echoes this paradox of the historical with the modern in his score.

A passage sung in Latin by soloists and a boys chorus and some of the festive music played by recorder and brass sound authentic while other sections of the score are dissonant and eerie. The love theme, heard on a lute with sustained violins, is delicate and evocative. The scoring for the suspense and political plotting sequences sound very contemporary, particularly when they use instruments unheard of in Renaissance England. But then there are selections from Mozart and Elgar tossed in as well, so the whole movie is a hodgepodge of music history. Perhaps all of Hirschfelder's movie music can be described as a delectable hodgepodge, which is just a way of saying he is as eclectic as he is accomplished. Official website: www.davidhirschfelder.com.

Credits

(all films Australia unless stated otherwise)

Year	Film	Director
1992	Strictly Ballroom (BAFTA)	Baz Luhrmann
1994	Dallas Doll	Ann Turner (Australia/UK)
1995	Tunnel Vision	Clive Fleury
1995	The Life of Harry Dare	Aleksi Vellis
1996	Shine (AAN; GGN; BAFTA-N)	Scott Hicks
1996	Dating the Enemy	Megan Simpson Huberman
1998	Sliding Doors	Peter Howitt (UK/USA)
1998	The Interview	Craig Monahan
1998	Elizabeth (AAN; BAFTA-N)	Shekhar Kapur (UK)
1999	What Becomes of the Broken Hearted?	Ian Mune (N. Zealand)
2000	Hanging Up	Diane Keaton (USA/Germany)
2000	The Weight of Water	Kathryn Bigelow (USA/France)
2000	Better Than Sex	Jonathan Teplitzky (Australia/France)
2003	Criminal Ways	Nick Giannopoulos
2004	Peaches	Craig Monahan
2006	Aquamarine	Elizabeth Allen (USA/Australia)
2006	Irresistible	Ann Turner
2007	Shakes Hands with the Devil	Roger Spottiswoode (Canada)
2008	The Children of Huang Shi	Roger Spottiswoode (Australia/China/Germany/USA)
2008	Salute	Matt Norman (Australia/USA)
2008	Australia	Baz Luhrmann (Australia/UK/USA)
2009	The Blue Mansion	Glen Goei (Singapore)
2010	I Love You Too	Daina Reid
2010	Legend of the Guardians: The Owls of Ga'Hoole	Zack Snyder (USA/Australia)
2011	Sanctum	Alister Grierson (USA/Australia)
2012	Beyond Right and Wrong: Stories of Justice and Forgiveness	Lekha Singh, Roger Spottiswoode (USA/UK/Rwanda/Palestine/Israel/Ireland)
2013	The Railway Man	Jonathan Teplitzky (Australia/UK)
2014	John Doe: Vigilante	Kelly Dolen
2014	Healing	Craig Monahan

HOLDRIDGE, Lee (b. 1944) A prolific composer for television, he has also written for the concert hall, ballet, opera house, and movies, most memorably feature documentaries.

He was born Lee Elwood Holdridge in Port-au-Prince, Haiti, the son of a botanist from the States and a Puerto Rican mother, and began violin lessons when he was ten. Holdridge began composing all kinds of music, from chamber pieces to rock songs, at the age of fifteen and later began his professional career writing and arranging music in New York City. Singer-songwriter Neil Diamond brought Holdridge to Los Angeles as his arranger and the two collaborated on a series of very popular recordings. He has also done arrangements and supervised albums by other top singers in show business, including Stevie Wonder, Barbra Streisand, Al Jarreau, Placido Domingo, John Denver, Diana Ross, Natalie Cole, and Dionne Warwick. Holdridge's first experience with movies was in 1970 when he contributed some original music to the low-budget drama *Pigeons*. Three years later he cowrote the score for another small drama, *Jeremy*. Holdridge's movie career finally took off when he collaborated with Diamond on the allegorical film *Jonathan Livingston Seagull*, arranging and adapting Diamond's eight songs and composing the background score. Although the movie was roundly castigated, the score was very popular and many offers followed. Unfortunately, few of the movies Holdridge has scored over the decades are of quality. Most are strained comedies, sappy melodramas, and unnecessary sequels. Among the better films are *American Pop*, *Splash*, *Mr. Mom*, *The Beastmaster*, *Pastime*, *The Twilight of the Golds*, *Old Gringo*, *Hell and Mr. Fudge*, and *Gunfighter's Moon*. Yet Holdridge has been fortunate enough to be associated with several outstanding documentary features, including *16 Days of Glory*, *The Long Way Home*, *In Search of Peace*, *Unlikely Heroes*, *Ever Again*, *Winston Churchill: Walking with Destiny*, and *Brothers at War*.

If Holdridge's movie credits have been uneven, he has enjoyed a very successful and lauded television career, scoring many TV series and over 130 miniseries and TV movies. His music for such series as *Moonlighting*, *Beauty and the Beast*, *Bob*, *One Life to Live*, *World of Discovery*, *Wizards and Warriors*, *Eight Is Enough*, and *American Family* have not only been highly praised and awarded but some of the themes became chart singles. Of the many outstanding TV movies and miniseries Holdridge scored,

the most notable ones include *Another Part of the Forest* (1972), *Gemini Man* (1976), *East of Eden* (1981), *I Want to Live* (1983), *I'll Take Manhattan* (1987), *The Tenth Man* (1988), *Do You Know the Muffin Man?* (1990), *Call of the Wild* (1993), *Heidi* (1993), *Buffalo Girls* (1995), *The Tuskegee Airmen* (1995), *A Christmas Memory* (1997), *Into Thin Air* (1997), *Mutiny* (1999), *The Mists of Avalon* (2001), *The Shunning* (2011), and *When the Heart Calls* (2013). Holdridge has scored several television documentaries and written extensively for the concert hall, including orchestral suites, concertos, elegies, sonatas, and art songs. He has also scored ballets and operas and has conducted his and others' music in all media.

There is a great deal of variety in Holdridge's television music because he has scored everything from silly sitcoms to disturbing documentaries. There is less diversity in his film scores but the quality is often high. His screen music tends to be lyrical, romantic, and atmospheric, even in the dumb comedies he was handed. His first important score, that for *Jonathan Livingston Seagull*, is quite extensive, almost the entire film is set to music. Much of this scoring consists of Diamond's songs but there are moments when Holdridge takes over. There is a quivering string passage that makes various attempts to climb the scale before finally resolving itself into a fluent flying theme that is graceful and majestic. This fits in neatly with the movie's premise of an ambitious seagull who wishes to fly beyond the ordinary. Also memorable is some quietly pounding music in which strings soar over the deep bass notes. The melodrama sequel *The Other Side of the Mountain: Part 2* has a heart-tugging love theme on piano, guitar, and woodwinds that rolls along with a firm stride without losing any of its delicate romanticism. A better movie and richer score can be found in *Old Gringo*, a character drama about an American schoolteacher (Jane Fonda) in Mexico and her relationship with a revolutionary (Jimmy Smits) and a dying writer (Gregory Peck). The score includes a moving theme featuring oboe and harp that is lyrical and heartfelt. When a guitar is added, the piece takes on the flavor of a Mexican folk ballad. There is also a wavering string passage with a sense of mystery and awe, and a mariachi band and symphony orchestra combine to play the felicitous love theme. Of the many comedies Holdridge scored, one of the best is the fantasy-farce *Splash*, which has a strong score. This offbeat tale about a human (Tom Hanks) who falls in love with a mermaid (Daryl Hannah) is far from subtle, but the score is quite elegant. The delicate and fluid main theme, heard on piano and strings, conveys the feeling of gentle waves. Its four-note motif is entrancing as it slowly rises in intensity like a wave hitting the shore. Another passage is violent and turbulent, suggesting a storm at sea, and there is a joyous theme with rhythmic percussion and cascading horns that seems to race along in an expansive mood. Even the fantasy action movie *The Beastmaster* has a surprisingly rich score. This tale of a son (Marc Singer) who sets out with animal cohorts to revenge the death of his father resembles a superhero adventure, yet it has its tender moments, as echoed in the score. The oboe and flute are featured in a bold main theme with harp accents, brass fanfares, and swaying strings. A reflective passage on flute and horns has a melancholy air that is contrasted by a rousing march theme played on brass and percussion that seems to erupt as it builds.

Some might argue that Holdridge's best screen music can be found in his finest movies, the documentaries. Certainly they contain his most emotional music. The subjects of the documentaries are often very sobering, hence the emotive music. One of the most moving of the documentaries is *Into the Arms of Strangers* about the Jewish children who were sent to Britain in order to survive the Holocaust. The main theme is a piano lullaby with a steady tempo that transitions into a fully orchestrated anthem of sorts. *The Long Way Home*, about the founding of the state of Israel, has a main theme that is a sorrowful string piece that moves along and slowly builds as horns are added. There is also a piano and woodwind passage that tentatively plays out a minor-key melody that retains its morose tone even when speeded up. *In Search of Peace*, which explores the first two decades of the nation of Israel, boasts a jarring main theme with propelling percussion that gives way to a soulful horn passage that suggests a call to Hebrew prayer. Also noteworthy is a poignant string lament that is picked up by woodwinds and grows more hopeful.

Less solemn is Holdridge's score for the documentary *16 Days of Glory*, an inside look at the 1984 Los Angeles Olympics. He provides an inspiring theme for the swimming competition, a piece that wavers in the air then explodes with a fully realized melodic line. The cycling competition is scored with nervous strings climbing the scale, finally reaching a sustained musical resolution. *Winston Churchill: Walking with Destiny* is also a more optimistic documentary. There is a quiet march with muted brass fanfares and ponderous percussion that builds into a full orchestra playing variations of a hopeful musical motif. Also effective is a processional that is melancholy yet filled with dignity. Perhaps the finest of the documentaries that Holdridge scored is *Brothers at War*, which examines an American family and how it is affected by having two sons serve in Iraq. The mixed emotions in the film are conveyed in the main theme, a piece of music that is so tentative at first that it seems reluctant to break into its gliding melody built around an evocative musical phrase. Television has used Holdridge better than the movies but he has managed to give the cinema some extraordinary music all the same. Official website: www.leeholdridge.com.

Credits

(all films USA unless stated otherwise)

Year	Film	Director
1973	*Jeremy* (aka *Jeremy Jones*)	Arthur Barron
1973	*Jonathan Livingston Seagull*	Hall Bartlett
1975	*Nothing by Chance*	William H. Barnett
1975	*e'Lollipop* (aka *Forever Young, Forever Free*)	Ashley Lazarus (S. Africa)
1976	*Mustang Country*	John C. Champion
1976	*Goin' Home*	Chris Prentiss
1977	*The Pack* (aka *The Long Hard Night*)	Robert Clouse
1978	*The Other Side of the Mountain: Part II*	Larry Peerce
1978	*Oliver's Story*	John Korty
1978	*Moment by Moment*	Jane Wagner
1979	*Tilt*	Rudy Durand
1979	*French Postcards*	Willard Huyck (France/W. Germany/USA)
1981	*American Pop*	Ralph Bakshi

Year	Film	Director
1982	The Beastmaster	Don Coscarelli (USA/W. Germany)
1983	Mr. Mom	Stan Dragoti
1984	Splash	Ron Howard
1984	Micki + Maude	Blake Edwards
1985	Sylvester	Tim Hunter
1986	16 Days of Glory	Bud Greenspan
1986	The Men's Club	Peter Medak
1987	Walk Like a Man	Melvin Frank
1987	Born in East L.A.	Cheech Marin
1987	A Tiger's Tale	Peter Douglas
1988	Big Business	Jim Abrahams
1988	The Explorers: A Century of Discovery	Cara Biega
1989	Old Gringo	Luis Puenzo
1990	Pastime	Robin B. Armstrong
1991	The Giant of Thunder Mountain	James W. Roberson
1994	Freefall	John Irvin (USA/S. Africa)
1996	The Twilight of the Golds	Ross Kagan Marks
1997	Gunfighter's Moon	Larry Ferguson (USA/Canada)
1997	The Long Way Home	Mark Jonathan Harris
1997	Family Plan	Fred Gerber
2000	Into the Arms of Strangers: Stories of the Kindertransport	Mark Jonathan Harris (UK/USA)
2001	In Search of Peace	Richard Trank
2003	Unlikely Heroes	Richard Trank
2004	Puerto Vallarta Squeeze	Arthur Allan Seidelman (Mexico/USA)
2006	Ever Again	Richard Trank
2007	I Have Never Forgotten You: The Life & Legacy of Simon Wiesenthal	Richard Trank
2009	Brothers at War	Jake Rademacher
2009	Against the Tide	Richard Trank
2010	Winston Churchill: Walking with Destiny	Richard Trank
2012	Hell and Mr. Fudge	Jeff Wood
2012	It Is No Dream: The Life of Theodor Herzl	Richard Trank
2013	The Prime Ministers: The Pioneers	Richard Trank
2013	Great Voices Sing John Denver	Kenneth Shapiro (USA/UK)
2014	Dulce Rosa	Kenneth Shapiro, Richard Sparks

HOLLANDER, Frederick (1896–1976) A prolific songwriter and composer who began and ended his career in Germany, he contributed music to many Hollywood movies between 1933 and 1954.

Born Friedrich Hollaender in London, England, he was the son of German operetta composer Victor Hollaender, who wrote music for the Berlin stage before going to England to be musical director for the Barnum and Bailey Circus. The family returned to Berlin in 1899 when the father took a job as a teacher at the Stern Conservatory (which was run by his brother Gustav) and young Hollander later studied music there under famed composer Engelbert Humperdinck. As a teenager he played piano in local silent movie houses where he improvised screen scores. When Hollander was eighteen he became a rehearsal pianist and vocal coach at the New German Theatre in Prague. During World War I he arranged entertainments for the German troops then returned to Berlin after the armistice to compose and conduct music for various theatres and cabarets. Hollander wrote scores for some German silent movies in the 1920s then found international recognition in 1930 for his music for Josef von Sternberg's early talkie classic *The Blue Angel* in which Marlene Dietrich introduced the torch standard "Falling in Love Again (Can't Help It)" (German lyric by Robert Liebermann, English lyric by Sammy Lerner). The movie was filmed in both German and English and the score and other songs were orchestrated and conducted by Franz Wachsmann. Hollaender and Wachsmann changed their names to Hollander and Waxman when they arrived in Hollywood in 1933 and, after working together on a handful of movies, each went on to have notable solo careers.

Hollander contributed music to over one hundred films during the next two decades, including some musicals for which he also wrote songs, such as *Man About Town*, *A Foreign Affair*, and *The 5,000 Fingers of Dr. T.* Among his many film scores are those for such acclaimed movies as *Every Night at Eight, Poppy, Desire, Midnight, Typhoon, Safari, The Great McGinty, Here Comes Mr. Jordan, The Man Who Came to Dinner, The Talk of the Town, Christmas in Connecticut, Born Yesterday, Androcles and the Lion, It Should Happen to You,* and *We're No Angels.* Hollander also wrote songs for films scored by others, such as *Thrill of a Lifetime* (1937) and *Destry Rides Again* (1939). He received Oscar nominations for Best Song for "Whispers in the Dark" (lyric by Leo Robin) from *Artists & Models* (1937) and "This Is the Moment" (lyric by Robin) from *That Lady in Ermine* (1948), as well as nominations for his scores for *The Talk of the Town* and *The 5,000 Fingers of Dr. T.* In 1956 Hollander returned to Germany, where he wrote for the theatre in Munich and scored some German TV movies before he died at the age of seventy-nine.

Many of Hollander's Hollywood scores were written with one or more other composers, but he has enough solo credits by which one can evaluate his screen music. In addition to four sultry songs sung by Dietrich in *The Blue Angel*, the film boasts a fine atmospheric score by Hollander. The opening music is a merry German polka that glides into an upbeat version of the now-famous "Falling in Love Again" theme. The world of the nightclub singer Lola (Dietrich) is scored with carefree and even mockingly frivolous tunes, whereas the academic milieu of Professor Rath (Emil Jennings) is deadly quiet with only the ringing of a bell or chiming of a clock to break the silence. When the teacher is reduced to playing a clown onstage, the music seems to laugh at him along with the audience. The heartbreaking ending, in which a broken Rath returns to his old classroom, is scored with a series of dying chimes. Hollander wrote the music for a handful of other Dietrich movies later in Hollywood, such as *Destry Rides Again*, which had a soundtrack score by Frank Skinner but three delectable songs for Dietrich by Hollander and Frank Loesser (lyrics). The wry and sassy "See What the Boys in the Back Room Will Have" became one of Dietrich's signature songs.

If there was a trace of the Teutonic in Hollander's music for Dietrich (even when she was in the Wild West), it disappears in his other American films. The W. C. Fields vehicle *Poppy* has a zippy score that suggests a slaphappy operetta. Calliope music is heard under many of the carnival scenes and frolicsome cartoonish tunes can be heard behind Fields's misadventures. The comedy classic *The Man Who Came to Dinner* has a brisk march as its main theme then Hollander adds some delicious musical commentary as a radio/newspaper celebrity (Monte Woolley) torments an entire Ohio town. For the stylish comedy *Midnight*, Hollander composed a waltzing main theme with a European flavor as befits its French setting. Some vigorous passages capture the hustle and bustle of Paris with honking brass while scenes at a French chateau are scored with happy strings playing a bucolic reverie. Another comedy classic, *Born Yesterday*, also uses a waltz for its main theme, but there is more American panache in it. Set in Washington, D.C., the character comedy centers on a smart-dumb blonde (Judy Holliday) who loves to listen to swing on the radio, and Hollander obliges with original Big Band passages that capture her spirited restlessness. Much of the seasonal favorite *Christmas in Connecticut* uses holiday songs throughout, but there is a pleasing swing theme for the titles and a warm domestic theme for the idyllic but manufactured Christmas in the country. Hollander wrote a very romantic score for the talky but engaging comedy of ideas, *The Talk of the Town*. He uses the full orchestral sound for what is basically a three-character piece, yet there is still something intimate about this glowing score filled with waltzing strings and twinkling woodwinds.

A Foreign Affair, a much darker comedy-drama set in Berlin after World War II, gave Hollander the opportunity one last time to write German cabaret songs for Dietrich. "Black Market," "Illusions," and "The Ruins of Berlin" may not have caught on like the earlier Hollander-Dietrich hits, but they are very potent in the context of the movie. The jaunty music heard outside of the cabarets has a vivacious tone that contrasts with the scenes of bombed-out Berlin. Sometimes a march, sometimes a Viennese waltz, the soundtrack is rich in atmosphere and color. Perhaps Hollander's most ambitious and unusual score was the one for the fantasy *The 5,000 Fingers of Dr. T.* Hans J. Salter and Heinz Roemheld assisted him on the score and there were seven songs with delightful lyrics by

Theodor Geisel (aka Dr. Seuss). A schoolboy (Tommy Rettig) has a colorful vision of his piano teacher (Hans Conried) as a maniacal villain and much of the tale takes place in his vivid imagination. The movie has marvelously surreal sets and costumes and the score matches them, using everything from circus themes to pseudo-avant-garde symphonic chaos. (See also Hans J Salter.) It is a one-of-a-kind Hollywood score that cleverly echoes German expressionism even as it remains lighthearted and silly in a Seussian way. Perhaps Hollander never totally abandoned his homeland and its music during his twenty-two years in America. Autobiographical novel: *Those Torn from the Earth* (1941). Official website: www.frederick hollandermusic.com.

Credits

(all films USA unless stated otherwise)

Year	Film	Director
1920	Sumurun	Ernst Lubitsch (Germany)
1926	The Wife's Crusade	Martin Berger (Germany)
1930	Murder for Sale	Hanns Schwarz (Germany)
1930	The Blue Angel	Josef von Sternberg (Germany)
1931	Looking for His Murderer	Robert Siodmak (Germany)
1931	Three Days of Love	Heinz Hilpert (Germany)
1931	Flagrant Délit	Hanns Schwarz, Georges Tréville (Germany)
1932	Storms of Passion	Robert Siodmak (Germany)
1932	Tumultes	Robert Siodmak (Germany/France)
1933	I Am Suzanne!	Rowland V. Lee
1934	The Only Girl	Friedrich Hollaender (Germany/UK/USA)
1935	College Scandal	Elliott Nugent
1935	Shanghai	James Flood
1935	Every Night at Eight	Raoul Walsh
1935	Accent on Youth	Wesley Ruggles
1935	Here Comes Cookie	Norman Z. McLeod
1936	Desire	Frank Borzage
1936	Till We Meet Again	Robert Florey
1936	Poppy	A. Edward Sutherland
1936	A Son Comes Home	Ewald André Dupont
1936	Valiant Is the Word for Carrie	Wesley Ruggles
1936	Hideaway Girl	George Archainbaud
1937	John Meade's Woman	Richard Wallace
1937	Angel	Ernst Lubitsch
1937	True Confession	Wesley Ruggles
1938	Bluebeard's Eighth Wife	Ernst Lubitsch
1938	Zaza	George Cukor
1939	Midnight	Mitchell Leisen
1939	Invitation to Happiness	Wesley Ruggles
1939	Man About Town	Mark Sandrich
1939	Honeymoon in Bali	Edward H. Griffith
1939	Disputed Passage	Frank Borzage
1940	Remember the Night	Mitchell Leisen
1940	Too Many Husbands	Wesley Ruggles
1940	Typhoon	Louis King
1940	The Biscuit Eater	Stuart Heisler
1940	Safari	Edward H. Griffith
1940	Queen of the Mob	James P. Hogan
1940	Golden Gloves	Edward Dmytryk, Felix E. Feist
1940	The Great McGinty	Preston Sturges
1940	Rangers of Fortune	Sam Wood
1940	South of Suez	Lewis Seiler
1940	Victory	John Cromwell

Year	Film	Director
1941	*Life with Henry*	Theodore Reed
1941	*Footsteps in the Dark*	Lloyd Bacon
1941	*Million Dollar Baby*	Curtis Bernhardt
1941	*Here Comes Mr. Jordan*	Alexander Hall
1941	*Manpower*	Raoul Walsh
1941	*You Belong to Me*	Wesley Ruggles
1942	*The Man Who Came to Dinner*	William Keighley
1942	*Wings for the Eagle*	Lloyd Bacon
1942	*The Talk of the Town* (AAN)	George Stevens
1943	*Background to Danger*	Raoul Walsh
1943	*Princess O'Rourke*	Norman Krasna
1943	*Once Upon a Time*	Alexander Hall
1945	*The Affairs of Susan*	William A. Seiter
1945	*Pillow to Post*	Vincent Sherman
1945	*Conflict*	Curtis Bernhardt
1945	*Christmas in Connecticut*	Peter Godfrey
1946	*Cinderella Jones*	Busby Berkeley
1946	*The Bride Wore Boots*	Irving Pichel
1946	*Janie Gets Married*	Vincent Sherman
1946	*Two Guys from Milwaukee*	David Butler
1946	*Never Say Goodbye*	James V. Kern
1946	*The Verdict*	Don Siegel
1947	*The Perfect Marriage*	Lewis Allen
1947	*That Way with Women*	Frederick De Cordova
1947	*Stallion Road*	James V. Kern, Raoul Walsh
1947	*The Red Stallion*	Lesley Selander
1948	*Berlin Express*	Jacques Tourneur
1948	*Wallflower*	Frederick De Cordova
1948	*A Foreign Affair*	Billy Wilder
1949	*Caught*	Max Ophüls
1949	*A Woman's Secret*	Nicholas Rey
1949	*Adventure in Baltimore*	Richard Wallace
1949	*Strange Bargain*	Will Price
1949	*Bride for Sale*	William D. Russell
1949	*A Dangerous Profession*	Ted Tatzlaff
1950	*Never a Dull Moment*	George Marshall
1950	*Born to Be Bad*	Nicholas Ray
1950	*Walk Softly, Stranger*	Robert Stevenson
1950	*Born Yesterday*	George Cukor
1951	*My Forbidden Past*	Robert Stevenson
1951	*Darling, How Could You!*	Mitchell Leisen
1952	*The First Time*	Frank Tashlin
1952	*Androcles and the Lion*	Chester Erskine, Nicholas Ray
1953	*The 5,000 Fingers of Dr. T.* (AAN)	Roy Rowland
1954	*It Should Happen to You*	George Cukor
1954	*Phffft*	Mark Robson
1955	*We're No Angels*	Michael Curtiz
1960	*The Haunted Castle*	Kurt Hoffmann (W. Germany)

HONEGGER, Arthur (1892–1955) A Swiss-born composer of the concert and opera stage and one of the giants of twentieth-century neoclassical music, he wrote thirty screen scores over a period of twenty-five years.

Oscar Arthur Honegger was born in Le Havre, France, the son of Swiss parents who were music lovers. He stud-ied the violin as a youth and later attended the Zurich Conservatory and the Paris Conservatory, writing his first quartets and orchestral pieces as a student. In Paris, Honegger became interested in the new movements in music and was soon labeled one of "The Six," young composers who were rebelling against classical Germanic music and advocating a simpler and more modern sound. Honegger found wide recognition and acclaim in the 1920s for his ballets and operas, later for his instrumental works as well. Perhaps his most important symphonic work was *Pacific 231*, an orchestral piece inspired by a steam locomotive, which premiered in 1923. His long collaboration with poet Paul Claudel resulted in some of his most famous works, most memorably the oratorio *Jeanne d'Arc au bûcher (Joan of Arc at the Stake)* in 1935. Honegger remained in Paris during the German occupation of World War II and continued to compose but, because of his sympathy for the National Front, his work was not permitted to be performed. After the war, Honegger embarked on an extensive tour of America, but it was cut short when he suffered a heart attack in 1947. He continued to write until his death in 1955 at the age of sixty-three. Honegger's output includes five symphonies, four oratorios, six operas, operettas, ballets, chamber music, and film scores. Honegger's sporadic career in movies began in 1923 when he scored the silent film *The Wheel* for French director Abel Gance. Four years later he wrote the extensive score for Gance's five-hour epic *Napoleon* requiring the longest symphonic score yet written for the cinema. Honegger's first sound film was the 1934 version of *Les Misérables* followed by several other French movies in the 1930s, most memorably *Mayerling, Crime and Punishment, Flight into Darkness,* and *Liberté*. He also scored the Swiss film *Demon of the Himalayas,* two American movies (*The Woman I Love* and *Storm over Tibet*), and the British screen adaptation of *Pygmalion,* arguably his most famous score.

While Honegger's "serious" music is studied and performed today, his screen compositions are usually ignored. Scholarly works and collections usually do not even mention the fact that he wrote music for thirty movies. Some of this is because this music is very difficult to locate. Honegger's concert music is characterized by its propulsive rhythms, Bach-like counterpoint, strong melodic lines, complex harmony, and a solemnity in tone that sets him apart from the other five composers of the Six. It is difficult to see much of this in his screen scores. They tend to be conventional and efficient. The *Napoleon* score is filled with everything from anthems and marches to romantic passages and vigorous symphonic battles. Because that silent epic has been rescored by Carl Davis and Carmine Coppola for restored versions now shown, few have heard Honegger's music for the movie. Fortunately a suite

taken from the score was made in 1926 and one can hear the highlights. A violin and French horn passage is delicate and entrancing, much in the flavor of Camille Saint-Saëns. A gliding waltz is used for some of the palace scenes. The way a sweeping military theme incorporates "La Marseillaise" is beautifully done. The memorable snowball fight with the boy Napoleon and his fellow students is scored with propulsive pizzicato strings and fluttering flutes racing up and down the scale. This is a superb score by any standards and one questions why those restoring the film in 1981 insisted on new music.

The French 1934 version of *Les Misérables* was Honegger's first talkie, and again he wrote quite an extensive score. A gloomy march that occasionally bursts into half-hearted fanfares sets the tone of the film very well, right down to a sour trumpet solo that cries with poverty. An oboe solo in one passage is echoed by violins, while a cafe scene is scored with flute and accordion; yet both pieces are in minor keys and have a melancholy undercurrent. The scenes at the barricade have the most rousing music in the score, the brass in a bold mood while the strings are similarly defiant. The love theme is restrained, even hesitant. In fact, the whole score impresses one with its emphasis on heartfelt emotion rather than passion or bombast. One Honegger movie that is still seen is *Pygmalion,* arguably the best movie ever made from a George Bernard Shaw play. This talky drawing room comedy was directed by Anthony Asquith on a small scale and Honegger's music is played by a small but lively orchestra. Horns and strings alternate in a sprightly manner during the opening theme that recalls a Gilbert and Sullivan frolic. There is a breezy theme for Eliza (Wendy Hiller) that suggests her carefree nature but also her romantic streak. When Professor Higgins (Leslie Howard) is demonstrating his recording equipment the music is frantic and modern, the piano striking keys stridently as the horns and strings go berserk. This theme is repeated as Eliza endures her vocal exercises and the nightmares that result from them. Honegger even has fun with the music at the ambassador's ball, turning a flowing waltz into a wry commentary with a lone clarinet in counterpoint to the strings. Higgins's frustration when Eliza leaves him is musicalized by a restless series of scales that mocks the vocal lessons used earlier in the film. Maybe the most remarkable aspect of this joyous but subtle score is how British it sounds, particularly coming from a Swiss composer who lived in France all his life. Yet all of

Honegger's music is amazingly eclectic and one shouldn't be surprised. He must have enjoyed composing for the screen for, as busy as he was, he always returned to the medium, especially between 1934 and 1946. If only his

movie music was taken as seriously as his other work. Autobiography: *I Am a Composer* (1951); biography: *Arthur Honegger*, Harry Halbreich (trans. Roger Nichols) (1999). Website: www.arthur-honegger.com.

Credits

(all films France unless stated otherwise)

Year	Film	Director
1923	The Wheel	Abel Gance
1927	Napoleon	Abel Gance
1934	Les Misérables	Raymond Bernard
1934	The Kidnapping	Dimitri Kirsanoff
1934	Roi de Camargue	Jacques de Baroncelli
1934	Cease Firing	Jacques de Baroncelli
1935	Demon of the Himalayas	Andrew Marton (Switzerland)
1935	Crime and Punishment	Pierre Chenal
1935	Flight into Darkness	Anatole Litvak
1936	Mayerling	Anatole Litvak
1936	Les mutinés de l'Elseneur	Pierre Chenal
1936	Nitchevo	Jacques de Baroncelli
1937	Mademoiselle Docteur	Georg Wilhelm Pabst
1937	The Woman I Love	Anatole Litvak (USA)
1937	Marthe Richard	Raymond Bernard
1937	Harvest	Marcel Pagnol
1937	Passeurs d'hommes	René Jayet
1937	Liberté	Jean Kemm
1938	Pygmalion	Anthony Asquith, Leslie Howard (UK)
1939	Farinet ou l'or dans la montagne	Max Haufler (Switzerland/France)
1940	Les musiciens du ciel	Georges Lacombe
1942	Le journel tombe a cinq heures	Georges Lacombe
1942	Huit hommes dans un château	Richard Pottier
1943	Secrets	Pierre Blanchar
1943	Captain Fracasse	Abel Gance (Italy/France)
1943	Mermoz	Louis Cuny
1943	Secrets of a Ballerina	Pierre Blanchar
1946	Dawn Devils	Yves Allégret
1946	A Friend Will Come Tonight	Raymond Bernard
1946	Un revenant	Christian-Jaque
1952	Storm over Tibet	Andrew Marton (USA)

HOOPER, Nicholas (b. 1952?) A British composer for television and movies, he has been much honored for his small-screen scores and more recently has found film recognition with his music for the fifth and sixth installments of the Harry Potter adventures.

Nicholas Hooper has successfully kept information about his birth, upbringing, education, and personal matters out of print. His movie career began in 1985 when he scored the American nature documentary *Land*

of the Tiger as a *National Geographic Special* shown in theatres. Over the next dozen years Hooper scored some film shorts and the 1993 television documentary *The Time Traveller* before returning to feature movies with the British historical drama *The Tichborne Claimant* in 1998. His music for the 2001 BBC miniseries *The Way We Live Now* was highly praised and led to many other television assignments, including such series as *The Future Is Wild*, *Blue Murder*, *Nature*, *Birdsong*, and *North*

America. Among his seventeen TV movies and miniseries are *The Secret* (2002), *Loving You* (2003), *State of Play* (2003), *The Young Visitors* (2003), *Messiah: The Promise* (2004), *The Girl in the Cafe* (2005), *Prime Suspect 7: The Final Act* (2006), *Einstein and Eddington* (2008), *Enid* (2009), and *The Escape Artist* (2013). Hooper was selected by director David Yates to score *Harry Potter and the Order of the Phoenix* and *Harry Potter and the Half-Blood Prince,* thereby reviving his movie career. His most acclaimed recent films have been the documentaries *African Cats* and *Chimpanzee* for Walt Disney Studios.

John Williams and Patrick Doyle had successfully scored the first four Harry Potter films, so expectations were high when Hooper was hired to write the music for *Harry Potter and the Order of the Phoenix.* He used some of Williams's music, particularly the theme for the owl Hedwig, but most of the score was original and quite thrilling. In this fifth installment, the loathsome Dolores Umbridge (Imelda Staunton) and the Ministry of Justice take over the Hogwarts school, Harry (Daniel Radcliffe) experiences violent dreams about Lord Voldemort (Ralph Fiennes), and Harry's friends secretly practice with their magic wands to prepare for an encounter with Voldemort's henchmen. The opening track is vigorous chase music with a tribal beat and a touch of a British folk song gone berserk when played on electric guitar. Hooper's theme for Umbridge is a quirky minor-key piece played on trombones, bassoons, oboe, and orchestral bells which has an odd rhythm, the tempo suddenly stopping short then jumping ahead. The romantic music under Harry's kiss with Cho Chang (Katie Leung) is quiet and mystical as bells softly provide the rhythm. The music for the students' practice session with the wands is lighthearted and even silly, as played on a xylophone, celesta, clarinet,

and bassoon punctuated with plucked strings. The darker sections of the score involve furious strings and pounding brass, and the climactic confrontation between Harry and Voldemort is scored mostly with sound effects, but a string passage is interwoven into the sections when Harry has visions of his family.

The sixth movie, *Harry Potter and the Half-Blood Prince,* is perhaps the darkest yet in the series as events from the far past come into play and Voldemort wreaks havoc on both the wizard and Muggle worlds. Hooper opens the film ominously with low rumbling strings and brass that steadily accelerate and break into a restless theme featuring a solo violin and sweeping orchestral accompaniment. A wordless chorus is added to various passages, often serving as another instrument rather than a featured melody or theme. There is a lovely but uncomfortable theme played on celesta, piano, strings, and sustained woodwinds that is reflective and very self-aware. Similarly, a solo on the viola matched by violins and harp is graceful and even serene but there is an unsettling tone as well. A lighter moment in the score is heard when the Wesley twins (Oliver and James Phelps) open their own magic shop and the music explodes in a rapid, unusually accented piece of delicious chaos. Hooper retains Williams's music for the Quidditch match but writes an original theme for the practice scene in which woodwinds and horns race across the scale in time to the quixotic sport. But most of this score is indeed dark, as brooding, minor-key music reflects Harry's inner turmoil and the fatalistic future he faces. Hooper rose to the challenge of continuing to provide high-quality music for the Harry Potter series, and it is hoped that he will return to screen scoring more frequently in the future.

Credits

Year	Film	Director
1985	*Land of the Tiger*	Dennis B. Kane, Thomas Skinner (USA)
1998	*The Tichborne Claimant*	David Yates (UK)
2002	*The Heart of Me*	Thaddeus O'Sullivan (UK/Germany)
2007	*Harry Potter and the Order of the Phoenix*	David Yates (UK/USA)
2009	*Harry Potter and the Half-Blood Prince*	David Yates (UK/USA)
2011	*African Cats*	Alastair Fothergill, Keith Scholey (USA)
2011	*Stella Days*	Thaddeus O'Sullivan (Ireland/Norway/Germany)
2012	*Chimpanzee*	Alastair Fothergill, Mark Linfield (Tanzania/USA)

HOPKINS, Kenyon (1912–1983) An outstanding jazz composer and arranger who worked with Big Bands, in films and television, and for the concert hall, he scored sixteen movies in the 1950s and 1960s, including some hard-hitting classic dramas.

Born in Coffeyville, Kansas, the son of a minister, Kenyon Hopkins grew up in Michigan. He studied music at Oberlin College and Temple University before going to New York City, where he worked as an arranger on radio, in the theatre, and for such bandleaders as Andre Kostelanetz and Paul Whiteman. After serving in the Coast Guard during World War II, Hopkins signed with Capitol Records and made a series of jazz and instrumental mood albums, some of which were very popular. During the 1950s he was head arranger and composer for Radio City Music Hall and in the early 1960s he was music director for CBS Radio. Hopkins wrote and arranged two symphonies and chamber pieces for the concert hall, recordings of international music, and a jazz ballet. He made an auspicious movie debut in 1956 when he composed a superb jazz score for the controversial drama *Baby Doll*, followed by such superior films as *12 Angry Men*, *The Fugitive Kind*, *The Strange One*, *Wild River*, *The Hustler*, *Lilith*, and *This Property Is Condemned*. Hopkins entered television in 1964 with his compelling music for the dramatic series *East Side/West Side*. Later that same year he scored the series *The Reporter*, followed by *Hawk* and some early TV movies. His television music was groundbreaking, using fewer instruments for a sharper and more intimate sound. Sometimes he utilized only a particular section of the orchestra, which gave his scores a distinctive sound. Hopkins's films in the later 1960s were disappointments, so he left movies in 1970 when he was named music director of Paramount's television division. It was there that he supervised, arranged, and/or wrote theme music for such TV series as *The Odd Couple*, *Barefoot in the Park*, *The Young Lawyers*, *Longstreet*, *The Brady Bunch*, *Mannix*, *Mission: Impossible*, and *Love, American Style*. Hopkins retired from television in 1973 and a decade later died at the age of seventy-one. Today he is most known for his television work and his many albums and soundtrack scores are waiting to be rediscovered.

In many ways Hopkins's first Hollywood score, *Baby Doll*, is his best because it contains so many interesting versions of jazz and blues. Tennessee Williams's tale of a sluttish virgin (Carroll Baker) and the two men (Eli Wallach and Karl Malden) who lust after her was so carnal in its tone that the movie was condemned as sinful even though there was hardly any sex in it. This naive and risqué paradox is captured in Hopkins's skillful score. The main theme is a languid yet sultry jazz piece with a lonely saxophone and lazy strings drifting over a bluesy harmonica. There is also a blues passage that repeats the same musical phrase, each time taking a half step up the scale, and an up-tempo theme with racing strings and rhythmic brass that sounds like a nightmarish chase. Hopkins brings more variety to the score with a down and dirty honky-tonk blues piece played on harmonica, saxophone, and electric guitar. Perhaps the most memorable music is one identified as the "Lemonade" theme. It is a rhythmic passage with an odd assortment of instruments (strings, saxophone, mandolin, and harmonica) that moves along in a breezy, carefree manner that suggests both innocent youth and lust. Few screen composers have understood the power of movie scoring so well in their first effort. Hopkins's second film, the taut and talky drama *12 Angry Men*, has a completely different tone and his music is more subtle with only a hint of jazz. This engrossing film, about a dozen jurors trying to reach a unanimous verdict, has little action, mostly takes place in one room, and is thick with dialogue. Director Sidney Lumet requested that there be little music but what is there is used effectively. The movie opens with no music as the camera takes the viewer from the street into the courthouse and eventually into the courtroom where the jury is charged by the judge to retire and decide on a verdict. Not until the jurors leave the courtroom and assemble in the jury room do the opening credits and music begin. It is a simple but melancholy flute theme that tries to ascend the scale but keeps falling back only to repeat itself and try again. At the end of the film, after the jury has come to a decision, the theme returns, this time played by a full but restrained orchestra. By the final moments of the movie the music finally climbs the scale and resolves itself.

Hopkins's other superior jazz score is the one he wrote for *The Hustler*, Robert Rossen's fascinating drama about the rivalry between a veteran pool champ (Jackie Gleason) and a young upstart (Paul Newman). One can feel the dark and smoky pool halls in Hopkins's music. There is a bluesy jazz theme with a wailing saxophone and expressive percussion, including a freewheeling bongo beat. In another passage, ascending xylophone, woodwinds, and brass each follow a different track and tempo, the effect being both casual and urgent at the same time. Also intriguing is a hot jazz piece featuring honky-tonk piano, muted brass, and a crystal-clear saxophone calling out with a mocking tone. *The Fugitive Kind*, based on a Tennessee Williams play, seethes with passion as a drifter (Marlon Brando) is pursued by an older woman (Anna Magnani) and by the town tramp (Joanne Woodward). For such a raw, lusty film, the music is rather subdued. The main theme is a gentle and evocative guitar and flute piece that hesitates as it flows unevenly until finally it transitions into a flowing musical line. Much of the rest of the score is in the blues mode, including two blues songs that Hopkins set to Williams's lyrics. *The Strange One*, a drama set in a Southern military school, has an up-tempo jazz piece with

echoing saxophones that play variations on a simple four-note climb. Hopkins's third Tennessee Williams movie was *This Property Is Condemned* though the melodrama bore little resemblance to the original one-act play. In a dying Mississippi town, a torrid romance springs up between the town flirt (Natalie Wood) and a visiting railroad official (Robert Redford). The highlight of Hopkins's score is a bustling travel theme with electric guitar, strings, and brass that sometimes slows down for a waltzing section, then continues racing along. After this movie, Hopkins was rarely given a high-quality project, so it is not surprising that four years later he left the movies for television. Yet during the period of 1956 to 1966, he scored some significant dramas and provided each one with a compelling score.

Credits

(all films USA)

Year	Film	Director
1956	*Baby Doll*	Elia Kazan
1957	*12 Angry Men*	Sidney Lumet
1957	*The Strange One*	Jack Garfein
1960	*The Fugitive Kind*	Sidney Lumet
1960	*Wild River*	Elia Kazan
1961	*Wild in the Country* (aka *Lonely Man*)	Philip Dunne
1961	*The Hustler*	Robert Rossen
1963	*The Yellow Canary*	Buzz Kulik
1964	*Lilith*	Robert Rossen
1966	*Mister Buddwing*	Delbert Mann
1966	*This Property Is Condemned*	Sydney Pollack
1967	*Doctor, You've Got to Be Kidding!* (aka *This Way Out, Please*)	Peter Tewksbury
1968	*A Lovely Way to Die*	David Lowell Rich
1969	*The Tree*	Robert Guenette
1969	*The First Time*	James Neilson
1969	*Downhill Racer*	Michael Ritchie

HORNER, James (b. 1953) A very successful American composer and conductor who has scored over one hundred movies since 1978, his *Titanic* soundtrack has sold more CDs than any other. Horner has written the music for some of the most popular movies of the last three decades yet some of his finest work has been for obscure films.

He was born James Roy Horner in Los Angles, the son of film and theatre producer-designer-director Harry

Horner, and grew up in England where he began piano lessons as a boy and later studied at the Royal College of Music in London. Horner returned to California as an adult and studied music at UCLA. While working on his PhD there, Horner was asked to score some short movies for the American Film Institute. He so much enjoyed composing for the screen, Horner left UCLA without finishing his degree and concentrated on screen music from then on. His first feature films were low-budget sci-fi movies for producer Roger Corman, but there were some fine early scores that he wrote for Oliver Stone and Wes Craven features. Recognition came with his dynamic score for *Star Trek II: The Wrath of Kahn* in 1982, and that same year he had another hit with *48 Hrs.* Horner quickly rose to the top of his profession, working with such directors as Norman Jewison, Ron Howard, Peter Yates, and James Cameron. Many of his successes over the years have been sci-fi movies or have had fantasy elements, such as *Krull, Star Trek III: The Search for Spock, Cocoon, Willow, Aliens, Field of Dreams, Honey I Shrunk the Kids, The Pagemaster, Jumanji, Deep Impact, Bicentennial Man,* and *Avatar.* Yet Horner's credits are very eclectic, including everything from historical movies such as *Glory, Legends of the Fall, The New World,* and *Troy* to animated films such as *An American Tail, The Land before Time, Balto,* and *We're Back! A Dinosaur Story.* Some projects have been big-budget blockbusters, such as *Titanic, Braveheart, Apollo 13, How the Grinch Stole Christmas,* and *The Amazing Spider-Man,* while exceptional scores can be found in such intimate films as *A Beautiful Mind, Iris, Searching for Bobby Fischer,* and *The Spitfire Grill.*

By the turn of the new century, Horner was one of the most in-demand composers in Hollywood. He has few television credits and, unlike many composers with a classical training, his works for the concert hall are infrequent. Horner puts all his energies into film. He often orchestrates and conducts the recordings of his scores so he does not accept as many projects as the more prolific screen composers. The score for *Avatar,* for example, took two years and during that time he worked on no other projects. He has been nominated for many awards and has won two Oscars but, more importantly, he is regarded as having a golden touch when it comes to movie projects. So many Horner-scored movies have been box office hits that producers sometimes credit the music for the pictures doing so well. There is no question that the luscious scores for *Fields of Dreams, Titanic,* and *Avatar* contributed greatly to those movies' success but most would agree that it is next to impossible for a musical score to turn a poor film into an excellent one. All the same, Horner's music has often made a mediocre movie seem much better than it is. Horner has stated that he is most influenced by Dmitri Shostakovich. There is definitely a Russian flavor in several Horner scores even if the movies have no connection to that culture. Yet there is just as much Celtic-like music

in his work as any other ethnic sound. Many of his scores use choral singing, particularly a female wordless chorus. Sometimes a solo voice is used instead. Like many composers, he uses very distinct musical motifs. His leitmotif for the villain in his movies is often a four-note phrase with a strong downbeat. He favors brass fanfares where appropriate, though a solo piano played fortissimo is a recurring element in his work, often used to denote inspiration or a turning point for a character. But these are all generalizations. One had best look at a handful of his many scores more carefully.

Horner first gained attention for his melodic main theme in *Star Trek II: The Wrath of Kahn.* French horns are featured as swirling strings attack with fervor, the music going from one heroic crescendo to another. It all suggests exploration and adventure not unlike the feeling that John Williams's *Star Wars* score manages to do. Another propulsive theme has violins circling furiously like angry bees. There is a radiantly idyllic passage with high-pitched noises playing against a harp, and pounding attack music in which both traditional and electronic percussion lead the way and various instruments follow. This was a score that was bound to get noticed. Horner's music for the lesser-known sci-fi movie *Krull* is even richer. Female voices compete with trumpet fanfares in the main theme, growing from a curious duet to a symphonic celebration of power and pride. A dreamy passage with twinkling chimes and swaying strings is inspiring in the way it grows in strength. Also memorable is a march sounded by French horns and strings, a felicitous lullaby in which an oboe echoes the sounds of a female choir, and a love theme played first on cellos then filled out by a celesta and piano accompaniment. Horner's innovative use of voices in *Brainstorm* is quite splendid. This rather convoluted sci-fi thriller about artificial realities manufactured by an electronics company leaves much to be desired, but it provided several opportunities for imaginative scoring. This time the high-pitched sound of a boys choir blends into the screeching of instruments at the top of the scale, all the while contrasted with low grinding chords from bass instruments. Another passage has musical instruments and synthesized sounds both rapidly descending the scale until they reverse and spring up like a geyser. At one point in the movie an inventor (Louise Fletcher) gets to electronically record her own heart attack and Horner's music is a frightening onslaught of brass and strings moving about in a dizzy manner as they climb the scale to an explosive climax.

The period movies that Horner scored gave him an opportunity to move away from so much tech music but he doesn't abandon his love of human voices as part of the orchestration. Perhaps the finest of his period films is *Glory*, a scintillating yet sobering true story about an all-black Union regiment fighting in the Civil War and their tragic plight during a battle in South Carolina. The unforgettable main theme has the innocent and celestial voices of the Boys Choir of Harlem singing the hymnlike melody against a military march, making the sound both patriotic and fatalistic. While this passage is the most stirring, the entire score is filled with similarly enthralling music. A doleful Christmas hymn played on lonesome reeds is so fragile that it aches with tenderness. The various marches heard throughout the movie have a melancholy subtext, often the mellow horns dictating the pace rather than the percussion. As the soldiers prepare for battle, the boys choir is heard again, their questioning voices joining the muted drum rolls and the fluid strings. The charge on Fort Wagner is scored with a double-time marching hymn sung by the boys' staccato voices, an urgent passage not unlike Carl Orff's opening of *Carmina Burana*. After the suicidal battle, the boys choir chants a simple but eloquent epitaph using a solemn variation of the opening theme. The epic melodrama *Legends of the Fall* is a period piece that gets less interesting the longer one spends with the characters. A Montana family is torn apart over jealousy, unrequited love, sibling rivalry, and just plain nastiness. Yet the movie is beautifully filmed and Horner's soundtrack is highly commendable. The score has a great deal of variety and does not rely on one major theme. The vast open landscape is musicalized with a rumbling passage in which a horn imitates the call of birds and the full orchestra has the fervor of wild horses racing across the horizon. There is a domestic theme that rolls and floats with a simple majesty, an agitated passage that sounds like a symphonic storm, and a memorable musical sequence in which a fiddle plays a furious waltz. For the thriller *The Devil's Own*, Horner turns to Celtic music and traditional Irish instruments. An American family is caught in the middle of terrorism when they take in an IRA gunman (Harrison Ford) in disguise. Horner uses a wood flute, bodhran, harp, steel-string guitar, and uilleann pipes to create an Irish score that moves from mournful ballads to vigorous action music.

The main theme is a haunting Irish air sung in Celtic with ethnic instruments mixed with a full orchestra. There is a spirited folk tune heard on a flute that grows in intensity as other instruments are added. As the tension in the story builds, the soothing Irish airs take on a menacing tone, the percussion getting more strident and the horns sounding more sinister.

What of those big hit movies that are so enhanced by Horner's music? *Field of Dreams* has a mostly restrained score that quietly creeps up on you. This offbeat film concerns a farmer (Kevin Costner) who turns part of his field into a baseball diamond because some strange voices have instructed him to do so. The gentle but ghostly theme for the deceased ballplayers who show up on the field defines the magic of this unusual fantasy. The combination of a solo French horn, a string orchestra, and a synthesizer in the main theme is refreshingly different and memorable. United by variations of the same musical idea, the music in *Field of Dreams* holds together thematically as well as musically. Also in the score is a delicate, rural ballad played on a reflective guitar that captures the beauty and simplicity of nature. A fluid string passage for domestic serenity is one of the most sweeping in the score, but just as effective is the unembellished piano solo that is so unpretentious it begs not to be noticed. *Braveheart*, about a medieval Scots warrior (Mel Gibson) who leads a resistance movement against the British, has the expected Scottish sound with its bagpipes, kena, whistles, and drums, but there is also electronic music in the mix. Horner makes fine use of rumbling percussion throughout this score which definitely feels epic. The main theme is a primitive folk tune played on a solo bagpipe that seems to cry out in loneliness; other instruments do variations on this music throughout the film. A sprightly dance on period instruments heard during a wedding celebration has a tribal quality while a funeral is scored with a fragile lament in which the orchestra echoes a solo horn. A slow but determined march passage mixes strings and brass with electronic percussion, which takes over as the piece accelerates. The love theme is one of Horner's best, a flowing rhapsody that waltzes along with a folk flavor even when it is given a lush symphonic treatment. Because the sci-fi blockbuster *Avatar* creates an original planet inhabited by a new race of creatures, Horner has no historical context to study as with *Braveheart* or *Glory*, so he opts for a score that is often more tribal than sci-fi. The main theme is an anxious percussion and chorus piece backed by traditional strings and horns. There is a primitive feel to it, but one hears Latin Gregorian chant as well. The planet's Na'vi people have their own language so Horner comes up with sounds musically that communicate on the simplest level. Various kinds of chimes, beating of sticks, electronic echoes, and high-pitched whistles are used right alongside a conventional orchestra. It is similar to New Age music but it is more dramatic. In one passage, a children's chorus is heard amid restless percussion, both sounds building on each other until it explodes in a full symphonic piece. The battle scenes are scored with an angry adult chorus, threatening brass, and furious drumming. This is contrasted by some lyrical themes that manage to glide along peacefully even though the beat is agitated.

As massive as everything about the movie *Titanic* is, the main theme is a simple Irish air played on ethnic instruments but filtered through a synthesizer. The voices heard throughout the movie are not those of a huge choir but rather the echoing of a few voices. The love theme in the film is a solo female voice accompanied by a wood flute, while the motif for the ship itself is an expansive melody played by Horner's favorite duet, French horn and strings. (This melody was turned into the Oscar-winning song "My Heart Will Go On" for the final credits.) How much impact does this score have on the success of *Titanic*? Much more than many people have acknowledged. Because Horner repeats musical ideas from one movie to another he has been accused of not being very versatile. The full body of work defies this accusation but it is no secret that he often returns to a good musical idea when it has worked in the past. Some may see this as a lack of originality but it might be more fair to say that certain elements are all part of Horner's musical style. One can scoff and dismiss his choral voices and dulcet French horns as a Horner cliché but others could just as easily call such effects the "Horner sound" and appreciate them as engaging screen music.

Credits

(all films USA unless stated otherwise; * for Best Song)

Year	Film	Director
1978	The Watcher	uncredited
1979	Up from the Depths	Charles B. Griffith (Philippines/USA)
1979	The Lady in Red	Lewis Teague
1980	Humanoids from the Deep	Barbara Peters
1980	Battle beyond the Stars	Jimmy T. Murakami
1981	The Hand	Oliver Stone
1981	Wolfen	Michael Wadleigh
1981	Deadly Blessing	Wes Craven
1981	The Pursuit of D. B. Cooper	Roger Spottiswoode
1982	Star Trek II: The Wrath of Khan	Nicholas Meyer
1982	48 Hrs.	Walter Hill
1983	Something Wicked This Way Comes	Jack Clayton
1983	Krull	Peter Yates (UK/USA)
1983	Space Raiders	Howard R. Cohen
1983	Brainstorm	Douglas Trumbull
1983	Testament	Lynne Littman
1983	The Dresser	Peter Yates (UK)
1983	Gorky Park	Michael Apted
1983	Uncommon Valor	Ted Kotcheff
1984	The Stone Boy	Christopher Cain
1984	Star Trek III: The Search for Spock	Leonard Nimoy
1985	Heaven Help Us	Michael Dinner
1985	Cocoon	Ron Howard
1985	Volunteers	Nicholas Meyer
1985	The Journey of Natty Gann	Jeremy Kagan
1985	Commando	Mark L. Lester
1985	Wizards of the Lost Kingdom	Héctor Olivera (Argentina/USA)

Year	Film	Director
1985	*In Her Own Time*	Lynne Littman
1985	*Barbarian Queen*	Héctor Olivera (USA/Argentina)
1986	*Off Beat*	Michael Dinner
1986	*Aliens* (AAN)	James Cameron (USA/UK)
1986	*Where the River Runs Black*	Christopher Cain
1986	*The Name of the Rose*	Jean-Jacques Annaud (W. Germany/Italy/France)
1986	*An American Tail* (AAN*; GGN*)	Don Bluth
1987	*P. K. and the Kid*	Lou Lombardo
1987	*Project X*	Jonathan Kaplan
1987	**batteries not included*	Matthew Robbins
1988	*Andy Colby's Incredible Adventure*	Deborah Brock
1988	*Willow*	Ron Howard
1988	*Red Heat*	Walter Hill
1988	*Vibes*	Ken Kwapis
1988	*The Land before Time*	Don Bluth (USA/Ireland)
1988	*Cocoon: The Return*	Daniel Petrie
1989	*Field of Dreams* (AAN)	Phil Alden Robinson
1989	*Honey, I Shrunk the Kids*	Joe Johnston
1989	*In Country*	Norman Jewison
1989	*Dad*	Gary David Goldberg
1989	*Glory* (GGN)	Edward Zwick
1990	*I Love You to Death*	Lawrence Kasdan
1990	*Another 48 Hrs.*	Walter Hill
1991	*Once Around*	Lasse Hallström
1991	*My Heroes Have Always Been Cowboys*	Stuart Rosenberg
1991	*Class Action*	Michael Apted
1991	*The Rocketeer*	Joe Johnston
1991	*An American Tail: Fievel Goes West* (GGN*)	Phil Nibbelink, Simon Wells
1992	*Thunderheart*	Michael Apted
1992	*Patriot Games*	Phillip Noyce
1992	*Unlawful Entry*	Jonathan Kaplan (USA/Japan)
1992	*Sneakers*	Phil Alden Robinson
1993	*Swing Kids*	Thomas Carter
1993	*A Far Off Place*	Mikael Salomon
1993	*Jack the Bear*	Marshall Herskovitz
1993	*Once Upon a Forest*	Charles Grosvenor (UK/USA)
1993	*House of Cards*	Michael Lessac (USA/Italy)
1993	*Searching for Bobby Fischer*	Steven Zaillian
1993	*The Man without a Face*	Mel Gibson
1993	*Bopha!*	Morgan Freeman
1993	*We're Back! A Dinosaur Story*	Phil Nibbelink, Simon Wells, Dick Zondag, Ralph Zondag
1993	*The Pelican Brief*	Alan J. Pakula
1994	*Clear and Present Danger*	Phillip Noyce
1994	*The Pagemaster*	Pixote Hunt, Joe Johnston
1994	*Legends of the Fall* (GGN)	Edward Zwick
1995	*Braveheart* (AAN; GGN; BAFTA-N)	Mel Gibson
1995	*Casper*	Brad Silberling
1995	*Apollo 13* (AAN)	Ron Howard
1995	*Jade*	William Friedkin
1995	*Jumanji*	Joe Johnston
1995	*Balto*	Simon Wells
1996	*The Spitfire Grill*	Lee David Zlotoff
1996	*Courage under Fire*	Edward Zwick
1996	*To Gillian on Her 37th Birthday*	Michael Pressman
1996	*Ransom*	Ron Howard
1997	*The Devil's Own*	Alan J. Pakula (USA/Ireland)
1997	*Titanic* (AA, AA*; GG, GG*; BAFTA-N)	James Cameron

Year	Film	Director
1998	*Deep Impact*	Mimi Leder
1998	*The Mask of Zorro*	Martin Campbell (USA/Germany)
1998	*Mighty Joe Young*	Ron Underwood
1999	*Bicentennial Man*	Chris Columbus (USA/Germany)
2000	*The Perfect Storm*	Wolfgang Petersen
2000	*How the Grinch Stole Christmas*	Ron Howard (USA/Germany)
2001	*Enemy at the Gates*	Jean-Jacques Annaud (USA/Germany/UK/Ireland)
2001	*A Beautiful Mind* (AAN; GGN)	Ron Howard
2001	*Iris*	Richard Eyre (UK/USA)
2002	*Windtalker*	John Woo
2002	*The Four Feathers*	Shekhar Kapur (USA/UK)
2003	*Beyond Borders*	Martin Campbell (USA/Germany)
2003	*Radio*	Michael Tollin
2003	*The Missing*	Ron Howard
2003	*House of Sand and Fog* (AAN)	Vadim Perelman
2004	*Bobby Jones: Stroke of Genius*	Rowdy Herrington
2004	*Troy*	Wolfgang Petersen (USA/Malta/UK)
2004	*The Forgotten*	Joseph Ruben
2005	*The Chumscrubber*	Arie Posin (USA/Germany)
2005	*Flightplan*	Robert Schwentke
2005	*The Legend of Zorro*	Martin Campbell
2005	*The New World*	Terrence Malick (USA/UK)
2006	*All the King's Men*	Steven Zaillian (Germany/USA)
2006	*Apocalypto*	Mel Gibson
2007	*The Life before Her Eyes*	Vadim Perelman
2008	*The Spiderwick Chronicles*	Mark Waters
2008	*The Boy in the Striped Pajamas*	Mark Herman (UK/USA)
2009	*Avatar* (AAN; GGN, GGN*; BAFTA-N)	James Cameron (USA/UK)
2010	*The Karate Kid*	Harald Zwart (USA/China)
2011	*Day of the Falcon* (aka *Black Gold*)	Jean-Jacques Annaud (France/Italy)
2012	*For Greater Glory* (aka *Christiada*)	Dean Wright (Mexico)
2012	*The Amazing Spider-Man*	Marc Webb

HOWARD, James Newton (b. 1951) One of the busiest and most in-demand movie composers today, he is also a successful songwriter, musician, conductor, and record producer.

James Newton Howard was born in Los Angeles into a musical family and began piano lessons when he was four years old. Howard studied music at the Music Academy of the West and the University of Southern California's School of Music but left college to work as a musician for recording artists such as Harry Nilsson, Ringo Starr, and Diana Ross. In 1975 Howard was hired as keyboard player for Elton John's band, touring with and doing arrangements for the pop star for seven years. He also worked with such groups as Toto and Crosby, Stills and Nash. Howard moved into record producing and in 1985 composed, arranged, and produced his own album, *James Newton Howard and Friends*. That same year he made his movie debut when he cowrote with Alan Howarth

the score for the comedy *Head Office*. After solo scoring fifteen mostly forgettable movies, Howard finally had a hit with the romantic comedy *Pretty Woman* in 1990. Although the music moviegoers most remembered was Roy Orbison's pop standard "Oh, Pretty Woman," the success of the film opened doors for Howard and he was given more prestigious projects, in particular *Prince of Tides* in 1991 which brought him his first Oscar nomination. Other nominations came with *The Fugitive, My Best Friend's Wedding, The Village, Michael Clayton*, and *Defiance*, as well as Best Song nominations for "Look What Love Has Done" (lyric by Carole Bayer Sager, James Ingram, and Patty Smyth) from *Junior* and "For the First Time" (lyric by Jud Friedman and Allan Dennis Rich) from *One Fine Day*.

Howard has scored *The Sixth Sense* and all of the other movies by director M. Night Shyamalan since 1999, most memorably *Unbreakable, Signs, Lady in the Water*, and the already-mentioned *The Village*. Among Howard's many other notable films are *Major League, Grand Canyon, Glengarry Glen Ross, Alive, Dave, Wyatt Earp, The Devil's Advocate, Snow Falling on Cedars, Peter Pan, Water for Elephants, The Hunger Games* and its sequels *Catching Fire* and *Mockingjay, Mumford, Waterhorse, Hidalgo, I Am Legend, Stir of Echoes, King Kong, Maleficent,* and the Disney animated features *Dinosaur, Treasure Planet,* and *Atlantis: The Lost Empire*. With composer Hans Zimmer he scored the popular *Batman Begins* and *The Dark Knight*. In all, since 1985 Howard has written the music for over 125 feature films, several of which he also orchestrated. He has also worked in television on occasion, scoring TV movies and some series, most significantly the theme and music for the long-running *ER*. More recently Howard has written a symphony, which debuted in California in 2009, and he has served as visiting professor of media composition at the Royal Academy of Music in London.

Howard's first important score, for the drama *The Prince of Tides*, is indicative of his work. Much of his music is in the classical form and he favors conventional instruments, in particular strings. Yet some of his scores are very modern and use rock, jazz, and high-tech innovations. The main theme for *The Prince of Tides* is a tender, nostalgic piece that avoids sentimentality by its lively variations on a three-note phrase. This story, about a psychiatrist (Barbra Streisand) who falls in love with a patient (Nick Nolte) as she delves into his haunted past, is also tender and nostalgic. There is a sensitive piano theme that is tentative as it repeats a simple phrase over sustained strings, a lovely reflective piece played on piano, and a mournful passage featuring an oboe that maintains its stride even as it holds on to certain notes. The movie's love theme is a lilting piece that slowly rises up to a crescendo only to build on it and rise further. In contrast, Howard's score for the action thriller *The Fugitive* demonstrates his more contemporary sound. The thrilling opening theme has gliding strings playing against a rumbling, restless countermelody that quietly suggests movement without breaking out into a chase. Once the wrongly accused fugitive (Harrison Ford) is on the run, more aggressive music follows, such as a pounding theme in which the downbeat is heavy yet the pace is light footed. The score also contains a frantic percussion and piano passage with a chaotic tempo, some soprano saxophone passages that have a jazz flavor, and the use of repeating French horns to create suspense.

Some of Howard's most effective music can be found in his movies for Shyamalan's ghostly thrillers. *The Sixth Sense*, in which a child psychologist (Bruce Willis) tries to help a youth (Haley Joel Osment) who sees ghosts, has a main theme that suggests both the boy's innocence and his strange powers: a macabre waltz played on strings and piano. There is also a graceful but eerie theme that repeats the same descending phrase, and for the most suspenseful scenes Howard employs high-pitched strings and electronic sound effects. For Shyamalan's *Unbreakable*, Howard scaled down his orchestra to strings, piano, a trumpet, and percussion. This score is more subtle as it quietly suggests something sinister afoot without revealing who the villain is until the end. A security guard (Willis again) seems to be immune to dangerous accidents while an art gallery owner (Samuel L. Jackson) suffers from a bone disease that makes him susceptible to any kind of accident. The two men meet and questions pile up until the revealing ending. The main theme for *Unbreakable* is a simple and delicate lullaby that moves from innocence to dark foreboding by changing key and tone but remaining slow and steady even when the percussion tries to push it along. A rock beat enters the score when the scenes become violent, and a four-note ascending motif on the trumpet returns throughout the movie as flashbacks are used to piece together the puzzle. The allegorical horror film *The Village* may be a disappointment after *The Sixth Sense* and *Unbreakable* but it has what is arguably Howard's best score for writer-director Shyamalan. An isolated community makes a pact with the demons who live in the surrounding woods in order to protect themselves but evil events occur anyway. The main theme has a solo violin playing a poignant lament that floats up and down the scale then a harp joins in to realize a folk melody which is picked up by a full orchestra. This lyrical music is contrasted with electronic sound effects and threatening music that accompanies the wrath of the demons. The score also contains a restless passage, played by various string instruments, that slowly becomes more frantic as it races along, and a serene theme featuring flutes that gracefully wavers until it resolves itself.

Two much more realistic dramas scored by Howard embrace the classical and the modern sound. The powerful historical drama *Defiance*, about four Jewish brothers (Daniel Craig, Liev Schreiber, Jamie Bell, and George MacKay) who join the Russian Resistance movement to thwart the Nazis, has a score that moves from the poetic to the harsh. Joshua Bell plays the solo violin heard in the main theme, a melancholy processional that keeps a steady pace even as it dwindles in sorrow. Later in the film a solo violin is also featured in a flowing passage that hints at klezmer music but is more agitated. Finally the music breaks out in a furious passage with frantic strings, blaring brass, and pounding percussion. The contemporary drama *Glengarry Glen Ross*, about cutthroat real estate salesmen, has a jazz score, mixing some jazz standards with Howard's original music. The main theme is a cool jazz piece played on saxophone and piano that conveys weariness even as the tempo suggests drive and confidence. There is also jazzy traveling music punctuated with clicks and piano chords as the saxophone pushes forward. Two westerns that Howard scored are also of interest. *Wyatt Earp* is the more conventional of the two as it chronicles the life of the famous lawman (Kevin Costner) and his family. The score is also conventional but exciting in its rich Americana and sense of the Old West. The main theme is a skipping theme heard on French horn in which a five-note phrase parades along with force as different parts of the orchestra pick up on a series of robust musical jumps. The long movie (212 minutes) has a lot of music with no less than six other distinct themes. Unfortunately most found the epic tedious and Howard's music went practically unnoticed. The more unorthodox western is *Hidalgo*, a (somewhat) true tale about a cowboy (Viggo Mortensen) who goes to the Middle East to race his mustang Hidalgo against the carefully bred Arabian horses. Howard's score mixes Western musical ideas with exotic Asian ones. The theme for the mustang is a somewhat mournful passage heard on flute and oboe that is evocative of nature and open spaces. This is contrasted with a more exotic theme with ethnic percussion and strings that commingle in a series of rhythmic crescendos. The movie opens with a race and several others follow; Howard scores these with zesty fanfares and thrilling acceleration. The most moving musical moment is when the cowboy and his mustang view the recently completed Statue of Liberty as they sail out of New York harbor. The music is a stirring anthem in which horns announce themselves with hope and confidence. Asian music can also be heard in *Snow Falling on Cedars*, a drama about a Japanese American (Rick Yune) accused of murder in an American town soon after World War II. Howard uses Asian instruments with a Western orchestra,

as in a sweeping theme with chorus and full orchestra moving from simple sustained notes to a pounding avalanche of music. A cello is featured in other passages, while a violin is teamed with the Japanese shakuhachi for the movie's delicate love theme.

It seems that much of Howard's later career has been filled with big-budget action movies with either supernatural or futuristic elements. The latter are quite evident in the nightmare world of *The Hunger Games* movies. Danny Elfman was contracted to score the music for this much-anticipated screen version of the best-selling trilogy. For reasons left to different interpretations, Elfman was out and Howard was hired at the last moment to quickly come up with a score. (Howard has a reputation as a fast worker and this was not the only time in his career that he was brought in late to score a film abandoned by another composer.) The opening theme for *The Hunger Games* is a reflective piece on guitar backed by various strings that grows in intensity and takes on a menacing yet sorrowful tone. The score is filled with touches of folk music, an interesting choice for this tale of a future society with televised fights to the death. One folklike theme played on strings and horns has a traveling beat. Another track sports a Celtic flavor when played on a fiddle and various percussion instruments that builds and turns into a fearful choral and orchestral march. The sequel *The Hunger Games: Catching Fire* boasts a delicate love theme featuring guitar and woodwinds with strings filling out the sound. Reverting to a fairy-tale past rather than the future, *Maleficent* is just as dark. This story of the early years of the famous Disney villainess (Angelina Jolie) from *Sleeping Beauty* (1959) has a main theme that starts quietly. Low brass play an echoing chant as high-pitched strings and voices join to create a mystical theme that entices as it builds into a grandiose anthem. There is a lively theme for the princess Aurora (Elle Fanning) that has the quality of a country dance, and the world of the fairies is scored with high-pitched pipes as chanting voices fill out the sound of the magical but melancholy passage. This fanciful kind of music can also be heard in the contemporary romantic comedy *My Best Friend's Wedding*. Howard has scored many comedies, but it is probably this score that is most intriguing. It has a rolling theme on strings and flute that takes delicate pauses then proceeds, something that echoes the indecision of the woman (Julia Roberts) who decides to woo her best friend (Dermot Mulroney) before he marries someone else. The score has a sparkling comic theme with dancing strings and woodwinds acting like frolicking fairies, and there is a restless passage in which the music races forward with a sense of wild abandon. In this case Howard's classical style is used for a modern tale. It is typical of the way he approaches screen scoring. The music can come from anywhere if it's right for the movie.

Credits

(all films USA unless stated otherwise; * for Best Song)

Year	Film	Director
1985	Head Office	Ken Finkleman
1986	Wildcats	Michael Ritchie
1986	8 Million Ways to Die	Hal Ashby
1986	Tough Guys	Jeff Kanew
1986	Nobody's Fool	Evelyn Purcell
1987	Campus Man	Ron Casden
1987	Promised Land	Michael Hoffman (USA/UK)
1987	Five Corners	Tony Bill (UK/USA)
1987	Russkies	Rick Rosenthal
1988	Off Limits (aka Saigon)	Christopher Crowe
1988	Some Girls	Michael Hoffman (USA/UK)
1988	Everybody's All-American	Taylor Hackford
1989	Tap	Nick Castle
1989	Major League	David S. Ward
1989	The Package	Andrew Davis
1990	Coupe de Ville	Joe Roth
1990	Pretty Woman	Garry Marshall
1990	Flatliners	Joel Schumacher
1990	Marked for Death (aka Screwface)	Dwight H. Little
1990	Three Men and a Little Lady	Emile Ardolino
1991	King Ralph	David S. Ward
1991	Guilt by Suspicion	Irwin Winkler
1991	Dying Young	Joel Schumacher
1991	The Man in the Moon	Robert Mulligan
1991	My Girl	Howard Zieff
1991	The Prince of Tides (AAN)	Barbra Streisand
1991	Grand Canyon	Lawrence Kasdan
1992	Diggstown	Michael Ritchie
1992	Glengarry Glen Ross	James Foley
1992	American Heart	Martin Bell
1992	Night and the City	Irwin Winkler
1993	Alive	Frank Marshall (USA/Canada)
1993	Falling Down	Joel Schumacher (France/USA/UK)
1993	Dave	Ivan Reitman
1993	The Fugitive (AAN)	Andrew Davis
1993	The Saint of Fort Washington	Tim Hunter
1994	Intersection (aka The Things of Life)	Mark Rydell
1994	Wyatt Earp	Lawrence Kasdan
1994	Junior (AAN*; GGN)	Ivan Reitman
1995	Just Cause	Arne Glimcher
1995	Outbreak	Wolfgang Petersen
1995	French Kiss	Lawrence Kasdan (UK/USA)
1995	Waterworld	Kevin Reynolds, Kevin Costner
1995	Restoration	Michael Hoffman (USA/UK)
1996	An Eye for an Eye	John Schlesinger
1996	The Juror	Brian Gibson
1996	Primal Fear	Gregory Hoblit

Year	Film	Director
1996	*The Trigger Effect*	David Koepp
1996	*Space Jam*	Joe Pytka
1996	*One Fine Day* (AAN*; GGN*)	Michael Hoffman
1997	*Romy and Michele's High School Reunion*	David Mirkin
1997	*Father's Day*	Ivan Reitman
1997	*My Best Friend's Wedding* (AAN)	P. J. Hogan
1997	*The Devil's Advocate*	Taylor Hackford (USA/Germany)
1997	*The Postman*	Kevin Costner
1998	*A Perfect Murder*	Andrew Davis
1999	*Runaway Bride*	Garry Marshall
1999	*Stir of Echoes*	David Koepp
1999	*The Sixth Sense*	M. Night Shyamalan
1999	*Mumford*	Lawrence Kasdan
1999	*Snow Falling on Cedars*	Scott Hicks
1999	*Wayward Son*	Randall Harris
2000	*Dinosaur*	Eric Leighton, Ralph Zondag
2000	*Unbreakable* (aka *No Ordinary Man*)	M. Night Shyamalan
2000	*Vertical Limit*	Martin Campbell (USA/Germany)
2001	*Atlantis: The Lost Empire*	Gary Trousdale, Kirk Wise
2001	*America's Sweethearts*	Joe Roth
2002	*Big Trouble*	Barry Sonnenfeld
2002	*Signs*	M. Night Shyamalan
2002	*Unconditional Love* (aka *Who Shot Victor Fox*)	P. J. Hogan
2002	*The Emperor's Club* (aka *The Palace Thief*)	Michael Hoffman
2002	*Treasure Planet*	Ron Clements, John Musker
2003	*Dreamcatcher*	Lawrence Kasdan (USA/Australia)
2003	*Peter Pan*	P. J. Hogan (Australia/USA/UK)
2004	*Hidalgo*	Joe Johnston (USA/Morocco)
2004	*The Village* (AAN)	M. Night Shyamalan
2004	*Collateral*	Michael Mann
2005	*The Interpreter*	Sydney Pollack (USA/UK/France/Germany)
2005	*Batman Begins* (aka *Batman 5*)	Christopher Nolan (USA/UK)
2005	*King Kong* (GGN)	Peter Jackson (N. Zealand/USA/Germany)
2006	*Freedomland*	Joe Roth
2006	*RV*	Barry Sonnenfeld (UK/Germany/USA)
2006	*Lady in the Water*	M. Night Shyamalan
2006	*Blood Diamond* (aka *Diamond*)	Edward Zwick (USA/Germany)
2007	*The Lookout*	Scott Frank
2007	*Michael Clayton* (AAN)	Tony Gilroy
2007	*The Water Horse*	Jay Russell (USA/UK/Australia)
2007	*I Am Legend*	Francis Lawrence
2007	*Charlie Wilson's War*	Mike Nichols (USA/Germany)
2007	*The Great Debaters*	Denzel Washington
2008	*Batman: The Dark Knight*	Clint Walker (UK)
2008	*Mad Money*	Callie Khouri
2008	*The Happening* (aka *Green Planet*)	M. Night Shyamalan (USA/India/France)
2008	*The Dark Knight* (aka *Batman Begins 2*) (BAFTA-N)	Christopher Nolan (USA/UK)
2008	*Yoyssou Ndour: I Bring What I Love*	Elizabeth Chai Vasarhelyi (Senegal/France/Egypt/USA)
2008	*Defiance* (AAN; GGN)	Edward Zwick
2009	*Confessions of a Shopaholic*	P. J. Hogan
2009	*Duplicity*	Tony Gilroy (USA/Germany)
2010	*Nanny McPhee Returns* (aka *Nanny McPhee and the Big Bang*)	Susanna White (UK/France/USA)
2010	*Avatar: The Last Airbender*	M. Night Shyamalan
2010	*Salt* (aka *Edwin A. Salt*)	Philip Noyce
2010	*Inhale* (aka *Run of Her Life*)	Baltasar Kormákur
2010	*Love & Other Drugs* (aka *Hard Sell*)	Edward Zwick

Year	Film	Director
2010	*The Tourist*	Florian Henckel von Donnersmarck (USA/France/Italy)
2011	*The Green Hornet*	Michel Gondry
2011	*Water for Elephants*	Francis Lawrence
2011	*Green Lantern* (aka *Emerald Dawn*)	Martin Campbell
2011	*Larry Crowne* (aka *Talk of the Town*)	Tom Hanks
2012	*Darling Companion*	Lawrence Kasdan
2012	*The Hunger Games*	Gary Ross
2012	*Snow White and the Huntsman*	Rupert Sanders
2012	*The Bourne Legacy* (aka *Marcher*)	Tony Gilroy
2013	*After Earth* (aka *1000 A.E.*)	M. Night Shyamalan
2013	*Parkland*	Peter Landesman
2013	*The Hunger Games: Catching Fire*	Francis Lawrence
2014	*Maleficent*	Dean DeBlois (USA/UK)
2014	*The Hunger Games: Mockingjay—Part 1*	Francis Lawrence
2014	*Cut Bank*	Matt Shakman
2014	*Pawn Sacrifice*	Edward Zwick
2015	*The Hunger Games: Mockingjay—Part 2*	Francis Lawrence
2015	*The American Can*	Edward Zwick

HYMAN, Dick (b. 1927) A prodigious American jazz composer, arranger, conductor, organist, and pianist, he has enjoyed a long career on records and in concerts and clubs, but he is most known in movies for his music supervision of many Woody Allen films.

He was born Richard Hyman in New York City and given a classical music training by his uncle, concert pianist Anton Rovinsky. While at Columbia University, Hyman became interested in jazz and swing and won an on-the-air radio contest that gave him lessons with the jazz and swing pianist Teddy Wilson. In the 1950s he played with the Benny Goodman Trio and later became the pianist for Goodman's famous band. Hyman was also interested in ragtime and other early forms of American popular music. Throughout his career he arranged, conducted, and performed (piano and organ) a wide variety of recordings, many as part of the Dick Hyman Trio. Embracing the new electronic sound of the 1960s, Hyman formed the group Dick Hyman and the Eclectic Electrics, doing many recordings and concerts and having a minor hit in 1968 with "The Minotaur," the first single ever to be entirely performed on a synthesizer. Hyman was also a performer and arranger for a handful of television shows, including *Sing Along with Mitch* (Miller) and *Beat the Clock*, and has composed music for the concert hall, ballets, and films, most memorably *Moonstruck* in 1987.

He first worked with director Woody Allen in 1983 on the mock documentary *Zelig*, arranging period music and writing new songs that pastiched the 1930s and 1940s. Because of Hyman's vast knowledge of different musical styles, Allen has often worked with the arranger on the soundtracks for his films. He composed an original score for *The Purple Rose of Cairo* but in most cases Hyman compiled, arranged, conducted, and performed old song standards for the Allen movies. The result is such beloved movie soundtracks as *Stardust Memories* (1980), *Broadway Danny Rose* (1984), *Hannah and Her Sisters* (1986), *Radio Days* (1987), *Bullets Over Broadway* (1994), *The Mighty Aphrodite* (1995), *Everyone Says I Love You* (1996), *Sweet and Lowdown* (1999), *The Curse of the Jade Scorpion* (2001), and *Melinda and Melinda* (2004). Hyman's recordings have been heard on the soundtracks of several movies over the years. Considered one of America's experts on jazz, Hyman was artistic director for the *Jazz in July* series at New York's 92nd Street Y for twenty years. He has been inducted into the Jazz Hall of Fame of Rutgers Institute of Jazz Studies and has received honorary degrees from four colleges. Although Hyman has limited movie composing credits, he has contributed much to the period sound of many films, resulting in some very popular soundtrack CDs.

Giacomo Puccini's music is important to the plot of *Moonstruck*, a superior romantic comedy about an Italian New Yorker (Cher) who is torn in her affections between her mousy fiancé (Danny Aiello) and his temperamental brother (Nicolas Cage). The characters make love to the sounds of *La Boheme* and later attend a performance of the Puccini opera at the Met. Hyman writes variations of Puccini's music and uses it throughout the movie. At different points there is a jazzy version of "Musetta's Waltz," an Italianate variation on accordion, and even a wry easy-listening adaptation. The pop songs "That's Amore" sung by Dean Martin and "It Must Be Him" sung by Vicki Carr are heard as part of the plotting in *Moonstruck*. Hyman was not left with much original music to score but he did create one of the best screen soundtracks for a comedy heard in the 1980s. For Allen's bittersweet romantic fantasy *The Purple Rose of Cairo*, Hyman wrote some delectable original music. This offbeat but charming film is about a neglected housewife (Mia Farrow) who escapes the Depression by going to the movies. The illusion of the cinema is broken when a dashing character (Jeff Daniels) in a movie literally comes off the screen and engages in a Hollywood romance with her. Some 1930s song standards are heard but most of the soundtrack is original Depression-era music by Hyman. There is a brisk and jazzy foxtrot which bounces along with carefree abandon as different instruments in a modest-sized band are featured. There is also a chipper dance theme that resembles a Charleston in tempo but is pure 1930s in sentiment. For the movie-within-a-movie that is shown over and over, Hyman writes some pseudoexotic passages for an Egyptian expedition and some swank cocktail music for the penthouse scenes. After writing pastiche 1930s songs for *Zelig*, it must have been satisfying for Hyman to write period jazz and dance music that was not a joke.

Credits

(all films USA)

Year	Film	Director
1978	*French Quarter*	Dennis Kane
1983	*Zelig*	Woody Allen
1985	*The Purple Rose of Cairo*	Woody Allen
1987	*Moonstruck* (BAFT-N)	Norman Jewison
1988	*Leader of the Band*	Nessa Hyams
1989	*The Lemon Sisters*	Joyce Chopra
1992	*Alan & Naomi*	Sterling Van Wagenen

ISHAM, Mark (b. 1951) A pioneer in the use of electronic music and a renowned jazz trumpet player and music producer, he has scored over one hundred feature films since 1983.

Born Mark Ware Isham in New York City, his mother a violinist and father a professor of humanities, he grew up there and in San Francisco, where he studied piano and voice at a young age. Isham soon discovered that the trumpet was his instrument of choice and by the time he was fifteen he was playing in jazz clubs, in the Oakland and San Francisco Symphony Orchestras, and for different bands, including his own Group 87. Fascinated by jazz and New Age music, he started making musical arrangements using electronic instruments and both performed and recorded his work, most memorably in the groundbreaking album *Vapor Drawings* in 1983. Isham's unique synthesized sound was widely acclaimed, and he worked with top singers and jazz artists as he continued to produce top-selling albums. Director Carroll Ballard was among the many impressed with Isham's music and hired him to score his nature drama *Never Cry Wolf* in 1983. Both the film and the score were well received, and Isham's prodigious screen career was launched. The next year he scored the Oscar-winning documentary *The Times of Harvey Milk*. Throughout his career, Isham would return to the documentary genre in both movies and television. He first worked with actor-director Robert Redford on the rural drama *A River Runs Through It* in 1992, receiving an Academy Award nomination for his score. The two men have since collaborated on three other movies, *Quiz Show*, *Lions for Lambs*, and *The Conspirator*. Isham has worked with most of the top directors of his day, most often with Alan Rudolph. Their nine movies together include *Made in Heaven*, *Afterglow*, *The Moderns*, *Mortal Thoughts*, and *Mrs. Parker and the Vicious Circle*. Over the decades Isham has written music for just about every type of genre, making him one of the most eclectic Hollywood composers of his era. Among his many noteworthy films are *The Beast of War*, *Reversal of Fortune*, *Little Man Tate*, *Of Mice and Men*, *Short Cuts*,

The Browning Version, *Fly Away Home*, *The Education of Little Tree*, *Nell*, *October Sky*, *The Majestic*, *Miracle*, *Crash*, *Running Scared*, *Eight Below*, *Invincible*, *Bobby*, *The Mist*, *The Secret Life of Bees*, *Warrior*, *Dolphin Tale*, and *42: The Jackie Robinson Story*. Isham has also had a substantial television career, scoring series, TV movies, and miniseries, but he is most known for his music for the popular *Once Upon a Time*.

It is interesting that Carroll Ballard wanted Isham to score *Never Cry Wolf*, a documentary-like drama about a government researcher (Charles Martin Smith) who lives with the wolves in the Canadian tundra and dispels several myths about the creatures. Not only had Isham never scored a film before but this did not seem like a project that called for jazz or synthesized music. Yet Isham's New Age music, just coming into prominence in 1983 when the film was completed, was ideal for this beautifully photographed movie. The opening theme, heard as a plane flies over the Canadian mountains, is solemn yet emotive as the synthesized instruments use sustained, echoing notes to convey the vastness of the snowy landscape. Because there is little dialogue in the film, there is a great deal of music and all of it is entrancing. Most memorable is the ending when the lone human sits on a cliff and plays notes on a bassoon to call out to the wolves. Isham's underscoring supports him with a slow, reflective theme that wavers around him, making for a unique and unforgettable duet. A dozen years later Ballard and Isham worked again on another nature drama, *Fly Away Home*. Many consider it Isham's finest score yet it utilizes neither New Age nor jazz. This unusual drama is about a Canadian inventor (Jeff Daniels) and his young daughter (Anna Paquin) who help some orphaned geese fly south for the winter by guiding them on a motorized glider. The film has the expansive spirit of *Never Cry Wolf* and Isham's music is even more poetic. He uses a full conventional orchestra and highlights solo instruments in different passages. The main theme features a solo clarinet that seems to wail out a three-note phrase as strings join in and fill out the sound, turning it into a stirring anthem with a tribal flavor. There is a playful passage heard on clarinet and violin while the girl cavorts with the young goslings, as well as a warm domestic theme with a female voice chanting alongside a solo cello. The score also includes a lively rhythmic passage on fiddle and accordion that has a folk dance quality. For the climactic flight, there is propulsive traveling music that races along with trumpet fanfares, vigorous strings, robust percussion, and an expansive sense of freedom. This same music is used for the song "10,000 Miles" which is sung twice on the soundtrack by Mary Chapin Carpenter.

Folk music can be heard in other Isham scores, among them *Nell* and *A River Runs Through It*. Nell (Jodie Foster) is a woman who has been raised in the North Carolina woods without any outside communication and speaks a mangled kind of language which a local doctor (Liam Neeson) tries to decipher. Isham's music is contemporary but laced with folk instruments and tunes. There is a vigorous passage on primitive horn and string instruments that suggests a berserk folk dance that grows in intensity then transitions to a kind of gentle minuet. Also of interest: a mournful theme on a solo horn with string accents, as well as an up-tempo folk tune that repeats a simple musical phrase but still grows and develops until it blossoms into a full musical resolution. *A River Runs Through It* is about two very different brothers (Brad Pitt and Craig Sheffer) growing up in rural Montana who disagree about everything except fly-fishing. Isham's main theme is a graceful and flowing dance tune with a folk flavor that builds nicely without getting too loud or bombastic. There is also a sparkling passage in which strings and horns flow freely with accents from other instruments giving it further life, a solo violin backed by a harp that plays a simple folk melody that glides along with pride, and a solo horn featured in a melancholy but not morose folk tune with delicate rises and falls. Less folk and more New Age is the score for *October Sky* about a youth (Jake Gyllenhaal) in a West Virginia coal mining community who is inspired by the Russian satellite Sputnik to build his own rocket. The story is set in 1957 and the soundtrack is filled with over a dozen song standards from the period. It is up to Isham's music to move beyond the 1950s and express the young inventor's eye on the future. The main theme features a solo violin backed by woodwinds that plays a simple melody with a warm and evocative feel for domestic happiness; when the full orchestra comes in, it takes on a rich feel of an anthem. There is also a tentative theme featuring a

violin that repeats a musical phrase before developing into a fully resolved musical line. The most moving passage in the score is a flute and orchestra theme that seems in awe of the night sky as different instruments add twinkling accents to suggest stars.

If one wants to experience Isham's jazz and synthesized musical powers, there are the superior scores for *The Moderns* and *Crash*. Alan Rudolph's *The Moderns* is set among expatriate American artists and art dealers in Paris in the 1920s. Isham scores this Jazz Age tale not only with jazz music but gives it a pop techno feel by using a synthesized format. The title theme is a languid jazz piece featuring violin and marimba that is sensual in its long musical lines. Filtered through a synthesizer, the pseudo period music has a very modern feel. There is a marvelous smooth jazz passage with the percussion marching while the strings and electronic instruments take their time. A piano and violin slow jazz theme has a mysterious tone while in another piece electric guitar, clarinet, and trumpet play a blues theme that is casual yet full of attitude. The contemporary drama *Crash* is an intricate and complex look at a handful of very diverse people in Los Angeles over a thirty-six-hour period. The city's many highways are important to the plot and theme of the drama and Isham's music sets the tone with his synthesized score that has the pulse of an urban highway. Just about all of the music in *Crash* is electronic and there is little melody or fully resolved musical phrases. Instead Isham creates sounds that overwhelm the music. All the same it is still a fully developed score. The title theme consists of electronic echoes and reverberating notes that quietly but steadily rush over the moviegoer; it is both a seductive and sinister assault on the ears. There is a furious electronic percussion theme with a wild guitar riff and frantic keyboard playing. In contrast is a low and seething theme with long sustained notes and echoing chords. The most intriguing passage in the score has a female voice chanting in an indecipherable language as the music takes on an eerie yet religious tone, a kind of synthesized Gregorian chant. For the climactic car crash scene, Isham provides a rapid, busy passage in which electronic sounds weave in and out of percussive chase music. For the many who consider Isham the father of the New Age sound, the *Crash* score is probably his most exciting. Official website: www.isham.com.

Credits

(all films USA unless stated otherwise)

Year	Film	Director
1983	Never Cry Wolf	Carroll Ballard
1984	The Times of Harvey Milk	Rob Epstein
1984	Mrs. Soffel	Gillian Armstrong
1985	Portraits of Anorexia	Wendy Zheutlin
1985	Trouble in Mind	Alan Rudolph
1986	The Hitcher	Robert Harmon
1987	Made in Heaven	Alan Rudolph
1988	The Moderns	Alan Rudolph
1988	The Beast of War	Kevin Reynolds
1990	Everybody Wins	Karel Reisz (UK/USA)
1990	Love at Large	Alan Rudolph
1990	Reversal of Fortune	Barbet Schroeder (USA/Japan/UK)
1991	Mortal Thoughts	Alan Rudolph
1991	Crooked Hearts	Michael Bortman
1991	Point Break (aka Johnny Utah)	Kathryn Bigelow (USA/Japan)
1991	Little Man Tate	Jodie Foster
1991	Billy Bathgate	Robert Benton
1992	A Midnight Clear	Keith Gordon
1992	Cool World	Ralph Bakshi
1992	A River Runs Through It (AAN)	Robert Redford
1992	The Public Eye	Howard Franklin
1992	Of Mice and Men	Gary Sinise
1993	Nowhere to Run (aka Crossing the Line)	Robert Harmon
1993	Fire in the Sky	Robert Lieberman
1993	Made in America	Richard Benjamin (France/USA)
1993	Short Cuts	Robert Altman
1993	Romeo Is Bleeding	Peter Medak (UK/USA)
1994	The Getaway	Roger Donaldson (USA/Japan)
1994	Thumbelina	Don Bluth, Gary Goldman (Ireland/USA)
1994	The Browning Version	Mike Figgis (UK)
1994	Mrs. Parker and the Vicious Circle	Alan Rudolph (USA/Canada)
1994	Quiz Show	Robert Redford
1994	Timecop	Peter Hyams (Canada/USA/Japan)
1994	Safe Passage	Robert Allan Ackerman
1994	Nell (GGN)	Michael Apted
1995	Miami Rhapsody	David Frankel
1995	Losing Isaiah	Stephen Gyllenhaal
1995	The Net	Irwin Winkler
1995	Home for the Holidays	Jodie Foster
1996	Last Dance	Bruce Beresford
1996	Fly Away Home	Carroll Ballard (USA/Canada)
1996	Night Falls on Manhattan	Sidney Lumet
1997	Afterglow	Alan Rudolph
1997	Kiss the Girls	Gary Fleder
1997	The Education of Little Tree	Richard Friedenburg (Canada)
1998	The Gingerbread Man	Robert Altman
1998	Blade, the Vampire Slayer	Stephen Norrington
1998	Free Money	Yves Simoneau (Canada)
1999	At First Sight (aka Sight Unseen)	Irwin Winkler
1999	Varsity Blues	Brian Robbins
1999	Breakfast of Champions	Alan Rudolph
1999	October Sky (aka Rocket Boys)	Joe Johnston
1999	Body Shots (aka Jello Shots)	Michael Cristofer
2000	Rules of Engagement	William Friedkin

Year	Film	Director
2000	*Where the Money Is*	Marek Kanievska (Germany/USA/UK/Canada)
2000	*Trixie*	Alan Rudolph
2000	*Men of Honor* (aka *Navy Diver*)	George Tillman Jr.
2001	*Save the Last Dance*	Thomas Carter
2001	*Life as a House*	Irwin Winkler
2001	*Hard Ball*	Brian Robbins (USA/Germany)
2001	*Don't Say a Word*	Gary Fleder (USA/Australia/Switzerland/Canada)
2001	*Impostor*	Gary Fleder
2001	*The Majestic* (aka *The Bijou*)	Frank Darabont (USA/Australia)
2002	*Moonlight Mile* (aka *Baby's in Black*)	Brad Silberling
2003	*The Cooler*	Wayne Kramer
2004	*Spartan*	David Mamet (USA/Germany)
2004	*Miracle*	Gavin O'Connor
2004	*Highwaymen*	Robert Harmon (USA/Canada)
2004	*Twisted* (aka *The Blackout Murders*)	Philip Kaufman (USA/Germany)
2004	*Crash*	Paul Haggis (USA/Germany)
2005	*Racing Stripes*	Frederik Du Chau
2005	*Kicking & Screaming*	Jesse Dylan
2005	*In Her Shoes*	Curtis Hanson (USA/Germany)
2006	*Running Scared*	Wayne Kramer (Germany/USA)
2006	*Eight Below* (aka *Antarctica*)	Frank Marshall
2006	*The Black Dahlia*	Brian De Palma (Germany/USA/France)
2006	*Invincible*	Ericson Core
2006	*Bobby*	Emilio Estevez
2007	*Freedom Writers*	Richard LaGravenese (Germany/USA)
2007	*Gracie* (aka *Finding Gracie*)	Davis Guggenheim
2007	*Next*	Lee Tamahori
2007	*In the Valley of Elah* (aka *Death and Dishonor*)	Paul Haggis
2007	*Reservation Road*	Terry George (USA/Germany)
2007	*Lions for Lambs*	Robert Redford
2007	*The Mist*	Frank Darabont
2008	*The Women*	Diane English
2008	*The Secret Life of Bees*	Gina Prince-Bythewood
2008	*Pride and Glory*	Gavin O'Connor (USA/Germany)
2008	*The Express: The Ernie Davis Story*	Gary Fleder (USA/Germany)
2009	*Not Forgotten*	Dror Soref
2009	*My One and Only*	Richard Loncraine
2009	*Crossing Over*	Wayne Kramer
2009	*The Bad Lieutenant: Port of Call—New Orleans*	Werner Herzog
2009	*Fame*	Kevin Tancharoen
2010	*The Crazies*	Breck Eisner (USA/United Arab Emirates)
2010	*The Conspirator*	Robert Redford
2011	*The Mechanic*	Simon West
2011	*Warrior*	Gavin O'Connor
2011	*Dolphin Tale*	Charles Martin Smith
2012	*The Lucky One*	Scott Hicks
2012	*Stolen* (aka *Medallion*)	Simon West
2012	*The Factory*	Morgan O'Neill (USA/Canada/France)
2013	*The Inevitable Defeat of Mister & Pete*	George Tillman Jr.
2013	*42: The Jackie Robinson Story*	Brian Helgeland
2013	*Homefront*	Gary Fleder

JABLONSKY, Steve (b. 1970) A more recent and successful composer for television and video games, he has been very busy in movies since 2003 scoring action and horror films.

Steve Jablonsky has kept details of his life private, including the place of his birth and information about his early years. He studied music composition at the University of California, Berkeley, then worked for Hans Zimmer's Remote Control Productions for several years. With Zimmer as his mentor, Jablonsky got jobs writing additional music for such movies as *Armageddon* (1998), *Antz* (1998), *The Tigger Movie* (2000), *Chicken Run* (2000), *Pearl Harbor* (2001), and *Pirates of the Caribbean: Curse of the Black Pearl* (2003). His first solo score was for the comic adventure *Border to Border* in 1998. Five years later he found recognition when he wrote the music for the remake of the horror thriller *The Texas Chainsaw Massacre*. Because of the success of that movie, Jablonsky was hired to score other remakes, including *The Amityville Horror*, *Friday the 13th*, and *The Nightmare on Elm Street*. His career took a favorable turn with his dynamic score for the action film *Transformers* in 2007 and he has scored the *Transformers* sequels since then. Among his other notable movies are *The Island*, *The Hitcher*, *Gangster Squad*, *Pain & Gain*, *Ender's Game*, *Lone Survivor*, and the animated Japanese adventure *Steamboy*. Jablonsky has scored a handful of television series, most memorably *Desperate Housewives*, and five TV movies. He has also written the music for several video games, some based on *Transformers* and other movies that he has scored.

Transformers, a sci-fi adventure about two races of mechanized creatures coming to Earth to fight over a mystical talisman, is filled with action and also uses the most up-to-date digital technology, so it is a visual feast as well. Jablonsky's exciting score is also very technical. There is a restless, rapid theme with riveting synthesized percussion that attacks with a series of reverberating crescendos. Later in the track, voices and horns are added as the piece intensifies into a vigorous call to arms. When the robotic forces arrive on Earth, the music is a rumbling

percussion piece with electronic noises that build into a full-fledged anthem with swaying strings, deep pounding percussion, and a high-pitched chorus. Also of interest is a half-time march with celestial voices, vibrant piano, and twinkling strings with waves of electronic music that seems to go in and out of focus. Moviegoers were so entranced with the *Transformers* score that when months went by and no soundtrack CD was issued, a massive online campaign was formed to get the music released. Similar but not quite as thrilling is *Ender's Game*, a sci-fi action movie about a battle to save Earth from an attack by an alien race. This time the restless main theme is heard on rapid violins against a slow melodic line played by a cello; the piece then transitions into a forceful march with full orchestra and rumbling synthesized percussion. A quiet and graceful section of this theme features a solo violin with fluid electronic accompaniment. The battle scenes are scored with pounding percussion and frenzied synthesized noise that is more chaotic than musical. A more interesting sci-fi thriller is *The Island*, about a man (Ewan McGregor) living in an idyllic community who discovers that he is a clone who was born and bred to provide body parts for others. The theme for the island where the clones are sent has solemn and foreboding music. Wavering voices and electronic instruments form a series of modest crescendos as synthesized noise surrounds and moves through the piece. The hero's theme is a slow and flowing passage in which voices and electronic waves of sound play under rhythmic traveling music. Also memorable is a propulsive track with a rock beat in which echoing percussion and electric guitar chords move forward with a dark purpose.

Jablonsky relies on high-tech music even when he scores a non-sci-fi period film, as with *Gangster Squad*. This crime drama, about cops trying to bring down a mobster (Sean Penn) in 1949 Los Angeles, has the music of a sci-fi movie flavored with the sound of a film noir. The theme for the mobster is a low, heavy piece with sustained organ chords and rhythmic percussion that suggests a powerful heartbeat that speeds up when angered. Los

Angeles itself is scored with a percussion theme with string accents that has the tempo of a feverish folk dance. There is also a slow passage on piano and sustained strings that moves carefully through a simple melody with such cau- tion that it seems hesitant and fearful. Jablonsky has not been given a wide variety of movies to score in his young career, but his music suggests that he can and will explore new ways to musicalize new genres.

Credits

(all films USA unless stated otherwise)

Year	Film	Director
1998	Border to Border	Thomas Whelan
2003	The Texas Chainsaw Massacre	Marcus Nispel
2004	Steamboy	Katsuhiro Ohtomo (Japan)
2005	The Amityville Horror	Andrew Douglas
2005	The Island	Michael Bay
2006	The Texas Chainsaw Massacre: The Beginning	Jonathan Liebesman
2007	The Hitcher	Dave Meyers
2007	Transformers (aka Prime Directive)	Michael Bay
2007	Dragon Wars: D-War	Hyung-rae Shim (S. Korea)
2009	Friday the 13th	Marcus Nispel
2009	Transformers: Revenge of the Fallen	Michael Bay
2010	A Nightmare on Elm Street	Samuel Bayer
2011	Your Highness	David Gordon Green
2011	Transformers: Dark of the Moon	Michael Bay
2012	Battleship	Peter Berg
2013	Gangster Squad	Ruben Fleischer
2013	Pain & Gain	Michael Bay
2013	Ender's Game	Gavin Hood
2013	Lone Survivor	Peter Berg
2014	Transformers: Age of Extinction	Michael Bay (USA/China)

JACKSON, Howard (1900–1966) A very prolific movie composer and arranger who worked on over four hundred Hollywood films, many of them shorts and B movies, he was rarely credited for his work and is all but forgotten today except for a handful of memorable Frank Capra comedies.

Very little is known about the man who was born How- ard Manucy Jackson in St. Augustine, Florida, and sixty- six years later he died there as well. In between he had a very active movie career, though he is little mentioned in accounts of the time. Jackson arrived in Hollywood soon after the birth of the talkies. By 1929 he was work- ing as a music arranger and composer of music cues and incidental music at Universal. His first solo score was for that studio's 1929 feature *Broadway*, based on the popular Broadway melodrama. By the next year Jackson was writ- ing screen scores for Paramount, such as the incidental music between all the acts in the all-star revue *Paramount on Parade*. For some of his films he was asked to provide songs and a few of them enjoyed a brief popularity, such as "Push 'Em Up," "Let's Be Frivolous," "Hearts in Dixie," and "Love Me Ever." After scoring the popular movies *True to the Navy* and *College Humor*, Jackson collaborated with director Frank Capra for the first time. The 1933 comedy *Lady for a Day* was an early hit for Capra and put him in the front ranks of Hollywood directors; Jackson was not even credited for his score. Capra and Jackson had an even bigger hit the next year with *It Happened One Night* but again Jackson was not credited. Two other Capra- Jackson features, *Broadway Bill* and *Mr. Deeds Goes to Town*, secured the director's reputation but seemed to do little for Jackson's career. He did the scores for a series of musicals in which all the attention was on the songwriters, as in *We're Not Dressing*, *One Night of Love*, and *Belle of the Nineties*. By 1937 Jackson was scoring only B mov- ies and comedy shorts. He rarely worked with a name director, as he scored dozens of low-budget melodramas, detective films, comedies, and westerns. When World War II broke out he wrote music for low-budget war films but spent more time scoring documentary shorts about war events, many of them with Capra. Between 1940 and 1946, Jackson scored over one hundred shorts and was credited for only ten of them.

After the war he was again only hired for B movies and shorts, although by then the studios were crediting all composers and music arrangers. By the mid-1950s he occasionally got to score a first-class project, such as *China Gate, Yellowstone Kelly, Merrill's Marauders*, and *Sergeant Rutledge*, and he did the soundtrack score (but not the songs) for a series of Doris Day musicals, including *Calamity Jane, April in Paris, Lucky Me*, and *The Pajama Game*. By the early 1960s Jackson turned to television and contributed music to the series *The Gallant Men, The Dakotas*, and *Hawaiian Eye*. By 1964 he was no longer active and he died two years later, as obscure and uncredited as ever. Between his composing and music arranging work, Jackson is one of Hollywood's most prolific artists with over 150 features and 250 shorts to his credit. One can only guess at the other movies he worked on that no record of his contribution exists. Why such a busy composer was always kept in the lower ranks is a puzzle. He worked with some top directors on occasion but then seemed to be passed over for their later projects. Jackson was probably not temperamental or difficult to work with because he was constantly employed. Could it be that his music was routine and not good enough for better movies?

Listening to Jackson's Capra film scores, one discovers a possible reason. There is very little original music in these comedies. *Lady for a Day* is filled with street songs such as "Sidewalks of New York" and "Santa Lucia." For one of the most tender scenes, in which Apple Annie (May Robson) writes a loving letter to her daughter, the music comes from her phonograph which is playing a delicate selection from Tchaikovsky's Fifth Symphony. The nightclub and restaurant scenes also use existing music arranged by Jackson. The few times original music is heard it is brief and functional, such as the big party in which they try to pass Annie off as a moneyed lady. The opening theme for *It Happened One Night* is a piquant waltz as one might hear in a high-society tea salon and it is very catchy; it is rarely heard again in the movie. The most memorable scenes, such as the blanket serving as the walls of Jericho or the hitchhiking sequence, are presented without music. The only time music becomes an important element is during a bus ride when the journalist Peter (Clark Gable) leads everyone in a sing-along and the old favorite "The Daring Young Man on the Flying Trapeze" is used. *Meet John Doe* uses a comic version of "Roll Out the Barrel" and other standards for its opening montage of the Depression and later other familiar tunes pop up, even the Disney ditty "Hi-Diddle-Dee-Dee." Not until the comedy turns serious in the last reels does Jackson provide some atmospheric background music. But it is clear that Capra did not want much original music in his films and Jackson complied, either willingly or resignedly.

Director John Ford thought differently and requested more original music when Jackson scored his western *Sergeant Rutledge*. One of the few movies of the era to look at African Americans in the West, this powerful drama has some arresting musical passages but too often Jackson quotes songs from American folklore. *Yellowstone Kelly*, another western, has a traditional action score with fewer interpolations from folk songs. There is a cocky and sprightly theme for the title character (Clint Walker) and some energetic passages for the action scenes.

For Mervyn LeRoy's comedy *Three Men on a Horse*, such Americana was not appropriate so Jackson came up with a silly theme song based on the trumpet call at a horse race. (The comedy is about a system to bet on the horses.) The gangster drama *Broadway* takes place mostly in a nightclub so most of the music comes from the onstage acts, but there is a robust opening theme that suggests the glitter of Broadway and the hoodlums that are in every dark corner. The drama *China Gate*, about Indonesia in the early days of the Vietnam War, has a memorable title song by Victor Young and Harold Adamson which is sung by Nat King Cole on the soundtrack. Jackson's score has the flavor of Asian music at times but most of it is standard wartime action music. The more one looks at the Jackson movie scores, the clearer it becomes that his real talent lay in his music arrangements. He took existing music or, in the case of the many musicals he worked on, new songs and created a unified soundtrack. In an age when the studios did not want to feature the composers (or even credit them), Jackson was kept very busy. Perhaps a career mostly in B movies is not very impressive but one has to admire the way he made effective scores from music by others.

Credits

(all films USA)

Year	Film	Director
1929	*Broadway*	Pál Fejos
1930	*Paramount on Parade*	Victor Schertzinger, etc.
1930	*True to the Navy*	Frank Tuttle
1930	*The Social Lion*	A. Edward Sutherland
1930	*Love among the Millionaires*	Frank Tuttle
1930	*Playboy of Paris*	Ludwig Berger
1933	*Goldie Gets Along*	Malcolm St. Clair
1933	*Central Airport*	William A. Wellman, Alfred E. Green
1933	*Man Hunt*	Irving Cummings
1933	*College Humor*	Wesley Ruggles
1933	*Midnight Club*	Alexander Hall, George Somnes
1933	*Lady for a Day*	Frank Capra
1933	*Big Executive*	Erie C. Kenton
1933	*Girl without a Room*	Ralph Murphy
1933	*Hell and High Water*	Grover Jones, William Slavens McNutt
1934	*Beloved*	Victor Schertzinger
1934	*It Happened One Night*	Frank Capra
1934	*Glamour*	William Wyler
1934	*Bottoms Up*	David Butler
1934	*We're Not Dressing*	Norman Taurog
1934	*Thirty Day Princess*	Marion Gering
1934	*I Give My Love*	Karl Freund
1934	*One Night of Love*	Victor Schertzinger
1934	*Belle of the Nineties*	Leo McCarey
1934	*Broadway Bill*	Frank Capra
1935	*The Best Man Wins*	Erie C. Kenton
1935	*Eight Bells*	Roy William Neill
1935	*Air Hawks*	Albert S. Rogell
1935	*Dizzy Dames*	William Nigh
1935	*The Old Homestead*	William Nigh
1935	*The Widow from Monte Carlo*	Arthur Greville Collins
1935	*The Lone Wolf Returns*	Roy William Neill
1936	*The Music Goes 'Round*	Victor Schertzinger
1936	*Mr. Deeds Goes to Town*	Frank Capra
1936	*Devil's Squadron*	Erie C. Kenton
1936	*And So They Were Married*	Elliott Nugent
1936	*The King Steps Out*	Josef von Sternberg
1936	*Counterfeit*	Erie C. Kenton
1936	*Meet Nero Wolfe*	Herbert J. Biberman
1936	*Earthworm Tractors*	Ray Enright
1936	*Bengal Tiger*	Louis King
1936	*Love Begins at Twenty*	Frank McDonald
1936	*Trailin' West*	Noel M. Smith
1936	*Down the Stretch*	William Clemens
1936	*Here Comes Carter*	William Clemens
1936	*Polo Joe*	William C. McGann
1936	*The Captain's Kid*	Nick Grinde, Tom Reed
1936	*California Mail*	Noel M. Smith
1936	*Three Men on a Horse*	Mervyn LeRoy
1936	*Fugitive in the Sky*	Nick Grinde
1936	*Conflict*	David Howard
1936	*King of Hockey*	Noel M. Smith
1937	*Guns of the Pecos*	Noel M. Smith
1937	*Her Husband's Secretary*	Frank McDonald

Year	Film	Director
1937	*Penrod and Sam*	William C. McGann
1937	*That Man's Here Again*	Louis King
1937	*The Cherokee Strip*	Noel M. Smith
1937	*Blazing Sixes*	Noel M. Smith
1937	*Fly Away Baby*	Frank McDonald
1937	*Empty Holsters*	B. Reeves Eason
1937	*Talent Scout*	William Clemens
1937	*The Devil's Saddle Legion*	Bobby Connolly
1937	*Dance Charlie Dance*	Frank McDonald
1937	*The Footloose Heiress*	William Clemens
1937	*Prairie Thunder*	B. Reeves Eason
1937	*The Adventurous Blonde*	Frank McDonald
1938	*Sergeant Murphy*	B. Reeves Eason
1938	*Blondes at Work*	Frank McDonald
1938	*Daredevil Drivers*	B. Reeves Eason
1938	*Penrod and His Twin Brother*	William C. McGann
1938	*Accidents Will Happen*	William Clemens
1938	*Torchy Blane in Panama*	William Clemens
1938	*The Beloved Brat*	Arthur Lubin
1938	*Little Miss Thoroughbred*	John Farrow
1938	*My Bill*	John Farrow
1938	*Penrod's Double Trouble*	Lewis Seiler
1938	*Girls on Probation*	William C. McGann
1938	*Torchy Gets Her Man*	William Beaudine
1939	*Devil's Island*	William Clemens
1939	*Torchy Blane in Chinatown*	William Beaudine
1939	*The Adventures of Jane Arden*	Terry O. Morse
1939	*The Man Who Dared*	Crane Wilbur
1939	*Torchy Runs for Mayor*	Ray McCarey
1939	*Sweepstakes Winner*	William C. McGann
1939	*The Cowboy Quarterback*	Noel M. Smith
1939	*Torchy Blane . . . Playing with Dynamite*	Noel M. Smith
1939	*Everybody's Hobby*	William C. McGann
1939	*Pride of the Blue Grass*	William C. McGann
1939	*On Dress Parade*	William Clemens, Noel M. Smith
1939	*Kid Nightingale*	George Amy
1940	*Granny Get Your Gun*	George Amy
1940	*An Angel from Texas*	Ray Enright
1940	*A Fugitive from Justice*	Terry O. Morse
1940	*Gambling on the High Seas*	George Amy
1940	*Ladies Must Live*	Noel M. Smith
1940	*River's End*	Ray Enright
1940	*Calling All Husbands*	Noel M. Smith
1940	*East of the River*	Alfred E. Green
1940	*She Couldn't Say No*	William Clemens
1941	*Father's Son*	D. Ross Lederman
1941	*Here Comes Happiness*	Noel M. Smith
1941	*Knockout*	William Clemens
1941	*Strange Alibi*	D. Ross Lederman
1941	*Bad Men of Missouri*	Ray Enright
1941	*Three Sons o' Guns*	Benjamin Stoloff
1941	*Law of the Tropics*	Ray Enright
1941	*The Body Disappears*	D. Ross Lederman
1941	*You're in the Army Now*	Lewis Seiler
1942	*Wild Bill Hickok Rides*	Ray Enright
1942	*Bullet Scars*	D. Ross Lederman
1942	*Lady Gangster*	Robert Florey
1942	*I Was Framed*	D. Ross Lederman

Year	Film	Director
1942	*Murder in the Big House*	B. Reeves Eason
1942	*Secret Enemies*	Benjamin Stoloff
1942	*Busses Roar*	D. Ross Lederman
1943	*Truck Busters*	B. Reeves Eason
1943	*The Mysterious Doctor*	Benjamin Stoloff
1943	*Murder on the Waterfront*	B. Reeves Eason
1943	*The Battle of Britain*	Frank Capra, Anthony Veiller
1944	*Casanova Brown*	Sam Wood
1945	*Club Havana*	Edgar G. Ulmer
1945	*How Doooo You Do!!!*	Ralph Murphy
1950	*Fifty Years Before Your Eyes*	Robert Youngson
1950	*The Breaking Point*	Michael Curtiz
1951	*Lullaby of Broadway*	David Butler
1951	*Starlift*	Roy Del Ruth
1952	*Where's Charley?*	David Butler
1952	*April in Paris*	David Butler
1953	*Appointment in Honduras*	Jacques Tourneur
1953	*Calamity Jane*	David Butler
1954	*Lucky Me*	Jack Donohue
1954	*Silver Lode*	Allan Dwan
1954	*Tobor the Great*	Lee Sholem
1954	*Passion*	Allan Dwan
1955	*Escape to Burma*	Allan Dwan
1955	*Run for Cover*	Nicholas Ray
1955	*Pearl of the South Pacific*	Allan Dwan
1955	*Tennessee's Partner*	Allan Dwan
1956	*Slightly Scarlet*	Allan Dwan
1957	*Deep Adventure*	Scotty Welbourne
1957	*China Gate*	Samuel Fuller
1957	*The Pajama Game*	George Abbott, Stanley Donen
1958	*Manhunt in the Jungle*	Tom McGowan
1958	*Cry Terror!*	Andrew L. Stone
1958	*Girl on the Run*	Richard L. Bare
1959	*Yellowstone Kelly*	Gordon Douglas
1960	*Noose for a Gunman*	Edward L. Cahn
1960	*Sergeant Rutledge*	John Ford
1961	*Gold of the Seven Saints*	Gordon Douglas
1961	*Claudelle Inglish*	Gordon Douglas
1962	*Merrill's Marauders*	Samuel Fuller
1962	*House of Women*	Walter Doniger, Crane Wilbur
1962	*Black Gold*	Leslie H. Martinson

JANSSEN, Werner (1899–1990) A respected conductor who was heard in concert halls around the world, he was also a songwriter and composer who scored a dozen feature films spread over a period of two decades.

Werner Janssen was born in New York City, the son of a successful restaurateur. When Janssen refused to go into the family business and wanted to study music, he had to pay for his tuition by working as a waiter and then got jobs performing in clubs and cabarets. Janseen studied music

education at Dartmouth College and the New England Conservatory of Music, but his schooling was interrupted when he served in the infantry during World War I. His music career began in Tin Pan Alley, where he wrote some popular songs, some of which were interpolated into such Broadway shows as *Love Dreams* (1921), *Letty Pepper* (1922), *Lady Butterfly* (1923), *Ziegfeld Follies of 1925*, *Luckee Girl* (1928), and *Boom Boom* (1929). The money he earned from sheet music royalties and records allowed him to go to Europe for further music study in Switzerland and Italy. In 1929 his first jazz concert piece, *New Year's Eve in New York*, was performed in the States followed by other symphonic works by major American orchestras. By the 1930s Janssen had gained a reputation as a fine conductor and worked all over Europe and America, serving as conductor for the New York Philharmonic and the Baltimore Symphony Orchestra for a time. In 1940 he founded the Janssen Symphony in Los Angeles, a rival to that city's philharmonic, and continued to compose and record over the next four decades. Janssen's conducting career also flourished as he worked with major orchestras in Europe and the States, becoming one of the most in-demand and highly paid conductors of his time.

Janssen first got involved in movies in 1936 when he was asked to score the melodrama *The General Died at Dawn*. He then began a long association with producer Walter Wanger, resulting in such films as *Blockade* and *Eternally Yours*. Both movie scores were nominated for an Oscar, as were Janssen's scores for *Guest in the House*, *The Southerner*, and *Captain Kidd*. After World War II, he scored the Marx Brothers vehicle *A Night in Casablanca* and the film noir thriller *Ruthless* before retiring from movies in 1948. He returned a decade later to write the score for the screen version of the Anton Chekhov play *Uncle Vanya* for actor-producer-director Franchot Tone. Janssen remained active in the musical world for another two decades and continued to compose until his death at the age of ninety. His concert works include orchestral suites, string quartets, various quintets and fugues, and scores for film shorts. He received several music awards and honorary degrees during his lifetime and some of his recordings of classical works are still esteemed today.

Because of his concert reputation, Janssen was treated well by Hollywood. During a period of seven years he was nominated for a Best Score by the Academy five times. Considering these were not extremely popular films, this recognition is remarkable. The comedy-drama *Eternally Yours* has a gushing title song (lyric by L. Wolfe Gilbert) heard over the opening credits and there is a flowing waltz for the stage act by an illusionist (David Niven) but the most interesting music in the score is the darker theme be-

hind the troubled romance and some passages during the hypnosis scenes. For the film noir gem *Guest in the House*, Janssen alternates the driving theme for the psychopathic heroine (Ann Baxter) with some lighthearted passages for the domestic world she invades. French director Jean Renoir hired Janssen to score his Hollywood drama *The Southerner* and much of that movie's power can be attributed to the score. The main theme is a restless piece of frenzy that turns into a homespun passage with a slight Southern flavor. As the farming Tucker family struggles against misfortune, the music captures the durability of the human spirit and the overwhelming forces of nature. A distant chorus is sometimes used in both the warm and oppressive themes. Just as Renoir's film is an Emile Zola–like portrait of rural life, Janssen's score is a kind of tone poem on the same subject.

Ruthless is a 1948 drama about a Machiavellian businessman (Zachary Scott) who claws his way to the top. The film has been compared to *Citizen Kane* in its subject and intent and Janssen's score is sometimes reminiscent of Bernard Herrmann's music for that classic. The menacing opening theme features a solo violin playing against ominous chords. Flashbacks are introduced with an eerie theme that has a science fiction musical flavor. Much of the rest of the score is brooding and fatalistic, even the love theme being more melancholy than romantic. Another minor-key score by Janssen is the one he wrote for the comic thriller *Slightly Honorable*. The opening theme is sarcastic, spoofing both the high-tension music of film noir and the sentimental music of weepies. The rest of the score keeps up this frivolous tone with some delightful passages with squawking brass and irreverent woodwinds. Janssen's most symphonic score is the rousing soundtrack he composed for the adventure *Captain Kidd*. There is little satire in the music, from the seafaring opening theme to the dramatic music for the action scenes to the growling passages used in the dastardly plotting scenes. This is unabashed Hollywood scoring with full orchestral sound and a sweeping climax. Although Janssen scored only a dozen feature films, the variety in subject matter and tone is matched by how different the scores are. For a famous conductor who worked in movies only occasionally, he managed to leave quite a legacy.

Credits

(all films USA)

Year	Film	Director
1936	*The General Died at Dawn*	Lewis Milestone
1938	*Blockade* (AAN)	William Dieterle
1939	*Winter Carnival*	Charles Reisner
1939	*Eternally Yours* (AAN)	Tay Garnett
1939	*Slightly Honorable*	Tay Garnett
1940	*The House across the Bay*	Archie Mayo
1944	*Guest in the House* (AAN)	John Brahm, André De Toth, Lewis Milestone
1945	*The Southerner* (AAN)	Jean Renoir
1945	*Captain Kidd* (AAN)	Rowland V. Lee
1946	*A Night in Casablanca*	Archie Mayo
1948	*Ruthless*	Edgar G. Ulmer
1957	*Uncle Vanya*	John Goetz, Franchot Tone

JARRE, Maurice (1924–2009) A truly international composer and conductor who scored dozens of movies on four continents, the French-born Jarre is most known for his music in epic films directed by David Lean.

Born Maurice-Alexis Jarre in Lyon, France, he was the son of a radio technician who sent his son to the Sorbonne in Paris to study engineering. Although Jarre didn't become interested in music until his university days, he decided to change his career goals and studied at the Conservatoire de Paris. Jarre had a particular interest in percussion, so when he studied composition he used percussion instruments prominently in his work. This approach to music would continue throughout his lifetime. Jarre was also one of the first students to become proficient on the Martenot Waves, an early form of synthesizer. This electronic instrument was another aspect of music that he would pursue in his later career. Jarre's first compositions were not for film but for the theatre. Director-actor Jean Vilar asked him to create an original score for a stage production of *The Prince of Homburg* in 1950 and the result was so successful that Vilar hired the young composer to write music for all the productions at his newly formed Theatre National Populaire. Jarre continued to score for the theatre company for twelve years, even as his movie career took off. His first film scores were for documentary shorts directed by Georges Franju. The same director hired Jarre for the feature *Head against the Wall* in 1959 but his first recognition came the next year with Franju's popular horror movie *Eyes without a Face*. Other European movies followed as well as his first American feature, the 1960 crime

drama *Crack in the Mirror*. In 1962, Jarre found international recognition from three scores: the French-Austrian character drama *Sundays and Cybele* (which earned him an Oscar nomination), the D-Day spectacular *The Longest Day*, and the biopic epic *Lawrence of Arabia* (which won him an Academy Award). This last was directed by David Lean who used Jarre on all of his films for the rest of the British artist's career. Although Jarre was in great demand in Hollywood, he did not forsake foreign-language films, returning to Europe frequently throughout his career to score movies by Franju, Henri Verneuil, Frédéric Rossif, Luchino Visconti, René Clément, Volker Schlöndorff, and other distinguished directors. He also scored several Canadian and Australian movies and even wrote music for Libyan and Japanese films. The list of directors who worked with Jarre during his forty-year career reads like a *Who's Who* in the directing field, including such diverse artists as Alfred Hitchcock, Paul Newman, John Frankenheimer, Clint Eastwood, John Huston, Peter Weir, Paul Mazursky, William Wyler, and Elia Kazan.

Yet despite such diversity, Jarre is best known for his music for four Lean films: *Lawrence of Arabia, Doctor Zhivago, Ryan's Daughter*, and *A Passage to India*. His other outstanding scores include those for *The Train, The Collector, The Fixer, The Damned, The Man Who Would Be King, The Tin Drum, Witness, Gorillas in the Mist, Dead Poets Society*, and *Ghost*. Jarre was extremely prolific, scoring over one hundred feature films as well as twenty TV movies and miniseries, such as *Great Expectations* (1974), *Jesus of Nazareth* (1977), *Shogun* (1980), and *Uprising*

MAURICE JARRE. One of the truly international composers, the Frenchman Jarre scored movies and television programs for many different countries during his productive career. He is pictured here in 1980 conducting his soundtrack recording for the American TV miniseries *Shogun. NBC / Photofest © NBC*

(2001), his last composing credit. He had also written the score for Lean's *Nostromo*, but the director died in 1991 and the movie was never made. Jarre was active to the end of his life, usually composing at least two scores a year until he died in 2009 at the age of eighty-four. Although he was often awarded during his lifetime and was considered by Hollywood to be one of the most accomplished of movie composers, many moviegoers only thought of Jarre as the creator of "Lara's Theme" from *Doctor Zhivago* and other grandiose themes in David Lean epics.

As diverse as Jarre's music is, one can often pick out distinct musical characteristics in many of his scores. The use of percussion is one of the most evident, as heard in the various tracks in *The Longest Day*, *Doctor Zhivago*, *The Man Who Would Be King*, and *Lawrence of Arabia*, but also in more subtle ways in *Behold a Pale Horse*, *The Only Game in Town*, *The Professionals*, and *Gorillas in the Mist*. Yet there are just as many Jarre scores that forgo strong percussion and emphasize other solo instruments, such as the mournful oboe in *Enemy Mine*, the melancholy piano in *Jacob's Ladder*, the floating flute in *Dead Poets Society*, or the almost-painful cry of the violin in *The Fixer*. He was particularly interested in ethnic instruments, such as using the ancient stringed kithara in *Lawrence of Arabia*, the balalaika throughout *Doctor Zhivago*, and a medieval Slovak flute called a fujara in *The Tin Drum*. He also was inventive in the way he utilized synthesized sounds in his scores. Jarre's fascination with the synthesizer never waned and he returned to it often. His 1982 score for *The Year of Living Dangerously* is believed to be the first to be performed completely on the synthesizer and his hymn-like music for *Witness* is one of those rare occasions when a synthesizer has a folk flavor. Similar synthesized music can be heard in *Prancer*, *The Bride*, and TV's *Jesus of Nazareth*. Jarre was adept at coming up with highly romantic music as required, some memorable examples being *A Walk in the Clouds*, *Ryan's Daughter*, *The Mosquito Coast*, *Fatal Instinct*, *Ghost*, and *Enemies: A Love Story*. When Hollywood called for a big sound, he was able to oblige with a rousing composition. *Grand Prix* has such a violent urgency that it is unnerving and for *Mad Max Beyond Thunderdome* Jarre utilized a full chorus to compete with four grand pianos, a pipe organ, and three synthesizers.

Perhaps the essence of Jarre's talent for memorable music was his ability to create melodic themes that echo

in one's ear like a song. Although he only wrote a handful of songs in his career, his scores often have themes that are structured like a popular song and are reinforced in the ear. It is not surprising that two of Jarre's themes later became popular songs: "Lara's Theme" from *Doctor Zhivago* was given a lyric by Paul Francis Webster and was a best seller as "Somewhere My Love"; and "Rosy's Theme" from *Ryan's Daughter* later surfaced as the spirited song "It Was a Good Time" (lyric by Mack David and Mike Curb). Other musical themes linger on as if they were popular songs. The main theme from *Lawrence of Arabia*, for example, needs no words to sweep over one and conjure up the vast desert, the pseudo-Arabian music returning like a song one has heard since childhood. Its series of repeating descending notes is played on strings, horns, and other Western instruments yet the effect is as if it were heard on ethnic flutes and drums. Part of the theme is very British as a pompous military march sets out at a brisk pace but is overwhelmed by the long, sustained notes of the Arabian section. Yet there is so much more to this superb score that brings the world of World War I hero T. E. Lawrence (Peter O'Toole) to life. The theme for the British aspect of the movie is very Victorian in its brass, piccolo, and string promenades and marches. The desert theme is slow and exotic as a native flute caresses a simple tune then the climbing string chords on the ancient kithara leads up the scale where the full orchestra returns to the film's principal theme. Another passage is all percussion as Western and tribal drums compete with each other, while an Arabian march is percussive with horns giving the beat an unexpected pattern. There is also a sprightly passage in which strings and horns race with a confident air. Jarre was a not a Hollywood heavy hitter when he was hired to provide some music for *Lawrence of Arabia*. Producer Sam Spiegel's plan was to have Benjamin Britten, Aram Khachaturian, and even Broadway composer Richard Rodgers do different parts of the score. But when director Lean heard Jarre's opening theme, he insisted that the French composer do the whole score. Jarre obliged, completing all the music and conducting most of it in four weeks. The soundtrack album was on the charts for over a year, won an Oscar for Jarre, and secured his Hollywood career.

The other Lean films that Jarre scored are each very different but all have the big symphonic sound for which he became famous. *Doctor Zhivago* has a sprawling story with many characters who struggle with love and survival before, during, and after the Russian Revolution. Jarre's score is expert at capturing the historical sweep of the tale as well as the intimate love story between the married doctor-poet of the title (Omar Sharif) and his mistress Lara (Julie Christie) who is wed to a radical Bolshevik (Tom Courtenay). The resulting score has more music and greater variety than that in *Lawrence of Arabia*. The overture, a complete musical piece in itself, quotes the ancient Russian anthem "God Save the Czar" and includes a variety of passages from the score, from a deep-voiced male chorus chanting a ponderous march to zesty traveling music with vivacious strings and horns. For the opening credits, two dozen busy balalaikas strum out a rustic folk tune as they are echoed by violins; then "Lara's Theme" is heard for the first time in a brisk, dancing version. Among the many memorable tracks in the *Doctor Zhivago* score are an elegant waltz for the aristocrats, a simple and cheery dance tune for the students, expansive traveling music for the arrival at the country estate at Varykino, a robust anthem for the street protestors, and piercing percussion and brass for the various military confrontations. At the funeral of the young Yuri's mother, the Russian Orthodox hymn "Kontakion" is chanted and then is overwhelmed by a haunting passage in which deep percussion and strings pound away with a fearsome power. The theme for Lara was originally to be a familiar Russian folk tune, but when it was discovered that the tune was not all that old and still under copyright, Jarre composed an original melody, one that ended up being one of the most famous of all movie tunes. It is a simple waltz that gracefully climbs the scale, only to slide back down in a beguiling fashion. "Lara's Theme" returns several times throughout the score played by different instruments and in different moods, from the delicately romantic to the fervently passionate. If the score for *Doctor Zhivago* sounds not quite like any other, it is because Jarre gathered a large and unusual orchestra for the recording. In addition to the conventional instruments and the many balalaikas, the ensemble for the recording sessions also included a harpsichord, electric piano, zither, Japanese lute, organ, gong, novachord, and Moog synthesizer. Jarre's exhaustive ideas paid off. The score not only won him another Oscar but the soundtrack album remained on the *Billboard* charts for three years.

Many complained that the big epic sound Jarre created for *Ryan's Daughter* was too big this time. This is a simple tale of an Irish lass (Sylvia Miles) in a small coastal town who weds the local schoolmaster (Robert Mitchum) then has an affair with a wounded British office (Christopher Jones). Yet the story was directed by Lean as a grand-opera romance set against a vast landscape. The emotions ran as high as the crashing waves and a little story was blown out of proportion. Lean wanted a score just as oversized and Jarre came up with music that seemed more appropriate for an Irish historical epic. The main theme is a catchy tune in which a musical idea is repeated, each time a bit higher on the scale. When this is played on a harp and Irish flute, it is quite engaging. When the full orchestra turns the theme into bombastic onslaught, one wonders what kind of movie this is. Also in the score is a rousing military march for the British, a swirling waltz with a folk flavor for the Irish, jaunty traveling music played on pipes and organ with a circus temperament, and a radiant "Rosie's Theme" that is as spunky and feisty as the title heroine. *Ryan's Daughter* is an exceptional score but suffers from the excess of the movie it supports. Lean's last film, *A Passage to India*, is more balanced. The story of an Englishwoman (Judy Davis) who is bewitched and seduced by the strange and exotic world of India is told without excess, the scale appropriate for E. M. Forster's tale. (It was Lean's first film since 1955 not to use a widescreen process.) There is relatively little music in the 164-minute film, but what is there is commendable if not outstanding. In the film, India is seen from an imperial British point of view; similarly, much of the music is also very European. The opening theme is an agitated double-time waltz that sounds very Western and doesn't hint at the Asian setting to follow. The melody is very close to the main theme for *Ryan's Daughter* but at a faster tempo and with some different accents. This also serves as the theme for the confused heroine, the swirling strings and brass crescendos sometimes coming across as more chaotic than lively. A bicycle ride though the Indian landscape is scored with a sparkling passage featuring a solo trumpet rather than a sitar. Even when some of the British go on an outing to the mysterious Marabar Caves, the music remains European with some Asian instruments providing Hindu accents without overpowering the Western melody. Jarre's *A Passage to India* score won an Oscar, perhaps more in tribute to the veteran composer and director rather than for its own merits.

One needs to look at Jarre's music for small movies to appreciate his versatility. The romantic fantasy *Ghost*, about a murdered man (Patrick Swayze) who returns to help his lover (Demi Moore) and a psychic (Whoopi Goldberg) catch the culprit, was a surprise hit. The soundtrack album was also an unexpected success, mostly because of the contagious song "Unchained Melody" that was played during an erotic clay-modeling scene. The tune was by Alex North and Hy Zaret and was written in 1955 for the prison film *Unchained*. Jarre used the song so often in his score that North was given co-composer credit for *Ghost*. Both a traditional orchestra and electronic instruments were used in the original music Jarre wrote for the movie. The love theme is a gliding passage featuring strings and horns with some electronic touches in the background. Synthesized music dominates the supernatural tracks that range from eerie high-frequency echoes to harsh pulsating pounding and chaotic crescendos. There is even more synthesized music in *Witness*, a thriller about a cop (Harrison Ford) who takes refuge in an Amish community to solve a murder. The main theme is a slow and brooding passage with sustained electronic notes and a simple melody played on an electric keyboard with lots of reverberation. Another disturbing passage is a series of low echoing chords and a languid melody played on synthesized reeds. The love theme is a solemn piece featuring an electronic flute that climbs the scale in a relaxed and serene manner. The musical highlight of the movie is a barn-raising sequence in which synthesized bass notes play a simple pattern while Bach-like melodies on organ enter and overlap each other in a resplendent way. For the inspiring melodrama *Dead Poets Society*, Jarre adds bagpipe sounds to electronic and conventional orchestrations. In 1959, a charismatic and unorthodox English teacher (Robin Williams) cultivates a love for poetry and builds self-esteem for his male students at a New England boarding school. The stirring main theme, with more than a touch of Gaelic flavor, is played on electric keyboard, strings, drums, and bagpipes, the piece growing in intensity and speed as more instruments are added.

There is also a poignant passage heard on Celtic harp and flute that serves as a funeral dirge, and a growling theme with low echoing noises as electronic glissandos on various instruments perform a mystical dance in the high register.

The eccentric German film *The Tin Drum* calls for an unorthodox score, and Jarre provided one filled with odd sounds that somehow remain musical. When the Nazis take over Germany in the late 1920s, a twelve-year-old boy (David Bennent) stops growing and protests the changes taking place around him by furiously beating on a toy tin drum. One of Jarre's themes features a distorted electronic horn; another is a frantic percussion passage that seems to move in different directions at the same time. A flowing rhapsody played on violins is punctuated by electronic squawks and a jazzy saxophone. Grumbling brass and a wailing clarinet seem to float back and forth in an arresting track that climaxes with a solo tin drum. This is creative screen scoring on an almost surreal level. *Gorillas in the Mist*, a biopic about Dian Fossey who studied rare African mountain gorillas and then dedicated her life to protecting them, has some electric instruments but the result is much less eccentric. The beauty and mystery of the African jungle is conveyed in the opening theme in which a symphonic orchestra plays a vivid pastoral while tribal drums and native chanting take over and the two opposing sounds blend harmonically. Sometimes in the score, electronic horns and percussion take the place of authentic instruments; other times electric piano, a high-pitched pipe, and a conventional violin overlap in a lilting manner. Another intriguing combination consists of synthesized drums and keyboard playing a rhythmic duet that is surprisingly authentic sounding. Also memorable is a passage in which a solo cello plays a sonorous air with electronic accompaniment. The *Gorillas in the Mist* soundtrack was mostly performed by nine keyboard musicians who were listed as the Maurice Jarre Electronic Ensemble. This is a far cry from the 110 musical instruments needed to make the *Doctor Zhivago* recording. Although he is most remembered for those big epic scores, there is so much more to Jarre than that. Biography: *Maurice Jarre*, Flessas Giannis (in Greek) (2009).

Credits

(* for Best Song)

Year	Film	Director
1959	Head against the Wall	Georges Franju (France)
1959	The Chasers	Jean-Pierre Mocky (France)
1959	Beast at Bay	Pierre Chenal (France)
1959	Stars at Noon	Jacques Ertaud, Marcel Ichac (France)
1959	Vous n'avez rein à déclarer?	Clément Duhour (France)
1960	Eyes without a Face	Georges Franju (France/Italy)
1960	The Itchy Palm	Gérard Oury (France/Italy)
1960	Lovers on a Tightrope	Jean-Charles Dudrumet (France)
1960	Crack in the Mirror	Richard Fleischer (USA)
1960	Recourse in Grace	Laslo Benedek (France/Italy)
1961	The President	Henri Verneuil (France/Italy)
1961	Spotlight on a Murderer	Georges Franju (France)
1961	The Big Gamble	Richard Fleischer, Elmo Williams (USA)
1961	Le puits aux trois vérités	François Villiers (Italy/France)
1961	Famous Love Affairs	Michel Boisrond (France/Italy)
1961	Le temps du ghetto	Frédéric Rossif (France)
1962	Les oliviers de la justice	James Blue (France)
1962	Sun in Your Eyes	Jacques Bourdon (France)
1962	Therese	Georges Franju (France)
1962	The Longest Day	Andrew Marton, etc. (USA)
1962	Sundays and Cybele (AAN)	Serge Bourguignon (France/Austria)
1962	Lawrence of Arabia (AA; GGN)	David Lean (UK/USA)
1963	Mourir à Madrid	Frédéric Rossif (France)
1963	L'oiseau de paradis	Marcel Camus (France)
1963	Ton ombre est la mienne	André Michel (Italy/France)
1963	A King without Distraction	François Leterrier (France)
1963	Judex	Georges Franju (France/Italy)
1964	Behold a Pale Horse	Fred Zinnemann (USA)
1964	The Train	John Frankenheimer (France/Italy/USA)
1964	Weekend at Dunkirk	Henri Verneuil (France/Italy)
1965	The Animals	Frédéric Rossif (France)
1965	The Collector	William Wyler (UK/USA)
1965	Doctor Zhivago (AA; GG)	David Lean (USA/Italy)
1966	Is Paris Burning? (GGN)	René Clément (France)
1966	The Professionals	Richard Brooks (USA)
1966	Gambit	Ronald Neame (USA)
1966	Grand Prix	John Frankenheimer (USA)
1967	The Night of the Generals	Anatole Litvak (UK/France)
1967	The 25th Hour	Henri Verneuil (France/Italy)
1968	Villa Rides	Buzz Kulik (USA)
1968	5 Card Stud	Henry Hathaway (USA)
1968	The Fixer	John Frankenheimer (UK)
1968	Isadora	Karel Reisz (UK/France)
1968	The Extraordinary Seaman	John Frankenheimer (USA)
1969	The Damned	Luchino Visconti (Italy/W. Germany)
1969	Topaz	Alfred Hitchcock (USA)
1970	Una stagione all'inferno	Giovanna Gagliardo (Italy/France)
1970	The Only Game in Town	George Stevens (USA)
1970	El Condor	John Guillermin (USA)
1970	Ryan's Daughter	David Lean (UK)
1971	Plaza Suite	Arthur Hiller (USA)
1971	Red Sun	Terence Young (France/Italy/Spain)
1971	Jean Vilar, une belle vie	Jacques Rutman (France)
1972	Pope Joan	Michael Anderson (UK)

Year	Film	Director
1972	*The Life and Times of Judge Roy Bean* (AAN*; GGN*)	John Huston (USA)
1972	*The Effect of Gamma Rays on Man-in-the-Moon Marigolds*	Paul Newman (USA)
1973	*The MacKintosh Man*	John Huston (UK/USA)
1973	*Ash Wednesday*	Larry Peerce (USA)
1974	*Grandeur Nature*	Luis García Berlanga (France/Italy/Spain)
1974	*The Island at the Top of the World*	Robert Stevenson (USA)
1975	*Mandingo*	Richard Fleischer (USA)
1975	*Posse*	Kirk Douglas (USA)
1975	*Mr. Sycamore*	Pancho Kohner (USA)
1975	*The Man Who Would Be King* (GGN)	John Huston (UK/USA)
1976	*Al-risâlah*	Moustapha Akkad (Libya)
1976	*Shout at the Devil*	Peter R. Hunt (UK)
1976	*The Last Tycoon*	Elia Kazan (USA)
1977	*The Message* (AAN)	Moustapha Akkad (Lebanon, Libya)
1977	*Crossed Swords*	Richard Fleischer (UK/USA)
1977	*March or Die*	Dick Richards (UK)
1978	*Like a Turtle on Its Back*	Luc Béraud (France)
1978	*Two Solitudes*	Lionel Chetwynd (Canada)
1979	*The Tin Drum*	Volker Schlöndorff (W. Germany)
1979	*Winter Kills*	William Richert (USA)
1979	*The Magician of Lublin*	Menahem Golan (Israel/W. Germany)
1980	*The Black Marble*	Harold Becker (USA)
1980	*The American Success Company*	William Richert (USA)
1980	*The Last Flight of Noah's Ark*	Charles Jarrott (USA)
1980	*Resurrection*	Daniel Petrie (USA)
1981	*Lion of the Desert*	Moustapha Akkad (Libya/USA)
1981	*Die Fälschung*	Volker Schlöndorff (W. Germany/France)
1981	*Taps*	Harold Becker (USA)
1982	*Firefox*	Clint Eastwood (USA)
1982	*Young Doctors in Love*	Garry Marshall (USA)
1982	*Don't Cry, It's Only Thunder*	Peter Werner (USA)
1982	*The Year of Living Dangerously*	Peter Weir (Australia/USA)
1983	*For Those I Loved*	Robert Enrico (France/Canada)
1984	*Top Secret*	Jim Abrahams, David/Jerry Zuker (USA/UK)
1984	*Dreamscape*	Joseph Ruben (USA)
1984	*A Passage to India* (AA; GG; BAFTA-N)	David Lean (UK/USA)
1985	*Witness* (AAN; GGN; BAFTA)	Peter Weir (USA)
1985	*Mad Max Beyond Thunderdome*	George Miller, George Ogilvie (Australia)
1985	*The Bride*	Franc Roddam (UK/USA)
1985	*Enemy Mine*	Wolfgang Petersen (USA)
1986	*Tai-Pan*	Daryl Duke (USA)
1986	*The Mosquito Coast* (GGN)	Peter Weir (USA)
1986	*Solarbabies*	Alan Johnson (USA)
1987	*Le palanquin des larmes*	Jacques Dorfmann (France/Canada/China)
1987	*Shuto shôshitsu*	Toshio Masuda (Japan)
1987	*No Way Out*	Roger Donaldson (USA)
1987	*Julia and Julia*	Peter Del Monte (Italy)
1987	*Fatal Attraction*	Adrian Lyne (USA)
1987	*Gaby: A True Story*	Luis Mandoki (USA/Mexico)
1988	*Wildfire*	Zalman King (USA)
1988	*Moon over Parador*	Paul Mazursky (USA)
1988	*Gorillas in the Mist* (AAN; GG)	Michael Apted (USA)
1988	*Distant Thunder*	Rick Rosenthal (USA/Canada)
1989	*Chances Are*	Emile Ardolino (USA)
1989	*Dead Poets Society* (BAFTA)	Peter Weir (USA)
1989	*Prancer*	John D. Hancock (USA/Canada)
1989	*Enemies: A Love Story*	Paul Mazursky (USA/Canada)

Year	Film	Director
1990	*Ghost* (AAN)	Jerry Zucker (USA)
1990	*Solar Crisis*	Richard C. Sarafian (Japan/USA)
1990	*After Dark, My Sweet*	James Foley (USA)
1990	*Jacob's Ladder*	Adrian Lyne (USA)
1990	*Almost an Angel*	John Cornell (USA)
1991	*Only the Lonely*	Chris Columbus (USA)
1991	*Fires Within*	Gillian Armstrong (USA)
1992	*The Setting Sun*	Rou Tomono (Japan)
1992	*School Ties*	Robert Mandel (USA)
1992	*Shadow of the Wolf*	Jacques Dorfmann, Pierre Magny (France/Canada)
1993	*Mr. Jones*	Mike Figgis (USA)
1993	*Fearless*	Peter Weir (USA)
1995	*A Walk in the Clouds* (GG)	Alfonso Arau (USA/Mexico)
1996	*The Sunchaser*	Michael Cimino (USA)
1997	*Le jour et la nuit*	Bernard-Henri Lévy (France/Canada)
1999	*Sunshine* (GGN)	István Szabó (Germany/Hungary)
2000	*I Dreamed of Africa*	Hugh Hudson (USA)

JAUBERT, Maurice (1900–1940) A French journalist and lawyer who turned to music and worked with the most experimental French directors of the 1930s, he completed only nineteen feature films during his short life but they include some of the most innovative scores of the period.

Maurice Jaubert was born in Nice, France, the son of a lawyer who wanted him to follow in his footsteps. Jaubert received a law degree from the Sorbonne in Paris and practiced for a time but eventually broke away from his conventional family and pursued a music career. After studying composition and music theory at the Nice Conservatory, he became the music director for Pleyela Records in 1925, then five years later took on the same duties for the Pathé-Nathan Studios. As music critic for the journal *Esprit*, he met the leading composers of the day and wrote reviews and articles, promoting the music of Maurice Ravel, Arthur Honegger, Georges Auric, Kurt Weill, Darius Milhaud, and others. His first film project was writing music for Jean Renoir's silent movie *Nana* in 1926. After contributing music to some other silents and early sound shorts, Jaubert wrote the score for the German talkie *The Wonderful Lies of Nina Petrovna* in 1929. He collaborated with director René Clair on two unusual movies, *July 14* and *The Last Billionaire*, and composed unconventional music for their scores. He wrote similarly experimental scores for Jean Vigo's classic films *Zero for Conduct* and *L'Atalante*, then collaborated with Marcel Carné on four movies in the late 1930s. Jaubert was also very active in theatre, writing incidental music for several

plays, particularly for playwright Jean Giraudoux, and for the concert hall he composed art songs, sonatas, tone poems, and piano pieces. He usually conducted his film music and was musical director for other movies. When World War II broke out, Jaubert enlisted and was killed in combat early in the conflict. He was only forty years old. Over the decades a new appreciation for the films of Jean Vigo, Marcel Carné, and others has brought more attention to Jaubert's screen music. Later director Francois Truffaut was greatly influenced by these directors and Jaubert's scores. Truffaut utilized the long-deceased composer's concert pieces and stage music to create the scores for his movies *The Story of Adele H* (1971), *Small Change* (1976), *The Man Who Loved Women* (1977), and *The Green Room* (1978). Jaubert was the subject of François Porcile's 1985 documentary *A Composer for the Cinema: Maurice Jaubert*.

From the beginning of his screen career, Jaubert showed an uncanny understanding of the medium and how music can express dramatic ideas. By 1933 he was experimenting with new musical ideas. With Jean Grémillon he co-composed and arranged a marvelous score for *July 14*, the main theme an intoxicating piece of lighter-than-air happiness. It is not surprising that the music was turned into the popular song "A Paris dans chaque faubourg." That same year, Jaubert worked with young director Vigo on the brilliant *Zero for Conduct*, a surreal look at a boys' boarding school as seen through the eyes of four mischievous youths. Music flows through just about all of the forty-minute comedy. Many sequences have no dialogue at all and the music says it all. A rousing school song is sung by the boys with sarcastic ardor. The music during a train ride rhythmically chugs along with the starting and stopping of the engine, the horns and strings getting sillier the faster the train goes. When the students go on a free-for-all outing, a cockeyed march accompanies them. For the memorable slow-motion sequence in which the boys celebrate their rebellion, Jaubert inverted some of his music heard previously in the movie, the effect as dazzling musically at it is visually. Such surreal sequences in Vigo's *L'Atalante* the next year are even more compelling. An erotic dream is scored with an alto saxophone playing a lyrical melody, and when the separated newlyweds (Dita Parlo and Jean Dasté) toss and turn as they sleep in different beds the music has a slight circus feel to it. The rhythm of the engine of the barge, on which the young couple live, is captured in the pulsating music. The accordion joins the alto saxophone for the luscious song "Le chant des mariniers." In another sequence, a solo horn accompanies the wife as she wanders the town. The main theme for *L'Atalante* is a flowing waltz that has an otherworldly quality. Strings waver while the woodwinds etch out a simple tune that is delectable. This is screen music at its best.

While Jaubert never got to score any other films as superior as the two Vigo pieces, he worked on some very interesting projects with top directors and his scores are filled with little personal touches that still please. In Clair's *The Last Billionaire*, the music satirizes the royal court by playing a bizarre spoof of a national anthem. A more somber approach can be found in his music for Marcel Carné's dark films of the late 1930s. The dreariness of the down-and-out *Hotel du Nord* is conveyed by a very melancholy score while the pessimistic *Daybreak* has music with an edge, a tragedy waiting to happen. When Jaubert's music returned to the screen in the 1970s, it was as if he never left. Truffaut's selection and use of Jaubert's music in his films is masterful. The chapel music in *The Green Room* is reverent yet secular and sensual. The pseudoclassical music for the period film *The Story of Adele H* is as restless and feverish as the title heroine (Isabelle Adjani). The whimsical *Small Change*, about the resilience of children, has an exuberant score with some delightful songs. *The Man Who Loved Women* has a vigorous score with a classical flavor. This cinema quartet is an opportunity to see how one of France's finest directors worked with one of its best screen composers even though they are from separate time periods. Truffaut was New Wave cinema but that wave was started decades earlier in movies scored by Jaubert.

Credits

(all films France unless stated otherwise)

Year	Film	Director
1926	Nana	Jean Renoir
1929	The Wonderful Lies of Nina Petrovna	Hanns Schwarz (Germany)
1930	Little Red Riding Hood	Alberto Cavalcanti
1932	The Amazon Head Hunters	Marquis de Wavrin (Belgium/France)
1932	L'affaire est dans le sac	Pierre Prévert
1933	July 14	René Clair
1933	Zero for Conduct	Jean Vigo
1934	L'Atalante	Jean Vigo
1934	The Last Billionaire	René Clair
1936	The Parisian Life	Robert Siodmak
1937	Dance Program	Julien Duvivier
1937	Drole de Drame (aka The Strange Adventure of Doctor Molyneux)	Marcel Carné
1938	Les filles du Rhone	Jean-Paul Paulin
1938	Port of Shadows	Marcel Carné
1938	Youth in Revolt (aka Altitude 3.200)	Jean Benoit-Levy, Marie Epstein
1938	Hotel du Nord	Marcel Carné
1939	Pasha's Wives	Marc Sorkin, Georg Wilhelm Pabst
1939	The End of the Day	Julien Duvivier
1939	Daybreak	Marcel Carné

JOHNSON, Laurie (b. 1927) A busy British conductor, arranger, and composer for television in the 1960s and 1970s, he made many records and scored an odd assortment of movies between 1958 and 1987.

Born Laurence Reginald Ward Johnson in the London section of Hampstead, he was educated at the Royal College of Music, later teaching there. After serving in the military, Johnson began his professional career as a composer and arranger for the Ted Heath Band. During the 1950s he worked with several of the Big Bands and made dozens of recordings. He found wider recognition on television in 1961 with his theme music for the British series *Top Secret*, the song "Sucu Sucu" hitting the charts. Over the next two decades Johnson composed theme songs and music for over forty series, including *This Is Your Life*, *Animal Magic*, *Shirley's World*, *Thriller*, *Jason King*, *The Professionals*, and the original *The Avengers* for which he composed the famous theme and scored 156 episodes throughout the 1960s. He also wrote music for some notable TV movies, in particular *Mister Jerico* (1970) and the popular adaptations of Barbara Cartland romance novels: *A Hazard of Hearts* (1987), *The Lady and the Highwayman* (1989), *A Ghost in Monte Carlo* (1990), and *Duel of Hearts* (1991). Johnson's movie career has been more sporadic and uneven. His first score was for the historical adventure *The Moonraker* in 1958, followed by a scattered collection of broad comedies, dark dramas, and horror and sci-fi thrillers. The only film to find international success was the dark comedy classic *Dr. Strangelove*, but his credits also include such quality movies as *Tiger Bay*, *Spare the Rod*, *Bitter Harvest*, *First Men in the Moon*, *Hot Millions*, *Captain Kronos—Vampire Hunter*, *The Belstone Fox*, *And Soon the Darkness*, *The Maids*, and *Hedda*. Johnson's screen music has often been used in other films and television series ranging from *Benny Hill Down Under* (1977) to *SpongeBob SquarePants* (2009). His concert hall works include musical suites, tone poems, and a symphony, and his London stage musicals include *Lock Up Your Daughters* (1959), *Pieces of Eight* (1959), *Little Old King Cole* (1961), and *The Four Musketeers* (1967). In 1972 he cofounded his own film production company and six years later cofounded Gainsborough Pictures. Still active in the 1990s, Johnson founded the London Big Band in 1997 and produced festivals of jazz and Big Band music that were televised throughout the United Kingdom.

Johnson's classical music training shows up in his television and screen scores. He favors the string section but creates a unique sound by writing unusual chord combinations in his scores. He sometimes adds electric guitar and bass to his music, the modern sound mixing with the classical one. For example, the famous theme for *The Avengers* is a jazz piece with strings and brass that are slightly distorted on some sustained notes. The catchy "Sucu Sucu" theme from *Top Secret* is a bossa nova piece heard on zesty trumpets with electric keyboard and guitar accompaniment. While Johnson's movie scores are not as well known, they also have a sparkling modern sentiment with classical touches. *Hot Millions*, a comic crime caper about a con artist (Peter Ustinov) who attempts to swindle a big insurance company, has a zippy main theme that is an allegro piece with rapid brass and reeds underscored with bubbly strings. The rest of the score is equally jocular except for a fluid love theme played on piano and strings that is restrained and lyrical. The score for the drama *Bitter Harvest* utilizes Johnson's considerable experience with jazz composing and arranging. This tale of a restless Welsh girl (Janet Munro) who tries to find fulfillment in swinging London has a bluesy theme in which a solo clarinet floats over a string accompaniment at a languid pace. Another tripping passage has a jazzy clarinet playing sustained notes while the strings move at a faster tempo. More upbeat but still with a somber subtext is a sprightly theme for piano and percussion that has a Latin beat even though the strings move slowly and smoothly underneath. A more romanticized score can be found in *The Belstone Fox*, which concerns the rivalry between a hunter (Eric Porter) and a fox but told from the animal's point of view. Johnson provides a gliding theme featuring an oboe and muted brass over a full orchestra with the suggestion of a fox horn call at certain points.

Perhaps Johnson's finest film score is the lush and symphonic one he wrote for *First Men in the Moon*, a fanciful Victorian tale, based on an H. G. Wells novel, about the discovery of an underground city on the moon. The main theme is a grand but ponderous piece with blaring brass and percussive crescendos that suggest something dangerous and important is coming. The moon landing is scored with a series of descending brass phrases and twinkling chimes that is both mysterious and magical. There is a quiet passage on electric keyboard with long descending glissandos that have an eerie tone, as well as a flowing romantic theme on strings and French horn that is as graceful as it is delicate. As for Johnson's most famous movie, *Dr. Strangelove* is more an opportunity for skillful musical arranging than composing. Director Stanley Kubrick wanted the score to include popular songs that would wryly comment on the action, so there is very little original music in the comedy. Johnson arranged a serene orchestra version of the 1932 standard "Try a Little Tenderness" (by Harry M. Woods, Reginald Connelly, and Jimmy Campbell) to play over the opening credits when bombers are being refueled in midair. The traditional Irish antiwar ballad "Johnny I Hardly Knew Ye" is heard under one scene in flight. And for the tragicomic ending, in which atomic bombs explode in slow motion, a recording of Vera Lynn singing "We'll Meet Again" (by Ross Parker and Hugh Charles) is heard. Johnson's original theme music consists of military drums in the distance as two trumpets quietly announce themselves then break into a merry march. Yet even this theme is heard in counterpoint with a male chorus humming the traditional march "When Johnny Comes Marching Home" to a harmonica accompaniment. *Dr. Strangelove* has a very effective score but it is hardly a good sample of Johnson's composition talents. He may be little known today except for his television music, but Johnson has written some splendid screen scores. Unfortunately most of the films are long forgotten. Official website: www.lauriejohnson.co.uk.

Credits

(all films UK unless stated otherwise)

Year	Film	Director
1958	*The Moonraker*	David MacDonald
1958	*Girls at Sea*	Gilbert Gunn
1959	*Tiger Bay* (aka *Mystery at Tiger Bay*)	J. Lee Thompson
1959	*No Trees in the Street*	J. Lee Thompson
1959	*Operation Bullshine*	Gilbert Gunn
1960	*I Aim at the Stars*	J. Lee Thompson (USA/W. Germany)
1961	*Spare the Rod*	Leslie Norman
1961	*What a Whopper*	Gilbert Gunn
1963	*Siege of the Saxons*	Nathan Juran
1963	*Bitter Harvest*	Peter Graham Scott
1964	*Dr. Strangelove or: How I Learned to Stop Worrying and Love the Bomb*	Stanley Kubrick (USA/UK)
1964	*First Men in the Moon*	Nathan Juran
1964	*Contest Girl* (aka *The Beauty Jungle*)	Val Guest
1964	*East of Sudan*	Nathan Juran
1965	*You Must Be Joking!*	Michael Winner
1968	*Hot Millions*	Eric Till (USA/UK)
1970	*And Soon the Darkness*	Robert Fuest
1971	*The Firechasers*	Sidney Hayers
1973	*The Belstone Fox*	James Hill
1974	*Captain Kronos—Vampire Hunter*	Brian Clemens
1975	*The Maids*	Christopher Miles (UK/USA)
1975	*Hedda*	Trevor Nunn
1975	*Diagnosis: Murder*	Sidney Hayers
1977	*It Shouldn't Happen to a Vet*	Eric Till
1980	*Tvingad att leva*	Mats Helge (Sweden)
1987	*It's Alive III: Island of the Alive*	Larry Cohen (USA)

JOHNSTON, Adrian (b. 1961) A recent but prolific British composer for television, he has written music for the theatre and has scored over thirty feature films since 1991.

Adrian Johnston was born in rural Cumbria, Great Britain, and was educated at Edinburgh University, graduating with a degree in English. Johnston began his music career as a drummer for rock and pop bands in the 1980s, including Moles for Breakfast, The Waterboys, and The Mike Flowers Pops. He then moved into composing, writing music for the theatre, and having his work heard at the

Royal Shakespeare Company, the Glasgow Citizens Theatre, the Royal National Theatre, and other prestigious companies. Johnston first got involved with movies when he worked as an accompanist at film festivals showing silent movies. He began writing original music for these early movies, scoring dozens of shorts then writing complete scores for the 1921 French drama *La Terre* and the 1924 Harold Lloyd comedy *Hot Water*. Johnston's first score for a new film was for the 1996 version of Thomas Hardy's *Jude the Obscure* titled *Jude*. Since then he has scored a wide variety of British and Irish movies, as well as the occasional American production. Among his notable films are *Enter Achilles, Welcome to Sarajevo, Divorcing Jack, The Debt Collector, Some Voices, Lawless Heart, Me Without You, If Only, The Mighty Celt, Kinky Boots, Lassie, Becoming Jane, The Scapegoat*, and *Brideshead Revisited*. Johnston has been even busier working in television where he has gained more notoriety and many awards. *Touching Evil, Perfect Strangers, Meadowlands, The Street, White Heat, Accused, The Tunnel*, and *Dancing on the Edge* are his most well-known TV series. He has written scores for over forty TV movies and miniseries, including *Broken Glass* (1996), *Death of a Salesman* (1996), *Our Mutual Friend* (1998), *All the King's Men* (1999), *Turn of the Screw* (1999), *Crime and Punishment* (2002), *The Mayor of Casterbridge* (2003), *Byron* (2003), *The Lost Prince* (2003), *Sherlock Holmes and the Case of the Silk Stocking* (2004), *Gideon's Daughter* (2005), *Capturing Mary* (2007), *Diamonds* (2009), *Zen* (2011), *The Politician's Husband* (2013), and *Klondike* (2014). He has also scored several documentaries for television, most memorably *7Up 2000* (2000), *Shackleton: Breaking the Ice* (2001), and *Elizabeth: Queen, Wife, Mother* (2012).

Has Johnston become so proficient with scores in the style of romanticism because he has done so many period pieces for film and television? More likely it is the other way around. He is hired for such movies because from the start he has written sterling music in the romantic style. His first movie, *Jude*, has the polish and confidence of a veteran. This dark tale concerns a married sculptor (Christopher Eccleston) and his married cousin (Kate Winslet) who fall in love and attempt to live together out of wedlock but are tormented by society and their own guilt. Thomas Hardy's tragic look at nineteenth-century rural life is reflected in Johnston's poignant score. The principal theme features a high-pitched violin that lingers

on each musical phrase so achingly that it seems to wail. When other strings and some pipes join in, the folk quality of the music comes out, but the sorrow remains. Among the other effective themes are a lilting folk tune on pipes and guitar that feels free and joyous, a somber but provocative lament on pipes and various strings that does not drag yet is still very morose, a twinkling passage on horn and harp that is fresh and clear as it takes its time with a merry tune, a dramatic theme that is agitated and turbulent like unpredictable waves at sea, and a funeral dirge played on slightly off-pitch strings that is truly haunting. With such an auspicious debut no wonder both television and filmmakers wanted Johnston to score everything from Charles Dickens to Evelyn Waugh. The latter's *Brideshead Revisited* afforded Johnston the chance to write a score set in the 1920s but the arresting music in this 2008 adaptation is still deeply entrenched in romanticism. Perhaps the most memorable music in the film is a sweeping theme featuring a solo violin that is restless and confused, repeating itself on a different key but still aimless. There is also a busy piano theme with hesitant strings that glitters with sunshine; a sparkling passage on strings and horns that moves like a gentle wind, gaining and losing speed in the process; and a moody piece on strings and piano that maintains a steady tempo but cannot lift from its minor-key mood. The Jazz Age is represented by some 1920s standards heard at parties and bars and an original jazz piece on violin and guitar that is brisk but jaded. The score for *Becoming Jane*, a highly fictionalized look at the early life and romances of Jane Austen (Anne Hathaway), is arguably Johnston's finest piece of romanticism. Most of the music is orchestrated with a small ensemble featuring piano, harp, flute, and violin. The main theme is a graceful adagio for piano and violin with a leisurely and long melodic line. A harp sets the tone for another theme that is scintillating in its simplicity, moving at a languid pace but still full of life. There is a lush passage that moves with a restrained frivolity, the piano accompaniment acting giddy while the strings are solemn. The livelier themes include a vivacious piece heard during a cricket match with restless strings and fluttering reeds that seems to skip and run, and a whirling dance tune for the London scenes played on vigorous strings and reeds with busy piano embellishments. Perhaps the most moving track is for a love scene in a rose garden. It is a reflective passage played on piano with strings surrounding the delicate lament-like sound; then the piece grows, the fingering of piano and harp getting more complex and the passion of the music rising.

Johnston has scored many movies with a modern setting, and some are very laudable. *If Only*, a romantic melodrama with fantasy elements, is about a London businessman (Paul Nicholls) who gets to relive one day in his past with the hope of saving his deceased girlfriend (Jennifer Love Hewitt). The score opens with an up-tempo opening theme with nervous percussion and a freewheeling piano that sounds very contemporary but still romantic. There is also in the score a pulsating passage with anxious percussion and synthesized chords that races along in an urban manner, bouncy traveling music heard on piano and backed by a restrained rock band, and a flowing string passage with sustained notes on an electric keyboard. For the love scenes, Johnson returns to romanticism with a dulcet theme on piano with graceful strings. More edgy is the cult favorite *Kinky Boots* about a struggling shoe company that finds new life when it starts to manufacture sexy footwear for drag queens. The soundtrack includes several pop and rock song favorites but Johnston provides some original disco music heard on a synthesizer, a rhythm and blues theme, a jazz piano and saxophone piece that is slow and sultry but doesn't take itself too seriously, and a mix of electronic and conventional instruments for the more inspiring moments in the film. While all this is commendable, the modern scores don't match the period ones. When it comes to the romantic style, Johnston is in a class by himself.

Credits

(all films UK unless stated otherwise)

Year	Film	Director
1991	La Terre (1921)	André Antoine (France)
1992	Hot Water (1924)	Fred C. Newmeyer, Sam Taylor (USA)
1996	Jude	Michael Winterbottom
1996	Enter Achilles	Clara van Gool (Netherlands)
1997	Welcome to Sarajevo	Michael Winterbottom (UK/USA)
1997	Food of Love	Stephen Poliakoff (France/UK)
1998	I Want You	Michael Winterbottom
1998	The Tribe	Stephen Poliakoff
1998	Divorcing Jack	David Caffrey
1999	The Debt Collector	Anthony Neilson
1999	The Darkest Light	Simon Beaufoy, Bille Eltringham (France/UK)
1999	With or Without You	Michael Winterbottom
1999	The Last Yellow	Julian Farino
2000	The Suicide Club (aka Game of Death)	Rachel Samuels (USA)
2000	About Adam	Gerard Stembridge (Ireland/UK/USA)
2000	Some Voices	Simon Cellan Jones
2001	Lawless Heart	Tom Hunsingert, Neil Hunter (UK/France)
2001	Me without You	Sandra Goldbacher (UK/Germany)
2002	This Is Not a Love Song	Billie Eltringham
2004	If Only	Gil Junger (USA/UK)
2005	The Mighty Celt	Pearse Elliott (Ireland)
2005	Picadilly Jim	John McKay (Isle of Man)
2005	Isolation	Billy O'Brien (UK/Ireland/USA)
2005	Kinky Boots	Julian Jarrold (USA/UK)
2005	Lassie	Charles Sturridge (USA/France/Ireland/UK)
2007	Sparkle	Tom Hunsinger, Neil Hunter
2007	Becoming Jane	Julian Jarrold (UK/Ireland)
2008	Brideshead Revisited	Julian Jarrold (UK/Italy/Morocco)
2009	Glorious 39	Stephen Poliakoff
2012	The Scapegoat	Charles Sturridge
2014	Scintilla	Billy O'Brien

JONES, Quincy (b. 1933) A multihyphenate impresario who has composed, conducted, arranged, performed, and produced music in every medium, the African American artist wrote the scores for thirty-four feature films in the 1960s and 1970s. Just as Jones's talents have triumphed in all forms of show business, so does his music encompass many forms, including jazz, hip-hop, soul, African, Brazilian, swing, rock, rhythm and blues, funk, and even classical.

Quincy Delight Jones Jr. was born in Chicago's South Side, the son of a baseball player and carpenter. Because his mother suffered from schizophrenia, Jones's childhood was a difficult one. After his mother was institutionalized, his father remarried and moved to Bremerton, Washington, to work in a defense plant during World War II. Jones studied trumpet in high school and formed his own jazz band, making arrangements and performing throughout the Seattle area. In 1951 he received a scholarship to study at Schillinger House (today Berklee College of Music) in Boston but did not remain there long because he was offered a job as trumpeter in Lionel Hampton's band. Jones often did arrangements for the band, which led to jobs arranging music for Gene Krupa, Count Basie, Sarah Vaughan, Duke Ellington, and the up-and-coming Ray Charles, whom he knew from Seattle. With Hampton's band and then with Dizzy Gillespie, Jones toured Europe, the Middle East, and South America, learning about new musical forms particularly in Latin America. ABC-Paramount Records signed Jones up in 1956 to make recordings with his own band. The next year he went to Paris, where he studied music theory and composition with the renowned teacher Nadia Boulanger. He continued to perform with his jazz band throughout Europe, returning to the States to make records and take on interesting jobs, such as being musical director for Harold Arlen's jazz musical *Free and Easy* on tour and writing the score for the Swedish movie *The Boy in the Tree* in 1961. By the 1960s Jones was producing records and quickly found success with hit singles by Lesley Gore. He went on to produce albums by Frank Sinatra, Michael Jackson, and other top names in show business. Many of these featured arrangements by Jones, who was now one of the most acclaimed arrangers in the business.

Jones's screen composing career took off when he scored Sidney Lumet's celebrated film *The Pawnbroker* in 1964 and offers for other films poured in. While many of these were movies with an African American subject matter and with such stars as Sidney Poitier, there were also light comedies, cop thrillers, romantic melodramas, and action films. Among the popular movies he scored are *Mirage*, *Walk Don't Run*, *In the Heat of the Night*, *The Slender Thread*, *Mackenna's Gold*, *Bob & Carol & Ted & Alice*, *In Cold Blood*, *The Out of Towners*, *The New Centurions*, *Cactus Flower*, *The Getaway*, and *The Color Purple*. For the 1967 film *Banning*, Jones became the first African American ever nominated for the Oscar for Best Song with "The Eyes of Love" (lyric by Bob Russell). He did the musical adaptation of the stage score for the film version of *The Wiz* (1978) and composed music for the television series *Ironside*, *The Bill Cosby Show*, and *Hey, Landlord*, as well as the TV movies and miniseries *Ironside* (1967), *Split Second to an Epitaph* (1968), *Killer by Night* (1972), and one episode of *Roots* (1977). Songs composed by Jones for records often were on the charts, such as "Ai No Corrida," "One Hundred Ways," "Just Once," "Streetbeater" (which was used as the theme song for the sitcom *Sanford and Son*), and his fusion hit "Soul Bossa Nova," which later showed up everywhere, including World Cup competitions, quiz shows, Woody Allen's 1969 comedy *Take the Money and Run*, and the Austin Powers movies. By the mid-1970s Jones left screen composing to concentrate on his show business empire, Quincy Jones Entertainment, which has produced TV shows, concerts, records, awards shows, fund-raisers, music videos, and podcasts. He returned to movie composing in 1985 for his most famous score, *The Color Purple*, later coproducing the Broadway version in 2005, the same year he contributed some music to the Hollywood/Canadian film *Get Rich or Die Tryin'*. He was the subject of the 1990 documentary film *Listen Up: The Lives of Quincy Jones*, and over the years has received countless entertainment and humanitarian awards.

Although Jones may be labeled as primarily a jazz musician and composer, his movie scores are representative of his eclectic approach to music. *The Pawnbroker* is a disturbing drama about a Jewish New Yorker (Rod Steiger) whose memories of the Holocaust have dried up all his emotions and interest in life. This is definitely a jazz score, the main theme surprisingly lively for such a somber subject. Yet the solo saxophone has a wailing tone at times and conveys the pain the pawnbroker hides. A rapid theme titled "Rack 'Em Up" is restless, the vocal

QUINCY JONES. The multihyphenate Jones began as a trumpet player and ended up creating a music empire that encompasses all kinds of music. Pictured here is the young Jones in Paris in the 1950s, already totally in charge and making beautiful music. *Photofest*

scat singing suggesting the noisy urban setting that surrounds the pawnbroker. Jazz is also prevalent in the semidocumentary drama *In Cold Blood* about a Kansas family senselessly murdered by two young men (Robert Blake and Scott Wilson). The victims' theme is a simple and unembellished waltz played by woodwinds and strings. But for the main theme dissonant jazz music is used and the killers are identified by a cool jazz motif punctuated by striking different sized bottles to hit various notes. The flashback to the murder itself is scored with sustained pipe organ chords and low strings, a truly odd and upsetting sound. The mystery *Mirage* has an easy and languid kind of jazz with a touch of the bossa nova flavor in it. The jazz in the drama *The Slender Thread* is not easy, but hesitant, unpredictable, and suspenseful, the music this time punctuated by gongs, chimes, electric guitar, and piano. Electric keyboard and synthesized instruments play the hip jazz theme in *The Anderson Tapes*, a heist movie with a cockeyed sense of humor. All of these scores are clearly in the jazz mode yet each is very different and distinctive.

For the popular police drama *In the Heat of the Night* set in a small Mississippi town, Jones utilizes blues, funk, and folk. The title theme is a lazy country blues with a bit of gospel heard in the background singers and the electric organ that accompanies them. Ray Charles sings the title song (lyric by Marilyn and Alan Bergman) on the soundtrack, and it went on to become a hit, recorded by Count Basie and others. The score also contained some first-class folk and country passages as well as other songs sung by notable Nashville artists. The music for the dramatic confrontation scenes is a funky theme on various strings and drums with some clever mixing on the synthesizer. Jones composed, arranged, and conducted the music in *The Heat of the Night* and did superior work in all three jobs. It is arguably his finest score. Some award that distinction to *The Color Purple*, the acclaimed film about the blossoming of an African American woman (Whoopi Goldberg) over the decades. Also set in the South, the film has a lot of rural blues. The main title is a bucolic waltz, but it is the blues theme "Miss Celie's Blues" that is more typical of this wonderfully evocative score. Unlike the *In the Heat of the Night* score which was all Jones, several artists collaborated with him on the music for *The Color Purple*. Rod Templeton, Lionel Richie, Sonny Terry, and Jeremy Lubbock all had a hand in different parts of the score, but it was Jones who coordinated and arranged it all into a seamless whole. Since he also was one of the producers of the movie, you might say *The Color Purple* represents Jones as the ultimate impresario. Autobiography: *Q: The Autobiography of Quincy Jones* (2001); biography: *Quincy Jones: His Life in Music*, Clarence Bernard Henry (2013). Official website: www.quincyjones.com.

Credits

(all films USA unless stated otherwise; * for Best Song)

Year	Film	Director
1961	*Pojken i trädet (aka The Boy in the Tree)*	Arne Sucksdorff (Sweden)
1964	*The Pawnbroker*	Sidney Lumet
1965	*Mirage*	Edward Dmytryk
1965	*The Slender Thread*	Sydney Pollack
1966	*Walk Don't Run*	Charles Walters
1966	*The Deadly Affair*	Sidney Lumet (UK)
1967	*Enter Laughing*	Carl Reiner
1967	*Banning* (AAN*)	Ron Winston
1967	*In the Heat of the Night*	Norman Jewison
1967	*In Cold Blood* (AAN)	Richard Brooks
1968	*A Dandy in Aspic*	Anthony Mann, Laurence Harvey (UK)
1968	*The Counterfeit Killer*	Joseph Lejtes
1968	*Jigsaw*	James Goldstone
1968	*For Love of Ivy* (AAN*)	Daniel Mann
1968	*The Hell with Heroes*	Joseph Sargent
1968	*The Split*	Gordon Flemyng
1969	*Mackenna's Gold*	J. Lee Thompson
1969	*The Italian Job*	Peter Collinson (UK)

Year	Film	Director
1969	*The Lost Man*	Robert Alan Aurthur
1969	*Bob & Carol & Ted & Alice*	Paul Mazursky
1969	*John and Mary*	Peter Yates
1969	*Cactus Flower* (GGN*)	Gene Saks
1970	*Last of the Mobile Hot Shots*	Sidney Lumet
1970	*The Out of Towners*	Arthur Hiller
1970	*They Call Me Mister Tibbs*	Gordon Douglas
1970	*Up Your Teddy Bear*	Don Joslyn
1971	*Brother John*	James Goldstone
1971	*The Anderson Tapes*	Sidney Lumet
1971	*Honky* (GGN*)	William A. Graham
1971	*$ (aka Dollars)*	Richard Brooks
1972	*The Hot Rock*	Peter Yates
1972	*The New Centurions*	Richard Fleischer
1972	*The Getaway* (GGN)	Sam Peckinpah
1985	*The Color Purple* (AAN, AA*; GGN)	Steven Spielberg

JONES, Trevor (b. 1949) An internationally successful composer for movies and television, since 1980 he has scored over fifty feature films of very diverse subjects but he is most known for his dynamic music for fantasy adventures.

He was born Trevor Alfred Charles Jones in Cape Town, South Africa, to a family involved in local theatre and movies. Jones lived across the street from a neighborhood cinema that was so poorly equipped that sometimes there was no sound during the movies played, helping the youth to understand the importance of screen music. When he was only five years old, Jones decided he wanted to become a movie composer. He attended London's Royal Academy of Music on scholarship then began his career reviewing radio and television music for the BBC. In 1974 Jones returned to school, eventually getting a graduate degree in film and media music from the University of York and pursued further study of scoring and sound from the National Film and Television School. (Years later he returned to the NFTVS as a teacher, eventually becoming chair of music.) While still studying at this last institution, Jones scored many student films, then in 1979 he wrote music for the documentary short *Brittania: The First of the Last*. Although he scored two feature films in 1980 it was his score the next year for the Oscar-winning short *The Dollar Bottom* that launched his career. Director John Boorman had a limited budget for his independent adventure film *Excalibur* and planned to use classical music throughout the movie. But he found that some scenes still needed original music so he

hired the unknown Jones, who ended up writing fifty-five minutes of music for the movie. *Excalibur* was a surprise success and Jones's work was noticed by director-puppeteer Jim Henson, who hired him to score his fantasy movie *The Dark Crystal*. He worked with Henson again on the similarly fantastical *Labyrinth*. The popularity of these two American-British works opened the door to Hollywood and for the rest of his career Jones has worked on both sides of the Atlantic as well as in his homeland of South Africa. His other notable movies include *Runaway Train*, *Angel Heart*, *Dominick and Eugene*, *Mississippi Burning*, *The Last of the Mohicans*, *In the Name of the Father*, *Richard III*, *Brassed Off*, *G.I. Jane*, *Cliffhanger*, *Lawn Dogs*, *Dark City*, *Notting Hill*, *Thirteen Days*, *From Hell*, and *Chaos*. Jones has frequently written music for television, scoring such series as *Dinotopia*, *Jozi-H*, and *Labyrinth*. Among his many TV movies and miniseries are *The Last Days of Pompeii* (1984), *The Last Place on Earth* (1985), *By Dawn's Early Light* (1990), *Gulliver's Travels* (1996), *Merlin* (1998), *Cleopatra* (1999), and *Blood and Oil* (2010). Jones has also written music for the theatre, ballet, and the concert hall where orchestral suites from his movies have been performed around the world.

Jones has a more extensive music education than most screen composers, so one might expect his film scores to favor the classical mode. But he got very interested in acoustic, electronic, and synthesized music around the time he was first hired to score films and television so most of his work is modern with traces of the classical here and there. He was competing with the classics when he was hired to write extra music for *Excalibur*. Before Jones was brought into the project, director Boorman had already chosen Carl Orff's opening of *Carmina Burana* as the theme for the sword Excalibur and had earmarked passages from Richard Wagner's *Parsifal*, *Tristan und Isolde*, and *Die Götterdämmerung* for other scenes. Boorman presents the saga of King Arthur (Nigel Terry) and his knights as a stylistic pageant on a grand opera level so such bombastic music was not out of place. Jones followed suit writing an opening theme with foreboding percussion, threatening brass, and determined strings that lead up to a stirring crescendo with horns making a bold announcement. The land of Camelot is scored with a vibrant dance theme that has primitive drums but elaborate recorders and other period instruments, all moving to an aggressive beat. The theme for the ambivalent Arthur is a powerful anthem in which the brass are warlike but the recorders and strings are serene and lyrical. Other memorable passages include a high tenor and a deep male choir chanting a harsh Kyrie Eleison, and a vivacious court dance on period instruments that is so fervent it almost seems oppressive. Jones was able to hold his own, musically speaking, and he was noticed.

His two movies with Jim Henson, *The Dark Crystal* and *Labyrinth*, are also stylistic pageants that require dynamic music. The former is a fanciful Tolkien-like saga about an orphan (a puppet voiced by Henson) who seeks to recover a lost portion of the mighty Dark Crystal in order to restore harmony on his ancient planet. Jones assembled an unusual musical ensemble that included both synthesizers and conventional orchestra, with such oddities as crumhorns, recorders, and the rare double-flageolet (an early form of recorder). The result is a score that sometimes uses high-tech methods to sound very primitive. There is a delicate and mysterious theme with high-pitched female chanting and lilting string accompaniment that returns throughout the film. The score also includes a propulsive march with full orchestra repeating a vigorous five-note phrase with determination; a racing theme with frantic strings and blaring brass; an eerie passage with oboe, recorders, and voices that is enchanting instead of frightening; and a love theme featuring recorder and piano with long flowing lines that convey a sense of wonder and discovery rather than passion. Even more high tech is the score for *Labyrinth*, a fable about a teenager (Jennifer Connelly) who must get through the enchanted labyrinth of the Goblin King Jareth (Sting) in order to rescue her little brother (Toby Froud). Singer-songwriter-actor Sting wrote and sang five songs in the movie and Jones provided a soundtrack score that is often hard rock in order to match Sting's style. The film opens with synthesized trumpet fanfares supported by crashing percussion. The theme for the labyrinth consists of echoing high-frequency sounds, electric guitar riffs, and odd percussion sounds, all of which has the feel of a unified musical piece without ever breaking into a melody. There is also a pounding heavy metal passage that has a disco beat but a New Age sound, and a hallucinatory theme with descending glissandos on the synthesizer, distant voices, and electric guitars that move into a blues mode. The theme for the heroine is somewhat less rocking. It is an up-tempo passage that moves in a lyrical but steady pace as it keeps returning to an engaging series of descending notes.

Jones often uses electronic and synthesized music in his realistic movies as well. The disturbing drama *Mississippi Burning*, about two FBI agents (Gene Hackman and Willem Dafoe) who investigate the death of three civil rights workers in a small Southern town in 1964, is filled with tension, and Jones's score is perhaps his most oppressive, a mix of jazz, blues, and high-tech musical sounds. The recurring theme has a rhythmic bass line with slow and strained notes on a synthesizer and a mournful saxophone solo that seems to wail and question as it reaches up the scale higher and higher without resolution. Some of the most sobering scenes are scored with a high-pitched chorus heard over weeping strings. Equally disturbing is the Irish drama *In the Name of the Father* about a petty thief (Daniel Day-Lewis) wrongly accused of an IRA bombing in London and his attempts to clear his name and that of his implicated father (Pete Postlethwaite). Jones's score is searing and uncompromising. In the main theme, sustained violin notes creep up the scale as rumbling percussion in the background suggests something sinister. A piano and trumpet passage, with echoing notes and electronic embellishments, repeats a simple musical phrase with a sense of weariness and despair. There is a pounding track on drums and electric guitar that is threatening and harsh, as well as a slow and ponderous theme with high-strung strings, echoing electronic chords, and a morose solo piano. A slightly lighter touch can be heard in a gliding theme with facile strings and horns, but it too has a somber subtext. Less realistic but just as uncomfortable is Richard Loncraine's unforgettable 1995 screen version of Shakespeare's *Richard III* set in 1930s Fascist Britain with a cunning performance by Ian McKellen as the diabolical title monarch. The decor is a stylized picture of the period and Jones's music is a high-tech rearrangement of prewar popular music. The film opens with a jazz band, featuring a nimble piano and confident bass, playing a breezy 1930s foxtrot for a royal gathering. The same music is then set to a paraphrase of Christopher Marlowe's poem "The Passionate Shepherd to His Love" and sung by Stacey Kent as a smooth nightclub number. This is the society that Richard loathes and sets out to destroy. The rest of the score is more electronic and chilling. There is a heavyhearted lament heard on a bluesy saxophone with agitated strings underneath that feels like danger is just around the corner. The battle scenes are scored with rapid percussion, ponderous brass, and frantic strings, all of it filtered through a synthesizer to make it all the more oppressive. *Richard III* is one of Jones's most potent scores.

Of the broad farces and romantic comedies Jones has scored, none were as popular in Britain and the States as *Notting Hill*. This inconsequential but charming tale, about a London bookshop owner (Hugh Grant) whose life is turned upside down when he meets and romances a famous Hollywood star (Julia Roberts), has a dozen popular songs on the soundtrack to make the movie sound contemporary, but the heart of the tale is in Jones's lightweight but delectable music. There is a simple and expressive theme played on two acoustic guitars that is unsentimental yet reflective and heartfelt. It suggests romance without overdoing it. Also memorable is a rhythmic folk passage featuring piano and guitars that moves in a freewheeling manner. For the more tender scenes there is a warm, romantic theme with sustained synthesized notes heard under a solo guitar. If the use of electronic music is scarce in *Notting Hill*, it pretty much disappears in the action adventure *Cliffhanger*. There are stunts and thrills a minute in this story of a professional mountain climber (Sylvester Stallone) who embarks on a perilous rescue in the Colorado Rockies to save some stranded hikers and finds himself involved in a mission of greed. The main theme is a symphonic piece with full orchestra moving with majesty through an inspiring musical phrase that seems to celebrate nature and man's quest to conquer it. This musical motif is repeated later in the film with different orchestrations, becoming intimate on strings and melancholy on horns. Much of the score is as big and grandiose as the visual panorama, though there is a quieter passage on electronic keyboard and conventional orchestra that features a solo trumpet mourning quietly.

Many would agree that Jones's finest score is the one he wrote for the 1992 version of *The Last of the Mohicans*. Unfortunately there is much confusion and misunderstanding over just who wrote what in this splendid score which, surprisingly, sounds like the work of one composer. Jones was hired by director Michael Mann to score the oft-filmed novel by James Fenimore Cooper. The large and complicated production went over budget and cutting the three-hour rough cut forced the studio to delay the release of the movie a few months. Either because Jones had to move on to another project or wanted to get out of the messy situation, composer Randy Edelman was hired to finish the score. How much of Edelman's music is in the final score has been debated but most likely he contributed about a quarter of the music. The fact that Jones's and Edelman's portions are not distinguishable attests to the unity of the score for *The Last of the Mohicans*. Jones's brooding main theme has low brass and rambunctious drums that explode into a slow and fervent horn and string melody with a fatalistic tone. He also wrote a brisk folk theme on strings (performed by the esteemed Scottish fiddler Alasdair Fraser) that moves like a festive dance; an action theme with restless violins and sustained brass for chase and hunting scenes; an expansive nature track in which a rhythmic guitar is backed by a full orchestra; battle scenes scored with pounding percussion, furious strings, and ominous brass that climb the scale with a purpose; and a graceful love theme featuring pipes playing a simple folk melody. The film ends on a haunting note as a solo female chants a slow dirge over a muted but vigorous percussion. Both Jones and Edelman received composer credit for *The Last of the Mohicans* and shared in the praise and awards the score received. It was a highpoint in Jones's career but just one of many. He has written so much outstanding music for the screen that his contribution cannot be measured by one movie. Official website: www.trevorjonesfilmmusic.com.

Credits

(* for Best Song)

Year	Film	Director
1980	Brothers and Sisters	Richard Woolley (UK)
1980	The Beneficiary	Carlo Gebler (UK)
1981	Excalibur (aka The Knights)	John Boorman (USA/UK)
1981	The Appointment	Lindsey C. Vickers (UK)
1982	The Sender	Roger Christian (UK)
1982	The Dark Crystal	Jim Henson, Frank Oz (USA/UK)
1983	Nate and Hayes (aka Savage Islands)	Ferdinand Fairfax (USA/New Zealand)
1985	Runaway Train	Andrey Konchalovskiy (USA)
1986	Labyrinth	Jim Henson (UK/USA)
1987	Angel Heart	Alan Parker (USA/Canada/UK)
1988	Dominick and Eugene	Robert M. Young (USA)
1988	Diamond's Edge (aka Just Ask for Diamond)	Stephen Bayly
1988	Mississippi Burning (BAFTA-N)	Alan Parker (USA)
1988	Sweet Lies	Nathalie Delon (France/USA)
1989	Sea of Love	Harold Becker (USA)
1990	Bad Influence	Curtis Hanson (USA)
1990	Arachnophobia	Frank Marshall (USA/Venezuela)
1991	True Colors	Herbert Ross (USA)
1991	Chains of Gold	Rod Holcomb (USA)
1992	Freejack	Geoff Murphy (USA)
1992	Blame It on the Bellboy	Mark Herman (UK/USA)
1992	CrissCross	Chris Menges (USA)
1992	The Last of the Mohicans (GGN; BAFTA-N)	Michael Mann (USA)
1993	Cliffhanger	Renny Harlin (Italy/France/USA)
1993	In the Name of the Father	Jom Sheridan (Ireland/UK/USA)
1995	Hideaway	Brett Leonard (USA)
1995	Kiss of Death	Barbet Schroeder (USA)
1995	Richard III	Richard Loncraine (UK/USA)
1996	Loch Ness	John Henderson (UK/USA)
1996	Brassed Off (BAFTA-N)	Mark Herman (UK/USA)
1997	Roseanna's Grave (aka For Roseanna)	Paul Welland (USA/Italy)
1997	G.I. Jane (aka A Matter of Honor)	Ridley Scott (USA/UK)
1997	Lawn Dogs	John Duigan (UK)
1998	Desperate Measures	Barbet Schroeder (USA)
1998	Dark City	Alex Proyas (Australia/USA)
1998	The Mighty (aka Freak the Mighty) (GGN*)	Peter Chelsom (USA)
1998	Titanic Town	Roger Michell (UK)
1998	Talk of Angels	Nick Hamm (USA)
1999	Notting Hill	Roger Michell (UK/USA)
1999	Molly (aka Rescue Me)	John Duigan (USA)
2000	Thirteen Days	Roger Donaldson (USA)
2001	The Long Run	Jean Stewart (So. Africa)
2001	From Hell (aka Jack)	Albert and Allen Hughes (USA)
2002	Crossroads (aka Not a Girl)	Tamra Davis (USA)
2003	I'll Be There (aka The Family Business)	Craig Ferguson (USA/UK)
2003	The League of Extraordinary Gentlemen	Stephen Norrington (USA/Germany/ Czech Republic/ UK)
2004	Around the World Days	Frank Coraci (USA/Germany/Ireland/UK)
2005	Aegis	Junji Sakamoto (Japan)
2005	Chaos	Tony Giglio (Canada/UK/USA)
2006	Fields of Freedom	David de Vries (USA)
2008	A Deal Is a Deal	Jonathan Gershfield (UK)
2011	How to Steal 2 Million	Charlie Vundla (So. Africa)
2014	To Tokyo	Caspar Seale Jones (UK)

KACZMAREK, Jan A. P. (b. 1953) A Polish-born, internationally recognized composer for the theatre, concert hall, television, and movies, he has scored over thirty feature films for ten different countries.

Born Jan Andrzej Pawel Kaczmarek in Konin, Poland, although he studied music from the time he was a child, he pursued a law degree at Adam Mickiewicz University in Poznan with the hopes of someday becoming a diplomat. In the late 1970s Kaczmarek became disillusioned with world politics and became interested in theatre, specifically Jerzy Grotowski's experimental Theatre Laboratory. He wrote music for theatre productions and for small recording ensembles. His 1977 work *Orchestra of the Eighth Day* found success in Poland then toured throughout Europe, bringing attention to both Kaczmarek and his music. Kaczmarek's tour took him to the United States in 1982 and while there he recorded his *Music for the End* album for Flying Fish Records. Also while in America, he wrote music for different theatre companies in Chicago, Los Angeles, and New York, winning awards for his efforts. Kaczmarek began his television career in 1984 when he scored a TV movie for Polish television. Two years later he wrote the music for his first feature film, the Polish drama *Playing the Blind*, and in 1990 he scored the Hong Kong–American thriller *Pale Blood*, getting the attention of Hollywood. Over the decades Kaczmarek has worked on all kinds of movies, from intimate character dramas to biblical epics, although very few of his films are well known in the States. His only major international success is the biographical *Finding Neverland* but Kaczmarek has scored many other reputable movies, including *Gospel according to Harry*, *Total Eclipse*, *Washington Square*, *Aimee & Jaguar*, *The Third Miracle*, *Unfaithful*, *The Visitor*, *Evening*, *The Karamazov Brothers*, *City Island*, *Hachi: A Dog's Tale*, *Get Low*, and *Inbetween Worlds*. He has also scored documentaries and many TV movies, including a popular European miniseries based on *War and Peace* (2007). Among Kaczmarek's concert works are *Cantata for Freedom* in 2005 to commemorate the twenty-fifth anniversary of the Solidarity movement in Poland, and *Oratorio 1956* (2006) to honor the Polish uprising against the Communist government fifty years earlier. Inspired by the Sundance Institute that Robert Redford set up in America in the 1980s, Kaczmarek spent years setting up a similar arts organization in Poland. Named the Rozbitek Institute, it finally opened in 2010. He also founded the Poznan International Film and Music Festival in 2011.

Since *Finding Neverland* is the only movie Kaczmarek scored that found wide recognition, it is appropriate that its superb music is a good representation of his talents. The mostly accurate movie chronicles how playwright James M. Barrie (Johnny Depp) befriended the Llewelyn family and wrote *Peter Pan* using the son Peter (Freddie Highmore) as his inspiration for the youth who never grows old. Kaczmarek's music is not slavishly Victorian but suggests a classical tone as it uses a small musical ensemble with an intimate sound. The Llewelyn boys are scored with a twinkling, spirited piano theme that has a playful tone as it jumps about the scale like fairies flying about. A fully orchestrated version of this music is heard when the play *Peter Pan* is eventually staged in London. Barrie's Neverland has its own theme as he and the children enter it in their playing and in his imagination. It is a solemn adagio heard on a primitive flute as sustained strings play underneath; the piece gains in intensity when a full orchestra is added and a mandolin is featured. The fragile theme for the shy Peter is a tentative passage with a reluctant piano melody and caressing strings. Everyday events become magical with Kaczmarek's music. A trip to the park is scored with a graceful and melodic theme featuring reeds in an elegant dance. And a kite-flying sequence has hesitant music at first, but as the kite takes to the wind the orchestra is added and the music becomes expansive and free flowing. There is also delightful music for the children playing pirates with Barrie: a merry march featuring accordion and oboes with cymbals for the sword fighting. The piano soloist throughout the soundtrack is Leszek Mozdzer who, during the recording sessions, improvised on one of Kaczmarek's themes. The music was so intoxicating that the track was retained and played under the final credits. Kaczmarek's wonderful score for *Finding Neverland* won the Oscar, and he was rightfully recognized by Hollywood even if his other movies were not.

While the music in his other scores tends to be in the style of romanticism, each score embraces different forms as needed. The offbeat drama *Get Low*, set in rural Tennessee in the 1930s, uses American folk music. This tale, about an eccentric old hermit (Robert Duvall) who decides to hold his own funeral while he is still alive, is scored with both authentic and electronic instruments. The main theme is a slow country tune played on a synthesizer with lingering notes and the sound of wind rushing through the music. A solo fiddle is featured in a morose passage with heavy percussive chords; even when the melody is picked up by an oboe and strings, the piece maintains its reflective tempo. There is also a lively tune played on guitar and horns, another on banjo and Jew's harp, and a very timid piano track that sounds like a delicate but hesitant sunrise. The character drama *Evening* is set in the present and the past as an old woman (Vanessa Redgrave) tells her daughters (Natasha Richardson and Toni Collette) about a love affair in the 1950s. Kaczmarek's recurring motif is a reflective theme in which a harp, piano, violin, oboe, and a female voice are each featured as strings gracefully descend the scale then manage to find new life as they climb back up. There is an animated piano and violin passage that moves forward elegantly but with a purpose, and a sunny jazz track on piano with a sprightly tempo and a gleeful sense of freedom. *Unfaithful* is a contemporary drama, but the score is still romantic in a classical mode. The story of a married couple (Diane Lane and Richard Gere) whose marriage is torn apart by her infidelity is scored with a melancholy piano and harp piece with a moody yet not depressing tone; strings are added without destroying the fragile nature of the piece. Less glum is a romantic theme played on an accordion and strings which is unsentimental in its simple and forthright manner. Kaczmarek wrote three art songs as well as the soundtrack score for *Washington Square*, a movie based on Henry James's novel (previously filmed as *The Heiress* in 1949). The shy spinster Catherine (Jennifer Jason Leigh) in nineteenth-century New York City is wooed by the handsome Morris (Ben Chapin) over the objections of her stern father (Albert Finney) who believes the suitor is only after her money. The score is accurate to the period, including the light-opera Italian song "Tu chiami una vita" (lyric by Salvatore Quasimodo) which Catherine and Morris play and sing at the piano. The main theme, a very hesitant lament, is heard on solo violin and piano at different points in the movie. There is also a theme for Catherine that is a lovely and emotive nocturne with a melancholy subtext. The film ends with a mournful opera-like aria "L'absence" (lyric by Théophile Gautier) sung with heartbreaking clarity by Marissa Anna Muro on the soundtrack. Kaczmarek continues to write exceptional music for the screen. Let us hope another one of his films becomes successful enough that the public will be reminded of his considerable composition talents. Official website: www.jan-ap-kaczmarek.com.

Credits

Year	Film	Director
1986	*Playing the Blind*	Dominik Wieczorkowski-Rettinger (Poland)
1990	*Pale Blood*	V. V. Dachin Hsu, Michael W. Leighton (Hong Kong/USA)
1992	*White Marriage*	Magdalena Lazarkiewicz (Poland)
1993	*Doppelganger* (aka *The Evil Within*)	Avi Nesher (USA)
1994	*Gospel according to Harry* (aka *Waiting for Halley's Comet*)	Lech Majewski (Poland/USA)
1995	*Felony*	David A. Prior (USA)
1995	*Total Eclipse*	Agnieszka Holland (UK/France/Belgium)
1996	*Dead Girl*	Adam Coleman Howard (USA)
1997	*Bliss*	Lance Young (Canada/USA)
1997	*Washington Square*	Agnieszka Holland (USA)
1999	*Aimee & Jaguar*	Max Färberböck (Germany)
1999	*The Third Miracle*	Agnieszka Holland (USA)
2000	*Lost Souls*	Janusz Kaminski (USA)
2001	*Quo Vadis*	Jerzy Kawalerowicz (Poland/USA)
2001	*Edges of the Lord*	Yurek Bogayevicz (USA/Poland)

Year	Film	Director
2002	*Unfaithful*	Adrian Lyne (USA/Germany/France)
2004	*Finding Neverland* (AA; GGN; BAFTA-N)	Marc Forster (USA/UK)
2006	*Who Never Lived*	Andrzej Seweryn (Poland)
2007	*Evening*	Lajos Koltai (USA/Germany)
2007	*The Visitor*	Thomas McCarthy (USA)
2007	*Hamia*	Janusz Kaminski (Poland)
2008	*The Karamazov Brothers*	Petr Zelenka (Czech Republic/Poland)
2008	*Passchendaele*	Paul Gross (Canada)
2009	*Horsemen*	Jonas Akerlund (USA)
2009	*City Island*	Raymond De Felitta (USA)
2009	*Hachi: A Dog's Tale*	Lasse Hallström (USA/UK)
2009	*Get Low*	Aaron Schneider (USA/Germany/Poland)
2010	*Leonie*	Hisako Matsui (France/USA/Japan/UK)
2010	*The Officer's Wife* (aka *Goats Hill*)	Piotr Uzarowicz (USA)
2012	*The Time Being*	Nenad Cicin-Sain (USA)
2013	*1939 Battle of Westerplatte*	Pawel Chochlew (Lithuania/Poland)
2013	*Joanna*	Aneta Kopacz (Poland)
2014	*Inbetween Worlds*	Feo Aladag (Germany)

KAMEN, Michael (1948–2003) A very successful musician, arranger, conductor, songwriter, and composer for ballet, rock albums, television, and movies, he scored sixty-five feature films of a wide variety but is most known for his action thrillers, including three *Die Hard* and four *Lethal Weapon* movies.

Michael Arnold Kamen was born in New York City, the son of a dentist and a schoolteacher, and was interested in all kinds of music as a youth. Kamen attended Manhattan's High School of Music and Art and then Juilliard School of Music. While a student at the latter, he studied the oboe and formed his own group, the New York Rock & Roll Ensemble, which played everything from hard rock to classical oboe duets. Kamen began his composing career writing music for ballet then did a complete about-face and worked as an arranger and keyboardist for rock bands and singers, including Aerosmith, Roger Daltrey, Bon Jovi, Eric Clapton, Queen, Tom Petty, Janis Ian, Rush, Bob Dylan, Metallica, Jim Croce, Sting, and David Bowie. Perhaps his two most important works in pop-rock music are the arrangements for Pink Floyd's *The Wall* and Kate Bush's *The Red Shoes* album. Even as Kamen was involved in the rock scene, he composed more ballets and works for the concert hall, including concertos for saxophone and for electric guitar. He also gained a high reputation as a conductor of both rock ensembles and symphony orchestras.

Kamen's first association with movies was in 1971 when his college group New York Rock & Roll Ensemble played a number on the soundtrack for the comic rock western *Zachariah*. He played the synthesizer on the soundtrack of *Godspell* (1973) before writing the score for the dance short *Rodin mis en vie* in 1976. That same year he composed the music for his first feature film, the action thriller *The Next Man*. During the next ten years he scored such offbeat and/or cult movies as *Between the Lines*, *Polyester*, *Highlander*, *Brazil*, and *Mona Lisa* before finding fame for his score for the action hit *Lethal Weapon* in 1987. Other similar thrillers followed, including the sequels to *Lethal Weapon*, *Die Hard* and its sequels, *License to Kill*, *Hudson Hawk*, *Last Action Hero*, and *X-Men*. While these movies got the most attention, Kamen was praised for his scores for a variety of other films ranging from period pieces, like *Robin Hood: Prince of Thieves* and *The Three Musketeers*, to contemporary dramas, as with *Don Juan DeMarco* and *Mr. Holland's Opus*. Among his many other notable movies are *The Dead Zone*, *Adventures in Babysitting*, *For Queen & Country*, *The Adventures of Baron Munchausen*, *The Last Boy Scout*, *Circle of Friends*, *Stonewall*, *The Winter Guest*, *The Iron Giant*, *Open Range*, and *What Dreams May Come*. Kamen's television credits include some TV movies and miniseries, most memorably *Liza's Pioneer Diary* (1976), *Edge of Darkness* (1985), *From the Earth to the Moon* (1998), and *Band of Brothers* (2001). After the success of *Mr. Holland's Opus*, he founded the Mr. Holland's Opus Foundation in 1996 that provides new and refurbished musical instruments for school and community music programs in need. Kamen was also one of the cofounders in 2002 of the Music Education Consortium in Great Britain, which provides funds for music programs in schools. Although he was diagnosed with multiple sclerosis in 1997, Kamen remained active writing, conducting, and performing until his death six years later from a heart attack at the age of fifty-five.

Although Kamen's career really took off with *Lethal Weapon*, that score was written with guitarist Eric Clapton, as were the other three movies in the series, with an assist by saxophone artist David Sanborn. It was in the third outing of the mismatched cops (Mel Gibson and Danny Glover) that the trio wrote their most dynamic score. Once again Clapton provides the guitar sound for Gibson's character while Sanborn's saxophone musicalized Glover's character. The bluesy saxophone and trumpet theme from the first film is heard again and there is plenty of new music, including a cool jazz love theme that became the hit song "It's Probably Me" sung by Sting who also wrote the lyric. Kamen worked alone on the score for *Die Hard*, the popular action film about a cop (Bruce Willis) out to rescue his wife and others who have been taken hostage by a terrorist (Alan Rickman). Interestingly for an action movie, the score is mostly quiet and seething rather than explosive. There is a slightly echoing guitar theme with tentative strings and horns that has a casual air but a moody subtext. Nervous strings and quirky horns are heard in a suspense theme that takes its time before gathering speed and volume, while a ponderous organ and strings passage slowly moves forward with caution. The action scenes are scored with frantic percussion and rapid horn glissandos, while the gripping assault on a tower is accompanied by a march with barking horns, uneven percussion, and menacing strings that change tempo as they push ahead with stealthy purpose. Kamen scored so many action thrillers that one marvels at his ability to find something fresh with each outing.

Most musicologists find Kamen's nonaction scores more interesting. The period adventure *Robin Hood: Prince of Thieves*, with Kevin Costner as a rather modern and very American bandit-hero, met with mixed reactions from critics and audiences, but there was little disagreement over Kamen's splendid score. A gentle French horn, harp, and string theme floats up and down the scale with a serene tone and a touch of a medieval flavor. There are horn fanfares with low strings and drums that march ahead with pomp and confidence, and a growling passage in which various strings wearily climb the scale where they are met by expressive harp chords and a horn melody that trips along casually. Most memorable is the entrancing love theme, at first played on solo horn and flute, which flows so smoothly that it hardly seems to rise and fall as it sweeps forward. This melody was used for the Oscar-nominated pop ballad "(Everything I Do) I Do It for You" by Kamen, Robert John Lange, and Bryan Adams and sung by Adams over the closing credits. A song from *Don Juan DeMarco* was also nominated for an Academy Award, this time the Spanish-flavored ballad "Have You Ever Really Loved a Woman?" written by the same three men. It is a rhythmic, romantic piece, sung three times in the movie (twice in Spanish), that takes its time but is still full of life. *Don Juan DeMarco* is an odd romantic drama about a suicidal young man (Johnny Depp), who believes he is the fabled Spanish lover Don Juan, and the psychiatrist (Marlon Brando) who attempts to cure him. The Latin-influenced score includes a playful, expressive habanera, heard on precise strings and bouncy reeds, that doesn't take itself too seriously; a vivacious Latin dance on bubbly violins and Spanish percussion with female chanting accents; and a casual guitar and violin passage that skips along with a cheery disposition.

Kamen's most ambitious and arguably best score is the extensive one he wrote for *Mr. Holland's Opus*, a drama about a failed composer (Richard Dreyfuss) who has taught music in high school for thirty years. During that time he has struggled to complete a full symphony and the movie climaxes with the school's former and present musicians performing his "American Symphony." Kamen wrote the eight-minute symphonic work before the movie was filmed then composed various themes for different characters and scenes. The movie overflows with music, everything from selections by Bach and Beethoven to pop-rock songs by John Lennon and Stevie Wonder to Tin Pan Alley standards by Sigmund Romberg and the Gershwins. Kamen wrote the ballad "Cole's Song" (lyric by Julian Lennon and Justin Clayton) which was sung by Lennon, as well as "Rowena's Theme," an unfinished song that is a clarinet lament that lingers over each note so that it barely seems to be moving. It is later heard in its complete form as a cello piece. But the musical highlight of *Mr. Holland's Opus* is the "American Symphony," a piece of romanticism with touches of rock that includes bits and pieces of music heard previously in the film. In fact, the symphony is a musical montage of Mr. Holland's life. The symphony includes tentative sections on strings and reeds, a rumbling and agitated movement heavy on percussion and brass, a delicate and lyrical theme featuring a solo clarinet, and a bombastic allegro that seems to be racing to the finish line. Few movies are as musically and thematically united as *Mr. Holland's Opus*.

Two very bizarre films directed by Terry Gilliam opened up interesting and new opportunities for Kamen. *Brazil* is a surreal sci-fi comedy-drama about a mousy bureaucrat (Jonathan Pryce) in a high-tech future world who rebels against the system with tragic results. The film has nothing to do with the South American country of the title but the popular samba song "Brazil" by Ary Barroso is used throughout the movie as a leitmotif. Kamen arranged and conducted the various versions of the song, heard on electric guitar with whistling accompaniment in one scene, another time set to the clicking of typewriters, played by a sultry saxophone on a different track, and sung by Geoff and Maria Muldaur during a dream sequence in which the hero flies away to freedom. Kamen's original music for *Brazil* includes a breezy foxtrot theme on reeds that suggests a 1930s jazz nightclub, a patriotic march on electric organ with a wry subtext, and a waltzing passage in double time that sounds frantic and confused.

While *Brazil* immediately became a cult favorite, the cockeyed epic *The Adventures of Baron Munchausen* was an expensive box office failure whose sense of satire and stylized spectacle was not for all tastes. The eighteenth-century aristocrat Baron von Munchausen (John Neville) and his misfit companions get caught up in wars, are swallowed by a giant sea monster, dally with Venus (Uma Thurman), visit the moon and the inside of a volcano, and outwit the Grim Reaper himself. Kamen scores this fantastical romp with lively and sardonic music. There is a joyous orchestral parade that swirls and marches up and down the scale with glee; a furious gavotte played on a giddy violin and buffoonish oboe; a silly march played on pizzicato strings and high reeds with brass instruments that seem to be laughing at themselves; a theme for Venus, played on harpsichord, harp, and clarinet, which is an elegant but gushing minuet that turns into a lush waltz when a full orchestra is added; and a triumphal march on blaring brass, busy strings, and vigorous percussion that cannot be taken seriously. It is difficult to believe that this is the same composer who scored all those *Lethal Weapon* movies. What a diverse talent for composition Kamen had, and how fortunate that he found time in his busy career to score so many movies. Official website: www. michaelkamen.com.

Credits

(all films USA unless stated otherwise; * for Best Song)

Year	Film	Director
1976	*The Next Man*	Richard C. Sarafian
1977	*Between the Lines*	Joan Micklin Silver
1977	*Stunts*	Mark L. Lester
1979	*S+H+E: Security Hazards Expert*	Robert Michael Lewis (W. Germany/USA)
1981	*Polyester*	John Waters
1981	*Venom*	Piers Haggard, Tobe Hooper (UK)
1983	*Angelo My Love*	Robert Duvall
1983	*The Dead Zone*	David Cronenberg
1985	*Brazil*	Terry Gilliam (UK)
1986	*Highlander*	Russell Mulcahy (UK)
1986	*Mona Lisa*	Neil Jordan (UK)
1986	*Shanghai Surprise*	Jim Goddard (UK)
1987	*Lethal Weapon*	Richard Donner
1987	*Rita, Sue and Bob, Too!*	Alan Clarke (UK)
1987	*Adventures in Babysitting*	Chris Columbus
1987	*Someone to Watch Over Me*	Ridley Scott
1987	*Suspect*	Peter Yates
1988	*Action Jackson*	Craig R. Baxley
1988	*For Queen & Country*	Martin Stellman (UK/USA)

Year	Film	Director
1988	Crusoe	Caleb Deschanel (UK/USA)
1988	Die Hard	John McTiernan
1988	Homeboy	Michael Seresin
1988	The Raggedy Rawney	Bob Hoskins (UK)
1988	The Adventures of Baron Munchausen	Terry Gilliam (UK/Italy)
1989	Rooftops	Robert Wise
1989	Road House	Rowdy Herrington
1989	Renegades (aka Lakota)	Jack Sholder
1989	License to Kill	John Glen (UK/USA)
1989	Lethal Weapon 2	Richard Donner
1990	The Krays	Peter Medak (UK)
1990	Die Hard 2	Renny Harlin
1990	Cold Dog Soup	Alan Metter (UK)
1991	Nothing But Trouble (aka Git)	Dan Aykroyd
1991	Hudson Hawk	Michael Lehmann
1991	Robin Hood: Prince of Thieves (AAN*; GGN; GGN*)	Kevin Reynolds
1991	Company Business (aka Dinosaurs)	Nicholas Meyer
1991	Let Him Have It	Peter Medak (France/UK)
1991	The Last Boy Scout	Tony Scott
1992	Shining Through	David Seltzer (USA/UK)
1992	Lethal Weapon 3	Richard Donner
1992	Blue Ice	Russell Mulcahy (UK/USA)
1993	Splitting Heirs	Robert Young (UK)
1993	Last Action Hero (aka Extremely Violent)	John McTiernan
1993	Wilder Napalm	Glenn Gordon Caron
1993	The Three Musketeers	Stephen Herek (Austria/UK/USA)
1994	Don Juan DeMarco (AAN*; GGN; GG*)	Jeremy Leven
1995	Circle of Friends	Pat O'Connor (Ireland/USA/UK)
1995	Die Hard: With a Vengeance	John McTiernan
1995	Stonewall	Nigel Finch (UK/USA)
1995	Mr. Holland's Opus	Stephen Herek
1996	Jack	Francis Ford Coppola
1996	101 Dalmatians	Stephen Herek
1997	Inventing the Abbotts	Pat O'Connor
1997	Remember Me?	Nick Hurran (UK)
1997	Event Horizon (aka The Stars My Destination)	Paul W. S. Anderson (UK/USA)
1997	The Winter Guest	Alan Rickman (UK/USA)
1998	Lethal Weapon 4	Richard Donner
1998	What Dreams May Come	Vincent Ward (USA/New Zealand)
1999	The Iron Giant	Brads Bird
2000	Frequency	Gregory Hoblit
2000	X-Men	Bryan Singer
2003	Open Range	Kevin Costner
2004	Against the Ropes (aka The Jackie Kallen Story)	Charles S. Dutton (USA/Germany)
2004	Boo, Zino & the Snurks (aka Back to Gaya)	Lenard Fritz Krawinkel, Holger Tappe (Germany/Spain)
2004	First Daughter	Forest Whitaker

KAPER, Bronislau (1902–1983) A Polish-born composer and songwriter who began his career in Europe, he quickly established himself in Hollywood for his songs and then for his scores.

Born Bronislaw Kaper in Warsaw, Poland, he played the piano by ear as a boy. Even though he was accepted at the Warsaw Conservatory where he studied composition and piano, he pursued a degree in law at Warsaw University to please his father. After graduation he went to Berlin where he became involved with the cabaret scene and the German film industry. Kaper befriended the young Austrian composer Walter Jurmann and the two began to score German and Austrian movies, sometimes together, other times as solo composers. The rise of the Nazi Party prompted Kaper and Jurmann to go to Paris where they soon found work through other émigrés in France. The music from one of Kaper's French films was turned into the hit song "Ninon" which was soon being played all over Europe. Hollywood producer Louis B. Mayer, who was vacationing in Europe, heard the catchy song everywhere he went. He inquired as to the composer, arranged to meet him in Paris, and offered him a contract at MGM. Both Kaper and Jurmann arrived in Hollywood in 1935 and soon found recognition writing the ditty "Cosi-Cosa" (lyric by Ned Washington) for the Marx Brothers' *A Night at the Opera*. The two composers' first movie score in America was *Escapade*, which also included a song, "You're All I Need" (lyric by Gus Kahn and Harold Adamson). Soon Kaper was scoring films on his own but often teamed with Jurmann for songs either in his or other artists' movies.

Kaper's most productive years in Hollywood were between 1941 and 1965. His score for the thriller *Gaslight* in 1944 put him in the top rank of Hollywood composers. Kaper remained at MGM until the early 1960s, working with a variety of top directors and scoring such notable films as *The Stranger*, *Our Vines Have Tender Grapes*, *A Yank at Eton*, *White Cargo*, *Mrs. Parkington*, *Green Dolphin Street*, *The Secret Garden*, *The Red Badge of Courage*, *Lili*, *Them!*, *The Swan*, *Green Mansions*, *Auntie Mame*, *The Brothers Karamazov*, *BUtterfield 8*, *Lord Jim*, and the 1962 remake of *Mutiny on the Bounty*. He also wrote many songs for movies he did not score, such as "All God's Chillun Got Rhythm" for *A Day at the Races* (1937), "While My Lady Sleeps" for *The Chocolate Soldier* (1941), "My Heart Is Singing" for *Three Smart Girls* (1936), "The One I Love" from *Everybody Sing* (1938), and the title number for *San Francisco* (1936). Kaper adapted Chopin's music for the Broadway operetta *Polonaise* (1945) and near the end of his career he also wrote for television, most memorably the theme for *The F.B.I.* When the studio system fell apart in the 1960s, Kaper started to lose interest in movies and retired in 1968, returning only once four years later to score the thriller *The Salzburg Connection*. He remained in Hollywood and was very active on the board of the Los Angeles Philharmonic. After Kaper's death from cancer at the age of eighty-one, the Philharmonic created the Bronislau Kaper Awards for Young Artists, honoring not film composers but piano and string musicians.

Unlike many of his fellow screen composers, Kaper did not conduct his scores at the recording sessions yet he used his expert piano skills to coach the studio musical director. These conductors were often astonished at Kaper's ability to capture the rhythm of filmed scenes in his music, whether it was filled with dialogue, as in much of *Auntie Mame*, or unspoken, as in lengthy sections of *The Red Badge of Courage*. His other strength was melody, one of the reasons so many memorable songs have come from his scores. Ironically, he wrote few musicals for Hollywood. *Lili* is categorized as a musical even though it has only one song but plenty of dance music. The waltz ditty "Hi-Lili, Hi-Lo" (lyric by Helen Deutsch) is embarrassingly simple and unforgettable, especially as sung by a French waif (Leslie Caron) and some puppets, but Kaper expands on the tune in the movie's imaginative dream sequence, finding many variations in the little piece. There is another enchanting song, "Take My Love" (lyric also by Deutsch), in another Caron movie, *The Glass Slipper*, a charming version of the Cinderella tale which, although it too has only one song, feels very much like a musical. Again Kaper plays with variations of the ballad in other parts of the score. Both movies, though pure Hollywood products, have the look, tone, and sound of a European film. That can also be said for a very different Kaper project, *The Brothers Karamazov*. The Dostoyevsky tale interested the Eastern European Kaper, and he filled the score with Russian folk songs, gypsy dances, and some Prokofiev-like symphonics. The main title theme is extraordinarily harsh, which also gives this movie a very European feel. The gentle period comedy *The Swan*, a romance set in a fictional European duchy, is possibly the antithesis of the Karamazov tale. Kaper wrote a delectable if understated score that has a fairy-tale quality to it. Near the end of Kaper's career he again explored a very Continental sound for the farce *A Flea in Her Ear*. This unsuccessful screen adaptation of a French farce overflows with Offenbach-like music, from giddy waltzes to vibrant bistro music to a silly march.

Kaper enjoyed the exotic, and movies set in faraway lands held a fascination for him. When the Brazilian composer Heitor Villa-Lobos scored the jungle fantasy *Green Mansions* there were many problems, mostly a result of the famed South American's inexperience with screen music. He left the project and Kaper was hired to write a new one, but he insisted on using some of the Villa-Lobos music. The film is an awkward thing but the music is entrancing. It is next to impossible to pick out what is Kaper and what is Villa-Lobos, though the dreamy title song (lyric by Paul Francis Webster) is pure Kaper. Another movie that is awkward, if not a little ridiculous, is the 1962 remake of *Mutiny on the Bounty* but again the Kaper score is exceptional. The main theme and the music for the scenes aboard the ship are very Western and very grandiose. Although there is nothing very dramatic about the *Bounty* setting sail from England, Kaper's music turns the departure into a thrilling event. When the story reaches Tahiti, Kaper's music embraces the exotic. Tribal drums, primitive horns, native chanting, and a flowing love theme take over and the beautiful location cinematography is matched by Kaper's delectable music. Titled "Follow Me" or "Love Song from *Mutiny on the Bounty*," the song version (lyric by Webster) became an unlikely hit. Kaper returned to that exotic part of the world for *Lord Jim*. Again the music is very Western at first as the brass instruments blare and the strings splash in time with the sea. But once the British captain Jim (Peter O'Toole) is among the people of Southeast Asia, the score includes Javanese gamelan instruments that clink and clank and compete with the symphonic orchestra.

The historic melodrama *Green Dolphin Street* is one of Kaper's more romantic scores. The story featured a massive earthquake, which he scored in an unusual way. The music leading up to the eruption is filled with tension, but once the quake hits there is no music. As the rumbling subsides, the music quietly enters again. The mellow love theme from the film became a popular song under the title "On Green Dolphin Street" (lyric by Washington). In the 1950s it became a favorite of Miles Davis and other jazz artists who liked Kaper's musical phrases, ripe for improvisation. Another Kaper song to find a home with jazz musicians is the haunting "Invitation." The music was first heard as part of Kaper's score for the Lana Turner melodrama *A Life of Her Own* in 1952. Two years later he reused it in another melodrama, *Invitation*. This time it caught on as an instrumental single.

Four Kaper scores that eschew the exotic and capture an American sound should be mentioned. The fine Civil War film *The Red Badge of Courage* uses music not so much to tell the story as to relate the emotions that the young hero (Audie Murphy) is experiencing. The percussive sounds of military drills and battle may surround the youth, but his own thoughts often override them, such as a banjo tune as he writes a letter home. The music is often chaotic and choppy, just as the soldier is confused and bewildered. It took years for John Huston's screen version of the classic novel to be appreciated and along with it Kaper's score. Orson Welles's World War II home-front melodrama *The Stranger* relies on Kaper's music to break through the domestic surface and suggest the sinister underneath. A Nazi criminal (Welles) takes on a new identity and lives in a small American town. He is very effective in fooling everyone but the score tells us that he is an impostor. The climactic scene in which Welles is killed by a clock figure is scored with robust music that matches the macabre finale. The 1960 melodrama *BUtterfield 8*, with Elizabeth Taylor as the immoral heroine, has a very contemporary score by Kaper that sometimes moves into cool jazz and blues. The opening minutes of the movie, in which Taylor wakes up alone in a man's apartment, gets dressed, and realizes she has been mistaken as a call girl, has no dialogue. It is Kaper's music that conveys her shifting moods, every move accented with the appropriate tone. Scores for comedies are tricky because dialogue is often so tightly packed that music just gets in the way. Yet Kaper came up with a sparkling score for *Auntie Mame*, a very talky comedy indeed. The fast-talking Mame (Rosalind Russell) is over the top and the temptation to give her a silly theme must have been great. But Kaper wrote a regal waltz for her theme, suggesting the splendid way she sees herself. The music is still comic as the piano races up and down the keyboard and the strings sway elegantly. This theme returns throughout the movie, although in altered forms. For the film's most farcical scene, the fox hunt at a Southern plantation, Kaper departs from the waltz and provides a delightful pastiche of rural chase music.

It is interesting that Kaper, unlike his fellow émigrés from Europe, did not compose for the concert stage, ballet, or opera. Writing music for the movies was satisfying enough for him. He was very practical about composing for Hollywood and did not complain about how little attention movie composers and their music received. Kaper argued that music in a dark cinema has a subliminal power and need not be noticed and applauded. He was also very apt to talk a director out of using too much music in a film. It was not that he felt screen music was unimportant but he had a very real grasp of the essence of his art form.

Credits

(all films USA unless stated otherwise; * for Best Song)

Year	Film	Director
1930	Alraune	Richard Oswald (Germany)
1930	Laubenkolonie	Max Obal (Germany/Netherlands)
1931	Her Majesty Love	Rudolph Bernauer, Adolf Lantz (Germany)
1931	His Highness Love	Robert Péguy, Erich Schmidt (Germany)
1931	Marriage with Limited Liability	Franz Wenzler (Germany/Austria)
1932	The Man Who Doesn't Know to Say No	Heinz Hilpert (Germany)
1932	Things Are Getting Better Already	Kurt Gerron (Germany)
1932	Skandal in der Parkstrasse	Franz Wenzler (Germany)
1932	Right to Happiness	Georg Jacoby (Germany)
1932	Ein Toller Einfall	Kurt Gerron (Germany)
1932	Schuss im Morgengrauen	Alfred Zeisler (Germany)
1932	Three on a Honeymoon	Erich Schmidt, Joe May (Austria)
1933	Mariage à responsabilité limitée	Jean de Limur (France)
1933	Honeymoon Trip	Germain Fried, Joe May (France/Austria)
1933	I Will Teach You to Love	Heinz Hilpert (Germany)
1933	A Song for You	Joe May (Germany)
1933	Une femme au volant	Pierre Billon, Kurt Gerron (France)
1933	Tout pour l'amour	Henri-Georges Clouzot, Joe May (Germany)
1933	Abenteuer am Lido	Richard Oswald (Austria)
1934	Man Stolen	Max Ophüls (France)
1934	A Sensitive Lad	Jean Choux (Germany)
1934	Moscow Nights	Alexis Granowsky (France)
1935	Escapade	Robert Z. Leonard
1935	I Stand Condemned (aka Moscow Nights)	Anthony Asquith (UK)
1936	Le chant du destin	Jean-René Legrand (Austria)
1940	I Take This Woman	W. S. Van Dyke
1940	The Mortal Storm	Frank Borzage
1940	The Captain Is a Lady	Robert B. Sinclair
1940	We Who Are Young	Harold S. Bucquet
1940	Dulcy	S. Sylvan Simon
1940	Comrade X	King Vidor
1941	Blonde Inspiration	Busby Berkeley
1941	Rage in Heaven	W. S. Van Dyke
1941	Barnacle Bill	Richard Thorpe
1941	A Woman's Face	George Cukor
1941	I'll Wait for You	Robert B. Sinclair
1941	Whistling in the Dark	S. Sylvan Simon
1941	Dr. Kildare's Wedding Day	Harold S. Bucquet
1941	When Ladies Meet	Robert Z. Leonard
1941	Two-Faced Woman	George Cukor
1941	H. M. Pulham, Esq.	King Vidor
1941	Johnny Eager	Mervyn LeRoy
1942	Nazi Agent	Jules Dassin
1942	Fingers at the Window	Charles Lederer
1942	We Were Dancing	Robert Z. Leonard
1942	The Affairs of Martha	Jules Dassin
1942	Crossroads	Jack Conway
1942	Somewhere I'll Find You	Wesley Ruggles
1942	A Yank at Eton	Norman Taurog
1942	Keeper of the Flame	George Cukor
1942	White Cargo	Richard Thorpe
1943	Slightly Dangerous	Wesley Ruggles
1943	Above Suspicion	Richard Thorpe
1943	Bataan	Tay Garnett

Year	Film	Director
1943	The Cross of Lorraine	Tay Garnett
1944	The Heavenly Body	Alexander Hall, Vincente Minnelli
1944	Gaslight	George Cukor
1944	Maisie Goes to Reno	Harry Beaumont
1944	Marriage Is a Private Affair	Robert Z. Leonard
1944	Mrs. Parkington	Tay Garnett
1945	The Thin Man Goes Home	Richard Thorpe
1945	Without Love	Harold S. Bucquet
1945	Bewitched	Arch Oboler
1945	Our Vines Have Tender Grapes	Roy Rowland
1946	The Stranger	Orson Welles
1946	Courage of Lassie	Fred M. Wilcox
1946	Three Wise Fools	Edward Buzzell
1946	The Secret Heart	Robert Z. Leonard
1947	Cynthia	Robert Z. Leonard
1947	Green Dolphin Street	Victor Saville
1947	High Wall	Curtis Bernhardt
1948	B.F.'s Daughter	Robert Z. Leonard
1948	Homecoming	Mervyn LeRoy
1948	The Secret Land	Orville O. Dull
1948	Act of Violence	Fred Zinnemann
1949	The Secret Garden	Fred M. Wilcox
1949	The Great Sinner	Robert Siodmak
1949	That Forsyte Woman	Compton Bennett
1949	Malaya	Richard Thorpe
1950	Key to the City	George Sidney
1950	The Skipper Surprised His Wife	Elliott Nugent
1950	A Life of Her Own (GGN)	George Cukor
1950	To Please a Lady	Clarence Brown
1950	Kim	Victor Saville
1951	Grounds for Marriage	Robert Z. Leonard
1951	Three Guys Named Mike	Charles Walters
1951	Mr. Imperium	Don Hartman
1951	The Red Badge of Courage	John Huston
1952	The Wild North	Andrew Marton
1952	Invitation	Gottfried Reinhardt
1952	Shadow in the Sky	Fred B. Wilcox
1953	The Naked Spur	Anthony Mann
1953	Lili (AA)	Charles Walters
1953	Ride, Vaquero!	John Farrow
1953	Saadia	Albert Lewin
1954	Them!	Gordon Douglas
1954	Her Twelve Men	Robert Z. Leonard
1955	The Prodigal	Richard Thorpe
1955	The Glass Slipper	Charles Walters
1955	Quentin Durward	Richard Thorpe
1956	Forever, Darling	Alexander Hall
1956	The Swan	Charles Vidor
1956	Somebody Up There Likes Me	Robert Wise
1956	The Power and the Prize	Henry Koster
1957	The Barretts of Wimpole Street	Sidney Franklin
1957	Jet Pilot	Josef von Sternberg, Jules Furthman
1957	Don't Go Near the Water	Charles Walters
1958	The Brothers Karamazov	Richard Brooks
1958	Auntie Mame	Morton DaCosta
1959	Green Mansions	Mel Ferrer
1959	The Scapegoat	Robert Hamer (UK/USA)
1960	Home from the Hill	Vincente Minnelli

Year	Film	Director
1960	The Angel Wore Red	Nunnally Johnson (Italy/USA)
1960	BUtterfield 8	Daniel Mann
1961	Two Loves	Charles Walters
1961	Ada	Daniel Mann
1962	Mutiny on the Bounty (AAN, AAN*; GGN)	Lewis Milestone, Carol Reed
1964	Kisses for My President	Curtis Bernhardt
1965	Lord Jim	Richard Brooks (UK/USA)
1967	Tobruk	Arthur Hiller
1967	The Way West	Andrew V. McLaglen
1967	Counterpoint	Ralph Nelson
1968	A Flea in Her Ear	Jacques Charon (France/USA)
1972	The Salzburg Connection	Lee H. Katzin

KAPLAN, Sol (1919–1990) A respected conductor, concert pianist, and busy composer for television and movies, he was most active in Hollywood during the late 1940s and early 1950s, scoring twenty-five films in four years.

He was born Solomon Kaplan in Philadelphia, and was a child prodigy on the piano, performing with the Philadelphia Orchestra when he was twelve and at Carnegie Hall when he was twenty-one. Soon after that, Kaplan got involved with movies as a conductor and composer. He contributed some music to a handful of features in the early 1940s then was hired as sole composer for the popular comedy-drama *Tales of Manhattan* in 1942. During World War II, Kaplan wrote music for film shorts produced by the Office of Strategic Services and the Army Signal Corps, as well as the feature documentary *Appointment in Tokyo*. He was in great demand in Hollywood after the war, scoring several films each year. Among his many notable movies from this period are *Hollow Triumph, Reign of Terror, 711 Ocean Drive, Halls of Montezuma, I'd Climb the Highest Mountain, Rawhide, I Can Get It for You Wholesale, The House on Telegraph Hill, Return of the Texan, Deadline—U.S.A., Niagara, Diplomatic Courier, Destination Gobi,* and *Titanic.* Kaplan's career collapsed in 1953 when he was accused of being a Communist and was blacklisted. The only job he could get was scoring the controversial drama *Salt of the Earth,* which was produced by members of the blacklisted "Hollywood Ten." Kaplan turned to the theatre and wrote incidental music for seven Broadway plays in the late 1950s and early 1960s, as well as the score for the Off-Broadway musical *The Banker's Daughter* (1962). By the mid-1960s he started to get work again in the movies, scoring such films as *The Victors, The Guns of August, The Spy Who Came In from the Cold,* and *Judith.* Kaplan was

also hired to write music for television movies and series. His music for two episodes of *Star Trek* in 1966 was so dynamic that it was reused for other episodes for years. He was less active during the 1970s, although he was praised for his score for the Canadian drama *Lies My Father Told Me.* Kaplan's last score was for the crime drama *Over the Edge,* which was directed by his son Jonathan Kaplan. He retired from movies in 1980 and died of lung cancer ten years later at the age of seventy-one.

Kaplan's first solo score was one of his most challenging. *Tales of Manhattan* is an all-star anthology movie with five stories, all connected by a tailor-made tailcoat that is cursed and brings misfortune to its five owners. Kaplan's opening music is a furious and busy jazz piece that echoes the allegro sections of George Gershwin's *Rhapsody in Blue.* The score then changes its tone for each of the five tales, from a mournful march theme for the down-and-out lawyer (Edward G. Robinson) to a frolicsome piece on giggling flutes and reeds for a jealous society wife (Ginger Rogers). The dress coat has its own theme, a rapid humoresque on strings and reeds that seems to be mocking those who take possession of it. There is a lot of music in *Tales of Manhattan* and it is all quite splendid. More serious are three film noir scores that Kaplan wrote for some crime dramas. *Hollow Triumph* is about a crook (Paul Henreid) on the run from gangsters who takes on a new identity as a psychiatrist. The score has propulsive opening music with grinding percussion and a busy orchestra that is restless and agitated. This is followed by similarly harsh passages, including a rambunctious march with a heavy bass line and blaring brass. There is also a low and moody theme on woodwinds that keeps repeating the same anxious musical phrase, and a sentimental theme with softened violins and horns that conveys domestic warmth. Fake identity also figures in the noir mystery *The House on Telegraph Hill*. A concentration camp survivor (Valentina) takes the name of her deceased friend in order to get to America, only to find that the San Francisco family she has fooled may be out to murder her. The recurring theme includes eerie reeds, languid strings, ponderous brass, and pounding muted percussion that suggests a steady heartbeat as the music all around changes tempo and key. Perhaps Kaplan's most known movie today is *Niagara*, a gripping film noir starring Marilyn Monroe in one of her best performances. She plays a faithless wife who cheats on her husband (Joseph Cotton) and, with her lover (Richard Allan), plots to murder him as well. The noir score is dark and often harsh but because of Monroe the music can also be sultry and sensual. There is a mellow and jaded theme played on reeds and strings that is filled with resignation, another that is sharp and demanding as the brass intimidate and the strings get nervous. The most important piece of music in the melodrama is not by Kaplan but the sexy song "Kiss" by Lionel Newman (music) and Haven Gillespie (lyric). It is heard on a record player, Monroe sings along with it, and the melody is played on a carillon as a signal for the lovers.

Two exceptional war films allowed Kaplan to compose dramatic music in a different mode. *The Victors* is a taut, cliché-free drama that follows a group of American soldiers in Europe during World War II. The movie opens with a disturbing montage of images of war with a low, minor-key march heard in the background. The credits that follow are scored with a military victory march on brass and drums with a simple four-note phrase that keeps up its spirit as it is tossed back and forth. There is also a tripping string theme for the quieter moments and romantic scenes, a lyrical Italianate passage on mandolins, as well as three songs (lyrics by Freddy Douglass and Howard Greenfield)

heard in the background. One of the most unforgettable scenes in *The Victors* features a rapid blues passage with wild trumpet and bongos that is heard when some kids are looting the bodies of dead soldiers. Another intelligently made World War II film is *Destination Gobi* about some U.S. Navy weathermen in Mongolia's Gobi Desert recruiting the help of Mongol nomads against the Japanese. Kaplan wrote a very unusual march for the movie. It is played on violins with brass and percussion accompaniment, and some gongs and high-pitched Asian musical phrases are added to convey the America-Mongol alliance. This is made all the more interesting when it is mixed with "Anchors Aweigh" for a kind on intercultural montage. Just as *The Victors* and *Destination Gobi* are realistic presentations of war, *The Spy Who Came In from the Cold* is one of the most realistic movies about espionage. Based on John le Carré's Cold War novel, the very nonromanticized drama concerns a burnt-out British Secret Service agent (Richard Burton) who refuses to resign and goes on a mission to East Germany where he begins to question exactly who the enemy really is. The black-and-white film directed by Martin Ritt is stark, sullen, and very low key. Kaplan's score captures the tone and atmosphere very well. A gloomy and reflective piano solo wearily climbs the scale then slips back down without a struggle. There is a growling, restless theme on reeds and percussion that is aggressive and threatening, a clarinet and violin duet with agitated percussion that sounds like it is grumbling, a horn and percussion passage that marches forward slowly but with dreadful purpose, and for contrast a perky jazz passage with saxophone and electric guitar that is lively but detached and chilly. Many consider this Kaplan's finest score. It is certainly the work of a masterful composer who is too little known today.

Credits

(all films USA unless stated otherwise)

Year	Film	Director
1942	Tales of Manhattan (aka Stars Over Manhattan)	Julien Duvivier
1942	Apache Trail	Richard Thorpe, Richard Rosson
1945	Appointment in Tokyo (aka Appointment at Corregidor)	Jack Hively
1948	Hollow Triumph (aka The Scar)	Steve Sekely
1949	Alice in Wonderland	Dallas Bower (USA/France/UK)
1949	Down Memory Lane	Phil Karlson
1949	Trapped	Richard Fleischer

Year	Film	Director
1949	*Reign of Terror* (aka *The Black Book*)	Anthony Mann
1949	*Port of New York*	Laslo Benedek
1950	*711 Ocean Drive*	Joseph M. Newman
1950	*Mister 880* (aka *Old 880*)	Edmund Goulding
1950	*Halls of Montezuma*	Lewis Milestone
1951	*I'd Climb the Highest Mountain*	Henry King
1951	*Rawhide* (aka *Desperate Siege*)	Henry Hathaway
1951	*I Can Get It for You Wholesale* (aka *Only the Best*)	Michael Gordon
1951	*The House on Telegraph Hill*	Robert Wise
1951	*The Secret of Convict Lake*	Michael Gordon
1952	*Red Skies of Montana* (aka *Smoke Jumpers*)	Joseph M. Newman
1952	*Return of the Texan*	Delmer Daves
1952	*Deadline—U.S.A.*	Richard Brooks
1952	*Kangaroo* (aka *The Australian Story*)	Lewis Milestone
1952	*Diplomatic Courier*	Henry Hathaway
1952	*Something for the Birds*	Robert Wise
1952	*Way of a Gaucho*	Jacques Tourneur
1953	*Niagara*	Henry Hathaway
1953	*Treasure of the Golden Condor* (aka *Condor's Nest*)	Delmer Daves
1953	*Destination Gobi* (aka *Gobi Outpost*)	Robert Wise
1953	*Titanic* (aka *Nearer My God to Thee*)	Jean Negulesco
1954	*Salt of the Earth*	Herbert J. Biberman
1957	*The Burglar*	Paul Wendkos
1959	*Happy Anniversary*	David Miller
1960	*Girl of the Night*	Joseph Cates
1963	*The Victors*	Carl Foreman
1964	*The Young Lovers*	Samuel Goldwyn Jr.
1964	*The Guns of August*	Nathan Kroll
1965	*The Spy Who Came In from the Cold*	Martin Ritt (UK)
1966	*Judith* (aka *Conflict*)	Daniel Mann (Israel/UK/USA)
1969	*Explosion*	Jules Bricken (Canada/USA)
1972	*Living Free*	Jack Couffer (UK)
1975	*Lies My Father Told Me*	Ján Kadár (Canada)
1979	*Over the Edge* (aka *On the Edge*)	Jonathan Kaplan

KARLIN, Fred (1936–2004) An American trumpet virtuoso and composer who wrote the scores for over one hundred TV movies, he had a less busy but still impressive career scoring feature films.

Frederick James Karlin was born in Chicago and became interested in music when as a teenager he saw the movie *Young Man with a Horn*. Harry James's trumpet playing on the soundtrack inspired him to learn to play the instrument, which he did throughout high school and during his four years at Amherst College. While in school, Karlin changed his major from literature to music and composed a string quartet as part of his studies. He began his music career playing jazz trumpet in Chicago then moved to New York City where he arranged music for various bands (including Harry James's), Radio City Music Hall, and television commercials. Producer Alan J.

Pakula was impressed with Karlin's work and hired him in 1967 to score *Up the Down Staircase*, a high-profile movie about an inner-city high school. The result was a jazzy score flavored with rock that was much applauded. When Pakula directed his first movie in 1969, the delicate love story *The Sterile Cuckoo*, he again used Karlin, who came up with an entrancing, evocative score that included the hit song "Come Saturday Morning" (lyric by Dory Previn). The folk ballad was nominated for an Academy Award; the next year Karlin won the Oscar for the song "For All We Know" (lyric by Robb Wilson and Arthur James) from his score for the comedy *Lovers and Other Strangers*. Both songs became chart records and helped solidify Karlin's stature in Hollywood. Yet he never really found a successful niche in Tinseltown. Most subsequent features were critical or financial flops, the major exceptions being the sci-fi movies *Westworld* and *Futureworld* and the biopic *Leadbelly*. By the late 1970s, Karlin was offered some dreadful movies to score so he concentrated on television. After winning the Emmy for his score for *The Autobiography of Miss Jane Pittman* (1974), Karlin became an A-list composer for the small screen, writing music for dozens of TV movies and miniseries, including *Death Be Not Proud* (1975), *Minstrel Man* (1977), *The Life and the Assassination of the Kingfish* (1977), *Forever* (1978), *The Awakening Land* (1978), *Ike: The War Years* (1979), *Homeward Bound* (1980), *Inside the Third Reich* (1982), *Robert Kennedy and His Times* (1985), *Bridge to Silence* (1989), *Her Wicked Ways* (1991), and *Survive the Savage Sea* (1992). In all, he received eleven Emmy nominations and was kept busy working in television until his death at the age of sixty-seven.

A true measure of Karlin's composing skill would have to concentrate on his TV work, but he has some exceptional feature film scores that are worth examining. His first screen score is one of his best: *Up the Down Staircase*, with its melodic and rhythmic main theme. Karlin used soprano recorders in the music, an interesting choice for a contemporary urban film. Yet appropriate because the new teacher tries to interest her students in classic literature. The high-pitched recorders are broken up by rock passages played on electric guitar and organ. The score for *The Sterile Cuckoo* is built around the main theme "Come Saturday Morning," an enticing song that is romantic and yet oddly melancholy. Similarly, the song "For All We Know" is the centerpiece of the quirky comedy *Lovers and Other Strangers*. It also has a somber subtext but when recorded out of context of the movie is a poignant love song. The rather forgettable movie *The Baby Maker* has gentle, contemporary music played on guitar while the score for *Westworld* is a lively combination of hillbilly fiddling, sweeping prairie themes, honky-tonk piano, and

creepy echoing music that reflects the sci-fi elements in the story. For the follow-up movie *Futureworld*, Karlin came up with an interesting score in which tense violins played a classical theme with a pulsating tempo. Karlin's favorite instrument, the trumpet, plays the mournful theme in the little-known futuristic fable *Ravagers*. The score also has some lyrical sections in which the clarinet has lovely emotive passages. The biopic *Leadbelly* is filled with songs that were sung and recorded by blues and folk legend Huddie Leadbetter but Karlin wrote a scintillating country soundtrack score that complemented the famous tunes nicely. His main theme for the western *The Stalking Moon* is also country flavored with a whistling solo that suggests roaming in wide-open spaces. Similarly, the theme for the Seminole tale *Joe Panther* features a solo folk voice that celebrates the rural life in the Everglades. For the aviation film *Cloud Dancer*, Karlin's score highlights a solo guitar and piano to create a simple dreamy theme that moves into a rhythmic folk song about soaring. A solo harmonica plays against flutes for the main theme in *Mixed Company*. Most of these movies are small pictures with limited budgets and few pretensions. Karlin's music is equally unpretentious and engaging.

Karlin never abandoned performing and was an acclaimed jazz trumpeter who played and recorded with various groups. In 1988 he founded the ASCAP/Fred Karlin Film Scoring Workshop which allows young composers to write and hear their compositions performed. Karlin also taught film and television scoring at the University of Southern California and wrote two books on screen music: *On the Track: A Guide to Contemporary Film Scoring* (with Rayburn Wright) and *Listening to Movies: The Film Lover's Guide to Film Music*. While Karlin's movie work was limited in quantity and he never found wide public recognition, in the music business he was considered an expert musician and masterful composer.

Credits

(all films USA unless stated otherwise; * for Best Song)

Year	Film	Director
1967	*Up the Down Staircase*	Robert Mulligan
1968	*Yours, Mine and Ours*	Melville Shavelson
1968	*The Stalking Moon*	Robert Mulligan
1969	*The Sterile Cuckoo* (AAN*)	Alan J. Pakula
1970	*Lovers and Other Strangers* (AA*)	Cy Howard

Year	Film	Director
1970	The Baby Maker (AAN)	James Bridges
1970	Cover Me Babe	Noel Black
1971	The Marriage of a Young Stockbroker	Lawrence Turman
1971	Believe in Me	Stuart Hagmann
1972	The Little Ark (AAN*)	James B. Clark
1972	Every Little Crook and Nanny	Cy Howard
1973	Westworld	Michael Crichton
1974	Goodnight Jackie	Jerry London
1974	The Spikes Gang	Richard Fleischer
1974	Zandy's Bride	Jan Troell
1974	Chosen Survivors	Sutton Roley (Mexico/USA)
1974	The Take	Robert Hartford-Davis (UK)
1974	The Gravy Train (aka The Dion Brothers)	Jack Starrett
1974	Mixed Company	Melville Shavelson
1976	Mastermind	Alex March
1976	Baby Blue Marine	John D. Hancock
1976	Leadbelly	Gordon Parks
1976	Futureworld	Richard T. Heffron
1976	Joe Panther	Paul Krasny
1977	Greased Lightning	Michael Schultz
1978	Mean Dog Blues	Mel Stuart
1979	Ravagers	Richard Compton
1979	California Dreaming	John D. Hancock
1980	Cloud Dancer	Barry Brown
1980	Loving Couples	Jack Smight
1986	Vasectomy: A Delicate Matter	Robert Burge
1991	Strawberry Road	Koreyoshi Kurahara (Japan/USA)

KENT, Rolfe (b. 1963) A British composer very much in demand for contemporary film comedies, he has scored a variety of movies since 1994, mostly for independent filmmakers.

Born in St. Albans, England, although his family was not musical and he received very little formal training, Rolfe Kent decided at the age of twelve that he wanted to be a screen composer. His mother was a trained psychologist and Kent studied psychology at the University of Leeds. After graduation he taught the same subject at Leeds Polytechnic before pursuing a music career by writing for theatre groups and dance clubs in London. Kent began scoring television series in 1989 and over the decades has written music for such series as *So Haunt Me*, *The Jury*, *The Jury II*, and *The High Bar*, but he is most known for his main theme for the internationally popular series *Dexter*. His film career began in the States when he scored the thriller *Dead Connection* in 1994 and the next year he worked with independent director Richard Shepard for the first time when he scored the crime drama *Mercy*. Over the decades Kent has continued to collaborate

with Shepard and other notable independent filmmakers, such as Alexander Payne, Mark Waters, Jason Reitman, and Daniel Waters. His first box office success was the satiric comedy *Election* in 1999, followed by such notable hits as *Legally Blonde*, *About Schmidt*, *Sideways*, *Killers*, *Labor Day*, *Up in the Air*, *Mean Girls*, *Wedding Crashers*, and *Thank You for Smoking*. Yet some of Kent's best music can be found in the many small and lesser known movies of high quality, including *Citizen Ruth*, *The House of Yes*, *Slums of Beverly Hills*, *The Theory of Flight*, *Just Like Heaven*, *The Hunting Party*, *Reign Over Me*, *Men Who Stare at Goats*, *The Lucky Ones*, and *Bad Words*, as well as such documentaries as *Left Behind: The Story of the New Orleans Public Schools* and *Troupers*.

It is not surprising that Kent is much sought after for comedies, particularly quirky contemporary comedies, because he has a talent for writing music that is offbeat, catchy, and actually funny. More than a little of the success of *Sideways* can be attributed to Kent's delightful score. This unorthodox road picture, about two middle-aged oafs (Paul Giamatti and Thomas Haden Church) on a tour of California wine country, has an oddball tone and it is captured in the music, as with the sunny and goofy theme on electric keyboard and harmonica that is jaunty and freewheeling if not a little haphazard. There is some bouncy travel music on saxophone and flute that is carefree and rhythmic, another driving theme on trumpet and saxophone with keyboard solo riffs, and a jazz passage featuring saxophone and bass that is breezy and casual. On the quieter side is a cool jazz piece played on piano, flute, accordion, and electronic chimes, and a melancholy track that has a touch of the blues. The sarcastic comedy *Election*, about the efforts of three students (Reese Witherspoon, Jessica Campbell, and Chris Klein) to get elected president of a high school student council, has a sprightly and cheery theme on strings and horns that sounds like a silly parade as it mocks the political intrigue fueled by a teacher (Matthew Broderick). Kent's score also has a funny cha-cha on saxophone and electric keyboard, a fun disco track, and a slow movement on strings and chimes heard under the farcical prayers of the three students. The crass comedy *Wedding Crashers*, about two wolves (Owen Wilson and Vince Vaughn) who pick up girls at weddings they are not invited to, has a slaphappy rumba theme with playful percussion, and a jittery allegro passage on piano that hints at the desperation behind these characters. There is also a reflective theme on plucked strings and reeds that doesn't drag but is still affecting. Kent wrote a comic score with some interesting variations for *Mean Girls* in which a high school student (Lindsay Lohan), raised in Africa, learns about a fiercer jungle when she crosses the members of a female clique. The main theme is a rhythmic piece featuring banjo, electronic instrumentation, and vocal chanting with an African flavor that mocks *The Lion King* soundtrack. There is also a jaunty percussion passage with confused strings and low brass, a sparkling piece on electronic keyboard with wordless vocals that travel up and down in a dizzy manner, a propulsive percussion passage that is chaotic and furious, and a pizzicato string and electric keyboard theme that travels smoothly with a casual air. As many comedies as Kent has scored, he doesn't seem to run out of original musical ideas. In *Slums of Beverly Hills*, an incongruous farce about a family of lowlifes in an upscale community, he provides a Greek dance theme with a cockeyed rhythm played on a fiery violin. The very popular *Legally Blonde*, in which a supposed dumb blonde (Reese Witherspoon) enrolls at Harvard Law School to get even with the prig (Matthew Davis) who dumped her, is scored with pseudoclassical music to comment on the Ivy League world that is being debunked. There is a memorable slapstick passage featuring rat-a-tat woodwinds and plucked strings that seem to ricochet up and down the scale.

Some of the more serious films Kent scored also have superior music, often with a bit of an edge to it. *Up in the Air* is a romantic drama about a soulless executive (George Clooney) who softens when faced with romance. The score is not very sentimental but rather testy and agitated. There is an echoing percussion theme with various drums and bells that conveys the hero's hectic life, as well as a steady and rapid electric guitar and bass theme with synthesized strings that suggests even love has a sharp subtext. Another romantic comedy with a tough side, *Killers* is about a pair of newlyweds (Katherine Heigl and Ashton Kutcher) who learn that one of their neighbors has a contract to kill them. Kent's score walks the line between farce and melodrama quite well. There is a zesty accordion and piano dance theme with sustained strings underneath that has a propulsive tone and a touch of frustration implied. The score also features rapid chase music on nervous strings, wailing brass, and pounding percussion; a flowing guitar, piano, strings, and reeds passage that is graceful but still has a tough attitude; an exotic dance tune featuring harmonica that is casual yet sultry; and a vivacious flamenco track on guitar and synthesized sustained notes with a frustrated subtext. A heavy melodrama that manages to find some humor in its sobering situation, *The Hunting Party* is about some journalists searching for a war criminal in Bosnia. The main theme features sustained strings with restless percussion and angry brass. There is also a solemn piece with strings that repeat the same musical phrase as if stuck, a vibrant percussion track with electronic chords, and a guitar and strings love theme that is quiet and delicate. Perhaps Kent's finest score is for the unconventional comedy-drama *About Schmidt*. A retired insurance man (Jack Nicholson) journeys from Omaha to Denver in an RV to attend the wedding of his somewhat-estranged daughter (Hope Davis) and along the way is forced to reexamine his life. The movie has an ambiguous tone, which is captured in the main musical theme played on strings and reeds as it moves at a steady pace then slows down for a reflective section on piano. The superb score has some traveling music with lively strings and a solo clarinet repeating a hopping musical phrase but it keeps getting interrupted by accordion chords and a mocking bassoon. Also interesting are an odd passage on banjo, strings, and electronic flourishes with an Asian flavor; a sweeping waltz on strings and reeds that sounds more European than midwestern; a cheerful passage on strings and bassoon that trips along merrily; a troubled and inde-

cisive harp theme accompanied by wavering violins, the same combination used for a quiet and heavyhearted section; and an angry passage featuring restless strings and a complaining bassoon. The way Kent is able to score such complex films as *About Schmidt* is a major part of his considerable talent for movie music. Official website: www. rolfekent.com.

Credits

(all films USA unless stated otherwise)

Year	Film	Director
1994	Dead Connection	Nigel Dick
1994	Finding Interest	Samer Daboul, Trevor Sands
1995	Mercy	Richard Shepard
1996	Citizen Ruth (aka Meet Ruth Stoops)	Alexander Payne
1997	The House of Yes	Mark Waters
1998	Slums of Beverly Hills	Tamara Jenkins
1998	The Theory of Flight	Paul Greengrass (UK)
1999	Don't Go Breaking My Heart	Willi Paterson (UK)
1999	Election	Alexander Payne
1999	Oxygen (aka Dying to Escape)	Richard Shepard
2000	Gun Shy	Eric Blakeney
2000	Nurse Betty	Neil LaBute (Germany/USA)
2000	Mexico City	Richard Shepard (Mexico/USA)
2001	Happy Campers	Daniel Waters
2001	Someone Like You . . . (aka Animal Husbandry)	Tony Goldwyn
2001	Town & Country	Pater Chelsom
2001	Legally Blonde	Robert Luketic
2001	Kate & Leopold	James Mangold
2002	40 Days and 40 Nights	Michael Lehmann (USA/UK/France)
2002	About Schmidt	Alexander Payne
2003	Legally Blonde 2: Red, White & Blonde	Charles Herman-Wurmfeld
2003	Freaky Friday	Mark Waters
2004	Mean Girls (aka Queen Bees and Wannabes)	Mark Waters (USA/Canada)
2004	Sideways (GGN)	Alexander Payne (USA/Hungary)
2004	The Last Shot (aka Providence)	Jeff Nathanson
2005	The Matador	Richard Shepard (USA/Germany/Ireland)
2005	Wedding Crashers	David Dobkin
2005	Thank You for Smoking	Jason Reitman
2005	Just Like Heaven (aka If Only It Were True)	Mark Waters
2006	Failure to Launch	Tom Dey
2007	Reign Over Me (aka Empty City)	Mike Binder
2007	Sex and Death 101	Daniel Waters
2007	The Hunting Party (aka Spring Break in Bosnia)	Richard Shepard (USA/Croatia/ Bosnia and Herzegovina)
2008	Left Behind: The Story of the New Orleans Public Schools	Vincent Morelli, Jason Berry
2008	The Lucky Ones (aka The Return)	Neil Burger
2009	17 Again	Burr Steers
2009	Ghosts of Girlfriends Past	Mark Waters
2009	Up in the Air	Jason Reitman
2009	The Men Who Stare at Goats	Grant Heslov (USA/UK)
2010	Killers (aka Five Killers)	Robert Luketic
2010	Charlie St. Cloud	Burr Steers (USA/Canada)

Year	Film	Director
2011	*Troupers*	Sara Ballantine, Dea Lawrence
2011	*Mr. Popper's Penguins*	Mark Waters
2011	*Young Adult*	Jason Reitman
2012	*Gambit*	Michael Hoffman
2013	*The Scapegoat*	Nicolas Bary (France)
2013	*Labor Day*	Jason Reitman
2013	*Bad Words*	Jason Bateman
2013	*Dom Hemingway*	Richard Shepard (UK)
2014	*Vampire Academy*	Mark Waters (USA/UK/Romania)

KHACHATURIAN, Aram (1903–1978) The most acclaimed Armenian composer and conductor of the twentieth century, he ranks among the finest Soviet artists of his era because of his exotic music for the concert hall, theatre, and the ballet. Khachaturian also scored ten feature films in Russia, producing music that continues to live in the concert hall.

Aram Ilyich Khachaturian (sometimes spelled Kachaturyan) was born in Tiflis, Russia (now Tbilsi in the Republic of Georgia), into an Armenian family, the son of a bookmaker. As a youth he got to experience the most recent Russian music when Fyodor Shalyapin, Sergei Rachmaninoff, and other composers/conductors came to Tiflis to perform at the local branch of the Russian Musical Society. Khachaturian did not begin his formal musical training until he was nineteen and studied cello at the Gnesin Music School in Moscow even while he pursued a degree in biology at the Moscow State University. He then studied composition at the Moscow National Conservatory, where his work was so advanced that visiting composer Sergey Prokofiev took some of Khachaturian's pieces to Paris where he saw to it that they were performed. His career blossomed in the 1930s as both his short works and extended compositions were published and performed in Russia and then across Europe. Among his many dance compositions, orchestral suites, symphonies, concertos, ballets, piano pieces, art songs, and chamber works, one stands out as the most famous: the fiery "Sabre Dance" from the ballet *Gayane* (1942) which has been frequently recorded and performed around the world and heard in dozens of movies and television programs. (The beautiful adagio section from the same ballet was used effectively in *2001: A Space Odyssey*.)

Khachaturian also wrote for the theatre and the Russian cinema. His first screen score was for the drama *Pepo* in 1935, followed by nine other feature films over the next twenty-four years: the two-part *The Battle of Stalingrad*, *Attack from the Sea*, *The Russian Question*, *Secret Mission*, *Zangezur*, *Admiral Ushakov*, *Othello*, and *On the Eve*. Khachaturian later turned his scores for *The Battle of Stalingrad* and *Othello* into symphonic suites that have been performed and recorded. He also wrote the Armenian national anthem. Although Khachaturian was praised by the Communist Party in the 1930s and during the war years, his music was declared too "formalist" by Stalin in 1948. Khachaturian was denied commissions, so he taught at the Gnesin Music School and the Moscow National Conservatory and also conducted extensively. After the death of Stalin, Khachaturian and other denounced composers were once again approved of by the state. He continued to write, received many awards and honors, and served as secretary of the Union of Soviet Composers until his death in 1978 at the age of seventy-four. A national hero and source of pride in Armenia, Khachaturian is now considered one of the giants in twentieth-century music.

Because he often used folk tunes from his native land and was fascinated by Oriental and Eastern European music, Khachaturian is grouped with Alexander Borodin and Nikolai Rimsky-Korsakov as a composer of exotic music. Yet he is firmly entrenched in classical traditions and much of his work is more Western than Eastern. In fact, most of Khachaturian's music can be classified as "modern," which is why he ran afoul of the party line in the Soviet Union. Because of the Cold War and the propagandist subject matter of the movies he scored, few of the films were seen in the States. Yet his music from those movies has traveled. In *Popi*, the first sound movie made in Armenia, there is a simple peasant song by Khachaturian that is widely known today, although most assume it is an authentic folk song from the nineteenth century. He also has a march in *Zangezur* that is also performed as a traditional piece of Armenian folklore. Because of the orchestral suites fashioned from *The Battle of Stalingrad* and *Othello*, these are Khachaturian's most known cinema scores. The former film is an epic presentation of the 1942–1943 battle that served as the turning point in World War II in Russia. The movie is not modest or subtle in its praise of the Soviet forces and the leadership of Stalin. Khachaturian's music has its bombastic passages, particularly a march on brass and strings that has more cymbal crashes than any World War II battle. An invasion theme on trumpets and flutes seems to rush ahead without fear. There are also quieter and more reflective passages, such as a solemn yet flowing theme for strings that climbs the scale with a purpose before exploding into a stormy section of strings and horns. *The Battle of Stalingrad* score ends with a

bang, but it is more in the spirit of an anthem and a victory march. Because *Othello* is not a patriotic propaganda film, its score is less grandiose and quite moving. The most memorable theme is the music for the song Desdemona (Irina Skobtseva) sings before her death, a lyrical piece that timidly moves up and down the scale. The theme for the title Moor (Sergei Bondarchuk) is also lovely, played on a solo violin with such heartache and passion that Shakespeare's character is laid bare. While Khachaturian's screen music cannot compete with his concert work, it is still notable. If only he had been given better movies to score, there might have been a cinema music masterwork. Biography in English: *Aram Khachaturian: A Biography*, Viktor A. Yuzefovich; Nicholas Kournokoff, Vladimir Bobrov, translators (1985). Official English website: www. khachaturian.am/eng.

Credits

(all films USSR unless stated otherwise)

Year	Film	Director
1935	Pepo	Amo Bek-Nazaryan, Armen Gulakyan
1938	Zangezur	Amo Bek-Nazaryan, Y. Dukor
1947	The Russian Question	Mikhail Romm
1949	The Battle of Stalingrad I	Vladimir Petrov
1949	The Battle of Stalingrad II (aka The Victors and the Vanquished)	Vladimir Petrov
1950	Secret Mission	Mikhail Romm
1953	Attack from the Sea	Mikhail Romm
1953	Admiral Ushakov	Mikhail Romm
1955	Othello	Sergei Yutkevich
1959	On the Eve	Vladimir Petrov (USSR/Bulgaria)

KILAR, Wojciech (1932–2013) A prolific Polish composer for the concert hall who scored over eighty movies in his homeland before finding an international reputation, he worked with the top Polish directors of his era.

Born in Lwowskie, Poland (which is now Lviv in the Ukraine), Wojciech Kilar was the son of a physician and a theatre actress. He studied piano and composition at the State College of Music in Katowice and the Music Academy at Kraków, as well as with Nadia Boulanger in Paris. In the 1960s, Kilar was noticed as one of the Polish avant-garde composers of chamber works, symphonies, solo piano compositions, and choral pieces. He later abandoned

the modernist approach and concentrated on folk songs, religious music, and patriotic pieces. Kilar first became involved with movies in 1958 when he scored the documentary short *Narciarze*, then two years later he wrote music for his first feature film *Lunatycy/The Moonwalkers*. For the next four decades he scored four or five movies each year and became the preeminent screen composer in Poland. In 1973 he worked with director Krzysztof Zanussi for the first time, scoring his drama *The Illumination*. The two men went on to collaborate on twenty-five subsequent features, one of the longest director-composer relationships in cinema. Among the other notable Polish directors

Kilar worked with are Kazimierz Kutz, Krzysztof Kies-lowski, Andrzej Wajda, and Roman Polanski. His most acclaimed Polish films include *Jump, Skinny and Others, Our Folks, The Structure of Crystal, Salt of the Black Earth, Pearl in the Crown, The Promised Land, A Trip Down the River, Camouflage, Blind Chance,* and *Chronicle of Love Affairs.* After 1976, Kilar was sought out by other European film directors, resulting in such movies as *The King and Mister Bird, From a Far Country, Imperative, A Year of Quiet Sun, The Turning Table,* and *The Pianist.* His first American movie, *Bram Stoker's Dracula* directed by Francis Ford Coppola, was a resounding international hit in 1992, and Kilar became widely known in the States. His other American movies include *Death and the Maiden, We Own the Night, The Ninth Gate,* and *The Portrait of a Lady.* By the turn of the new century, Kilar scored fewer movies and concentrated on writing and conducting music for the concert hall. He also scored some Polish television programs and documentaries, and wrote music for special occasions, such as the hundredth anniversary of the Warsaw National Philharmonic. Kilar was much awarded and honored during his lifetime, as he served on committees and supported arts institutions in Poland. He died at the age of eighty-one from complications after having a brain tumor removed.

Although Kilar was labeled an avant-gardist for a time, much of his music is in the style of romanticism. He favors cellos and basses in his orchestrations, and later in his career he strived for simplicity in his work, some of his music moving close to minimalism. (Kilar stated that John Cage's approach to music had a great impact on his later work.) His scores for some of the Polish films of the 1960s reveal the modernist side of Kilar. The compelling 1965 drama *Salto,* known as well by its English title, *Jump,* is about a young drifter (Zbigniew Cybulski) who comes to a small town and has a startling effect on the inhabitants before he continues on. The James Dean–like Cybulski manages to be seductive and threatening at the same time, as does some of Kilar's music. The film's score opens with metronome-like plucked bass strings that are joined by various percussion instruments and brass chords to build from a ticktock pattern to a complex piece of modern music. There is a slow and languid tango played on bass strings and solo clarinet that is so jaded it seems to be mocking. A highlight in *Jump* is a marvelous dance sequence in the town hall in which Cybulski improvises an interpretive

jazz dance and soon all the townspeople are caught up in an expressionistic modern ballet that is all rhythm and no melody. Kilar scores the scene with a solo bass fiddle that sets the tempo for the dance then adds simple percussion to allow it to build into a fully satisfying musical number. A decade after *Jump,* Kilar was still using avant-garde techniques but embracing classical forms as well. Both can be seen in *The Promised Land,* a drama about an odd trio of young entrepreneurs who hope to make a fortune with their factory in Lodz during the first decade of the twentieth century. The opening music consists of a percussive heartbeat with different mechanical noises added in irregular patterns. Yet later in the movie there is a sweeping waltz on strings, harp, and reeds that moves swiftly and carelessly but always in a classical format. Also memorable is a zesty and frantic march played on hyperactive strings, giddy woodwinds, and pompous brass that is so earnest it is comic. Of all the Polish films Kilar scored, the one probably seen most outside his homeland was Polanski's *The Pianist.* This engrossing true tale of a Polish musician (Adrien Brody) living in the Warsaw ghetto during World War II is filled with piano selections by Fredric Chopin (played on the soundtrack by Janusz Olejniczak) and some other classical music. Kilar wrote the main theme for the drama, a minor-key march played on a solo clarinet and plucked strings that has the tempo of a slow dance but the temperament of a death march. When this theme is later repeated by full orchestra it is even more sinister and even oppressive.

Kilar's first American movie, Coppola's *Bram Stoker's Dracula,* is less avant-garde and more classical, although a minimalist kind of classical. As the title suggests, this version follows the original book more closely than other screen adaptations. All the action is set in England and Count Dracula is played by Gary Oldman as a dark but romantic Victorian villain. Kilar's music throughout is more subtle and cerebral than the expected horror score. A recurring theme features string bass with percussion pounding like a funeral march as they repeat a sliding phrase. Then this phrase is picked up by violins and brass so that it almost becomes dancelike, a Victorian dance of death. There is also a restless theme that pushes forward through a series of blaring crescendos on brass and percussion, and a theme for the hapless heroine Mina (Winona Ryder) which is a slow and eerie string passage with a female chanting high above a growling bass pattern. The love theme in the movie is Gothic romanticism: gently falling phrases played on reeds and strings that reach up only to descend again in a graceful manner. Another quiet but emotional classically flavored score can be heard in the 1996 version of *The Portrait of a Lady*. This is far from a fully satisfying version of Henry James's enigmatic novel, but Kilar's score is exceptional. The main theme for the film is a hesitant piano piece that is reflective but the underscoring of strings gives it some weight. Then two wooden recorders are added, giving the theme the feel of a muted folk song. The theme for the confused American heroine (Nicole Kidman) is a lyrical passage heard on strings and piano that moves forward elegantly but with a doleful subtext. Also in the score is a haunting minor-key orchestral theme that is indecisive even as it climbs the scale with steady movement, a melancholy nocturne played on cellos that is stately but moody, and a solo oboe that is featured in a heavyhearted theme that stops just short of wailing. Classical selections by Franz Schubert and Johann Strauss are used on the soundtrack to support the European atmosphere, but it is Kilar's music that captures the ambiguous quality of James's characters.

Two less subtle American dramas that Kilar scored have music that is more fiery. *The Ninth Gate* is a mystery thriller about a rare book dealer (Johnny Depp) who gets caught up in all kinds of intrigues when he searches for a demonic book from the seventeenth century. The opening music is an ominous waltz in half time in which the violins and reeds are filled with dread. A recurring theme features a female *vocalise*, a creepy wordless aria that rises and falls with passion as strings and piano calmly play underneath. There is an agitated passage filled with heavy repetition played on shrill strings and strident piano, some chase music heard on dizzy strings going in circles with woodwind accents, and a rhythmic march played on high-pitched woodwinds, sustained strings, and nervous piano scales. More cerebral is the political thriller *Death and the Maiden* about a South American wife (Sigourney Weaver) who suspects that her houseguest (Ben Kingsley) is the same man who tortured her during a previous political regime. Piano and reeds are featured in a flowing lament that is heavy with remorse yet is still pleasing; a lilting phrase played on strings and orchestra is added, but the piece remains very intimate. The score also includes a ponderous minor-key passage with sour strings and foreboding piano chords, and a chilling theme utilizing plucked strings, a march drumbeat, and echoing electronic sounds. The most minimal track in the score is heard during a confession scene. A wavering musical phrase is repeated with only the most subtle variations and key changes. This 1994 movie shows that the avant-garde Kilar from the 1960s was still very much alive three decades later. Official English website: www.wojciechkilar.pl.

Credits

(all films Poland unless stated otherwise)

Year	Film	Director
1960	The Moonwalkers	Bohdan Poreba
1960	Nobody's Calling	Kazimierz Kutz
1961	Silent Traces	Zbigniew Kuzminski
1962	And You Will Become an Indian	Konrad Nalecki
1962	The Voice from Beyond	Stanislaw Rózewicz
1962	The Milczarek Family	Jósef Wyszomirski
1962	Cafe from the Past	Jan Rybkowski
1962	Tarpany	Kazimierz Kutz
1963	Red Berets	Pawel Komorowski
1963	Far Is the Road	Bohdan Poreba
1963	Silence	Kazimierz Kutz
1963	The Penthouse	Konrad Nalecki
1963	Codename Nectar	Leon Jeannot
1964	Giuseppe in Warsaw	Stanislaw Lenartowicz
1964	Echo	Stanislaw Rózewicz
1964	Five	Pawel Komorowski

Year	Film	Director
1965	By the Truth	Janusz Weychert
1965	The Island of Delinquents	Stanislaw Jedryka
1965	Jump	Tadeusz Konwicki
1965	Three Steps on Earth	Jerzy Hoffman, Edward Skórzewski
1966	Mexico Tomorrow	Aleksander Scibor-Rylski
1966	Catastrophe	Sylwester Checinski
1966	Hell and Heaven	Stanislaw Rózewicz
1966	Maria and Napoleon	Leonard Buczkowski
1966	Whoever May Know	Kazimierz Kutz
1966	Boomerang	Leon Jeannot
1967	Return to Earth	Stanislaw Jedryka
1967	Skinny and Others	Henryk Kluba
1967	Full Ahead	Stanislaw Lenartowicz
1967	Westerplatte	Stanislaw Rózewicz
1967	God's Whip	Maria Kaniewska
1967	The Murderer Leaves a Clue	Aleksander Scibor-Rylski
1967	Our Folks	Sylwester Checinski
1967	Stall on Salvador	Pawel Komorowski
1967	Late Afternoon	Aleksander Scibor-Rylski
1968	Dreaming Tablet	Zbigniew Chmielewski
1968	Wolves' Echoes	Aleksander Scibor-Rylski
1968	Last After the God	Pawel Komorowski
1968	The Doll	Wojciech Has
1969	Loneliness for Two	Stanislaw Rózewicz
1969	Man with an Apartment	Leon Jeannot
1969	The Neighbors	Aleksander Scibor-Rylski
1969	The Red and the Gold	Stanislaw Lenartowicz, etc.
1969	The Criminal Who Stole a Crime	Janusz Majewski
1969	The Structure of Crystal	Krzysztof Zanussi
1969	Only the Dead Can Answer	Sylwester Checinski
1969	The Pier	Wojciech Solarz
1970	Salt of the Black Earth	Kazimierz Kutz
1970	The Bear	Janusz Majewski
1970	A Trip Down the River (aka The Cruise)	Marek Piwowski
1970	Family Life	Krzysztof Zanussi
1970	Romantic People	Stanislaw Rózewicz
1971	Haven	Pawel Komorowski
1971	Dancing Party in Hitler's Headquarters	Jan Batory
1971	The Ring of Queen Ann	Maria Kaniewska
1971	Calm Flat	Stanislaw Lenartowicz
1972	Pearl in the Crown	Kazimierz Kutz
1972	Diamonds of Mrs. Zuza	Pawel Komorowski
1972	Crystal Ball	Stanislaw Rózewicz
1972	King Boleslaus the Bold	Witold Lesiewicz
1973	Obsession	Stanislaw Lenartowicz
1973	Major Hubal	Bohdan Poreba
1973	Jealousy and Medicine	Janusz Majewski
1973	The Illumination	Krzysztof Zanussi
1974	The Wicket Gate	Stanislaw Rózewicz
1975	A Woman's Decision	Krzysztof Zanussi
1975	The Promised Land	Andrzej Wajda
1975	The Line	Kazimierz Kutz
1975	From Nowhere to Nowhere	Kazimierz Kutz
1975	The Catamount Killing	Krzysztof Zanussi
1975	Jaroslaw Dabrowski	Bohdan Poreba
1976	The Shadow Line	Andrzej Wajda (UK/Poland)
1976	Leper	Jerzy Hoffman
1977	Camouflage	Krzysztof Zanussi

Year	Film	Director
1977	Birds to Birds	Pawel Komorowski
1978	Spiral	Krzysztof Zanussi
1979	David	Peter Lilienthal (W. Germany)
1980	The King and Mister Bird	Paul Grimault (France)
1980	The Beads of One Rosary	Kazimierz Kutz
1980	The Constant Factor	Krzysztof Zanussi
1981	From a Far Country	Krzysztof Zanussi (Italy/UK/Poland)
1982	Imperative	Krzysztof Zanussi (W. Germany)
1984	A Year of the Quiet Sun	Krzysztof Zanussi (Poland/USA/W. Germany)
1984	I Shall Always Stand Guard	Kazimierz Kutz
1984	Marynia	Jan Rybrowski
1985	Power of Evil	Krzysztof Zanussi (France/W. Germany/Italy)
1986	The Brothers Will Come Soon	Kazimierz Kutz
1986	Chronicle of Love Affairs	Andrzej Wajda
1987	Blind Chance	Krzysztof Kieslowski
1988	Salsa	Boaz Davidson (USA)
1988	Wherever You Are . . .	Krzysztof Zanussi (Poland/W. Germany/ UK/France/ Italy)
1988	The Turning Table	Paul Grimault, Jacques Demy (France)
1989	Inventory	Krzysztof Zanussi (Poland/W. Germany)
1990	Korczak	Andrzej Wajda (Poland/Germany/UK)
1991	Life for Life	Krzysztof Zanussi (Poland/Germany)
1992	The Touch	Krzysztof Zanussi (Poland/UK/Denmark)
1992	Bram Stoker's Dracula	Francis Ford Coppola (USA)
1994	Death as a Slice of Bread	Kazimierz Kutz
1994	Faustyna	Jerzy Lukaszewicz
1994	Death and the Maiden	Roman Polanski (UK/USA/France)
1995	Legenda Tatr	Wojciech Solarz
1996	Ghost with Driver	Gérard Oury (France)
1996	At Full Gallop	Krzysztof Zanussi
1996	The Portrait of a Lady	Jane Campion (UK/USA)
1996	Deceptive Charm	Krzysztof Zanussi
1996	A Woman's Business	Krzysztof Zanussi
1997	Our God's Brother	Krzysztof Zanussi
1999	The Ninth Gate	Roman Polanski (Spain/France/USA)
1999	A Week in the Life of a Man	Jerzy Stuhr
1999	Pan Tadeusz: The Last Foray in Lithuania	Andrzej Wajda (Poland/France)
2000	Life as a Fatal Sexually Transmitted Disease	Krzysztof Zanussi (Poland/France)
2001	The Soul Sings	Krzysztof Zanussi
2001	Hidden Treasures of the Weekend Stories Cycle	Krzysztof Zanussi
2002	The Supplement	Krzysztof Zanussi
2002	The Pianist (BAFTA-N)	Roman Polanski (France/Poland/Germany/UK)
2002	The Revenge	Andrzej Wajda
2005	Persona Non Grata	Krzysztof Zanussi (Poland/Italy/Russia/France)
2007	We Own the Night	James Gray (USA)
2007	Black Sun	Krzysztof Zanussi (Italy/France)
2008	And a Warm Heart	Krzysztof Zanussi
2009	Revisited	Krzysztof Zanussi

KNOPFLER, Mark (b. 1949) A popular Scottish singer, musician, songwriter, and record producer who became famous as the lead singer, guitarist, and composer for the British rock band Dire Straits, he has scored seven feature films and is heard on the soundtrack of several others.

Mark Freuser Knopfler was born in Glasgow, Scotland, the son of a Hungarian refugee and an English mother, and the family moved to Blyth, Northumberland, in England when he was seven. Knopfler sang and played guitar in school bands as a teenager then studied journalism at Harlow Technical College for a year. For two years he worked as a reporter for the *Yorkshire Evening Post*, then gave it up to further his education at Leeds University, where he received a degree in English. Yet Knopfler most loved writing and performing rock and Celtic music. To earn a living he taught at Loughton College while performing with different bands in clubs and pubs. In 1977 Knopfler formed the group Dire Straits with his younger brother David, Pick Withers, and John Illsley. One of the rock band's demo tapes was picked up by a radio station and soon Dire Straits was making albums that climbed the charts in Britain, Australia, the United States, and France. The group toured and recorded for nearly twenty years before disbanding in 1995. Knopfler's solo career since then has included seven albums, international tours, and many awards. The first movie to include a Knopfler song ("Walk of Life") was the Italian comedy *Amorevolmente* (1980), followed by dozens of others, including *An Officer and a Gentleman* (1982), *The Color of Money* (1986), *Twister* (1996), *Michael* (1996), *Can't Hardly Wait* (1998), *Bandits* (2001), *Two Tickets to Paradise* (2006), and *Argo* (2012). His first screen score is his most famous, *Local Hero* in 1983. The small Scottish film by Bill Forsyth was not a success at first but later became a very popular cult favorite. Knopfler's soundtrack, on the other hand, was an immediate hit. He went on to score Forsyth's *Comfort and Joy* as well as two successful American movies, *The Princess Bride* and *Wag the Dog*. His other feature films are *Cal*, *Last Exit to Brooklyn*, and *A Shot at Glory*.

Initially known as a rock singer-songwriter, Knopfler has over the years embraced country, jazz, blues, and Scottish folk in his work, particularly in his screen music. This can be heard in his first score, the wonderful collection of the old and new in *Local Hero*. The quirky little film, about an American oilman (Peter Riegert) from Texas who is quietly seduced away from the modern world by an oddball Scottish town, calls for music that has a foot in both worlds. There is an easygoing song titled "The Way It Always Starts" (vocal by Gerry Rafferty) that is modern folk-rock, then the rest of the score is instrumental. The main theme is a gentle Scottish air heard on guitar and electric keyboard with a subdued rock beat that slowly builds and entices one, just as Scotland does to the main character in *Local Hero*. The Houston, Texas, scenes are scored with a furious, hard rockabilly sound while the Gaelic town has a lazy, reflective folk sound. At the local Ceiligh (dance),

lively folk dancing is heard, then one of the punk rockers in the band plays a heartbreaking dirge on a high-pitched pipe, a musical highlight in this beguiling movie. The music that accompanies the Northern Lights is a mystical, heavenly hymn played on a pipe organ while the seashore is scored with vibrating sustained chords that have a majestic feel. Knopfler's years of writing and performing rock music would not lead one to expect such a score from him. Just as *Local Hero* is a one-of-a-kind movie, so too is the score a unique marvel.

Comfort and Joy, Knopfler's other Scottish movie, has an urban setting (Knopfler's hometown of Glasgow) and a jazz-blues-rock score. Some passages are upbeat and celebratory, but much of the music reflects the loneliness of a radio DJ (Bill Patterson) who is depressed during the Christmas holidays. One melancholy theme, titled "A Fistful of Ice Cream," is dreamy and surprisingly melodic even as it is used to underscore the rivalry of two ice cream truck companies. Also urban but more brutally realistic is *Last Exit to Brooklyn* based on Hubert Selby Jr.'s novel about life on the streets in 1952 in the New York borough of the title. The main theme is a morose piece of slow jazz that warns the audience that there is very little to laugh about with these lowlife characters. Knopfler uses orchestral strings throughout rather than his trademark guitar, so the score often sounds like it comes from 1950s Hollywood. While *Last Exit to Brooklyn* is difficult to warm up to, there is much to recommend in the music. The sly political satire *Wag the Dog* is very American in setting and tone, and there is more than a bit of American folk in the score. The main theme is an up-tempo bluegrass piece with some fancy guitar playing, the title song (sung by Knopfler) is a sarcastic urban folk ditty, and there is even a passage that plays a weary patriotic tune with military drumming in the background.

For *The Princess Bride*, a cult film that surpasses *Local Hero* in popularity, Knopfler wrote six songs as well as the soundtrack score. The theme song for this daffy spoof of swashbuckling romances is the ballad "Storybook Love" (sung by Knopfler), a sincere folk love song. More in keeping with the spirit of fun is the sword fight music with quivering strings, mocking brass fanfares, and a frantic pipe organ. There is also sprightly folk dance music played on pipe and tabor, a symphonic minuet for strings and woodwinds, and a romantic theme with flute and plucked strings that is warm and engaging. Listening to the soundtrack of *The Princess Bride* is like hearing a Hollywood swashbuckler score filtered through a large grin. From rock to Scottish folk to satire is quite an unusual path, but that is the one Knopfler's career has taken. If only that path would lead to more movies. Official website: www.markknopfler.com.

Credits

Year	Film	Director
1983	*Local Hero* (BAFTA-N)	Bill Forsyth (UK)
1984	*Cal*	Pat O'Connor (UK)
1984	*Comfort and Joy*	Bill Forsyth (UK)
1987	*The Princess Bride*	Rob Reiner (USA)
1989	*Last Exit to Brooklyn*	Uli Edel (USA/UK/W. Germany)
1997	*Wag the Dog* (aka *Bite the Bullet*)	Barry Levinson (USA)
2000	*A Shot at Glory*	Michael Corrente (USA/UK)

KOMEDA, Christopher (1931–1969) A Polish musician and composer who scored two dozen feature films in his brief, nine-year movie career, he is most known for his scores for director Roman Polanski.

Born Krzysztof Komeda-Trzcinski in Poznan, Poland, he began piano lessons at a very early age, studying at the Poznan Conservatory at the age of eight. Although Komeda pursued musical activities in high school, after graduation he attended the local Medical Academy and received a diploma to practice ear, nose, and throat medicine. He did not abandon his pianist skills, however, and became particularly interested in jazz, playing with various groups in the 1950s including his own Komeda Sextet. The Communist government was suspicious of jazz, but the Komeda Sextet became very popular across Europe and opened doors for modern jazz in the Eastern Bloc. Komeda toured the Continent, made some legendary recordings, and was soon internationally acclaimed as a leader of European jazz and its distinction from American jazz. He became involved in movies when young director Polanski asked him to score his 1958 short *Dwaj ludzie z szafa* (*Two Men and a Wardrobe*). In 1960 Komeda scored his first feature movie but recognition for his screen music did not come until two years later with Polanski's sexual thriller *Knife in the Water*. The two men would go on to collaborate on four other films: *Cul-de-Sac*, *The World's Most Beautiful Swindlers*, *The Fearless Vampire Killers*, and *Rosemary's Baby*. With other European directors he scored such movies as *My Old Man*, *Hunger*, *Epilogue*, *Barrier*, and *The Departure*. By the late 1960s Komeda was working in Hollywood. After completing the score for *The Riot*, he died from complications from a head injury received when he fell during a drunken spree. Komeda was only thirty-seven years old and was mourned as one of the finest jazz pianists of his day. Since 1995 the Komeda Jazz Festival in Poland has been held annually in his memory. A German-Polish documentary about the musician-composer and his music, titled *Komeda: A Soundtrack for a Life*, was released in 2010.

Komeda was a very influential musician and composer in the world of international jazz and his screen music was just starting to be appreciated when he died. He was very active in the movies during the 1960s, scoring European and American films at the rate of three a year. In addition to his twenty-four features, Komeda wrote music for fourteen shorts. His best known scores in the States and Great Britain are those for the Polanski films. The breezy jazz score for *Knife in the Water* starts out carefree as the boat travels along with saxophone accompaniment. A later passage is a sexy cool jazz played on piano and saxophone. When events take an odd and deadly turn, the music is a pulsating, anti-melodic march with various percussion instruments picking up the tempo. Komeda uses high-pitched woodwinds and brass for the main theme for the bizarre hostage melodrama *Cul-De-Sac*, the effect not unlike a mocking kazoo. There is a similarly satiric sound in the score for the stylish spoof *The Fearless Vampire Killers*. The main theme features a wordless chorus chanting an irreverent hymn with a rock beat. Some passages are lighthearted and casual like a television commercial, while the suspense theme recalls cheap 1950s horror music. Komeda also playfully uses some pseudo avant-garde music for this period movie with a very modern sensibility. An eerie lullaby is the most memorable aspect of the score for the satanic drama *Rosemary's Baby*. It is gentle theme that repeats variations of a simple musical phrase. The movie's star Mia Farrow sings a series of "la la la" chants over the strings and the effect is not so much comforting as haunting. A different kind of chanting is heard in the theme for the movie's coven of devil worshippers. A wailing trumpet and abrupt strings play one of the film's surreal passages, and the nightmare sequence in which Rosemary is impregnated by Satan is scored with a complex modern composition with sustained notes, screeching strings, and harsh rhythmic whispering. *Rosemary's Baby* is a unique thriller in that it focuses on character rather than action and Komeda's score is equally distinctive for its restraint and weird delicacy.

The scores for Komeda's non-Polanski movies are less known but often as fascinating. The character drama *My Old Man* has a lyrical yet rhythmic score that features different kinds of jazz. The zesty main theme, played on accordion and woodwinds, is carefree and engaging. A pas-sage performed on a harmonica is equally spirited while a bluesy theme behind the scenes reminiscing about the past is a resigned but tripping saxophone solo. Bill Medley sings the song "One Hundred Years" (lyric by Robert Wells) on the soundtrack for *Riot*, an American film about a tragic prison break. It is an upbeat piece with a blues mentality but a felicitous tempo. The rest of the score also has that kind of complex nature, moving from harmonica to strings effortlessly. The score for *Hunger*, a Scandinavian movie classic of social realism, has a merry but cockeyed carousel waltz that leads into atonal sections filled with repetition and suspense. A wandering clarinet and piano fragments are used effectively in several scenes. Perhaps as in no other of Komeda's film scores, jazz blends into various forms of background music in *Hunger*. Such a fine score is a painful reminder of what Komeda might have accomplished had his movie career and his life not ended so prematurely. Official website: www.komeda.pl.

Credits

(all films Poland unless stated otherwise)

Year	Film	Director
1960	*Goodbye, Till Tomorrow*	Janusz Morgenstern
1960	*Innocent Sorcerers*	Andrzej Wajda
1960	*Szklana góra*	Pawel Komorowski, Barbara Sass
1962	*The Verdict*	Jerzy Passendorfer
1962	*Knife in the Water*	Roman Polanski
1962	*Opening Tomorrow*	Janusz Morgenstern
1962	*My Old Man*	Janusz Nasfeter
1963	*Smarkula*	Leonard Buczkowski
1963	*Epilogue*	Henning Carlsen (Denmark)
1963	*The Criminal and the Lady*	Janusz Nasfeter
1964	*Ubranie prawie nowe*	Wlodzimierz Haupe
1964	*The World's Most Beautiful Swindlers*	Roman Polanski, etc. (France/Italy/ Japan/Netherlands)
1964	*The Law and the Fist*	Jerzy Hoffman, Edward Skórzewski
1964	*Przerwany lot*	Leonard Buczkowski
1965	*The Cats*	Henning Carlsen (Sweden)
1965	*Penguin*	Jerzy Stefan Stawinski
1966	*Evening before Christmas*	Helena Amiradzibi, Jerzy Stefan Stawinski
1966	*Unloved*	Janusz Nasfeter
1966	*Hunger*	Henning Carlsen (Denmark/Norway/Sweden)
1966	*Cul-de-Sac*	Roman Polanski (UK)
1966	*Barrier*	Jerzy Skolimowski
1967	*The Fearless Vampire Killers* (aka *Dance of the Vampires*)	Roman Polanski (USA/UK)
1967	*The Departure*	Jerzy Skolimowski (Belgium)
1967	*People Meet and Sweet Music Fills the Heart*	Henning Carlsen (Denmark/Sweden)
1968	*Rosemary's Baby* (GGN)	Roman Polanski (USA)
1969	*Riot*	Buzz Kulik (USA)

KORNGOLD, Erich Wolfgang (1897–1957) A world-class composer for the opera and concert hall, he reluctantly entered into movie scoring but wrote a handful of brilliant scores before abandoning Hollywood. Korngold was so famous and in such demand that few Hollywood composers were as wooed and pampered. And few have made such an impact in so short a screen career.

Erich Wolfgang Korngold was born in the Austria-Hungary city of Brno (today in the Czech Republic), the son of a music critic, and started composing music at the age of nine. A child prodigy on the piano, Korngold moved with his family to Vienna, where he was praised by Gustav Mahler and Richard Strauss for his compositions. By the time he was eleven, his ballet *The Snowman* was performed at the Vienna Court Opera to wide acclaim. This was followed by piano sonatas, symphonies, and operas all before he was twenty-one. As a young adult, Korngold arranged and conducted operettas by Johann Strauss and taught composition at the Vienna Staatsakademie, earning the rank of professor *honor causa*. He served in the Austria-Hungarian army during World War I but spent most of his enlistment composing marches for military bands. After the war he returned to Vienna where he continued to write for the concert hall and the opera. Because Korngold was Jewish and started to feel the pressure exerted by the Nazi Party, he willingly accepted an invitation by director Max Reinhardt to go to Hollywood in 1934 to arrange Felix Mendelssohn's music for a film version of *A Midsummer Night's Dream*. Korngold remained in the States where he started composing for the screen and was quickly recognized as a major force in the art form. His scores for such adventure movies as *Captain Blood*, *Anthony Adverse*, *The Prince and the Pauper*, *The Adventures of Robin Hood*, *The Sea Wolf*, and *The Sea Hawk* set a new standard for the genre and he also excelled at writing music for dramas, most memorably *The Private Lives of Elizabeth and Essex*, *King's Row*, *Devotion*, and *Of Human Bondage*. Sadly, the quality of the films that Korngold scored waned the longer he stayed in Hollywood. Many felt his music was also getting less and less rewarding. In 1943 Korngold became an American citizen and after the war ended he stayed in America but he was disillusioned with Hollywood and the kinds of movies he was given to score. He gave up screen composing in 1947 in order to write for the concert hall. He only returned to films once in 1955 when he arranged the music of Richard Wagner for the biopic *Magic Fire* and composed some original incidental music as well. Korngold continued to live in Hollywood until his death in 1957 of a cerebral thrombosis at the age of sixty. When he died, Korngold's romantic style of music was considered old fashioned and a remnant of the past. It wasn't until the 1970s that his film and concert music was rediscovered, performed, and recorded. His legacy includes operas, symphonies, piano works, violin concertos, string quartets, and concert versions of his film scores.

Although he contributed to only twenty movies, Korngold is ranked as one of the giants of American screen music. He was one of the first Hollywood composers to create an individual musical motif for each of the main characters, a device he was very familiar with in opera. In fact, many of his best films have been described as operas without singing. Korngold favored strong string sections, particularly in his adventure film scores, and was an advocate of nineteenth-century romanticism. His music is also influenced by that of Mahler, Richard Strauss, and Giacomo Puccini, all three of whom met Korngold as a youth and declared his genius. Yet Korngold could be very modern in his thinking. He thoroughly understood the movie medium and had an uncanny instinct for what worked on the screen. He often composed at a piano while a projectionist ran the film footage for him. Other times he timed the filmed sequences down to the second and wrote music accordingly. He understood how music could unite a movie thematically and how the rhythm of the action on-screen must be supported by the music. This is somewhat remarkable since he came from the world of classical music and had little experience with moviemaking when he wrote his first screen score. That score was for *Captain Blood* and what an auspicious debut it was! (Actually, Korngold had earlier written the music for a trite movie musical titled *Give Us This Night* which was so weak it was not released by the studio for two years.) Legend has it that Korngold had no desire to compose again for Hollywood, but when he saw the rough cut of *Captain Blood* with Errol Flynn's grandiose and funny performance, he thought it would make a fun opera. With such an approach in mind he agreed to score the movie. When told the score was needed in three weeks, Korngold panicked. He hired his trusted composer friend Hugo Friedhofer to orchestrate the music as he furiously composed it. For the extended duel between Flynn and Basil Rathbone and later for the naval battle the composer was so stretched for

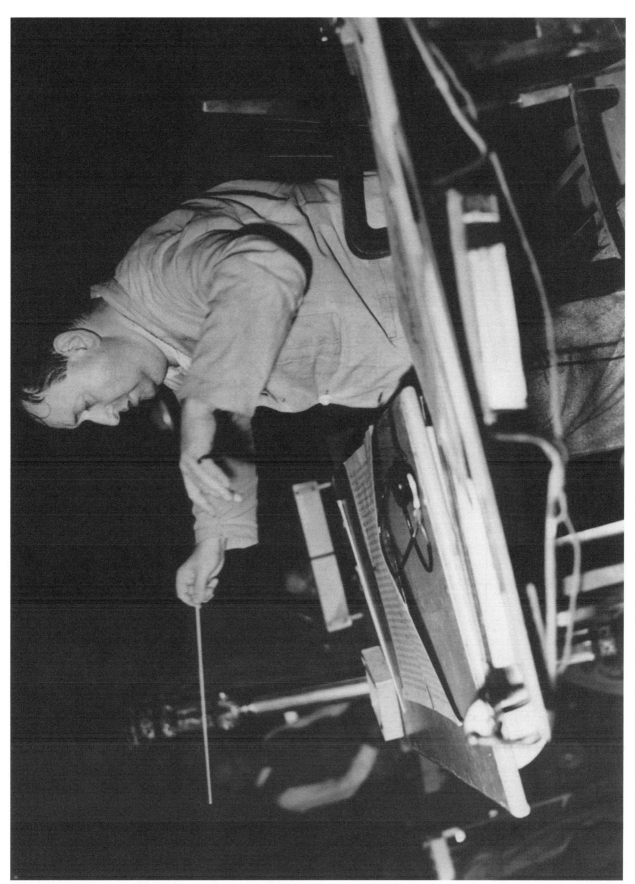

ERICH WOLFGANG KORNGOLD. Although he worked in Tinseltown only from 1935 to 1955, it was enough time for Korngold to single-handedly establish the sound of the Hollywood swashbuckler. In this undated photo, he conducts the vigorous screen music for which he was most known for. *Photofest*

time that he took some themes from Liszt and worked with Friedhofer in turning them into background music. The music throughout *Captain Blood* is stirring yet playful, grandiose yet accessible, romantic yet satiric. Horns blare and strings race in the main theme as the fanfares seem to mock their own majesty. The love theme for Flynn and Olivia de Havilland is full throttle rather than coy, with arresting hesitations built into the tempo. For the action scenes, sometimes drums set the pace as fluttering flutes and piccolos dance throughout. Other times the violins scamper along with the actors, both showing off their bravado shamelessly. *Captain Blood* was a hit for Flynn, Warner Brothers, and the composer; Korngold had pretty much invented the "swashbuckler score."

Anthony Adverse was a period piece of a very different sort. The long episodic film has little humor and both the romantic and the action sequences are never playful but rather earnest and noble. Korngold's score is long and complex, just as the plot covers decades and three continents. *Anthony Adverse* runs two hours and twenty minutes and just about all of that is scored. There are over forty-three different musical motifs, including several character themes, ballroom dancing in Paris, tribal rituals in Africa, Italian street festivals, Havana moonlight dancing, and sequences from real and fictitious operas. It is a romantic score, not to mention an ambitious one, but one misses the sly twinkle from the *Captain Blood* soundtrack. That wry quality can be found again in Korngold's most famous score, his Oscar-winning one for the 1938 version of *The Adventures of Robin Hood*. While not on an epic scale like *Anthony Adverse*, the score is filled with variety as each sequence has its own new and delightful flavor. The main theme is a merry march for Robin's band of comrades. When they disguise themselves as monks and head to the king's coronation, Korngold gives them a silly march that mocks the solemnity of the occasion. Villains Basil Rathbone and Claude Rains have their sinister themes and King Richard (Ian Hunter) has his regal air. The love theme for Flynn and de Havilland is warm and intoxicating while being a bit tentative and restrained. One can practically hear the birds in Sherwood Forest in the chirping flutes. But like all swashbucklers, the most memorable scenes in *The Adventures of Robin Hood* are the action ones and in each case the music does not disappoint. The military music behind the battle in the forest builds in an ominous way then breaks into a thrilling release as the

outlaws leap from the trees down on the sheriff's troops. When the merry men hold a bucolic banquet in the woods, the frolicsome waltz is practically giddy. The archery tournament is scored with gloriously pompous fanfares. As for the climactic duel between Rathbone and Flynn, perhaps the best scene of its kind in the movies, the music not only captures the pattern of the two clinking swords but also the rhythm of the encounter as the two men jockey for the high ground. Korngold seems to be at his energetic and creative peak with this marvelous score.

The third of his famous swashbucklers is *The Sea Hawk*, another Flynn adventure but this time set mostly at sea. From the opening fanfares one gets a sense of water as the music seems to rise and fall with the waves. This theme returns later in the film as Flynn's men escape by ship and burst into a sea chantey version called "Strike for the Shores of Dover" (lyric by Jack Scholl and Howard Koch). If the Korngold adventure scores are a form of opera, why not have the actors sing? The romantic theme in *The Sea Hawk* is one of Korngold's loveliest. It too has a maritime flow as it cautiously repeats a gliding three-note phrase. When the sailors trudge through the forests of Panama, the march theme is a curious blend of piano and saxophone. There is another classic duel in the film, this time between Flynn and Henry Daniell, and again it is scored with furious confidence and panache.

In comparison to this trio of swashbucklers, the rest of Korngold's scores may be classified as quieter and more intimate. Perhaps the finest of this type is *The Private Lives of Elizabeth and Essex*. This is a large-scale period piece and it has its lavish fanfares and regal pomp yet the heart of the score (and the film) is a romance. The love theme is a graceful piece that resounds in the ear because of the way the musical phrases double back on each other. *Juarez*, another historical piece, also has a memorable love theme, this time more insistent and, appropriately, with a Latin flavor. Korngold's score for *The Sea Wolf* is not only quieter but actually somber and, at times, dissonant. The opening theme captures the chaos of the wilderness in the North but soon the score seems to be enveloped in a fog (as are the characters) and everything becomes morose and haunting. *King's Row* is a small-town melodrama that contains perhaps his most American score. It too starts with the familiar Korngold fanfare but quickly becomes patriotic then folklike as it turns into a children's song. There are various themes for the central characters, most memorably one for the grandmother that aches with domesticity and warmth. The heavenly choir heard behind an amputee's declaration to live may strike modern audiences as Korngold corn but it is exactly the kind of ending one might experience in an opera house.

Did Korngold's music diminish as the quality of his films did? There are some pleasing musical moments in *Of Human Bondage* and certainly the scores for *Escape Me Never* and *Devotion* are better than what appears onscreen. The melodrama *Deception*, about a concert cellist (Paul Henreid), has a plot that centers on a new concerto for cello and orchestra written by an egotistical composer (Claude Rains). Korngold wrote a complete concerto for the film and it ranks highly with his other concert work.

But this was not the kind of music Hollywood was asking for in 1946. It was not so much Korngold's music that changed as much as the times. The swashbuckling fantasy faded with the 1940s and World War II, and the highly romantic Korngold sound went out of favor. It returned with the 1950s epics but by then Korngold had abandoned Hollywood. That sound would be revived again in the 1970s when John Williams took up Korngold's mantle and wore it to write the *Star Wars* and *Indiana Jones* movies. On the ocean with Errol Flynn in *The Sea Hawk* or in space with Luke Skywalker, the Korngold legacy lives on. Official website: www.korngold-society.org. Biographies: *The Last Prodigy*, Brenden G. Carroll (1997); *Erich Wolfgang Korngold*, Jessica Duchen (1996).

Credits

(all films USA)

Year	Film	Director
1935	Captain Blood	Michael Curtiz
1936	Give Us This Night	Alexander Hall
1936	The Green Pastures	Marc Connelly, William Keighley
1936	Anthony Adverse	Mervyn LeRoy
1937	The Prince and the Pauper	William Keighley
1937	Another Dawn	William Dieterle
1938	The Adventures of Robin Hood (AA)	Michael Curtiz, William Keighley
1939	Juarez	William Dieterle
1939	The Private Lives of Elizabeth and Essex (AAN)	Michael Curtiz
1940	The Sea Hawk (AAN)	Michael Curtiz
1941	The Sea Wolf	Michael Curtiz
1942	King's Row	Sam Wood
1943	The Constant Nymph	Edmund Golding
1944	Between Two Worlds	Edward A. Blatt
1945	San Antonio	David Butler
1946	Devotion	Curtis Bernhardt
1946	Of Human Bondage	Edmund Golding
1946	Deception	Irving Rapper
1947	Escape Me Never	Peter Godfrey
1955	Magic Fire	William Dieterle

KOSMA, Joseph (1905–1969) A prodigious Hungarian-born composer who wrote music for over one hundred French films, he scored some outstanding movies directed by Marcel Carné and Jean Renoir.

He was born József Kozma in Budapest, Hungary (then Austria-Hungary), the son of parents who taught stenography, and began playing the piano without lessons when he was five. By the time Kosma was eleven, he was writ-

ing original music, including an opera. He later studied composition and conducting at the Academy of Music in Budapest and at the Franz Liszt Academy, where he was mentored by Béla Bartók. While continuing private instruction in Berlin, Kosma met director-playwright Bertolt Brecht and got involved in theatre. With the rise of the Nazi Party, Brecht left Germany and the Jewish Kosma immigrated to Paris in 1933. The poet-screenwriter Jacques

Prévert introduced the young composer to director Jean Renoir, who hired Kosma to cowrite with Jean Wiener the score for his comic thriller *The Crime of Monsieur Lange* in 1936. Later that same year, Kosma was sole composer for Marcel Carné's drama *Jenny*. After scoring Renoir's celebrated film short *A Day in the Country*, the two men collaborated on the landmark antiwar movie *La grande illusion*, arguably the greatest French film of all time. Kosma and Renoir worked together on six subsequent movies: *La Marseillaise*, *The Rules of the Game*, *La bête humaine*, *Elena and Her Men*, *Picnic on the Grass*, and *The Elusive Corporal*. He collaborated with Carné again on *Les visiteurs du soir*, *Les portes de la nuit*, *La fleur de l'âge*, *La marie du port*, and *Julliette, or Key of Dreams*.

When the Nazis occupied France, Kosma was placed under house arrest and banned from writing music. Prévert managed to get some of Kosma's compositions to different filmmakers during the war and they were used under other composers' names. Although Carné's 1945 masterpiece *Les enfants du paradis* (*Children of Paradise*) was scored by Maurice Thiriet, Kosma's music was used for a famous pantomime sequence. After the war, Kosma's screen career flourished in France as he also scored other European movies and even a few American productions. Among his many other notable films are *La dame d'onze heures*, *The Lovers of Verona*, *The Farm of Seven Sins*, *Huis-clos*, *The Ragpickers of Emmaus*, *Main Street*, *The Eighth Day*, *People of No Importance*, and *L'inspecteur aime la bagarre*. Kosma's most famous piece of music is the song "Les feuilles mortes," a jazz ballad with a classical flavor. It was written for the movie *Les portes de la nuit/ Gates of Night* in 1946 with a lyric by Prévert. With an English lyric by Johnny Mercer it became a song standard in the States as "Autumn Leaves." Kosma and Prévert wrote approximately eighty songs together, some heard in movies, others onstage, in cabarets, and on records. In his later years, Kosma returned to writing music for the theatre and also scored two operas and some movies for French television. He continued to work in films until two years before his death at the age of sixty-three.

It is unfortunate that the two greatest films Kosma scored, Renoir's *La grande illusion* and *The Rules of the Game*, have so little original music in them. The former movie, which follows the tragicomic plight of some French prisoners of war during World War I, is also about the waning of a class system and an old way of life. Yet this is not told through music. Kosma wrote some military march music and some underscoring for character scenes but much of the score consists of familiar songs ranging from "La Marseillaise" to a traditional children's ditty to "It's a Long Way to Tipperary." Popular French songs are heard during the amateur theatricals the prisoners perform and during a wry sequence in which the POWs play a silly tune on homemade flutes, much to the annoyance of their German captors. *The Rules of the Game* has a bit more original music. This astute tragicomedy of manners is also about the end of an era. The wealthy people gathered for a weekend house party are immoral, foolish, endearing, and doomed. This time the ideas in the movie are expressed in the music. Kosma's score opens with a vigorous waltz played on strings and brass in such an aggressive manner that it feels like a march. There is a muted trumpet solo under a hunting scene that is a jazzy version of a call to arms, a furious allegro heard on a player piano for a pantomime put on by the guests, and the movie ends with a sour version of the opening theme. In between are again popular songs and dance music of the time as well as selections from Mozart, Chopin, Saint-Saëns, and Strauss. Perhaps Kosma's first fully realized screen score can be heard in Renoir's *La bête humaine* based on Emile Zola's tragic tale of a train engineer (Jean Gabin) and his love affair with a married woman (Simone Simon) who is also a murderer. The score opens with a fluid string passage that has an agitated subtext as it moves back and forth from serene musical phrases to nervous crescendos. This same music is repeated as the love theme, but it is still high strung as it gets very passionate. There is also a less strained passage on strings and woodwinds that dances without care, and a waltz played by a dance band that has a jazzy flavor. Zola's ideas and Renoir's dramatization are reflected in Kosma's compelling music. This is expert screen scoring.

A wide variety of first-rate music can be heard in different Kosma scores. *People of No Importance* is about another doomed love affair, this time between a discontented waitress (Françoise Arnoul) and a married truck driver (Jean Gabin). The main theme consists of quivering strings and a solo violin playing a melancholy lullaby that slowly descends the scale with resignation. The Spanish-French drama *Main Street* (known as *Calle Mayor* in Spain and *Grand Rue* in France) is about two small-town rascals (José Suárez and Yves Massard) who pretend to love a married woman (Betsy Blair) with heartbreaking results.

Kosma's main theme is lively and cruel as fluttering wood-winds dance above swaying strings and some rumbling percussion and brass. *Huis-clos*, an opened-up screen version of Jean-Paul Sartre's existentialist drama *No Exit*, is an allegory of hell, so it is interesting that Kosma scores the movie with a carousel waltz played on muted pipes that is mockingly cheerful. Renoir's *Picnic on the Grass* is an offbeat comedy of manners with political overtones. The most memorable music in the film is when a shepherd's high-pitched pipes plays and echoes the strong wind that scatters the participants of a celebratory picnic. The score also includes a jazzy piece heard on clarinet that swings in a carefree manner, and a flute featured in a lyrical passage filled with harp glissandos. Perhaps Kosma's finest score for Carné is the fantasy drama *Les portes de la nuit* which became better known as *Gates of the Night*. This is the movie that introduced the "Autumn Leaves" melody, but the entire score is masterful. Prévert's story involves a young man (Yves Montand) who is told by a tramp that he will meet and fall in love with a beautiful woman. When he meets Malou (Nathalie Nattier), he does fall in love with her, but connections to the past threaten to destroy the romance. Kosma provides brisk but moody opening music on low and high strings that climb the scale only to tumble back down. This transitions into the haunting "Autumn Leaves" theme which returns throughout the film, sometimes with a mournful tone, other times as a more aggressive piece. There is also a vigorous waltz that speeds ahead like a race rather than a dance, a solemn chant performed by a wordless choir that is filled with despair, a sidewalk cafe tune played on accordion that is unsettling, and a march played on woodwinds and brass that is threatening and suspenseful. Finally, one must acknowledge Kosma's wonderful ballet music for a sequence in Carné's *Children of Paradise*. It is a glittering piece for strings and woodwinds that seems to float on a summer breeze. Then a new section stirs itself up like a storm with musical flourishes on brass. It then calms down to return to the original theme again. Here is a case in which Kosma's music is as sterling as the movie classic for which it was written.

Credits

(all films France unless stated otherwise)

Year	Film	Director
1936	The Crime of Monsieur Lange	Jean Renoir
1936	Jenny	Marcel Carné
1937	La grande illusion	Jean Renoir
1938	The Time of the Cherries	Jean-Paul Le Chanois
1938	La Marseillaise	Jean Renoir
1938	La bête humaine	Jean Renoir
1939	The Rules of the Game	Jean Renoir
1942	Les visiteurs du soir	Marcel Carné
1943	A Woman in the Night	Edmond T. Gréville
1943	Adieu Léonard	Pierre Prévert
1946	Messieurs Ludovic	Jean-Paul Le Chanois
1946	Pétrus	Marc Allégret
1946	Gates of the Night	Marcel Carné
1947	The Royalists	Henri Calef
1947	Voyage Surprise	Pierre Prévert
1947	Noah's Ark	Henry Jacques
1947	L'amour autour de la maison	Pierre de Hérain
1947	Bethsabée	Léonide Moguy
1947	La fleur de l'âge	Marcel Carné
1948	La dame d'onze heures	Jean-Devaivre
1948	Crossroads of Passion	Ettore Gianni, Henri Calef (Italy/France)
1948	Man to Men (aka Heroes in White)	Christian-Jaque (France/Switzerland)
1948	Wench	Henri Calef
1949	The Lovers of Verona	André Cayatte
1949	L'école buissonnière	Jean-Paul Le Chanois

Year	Film	Director
1949	*The Hell of Lost Pilots*	Georges Lampin
1949	*The Farm of Seven Sins*	Jean-Devaivre
1949	*Wicked City*	François Villiers
1949	*Au grand balcon*	Henri Decoin
1950	*The Big Meeting*	Jean Dréville
1950	*La marie du port*	Marcel Carné
1950	*Here Is the Beauty*	Jean-Paul Le Chanois
1950	*Vendetta en Camargue*	Jean-Devaivre
1950	*Paris Incident*	Henri Decoin
1950	*Lost Souvenirs*	Christian-Jaque
1950	*Fugitive from Montreal*	Jean-Devaivre
1950	*Captain Blackjack*	Julien Duvivier, José Antonio Nieves Conde(Spain/ USA/France)
1951	*Sans laisser d'adresse*	Jean-Paul Le Chanois
1951	*Juliette, or Key of Dreams*	Marcel Carné
1951	*Shadow and Light*	Henri Calef
1951	*Sins of Madeleine*	Henri Lepage
1951	*Pardon My French*	Bernard Vorhaus (USA/France)
1951	*The Cape of Hope*	Raymond Bernard (France/Italy)
1951	*Paris Is Always Paris*	Luciano Emmer (Italy/France)
1951	*Perfectionist*	Yves Ciampi
1952	*The White Road (aka The Green Glove)*	Rudolph Maté (USA/France)
1952	*Wolves Hunt at Night*	Bernard Borderie (France/Italy)
1952	*Matrimonial Agency*	Jean-Paul Le Chanois
1952	*Dans la vie tout s'arrange*	Marcel Cravenne (France/UK)
1952	*Judgment of God*	Raymond Bernard
1952	*The Curious Adventures of Mr. Wonderbird*	Paul Grimault
1952	*Crimson Curtain*	André Barsacq
1953	*Opération Magali*	Laszló V. Kish
1953	*Innocents in Paris*	Gordon Parry (UK)
1953	*Children of Love*	Léonide Moguy
1953	*Rhine Virgin*	Gilles Grangier
1953	*Alarm in Morocco*	Jean-Devaivre (France/Italy)
1954	*Wild Fruit*	Hervé Bromberger
1954	*Huis-clos*	Jacqueline Audry
1955	*Fantaisie d'un jour*	Pierre Cardinal
1955	*The Ragpickers of Emmaus*	Robert Darene
1955	*Magic Village*	Jean-Paul Le Chanois (France/Italy)
1955	*Pas de souris dans le business*	Henri Lepage
1955	*House on the Waterfront*	Edmond T. Gréville
1955	*The Fugitives*	Jean-Paul Le Chanois
1955	*M'sieur la Caille (aka No Morals)*	André Pergament
1955	*Pas de pitié pour les caves*	Henri Lepage
1955	*Lady Chatterley's Lover*	Marc Allégret
1956	*Maigret dirige l'enquête*	Stany Cordier
1956	*People of No Importance*	Henri Verneuil
1956	*Kiss of Fire*	Robert Darene (Italy/France)
1956	*Law of the Streets*	Ralph Habib
1956	*This Is the Dawn*	Luis Buñuel (France/Italy)
1956	*Diary of a Bad Girl*	Léonide Moguy (France/Italy)
1956	*Elena and Her Men*	Jean Renoir (Italy/France)
1956	*Main Street*	Juan Antonio Bardem (Spain/France)
1956	*Soupçons*	Pierre Billon
1956	*I'll Get Back to Kandara*	Victor Vicas
1957	*The Case of Dr. Laurent*	Jean-Paul Le Chanois
1957	*Demoniac*	Luis Saslavsky
1957	*L'inspecteur aime la bagarre*	Jean-Devaivre
1957	*Three Days to Live*	Gilles Grangier

Year	Film	Director
1958	*Tamango*	John Berry (France/Italy)
1958	*Un certain Monsieur Jo*	René Jolivet
1958	*The Cat*	Henri Decoin
1958	*The Doctor's Dilemma*	Anthony Asquith (UK)
1959	*Quai des illusions*	Émile Couzinet (France/Italy)
1959	*Picnic on the Grass*	Jean Renoir
1959	*Adorable Sinner*	Robert Siodmak
1960	*The Eighth Day*	Marcel Hanoun
1960	*Spy Is a Girl*	Henri Decoin
1960	*Croesus*	Jean Giono
1961	*Le pavé de Paris*	Henri Decoin (Italy/France)
1961	*El secreto de los hombres azules*	Edmond Agabra (France/Spain)
1961	*Man Wants to Live*	Léonide Moguy (France/Italy)
1962	*Dawn on the Third Day*	Claude Bernard-Aubert (France/Greece)
1962	*The Elusive Corporal*	Jean Renoir
1962	*La poupée*	Jacques Baratier (Italy/France)
1962	*Snobs!*	Jean-Pierre Mocky
1962	*À fleur de peau*	Claude Bernard-Aubert
1963	*Heaven Sent* (aka *Light-Fingered George*)	Jean-Pierre Mocky
1963	*In the French Style*	Robert Parrish (USA/France)
1966	*Pitzutz B'Hatzot*	Hervé Bromberger (Israel/France)
1967	*Bitter Fruit*	Jacqueline Audry
1967	*Kitosch, the Man Who Came from the North*	José Luis Merino (Italy/Spain)

LAI, Francis (b. 1932) A prolific French songwriter and composer for the movies, he has scored over one hundred feature films, many with director Claude Lelouch.

Francis Albert Lai was born in Nice, France, and was interested in music at a young age. Lai took lessons in piano and accordion and discovered jazz in cabarets in nearby Marseilles. He began his career in 1950 as a musician for various orchestras then met up with singer-songwriter Claude Goaty and became her accompanist. Settling in the Montmarte district of Paris, Lai was soon writing songs for Goaty, Edith Piaf, Yves Montand, and others. He met film director Claude Lelouch, who was impressed with Lai's songs and in 1966 asked him to write a complete score for his romantic drama *A Man and a Woman*. Both the film and the music became an international phenomenon, the love theme from the movie becoming one of the most recognized tunes of the decade. Lelouch and Lai have since worked together on over thirty films, perhaps the longest director-composer collaboration in movies. Among their most notable credits are *Live for Life, Grenoble, Life Love Death, The Good and the Bad, And Now My Love, Robert et Robert, Bolero, Itinerary of a Spoiled Child, Chance or Coincidence*, and *L'aventure, c'est l'aventure*. After the success of *A Man and a Woman*, Lai was in demand for European and American movies. His most popular Hollywood film was *Love Story* which brought Lai an Oscar for Best Score, a best-selling song, and a soundtrack album that climbed the charts. Among his many other noteworthy movies on both sides of the Atlantic are *Rider on the Rain, I'll Never Forget What's'isname, Tender Moment, And Hope to Die, Merry-Go-Round, Happy New Year, Anima Persa, International Velvet, Bilitis, My New Partner*, and *Dark Eyes*. Lai composed several songs for his movie scores and outside of the cinema he has written hundreds of other songs. He has also written music for documentaries and television.

Although Lai began his career as a songwriter of pop hits, many of his film scores are not in the pop mode. He had little formal education in music, yet he often turns to classical models in his scores. Perhaps the primary characteristic of Lai's music is his ability to create a catchy musical idea and sustain it through repetition and variations. The fact that he does this without relying on melody is unusual and unique. A good example is the insistently memorable main theme for Lai's first feature film score, *A Man and a Woman*. This simple but affecting tale is about the romance between a race car driver (Jean-Louis Trintignant) and a script supervisor (Anouk Aimée) for the movies, both of them widowed and with children. The famous title theme moves like a samba with repeated notes that take their time before they move to a new key and repeat elsewhere on the scale. The theme is heard in different variations throughout the movie. As played on electric keyboard and guitar with wordless vocals by Nicole Croisille and Pierre Barouh, the theme is suave and modern. When it is speeded up, the theme takes on a jazz temperament. At another point in the movie Croisille and Barouh sing a duet version (lyric by Barouh) which later became a hit song. Yet there is more to the score for *A Man and a Woman* than its celebrated theme. Lai wrote three other themes/songs (lyrics by Barouh) for the soundtrack, including a slow jazz track on woodwinds and strings with a solo trumpet that is melancholy yet lyrical. Interpolated into the score is a breezy samba on guitar written by Baden Powell (with Barouh singing his own French lyric) that fits in seamlessly with the rest of Lai's music. *A Man and a Woman* was one of the most popular foreign films in America during the 1960s and Lai's soundtrack album and theme song were on the charts for a long time. Along with composer Michel Legrand, Lai became the voice of modern French music in the States.

Lelouch and Lai's *Live for Life*, while not nearly as popular as *A Man and a Woman*, is very similar to it. The love story this time is a triangle consisting of a self-centered television newscaster (Yves Montand), his wife (Annie Giradot), and his mistress (Candice Bergen). The breezy main theme, played on electric keyboard with synthesized effects, is not unlike the love theme from *A Man and a Woman*. It also repeats notes and moves at a steady, samba beat. The difference lies in the way this casual travel theme has a carefree nature rather than a romantic one. The musical motif for the wife is a bluesy passage on electric organ that has interesting pseudobaroque sections. This music is heard later played on an accordion and it becomes the movie's love theme. Although the soundtrack for *Live for Life* was not a best seller, two other French movies scored by Lai did produce chart-selling albums. *Le passager de la pluie*, known outside France as *Rider on the Rain*, is an expert crime thriller directed by René Clément about an American colonel (Charles Bronson) who gets involved in a murder case in the South of France. Lai's score is far from the romantic, easy-listening temperament of *A Man and a Woman* and *Live for Life*. The opening music is a rock theme on electronic instruments and woodwinds and strings that moves like a rapid dance, yet the whole piece has a jaded air about it. There is a cool jazz passage played on a synthesizer with a steady beat that is later used for the title song (lyric by Sébastien Japrisot) sung by Séverine on the soundtrack. Also in this commendable score is a moody accordion passage that lingers over most notes while sustained strings float above, an echoing theme on synthesized instruments that repeats a simple phrase with interesting variations, and a slow and rather morose track played on guitar that is so tentative it seems to be afraid of itself. Another French film with a popular soundtrack album is *Bilitis*, an erotic tale of a girls' boarding school teen (Patti D'Arbanville) who discovers sex one summer when she has an affair with a woman and then a man. Not much above a soft porn flick, the movie and its sensual music had such great appeal that moviegoers (who could not purchase a copy of the film in 1977) bought the soundtrack album. Lai's slow and sensuous main theme uses an echoing synthesizer with high notes for the melody, sustained strings beneath. Some passages in the score utilize high-pitched female *vocalise* accompanied by a dreamlike harp. The whole movie is a sexual fantasy of sorts and most of the music is along those lines. There is some sprightly traveling music played on electronic instruments that bounces along happily and it seems like a breath of fresh air after all that erotic chanting.

An ambitious French movie with an outstanding score by Lai and Michel Legrand is Lelouch's *Les uns et les autres*, better known internationally as *Bolero* or even *Dance of Life*. Three generations of dancers and musicians from Germany, France, Russia, and the United States are chronicled from the late 1930s to the 1980s in this sprawl-ing film filled with music. The characters include a violinist, conductor, pianist, singers, ballerinas, and even a blind accordionist (played by Lai himself). Much of the plotting is held together by music, the score and the songs pretty much equally divided between Lai and Legrand. Lai wrote the title theme, an accordion and string waltz that has the feeling of cafe music but, as orchestrated by Legrand, is more expansive. It also serves as the title song (lyric by Barouh) sung by Croisille on the soundtrack. Among the many highlights in this wonderful score are a waltz on woodwinds and strings that is light footed and romantic, a Big Band piece with unexpected strings among the brass and reeds, a vivacious Folies Bergere number, a jazz track with swinging woodwinds but a relaxed and casual brass section, and a dramatic string theme that climbs the scale with passion. The film ends at a benefit performance in Paris in which Ravel's "Bolero" is used. Legrand did not contribute music to Lai's biggest hit, *Love Story*, yet many have pointed out that Lai's main theme is uncomfortably close to Legrand's Oscar-winning song "The Windmills of Your Mind" from the movie *The Thomas Crown Affair* two years earlier. All the same, the *Love Story* score is very effective, was extremely popular, and is surprisingly classical. The tearjerking tale of the doomed romance between a wealthy Harvard "preppie" (Ryan O'Neal) and a working-class girl (Ali MacGraw) could have been scored with sappy pop music or even a rock ballad. Lai opted to go with a minor-key classical theme on piano and strings. The piece has repeated notes like in *A Man and a Woman* but, rather than being smooth and modern, the tone is decidedly old fashioned. As with many of Lai's other movie themes, this one made for a good song. After the movie was released, a lyric by Carl Sigman was added and under the title "Where Do I Begin" it was a popular single for several singers. The rest of the *Love Story* score is also classically flavored. A playful scene with the lovers frolicking in the snow is scored with an upbeat passage played on electric instruments that races forward happily as a female vocalizes a wordless chant. There is an elaborate classical piece heard on a harpsichord with Scarlatti-like flourishes even though the track has a rock beat. Also enticing is a skating waltz played on strings and woodwinds that is zesty and expansive as it easily moves up and down the scale with giddy glee.

Lai's music has often been compared to that of Henry Mancini because both captured an easy jazz style with pop accents that define 1960s pop. Yet Mancini's music is strong on melody and his catchy tunes stick in the ear because they are so hummable. Lai's music also is catchy but it is through its rhythmic and harmonic ideas. Of course there is still melody, otherwise so many of his themes would not make such popular songs. But even in song form, Lai's music is memorable because of the way it intrigues and seduces the ear with its musical progressions and harmonics. Official website: www.francis-lai.com.

Credits

(all films France unless stated otherwise; * for Best Song; ** score nominated for César Award)

Year	Film	Director
1966	A Man and a Woman (GGN*)	Claude Lelouch
1967	My Love, My Love	Nadine Trintignant
1967	Action Man	Jean Delannoy
1967	Live for Life (GGN; GGN*; BAFTA-N)	Claude Lelouch (France/Italy)
1967	The Bobo	Robert Parrish (USA)
1967	I'll Never Forget What's'isname	Michael Winner (UK)
1968	The Golden Claws of the Cat Girl	Edouard Logereau (France/Italy)
1968	Grenoble	Claude Lelouch, François Reichenbach
1968	House of Cards	John Guillermin (USA)
1968	Mayerling	Terence Young (France/UK)
1968	Tender Moment	Michel Boisrond
1969	Life Love Death	Claude Lelouch (France/Italy)
1969	Hannibal Brooks	Michael Winner (UK)
1969	Three Into Two Won't Go	Peter Hall (UK)
1969	Love Is a Funny Thing	Claude Lelouch (France/Italy)
1970	Rider on the Rain (aka Rain)	René Clément (France/Italy)
1970	I Want You Now	Michel Boisrond
1970	With Love in Mind	Robin Cecil-Wright (UK)
1970	The Games	Michael Winner (UK)
1970	Hello-Goodbye	Jean Negulesco, Ronald Neame (UK)
1970	The Modification	Michel Worms (Italy/France)
1970	The Crook	Claude Lelouch (France/Italy)
1970	Love Story (AA; GG)	Arthur Hiller (USA)
1970	The Love Mates (aka Madly)	Roger Kahane (Italy/France)
1971	Early Morning	Jean-Gabriel Albicocco
1971	Smic Smac Smoc	Claude Lelouch
1972	L'odeur des fauves (aka Scandal Man)	Richard Balducci (France/Italy)
1972	L'aventure, c'est l'aventure	Claude Lelouch (France/Italy)
1972	Dust in the Sun	Richard Balducci (Spain/France)
1972	And Hope to Die	René Clément (France/Italy)
1972	Tom Thumb	Michel Boisrond
1973	Merry-Go-Round (aka Dance of Love)	Otto Schenk (W. Germany)
1973	Killing in the Sun	Daniel Vigne (France/Italy)
1973	Happy New Year (BAFTA-N)	Claude Lelouch (France/Italy)
1973	A Free Man	Roberto Muller
1974	Par le sang des autres	Marc Simenon (France/Canada)
1974	Visit to a Chief's Son	Lamont Johnson (USA)
1974	Loving in the Rain	Jean-Claude Brialy (France/Italy/W. Germany)
1974	And Now My Love	Claude Lelouch (France/Italy)
1974	Love Child (aka Child Under a Leaf)	George Bloomfield (Canada)
1974	Marriage	Claude Lelouch
1975	Cat and Mouse	Claude Lelouch
1975	Scar Tissue (aka The Baby Sitter)	René Clément (France/Italy/W. Germany)
1975	Emmanuelle II	Francis Giacobetti
1976	The Good and the Bad	Claude Lelouch

Year	Film	Director
1976	*Second Chance*	Claude Lelouch
1976	*Body of My Enemy*	Henri Verneuil
1976	*Striptease*	Germán Lorente (Spanish)
1977	*Anima Persa*	Dino Risi (Italy/France)
1977	*Bilitis***	David Hamilton (France/Italy)
1977	*Another Man, Another Chance*	Claude Lelouch (France/USA)
1977	*Widow's Nest*	Tony Navarro (Spain/USA)
1978	*Boarding School*	André Farwagi (W. Germany)
1978	*Robert et Robert*	Claude Lelouch
1978	*International Velvet*	Bryan Forbes (USA)
1978	*The Small Timers*	Robert Pouret
1978	*Oliver's Story*	John Korty (USA)
1979	*Us Two*	Claude Lelouch (France/Canada)
1980	*Les Borsalini*	Michel Nerval
1980	*Beyond the Reef* (aka *Sharkboy of Bora Bora*)	Frank C. Clarke (USA)
1981	*Bolero* (aka *Dance of Life*)**	Claude Lelouch
1981	*Madame Claude 2*	François Mimet
1983	*Salut la puce*	Richard Balducci
1983	*Edith and Marcel*	Claude Lelouch
1984	*Dog Day*	Yves Boisset
1984	*My New Partner*	Claude Zidi
1984	*I Believe in Santa Claus*	Christian Gion
1985	*No More God, No More Love*	Tôru Murakawa (Japan)
1985	*Marie: A True Story*	Roger Donaldson (USA)
1985	*AIDS: Love in Danger*	Hans Noever (W. Germany/France)
1986	*A Man and a Woman: Twenty Years Later*	Claude Lelouch
1986	*Attention Bandits!*	Claude Lelouch
1987	*Association de malfaiteurs*	Claude Zidi
1987	*Dark Eyes*	Nikita Mikhailkov (Italy/USA/USSR)
1988	*Bernadette* (aka *The Passion of Bernadette*)	Jean Delannoy (Switzerland/France/ Luxembourg)
1988	*Les pyramides bleues* (aka *Paradise Calling*)	Arielle Dombasle (France/Mexico)
1988	*Itinerary of a Spoiled Child***	Claude Lelouch (France/W. Germany)
1988	*Keys to Freedom*	Steve Feke (USA)
1988	*The Spirit*	Niklaus Schilling (W. Germany)
1990	*My New Partner II*	Claude Zidi
1990	*I'll Be Going Now*	Dino Risi (Italy/France)
1990	*Those Were the Days . . . and Moons*	Claude Lelouch
1990	*Le provincial*	Christian Gion
1991	*The Keys to Paradise*	Philippe de Broca
1992	*La belle histoire*	Claude Lelouch
1992	*Stranger in the House*	Georges Lautner
1993	*All That . . . for This?*	Claude Lelouch (France/Canada)
1994	*The Thief and the Liar*	Paul Boujenah
1996	*Men, Women: A User's Manual*	Claude Lelouch
1997	*Le serment sous la lune*	Regis Ghezelbash (S. Korea/France)
1998	*Chance or Coincidence***	Claude Lelouch (France/Canada)
1999	*Une pour toutes*	Claude Lelouch
2000	*Les Insaisissables*	Christian Gion
2003	*Plastic Tree*	Il-Seon Eo (S. Korea)
2003	*Ripoux 3*	Claude Zidi
2004	*Le genre humain—1ere partie: Les Parisiens*	Claude Lelouch
2005	*Le courage d'aimer*	Claude Lelouch
2006	*Amore e liberta—Masaniello*	Angelo Antonucci (Italy)
2010	*What War May Bring*	Claude Lelouch

LANGE, Arthur (1889–1956) A top musical director, arranger, songwriter, conductor, bandleader, and composer for theatre, dance bands, records, and movies, he contributed original music to over one hundred feature films but usually worked with other composers and was uncredited.

Arthur Lange was born in Philadelphia and privately educated, studying piano and later playing it and the banjo for local orchestras. As a teenager Lange went to New York City and found work writing and arranging music for music publishers and record companies. With lyricist Andrew B. Sterling, he wrote many songs for Tin Pan Alley. In the 1920s he orchestrated such Broadway musicals as *Maid of Athens* (1914), *Little Miss Charity* (1920), *The Right Girl* (1921), *Helen of Troy, New York* (1923), *Earl Carroll Vanities* (1923), and *Sidewalks of New York* (1927). Lange formed his own band in 1923 and conducted it onstage and on records. He was also considered one of the finest arrangers of dance music in the business and his stock arrangements were used by dozens of orchestras across the country. In 1926 his book *Arranging for the Modern Dance Orchestra* was published and for many years was the preeminent work on the subject. By 1929 Lange was in Hollywood and was hired to head the new music department at MGM. He not only arranged all the music for the all-star production *The Hollywood Revue of 1929* but composed the incidental music as well. Over the next twenty-five years, he contributed music to musicals, dramas, comedies, and thrillers for different studios. Lange was the sole composer for approximately thirty feature films, but he cowrote or contributed to at least

one hundred other movies even as he conducted and/or arranged many more. He received Oscar nominations for his scores for *The Great Victor Herbert*, *Lady of Burlesque*, *Casanova Brown*, *Belle of the Yukon*, and *The Woman in the Window*, all shared with co-composers. Among his many other significant scores are those for *Dynamite*, *Rebound*, *Lady with a Past*, *Rebecca of Sunnybrook Farm*, *The Golden West*, *The Lottery Lover*, *Thanks a Million*, *In Old Kentucky*, *The Great Ziegfeld*, *Kidnapped*, *Woman on the Run*, *Japanese War Bride*, *Queen for a Day*, and *99 River Street*. In 1947 Lange became resident conductor for the Santa Monica Civic Symphony, a position he held for ten years. He was just beginning to work in television in 1956 when he died at the age of sixty-seven.

Hollywood never considered Lange an important composer and perhaps he himself didn't hold his original music very highly except for his Tin Pan Alley songs. It is most likely he contributed original music to the movies for which he was doing the arrangements because it was faster and more efficient when turning out so many movies for MGM, Warners, and the other studios he worked for. For the most part, the thirty films Lange scored alone were not major projects or were musicals in which the bulk of the music was heard in songs written by others. Listening to his solo scores for his better-known nonmusicals, such as *Rebound*, *In Old Kentucky*, and *Thanks a Million*, one is more impressed by the arrangements than the original music. As a screen composer. Lange might be dismissed as negligible; as an arranger, he was a powerhouse.

Credits

(all films USA)

Year	Film	Director
1929	The Hollywood Revue of 1929	Charles Reisner
1929	Our Modern Maidens	Jack Conway
1929	Dynamite	Cecil B. DeMille
1931	Millie	John Francis Dillon
1931	A Woman of Experience	Harry Joe Brown
1931	The Common Law	Paul L. Stein
1931	Rebound	Edward H. Griffith
1931	The Big Gamble	Fred Niblo
1931	Bad Company (aka The Gangster's Wife)	Tay Garnett
1931	Suicide Fleet	Albert S. Rogell
1931	The Big Shot	Ralph Murphy
1932	Prestige	Tay Garnett

Year	Film	Director
1932	*Lady with a Past*	Edward H. Griffith
1932	*Week Ends Only*	Alan Crosland
1932	*Rebecca of Sunnybrook Farm*	Alfred Santell
1932	*Hat Check Girl*	Sidney Lanfield
1932	*Rackety Rax*	Alfred L. Werker
1932	*The Golden West*	David Howard
1932	*Call Her Savage*	John Francis Dillon
1933	*Smoke Lightning*	David Howard
1933	*Broadway Bad*	Sidney Lanfield
1933	*Hello, Sister!*	Alan Crosland, etc.
1933	*Adorable* (aka *Princess at Your Orders*)	William Dieterle
1933	*My Weakness*	David Butler
1933	*Jimmy and Sally*	James Tinling
1934	*Stand Up and Cheer!*	Hamilton MacFadden
1934	*Now I'll Tell*	Edwin J. Burke
1934	*Servants' Entrance*	Frank Lloyd, Walt Disney
1934	*Marie Galante*	Henry King
1935	*The Lottery Lover* (aka *Love Can Be Fun*)	Wilhelm Thiele
1935	*One More Spring*	Henry King
1935	*It's a Small World*	Irving Cummings
1935	*Thanks a Million*	Roy Del Ruth
1935	*In Old Kentucky*	George Marshall
1936	*The Great Ziegfeld*	Robert Z. Leonard
1936	*Magnificent Brute*	John G. Blystone
1936	*Under Your Spell*	Otto Preminger
1936	*White Hunter*	Irving Cummings
1937	*This Is My Affair*	William A. Seiter
1937	*Love under Fire*	George Marshall
1937	*Wife, Doctor and Nurse*	Walter Lang
1937	*Lancer Spy*	Gregory Ratoff
1938	*Kidnapped*	Alfred L. Werker, Otto Preminger
1938	*Hold That Co-ed*	George Marshall
1938	*Submarine Patrol* (aka *Suicide Fleet*)	John Ford
1939	*Let Freedom Ring* (aka *Song of the West*)	Jack Conway
1939	*The Great Victor Herbert* (AAN)	Andrew L. Stone
1940	*Married and in Love*	John Farrow
1942	*That Other Woman* (aka *Leap Year*)	Ray McCarey
1943	*Lady of Burlesque* (AAN)	William A. Wellman
1943	*The Dancing Masters* (aka *A Matter of Money*)	Malcolm St. Clair
1944	*Belle of the Yukon* (AAN)	William A. Seiter
1944	*Pin Up Girl* (aka *Imagine Us*)	H. Bruce Humberstone
1944	*Woman in the Window* (AAN)	Fritz Lang
1944	*Bermuda Mystery*	Benjamin Stoloff
1944	*Casanova Brown* (AAN)	Sam Wood
1945	*It's a Pleasure*	William A. Seiter
1946	*Rendezvous 24*	James Tinling
1946	*The Fabulous Suzanne*	Steve Sekely
1948	*Texas, Brooklyn and Heaven*	William Castle
1948	*Jungle Patrol* (aka *West of Tomorrow*)	Joseph M. Newman
1950	*The Vicious Years*	Robert Florey
1950	*The Golden Gloves Story*	Felix E. Feist
1950	*Woman on the Run*	Norman Foster
1951	*The Groom Wore Spurs*	Richard Whorf
1951	*Queen for a Day*	Arthur Lubin
1951	*The Lady Says No*	Frank Ross
1952	*Japanese War Bride* (aka *East Is East*)	King Vidor
1952	*The Pride of St. Louis*	Harmon Jones
1953	*Down Among the Sheltering Palms*	Edmund Goulding

Year	Film	Director
1953	*War Paint*	Lesley Selander
1953	*99 River Street*	Phil Karlson
1953	*The Steel Lady*	Ewald André Dupont
1954	*Beachhead*	Stuart Heisler
1954	*Southwest Passage*	Ray Nazarro
1954	*The Mad Magician*	John Brahm

LEGRAND, Michel (b. 1932) An internationally acclaimed French composer, conductor, pianist, and songwriter, he was already famous before he scored his first movie because of his popular jazz, pop, and classical albums. A busy career in concert, records, and television has not kept him from scoring over 150 feature films.

He was born Michel Jean Legrand in Bécon-les-Bruyères, a suburb of Paris, the son of composer, conductor, and actor Raymond Legrand. He received a thorough musical education at the Paris Conservatoire and under the notable teachers Henri Challan and Nadia Boulanger. Legrand was awarded prizes for his classical piano skills and early compositions, but in 1947, after attending a concert by Dizzy Gillespie, he became interested in jazz. His first jobs were as accompanist for singers, but in 1954 he gained wide recognition for his album *I Love Paris*, followed by other best-selling records, including some with Gillespie. His 1957 album *Michel Legrand Plays Cole Porter* distinguished him as a superb pianist and interpreter of song standards. After writing the music for two French documentaries, Legrand scored his first feature film, the comedy *Le triporteur* (*The Tricyclist*) in 1957. He immediately got involved with the young French directors who comprised the New Wave cinema, particularly Claude Lelouch, Jean-Luc Godard, and Jacques Demy. It was his modern operatic score for Demy's *The Umbrellas of Cherbourg* in 1964 that got international attention. Not only was the movie and the score praised, but it afforded Legrand his first hit song, "I Will Wait for You," which became popular around the world.

Hollywood was interested, and after scoring a few American movies in the early 1960s, Legrand moved to Los Angeles. Throughout his fifty-year film career, he has often returned to Europe and worked with French and Italian artists. Yet it was his American films that found success around the globe and made Legrand an internationally beloved songwriter and composer. *The Thomas Crown Affair* in 1968 and its theme song "The Windmills of Your Mind"

brought him his first Oscar, followed by many other awards over the years. Among Legrand's best scores from the 1960s and 1970s are those for *The Young Girls of Rochefort*, *Ice Station Zebra*, *The Picasso Summer*, *The Go-Between*, *Pieces of Dreams*, *Summer of '42*, *Le Mans*, *Lady Sings the Blues*, *The Three Musketeers*, *Gable and Lombard*, *The Happy Ending*, and *The Other Side of Midnight*. Only a few of these movies were box office successes, and Legrand's screen career has been filled with outstanding scores in mediocre or poor pictures. During the 1980s and 1990s, he continued to score four or five feature films a year, producing fine scores for *Atlantic City*, *Best Friends*, *Yentl*, *Never Say Never Again*, and *Dingo*. Legrand has concentrated on concerts, theatre, and other projects in the new century.

Legrand was one of the first of the A-list Hollywood composers to score TV movies. His score for *Brian's Song* in 1971 was one of the few small screen scores to produce a best-selling album. His other television films and miniseries include *It's Good to Be Alive* (1974), *Cage Without a Key* (1975), *A Woman Called Golda* (1982), *The Jesse Owens Story* (1984), *Promises to Keep* (1985), *Not a Penny More, Not a Penny Less* (1990), and *The Ring* (1996), as well as several others for European television. Legrand's love for jazz never waned, and throughout his career he has made many jazz recordings of his own works and music by others. He has also been in demand as a conductor, appearing in many classical and pop concerts over the years. Legrand became more interested in theatre when *The Umbrellas of Cherbourg* was turned into an Off-Broadway musical play in 1979. His original musical *Amour* had a brief run on Broadway in 2002 and his musical stage version of *La Dame aux Camélias* titled *Marguerite* premiered in London in 2008. None of these stage works was a long-running hit, but the latter two shows were recorded and Legrand's scores have been widely praised.

While Legrand's screen music is often steeped in romanticism there is always something very modern about his scores. Perhaps it is his method of beginning a piece in

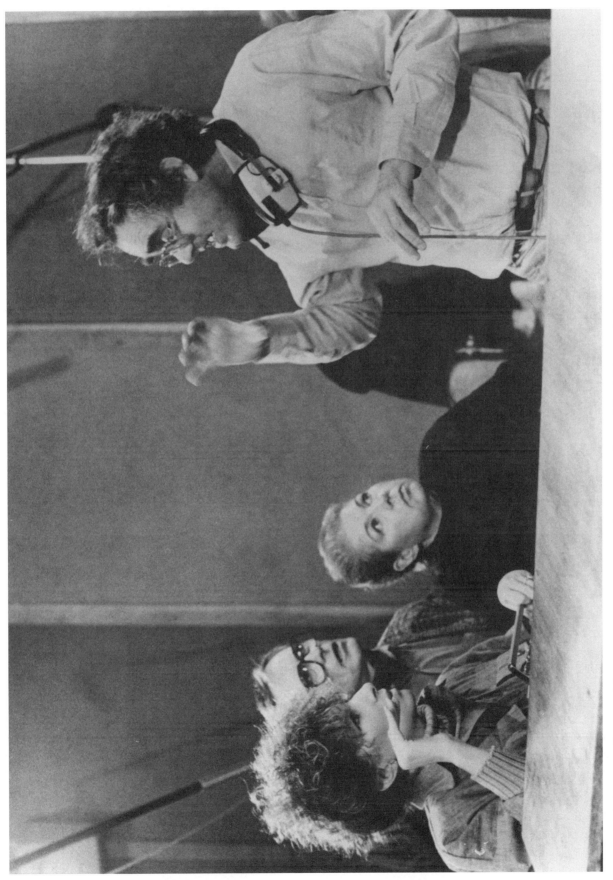

MICHEL LEGRAND. Equally successful as a screen score composer and a songwriter, Legrand (far right) wrote both the soundtrack and the music for the songs for *Yentl* (1983). Here he confers with his lyricists Marilyn and Alan Bergman and the movie's director and star, Barbra Streisand. *MGM / Photofest © MGM*

a minor key then building up into a more expansive major key, only to return to the original tone at the end. He favors violins but he sometimes uses them in a strident or even abrasive manner, as in his disturbing score for *The Go-Between*. Legrand also is adept at building an entire composition on a simple two- or three-note phrase, varying it and letting it build from a solo piece into a fully orchestrated one. A good example is the plaintive musical phrase that is the center of his *Summer of '42* score. Usually such compositions do not lend themselves to a songlike structure but the music from that movie was later turned into the very popular "The Summer Knows" (lyric by Alan and Marilyn Bergman). Over the years, Legrand saw several songs from his films become hits even though few of these movies were musicals. But in three cases the movies were very much musicals. *The Umbrellas of Cherbourg* was a bold experiment on many levels. A modern opera with no spoken dialogue, the movie was highly romantic in its look as well as its music. Several musical themes were introduced during the bittersweet story, the two most memorable being "I Will Wait for You" and "Watch What Happens" (English lyrics by Norman Gimbel). Both are highly lyrical yet have some disarming minor-key sections that make the score sound far from old fashioned. Less successful was Demy's second opera film *The Young Girls of Rochefort*, although some of the music has a pleasant 1960s feel even as it apes old-time musicals. Years later Legrand collaborated with lyricists Marilyn and Alan Bergman (who had written the words to a handful of his hit songs) on *Yentl*, more a musical than an opera. This tale, about a Jewish girl (Barbra Streisand) disguising herself as a man so that she can study at a yeshiva, is an engaging comedy-drama set in Eastern Europe at the turn of the twentieth century. Not only was the period movie filled with superior songs, the score was rich in European sounds that are so important to the setting and characters. Another form of musical, the bio-drama *Lady Sings the Blues*, is filled with Billie Holiday standards. Yet one is still impressed by Legrand's jaunty love theme that is not a song.

Among the many other Legrand scores that deserve mention is that for the 1974 version of *The Three Musketeers*. Director Richard Lester's fast and furious take on the old tale was vividly reinforced by Legrand's bombastic yet comic score with a full brass sound that often suggested a cartoon. Also fast and furious at times is the jazzy score he wrote for the racing movie *Le Mans*. This is contrasted

nicely with the violins playing the movie's lilting love theme. The haunting theme from *The Happy Ending* lends itself to one of Legrand's most beguiling songs, "What Are You Doing for the Rest of Your Life?" (lyric by the Bergmans). Audiences and critics dismissed the pseudobiopic *Gable and Lombard* and Legrand's scintillating score was neglected. The love theme is sultry and low key yet is also used effectively at a faster tempo at times, giving the movie the lift it so desperately needs. Another box office disaster, *Ice Station Zebra* has an eerie and almost surreal theme that is very unusual for what attempted to be an action movie. As unsuccessful as these films were, at least the public got to see them. Not so for the movie that has what is arguably Legand's most fascinating score, *The Picasso Summer*. As a restless and young married couple (Albert Finney and Yvette Mimieux) searches for Pablo Picasso in France and Spain, the main musical theme conveys an expansive spirit and, at the same time, its own kind of restlessness. It is a catchy and satisfying theme even though it is overplayed in the film and starts to grate on one after a dozen different variations. (The music later found success as the song "Summer Me, Winter Me.") More interesting are the three musical suites that Legrand composed to accompany the movie's trio of animated sequences in which Picasso's artwork is given movement. The subjects are lust, bullfighting, and war and peace, and Legrand's music is as vibrant as the images created from Picasso's works. The American film was directed by the Frenchman Serge Bourguignon and the studio was so unhappy with the quirky, odd little movie that Robert Sallin was brought in to reshoot and recut the footage. Still unsatisfied, the studio released *The Picasso Summer* only in Europe. In the States it was kept on the shelf for three years then shown on American television. Luckily much of the score was included on the B side of the *Summer of '42* album so the music got some recognition.

Legrand was not the only European composer to find favor in America in the 1960s but he was by far the most popular and influential. He brought a French flavor to Hollywood movies without slipping into the sidewalk accordion cliché. His music was the new European sound made accessible because it was melodically and harmonically so appealing. While much of his film music might be dismissed as pop, the work is seldom garish or pandering. Legrand has been able to prove that romanticism is not only not dead but it could be popular. Official website: www.michellegrandofficial.com.

Credits

(* for Best Song; ** nominated for France's César Award for music)

Year	Film	Director
1957	The Tricyclist	Jacques Pinoteau (France)
1958	Sinners of Paris	Pierre Chenal (France)
1960	America as Seen by a Frenchman	François Reichenbach (France)
1960	Wasteland	Marcel Carné (Italy/France)
1960	Jack of Spades	Yves Allégret (France)
1960	The Door Slams	Michel Fermaud, Jacques Poitrenaud (France)
1961	Lola	Jacques Demy (Italy/France)
1961	Me faire ça à moi	Pierre Grimblat (France)
1961	The Counterfeiters of Paris	Gilles Grangier (France/Italy)
1961	A Woman Is a Woman	Jean-Luc Godard (France/Italy)
1961	Le coeur battant	Jacques Doniol-Valcroze (France)
1961	Keep Talking, Baby	Guy Lefranc (France)
1961	Un coeur gros comme ça	François Reichenbach (France)
1962	A Swelled Head	Claude de Givray (France)
1962	The Seven Deadly Sins	Jacques Demy, Jean-Luc Godard, Edouard Molinaro, etc. (Italy/France)
1962	Cleo from 5 to 7	Agnés Varda (France/Italy)
1962	Comme un poisson dans l'eau	André Michel (France)
1962	Vivre sa vie	Jean-Luc Godard (France)
1962	Le Gentleman d'Epsom	Gilles Grangier (France/Italy)
1962	Eva	Joseph Losey (France/Italy)
1962	The Empire of Night	Pierre Grimblat (France)
1963	La douceur du village	François Reichenbach (France)
1963	Bay of Angels	Jacques Demy (France)
1963	Love Is a Ball	David Swift (USA)
1963	Le joli mai	Pierre Lhomme, Chris Marker (France)
1963	Maigret voit rouge	Gilles Grangier (France/Italy)
1964	The Umbrellas of Cherbourg (AAN, AAN*)	Jacques Demy (France/W. Germany)
1964	Agent 38-24-36	Edouard Molinaro (France/Italy)
1964	The Lovers of the France	Pierre Grimblat, François Reichenbach (France/Italy)
1964	Band of Outsiders	Jean-Luc Godard (France)
1964	The World's Most Beautiful Swindlers	Jean-Luc Godard, etc. (France/Italy)
1965	The Plastic Dome of Norma Jean	Juleen Compton (USA)
1965	Code Name: Jaguar	Maurice Labro (Spain, France, W. Germany)
1965	When the Peasants Pass	Edouard Molinaro (France)
1966	A Matter of Resistance	Jean-Paul Rappeneau (France)
1966	Monkey Money	Yves Robert (France/Italy/Spain)
1966	L'or et le plomb	Alain Cuniot (France)
1966	Et la femme créa l'amour	Fabien Collin (France)
1966	Tender Scoundrel	Jean Becker (France/Italy)
1966	Who Are You, Polly Magoo?	William Klein (France)
1967	The Young Girls of Rochefort (AAN)	Jacques Demy (France)
1967	The Oldest Profession	Claude Autant-Lara, Jean-Luc Godard, etc. (France/Italy/W. Germany)
1967	A Matter of Innocence (aka Pretty Polly)	Guy Green (UK)
1968	The Man in the Buick	Gilles Grangier (France)
1968	How to Save a Marriage and Ruin Your Life	Fielder Cook (USA)
1968	Sweet November	Robert Ellis Miller (USA)
1968	The Thomas Crown Affair (AA*; GG*; GGN; BAFTA-N)	Norman Jewison (USA)
1968	Ice Station Zebra	John Sturges (USA)
1969	Play Dirty	André De Toth (UK)
1969	The Picasso Summer	Serge Bourguignon, Robert Sallin (USA)
1969	The Swimming Pool	Jacques Deray (Italy/France)

Year	Film	Director
1969	*Castle Keep*	Sydney Pollack (USA)
1969	*Call Me Mathilde*	Pierre Mondy (France)
1969	*The Happy Ending* (AAN*; GGN, GGN*)	Richard Brooks (USA)
1970	*To Catch a Pebble*	James F. Collier (USA)
1970	*Wuthering Heights* (GGN)	Robert Fuest (UK)
1970	*Pieces of Dreams* (AAN*; GGN*)	Daniel Haller (USA)
1970	*The Lady in the Car with Glasses and a Gun*	Anatole Litvak (France/USA)
1970	*Donkey Skin*	Jacques Demy (France)
1970	*The Scoundrel*	Jean-Paul Rappeneau (France/Italy)
1971	*Summer of '42* (AA; GGN; BAFTA)	Robert Mulligan (USA)
1971	*Le Mans* (GGN)	Lee H. Katzin (USA)
1971	*La ville-bidon*	Jacques Baratier (France/W. Germany)
1971	*The Go-Between*	Joseph Losey (UK)
1971	*Touch and Go*	Philippe de Broca (France/Italy)
1971	*A Few Hours of Sunlight*	Jacques Deray (France/Italy)
1972	*The Old Maid*	Jean-Pierre Blanc (France/Italy)
1972	*A Time for Loving*	Christopher Miles (UK)
1972	*Hearth Fires*	Serge Korber (France/Italy)
1972	*Two Is a Happy Number*	Mel Stuart (USA)
1972	*Portnoy's Complaint*	Ernest Lehman (USA)
1972	*Lady Sings the Blues* (GGN)	Sidney J. Furie (USA)
1972	*Not Dumb, the Bird*	Jean Delannoy (France/Italy/W. Germany)
1972	*The Outside Man*	Jacques Deray (Italy/France/USA)
1973	*Le gang des otages*	Edouard Molinaro (Italy/France)
1973	*The Nelson Affair*	James Cellan Jones (UK)
1973	*Story of a Love Story*	John Frankenheimer (France/Italy)
1973	*40 Carats*	Milton Katselas (USA)
1973	*Cops and Robbers*	Aram Avakian (USA)
1973	*A Doll's House*	Joseph Losey (UK/France)
1973	*A Slightly Pregnant Man*	Jacques Demy (France/Italy)
1973	*F for Fake*	Orson Welles (France/Iran/W. Germany)
1973	*Breezy* (GGN, GGN*)	Clint Eastwood (USA)
1973	*The Three Musketeers* (BAFTA-N)	Richard Lester (Spain/USA/Panama/UK)
1974	*Our Time*	Peter Hyams (USA)
1975	*Sheila Levine Is Dead and Living in New York*	Sidney J. Furie (USA)
1975	*Le sauvage*	Jean-Paul Rappeneau (France/Italy)
1975	*Gable and Lombard*	Sidney J. Furie (USA)
1976	*The Honeymoon Trip*	Nadine Trintignant (Italy/France)
1976	*Ode to Billy Joe*	Max Baer Jr. (USA)
1976	*The Smurfs and the Magic Flute*	Peyo (France/Belgium)
1977	*Gulliver's Travels*	Peter R. Hunt (UK/Belgium)
1977	*The Other Side of Midnight*	Charles Jarrott (USA)
1978	*One Can Say It without Getting Angry*	Roger Coggio (France/Italy)
1978	*Roads to the South*	Joseph Losey (France/Spain)
1978	*Firebird: Daybreak Chapter*	Kon Ichikawa (Japan)
1978	*Mon premier amour*	Élie Chouraqui (France)
1979	*Je vous ferai aimer la vie*	Serge Korber (France)
1979	*Lady Oscar*	Jacques Demy (Japan)
1979	*Les fabuleuses aventures du légendaire Baron de Munchausen*	Jean Image (France)
1980	*The Mountain Men*	Richard Lang (USA)
1980	*The Hunter*	Buzz Kulik (USA)
1980	*Atlantic City* **	Louis Malle (Canada/France)
1980	*Falling in Love Again* (GGN*)	Steven Paul (USA)
1981	*Bolero* **	Claude Lelouch (France)
1981	*Your Ticket Is No Longer Valid*	George Kaczender (Canada)
1982	*Bankers Also Have Souls*	Michel Lang (France/Italy)
1982	*Qu'est-ce qui fait courir David?*	Élie Chouraqui (France)

Year	Film	Director
1982	*Slapstick (of Another Kind)*	Steven Paul (USA)
1982	*Best Friends (AAN*)*	Norman Jewison (USA)
1983	*Revenge of the Humanoids*	Albert Barillé (France)
1983	*A Love in Germany*	Andrzej Wajda (France/W. Germany)
1983	*Never Say Never Again*	Irvin Kershner (UK/USA/W. Germany)
1983	*Yentl (AA, AAN*; GGN, GGN*)*	Barbra Streisand (UK/USA)
1984	*Secret Places*	Zelda Barron (UK)
1984	*Paroles et musique ***	Élie Chouraqui (France/Canada)
1985	*Hell Train*	Roger Hanin (France)
1985	*Palace*	Edouard Molinaro (France/W. Germany)
1985	*Partir, revenir*	Claude Lelouch (France)
1985	*Parking*	Jacques Demy (France)
1987	*Club de rencontres*	Michel Lang (France)
1987	*Spiral*	Christopher Frank (France)
1988	*Switching Channels*	Ted Kotcheff (USA)
1988	*Trois places pour le 26*	Jacques Demy (France)
1989	*Cinq jours en juin*	Michel Legrand (France)
1989	*The Jeweller's Shop*	Michael Anderson (Italy/Austria/W. Germany/Canada)
1990	*Fate*	Stuart Paul (USA)
1990	*Flight from Paradise*	Ettore Pasculli (Germany/France/Italy)
1990	*Eternity*	Steven Paul (USA)
1990	*Gaspard et Robinson*	Tony Gatlif (France)
1991	*Dingo*	Rolf de Heer (Australia/France)
1993	*The Pickle*	Paul Mazursky (USA)
1993	*Les demoiselles ont eu 25 ans*	Agnés Varda (France)
1994	*Prêt-a-Porter*	Robert Altman (USA)
1995	*L'univers de Jacques Demy*	Agnés Varda (France/Belgium/Spain)
1995	*Les misérables*	Claude Lelouch (France)
1995	*Les enfants de lumiere*	André Asséo (France)
1995	*Aaron's Magic Village (aka The Real Shlemiel)*	Albert Hanan Kaminski (France/Germany/ Hungary)
1998	*Madeline*	Daisy von Scherler Mayer (France/USA)
1999	*Doggy Bag*	Frédéric Comtet (France)
1999	*La bûche*	Daniele Thompson (France)
2002	*And Now . . . Ladies and Gentlemen*	Claude Lelouch (France/UK)
2003	*Yantarnye Krylya*	Andrei Razenkov (Russia)
2005	*Cavalcade*	Steve Suissa (France)
2006	*The Legend of Simon Conjurer*	Stuart Paul (New Zealand/USA)
2008	*Disco*	Fabien Onteniente (France)
2009	*Oscar and the Lady in Pink*	Eric-Emmanuel Schmitt (France/Belgium/Canada)
2013	*Max Rose*	Daniel Noah (USA)

LURIE, Deborah (b. 1974) An up-and-coming film composer who is also a respected orchestrator, she has scored over twenty feature films and several shorts.

Deborah Ruth Lurie was born with a rare condition called synesthesia that even as a child allowed her to identify any note on the scale by seeing a corresponding color in her mind. Such a gift meant Lurie had perfect pitch and understood music theory at a young age. While she was growing up in Palo Alto, California, she was involved in music, dance, and theatre. As a pianist, Lurie studied and performed both classical and jazz pieces, as well as com-

posing original music, such as a score for her high school production of *A Midsummer Night's Dream*. She studied composition at the University of Southern California and then began orchestrating film and television scores, sometimes composing additional music. Lurie's first original scores were for the shorts *The Promise* (1997) and *George Lucas in Love* (1999), followed by her first feature *Best Man in Grass Creek* that same year. She has often been pigeonholed into scoring teen movies, such as *Sleepover*, *Sydney White*, *Spring Breakdown*, *Whirlygirl*, *Prom*, *Fun Size*, and the remake of *Footloose*. But Lurie has also written scores for adult melodramas, such as *Dear John, Mozart and the Whale*, and *An Unfinished Life*, action films as with *My Name Is Modesty* and *9*, and unique character movies such as *The Betrayed, The Little Traitor*, and *Imaginary Heroes*. Her credits also include the celebrity documentaries *Justin Bieber: Never Say Never* and *Katy Perry: Part of Me*, and the TV movie *The Year without a Santa Claus* (2006). Lurie has arranged music for various pop groups, stage works, and major film musicals such as *Dreamgirls* (2006), the remake of *Fame* (2009), and *Alice in Wonderland* (2010), and action movies, as with *Spider-Man 2* (2004) and *Spider-Man 3* (2007).

Perhaps the most popular movie that Lurie scored is the romantic *Dear John* about the unfulfilled love between a student (Amanda Seyfried) and a soldier (Channing Tatum). The main theme is a flowing piece played by piano and orchestra that has classical roots. Much of the rest of the score is equally graceful and romantic without wallowing in sentimentality as the movie itself does. Lurie wrote a poignant score for the rural character drama *An Unfinished Life*. There is a folk quality to the main theme even though the guitar and folk instruments are backed by a symphonic sound. The Wyoming farm setting is beautifully conveyed by the entire score which sounds rustic even as it is elegant. Both of these films were directed by Swedish-born Lasse Hallström, as was the restrained drama *Safe Haven* which has a pleasing score by Lurie. The setting is a North Carolina town where a woman (Julianne Hough) with a past tries to start over again. While the movie is filled with blues, folk, and rock songs by others, the soundtrack itself is breezy, fluid, and very contemporary even as it has one foot in the classical mode. Of the handful of teen movies directed by Joe Nussbaum, perhaps the most interesting is that for *Sydney White*, an updating of the Cinderella tale.

The score has lite-rock, jazz, bluegrass, rhythm and blues, a gliding love theme, and some magical suspense music. Yet what might have become a hodgepodge is surprisingly unified and winning.

The Little Traitor, an engrossing drama set in 1947 Jerusalem, has a rhythmic main theme that echoes Middle Eastern music with its strings and percussion. The contemporary crime comedy *One for the Money* has a jazz-rock-blues score with some skillful passages on electric organ. The sci-fi action film *9* has an eclectic score that ranges from the brooding and mystical to the vigorous. The main theme is a pounding piece with sustained notes and a wordless chorus. Also impressive is the theme for a winged beast in which the music repeats a marching musical phrase effectively, a hard-rock passage in which electric keyboard and percussion compete furiously, and a tender theme for the movie's quieter moments features aching woodwinds and harp. Danny Elfman contributed some passages to *9* and one is reminded of some of his sci-fi scores, but Lurie received sole composer credit and the movie is mostly hers. Finally, one must mention the laudable score Lurie wrote for *Mozart and the Whale*, an offbeat but memorable movie about the romance between two people (Radha Mitchell and Josh Hartnett) with Asperger's syndrome. The main theme is a delicate and reflective piece in which woodwinds and piano seem to dance together gracefully. Some passages are minor-keyed waltzes with awkward rests; others are more flowing and sprightly. Yet the whole has a restrained yet sparkling quality that avoids cliché. While some of Lurie's movies have been successful and beloved, she has yet to score a breakout screen hit that will bring her the recognition she deserves. Official website: www. deborahlurie.com.

Credits

(all films USA unless stated otherwise)

Year	Film	Director
1999	*Best Man in Grass Creek*	John Newcombe
2004	*My Name Is Modesty: A Modesty Blaise Adventure*	Scott Spiegel
2004	*Sleepover*	Joe Nussbaum
2004	*Imaginary Heroes*	Dan Harris (USA/Germany/Belgium)
2005	*Drop Dead Sexy*	Michael Philip
2005	*An Unfinished Life*	Lasse Hallström (USA/Germany)
2005	*Mozart and the Whale*	Petter Naess

Year	Film	Director
2006	*Whirlygirl*	Jim Wilson
2007	*Sydney White*	Joe Nussbaum
2007	*The Little Traitor*	Lynn Roth (Israel/USA)
2008	*The Betrayed*	Amanda Gusack
2009	*Spring Breakdown*	Ryan Shiraki
2009	*9*	Shane Acker
2010	*Dear John*	Lasse Hallström
2011	*Justin Bieber: Never Say Never*	Jon M. Chu
2011	*Prom*	Joe Nussbaum
2011	*Footloose*	Craig Brewer
2012	*One for the Money*	Julie Anne Robinson
2012	*Katy Perry: Part of Me*	Dan Cutforth, Jane Lipsitz
2012	*Fun Size*	Josh Schwartz
2013	*Safe Haven*	Lasse Hallström

MANCINA, Mark (b. 1957) A versatile performer and composer who started in the world of rock music, he has scored a wide variety of movies, ranging from nail-biting action films to Disney animated features.

Born Mark Alan Mancina in Santa Monica, California, as a youth he studied classical guitar and piano as well as composition. After further study at California State University at Fullerton, Mancina wrote songs, arranged music, and produced records for Trevor Rabin, Yes, and Emerson, Lake and Palmer. Between 1987 and 1991, he collaborated with fellow composers Tim James and Steve McClintock on ten action movies. He made his solo composing debut with the melodrama *Crossing the Line* in 1990 and the next year collaborated with Hans Zimmer on the thriller *Where Sleeping Dogs Lie*. Mancina's first box office hit was *Speed* and by the mid-1990s he was in demand for all kinds of movies. Among the most notable are *Twister, Con Air, Bad Boys, August Rush, Moll Flanders, Born Wild, Training Day, Asylum,* and the animated movies *Brother Bear, Tarzan,* and *Planes*. For television, he has written music for many commercials and such series as *The Outer Limits, The Strip, Space Rangers, Blood+,* and *Criminal Minds*. Even after finding fame for writing solo, Mancina has continued to collaborate with other composers on screen and stage projects. He worked with Elton John, Hans Zimmer, and Lebo M on the 1997 Broadway version of *The Lion King* and with Phil Collins on the music for the screen and 2006 stage version of *Tarzan*.

Mancina burst on the scene with his riveting score for *Speed*, a far-from-subtle work but a score more than appropriate for this action thriller about a city bus triggered to explode if it slows down. Much of the music can be described as hyperjazz on electric instruments with sound effects added. Once the chase starts in *Speed* there are few moments of respite, so there are few chances for quieter moments in the score. Those that are there seem like bliss, but they cannot last long before we are back to the pounding chase music. *Twister*, another action piece, is about tracking and studying a series of tornadoes, so Mancina is able to score both scenes of destruction and calm. Again

sound effects are added to the music, which uses both electric guitar and conventional orchestra. Some passages have a wordless choir and a fervent tone, as if in awe of these powerful storms. Mancina collaborated with Trevor Rabin on the score for *Con Air*, a star-studded action film about convicts hijacking a plane. The plot and characters take a backseat to explosions. Not surprisingly, the main theme is a series of explosive sound effects battling a riff on an electric guitar. Most of what follows is equally propulsive with a few passages toned down for variety's sake, such as a flowing romantic "Triahs" theme. Somewhat more coherent is the cop thriller *Bad Boys* which has a driving main theme with a rock beat and an unrelenting series of repeated musical phrases. Other passages include unsung rap, mysterious mood music, manic hip-hop, sultry salsa, and an electric guitar lament.

All of those action films were directed with a sledgehammer touch and, because Mancina scored them with the same sensibility, one suspects that his composition abilities are limited. For contrast, perhaps the Disney projects offer a different perspective. The animated *Tarzan* might be described as an action movie of sorts and the rhythmic opening music using accelerated drums might lead one to think this will be a jungle version of *Speed*. But both the film and the score are much richer, more engrossing, and more exhilarating than any chase. Phil Collins wrote and sang the rock-pop songs and Mancina filled in with a masterful soundtrack score. He does not overdo the African aspect of the setting, allowing drums and high-pitched pipes at times but mostly conveying the majesty of the jungle with reflective music filled with wonderment. Choral voices are used in some passages while a solo oboe or flute suffices in others. Even the action scenes have a robust, rhythmic sound that remains pastoral and can never be mistaken for a car chase. Disney's animated *Brother Bear*, set among Native Americans in a cold northern climate, has a similarly bucolic score. Tribal chanting, the rumbling of drums, delicate primeval passages, and sweeping symphonic music that captures the grandeur of nature fill the score by Mancina collaborating again with Collins. The parts of the movie dealing with the Great Spirits are the most enchanting and the music for those scenes is mystical and haunting. The animated *Planes*, in which each flying machine becomes a character much as automobiles did in *Cars*, is far from inspired film-making yet Mancina's score treats the subject with playful awe. The glory of flying is the cue for much of the music, whether it be grand and expansive or quiet and poignant. The choral chanting here resembles a heavenly kind of scat singing while the action scenes sometimes use trumpet fan-fares and racing strings. Even more playful is the score for the Disney live-action spoof *The Haunted Mansion*. Like the theme park attraction it is based on, the movie is far from actually scary and Mancina's music enjoys using hor-ror clichés while balancing them with merry minuets, jocu-lar vocals, mischievous woodwinds, moody organ chords, and metronome-like percussion. Except for *Tarzan*, none of the above Disney projects are totally satisfying, but one cannot help admire their splendid scores.

Most would agree that Mancina's finest screen music can be found in *August Rush*, a sentimental movie about a child musical prodigy (Freddie Highmore) who searches for his birth parents. The film is filled with different kinds of music ranging from classical to atonal. The main theme is a New Age piece accented by sound effects. It is celestial and reverent in a restrained manner. Cello and guitar solos are featured in later passages, those being the two instruments the boy's parents played. There is an emotive lullaby heard on piano but echoed electroni-cally, selections with avant-garde mixes of manufactured sounds and piano, and a resplendent arpeggio that seems to blossom as it goes along. The highlight of the score is the concert in Central Park in which "August Rhapsody in C Major" is played. All of the earlier elements of the score return in this delectable piece that includes sym-phonic bombast, vivid solos for guitar, cello, and piano, jazzy scat singing, a rhythmic string serenade, and some glittering orchestral passages that soar. Because *August Rush* was a flawed and unpopular movie, Mancina's best score is not as well known as it should be. Perhaps it will find new life in the concert hall. Official site: www. markmancina.com.

Credits

(all films USA unless stated otherwise)

Year	Film	Director
1990	Crossing the Line	Gary Graver
1991	Where Sleeping Dogs Lie	Charles Finch
1993	Taking Liberty	Stuart Gillard
1994	Monkey Trouble	Franco Amurri (USA/Japan)
1994	Speed	Jan de Bont
1995	Man of the House	James Orr
1995	Bad Boys	Michael Bay
1995	Assassins	Richard Donner (USA/France)
1995	Fair Game	Andrew Sipes
1995	Money Train	Joseph Ruben
1995	Born Wild	Philippe Blot
1996	Twister	Jan de Bont
1996	Moll Flanders	Pen Densham
1997	Con Air	Simon West
1997	Speed 2: Cruise Control	Jan de Bont
1998	Return to Paradise	Joseph Ruben
1999	Tarzan	Chris Buck, Kevin Lima
2000	Auggie Rose	Matthew Tabak
2000	Bait	Antoine Fuqua (Canada/Australia/USA)
2001	Training Day	Antoine Fuqua (USA/Australia)
2001	Domestic Disturbance	Harold Becker
2002	The Reckoning	Paul McGuigan (USA/Spain)
2003	Brother Bear	Aaron Blaise, Robert Walker
2003	The Haunted Mansion	Rob Minkoff

Year	Film	Director
2005	*Asylum*	David Mackenzie (UK/Ireland)
2007	*Shooter*	Antoine Fuqua
2007	*August Rush*	Kirsten Sheridan
2008	*Camille*	Gregory Mackenzie (USA/UK)
2009	*Imagine That*	Karey Kirkpatrick (USA/Germany)
2009	*Hurricane Season*	Tim Story
2011	*The Templar Code*	Daniel Kult, Austin Anthofer
2013	*Penthouse North*	Joseph Ruben
2013	*Planes*	Klay Hall
2014	*Planes: Fire & Rescue*	Jeffrey M. Howard

MANCINI, Henry (1924–1994) One of the most successful and recognized American film composers of the postwar era, Mancini was a versatile songwriter as well with many hit songs and scores. Because of his popular film and television theme songs, he was one of only a handful of Hollywood composers who was widely known to the general public during his lifetime.

He was born Enrico Nicola Mancini in Cleveland, Ohio, the son of an Italian immigrant who moved his family to Pennsylvania and worked in the steel mills outside of Pittsburgh. As a boy he studied the piccolo and then later the piano. Mancini's education at Juilliard School of Music in New York City was interrupted by service in the army during the last two years of World War II. His first music jobs after the war were as arranger and pianist, soon doing both for the Glenn Miller Orchestra as re-formed by Tex Beneke. His film career started in 1952 when he was hired by Universal Pictures to write and cowrite musical themes, often without receiving screen credit. Scoring such notable movies as *Touch of Evil* and *The Creature from the Black Lagoon* did little to bring him recognition, although his arrangements for *The Glenn Miller Story* did warrant an Academy Award nomination. By the time Mancini left Universal in 1958 to become an independent composer and arranger, he had honed his craft working on dozens of movies, many cowritten with Herman Stein.

It was television that first brought Mancini fame. His jazz-flavored theme song for the series *Peter Gunn* in 1958 quickly became a musical hit and remained a familiar favorite long after the series ended in 1961. The program also gave Mancini his first contact with the series' writer and producer Blake Edwards. Mancini would have his greatest successes with Edwards's films, the two working on over thirty movies during the next thirty-five years. The

first Edwards-Mancini hit film was *Breakfast at Tiffany's* which introduced the Oscar-winning song "Moon River" (lyric by Johnny Mercer) and brought Mancini his first of twenty Grammy Awards. Other outstanding Edwards films of the 1960s that Mancini scored include *Days of Wine and Roses*, *The Great Race*, and *The Pink Panther*. This last introduced Mancini's most famous musical piece, the odd and funny "Pink Panther Theme" which is one of the most recognized compositions in the history of American film. The theme was reprised in the many *Panther* sequels, a television animated series, and in dozens of animated shorts. Another Mancini composition that was a surprise hit was the quixotic "Baby Elephant Walk," which he wrote for a short sequence in the Howard Hawks movie *Hatari!* The piece became a favorite on the radio and with orchestras around the world.

By the mid-1960s, Mancini was one of Hollywood's most distinctive composers, creating a cool jazz sound that epitomized the nonrock musical flavor of the decade. He worked with a variety of directors in the next decades, but he often reunited with Edwards for the newest *Panther* sequel or in two movie musicals, *Darling Lili* and *Victor/Victoria*, both of which called for full musical comedy scores. (Mancini's other film musical was the animated *The Great Mouse Detective* for Disney.) For television, he wrote the theme songs for such series as *Mr. Lucky* and *The Invisible Man* and scored TV movies, most memorably *The Shadow Box* (1980), and miniseries, in particular *The Thorn Birds* (1983). At the time of his death he was working on the Broadway version of *Victor/Victoria*, which later opened in New York in 1995. It is estimated that during his forty-year career, Mancini had a hand in the scores of over 150 movies. In addition to those already mentioned, his noteworthy films include *It Came from Outer Space*, *So This Is Paris*,

HENRY MANCINI. Because he had so many hit songs, Mancini was too often thought of as a songwriter rather than a composer. He is pictured here conducting the score for the torrid romance *Moment to Moment* (1965) which, not surprisingly, has a title song by Mancini that was popular. *Universal Pictures / Photofest © Universal Pictures*

Ain't Misbehavin', The Private War of Major Benson, Operation Petticoat, High Time, Imitation of Life, Mr. Hobbs Takes a Vacation, Charade, Dear Heart, Two for the Road, Wait until Dark, The Molly Maguires, Sometimes a Great Notion, Silver Streak, 10, Mommie Dearest, The Glass Menagerie, and *A Fine Mess.*

While it is easy to recognize the Mancini sound in much of his music, he was much more versatile that one might assume. Using the genre of jazz, he was able to expand on jazz themes and used riffs in a surprisingly agile way. Perhaps no one has better mastered the art of making jazz comic, as seen in the "Pink Panther Theme" and dozens of other compositions. While much of his music can be described as sleek and cool, there are just as many highly romantic themes, as heard in the scores for *Charade, The Molly Maguires, Two for the Road,* and *Arabesque.* Although he was not given as many dramas to score as other composers of his day, Mancini was still able to come up with some highly charged scores, such as those for *Wait until Dark, Angela,* and *The Glass Menagerie.* (Mancini wrote a very heavy organ and strings composition for Alfred Hitchcock's *Frenzy* in 1972, but it was replaced by a more conventional score by Ron Goodwin.) Another distinctive aspect of Mancini's film scores is his preference for composing several separate themes for a nonmusical movie. Multitheme scores for epic films and historical spectacles are common; for simple comedies and romances, it is rare. While many screen composers will come up with a single main theme and then do variations of it throughout the film, Mancini often approached each movie as a musical with a variety of different compositions. For example, his score for the intimate romantic comedy–drama *Two for the Road* has nine separate and distinct musical themes, ranging from the lushly romantic to the silly and eccentric. The changing relationship between a married couple (Audrey Hepburn and Albert Finney) is seen before and during their ten-year marriage as different road trips they took across provincial France are witnessed in a nonsequential manner. It is a stylish and adult romantic movie that hits various emotions, all beautifully captured in the music. The captivating title theme moves like travel music, yet its simple rising and falling make it also a bewildering waltz. At one point it is sung by a choir on the soundtrack, but Leslie Bricusse's lyric is so uninspired that it kept the song from becoming a hit. Also in the *Two for the Road* score is some warm and casual French sidewalk cafe music

played on accordions, guitar, and a solo clarinet; a cool jazz piece on woodwinds and xylophone with a tricky but catchy rhythm; a breezy theme on electric organ and saxophone that is so carefree it is almost slaphappy; and a fluid, French-flavored passage on accordion, woodwinds, and guitar that moves so smoothly it is irresistible. This is a typical, yet special, Mancini score from the 1960s and is a fine example of the Mancini sound.

Because the theme from *The Pink Panther* is so famous, many forget that it came from a romantic heist movie and not one of the broad Peter Sellers comedies that followed. In fact Sellers's hilarious Inspector Clouseau is a supporting character in this crime film about the romantic jewel thief called the Phantom (David Niven). Most of the music is more romantic than comic, such as a casual slow-jazz passage with muted trumpet, saxophone, accordion, and piano that is sensual as it takes its time and waits for the strings and voices to enter and fill out the melody. There is also an easygoing instrumental with a slight cha-cha beat, an accordion solo with strings that is nonchalant yet appealing, and a lovely piano and strings foxtrot that is very tentative and consequently highly romantic. Yet the now-famous animated opening credits were scored by Mancini with a comic theme he wrote with saxophonist Plas Johnson in mind. The music is a cool jazz piece featuring a sly saxophone with sustained notes that are sassy and flippant. When a full orchestra enters for a fuller sound, the theme loses some its comic punch and becomes a catchy and melodic tune that cannot be forgotten. One of the distinctive aspects in the "Pink Panther Theme" is the way all the instruments tumble down the scale at times, foreshadowing the farcical humor to follow. Another Mancini score forgotten except for its hit song is *Breakfast at Tiffany's* which introduced what is arguably Mancini's most known song, "Moon River." This much-altered version of Truman Capote's novella was built around star Audrey Hepburn, who was miscast but so utterly charming that no one cared. (Capote's Holly Golightly is a brash, somewhat uncouth blonde.) The script called for Hepburn to quietly sing a song as she accompanied herself on the guitar. The studio hired Mancini for the score but wanted a more established songwriter for the song. Director Blake Edwards convinced the producers to let Mancini compose the song, his argument probably supported by the fact that veteran lyricist Johnny Mercer would provide the words. "Moon River" had to conform to Hepburn's limited vocal range, so the music is rather simple in terms of pitch and scale. Yet the music is so flexible and indelible that it works as a score as well as a song. The movie opens with a solo harmonica and guitar version of "Moon River" then a chanting chorus is added. The sound is rustic, like an old folk tune with a 1960s sensibility, but once the strings are added it becomes more sophisticated. In addition to Hepburn's vocal, the tune is also heard as a lively cha-cha version that surprisingly works effectively, and at another point in the film there is a somber version on low woodwinds and brass that conveys the heavily disguised sadness inside Holly. Other music in the score includes a cool jazz piece with humming voices that is slow but cheerful, and a cool and lazy jazz theme featuring bass strings and percussion with a slow but steady beat. Yet it is "Moon River" that dominates the score and no one left the movie theatre without humming it.

Even when the featured song did not become a chart hit, Mancini managed to please with a score filled with variety and musical panache. *The Great Race* is a live-action cartoon that spoofed everything from silent movies to women's liberation. Using the structure of a car race that stretches across three continents from New York City westward to Paris, the comic epic finds time for exaggerated adventure, superficial romance, dastardly plots, and the biggest pie fight on record. Mancini scores this extravaganza like a comic operetta. The waltzing song "The Sweetheart Tree" may have been an attempt for another "Moon River" (a dubbed Natalie Wood sings it as she accompanies herself on the guitar) but it did not repeat the earlier song's success. Yet the music is charming, especially when played on a player piano on the soundtrack. Among the other musical delights in this score is a recurring theme for the comic villain (Jack Lemmon) which is a slow, off-key tune played on a languid horn with electric piano accents; a brisk royal waltz with a hint of an Eastern European ethnic sound in the way the strings suggest gypsy music; and a theme for the racing cars in which various instruments speed ahead as the low brass instruments make snide musical comments. The giant pie fight is scored with a vigorous polka featuring a frantic accordion and a lot of squawking brass and frazzled strings. "The Sweetheart Tree" may not have caught fire, but *The Great Race* score triumphs all the same.

Two other Mancini scores built around a potent song are those for *Charade* and *The Days of Wine and Roses.*

The former is another Audrey Hepburn romance, this time in the guise of a mystery. After her husband is murdered, a Parisian (Hepburn) is tormented by various villains looking for money the dead man owed them. She is aided by a mysterious man (Cary Grant) who is forever changing his name because he has so much to hide from her. *Charade* is one of the most romantic movies of the 1960s and the title song can take some of the credit. Mercer again provided an expert lyric for Mancini's slow but intoxicating waltz music. The movie opens with a rhythm version of the tune played on various percussion instruments as different instruments take turns playing the melody, all with the slightly sinister sound of a spy movie. Once a romance develops between the two main characters, the title theme becomes more romantic with strings as the predominant instrument. Yet there is other music in *Charade*, such as a sensual theme played on accordion that is jazzy and slow and lends the piece a sense of mystery, a vivacious polka with a heavy beat and nimble accordion playing, and a quiet but suspenseful theme on low woodwinds and brass punctuated with ominous piano chords. *The Days of Wine and Roses* also boasts a hit Mancini-Mercer song but this disturbing drama could not be more different from the easy romance of *Charade*. An ambitious businessman (Jack Lemmon) introduces his young wife (Lee Remick) to alcohol and gradually their addiction destroys his career and their marriage. The title theme is a delicate yet rhapsodic piece of music with an old-fashioned sense of romance. The way Mancini uses this throughout the movie to express the powerful emotions of the story is very accomplished. For the opening credits, a slow and dreamy version of the theme is sung by a chorus and the effect is almost sentimental. As the drama deepens, the music takes on different colors. By the heartbreaking end of the movie, a minor-key version is heard that is even slower, more reflective, and full of sorrow. In the case of *The Days of Wine and Roses*, one song says it all.

Among Mancini's many dramatic scores, two movies can illustrate his versatility. His jazzy film noir score for *Touch of Evil* first brought him some recognition in 1958, the same year his TV theme from *Peter Gunn* became a hit. There is no chart-topping song or catchy tune in *Touch of Evil* yet the score is enthralling all the same. Orson Welles's dark and stylistic crime drama is about everything from police corruption to lust to murder in a Mexican border town. The look and sound of the film is noir with some interesting variations on Mancini's part. The main theme is a percussive jazz piece with a Latin rhythm, but a dissonant and harsh sound even when it moves into a sultry dance played by a sensual saxophone. The score also includes a mambo track featuring brass and bongos that repeats the same teasing phrases even when more instruments are added to the mix, a boogie-woogie passage played by a jazz band with nimble solos on electric guitar and saxophone, and a rhythmic theme that has the flavor of early rock and roll, especially when an electric guitar is featured. *Touch of Evil* often resembles a booze-soaked nightmare, and Mancini captured it all in his music. A very different sound can be found in *The Molly Maguires*, a period drama about the plight of immigrant coal miners in 1876 Pennsylvania and the efforts by the radical group, known as the Molly Maguires, to sabotage the uncaring coal company. Many of the immigrants are Irish, so the score is richly flavored with original Celtic music. The opening music is a gentle folk song played on a high-pitched instrument called an ocarina. Low strings repeat an enticing musical phrase that is eventually picked up by a full orchestra, but still the piece remains intimate and delicate. Another notable theme is a merry jig played on a

pennywhistle that seems simple but carefully develops as it moves on. The score also includes some restless, agitated music with demanding brass and piercing pipes that have an Irish jig flavor; a rustic passage, featuring a solo oboe and dulcimer, that flows along with grace and dignity; and a love theme played on flute and dulcimer that is primitive yet fully captivating.

Mancini was honored with many awards during his career, including four Oscars from eighteen nominations and a record-setting seventy-two Grammy nominations (winning twenty). He responded by giving much attention to the industry and young composers. He left his archives (and a scholarship) to UCLA. In 1996 the Henry Mancini Institute was founded with his money; the Henry Mancini Arts Academy in his hometown of Aliquippa, Pennsylvania, was founded by his estate; and the composers' union ASCAP has offered a Henry Mancini Scholarship annually since 2001. Mancini wrote an autobiography—*Did They Mention the Music?* (revised) with Gene Lees (2002)—and the instructional manual *Sounds and Scores: A Practical Guide to Professional Orchestration* (1962). Biography: *Henry Mancini: Reinventing Film Music*, John Caps (2012). Official website: www.henrymancini.com.

Credits

(all films USA unless stated otherwise; * for Best Song)

Year	Film	Director
1952	Sally and St. Anne	Rudolph Maté
1952	Lost in Alaska	Jean Yarbrough
1952	Horizons West	Budd Boetticher
1952	Back at the Front	George Sherman
1952	The Raiders	Lesley Selander
1953	Girls in the Night	Jack Arnold
1953	Seminole	Budd Boetticher
1953	Column South	Frederick De Cordova
1953	The Lone Hand	George Sherman
1953	All I Desire	Douglas Sirk
1953	The Veils of Bagdad	George Sherman
1953	Walking My Baby Back Home	Lloyd Bacon
1954	The Glenn Miller Story (AAN)	Anthony Mann
1954	Drums across the River	Nathan Juran
1955	So This Is Paris	Richard Quine
1955	Ma and Pa Kettle at Waikiki	Lee Sholem
1955	The Private War of Major Benson	Jerry Hopper
1955	Ain't Misbehavin'	Edward Buzzell
1955	One Desire	Jerry Hopper
1955	The Second Greatest Sex	George Marshall
1955	The Square Jungle	Jerry Hopper

Year	Film	Director
1956	The Benny Goodman Story	Valentine Davies
1956	World in My Corner	Jesse Hibbs
1956	The Kettles in the Ozarks	Charles Lamont
1956	A Day of Fury	Harmon Jones
1956	Congo Crossing	Joseph Pevney
1956	The Great Man	José Ferrer
1956	Rock, Pretty Baby	Richard Bartlett
1957	Mister Cory	Blake Edwards
1957	The Tattered Dress	Jack Arnold
1957	Kelly and Me	Robert Z. Leonard
1957	Man Afraid	Harry Keller
1958	The Big Beat	Will Cowan
1958	Flood Tide	Abner Biberman
1958	Damn Citizen	Robert Gordon
1958	Summer Love	Charles F. Haas
1958	Touch of Evil	Orson Welles
1958	The Thing That Couldn't Die	Will Cowan
1958	Voice in the Mirror	Harry Keller
1959	Imitation of Life	Douglas Sirk
1959	Operation Petticoat	Blake Edwards
1960	High Time	Blake Edwards
1961	The Great Impostor	Robert Mulligan
1961	Breakfast at Tiffany's (AA*)	Blake Edwards
1961	Bachelor in Paradise (AAN*)	Jack Arnold
1962	Experiment in Terror	Blake Edwards
1962	Mr. Hobbs Takes a Vacation	Henry Koster
1962	Hatari!	Howard Hawks
1963	Days of Wine and Roses (AA*)	Blake Edwards
1963	Soldier in the Rain	Ralph Nelson
1963	Charade (AAN*)	Stanley Donen
1964	Man's Favorite Sport?	Howard Hawks
1964	Dear Heart (AAN*; GGN*)	Delbert Mann
1964	The Pink Panther (AAN)	Blake Edwards
1964	A Shot in the Dark	Blake Edwards
1965	The Great Race (AAN*; GGN*)	Blake Edwards
1965	Moment to Moment	Mervyn LeRoy
1966	Arabesque	Stanley Donen
1966	What Did You Do in the War, Daddy?	Blake Edwards
1967	Two for the Road (GGN)	Stanley Donen (UK)
1967	Wait until Dark	Terence Young
1968	The Party	Blake Edwards
1969	Me, Natalie	Fred Coe
1969	I girasoli (Sunflower) (AAN)	Vittorio De Sica (Italy)
1969	Gaily Gaily	Norman Jewison
1970	The Molly Maguires	Martin Ritt
1970	The Hawaiians	Tom Gries
1970	Darling Lili (AAN*; GG*)	Blake Edwards
1971	Sometimes a Great Notion (AAN*)	Paul Newman
1971	The Night Visitor	Laslo Benedek (USA/Sweden)
1973	The Thief Who Came to Dinner	Bud Yorkin
1973	Oklahoma Crude (GGN*)	Stanley Kramer
1974	The White Dawn	Philip Kaufman
1974	The Girl from Petrovka	Robert Ellis Miller
1974	99 and 44/100% Dead	John Frankenheimer
1975	The Great Waldo Pepper	George Roy Hill
1975	The Return of the Pink Panther (GGN)	Blake Edwards
1975	Once Is Not Enough	Guy Green
1976	W. C. Fields and Me	Arthur Hiller

Year	Film	Director
1976	Alex and the Gypsy	John Korty
1976	Silver Streak	Arthur Hiller
1976	The Pink Panther Strikes Again (AAN*)	Blake Edwards
1978	House Calls	Howard Zieff
1978	Angela	Boris Sagal (Canada/USA)
1978	The Revenge of the Pink Panther	Blake Edwards
1978	Who Is Killing the Great Chefs of Europe?	Ted Kotcheff
1979	The Prisoner of Zenda	Richard Quine
1979	Nightwing	Arthur Hiller
1979	10 (AAN*; GGN)	Blake Edwards
1980	Little Miss Marker	Walter Bernstein
1980	A Change of Seasons	Richard Lang
1981	Back Roads	Martin Ritt
1981	Condorman	Charles Jarrott (UK)
1981	S.O.B.	Blake Edwards
1981	Mommie Dearest	Frank Perry
1982	Victor/Victoria(AA; GGN)	Blake Edwards
1983	Second Thoughts	Lawrence Turman
1982	Trail of the Pink Panther	Blake Edwards
1983	Better Late Than Never	Bryan Forbes (UK)
1983	Curse of the Pink Panther	Blake Edwards
1983	The Man Who Loved Women	Blake Edwards
1984	Harry & Son	Paul Newman
1985	Lifeforce	Tobe Hooper (UK/USA)
1985	Santa Claus: The Movie	Jeannot Szwarc (UK/USA)
1986	The Great Mouse Detective	Ron Clements, Burny Mattison
1986	A Fine Mess	Blake Edwards
1986	That's Life! (AAN*; GGN*)	Blake Edwards
1987	Blind Date	Blake Edwards
1987	The Glass Menagerie(GGN)	Paul Newman
1987	Sunset	Blake Edwards (USA/Italy)
1988	Without a Clue	Thom E. Eberhardt (UK)
1989	Physical Evidence	Michael Crichton
1989	Skin Deep	Blake Edwards
1989	Welcome Home	Franklin J. Schaffner (UK/USA)
1990	Ghost Dad	Sidney Poitier
1990	Fear	Rockne S. O'Bannon
1991	Switch	Blake Edwards
1991	Married to It	Arthur Hiller
1992	Tom and Jerry: The Movie	Phil Roman
1993	Son of the Pink Panther	Blake Edwards

MANDEL, Johnny (b. 1925) A successful Hollywood and television composer, songwriter, arranger, and conductor, he is considered one of the giants of jazz, a style of music which he used in some of his thirty-two movie scores.

John Alfred Mandel was born in New York City, the son of a garment manufacturer and a professional singer, and studied piano and trumpet as a child. After a music education at the Manhattan School of Music and Juilliard, Mandel began his professional career as trumpet player for Joe Venuti's band. He soon switched to the trombone and played that instrument in bands conducted by Buddy Rich, Chubby Jackson, Jimmy Dorsey, and others. Mandel took up music arranging and then composing for Woody Herman, Count Basie, Zoot Sims, Stan Getz, and Chet Baker. By 1954 he was turning out hit songs, among them "Low Life," "Tommyhawk," "Straight Life," "Pot Luck," and "Not Really the Blues." Although he had arranged, conducted, and contributed some music to television shows and movies in the 1950s, his first solo film score was for the melodrama *I Want to Live* in 1958. The jazz score won a Grammy Award and the album became a chart seller. Although Mandel was in demand for compositions and arrangements for Tony Bennett, Frank Sinatra, and other artists, he consistently returned to films over the next three decades. Many of his screen scores produced hit songs, such as the Oscar-winning "The Shadow of Your Smile" (lyric by Paul Francis Webster) from *The Sandpiper*, "Emily" (lyric by Johnny Mercer) from *The Americanization of Emily*, "Suicide Is Painless" (lyric by Mike Altman) from *M*A*S*H*, "A Time for Love" (lyric by Webster) from *An American Dream*, and "Take Me Home" (lyric by Marilyn and Alan Bergman) from *Molly and Lawless John*. Mandel's other noteworthy movies include *Harper*, *Pretty Poison*, *The Russians Are Coming, the Russians Are Coming*, *The Last Detail*, *Being There*, *Freaky Friday*, *Escape to Witch Mountain*, *Agatha*, *Caddyshack*, and *The Verdict*. By the 1980s Mandel did less screen work and concentrated on jazz recordings and working with Shirley Horn, Barbra Streisand, Diana Krall, and other singers on albums. He also continued to write music for television into the 1990s. His most famous TV theme was that for the long-running *M*A*S*H*, and he scored such TV movies as *Under the Yum Yum Tree* (1969), *The Trackers* (1971), *Call Holme* (1972), *The Turning Point of Jim Malloy* (1975), *Evita Peron* (1981), *A Letter to Three Wives* (1985), *Foxfire* (1987), *Single Women Married Men* (1989), and *Kaleidoscope* (1990).

Mandel's first jazz score for the movies, *I Want to Live*, is considered his best. The Robert Wise film, about a woman (Susan Hayward) on death row, is gritty and powerful. Mandel's score conjures up an urban landscape with cool and bluesy jazz played by celebrated jazz musicians Gerry Mulligan, Pete Jolly, Art Farmer, Bud Shank, Red Mitchell, Frank Rosolino, and Shelly Manne. The impassioned story was regulated by this restrained and moody score, helping the movie avoid the melodramatics that would have cheapened it. A more romantic jazz score could be found in the uneven romantic drama *The Sandpiper*. While "The Shadow of Your Smile" quickly became a song standard, its music holds its own as a screen theme, conveying a romance that is distant and even melancholy. The jazz in *The Americanization of Emily* is in the classic mode, the story being set during World War II. The three-note phrase in the main theme "Emily" is enticing and remains intoxicating as Mandel arranges many different variations of it. The jazz in the private-eye drama *Harper* is more contemporary, using electronic instruments and a 1960s beat. This jazz swings in a way

that ironically comments on the cold and disenfranchised title antihero (Paul Newman). The satiric comedy *Being There* uses a classically flavored score, utilizing Erik Satie's *Gnossienne No. 4* but letting the piano sometimes ease into a jazz idiom. The main theme for the war comedy *M*A*S*H* is an easygoing jazz piece that is used as a choral number and as an orchestrated passage, the casual sound contrasts to the chaos going on in the story. Even the broad comedy *Caddyshack* has a breezy jazz theme that lets the strings flow against a rhythmic combo of piano, bass, and percussion, while the thriller *Point Blank* has a jazzy bossa nova theme with a flute and piano providing the seductive melody.

There are some expert scores written by Mandel that are not in the jazz genre. The music in the courtroom drama *The Verdict* is oddly menacing, the strings anticipating something dreadful. The movie is about a jaded ambulance-chasing lawyer (Paul Newman) who gets involved with a case that revitalizes him. This internal action is expressed in a stirring and dramatic score that relies on no jazz techniques. For the Disney adventure movie *Escape from Witch Mountain*, Mandel wrote an urgent James Bond–like main theme with rapid strings and pounding brass. Yet, being a family film, most of the score is more playful than oppressive. There is a delightful harmonica march for a scene in which marionettes come to life, and even the supernatural scenes are scored with sprightly and optimistic music. Even more fun is the Cold War farce *The Russians Are Coming, the Russians Are Coming* about the hysteria that breaks out on a small American island when a Russian submarine goes aground. The main theme is a daffy fusion of patriotic American tunes, played on fife and drum, and Russian folk songs, sung by a robust male choir. The shenanigans that follow are scored with silly marches, both Soviet and American. The crime drama *An American Dream* has a score most remembered for Mandel and Webster's ballad "A Time to Love" yet parts of the rest of the score are similarly romantic and entrancing. The romantic mystery *Agatha* has a subdued theme in which the piano and oboe echo the tentative and shy world of mystery writer Agatha Christie (Vanessa Redgrave). The movie is not so much a whodunnit as a character study and Mandel's minor-key score gives the story the ambiance the period drama needs. Although Mandel is first and foremost a jazz man, on-screen his music goes far beyond one genre.

Credits

(all films USA unless stated otherwise; * for Best Song)

Year	Film	Director
1958	*I Want to Live*	Robert Wise
1960	*The 3rd Voice*	Hubert Cornfield
1961	*The Lawbreakers*	Joseph M. Newman
1963	*Drums of Africa*	James B. Clark
1964	*The Americanization of Emily*	Arthur Hiller
1965	*The Sandpiper* (AA*; GGN; GGN*)	Vincente Minnelli
1966	*Harper*	Jack Smight
1966	*The Russians Are Coming, the Russians Are Coming*	Norman Jewison
1966	*An American Dream* (aka *See You in Hell, Darling*) (AAN*)	Robert Gist
1967	*Point Blank*	John Boorman
1968	*Pretty Poison*	Noel Black
1969	*Heaven with a Gun*	Lee H. Katzin
1969	*That Cold Day in the Park*	Robert Altman (USA/Canada)
1969	*Some Kind of a Nut*	Garson Kanin
1970	*M*A*S*H*	Robert Altman
1970	*The Man Who Had Power Over Women*	John Krish (UK)
1972	*Journey through Rosebud*	Tom Gries
1972	*Molly and Lawless John* (GG*)	Gary Nelson
1973	*Summer Wishes, Winter Dreams*	Gilbert Cates
1973	*The Last Detail*	Hal Ashby
1974	*W*	Richard Quine
1975	*Escape to Witch Mountain*	John Hough
1976	*The Sailor Who Fell from Grace with the Sea*	Lewis John Carlino (UK)
1976	*Freaky Friday*	Gary Nelson
1979	*Agatha*	Michael Apted (UK)
1979	*Being There*	Hal Ashby
1980	*The Baltimore Bullet*	Robert Ellis Miller
1980	*Caddyshack*	Harold Ramis
1982	*Deathtrap*	Sidney Lumet
1982	*Lookin' to Get Out*	Hal Ashby
1982	*The Verdict*	Sidney Lumet
1989	*Brenda Starr*	Robert Ellis Miller

MANSELL, Clint (b. 1963) A more recent but already accomplished British composer who started as a singer and musician in rock, he has scored some very unusual films since 1998.

He was born Clinton Darryl Mansell in Coventry, England, and was interested in rock music as a youth, learning the guitar and playing in amateur bands. Mansell first found recognition as the guitarist and lead singer for the alternative rock band Pop Will Eat Itself, which was formed in 1986 and for a decade was very active in concert and on records. (The group reunited briefly in 2005 and put out a new recording in 2010.) He also worked with other bands,

most memorably as a backup vocal on the album *The Fragile* by Nine Inch Nails. When the innovative American film director Darren Aronofsky was preparing his first feature, *Pi*, in 1997, he asked Mansell to score the entire sci-fi thriller even though the British rocker had no film experience. The low-budget *Pi* was a surprise success and Mansell has scored every Aronofsky movie since then. Their second collaboration, the psychological drama *Requiem for a Dream*, includes in its score a string piece titled "Lux Aeterna" performed by the Kronos Quartet. The movie has become a cult favorite and different versions of "Lux Aeterna" have been heard on recordings, for movie trailers, and in television programs ranging from *Soccer Saturday* to *America's Got Talent*. The other Aronofsky-Mansell collaborations include *The Fountain*, *The Wrestler*, *Black Swan*, and *Noah*. With other directors, Mansell has scored such diverse movies as *Smokin' Aces*; *11:14*; *Definitely, Maybe*; *Dream from Leaving*; *Moon*; *Farewell*; *United*; *Stoker*; and *Filth*. He has also written music for TV movies, film shorts, and video games.

Coming from an alternative and industrial rock background, it is not surprising that Mansell's scores are very electronic and use mechanized sounds not associated with a conventional soundtrack ensemble. This is certainly true for his first score, *Pi*. The story concerns a mathematics whiz (Sean Gullette) who uses his homebuilt supercomputer to try and discover the numerical pattern that fuels the universe. Such a plot could not be scored with traditional music. Mansell skips over the rock possibility and goes directly to industrial sounds, a kind of symphony of noise that a computer might create and enjoy. The opening music is an electronic percussion theme with synthesized echoes, blasts of sound, heartbeats, explosions, and high-frequency vibrations. Later there is a slow theme on a synthesized keyboard with all kinds of electronic noises that punctuate the long, sustained notes that refuse to form a melody. This exciting score also has a chaotic passage in which the percussion instruments compete with various nonmusical sounds; a suspenseful theme with quivering electronic notes, vocal interruptions, and drum riffs; and a quieter track on electric organ that rapidly repeats a musical phrase as it fades in and out. Mansell's most recent score is that for the biblical epic *Noah*, yet even this tale from Genesis used high-tech music. The main theme is a solemn march played on synthesized chords and sustained strings that gently rise up the scale gaining strength and purpose on the way. When Noah (Russell Crowe) contemplates the future God has decreed for mankind, the music is a rumbling passage with nervous percussion and synthesized high notes that suggest something overwhelming to come. The score also includes a suspenseful theme with echoing percussive pounding, low restless strings, and a melancholy air played on electronic horns. Also memorable is a mesmerizing passage with flowing violins and muted percussion that grows into an anthem with each added electronic sound. *Pi* is a low-budget thriller that in-

trigues; *Noah* is a big-budget spectacular that disappoints. Yet both have superior scores.

It is ironic that the most famous piece of music written by a rocker turns out to be in the classical vein. With all of its different variations and adaptations, Mansell's "Lux Aeterna" is basically a string chamber work. In the film *Requiem for a Dream*, where it was first introduced, "Lux Aeterna" is played by a string quartet with electronic accents and flourishes. It moves at a steady tempo but with a woeful subtext. The movie is a disturbing drama about four very different addicts each with their individual dependency. The "Lux Aeterna" theme is pliable enough that it can be applied to each of the characters. When the piece accelerates and a choir is added, the somber mood changes to a downright sinister one. When a moaning vocal is added for certain scenes, the effect is surreal and nightmarish. *Requiem for a Dream* has another theme that is quite compelling: a propulsive piece with agitated synthesized strings and horns, angry percussion, and an ominous chanting choir. We are no longer inside a computer but inside these damaged characters and the music tells us that it is a very human nightmare. Because the mystery thriller *Black Swan* concerns characters in a ballet company performing *Swan Lake*, a good deal of music by Tchaikovsky is heard. How this famous ballet score is reinterpreted and arranged so that it takes on a deadly persona is what makes the music so effective. (Matt Dunkley orchestrated and conducted both the Tchaikovsky and Mansell music.) Mansell's original music is often interwoven with selections from the ballet but there are several tracks that stand on their own without any interference from Tchaikovsky. There is a quietly threatening theme played on piano and strings that repeats a simple musical phrase as it grows from a distant sound to an oppressive lullaby of sorts. The *Black Swan* score also includes a gentle but creepy passage with ascending piano chords and delicate string flourishes, a minor-key promenade on strings and woodwinds that moves in a stately fashion from a processional to a rhythmic folk dance in half time, and a slow march played on piano and strings that is very fragile as it pauses in unexpected places. This is a quieter score than one expects from Mansell but then his career so far has been filled with surprises. Official website: www.clintmansell.com.

Credits

(all films USA unless stated otherwise)

Year	Film	Director
1998	Pi	Darren Aronofsky
2000	Requiem for a Dream	Darren Aronofsky
2001	The Hole	Nick Hamm (UK)
2001	Rain	Katherine Lindberg (USA/Germany/Spain)
2001	World Traveler	Bart Freundlich (Canada/USA)
2001	Knockaround Guys	Brian Koppelman, David Levien
2002	Abandon	Stephen Gaghan (USA/Germany/Canada)
2002	Murder by Numbers (aka Foolproof)	Barbet Schroeder
2002	Every Night the Same Thing	David Huynh (Canada)
2002	Sonny (aka Pony Rides)	Nicolas Cage
2003	11:14	Greg Marcks (USA/Canada)
2004	Suspect Zero	E. Elias Merhige
2005	Sahara	Breck Eisner (UK/Spain/Germany/USA)
2005	Trust the Man	Bart Freundlich
2005	Doom	Andrzej Bartkowiak (UK/Czech Republic/ Germany/ USA)
2006	The Fountain (aka The Last Man) (GGN)	Darren Aronofsky (USA/Canada)
2006	Smokin' Aces	Joe Carnahan (UK/France/USA)
2007	Wind Chill	Gregory Jacobs (USA/UK)
2008	Definitely, Maybe	Adam Brooks (Germany/UK/USA/France)
2008	The Wrestler	Darren Aronofsky (USA/France)
2008	Dream from Leaving	Nathan Cox, etc.
2009	Moon	Duncan Jones (UK)
2009	Blood: The Last Vampire	Chris Nahon (Hong Kong/France/China)
2009	Farewell	Christian Carion (France)
2009	The Rebound	Bart Freundlich
2010	Black Swan	Darren Aronofsky
2010	Last Night (aka Tell Me)	Massy Tadjedin (USA/France)
2011	United	James Strong (UK)
2013	Stoker	Chan-wook Park (UK/USA)
2013	Filth	Jon S. Baird (UK)
2014	Noah	Darren Aronofsky

MARIANELLI, Dario (b. 1963) A highly respected Italian composer for the theatre, concert hall, ballet, television, and movies, he has scored nearly forty feature films since 1994, almost all of them English-language movies.

Born in Pisa, Italy, Dario Marianelli studied piano and composition privately in Florence and then at London's Guildhall School of Music and the National Film and Television School. While still a student at the latter institution, Marianelli scored three feature films for the Irish director Paddy Breathnach. After graduation in 1997, he remained in England where he wrote music for the theatre and ballet, choral pieces for the BBC Singers, and orchestral works that were premiered by the London Philharmonic, BBC Symphony Orchestra, Britten-Pears Orchestra, London Symphony, and other renowned ensembles. Marianelli's first movie project after he finished his training at the National Film and Television School was the action comedy *I Went Down* in 1997. A number of diverse films followed but wide recognition did not come until he wrote the music for the 2005 version of *Pride & Prejudice*, which was a hit on both sides of the Atlantic. The director was Joe Wright who has since worked with Marianelli on *Atonement* (which brought Marianelli an Oscar), *The Soloist*, *Anna Karenina* (an Oscar nominee for Best Score), and *Pan*. With other directors Marianelli has scored such notable films as *Ailsa*, *The Warrior*, *In This*

World, I Capture the Castle, V for Vendetta, The Color of Freedom, The Brave One, Agora, Jane Eyre, Salmon Fishing in Yemen, and *Quartet.* He has also written for television, scoring TV movies and documentaries. Marianelli is a respected pianist and conductor and has done both jobs for many of his movies.

Because Marianelli has scored so many period movies so effectively, he is thought of as a classicist. Yet even his music for screen versions of literary classics are much more than pastiche. Marianelli favors a traditional orchestra or chamber ensemble and avoids synthesized or electronic music. All the same, his screen music never seems old fashioned. His most awarded score, that for the mystery-romance *Atonement,* is a fine example of Marianelli's talents. This disturbing tale is about a precocious teenager (Saoirse Ronan) who destroys the lives of several people because of her lies. The opening music over the credits is a zesty piano and typewriter duet with anxious strings pushing the piece ahead. A soulful clarinet is featured in a melancholy piece that glides along on sustained notes, while a cheerful piano, oboe, and strings passage moves up and down the scale with such glee that it is contagious. The score also includes a mournful farewell theme featuring solo viola, harmonica, and reeds that is stirring while never totally letting go of its emotions. A series of love letters is scored with a jittery theme on piano and strings that is passionate but equally nervous and confused. There is little in Marianelli's score to convey the 1940s period. Instead he writes music for the character and the situation. The same cannot be said for his score for *Pride & Prejudice,* which is filled with eighteenth-century musical touches. The principal theme is a reflective piece featuring piano and reeds that is so serene it seems otherworldly. This is contrasted with a lively yet elegant dance on various strings that is Vivaldi-like. There is a solo violin passage that has a brisk pace and a long melodic line; other strings provide a subdued accompaniment as the music develops into a fully orchestrated composition. The *Pride & Prejudice* score is filled with memorable tracks, including a tender piano nocturne that takes its time as violins waver in the background; a restless piece with jittery strings and frantic brass that alternates with a quiet piano and cello section that is doleful; a sparkling folk dance on pipes and strings that accelerates toward a frenzied climax; a vivid piano and string passage that is curious as it explores different versions of its musical idea; and a busy piano and orchestra

piece that moves in a baroque manner as it speeds up and gets excited. This film is a rather traditional version of Jane Austen's beloved novel, and Marianelli's music re-creates the period beautifully.

The 2012 screen version of *Anna Karenina* does not take a traditional approach. The Tolstoy novel is re-created in artificial settings with theatrical techniques that did not please most moviegoers. Marianelli again musically re-creates the eighteenth century, but the score is also theatrical, some of the music exaggerated or presented as in a cabaret or theatre rather than part of Tolstoy's aristocratic world. The opening music is a spirited piece played on accordion, strings, and woodwinds that moves like a dance tune but has a more questioning tone, as if something is not right with this pretty theatre setting. There is a rapid passage on clarinet and accordion, with agitated strings, whistling, and furtive vocals underneath, that seems to be running away from something. One period waltz seems carefree and even careless, while another waltz is more elegant and maintains its poise. The score is full of big emotions: a cancan track with laughing brass, frivolous accordion, and a fiery fiddle; a sorrowful passage with high-pitched strings floating over low sustained strings; a morose folk song sung in Russian; and a drunken tango played like a march as various instruments are featured, each one with a mocking tone. This *Anna Karenina* was not much appreciated by the public but Marianelli's score was noticed and praised.

Not all of Marianelli's movies are period pieces. *V for Vendetta* is actually set in the future when Britain is ruled by a Fascist government. The sci-fi thriller is about a freedom fighter (Hugo Weaving) who tries to topple the system. As futuristic as the movie is, Marianelli still relies on a conventional orchestra, though he uses some synthesized touches here and there. The main theme consists of ominous pounding percussion, low and threatening brass, choral chanting, sustained electronic chords, and a racing melodic line that reaches up, pulls back, then pushes ahead again. The score has some seething suspense music in which waves of music rise and fall as distant percussion sounds like thunder. There is a lyrical theme on strings and reeds that moves tentatively but with heartfelt emotion, and the action scenes are scored with an aggressive march played on brass, strings, and percussion that builds as a vigorous chorus is added and the tempo moves into furious mode. Perhaps the most memorable track in the score is the music heard during a scene in an abbey. There is muted Gregorian chant in the background as a very sensual orchestra and choral section enters, builds, and overwhelms it. During his

relatively recent career, Marianelli has moved in many directions, musically speaking. As he does so, it is hoped that he does not abandon writing period scores, for they are unusually skillful.

Credits

(all films UK unless stated otherwise)

Year	Film	Director
1994	Ailsa	Paddy Breathnach (Ireland)
1995	The Long Way Home	Paddy Breathnach (Ireland)
1997	I Went Down	Paddy Breathnach (Ireland/UK/USA)
1999	Southpaw: The Francis Barrett Story	Liam McGrath (UK/Ireland)
2000	Being Considered	Jonathan Newman
2000	Pandaemonium	Julien Temple
2001	Happy Now	Philippa Cousins
2001	The Warrior	Asif Kapadia (UK/France/Germany/India)
2002	In This World	Michael Winterbottom
2003	I Capture the Castle	Tim Fywell
2003	September	Max Färberböck (Germany)
2003	Cheeky	David Thewlis (UK/France)
2005	Pride & Prejudice (AAN)	Joe Wright (France/UK/USA)
2005	The Brothers Grimm	Terry Gilliam (USA/Czech Republic/UK)
2005	Beyond the Gates (aka Shooting Dogs)	Michael Caton-Jones (UK/Germany)
2005	Burnt Out	Fabienne Godet (France)
2005	V for Vendetta	James McTeigue (USA/UK/Germany)
2006	Opal Dream	Peter Cattaneo (Australia/UK)
2006	The Return (aka Revolver)	Asif Kapadia (USA)
2007	The Color of Freedom (aka Goodbye Bafana)	Billie August (Germany/France/ Belgium/S. Africa/Italy/UK/Luxembourg)
2007	Shrooms	Paddy Breathnach (Ireland/UK/Denmark)
2007	Atonement (AA; GG; BAFTA-N)	Joe Wright (UK/France/USA)
2007	Far North	Asif Kapadia (UK/France)
2007	The Brave One	Neil Jordan (USA/Australia)
2009	The Soloist (aka Imagining Beethoven)	Joe Wright (UK/USA/France)
2009	Agora	Alejandro Amenábar (Spain)
2009	Everybody's Fine	Kirk Jones (USA)
2010	Eat Pray Love	Ryan Murphy (USA)
2011	Jane Eyre	Cary Fukunaga (UK/USA)
2011	Salmon Fishing in Yemen	Lasse Hallström
2012	Anna Karenina (AAN; GGN; BAFTA-N)	Joe Wright
2012	Quartet	Dustin Hoffman
2013	Redemption (aka Hummingbird)	Steven Knight (UK/USA)
2013	Third Person	Paul Haggis (UK/USA/Germany/Belgium)
2014	A Long Way Down	Pascal Chaumeil (UK/Germany)
2014	The Boxtrolls (aka Here Be Monsters)	Graham Annable, Anthony Stacchi (USA)
2014	Wild Card (aka Heat)	Simon West (USA)
2015	Pan	Joe Wright (USA)

MAYUZUMI, Toshiro (1929–1997) An experimental Japanese composer who blended traditional Asian music with Western techniques and instruments, he scored over one hundred movies, some of which found success in the West.

Toshiro Mayuzumi was born in Yokohama, Japan, and educated at the National University of Fine Arts and

Music in Tokyo and at the Paris Conservatory. While in Europe, Mayuzumi discovered modern Western music by Olivier Messiaen, Pierre Boulez, John Cage, and other avant-gardists. When he returned to Japan in 1950 he introduced the new sound to Japanese culture and composed his own works that were influenced by it. Mayuzumi began his screen career in 1951 with his score for *As Seishun* which has been translated as *Ah, Youth* or *It's Great to Be Young*. During the 1950s and 1960s he was very active in cinema, scoring five or more Japanese films each year. A handful of these found success in the West, particularly *The Big Wave* in 1961. Director John Huston hired Mayuzumi to write experimental scores for his Hollywood movies *Reflections in a Golden Eye* and *The Bible: In the Beginning . . .* , winning an Oscar nomination for the latter. He only scored a handful of other foreign movies, as he continued to work in the Japanese cinema until 1984 even as his career as a concert composer flourished. Mayuzumi first found international acclaim for his *Nirvana Symphony* in 1958 and furthered his reputation with his ballet *Bugaku*, which was performed by the New York City Ballet in 1962. Among his other renowned works are the opera *Kinkakuji* (*The Temple of the Golden Pavilion*), the *Mandala Symphony*, the jazz piece *Hors d'Oeuvres*, *Rhumba Rhapsody*, *Xylophone Concertino*, and his electronic score for the 1964 Tokyo Olympics. Mayuzumi frequently wrote music for the Japanese theatre and composed many chamber works and small instrumental pieces for both Asian and Western instruments even though he publicly criticized Japan for its obsession with Western music and abandoning traditional Japanese forms. He was host of the Japanese television program *Concert without a Name*, which ran thirty years, produced the documentary *The Birth and Death of Japanese Music* (1968), and served as president of the Japan Federation of Composers. When he died in 1997 at the age of sixty-eight, Mayuzumi was perhaps the most internationally acclaimed Japanese composer.

To say that Mayuzumi's music is eclectic is an understatement. He composed so many forms of music, used such a wide variety of instruments, and drew from so great a multitude of cultures that his style might be better described as world music. He was one of the first composers to combine Asian and Western music with an avant-garde sensibility. It is not uncommon in his music to find primitive instruments in the same work with electronic tape manipulation, and to hear jazz and Balinese sounds, Buddhist temple bells, and electronic keyboard. Yet this kind of experimentation was not needed for the many comedies, thrillers, war dramas, and spy and action films he scored. For most of his movies, Mayazumi looked back to age-old Japanese musical forms and continued a tradition rather than deconstructed it. There are a handful of movies in which he was allowed or

even asked to re-create his bold and modern concert music. The score for *Street of Shame*, with its distorted strings, electronically altered instruments, and scat-like vocals is a good example. The comedy *Good Morning* about a Japanese family's obsession with the new invention of television has a mocking score in which cheerful Western TV-commercial music takes on an Asian flavor.

Huston was familiar enough with this side of Mayuzumi to hire him to score the giant Hollywood spectacle *The Bible: In the Beginning . . .* The main theme is a bombastic rhapsody very much in the Western symphonic tradition, the sort of thing Hollywood did so well in the 1950s biblical epics. Yet when the creation of the world comes, Mayuzumi abandons the conventional sounds and experiments with the techniques for which he was famous. The music becomes atonal, the melody dissolves into various motifs, and the instruments are altered or filtered to come up with strange, hypnotic, and very Stravinsky-like effects. The creation of Adam is scored with electronic chords, echoing strings, and a forbidding bass choir that is eventually overwhelmed by more optimistic voices and celebratory strings. The creation of Eve brings on a gentle and flowing theme that is sung by a female chorus and accompanied by fluttering bird-flutes until the full orchestra picks up the theme. The parade of animals into Noah's Ark has primitive flutes playing over an oboe bass line and then a merry march that suggests both a snake charmer and a carnival. This is all what Huston must have had in mind for *The Bible* and Mayuzumi was indeed the right person for the job. He hired Mayuzumi again for a very different kind of film, the dark psychological drama *Reflections in a Golden Eye*. Based on an offbeat Carson McCullers story, this look at obsession and repression among a handful of characters at a Georgia military base was filled with various sexual confusions and surreal scenes, some dreamed and others real. Mayuzumi's score is as daring as the movie. Jazz passages are accompanied by Asian flutes and percussion, military music goes berserk, synthesized chords are distorted and repeated, and a Southern blues theme moves from the languid to the oppressive. It was a challenging movie that never could have been very popular but for Western audiences it was an opportunity to hear a Mayuzumi score in a Hollywood movie. It is the concert hall and not the cinema that has kept Mayuzumi's music alive, for he is very much performed and recorded today. Yet some of his screen music deserves more attention because it is so stubbornly modern.

Credits

(all films Japan unless stated otherwise)

Year	Film	Director
1951	*Ah, Youth* (aka *It's Great to Be Young*)	Shin Saburi
1951	*Carmen Comes Home*	Keisuke Kninoshita
1952	*Home Sweet Home*	Noboru Nakamura
1952	*The Woman Who Touched the Legs*	Kon Ichikawa
1952	*Carmen Falls in Love*	Keisuke Kinoshita
1952	*This Way, That Way*	Kon Ichikawa
1953	*Sunflower Girl*(aka *Love in a Teacup*)	Yasuki Chiba
1953	*Mr. Pu*	Kon Ichikawa
1953	*The Blue Revolution*	Kon Ichikawa
1953	*Youth of Heiji Senigata*	Kon Ichikawa
1953	*Kofuku-san*	Yasuki Chiba
1953	*The Lovers*	Kon Ichikawa
1953	*Yassamossa*	Minoru Shibuya
1954	*Between Yesterday and Tomorrow*	Yuzo Kawashima
1954	*The Woman in the Rumor*	Kenji Mizoguchi
1954	*Mother's First Love*	Seiji Hisamatsu
1954	*Aku no tanoshisa*	Yasuki Chiba
1954	*The Surf*	Senkichi Taniguchi
1954	*Nyonin no yakata*	Masahisa Sunohara
1954	*Niwatori wa futatabi naku*	Heinosuke Gosho
1954	*Wakaki hi no takuboku: Kumo wa tensai*	De Nobuo Nakagawa
1954	*Twelve Chapters on Women*	Kon Ichikawa
1955	*Burden of Love*	Yuzo Kawashima
1955	*Ghost Story of Youth*	Kon Ichikawa
1955	*Till We Meet Again*	Yuzo Kawashima
1956	*Onna no ashi ato*	Minoru Shibuya
1956	*Christ in Bronze*	Minoru Shibuya
1956	*Fusen*	Yuzo Kawashima
1956	*Street of Shame*	Kenji Mizoguchi
1956	*Brother and Sister*	Shue Matsubayashi
1957	*Kao*	Tatsuo Osone
1957	*A Sun-Tribe Myth from the Bakumatsu Era* (aka *Sun in the Last Days of the Shogunate*)	Yuzo Kawashima
1957	*Yuwaku*	No Nakahira
1957	*Bitoku no yoromeki*	Ko Nakahira
1957	*The Unbalanced Wheel* (aka *Crazy Society*)	Minoru Shibuya
1958	*The Chase* (aka *Stakeout*)	Yoshitaro Nomura
1958	*The Young Beast*	Shintaro Ishihara
1958	*Conflagration* (aka *Flame of Torment*)	Kon Ichikawa
1958	*Kami no taisho*	Hiromichi Horikawa
1958	*The Naked General*	Hiromichi Horikawa
1958	*Endless Desire*	Shohei Imamura
1958	*Season of the Witch*	Minoru Shibuya
1958	*Stolen Desire*	Shohei Imamura
1958	*Onna de aru koto*	Yuzo Kawashima
1959	*Kiri aru jyoji*	Minoru Shibuya
1959	*Immoral Lecture*	Katsumi Nishikawa
1959	*Good Morning*	Yasujiro Ozu
1959	*Yaju shisubeshi*	Eizo Sugawa
1960	*Banana*	Minoru Shibuya
1960	*When a Woman Ascends the Stairs*	Mikio Naruse
1960	*Yakuza no uta*	Toshio Masuda
1960	*Mystery of the Himalayas*	Suketaro Shimada
1960	*My Second Brother*	Shohei Imamura

Year	Film	Director
1960	Onna no saka	Kozaburo Yoshimura
1960	The Dangerous Kiss	Yuzo Kawashima
1960	The Warped Ones	Koreyoshi Kurahara
1960	A False Student	Yasuzo Masumura
1960	Seinen no ki	Toshiro Masuda
1961	Kojin kojitsu	Minoru Shibuya
1961	Pigs and Battleships	Shohei Imamura
1961	The Big Wave	Tad Danielewski (USA/Japan)
1961	He and I	Ko Nakahira
1961	The End of Summer (aka Autumn for the Kohayagawa Family)	Yasujiro Ozu
1961	Arabu no arashi	Ko Nakahira
1962	Yopparai tengoku	Minoru Shibuya
1962	Black Lizard	Umetsugu Inoue
1962	Foundry Town	Kiriro Urayama
1962	Wakakute warukute sugoi koitsura	Ko Nakahira
1962	Born in Sin	Yasuki Chiba
1962	I Hate but Love	Loreyoshi Kurahara
1963	Dorodarake no jungo	Ko Nakahira
1963	Sensation Seekers	Jun Fukuda
1963	Nanika omoroi koto nai ka	Koreyoshi Kurahara
1963	Hiko shojo	Kiriro Urayama
1963	Futari dake no toride	Minoru Shibuya
1963	Bushido (aka Cruel Tales of Bushido)	Tadashi Imai
1963	Miren	Yasuki Chiba
1963	Keirin shonin gyojyoki	Shogoro Nishimura
1963	The Insect Woman	Shohei Imamura
1963	Bright Sea	Ko Nakahira
1964	Monro no youna onna	Minoru Shibuya
1964	Black Sun	Koreyoshi Kurahara
1964	Only on Mondays	Ko Nakahira
1964	Intentions of Murder	Shohei Imamura
1964	Brand of Evil	Hiromichi Horikawa
1964	Plants from the Dunes	Ko Nakahira
1964	Revenge	Tadashi Imai
1964	The Flame of Devotion	Koreyoshi Kurahara
1964	You Can Succeed, Too	Eizo Sugawa
1964	The Hunter's Diary	Ko Nakahira
1965	Shirotori	Toshio Masuda
1965	Miseinen—Zoku cupola no aru machi	Takashi Nomura
1965	Radishes and Carrots	Minoru Shibuya
1965	Tokyo Olympiad	Kon Ichikawa
1966	Asiapol Secret Service	Akinori Matsuo (Hong Kong/Japan)
1966	The Pornographers (aka The Amorists)	Shohei Imamura
1966	Watashi, Chigatteiru kashira	Akinori Matsuo
1966	The Heart of Hiroshima	Koreyoshi Kurahara
1966	The Bible: In the Beginning . . . (AAN; GGN)	John Huston (USA/Italy)
1966	The Daphne	Yasuki Chiba
1967	Longing for Love	Koreyoshi Kurahara
1967	Reflections in a Golden Eye	John Huston (USA)
1968	The Sands of Kurobe (aka Tunnel to the Sun)	Kei Kumai
1968	Neon taiheiki	Tadahiko Isomi
1968	Farewell, Moscow Outpost	Hiromichi Horikawa (Japan/France)
1968	Profound Desires of the Gods	Shohei Imamura
1969	5,000 Kilometers to Glory	Koreyoshi Kurahara
1969	The Girl I Abandoned	Kiriro Urayama
1970	Fuji sancho	Tetsutaro Murano
1971	A Soul to Devils	Ko Nakahira

Year	Film	Director
1977	*Yakuza War: The Japanese Don*	Sadao Nakajima
1977	*The Godfather: Ambition*	Sadao Nakajima
1978	*The Godfather: Resolution*	Sadao Nakajima
1980	*Tokugawa ichizoku no houkai*	Kosaku Yamashita
1984	*Jo no mai*	Sadao Nakajima

MENDOZA, David (1894–1975) A radio and movie composer virtually unknown today, he was involved with some landmark films during the silent period and with early talkies.

Little is known about Mendoza, who was born in New York City and began his career conducting dance bands in his hometown. He was musical director for some Manhattan theatre productions before heading west to Hollywood, where he was conductor and sometime composer for silent films. Mendoza was one of three composers to write the score for the 1919 German historical drama *Madame DuBarry* when it was released in the States in 1920. Four years later he was teamed with William Axt to write the music for the adventure silent *The Sea Hawk*, and the two composers worked so well together they were teamed for a series of important silent movies, including *The Big Parade, Ben-Hur, La Boheme, Camille, The Fire Brigade, Annie Laurie, The Garden of Allah*, and *The Student Prince in Old Heidelberg*. In 1926 Mendoza and Axt composed the score for *Don Juan*, the first movie to have music and sound effects synchronized to the film stock. There was no recorded dialogue in *Don Juan*, but in the Vitaphone process the sound effects and music were put on discs that matched each reel of the movie. It was the success of *Don Juan* that encouraged Warner Brothers to continue to experiment with sound, and in 1927 they offered *The Jazz Singer*. The first talkie that Mendoza scored on his own was *Glorious Betsy* in 1928. During the early years of talking movies, he wrote the music (sometimes with others) for such memorable films as *Disraeli, The Public Enemy, Little Caesar, Svengali*, and *Alexander Hamilton*. By 1932 Mendoza stopped composing and musical directing featured films and for the next eight years concentrated on film shorts, mostly musicals. He appeared on-screen as the conductor in the musical short *Home Run on the Keys* (1937) and that same year he and his band were featured in the movie short *David Mendoza & His Orchestra*. By 1940 Mendoza left movies and worked in radio, with dance bands, and in the theatre, including conducting a series of five ice shows on Broadway during the 1940s. After that he pretty much disappears from the public record until his death in New York City in 1975 at the age of eighty-one.

Just as details about Mendoza's life and career are hard to come by, finding music that he, and he alone, wrote is also difficult. All of the silent film scores he wrote were with Axt or other composers, sometimes four men working on the same movie. (See William Axt entry for a discussion of the *Don Juan* score.) Once sound came in and the music was put right onto the film stock, the use of multiple composers was still common. As far as can be determined, Mendoza was the sole composer for sixteen talkies, some of which are lost. Others have very little original music, relying on stock studio music and public domain tunes. No composer is listed for two early gangster classics, *Little Caesar* and *The Public Enemy*. Yet Mendoza is credited for writing the opening music for both. The latter melodrama opens with two pieces of music that alternate back and forth during the brief credits. There is a cocky theme on horns and drums and there is a soft, sentimental passage on strings. These obviously represent the two sides of the law that are at odds in *The Public Enemy*. The opening music for *Little Caesar* is a robust theme played on strings and horns, a series of barking chords that climb the scale with self-important pomp. This is clearly a motif for the central character of Rico (Edward G. Robinson), but it is not repeated later in the movie. All the same, these two pieces of music hint at Mendoza's understanding of screen scoring.

A movie that has a slightly more extensive score is *Svengali*, the tale of a diabolical music maestro (John Barrymore) who uses his hypnotic powers to take total control of his pretty protégé, Trilby (Marian Marsh). Like many of the early talkies, there is not a great deal of underscoring in *Svengali*. Trilby sings opera arias and art songs and Svengali plays other pieces on the piano but none are by Mendoza. His contribution to the score includes the opening music, a flowing passage played on strings and reeds that is accompanied by mysterious harp glissandos and overshadowed by some ominous chords on horns. This time the music does return later in the movie as a leitmotif. When Svengali uses telepathy to control Trilby, the only music is a distant chime and the sound of the wind. His hypnotizing her is also done mostly in silence. There is a romantic theme for Trilby and her love for the handsome artist Billee (Bramwell Fletcher). It is a sentimental piece

with descending musical phrases heard on strings. All this is far from a full score as we think of one today but was considered complete enough in its day. Mendoza probably thought of himself as a musical director and conductor rather than a composer. It certainly seems Hollywood saw him that way. Just as movie scoring was beginning to come into its own in the 1930s, Mendoza quit feature films. Yet he was there when it all began and played a significant role in the development of the film soundtrack.

Credits

(all films USA)

Year	Film	Director
1924	The Sea Hawk	Frank Lloyd
1925	The Big Parade	King Vidor, George W. Hill
1925	Ben-Hur: A Tale of the Christ	Fred Niblo, etc.
1926	Mare Nostrum (aka Our Sea)	Rex Ingram
1926	La Boheme	King Vidor
1926	Don Juan	Alan Crosland
1926	The Scarlet Letter	Victor Sjöström
1926	Camille	Fred Niblo
1926	The Fire Brigade	William Nigh
1927	Slide, Kelly, Slide	Edward Sedgwick
1927	Annie Laurie	John S. Robertson
1927	The Garden of Allah	Rex Ingram
1927	The Student Prince in Old Heidelberg	Ernst Lubitsch, John M. Stahl
1928	The Trail of '98	Clarence Brown
1928	Glorious Betsy	Alan Crosland
1929	The Careless Age	John Griffith Wray
1929	Disraeli	Alfred E. Green
1930	The Song of the Flame	Alan Crosland
1930	Mothers Cry	Hobart Henley
1931	God's Gift to Women (aka The Devil Was Sick)	Michael Curtiz
1931	My Past	Roy Del Ruth
1931	Little Caesar	Mervyn LeRoy
1931	The Public Enemy	William A. Wellman
1931	Svengali	Archie Mayo
1931	Men of the Sky	Alfred E. Green
1931	Gold Dust Gertie	Lloyd Bacon
1931	Children of Dreams	Alan Crosland
1931	The Bargain (aka You and I)	Robert Milton
1931	Alexander Hamilton	John G. Adolfi
1931	The Mad Genius	Michael Curtiz
1931	Compromised (aka We Three)	John G. Adolfi

MENKEN, Alan (b. 1949) Although his screen credits are relatively few, the theatre and movie composer and songwriter is one of Hollywood's most successful (and awarded) composers because of his scores and songs for Disney animated movie musicals. For his fourteen screen scores,

he has won eight Academy Awards (out of nineteen nominations), sometimes getting four nominations per movie.

Born in New Rochelle, New York, the son of a Jewish dentist, Alan Menken studied violin and piano as a boy. He enrolled in the premed program at New York

University with the intention of becoming a doctor but soon switched to music studies. He began his career writing songs for Manhattan nightclubs and Off-Broadway revues. With lyricist-librettist Howard Ashman, he wrote the score for the offbeat musical *God Bless You, Mr. Rosewater* in 1979. Three years later the team had a long-running Off-Broadway hit, the musical sci-fi spoof *Little Shop of Horrors*. When the musical was filmed in 1986, Menken wrote a new song ("Mean Green Mother from Outer Space") with Ashman that was nominated for an Oscar. The team was hired by the Disney studio in 1989 to score the animated musical *The Little Mermaid*, resulting in not only an outstanding movie but the beginning of a renaissance in animation for Disney and other companies. Menken wrote the music for the celebrated songs in *The Little Mermaid* and did the soundtrack score as well, his first screen effort. The score and two songs were nominated for Oscars; the score and "Under the Sea" won. Menken and Ashman had equal success with *Beauty and the Beast*, winning four nominations and two awards for the score and the title song. After only two films, Menken was one of the top composers in the business.

Ashman died from complications from AIDS while working on *Aladdin* so British lyricist Tim Rice collaborated with Menken on the uncompleted songs and again the movie was a critical and popular success. Working with Stephen Schwartz, Menken scored the songs for *Pocahontas* and *The Hunchback of Notre Dame*, winning further kudos and awards. His lyricist-collaborator for *Hercules* was David Zippel and Menken worked with Glenn Slater on the songs for *Home on the Range, Enchanted*, and *Tangled*. Because all of these films boasted such memorable songs, it was often overlooked by the public that Menken had written the soundtrack music as well, giving each film a melodic and dramatic score that supported the action so well. Also, his nonanimated scores have gotten little attention. *Life with Mikey, The Shaggy Dog, Noel*, and *Mirror Mirror* have highly crafted scores in the lighter vein but only the music in *Enchanted* received much notice and that again was because of the songs. Menken also contributed songs to several films that he did not score, including *Who Framed Roger Rabbit* (1988), *Rocky V* (1990), *Home Alone 2: Lost in New York* (1992), *Newsies* (1992) *Captain America: The First Avenger* (2011), and *Jock of the Bushveld* (2012). In the 1990s Menken began to concentrate on the theatre again. He wrote new music

for the Broadway productions of his film musicals: *Beauty and the Beast* (1994), *The Little Mermaid* (2008), *Newsies* (2011), and *Aladdin* (2013). His other stage works, written with various collaborators, include *Diamonds* (1984), *Personals* (1986), *The Apprenticeship of Duddy Kravitz* (1987), *Weird Romance* (1992), *A Christmas Carol* (1994), *King David* (1997), *Sister Act* (2011), and *Leap of Faith* (2012). Menken has also written songs for various television shows, most memorably some tunes for *Sesame Street* in the late 1980s.

Menken's songs have been accurately described as being in the classic Broadway style. His songs may utilize calypso, French cafe music, seafaring chanteys, gospel, rhythm and blues, western folk, Motown, or exotic Middle Eastern themes, but all still have a bright and brash Broadway sensibility. The same can be said for his movie scores, although often he can use a more subtle and softer approach than the song score allows. For example, the cancan and other popular French styles fill the songs in *Beauty and the Beast*, but in the soundtrack score there are nods to Camille Saint-Saëns and Claude Debussy. The songs in *Aladdin* use everything from the Charleston to pop-rock, yet the soundtrack score is rich with enticing music inspired by Alexander Borodin and Nikolai Rimsky-Korsakov. The music throughout *The Little Mermaid* often returns to masculine sea chanting while themes in the *Pocahontas* soundtrack evoke tribal chanting. None of these uses of pastiches approach pretentiousness because the scores and the films are lightweight. Yet in *The Hunchback of Notre Dame*, perhaps the most serious and darkest of his Disney movie musicals, Menken provides some stirring and disturbing music to match the sinister tone of much of the story. It is arguably Menken's most complex score. Yet the nature of animated musicals is often satiric in tone and the music in the Menken scores has a great deal of fun with this. The rousing music in *Home on the Range* pokes fun at every vigorous western score. *Hercules* spoofs gospel, rock, and jazz, never even thinking of using Greek music to tell this very ancient tale anachronistically. The soundtrack for the partially animated *Enchanted* is as pastiched as the cartoon adventure, exaggerating both the romantic music and the dramatic themes. This is not to dismiss Menken as a glib and clever musical craftsman. His talent for catchy melody and harmony cannot be overlooked. Audiences respond to his music and, when put in the form of songs, they quickly become popular favorites.

Menken's Oscar-winning songs "A Whole New World," "Beauty and the Beast," "Colors of the Wind," and "Under the Sea" have become movie song standards because

they are timeless in their theatricality. Much the same can be said about his soundtrack scores. Unofficial website: www.alanmenken.info.

Credits

(all films USA unless stated otherwise; * for Best Song)

Year	Film	Director
1986	Little Shop of Horrors (AAN*)	Frank Oz
1989	The Little Mermaid (AA; AA*; AAN*; GG; GG*; GGN*)	Ron Clements, John Musker
1991	Beauty and the Beast (AA*; AAN*; GG; GG*; GGN*; BAFTA-N)	Gary Trousdale, Kirk Wise
1992	Aladdin (AA*; AAN*; GG*; GG*; GGN*; BAFTA-N)	Ron Clements, John Musker
1993	Life with Mikey	James Lapine
1995	Pocahontas (AA*; GG*; GGN)	Mike Gabriel, Eric Goldberg
1996	The Hunchback of Notre Dame (AAN; GGN)	Gary Trousdale, Kirk Wise
1997	Hercules (AAN*; GGN*)	Ron Clements, John Musker
2004	Home on the Range	Will Finn, John Sanford
2004	Noel	Chazz Palminteri
2006	The Shaggy Dog	Brian Robbins
2007	Enchanted (AAN*; GGN*)	Kevin Lima
2010	Tangled (AAN*; GGN*)	Nathan Greno, Byron Howard
2012	Mirror Mirror	Tarsem Singh (USA/Canada)

MILHAUD, Darius (1892–1974) A French modernist composer and celebrated teacher who was greatly influenced by jazz, he scored fifteen feature films over a long range of fifty years.

Born in Marseilles, France, Darius Milhaud grew up in Aix-en-Provence, the son of a prosperous Jewish family that made their fortune as dealers in the almond trade but were also music enthusiasts. Milhaud studied violin and piano as a boy and even as a youth began composing. He attended the Paris Conservatory of Music where he befriended such artists as Erik Satie, Jean Cocteau, and Paul Claudel. During World War I he went to Brazil as an aide to Claudel and became fascinated by the music, which was so different from what he was hearing and studying in Europe. Returning to Paris after the war, Milhaud was joined by five other young composers (Satie, Arthur Honegger, Francis Poulenc, Georges Auric, and Louis Durey) who revolted against the Germanic classical form and wrote music with simpler textures, clearer musical lines, and a more modern tone. Dubbed "The Six" by the press, these outspoken young composers received a great deal of attention, most of them going on to significant mu-

sical careers. Milhaud was perhaps the most experimental of the group. He utilized Brazilian music and jazz in his compositions and adopted the concept of polytonality (the use of two signature keys at the same time) in his many works. As he traveled all over Europe and America, he conducted, performed on the piano, and taught music even as he enjoyed a prolific composing career. His over four hundred works include twelve symphonies, eighteen string quartets, ballets, operas, chamber music, piano pieces, theatre scores, jazz compositions, and silent and talking films. When the Nazis occupied France during World War II, Milhaud was able to escape to Lisbon and then on to the United States where he taught at Mills College in California. After the war he divided his time between the States and Paris, teaching and conducting in both places. The list of Milhaud's students reads like a *Who's Who* in twentieth-century music, ranging from Jean Coulthard and Ramon Sender to Dave Brubeck and Philip Glass. Milhaud retired from teaching in 1971 and died three years later in Geneva, Switzerland.

Milhaud's movie career began when he was only twenty-three years old, writing music for the 1915 American silent film *The Beloved Vagabond*. His first sound film was Jean Renoir's *Madame Bovary* in 1934, and most of his subsequent movie projects were French, including *Tartarin de Tarascon*, *Rasputin*, *The Citadel of Silence*, *Cavalcade of Love*, and *The Mayor's Dilemma*. His two American scores are for *The Private Affairs of Bel Ami* and one segment in the surreal anthology *Dreams That Money Can Buy*. Of Milhaud's many talents, his screen compositions have gotten the least amount of attention. Some of this is because he never scored a famous or influential film, though *Madame Bovary* and *The Private Loves of Bel Ami* come close. The former originally ran nearly three hours and was cut by more than a third before it was released. The surviving movie is a bit of a shambles and uneven to say the least, but enough of Milhaud's music is still there to enjoy. It is a simple, minimalist score often with a leisurely tempo and a melancholy tone, taking its cue from the lonely and frustrated title heroine (Valentine Tessier). The scenes of small village life are scored with an artificial joie de vivre and there is a lovely hesitation waltz for the ball scene. Although *Madame Bovary* is a period piece, the score strikes one as modern because of its lack

of flourishes and sentiment. *The Private Affairs of Bel Ami* is a droll tragicomedy, based on a Guy Maupassant story, about a womanizer (George Sanders) who misses out on the one true love of his life (Angela Lansbury). The opening music is a frivolous march with a French flair, exuding pomp and silliness at the same time. The scoundrel's theme is a quirky piece with various woodwinds in competition. There is some lovely salon music and the 1880s milieu is captured in other passages as well. For the true modernist Milhaud in a movie, one has to look at the "Ruth, Roses, and Revolvers" segment of Hans Richter's *Dreams That Money Can Buy*. In this bizarre section of a very Daliesque movie, two mannequins seem to court and dance to Milhaud's carnival-like music. The surreal piece then bursts into the cockeyed song "The Girl with the Pre-Fabricated Heart" (lyric by John La Touche) which is sung on the soundtrack by Libby Holman. This is probably as avant-garde as Milhaud ever gets on-screen and it makes one wonder what he might have done with more adventurous film projects. Autobiographies: *Notes without Music* (1953); *My Happy Life* (1973); biography: *Darius Milhaud*, Paul Collaer (1947).

Credits

(all films France unless stated otherwise)

Year	Film	Director
1915	*The Beloved Vagabond*	Edward José (USA)
1922	*Le roi de Camargue*	André Hugon
1934	*Madame Bovary*	Jean Renoir
1934	*Tartarin de Tarascon*	Raymond Bernard
1936	*The Beloved Vagabond*	Curtis Bernhardt (UK)
1937	*The Citadel of Silence*	Marcel L'Herbier
1938	*Hatred*	Robert Siodmak
1938	*Rasputin*	Marcel L'Herbier
1939	*The Mayor's Dilemma*	Raymond Bernard
1940	*Cavalcade of Love*	Raymond Bernard
1945	*L'espoir*	André Malraux, Boris Peskine (Spain/France)
1947	*The Private Affairs of Bel Ami*	Albert Lewin (USA)
1947	*Dreams That Money Can Buy*	Hans Richter (USA)
1950	*Life Begins Tomorrow*	Nicole Védres
1969	*God Chose Paris*	Philippe Arthuys, Gilbert Prouteau

MOCKRIDGE, Cyril J. (1896–1979) A very busy British-born Hollywood arranger and composer who was on the staff at Twentieth Century-Fox for many years, he contributed music to over 225 feature films

that include everything from westerns to Shirley Temple vehicles.

Cyril Mockridge was born in London and took piano lessons as a boy. He studied at the Royal Academy of

Music then served in the London Rifle Brigade during World War I. He was captured by the Germans and spent a portion of the war in a POW camp. Mockridge began his career as pianist and arranger for bands in England then in 1922 immigrated to the United States, where he worked with dance bands and played in the pit for Broadway musicals. By 1933 he was in Hollywood where he arranged music for the movies. Mockridge contributed some original music to the 1933 musical *My Weakness* and a few other films before going to Fox in 1935 as a staff composer-arranger; he remained there for twenty-six years. The first movie that Mockridge scored by himself was the romantic comedy *The Man Who Broke the Bank at Monte Carlo* in 1935. Over the next three decades he usually worked with at least one other composer each film. All the same, that leaves approximately 125 movies that he scored by himself. Mockridge worked on all kinds of films at Fox, sometimes writing soundtrack filler for musicals with songs by others and other times writing a complete score for comedies, westerns, and melodramas. He contributed music to all of the Shirley Temple films, most memorably *The Little Colonel, Captain January, The Littlest Rebel, Poor Little Rich Girl*, and *The Little Princess*. Among the dozens of other musicals he scored are such memorable movies as *On the Avenue, Down Argentine Way, Sun Valley Serenade, Stormy Weather, Wabash Avenue, The Farmer Takes a Wife, Daddy Long Legs*, and *Guys and Dolls*, getting an Oscar nomination for the last. Working alone or with others, Mockridge scored some of the best Fox nonmusicals from the golden age, including *King of Burlesque, Seventh Heaven, In Old Chicago, I'll Give a Million, Johnny Apollo, Charley's Aunt, The Ox-Bow Incident, Heaven Can Wait, The Dark Corner, Cluny Brown, My Darling Clementine, The Late George Apley, Miracle on 34th Street, Desk Set, I Was a Male War Bride, River of No Return, Cheaper by the Dozen, Where the Sidewalk Ends, How to Marry a Millionaire, The Solid Gold Cadillac, North to Alaska*, and *The Man Who Shot Liberty Valance*. In the early 1960s Mockridge left Fox and began a new career in television, writing music for such series as *Margie, Laramie, Going My Way, Wagon Train, McHale's Navy, Daniel Boone*, and *Lost in Space*. He retired in 1969 and died ten years later at the age of eighty-two.

A good number of the movies Mockridge scored on his own were musicals or vehicles for singing stars such as Shirley Temple and Betty Grable. Very little original music was required, as Mockridge filled in with orchestral arrangements of the songs written by others. Of the nonmusicals, the westerns often had the most-noticed music, although too often that music was already familiar to moviegoers. *My Darling Clementine*, John Ford's version of the famous shoot-out at the O.K. Corral, is a good example. The title song dates back to 1884 and is used throughout the film in different forms: performed on a sluggish church organ, a casual banjo, a vivacious fiddle, and with gusto by a mixed chorus. Some Stephen Foster tunes are also used as underscoring. Mockridge provided some saloon piano music under a Shakespearean actor (Alan Mowbray) as he recites from *Hamlet*, a strings and harmonica passage that moves like a hymn yet has a lazy cowboy feel to it, and a dramatic theme on wailing horns and descending strings that is used for a death scene. A very different kind of western, *The Ox-Bow Incident*, has a very nonwestern score. This disturbing tale about a lynch mob is more psychological than action packed and Mockridge's music avoids a prairie sound. There is a dramatic theme on strings and brass that has an urgency about it. It comes across more like film noir music than rural. Even when the posse is on the move across the plains, the music is a dissonant series of falling chords that seems almost urban. A few times throughout the movie, high-pitched celestial voices are heard softly in the distance. The only touch of musical cliché in *The Ox-Bow Incident* is the use of "Red River Valley" at different points in the film, usually played on a harmonica. Yet even this works effectively, particularly when the members of the posse realize they have killed innocent men and the traditional old tune is quietly used to break their uncomfortable silence.

Mockridge scored some actual film noirs and came up with powerful music for them. *Nightmare Alley*, a dark melodrama about blackmail and murder among the workers in a carnival sideshow, has an explosive main theme in which furious strings keep crashing up and down the scale and angry brass blare out fanfares that announce trouble. There is plenty of carnival music underscoring, most of it sour and mocking, and the minor-key love theme is played on strings that seem nervous. For the climactic confrontation, pounding percussion and distorted harp glissandos go berserk. Also quite exciting is the music in *The Dark Corner*, a noir thriller about a private eye (Mark Stevens) being framed for murder. Jazzy trumpets and bluesy strings overlap in the main theme, which repeats a simple melody with strident fury. There is also a jazz combo heard in a club and the music is footloose and playful. Even the Charlie Chan (Sidney Toler) mystery *Murder over New York* has a touch of noir scoring. Blasts of horns are matched by Oriental gongs in the opening music. Later there is a flowing foxtrot that moves smoothly and a blues passage that is very urban and Gershwinesque.

Of the many comedies and family films Mockridge scored, none has proven as beloved and popular as the original *Miracle on 34th Street*. This whimsical tale of the real Kris Kringle (Edmund Gwenn) and how he deals with the commercialization of Christmas is captured in Mockridge's robust opening music that bounces and races along in a busy urban way. It suggests a frantic Christmas season and the commercial side of the holiday yet is merry enough to convey a lot of heart as well. There is a twinkling theme on harp, strings, and woodwinds that serves as the theme for the dream house young Susan (Natalie Wood) imagines. It is a warm lullaby with long melodic lines but not too sentimental. The score often quotes from "Jingle Bells" in many different variations, from a highstrung race to a melancholy lament. It sometimes seems that every Mockridge score has at least one song standard hidden somewhere. More often than not, this is true, be it nineteenth-century ditties in *In Old Chicago* or Tin Pan Alley favorites in *Cheaper by the Dozen* or swing numbers in *Four Jills in a Jeep*. Maybe Hollywood didn't trust Mockridge to score a whole movie without some tuneful insurance. But judging by the pieces of original music he wrote for the screen, he was capable of much more.

Credits

(all films USA)

Year	Film	Director
1933	My Weakness (aka That's My Weakness)	David Butler
1935	The Little Colonel	David Butler
1935	The Man Who Broke the Bank at Monte Carlo	Stephen Roberts
1935	The Littlest Rebel	David Butler
1936	King of Burlesque	Sidney Lanfield
1936	The Country Doctor	Henry King
1936	Everybody's Old Man	James Flood
1936	Captain January	David Butler
1936	Private Number	Roy Del Ruth
1936	Poor Little Rich Girl	Irving Cummings
1936	To Mary—with Love	John Cromwell
1936	Sing, Baby, Sing	Sidney Lanfield
1936	Reunion	Norman Taurog
1937	On the Avenue	Roy Del Ruth
1937	Nancy Steele Is Missing!	George Marshall
1937	Seventh Heaven	Henry King
1937	Café Metropole	Edward H. Griffith
1937	You Can't Have Everything	Norman Taurog
1937	Wake Up and Live	Sidney Lanfield
1937	Danger—Love at Work	Otto Preminger
1937	Second Honeymoon	Walter Lang
1937	In Old Chicago	Henry King
1938	Always Goodbye	Sidney Lanfield
1938	I'll Give a Million	Walter Lange
1938	Gateway	Alfred L. Werker
1939	The Little Princess	Walter Lang. William A. Seiter
1939	Inside Story	Ricardo Cortez
1939	Second Fiddle	Sidney Lanfield
1939	Hotel for Women	Gregory Ratoff
1939	Hollywood Cavalcade	Irving Cummings, etc.
1939	Everything Happens at Night	Irving Cummings
1940	Johnny Apollo (aka Dance with the Devil)	Henry Hathaway

Year	Film	Director
1940	*Girl in 313*	Ricardo Cortez
1940	*Lucky Cisco Kid*	H. Bruce Humberstone
1940	*Manhattan Heartbeat* (aka *Marriage in Transit*)	David Burton
1940	*Pier 13*	Eugene Forde
1940	*Girl from Avenue A*	Otto Brower
1940	*Young People*	Allan Dwan
1940	*The Great Profile*	Walter Lang
1940	*Charlie Chan at the Wax Museum*	Lynn Shores
1940	*Yesterday's Heroes*	Herbert I. Leeds
1940	*Down Argentine Way*	Irving Cummings
1940	*Youth Will Be Served*	Otto Brower
1940	*Tin Pan Alley*	Walter Lang
1940	*Murder over New York*	Harry Lachman
1940	*Michael Shayne: Private Detective*	Eugene Forde
1940	*Jenny*	David Burton
1941	*Romance of the Rio Grande*	Herbert I. Leeds
1941	*Tall, Dark and Handsome* (aka *Ready, Willing and Beautiful*)	H. Bruce Humberstone
1941	*Golden Hoofs*	Lynn Shores
1941	*Murder among Friends*	Ray McCarey
1941	*Sleepers West* (aka *Sleepers East*)	Eugene Forde
1941	*Scotland Yard*	Norman Foster
1941	*The Great American Broadcast*	Archie Mayo
1941	*The Cowboy and the Blonde*	Ray McCarey
1941	*A Very Young Lady*	Harold D. Schuster
1941	*Accent on Love*	Ray McCarey
1941	*Dance Hall*	Irving Pichel
1941	*Charley's Aunt*	Archie Mayo
1941	*Dressed to Kill* (aka *The Dead Take No Bows*)	Eugene Forde
1941	*Sun Valley Serenade*	H. Bruce Humberstone
1941	*We Go Fast*	William C. McGann
1941	*Riders of the Purple Sage*	James Tinling
1941	*Moon over Her Shoulder*	Alfred L. Werker
1941	*I Wake Up Screaming* (aka *Hot Spot*)	H. Bruce Humberstone
1941	*Marry the Bo$$'$ Daughter*	Thornton Freeland
1941	*The Perfect Snob*	Ray McCarey
1942	*Red, White and Perfect*	Herbert I. Leeds
1942	*Castle in the Desert*	Harry Lachman
1942	*Song of the Islands*	Walter Lang
1942	*The Night before the Divorce*	Robert Siodmak
1942	*Rings on Her Fingers* (aka *Double or Nothing*)	Rouben Mamoulian
1942	*Lone Star Ranger*	James Tinling
1942	*Sundown Jim*	James Tinling
1942	*Moontide*	Archie Mayo, Fritz Lang
1942	*My Gal Sal*	Irving Cummings
1942	*The Mad Martindales*	Alfred L. Werker
1942	*It Happened in Flatbush*	Ray McCarey
1942	*Thru Different Eyes*	Thomas Z. Loring
1942	*A-Hunting We Will Go*	Alfred L. Werker
1942	*The Man in the Trunk*	Malcolm St. Clair
1942	*Over My Dead Body*	Malcolm St. Clair
1943	*The Meanest Man in the World*	Sidney Lanfield
1943	*Tonight We Raid Calais*	John Brahm
1943	*The Ox-Bow Incident*	William A. Wellman
1943	*Coney Island*	Walter Lang
1943	*Stormy Weather*	Andrew L. Stone
1943	*Heaven Can Wait*	Ernst Lubitsch
1943	*Holy Matrimony*	John M. Stahl

Year	Film	Director
1943	*Happy Land*	Irving Pichel
1943	*The Fighting Sullivans*	Lloyd Bacon
1943	*Pin Up Girl* (aka *Imagine Us*)	H. Bruce Humberstone
1944	*The Eve of St. Mark*	John M. Stahl
1944	*Ladies of Washington*	Louis King
1944	*Take It or Leave It*	Benjamin Stoloff
1944	*Sweet and Low-Down*	Archie Mayo
1944	*In the Meantime, Darling* (aka *Army Wives*)	Otto Preminger
1944	*Irish Eyes Are Smiling*	Gregory Ratoff
1944	*Something for the Boys*	Lewis Seiler
1945	*Thunderhead—Son of Flicka*	Louis King
1945	*Molly and Me*	Lewis Seiler
1945	*Captain Eddie*	Lloyd Bacon
1945	*Doll Face* (aka *Here's a Kiss*)	Lewis Seiler
1945	*Colonel Effingham's Raid*	Irving Pichel
1946	*Claudia and David*	Walter Lang
1946	*Sentimental Journey* (aka *The Little Horse*)	Walter Lang
1946	*The Dark Corner*	Henry Hathaway
1946	*Cluny Brown*	Ernst Lubitsch
1946	*If I'm Lucky*	Lewis Seiler
1946	*Three Little Girls in Blue*	H. Bruce Humberstone
1946	*My Darling Clementine*	John Ford
1946	*Wake Up and Dream*	Lloyd Bacon
1947	*The Late George Apley*	Joseph L. Mankiewicz
1947	*Miracle on 34th Street*	George Seaton
1947	*Thunder in the Valley* (aka *Bob, Son of Battle*)	Louis King
1947	*Nightmare Alley*	Edmund Goulding
1947	*You Were Meant for Me*	Lloyd Bacon
1948	*Scudda Hoo! Scudda Hay!*	F. Hugh Herbert
1948	*Green Grass of Wyoming*	Louis King
1948	*Deep Waters*	Henry King
1948	*The Walls of Jericho*	John M. Stahl
1948	*That Lady in Ermine* (aka *This Is the Moment*)	Ernst Lubitsch, Otto Preminger
1948	*The Luck of the Irish* (aka *Leave It to the Irish*)	Henry Koster
1948	*Road House*	Jean Negulesco
1948	*That Wonderful Urge*	Robert B. Sinclair
1949	*The Beautiful Blonde from Bashful Bend*	Preston Sturges
1949	*Come to the Stable*	Henry Koster
1949	*Slattery's Hurricane*	André De Toth
1949	*I Was a Male War Bride*	Howard Hawks
1949	*Thieves' Highway* (aka *Collision*)	Jules Dassin
1949	*Father Was a Fullback*	John M. Stahl
1949	*Dancing in the Dark*	Irving Reis
1950	*Mother Didn't Tell Me*	Claude Binyon
1950	*Wabash Avenue*	Henry Koster
1950	*Cheaper by the Dozen*	Walter Lang
1950	*A Ticket to Tomahawk*	Richard Sale
1950	*Love That Brute*	Alexander Hall
1950	*Where the Sidewalk Ends*	Otto Preminger
1950	*Stella*	Claude Binyon
1950	*I'll Get By*	Richard Sale
1950	*American Guerrilla in the Philippines*	Fritz Lang
1951	*You're in the Navy Now* (aka *U.S.S. Teakettle*)	Henry Hathaway
1951	*Follow the Sun*	Sidney Lanfield
1951	*Half-Angel*	Richard Sale
1951	*The Frogmen*	Lloyd Bacon
1951	*As Young as You Feel* (aka *Will You Love Me in December?*)	Harmon Jones

Year	Film	Director
1951	Mr. Belvedere Rings a Bell (aka Mr. Belvedere Blows His Whistle)	Henry Koster
1951	Love Nest	Joseph M. Newman
1951	Let's Make It Legal	Richard Sale
1951	The Model and the Marriage Broker	George Cukor
1951	Golden Girl	Lloyd Bacon
1951	Elopement	Henry Koster
1952	Deadline—U.S.A.	Richard Brooks
1952	Belles on Their Toes	Henry Levin
1952	We're Not Married!	Edmund Goulding
1952	Dreamboat	Claude Binyon
1952	Night without Sleep	Roy Ward Baker
1953	The Farmer Takes a Wife	Henry Levin
1953	Mister Scoutmaster	Henry Levin
1953	City of Bad Men	Harmon Jones
1953	How to Marry a Millionaire	Jean Negulesco
1954	Night People	Nunnally Johnson
1954	Siege at Red River	Rudolph Maté
1954	River of No Return	Otto Preminger, Jean Negulesco
1954	Woman's World	Jean Negulesco
1955	Many Rivers to Cross	Roy Rowland
1955	Daddy Long Legs	Jean Negulesco
1955	Guys and Dolls (AAN)	Joseph L. Mankiewicz
1955	How to Be Very, Very Popular	Nunnally Johnson
1956	The Lieutenant Wore Skirts (aka I Lost My Wife to the Army)	Frank Tashlin
1956	The Solid Gold Cadillac	Richard Quine
1956	Bus Stop	Joshua Logan
1957	Oh, Men! Oh, Women!	Nunnally Johnson
1957	Desk Set	Walter Lang
1957	Will Success Spoil Rock Hunter?	Frank Tashlin
1957	Kiss Them for Me	Stanley Donen
1958	The Gift of Love	Jean Negulesco
1958	I Married a Woman	Hal Kanter
1958	Rally 'Round the Flag, Boys!	Leo McCarey
1959	Thunder in the Sun	Russell Rouse
1959	A Private's Affair	Raoul Walsh
1960	Tall Story (aka The Way the Ball Bounces)	Joshua Logan
1960	Wake Me When It's Over	Mervyn LeRoy
1960	North to Alaska (aka Go North)	Henry Hathaway
1960	Flaming Star (aka Black Heart)	Don Siegel
1962	The Man Who Shot Liberty Valance	John Ford
1963	Donovan's Reef	John Ford

MORLEY, Angela (aka Wally Stott) (1924–2009) A successful British musician, arranger, conductor, and composer for television, radio, and movies, the transsexual woman artist had a busy career in the recording industry but managed to score thirteen films over the course of thirty-six years.

Angela Morley was born Walter Stott in Leeds, England, the son of a watchmaker who played the ukulele and a mother who was a singer. Stott began piano lessons at the

age of eight but when his father died unexpectedly the family suffered financial woes and the lessons ended. He continued on the piano on his own, later learning how to play the accordion, violin, clarinet, and saxophone as well. It was as a saxophonist that Stott found work and left school to tour with a band, learning also to write arrangements for the group. With the outbreak of World War II and the shortage of musicians not in the military, he found plenty of work performing on tour, on radio, and on records.

Wally Stott (as he was billed) was only twenty when he was hired to play in the Geraldo Orchestra, the top band in Britain at the time. Even as he wrote arrangements for the orchestra, Stott took private instruction on composition and started to write his own music. By 1950 he gave up performing and concentrated on composing and arranging. As music director for Philips Records, Stott worked with celebrated singers such as Rosemary Clooney and Mel Tormé and presented his own albums of "easy listening," or what was then called mood music. On television, he conducted and arranged music for two very popular programs, *Hancock's Half Hour* and *The Goon Show*.

Stott's first movie credit was cowriting with Stanley Black the music for the 1952 romantic drama *Holiday Week*. His first solo effort was the comedy *Will Any Gentleman . . . ?* the next year. But Stott was not happy writing for the movies and concentrated on records, concerts, and television, although he wrote arrangements for films scored by John Williams, Miklós Rózsa, Alex North, Bill Conti, Richard Rodney Bennett, and others. In 1972 Stott underwent a sex change operation, took the name Angela Morley, and remained married to Christine Parker for the rest of her life. During the 1970s Morley was conductor of the BBC Radio Orchestra and the BBC Big Band. She occasionally returned to movies, receiving Oscar nominations for two musicals, *The Little Prince* and *The Slipper and the Rose: The Story of Cinderella*. There was also high praise for her score for the animated movie *Watership Down*, her last feature film. Morley's other movies of note are *Cocktails in the Kitchen*, *The Looking Glass War*, *Captain Nemo and the Underwater City*, and *When Eight Bells Toll*. In the 1980s she turned to writing music for American television series, such as *Wonder Woman*, *McClain's Law*, *Hotel*, *The Colbys*, *Dynasty*, *Falcon Crest*, and *Dallas*. She relocated to Scottsdale, Arizona, in 1994 and founded the Chorale of the Alliance Française of Greater Phoenix for which she wrote many arrangements of French songs. Morley remained active as an arranger and conductor until her death in 2009 from a heart attack at the age of eighty-four.

Although the musicals *The Little Prince* and *The Slipper and the Rose* are Morley's most acknowledged movies, neither have very much of her music. The former is a widely castigated version of Antoine de Saint-Exupéry's popular story, an allegorical tale of a pilot (Richard Kiley) who travels the universe with a boy prince (Steven

Warner). The original songs by Frederick Loewe (music) and Alan Jay Lerner (lyrics) were wanting, and Loewe and Morley cowrote the soundtrack music which was mostly based on the songs. *The Slipper and the Rose* is a much better film. The songs are by the Disney songwriters Robert B. and Richard M. Sherman and the soundtrack score is by Morley. Again the underscoring is based on the songs and Morley's work as orchestrator and conductor is her real contribution to the movie. Two action thrillers that Morley scored on her own are good examples of her screen composition skills. *When Eight Bells Toll* is a James Bond–like adventure and Morley provides a Bond-like score. A British agent (Anthony Hopkins) is on the hunt for a ship that has disappeared off the coast of Scotland and his various exploits are scored with jazz, Big Band, and synthesized music. The main theme begins with strings sliding up the scale with a vengeance then propulsive music is heard on electric guitar, and brass instruments push forward with confidence and a bit of cockiness. For the suspense scenes, high-frequency sustained notes on a synthesizer are contrasted with low brass underneath. There is also a raucous chase theme with a Big Band sound in which brass and percussion seem to be running ahead of themselves. Morley's music for *When Eight Bells Toll* may lack the sexiness of the Bond scores but so does the plot, which is based on an Alistair MacLean novel. Also more cerebral than the Bond adventures is *The Looking Glass War*, a thriller based on a John le Carré novel. During the Cold War, a British spy (Christopher Jones) infiltrates East Germany to find hidden missiles aimed at free Europe. Morley's opening music for the thriller is a superb cool jazz piece. A muted solo trumpet plays a smooth yet expressive melody that is punctuated with electronic vibrations, echoing pounding on various percussion, and exotic sitar and piano glissandos. As was often the case, Morley arranged and conducted the music and her years of experience with bands is quite evident.

Morley's most famous film, the animated *Watership Down*, is arguably her best score, although it is a low-key and rather quiet series of tracks that might serve for a nature ballet. Ironically, this allegorical tale about Fascism is very violent and far from a children's cartoon. Based on the Richard Adams novel, the plot follows some members of a rabbit warren who foresee terrible destruction coming and so set out on a journey to find a safe haven. The locations in the movie are bucolic and vividly rendered, but what happens is often vicious and disturbing. Morley's score is subtle, suggesting fear and terror without overtly dramatic music. The prologue and main theme, a melancholy yet lyrical piece featuring woodwinds, was written by Malcolm Williamson. The rest of the score was composed by Morley, who orchestrated it as well. Among the more peaceful passages is a delicate theme on flute and harp that seems to be tossed about on a gentle wind. There is also a mystical track with harp glissandos, marching brass, and swirling strings. On the darker side are a nightmarish theme with wavering strings, frantic brass below, and a lonesome flute solo above; a heartfelt lament featuring a solo flute with gentle accompaniment by reeds; and a march on pizzicato strings, gurgling woodwinds, and rhythmic percussion that is somewhat oppressive. One of the few outright jubilant passages is a slightly swinging theme for the seagull Kehaar in which the woodwinds merrily bounce about the scale. Either as Wally Stott or Angela Morley, this outstanding arranger was little known to the public, but in the music business she was highly respected. It is unfortunate that she did not score more movies. Official website: www.angelamorley.com.

Credits

(all films UK unless stated otherwise)

Year	Film	Director
1952	*Holiday Week* (aka *Hindle Wakes*)	Arthur Crabtree
1953	*Will Any Gentleman . . . ?*	Michael Anderson
1954	*Cocktails in the Kitchen* (aka *For Better, for Worse*)	J. Lee Thompson
1956	*It's Never Too Late*	Michael McCarthy
1957	*Let's Be Happy*	Henry Levin
1959	*The Heart of a Man*	Herbert Wilcox
1959	*The Lady Is a Square*	Herbert Wilcox
1969	*Captain Nemo and the Underwater City*	James Hill
1969	*The Looking Glass War*	Frank Pierson
1971	*When Eight Bells Toll*	Etienne Périer
1974	*The Little Prince* (AAN)	Stanley Donen (UK/USA)
1976	*The Slipper and the Rose: The Story of Cinderella* (AAN)	Bryan Forbes
1978	*Watership Down*	Martin Rosen

MORODER, Giorgio (b. 1940) A celebrated Italian songwriter, record producer, singer, musician, and composer who has been a major force in pop music for over three decades and is often cited as the Father of Disco, he has scored only sixteen feature films, but they include some very popular songs and scores.

Born Hansjörg Moroder in Urtijëi, Italy, he took up the guitar at a young age, later playing and singing in local rock groups. Moroder began his professional music career as a bass player and guitarist for different bands that toured Europe. He got involved with the discotheque scene in Aachen, Germany, at the Scotch-Club, considered the first disco club in Europe. Moroder sang (in many languages) and played guitar there, also making single records for different recording companies in Germany. His first hit single, "Looky Looky," was released in 1969, followed by many others that found success in Europe and later America. Moroder's fame climbed when he cowrote and produced the Donna Summer hits "I Feel Love" and "Love to Love You Baby." In the 1970s, Moroder founded Oasis Records and established Musicland Studios, which became a studio home for Elton John, Queen, Led Zeppelin, and the Electric Light Orchestra. Since then he has written for and produced many records for such diverse artists as Melissa Manchester, David Bowie, Barbra Streisand, the Three Degrees, Kenny Loggins, Olivia Newton-John, Sparks, Adam Ant, Bonnie Tyler, Blondie, and Pat Benatar. He has also written music for video games, sporting events (including three Olympics), and television commercials.

Moroder's screen career began inauspiciously when he scored the German drama *Sex Life in a Convent* in 1972.

He did not return to the cinema until six years later when director Alan Parker asked him to write the music for the powerful prison thriller *Midnight Express*. Moroder's totally synthesized score was a sensation, winning the Oscar and the album becoming a best seller. One track from the recording, "The Chase," became famous on its own and has been used for everything from radio talk shows to wrestling exhibitions. Moroder's next three films produced hit songs as well. *American Gigolo* featured Blondie singing "Call Me" (written with Debbie Harry), Donna Summer's "On the Radio" (lyric by Summer) came from *Foxes*, and David Bowie and Moroder had a hit with the title number from *Cat People*. Both songs and score for *Flashdance* were also popular, as was the movie itself. Moroder's other notable films include *Scarface*, *Electric Dreams*, and *Let It Ride*. In 1984 he composed a new soundtrack for the 1927 silent film classic *Metropolis* and changed the speed of the movie to match the synthesized score. The controversial result featured such artists as Benatar, Tyler, Jon Anderson, Freddie Mercury, and Billy Squier on the soundtrack. Moroder's songs have been used in dozens of movies, ranging from *Looking for Mr. Goodbar* (1977) to *American Hustle* (2013), and he has written new songs for movies he did not score, most memorably the Oscar-winning "Take My Breath Away" (with Tom Whitlock) from *Top Gun* (1986). His other Oscar for Best Song was for "Flashdance . . . What a Feeling." Moroder has remained active in many phases of music, including acting as DJ, but has not scored a movie since the German nature documentary *Underwater Impressions* in 2003, the last work of controversial filmmaker Leni Riefenstahl.

One of the characteristics of Moroder's music is the way he moves from acoustic to synthesized instruments within one musical piece. Although he was one of the pioneers in using the synthesizer, Moroder was not slavish to the device and early on experimented with other techno and electronic sounds. Much emphasis has been put on the many hit songs he wrote for the movies but a close look at his soundtrack scores is more useful in examining Moroder the screen composer. *Flashdance*, for example, has over a dozen songs, most written for the film and others from the classical or Tin Pan Alley repertory. *Midnight Express*, on the other hand, has only one: a blues number written by David Castle. This harrowing story of an American (Brad Davis) and his attempt to escape from a Turkish prison is energized by Moroder's penetrating score, which utilized the Moog synthesizer to a degree not yet heard in an American movie. The main theme is a slow disco piece with synthesized horns in the upper range and echoing sound effects below. It is mysterious, uncomfortable, and just a bit threatening. Also subdued is the flowing love theme on electronic keyboard with high-pitched sustained notes lingering above. The rest of the score is high energy, as with a restless passage with high-pitched electronic chimes, wavering synthesized horns, and pounding percussion, all set to a disco beat. The famous chase theme, which runs eight minutes in the film, has several movements, making a kind of wired symphony. The track opens with electronic notes that slowly slide up and down the scale while percussion and electric guitar move to a disco beat. Another section is a rhythmic piece in which a repeated musical phrase echoes as mechanical sounds enter at unexpected points. Also part of this chase sequence is a percussion passage, with chimes, bells, whistles, and lots of vibrato, and a passage in which synthesized horns play a repeated fanfare that eventually breaks into a melody. It is little wonder why such a refreshing and dynamic score got so much attention in 1978.

American Gigolo is a negligible thriller about a male escort (Richard Gere) who gets on the wrong side of the law when one of his clients is found murdered. There is little drive in the plotting, but Moroder's music moves with a disco beat while still including a good deal of variety. One theme features electronic bass guitar and synthesized organ chords that move at a steady pace even as the piece carefully accelerates and the pitch rises. Another passage consists of repeating electronic frequency noise with a bongo drum and a rapid guitar riff underneath. The love theme, played on conventional piano and vibrating bass sounds, has a casual and breezy temperament as it flows forward at a moderate tempo. The score (and movie) ends with a hymnlike passage played on electric organ with a rock accompaniment that remains subdued even when electric guitar riffs are added. A melodrama that is certainly driven is *Scarface*, a tough and ferocious film about the rise and fall of a Cuban gangster (Al Pacino) in Miami in the 1980s. This violent movie keeps the viewer uncomfortably on the edge, helped by Moroder's compelling score. The main theme has electronic crashes and wavering keyboard chords that move like a funeral dirge until the tempo changes to a more propulsive disco beat and the instruments perk up. The theme for the antihero is a pounding passage with determined but restrained drumbeats and electric organ chords, the effect being as seething and dangerous as the man. The final musical track is a kind of processional played on synthesized organ chords with echoing brass acting like percussion. Moroder wrote ten

songs for *Scarface*, but it is the soundtrack score that most impresses. His career is filled with dozens of hit songs, but scores like those for *Midnight Express* and *Scarface* deserve their own place of honor. Official website: www. moroder.net.

Credits

(all films USA unless stated otherwise; * for Best Song)

Year	Film	Director
1972	Sex Life in a Convent	Eberhard Schröder (W. Germany/France)
1978	Midnight Express (AA)	Alan Parker (UK/USA)
1980	American Gigolo (GGN*)	Paul Scharder
1980	Foxes	Adrian Lyne
1982	Cat People (GGN; GGN*)	Paul Schrader
1983	Flashdance (AA*; GG; GG*; BAFTA-N; BAFTA-N*)	Adrian Lyne
1983	Scarface (GGN)	Brian De Palma
1983	D.C. Cab (aka Capitol Cab)	Joel Schumacher
1984	Electric Dreams (BAFTA-N*)	Steve Barron (USA/UK)
1984	Metropolis (1927)	Fritz Lang (Germany)
1987	Over the Top (aka Meet Me Half Way)	Menahem Golan
1988	Fair Game (aka Mamba)	Mario Orfini (Italy)
1989	Let It Ride	Joe Pytka
1992	Cyber Eden (aka Jackpot)	Mario Orfini (Italy/France)
1996	Pepolino und der Schatz der Meerjungfrau	János Uzsák (Germany/Hungary/Canada)
2003	Underwater Impressions	Leni Riefenstahl (Germany)

MOROSS, Jerome (1913–1983) A unique composer and arranger of ballet, operas, concert hall works, and the theatre, he managed to score fifteen feature films during his varied and impressive career.

Jerome Moross was born in the New York City borough of Brooklyn, the son of Russian immigrants, and was a child prodigy on the piano, performing in public at the age of five and writing his own music three years later. As a teenager, Moross's orchestral compositions were performed by professionals in various Manhattan venues. At this time he befriended composer-conductor Bernard Herrmann, who conducted some of Moross's pieces, the two becoming lifelong friends. Many of these compositions, and several of his subsequent works, used traditional American folk music which he arranged and orchestrated in unique ways. Moross attended New York University, graduating at the age of eighteen, and he also studied music at Juilliard. The young composer-arranger already had a glowing reputation by the time he finished his formal

education. In 1934 he was hired by CBS Radio to write the theme song for *American School of the Air: Folk Music of America*. The piece, titled "Ramble on a Hobo Tune," later became the basis of his only symphony. Moross also wrote music for the popular radio program *March of Time*. He began composing for the stage in 1934 when he wrote the ballet *Paul Bunyan: An American Saga*. The next year he wrote incidental music for the Maxim Gorky play *Mother*. But he made his living mostly by conducting and arranging. He was musical director for the unsuccessful New York premiere of the Bertolt Brecht–Kurt Weill German musical *The Threepenny Opera* in 1933 and George Gershwin was so impressed with the young pianist that he hired Moross for the pit for the tour of *Porgy and Bess*. His career took an important turn when he wrote the music for the leftist musical revue *Parade* in 1935. This led to more ballet commissions, most memorably *Frankie and Johnny*, choreographed by Ruth Page, which found success in New York and Chicago and today is considered an

American masterwork. Moross returned to the New York theatre later in his career, scoring such unusual musicals as the dance program *Broadway Ballads* (1948), the cult favorite *The Golden Apple* (1954), and the controversial *Gentlemen, Be Seated* (1963).

Having befriended composer Aaron Copland in Manhattan, Moross was invited out to Hollywood in 1940 to orchestrate Copland's score for the screen version of *Our Town*. He stayed on to arrange the music for many other films, including such notable works as *They Drive by Night* (1940), *Since You Went Away* (1944), *Christmas in Connecticut* (1945), *The Best Years of Our Lives* (1946), *The Bishop's Wife* (1947), and *Hans Christian Andersen* (1952). Before returning to New York, Moross scored his first feature film, the thriller *Close-Up*, in 1948. The movie was not a success and neither were his other early efforts. But his score for *The Big Country* in 1948 was nominated for an Oscar and for the next two decades he returned to California on occasion and scored an eclectic group of movies, including *The Adventures of Huckleberry Finn*, *The Cardinal*, *Five Finger Exercise*, *The War Lord*, and *Rachel, Rachel*. Moross also wrote music for such television series as *Gunsmoke*, *Have Gun—Will Travel*, *Lancer*, and *Wagon Train*. His legacy also includes four one-act operas, a handful of ballets, and many orchestral and chamber pieces.

Although Moross's screen career was only a small part of his life, one can find important aspects of his musical talent in his movie scores. His interest in American folk music shaped the music in Moross's most famous score, the western *The Big Country*. The main theme is lushly symphonic but is actually a simple tune that could be played effectively on guitar or harmonica. The melody is catchy yet leisurely and even reflective. There are urgent passages in the score in which the brass seem to be chomping at the bit, other sections that have a slow majesty. One theme recalls a merry folk dance which speeds up in a challenging way. In fact, the score reminds one of a robust ballet in which images of Americana dance before you. Some have compared Moross's music to an opera. Describe it as you may, this is a masterful piece of American music and one of the triumphs of screen scoring. It was also very

influential. Most western scores written after 1948 seem to be inspired, at least in part, by *The Big Country*.

Twenty years later, Moross scored the intimate character drama *Rachel, Rachel* by first-time director Paul Newman. The film, about a spinster teacher (Joanne Woodward) facing a midlife crisis, has an emotive main theme patterned after a children's ditty. Flutes and strings delicately intertwine as the melody carefully explores the scale and an oboe floats overheard. The story of *Rachel, Rachel* is a contemporary one, but the score has a timeless folk quality. Had it been orchestrated like *The Big Country*, it might pass for a western soundtrack. Also contemporary, the drama *The Cardinal* has a splendid score. The opening music is both ponderous and romantic with a classical flavor. A sweeping five-note phrase is repeated as it gains stature. As a curate (Tom Tryon) moves up the liturgical ladder to become a powerhouse in the Church, the music seems to gain weight. There is a vivid passage that captures the hustle and bustle of Rome as well as grandiose music for the pomp and ceremony at the Vatican. A tripping waltz is also used effectively to convey the world of the privileged class, and a melancholy piece for the muted romance in the tale. *The Cardinal* is far from an "Americana" score yet it still has Moross's richness and melodic sense. The same might be said for his vivacious score for the formulaic dinosaur movie *The Valley of the Gwangi*. A circus troupe discovers a prehistoric monster in Mexico and try to turn it into a big-top attraction. The music has the energetic verve of a big western, particularly its main theme in which fanfares of brass and restless strings try to outrun each other. You can take Moross out of the American landscape but it seems you cannot take the folk heritage out of this remarkable composer. When Moross died from a stroke at the age of sixty-nine, he left several unfinished projects. He had ventured into many areas of music but did not find widespread fame in any one genre. At least not during his lifetime. Today his music is greatly admired and some of his works are viewed as American originals. But, sadly, Hollywood did not use him well and a great opportunity was missed. Official website: www.moross.com.

Credits

(all films USA)

Year	Film	Director
1948	*Close-Up*	Jack Donohue
1951	*When I Grow Up*	Michael Kanin
1952	*The Captive City*	Robert Wise
1956	*The Sharkfighters*	Jerry Hopper
1958	*The Proud Rebel*	Michael Curtiz
1958	*The Big Country* (AAN)	William Wyler
1959	*The Jayhawkers!*	Melvin Frank
1960	*The Adventures of Huckleberry Finn*	Michael Curtiz
1960	*The Mountain Road*	Daniel Mann
1962	*Five Finger Exercise*	Daniel Mann
1963	*The Cardinal*	Otto Preminger
1965	*The War Lord*	Franklin J. Schaffner
1968	*Rachel, Rachel*	Paul Newman
1969	*The Valley of Gwangi*	Jim O'Connolly
1969	*Hail, Hero!*	David Miller

MORRICONE, Ennio (b. 1928) One of the most renowned composers of international cinema, with over 350 feature films to his credit, the Italian-born composer, conductor, arranger, and musician has also written over one hundred pieces for the concert hall and dozens of popular songs, making him possibly the most prolific composer of the twentieth century. Although Morricone is mostly known for his scores for a series of "spaghetti" westerns in the 1960s and 1970s, his output is much more encompassing, taking in a variety of genres, many famous directors, and several countries.

He was born in Rome, the son of a trumpet player who performed in various orchestras in the capital city. By the time he was six years old, Morricone was composing original musical pieces on the family piano. His father taught the boy how to read music and gave him experience playing a handful of musical instruments. At the age of nine, Morricone took trumpet lessons at the prestigious National Academy of Santa Cecilia, enrolling as a full-time student three years later. He also studied composition, choral and symphonic music, and conducting there. After graduation, Morricone pursued a career writing for the concert stage, radio, and the theatre, as well as playing in jazz bands. He first found recognition for a pop song (lyric by Roby Ferrante) titled "Ogni volta" ("Every Time") which was recorded by Paul Anka and sold over three million copies internationally. This was followed by several song hits that he composed and arranged for various art-

ists in Europe and the States. Morricone first contributed music to films in the late 1950s as a ghostwriter, adding incidental music to soundtrack scores by others. The few times he was credited, he used the pen names Leo Nichols or Dan Savio. His first complete screen score was for the Italian drama *Il Federale* (*The Fascist*) in 1961 for director Luciano Salce. It was a conventional score, but for Salce's *La voglia matta* (*Crazy Desire*) the next year Morricone wrote a jazz score that was noticed by the critics. By this time he was heavily involved in avant-garde music, writing improvisational pieces for concerts and clubs and becoming active in the Gruppo di Improvvisazione di Nuova Consonanza (G.I.N.C. or "Il Gruppo"), recording many albums with the experimental group. The Rome-based organization gave Morricone the opportunity to mix classical music with jazz and abstract music, creating a sound that would later get so much attention in his screen scores.

Morricone scored his first western, *Gunfight at Red Sands*, in 1963, but it was his music for *A Fistful of Dollars* the next year that launched his remarkable screen career. Directed by his college friend Sergio Leone, the movie changed the look and sound of the western genre, soon labeled the "spaghetti western." These bleak, nihilistic westerns, with a cold antihero who uses trickery as well as his gun to find justice, immediately found favor in Europe and around the world. The cast was usually international, the production simple and austere, and the tone cynical and deadly. A major element in the spaghetti western was the soundtrack, which differed from conventional prairie music. Morricone defined the new sound with his brilliant score for *A Fistful of Dollars*, using echoing sounds, modern music, and a highly stylized sense of drama. Leone, Morricone, and their star, a young and little-known Clint Eastwood, re-teamed for some of the best examples of the new genre, most memorably *For a Few Dollars More* and *The Good, the Bad, and the Ugly*. The main theme for the last of this "Dollars" trilogy, with its chilling echoes and startling howls, quickly became one of the most recognized musical themes around the world. A version by bandleader Hugo Montenegro sold over a million records and the theme has since been heard in many other films and television shows. Although Morricone was quickly associated with westerns, he broke away from the genre when he scored the politically potent *The Battle of Algiers* in 1966. That same year he coscored his first Hollywood movie, John Huston's epic *The Bible: In the Beginning . . .*, and was now regarded an international composer. Among his notable American movies over the next five decades are *Once Upon a Time in the West, Two Mules for Sister Sara, Orca, Days of Heaven, Bloodline, The Island, The Thing, The Untouchables, Bulworth, Bugsy, Mission to Mars, Disclosure, Wolf, In the Line of Fire, Exorcist II: The Heretic, Lolita, Love Affair*, and *Hamlet*. Yet some of Morricone's greatest successes were from European countries, as with *The Mission, La Cage aux Folles, The Decameron, 1900, Burn!, The Canterbury Tales, Malena, The Serpent, Arabian Nights, Once Upon a Time in America, Legend of 1900*, and *Cinema Paradiso*. Such an international career is even more remarkable in the fact that Morricone remains in Rome, refuses to fly in an airplane, and that the filmmakers always have had to come to him. He has also composed for television movies and miniseries in several countries even though he only speaks Italian.

His conducting career is significant, having given hundreds of concerts around the world. It seems Morricone's aversion to air travel is overcome by the opportunity to go by boat or train to conduct the great symphonic orchestras on four continents. Some of these concerts featured his screen scores but most have consisted of his own symphonies, concertos, choral works, requiems, sonatas, and small ensemble pieces. In addition to over three hundred soundtrack albums, Morricone has many jazz, classical, and avant-garde recordings. For his screen music, concert compositions, and recordings, Morricone has won awards across the globe. Yet he has never been fully embraced by

Hollywood because he would not sign long-term contracts, agree to certain conditions, or play the Tinseltown game. For his hundreds of movies (some of them extremely popular in the United States), he was nominated for the Oscar only five times and never won. In 2007 the Academy finally was embarrassed enough by its long-term neglect and gave him an honorary Oscar. Being arguably the world's most popular movie composer has sometimes kept Morricone from being taken seriously by music critics. But enough time has passed since his splashing debut in the 1960s that today his work is studied and appreciated as well as enjoyed.

The spaghetti western scores, in particular, have gone from being a hot fad to a cult favorite, and are now considered landmark screen music. *A Fistful of Dollars*, made on a low budget in Spain, has little dialogue, so the music becomes more essential. The main theme is minimalist: a solo guitar, a lone whistling voice, the rhythmic beating of a whip, then voices added to a restless melody played on an electric guitar. In another passage, a trumpet calls out forlornly as voices and strumming guitars provide the tempo. There is also a chase theme that suggests the galloping of horses but the blaring trumpets and male voices also convey a frenzied religious rite. Director Leone created this new kind of western in which good and evil are unclear and violence springs up like a dust storm. Morricone captures this in his music and the effect is penetrating. A twanging guitar and a lone flute sets the tempo for the soundtrack of the sequel *For a Few Dollars More*. Again whistling, electric guitar, and male voices are used, but violins play against the twang for a cockeyed kind of majesty. For the final shootout, the music is surprisingly serene, as if the duel was an occasion for mourning. The most interesting passage, titled "Clock Music," involves the unlikely combination of a pipe organ, ticking chimes, and a morose trumpet. *The Good, the Bad, and the Ugly* is the most famous entry in the "Dollars" trilogy and it has the most famous score. The celebrated main theme utilizes bird sounds, howling echoes, electronic sounds, a chorus, and gunshots, creating an unforgettable montage that is both threatening and rhythmically enticing. The rest of the score does not disappoint. A Spanish guitar quietly reflects the sadness of a sunset, furious strings build to a deadly quiet, a nervous guitar and chimes forecast danger, sorrowful trumpets at different tempos and pitches convey loneliness, whistling and a harmonica are used for a lighter theme, and a romantic passage relies on harmonica and low strings. The lyrical

"Ecstasy of Gold" theme has a solo female voice that manages to sing over and above the full rumbling orchestra as it pushes forward in a deliberate march. *The Good, the Bad, and the Ugly* is probably Morricone's masterpiece. How does one score another western after this? The surprise is that *Once Upon a Time in the West* is perhaps as strong a movie as *The Good, the Bad, and the Ugly* and its score equally accomplished. The main theme does not attack as in the trilogy. Instead a female voice sings a wordless hymn and then a conventional orchestra and choir pick up on the flowing melody. There is a menacing theme that consists only of reverberating guitar chords, a massacre is presented with heavy electronic notes that are answered by strings and high-pitched vibrations, some lively saloon music uses a slide whistle sardonically, a solo harmonica gives way to a melancholy oboe for the score's saddest selection, and a lazy but rhythmic banjo pokes along in the "Cheyenne" theme. Later westerns by other composers would imitate Morricone, sometimes effectively but rarely as memorably as in these four quintessential films.

Of his many other scores worthy of study, it is difficult to choose which ones convey his variety and creativity. Certainly the American movie *Days of Heaven* must be included. The story of three Chicago runaways (Richard Gere, Brooke Adams, and Linda Manz) who find refuge on the open prairie is leisurely plotted and beautifully photographed. The poetic nature of the landscape inspired Morricone to write perhaps his most lyrical score. For the main theme he boldly uses Camille Saint-Saens's piece "The Aquarium" even though there is no significant body of water on the farm where most of the action takes place. But the French master's gliding music is picked up by the waves of grain and the slow-moving clouds so easily that it seems the classical piece was created just for this film. A waltzing theme titled "Happiness" floats on the air as it builds in intensity, a flute echoed by a full orchestra. A solo guitar is used for a plaintive theme that meanders cautiously for the tentative romance between the young farmer (Sam Shepard) and one of his laborers (Adams). More nostalgic but just as lyrical is Morricone's score for the Italian film *Cinema Paradiso*. The main theme conjures up the past as its simple piano tune is enhanced by strings and a jaunty clarinet. The young boy (Salvatore Cascio) who befriends the old projectionist (Philippe Noiret) at the local cinema has his own theme, a lively violin piece that seems to bounce up and down the scale. The love theme in the movie is not by Morricone but by his son Andrea whose poignant melody blends in with the rest of this heartfelt score.

The complex parable *The Mission*, about the clash between Christian ideals and the natives in eighteenth-century South America, inspired a very powerful score from Morricone. The story is feverish and passionate and so is the score, mixing European religious music with tribal sounds. In the main theme a heavenly choir competes with simple drums. The religious music gets more aggressive as the drums recede, conveying the point of the film musically within the first few minutes. In one scene a Jesuit priest (Jeremy Irons) plays an oboe to get the attention of the natives. It is a mesmerizing melody and one that could believably soothe the savages. Guaranteed to have the opposite effect is the score for *The Untouchables*. From its first notes, the propulsive music pounds and struggles even though a mellow harmonica plays in the background. Gunshots punctuate the main theme as in the spaghetti westerns but this sound is urban, strident, and overpowering. The theme for mobster Al Capone (Robert De Niro) has a slight Neapolitan flavor and is played on echoing keyboard. During the climactic gun battle between the G-men and the bootleggers, trumpets also battle it out as musical lines overlap and a frenzy of brass drowns out the gunshots. For another gangster film, *Bugsy*, about the 1950s racketeer Bugsy Siegel (Warren Beatty), Morricone takes a gentler approach, the suspense coming from sustained violins and a steady pattern of bass notes. This score has some marvelous blues and jazz passages as befits the era and the nightclub atmosphere pervades even the love theme, played on a sultry trumpet at times, on the clarinet other times. Finally, the chilling score for *Casualties of War* must be mentioned. This very grim Vietnam War movie has a graceful score that makes the horrors on the screen more upsetting. A wordless choir and full orchestra create a fervent hymnlike sound but the brutal actions of an American platoon seem oblivious to anything so sacred as music.

The more one studies the screen scores of Morricone, the more one realizes that his work defies simple definition or explanation. There may be various Morricone trademarks, ranging from frequent choral music to the use of sound effects, but there is no one style. He is perhaps the most eclectic composer in a field that demands variety and endless creativity. Music theory book: *Composing for the Cinema*, Morricone and Gillian B. Anderson (2013). Official website: www.enniomorricone.it.

Credits

(all films Italy unless stated otherwise; * for Best Song)

Year	Film	Director
1961	The Fascist	Luciano Salce (France/Italy)
1962	La cuccagna	Luciano Salce
1962	Crazy Desire	Luciano Salce
1962	I motorizzati	Camillo Mastrocinque (Italy/Spain)
1963	The Little Nuns	Luciano Salce
1963	I basilischi	Lina Wertmüller
1963	Gunfight at Red Sands	Ricardo Blasco (Spain/Italy)
1963	Il Successo	Mauro Morassi, Dino Risi (Italy/France)
1964	Full Hearts and Empty Pockets	Camillo Mastrocinque (Italy/W. Germany)
1964	I maniaci	Lucio Fulci (Spain/Italy)
1964	Before the Revolution	Bernardo Bertolucci
1964	I marziani hanno 12 mani	Franco Castellano, Giuseppe Moccia (Italy/Spain)
1964	Tutto e musica	Domenico Modugno
1964	Two Escape from Sing Sing	Lucio Fulci
1964	A Fistful of Dollars	Sergio Leone (Italy/Spain/W. Germany)
1964	Bullets Don't Argue	Mario Caiano (Spain/Italy/W. Germany)
1964	Eighteen in the Sun	Camillo Mastrocinque
1964	In ginocchio da te	Ettore Maria Fizzarotti
1965	Se non avessi piu te	Ettore Maria Fizzarotti
1965	Non son degno di te	Ettore Maria Fizzarotti
1965	A Pistol for Ringo	Duccio Tessari (Spain/Italy)
1965	Nightmare Castle	Mario Caiano
1965	Highest Pressure	Enzo Trapani
1965	Slalom	Luciano Salce (Italy/France/Egypt)
1965	Thrilling	Carlo Lizzani, etc.
1965	Fists in the Pocket	Marco Bellocchio
1965	Idoli Controluce	Enzo Battaglia
1965	The Return of Ringo	Duccio Tessari (Spain/Italy)
1965	For a Few Dollars More	Sergio Leone (Italy/Spain/W. Germany)
1966	Mi vedrai toenare	Ettore Maria Fizzarotti
1966	Seven Guns for the MacGregors	Franco Giraldi (Spain/Italy)
1966	Svegliati e Uccidi	Carlo Lizzani (Italy/France)
1966	Agent 505: Death Trap Beirut	Manfred R. Köhler (W. Germany/Italy)
1966	The Hawks and the Sparrows	Pier Paolo Pasolini
1966	El Greco	Luciano Salce (Italy/France/Spain)
1966	The Battle of Algiers	Gillo Pontecorvo (Italy/Algeria)
1966	The Hills Run Red	Carlo Lizzani
1966	Un uomo a metà	Vittorio De Seta (Italy/France)
1966	The Bible: In the Beginning	John Huston (USA/Italy)
1966	Come Imparai ad Amare le Donne	Luciano Salce (Italy/France/W. Germany)
1966	Navajo Joe	Sergio Corbucci (Italy/Spain)
1966	The Big Gundown	Sergio Sollima (Spain/Italy)
1966	A Bullet for the General	Damiano Damiani
1966	The Good, the Bad and the Ugly	Sergio Leone (Italy/Spain/W. Germany)
1967	Il giardino delle delizie	Silvano Agosti
1967	Dirty Heroes	Alberto De Martino (Italy/France)
1967	Hellbenders	Sergio Corbucci (Italy/Spain)
1967	The Witches	Vittorio De Sica, etc. (Italy/France)
1967	Long Days of Vengeance	Florestano Vancini (Italy/Spain/France)
1967	Up the MacGregors	Franco Giraldi (Spain/Italy)
1967	Soldier's Girl	Alessandro Blasetti
1967	Operation Kid Brother (aka OK Connery)	Alberto De Martino
1967	Sugar Colt	Franco Giraldi (Spain/Italy)
1967	Matchless	Alberto Lattuada

Year	Film	Director
1967	Death Rides a Horse	Giulio Petroni
1967	The Rover	Terence Young
1967	China Is Near	Marco Bellocchio
1967	Grand Slam	Giuliano Montaldo (Italy/Spain)
1967	The Girl and the General	Pasquale Festa Campanile (Italy/France)
1967	Her Harem	Marco Ferreri (Italy/France)
1967	Destino: Estambul 68	Miguel Inglesias (Spain/Italy)
1967	Face to Face	Sergio Sollima (Spain/Italy)
1967	Arabella	Mauro Bolognini
1968	Ecce Homo	Bruno Gaburro
1968	Eat It	Francesco Casaretti
1968	Sanger: Diabolik	Mario Bava (Italy/France)
1968	Escalation	Roberto Faenza
1968	Guns for San Sebastian	Henri Verneuil (France/Italy/Mexico)
1968	Comandamenti per un gangster	Alfio Caltabiano
1968	Grazie Zia	Salvatore Samperi
1968	Run, Man, Run	Sergio Sollima (Italy/France)
1968	A Professional Gun (aka The Mercenary)	Sergio Corbucci (Italy/Spain)
1968	A Sky Full of Stars for a Roof	Giulio Petroni
1968	Teorema	Pier Paolo Pasolini
1968	Galileo	Liliana Cavani (Italy/Bulgaria)
1968	The Magnificent Tony Carrera	José Antonio de la Loma (Spain/W. Germany/Italy)
1968	Listen, Let's Make Love	Vittorio Caprioli (Italy/France)
1968	Partner	Bernardo Bertolucci
1968	A Fine Pair	Francesco Maselli
1968	A Quiet Place in the Country	Elio Petri (Italy/France)
1968	The Great Silence	Sergio Corbucci (Italy/France)
1968	Bandits in Rome	Alberto De Martino
1968	Once Upon a Time in the West	Sergio Leone (Italy/USA)
1969	He and She	Mauro Bolognini
1969	Giotto	Luciano Emmer
1969	Dirty Angels	Mauro Severino
1969	Fraulein Doktor	Alberto Lattuada (Italy/Yugoslavia)
1969	Mother's Heart	Salvatore Samperi
1969	Tepepa	Giulio Petroni (Italy/Spain)
1969	Alibi	Adolfo Celi, Vittorio Gassman
1969	The Lady of Monza	Eriprando Visconti
1969	Machine Gun McCain	Giuliano Montaldo
1969	Metti, una sera a cena	Guiseppe Patroni Griffi
1969	That Splendid November	Maura Bolognini (Italy/France)
1969	H2S	Roberto Faenza
1969	What Did Stalin Do to Women?	Maurizio Liverani
1969	The Five Man Army	Don Taylor, Italo Zingarelli
1969	La stagione dei sensi	Massimo Franciosa (Italy/W. Germany)
1969	Senza sapere niente di lei	Luigi Comencini
1969	A Brief Season	Renato Castellani
1969	The Sicilian Clan	Henri Verneuil (France)
1969	The Invisible Woman	Paolo Spinola
1969	Zenabel	Ruggero Deodato (Italy/France)
1969	Burn!	Gillo Pontecorvo (Italy/France)
1969	The Red Tent	Mikhail Kalatozov (USSR/Italy)
1970	Kill the Fatted Calf and Roast It	Salvatore Samperi
1970	Investigation of a Citizen Above Suspicion	Elio Petri
1970	Two Mules for Sister Sara	Don Siegel (USA/Mexico)
1970	The Bird with the Crystal Plumage	Dario Argento (Italy/W. Germany)
1970	The Most Beautiful Wife	Damiano Damiani
1970	Death of a Friend	Franco Rossi
1970	Metello	Mauro Bolognini

Year	Film	Director
1970	The Fifth Day of Peace	Giuliano Montaldo (Italy/Yugoslavia)
1970	Hornets' Nest	Phil Karlson, Franco Cirino (Italy/USA)
1970	The Family	Sergio Sollima (Italy/France)
1970	The Year of the Cannibals	Liliana Cavani
1970	When Women Had Tails	Pasquale Festa Campanile
1970	Forbidden Photos of a Lady Above Suspicion	Luciano Ercoli (Spain/Italy)
1970	The Voyeur	Franco Indovina (Italy/France)
1970	Companeros	Sergio Corbucci (Italy/W. Germany/Spain)
1970	La califfa	Alberto Bevilacqua (France/Italy)
1971	Incontro	Piero Schivazappa
1971	Tre nel mille	Franco Indovina
1971	The Cat o' Nine Tails	Dario Argento (Italy/France/W. Germany)
1971	A Lizard in a Woman's Skin	Lucio Fulci (Italy/Spain/France)
1971	Sacco & Vanzetti	Giuliano Montaldo (Italy/France)
1971	Veruschka	Franco Rubartelli
1971	Cold Eyes of Fear	Enzo G. Castellari (Italy/Spain)
1971	The Decameron	Pier Paolo Pasolini (Italy/France/W. Germany)
1971	Black Belly of the Tarantula	Paolo Cavara (Italy/France)
1971	Giornata nera per l'ariete (aka The Fifth Cord)	Luigi Bazzoni
1971	Day of Judgment	Mario Gariazzo, Robert Paget (Italy/UK)
1971	Sans mobile apparent	Philippe Labro (France/Italy)
1971	Lulu the Tool	Elio Petri
1971	Tis Pity She's a Whore	Giuseppe Patroni Griffi
1971	Menage Italian Style	Franco Indovina
1971	Duck, You Sucker	Sergio Leone
1971	The Burglars	Henri Verneuil (France/Italy)
1971	L'istruttoria e chiusa: Dimentichi	Damiano Damiani (Italy/France)
1971	La corta notte delle bambole di vetro	Aldo Lado (Italy/W. Germany/Yugoslavia)
1971	Maddalena	Jerzy Kawalerowicz (Italy/Yugoslavia)
1971	Four Flies on Grey Velvet	Dario Argento (Italy/France)
1971	Don't Turn the Other Cheek	Duccio Tessari (Italy/W. Germany/Spain)
1972	Quando la preda è l'uomo	Vittorio De Sisti
1972	Lui per lei	Claudio Rispoli
1972	For Love One Dies	Carlo Carunchio
1972	Fiorina la vacca	Vittorio De Sisti
1972	Anche se volessi lavorare, che faccio?	Flavio Mogherini
1972	1870	Alfredo Giannetti
1972	My Dear Killer	Tonino Valerii (Italy/Spain)
1972	La violenza: Quinto potere	Florestano Vancici
1972	Chronicle of a Homicide	Maura Bolognini
1972	Questa specie d'amore	Alberto Bevilacqua
1972	When Women Lost Their Tails	Pasquale Festa Campanile (Italy/W. Germany)
1972	What Have You Done to Solange?	Massimo Dallamano (Italy/W. Germany)
1972	Il diavolo nel cervello	Sergio Sollima (Italy/France)
1972	Who Saw Her Die?	Aldo Lado (Italy/W. Germany)
1972	The Canterbury Tales	Pier Paolo Pasolini (Italy/France)
1972	The Master and Margaret	Aleksandar Petrovic (Italy/Yugoslavia)
1972	Winged Devils	Duccio Tessari
1972	Sonny and Jed	Sergio Corbucci (Italy/W. Germany/Spain)
1972	Bluebeard	Edward Dmytryk, Luiano Sacripanti (France/Italy/W. Germany)
1972	The Assassination	Yves Boisset (France/Italy/W. Germany)
1972	Slap the Monster on Page One	Marco Bellocchio (Italy/France)
1972	Life Is Tough, Eh Providence?	Giulio Petroni (Italy/France/W. Germany)
1972	La cosa buffa	Aldo Lado
1972	I figli chiedono perché	Nino Zanchin
1972	The Master Touch	Michele Lupo (Italy/W. Germany)
1972	Il Ritorno di Clint il silitario	Alfonso Balcázar (Spain/Italy)

Year	Film	Director
1972	What Am I Doing in the Middle of the Revolution?	Sergio Corbucci (Italy/Spain)
1973	Sepolta viva	Aldo Lado (France/Italy)
1973	Crescete e moltiplicatevi	Giulio Petroni
1973	The Serpent	Henri Verneuil (France/Italy/W. Germany)
1973	Property Is No Longer a Theft	Elio Petri (Italy/France)
1973	Blood in the Streets (aka Revolver)	Sergio Sollima (Italy/France/W. Germany)
1973	Massacre in Rome	George P. Cosmatos (Italy/France)
1973	The Romantic Agony	Guido Pieters (Netherlands)
1973	Here We Go Again, Eh Providence?	Alberto De Martino (Spain/Italy/France)
1973	Giordano Bruno	Guiliano Montaldo (Italy/France)
1973	My Name Is Nobody	Tonino Valerii, Sergio Leone (Italy/France/W. Germany)
1974	The Devil Is a Woman	Damiano Damiani (UK/Italy)
1974	Sarah's Last Man	Maria Virginia Onorato
1974	Spasmo	Umberto Lenzi
1974	The Last 4 Days (aka Last Days of Mussolini)	Carlo Lizzani
1974	Arabian Nights	Pier Paolo Pasolini (Italy/France)
1974	The Infernal Trio	Francis Girod (France/W. Germany/Italy)
1974	The Cousin	Aldo Lado
1974	Almost Human	Umberto Lenzi
1974	Allonsanfan	Paolo and Vittorio Taviani
1974	The Murri Affair	Mauro Bolognini (Italy/France)
1974	The Secret	Robert Enrico (France/Italy)
1974	The Antichrist (aka The Tempter)	Alberto De Martino
1975	Autopsy	Armando Crispino
1975	The Two Seasons of Life	Samy Pavel (Belgium)
1975	Liber, amore, mio . . .	Mauro Bolognini
1975	The Teenage Prostitution Racket	Carlo Lizzani, Mino Giarda
1975	Last Stop on the Night Train	Aldo Lado
1975	The Night Caller	Henri Verneuil (France/Italy)
1975	Weak Spot	Peter Fleischmann (France/Italy/W. Germany)
1975	Down the Ancient Stairs	Mauro Bolognini (Italy/France)
1975	End of the Game	Maximilian Schell (W. Germany/Italy)
1975	Leonor	Juan Luis Buñuel (Spain/France/Italy)
1975	The Divine Nymph	Giuseppe Patroni Griffi
1975	Labbra di lurido blu	Giulio Petroni
1975	The Flower in His Mouth	Luigi Zampa
1975	The "Human" Factor	Edward Dmytryk (UK)
1975	Saló, or the 120 Days of Sodom	Pier Paolo Pasolini (Italy/France)
1975	A Genius, Two Friends, and an Idiot (aka Nobody's the Greatest)	Damiano Damiani, Sergio Leone (Italy/France/W. Germany)
1975	Eye of the Cat	Alberto Bevilacqua
1975	The Sunday Woman	Luigi Comencini (Italy/France)
1976	The Thruster	Samy Pavel (Belgium/France)
1976	Per amore	Mino Giarda
1976	San Babila—8 P.M.	Carlo Lizzani
1976	Todo Modo	Elio Petri (Italy/France)
1976	1900	Bernardo Bertolucci (Italy/France/W. Germany)
1976	And Agnes Chose to Die	Giuliano Montaldo
1976	The Inheritance	Mauro Bolognini
1976	The Desert of the Tartars	Valerio Zurlini (Italy/France/W. Germany)
1977	Stato interessante	Sergio Nasca
1977	Rene the Cane	Francis Girod (Italy/France)
1977	The Man from Chicago	Sohban Kologlu, etc. (France/Turkey)
1977	Exorcist II: The Heretic	John Boorman (USA)
1977	Orca	Michael Anderson (USA)
1977	Il prefetto di ferro	Pasquale Squitieri

Year	Film	Director
1977	*Il mostro*	Luigi Zampa
1977	*Hitch Hike*	Pasquale Festa Campanile
1977	*Holocaust 2000*	Alberto De Martino (Italy/UK)
1977	*Il gatto*	Luigi Comencini (Italy/France)
1978	*Corleone*	Pasquale Squitieri
1978	*Una vita venduta*	Aldo Florio
1978	*One Two Two*	Christian Gion (France)
1978	*Pedro Páramo*	José Bolaños (Mexico)
1978	*Days of Heaven* (AAN; BAFTA)	Terrence Malick (USA)
1978	*Stay as You Are*	Alberto Lattuada (Italy/Spain)
1978	*La cage aux folles*	Edouard Molinaro (France/Italy)
1978	*L'immoralita*	Massimo Pirri
1979	*Footloose*	Stefano Rolla
1979	*Dedicato al mare Egeo*	Masuo Ikeda (Italy/Japan)
1979	*Buone notizie*	Elio Petri
1979	*Il giocattolo*	Giuliano Montaldo
1979	*The Humanoid*	Aldo Lado
1979	*Viaggio con anits* (aka *Lovers and Liars*)	Mario Monicelli (Italy/France)
1979	*Bloodline*	Terence Young (USA/W. Germany)
1979	*Luna*	Bernardo Bertolucci (Italy/USA)
1979	*Ogro*	Gillo Pontecorvo (Spain/France/Italy)
1979	*Il Prato*	Paolo and Vittorio Taviani
1979	*I as in Icarus*	Henri Verneuil (France)
1980	*Si salvi chi vuole*	Roberto Faennza
1980	*Windows*	Gordon Willis (USA)
1980	*Fun Is Beautiful*	Carlo Verdone
1980	*Il ladrone*	Pasquale Festa Campanile (Italy/France)
1980	*Stark System*	Armenia Balducci
1980	*Nouvelles rencontres*	Jean Luret (Canada/France)
1980	*The Island*	Michael Ritchie (USA)
1980	*L'oeil pervers*	Jean Luret (Canada/France)
1980	*The Blue-Eyed Bandit*	Alfredo Giannetti
1980	*The Lady Banker*	Francis Girod (France)
1980	*La cage aux folles II*	Edouard Molinaro (France/Italy)
1981	*Bianco, rosso e Verdone*	Carlo Verdone
1981	*Lady of the Camelias*	Mauro Bolognini (France/Italy)
1981	*Buddy Goes West*	Michele Lupo
1981	*Tragedy of a Ridiculous Man*	Bernardo Bertolucci
1981	*La disubbidienza*	Aldo Lado (Italy/France)
1981	*So Fine*	Andrew Bergman (USA)
1981	*The Professional*	Georges Lautner (France)
1981	*Men or Not Men*	Valentino Orsini
1982	*When Love Is Lust*	Vittorio De Sisti
1982	*Porca vacca*	Pasquale Festa Campanile
1982	*Espion, leve-toi*	Yves Boisset (France/Switzerland)
1982	*Butterfly* (GGN*)	Matt Cimber (USA)
1982	*The Thing*	John Carpenter (USA)
1982	*White Dog*	Samuel Fuller (USA)
1982	*Blood Link*	Alberto De Martino (Italy/USA/W. Germany)
1983	*Le ruffian*	José Giovanni (France/Canada)
1983	*Treasure of the Four Crowns*	Ferdinando Baldi (Spain/USA/Italy)
1983	*Order of Death* (aka *Copkiller*)	Roberto Faenza
1983	*Nana, the True Key of Pleasure*	Dan Wolman
1983	*Hundra*	Matt Cimber (Spain/USA)
1983	*The Key*	Tinto Brass
1983	*Le marginal*	Jacques Deray (France)
1983	*Sahara*	Andrew V. McLaglen (UK/USA)
1984	*Once Upon a Time in America* (GGN; BAFTA)	Sergio Leone (Italy/USA)

Year	Film	Director
1984	*Les voleurs de la nuit*	Samuel Fuller (France)
1984	*Code Name: Wild Geese*	Antonio Margheriti (Italy/W. Germany)
1985	*Red Sonja*	Richard Fleischer (Netherland/USA)
1985	*La gabbia*	Giuseppe Patroni Griffi (Italy/Spain)
1985	*The Repenter*	Pasquale Squitieri
1985	*La cage aux folles 3: The Wedding*	Georges Lautner (France/Italy)
1986	*The Venetian Woman*	Maura Bolognini
1986	*The Mission* (AAN; GG; BAFTA)	Roland Joffé (UK)
1987	*Farewell Moscow*	Mauro Bolognini
1987	*Control*	Giuliano Montaldo (Italy/France/Canada/USA)
1987	*The Untouchables* (AAN; GGN; BAFTA)	Brian De Palma (USA)
1987	*Rampage*	William Friedkin (USA)
1987	*Quartiere*	Silvano Agosti
1987	*Gli occhiali d'oro*	Giuliano Montaldo (Italy/France)
1988	*Il cuore di mamma*	Gioia Benelli
1988	*Frantic*	Roman Polanski (USA/France)
1988	*A Time of Destiny*	Gregory Nava (USA/Yugoslavia)
1988	*Cinema Paradiso* (BAFTA)	Giuseppe Tornatore (Italy/France)
1989	*Casualties of War* (GGN)	Brian De Palma (USA)
1989	*Tempo di Uccidere*	Giuliano Montaldo (Italy/France)
1989	*Fat Man and Little Boy*	Roland Joffé (USA)
1990	*Tie Me Up! Tie Me Down!*	Pedro Almodóvar (Spain)
1990	*Dimenticare Palermo*	Francesco Rosi (Italy/France)
1990	*Tre colonne in cronaca*	Carlo Vanzina
1990	*The Bachelor*	Roberto Faenza (Italy/Hungary)
1990	*Crossing the Line* (aka *The Big Man*)	David Leland (UK)
1990	*Everybody's Fine*	Giuseppe Tornatore (Italy/France/USA)
1990	*Tracce di vita amorosa*	Peter Del Monte
1990	*State of Grace*	Phil Joanou (UK/USA)
1990	*Hamlet*	Franco Zeffirelli (USA/UK/France)
1991	*Money*	Steven Hilliard Stern (France/Canada)
1991	*Husbands and Lovers*	Mauro Bolognini
1991	*Especially on Sunday*	Tonino Guerra (Italy/France/Belgium)
1991	*La thune*	Philippe Galland (France)
1991	*Bugsy* (AAN; GGN)	Barry Levinson (USA)
1992	*Beyond Justice*	Duccio Tessari
1992	*City of Joy*	Roland Joffé (France/UK)
1992	*La signora delle camelie* (1915)	Gustavo Serena
1992	*A csalás gyönyöre*	Livia Gyarmathy (Hungary)
1992	*Ilona und Kurti*	Reinhard Schwabenitzky (Austria)
1993	*Estasi*	Maria Carmel Cicinnati, Peter Exacoustos
1993	*Il lungo silenzio*	Margarethe von Trotta (Italy/Germany)
1993	*Jona che visse nella balena*	Roberto Faenza (Italy/France/Hungary)
1993	*La scorta*	Ricky Tognazzi
1993	*In the Line of Fire*	Wolfgang Petersen (USA)
1994	*A Pure Formality*	Giuseppe Tornatore (Italy/France)
1994	*Wolf*	Mike Nichols (USA)
1994	*Genesis: The Creation and the Flood*	Ermanno Olmi (Italy/Germany)
1994	*Love Affair*	Glenn Gordon Caron (USA)
1994	*Disclosure*	Barry Levinson (USA)
1995	*L'uomo proiettile*	Silvano Agosti
1995	*According to Pereira*	Roberto Faenza (Italy/Portugal)
1995	*The Night and the Moment*	Anna Maria Tato (UK/France/Italy)
1995	*Who Killed Pasolini?*	Marco Tullio Giordana (Italy/France)
1995	*The Star Maker*	Giuseppe Tornatore
1996	*The Stendhal Syndrome*	Dario Argento
1996	*Vite strozzate*	Ricky Tognazzi (Italy/France/Belgium)
1996	*The Nymph*	Lina Wertmüller

Year	Film	Director
1996	*We Free Kings*	Sergio Citti (Italy/France/Germany)
1996	*La lupa*	Gabriele Lavia
1997	*Naissance des stéréoscopages*	Stéphane Marty (France)
1997	*Con rabbia e con amore*	Alfredo Angeli
1997	*U Turn*	Oliver Stone (France/USA)
1997	*Lolita*	Adrian Lyne (USA/France)
1998	*Bulworth*	Warren Beatty (USA)
1998	*The Legend of 1900* (GG)	Guiseppe Tornatore
1998	*The Phantom of the Opera*	Dario Argento
2000	*Canone inverso*	Ricky Tognazzi
2000	*Mission to Mars*	Brian De Palma (USA)
2000	*Vatel*	Roland Joffé (France/UK/Belgium)
2000	*Malena* (AAN; GGN)	Giuseppe Tornatore (Italy/USA)
2001	*The Sleeping Wife*	Silvano Agosti
2001	*Aida of the Trees*	Guido Manuli (Italy/UK)
2002	*Black Angel*	Tinto Brass
2002	*Ripley's Game*	Liliana Cavani (Italy/UK/USA)
2002	*Il diario di Matilde Manzoni*	Lino Capolicchio
2003	*The End of a Mystery*	Miguel Hermoso (Spain)
2003	*Alla fine della notte*	Salvatore Piscielli
2003	*Al cuore si comanda*	Giovanni Morricone
2004	*72 Meters*	Vladimir Khotineko (Russia)
2004	*Cartoni animati*	Franco and Sergio Citti
2004	*Guardiani delle nuvole*	Luciano Odorisio
2005	*Fateless*	Lajos Koltai (Hungary/Germany)
2005	*E ridendo l'uccise*	Florestano Vancini
2006	*A Crime*	Manuel Pradal (France/USA)
2006	*The Unknown Woman*	Giuseppe Tornatore (Italy/France)
2008	*The Demons of St. Petersburg*	Giuliano Montaldo
2009	*Baaria*	Giuseppe Tornatore (Italy/France)
2010	*Angelus Hiroshimae*	Giancarlo Planta
2013	*The Best Offer*	Giuseppe Tornatore
2013	*L'enfant du Sahara*	Laurent Merlin (France)

MORRIS, John (b. 1926) An in-demand musical arranger in theatre and composer of mostly movie comedies, he scored thirty films between 1967 and 1991, including nine directed by Mel Brooks.

Born John Leonard Morris in Elizabeth, New Jersey, he began his career as an arranger and pianist in the theatre. Morris was musical director and/or contributed dance music for two dozen Broadway musicals between 1952 and 1974, including *Shinbone Alley* (1957) and *All American* (1962), both of which had books by Mel Brooks. In 1967 Morris and Brooks worked together on *The Producers*, the first film for each of them. The two men went on to collaborate on such popular comedies as *The Twelve Chairs*, *Blazing Saddles*, *Young Frankenstein*, *Silent Movie*, *High Anxiety*, and *Spaceballs*, as well as the Brooks-produced movies *The Elephant Man* and *To Be or Not to Be*. Morris also scored comedies for two of Brooks's fellow comedi-

ans, Gene Wilder and Marty Feldman. His other movies of note include *The Gambler*, *The Adventures of Sherlock Holmes' Smarter Brother*, *The Woman in Red*, *Dirty Dancing*, *The Wash*, and *Ironweed*. Morris also wrote for television, composing scores for twenty TV movies and miniseries, including *The Scarlet Letter* (1979), *Doctor Franken* (1980), *The Mating Season* (1980), *Splendor in the Grass* (1981), *Ghost Dancing* (1983), *Fresno* (1986), *The Last Best Year* (1990), *Scarlett* (194), *With God on Our Side: George W. Bush and the Rise of the Religious Right in America* (1996), *The Lady in Question* (1999), and *The Blackwater Lightship* (2004), as well as the theme songs for *The French Chef* (1963) and the long-running sitcom *Coach* in the 1990s. He returned to Broadway to write book, music, and lyrics for the short-lived musical *A Time for Singing* (1966). Morris left films in 1991 and concentrated on music for TV movies until 2006 when he retired.

Although most of his film work was in broad comedies, Morris found a good deal of variety and creativity in scoring movies in that genre. Because almost all of these comedies were spoofs of different genres, from westerns to sci-fi flicks, Morris got to compose all kinds of music, though usually in a satiric vein. *Blazing Saddles* has a silly robust title song (lyric by Mel Brooks) that lampoons the western ballads usually sung by Gene Autry or Frankie Laine in 1950s oaters. In fact, Laine himself sings the ribald number that is punctuated by the lash of a whip. When the music quiets down for a harmonica section, it is almost touching in spite of itself. There is plenty of music in *Blazing Saddles*, including standards such as "April in Paris" and "I Get a Kick Out of You," sung for comic contrast, and original tunes (music and lyrics by Brooks) like the daffy chorus line number "The French Mistake" and a roguish Marlene Dietrich spoof "I'm Tired" sung by a saloon gal (Madeline Kahn). There is a wry ballad about the town of Rock Ridge, a merry theme for a wagon train, and some glitzy music for the extended chase scene in a Hollywood studio. The score for *Young Frankenstein* is more subtle even if the spoofing of classic horror films is still wickedly funny. Morris's main theme is a clever pastiche of the genre's suspense music yet the principal violin theme is actually quite lyrical and it is given a restrained interpretation at different points in the movie. *Young Frankenstein* is arguably the most atmospheric of all of Brooks's film spoofs and some of that can be attributed to the splendid decor (using some of the original Universal sets) and the score by Morris. *High Anxiety* is a takeoff on various Alfred Hitchcock thrillers but mostly *Spellbound* (1945). The score is not as focused because the spoofing is uneven. Morris provides some foreboding in the suspense music and copies the shrill Bernard Herrmann sound from *The Birds* (1963), yet the title song (music and lyric by Brooks) is a breezy and accurate send-up of a 1960s lounge number. The comedy and the music is more pointed in *Spaceballs*, a not-so-subtle but consistently funny ribbing of the *Star Wars* films. Morris offers his own John Williamsesque theme, which is kept from becoming too majestic by the sound of video game–like lasers. The "Dark Helmet" theme is as heavy as the Darth Vadar music so when diminutive Rick Moranis shows up as the villain the contrast is delightful. There are not too many action scenes in *Spaceballs* but those that are there are scored with panache even as the quieter sections of

the score touch on the poetic. This is musical spoofing at its finest.

Other comedies that Morris scored are not so much satire as homage. Consider the wonderful Eastern European folk music in *The Twelve Chairs*. Vigorous fiddling, ethnic dances, Russian drinking tunes, and klezmer woodwinds fill the score, which has a furious tempo and frantic melodies. *The Adventures of Sherlock Holmes' Smarter Brother* pays tribute to British pluck with a regal march while *The Last Remake of Beau Geste* has a happy march with a French cancan flavor. *Silent Movie* required almost nonstop music and Morris filled the eighty-six minutes with circus themes, sprightly marches, a tangy bolero, dandy foxtrots, cockeyed calliope tunes, and sentimental waltzes. Brooks may not have recaptured the humor of those classic silents but musically the movie is a marvel. Morris got to ape all kinds of music in *The History of the World: Part I*, from ancient Roman processional pomp to a King Louis XIV minuet. Again the humor was uneven but Morris seemed to find delicious musical ideas throughout history. When he was asked by Gene Wilder to score his comic horror movie *Haunted Honeymoon*, Morris wrote lush and dramatic music that did not recall *Young Frankenstein* at all. A pipe organ and full brass section perform the main theme which plays it straight for the most part. The suspenseful music that follows is also quite effective, especially in its use of wavering organ chords and screaming electronic motifs. This is not a comic score by a long shot and probably did not help the movie which was a critical and popular failure. *Clue*, another unsuccessful spoof, has a nimble, giggling main theme that sets the tone for the murder satire. The music throughout is giddy and mocking with no attempt to be scary or suspenseful.

Morris rarely got to score romantic comedies. It is unfortunate because *The Woman in Red* has a sassy, contemporary score with some pulsating disco music and intoxicating romantic passages. He did get to write music for a handful of melodramas and proved just as proficient, as with *Stella*, a 1990 remake of *Stella Dallas* (1937). The main theme is a rhythmic jazz piece featuring a piano and saxophone that establishes the contemporary setting for the age-old story. The love theme is warm and flowing but not sentimental. The tearful ending is scored gracefully, taking on a more optimistic tone than one expects. The score for the romance *Dirty Dancing* consists mostly of pop songs but Morris wrote an entrancing theme in which a piano cautiously spells out a lovely melody. There is also some vibrant dance music that moves from pop to rock to jazz. The 1930s drama *Ironweed* has a nostalgic score led by a heartfelt theme heard on a lone horn with a female humming on the soundtrack. Another passage, played on a piano, has a spirited tempo but still aches with remorse. Probably Morris's finest score in a serious vein is that for *The Elephant Man*, a movie about a grotesque individual (John Hurt) but scored with delicate music. The main theme is a somber waltz played by a solo flute then a solo oboe as strings and harp come in. It is quite a haunting piece and is easily recognized even when played on handbells behind the carnival scene where the "elephant man"

is discovered. There is some sparkling Victorian music as the plot includes famous theatre folk, and a dulcet flute passage that is associated with the poetry that brings solace to the creature. The death of the elephant man, caused by his deliberate decision to lie back on a bed like normal people and thereby suffocate, is scored with Samuel Barber's "Adagio for Strings," creating a funeral hymn for his passing. A score like *The Elephant Man* makes one wonder if the movies might not have been better served if Morris had not concentrated mostly on comedies and more on "serious" projects. But then moviegoers might have been denied several outstanding scores in the comic genre and there are fewer composer giants in that arena.

Credits

(all films USA unless stated otherwise; * for Best Song)

Year	Film	Director
1967	The Producers	Mel Brooks
1970	The Gamblers	Ron Winston (USA/Yugoslavia)
1970	The Twelve Chairs	Mel Brooks
1974	Blazing Saddles (AAN*)	Mel Brooks
1974	Bank Shot	Gower Champion
1974	Young Frankenstein	Mel Brooks
1975	The Adventures of Sherlock Holmes' Smarter Brother	Gene Wilder (USA/UK)
1976	Silent Movie	Mel Brooks
1977	The Last Remake of Beau Geste	Marty Feldman
1977	The World's Greatest Lover	Gene Wilder
1977	High Anxiety	Mel Brooks
1979	The In-Laws	Arthur Hiller
1980	In God We Tru$t (aka Gimme That Prime Time Religion)	Marty Feldman
1980	The Elephant Man (AAN)	David Lynch
1981	History of the World: Part I	Mel Brooks
1983	Table for Five	Robert Lieberman
1983	Yellowbeard	Mel Daminski (UK)
1983	To Be or Not to Be	Alan Johnson
1984	The Woman in Red	Gene Wilder
1984	Johnny Dangerously	Amy Heckerling
1985	The Doctor and the Devils	Freddie Francis (UK/USA)
1985	Clue	Jonathan Lynn
1986	Haunted Honeymoon	Gene Wilder
1987	Dirty Dancing	Emile Ardolino
1987	Spaceballs	Mel Brooks
1987	Ironweed	Hector Babenco
1988	The Wash	Michael Toshiyuki Uno
1989	Second Sight	Joel Zwick
1990	Stella	John Erman
1991	Life Stinks (aka Life Sucks)	Mel Brooks
2006	Kansas to Kandahar	Calvin Skaggs

MYERS, Stanley (1933–1993) A widely admired British conductor and composer for television and movies, he scored over eighty feature films on both sides of the Atlantic, working on everything from Disney adventures to cult horror flicks to controversial and provocative screen versions of James Joyce and D. H. Lawrence.

Stanley Myers was born in Birmingham, England, and educated at the nearby King Edward's School and at Oxford University. In the 1950s he wrote songs and worked in the theatre, directing and conducting the music for stage musicals. Myers first worked in film in 1958 when he contributed some music to the low-budget movie *Murder Reported*. By the 1960s he was busy writing scores for television, then returned to the movies to compose some of the music for *Diary of a Young Man* (1964). Two years later Myers was a solo composer in the British film industry and by 1970 was famous for his musical theme "Cavatina," which was played on the soundtrack for *The Walking Stick*. As a song and an instrumental piece, "Cavatina" went on to become one of the most popular tunes of the era; Myers revised the piece in 1978 as the main theme for his score for *The Deer Hunter*. Over the years he continued working as a conductor and arranger as he scored a wide variety of movies in Britain and America. Myers was often hired to write music for cutting edge or sexually adventurous projects, including movies such as *Prick Up Your Ears*, *Ulysses*, *Lady Chatterly's Lover*, *Sammy and Rosie Get Laid*, *The Tropic of Cancer*, *Little Malcolm*, *Conduct Unbecoming*, and *House of Whipcord*. Yet his credits also include *The Watcher in the Woods*, *The Witches*, and other family suspense films, and several comedies, as with *Otley*, *Wish You Were Here*, *Scenes from the Class Struggle in Beverly Hills*, *Stars and Bars*, and *Take a Girl Like You*. Myers scored many horror films, ranging from low-budget slashers to star-studded Hollywood chillers. Among them are *Iron Maze*, *Track 29*, *The Zero Boys*, *The Incubus*, *Cover Up*, and *Schizo*. Among Myers's other movies are such diverse works as *The Greek Tycoon*, *Rosencrantz and Guildenstern Are Dead*, *Absolution*, *The Night of the Following Day*, *Dreamchild*, *No Way to Treat a Lady*, *Sarafina!*, *A Portrait of the Artist as a Young Man*, *Insignificance*, and *X, Y and Zee*.

Myers was also a prolific television composer. He scored twenty-six TV movies, including *Divorce His—Divorce Hers* (1973), *Summer of My German Soldier* (1978), *A Pattern of Roses* (1983), *Black Arrow* (1985), *Florence*

Nightingale (1985), *Scoop* (1987), *A Pack of Lies* (1987), *Harry's Kingdom* (1987), *Christabel* (1988), *Tidy Endings* (1988), *Roald Dahl's Danny the Champion of the World* (1989), *A Murder of Quality* (1991), *Mrs. 'Arris Goes to Paris* (1992), *Heart of Darkness* (1993), and *Stalag Luft* (1993). He also composed music for such series and miniseries as *Doctor Who* (1964), *Diary of a Young Man* (1964), *All Gas and Gaiters* (1967–1971), *Shoulder to Shoulder* (1974), *The Legend of Robin Hood* (1975), *The Martian Chronicles* (1980), *Nancy Astor* (1982), *The Singing Detective* (1986), and *Middlemarch* (1994).

Myers was still very much in demand and very active when he died at the age of sixty.

"Cavatina" is a lovely and intriguing piece of music, delicate and romantic, and it is not surprising to understand why it remains so popular. Its use in *The Deer Hunter* is particularly potent, allowing the moviegoer to understand the soft side to these mostly rough and inarticulate characters. Yet there are other musical passages by Myers in the movie that are also expert. A theme titled "Sarabande" featuring flute and guitar is mystical and haunting as it quietly suggests chaos under a calm surface. His adaptation of Russian folk tunes in *The Deer Hunter* is very effective, particularly the chanting of a Greek Orthodox hymn under the shooting of a deer. The lone trumpet heard during some of the Vietnam sequences is also very effective. Myers rarely got to score big epic projects like *The Deer Hunter* but he proved to be up to the task with this potent score. The screen version of James Joyce's *Ulysses* is another kind of epic but there is not very much music needed and that which is there comes in brief snatches, as appropriate for the stream-of-consciousness tale. There is a quivering theme played on Irish pipes for the Jewish Dubliner Leopold Bloom (Milo O'Shea) and other Irish-flavored passages appear on occasion, but for the most part the inner thoughts of these characters are not musical. For a flowing score, one has to turn to *The Greek Tycoon*, a thinly disguised story about Jackie Kennedy's romance and marriage with Aristotle Onassis (Anthony Quinn). Myers doesn't overdo the Greek ethnic music, instead presenting a romantic main theme featuring a bouzouki and trumpet over a gushing orchestra. There is also a reflective theme played on guitar and piano that is as tentative as it is melancholy. These characters seem to have no deep thoughts as in *Ulysses* so the music tries to help raise them above tabloid stereotypes.

No Way to Treat a Lady, about a serial killer (Rod Steiger) who dresses in different guises to get to his victims, has a breezy contemporary score with touches of rock and jazz as well as a quirky passage with electric guitar and church organ. The movie's suspense and offbeat sense of humor are both served in Myers's loose urban music. Even the love theme, "A Quiet Place" (lyric by Andrew Belling), is rhythmic in a bouncy Burt Bacharach manner. Also funky and carefree is the music in the oddball comedy *Otley* which spoofs the spy film genre. A harmonica joins the strings for a sprightly theme called "Homeless Bones" (lyric by Don Partridge). Also fun is a silly theme played on electric organ, brass, and high-pitched woodwinds and a pastiche of baroque music, the strings undercut by a rock band. Myers's first full film score, the lightweight crime comedy *Kaleidoscope*, has a bouncy main theme that moves along steadily as it segues into different musical ideas ranging from circus music to bossa nova. Another theme uses electric guitar to tie together all kinds of instrumental solos. Myers took the title literally when he wrote the score for this comic caper. The thriller *Sitting Target* has an interesting score that uses electronic sounds over a pulsating bass line and distorted violins. The more romantic side of the story is scored with a cautious love theme played on piano and muted saxophone, the melody veering off into pauses before continuing on. The hip character melodrama *X, Y and Zee* uses a high-pitched pipe against lite-rock music and the result is surprisingly effective. This story of a swinging ménage a trois is pretty contrived but the music is more convincing than the people.

Two of Myers's most satisfying scores were written for conventional suspense adventures. *The Witches*, based on a Roald Dahl book, has an enticing main theme that suggests evil but fun doings. The racing strings and pounding brass seem to be laughing at each other. When the evil overcomes the fun, the music is indeed sinister as high choral voices are heard over a percussive march. There is a mysterious passage that seems to offer some comfort, a warm and sublime theme that is used for domestic nostalgia, and a furious track in which one can sense magical creatures running all around the place. *The Witches* is a dark tale, to say the least, yet the music helps remind us that this is still a children's adventure. The Disney haunted-house thriller *The Watcher in the Woods* has a beguiling main theme. A delicate music box motif is interrupted by deep chords or nervous strings. As the expected ghost is sensed, the music mixes classic organ motifs with some high-tech electronic instrumentation. This may not be innovative screen scoring for a composer usually working in alternative filmmaking but Myers displays a talent for fitting the music to the movie, something that should not be underestimated.

Credits

(all films UK unless stated otherwise)

Year	Film	Director
1966	*Kaleidoscope* (aka *The Bank Breaker*)	Jack Smight
1967	*Ulysses*	Joseph Strick (UK/USA)
1968	*No Way to Treat a Lady*	Jack Smight (USA)
1968	*Separation*	Jack Bond
1968	*Otley*	Dick Clement
1968	*The Night of the Following Day*	Hubert Cornfield, Richard Boone (USA)
1969	*Man on Horseback*	Volker Schlöndorff (W. Germany)
1969	*Age of Consent*	Michael Powell (Australia)
1969	*Two Gentlemen Sharing*	Ted Kotcheff
1970	*Tropic of Cancer*	Joseph Strick (USA)
1970	*The Walking Stick*	Eric Till
1970	*Underground*	Arthur H. Nadel (UK/USA)
1970	*The Devil's Widow* (aka *The Ballad of Tam Lin*)	Roddy McDowall
1970	*A Severed Head*	Dick Clement
1970	*Take a Girl Like You*	Jonathan Miller
1971	*Long Ago, Tomorrow* (aka *The Raging Moon*)	Bryan Forbes

Year	Film	Director
1972	*X, Y and Zee* (aka *Zee and Co.*)	Brian G. Hutton
1972	*Sitting Target*	Douglas Hickox (UK/USA)
1972	*King, Queen, Knave*	Jerzy Skolimowski (W. Germany/USA)
1972	*A Free Woman*	Volker Schlöndorff (W. Germany)
1973	*Anyone for Sex?* (aka *The Love Ban*)	Ralph Thomas
1973	*The Blockhouse*	Clive Rees
1974	*Road Movie* (aka *Janice*)	Joseph Strick (USA)
1974	*House of Whipcord*	Pete Walker
1974	*Little Malcolm*	Stuart Cooper
1974	*Caravan to Vaccares*	Geoffrey Reeve (UK/France)
1974	*Cover Up* (aka *Frightmare*)	Pete Walker
1975	*The Wilby Conspiracy*	Ralph Nelson
1975	*Conduct Unbecoming*	Michael Anderson
1976	*The Confessional* (aka *House of Mortal Sin*)	Pete Walker
1976	*Coup de Grâce*	Volker Schlöndorff (France/W. Germany)
1976	*Schizo*	Pete Walker
1977	*A Portrait of the Artist as a Young Man*	Joseph Strick (Ireland)
1978	*The Greek Tycoon*	J. Lee Thompson (USA)
1978	*The Comeback*	Pete Walker
1978	*Absolution* (aka *Murder by Confession*)	Anthony Page
1978	*The Deer Hunter*	Michael Cimino (UK/USA)
1979	*The Class of Miss MacMichael*	Silvio Narizzano
1979	*Yesterday's Hero*	Neil Leifer (UK/Australia)
1979	*The Great Riviera Bank Robbery* (aka *Dirty Money*)	Francis Megahy
1979	*A Nightingale Sang in Berkeley Square*	Ralph Thomas (USA)
1980	*The Watcher in the Woods*	John Hough, Vincent McEveety (USA/UK)
1980	*Border Cop* (aka *The Border*)	Christopher Leitch
1981	*Lady Chatterley's Lover*	Just Jaeckin (UK/France/W. Germany)
1982	*The Incubus*	John Hough (Canada)
1982	*Moonlighting*	Jerzy Skolimowski
1983	*Eureka*	Nicolas Roeg (UK/USA)
1983	*Beyond the Limit* (aka *The Honorary Consul*)	John Mackenzie
1984	*Success Is the Best Revenge*	Jerzy Kolimowski (France/UK)
1984	*Blind Date* (aka *Deadly Seduction*)	Nico Mastorakis (USA/Greece)
1984	*The History of O: Chapter 2*	Éric Rochat (France/Spain/Panama)
1984	*The Next One* (aka *The Time Traveller*)	Nico Mastorakis (USA/Greece)
1984	*The Chain*	Jack Gold
1985	*Insignificance*	Nicolas Roeg
1985	*The Lightship* (aka *Killers at Sea*)	Jerzy Skolimowski (USA)
1985	*Dreamchild*	Gavin Millar
1986	*Separate Vacations*	Michael Anderson (Canada/USA)
1986	*Castaway*	Nicolas Roeg
1986	*The Zero Boys* (aka *Hero Boys*)	Nico Mastorakis (USA)
1987	*Prick Up Your Ears*	Stephen Frears
1987	*The Second Victory*	Gerald Thomas (UK/W. Germany)
1987	*Wish You Were Here* (aka *Too Much*) (BAFTA-N)	David Leland
1987	*Sammy and Rosie Get Laid*	Stephen Frears
1988	*The Nature of the Beast*	Franco Rosso
1988	*Taffin*	Francis Megahy (UK/Ireland/USA)
1988	*Trading Hearts*	Neil Leifer (USA)
1988	*Stars and Bars*(aka *Englishman in New York*)	Pat O'Connor (USA)
1988	*Track 29*	Nicolas Roeg (USA/UK)
1988	*Death Street USA* (aka *Nightmare at Noon*)	Nico Mastorakis (UK/USA)
1988	*Paperhouse*	Bernard Rose
1988	*The Boost*	Harold Becker (USA)
1989	*Torrents of Spring*	Jerzy Skolimowski (UK/France/Italy)

Year	Film	Director
1989	*Scenes from the Class Struggle in Beverly Hills*	Paul Bartel (USA)
1990	*Ladder of Swords*	Norman Hull
1990	*The Witches*	Nicolas Roeg (UK/USA)
1990	*Rosencrantz & Guildenstern Are Dead*	Tom Stoppard (UK/USA)
1991	*Iron Maze*	Hiroaki Yoshida (Japan/USA)
1991	*Voyager*	Volker Schlöndorff (France/Germany)
1991	*Cold Heaven*	Nicolas Roeg (USA)
1992	*Sarafina!*	Darrell Roodt (S. Africa/UK/France/USA)
1993	*Claude* (aka *Trusting Beatrice*)	Cindy Lou Johnson (USA)
1993	*The Summer House*	Waris Hussein

NASCIMBENE, Mario (1913-2002) A prolific Italian conductor and composer who had an international career scoring concert works and over 120 feature films on three continents, he was one of the first European movie composers to be hired by Hollywood for major projects.

Born Mario Ernesto Rosolino Nascimbene in Milan, Italy, he studied composition and conducting at the Giuseppe Verdi Conservatory of Music in his hometown. Nascimbene began his career writing music for chamber groups and the ballet and by the age of twenty-eight was gaining a reputation throughout Europe. In 1943 he was asked by movie director Ferdinando Maris Poggioli to write the score for his romantic comedy *L'amour canta* (released worldwide as *Love Song*). The experience so exhilarated Nascimbene and the reaction to his music was so encouraging that he decided to concentrate on screen scoring from then on. While most serious composers in Europe looked at movie music as second rate, Nascimbene was one of the first Italian artists of rank to embrace the cinema. Filmmaking during World War II in Italy was problematic but he managed to work on six more movies before the country was liberated and a fertile period of Italian movies began. Among the notable postwar movies that Nascimbene scored are *Fantasmi del mare*, *Rome 11:00*, *Too Young for Love*, *O.K. Nero*, *Il viale della speranza*, *La valigia dei sogni*, *Prima di sera*, and *Vacation with a Gangster*.

Although none of these were international hits, Hollywood became interested in Nascimbene. In 1954 United Artists and director Joseph L. Mankiewicz hired him to score the Humphrey Bogart–Ava Gardner mystery-melodrama *The Barefoot Contessa*; it is believed it was the first time a major studio opted to use an Italian composer rather than an established Hollywood one for such an important project. Although Nascimbene continued to score Italian and other Continental films, he was frequently hired for British and American movies as well. He was most known for his music for biblical epics, such as *Solomon and Sheba* and *Barabbas*; prehistoric adventures, as with *One Million B.C.* and *When Dinosaurs Ruled the*

Earth; and history movies, including *Alexander the Great* and *The Vikings*. Among Nascimbene's other English-language credits are such diverse films as *Room at the Top*, *A Farewell to Arms*, *Child in the House*, *The Quiet American*, *Romanoff and Juliet*, *Light in the Piazza*, *Doctor Faustus*, and *Sons and Lovers*. The memorable foreign-language movies he scored in the later part of his five-decade career include *Violent Summer*, *Nel blu dipinto di blu*, *La banda Casaroli*, *The Verona Trial*, *The Camp Follower*, *Indian Summer*, *The Messiah*, and *The Mummy/The Night of Counting the Years*, the last considered by some to be the greatest Egyptian movie ever made. In the late 1960s and early 1970s, Nascimbene wrote music for several Italian television movies. He retired in 1975, returning to work in 1990 to score the sequel *Blue Dolphin—l'avventura continua*. Nascimibene died twelve years later at the age of eighty-eight, one of the most awarded and honored figures in Italian cinema.

Hollywood probably hired Nascimbene for *The Barefoot Contessa* because of its Italian setting and Mediterranean atmosphere and because the movie was shot in Italy. He did not disappoint them, for the score is wonderfully romantic and very European. The story is a series of flashbacks as different men in the life of Maria Vargas (Ava Gardner) attend her funeral and remember how she changed their lives. The main theme is a tender lament on solo clarinet and nervous strings that is romantic but also woeful. When this same music is later given a full orchestral treatment, it becomes lush and passionate. The film's love theme, played on guitar, flute, and accordion, has a languid tone that adds to the mystery of Maria. At one point in the movie Gardner dances to a sultry Spanish folk tune, and when the story returns to the funeral there is a somber piano, violin, and clarinet version of the opening theme. Nascimbene's score for *The Barefoot Contessa* had the authentic sound of Europe but filtered through a Hollywood sensibility. No wonder other studios came calling. Yet it was Nascimbene's next score for an American film that brought him even wider recognition in the States.

The 1957 screen version of Ernest Hemingway's novel *A Farewell to Arms* is lacking in most departments, from the script to the acting, but the music is first rate. The story, about the tragic romance between a British nurse (Jennifer Jones) and an American ambulance driver (Rock Hudson) working for the Italian army during World War I, is devoid of sentiment in Hemingway's novel, but the movie milks it shamelessly. Not so the score, which is romantic without turning to mush. The main theme is a slow march with weary percussion but eager brass that transitions into a felicitous passage that moves at a spirited tempo as strings and woodwinds easily glide up and down the scale. This same passage serves as the movie's love theme when later played on mandolins, harp, and violins, yet it maintains the earlier spirit. Another memorable track in the score is that for the retreat of the army: dreary percussion, resigned trumpet fanfares, and uncertain orchestral flourishes.

It is interesting that Nascimbene scored so many British movies which did not want the romantic Hollywood sound. The best of them is *Room at the Top*, an unsentimental look at a scheming accountant (Laurence Harvey) who tries to climb the corporate ladder by wooing the boss's daughter (Heather Sears) even as he is sleeping with an older married woman (Simone Signoret). Nascimbene scores this gritty and realistic tale with film noir music. The opening theme has strident strings, threatening percussion, and harsh trumpet phrases, all recklessly climbing the scale. There is a passage with descending strings and piano phrases that is oddly uncomfortable, and the love theme on strings and woodwinds is waltzing yet casual and a touch insincere. A very different British film is the 1967 screen adaptation of Christopher Marlowe's Elizabethan play *Doctor Faustus*, which Richard Burton coproduced, codirected, and starred in. This morality drama, about the title professor who sells his soul to the devil to achieve ultimate knowledge, is scored with horror film music, albeit less obvious and more religious than the standard Hollywood approach. The gloomy recurring theme has sorrowful strings, high-frequency electronic noises, and a ghoulish choir chanting in time to heavy bass notes. The scenes with Satan's emissary Mephistophilis (Andreas Teuber) is scored with eerie music played on electronic keyboard and percussive gongs that beat slowly like a funeral dirge. The theme for the lusty Helen of Troy (Elizabeth Taylor) consists of a solo flute phrase, guitar chords, and a high-pitched female chant.

The movie that set Nascimbene's Hollywood career off in a new direction in 1956 was the failed epic *Alexander the Great* which must have sounded good on paper: a strong cast headed by Richard Burton as the title hero, an intelligent script by reputable director Robert Rossen, and a big budget to shoot the historical adventure in Spain. How it all ended up being so ineffective is still a matter of discussion. The movie was a major disaster at the box office but no one blamed Nascimbene's splendid score. The music for the opening credits includes forceful drums and trumpet blasts that play a minor-key march that trudges along in a solemn manner. There is a lyrical theme on woodwinds that is serene and exotic as it moves slowly as if in a dream. The battle scenes are scored with rapid trumpet phrases and fiery drum riffs. There is also a sorrowful lament with a solo horn chanting then frantic percussion enters and the simple horn melody speeds up. Perhaps this score encouraged United Artists to hire Nascimbene for *The Vikings*, an adventure drama with a surprisingly strong story and vivid characters. Two Viking half brothers (Tony Curtis and Kirk Douglas) vie to become king of Northern Britain not knowing they are blood relations. Since no one knows what kind of music the primitive Vikings might have had, Nascimbene had free rein and came up with an exhilarating score that was primitive yet melodically catchy. The opening theme is a simple but unforgettable three-note call on brass that makes a full-octave jump. It is so simple and yet, once heard, cannot be dismissed. Throughout the film this basic theme returns and it can be swift and rousing, flowing and inspiring, or slow and haunting, as it is used for everything from a march to a battle to a funeral. Yet one does not tire of it because of the way Nascimbene arranges the music. At a few points the theme is chanted by a mixed chorus and one starts to believe that this is what Viking music must have been like. Also in the score is a gliding passage on woodwinds and strings that is regal yet has a primitive folk flavor, a plodding march with heavy pounding percussion and anxious horns, and a string passage with a flute solo that is slow and bucolic. *The Vikings* was a hit at the box office and the score was so praised and embraced that every studio wanted Nascimbene for their big historical and/or biblical epics. Few were as satisfying as *The Vikings* but often the music was commendable. The rather silly, overheated *Solomon and Sheba* boasted a giant production which Nascimbene scored with a large orchestra at full throttle, plenty of fervent horn fanfares, blaring processional music, primitive drumming, robust choral passages, Hebrew chanting, and exotic dance music. The movie opens with a grandiose and sweeping theme with a chanting chorus reaching higher and higher as it competes with brass fanfares and harp glissandos. There is a grinding march on horns and percussion that seems to chew up the music; later a jaunty march for a battle with fluttering pipes, cymbal crashes, and brass flourishes that all speed up as the action does; and a love theme that is solemn and majestic and perhaps more reverent than romantic.

There is so much more to Nascimbene's career than his Hollywood projects. Two outstanding foreign-language films might represent his Continental screen work. The Italian-French drama *Violent Summer* was set in 1943 and followed some residents of the Riccione district of Italy before and once the war catches up with them. The main theme is filled with drum crashes, trumpets that play an oppressive march, and passionate strings that saw away at a melodramatic melody with lots of crescendos. The rest of the score is more varied. There is a restrained tango on guitar and violin that the residents dance to; a bluesy passage with a solo clarinet that is very seductive; and a leisurely but emotive love theme, featuring a solo mandolin with other strings, that avoids Italianate clichés. This same romantic music returns in a passionate, fully orchestrated version when events turn tragic. *Violent Summer* was made in 1959 when Italian postwar neorealism was giving

way to more romantic movies. Nascimbene was by then considered a master of this kind of screen music. A decade later he was simplifying his romanticism and using some electronic techniques in his scores. A powerful example of Nascimbene at his most minimalist is his music for the 1969 Egyptian drama *The Mummy*, which is better known by its subtitle *The Night of Counting the Years*. Based on a true story, the film recounts the 1881 conflict between Horbat tribesmen, who are raiding the ancient Egyptian tombs for treasures to sell, and the government's Antiquities Organization who are trying to stop them. The movie is also filled with ancient philosophy and reflections on the past. It is slow going for most contemporary viewers but others rank *The Mummy* very high. Nascimbene's score is a masterwork of restraint. Much of the soundtrack is distant chanting or sustained notes or rumbling percussion overwhelmed by wind and other natural sounds. The film opens with echoing noises and high-pitched strings. Later sections feature growling brass and low strings that roll along with weight and sorrow. There is also a gloomy dirge that seems to carry the weight of the world, and a grim chant with vibrating noises and low-register electronic chords. This is all a far cry from the music Nascimbene wrote for the ancient days of Alexander or the Vikings. Like many a painter or poet at the end of their careers, he seemed to return to the simplest of forms to express himself.

Credits

(all films Italy unless stated otherwise)

Year	Film	Director
1941	Love Song	Ferdinando Maria Poggioli
1941	Solitudine	Livio Pavanelli
1942	Girl of the Golden West	Carl Koch
1942	Se io fossi onesto	Carlo Ludovico Bragaglia
1942	Margherita and Her Three Uncles	Ivo Pirelli
1943	Redenzione	Marcello Albani
1945	Incontro con Laura	Carlo Alberto Felice
1946	Inquietudine	Vittorio Carpignano, Emilio Cordero
1946	Il piccolo ribelle	Emilio Cordero
1948	L'ultima cena	Luigi Gischino, Charles Resiner
1948	Fantasmi del mare	Francesco De Roberts
1950	Captain Demonio	Carlo Borghesio
1951	E l'amor che mi rovina	Mario Soldati
1951	O.K. Nero	Mario Soldati
1951	Operazione Mitra	Giorgio Cristallini
1951	Love I Haven't . . . But . . . But	Giorgio Bianchi
1952	Rome 11:00	Guiseppe De Santis (Italy/France)

Year	Film	Director
1952	Don Juan's Night of Love	Mario Soldati (Italy/France)
1952	Zorro's Dream	Mario Soldati
1953	Il viale della speranza	Dino Risi
1952	Cronaca di un delitto	Mario Sequi
1953	Too Young for Love	Lionello De Felice (Italy/France)
1953	La valigia dei sogni	Luigi Comencini
1953	Love in the City	Michelangelo Antonioni, etc.
1953	It Happened in the Park	Gianni Franciolini, Vittorio De Sica (Italy/France)
1953	Prima di sera	Piero Tellini
1953	Lasciateci in pace	Marino Girolami
1954	100 Years of Love	Lionello De Felice
1954	Cose da pazzi	Georg Wilhelm Pabst
1954	The Bed	Henri Decoin, etc. (France/Italy)
1954	The Barefoot Contessa	Joseph L. Mankiewicz (USA/Italy)
1954	Days of Love	Guiseppe De Santis, Leopoldo Savona (Italy/France)
1954	Angela	Edoardo Anton, Dennis O'Keefe (USA/Italy)
1954	Scuola elementare	Alberto Lattuada
1954	Knights of the Queen	Mauro Bolognini, Joseph Lerner
1954	Vacation with a Gangster	Dino Risi
1954	Ballata tragica	Luigi Capuano
1955	New Moon	Luigi Capuano
1955	The Widow	Lewis Milestone (Italy/France)
1955	Roman Tales	Gianni Franciolini (Italy/France)
1955	Io Sono la Primula Rossa	Giorgio Simonelli
1956	Alexander the Great	Robert Rossen (USA/Spain)
1956	Child in the House	Cy Endfield (UK)
1956	Noi siamo le colonne	Luigi Filippo D'Amico
1957	Men and Wolves	Giuseppe De Santis, Leopoldo Savona (Italy/France)
1957	The King's Musketeers	Joseph Lerner
1957	Night Operation	Giuseppe Bennati
1957	La spada imbattibile	Hugo Fregonese
1957	That Night! (aka Brave Tomorrow)	John Newland (USA)
1957	A Farewell to Arms	Charles Vidor, John Huston (USA)
1957	The Latest Violence	Raffaello Matarazzo, Silvio Amadio
1957	Honor Among Thieves	Nanni Loy, Gianni Puccini
1958	Love and Chatter	Alessandro Blasetti (Italy/Spain)
1958	The Quiet American	Joseph L. Mankiewicz (USA)
1958	Le imprese di una spada leggendaria	Nathan Juran, Frank McDonald
1958	The Vikings	Richard Fleischer (USA)
1959	Room at the Top	Jack Clayton (UK)
1959	Desert Desperados	Steve Sekely, Gianni Vernuccio (Italy/USA)
1959	Mantelli e spade insanguinate	Nathan Juran, Frank McDonald
1959	Solomon and Sheba	King Vidor (USA)
1959	Subway in the Sky	Muriel Box (UK)
1959	Violent Summer	Valerio Zurlini (Italy/France)
1959	Nel blu dipinto di blu	Piero Tellini
1959	Death of a Friend	Franco Rossi
1960	Scent of Mystery	Jack Cardiff (USA)
1960	Carthage in Flames	Carmine Gallone (Italy/France)
1960	Sons and Lovers	Jack Cardiff (UK)
1960	La garçonniere	Guiseppe De Santis
1961	Bondage Gladiator Sexy	Giorgio Ferroni (Italy/France)
1961	Love, Freedom and Treachery (aka Law of War)	Bruno Paolinelli (Italy/France/W. Germany)
1961	Romanoff and Juliet	Peter Ustinov (USA)
1961	Francis of Assisi	Michael Curtiz (USA)
1961	The Mongols	André De Toth, etc. (Italy/France)
1961	Constantine and the Cross	Lionello De Felice (Italy/Yugoslavia)
1961	The Happy Thieves	George Marshall (USA)

Year	Film	Director
1961	*Barabbas*	Richard Fleischer (Italy/USA)
1962	*Jessica*	Jean Negulesco, Oreste Palella (France/USA/Italy)
1962	*Light in the Piazza*	Guy Green (USA)
1962	*Disorder*	Franco Brusati (Italy/France)
1962	*Charge of the Black Lancers*	Giacomo Gentilomo (Italy/France)
1962	*The Golden Arrow*	Antonio Margheriti
1962	*Story of San Michele*	Giorgio Capitani, etc. (France/Italy/ W. Germany)
1962	*The Changing of the Guard*	Giorgio Bianchi, Sergio Leone (Italy/France)
1962	*War Gods of Babylon*	Silvio Amadio
1962	*The Story of Joseph and His Brethren*	Irving Rapper, Luciano Ricci (Yugoslavia/Italy)
1962	*Swordsman of Siena*	Baccio Bandini, Etienne Périer (Italy/France)
1962	*La banda Casaroli*	Florestano Vanici (Italy/France)
1962	*Desert War*	Luigi Filippo D'Amico
1963	*The Verona Trial*	Carlo Lizzani (Italy/France)
1965	*Where the Spies Are*	Val Guest (UK)
1965	*The Camp Followers*	Valerio Zurlini (Italy/France/ W. Germany/Yugoslavia)
1966	*Kiss the Girls and Make Them Die*	Henry Levin, Arduino Maiuri
1966	*One Million Years B.C.*	Don Chaffrey (UK)
1967	*Dick Smart 2007*	Franco Prosperi
1967	*Doctor Faustus*	Richard Burton, Nevill Coghill (UK)
1967	*Pronto . . . c'e una certa Giuliana per te*	Massimo Franciosa
1968	*The Vengeance of She*	Cliff Owen (UK)
1968	*Summit*	Giorgio Bontempi
1968	*Commandos*	Armando Crispino (Italy/W. Germany)
1969	*Togli le gambe dal parabrezza*	Massimo Franciosa
1969	*The Mummy* (aka *The Night of Counting the Years*)	Chadi Abdel Salam (Egypt)
1970	*When Dinosaurs Ruled the Earth*	Val Guest (UK)
1970	*Gradiva*	Giorgio Albertazzi
1971	*Creatures the World Forgot*	Don Chaffey (UK)
1972	*Indian Summer*	Valerio Zurlini (Italy/France)
1974	*Year One*	Roberto Rossellini
1975	*The Messiah*	Roberto Rossellini (Italy/France)
1990	*Blue Dolphin l'avventura continua*	Giorgio Moser

NEWMAN, Alfred (1901–1970) With a career that covers the golden age of Hollywood, composer, arranger, and conductor Alfred Newman may be the quintessential American movie composer. As music director at United Artists and then Twentieth Century-Fox, he supervised hundreds of feature films and composed scores for 225 movies. Newman won a record number of Oscars (forty-five nominations and nine wins) and was considered the premier screen composer in the business. Yet his impact goes beyond statistics. He brought a polish and dedication to film scoring that helped make the golden age so special.

Alfred Newman was born in New Haven, Connecticut, the son of an impoverished produce dealer. As the eldest in a family of ten children, Newman had a limited education but was encouraged by his mother to study piano. He was only eight years old when he began working as a piano player in restaurants and clubs in order to support his family. It was soon clear to many that Newman was something of a child prodigy. As a teenager he toured in vaudeville billed as "The Marvelous Boy Pianist" and he was only seventeen when he began conducting musicals on Broadway. During the 1920s, Newman was conductor for a dozen musicals composed by Jerome Kern, George Gershwin, Richard Rodgers, and others. Songwriter Irving Berlin was so impressed with Newman's work that he insisted the conductor be brought to Hollywood in 1930 to be musical director on his film *Reaching for the Moon*. That same year Newman scored as well as conducted his first movie, and so began one of the most remarkable of Hollywood careers.

Producer Samuel Goldwyn was the first to recognize Newman's talent and saw to it he got more composing

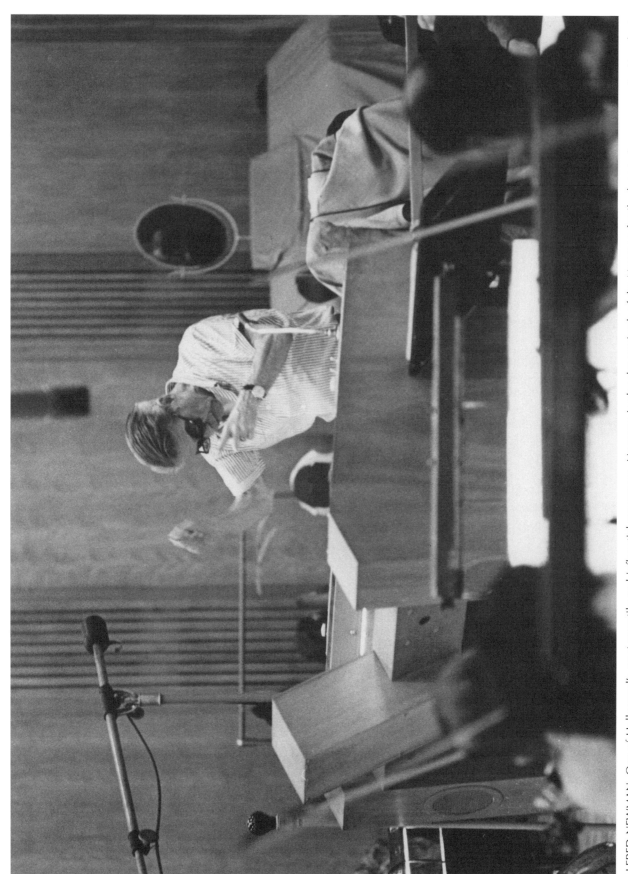

ALFRED NEWMAN. One of Hollywood's most versatile and influential composers, Newman is also the patriarch of the Newman family dynasty in screen music. Here he is conducting the soundtrack recording of his last film, *Airport* (1970), a score as vigorous and exciting as his first film music forty years earlier. *Universal Pictures / Photofest © Universal Pictures*

work. Newman's music for Goldwyn's *Street Scene* was noticed by the studios and soon he was in demand. Throughout the 1930s he scored such outstanding films as *Rain, Hallelujah I'm a Bum, The Count of Monte Cristo, Les Misérables, Dodsworth, Stella Dallas, The Prisoner of Zenda, The Hurricane, Drums Along the Mohawk, Wuthering Heights, Alexander's Ragtime Band*, and *The Hunchback of Notre Dame*. In 1940 he became the musical director at Twentieth Century-Fox, a position he held for twenty years as he oversaw dozens of movies, scoring a good number of them. For the studio he wrote the musical fanfare for the Fox logo which continues to be used to this day. Among the many notable Fox films that he scored are *The Grapes of Wrath, Foreign Correspondent, Tin Pan Alley, How Green Was My Valley, The Song of Bernadette, State Fair, Gentleman's Agreement, The Snake Pit, Twelve O'Clock High, All About Eve, The Robe, Love Is a Many-Splendored Thing, With a Song in My Heart, The King and I, Anastasia, The Diary of Anne Frank*, and *South Pacific*. In 1960 Newman left Fox and worked as a freelance composer and conductor for the next ten years, scoring such movies as *Flower Drum Song, How the West Was Won, The Greatest Story Ever Told*, and *Airport*. Suffering from ill health, Newman retired in 1970 and died of emphysema later that same year at the age of sixty-eight.

Newman's numerous screen credits include many musicals. Very rarely did he write songs for these films but instead scored the music that surrounded numbers by Rodgers and Hammerstein, Berlin, Gershwin, Cole Porter, and others. Because of his experience arranging and conducting music on Broadway, he was expert at giving a musical its tone and polish. Consequently, Newman was in great demand for movie musicals and some of his finest work was scoring them even though the attention often went to the songwriters. Newman stated once that he preferred arranging and conducting over composing because the latter was lonely and toilsome work. He was a meticulous and demanding worker, insisting on the best from himself and others. Arriving in Hollywood just as talkies were getting more technically sophisticated, he contributed to creating the musical sound of the era and was at the heart of the studio system at its peak. His waning years were also the declining years of this system. The passing of Newman was symbolic of the end of a golden age.

Unlike his contemporary Max Steiner who favored leitmotifs in his movie scores, Newman usually wrote mood music in the operatic manor. While some of his themes did stand out and later became popular as songs, much of his music is underscoring used for atmosphere. In *Street Scene*, his first notable score, Newman created an extended musical sequence that mirrored everyday life in a Lower East Side neighborhood in Manhattan. The music is bluesy yet frantic, capturing the excitement and weariness of the city. Although this sequence is not a song, it has some very catchy musical themes in it and it quickly caught the attention of moviegoers and critics. Newman later arranged the sequence into the orchestral piece "Sentimental Rhapsody," a title that pays homage to Gershwin's "Rhapsody in Blue" which it resembles at times. Newman would later use the theme again in some of his scores at Fox. He was not averse to reusing material throughout his career. His tender theme from the melodrama *These Three* later showed up as the love theme in his score for *The Razor's Edge*. Similarly, the lovely theme used for an ocean voyage in *Dodsworth* was turned into the main theme for *The Hurricane*, finding popularity when it was turned into the song "The Moon of Manakoora." Newman also used old folk melodies as the basis for his scores. The lyrical tune "Aura Lee" was used effectively throughout *Come and Get It*. (Many years later Elvis Presley popularized the song again when he sang it as the title number in *Love Me Tender*.) For *The Grapes of Wrath*, he brought in the folk favorite "Red River Valley" throughout the score. Welsh hymns were incorporated into the score for *How Green Was My Valley*. Because Newman was such a proficient arranger, the use of these familiar tunes was masterfully done and the scores felt both old and new.

There are so many Newman scores worth examining that it is only possible to give samplings of his virtuosity. It was the music in his dramas that first brought him recognition so they are a good place to begin. His score for the 1939 screen version of Emily Bronte's *Wuthering Heights* is unique in the way the different musical themes help clarify the story within a story and all the flashbacks. The tormented love between the rustic, earthy Heathcliff (Laurence Olivier) and the aristocratic but wild Cathy (Merle Oberon) is told in bits and pieces by other characters, so Newman created different motifs for the principals as a way of framing the action. The most famous theme is that for Cathy, a glowing pastoral with strings that slide up and down the scale with ease, pausing at times before continuing on with new life. Heathcliff's theme is much darker and strained; the music for his wealthy rival (David Niven) is elegant and genteel. All this is held together because Newman's music (and his expert conducting of the score) seems to breathe the same passionate air. *Wuthering Heights* is like grand opera with big emotions, and it has aggressive, full-bodied music to make it work. This is not the sound of Newman's score for *The Song of Bernadette*, a restrained telling of the French teenager (Jennifer Jones) who experienced visions of a "beautiful lady" in 1858. If *Wuthering Heights* is grand opera, this biopic is more in the form of an oratorio. A women's chorus is used effectively throughout the film without overpowering the action on the screen or turning the score into a religious ceremony. Newman uses the sound of the wind and the scampering of leaves to lead into the ethereal music on strings for Bernadette's vision of the Blessed Virgin. Moviegoers never see the "beautiful lady" so the music has to create the aura and warmth of her personage. The film opens with portentous descending notes that lead into a solemn but lively melody with brass accents and some woodwind solos. Also in the score are a reflective passage with little melody as it imitates a slight breeze in the air, a stirring theme with full orchestra slowly gathering strength and reaching a blossoming climax, and a lonely woodwind track with wavering strings that seem to cry out to be noticed.

Another biopic with a sensitive subject matter is *The Diary of Anne Frank*. The title teenager (Millie Perkins) this time speaks her own words as the famous diary is used for Perkins's engaging narration. While her Jewish family hides from the Nazis in occupied Amsterdam during World War II, life continues and the details of such a life are what make the story so honest and compelling. Newman's quiet yet full-spirited score is masterful. Resisting a gloomy or fatalistic tone, he uses uplifting violins that seem to climb the scale to be free. The old European sound is hopeful and even optimistic, as expressed in the title character's philosophy. The main theme is a lively horn passage with intricate woodwinds fluttering away then transitioning into a long melodic line that is serene and soothing as it gently floats up the scale and then just as easily descends. There is also a reflective and melancholy theme on various strings and horns that has a restlessness about it. Although never seen, the Nazis are scored with an oppressive march in half time in which brass and strings create a fearsome sound.

Confinement of another kind is the subject of *The Snake Pit* in which a woman (Olivia de Havilland) finds herself in a state mental asylum and cannot remember the circumstances that led her there. Newman's potent score suggests fragility and torment without slipping into turgid melodramatics. The harsh opening theme with threatening low brass softens into a string passage that is restless and nervous as the musical notes seems to tumble down the scale helplessly. This is one of several movies scored by Newman that has a documentary feel to it. The World War II drama *Twelve O'Clock High*, about a driven general (Gregory Peck) who uses ruthless means to whip his bomber squad into shape, is more about character than action. Music is used sparingly throughout the movie and most of that is the soldiers' singing of popular songs of the era. Newman's main theme is a series of repeated musical phrases played on brass and strings that are filled with awe and danger. There is a melodic passage with lively strings punctuated by brass fanfares, as well as an eerie and unsettling theme played on brass instruments that is more about the main character's obsession than patriotic fervor. Interestingly, the documentary-like dramas *Gentlemen's Agreement* and *Call Northside 777* have no music except during the opening and closing credits.

Newman's scores for period adventure movies often include his most vigorously melodic music. *Beau Geste* and *How the West Was Won* are good examples from early and late in his career. The three Geste brothers (Gary Cooper, Ray Milland, and Robert Preston) struggle in the Foreign Legion under the command of their sadistic commander (Brian Donlevy) as they battle the desert hordes. Newman wrote a sparkling score, beginning with the opening music: explosive chords that lead into an exotic musical phrase then into a brisk march with strings overpowering the brass as they scamper up and down the scale. There is also a slow and sultry theme filled with the mystery of the desert, a ponderous death march with pounding percussion and sorrowful horns, and a passage in which nervous strings and repeating woodwinds create a sense of unseen danger. The music softens considerably for the scenes back in England and for a touching death scene that features a solo violin wailing quietly. The wide-screen spectacular *How the West Was Won* called for a big sound, and Newman provided it with a score filled with thrilling marches, lush romantic themes, and rousing action music. This fifty-year epic centers on a family that gets involved in such major nineteenth-century events as the gold rush, the Civil War, the settling of the prairie, and the building of the railroads. Newman wrote a long and sweeping score that incorporated familiar American folk songs, stirring choral sections, and a rousing march theme with French horns, string flourishes, and invigorating percussion that conveys the sweeping panorama of the land. Unfortunately, the studio also added sections from Verdi's *Requiem* and Handel's *Messiah*, overloading the score and making the movie pretentious at times. Newman complained and tried to get his name off the picture but, as always, the studio won. All the same, the score is a substantial accomplishment and its recurring theme is one of Newman's most exciting pieces of music.

A different kind of excitement can be found in his scores for two biblical epics: *The Robe* and *The Greatest Story Ever Told*. The former is a passionate, perhaps even overwrought, tale about various Romans who are changed and obsessed by the robe that Jesus wore to his crucifixion. This first CinemaScope movie was oversized in many ways but Newman's score was a skillful combination of bombast and restraint. The principal theme is a weighty, reverent series of brass chords with a wordless chorus that leads into a majestic, stately minor-key theme in which each musical phrase builds on the previous one. In another passage, various horns echo each other in a teasing way until a fluid melody forms on high woodwinds. Also memorable is a track in which a solo flute plays an exotic folk tune that is simple yet mysterious; the melody is then picked up by strings and the flowing musical line turns into a sophisticated adagio piece. The love theme is unusual in that it is a minor-key piece in which a solo cello rises above the other strings in a marvelous manner. The score also includes a brisk military march with boastful horns and eager percussion that builds into a frenzy, and a stirring finale with a choral "Hallelujah" matched by a swelling orchestra. Many consider *The Robe* one of Newman's finest achievements. Ironically, it was not even nominated for an Oscar. Twelve years later, when Newman scored the biblical *The Greatest Story Ever Told*, he wrote more subtle and atmospheric music. Unfortunately director George Stevens and the studio thought this life of Christ needed a bigger sound and again substituted selections from Verdi's *Requiem*

and Handel's *Messiah* in place of some of Newman's tracks. (Fortunately the original soundtrack survives and today one can hear Newman's complete and unadulterated score.) There is still much in the released score that is first rate. The recurring theme for Jesus (Max von Sydow) is a simple series of chords that lead into flowing strings that are reverent yet lively. In another theme various flutes and reeds play a round of overlapping musical phrases that is complicated yet straightforward enough to sound period. Also of interest is a track that starts with low chanting and cautious strings, then the chorus finds its power and the orchestra follows suit. While *The Robe* was a popular hit, *The Greatest Story Ever Told* was a star-studded flop. At least this time Newman's score was nominated for an Oscar.

Newman's last score, for the high-flying soap opera *Airport*, was written when he was very ill (he died before the movie was released) yet it has the vitality of a young composer. This popular disaster film, the first in a long line of airborne melodramas, follows the ground staff, flight crew, and passengers on a jet carrying a suicidal man (Van Heflin) with a bomb. Contrived and plodding, the movie boasts a score that has an urgency that is often more involving than the action on the screen. The main theme consists of brass instruments that echo themselves in a fast and agitated march with short, potent musical phrases that suggest something crucial is happening. The suspense music is sharp and modern while the love theme is a slow and sensual foxtrot played on strings and muted trombone that is somewhat languid but doesn't drag. Here is a score that really takes flight. Although Newman always considered himself a conductor rather than a composer, history has thought otherwise. Along with Max Steiner and Dimitri Tiomkin, Newman is considered one of Hollywood's three "Godfathers of film music." He helped establish the standards of effective screen scoring and served as the inspiration and model for dozens of movie composers to follow. He is also a figurehead in the "first family" of film scoring. His brothers Lionel and Emil are also prodigious composers in Hollywood, his sons David and Thomas Newman each have approximately one hundred movie soundtracks to his credit, his nephew Randy Newman is one of the top songwriters and screen composers in movies today, and various other relatives are in the music business as well.

Credits

(all films USA; * for Best Song; ** for Musical Direction)

Year	Film	Director
1930	The Devil to Pay!	George Fitzmaurice
1931	Kiki	Sam Taylor
1931	Street Scene	King Vidor
1931	Palmy Days	A. Edward Sutherland
1931	The Age for Love	Frank Lloyd
1931	The Unholy Garden	George Fitzmaurice
1931	Around the World with Douglas Fairbanks	Douglas Fairbanks, Victor Fleming
1931	Corsair	Roland West
1931	Arrowsmith	John Ford
1931	Tonight or Never	Mervyn LeRoy
1932	Cock of the Air	Tom Buckingham
1932	The Greeks Had a Word for Them	Lowell Sherman
1932	Sky Devils	A. Edward Sutherland
1932	Night World	Hobart Henley
1932	Movie Crazy	Clyde Bruckman
1932	Mr. Robinson Crusoe	A. Edward Sutherland
1932	Rain	Lewis Milestone
1932	The Kid from Spain	Leo McCarey
1932	Flesh	John Ford
1932	Cynara	King Vidor
1933	Hallelujah I'm a Bum	Lewis Milestone
1933	Secrets	Frank Borzage
1933	I Cover the Waterfront	James Cruze
1933	The Masquerader	Richard Wallace
1933	The Bowery	Raoul Walsh
1933	Broadway Thru a Keyhole	Lowell Sherman
1933	Blood Money	Rowland Brown
1933	Roman Scandals	Frank Tuttle
1933	Advice to the Lovelorn	Alfred L. Werker
1933	Gallant Lady	Gregory La Cava
1934	Nana	Dorothy Arzner, George Fitzmaurice
1934	The House of Rothschild	Alfred L. Werker
1934	Looking for Trouble	William A. Wellman
1934	The Last Gentleman	Sidney Lanfield
1934	Born to Be Bad	Lowell Sherman
1934	The Cat's-Paw	Sam Taylor
1934	Our Daily Bread	King Vidor
1934	The Count of Monte Cristo	Rowland V. Lee
1934	Bulldog Drummond Strikes Back	Roy Del Ruth
1934	The Affairs of Cellini	Gregory La Cava
1934	We Live Again	Rouben Mamoulian
1934	Transatlantic Merry-Go-Round	Benjamin Stoloff
1934	Kid Millions	Roy Del Ruth
1934	The Mighty Barnum	Walter Lang
1935	Clive of India	Richard Boleslawski
1935	Folies Bergere de Paris	Roy Del Ruth
1935	The Wedding Night	King Vidor
1935	Les Misérables	Richard Boleslawski
1935	Cardinal Richelieu	Rowland V. Lee
1935	The Call of the Wild	William A. Wellman
1935	The Dark Angel	Sidney Franklin
1935	Red Salute	Sidney Lanfield
1935	Barbary Coast	Howard Hawks
1935	The Melody Lingers On	David Burton

Year	Film	Director
1935	*Splendor*	Elliott Nugent
1936	*Strike Me Pink*	Norman Taurog
1936	*These Three*	William Wyler
1936	*One Rainy Afternoon*	Rowland V. Lee
1936	*Dancing Pirate*	Lloyd Corrigan
1936	*Dodsworth*	William Wyler
1936	*Ramona*	Henry King
1936	*The Gay Desperado*	Rouben Mamoulian
1936	*Come and Get It*	Howard Hawks, William Wyler
1936	*Beloved Enemy*	H. C. Potter
1937	*You Only Live Once*	Fritz Lang
1937	*When You're in Love*	Robert Riskin
1937	*History Is Made at Night*	Frank Borzage
1937	*Woman Chases Man*	John G. Blystone
1937	*Slave Ship*	Tay Garnett
1937	*Wee Willie Winkie*	John Ford
1937	*Stella Dallas*	King Vidor
1937	*Dead End*	William Wyler
1937	*The Prisoner of Zenda* (AAN)	John Cromwell
1937	*The Hurricane*	John Ford
1937	*52nd Street*	Harold Young
1938	*The Cowboy and the Lady* (AAN)	H. C. Potter
1938	*Alexander's Ragtime Band* (AA**)	Henry King
1938	*Trade Winds*	Tay Garnett
1938	*The Goldwyn Follies* (AAN**)	George Marshall
1939	*Gunga Din*	George Stevens
1939	*Wuthering Heights* (AAN)	William Wyler
1939	*Young Mr. Lincoln*	John Ford
1939	*Beau Geste*	William A. Wellman
1939	*The Star Maker*	Roy Del Ruth
1939	*The Rains Came* (AAN)	Clarence Brown
1939	*They Shall Have Music* (AAN)	Archie Mayo
1939	*The Real Glory*	Henry Hathaway
1939	*Drums along the Mohawk*	John Ford
1939	*The Hunchback of Notre Dame* (AAN)	William Dieterle
1940	*The Blue Bird*	Walter Lang
1940	*The Grapes of Wrath*	John Ford
1940	*Little Old New York*	Henry King
1940	*Vigil in the Night*	George Stevens
1940	*Lillian Russell*	Irving Cummings
1940	*Earthbound*	Irving Pichel
1940	*Maryland*	Henry King
1940	*Foreign Correspondent*	Alfred Hitchcock
1940	*Brigham Young*	Henry Hathaway
1940	*Public Deb No. 1*	Gregory Ratoff
1940	*The Westerner*	William Wyler
1940	*They Knew What They Wanted*	Garson Kanin
1940	*The Mark of Zorro* (AAN)	Rouben Mamoulian
1940	*Tin Pan Alley* (AA)	Walter Lang
1941	*Hudson's Bay*	Irving Pichel
1941	*That Night in Rio*	Irving Cummings
1941	*Blood and Sand*	Rouben Mamoulian
1941	*Man Hunt*	Fritz Lang
1941	*Moon over Miami*	Walter Lang
1941	*Charley's Aunt*	Archie Mayo
1941	*Wild Geese Calling*	John Brahm
1941	*Belle Starr*	Irving Cummings
1941	*A Yank in the R.A.F.*	Henry King

Year	Film	Director
1941	*Week-End in Havana*	Walter Lang
1941	*How Green Was My Valley* (AAN)	John Ford
1941	*Rise and Shine*	Allan Dwan
1941	*Ball of Fire* (AAN)	Howard Hawks
1941	*Remember the Day*	Henry King
1942	*Son of Fury: The Story of Benjamin Blake*	John Cromwell
1942	*Roxie Hart*	William A. Wellman
1942	*Secret Agent of Japan*	Irving Pichel
1942	*To the Shores of Tripoli*	H. Bruce Humberstone
1942	*This Above All*	Anatole Litvak
1942	*Prelude to War*	Frank Capra, Anatole Litvak
1942	*My Gal Sal* (AAN**)	Irving Cummings
1942	*Ten Gentlemen from West Point*	Henry Hathaway
1942	*The Pied Piper*	Irving Pichel
1942	*The Loves of Edgar Allan Poe*	Harry Lachman
1942	*Orchestra Wives*	Archie Mayo
1942	*Girl Trouble*	Harold D. Schuster
1942	*Springtime in the Rockies*	Irving Cummings
1942	*The Black Swan* (AAN)	Henry King
1942	*Life Begins at Eight-Thirty*	Irving Pichel
1943	*December 7th*	John Ford, Gregg Toland
1943	*Claudia*	Edmund Goulding
1943	*Coney Island* (AAN**)	Waltere Lang
1943	*The Moon Is Down*	Irving Pichel
1943	*My Friend Flicka*	Harold D. Schuster
1943	*Heaven Can Wait*	Ernst Lubitsch
1943	*The Song of Bernadette* (AA)	Henry King
1944	*The Gang's All Here*	Busby Berkeley
1944	*The Purple Heart*	Lewis Milestone
1944	*Wilson*	Henry King
1944	*Irish Eyes Are Smiling* (AAN)	Gregory Ratoff
1944	*Sunday Dinner for a Soldier*	Lloyd Bacon
1944	*The Keys of the Kingdom* (AAN)	John M. Stahl
1945	*A Tree Grows in Brooklyn*	Elia Kazan
1945	*A Royal Scandal*	Otto Preminger
1945	*A Bell for Adano*	Henry King
1945	*State Fair* (AAN)	Walter Lang
1945	*The Dolly Sisters*	Irving Cummings
1945	*Leave Her to Heaven*	John M. Stahl
1946	*Dragonwyck*	Joseph L. Mankiewicz
1946	*Centennial Summer* (AAN)	Otto Preminger
1946	*Margie*	Henry King
1946	*The Razor's Edge*	Edmund Goulding
1947	*I Wonder Who's Kissing Her Now*	Lloyd Bacon
1947	*Mother Wore Tights* (AA**)	Walter Lang
1947	*Gentleman's Agreement*	Elia Kazan
1947	*Captain from Castile* (AAN)	Henry King
1948	*Call Northside 777*	Henry Hathaway
1948	*Sitting Pretty*	Walter Lang
1948	*Give My Regards to Broadway*	Lloyd Bacon
1948	*Deep Waters*	Henry King
1948	*When My Baby Smiles at Me* (AAN**)	Walter Lang
1948	*The Walls of Jericho*	John M. Stahl
1948	*That Lady in Ermine*	Ernst Lubitsch
1948	*Road House*	Jean Negulesco
1948	*Cry of the City*	Robert Siodmak
1948	*The Snake Pit* (AAN)	Anatole Litvak
1948	*Yellow Sky*	William A. Wellman

Year	Film	Director
1949	Chicken Every Sunday	George Seaton
1949	A Letter to Three Wives	Joseph L. Mankiewicz
1949	Down to the Sea in Ships	Henry Hathaway
1949	Mother Is a Freshman	Lloyd Bacon
1949	Mr. Belvedere Goes to College	Elliott Nugent
1949	You're My Everything	Walter Lang
1949	Thieves' Highway	Jules Dassin
1949	Pinky	Elia Kazan
1949	Prince of Foxes	Henry King
1949	Twelve O'Clock High	Henry King
1949	Come to the Stable (AAN*)	Henry Koster
1950	When Willie Comes Marching	John Ford
1950	Cheaper by the Dozen	Walter Lang
1950	The Big Lift	George Seaton
1950	Panic in the Streets	Elia Kazan
1950	The Gunfighter	Henry King
1950	No Way Out	Joseph L. Mankiewicz
1950	All About Eve (AAN)	Joseph L. Mankiewicz
1950	For Heaven's Sake	George Seaton
1951	Fourteen Hours	Henry Hathaway
1951	On the Riviera (AAN)	Walter Lang
1951	Take Care of My Little Girl	Jean Negulesco
1951	David and Bathsheba (AAN)	Henry King
1951	Golden Girl	Lloyd Bacon
1951	Elopement	Henry Koster
1952	With a Song in My Heart (AA)	Walter Lang
1952	Wait Till the Sun Shines, Nellie	Henry King
1952	What Price Glory	John Ford
1952	Full House (aka O. Henry's Full House)	Henry Hathaway, etc.
1952	The Prisoner of Zenda	Richards Thorpe
1952	Stars and Stripes Forever	Henry Koster
1953	Tonight We Sing	Mitchell Leisen
1953	Call Me Madam (AA)	Walter Lang
1953	The President's Lady	Henry Levin
1953	The Robe	Henry Koster
1954	Hell and High Water	Samuel Fuller
1954	The Egyptian	Michael Curtiz
1954	There's No Business Like Show Business (AAN)	Walter Lang
1955	A Man Called Peter	Henry Koster
1955	Daddy Long Legs (AAN)	Jean Negulesco
1955	The Seven Year Itch	Billy Wilder
1955	Love Is a Many-Splendored Thing (AA)	Henry King
1956	Carousel	Henry King
1956	The King and I (AA)	Walter Lang
1956	Bus Stop	Joshua Logan
1956	Anastasia (AAN)	Anatole Litvak
1958	The Gift of Love	Jean Negulesco
1958	South Pacific (AAN)	Joshua Logan
1958	The Bravados	Henry King
1958	A Certain Smile	Jean Negulesco
1959	The Diary of Anne Frank (AAN)	George Stevens
1959	The Best of Everything (AAN*)	Jean Negulesco
1961	The Pleasure of His Company	George Seaton
1961	Flower Drum Song (AAN)	Henry Koster
1962	State Fair	José Ferrer
1962	The Counterfeit Traitor	George Seaton
1962	How the West Was Won (AAN)	John Ford, etc.
1965	The Greatest Story Ever Told (AAN)	George Stevens

Year	Film	Director
1966	*Nevada Smith*	Henry Hathaway
1967	*Camelot* (AA)	Joshua Logan
1968	*Firecreek*	Vincent McEveety
1970	*Airport* (AAN; GGN)	George Seaton

NEWMAN, David (b. 1954) A busy member of the Newman family of screen composers, he has scored close to one hundred feature films, almost all of them contemporary comedies.

David Louis Newman was born in Los Angeles, the eldest son of famed movie composer Alfred Newman and the elder brother of Thomas and Maria Newman, also composers. David Newman was very proficient on the violin at a young age and as a teenager and young adult he played in the American Youth Symphony. He studied conducting and violin at the University of Southern California before beginning his career in movies as a musician on soundtracks, most memorably his violin solo for *E.T., the Extra-Terrestrial* (1982). Newman also orchestrated and/or conducted film scores by others, something he would later do for several of his own scores. His career as a screen composer began in 1984 with the Tim Burton short *Frankenweenie* (not to be confused with the 2012 animated feature of the same title). Newman's first feature film was the comic horror spoof *Critters* two years later. Since then he has scored an average of four movies per year, many of them low-budget, independent films at first, but later major projects with name directors and stars. Although Newman's credits include some horror, mystery, and dramatic works, about 90 percent of his films are broad, modern comedies. Not many of these have been critical successes but several were box office hits and frequently his music was praised. Among the most notable of his movies are *Heathers, Throw Mama from the Train, Bill & Ted's Excellent Adventure, The War of the Roses, The Freshman, Paradise, Other People's Money, The Mighty Ducks, Hoffa, The Sandlot, The Nutty Professor, Matilda, Galaxy Quest, Bowfinger, Death to Smoochy, The Spirit,* and *Serenity,* as well as the animated features *The Brave Little Toaster, DuckTails the Movie: Treasure of the Lost Lamp, Ice Age,* and *Anastasia,* getting an Oscar nomination for the last. Newman has written music for television series and TV movies and for the concert hall, in particular his "Concerto for Winds," *1001 Nights,* and a musical suite written for the silent film classic *Sunrise* (1927). He was named music director of the Sundance Institute in 1997 and a decade later was elected president of the Film Music Society. Newman has a distinguished reputation as a conductor, leading such ensembles as the American Symphony, Los Angeles Philharmonic, National Orchestra of Belgium, New Japan Philharmonic, and the ORF Vienna Radio Symphony.

Any discussion of Newman as a screen composer seems to concentrate on his handful of dramas and not his many comedies. This is to be expected since serious movies (even sci-fi and horror works) are supposed to have serious music. Comedy scores are dismissed as negligible, particularly those from very poor comedies of which Newman has scored plenty. *Hoffa,* the biopic about teamster kingpin Jimmy Hoffa (Jack Nicholson) is indeed serious and Newman's score captures both the heroic and the sinister side of the title character. There is a slow and stately horns passage with swirling strings that has a touch of pathos as it returns throughout the movie. In contrast is a gliding theme on strings and brass that spirals up the scale to erupt in expansive crescendos. Two other memorable passages in this very moody score are a heavy theme with restless percussion and forceful orchestral sweeps, and an urgent track with furious strings, bombastic brass, and percussive pounding that sets the pace. The music in *Hoffa* is so atmospheric that it is not difficult to understand why it has been used in dozens of film trailers for other movies. The action-packed sci-fi thriller *Serenity* also has a commendable "serious" score. This tale about intrigue inside and the aliens outside a spacecraft traveling in the future has suspenseful music that avoids sci-fi and horror film clichés. The compelling main theme begins with a solemn solo violin then intricate electric guitar fingering and energetic strings are added and the music pushes forward as the brass shout out with fervor. On the quieter side are a hesitant passage in which strings and horns move carefully ahead with short musical phrases, and a morose violin lament that seems to lose its will to continue on. The many action scenes are scored with a pounding march with hammering percussion and boastful brass. A similarly penetrating score can be found in *The Phantom*, a comic book–like adventure featuring an action hero (Billy Zane) and a wry sense of humor. Yet there is little levity in Newman's score, which has a seething main theme with harkening brass, nervous strings, an ominous male chorus, and explosive percussion that breaks out into a furious run. There is also an expansive theme with full orchestra that builds like an anthem as it climbs the scale, gaining power along the way. On the more gentle side is a lyrical passage featuring a primitive flute and piano with support by glowing strings.

To concentrate on these serious scores is to ignore most of Newman's career. What most impresses one about his so-called "lightweight" music is the ability to come up with imaginative and risible scores for so many comedies that seem too much like one another. The Arnold Schwarzenegger vehicle *Jingle All the Way* has a delicious main theme, a furious race with parading drums and brass that could serve for a sporting event but is more neurotic and confused. The endlessly similar Eddie Murphy comedies have exceptionally fun scores. *The Nutty Professor* opens with a cockeyed march with slaphappy woodwinds alternating with frantic brass. To add to the merriment, a solo bassoon interrupts on occasion, then the whole thing speeds up into a wild circus parade. *Dr. Seuss' The Cat in the Hat* has a score as lively as the comedy is sterile. Pizzicato strings and fluttering flutes compete against a piano and xylophone while the percussion goes berserk. There is a theme that has the tune of a lullaby but the pace and temperament of a sleigh ride down a mountain. While there is little wit in *The Flintstones*, Newman's music is very witty. The score begins with lumbering brass, woodwinds, and percussion that suggest a wooly mammoth slowly moving along. This transitions into a jazzy blues passage that is languid and a little drunk as notes are slurred. The farce *The War of the Roses*, in which a battling married couple (Michael Douglas and Kathleen Turner) duke it out as if in a cartoon, has an exceptional offbeat main theme. Grumbling brass, twittering woodwinds, vivacious piano, and sprightly strings all move from an angry march tempo to a tango-like frolic.

When Newman is handed a better comedy or one that has some substance, the scores get even better. The animated *Ice Age*, about some prehistoric animals making a journey to return an infant human to its tribe, is rich with different emotions. The score is equally diverse and engaging. The opening theme is jaunty traveling music on synthesized banjo with various percussion instruments contributing to its carefree spirit. A herd of rhinos is scored with alternating slow horns and frantic woodwinds and percussion, there is a funny woodwind and string theme that seems to quickly tiptoe along with delight, and a furious comic march is played on xylophone and brass and speeds forward with the tempo of wild laughter. The music for the more sobering scenes is just as pleasing, such as a lyrical passage with flowing woodwinds and chanting voices that has a primitive folk flavor, and a bassoon and piano theme that moves from silly to heartbreaking before you know it. *Matilda* is a dark comedy about a young girl (Mara Wilson) who possesses magical powers and uses them to correct injustices done to herself, her fellow students, and her teacher (Embeth Davidz). There is a beguiling piano and string theme that is childlike and has a sense of mischief. Also sparkling is a sprightly theme on woodwinds, strings, and bells that dances along without a care. The horrible school principal (Pam Ferris) has her own theme which is menacing in a silly way with dizzying strings and sour brass notes. Among the fine quiet passages is a gentle theme on clarinet and strings that is melancholy yet still hopeful. The nostalgic comedy *The Sandlot*, about a neighborhood boys' baseball team, is an episodic charmer that hits all the tender emotions. Newman wrote one of his finest and most varied scores for this coming-of-age movie. In one theme an electric keyboard and guitar ramble along in a freewheeling manner, in another high strings, rapid percussion, and racing brass combine for some quirky chase music. There is a honky-tonk blues passage on electric organ, harmonica, Jew's harp, and banjo that takes its time as it bounces along, and a scampering march with frivolous woodwinds, schizophrenic percussion, and odd vocal accents. The score also has a lazy theme on harmonica, electronic guitar, and echoing synthesized chords, and a whistling track with electric keyboard and vibrating guitar chords that spoofs Ennio Morricone's *The Good, the Bad, and the Ugly* music.

It is a bit unexpected that Newman's most awarded and perhaps best score was written neither for a comedy nor a drama but an animated romantic movie, *Anastasia*. This softened version of the legend of a Russian waif who may be the surviving member of the Romanoff family is a full-scale musical with six excellent songs by Stephen Flaherty (music) and Lynn Ahrens (lyrics). Newman uses the music from some of these in his soundtrack score but there is some original themes that are superb as well. A recurring theme taken from Flaherty is a delicate lullaby played on a balalaika with the twinkling sound of a music box. Newman turns the simple tune into a leitmotif as it becomes important to the plot. The score opens with a pompous royal march that overflows with a sense of pride and entitlement. The villain Rasputin has a sinister theme with heavy brass and percussion chords. There is a swirling waltz that moves too fast to be totally happy. In fact, a sense of doom arises when a chanting chorus is added. The musical highlight of *Anastasia* is the finale which required an orchestra

of ninety pieces and a chorus of thirty voices. It begins as a graceful passage featuring French horns with a children's chorus that is full of magic. It then builds into a rousing anthem with an adult choir and soaring brass fanfares rising over the full orchestra. The track recalls the musical proficiency of Newman's father Alfred and of his mentor Jerry Goldsmith. Yet it is pure David Newman in the way it rises to the occasion. Too often throughout Newman's career the project he has been handed has been mediocre or worse. Yet he and his music seem to be undeterred and proceed as if each film were a masterpiece. Official website: www.davidnewmancomposer.com.

Credits

(all films USA unless stated otherwise)

Year	Film	Director
1986	Critters	Stephen Herek
1986	Vendetta (aka Angels Behind Bars)	Bruce Logan
1987	The Kindred	Stephen Carpenter, Jeffrey Obrow
1987	My Demon Lover	Charlie Loventhal
1987	Malone	Harley Cokeliss
1987	The Brave Little Toaster	Jerry Rees (USA/Taiwan/Japan)
1987	Throw Mama from the Train	Danny DeVito
1988	Heathers (aka Fatal Game)	Michael Lehmann
1989	Bill & Ted's Excellent Adventure (aka Dudes)	Stephen Herek
1989	Disorganized Crime	Jim Kouf
1989	Little Monsters	Richard Greenberg
1989	Gross Anatomy	Thom Eberhardt
1989	The War of the Roses	Danny DeVito
1990	Madhouse	Tom Ropelewski
1990	Fire Birds	David Green
1990	The Freshman	Andrew Bergman
1990	DuckTales the Movie: Treasure of the Lost Lamp	Bob Hathcock (France/USA)
1990	Mr. Destiny	James Orr
1990	Meet the Applegates (aka The Applegates)	Michael Lehmann
1991	The Marrying Man	Jerry Rees
1991	Talent for the Game	Robert M. Young
1991	Michael & Mickey	Jerry Rees
1991	Don't Tell Mom the Babysitter's Dead	Stephen Herek
1991	Rover Dangerfield	James L. George, Bob Seeley
1991	Bill & Ted's Bogus Journey	Peter Hewitt
1991	The Runestone	Willard Carroll
1991	Paradise	Mary Agnes Donoghue
1991	Other People's Money	Norman Jewison
1992	Honeymoon in Vegas	Andrew Bergman
1992	The Mighty Ducks	Stephen Herek
1992	That Night	Craig Bolotin (France/USA)
1992	Hoffa	Danny DeVito (France/USA)
1993	The Sandlot	David M. Evans
1993	Coneheads	Steve Barron
1993	Undercover Blues (aka Cloak and Diaper)	Herbert Ross
1994	The Air up There	Paul Michael Glaser
1994	My Father the Hero	Steve Miner (France/USA)

Year	Film	Director
1994	*The Flintstones*	Brian Levant
1994	*The Cowboy Way*	Gregg Champion
1994	*I Love Trouble*	Charles Shyer
1995	*Boys on the Side*	Herbert Ross (USA/France)
1995	*Tommy Boy*	Peter Segal
1995	*Operation Dumbo Drop*	Simon Wincer
1996	*Big Bully*	Steve Miner
1996	*The Phantom*	Simon Wincer (Australia/USA)
1996	*The Nutty Professor*	Tom Shadyac
1996	*Matilda*	Danny DeVito
1996	*Jingle All the Way*	Brian Levant
1997	*Out to Sea*	Martha Coolidge
1997	*Anastasia* (AAN)	Don Bluth, Gary Goldman
1999	*Never Been Kissed*	Raja Gosnell
1999	*Brokedown Palace* (aka *Two Girls*)	Jonathan Kaplan
1999	*Bowfinger* (aka *Bowfinger's Big Thing*)	Frank Oz
1999	*Galaxy Quest* (aka *Captain Starshine*)	Dean Parisot
2000	*The Flintstones in Viva Las Vegas*	Brian Levant
2000	*Nutty Professor II: The Klumps*	Peter Segal
2000	*Duets*	Bruce Paltrow
2000	*Bedazzled*	Harold Ramis (USA/Germany)
2000	*102 Dalmatians*	Kevin Lima (USA/UK)
2001	*Dr. Dolittle 2*	Steve Carr
2001	*The Affair of the Necklace*	Charles Shyer
2002	*Death to Smoochy*	Danny DeVito (USA/UK/Germany)
2002	*Ice Age*	Chris Wedge, Carlos Saldanha
2002	*Life or Something Like It*	Stephen Herek
2002	*Scooby-Doo*	Raja Gosnell (USA/Australia)
2003	*How to Lose a Guy in 10 Days*	Donald Petrie (USA/Germany)
2003	*Daddy Day Care*	Steve Carr
2003	*Duplex*	Danny DeVito (USA/Germany)
2003	*Dr. Seuss' The Cat in the Hat*	Bo Welch
2004	*Scooby-Doo 2: Monsters Unleashed*	Raja Gosnell (USA/Canada)
2005	*Are We There Yet?*	Brian Levant (USA/Canada)
2005	*Man of the House* (aka *Cheer Up*)	Stephen Herek
2005	*Monster-in-Law*	Robert Luketic (Germany/USA)
2005	*Serenity* (aka *Firefly*)	Joss Whedon
2007	*Norbit*	Brian Robbins
2008	*Welcome Home, Roscoe Jenkins*	Malcolm D. Lee
2008	*The Spirit*	Frank Miller
2009	*My Life in Ruins*	Donald Petrie (USA/Spain)
2009	*Alvin and the Chipmunks: The Squeakquel*	Betty Thomas
2010	*Crazy on the Outside*	Tim Allen
2010	*The Spy Next Door*	Brian Levant
2010	*Animals United*	Reinhard Klooss, Holger Tappe (Germany)
2011	*Big Mommas: Like Father, Like Son*	John Whitesell
2013	*Tarzan*	Reinhard Klooss (Germany)
2014	*Behaving Badly*	Tim Garrick

NEWMAN, Emil (1911–1984) A busy conductor, arranger, and composer member of the famed Newman dynasty who was music director for over 175 films, his screen compositions are fewer and less substantial than those of his illustrious relatives.

He was born in New Haven, Connecticut, one of ten children of a fruit peddler and his wife who emigrated from Russia. Newman grew up in the shadow of his elder brother Alfred who was a child prodigy and later an important Hollywood composer. Like his younger brother Lionel, he got into the film business through the help of Alfred who worked at Twentieth Century-Fox. By 1936 Newman was musical director for B movies at Fox and by the 1940s was one of the studio's busiest and most respected arrangers and conductors. Over the next decade he was in charge of the music for such notable movies as *Down Argentine Way* (1940), *Riders of the Purple Sage* (1941), *Hello Frisco, Hello* (1943), *Stormy Weather* (1943), *Guadalcanal Diary* (1943), *Lifeboat* (1944), *Four Jills in a Jeep* (1944), *Laura* (1944), *Junior Miss* (1945), *The Best Years of Our Lives* (1946), *The Bishop's Wife* (1947), and *My Foolish Heart* (1949). As a composer, Newman contributed music to about fifty movies but most were in collaboration with several others. Of the films scored with just one other composer, almost all were forgettable B movies. Records show that Newman was sole composer on only four movies during his entire career and these are minor works, to say the least. Yet as a musical director and conductor he was one of the best in his field. His only Oscar nomination

was for arranging the music in the Big Band musical *Sun Valley Serenade* (1941). Newman moved into television in the mid-1950s and composed music for a few series, including *The Count of Monte Cristo*, *The Adventures of Tugboat Annie*, and *New York Confidential*. He retired in 1965 and died of lung cancer nineteen years later at the age of seventy-three.

Like his brother Lionel, his significant musical contribution to Hollywood was not as composer but as conductor and arranger. The list of movies he wrote music for is generally unimpressive; the same can be said for the music. The exceptions are *A Song Is Born*, *Island in the Sky*, and *Hondo*, and those each had two credited composers. Newman's solo efforts—*Quiet Please: Murder*, *Chicago Confidential*, *Unwed Mother*, and *Riot in Juvenile Prison*—are B movies of the most undistinguished kind. Yet before one dismisses Emil Newman as the underachiever in a prominent family, it is best to recall that he directed the music for dozens of movies, some of them enduring classics.

Credits

(all films USA)

Year	Film	Director
1942	Careful, Soft Shoulder	Oliver H. P. Garrett
1942	Dr. Renault's Secret	Harry Lachman
1942	Quiet Please: Murder	John Larkin
1942	Time to Kill	Herbert I. Leeds
1942	Over My Dead Body	Malcolm St. Clair
1943	Tonight We Raid Calais	John Brahm
1948	A Song Is Born	Howard Hawks
1948	Jungle Patrol	Joseph M. Newman
1950	Guilty of Treason	Felix E. Feist
1950	Woman on the Run	Norman Foster
1951	The Groom Wore Spurs	Richard Whorf
1951	The Lady Says No	Frank Ross
1952	Japanese War Bride	King Vidor
1953	War Paint	Lesley Selander
1953	Island in the Sky	William A. Wellman
1953	99 River Street	Phil Karlson
1953	The Steel Lady	Ewald André Dupont
1953	Hondo	John Farrow
1954	Beachhead	Stuart Heisler
1954	Southwest Passage	Ray Nazarro
1954	The Mad Magician	John Brahm
1954	Ring of Fear	James Edward Grant, William
1955	The Naked Street	Maxwell Shane
1957	The Iron Sheriff	Sidney Salkow
1957	Chicago Confidential	Sidney Salkow
1957	Death in Small Doses	Joseph M. Newman
1958	Hong Kong Confidential	Edward L. Cahn
1958	Unwed Mother	Walter Goniger
1959	Riot in Juvenile Prison	Edward L. Cahn
1965	The Great Sioux Massacre	Sidney Salkow

NEWMAN, Lionel (1916–1989) A prominent musical arranger, conductor, songwriter, and composer from the distinguished musical family of Hollywood, he may have scored fewer films than his brothers but he had a prolific career supervising the music in over 250 movies.

Lionel Newman was born in New Haven, Connecticut, the youngest son of poor Russian immigrant parents. Newman dropped out of school at the age of fifteen to work as a pianist accompanying singers (including Mae West) in vaudeville and was still in his teens when he conducted Manhattan stage productions by impresario Earl Carroll. After working as a pianist and conductor of Newman's Society Orchestra on an ocean liner, he went to Hollywood where his elder brother Alfred was composing scores at Twentieth Century-Fox. He rose from rehearsal pianist to musical director and studio vice president during his forty-six years at Fox, taking over the music for television production as well from 1959 to 1985. Newman's first solo composing credit at the studio was the James Stewart comedy *The Jackpot* in 1950, followed by others but Fox was more interested in his conducting and arranging skills than his original compositions. Despite the greater fame his brother Alfred received, Newman was not overlooked by Hollywood. He received Academy Award nominations for adapting and arranging music for the musicals *I'll Get By* (1950), *There's No Business Like Show Business* (1954), *The Best Things in Life Are Free* (1956), and *Doctor Doolittle* (1967), for the songs "The Cowboy and the Lady" (lyric Arthur Quenzer) from the 1938 film of the same name and "Never" (lyric by Eliot Daniel) in *Golden Girl* (1951), and for his soundtrack scores for *Mardi Gras*, *Say One for Me*, *Let's Make Love*, and *The Pleasure Seekers* (1964). Newman's only Oscar win from a dozen nominations was his arranging (with Lennie Hayton) and conducting of the music for *Hello, Dolly!* (1969). Among the other movies he scored are *A Kiss Before Dying*, *Love Me Tender*, *Kiss Them for Me*, *The Girl Can't Help It*, *Bernadine*, *Compulsion*, *North to Alaska*, and *The Boston Strangler*. He supervised the music in hundreds of television episodes and composed the theme song for a handful of them. Newman was also a successful songwriter whose hit songs include "Again," "Daniel Boone," and "As If I Didn't Have Enough on My Mind." In the 1980s he took up conducting symphony orchestras around the world then retired in 1985 and died four years later at the age of seventy-three. A scholarship for young classical conductors is named in his honor, as is the music building at Twentieth Century-Fox.

While Alfred Newman was known as the pioneering Hollywood composer, Lionel was considered one of the sharpest, most dedicated, and best music men in the business. He was a perfectionist who raised the level of musicianship at Fox to a high level, making its studio orchestra arguably the best in Hollywood. Of the thirty feature films he contributed original music to, many were in collaboration with others so it is difficult to assess Newman the composer. Most of his solo efforts were comedies or westerns and often it is the arrangement of the music that impresses more than the originality of the score. In the Civil War drama, *Love Me Tender*, for example, Newman takes some traditional American folk songs and arranges them into an effective score. His stirring rendition of "Aura Lee" sounded new and, turned into the title song, it provided a hit for Elvis Presley in his screen debut. From square dances and military marches to romantic passages and solemn hymns, the score is pure Americana, although only sections are original. *Mardi Gras*, another musical featuring a pop chart singer (Pat Boone), is set in contemporary New Orleans and Newman again uses traditional jazz and blues in his score. Sammy Fain and Paul Francis Webster wrote eight forgettable songs for the movie, which slow the story down while Newman's soundtrack score tries to keep the locale alive. There is even sassy striptease music for Barrie Chase's nightclub act that sounds more like the Big Easy than all of Boone's singing about Bourbon Street. Another Boone vehicle, *Bernadine*, was supposedly a candid look at teenagers in 1956 but it was mostly a string of pop songs written for Boone. Newman's soundtrack score is more substantial with themes that better reflected the older generation than the kids.

The Pleasure Seekers, a remake of *Three Coins in the Fountain* but set in Madrid instead of Rome, has a spunky jazz score with touches of Spanish trumpets, guitars, and maracas to maintain the right atmosphere. Newman wrote some lovely romantic passages for the film, including a dreamy theme heard at the Prado Museum that is as beguiling as the paintings. The Jayne Mansfield musical *The Girl Can't Help It* is filled with pop-rock numbers sung by Little Richard, the Platters, Fats Domino, and others, while the soundtrack score by Newman is more interested in blues and jazz. The same kind of sound can be found in his scores for the Doris Day vehicles *Do Not*

Disturb and *Move Over Darling* and Marilyn Monroe's last outing, *Let's Make Love*. Newman was able to be a bit more ambitious with his noncomedies. The thriller *A Kiss Before Dying* has romantic passages with a somber subtext, just as the psychotic killer (Robert Wagner) has a charming demeanor and a deadly purpose. Yet when he strikes, the music is all harsh brass and screaming violins. Two similarly psychotic murderers (Dean Stockwell and Bradford Dillman) are examined in *Compulsion* based on the Leopold and Loeb case of a thrill killing. The jazzy main theme picks up on the dangerously carefree attitude of the young killers as trumpets blare senselessly and

saxophones laugh. Much of *Compulsion* is unscored as dictated by the documentary look and feel of the movie but when music hits it does so with a wallop. The main theme for *The St. Valentine's Day Massacre* is a chaotic jazz piece for piano and percussion. The violent scenes are mostly done without music and again Newman adapts some period tunes to fit into the melodrama. After all those comedies and musicals, Newman must have enjoyed sinking his teeth into grittier stuff. Yet legend has it that he was such a perfectionist that every project was important to him. Perhaps that, rather than his original music, is his legacy.

Credits

(all films USA)

Year	Film	Director
1950	The Jackpot	Walter Lang
1953	The Silver Whip	Harmon Jones
1953	Powder River	Louis King
1954	Siege at Red River	Rudolph Maté
1954	The Rocket Man	Oscar Rudolph
1954	Princess of the Nile	Harmon Jones
1954	The Gambler from Natchez	Henry Levin
1956	The Killer Is Loose	Budd Boetticher
1956	The Proud Ones	Robert D. Webb
1956	A Kiss Before Dying	Gerd Oswald
1956	The Last Wagon	Delmer Daves
1956	Love Me Tender	Robert D. Webb
1956	The Girl Can't Help It	Frank Tashlin
1957	The Way to the Gold	Robert D. Webb
1957	Bernadine	Henry Levin
1957	Kiss Them for Me	Stanley Donen
1958	Sing Boy Sing	Henry Ephron
1958	The Bravados	Henry King
1958	Mardi Gras (AAN)	Edmund Goulding
1959	Compulsion	Richard Fleischer
1959	Say One for Me	Frank Tashlin
1960	Let's Make Love (AAN)	George Cukor
1960	North to Alaska	Henry Hathaway
1963	Move Over, Darling	Michael Gordon
1964	The Pleasure Seekers (AAN)	Jean Negulesco
1965	Do Not Disturb	Ralph Levy
1967	The St. Valentine's Day Massacre	Roger Corman
1968	The Boston Strangler	Richard Fleischer

NEWMAN, Randy (b. 1943) Although he has not scored nearly as many movies as other members of his illustrious musical family, the pop songwriter, singer, and composer has written some outstanding film scores and has been duly recognized for his work.

Born Randall Stuart Newman in Los Angeles, he is the son of Irving Newman, a physician in the military who liked to write songs on occasion. The young Newman was born into Hollywood's most celebrated musical family. His uncles Alfred, Lionel, and Emil Newman were prolific

RANDY NEWMAN. Although he made a name for himself as a pop singer-songwriter, the Newman family's gravitation to screen scoring must have been strong and he ended up writing for Hollywood and doing very well for himself. His two dozen movies have brought him sixteen Oscar nominations and two wins. *Dreamworks / Photofest © Dreamworks LLC*

screen composers and his cousins Thomas, Joey, Maria, Tim, and David Newman also made their mark in movie music. Newman was only a week old when the family moved to a military base near New Orleans, his mother's hometown. When Newman was seven years old, his father left the military and the family returned to Los Angeles, where he became a noted physician to Hollywood stars. Young Newman took piano lessons as a child and started writing pop songs when he was a teenager. Before he graduated from high school, he already had a contract as a staff composer at Liberty Records. He went on to study music theory and composition at UCLA before having his first song hit, "I Think It's Going to Rain Today," recorded by Judy Collins and many others. Other song hits recorded by famous singers followed, as well as albums featuring Newman as composer, arranger, and singer.

Television producer Norman Lear hired Newman to score his feature film comedy *Cold Turkey* in 1971 but the movie was a flop and the experience soured Newman on screen scoring so he returned to pop music. A decade later he scored the West German film *Herbstkatzen*, then had success later that same year with the film *Ragtime*. Newman not only wrote the score but created the ragtime tunes that the main character (Howard E. Rollins Jr.) plays in a Harlem nightclub. The score and the song "One More Hour" were nominated for Oscars and Newman was now in the family business of screen music. Praise for his music in *The Natural, Parenthood, Avalon, Awakenings*, and other movies secured his career but it was Newman's scores for Pixar Animation that pushed him to the top ranks of Hollywood success. For the first Pixar feature, *Toy Story*, Newman wrote an exciting score as well as such delectable songs as "I Will Go Sailing No More" and "You've Got a Friend in Me." He also scored the two *Toy Story* sequels as well as the Pixar hits *A Bug's Life, Monsters, Inc., Cars*, and *Monsters University*. For the Disney animated movies *James and the Giant Peach* and *The Princess and the Frog*, Newman wrote radiant scores and several sparkling songs. His other live-action movies include *Pleasantville, Meet the Parents*, and its sequel *Meet the Fockers*. Newman has not turned out movie scores as frequently as his uncles or cousins because of his extensive recording and concert career but his contribution to cinema music is substantial.

Because he grew up in New Orleans clubs and Hollywood recording studios and heard a good deal of jazz in the former and movie scores in the latter, Newman's music for the screen is a pleasant blending of both sounds. Certainly both can be found in his lovely score for *Ragtime*, which has twinkling waltzes, soft and aggressive rags, and a felicitous love theme. Although the baseball fairy tale *The Natural* is set in the 1920s and 1930s, the music evokes a timeless fantasy world rather than the real one. The score encompasses many different moods, but it is all of one piece as a symphony with different movements. The simple, grassroots theme for the innocent boy on the farm develops into the more romantic love theme, which then expands into the inspiring main theme that lives and breathes victory. The nostalgic *Avalon*, about growing up in Baltimore in the 1940s, uses a simple minor-key waltz played on a piano. Strings are added for the more dramatic sequences but it remains a quiet and entrancing score. The music for *Awakenings* is similarly low key with another minor-key waltz. The score begins with a melancholy tone as the catatonic patients are portrayed with tender affection. As the miracle drug allows them (temporarily) to become normal, the music grows more optimistic. Newman's score for the western *Maverick* avoids Wild West clichés and opts instead for a mellow score that seems inspired by Aaron Copland's rural music. Jazz is predominant in his score for the urban comedy-drama *The Paper*. Interestingly, none of these scores suggest that Newman was a very popular pop singer and songwriter. They are all masterful in the conventional movie music tradition.

It is in his scores for the Pixar films that Newman the pop icon emerges. Jazz can be found in most of them but also a lot of Broadway, pop, blues, and old-time Tin Pan Alley are used effectively. Since the attention usually goes to the songs in these computer-animated movies, one sometimes forgets how delightful the soundtrack scores are. The three *Toy Story* movies are filled with farcical and slapstick music that comments on the films' comedy and action. But each also has at least one heartbreaking theme, such as the "I Will Go Sailing No More" theme in the first installment, the torchy "When She Loved Me" theme in the second, and the nostalgic "We Belong Together" theme in the third, which aches with bittersweet emotion. The two *Monsters, Inc.* movies concentrate more on comedy than pathos and both have a lively, fun-filled score. The first film uses Dixieland jazz, while the second, *Monsters University*, is filled with collegiate musical pastiches, including a fight song, a marching band piece, frat house party music, and an alma mater, all done tongue in cheek and with glee. Perhaps Newman's finest score for an animated movie is the rich and flavorful one he wrote for Disney's *The Princess and the Frog*. Since the story is set in New Orleans and the surrounding bayou, Newman was on his home turf, so to speak. The songs embrace Cajun folk, Dixieland jazz, gospel, Creole chanting, hillbilly ditties, and other sounds he grew up with in Louisiana. The soundtrack score encompasses some of these but also contains gliding waltzes, mystical hymns, vivacious suspense music, and comic passages. It many ways the score for *The Princess and the Frog* summarizes the essence of Newman's musical talents.

One must keep in mind that movie music is only one portion of Newman's career. He has written songs for television, other composers' films, and special occasions, such as his album *Louisiana 1927* as a fund-raiser after Hurricane Katrina in his beloved New Orleans. Newman has even attempted theatre scoring, writing the rock-pop opera *Randy Newman's Faust*, which premiered in California in 1995. A sly biographical musical, *The Education of Randy Newman*, and the theatre revues *Maybe I'm Doing It Wrong* (1982) and *Harps and Angels* (2010) were composed of Newman's songs from his albums and movies. Until the Pixar films, he was considered more a pop artist than a screen composer. Today he is among Hollywood's top music makers. Biographies: *Randy Newman's American Dreams*, Kevin Courrier (2005); *Randy Newman in Person*, Mat Snow (2011). Official website: www.randynewman.com.

Credits

(all films USA unless stated otherwise; * for Best Song)

Year	Film	Director
1971	Cold Turkey	Norman Lear
1981	Herbstkatzen	Rainer Klaholz (W. Germany)
1981	Ragtime (AAN, AAN*; GGN*; BAFTA-N*)	Milos Forman
1984	The Natural (AAN)	Barry Levinson
1989	Parenthood (AAN*; GGN*)	Ron Howard
1990	Avalon (AAN; GGN)	Barry Levinson
1990	Awakenings	Penny Marshall
1994	The Paper (AAN*)	Ron Howard
1994	Maverick	Richard Donner
1995	Toy Story (AAN, AAN*; GGN*)	John Lasseter
1996	James and the Giant Peach (AAN)	Henry Selick (UK/USA)
1996	Michael	Nora Ephron
1998	Pleasantville (AAN)	Gary Ross
1998	Babe: Pig in the City (AAN*)	George Miller (Australia)
1998	A Bug's Life (AAN; GGN)	John Lasseter, Andrew Stanton
1999	Toy Story 2 (AAN*; GGN*)	Ash Brannon, John Lasseter, Lee Unkrich
2000	Meet the Parents (AAN*)	Jay Roach
2001	Monsters, Inc.(AA*, AAN)	Pete Docter, David Silverman, Lee Unkrich
2003	Seabiscuit	Gary Ross
2004	Meet the Fockers	Jay Roach
2006	Cars (AAN*)	John Lasseter, Joe Ranft
2008	Leatherheads	George Clooney (USA/Germany)
2009	The Princess and the Frog (AAN*)	Ron Clements, John Musker
2010	Toy Story 3 (AA*)	Lee Unkrich
2013	Monsters University	Dan Scanlon

NEWMAN, Thomas (b. 1955) A second-generation member of the celebrated Newman family of screen composers, he has scored nearly one hundred feature films since 1984 and has been nominated for Oscars eleven times.

Thomas Montgomery Newman was born in Los Angeles, the youngest son of acclaimed Hollywood composer Alfred Newman. (His siblings are composers-musicians David and Maria Newman; his uncles are screen composers

Lionel and Emil Newman; and his cousins are movie-television composers Randy and Joey Newman.) He took violin and piano lessons as a boy and later studied music at the University of Southern California and Yale University. Newman began his career writing musicals Off-Broadway then played keyboard for the rock band Innocents and the improv combo Tokyo 77. He first worked in television when his uncle Lionel hired him to score an episode of the series *The Paper Chase* in 1979. Composer John Williams, a friend of the Newman family, then asked him to help orchestrate parts of his score for *Star Wars: Episode VI—Return of the Jedi* (1983). The next year Newman wrote his first feature film score, composing the music for the teen comedy-drama *Reckless*. But it was his score for the quirky *Desperately Seeking Susan* in 1985 that brought Newman his first wide recognition. Unfortunately he was subsequently given mediocre movies to score and did not have another success until *Fried Green Tomatoes* in 1991. Newman's luck changed and over the next two decades he was handed many first-class projects, including *The Player, Scent of a Woman, The Shawshank Redemption* (which earned him his first of many Oscar nominations), *Little Women, The Horse Whisperer, American Beauty, The Green Mile, Erin Brockovich, Road to Perdition, Lemony Snicket's A Series of Unfortunate Events, Cinderella Man, The Good German, The Help, The Iron Lady, The Best Exotic Marigold Hotel, Skyfall,* and *Saving Mr. Banks,* as well as the Pixar animated hits *Finding Nemo* and *WALL-E.* He has also composed music for television series, such as *Amazing Stories, Six Feet Under,* and *The Newsroom,* and TV movies, as with *Citizen Cohn* (1992) and *Angels in America* (2003). Newman has also written for the concert hall, most memorably his orchestral work *It Got Dark* (2009).

Newman's screen music is characterized by a fusion of a full orchestral sound with the modern sound of the synthesizer. He favors the percussion section in much of his music and he has a special interest in the zither, hammered dulcimer, and other nonorchestral instruments. For quieter sections in his score he often features the piano which he insists on playing himself during the recording sessions. Generally his scores tend to be subtle rather than dramatic, atmospheric rather than melodic. Newman's music may not jump out at one and, because of this, his work is often nominated but has not won an Oscar. Even his first score, for *Reckless,* has some interesting experi-

ments. Chimes and bells are worked into the rock score and the strong percussion line is vigorous and bold with variations in color. The contemporary comedy-drama *Desperately Seeking Susan* is filled with inventive touches. Again the score is rock but the unexpected use of percussion (xylophone, tin cans, hammer on metal, cow bells, clanging pipes, etc.) give this offbeat movie a musical edginess. Synthesized chords and scales are added for some passages and an electric keyboard conveys the loose-living kind of romance in the story. By the time Newman scored the rural melodrama *Fried Green Tomatoes,* he had turned to a more conventional orchestra but avoided the symphonic grandeur that was inappropriate for the setting and the characters. There are some delightful honky-tonk passages, a lovely theme heard on woodwinds and harp, some blues sections that move briskly, and piano and guitar solos that are extremely lyrical and engaging. *The Player,* on the other hand, is an urban and slick tale about Hollywood, and the jazzy score is often chaotic and dissonant. The percussion used this time is rapid and tribal, mixed with a furious piano and plenty of electric sounds. If it wasn't so rhythmic and satisfying, it might even be described as atonal and avant-garde. For the period piece *Little Women,* Newman let a trumpet and strings carry the simple, hymnlike main theme. While not quite a pastiche of nineteenth-century parlor songs, the music draws one into the period all the same. The score also has some spirited passages that echo the life-affirming personality of Jo March (Wynona Ryder) and a sparkling theme in which the flutes imitate the chirping of birds.

The score for the prison drama *The Shawshank Redemption* was a turning point in some ways for Newman. The music is a series of somber themes that rarely break out into melody. The low bass strings heard under sorrowful violins are poetic rather than depressing, as are the tender passages played on the piano. The quiet frustration and resignation of prison life is conveyed through sustained notes that linger before trying to resolve themselves into a conclusion. Only at the end of the movie, when the wrongly accused hero (Tim Robbins) is free, does the score soar and complete the musical ideas that were heard earlier in fragments. Just as *The Shawshank Redemption* was not a success when first released and later became a cult favorite, so too the score was not fully appreciated in 1994 (though it was nominated by the Academy) and is now considered one of Newman's best. A movie and score that was an immediate hit with audiences was *American Beauty*, a sardonic look at empty lives in suburbia. Newman scores this tragicomic tale with a percussive sound. The main theme is a five-note musical phrase played on a marimba with accompaniment by steel guitar, mandolin, tabula, and other strident instruments. The repetitive pattern is structured like an improv jazz piece, building in intensity in its own meandering way. When the antihero (Kevin Spacey) fantasizes about the teenage nymphet he has met, the percussion shifts to harp, piano, and softer instruments. What makes the *American Beauty* score so satisfying is how Newman finds endless variety within his limiting the music to the percussion section. *The Green Mile*, another prison film, is scored with little percussion and relies mostly on strings with some help from a solo flute, oboe, and piano sections. The main theme is a graceful lament with a touch of mystery to it, setting up the mystical powers of the inmate John Coffey (Michael Clarke Duncan). The long sustained strings and the wavering woodwinds provide a vivid contrast to the desolate setting yet hint that something magical can happen here. The scoring for an execution scene is a series of sharp and oppressive chords that are perhaps too effective. In contrast, there is a lighter and frolicsome theme for the pet mouse Mr. Jingles that is played on the xylophone with plucked strings joining in. The Depression-era gangster movie *Road to Perdition* is also heavy moviegoing and it also has a superior score. The main theme is a flowing and evocative piece of romanticism built around a four-note phrase. The same theme is speeded up later in the film to accommodate the revenge plot. Once again Newman introduces an Irish harp, penny whistles, and other unconventional instruments into an orchestral score.

The lighter side of Newman's music can be heard in the cartoonish *Lemony Snicket's A Series of Unfortunate Events*. This unorthodox children's tale is often scored with Middle Eastern instruments, giving the darkly comic events an exotic quality and adding to the fairy-tale nature of the plot. The sinister Count Olaf (Jim Carrey) is scored with scampering woodwinds and plucked violins, suggesting a playful kind of evil. When Olaf tries to eliminate the Baudelaire orphans by locking them in a car left on the railroad tracks, Newman uses electric static, quivering strings, and chimes to score the approaching train. Less gruesome is the animated adventure *Finding Nemo*, which takes place mostly underwater. At times Newman's score cleverly echoes and reverberates as sound does when it travels in water. There are many aquatic characters in the movie and several are given their own theme. The scatterbrained blue tang fish Dory (voice of Ellen Degeneres) has a daffy motif in which strings and brass jump all over the scale. The comic sharks are scored with kettle drums and low strings, a spoof of the famous shark theme John Williams wrote for *Jaws* (1975). A forest of jellyfish has a swirling theme in which strings dance a furious exotic dance, a stream of sea turtles is given a lazy habanera, and so on in an endlessly imaginative way. Music plays an unusually important role in another Pixar film, *WALL-E*, which has little dialogue in its first half. The tireless little robot WALL-E is left on the abandoned planet Earth to collect and compact mountains of trash. Newman gives this plucky character a rhythmic theme that is plucked on strings while an oboe works its way up and down the scale. The feminine space probe EVE who steals his heart has a lilting theme played on strings and harp. Their romance is scored with passionate music that humanizes the mechanical characters. Newman spoofs the famous *2001: A Space Odyssey* opening, pastiches a Burt Bacharach bossa nova, and adds electronic sounds and voices to the music, giving *WALL-E* a silly side to offset the film's serious message about wasting the planet. Whether scoring a grim drama or an animated fantasy, Newman's creativity and experimentation is unflagging. He may not turn out "hit" scores that are easily consumed by the public but filmmakers know that he is among the best contemporary composers when it comes to serving the movie.

Credits

(all films USA unless stated otherwise; * for Best Song)

Year	Film	Director
1984	*Reckless*	James Foley
1984	*Revenge of the Nerds*	Jeff Kanew

Year	Film	Director
1984	*Grandview, U.S.A.*	Randal Kleiser
1985	*Desperately Seeking Susan*	Susan Seidelman
1985	*Girls Just Want to Have Fun*	Alan Metter
1985	*The Man with One Red Shoe*	Stan Dragoti
1985	*Real Genius*	Martha Coolidge
1986	*Gung Ho*	Ron Howard
1986	*Jumpin' Jack Flash*	Penny Marshall
1987	*Light of Day* (aka *Born in the U.S.A.*)	Paul Schrader
1987	*The Lost Boys*	Joel Schumacher
1987	*Less Than Zero*	Marek Kanievska
1988	*The Prince of Pennsylvania*	Ron Nyswaner
1988	*The Great Outdoors* (aka *Big Country*)	Howard Deutch
1989	*Cookie*	Susan Seidelman
1990	*Men Don't Leave*	Paul Brickman
1990	*Naked Tango*	Leonard Schrader (Argentina/Switzerland/Japan/USA)
1990	*Welcome Home, Roxy Carmichael*	Jim Abrahams (UK/USA)
1991	*Career Opportunities*	Bryan Gordon
1991	*The Rapture*	Michael Tolkin
1991	*Deceived*	Damian Harris
1991	*The Linguini Incident*	Richard Shepard
1991	*Fried Green Tomatoes*	Jon Avnet
1992	*The Player*	Robert Altman
1992	*Whispers in the Dark*	Christopher Crowe
1992	*Scent of a Woman*	Martin Brest
1993	*Flesh and Bone*	Steve Kloves
1993	*Josh and S.A.M.*	Billy Weber
1994	*Threesome*	Andrew Fleming
1994	*The Favor*	Donald Petrie
1994	*The Shawshank Redemption* (AAN)	Frank Darabont
1994	*The War*	Jon Avnet
1994	*Little Women* (AAN)	Gillian Armstrong (USA/Canada)
1995	*Unstrung Heroes* (AAN)	Diane Keaton
1995	*How to Make an American Quilt*	Jocelyn Moorhouse
1996	*Up Close & Personal* (aka *Golden Girl*)	Jon Avnet
1996	*Phenomenon*	Jon Turteltaub
1996	*American Buffalo*	Michael Corrente (UK/USA)
1996	*The People vs. Larry Flynt*	Milos Forman
1997	*Mad City*	Costa-Gavras
1997	*Red Corner*	Jon Avnet
1997	*Oscar and Lucinda*	Gillian Armstrong (USA/Australia/UK)
1998	*The Horse Whisperer*	Robert Redford
1998	*Meet Joe Black*	Martin Brest
1999	*American Beauty* (AAN; GGN; BAFTA)	Sam Mendes
1999	*The Green Mile*	Frank Darabont
2000	*Erin Brockovich*	Steven Soderbergh
2000	*My Khmer Heart*	Janine Hosking (Australia)
2000	*Pay It Forward*	Mimi Leder
2001	*In the Bedroom*	Todd Field
2002	*The Execution of Wanda Jean*	Liz Garbus
2002	*The Salton Sea*	D. J. Caruso
2002	*Road to Perdition* (AAN)	Sam Mendes
2002	*White Oleander*	Peter Kosminsky
2003	*Finding Nemo* (AAN)	Andrew Stanton, Lee Unkrich
2004	*Lemony Snicket's A Series of Unfortunate Events* (AAN)	Brad Silberling (USA/Germany)
2005	*Cinderella Man*	Ron Howard
2005	*Jarhead*	Sam Mendes (Germany/USA)
2006	*Little Children*	Todd Field

Year	Film	Director
2006	*The Good German* (AAN)	Steven Soderbergh
2007	*Towelhead* (aka *Nothing Is Private*)	Alan Bell
2008	*WALL-E* (AAN*; GGN*; BAFTA-N)	Andrew Stanton
2008	*Revolutionary Road*	Sam Mendes (USA/UK)
2009	*Brothers*	Jim Sheridan
2010	*The Debt*	John Madden (USA/UK/Hungary)
2011	*The Adjustment Bureau*	George Nolfi
2011	*The Help* (GGN*)	Tate Taylor (USA/India/United Arab Emirates)
2011	*The Best Exotic Marigold Hotel*	John Madden (UK/USA/United Arab Emirates)
2011	*The Iron Lady*	Phyllida Lloyd (UK/France)
2012	*Skyfall* (AAN; BAFTA)	Sam Mendes (UK/USA)
2013	*Saving Mr. Banks* (AAN; BAFTA-N)	John Lee Hancock (USA/UK/Australia)
2013	*Side Effects*	Steven Soderbergh

NIEHAUS, Lennie (b. 1929) A celebrated jazz saxophonist, arranger, and composer, he has written scores for eighteen feature films, almost all of them directed by Clint Eastwood.

Born Leonard Niehaus in St. Louis, Missouri, his father was an accomplished violinist and his sister a concert pianist. Niehaus began violin lessons when he was seven, later studied the bassoon, then as a teenager took up the clarinet and saxophone. After studying music at Los Angeles City College and Los Angeles State College, Niehaus began his music career playing in jazz clubs in Southern California. His first job with a name band was touring with Stan Kenton, with whom he performed for five years (interrupted by a two-year stint in the army) and for whom he also wrote arrangements and original music. In 1959, Niehaus began arranging music for record studios, working with such popular singers as Mel Tormé, the King Sisters, and Dean Martin. He later created a series of esteemed jazz recordings with such prominent artists as Mel Lewis, Shelly Manne, Hampton Hawes, and Jimmy Giuffre. Niehaus first got involved with movies in 1962 when he started doing arrangements for film composer Jerry Fielding. Soon he was in great demand in Hollywood, doing the arrangements and conducting the music for dozens of movies and television shows. Niehaus met Clint Eastwood in the 1950s while both were serving in the military. Their mutual admiration for jazz made them friends as each pursued different careers. Decades later, when Eastwood was coproducer for the crime mystery *Tightrope*, he asked Niehaus to write the music. The 1984 film was his first screen score and was followed by thirteen more movies with Eastwood as director, among them *Pale Rider*, *Heartbreak Ridge*, *The Rookie*, *Bird*, *Unforgiven*, *A Perfect World*, *Midnight in the Garden of Good and Evil*, *Absolute Power*, *The Bridges of Madison County*, and *Space Cowboys*. When Eastwood started composing his own scores for his movies, Niehaus continued to orchestrate and conduct some of them, as with *Mystic River* (2003), *Million Dollar Baby* (2004), *Flags of Our Fathers* (2006), and *Changeling* (2008). He has scored a few movies for other directors, most memorably *City Heat* and *Sesame Street Presents: Follow That Bird*, as well as some television series and nine TV movies, including *The Child Saver* (1988), *Lush Life* (1993), *Crazy Horse* (1996), *Titanic* (1996), *No Laughing Matter* (1998), *Jack Bull* (1999), and *Mitch Albom's For One Day More* (2007). Niehaus has written, arranged, and/or played alto saxophone for many acclaimed jazz pieces, among them *Spiritual Jazz Suite*, three *Christmas Jazz* suites, saxophone duets and quartets, and *I Swing for You*.

As one might expect, some of Niehaus's screen scores utilize wonderful jazz, some of it original music and some consisting of jazz standards. The score for *Bird*, the commendable biopic about jazz saxophone great Charlie "Bird" Parker (Forest Whitaker), is almost completely the latter. Although Niehaus was listed as composer for the movie, there was very little original music. Instead he arranged new versions of some jazz favorites and played alto saxophone on some of them. Actual recordings by Parker filled out the score. Much the same thing happened in *City*

Heat, a comic action film in which a cop (Eastwood) and his rival, a private eye (Burt Reynolds), are forced to team up to solve a murder. Niehaus arranged some new jazz vocals that were sung by Irene Cara and Al Jarreau and even used an old Rudy Vallee recording on the soundtrack. Yet there is a marvelous "Montage Blues" that he wrote for the film, a silky smooth jazz-blues featuring three pianos and a soulful saxophone. There is plenty of original jazz in *The Rookie*, although much of it is a variation of the main theme. Eastwood again plays a seasoned cop but this time he is saddled with a rookie cop (Charlie Sheen) to chase down a German underworld figure (Raul Julia). The recurring theme is a rhythmic jazz piece featuring a solo trumpet and lots of Latin percussion that is zesty and lighthearted. The tempo is frantic and, since much of the film is an extended chase, the music propels the less-than-satisfying movie. Although not a jazz score, the music in *Midnight in the Garden of Good and Evil* is also made up of song standards. Niehaus is credited as composer for this murder mystery set in Savannah, Georgia, but again there is very little original music. Instead there are new versions and old recordings of songs by lyricist Johnny Mercer, Savannah's favorite son.

Surprisingly, some of Niehaus's most complete and pleasing screen scores do not use jazz at all. Instead they tend toward old-fashioned romanticism. *The Bridges of Madison County*, about a brief but passionate romance between a farmwife (Meryl Streep) and an itinerant photographer (Eastwood), has a romantic, low-key score, so beautifully presented that it gives the sentimental movie some class. Set in 1965, the film's soundtrack includes several hit recordings of the day, but it is Niehaus's love theme that is so splendid. It begins as a hesitant piano passage that is so shy it needs strings to play the full melody, a series of descending phrases. As the theme progresses, it grows in strength to become a no-holds-barred piece of romanticism. Eastwood assisted Niehaus in writing the instrumental piece which, as it returns throughout the film, is just about the whole original score. A crime drama with a nonjazz score is *A Perfect World*. Eastwood again represents the law as a U.S. Marshal but the heart of the movie is the relationship between an escaped convict (Kevin Costner) and the young boy

(T. J. Lowther) he kidnaps and then bonds with. The focal point of the score is a sweeping orchestral passage that repeats a catchy six-note phrase at different pitches and keys as it pulls the listener along. At one point a solo trumpet then oboe are featured in a gliding version of the theme that is soothing and comforting. There is also a track in which various strings slide up and down the scale with ease, then it is repeated on a harmonica. The tale is set in Texas, so one is not surprised to hear a jaunty theme played by a country-western band that moves at a carefree trot, a kind of oddball traveling music for this very unique film.

Unforgiven has been described as a nihilistic western or an antiwestern. It is certainly a dark, unromantic view of the Old West. It also inspired Niehaus to write what some consider his finest movie score. A jaded gunslinger (Eastwood) comes out of retirement and, with his old partner (Morgan Freeman) and a young blade (Jaimz Woolvett), sets out to get the cowboys who cut up a prostitute. The story and characters have a resigned tone, which Niehaus picks up on in his music. It is mostly a quiet, moody score with little of the expected western music, though on one track an echoing harmonica and strings play a lonely lament that has a touch of the folk song in it. The rest of the music is not very rural. There is a seething, restless theme with low woodwinds and reverberating electronic sounds; suspense music played by squawking brass, grumbling percussion, sustained strings, and some electronic accents; and a rambunctious passage with galloping percussion and angry brass. The villains are scored with sinister music played on weary strings, repeating brass phrases, and chime accents. More serene is a fully orchestrated theme with a sense of contentment as the music subtly flows up and down the scale.

The most memorable piece of music in *Unforgiven* is "Claudia's Theme" which was composed by Eastwood and Niehaus. It is a delicate ballad featuring a guitar duet that tentatively plays its simple but engaging melody. As Eastwood got more and more involved with writing music, it was not surprising that he began to score some of his own movies. As for Niehaus, he continued to arrange music for Eastwood and continued his estimable jazz career.

Credits

(all films USA and directed by Clint Eastwood unless stated otherwise)

Year	Film	Director
1984	*Tightrope*	Richard Tuggle
1984	*City Heat* (aka *Kansas City Heat*)	Richard Benjamin
1985	*Pale Rider*	
1985	*Sesame Street Presents: Follow That Bird*	Ken Kwapis
1986	*Never Too Young to Die*	Gil Bettman
1986	*Ratboy*	Sondra Locke
1986	*Heartbreak Ridge*	
1987	*Emanon*	Stuart Paul
1988	*Bird* (BAFTA-N)	
1990	*White Hunter Black Heart*	
1990	*The Rookie*	
1992	*Unforgiven*	
1993	*A Perfect World*	
1995	*The Bridges of Madison County*	
1997	*Absolute Power*	
1997	*Midnight in the Garden of Good and Evil*	
1999	*True Crime*	
2000	*Space Cowboys*	(USA/Australia)
2002	*Blood Work*	

NORDGREN, Erik (1913–1992) A Swedish conductor, musician, and composer who scored forty movies between 1945 and 1971, he is most known for his music in thirteen films by acclaimed director Ingmar Bergman.

He was born Herman Erik Nordgren in Sireköpinge, Sweden, and played violin as a child. Nordgren studied composition, conducting, and violin at the Royal Academy of Music in Stockholm, and after graduating in 1941 he became a music teacher. He was hired to score a Swedish screen version of *Crime and Punishment* in 1945 and two years later took up movie music in earnest, scoring *Woman without a Face* for director Gustaf Molander. Nordgren went on to collaborate with Molander on six more movies but his most famous collaboration was with Bergman, beginning with *Three Strange Love*s in 1949. The two men would be reunited for such screen classics as *Smiles of a Summer Night*, *The Seventh Seal*, *Secrets of Women*, *Wild Strawberries*, *The Magician*, *The Virgin Spring*, and *Through a Glass Darkly*. Beginning in 1948, Nordgren served as a music consultant for the record company EMI-HMV and four years later was named music director for the film studio Svensk Filmindustri, a position he retained until 1967. Nordgren left movies in the late 1960s to conduct the orchestra for the Swedish Broadcasting Corporation. He returned to the cinema one last time in 1971 to write the score for Jan Troell's international success *The Emigrants*. For the concert hall, Nordgren wrote a symphony, chamber music, string quartets, clarinet and bassoon concertos, and art songs. He retired from television conducting in 1976 but remained active writing music for the concert hall until his death sixteen years later.

While Nordgren's music might be labeled chilly and Nordic, particularly in Bergman's darker movies, he is often attracted to vigorous marches, lively dance music, and spirited string movements. One element found throughout much of his work is the use of the harp for the main melody line or to add color to otherwise bleak passages. Nordgren has been favorably compared to Finnish composer Jean Sibelius, not just because both are Scandinavian but for a similarity of tone in their chamber and small-scale musical pieces. *The Seventh Seal* is the movie that brought Bergman international celebrity. There is relatively little music in the movie, and when it appears it is reduced to short passages. The film opens with a brief choral quotation from the "Dies Irae" then a few chords return for the various appearances of Death. The Knight (Max von Sydow) has a restrained medieval theme that suggests the plodding of horse hooves. In the midst of this very quiet allegory is a very musical section: a traveling player performs a zesty dance tune on a simple pipe, a lusty and crude folk song is sung by two revelers imitating animal sounds, and a procession of peasants sing a fervent religious chant pleading for refuge from the plague. *The Seventh Seal* ends with the memorable Dance of Death, but it is a nearly silent dance and the movies concludes with a few measures of celestial singing. Quiet in a different way is the memory drama *Wild Strawberries*, which Nordgren scored with Göte Lovén. Music is sometimes used to jar memories, other times to re-create them. The score takes its cue from the ticking of a clock and the tolling of bells. An aged professor (Victor Sjöström) travels to the past even as he travels across the countryside. Scenes from his younger days are scored with lyrical passages, alternately warm and somber. A piano is sometimes used; a solo harp or violin enter at other moments. When the professor is given an honorary degree, there is a march and a processional, but both seem empty. These two films might be described as examples of muted scoring at its chilliest.

Even Bergman's period comedy *Smiles of a Summer Night* is stingy with its music, although most of it is very sprightly and engaging. This delicious comedy of manners about love lost, strayed, and recovered among a group of nineteenth-century Swedes has a bittersweet tone that makes it uniquely beguiling. The opening credits are accompanied by a waltzing art song sung by a choir. A ride in a carriage is given a robust and regal treatment, while a ride in a rowboat is given a romantic string passage. There is a satirical march theme for a pompous count (Jarl Kulle) and a sorrowful lament played under a scene when two women (Ulla Jacobsson and Margit Carlqvist) weep over the inconstancy of their husbands. A harp is used to convey the elegance and the tension of a formal dinner in the country. Nordgren's score for Bergman's *The Magician*, about a traveling magic show, is more distant yet suspenseful with lonesome guitar chords and the occasional beating of tympani used throughout the movie. But again music is used sparingly. One starts to suspect that the true score for a Bergman film is silence broken with sound effects such as waves crashing on the shore, clocks ticking, thunder exploding, birds chirping, or a mournful wind blowing. Ironically, after Nordgren and the director parted ways in 1961, Bergman married a musician and started using classical music in his movies, so much so that in 1974 he made his glorious film version of Mozart's *The Magic Flute*. As for Nordgren, one has to look at the non-Bergman films to hear a substantial musical score. Jan Troell's *The Emigrants* gives one that opportunity. This leisurely but potent movie, about how a group of Swedish farmers struggle in vain before deciding to immigrate to America, is hardly overflowing with music but what is there is effective. A stern church hymn sets up the stubborn, proud temperament of the people, then Nordgren introduces some minor-key themes that express the difficulty of their lives. A rhythmic folk song helps relieve some of the tension and the arrival in America is scored with optimism, though it is clear that difficulties lie ahead. Troell's drama *Here's Your Life*, a coming-of-age tale set among the working-class folk during World War I, also uses a church organ, although it is not so oppressive. Nordgren experiments with distorted music and sound effects in this score, something he also did in his concert work. Perhaps the concert hall is the correct venue for Nordgren. His movie music is not overwhelming enough to be much noticed, which is perhaps the way he and his directors wanted it.

Credits

(all films Sweden unless stated otherwise)

Year	Film	Director
1945	Crime and Punishment	Hampe Faustman
1947	Woman without a Face	Gustaf Molander
1948	Life Starts Now	Gustaf Molander
1948	Eva	Gustaf Molander
1949	Three Strange Loves (aka Thirst)	Ingmar Bergman
1949	Love Will Conquer	Gustaf Molander
1950	This Can't Happen Here (aka High Tension)	Ingmar Bergman
1951	Summer Interlude (aka Illicit Interlude)	Ingmar Bergman
1951	Divorced	Gustaf Molander

Year	Film	Director
1952	*Defiance*	Gustaf Molander
1953	*Waiting Women*	Ingmar Bergman
1953	*Dance, My Doll*	Martin Soderhjelm
1953	*Hidden in the Fog*	Lars-Eric Kjellgren
1953	*Unmarried*	Gustaf Molander
1954	*Gabrielle*	Hasse Ekman
1955	*Vald*	Lars-Eric Kjellgren
1955	*Smiles of a Summer Night*	Ingmar Bergman
1956	*Egen ingang*	Hasse Ekman
1957	*The Seventh Seal*	Ingmar Bergman
1957	*Wild Strawberries*	Ingmar Bergman
1958	*Bock i örtagard*	Gösta Folke
1958	*Playing on the Rainbow*	Lars-Eric Kjellgren
1958	*The Magician*	Ingmar Bergman
1959	*Face of Fire*	Albert Band (Sweden/USA)
1959	*Crimes in Paradise*	Lars-Eric Kjellgren
1960	*The Virgin Spring*	Ingmar Bergman
1960	*Kärlekens decimaler*	Hasse Ekman
1960	*The Devil's Eye*	Ingmar Bergman
1960	*Pa en bänk i en park*	Hasse Ekman
1961	*Two Living, One Dead*	Anthony Asquith (Sweden/UK)
1961	*Hällebäcks gard*	Bengt Blomgren
1961	*Through a Glass Darkly*	Ingmar Bergman
1961	*The Pleasure Garden*	Alf Kjellin
1964	*All These Women*	Ingmar Bergman
1964	*The Dress*	Vilgot Sjöman
1965	*4 x 4*	Jan Troell, etc.
1966	*Here's Your Life*	Jan Troell
1971	*The Emigrants*	Jan Troell

NORTH, Alex (1910–1991) A gifted and dedicated film composer and conductor who worked meticulously and carefully within the Hollywood system, he scored everything from spectacular epics to quiet character dramas during his forty-year career.

Born Isadore Soifer in Chester, Pennsylvania, of impoverished Russian-born immigrants who loved classical music, Alex North received a scholarship to study piano at the Curtis Institute in nearby Philadelphia then did further study at Juilliard in New York City, working nights as a telegraph operator to pay his tuition bills. Because he loved the music of Sergei Prokofiev and other Russian composers, North wanted to study music in his parents' homeland. He used his telegraph skills to interest the Soviets in hiring him as part of their campaign to recruit Americans to help the developing nation. North's telegraph work in Moscow did not last long, but it gave him the opportunity to study music at the Moscow Conservatory and to conduct music for various theatre groups. Returning to America in 1936 he studied under Aaron Copland and wrote music for dance, including Martha Graham's company, and theatre, mostly at the Federal Theatre Project. North went to Mexico with Graham's troupe and stayed there two years, studying with Mexican composer Silvestre Revueltas, who taught him about film scoring. North first worked in movies when he collaborated with director Elia Kazan on the documentary short *People of the Cumberland* in 1936, which led to his scoring dozens of shorts for the government. In the 1940s his concert pieces were performed in New York, and he wrote the background music for several Broadway plays. It was his haunting score for Arthur Miller's acclaimed drama *Death of a Salesman*, which Kazan directed, that brought North to Hollywood. Kazan was so pleased with North's work that he insisted the studio hire him to do the music for the screen version of *A Streetcar Named Desire* in 1951. Not only was the film a great success but the score was considered a breakthrough piece, utilizing jazz throughout in a psychological manner and influencing a new generation of screen composers.

North remained in Hollywood and went on to score dozens of features, shorts, and television shows. He shunned publicity and preferred to work quietly on his own. Because Kazan and other top directors liked working with him, North was given many quality movies to score. Among the Broadway play adaptations he wrote screen scores for are *Death of a Salesman*, *The Member of the Wedding*, *The Rainmaker*, *The Rose Tattoo*, *The Children's Hour*, *The Bad Seed*, and *Who's Afraid of Virginia Woolf?* He also wrote the music for such literary classic adaptations as *Les Miserables*, *The Dead*, *The Sound and the Fury*, *Sanctuary*, and *The Long, Hot Summer*. Although he preferred small-scale character dramas, he was assigned such big-budget spectaculars as *Spartacus*, *The Agony and the Ecstasy*, and *Cleopatra*. In his later years he worked with young directors and new acting talents in such varied movies as *Dragonslayer*, *Carny*, and *Good Morning, Vietnam*. Of the handful of television projects he scored, most memorable was his music for the 1976 miniseries *Rich Man, Poor Man*. Because he took screen composition so seriously, he was often mistreated or even humiliated by crass studios and directors. The supreme insult came in 1968 when he wrote an ambitious and lengthy score for Stanley Kubrick's sci-fi movie *2001: A Space Odyssey*. For the rough cut, selections of classical music were inserted before North and the studio brass viewed it. North spent months writing the score, only to attend the premiere and find that none of his music was used and that the classical pieces remained. Although he was nominated for an Oscar fifteen times over the period of three decades, he never won one. In 1986 the Academy presented North with an honorary Oscar for his years of superb music, the first time a composer was so honored.

The outstanding element in North's music is its strong connection to character. He strove to score people, not movies. He relished projects that had strong and fascinating characters, be they as different as Michelangelo and Emilio Zapata. Consequently, some of his finest work can be found in the screen versions of some renowned American plays. New Orleans jazz seems to infiltrate everything in *A Streetcar Named Desire*, but careful study of the score shows that it is the contrasting characters of the brute Stanley (Marlon Brando) and the fragile impostor Blanche (Vivien Leigh) that are musically holding the film together. The main theme is a sexy passage featuring a solo trumpet. It is heard as Blanche moves through crowded New

Orleans, the music picking up not on the crowds but on her personal disorientation. The theme for Stanley is quiet but restless and seething. When these two characters are together, the music suggests dangerous fireworks about to explode. The music in such scenes was so smoldering, especially the sections with a solo saxophone, that the Legion of Decency denounced it as "carnal music" and demanded that some sections of the score be removed. It seems surprising that a classically educated composer could embrace jazz so thoroughly and uniquely in his first major feature film. Yet North's experience with theatre and ballet music had already started to explore the various aspects of jazz. *A Streetcar Named Desire* is the first time such experimentation had been used in a Hollywood feature. There is surprisingly little music in the film, but when it is used the result is compelling.

North's score for another stage classic, *Death of a Salesman*, is more traditional, although it does include the haunting theme he wrote for the Broadway version. This motif for the defeated salesman Willie (Fredric March) is a solo flute and rarely has such a subtle sense of melancholy been heard. The main heroine in *The Rose Tattoo*, the fiery Neapolitan Serafina (Anna Magnani), is the opposite of Willy. She is a fierce fighter who underneath is quite vulnerable. The way North illustrates both aspects of the character in his music is masterful. For the screen version of Carson McCullers's drama *The Member of the Wedding*, North used little music, and what is there is very quiet and subtle. This is a small and intimate story, the kind that North favored, and the gentle woodwinds enter so carefully that many do not even notice them. A movie adaptation of Edward Albee's searing drama *Who's Afraid of Virginia Woolf?* posed many difficulties, but a superior cast and skillful direction by Mike Nichols turned it into powerful moviegoing. Few films have so much dialogue, most of it vitriolic and tense. North wisely avoided music that would echo this verbal violence. Instead he wrote a quiet, restful theme, which was played by a solo guitar backed by strings and harp. The serenity of the score, usually heard between the characters' confrontations, hinted at their deeply troubled nature underneath.

North's other outstanding score with Elia Kazan is *Viva Zapata!*, the story of Mexican patriot Emilio Zapata (Marlon Brando). The composer's time spent in Mexico served him well in writing this enthralling score. The expected Latin rhythms are there, but so too are dissonant themes that suggest the chaos of the revolt, some mournful passages with a religious flavor, a festive theme that is almost comic, and a love theme that is so muted it is hardly noticed. There are two scenes in *Viva Zapata!* in which music is used in a particularly skillful manner. When Zapata is arrested and led away, the peasants pick up stones and start to beat them together in a defiant pattern. The music unobtrusively enters as more stones are beat and the music swells as the crowd does. For Zapata's execution by firing squad, Kazan and North opted to remove all sound effects from the soundtrack and let the music carry the scene. After Kazan, the director who seems to have inspired North the most is John Huston. Of their five movies together, three must be mentioned. They first worked on *The Misfits*, a drama most remembered for the last performances by Clark Gable and Marilyn Monroe. Set in Reno and then the desert, the music is not western flavored but instead a restless jazz theme with piano and violins cascading downward in a forceful way. For Huston's dark comedy *Prizzi's Honor*, about two Mafia killers (Jack Nicholson and Kathleen Turner) who fall in love with each other, the main theme is brisk and almost giddy. For the James Joyce tale *The Dead*, North incorporated some Irish airs as a group of Dubliners celebrate Christmas. But the main theme—sometimes played by a lonely clarinet, others times by a solo violin—is a gracefully sad piece that manages to avoid becoming morbid.

How odd that North, who reveled in small character dramas, would end up scoring so many large epics. These "cast of thousands" movies were not what he loved, so he approached them as character studies. For the Roman tale *Spartacus*, he sought to find the heart of the title character (Kirk Douglas) in his music. The main theme, with its blaring trumpets, military drums, and pulsating march tempo, seems to present the powerful Romans whom Spartacus revolts against. The man himself is better understood in the music for such action scenes as the slaves' march to the sea and later their escape from the Roman army. The love theme for Spartacus and Varinia (Jean Simmons) is a birdlike waltz in which violins call to chirping woodwinds. The *Spartacus* soundtrack is filled with delightful surprises and it is easy to see why many consider it North's best Hollywood score. The wide-screen spectacle *The Agony and the Ecstasy* is basically a two-character drama about the conflicted relationship between artist Michelangelo (Charlton Heston) and Pope Julius II (Rex Harrison)

who commissioned him to paint the ceiling of the Sistine Chapel. The score is by North and Jerry Goldsmith, each one providing music for different sequences. Much of the background music is by North. It is sometimes in the Renaissance style with simple period instruments, other times in a more grandiose baroque fashion using pipe organ and harpsichord. North returned to the Vatican setting for the contemporary drama *The Shoes of the Fisherman* about a Russian-born pope (Anthony Quinn). The studio demanded that the score have a Russian feeling even though North argued that nationality was not what the movie was about. Since the composer rarely wins such battles, the score has some Russian touches but the most impressive sections are those dealing with the Vatican, such as the election of the new pope (swirling regal themes) and the loneliness of the job (mournfully touching passages). The movie was a critical and box office failure, but there is much to admire in North's rich score. The most expensive of all the spectaculars of the 1960s was *Cleopatra*, still on the books as one of the most unprofitable movies of all time. Ironically, this overheated costume drama greatly interested North, who enjoyed researching Roman and Egyptian music. He was particularly interested in trying to capture the tempestuous love affair between the Egyptian queen (Elizabeth Taylor) and the Roman Marc Antony (Richard Burton) musically. *Cleopatra* may still be considered an expensive joke, but North's score is nothing to be ashamed of. The musical motif for the queen is an exotic and shimmering string theme, suggesting small objects being dropped into water and causing ripples. The love scenes are scored with a very tentative theme that contrasts with the unhesitating passion of the two lovers. One of the film's most ridiculous yet memorable scenes is Cleopatra's arrival in Rome. The overly long and overproduced sequence is scored with boastful fanfares, tribal dances, an exotic march, and a heavy series of chords as the queen's float is dragged in by hundreds of slaves. This may not be North at his best, but it is surely at his most splendiferous.

The prison movie *Unchained* provided the opportunity for North to write his only hit song, but what a hit it was. The elegant "Unchained Melody" has been recorded by so many artists in so many versions that it has become widely recognized. The song (lyric by Hy Zaret) has been used in over forty films and television programs. In fact, it was used so extensively throughout the romantic mystery movie *Ghost* that the film's composer Maurice Jarre insisted that North be given co-composer credit. North got to score only a few westerns but one of them produced some fine music. John Ford's *Cheyenne Autumn* is something of an antiwestern about the plight of Native Americans. North studied the music of the plains Indians but did not copy it for his score. Instead he retained a native music sensibility as he musicalized the open country and the power of nature. Deeps chords give way to fluttering flutes in the main theme but later in the score there are sorrowful passages relating to the tragic migration of the tribal people. Finally, there is the sterling movie score by North that was never heard in theatres. When Kubrick discarded North's *2001: A Space Odyssey* music, the composer was so upset he put the sheet music away and refused to show it to anyone. Near the end of his life, North (encouraged by fellow composer Jerry Goldsmith) agreed to a recording of the score. Goldsmith conducted the London National Philharmonic in the recording session and the result was so thrilling that the rejected score has been placed among North's finest achievements. Listening to the recording, one can hear moments when North echoes some of the famous classical selections. Yet there is something thrilling about original music under the dawn of man sequence or the space station docking. North avoids any electronic or sci-fi sounds. If anything, the music recalls Holst's *The Planets* suite. One can argue that Kubrick's use of classical music is more quirky and creates a startling contrast between the space age and music from a romantic era. But North's score for *2001: A Space Odyssey* is exceptional film music and further evidence of how distinguished a talent he was. Biography: *Alex North, Film Composer*, Sanya Shoilevska Henderson (2009). Official website: www.alexnorthmusic.com.

Credits

(all films USA unless stated otherwise; * for Best Song)

Year	Film	Director
1941	The Golden Fleece	Thomas Bouchard (Canada/USA)
1951	The 13th Letter	Otto Preminger
1951	A Streetcar Named Desire (AAN)	Elia Kazan
1951	Death of a Salesman (AAN)	Laslo Benedek
1952	Viva Zapata! (AAN)	Elia Kazan
1952	Les Miserables	Lewis Milestone
1952	Pony Soldier	Joseph M. Newman
1952	The Member of the Wedding	Fred Zinnemann
1954	Go Man Go	James Wong Howe
1954	Désirée	Henry Koster
1955	Unchained (AAN*)	Hall Bartlett
1955	The Racers	Henry Hathaway
1955	Man with the Gun	Richard Wilson
1955	The Rose Tattoo (AAN)	Daniel Mann
1955	I'll Cry Tomorrow	Daniel Mann
1956	The Bad Seed	Mervyn LeRoy
1956	The Rainmaker (AAN)	Joseph Anthony
1956	The King and Four Queens	Raoul Walsh
1957	Four Girls in Town	Jack Sher
1957	The Bachelor Party	Delbert Mann
1958	The Long, Hot Summer	Martin Ritt
1958	Stage Struck	Sidney Lumet
1958	Hot Spell	Daniel Mann, George Cukor
1958	South Seas Adventure	Carl Dudley, etc.
1959	The Sound and the Fury	Martin Ritt
1959	The Wonderful Country	Robert Parrish
1960	Spartacus (AAN; GGN)	Stanley Kubrick
1961	The Misfits	John Huston
1961	Sanctuary	Tony Richardson
1961	The Children's Hour	William Wyler

Year	Film	Director
1962	All Fall Down	John Frankenheimer
1963	Cleopatra (AAN)	Joseph L. Mankiewicz, Rouben Mamoulian, Darryl F. Zanuck (UK/USA/Switzerland)
1964	Cheyenne Autumn	John Ford
1964	The Outrage	Martin Ritt
1965	The Agony and the Ecstasy (AAN)	Carol Reed (USA/Italy)
1966	Who's Afraid of Virginia Woolf? (AAN)	Mike Nichols
1968	The Devil's Brigade	Andrew V. McLaglen
1968	The Shoes of the Fisherman (AAN; GG)	Michael Anderson
1969	Hard Contract	S. Lee Pogostin
1969	A Dream of Kings	Daniel Mann
1971	Willard	Daniel Mann
1972	Pocket Money	Stuart Rosenberg
1974	Once Upon a Scoundrel	George Schaefer (USA/Mexico)
1974	Shanks (AAN)	William Castle
1975	Bite the Bullet(AAN)	Richard Brooks
1975	Journey into Fear	Daniel Mann (Canada)
1976	The Passover Plot	Michael Campus (Israel/USA)
1978	Somebody Killed Her Husband	Lamont Johnson
1979	Wise Blood	John Huston (USA/West Germany)
1980	Carny	Robert Kaylor
1981	Dragonslayer (AAN)	Matthew Robbins
1984	Under the Volcano (AAN)	John Huston (USA/Mexico)
1985	Prizzi's Honor	John Huston
1987	John Huston and the Dubliners	Lilyan Sievernich
1987	The Dead	John Huston (UK/Ireland/USA)
1987	Good Morning, Vietnam	Barry Levinson
1988	The Penitent	Cliff Osmond (USA/Mexico)
1991	Poslední motyl (aka The Last Butterfly)	Karel Kachyna (Czechoslovakia/France/UK)

NYMAN, Michael (b. 1944) An esteemed British musician, conductor, and composer for the opera, concert hall, ballet, and movies, he has scored over forty feature films for twenty countries on five continents.

Michael Laurence Nyman was born in London and studied piano and composition at King's College and the Royal Academy of Music before spending a year in Romania to study Eastern European folk music. Nyman began his music career not as a pianist or composer but as a music critic writing for various journals and newspapers. While discussing the avant-garde composer Cornelius Cardew in *The Spectator* in 1968, Nyman used the word "minimalism" to describe Cardew's work, the first time the term had been utilized in a music context. His 1974 book *Experimental Music: Cage and Beyond* is considered one of the best in the field. Although he was praised for his writings about past and present music, Nyman left criticism and turned to composing. As he wrote for the concert hall and opera house, he also began his movie composing career. Nyman had scored the film short *5 Postcards from Capital*

Cities back in 1967, but he did not write a full score for a feature film until the comedy *Keep It Up Downstairs* in 1976. That same year he worked with artist and film director Peter Greenaway for the first time, scoring the short *Goole by Numbers*. The innovative Greenaway and the experimental Nyman agreed on many aspects of art and later collaborated on the unorthodox features *The Falls, The Draughtsman's Contract, A Zed and Two Noughts, Drowning by Numbers, Prospero's Books,* and *The Cook, the Thief, His Wife & Her Lover.* For other directors, Nyman scored such diverse movies as *The Piano, Monsieur Hire, The Hairdresser's Husband, Carrington, Gattaca, The Ogre, Wonderland, The End of the Affair, Ravenous, I Am, Miradas múltiples,* and *The Trip,* as well as such acclaimed documentaries as *Man on Wire, 9 Months 9 Days,* and *The Mexican Suitcase.* He composed new scores for two experimental silent films, the French short *Ballet Méchane* (1924) and the Russian documentary *Man with a Movie Camera* (1929). Nyman has written music for some British television series, most memorably *Fairly Secret Army* and *Titch*, and several TV movies and documentaries. His music was used in the German documentary about him, *Michael Nyman in Progress* (2010). In 1976 he founded the Campiello Band which later became the better-known Michael Nyman Band, an ensemble made up of both old and modern instruments. The group made some esteemed recordings and many concert appearances. Nyman has also written six symphonies, numerous concertos and small ensemble pieces, song cycles, and ballet and modern dance music, but his greatest passion is writing for the opera stage. Among his acclaimed operas are *The Man Who Mistook His Wife for a Hat* (1986), *Noises, Sounds & Sweet Airs* (1987), *Facing Goya* (2000), *Man and Boy: Dada* (2003), and *Love Counts* (2005). Nyman is the recipient of many awards and honors, including the Commander of the Order of the British Empire (CBE) in 2008. His daughter Molly Nyman also writes music for the movies, in particular *The Road to Guantanamo* (2006) and *I Am Slave* (2010), both with Harry Escott.

Although Nyman is most associated with minimalism, a good portion of his work does not fall under that label and his screen music is more influenced rather than overwhelmed by the style. A good example is *The Piano* for which he wrote his most famous score. The somber plot concerns a mute woman (Holly Hunter) and her daughter (Anna Paquin) in 1850s New Zealand and the two men (Sam Neill and Harvey Keitel) who lust after the mother. A treasured family piano is key to the plot and the score utilizes the instrument in several of its passages. One restless theme features a minor-key piano playing some classical flourishes as it pushes forward as if driven. Another track is a lively piano piece that suggests a frantic dance moving out of control, and there is a tormented passage with rapid piano and fiery strings that is very modern. All of the score is influenced by minimalism, particularly with a recurring dissonant and mysterious passage that is unsettling even though it flows very smoothly. The sea is scored with frenzied strings and sustained woodwinds with calm sections on a solo violin, and there is a languid theme featuring a solo clarinet that doesn't drag but is still morose. In 1994 Nyman created a concerto from his *The Piano* score, recorded it, and it has been heard since in concert halls. Another period piece with modern music is *The End of the Affair*, a chilly romance in 1946 London involving a novelist (Ralph Fiennes) and his ex-mistress (Julianne Moore). The most conventional track in Nyman's score is a gliding fully orchestrated passage that wavers up and down as it keeps moving ahead with a world-weary tone. More minimal is a repetitive string and woodwind theme that keeps rising as if asking a musical question. Even the love theme for the movie is a tentative piano lament that is fragile and sad. The setting for the romantic drama *Carrington* is England during World War I, but again Nyman's music is modern, even when played by a classical string quartet. The difficult romance between writer Dora Carrington (Emma Thompson) and the homosexual author Lytton Strachey (Jonathan Pryce) is scored with a doleful main theme played on a high solo violin and low, mournful strings that picks up speed as it goes along and gets more frantic. The music is based on Nyman's String Quartet No. 3 and it captures the ambiguous nature of the love story very effectively. The score also has a passage that is a repetitive series of ascending phrases on various strings that is somewhat uplifting, and another in which a solo trumpet is featured in a vivacious dance band piece that bounces along like a silly march.

For some, Nyman's best screen score is the intricate one he wrote for the sci-fi drama *Gattaca*. This unusually cerebral futuristic tale is about a genetically inferior man (Ethan Hawke) categorized for menial work who deceives the authorities by altering his DNA and other tests to pass himself off as a superior human specimen. Nyman's minimalist music seems right at home in this thought-provoking sci-fi movie and critics who dismissed his earlier screen music were won over by this score. The gloomy main theme consists of tired strings, hesitant brass, and muted percussion that repeat a short descending musical phrase in different keys. Another passage features sustained strings with rhythmic woodwind accents that is used to build suspense, and more uplifting is a warm and serene piece featuring a solo French horn rising above the strings. The hero's romance with Irene (Uma Thurman) is scored with the pleasing "Irene's Theme," a flowing, expansive passage played by a full orchestra with lovely brass highlights. Just as *Gattaca* is a superior but little-known movie, so too is Nyman's outstanding score not as acknowledged as it should be.

Nyman is most often thought of in terms of his movies with the very daring and controversial Peter Greenaway. Ironically, Nyman's music for most of Greenaway's films is rather classical. In fact, some of these scores embrace the baroque style, which must be the most direct opposite to minimalism. *The Draughtsman's Contract* is set in 1694 on an English estate where a young artist (Anthony Higgins) is hired by the lady of the house (Janet Suzman) to do a series of drawings of the country home. He is soon involved in romance, intrigue, and murder. Nyman suggests the period using baroque music with dissonant or minor-key adjustments. One theme consists of harpsichord, brass, and strings playing a pompous processional that has a brisk tempo and many flourishes as it repeats one vigorous musical phrase. Another passage is a zesty string ensemble that is rapid but civilized. An adagio on pipe organ and strings moves in slow motion until horns are added and it becomes a graceful march. There is also a heavy horn and harpsichord theme that descends the scale with grief. Greenaway's bizarre but intriguing *The Cook, the Thief, His Wife & Her Lover* is set in the present but the music is classically flavored. This brutal tale of infidelity, murder, and cannibalism is given an ironic tone by Nyman's music. There is a classical theme on strings with the tempo of a stubborn metronome as repeated notes begrudgingly break away to play the sour melody which is picked up by other instruments. A high-pitched "Miserere" is sung by a youth (dubbed on soundtrack by Sarah Leonard) that is disturbing, as well as a low-key repetitive lament on woodwinds that is weary yet suspenseful. Some who complained that Nyman's modern music was inappropriate for his period movies also found fault with his pseudoclassical music being used in a contemporary film. Yet it is clear that both Greenaway and Nyman are not interested in the usual or the expected, one of the reasons the scores are so fascinating. Official website: www.michaelnyman.com.

Credits

(all films UK unless stated otherwise)

Year	Film	Director
1976	Keep It Up Downstairs	Robert Young
1980	The Falls	Peter Greenaway
1982	The Draughtsman's Contract	Peter Greenaway
1983	Frozen Music	Michael Eaton
1985	A Zed and Two Noughts	Peter Greenaway (UK/Netherlands)
1986	I'll Stake My Cremona to a Jew's Trump	Sara Jolly (Canada/UK)
1987	Le miraculé	Jean-Pierre Mocky (France)
1988	Drowning by Numbers	Peter Greenaway (UK/Netherlands)
1989	Monsieur Hire	Patrice Leconte (France)
1989	The Cook, the Thief, His Wife & Her Lover	Peter Greenaway (UK/France)
1990	The Hairdresser's Husband	Patrice Leconte (France)
1990	Men of Steel	Agnieszka Piotrowska
1991	Les enfants volants	Guillaume Nicloux (France)
1991	Prospero's Books	Peter Greenaway (UK/Netherlands/France/Italy/Japan)
1992	The Fall of Icarus	Jacques Bourton, Thonas De Norre (Canada/France)
1993	The Piano (GGN; BAFTA-N)	Jane Campion (N. Zealand/Australia/France)
1994	Mesmer	Roger Spottiswoode (Austria/Canada/UK)
1994	A la folie	Diane Kurys (France)
1995	Carrington	Christopher Hampton (UK/France)
1995	The Diary of Anne Frank	Akinori Nagaoka (Japan)
1996	The Ogre	Volker Schlöndorff (France/Germany/UK)
1997	Gattaca (aka The Eighth Day) (GGN)	Andrew Niccol (USA)
1999	Ravenous	Antonia Bird (Czech Republic/UK/USA)
1999	Wonderland	Michael Winterbottom
1999	Nabbie's Love	Yuji Nakse (Japan)
1999	The End of the Affair (GGN; BAFTA-N)	Neil Jordan (UK/USA)
2000	The Claim (aka Kingdom Come)	Michael Winterbottom (UK/France/Canada)
2002	24 Hours in the Life of a Woman	Laurent Bouhnik (France/Germany/UK)
2002	Man with a Movie Camera (1929)	Dziga Vertov (USSR)
2003	The Actors	Conor McPherson (UK/Germany/Ireland)

Year	Film	Director
2003	*Nathalie . . .*	Anne Fontaine (France/Spain)
2004	*Luminal*	Andrea Vecchiato
2004	*The Libertine*	Laurence Dunmore (UK/Australia)
2005	*Detroit: Ruin of a City*	George Steinmetz, Michael Chanan (USA/UK)
2005	*I Am*	Dorota Kedzierzawska (Poland)
2007	*Never Forever*	Gina Kim (So. Korea/USA)
2007	*Theresa: The Body of Christ*	Ray Loriga (Spain/France/UK)
2008	*Man on Wire*	James Marsh (UK/USA)
2009	*An Organization of Dreams*	Ken McMullen
2009	*9 Months 9 Days*	Ozcar Ramírez (Mexico)
2010	*The Trip*	Michael Winterbottom
2010	*Erasing David*	David Bond, Melinda McDougall
2010	*Krokodyle*	Stefano Bessoni (Italy)
2011	*The Mexican Suitcase*	Trisha Ziff (Mexico/Spain/USA)
2012	*White Elephant*	Pablo Trapero (Argentina/Spain/France)
2012	*On Landguard Point*	Robert Pacitti
2012	*Miradas múltiples*	Emilio Maillé (Mexico/France/Spain)
2012	*Everyday*	Michael Winterbottom
2012	*Fanny, Alexander & jag*	Stig Björkman (Sweden)
2013	*2 Graves*	Yvonne McDevitt (UK/Ireland)

ORTOLANI, Riz (1926–2014) A prolific Italian composer, songwriter, conductor, and arranger who found international success with some of his songs and movie music, he scored over two hundred movies between 1954 and 2010.

He was born Riziero Ortolani in Pesaro, Italy, into a musical family and took violin and flute lessons as a child. Ortolani studied at the Conservatorio Statale di Musica in his hometown before he began his career as a flautist with local orchestras. In 1948 he went to Rome and found work playing in dance halls before he was hired as a music arranger for the Italian state broadcasting network RAI. Ortolani first worked in movies when he cowrote the score for the Italian comedy *Le vacanze del Sor Clemente* in 1954. The next year he wrote his first solo score, followed by some other mostly forgotten movies in the 1950s. Ortolani formed his own orchestra and moved to Los Angeles in 1959, where they performed at the popular nightclub Circo's. By 1961 he was back in Italy and writing for the movies. His score for the shocking documentary *Mondo cane* the next year became world famous because of the lilting ballad "More" (with composer Nino Oliviero, lyric by Norman Newell) which went on to be recorded by dozens of international artists. Ortolani (who sometimes billed himself as Ritz Ortolani or Roger Higgins) was soon in great demand for European movies and later in Hollywood. He was a prodigious worker (in 1969 he scored eleven feature films, a television miniseries, and three documentary shorts) and over the next four decades scored all genres of movies, from sex comedies and westerns to historical films and horror thrillers. Among his memorable Continental films are *Il sorpasso*/*The Easy Life*, *Horror Castle*, *The Naked Hours*, *Castle of Blood*, *The Violent Four*, *Dead Men Don't Count*, *Night of the Serpent*, *His Name Was Madron*, *The Valachi Papers*, *The Assassin of Rome*, *The Ravine*, *Mondo Candido*, *Gunlaw*, *Submission*, *Atsalut pader*, *Mimi*, *Sahara Cross*, *Anni Struggenti*, *Valentina*, *Christmas Present*, *Incantata*, *In the Rose Garden*, *Magnificat*, and *Giovanna's Father*, as well as such praised documentary features as *Mediterranean Holiday*, *Africa addio*, and *Fangio: A Life at 300 an Hour*. Ortolani's many American and British movies include *The Seventh Dawn*, *The Yellow Rolls-Royce*, *The Glory Guys*, *Maya*, *The Bliss of Mrs. Blossom*, *The McKenzie Break*, and *Buona Sera, Mrs. Campbell*. He usually conducted the soundtrack recordings of his scores, as he did for many of his TV movies and miniseries for Italian television. Ortolani wrote many songs for his movies, such as the 1965 international hit "Forget Domani" (lyric by Norman Newell) from *The Yellow Rolls-Royce*. His screen music has been used by later filmmakers, most memorably in the Quentin Tarantino movies *Kill Bill Vol. 1* (2003), *Kill Bill Vol. 2* (2004), *Inglourious Basterds* (2009), and *Django Unchained* (2012). He founded the Pesaro Riz Ortolino Foundation that promotes music study and performance in his hometown. Active until the end, Ortolani died in Rome at the age of eighty-seven in 2014, the year his last miniseries was broadcast.

With its Italianate romanticism mixed with a pop, electronic presentation, the music of Ortolani was considered the new European sound of the 1960s. This sound first caught on in the States after *Mondo cane* was given an English narration and one of the musical themes was turned into the hit song "More." Ortolani and Nino Oliviero's music is smooth and sophisticated yet is given a slightly swinging beat when heard on the soundtrack. At one point there is a cool jazz version of "More" featuring piano, solo trumpet, and guitar that is so detached it seems almost uncaring. This low-key approach is ironic since the documentary, about strange sexual practices, disturbing bestial violence, and unorthodox cultish rituals, is far from smooth or serene. The rest of the score is more in keeping with the tone of *Mondo cane* (which can be translated as *A Dog's Life*). There is a slow and eerie passage with high-pitched female chanting and sustained strings that is dreamlike but unsettling. One jazz passage, featuring a solo trumpet with accordion accents, moves with a steady beat but has a sour sentiment. Another jazz track is carefree with squawking brass, nimble piano, and a forced sense of gaiety. Most haunting is a mixed chorus chanting a sinister dirge during some of the most upsetting scenes. Most of the millions who fell in love with "More" never saw the Italian movie. If they had, they might have had difficulty embracing the love song. A similar kind of musical irony can be found in the French-Italian crime drama *The Valachi Papers*. This violent and tense true story, about a small-time gangster (Charles Bronson) trying to survive once a Mafia kingpin (Lino Ventura) puts a price on his head, is scored with a sweeping string theme that is as tender and carefree as the action is oppressive and jarring.

A much lighter movie, though there is a dark subtext, is the Italian comedy *Il sorpasso*, which was released in English as *The Easy Life*. When the pleasure-loving Bruno (Vittorio Gassman) takes his younger friend Roberto (Jean-Louis Trintignant) on a road trip, the two have lots of laughs until Roberto discovers just how shallow his friend really is. Ortolani wrote a vivacious jazz score for this breezy movie. One rapid theme is played on vibrant clarinet and blaring brass as they race up the scale in time to a furious drum riff. There is also a cool jazz theme on electric organ that struts along with confidence but slows down for some reflective string sections. Also memorable is a jazzy and gliding foxtrot on strings and piano that moves with a romantic air. Some of Ortolani's most interesting electronic music can be found in the horror adventure *Cannibal Holocaust*. When a documentary film crew does not return from the Amazon rain forest, an American anthropologist (Robert Kerman) goes to South America to find out what happened. What he discovers is horrifying on several levels. Ortolani opens the score with a gentle guitar theme accompanied by distorted electronic sounds that are almost human as they repeat a catchy melody. At one point in the film, a synthesized violin plays a lyrical but foreboding melody as vibrating electronic bass and high-frequency accents add to the texture. There is a techno-rock passage on electric guitar with synthesized sound effects and distorted instruments, and an affecting love theme on acoustic guitar with synthesized accompaniment at various frequencies. Some of the most horrific scenes are scored with a heartbeat heard on different synthesized

instruments as an electronic keyboard plays chaotic and confusing chords. This is indeed a nightmarish score for a disturbing film.

Ortolani's British and Hollywood scores tend to be softer and less abrasive. The episodic comedy-drama *The Yellow Rolls-Royce* has a sprightly main theme that dances merrily as a simple musical phrase is repeated effectively. This music was also used for the song "Forget Domani" (sung on the soundtrack by Katina Ranieri) and for a zesty march that seems to laugh as it moves along. The offbeat comedy *The Bliss of Mrs. Blossom*, about a bored housewife (Shirley MacLaine) who keeps her longtime lover (James Booth) hidden up in her attic, has a cool jazz main theme that repeats a six-note phrase played by muted brass as a female vocalizes in a sexy yet nonchalant way. The film also has rhythmic piano and maraca track with sweeping strings that moves briskly yet is still romantic as it keeps returning to a catchy musical phrase. Perhaps Ortolani's most diverting yet pleasing American score is the one he wrote for the bittersweet comedy *Buona Sera, Mrs. Campbell*. For twenty years an Italian "widow" (Gina Lollabridgida) has been getting money from three American GIs to support her love child, each man thinking he is the father. An American-Italian reunion in the town threatens to expose her secret and her deception. The charming movie's main theme is a bouncy Neapolitan tarantella on mandolins and electric keyboard that is more jaunty than romantic. The title song (lyric by director/writer Melvin Frank) is an up-tempo ballad that is used in different ways throughout the film. The score also includes 1960s pop traveling music with a swinging beat, a string and electric keyboard theme that is gentle and nostalgic with the flavor of a hymn at times, and a romantic mandolin passage that keeps from becoming a cliché because of its melancholy subtext. Although the score is far from the hedonistic jazz heard in *Mondo cane*, this is the kind of music America wanted from Ortolani. By the 1980s, that sound was becoming a bit passé and Hollywood lost interest in Ortolani. He scored fewer and fewer English-language films but was still busy in Europe writing music for a wide variety of movies, many of which were never seen in America.

Credits

(all films Italy unless stated otherwise; * for Best Song)

Year	Film	Director
1954	*Le vacanze del Sor Clemente*	Camillo Mastrocinque
1955	*Processo all'amore*	Enzo Liberti
1956	*Accadde di notte*	Gian Paolo Callegari
1956	*I milliardari*	Guido Malatesta
1956	*Serenata al vento*	Luigi Latini de Marchi
1957	*Terror over Rome*	Anton Giulio Majano
1959	*Siempre estaré contigo*	Julián Soler (Mexico)
1961	*Valley of the Lions*	Carlo Ludovico Bragaglia
1961	*Malesia magica*	Lionetto Fabbri
1962	*Mondo cane* (AAN*)	Paolo Cavara, etc.
1962	*Il sorpasso* (aka *The Easy Life*)	Dino Risi
1962	*Mediterranean Holiday*	Hermann Leiter, Rudolf Nussgruber (W. Germany)
1963	*Women of the World*	Gualtiero Jacopetti, etc.
1963	*The Fall of Rome*	Antonio Margheriti
1963	*Horror Castle*	Antonio Margheriti
1964	*The Naked Hours*	Marco Vicario
1964	*Gunfight at High Noon*	Joaquín Romero Marchent (Spain/Italy)
1964	*Castle of Blood*	Sergio Corbucci (Italy/France)
1964	*Ecco* (aka *The Forbidden*)	Gianni Proia
1964	*Old Shatterhand*	Hugo Fregonese (W. Germany/Italy/France/ Yugoslavia)
1964	*The Seventh Dawn*	Lewis Gilbert (UK)
1964	*Ride and Kill*	José Luis Borau, Mario Caiano (Spain/Italy)
1964	*Hour of Death*	Joaquín Romero Marchent (Spain/Italy)
1964	*The Yellow Rolls-Royce* (GGN; GG*)	Anthony Asquith (UK)
1965	*El diablo también llora*	José Antonio Nieves Conde (Spain/Italy)
1965	*The Glory Guys*	Arnold Laven, Sam Peckinpah (USA)
1965	*Red Dragon*	Ernst Hofbauer (Italy/W. Germany)
1965	*Con rispetto parlando*	Marcello Ciorciolini
1965	*Spy in Your Eye* (aka *Berlin, Appointment for Spies*)	Vittorio Sala
1966	*Africa addio* (aka *Africa Blood and Guts*)	Gualtiero Jacopetti, Franco Prosperi
1966	*Lightning Bolt*	Antonio Margheriti (Italy/Spain)
1966	*Maya* (aka *Maya the Magnificent*)	John Berry (USA)
1966	*Special Code*	Pino Mercanti (Spain/Italy/France)
1966	*The Spy with a Cold Nose*	Daniel Petrie (UK)
1966	*Make Love, Not War*	Franco Rossi (Italy/Spain)
1967	*Kill and Pray* (aka *Resquiescant*)	Carlo Lizzani (Italy/W. Germany)
1967	*Soldier's Girl*	Alessandro Blasetti
1967	*Woman Times Seven*	Vittorio De Sica (Italy/France/USA)
1967	*Tiffany Memorandum*	Sergio Grieco (Italy/France)
1967	*On My Way to the Crusades, I Met a Girl Who . . .*	Pasquale Festa Campanile
1967	*Gunlaw*	Tonino Valerii (Italy/W. Germany)
1968	*The Biggest Bundle of Them All*	Ken Annakin (USA)
1968	*The Violent Four*	Carlo Lizzani
1968	*Beyond the Law*	Giorgio Stegani (Italy/W. Germany)
1968	*Anzio*	Edward Dmytryk, Duilio Coletti (Italy/USA)
1968	*The Bliss of Mrs. Blossom*	Joseph McGrath (UK)
1968	*The Girl Who Couldn't Say No* (aka *Tenderly*)	Franco Brusati
1968	*Mal d'Africa* (aka *The Final Prey*)	Stanis Nievo
1968	*Emma Hamilton*	Christian-Jaque (Italy/W. Germany/France/USA)
1968	*Buona Sera, Mrs. Campbell* (GGN*)	Melvin Frank (USA)
1968	*Dead Men Don't Count* (aka *Cry for Revenge*)	Rafael Romero Marchent (Spain/Italy)
1968	*The Last Roman*	Robert Siodmak, etc. (W. Germany/Italy Romania)
1969	*Sardinia Kidnapped*	Gianfranco Mingozzi

Year	Film	Director
1969	Fight for Rome II	Robert Siodmak, etc. (W. Germany/Italy/Romania)
1969	Bootleggers	Alfio Caltabriano (Italy/Spain)
1969	War Fever (aka The Liberators)	Tonino Ricci
1969	One on Top of the Other	Lucio Fulci (Italy/Spain/France)
1969	So Sweet . . . So Perverse	Umberto Lenzi (Italy/France/W. Germany)
1969	The Ravine	Paolo Cavara (Italy/Yugoslavia/USA)
1969	Night of the Serpent	Giulio Petroni
1969	La donna a una dimensione	Bruno Baratti
1970	Con quale amore, con quanto amore	Pasquale Festa Campanile
1970	Andrea Doria—74	Bruno Vailati
1970	Un caso di coscienza	Giovanni Grimaldi
1970	The Unholy Four	Enzo Barboni
1970	The Dove Must Not Fly	Sergio Garrone (Italy/W. Germany)
1970	Disperatamente l'estate scorsa	Silvio Amadio
1970	The Magnificent Bandits	Giovanni Fago (Italy/Spain)
1970	A Girl Called Jules	Tonino Valerii (France/Italy)
1970	The Adventures of Gerard	Jerzy Skolimowski (UK/Switzerland)
1970	The McKenzie Break	Lamont Johnson (Ireland/UK)
1970	His Name Was Madron (AAN*; GGN*)	Jerry Hopper (Israel)
1970	The Lovemakers	Giovanni Grimaldi
1971	The Statue	Rod Amateau (UK/USA)
1971	Say Hello to Yesterday	Alvin Rakoff (UK)
1971	Confessions of a Police Captain	Damiano Damiani
1971	The Hunting Party	Don Medford (USA/UK)
1971	Web of the Spider	Antonio Margheriti (Italy/France/W. Germany)
1971	Secret Fantasy	Pasquale Festa Campanile
1971	Goodbye Uncle Tom	Gualtiero Jacopetti, Franco Prosperi
1971	Non commettere atti impuri	Giulio Petroni
1972	The Valachi Papers	Terence Young (France/Italy)
1972	Seven Blood-Stained Orchids	Umberto Lenzi (Italy/W. Germany)
1972	Brother Sun, Sister Moon	Franco Zeffirelli (Italy/UK)
1972	Shadows Unseen	Camillo Bazzoni (Italy/France/W. Germany)
1972	The Dead Are Alive	Armando Crispino (Italy/W. Germany)
1972	All Brothers of the West Support Their Father	Sergio Grieco (Italy/Spain/W. Germany)
1972	The Assassin of Rome	Damiano Damiani
1972	Don't Torture a Duckling	Lucio Fulci
1972	A Reason to Live, a Reason to Die	Tonino Valerii (Spain/Italy/France/W. Germany)
1973	Dear Parents	Enrico Maria Salerno (Italy/France)
1973	The Heroes	Duccio Tessari (Italy/France/Spain)
1973	Mafia Junction	Massimo Dallamano (Italy/UK)
1973	Seven Dead in the Cat's Eye	Antonio Margheriti (France/Italy/W. Germany)
1973	Secrets of a Nurse	Luigi Zampa
1973	Fury	Antonio Calenda (Italy/UK)
1973	No, the Case Is Happily Resolved	Vittorio Salerno
1973	The African Deal (aka Carnal Contact)	Giorgio Bontempi (Italy/Ghana)
1973	Counselor at Crime	Alberto De Martino (Italy/Spain)
1973	One Way	Jorge Darnell (Italy/Mexico)
1973	La coppia	Enzo Siciliano
1973	Teresa the Thief	Carlo Di Palma (Italy/France)
1973	Mean Frank and Crazy Tony	Michele Lupo (Italy/France)
1973	The Amazons	Terence Young (Italy/France/Spain)
1974	There Is No 13	William Sachs (USA)
1974	The Real Cannibal Holocaust	Akira Ide (Italy/Japan)
1974	Erotomania	Marco Vicario
1975	Vieni, vieni amore mio	Vittorio Caprioli
1975	How to Kill a Judge	Damiano Damiani
1975	Mondo candido	Gualtiero Jacopetti, Franco Prosperi
1975	Blonde in Black Leather	Carlo Di Palma

Year	Film	Director
1976	Holiday Hookers	Armando Nannuzzi
1976	Mimi Bluette . . . fiore del mio giardino	Carlo Di Palma (Italy/France)
1976	Submission	Salvatore Samperi
1977	Sahara Cross	Tonino Valerii
1977	Death Steps in the Dark	Maurizio Prafeaux (Italy/Greece)
1977	Some Like It Cool (aka Casanova & Co.)	Frank Antel (Austria/France/Italy)
1977	I Am Afraid	Damiano Damiani
1977	Double Murder	Steno (France/Italy)
1977	The Girl in the Yellow Pajamas	Flavio Mogherini (Italy/Spain)
1978	Cyclone (aka Tender Storm)	René Cardona Jr. (Mexico/USA/Italy)
1978	Rings of Fear	Alberto Negrin (Italy/W. Germany/France)
1978	First Love	Dino Risi
1978	Brutes and Savages	Arthur Davis (USA)
1978	Le braghe del padrone	Flavio Mogherini
1978	Gegè Bellavita	Pasquale Festa Campanile
1979	From Hell to Victory	Umberto Lenzi (Italy/Spain/France)
1979	Tigers in Lipstick	Luigi Zampa (Italy/Spain)
1979	The Fifth Musketeer	Ken Annakin (Austria/W. Germany)
1979	Neapolitan Mystery	Sergio Corbucci
1979	Mimi	Florestano Vancini
1979	Il corpo della ragassa	Pasquale Festa Campanile
1979	Atsalut pader	Paolo Cavara
1979	Anni struggenti	Vittorio Sindoni
1980	Cannibal Holocaust	Ruggero Deodato
1980	Fangio: A Life at 300 an Hour	Hugh Hudson (Panama/Italy)
1980	Maria—Nur die Nacht war ihr Zeuge	Ernst Hofbauer (W. Germany/Italy)
1980	The Warning	Damiano Damiani
1980	House on the Edge of the Park	Ruggero Deodato
1981	Help Me to Dream	Pupi Avati
1981	Ghost of Love	Dino Risi (Italy/W. Germany/France)
1981	Honey	Gianfranco Angelucci (Italy/Spain)
1981	Nessuno e perfetto	Pasquale Festa Campanile
1981	And When She Was Bad (aka There Was a Little Girl)	Ovidio G. Assonitis
1981	Fear in the City	Gianni Manera
1982	The Girl from Trieste	Pasquale Festa Campanile
1982	Valentina	Antonio José Betancor (Spain)
1982	Mafalda	Carlos D. Marquez (Argentina)
1982	Porca vacca	Pasquale Festa Campanile
1982	Piu bello di cosi si muore	Pasquale Festa Campanile
1982	I camionisti	Flavio Mogherini (Italy/Spain)
1983	Revenge of the Dead	Pupi Avati
1983	1919, crónica del alba	Antonio José Betancor (Spain)
1983	A School Outing	Pupi Avati
1984	Warriors of the Year 2072	Lucio Fulci
1984	Tuareg: The Desert Warrior	Enzo G. Castellari (Spain/Italy/Israel)
1984	The Three of Us	Pupi Avati
1984	Giuseppe Fava: Siciliano come me	Vittorio Sindoni
1985	Impiegati	Pupi Avati
1985	Un foro nel parabrezza	Sauro Scavolini
1985	Graduation Party	Pupi Avati
1985	Miranda	Tinto Brass
1986	The Corruption	Salvatore Samperi (Italy/France)
1986	Christmas Present	Pupi Avati
1986	Una domenica si	Cesare Bastelli
1986	The Inquiry	Damiano Damiani (Italy/Spain/Tunisia)
1987	Capri Remembered	Tinto Brass
1987	Brothers in Blood	Tonino Valerii
1988	The Last Minute	Pupi Avati

Year	Film	Director
1988	*Bride and Groom*	Antonio Avati, etc.
1988	*I ragazzi di via Panisperna*	Gianni Amelio (Italy/W. Germany)
1989	*Le ciliege sono mature*	Fabio Del Bravo
1989	*Killer Crocodile*	Fabrizio de Angelis
1989	*The Story of Boys & Girls*	Pupi Avati
1989	*Massacre Play (aka The Wounded King)*	Damiano Damiani
1990	*The Dark Sun*	Damiano Damiani
1990	*In the Rose Garden*	Luciano Martino
1990	*One Cold May Morning*	Vittorio Sindoni
1990	*Killer Crocodile 2*	Giannetto De Rossi (Italy/USA)
1991	*Paprika*	Tinto Brass
1992	*Brothers and Sisters*	Pupi Avati
1992	*Angel with a Gun*	Damiano Damiani
1993	*Magnificat*	Pupi Avati
1994	*The Voyeur*	Tinto Brass
1995	*P.O. Box Tinto Brass*	Tinto Brass
1997	*The Best Man*	Pupi Avati
1998	*Grandes ocasiones*	Felipe Vega (Spain)
1999	*Midsummer Night's Dance*	Pupi Avati
2001	*The Knights Who Made the Enterprise*	Pupi Avati (Italy/France)
2003	*Incantato*	Pupi Avati
2004	*Christmas Rematch*	Pupi Avati
2005	*When Do the Girls Show Up?*	Pupi Avati
2005	*The Second Wedding Night*	Pupi Avati
2007	*A Dinner for Them to Meet*	Pupi Avati
2007	*The Hideout*	Pupi Avati (Italy/USA)
2008	*Giovanna's Father*	Pupi Avati
2010	*A Second Childhood*	Pupi Avati

OVCHINNIKOV, Vyacheslav (b. 1936) A Russian composer and conductor who is renowned throughout his country for his concert music, he is most known outside of Russia for his film scores, in particular that for the mammoth 1966 version of *War and Peace.*

Vyacheslav Aleksandrovich Ovchinnikov was born in Voronezh, Russia, to an impoverished family that loved music. Ovchinnikov took piano and violin lessons as a boy and by the age of nine was composing and performing his own works. He began his studies at the Music College of the Moscow Conservatory when he was only fifteen and by the time he graduated he had already completed two symphonies. For these and his overtures, tone poems, and other juvenile works he won some prestigious music competitions. As an adult, Ovchinnikov went on to write chamber pieces, violin and piano concertos, cantatas, oratorios, choral works, and symphonic music. His reputation as a conductor was made when he worked on Russian television; he would later conduct performances of the great classical pieces around the world. Ovchinnikov

was already a celebrated artist when director Andrei Tarkovsky approached him in 1961 to write the score for *The Steamroller and the Violin,* a small movie about a boy violinist (Igor Fomchenko) violinist who befriends the driver (Vladimir Zamanskiy) of a steamroller. The result was so satisfying that Tarkovsky worked with him again on *Ivan's Childhood,* another intimate drama about a boy (Nikolay Burlyaev) who acts as a spy on the eastern front during World War II. It was based on Ovchinnikov's scores for these two small-scale films that director-actor Sergey Bondarchuk hired him to score the longest, most expensive, and most prestigious movie ever made in Russia: a four-part version of Tolstoy's *War and Peace.* Ovchinnikov wrote eleven hours of music for the twelve-hour epic that was first seen outside of the Soviet Union in a two-part, eight-hour version. (Shorter versions were released later.) Both the movie and its score were praised around the world. He would return to films to score three more works by Bondarchuk as well as a half dozen movies for other Russian directors. In 1971 he also wrote a new score for the 1930 screen classic *Earth* by Aleksandr Dovzhenko. Ovchinnikov left movies in 1987 to concentrate on his concert career, traveling the world as an acclaimed conductor.

One tends to be overwhelmed by the size of the *War and Peace* score. There are themes for over a dozen major characters, dance music, marches, folk songs, hymns, and symphonic passages as grandiose as the cast of thousands on the screen. But once one focuses on just the most essential parts of the score, the true value of Ovchinnikov's accomplishment becomes more evident. The battle scenes have music that is as loud, vigorous, and sweeping as the visual images. These passages are in the classical style and one almost expects Tchaikovsky's *1812 Overture* to slip in without being noticed. Yet it is the less bombastic parts of the score that are more impressive. A grand processional for the entrance of the tzar at a St. Petersburg ball is as catchy as it is stirring. The resplendent waltz at the same ball, in which Natasha (Lyudmila Saveleva) and Andrei (Vyacheslav Tikhonov) fall in love, is swift and intoxicating as we experience the event through her point of view. This is contrasted with an infectious folk tune that

Natasha dances to in a country lodge, illustrating how the heroine captures the Russian spirit in its extremes. Similar extremes can be heard in the main theme: a splash of symphonic explosion that segues into a reflective choral passage, musically conveying both war and peace. A sprightly aristocratic mazurka is as pleasing as the gypsy music for a rural gathering. A race on sleighs has the energy of a Prokofiev chase while the burning of Moscow has a frenzied theme that sounds like a bizarre dance gone out of control. For the central character of Pierre (Bondarchuk) there is a somber and dreamy theme that is as introspective as he is. Natasha's theme is a beautiful slow waltz in which the strings seem to be suspended in space and time. The moody Prince Andrei has a wavering theme in which strings cannot seem to decide where to resolve themselves. Even the silent French drummer boy, captured by the Russians and fed by the teenage soldier Petya, has a lovely flute theme that aches with innocence. Ovchinnikov's score for *War and Peace* may be overwhelming but it is also filled with musical moments that are unforgettable. Official website (in English): www.vyacheslavovchinnikov.ru/en.

Credits

(all films USSR)

Year	Film	Director
1961	The Steamroller and the Violin	Andrei Tarkovsky
1962	Ivan's Childhood	Andrei Tarkovsky, Eduard Abalov
1965	War and Peace Part I	Sergey Bondarchuk
1965	Pervyy uchitel (aka The First Teacher)	Andrey Konchalovskiy
1966	War and Peace Part II	Sergey Bondarchuk
1966	Andrei Rublev	Andrei Tarkovsky
1966	Dolgaya schastlivaya zhizn (aka Long Happy Life)	Gennadi Shpalikov
1967	War and Peace Part III & IV	Sergey Bondarchuk
1969	A Nest of Gentry	Andrey Konchalovskiy
1970	Kat stat muzhchinoy	Khasan Khazhkasimov
1971	Earth (1930)	Aleksandr Dovzhenko
1972	Prishyol soldat s fronta (aka A Soldier Came Back from the Front)	Nikolai Gubenko, Vasiliy Shukshin
1973	That Sweet Word: Liberty!	Vytautas Zalakevicius
1974	Avariya	Vytautas Zalakevicius
1975	They Fought for Their Country	Sergey Bondarchuk
1979	Steppe	Sergey Bondarchuk
1986	Boris Gudunov	Sergey Bondarchuk
1987	Bagrationi	Giuli Chokhonelidze, Guguli Mgeladze

P

POLEDOURIS, Basil (1945–2006) A very successful television and movie composer and conductor, he is most known for his scores for action and adventure movies.

Born Basilis Konstantine Poledouris in Kansas City, Missouri, he was the son of devout Greek Orthodox parents who moved to California when he was still a baby. Poledouris grew up listening to music in his church, began piano lessons at the age of seven, played in bands and folk groups during his high school days, and studied filmmaking and music at the University of Southern California. Although he learned a great deal about music from screen composer and faculty member David Raksin, Poledouris concentrated on movie directing at USC. After graduation, he found work making short educational films, scoring them himself and providing music for other such movies. After working on over one hundred of these documentaries, Poledouris realized his talents lay in music, and he started composing for television in 1970. Two of his fellow film students at USC, John Milius and Randal Kleiser, were starting to make directing careers for themselves in Hollywood and Poledouris's first movie score was written for Milius's small-budget independent film *The Reversal of Richard Sun* in 1970. Eight years later Poledouris found more recognition for his score for Milius's surfing drama *Big Wednesday*. For Kleiser he scored the popular teen romance *The Blue Lagoon* then had one of the biggest hits of his career with Milius's action film *Conan the Barbarian*. Poledouris later reteamed with Milius and Kleiser for three subsequent movies each, most memorably for *Red Dawn* with Milius and *White Fang* with Kleiser.

The success of *Conan the Barbarian* and its sequel *Conan the Destroyer* labeled Poledouris an action movie composer. After he dazzled audiences with his score for the sci-fi action movie *RoboCop*, Poledouris was too rarely hired to score movies outside the action-adventure genre. Yet he managed to find a good deal of variety and creativity within that genre, as witnessed in such thrillers as *Flesh+Blood*, *On Deadly Ground*, *Iron Eagle*, *Under Siege 2*, *Starship Troopers*, and *The Hunt for Red October*. In stark contrast to these are the quieter, more optimistic movies that Poledouris got to score on occasion. Among the most accomplished of these are *Wind*, *Lassie*, *The Jungle Book*, *For Love of the Game*, and *Free Willy* and its sequel. There are also a surprising number of comedies among the credits of a composer most associated with violent thrillers. These range from routine comic tales, such as *Celtic Pride* and *Mickey Blue Eyes*, to outrageous satires and spoofs, as with *Serial Mom* and *Hot Shots! Part Deux*. Then there are a few first-class dramas that Poledouris scored, most memorably *The War at Home*, *Les Misérables*, *Breakdown*, and *It's My Party*, one of the first Hollywood movies about AIDS.

Some of Poledouris's finest work was written for television. For the miniseries *Amerika* (1987) and *Lonesome Dove* (1989), he wrote two very different but superior scores. Among his other TV movies and miniseries are *A Whale for the Killing* (1981), *Fire on the Mountain* (1981), *Amazons* (1984), *Intrigue* (1988), *Ned Blessing: The True Story of My Life* (1992), *Love and Treason* (2001), and *The Legend of Butch and Sundance* (2006). His bold and dramatic music for action movies appealed to organizations looking for such grandiose music for other events. Poledouris composed the invigorating music for the opening ceremony for the 1996 Olympics in Atlanta, rousing music for theme parks, and expansive soundtracks for IMAX films. After writing the music for the TV movie *The Legend of Butch and Sundance*, Poledouris retired to an island off the coast of the state of Washington where he battled cancer for four years before dying at the age of sixty-one.

If one screen score justifies Poledouris's high rank among Hollywood composers, that would be *Conan the Barbarian*. Because there is not a great deal of dialogue in this tale of ancient warriors, the musical soundtrack is more important than usual. Not only is the movie practically nonstop action but the score is also practically nonstop, so finding variety and freshness for the soundtrack was a challenge. Poledouris, composing only his seventh feature film, astonished everyone with his endless energy and resourcefulness. The main theme, titled "Anvil of Crom," takes its cue from the forging of a sword. Quiet pounding explodes into a passage with bombastic French horns and then into the flow of a full orchestral theme, suggesting both a primitive world and a classical epic tale. The vigorous theme for the hero Conan (Arnold Schwarzenegger) utilizes a Latin-chanting chorus in the style of Carl Orff's *Carmina Burana*. The romantic theme is surprisingly tender, starting off with only one oboe backed by muted strings then building until the strings take over. A solo oboe and lone flute alternate in another theme. The music for an orgy is more festive than sultry with music for primitive dancing as violins sweep back and forth and clarinets play a medieval air. Perhaps most intoxicating is the "Civilization" theme which turns this action cartoon into something poetic. With over two hours of extraordinary music, the *Conan the Barbarian* score could serve as any composer's finest moment.

It is a tribute to Poledouris that his other action film scores are not rehashes of his first hit. Even the sequel *Conan the Destroyer* has its own originality and excitement. The main theme this time is not so primitive as quick-fire. There is tribal drumming with a simple flute chorus, heavy brass, and strident violins all taking turns as they rush forward. The medieval adventure *Flesh+Blood* also has a main theme that pulsates with movement but the orchestration is fuller and more romanticized. The love theme is particularly dulcet with a solo recorder playing against a full orchestra. The futuristic *RoboCop* score uses a synthesizer and some electronic effects for the sci-fi tone but it is the main theme's five-note signature phrase and the minor-key accompaniment that make the music distinctive. There is a contrasting "Home" theme, in which the police officer turned robot (Peter Weller) thinks back on his human family. Voices call out hauntingly and this restless, fervent score mellows and flows freely for a while. Another sci-fi movie, *Starship Troopers*, makes many allusions to contemporary times and the military march in the opening theme recalls a World War II film score with some electric instruments added. *The Hunt for Red October*, an action movie with intelligence as well as a sense of adventure, has a splendid score that draws on its Cold War subject. Poledouris's Russian hymn, sung by a robust but precise chorus, is a stirring and melodic main theme. Other sections of the score are also very Russian in flavor, which contrasts with the pounding, aggressive music for the American forces. A musical passage that explores the personal side of the Russian captain (Sean Connery) is a

beautifully melancholy piece played by woodwinds. The final confrontation at sea is scored more like a suspense thriller than an action movie, the chorus returning to compete with pulsating brass and drums. There are more brains than brawn in *The Hunt for Red October* and Poledouris's score reflects this.

Poledouris was a surfer and avid maritime outdoorsman, so he particularly relished scoring movies about the sea. His early feature *Big Wednesday* is about three surfer buddies but the Pacific and the waves are really the focus of the tale. Poledouris mixes jazz with some Hawaiian themes and crashing crescendos to portray the ocean majestically. For a movie that is essentially a comedy, the score is rather reverent. Sometimes the open sea is scored like a western movie that is in awe of nature. For the feature *Wind*, a film about building and racing a boat to win the America's Cup, the focus is on sailing, and with Poledouris's inspiring score and the outstanding photography, there is again a kind of reverence for the sea. Parts of the score are quiet and reflective as a solo piano captures the gentle aspect of the ocean. Other passages are rousing and exhilarating, particularly when wind and sails take flight. Again one hears musical elements from the western genre although the instrumentation is more New Wave than pioneer. *Free Willy* celebrates the open sea as well, but this time it is about the efforts to return a theme park Orca whale back to its natural habitat. Violins, harp, and a choir are used in the main theme, a waltzing piece of sublime music that sometimes turns stormy with kettle drums, brass, and electronic instruments. While many dismissed *The Blue Lagoon* as a soft-porn joke, this teen romance set on a desert island boasts a splendid score that is also inspired by the sea. Beautiful scenery and photogenic young bodies both seem more like a picture calendar than a movie but there is nothing manufactured about the score. The main theme is gentle and lyrical, slowly picking up the cadence of waves on the beach. The love theme tends to be more tentative than passionate, the long melodic lines pausing unexpectedly and effectively. The Poledouris who scored these maritime movies seems so far away from the man who musicalized Conan and the RoboCop.

Three atypical scores by Poledouris should be considered. He uses very little Hindu music in his score for the live-action *The Jungle Book*. Instead the adventure film is scored like a pastoral symphony with full orchestra stirring up mystery, grandeur, and even playfulness. The youth Mowgli (Jason Scott Lee) is given a delicate theme accompanied by a native flute that has a touch of wonder and curiosity in the melody. For all its primeval charm, the movie is an adventure and there is plenty of exciting music as well, usually with the violins screeching like forest creatures and the brass coming in like elephant calls. *Breakdown* is a contemporary thriller about a husband (Kurt Russell) looking for his kidnapped wife (Kathleen Quinlan). What makes the movie so involving is that nothing is exaggerated and everything seems uncomfortably believable. The percussive main theme, with a variety of drums playing at different tempos and electronic sounds echoing at a high pitch, makes it quite clear that danger lurks everywhere. Once the hunt is on, the score grows

even more intense until the husband's desperation and fury are musicalized with a vengeance. Not until the end credits does the music subside and a minor-key passage allows one to breathe again. The dark comedy-drama *It's My Party* is about a big-time designer (Eric Roberts) who is dying from AIDS and decides to throw himself a farewell bash. Poledouris scores this unusual film with piano only, playing variations of a single theme throughout the film. The music manages to be melancholy and determined at the same time, resulting in several ambiguous emotions. For an action movie composer (or any composer), this score is a masterful piece of restraint and quiet sincerity. There is so much more to Poledouris than one can imagine while watching his barbarians.

Credits

(all films USA unless stated otherwise)

Year	Film	Director
1970	The Reversal of Richard Sun	John Milius
1973	Hollywood 90028	Christine Hornisher
1973	Extreme Close-Up	Jeannot Szwarc
1977	Tintorera: Killer Shark	René Cardona Jr. (UK/Mexico)
1978	Big Wednesday	John Milius
1980	The Blue Lagoon	Randal Kleiser
1982	Conan the Barbarian	John Milius
1982	Summer Lovers	Randal Kleiser
1984	The House of God	Donald Wrye
1984	Making the Grade	Dorian Walker
1984	Conan the Destroyer	Richard Fleischer
1984	Red Dawn	John Milius
1984	Protocol	Herbert Ross
1985	Flesh+Blood	Pail Verhoeven (Spain/USA/Netherlands)
1986	Iron Eagle	Sidney J. Furie (USA/Israel/Canada)
1987	RoboCop	Paul Verhoeven
1987	No Man's Land	Peter Werner
1987	Cherry 2000	Steve De Jarnatt
1988	Spellbinder	Janet Greek
1988	Split Decisions	David Drury
1989	Intruder	Scott Spiegel
1989	Farewell to the King	John Milius
1989	Wired	Larry Peerce
1990	The Hunt for Red October	John McTiernan
1990	Quigley Down Under	Simon Wincer (Australia/USA)
1991	White Fang	Randal Kleiser
1991	Flight of the Intruder	John Milius
1991	Return to the Blue Lagoon	William A. Graham
1991	Harley Davidson and the Marlboro Man	Simon Wincer
1992	Wind	Carroll Ballard
1993	RoboCop 3	Fred Dekker
1993	Hot Shots! Part Deux	Jim Abrahams
1993	Free Willy	Simon Wincer (USA/France)

Year	Film	Director
1994	*Serial Mom*	John Waters
1994	*Lassie*	Daniel Petrie
1994	*The Jungle Book*	Stephen Sommers
1995	*Under Siege 2: Dark Territory*	Geoff Murphy
1995	*Free Willy 2: The Adventure Home*	Dwight H. Little (France/USA)
1996	*It's My Party*	Randal Kleiser
1996	*Celtic Pride*	Tom DeCerchio
1996	*The War at Home*	Emilio Estevez
1996	*Amanda*	Bobby Roth
1997	*Breakdown*	Jonathan Mostow
1997	*Switchback*	Jeb Stuart
1997	*Starship Troopers*	Paul Verhoeven
1998	*Les Misérables*	Bille August (UK/Germany/USA)
1999	*Mickey Blue Eyes*	Kelly Makin (UK/USA)
1999	*Kimberly*	Frederic Golchan
1999	*For Love of the Game*	Sam Raimi
2000	*Cecil B. DeMented*	John Waters (France/USA)
2001	*Crocodile Dundee in Los Angeles*	Simon Wincer (Australia/USA)
2002	*The Touch*	Peter Pau (China/Hong Kong/Taiwan/Japan)

PORTMAN, Rachel (b. 1960) A highly respected British composer very active in Hollywood since the 1980s, she is the first woman to win an Academy Award for a feature film score.

Rachel M. Portman, born in Haslemere, England, took lessons in piano, violin, and organ as a child, and started composing when she was fourteen years old. Portman studied music at Worcester College at Oxford University and as an undergraduate wrote music for student films and theatre productions. When one student movie, *Privileged*, was picked up and broadcast by the BBC, she began scoring dramas for that and other British television networks. Portman's first studio film was *Experience Preferred . . . but Not Essential* in 1982. After two other movies and lots of television work, she was named the Young Composer of 1988 by the British Film Institute. In 1992 Portman was brought to Hollywood by British director Beeban Kidron to score *Used People*, and she has returned to the States to compose music for a wide variety of movies. Among her many significant films are *Ethan Frome*, *Benny & Joon*, *The Joy Luck Club*, *The Road to Wellville*, *Smoke*, *Marvin's Room*, *The Manchurian Candidate*, *Oliver Twist*, *The Legend of Bagger Vance*, *Infamous*, *The Human Stain*, *Nicholas Nickleby*, *Mona Lisa Smile*, *The Duchess*, *Because of Winn-Dixie*, and *The Sisterhood of the Traveling Pants 2*. Her score for *Emma* won the Oscar, and she was nominated for her music in *The Cider House Rules* and *Chocolat*. Portman is the most prolific woman composer in film today, with forty-five feature films and twenty TV movies and miniseries, including *Sharma and Beyond* (1984), *Four Days in July* (1985), *A Little Princess* (1986), *The Storyteller* (1988), *The Woman in Black* (1989), *Precious Bane* (1989), *Living with Dinosaurs* (1989), *Shoot to Kill* (1990), *Elizabeth R* (1992), and *Grey Gardens* (2009), as well as the animated made-for-video *Beauty and the Beast: The Enchanted Christmas* (1997). Portman's other credits include the children's opera *The Little Prince* (2003), the concert piece *The Water Diviner's Tale* (2007), and the stage musical *Little House on the Prairie* (2008). Among the many honors she has received are the Richard Kirk Award from the BMI Film & TV Awards and Officer of the Order of the British Empire (OBE) in 2010.

Portman's music can be described as conventional and in the classical tradition. She rarely uses electronic or altered instrumentation, favoring strings and woodwinds in a flowing manner. For this reason she is not hired to score action or science fiction movies, but rather character pieces, adaptations of literary classics, romantic comedies, and costume dramas. While her music is often lighthearted and even ethereal, there is considerable variety in her scores. She is also open to various kinds of music, such as using African and tribal instruments for the score for *Beloved*. This tale of a former slave (Oprah Winfrey) in nineteenth-century America is filled with mysticism, and Portman's score is likewise fantastical and ghostlike. A solo voice wailing over a background choir conveys a haunted and mournful tone. Ancient flutes mix with primitive string instruments to create a simple yet elegant lament. *Beloved* may not succeed as a film, but the atmosphere is compelling and much of that must be attributed to the score. Most of Portman's other films are not so heavy handed. *Chocolat* is a whimsical tale set in a small French village, and her music is quaint and intimate. The main theme is a gentle minor-key passage played by a small ensemble of piano, strings, and woodwinds. Other sections of the score utilize accordion and harp, giving the music an elegant French flavor. The arrival of a band of gypsies in the town brings more exotic themes as guitar and recorder are added to the mix. One passage, in which a high oboe plays against strings, is delectable. A much more American sound can be found in *The Legend of Bagger Vance* about professional golf. Actor Robert Redford directed and the movie has more than a passing similarity to the 1984 baseball film *The Natural* that he starred in. Both movies have a mystical quality to them, raising sport to an almost-religious experience. In the main theme, a solo trumpet pierces the silence as voices and orchestra carefully ascend the scale. Other sections, using piano and sustained strings, are mesmerizing in their simplicity. *The Legend of Bagger Vance* score includes a good deal of music from other sources, from Gabriel Fauré's *Requiem* to Fats Waller's "My Best Wishes," but Portman's gliding, intoxicating soundtrack score is what carries the movie.

Also American is the quirky film *The Cider House Rules* which is set in Maine but is scored with a rather rural British Isles flavor. In fact, one passage is a bit reminiscent of "Loch Lomond." Yet this felicitous score seems correct for the story. The graceful main theme uses a six-note motif as a piano plays against strings in a classical manner. Central to the story is an apple orchard that has its own theme. Sometimes it is played by alternating oboe and flute, other times a clarinet is heard over strings. Another quirky tale is *The Emperor's New Clothes* about Napoleon (Ian Holm) and his efforts to escape St. Helena and return to France. The central theme is a sprightly chamber piece that suggests a cockeyed dance. For the romantic *One Day*, voices join the strings in a reverent musical theme. Even more liturgical is an enticing wedding theme in which a soprano soars over a children's choir. The period film *Mona Lisa Smile* about academia has a lyrical score that echoes classical themes throughout. A solo clarinet plays the sustained notes as strings play against it in the main theme. Even more classical is the score for the Parisian period piece *Bel Ami* which has a propulsive symphonic score, Portman's music suggesting a vigorous Mozart piece. Even the contemporary domestic drama *Marvin's Room* has a classically flavored score. The piano presides over the main theme then a clarinet takes over as a full orchestra provides a contrasting melody. One of the most unusual films Portman got to score is the seriocomic *Smoke*. The clapping of a wood block provides the tempo as a delicate harp plays the melody that revolves around a three-note phrase. Like the movie itself, it is beguiling and oddly fascinating.

A pair of Dickens's films are ideal for Portman's musical sensibility. *Nicholas Nickleby* has a resplendent main theme in which a solo clarinet plays against restless strings. Slowed down, this same passage is highly romantic and rich with Victorian sentiment. The darker parts of this saga are scored with low and high strings in competition, sometimes a menacing oboe joining them. *Oliver Twist* uses a solo trumpet to announce its main theme, a brisk march that suggests the hustle and bustle of London. The title character's loneliness is conveyed with a solo clarinet that seems close to weeping in its sustained notes. Even sadder is the sorrowful theme for Newgate Prison where Fagin (Ben Kingsley) awaits execution. Perhaps the most pleasing of Portman's literary classic movies is *Emma* in which Jane Austen's world is brought to life in the score. The main theme is a delicate waltz in which harp and flute carry the smooth melody. Most of the passages are lighter in tone, suggesting a dance in which the characters are always engaged. There is a wry theme for the pompous characters, a folk theme for the rustics, and a lovely, fluid theme for the romantic moments. Austen's tales are essentially comic and this score knows how to maintain a light touch and not get bogged down in period music. Like her music, Portman is a self-professed traditionalist and a bit old fashioned. She composes at the piano and writes on paper rather than using computer programs. She usually orchestrates her own scores but trusts the recording sessions to experienced cinema conductors. Portman has managed to find success outside of the Hollywood system, yet her scores represent the best of Old Hollywood in their romanticism and dramatic storytelling. Official website: www.rachelportman.co.uk.

Credits

(all films USA unless stated otherwise)

Year	Film	Director
1982	Privileged	Michael Hoffman (UK)
1982	Experience Preferred . . . but Not Essential (aka First Love)	Peter Duffell (UK)
1984	Reflections	Kevin Billington (UK)
1987	90 Degrees South	Alan Ravenscroft (UK)
1990	Life Is Sweet	Mike Leigh (UK)
1991	Where Angels Fear to Tread	Charles Sturridge (UK)
1992	Rebecca's Daughters	Karl Francis (Germany/UK)
1992	Used People	Beeban Kidron (USA/Japan)
1993	Ethan Frome	John Madden (UK/USA)
1993	Benny & Joon	Jeremiah S. Chechik
1993	Friends	Elaine Proctor (S. Africa/UK/France)
1993	The Joy Luck Club	Wayne Wang (USA/China)
1993	Sirens	John Duigan (Australia/UK)
1994	War of the Buttons	John Roberts (UK/France/Japan)
1994	Only You (aka Faith)	Norman Jewison (USA/Italy)
1994	The Road to Wellville	Alan Parker
1995	Smoke	Wayne Wang, Paul Auster (Germany/USA/Japan)
1995	A Pyromaniac's Love Story	Joshua Brand
1995	Palookaville	Alan Taylor
1995	To Wong Foo Thanks for Everything, Julie Newmar	Beeban Kidron
1996	Emma (AA)	Douglas McGrath (UK/USA)
1996	Marvin's Room	Jerry Zaks
1997	Addicted to Love	Griffin Dunne
1998	Home Fries	Dean Parisot
1998	Beloved	Jonathan Demme
1999	The Other Sister	Garry Marshall
1999	Ratcatcher	Lynne Ramsay (UK/France)
1999	The Cider House Rules (AAN)	Lasse Hallström
2000	The Closer You Get (aka American Women)	Aileen Ritchie (UK/Ireland)
2000	The Legend of Bagger Vance	Robert Redford
2000	Chocolat (AAN; GGN)	Lasse Hallström (UK/USA)
2001	The Emperor's New Clothes	Alan Taylor (Italy/UK/Germany)
2002	Hart's War	Gregory Hoblit
2002	The Truth about Charlie	Jonathan Demme (USA/Germany)
2002	Nicholas Nickleby	Douglas McGrath (UK/USA)
2003	The Human Stain	Robert Benton (USA/Germany/France)
2003	Mona Lisa Smile	Mike Newell
2004	The Manchurian Candidate	Jonathan Demme
2005	Because of Winn-Dixie	Wayne Wang
2005	Oliver Twist	Roman Polanski (UK/Czech Republic/France/Italy)
2006	The Lake House	Alejandro Agresti (USA/Australia)
2006	Infamous (aka Every Word Is True)	Douglas McGrath
2008	The Sisterhood of the Traveling Pants 2	Sanaa Hamri (USA/Greece)
2008	The Duchess	Saul Dibb (UK/Italy/France/USA)
2010	Never Let Me Go	Mark Romanek (UK/USA)
2011	Snow Flower and the Secret Fan	Wayne Wang (China/USA)
2011	One Day	Lone Scherfig (USA/UK)
2012	The Vow	Michael Sucsy (USA/France/Austria/UK/Germany)
2012	Bel Ami	Declan Donnellan, Nick Ormerod (UK/Italy)
2012	Private Peaceful	Pat O'Connor (UK)
2013	Paradise (aka Lamb of God)	Diablo Cody
2013	Still Life	Uberto Pasolini (UK/Italy)
2013	Belle	Amma Asante (UK)
2013	The Right Kind of Wrong (aka Sex and Sunsets)	Jeremiah S. Chechik (Canada)

POWELL, John (b. 1963) A busy British composer since 1994 who works mostly in Hollywood, he has become one of the most in-demand composers for animated films.

Born in London, John Powell took violin lessons as a child and later studied piano at London's Trinity College of Music. He began his professional career playing in jazz and rock bands and for a time played in a soul band called the Faboulists before giving up performing to compose music for television commercials. In 1995 Powell cofounded Independently Thinking Music, a music company that has over the years created dozens of commercials for British and French television as well as scores for independent films. He first got involved in feature films as an assistant to composer Patrick Doyle and as composer for two French film shorts. Powell moved to Los Angeles in 1997 to pursue a screen composing career and that same year made an encouraging debut when he scored the sci-fi crime drama *Face/Off*. The next year he worked on his first of many animated movies when he and Harry Gregson-Williams wrote the music for the comedy *Antz*. He has since scored over fifty feature films, about half of them animated movies. Either solo or with co-composers such as Gregson-Williams and Hans Zimmer, he has scored such popular animated features as *The Road to El Dorado*, *Chicken Run*, *Shrek*, three *Ice Age* sequels, *Robots*, *Kung Fu Panda* and its sequels, *Bolt*, *Happy Feet* and its sequel, *Rio* and its sequel, the Dr. Seuss movies *Horton Hears a Who!* and *The Lorax*, and *How to Train Your Dragon* and its sequel. Powell's live-action movies range from thrillers to silly comedies. Among his many notable films are *The Bourne Identity* and its two sequels, *The Italian Job*, *I Am Sam*, *United 93*, *Rat Race*, *X-Men: The Last Stand*, *P.S. I Love You*, *Mr. & Mrs. Smith*, and *Green Zone*. He has also composed music for television and video shorts and has conducted the recordings of several of his film and TV scores.

Powell's first feature score, for *Face/Off*, was a solo effort, as were most of his live-action movies. An FBI agent (John Travolta) impersonates a terrorist (Nicolas Cage) while the terrorist takes on the identity of the agent in this intriguing action movie with some sci-fi elements. Powell mixes conventional and synthesized music effectively in the high-energy score. There is a graceful but agitated theme on strings with twinkling accents until the music explodes into an angry and painful passage with horns and vocal chanting. A rumbling electronic track with echoing strings, vibrating noises, and determined percussion is contrasted by a poetic French horn theme with furious strings underneath. The film's many chase scenes are scored with rapid percussion and angry brass fanfares that alternate with celestial strings. A quiet, tentative piano passage is overwhelmed by electronic noises and waves of synthesized music, and a sort-of love theme is played on electronic keyboard with bold string crescendos and a soaring choir. Quite the opposite of *Face/Off* is the tear-jerker *P.S. I Love You*, a romantic drama about a young widow (Hilary Swank) who receives a series of letters that her husband (Gerard Butler) wrote to her before he died, knowing that they would help her cope with his absence. Powell features the acoustic guitar in this gentle score, which shuns high-tech music. There is a sparkling solo guitar theme with string and harmonica accompaniment that moves in a sprightly manner but when slowed down has a melancholy tone. The evocative score also includes a traveling theme on guitar and woodwinds that seems to float along without pauses, a felicitous guitar and strings passage that has a confident air as it slowly gains strength, a cockeyed theme played on various woodwinds and guitar that comes across as a bit drunk and carefree, and a piano solo lament that is somber yet full of life. It is clear from these two scores that Powell has a considerable musical range.

The most popular live-action films that Powell scored are the three thrillers based on Robert Ludlum novels. *The Bourne Identity*, about an amnesiac (Matt Damon) trying to discover his past as he is being hunted down, is in many ways one long chase and Powell's music is similarly accelerated. The main theme, consisting of eight sustained notes that are stretched out when each note is doubled, features a bassoon in a doleful lament. The mellow theme then catches fire when eruptive percussion and pizzicato and gliding strings are added and the tempo changes to a steady dash. This same music is later used for an adagio section, where it is surprisingly dreamlike and mesmerizing. The many chase sequences are scored on synthesized percussion, piano, and furious electronic instruments. There is a traveling theme on electric and acoustic guitar with synthesized keyboard and growling percussion. At one point in the score the music turns nervous with jittery percussion and string glissandos that are a bit sour and more than a little dizzy. This kind of dynamic scoring was continued in Powell's music for *The Bourne Supremacy* and *The Bourne Ultimatum.* It is likely his career might have concentrated on such action movies, but animation would end up playing the primary role in his Hollywood career, all because of studio rivalry. When DreamWorks was putting together its first animated movie, *Antz,* producer Jeffrey Katzenberg found out that the Disney studio was making the very similar *A Bug's Life.* In order to release his film before the Disney product, production was rushed and music producer Hans Zimmer was required to come up with a score in record time. He assigned two of his protégés, Powell and Gregson-Williams, to write the major themes for the *Antz* score and hired a handful of others to compose the fill-ins. The movie and the music were both popular and Powell found himself contributing to the clever score for the stop-action spoof *Chicken Run,* which pastiched *The Great Escape* and Elmer Bernstein's music for that 1963 prison camp film. Gregson-Williams and Powell also had a hit with their eclectic score for the sarcastic fairy tale *Shrek* and Zimmer teamed up with Powell for the Spanish-flavored music for *The Road to El Dorado* and the pseudo-Asian scores for the *Kung Fu Panda* comedies. As delightful as these scores are, it is difficult to pinpoint Powell's contribution. So for the sake of accurate discussion, it is best to look at some of the many animated features that Powell scored alone.

Bolt, the only Disney animated movie that Powell scored, is an endearing tale of the canine star of a television superhero show who believes he actually has superpowers. When Bolt believes his owner Penny has been kidnapped, he sets off on a journey to rescue her, thereby discovering the real world. Powell's score is a combination of mock–action movie music and softer, revealing themes for the character-driven story. The recurring main theme, used in a variety of ways throughout the film, is a surging march on strings and percussion that easily slows down to become a reflective passage at times. Electronic sounds and synthesized music race ahead to a pounding percussion tempo for one of the chase sequences. A chase on a scooter is scored with a furious percussion and electronic organ passage with both electric and traditional strings running along as well. On the tender side, there is a delicate yet playful piece on French horn, piano, and celesta that uses a flowing melody in a classical frame of mind; and a heartfelt slow march on horns and percussion that turns into an inspiring anthem. One of the most risible tracks in the score is that heard at an RV park. It is a tiptoeing

theme played on harp, horn, flute, and piano that is giddy and slaphappy even before it turns into mocking western hoedown music. It is a feathered hero that takes a journey in *Rio,* a comic adventure about a macaw living in Minnesota who has to go to Rio de Janeiro to mate and save his species. The score is often Latin but more often than not raucously eclectic. The opening music features a solo flute and strings welcoming the day with a sunrise passage that has a touch of folk. This quickly turns into zesty western travel music, played on pipes and strings, that gallops along with glee. The score also includes a silly tuba, woodwinds, and strings track that is awkward and fun as it tries to be smooth but keeps breaking into a Latin quickstep or a jaunty bossa nova; a incongruous flight theme that is sometimes high flying and expansive, other times a series of descending notes that are very lead footed; a flowing Spanish tune on flute that is eager and pleasing; and an eccentric tango played on horns and strings that moves from the sultry to the ridiculous then back again.

Also an eclectic mishmash of musical styles is the score for the Dr. Seuss fable *Horton Hears a Who!* This animated parable concerns an elephant who risks everything to protect a microscopic community of Whos from destruction by those who do not believe the tiny creatures exist. The magical main theme is played on piccolo and strings that move at a brisk pace as if marching in a speeded-up parade, especially once a forceful chorus is added. There is fiery dance music with synthesized and conventional instruments rushing forward like a rhythmic race, and an up-tempo lullaby on woodwinds and pizzicato strings that takes a while to settle into a soothing and enchanting theme. The village of Whoville is scored with classical strings, brass crescendos, and mixed choir. Then a mariachi band in full force is heard, followed by chaotic synthesized music that has an Asian flavor. The music for the swanky Club Nool is a pseudo-Hawaiian theme with gliding strings and bongo drums.

Powell's only score to date to get an Oscar nomination is the rich and encompassing one he wrote for the animated family adventure *How to Train Your Dragon.* While all the Vikings are happily hunting and destroying dragons, the youth Hiccup befriends a young dragon he names Toothless and together they try to change the combative relationship between humans and dragons. This problematic tale has some very serious scenes and Powell's music for the most part is more epic than comic. The opening music is a

Celt-like folk tune chanted as primitive pipes play a simple, moody melody. Then the music transitions into a rousing march with vibrant drumming and a robust male choir. The score includes a lot of reverent, reflective music with choral support that comes across as quite inspiring. There is a rapid chase theme with shouting brass, fervent strings, and determined percussion; a swift passage with anxious strings and chanting women's chorus that slows down to form a hymn; and a lighthearted track on woodwinds and strings that sounds like a silly folk dance. Perhaps this score was noticed by the Academy because it sounds more like a live-action fantasy epic than an animated one. Yet looking at Powell's scores, for all his animated movies, one realizes they are so much more rewarding than "cartoon" music.

Credits

(all films USA unless stated otherwise)

Year	Film	Director
1997	Face/Off	John Woo
1998	With Friends Like These . . .	Philip Frank Messina
1998	Antz	Eric Darnell, Tim Johnson
1999	Endurance	Leslie Woodhead, Bud Greenspan (USA/UK/ Germany)
1999	Forces of Nature	Bronwen Hughes
1999	Chill Factor	Hugh Johnson
2000	The Road to El Dorado	Bibo Bergeron, etc.
2000	Chicken Run	Peter Lord, Nick Park (UK/USA)
2001	Just Visiting	Jean-Marie Poiré (France/USA)
2001	Shrek (BAFTA-N)	Andrew Adamson, Vicky Jenson
2001	Evolution	Ivan Reitman
2001	Rat Race	Jerry Zucker (Canada/USA)
2001	I Am Sam	Jessie Nelson
2002	Eye See You (aka Detox)	Jim Gillespie (USA/Germany)
2002	The Bourne Identity	Doug Liman (USA/Germany/Czech Rep.)
2002	Drumline	Charles Stone III
2002	The Adventures of Pluto Nash	Ron Underwood (USA/Australia)
2002	Two Weeks Notice	Marc Lawrence (USA/Australia)
2003	Stealing Sinatra	Ron Underwood
2003	Agent Cody Banks	Harald Zwart (USA/Canada)
2003	The Italian Job	F. Gary Gray (USA/France/UK)
2003	Gigli (aka Tough Love)	Martin Brest
2003	Paycheck	John Woo (USA/Canada)
2004	The Bourne Supremacy	Paul Greengrass (USA/Germany)
2004	Mr. 3000	Charles Stone III
2005	Be Cool	F. Gary Gray
2005	Robots	Chris Wedge, Carlos Saldanha
2005	Mr. & Mrs. Smith	Doug Liman
2006	Ice Age: the Meltdown	Carlos Saldanha
2006	United 93 (aka Flight 93)	Paul Greengrass (France/UK/USA)
2006	X-Men: The Last Stand	Brett Ratner (Canada/USA/UK)
2006	Happy Feet (BAFTA-N)	George Miller, etc. (Australia/USA)
2007	The Bourne Ultimatum	Paul Greengrass (USA/Germany)
2007	P.S. I Love You	Richard LaGravenese
2008	Jumper	Doug Liman (USA/Canada)
2008	Horton Hears a Who!	Jimmy Hayward, Steve Martino
2008	Stop-Loss	Kimberly Peirce
2008	Kung Fu Panda	Mark Osborne, John Stevenson
2008	Hancock (aka John Hancock)	Peter Berg
2008	Bolt	Byron Howard, Chris Williams
2009	Ice Age: Dawn of the Dinosaurs	Carlos Saldanha, Mike Thurmeier
2010	Green Zone	Paul Greengrass (France/USA/Spain/UK)

Year	Film	Director
2010	*How to Train Your Dragon* (AAN; BAFTA-N)	Dean DeBlois, Chris Sanders
2010	*Fair Game*	Doug Liman (USA/United Arab Emirates)
2010	*Knight and Day* (aka *All New Enemies*)	James Mangold
2011	*Mars Needs Moms*	Simon Wells
2011	*Rio*	Carlos Saldanha
2011	*Kung Fu Panda 2*	Jennifer Yuh
2011	*Happy Feet Two*	George Miller, etc. (Australia)
2012	*The Lorax*	Chris Renaud, Kyle Balda
2012	*Ice Age: Continental Drift*	Steve Martino, Mike Thurmeier
2014	*Rio 2*	Carlos Saldanha
2014	*How to Train Your Dragon 2*	Dean DeBlois
2015	*Kung Fu Panda 3*	Jennifer Yuh (USA/China)
2015	*Robodog*	Henry F. Anderson III (Japan)
2016	*How to Train Your Dragon 3*	Dean DeBlois

PREVIN, André (b. 1929) An internationally acclaimed conductor, pianist, and composer, he was very active in Hollywood from the late 1940s to the 1970s, scoring forty movies and supervising and conducting the scores for many more.

Born Andreas Ludwig Prewin in Berlin, Germany, of Jewish Russian ancestry, his father was a lawyer and judge and his mother a music teacher. The family left Germany in 1939 to escape the Nazis and settled in Los Angeles because an uncle, Charles Previn, was there, serving as musical director at Universal. Previn studied piano as a youth and after graduation from high school in 1946 began working in films as a musician and arranger. Two years later he composed his first screen score, for the melodrama *Tenth Avenue Angel*, followed by a half dozen other features during the next two years, most memorably *The Sun Comes Up*, *Border Incident*, *Challenge to Lassie*, and *The Outriders*. Although Previn had conducted and contributed music to some musicals, in 1950 he got to compose the complete background soundtrack for the musical biopic *Three Little Words*. Much of the rest of Previn's Hollywood career would be in musicals, composing and/or conducting such popular movies as *Kiss Me Kate*, *Kismet*, *It's Always Fair Weather*, *Gigi*, and *My Fair Lady*. He was able to return to scoring nonmusicals on occasion, writing music for such memorable films as *Bad Day at Black Rock*, *Irma la Douce*, *Elmer Gantry*, *The Catered Affair*, *The Four Horsemen of the Apocalypse*, *Two for the Seesaw*, *Long Day's Journey into Night*, and *The Fortune Cookie*. Previn received Oscar nominations for Best Song for "Faraway Part of Town" (lyric by Dory Langdon) in *Pepe* (1960), for musical adaptations for *Bells Are Ringing* (1960), *Thor-oughly Modern Millie* (1967), and *Jesus Christ Superstar* (1973), and he won for his adaptation of the Gershwin music in *Porgy and Bess* (1959). In all, Previn has received eleven Oscar nominations and won for *Gigi*, *Porgy and Bess*, *Irma la Douce*, and *My Fair Lady*. By the mid-1960s the Hollywood musical was in decline and Previn found himself scoring some inconsequential movies. By 1975 he left Hollywood to concentrate on concert work, both conducting and composing.

Although Previn did not attend a music school, as an adult he studied piano with Pierre Monteux who had a profound effect on the young musician-composer. In between Hollywood jobs, Previn toured and recorded as a jazz pianist, arranged and accompanied famous singers on television and on records, and gained a reputation as a refreshing interpreter of classical piano works. He has written two operas—*A Streetcar Named Desire* (1997) and *Brief Encounter* (2007)—as well as the music for Tom Stoppard's theatre-concert piece *Every Good Boy Deserves Favour* (1977). Among his many other concert works are concertos and sonatas for various solo instruments, chamber pieces, piano selections, and song cycles. For the theatre, Previn composed the music for the Broadway musicals *A Party with Betty Comden and Adolph Green* (1958) and *Coco* (1969), as well as the London musical *The Good Companions* (1974). He has rarely written music for television, but he did score the miniseries *Jennie: Lady Randolph Churchill* (1974). Previn is one of the most famous and recognized conductors of his era because of his television broadcasts in Great Britain and the States, such as the series *Previn and the Pittsburgh* which featured his eight years as the musical director of the Pittsburgh Sym-

ANDRÉ PREVIN. Before his renowned career as a concert hall conductor and composer, Previn was a precocious kid who worked on many Hollywood musicals when he was still in his teens. Here he is in the mid-1950s working out an arrangement for an MGM soundtrack. *Photofest*

phony. Over the decades he has held the same position for the London Symphony Orchestra, the Royal Philharmonic Orchestra, the Houston Symphony Orchestra, and the Los Angeles Philharmonic. Previn has made dozens of recordings, ranging from classical works to jazz records, with the top musicians in both fields. Few artists in music have had such a prolific and varied career as Previn has enjoyed.

Although Previn worked on many Hollywood musicals, few of them contain substantial amounts of his original music. Often he adapted and arranged Broadway scores into film scores, composing incidental music when no existing material would suffice. Even with musicals conceived as movies, the songs were usually written by others. Previn did get to write nine songs (lyrics by Betty Comden and Adolph Green) for *It's Always Fair Weather*, five songs (lyrics by then wife Dory Previn) for *Valley of the Dolls* (1967), and additional songs (lyrics by Alan Jay Lerner) for *Paint Your Wagon* (1969), which had a stage score by Lerner and Frederick Loewe. For the biopic *The Music Lovers*, Previn is credited as writing the score but the soundtrack is actually his adaptation and arrangements of Tchaikovsky's music. Similarly, most of the score for *Rollerball* consists of Previn's handling of themes by Johann Sebastian Bach, Dmitri Shostakovich, and Tchaikovsky again. In order to recognize and appreciate Previn the screen composer, one needs to look at his nonmusical movies. Early in his career he scored two *Lassie* movies that have warm and pleasing scores. *The Sun Comes Up* has a nostalgic main theme based on a five-note motif that builds and breaks into optimistic crescendos. The period film *Challenge to Lassie*, set in Edinburgh, has a similarly engaging score with a Scottish flavor throughout. The main theme is a flowing piece accompanied by pipes and strings that never falls into ethnic clichés.

In 1949, the same year Previn scored these two family movies, he also revealed a very different side of his composition skills with the music in *Border Incident*, a gritty drama about the smuggling of Mexicans into the States. The score is harsh and dramatic, filled with strong brass passages that have ardent dissonant harmonies. Previn sometimes returned to this kind of jarring and propulsive music throughout his screen career. The disturbing drama *Bad Day at Black Rock* opens with a vigorous theme that keeps in time with a train racing across the desert. The Bette Davis melodrama *Dead Ringer* has explosive brass,

wavering strings, and (surprisingly) a furious harpsichord playing the main theme, which abrasively attacks the ear. This harpsichord returns throughout the melodrama and, as used so masterfully by Previn, becomes an instrument of suspense. The detective film noir movie *Tension* has a central theme that simmers then snaps, the music conveying the film's idea that humans can take only so much before they snap. This kind of aggressive scoring reaches its peak with *Elmer Gantry*, a potent drama about evangelists touring the country in the 1920s. The main theme also attacks the ear with brassy thrusts and chaotic strings, this time using a seven-note motif. Very sharp and dissonant, the theme suggests the fury that Gantry (Burt Lancaster) can conjure up in his revival meetings. Yet when this same theme is slowed down and reorchestrated it actually sounds romantic. The *Elmer Gantry* score is filled with surprises. There is a lyrical, rural passage that borders on the comic, some Igor Stravinsky–like sections in which fanfares turn into very modern musical sounds, and a satiric blues theme for the prostitute Lulu (Shirley Jones) in which a muted horn seems to be laughing at Lulu's broken heart.

Previn is a true Hollywood composer in that he can sometimes go off in new directions when the movie calls for it. For the 1962 remake of the adventure tale *The Four Horsemen of the Apocalypse*, he wrote a symphonic score in the Old Hollywood tradition. The main theme has a thundering march tempo with strings and brass that seem to be riding on air like the four dreaded horsemen. The film also has one of Previn's most entrancing love themes, a sublime piece featuring a solo violin that has a touch of Hebrew chanting in it. It is not surprising that the melody was later turned into the emotive song "More in Love with You" (lyric by Marilyn and Alan Bergman). The "beatnik" movie *The Subterraneans* has a marvelous cool-jazz score with some chilling passages as well as a sultry theme played by Previn on piano that is both romantic and distant. Previn and some of his favorite musicians actually appear in the film, which is a jazz lover's delight. A very different sound is heard in the Hollywood backstager *Inside Daisy Clover*. The recurring theme is an odd and disarming carousel waltz with calliope instrumentation but also a wry subtext that suggests the superficiality of Tinseltown, the point of this uneven but interesting movie. Previn also wrote two songs (lyrics by Dory Previn) for the film, the merry march "The Circus Is a Wacky World" and the fervent "You're Gonna Hear from Me" sung by the title tomboy (Natalie Wood, dubbed by Jackie Ward) as she climbs her way to celluloid success.

The comedy *Irma la Douce* was based on a French musical that found success in London and on Broadway. Yet for the movie version all the songs were cut and Previn was asked to fashion a soundtrack score using the original stage music by Marguerite Monnot. He ended up writing most of the music in the finished product and it is sparkling. A giddy cancan theme opens the movie, setting up the Gallic and comic nature of the comedy. There is the expected cafe music and unexpected passages with high woodwinds that seem to squeal with delight. The theme for the call girl Irma (Shirley MacLaine) is an engaging waltz played on flute, strings, and accordion. Two of the best movies Previn got to score came out in 1962: the bittersweet romance *Two for the Seesaw* and the Eugene O'Neill autobiographical tragedy *Long Day's Journey into Night*. The latter, about a dysfunctional family on a tragic level, has a beautifully melancholy main theme heard on piano with strings playing the countermelody. There is just the slightest touch of jazz in this period film but mostly it is scored with somber music that echoes the depths of this very disturbed family. *Two for the Seesaw*, about the unlikely romance between a lawyer (Robert Mitchum) and a dancer (Shirley MacLaine), has a score that suggests both romance and urban weariness. The central theme is a lazy jazz piece played on solo trumpet with a casual yet lonely tone. There is also a lively cha-cha passage, a bouncy jazz theme played by a small combo, and a mournful duet for viola and saxophone that aches with ennui. Previn not only conducted and performed on the soundtracks for his films, he often returned to the music and recorded them with his fellow jazz musicians, sometimes finding new interpretations of the music. This was possible because so much of his screen music is of such high quality. When Previn left Hollywood to devote all his time to the concert hall, it was a loss whose impact can only now, years later, be understood. Autobiography: *No Minor Chords: My Days in Hollywood* (1991). Biographies: *André Previn*, Martin Bookspan, Ross Yockey (1981); *Previn*, Helen Drees Ruttencutter (1987); *Andre Previn: The Authorized Biography*, Michael Freedland (1991). Official website: www.andre-previn.com.

Credits

(all films USA unless stated otherwise; * for Best Song)

Year	Film	Director
1948	Tenth Avenue Angel	Roy Rowland
1949	The Sun Comes Up	Richard Thorpe
1949	Scene of the Crime	Roy Rowland
1949	Border Incident	Anthony Mann
1949	Challenge to Lassie (aka Lassie in Not)	Richard Thorpe
1949	Tension	John Berry
1950	The Outriders	Roy Rowland
1950	Shadow on the Wall	Pat Jackson
1950	Three Little Words (AAN)	Richard Thorpe
1950	Dial 1119	Gerald Mayer
1950	Kim	Victor Saville
1951	Cause for Alarm!	Tay Garnett
1953	The Girl Who Had Everything	Richard Thorpe
1953	Small Town Girl	László Kardos
1953	Kiss Me Kate (AAN)	George Sidney
1953	Give a Girl a Break	Stanley Donen
1955	A Bad Day at Black Rock	John Sturges
1955	It's Always Fair Weather (AAN)	Stanley Donen, Gene Kelly
1955	Kismet	Vincente Minnelli, Stanley Donen
1956	The Catered Affair	Richard Brooks
1956	Invitation to the Dance	Gene Kelly
1956	The Fastest Gun Alive	Russell Rouse

Year	Film	Director
1957	*Hot Summer Night*	David Friedlin
1957	*Designing Woman*	Vincente Minnelli
1957	*House of Numbers*	Russell Rouse
1958	*Gigi* (AA)	Vincente Minnelli
1960	*Who Was That Lady?*	George Sidney
1960	*The Subterraneans*	Ranald MacDougall
1960	*Elmer Gantry* (AAN)	Richard Brooks
1961	*All in a Night's Work*	Joseph Anthony
1961	*One, Two, Three*	Billy Wilder
1962	*The Four Horsemen of the Apocalypse*	Vincente Minnelli (USA/Mexico)
1962	*Long Day's Journey into Night*	Sidney Lumet
1962	*Two for the Seesaw* (AAN*)	Robert Wise
1963	*Irma la Douce* (AA)	Billy Wilder
1964	*Dead Ringer*	Paul Henreid
1964	*My Fair Lady* (AA)	George Cukor
1964	*Goodbye Charlie*	Vincente Minnelli
1964	*Kiss Me, Stupid*	Billy Wilder
1965	*Inside Daisy Clover*	Robert Mulligan
1966	*The Fortune Cookie*	Billy Wilder
1970	*The Music Lovers*	Ken Russell (UK)
1975	*Rollerball*	Norman Jewison (UK)

PREVIN, Charles (1888–1973) An important music director at Universal Pictures for many years, he also scored some two dozen features but was only credited on one of them.

He was born in the Brooklyn borough of New York City, the son of a rabbi, and educated at Cornell University and the New York College of Music. Previn began his career in vaudeville as a musician and a conductor then moved up to legit shows on Broadway. Between 1915 and 1933 he was musical director and/or conductor for dozens of Broadway musicals, including the landmark Gershwin operetta *Of Thee I Sing* (1931). Previn conducted on the radio for a few years then began working for Universal in 1936. Over the next thirteen years he supervised the music for over three hundred feature films ranging from Deanna Durbin musicals to classic horror movies. Often he also composed (usually with others) music for Universal but was only credited on the comedy *Hi, Buddy*. In the 1940s Previn was also the director and conductor at Radio City Music Hall. About the same time that Previn retired from movies, his great-nephew André, whom he had gotten work arranging music in Hollywood, started composing film scores. Charles Previn was nominated for Academy Awards seven times, winning for his score for *One Hundred Men and a Girl*.

Although Previn established and nurtured the musical sound of Universal Pictures during its golden era, it is very difficult to evaluate his composing talents. He rarely scored a film alone, often working with one or more studio composers. In the many musicals he supervised, the soundtrack music was more incidental than central in the movies that had songs by others or in the public domain. Previn shared the Oscar for *One Hundred Men and a Girl* with his frequent collaborator Frank Skinner, but in reality the original music heard in the film is by unidentified staff composers. That popular Deanna Durbin vehicle has ten musical numbers, ranging from Tchaikovsky's Symphony No. 5 to the standard "For He's a Jolly Good Fellow." The award was more in honor of Previn's expert adaptation and conducting of the movie's score than the composing of it. In fact, for all seven of the movies for which Previn was nominated, he wrote very little if any of the music heard, but his musical supervision was Oscar worthy.

One needs to look at the handful of nonmusical features that Previn composed to get a better idea of his original music. Early in his career at Universal, Previn and Rudy Schrager cowrote the score for the screwball comedy classic *My Man Godfrey*. It is a glitzy and playful score filled with swank nightclub music and some bouncy swing passages. Yet this is a movie about fast-paced dialogue and broad performances, so music is often scarce, heard only under the credits and in the background at parties and supper clubs. Another popular comedy, the

W. C. Fields vehicle *Never Give a Sucker an Even Break*, has a score by Previn and Skinner. The cartoon credits have cartoonish music with laughing trombones and silly strings, suggesting both a circus and a drunken spree. Gloria Jean sings four songs in the film, including "Hot Cha Cha" with music and lyric by Previn, but comedian Fields's verbal and physical comedy calls for silence, so there is not much of a soundtrack score. The more Previn movies one examines, the clearer it becomes that Universal saw him as a music director and not a composer. His conducting and arrangement abilities kept him busy and Previn the composer only surfaced when a film needed some fill-in music or a comedy required an opening theme and little else. Yet this should not distract one from Previn's remarkable handling of music in hundreds of movies. Consider such memorable titles as *The Rage of Paris* (1938), *Destry Rides Again* (1939), *One Night in the Tropics* (1940), *The Wolf Man* (1941), *Saboteur* (1942), *Arabian Nights* (1942), *Shadow of a Doubt* (1943), *And Then There Were None* (1945), and *The Three Musketeers* (1948), and then consider the man who supervised their musical sound.

Credits

(all films USA)

Year	Film	Director
1936	*Parole!*	Lew Landers
1936	*My Man Godfrey*	Gregory La Cava
1936	*The Man I Marry*	Ralph Murphy
1937	*The Mighty Treve*	Lewis D. Collins
1937	*One Hundred Men and a Girl*(AA)	Henry Koster
1937	*Prescription for Romance*	S. Sylvan Simon
1938	*Forbidden Valley*	Wyndham Gittens
1938	*Mad About Music* (AAN)	Norman Taurog
1939	*First Love* (AAN)	Henry Koster
1938	*State Police*	John Rawlins
1939	*Scouts to the Rescue*	Alan James, Ray Taylor
1939	*For Love or Money*	Albert S. Rogell
1939	*Hero for a Day*	Harold Young
1939	*The Phantom Creeps*	Ford Beebe, Saul A. Goodkind
1940	*Spring Parade* (AAN)	Henry Koster
1941	*Never Give a Sucker an Even Break*	Edward F. Cline
1941	*It Started with Eve* (AAN)	Henry Koster
1941	*Buck Privates* (AAN)	Arthur Lubin
1942	*Get Hep to Love*	Charles Lamont
1943	*Hi, Buddy*	Harold Young
1943	*Rhythm of the Islands*	Roy William Neill
1944	*Song of the Open Road* (AAN)	S. Sylvan Simon
1949	*That Midnight Kiss*	Norman Taurog

PROKOFIEV, Sergei (1891–1953) The Russian pianist, conductor, and composer who is considered one of the giants of twentieth-century music, he scored only nine feature films but his music has been heard in over one hundred movies and television programs.

Sergei Sergeyevich Prokofiev was born in Sontsovka (now Krasne) in present-day Ukraine, the son of an agricultural engineer, and grew up listening to his profession-ally trained mother play classical pieces on the piano. By the age of five Prokofiev was composing piano pieces, and when he was eight he had completed his first opera. Five years later he was admitted to the St. Petersburg Conservatory when he showed the school his portfolio of piano pieces, four operas, two sonatas, and a symphony. Remaining at the Conservatory for ten years, Prokofiev studied composition and piano, making his professional debut with a piano concert when he was nineteen. He moved from being a child prodigy to a famous enfant terrible who dazzled Russia with his exciting, modern music. Some found his dissonant and overly chromatic works painful to the ear, while he was applauded by some music critics and fellow composers. While touring Europe in a series of piano concerts, he met impresario Sergei Diaghilev and the two went on to collaborate on several ballets. When World War I broke out, Prokofiev returned to his studies at the Conservatory and wrote a symphony and other works. Because of the turmoil after the Russian Revolution, he left Russia in 1918 and remained abroad for fifteen years. In New York City he gave concerts and continued composing but was not fully accepted by the conservative critics, so in 1920 he went to Paris where he fared better, though his work was not fully embraced there either. Prokofiev returned to Russia in 1936 and continued to work although he was watched carefully by the Soviet regime, which was suspicious of modern music.

His film career began in 1934 when he was asked by director Aleksandr Faintzimmer to score *Lieutenant Kije*, known in the West as *The Czar Wants to Sleep*. The satirical adventure movie was not a resounding hit and the primitive recording of Prokofiev's music did not impress. But when he turned the score into a concert suite, it became very popular not only in Russia but across Europe. Four years later he worked with the renowned director Sergei Eisenstein for the first time, writing the music for the historical film *Alexander Nevsky*. This time both the movie and the score were widely acclaimed and again Prokofiev arranged the music into a popular concert suite for chorus and orchestra. After working on three other Soviet movies, Prokofiev reunited with Eisenstein to collaborate on a huge cinema-music project: a three-part film about *Ivan the Terrible*. The first part was released in 1944, the second part was completed but, rousing Stalin's displeasure, was not released until 1958 (five years after Prokofiev's death), and the third installment was never made. Regardless, the *Ivan the Terrible* scores are considered hallmarks in screen music. He worked on only two other films, the Russian biography *Lermantov* and the French biopic *The Extraordinary Adventures of Jules Verne*. While his screen activities were sporadic, Prokofiev was very productive in the 1940s writing concert works and ballets despite the strictures put on him and other artists by the Communist Party. He continued to compose until

his death from a cerebral hemorrhage at the age of sixty-one. Because he died on the same day that Stalin's demise was announced, there was little recognition for the passing of arguably Russia's greatest composer of the century.

Prokofiev's first film score, *Lieutenant Kije* or *The Czar Wants to Sleep*, has none of the characteristics of a novice screen composer. The tragicomic tone of this story, about a fabricated hero created by the military to please the czar (Mikhail Yanshin), is matched by Prokofiev's delectable score. The invisible hero has his own theme, a mystical fanfare played by a solo cornet and used throughout the movie as a sarcastic leitmotif. The romantic theme is gently restrained as it slowly builds in intensity, the central musical phrase picked up by various instruments. The famous "Troika" theme is an exuberant march that is both valorous and silly. (No wonder Woody Allen used it decades later as the musical motif in his 1975 comedy *Love and Death*.) The wedding theme is pompous and quirky with a joyous melody filled with odd key changes and a trumpet solo that conjures up the image of a waddling of a duck rather than a bride. (This familiar theme was used effectively throughout the oddball British comedy *The Horse's Mouth* in 1958.) The military march is flippant and cockeyed with the high woodwinds removing any sense of gravity. The burial of the hero has a minor-key melancholy theme with sorrowful brass and woodwinds but the sadness is soon undercut by the return of the funny wedding theme and the hero's robust theme. The score has sixteen distinct passages, each one a splendid variation on the movie's wry commentary on patriotism and blind devotion to the czar. It is not difficult to see how such wonderful music has become one of Prokofiev's most performed concert suites.

Nothing could be more different in tone than Eisenstein's *Alexander Nevsky*, a powerful piece of propaganda filmmaking. The thirteenth-century invasion of Russian soil by the Teutonic Knights and the disastrous results for the German crusaders was a clear warning to Germany in 1938 as the Nazis captured Poland and looked east. In this case, propaganda came in the form of high art, for *Alexander Nevsky* is a masterwork of both visual and musical moviemaking. The film's credits are presented in silence; music enters quietly but firmly as the Knights capture the key Russian leader, the governor of Pskov (Vasili Novikov). As Nevsky (Nikolai Cherkasov) organizes his troops to pursue the Germans, the music grows in strength as he and his army does. The justly famous battle on ice, in which the German horsemen charge across the frozen Lake Chud only to have the ice collapse and they drown in the icy water, is scored so dramatically that one can hear the horses in the rhythmic music, sense the chaos in the frenzied choral passage, experience the freezing destruction in the vigorous crescendos, and sense the drowning in the descending music. The aftermath of the battle includes the chilling image of a girl looking through the field of corpses for the two men who both sought her love. Prokofiev's music for the sequence is a mournful lullaby sung by a solo mezzo. The movie and the score end with the title hero liberating the governor. The music is fervent, joyous, and unabashedly patriotic with chorus and orchestra at full throttle. *Alexander Nevsky* has one of the most integrated of all movie scores. Some of this is because Eisenstein asked Prokofiev to score some sections of the story before they were filmed then he staged the scenes with the completed music in mind. This brilliant score shows Prokofiev's uncanny sense of music drama and the way music can create its own stunning visuals.

While the scores for the two completed parts of *Ivan the Terrible* do not match the music in *Alexander Nevsky* in quality, they have some superior passages throughout the lengthy films. The story of Czar Ivan IV (Cherkasov again), his rise to power, his fall, his reinstatement, and his battle with opposing forces in sixteenth-century Russia, allowed Prokofiev more variety as music was needed for a coronation, court intrigue, a wedding, revolts, and battles. Also, the films are not patriotic propaganda but disturbing tales of power corrupted and abused. (It was the scenes involving Ivan's secret police that particularly upset Stalin.) While some sections of the score are filled with folk music and Russian Orthodox hymns, other passages sound very

modern. One finds some dissonance and more minor keys here than in the *Alexander Nevsky* score. Again Prokofiev uses choral singing (both solo and large ensemble) effectively and again the music sometimes conjures up visual images, such as the pounding of military feet during the Conquest of Kazan sequence. The second part of the saga may not be as satisfying as the first, but in many ways the music in this later part of the story is finer. Military marches blend into dancing mazurkas, fervent hymns are contrasted by explosive battle music, and the complicated portrayal of Ivan is given some adroitly ambiguous music. *Ivan the Terrible* is a triumph for filmmaking and screen music with both Prokofiev and Eisenstein at the peak of their powers.

As impressive as Prokofiev's screen music is, one must remember that it comprises a rather small portion of his life's work. His legacy is monumental: acclaimed operas such as *The Gambler, The Love for Three Oranges,* and *War and Peace;* beloved ballets such as *The Prodigal Son, Romeo and Juliet,* and *Cinderella;* seven symphonies, nine piano sonatas, string quartets, piano concertos, and dozens of special pieces, most memorably *Peter and the Wolf.* Prokofiev's music is heard in concert halls around the world, on hundreds of recordings, on countless radio and television broadcasts, and in numerous movies. It is estimated that his music has been heard more than any other twentieth-century composer. How fortunate that Prokofiev spent even a little of his time in movies. Autobiography: *Sergei Prokofiev: Autobiography, Articles, Reminiscences,* S. Shlifstein (ed.), (2000); biographies: *Sergei Prokofiev,* Harlow Robinson (1987); *Prokofiev,* Israel Nestyev, Florence Jonas (1960); music theory: *Composing for the Red Screen: Prokofiev and Soviet Film,* Kevin Bartig (2013).

Credits

(all films Russia/USSR unless stated otherwise)

Year	Film	Director
1934	*The Czar Wants to Sleep* (aka *Lieutenant Kije*)	Aleksandr Faintsimmer
1938	*Alexander Nevsky*	Sergei Eisenstein, Dmitri Vasilyev
1943	*Kotovskiy*	Aleksandr Faintsimmer, Dmitri Vasilyev
1943	*Partizany v stepyah Ukrainy*	Igor Savchenko
1943	*Boyevoy kinosbornik 13: Nashi devushki*	Mikhail Romm, Grigori Kozintsev
1944	*Ivan the Terrible, Part I*	Sergei Eisenstein
1947	*Lermontov*	Albert Gendelshtein
1952	*Les aventures extraordinaires de Jules Vern*	Jean Aurel (France)
1958	*Ivan the Terrible, Part II*	Sergei M. Eisenstein

R

RABIN, Trevor (b. 1954) A popular rock-pop singer-musician-songwriter who has worked with many bands and has had successful solo albums as well, he has scored over forty feature Hollywood films of diverse genres.

Born in Johannesburg, South Africa, the son of a lawyer-violinist and actress-pianist, Trevor Rabin began piano lessons when he was six years old and as a preteen took up guitar. By the time Rabin was thirteen he was performing professionally in his brother's band; later he formed his own band, Conglomeration, which toured music festivals throughout South Africa. His music career blossomed when he was hired as a sessions guitarist for a recording studio and soon Rabin was an in-demand musician for concerts, recordings, and such bands as Freedom's Children. For this band Rabin wrote the anti-apartheid song "Wake Up! State of Fear," which was a controversial hit. After serving in the military, he continued his career by joining the group Rabbitt, perhaps the most popular rock band to come out of South Africa. In 1976, he contributed some music to the South African crime movie *Death of a Snowman* but did not return to movies for twenty years. In 1978, Rabin moved to London where he wrote, performed, and produced his own albums. A few years later he went to Los Angeles, where he wrote and performed for the popular bands Yes and Cinema as he continued to release solo albums. Rabin became a naturalized U.S. citizen in 1991. Five years later he retired from Yes and began his Hollywood composing career with the comic crime film *The Glimmer Man*. With Mark Mancina, he scored the popular action thriller *Con Air* then had a hit on his own as the sole composer for the sci-fi movie *Armageddon*. Since then Rabin has scored all kinds of movies, from family films to taut action adventures. He has written music for many sports-related movies, including *Gridiron Gang*, *Coach Carter*, *Glory Road*, *Grudge Match*, and *Remember the Titans*; the music from the last has been heard in concerts, television broadcasts, Olympics coverage, and political conventions. Among his other notable films are *Enemy of the State*, *Gone in Sixty Seconds*, *Bad Company*, *National Treasure* and its sequel, *American Outlaws*, *The Great Raid*, *Snakes on a Plane*, *The Sorcerer's Apprentice*, *The Guardian*, and the acclaimed documentary *The Movement: One Man Joins an Uprising*. Rabin often orchestrates his own scores. His songs written for various rock bands have been heard in over thirty movies, in particular the hit song "Owner of a Lonely Heart." Rabin has written for television, most memorably the series *Zero Hour*, and theme parks, as with the attraction Mission: SPACE at EPCOT. He continues to perform and record with various bands.

Because Rabin has been such a major figure in rock for so many years, one expects his movie music to be high tech with a rock sensibility. Some movies are scored like that, of course, but just as many use a conventional orchestra and a few employ both techniques. His first major score, for the apocalyptic *Armageddon*, is indeed rock influenced. As an asteroid the size of Texas races toward Earth, NASA scientists and military heads come up with a daring plan to blow up the giant object from within. The high-pressure film is given an equally tense score by Rabin yet there are quieter moments as well. The opening theme has echoing percussion under synthesized horns, a celestial choir, and grumbling electronic sounds. This is contrasted by a delicate section with a guitar playing a simple melody as if all is right with the world. There is also a morose dirge played on synthesized pipes with chanting voices and a funeral march beat. In another theme, a solo electric guitar is featured with high-pitched frequency noises above and traditional strings below. Even when this builds to a stirring orchestral passage, the music retains its intimacy. For the many action and suspense scenes, Rabin writes a vigorous passage with exploding percussive noises and frenzied electric guitar riffs. A good example of mixing the rock and classical methods can be found in his score for *The Guardian*. This action drama, about a top Coast Guard swimmer (Kevin Costner) who trains a troubled youth (Ashton Kutcher) new in the squad, has a surprisingly gentle score. The most haunting passage features a solo female chant that rises over a solemn and stately theme with sustained strings and mournful horns creating an enticing and evocative piece of music. There is also a sensitive track with a muted trumpet wavering over the hesitant strings. This exceptional score also includes a restrained rock passage with electric guitar riffs weaving in and out of a traditional orchestra playing a spirited march; a heavyhearted lament played on strings and horns that is more optimistic than expected; and an expansive theme with full orchestra that climbs the scale with a triumphal air.

Perhaps Rabin's two most popular movies are *Remember the Titans* and *National Treasure*, both using little rock or electronic music in their scores. The latter adventure film is a complicated but involved treasure hunt in which a historian (Nicolas Cage) searches for a war chest hidden by the Founding Fathers two centuries ago. *National Treasure* has a swift pace as supported by the frantic main theme, played on guitar, strings, and various percussion instruments, which races ahead and then slows down for some magical passages on piano. Some of the suspense music features jittery strings, wailing horns, and choral chanting, and there is a restless piano and string track that accelerates into a full-blown chase. Just as the plot slows down for some quiet scenes of wonderment, so does the music. There is a mysti-

cal theme with repetitive piano chords and sustained strings that is quite beguiling. Also memorable is a lovely orchestral passage featuring French horns that is regal and subtly overwhelming. *Remember the Titans* is the most involving of Rabin's many sports films. An African American football coach (Denzel Washington) in 1971 suburban Virginia battles tradition and prejudice as he turns his integrated team into a symbol for racial understanding. Rabin's main theme is a sublime orchestral piece with some poignant pauses and a melancholy subtext. There is also a delicate, reflective passage featuring French horns and strings that is very moving, as well as a hymnlike theme featuring a solo flute gliding over flowing strings. The football games are scored with rambunctious music that slowly climbs the scale until it reaches a series of crescendos, and there is a rapid march with restrained but proud brass and anxious percussion that is quite exhilarating. The movie's famous "Titan Spirit" theme is a vigorous orchestral track with triumphal brass, aggressive percussion, and soaring strings and woodwinds that is invigorating. It is not difficult to understand why the passage has been used to inspire and celebrate. Official website: www.trevorrabin.net.

Credits

(all films USA unless stated otherwise)

Year	Film	Director
1996	The Glimmer Man	John Gray
1997	Con Air	Simon West
1998	Homegrown	Stephen Gyllenhaal
1998	Armageddon	Michael Bay
1998	Enemy of the State	Tony Scott
1998	Jack Frost	Troy Miller
1999	Deep Blue Sea	Renny Harlin (USA/Australia)
2000	Whispers: An Elephant's Tale	Dereck Joubert
2000	Gone in Sixty Seconds	Dominic Sena
2000	Remember the Titans	Boaz Yakin
2000	The 6th Day	Roger Spottiswoode
2001	Texas Rangers	Steve Miner
2001	American Outlaws (aka Jesse James)	Les Mayfield
2001	Rock Star (aka Metal God)	Stephen Herek
2001	The One	James Wong
2002	Bad Company(aka Black Sheep)	Joel Schumacher (USA/Czech Republic)
2002	The Banger Sisters (aka Groupies Forever)	Bob Dolman
2003	Kangaroo Jack	David McNally (USA/Australia)
2003	Bad Boys II	Michael Bay
2004	Torque	Joseph Kahn (USA/Australia)
2004	Exorcist: The Beginning	Renny Harlin
2004	National Treasure	Jon Turteltaub
2005	Coach Carter (aka All Day Long)	Thomas Carter (USA/Germany)

Year	Film	Director
2005	The Great Raid	John Dahl (USA/Australia)
2006	Glory Road	James Gartner
2006	Snakes on a Plane	David R. Ellis (Germany/USA/Canada)
2006	Gridiron Gang	Phil Joanou
2006	Flyboys	Tony Bill (UK/USA)
2006	The Guardian	Andrew Davis
2007	Hot Rod	Akiva Schaffer
2007	National Treasure 2: Book of Secrets	Jon Turteltaub
2008	Get Smart	Peter Segal
2009	Race to Witch Mountain	Andy Fickman
2009	12 Rounds	Renny Harlin
2009	G-Force	Hoyt Yeatman
2010	The Sorcerer's Apprentice	Jon Turteltaub
2011	I Am Number Four	D. J. Caruso
2011	5 Days of War	Renny Harlin
2011	The Movement: One Man Joins an Uprising	Greg Hamilton, Kurt Miller
2013	Grudge Match	Peter Segal

RAKSIN, David (1912–2004) A highly respected screen and television composer who rarely got the attention he deserved, many in Hollywood called him the "grandfather of film music."

He was born in Philadelphia, the son of a music store owner who conducted an orchestra for silent films in the city's movie palace. Raksin studied various instruments as a boy then went on to study composition at the University of Pennsylvania. He paid for tuition by performing in his own dance band and writing arrangements for the local CBS Radio affiliate. After graduation Raksin went to New York City where he continued to play and write arrangements for various bands. His arrangement of Gershwin's "I Got Rhythm" was played by Benny Goodman on the radio and was so well received that Raksin was hired by the powerful music publisher Harms/Chappell. His movie career began in 1936 when music director Alfred Newman needed someone to arrange Charles Chaplin's simple music notations into a score for *Modern Times*. Chaplin was not musically proficient but had an excellent sense of what sounded right; it was Raksin who turned Chaplin's musical ideas into the famous screen score. Raksin contributed music and arrangements for several Hollywood films in the late 1930s and early 1940s, often working with others and rarely getting any screen credit. Often he was hired to write the background music for musicals that had songs by others. It was Raksin's score for the mystery drama *Laura* in 1944 that was the turning point in his career. The studio did not have much confidence in the movie and did not even submit its score for consideration by the Academy Awards committee. But *Laura* turned into a huge hit and the haunting theme from the film was heard everywhere. It was not until the movie was a box office hit that a song version of the theme was made, Johnny Mercer writing a beguiling lyric that turned the musical theme into one of the most recorded songs of the decade.

Although *Laura* seemed to put Raksin in the forefront of movie composers, his Hollywood career was not a satisfying one. It was soon discovered that Raksin's music was often too subtle for the average listener. Instead of emphasizing melody, he often chose to use subtle sonorities in his composition. He was also stubborn, refusing to tailor his music to the uneducated musical tastes of directors and producers. Consequently he was rarely offered major projects and even the quality small pictures he worked on were not promoted well. All the same, Raksin has some outstanding scores to his credit and, occasionally, a hit movie as well. Among his most notable movies are *Forever Amber*, *Pat and Mike*, *Force of Evil*, *The Bad and the Beautiful*, *Carrie*, *The Magnificent Yankee*, *Two Weeks in Another Town*, *Apartment for Peggy*, and *Separate Tables*. He was also a very much in-demand composer for television, writing themes and scores for dozens of TV movies and series. Because he got little satisfaction in Hollywood, Raksin dedicated much of his life to composing and teaching, spending his later years at the University of California at Los Angeles where he not only taught music theory and compositions but wrote music for student theatre productions.

DAVID RAKSIN. Little known to the public but highly esteemed by music artists in Hollywood, Raksin's music has been described as too good for the average ear. Here he conducts his dramatic score for *Separate Tables* (1958). *Photofest*

He was a founder and served eight terms as president of the Composers and Lyricists Guild of America and won many laurels late in life, though he was nominated for an Oscar only twice and never won.

The score for *Laura* is movie music at its finest. The main theme defines the ambiguity of being both haunting and romantic. Director-producer Otto Preminger wanted the unseen heroine (Gene Tierney) to have a memorable theme so that every time the detective (Dana Andrews) saw her picture or thought about her, the music would conjure up her ghostly presence. Preminger tried to secure the music from George Gershwin's "Summertime" and then Duke Ellington's "Sophisticated Lady" as Laura's theme but Raksin talked him out of it, saying those songs came with their own associations. Instead he wrote a moody minor-key theme in the style of Maurice Ravel and Claude Debussy that conveyed both romance and mystery. Dialogue is not needed to explain how the detective felt; the music says it all. The rest of the score is also first rate, utilizing some dramatic passages for the murder investigation and a lighter theme for the eccentric character of Waldo Lydecker (Clifton Webb). But it is the way the "Laura" theme enters and exits the score without getting monotonous that makes *Laura* so musically bewitching. The heroine of *Forever Amber* also has a minor-key theme but there is nothing haunting about the ambitious Amber (Linda Darnell) who sleeps her way through Restoration England until she is Charles II's mistress. Raksin approaches the period with a wry smile, playing up the French flavor of Charles's court by writing music in the style of Domenico Scarlatti and Jean-Baptiste Lully. *Forever Amber*'s two most serious scenes, the aftermath of the Great Plague of 1665 and the next year's Great London Fire, are scored with daringly chaotic music for the latter and a penetrating funeral march for the former. Another period film with a commendable score by Raksin can be found in *Carrie*, the film version of Theodore Dreiser's novel *Sister Carrie*. The period this time is the turn of the twentieth century and Raksin uses waltzes and ragtime within a very romantic score to tell the story of a doomed extramarital love affair. Laurence Olivier gives a compelling performance which Raksin underscores dramatically with minor keys and mournful melodies.

Two contemporary dramas and a western that Raksin scored deserve special attention. The melodrama *The Bad and the Beautiful* looks at the dark side of Hollywood as a producer (Kirk Douglas) uses and abuses everyone to get what he wants. The main theme is forceful in an aggressive Tinseltown manner but there are also some zesty passages, such as a vivacious scherzo section, and other themes utilizing jazz. The love theme, later titled "Love Is for the Very Young," is rather sensual, especially as played by a solo saxophone. *Two Weeks in Another Town* is also about moviemaking, this time with Douglas as a washed-up actor on location in Rome. Raksin avoids overt Italian music and concentrates on the Americans with a piano theme that alternates between the romantic and the melancholy. *Will Penny* is an antiwestern of sorts, concentrating on the weary life of an aging cowboy (Charlton Heston). The main theme has a weariness of its own, the tempo stumbling along as the orchestra repeats a musical phrase that never seems to resolve itself. This theme is repeated with a dissonant twist when an insane preacher (Donald Pleasance) goes on a biblical rampage. The bittersweet ending of the movie, with Will deciding not to take up domestic life with a widow and her son, is scored very delicately, the music filling in what the characters cannot say to each other. *Will Penny* was a box office flop but, like so much of Raksin's work in Hollywood, its score was better than most could notice, much less appreciate. Autobiography: *The Bad and the Beautiful: My Life in a Golden Age of Film* (2012).

Credits

(all films USA unless stated otherwise)

Year	Film	Director
1937	*The Mighty Treve*	Lewis D. Collins
1937	*She's Dangerous*	Milton Carruth, Lewis R. Foster
1937	*Wings over Honolulu*	H. C. Potter
1937	*As Good as Married*	Edward Buzzell
1938	*The Kid Comes Back*	B. Reeves Eason

Year	Film	Director
1939	*Mr. Moto's Last Warning*	Norman Foster
1939	*Second Fiddle*	Sidney Lanfield
1940	*Two Girls on Broadway*	S. Sylvan Simon
1941	*Dead Men Tell*	Harry Lachman
1941	*Ride on Vaquero*	Herbert I. Leeds
1941	*The Men in Her Life*	Gregory Ratoff
1942	*Who Is Hope Schuyler?*	Thomas Z. Loring
1942	*The Man Who Wouldn't Die*	Herbert I. Leeds
1942	*Thru Different Eyes*	Thomas Z. Loring
1942	*The Postman Didn't Ring*	Harold D. Schuster
1942	*Just Off Broadway*	Herbert I. Leeds
1942	*Dr. Renault's Secret*	Harry Lachman
1942	*The Undying Monster*	John Brahm
1942	*Time to Kill*	Herbert I. Leeds
1943	*City without Men*	Sidney Salkow
1943	*Something to Shout About*	Gregory Ratoff
1943	*He Hired the Boss*	Thomas Z. Loring
1943	*I Dood It*	Vincente Minnelli
1944	*Tampico*	Lothar Mendes
1944	*Greenwich Village*	Walter Lang
1944	*Laura*	Otto Preminger
1944	*Belle of the Yukon*	William A. Seiter
1945	*Where Do We Go from Here?*	Gregory Ratoff, George Seaton
1945	*Don Juan Quilligan*	Frank Tuttle
1945	*Fallen Angel*	Otto Preminger
1946	*Smoky*	Louis King
1947	*The Shocking Miss Pilgrim*	George Seaton, Edmund Goulding
1947	*The Homestretch*	H. Bruce Humberstone
1947	*The Secret Life of Walter Mitty*	Norman Z. McLeod
1947	*Forever Amber* (AAN)	Otto Preminger, John M. Stahl
1947	*Daisy Kenyon*	Otto Preminger
1948	*Fury at Furnace Creek*	H. Bruce Humberstone
1948	*Apartment for Peggy*	George Seaton
1948	*Force of Evil*	Abraham Polonsky
1949	*Whirlpool*	Otto Preminger
1950	*The Reformer and the Redhead*	Melvin Frank, Norman Panama
1950	*The Next Voice You Hear . . .*	William A. Wellman
1950	*A Lady without Passport*	Joseph H. Lewis
1950	*Right Cross*	John Sturges
1950	*The Magnificent Yankee*	John Sturges
1951	*Kind Lady*	John Sturges
1951	*Across the Wide Missouri*	William A. Wellman
1951	*The Man with a Cloak*	Fletcher Markle
1952	*The Girl in White*	John Sturges
1952	*Pat and Mike*	George Cukor
1952	*Carrie*	William Wyler
1952	*The Bad and the Beautiful*	Vincente Minnelli
1954	*Apache*	Robert Aldrich
1954	*Suddenly*	Lewis Allen
1955	*The Big Combo*	Joseph H. Lewis
1956	*Jubal*	Delmer Daves
1956	*Seven Wonders of the World*	Tay Garnett, etc.
1956	*Hilda Crane*	Philip Dunne
1956	*Bigger Than Life*	Nicholas Ray
1957	*The Vintage*	Jeffrey Hayden
1957	*Man on Fire*	Ranald MacDougall
1957	*Gunsight Ridge*	Francis D. Lyon
1957	*Until They Sail*	Robert Wise

Year	Film	Director
1958	*Twilight for the Gods*	Joseph Pevney
1958	*Separate Tables* (AAN)	Delbert Mann
1959	*Al Capone*	Richard Wilson
1960	*Pay or Die*	Richard Wilson
1961	*Night Tide*	Curtis Harrington
1961	*Too Late Blues*	John Cassavetes
1962	*Two Weeks in Another Town*	Vincente Minnelli
1964	*The Patsy*	Jerry Lewis
1964	*Invitation to a Gunfighter*	Richard Wilson
1965	*Sylvia*	Gordon Douglas
1965	*The Redeemer* (1959)	Joseph Breen, Fernando Palacios (Spain/USA)
1965	*Love Has Many Faces*	Alexander Singer
1966	*A Big Hand for the Little Lady*	Fielder Cook
1968	*Will Penny*	Tom Gries
1971	*What's the Matter with Helen?*	Curtis Harrington
1972	*Glass Houses*	Alexander Singer

RAPEE, Erno (1891–1945) A busy conductor and arranger for the concert hall, radio, and movies, he was also a prolific composer who scored many silent films and early talkies.

Born in Budapest, Hungary, Erno Rapee studied piano and began his career as a musician in that city. Rapee was still a young man when he was made conductor for the Royal National Hungarian Academy of Music. His first major composition, a piano concerto, was premiered by the Philharmonic Orchestra of Vienna, leading to an international career as conductor, pianist, and composer. While touring the United States, Rapee attracted the attention of Hugo Riesenthal, the conductor and sometime composer for the Manhattan movie palace Rialto. Soon Rapee was composing and conducting concerts and silent films, most memorably at the Capitol Theatre where he scored for the house orchestra of seventy-seven musicians. Samuel "Roxy" Rothafel later hired Rapee as conductor for his Roxy Theatre which had the largest orchestra in America. In addition to his busy schedule at the Roxy, Rapee continued to conduct as guest maestro at renowned symphony orchestras in the States and in Europe. By the 1930s many of these concerts were broadcast on the radio and Rapee became known internationally. Yet he is most remembered as the musical director and head conductor at Roxy's Radio City Music Hall, a position he held from 1932 until his death thirteen years later.

Rapee continued his composing for the concert stage but in the 1920s concentrated on music for silent movies. In his efforts to improve the music heard in motion picture houses, he wrote a book filled with various kinds of incidental music that pianists and orchestras in cinemas everywhere could use. Titled *Motion Picture Moods for Pianists and Organists, a Rapid Reference Collection of Selected Pieces Adapted to Fifty-Two Moods and Situations*, the book was immediately embraced by musicians internationally. Ironically, only three years after publication, sound movies arrived and the musical scores came from the screen and not the orchestra pit. But in the heyday of the silent films with live music, Rapee composed many memorable scores. For the wartime drama *What Price Glory*, he wrote a romantic theme titled "Charmaine." The music captured the audience's favor and, when words by Lew Pollack were added to the melody, it became a best seller on sheet music and records. Rapee enjoyed similar success when "Diane" from *Seventh Heaven* and "Marion" from *4 Devils* were given lyrics by Pollack and the songs both became Tin Pan Alley hits as well. These three songs were still being sung and recorded in the 1960s. In the 1920s, Rapee returned to Europe many times to conduct orchestras and managed to find time to score seven German films. When sound came in and the scores could be recorded on the film stock, Rapee continued to write, arrange, and conduct music for the screen. In 1928 he scored nine movies and worked on the music for several others. He was also musical supervisor on many movies, serving as musical director on ten early talkies in 1931 alone. The next year he left the movies and concentrated on his conducting and compositions for the concert stage. He returned to film scoring at the end of the decade to write the music for three documentaries. Rapee was busier than ever when he died of a heart attack at the age of fifty-four. He left behind a handful of books, thousands of pages of sheet music for the concert hall and the movies, and about a dozen recorded film scores.

While firmly in the European romantic tradition, Rapee's music can still be very appealing to modern listeners. "Charmaine" still thrills with its lilting phrases and engaging fluidity. More often known as "I'm in Heaven When I See You Smile," the musical theme "Diane" is a waltzing delight that carefully avoids Viennese pastiche. The theme "Little Mother" from *Four Sons* is sentimental but lively. The "When Love Comes Stealing into My Heart" theme from *The Man Who Laughs* is shameless operetta and sounds like the gushing love themes that would later populate the talkies. Rapee was also proficient in creating the jazzy sound of the Roaring Twenties, as heard in *Dry Martini* and *The Missing Link*. The "My Angel" theme from *Street Angel* has a Latin flavor, hinting at a tango without fully surrendering to the form. Perhaps Rapee's finest screen music was written for director F. W. Murnau. His score for the silent masterpiece *Sunrise* captures the

hectic urban frenzy of a big city that contrasts with the more melodious theme for the two lovers. (A year after the film premiered in New York City in 1927, Hugo Riesenthal wrote a new score and other composers scored the San Francisco premiere.) Murnau's *Faust* had a score by Rapee and Werner R. Heymann and it is not clear which composer did what. But it is a dynamic score filled with bold musical excitement, some sections reminiscent of Rapee's style.

Rapee's legacy in movies centers on his use of a striking musical theme (or even a song) that is repeated throughout the film at important moments. Other composers had done this earlier but, because Rapee's themes were sometimes so memorable, the return of the melody reinforced the theme in the audience's mind. While this was very effective in the Rapee scores, subsequent movies would use this technique to excess, bombarding the audience with a piece of music over and over again. Rapee was one of the first movie composers to write music that translated into hit songs. How conscious he was of this at first is not known, but surely the surprise success of "Charmaine" must have influenced his scoring later on.

Credits

(all films USA unless stated otherwise)

Year	Film	Director
1920	Over the Hill to the Poorhouse	Harry F. Millarde
1921	A Connecticut Yankee in King Arthur's Court	Emmett J. Flynn
1921	The Queen of Sheba	J. Gordon Edwards
1922	Nero	J. Gordon Edwards (Italy/USA)
1923	If Winter Comes	Harry F. Millarde
1924	The Iron Horse	John Ford
1924	The Last Man on Earth	John G. Blystone
1925	A Man without a Country	Rowland V. Lee
1925	Jealousy	Ewald André Dupont (Germany)
1925	The Waltz Dream	Ludwig Berger (Germany)
1926	Manon Lescaut	Arthur Robison (Germany)
1926	Monte Carlo	Christy Cabanne
1926	Die Brüder Schellenberg	Karl Grune (Germany)
1926	Der Prinz und die Tänzerin	Richard Eichberg (Germany)
1926	Wehe Wenn Sie Losgelassen	Carl Frolich (Germany)
1926	Faust	F. W. Murnau (Germany)
1926	What Price Glory	Raoul Walsh
1927	The Missing Link	Charles Reisner
1927	Seventh Heaven	Frank Borzage
1927	Sunrise	F. W. Murnau
1928	Mother Machree	John Ford
1928	Four Sons	John Ford
1928	Street Angel	Frank Borzage

Year	Film	Director
1928	*The Man Who Laughs*	Paul Leni
1928	*Fazil*	Howard Hawks
1928	*The Red Dance*	Raoul Walsh
1928	*Mother Knows Best*	John G. Blystone
1928	*4 Devils*	F. W. Murnau
1928	*Dry Martini*	Harry d'Abbadie d'Arrast
1929	*Making the Grade*	Alfred E. Green
1929	*Whispering Winds*	James Flood
1930	*Those Who Dance*	William Beaudine
1931	*Men of the Sky*	Alfred E. Green
1937	*The Dead March*	Bud Pollard
1941	*Invasion*	Bud Pollard
1942	*Conquer by the Clock*	Frederic Ullman, Slavko Vorkapich

RIDDLE, Nelson (1921–1985) One of the top arrangers in the history of American popular music, he also composed scores for many television shows and feature films.

Born Nelson Smock Riddle Jr. in Oradell, New Jersey, he studied piano as a child and the trombone as a teenager. After serving in World War II, Riddle spent two years as trombonist for the Tommy Dorsey Orchestra, also writing arrangements for the band, then became staff arranger at NBC Radio. By 1951 he formed his own orchestra and recorded with Capitol Records. Although Riddle made some memorable arrangements of hit songs for Nat King Cole, it was his association with Frank Sinatra that became legendary. Riddle helped create a new sound for Sinatra, arranged and conducted some of his greatest recordings, and the two later worked together in films. Soon recognized as the arranger-conductor of choice in the music business, Riddle went on to work with such notable singers as Ella Fitzgerald, Rosemary Clooney, Peggy Lee, Dean Martin, Judy Garland, Johnny Mathis, Kiri Te Kanawa, and Linda Rondstadt. His Hollywood career began in 1953 when he arranged music for the musical *All Ashore*. For the rest of the 1950s he was kept busy arranging and conducting movie scores for such films as *Guys and Dolls* (1955), *Carousel* (1956), *Autumn Leaves* (1956), *High Society* (1956), *A Kiss Before Dying* (1956), *The Pajama Game* (1957), *The Joker Is Wild* (1957), and *Pal Joey* (1957). Riddle first worked in television in 1954, orchestrating and conducting musical programs and TV specials for singing stars.

Riddle's first original screen score was for the melodrama *Flame of the Islands* in 1956 but it received little attention. That same year Sinatra recommended Riddle as composer for his western vehicle *Johnny Concho*, followed by such later Sinatra movies as *A Hole in the Head, Ocean's Eleven, Come Blow Your Horn, 4 for Texas,* and *Robin and the 7 Hoods.* Among the other films Riddle composed music for are *Merry Andrew, St. Louis Blues, The Girl Most Likely, Lolita, Li'l Abner, El Dorado, How to Succeed in Business without Really Trying, On a Clear Day You Can See Forever,* and *Rough Cut.* He won an Oscar for his arranging of period songs in *The Great Gatsby* (1974) and was nominated for similar work in *Can-Can* (1960) and *Paint Your Wagon* (1969), as well as for his original music in *Li'l Abner* and *Robin and the 7 Hoods.* Riddle was equally busy and successful in television. After writing specialty material for stars in the 1950s, he began composing TV theme songs, the three most famous being *The Untouchables, Route 66,* and *Batman.* Among the many other series he scored are *Naked City, The Rogues, The Man from U.N.C.L.E., Emergency!,* and *Barnaby Jones.* Riddle usually arranged and conducted all of his film and television music. By the 1980s, Riddle's style of music was quite out of fashion and he was less involved in composing and arranging. Then in 1983 pop singer Linda Rondstadt approached him about doing an album of standards. The result was three best-selling albums that revived interest in Riddle and his importance to popular music. Before the third album was completed, Riddle died of cardiac arrest and kidney failure at the age of sixty-four.

Although Riddle's fame rests on his outstanding arrangements written over a period of four decades, his original music for the screen is worth examining. Many of his credits are musicals with songs by others. He wrote the connecting music on the soundtrack and, very importantly, orchestrated and conducted the songs. For

The Great Gatsby, for example, no composer of the score is listed yet Riddle created a marvelous soundtrack using standards of the period and tying it all together with variations of Irving Berlin's classic torch song "What'll I Do?" Musicals such as *Li'l Abner* and *Robin and the 7 Hoods* have sections of original scoring but the emphasis remains on the songs. It is in his scores for dramas and comedies where one can hear Riddle the composer. The controversial *Lolita*, about a nymphet (Sue Lyon) and an older man (James Mason), has a love theme that meanders in a detached way. The melody heard on a piano is lazy and sultry while the string accompaniment has a weariness that can only be described as languid. Quite different is the pop selection titled "Lolita Ya Ya" that is sassy and childish with a slight bossa nova beat. The female scat singing captures the disarming appeal of the young Lolita, sexy and immature. The biopic *Harlow* has a Roaring Twenties main theme that conveys the sexy and glamorous aspects of Jean Harlow (Carol Lynley) and her world. There is also a flowing lullaby passage and some bluesy sections when the darker side of the story takes over. *El Dorado*, one of a handful of Riddle's westerns, has a traveling theme with rhythmic guitars and a robust male chorus. It is all very competent but one senses that the prairie genre is not best suited to the Riddle sound.

Perhaps that sound is best expressed in the comedies. *Ocean's Eleven*, perhaps the most famous of Sinatra's "Rat Pack" movies, has a jazzy main theme that swings in a Big Band manner. Riddle uses strings as if they were slide trombones and made the brass sound as if plucked rather than blown. The whole score is invigorating and had much to do with the success of this very "hip" caper film. Another Sinatra vehicle, *Marriage on the Rocks*, has a pop score with touches of jazz, Latin, and rock and roll (which Riddle abhorred). Some might call it pure 1960s music but it seems more like Riddle was trying to cover all bases to represent all of the many strands of music heard in 1965. The music for the comedy *Paris When It Sizzles* is mostly slow jazz with some highly romantic passages as well as silly marches, chaotic chase music, and Parisian atmosphere tunes. A frustrating film about writing a movie script, the comedy runs out of ideas early on but the music remains inventive through to the end. *What a Way to Go!* is a clever comedy in which different episodes in the story are presented in the style of different movies, from silents to "Rat Pack" action films. Riddle got to compose all kinds of music and much of it is a lot of fun. The main title is a breezy foxtrot with the slick Riddle sound, from laughing brass to gleeful strings. The musical pastiches throughout are often spot on, such as the silent movie piano scoring for the poor girl (Shirley MacLaine) from the wrong side of the tracks scenes and the bebop jazz for the modern art section. As fine as all of Riddle's screen music is, it must be said that perhaps his best original music was written for television. It was certainly his most popular. But there was always that wonderful Riddle sound that is his true legacy. Biographies: *Nelson Riddle: The Man behind the Music*, David Morrell (2013); *September in the Rain: The Life of Nelson Riddle*, Peter J. Levinson (2005). Official website: www.nelsonriddlemusic.com.

Credits

(all films USA)

Year	Film	Director
1956	*Flame of the Islands*	Edward Ludwig
1956	*Johnny Concho*	Don McGuire
1956	*Lisbon*	Ray Milland
1958	*The Girl Most Likely*	Mitchell Leisen
1958	*Merry Andrew*	Michael Kidd
1958	*St. Louis Blues*	Allen Reisner
1959	*A Hole in the Head*	Frank Capra
1959	*Li'l Abner* (AAN)	Melvin Frank
1960	*Ocean's Eleven*	Lewis Milestone
1962	*Lolita*	Stanley Kubrick
1963	*Come Blow Your Horn*	Bud Yorkin
1963	*4 for Texas*	Robert Aldrich
1964	*Paris When It Sizzles*	Richard Quine

Year	Film	Director
1964	*What a Way to Go!*	J. Lee Thompson
1964	*Robin and the 7 Hoods* (AAN)	Gordon Douglas
1965	*Harlow*	Alex Segal
1965	*Marriage on the Rocks*	Jack Donohue
1965	*A Rage to Live*	Walter Grauman
1965	*Red Line 7000*	Howard Hawks
1966	*Batman*	Leslie H. Martinson
1966	*El Dorado*	Howard Hawks
1967	*The Spy in the Green Hat*	Joseph Sargent
1967	*How to Succeed in Business without Really Trying*	David Swift
1967	*Tarzan's Jungle Rebellion*	William Witney
1969	*The Maltese Bippy*	Norman Panama
1969	*The Great Bank Robbery*	Hy Averback
1970	*On a Clear Day You Can See Forever*	Vincente Minnelli
1976	*America at the Movies*	George Stevens Jr.
1978	*Harper Valley P.T.A.*	Richard C. Bennett, Ralph Senensky
1978	*Goin' Coconuts*	Howard Morris
1980	*Rough Cut*	Don Siegel, Peter R. Hunt
1980	*Rascal Dazzle*	Edward Glass
1984	*Chattanooga Choo Choo*	Bruce Bilson

RIESENFELD, Hugo (1879–1939) A prodigious Austrian composer, conductor, and musician who worked in opera, theatre, and movies, he wrote scores for dozens of films before the advent of sound and then scored many early talkies.

Hugo Riesenfeld was born in Vienna and studied violin and piano as a child, later attending the local Conservatory of Music and the University of Vienna. His music career began as a violinist for European orchestras, including the Vienna Philharmonic, and then conducting. After serving as conductor for the Imperial Opera House in Vienna, Riesenfeld was brought to New York City in 1907 by impresario Oscar Hammerstein I to be music director for his Manhattan Opera House. He also worked for the producing team of Klaw and Erlanger on Broadway musicals. Riesenfeld became interested in silent movies when he was hired by Jesse L. Lasky to conduct the orchestra for the 1915 version of *Carmen*. Soon he was in great demand as a conductor and was hired by Samuel "Roxy" Rothafel to be music director for his three Manhattan movie palaces, the Rivoli, the Rialto, and the Criterion. Riesenfeld not only conducted the large orchestras in each movie house but also composed original music starting in 1916. By the time sound arrived in 1927, he had written over forty screen scores. Among them were scores for such notable movies as the Lon Chaney vehicles *The Miracle Man*, *Dr. Jekyll and Mr. Hyde*, and *The Hunchback of Notre Dame*;

Cecil B. DeMille's *The Ten Commandments* and *The King of Kings*; as well as *The Covered Wagon*, *Monsieur Beaucaire*, *Les Misérables*, *Beau Geste*, *The Cat and the Canary*, *Sunrise*, and *Uncle Tom's Cabin*.

With the arrival of talkies, Riesenfeld was in even greater demand. He was hired as music director for United Artists in 1928 and scored approximately forty sound movies, most memorably *Ramona*, *The Iron Mask*, *Evangeline*, *The Taming of the Shrew*, *Abraham Lincoln*, *Hell's Angels*, *Tabu*, *Peck's Bad Boy*, and *Little Men*. Near the end of his career he scored a series of musicals for the child star Bobby Breen, including *Let's Sing Again*, *Hawaii Calls*, and *Make a Wish*, the last bringing him his only Academy Award nomination. Riesenfeld continued to conduct, not only for the movies but as maestro for the Los Angeles Symphony. He also wrote some nonmovie music, including a ballet, a comic opera, a stage musical, and instrumental pieces for the concert hall. By the time he died in 1939 at the age of sixty, Riesenfeld had written thousands of pages of music, much of it never recorded but played live in movie palaces and then discarded.

Yet enough of Riesenfeld's music for sound movies does exist and sheet music for some of his silents survive so it is possible to understand the impact he had on screen scoring. Because his movie palace orchestras were large (usually about seventy musicians), he can be credited with bringing the big symphonic sound to Hollywood. Far from the tinkling piano in small cinemas, the music Riesenfeld wrote gave movies a grandeur and prestige unimagined before. For example, the western *The Covered Wagon* did not limit itself to just folk songs and other rural music. Riesenfeld wrote a rhythmic Native American theme, made reference to "The Star Spangled Banner," and treated the prairie locale with a symphonic sweep. His music for the DeMille epics matched the spectacle on-screen and his musical themes for the Chaney vehicles provided a vigorous soundtrack for the actor's larger-than-life theatrics. Riesenfeld was also able to write intimate pieces for small-scale movies. Perhaps his finest music in this style is the engag-

ing score for F. W. Murnau's masterpiece *Sunrise*. When the Fox movie premiered in 1927, it had a score pieced together by four different composers. The following year, Riesenfeld wrote a new score that was more unified and coherent, not to mention lyrical and entrancing. In a different vein, the music for the thriller *The Cat and the Canary* is unsettling and nervous. Riesenfeld continued to promote the big sound when talkies came in and the large orchestras could be recorded. Yet he also showed restraint in some of the less grandiose talkies he scored. Dozens of later screen composers were able to build on what Riesenfeld began: giving movies a majestic musical voice.

Credits

(all films USA unless stated otherwise)

Year	Film	Director
1916	The Habit of Happiness	Allan Dwan
1916	Hoodoo Ann	Lloyd Ingraham
1916	Joan the Woman	Cecil B. DeMille
1916	The Aryan	Reginald Barker, William S. Hart, Clifford Smith
1918	The Blue Bird	Maurice Tourneur
1918	Woman	Maurice Tourneur
1919	The Miracle Man	George Loane Tucker
1919	Sahara	Arthur Rosson
1919	The Mystery of the Yellow Room	Emile Chautard
1920	Dr. Jekyll and Mr. Hyde	John S. Robertson
1920	Humoresque	Frank Borzage
1920	Conrad in Quest of His Youth	William C. de Mille
1920	Always Audacious	James Cruze
1920	Anna Boleyn	Ernst Lubitsch (Germany)
1921	Reputation	Stuart Paton
1921	La Tosca (1918)	Edward José
1922	The Loves of Pharaoh	Ernst Lubitsch (Germany)
1923	The Covered Wagon	James Cruze
1923	Bella Donna	George Fitzmaurice
1923	The Hunchback of Notre Dame	Wallace Worsley
1923	The Ten Commandments	Cecil B. DeMille
1924	Madame Sans-Gêne	Léonce Perret
1924	Monsieur Beaucaire	Sidney Olcott
1925	The Swan	Dimitri Buchowetzki
1925	Beggar on Horseback	James Cruze
1925	The Wanderer	Raoul Walsh
1925	The Pony Express	James Cruze
1925	The Vanishing American	George B. Seitz
1925	Les Misérables	Henri Fescourt (France)
1926	Three Faces East	Rupert Julian
1926	The Volga Boatman	Cecil B. DeMille
1926	The Flaming Frontier	Edward Sedgwick
1926	Beau Geste	Herbert Brenon
1926	The Sorrows of Satan	D. W. Griffith
1926	Old Ironsides	James Cruze
1926	Chang: A Drama of the Wilderness	Merian Cooper, Ernest Schoedsack

Year	Film	Director
1927	Old San Francisco	Alan Crosland
1927	The Cat and the Canary	Paul Leni
1927	The Rough Riders	Victor Fleming
1928	Lucky Boy	Norman Taurog, Charles C. Wilson
1928	Sunrise (1927)	F. W. Murnau
1928	Two Lovers	Fred Niblo
1928	The King of Kings (1926)	Cecil B. DeMille
1928	Uncle Tom's Cabin (1927)	Harry A. Pollard
1928	Ramona	Edwin Carewe
1928	Tempest	Sam Taylor
1928	Looping the Loop	Arthur Robison (Germany)
1928	The Woman Disputed	Henry King, Sam Taylor
1928	The Battle of the Sexes	D. W. Griffith
1928	Revenge	Edwin Carewe
1928	The Cavalier	Irvin Willat
1928	The Awakening	Victor Fleming
1928	Sins of the Fathers	Ludwig Berger
1929	The Rescue	Herbert Brenon
1929	Lady of the Pavements	D. W. Griffith
1929	The Iron Mask	Allan Dwan
1929	Molly and Me	Albert Ray
1929	The Godless Girl	Cecil B. DeMille
1929	Bulldog Drummond	F. Richard Jones
1929	My Lady's Past	Albert Ray
1929	Eternal Love	Ernst Lubitsch
1929	This Is Heaven	Alfred Santell
1929	New Orleans	Reginald Barker
1929	Coquette	Sam Taylor
1929	Two Men and a Maid	George Archainbaud
1929	Evangeline	Edwin Carewe
1929	Midstream	James Flood
1929	Three Live Ghosts	Thornton Freeland
1929	The Taming of the Shrew	Sam Taylor
1930	Lummox	Herbert Brenon
1930	The Bad One	George Fitzmaurice
1930	Abraham Lincoln	D. W. Griffith
1930	One Romantic Night	Paul L. Stein
1930	Hell's Angels	Howard Hughes
1931	Tabu: A Story of the South Seas	F. W. Murnau
1933	Thunder over Mexico	Sergei M. Eisenstein
1933	The Wandering Jew	Maurice Elvey
1934	Peck's Bad Boy	Edward F. Cline
1934	Two Heads on a Pillow	William Nigh
1934	Flirtation	Leo Birinsky
1934	The President Vanishes	William A. Wellman
1934	Little Men	Phil Rosen
1936	Let's Sing Again	Kurt Neumann
1936	Hearts in Bondage	Lew Ayres
1936	Follow Your Heart	Aubrey Scotto
1936	Tundra	Norman Dawn
1936	The President's Mystery	Phil Rosen
1936	The Devil on Horseback	Crane Wilbur
1936	Daniel Boone	David Howard
1936	White Legion	Karl Brown
1936	Robinson Crusoe of Clipper Island	Ray Taylor, Mack Wright
1936	Rainbow on the River	Kurt Neumann
1937	Circus Girl	John H. Auer
1937	Make a Wish (AAN)	Kurt Neumann

Year	Film	Director
1938	*Tarzan's Revenge*	D. Ross Lederman
1938	*Hawaii Calls*	Edward F. Cline
1938	*Sunset Murder Case*	Louis J. Gasnier
1938	*King of the Sierras*	Samuel Diege, Arthur Rosson

ROBBINS, Richard (1940–2012) An American composer who scored mostly European movies, he is most remembered for his twenty films for the producer/director team of Ismail Merchant and James Ivory.

Richard Stephen Robbins was born in South Weymouth, Massachusetts, and began taking piano lessons when he was five years old. Robbins was educated at the New England Conservatory in Boston before receiving a fellowship to study music in Vienna. In 1976, while serving as acting director of the Mannes College of Music in New York, Robbins gave piano lessons to the daughter of Ruth Prawer Jhabvala, the novelist who wrote many screenplays for Merchant and Ivory. Through Jhabvala, he met the filmmaking team and they worked together on a documentary short about the school called *Sweet Sounds*. Robbins's first feature film score was for the Merchant-Ivory period drama *The Europeans* based on a Henry James novel. The movie was only a modest success, but Robbins demonstrated how original music could be used effectively with selections by Verdi, Schubert, and Stephen Foster. For the next three decades Robbins scored just about every Merchant-Ivory film, including such notable works as *Heat and Dust*, *Quartet*, *A Room with a View*, *Mr. & Mrs. Smith*, *Maurice*, *Jefferson in Paris*, *The Golden Bowl*, *The White Countess*, *Howards End*, and *The Remains of the Day*, winning Oscar nominations for the last two. For other directors he composed music for a dozen movies, including *Cotton Mary*, *The Perfect Murder*, *The Ballad of the Sad Cafe*, *Le Divorce*, *A Soldier's Daughter Never Cries*, *Bail Jumper*, *Place Vendôme*, and *The Mystic Masseur*. Robbins directed and provided some original music for the feature documentary *Street Musicians of Bombay*. Suffering from Parkinson's disease, he retired from the movies in 2005 and died from the disease seven years later at the age of seventy-one.

Most of the movies Robbins scored for Merchant-Ivory were period pieces, and he successfully suggested each epoch with his original music, even when heard with authentic music of the period. In addition to different time frames in British history, Robbins provided Hindu-flavored music for the India setting for *Heat and Dust*, jazz for the 1927 Paris drama *Quartet*, a classical mode for the 1970s film *Jefferson in Paris*, rich Teutonic Richard Strauss–like themes for the nineteenth-century *The Golden Bowl* set in various European locales, and pseudo-Chinese music for 1930s Shanghai in *The White Countess*. Robbins selected all of the existing music used in the Merchant-Ivory films, from opera arias to pop songs. In some ways his talent as a composer was matched by his skill as a musical director. Robbins acknowledged the strong influence minimalists Philip Glass and Steve Reich had on his work, yet much of his screen music is rich and romantic, especially when dictated by the story. Perhaps the least minimalist of his scores is the one he wrote for *A Room with a View*, a beautifully filmed (if very abridged) version of the E. M. Forster novel. The story concerns an overprotected English girl (Helena Bonham Carter) whose feelings are caught between her proper but stuffy fiancé (Daniel Day-Lewis) and an impetuous free spirit (Julian Sands) who woos her unconventionally. Each episode in the film is labeled and accompanied by selections from Puccini operas, as are the opening and end credits. Robbins's contribution is a series of short tracks that explore character, as in a restless, confused passage with circling strings, restless woodwinds, and nervous piano that conveys the heroine's indecision. There is also a lovely minor-key waltz on mandolin and pizzicato strings, an oboe solo that is languid and serene, a troubled theme with busy woodwinds, and a slow string and woodwind passage consisting of uncomfortable sustained notes. *A Room with a View* is filled with entrancing music, but few moviegoers recall the sections written by Robbins.

Three Merchant-Ivory films set in Britain have outstanding Robbins scores. *The Remains of the Day*, about a country house butler (Anthony Hopkins), his misplaced loyalty to his master (James Fox), and his timid romance with a new housekeeper (Emma Thompson), is set during the rise of Fascism in continental Europe in the 1930s. Darlington Hall, the setting for most of the film, seems to exist in its own isolated world and little contemporary music is heard. The opening music consists of sustained strings and jittery woodwinds that suggests an oncoming storm. The theme for Darlington Hall has fluttering flutes, celesta accents, and scales played on strings and reeds that slowly resolve into a sweeping waltz. There is also a passionate passage with a full orchestra moving from one crescendo to another suggesting an internal storm, and a slow reflective theme with low reeds and strings that barely moves from one note to another. There is little overt action in *The Remains of the Day* and Robbins musicalizes the little nuances in the movie beautifully. Forster's *Maurice* is about self-repressed homosexuality during the Edwardian era and Robbins arranged some Tchaikovsky music for the film to suggest this fiery passion under the surface. His original music is again concentrated on character as three different males (James Wilby, Hugh Grant, and Rupert Graves) deal with their sexuality. The score opens with a facile theme with some British pomp to set the period but also some romanticism with a seething subtext. There is a lyrical piece featuring the oboe that moves along with some anxiety as the strings descend the scale in a confused manner. Also memorable are a delicately slow passage on piano and strings that is tentative and careful as it moves away from its repeated main musical phrase, and a bucolic and simple folk tune featuring woodwinds that keeps returning to a phrase of descending notes. *Howards End*, also based on a Forster novel, looks at characters from three social classes in Britain before World War I. Two sisters (Emma Thompson and Helena Bonham Carter) have humanist ideas that are challenged by romantic and tragic events. One of the finest Merchant-Ivory works, *Howards End* boasts a subtle but enthralling score by Robbins. There is a slow piano passage that lingers over every note as if fearful of melody, then reeds and strings enter and the piece gradually comes to life. Also tentative is a string and flute theme that manages to be both cautious and lyrical. One track consists of a series of piano scales and a repeated musical phrase that is anxious and even fearful, while another section features a French horn and piano in a doleful lament that aches with poignancy. Perhaps most intriguing is a hesitation waltz on strings that repeats so often it comes across as modern and even minimalist.

What of Robbins's music outside of the Merchant-Ivory movies? The films are rarely as accomplished, but the music is frequently of similar high quality. American and French attitudes are contrasted in the romantic comedy *Le Divorce*, although the film barely rises above clichés. There is a woeful theme with repeated phrases that very slowly vary as a solo violin carries a minor-key melody that borders on a lament. The music has a depth that eludes the movie's characters. The French crime drama *Place Vendôme* is more satisfying. An alcoholic widow (Catherine Deneuve) tries to sell some diamonds that her late husband acquired illegally, only to confront both his and her past. Robbins's main theme is a dissonant and mournful waltz on woodwinds and strings that keeps moving but cannot escape its sorrow. There is also a restless passage on pizzicato strings and wavering woodwinds that builds even as it repeats the same musical idea. A Hindu nurse (Madhur Jaffrey) takes over the care of a sickly British baby in *Cotton Mary*. Set on the Malabar Coast in 1954, there are suggestions of Asian music in the score, such as a restless passage on ethnic strings and echoing horns that is exotic and more than a little threatening. There is also a folk melody with a narrow range played on lush strings and whistling pipes. Yet much of the score reflects the troubled English family, as with a reluctant theme featuring a solo oboe, strings, woodwinds, and celesta that is timid about breaking away from a repeated phrase to explore a melodic line. Another troubled family is explored in *A Soldier's Daughter Never Cries*, perhaps the best non-Ivory-directed movie Robbins got to score. A war hero who has become a famous novelist (Kris Kristofferson) has lived with his family in France for several years and when they move to the States they find themselves clashing with the cultural change. The most memorable track in the score is a sunny waltz on piano, strings, and woodwinds that moves with a free spirit but not too fast, even when clarinet accents come tripping in with laughing chords. Much of the rest of the score conveys the family's frustrations, as with a quiet but unsettling passage in which isolated violin chords and sustained horns refuse to resolve into a melody, or in a foreboding theme on horns, bongo drums, and pizzicato strings that is serene yet unsettling as it forecasts trouble. The teaming of Merchant, Ivory, and Robbins was inspired and resulted in several exceptional movies with superior scores. How unfortunate that Robbins did not have an equally impressive career outside of that team.

Credits

(all films directed by James Ivory unless stated otherwise)

Year	Film	Director
1979	*The Europeans* (UK)	
1980	*Jane Austen in Manhattan* (UK/USA)	
1981	*Quartet* (UK/France)	
1983	*Heat and Dust* (UK)	
1984	*The Bostonians* (UK/USA)	
1985	*A Room with a View* (BAFTA-N)(UK)	
1986	*My Little Girl* (aka *Streetgirls*)	Connie Kaiserman (USA)
1987	*Sweet Lorraine*	Steve Gomer (USA)
1987	*Maurice* (UK)	
1988	*The Perfect Murder*	Zafar Hai (UK/India)
1989	*Slaves of New York* (USA)	
1990	*Bail Jumper*	Christian Faber (USA)
1990	*Mr. & Mrs. Bridge* (UK/USA)	
1991	*The Ballad of the Sad Café*	Simon Callow (UK/USA)
1992	*Howards End* (AAN)(UK/Japan)	
1993	*The Remains of the Day* (AAN)(UK/USA)	
1994	*Street Musicians of Bombay*	Richard Robbins (UK)
1995	*Jefferson in Paris* (France/USA)	
1996	*Surviving Picasso* (USA)	
1996	*The Proprietor*	Ismail Merchant (France/UK/USA)
1997	*The Hidden Dimension*	Paul Cox (USA)
1998	*Place Vendôme*	Nicole Garcia (France)
1998	*A Soldier's Daughter Never Cries* (France/UK/USA)	
1999	*Cotton Mary*	Ismail Merchant, Madhur Jaffrey (France/USA/UK)
2000	*The Golden Bowl* (USA/France/UK)	
2000	*The Girl*	Sande Zeig (USA/France)
2001	*The Mystic Masseur*	Ismail Merchant (UK/India/USA)
2003	*Le Divorce* (USA)	
2005	*The White Countess* (UK/USA/Germany/China)	

ROEMHELD, Heinz (1901–1985) A tireless arranger, conductor, songwriter, and arguably the most prolific Hollywood composer, he scored over three hundred feature films and his stock music was heard in another 350 movies.

He was born Heinrich Erich Roemheld in Milwaukee, Wisconsin, into a musical family of German immigrants, some of whom also had music careers. Roemheld was a child prodigy, highly proficient on the piano at the age of four and beginning studies at the Milwaukee College of Music when he was fifteen. After earning enough money playing piano in theatres, he went to Berlin where he studied privately and performed with the Berlin Philharmonic Orchestra. When Roemheld returned to the States, he found work as conductor and pianist for silent movies. In 1925, while conducting the orchestra for a showing of the silent *The Phantom of the Opera* in Milwaukee, he

impressed film producer Carl Laemmle who brought Roemheld to Hollywood. By 1929, as the studios began making talkies with soundtrack scores, he was in great demand as an arranger, conductor, and composer. The first talkie Roemheld contributed original music to was the 1929 adventure *Tarzan the Tiger*. After composing and recording new soundtracks for such silent classics as *All Quiet on the Western Front* and *The Hunchback of Notre Dame*, Roemheld concentrated on sound movies. He was busiest in the 1930s when he worked on numerous comedies, gangster melodramas, adventure movies, musicals, historical pieces, horror thrillers, and just about every other genre except (oddly) westerns. In 1935 alone, he contributed music to over fifty films. Roemheld often worked with one or more composers on a movie but just as many movies were solo efforts. Among the many notable movies before World War II that he scored solo are *Outside the Law*,

Too Much Harmony, The Invisible Man, Bombay Mail, Mandalay, The Black Cat, Side Street, Dames, Imitation of Life, The Lives of a Bengal Lancer, The Good Fairy, Gold Diggers of 1935, Broadway Gondolier, Miss Page Glory, Hearts Divided, The Story of Louis Pasteur, Cain and Mabel, Three Smart Girls, A Slight Case of Murder, Brother Rat, Knute Rockne All American, Brother Orchid, and *The Strawberry Blonde* (which was nominated for a Best Score Oscar). He and Ray Heindorf won the Academy Award for their scoring of *Yankee Doodle Dandy* in 1942.

There were also dozens of movies for which Roemheld contributed stock music or short cues when the assigned composer was overworked. For example, when Max Steiner was overwhelmed with the massive score for *Gone with the Wind,* Roemheld was hired to compose the music for the burning of Atlanta. Roemheld scored few Hollywood movies during World War II because he served as chief of film, theatre, and music for the government's Information Control Division in Europe. By 1946 he was active again and was busy in Hollywood until the late 1950s, scoring such memorable films as *Thank Your Lucky Stars, The Male Animal, Gentleman Jim, The Hard Way, The Desert Song, The Lady from Shanghai, The Fuller Brush Man, Miss Grant Takes Richmond, The Good Humor Man, Chicago Calling, Union Station, Decision at Sundown, Ride Lonesome,* and *Ruby Gentry,* the last introducing Roemheld's most famous song, "Ruby" (lyric by Mitchell Parish). When Roemheld was assigned to write music for such uninspiring projects as *The Creature Walks among Us* and *The Monster That Challenged the World,* he left Hollywood, wrote for television for a while, then retired. He continued to compose, but for the concert hall, writing numerous concertos, piano preludes, and other instrumental works. Roemheld died in 1985 at the age of eighty-three. Although his music is heard in many classic Hollywood films, very little of Roemheld's music has been recorded and most only exists on the film stock.

Because Roemheld was often arranger and conductor for the movies he scored, the way he used music in the early talkies is more interesting than the music itself. So many of his films are built around existing songs that Roemheld took more pains writing different variations of than on creating original music. His only two movies to be recognized by the Academy are good examples. The musical biopic *Yankee Doodle Dandy* has a score fashioned from the many songs by Broadway songwriter-performer George M. Cohan (James Cagney). In addition to the many musical numbers, Cohan's music from lesser-known songs is used by Roemheld to score comic sequences, montages, sentimental scenes, and patriotic moments. The romantic comedy *The Strawberry Blonde,* about a streetwise tough (Cagney again) who uses all of his muscle and wit to win the love of the widely admired Virginia (Rita Hayworth), is set in the 1890s. The title comes from the popular sing-along favorite "The Band Played On," one of the many period songs heard on the soundtrack score. Again, the way Roemheld uses these to score love scenes, fight sequences, parades, and rallies is quite accomplished. The original music in the film is scarce and unnoticed. The same can be said for the many musicals Roemheld worked on. Only by listening to his solo scores for dramatic movies with little or no existing songs can one hear Roemheld the composer. The 1933 classic *The Invisible Man,* with Claude Rains as the title character, is still surprisingly effective, even the primitive special effects making an impact. Just about all of the music in the score is original and quite varied while staying within a specific mood. The main dramatic theme has woodwinds and strings that bounce across the scale as the music moves from fluid phrases to slow menacing ones, sometimes imitating the wind of a storm in the process. There is a violin solo that is furious and out of control, a series of pounding chords heard under a fearsome march on brass instruments, and intriguing use of blue notes in a waltz theme that give it a creepy tone.

The biopic *The Story of Louis Pasteur* does not hold up as well, but the score is again varied and evocative. The difficulties the famous French scientist (Paul Muni) undergoes trying to get the medical world to accept his findings about microorganisms is scored with some powerful music. The vigorous main theme, with aggressive brass and fervent strings, has a hymnlike quality yet moves much faster and is more driven. There is an inspiring passage that is a march but with the sweep of a waltz; a symphonic minor-key lament with wailing woodwinds and descending strings; and a moody, reflective theme with mellow strings and descending chords played on the reeds. In contrast is a lighter passage on oboe and strings that bounces giddily, and at the end of the movie there is a triumphant theme with robust trumpets signaling victory. A hot-blooded romantic triangle serves as the plot for *Ruby Gentry,* the movie that introduced Roemheld's most famous piece of music. The poor, oversexed title character (Jennifer Jones) marries the town's richest man (Karl Malden) but lusts after a handsome aristocrat (Charlton Heston). The main theme, which became the hit song "Ruby," is immediately enticing. It is a gliding romantic piece that slowly winds its way up the scale, changes key, then repeats the process with unforgettable panache. For once Roemheld got to write different variations of his own song. There is a bombastic version with harmonica and full orchestra that is rhapsodic; yet when slowed down and heard on lazy harmonica, the music is very sultry and raw.

Two outstanding scores by Roemheld have more suspense in their music. The murder mystery *Bombay Mail* is about a British police inspector (Edmund Lowe) who solves the case of a government head who was killed in his train compartment while traveling from Calcutta to Bombay. The score opens with a pompous march that quickly turns sour with dissonant notes and transitions into a furious race with squawking brass, frantic reeds, and restless strings. This theme, which creates excitement and forecasts danger, is so effective that Universal later used it in several of their films, including a series of *Flash Gordon* adventures. The rest of the score is also proficient. There is a slow-paced march on brass instruments that has a solemn air yet moves with spirit, another march with some British pomp but comes across as rather sinister, a warm domestic theme with whistling piccolos and giddy strings, some suspense music on a solo bass bassoon that is very menacing, and a light-footed theme with laughing reeds. *Bombay Mail* is, unfortunately, too little known today but still intrigues and entertains. *The Lady from Shanghai*, on the other hand, is an Orson Welles cult classic. The passionate yet oddly unromantic affair between an Irish seaman (Welles) and the wife (Rita Hayworth) of a rich cripple (Everett Stone) gets more complicated when a convoluted murder plot is added. Very atmospheric and stylish in a Wellesian way, the film noir favorite has a score that Welles publicly castigated on several occasions. He put together a temp score from stock music but Columbia Pictures actively disliked it. Without consulting Welles, Roemheld was appointed to write one that pleased the studio heads. The main theme is a dramatic piano and orchestra piece with crashing waves of music that ascend and descend the scale with a marchlike progression. This catchy musical idea is used throughout the movie, sometimes played on a solo flute and strings for a warm and romantic tone, other times turned into a sinister theme with confused strings and low minor-key woodwinds. Some of the scenes in Mexico are scored with a rapid rumba with threatening drums and Roemheld quotes from the popular Spanish standard "Bahia" for local color. The film's most memorable scene, the climactic shoot-out in a funhouse full of mirrors, was intended by Welles to be shown without music, the gunshots and shattering glass being the only sounds. Roemheld was instructed to add music and he came up with a bizarre track with chaotic piano trills, squawking horns, descending woodwind glissandos, and frantic strings. It is quite compelling (though Welles hated it) but even that music is often overlooked. Has any Hollywood composer contributed to so many movies and left so little an impact on those who appreciate screen scoring?

Credits

(all films USA unless stated otherwise)

Year	Film	Director
1929	Hell's Heroes	William Wyler
1930	The Cohens and the Kellys in Scotland	William James Craft
1930	Captain of the Guard	John S. Robertson, Pál Fejös
1930	Hide-Out	Reginald Barker
1930	All Quiet on the Western Front	Lewis Milestone
1930	Czar of Broadway	William James Craft
1930	What Men Want	Ernst Laemmle
1930	The Leather Pushers	Albert H. Kelley
1930	Outside the Law	Tod Browning
1930	A Lady Surrenders	John M. Stahl
1930	East Is West	Monta Bell
1930	See America Thirst	William James Craft

Year	Film	Director
1930	*Oriente es Occidente*	George Melford, Enrique Tovar Ávalos
1930	*Free Love*	Hobart Henley
1930	*The Boudoir Diplomat*	Malcolm St. Clair
1930	*The Cohens and the Kellys in Africa*	Vin Moore
1930	*White Hell of Pitz Palu* (1929)	Arnold Fanck, G. W. Pabst (Germany)
1931	*The Hunchback of Notre Dame* (1923)	Wallace Worsley
1931	*Many a Slip*	Vin Moore
1931	*Seed*	John M. Stahl
1931	*Up for Murder*	Monta Bell
1933	*Too Much Harmony*	A. Edward Sutherland
1933	*The Invisible Man*	James Whale
1933	*The Sin of Nora Moran*	Phil Goldstone
1934	*Bombay Mail* (aka *Bombay Express*)	Edwin L. Marin
1934	*Easy to Love*	William Keighley
1934	*Cross Country Cruise*	Edward Buzzell
1934	*Mandalay*	Michael Curtiz
1934	*Madame Spy*	Karl Freund
1934	*Fashions of 1934*	William Dieterle
1934	*As the Earth Turns*	Alfred E. Green
1934	*Journal of a Crime*	William Keighley
1934	*A Modern Hero*	G. W. Pabst
1934	*Registered Nurse*	Robert Florey
1934	*The Black Cat*	Edgar G. Ulmer
1934	*Love Birds*	William A. Seiter
1934	*Merry Wives of Reno*	H. Bruce Humberstone
1934	*Dr. Monica*	William Keighley, William Dieterle
1934	*The Circus Clown*	Ray Enright
1934	*Side Streets*	Alfred E. Green
1934	*Midnight Alibi*	Alan Crosland
1934	*Housewife*	Alfred E. Green
1934	*Dames*	Ray Enright, Busby Berkeley
1934	*One Exciting Adventure*	Ernst L. Frank
1934	*You Belong to Me*	Alfred L. Werker
1934	*Desirable*	Archie Mayo
1934	*British Agent*	Michael Curtiz
1934	*The Pursuit of Happiness*	Alexander Hall
1934	*The Lemon Drop Kid*	Marshall Neilan
1934	*A Lost Lady*	Alfred E. Green, Phil Rosen
1934	*Happiness Ahead*	Mervyn LeRoy
1934	*Madame Du Barry*	William Dieterle
1934	*Gentlemen Are Born*	Alfred E. Green
1934	*Imitation of Life*	John M. Stahl
1934	*Ready for Love*	Marion Gering
1934	*Flirtation Walk*	Frank Borzage
1934	*Here Is My Heart*	Frank Tuttle
1934	*The Man Who Reclaimed His Head*	Edward Ludwig
1934	*Sweet Adeline*	Mervyn LeRoy
1934	*Enter Madame!*	Elliott Nugent
1935	*The Lives of a Bengal Lancer*	Henry Hathaway
1935	*Maybe It's Love*	William C. McGann
1935	*A Notorious Gentleman*	Edward Laemmle
1935	*The Good Fairy*	William Wyler
1935	*Wings in the Dark*	James Flood
1935	*All the King's Horses*	Frank Tuttle
1935	*Living on Velvet*	Frank Borzage
1935	*Private Worlds*	Gregory La Caba
1935	*Gold Diggers of 1935*	Busby Berkeley
1935	*Storm over the Andes*	Christy Cabanne

Year	Film	Director
1935	Four Hours to Kill!	Mitchell Leisen
1935	The Devil Is a Woman	Josef von Sternberg
1935	Love in Bloom	Elliott Nugent
1935	Mary Jane's Pa	William Keighley
1935	Dinky	Howard Bretherton, D. Ross Lederman
1935	The Girl from 10th Avenue	Alfred E. Green
1935	Paris in Spring	Lewis Milestone
1935	Oil for the Lamps of China	Mervyn LeRoy
1935	Stranded	Frank Borzage
1935	Going Highbrow	Robert Florey
1935	Front Page Woman	Michael Curtiz
1935	Broadway Gondolier	Lloyd Bacon
1935	Bright Lights	Busby Berkeley
1935	The Irish in Us	Lloyd Bacon
1935	We're in the Money	Ray Enright
1935	Miss Page Glory	Mervyn LeRoy
1935	Little Big Shot	Michael Curtiz
1935	The Goose and the Gander	Alfred E. Green
1935	I Live for Love	Busby Berkeley
1935	Stormy	Lew Landers
1935	The Last Outpost	Charles Barton, Louis J. Gasnier
1935	Dr. Socrates	William Dieterle
1935	Three Kids and a Queen	Edward Ludwig
1935	I Found Stella Parish	Mervyn LeRoy
1935	The Payoff	Robert Florey
1935	Nancy Burns, Fugitive	William K. Howard
1935	Stars over Broadway	William Keighley
1935	East of Java	George Melford
1935	Broadway Hostess	Frank McDonald
1935	The Great Impersonation	Alan Crosland
1935	The Widow from Monte Carlo	Arthur Greville Collins
1935	The Bride Comes Home	Wesley Ruggles
1936	Her Master's Voice	Joseph Santley
1936	Tough Guy	Chester M. Franklin
1936	The Story of Louis Pasteur	William Dieterle
1936	Road Gang	Louis King
1936	Boulder Dam	Frank McDonald
1936	Colleen	Alfred E. Green
1936	Brides Are Like That	William C. McGann
1936	Snowed Under	Ray Enright
1936	The Singing Kid	William Keighley, Busby Berkeley
1936	I Married a Doctor	Archie Mayo
1936	Dracula's Daughter	Lambert Hillyer
1936	Sons o' Guns	Lloyd Bacon
1936	The Law in Her Hands	William Clemens
1936	The Golden Arrow	Alfred E. Green
1936	Hearts Divided	Frank Borzage
1936	The Big Noise	Frank McDonald
1936	The White Angel	William Dieterle
1936	Satan Met a Lady	William Dieterle
1936	China Clipper	Ray Enright
1936	The Case of the Velvet Claws	William Clemens
1936	Stage Struck	Busby Berkeley
1936	Give Me Your Heart	Archie Mayo
1936	Cain and Mabel	Lloyd Bacon
1936	The Girl on the Front Page	Harry Beaumont
1936	The Luckiest Girl in the World	Edward Buzzell
1936	Kliou the Tiger	Henri de la Falaise

Year	Film	Director
1936	*Two in a Crowd*	Alfred E. Green
1936	*Three Smart Girls*	Henry Koster
1936	*Sing Me a Love Song*	Ray Enright
1936	*Gold Diggers of 1937*	Lloyd Bacon
1937	*Smart Blonde*	Frank McDonald
1937	*Once a Doctor*	William Clemens
1937	*Stolen Holiday*	Michael Curtiz
1937	*The Great O'Malley*	William Dieterle
1937	*Ready, Willing and Able*	Ray Enright
1937	*Marked Woman*	Lloyd Bacon, Michael Curtiz
1937	*Call It a Day*	Archie Mayo
1937	*Mountain Justice*	Michael Curtiz
1937	*Melody for Two*	Louis King
1937	*Draegerman Courage*	Louis King
1937	*Kid Galahad*	Michael Curtiz
1937	*The Case of the Stuttering Bishop*	William Clemens
1937	*Ever Since Eve*	Lloyd Bacon
1937	*The Singing Marine*	Ray Enright
1937	*Marry the Girl*	William C. McGann
1937	*San Quentin*	Lloyd Bacon
1937	*Varsity Show*	William Keighley
1937	*Back in Circulation*	Ray Enright
1937	*It's Love I'm After*	Archie Mayo
1937	*Alcatraz Island*	William C. McGann
1937	*Over the Goal*	Noel M. Smith
1937	*The Perfect Specimen*	Michael Curtiz
1937	*West of Shanghai*	John Farrow
1937	*Stand-In*	Tay Garnett
1937	*Expensive Husbands*	Bobby Connolly
1937	*Sh! The Octopus*	William C. McGann
1937	*Hollywood Hotel*	Busby Berkeley
1938	*I Met My Love Again*	Joshua Logan, etc.
1938	*A Slight Case of Murder*	Lloyd Bacon
1938	*Love, Honor and Behave*	Stanley Logan
1938	*Women Are Like That*	Stanley Logan
1938	*Gold Diggers in Paris*	Ray Enright
1938	*Men Are Such Fools*	Busby Berkeley
1938	*Four's a Crowd*	Michael Curtiz
1938	*Secrets of an Actress*	William Keighley
1938	*Garden of the Moon*	Busby Berkeley
1938	*Brother Rat*	William Keighley
1938	*Hard to Get*	Ray Enright
1938	*Nancy Drew: Detective*	William Clemens
1938	*Comet over Broadway*	Busby Berkeley, John Farrow
1938	*Going Places*	Ray Enright
1939	*King of the Underworld*	Lewis Seiler
1939	*Wings of the Navy*	Lloyd Bacon
1939	*Nancy Drew . . . Reporter*	William Clemens
1939	*Yes, My Darling Daughter*	William Keighley
1939	*You Can't Get Away with Murder*	Lewis Seiler
1939	*Nancy Drew . . . Trouble Shooter*	William Clemens
1939	*Naughty but Nice*	Ray Enright
1939	*Hell's Kitchen*	Ewald André Dupont, Lewis Seiler
1939	*Waterfront*	Terry O. Morse
1939	*Nancy Drew and the Hidden Staircase*	William Clemens
1939	*No Place to Go*	Terry O. Morse
1939	*On Your Toes*	Ray Enright
1939	*The Roaring Twenties*	Raoul Walsh

Year	Film	Director
1939	*A Child Is Born*	Lloyd Bacon
1939	*Invisible Stripes*	Lloyd Bacon
1940	*Brother Rat and a Baby*	Ray Enright
1940	*British Intelligence*	Terry O. Morse
1940	*'Till We Meet Again*	Edmund Goulding
1940	*Flight Angels*	Lewis Seiler
1940	*Brother Orchid*	Lloyd Bacon
1940	*The Man Who Talked Too Much*	Vincent Sherman
1940	*My Love Came Back*	Curtis Bernhardt
1940	*No Time for Comedy*	William Keighley
1940	*Knute Rockne All American*	Lloyd Bacon, William K. Howard
1940	*Lady with Red Hair*	Curtis Bernhardt
1941	*Four Mothers*	William Keighley
1941	*Honeymoon for Three*	Lloyd Bacon
1941	*Flight from Destiny*	Vincent Sherman
1941	*The Strawberry Blonde* (AAN)	Raoul Walsh
1941	*The Wagons Roll at Night*	Ray Enright
1941	*Thieves Fall Out*	Ray Enright
1941	*Affectionately Yours*	Lloyd Bacon
1941	*Out of the Fog*	Anatole Litvak
1941	*Navy Blues*	Lloyd Bacon
1941	*Blues in the Night*	Anatole Litvak
1942	*Wild Bill Hickok Rides*	Ray Enright
1942	*Bullet Scars*	D. Ross Lederman
1942	*The Male Animal*	Elliott Nugent
1942	*Always in My Heart*	Jo Graham
1942	*Yankee Doodle Dandy* (AA)	Michael Curtiz
1942	*Gentleman Jim*	Raoul Walsh
1943	*The Hard Way*	Vincent Sherman
1943	*Thank Your Lucky Stars*	David Butler
1943	*Adventure in Iraq*	D. Ross Lederman
1943	*Find the Blackmailer*	D. Ross Lederman
1943	*The Desert Song*	Robert Florey
1944	*Make Your Own Bed*	Peter Godfrey
1944	*Janie*	Michael Curtiz
1945	*Wonder Man*	H. Bruce Humberstone
1945	*Too Young to Know*	Frederick De Cordova
1946	*O.S.S.*	Irving Pichel
1946	*Mr. Ace*	Edwin L. Marin
1946	*The Bachelor's Daughters*	Andrew L. Stone
1947	*Curley*	Bernard Carr
1947	*The Hal Roach Comedy Carnival*	Bernard Carr, Harve Foster
1947	*The Fabulous Joe*	Harve Foster
1947	*Heaven Only Knows*	Albert S. Rogell
1947	*Christmas Eve*	Edwin L. Marin
1947	*The Flame*	John H. Auer
1947	*It Had to Be You*	Don Hartman, Rudolph Maté
1947	*The Lady from Shanghai*	Orson Welles
1947	*On Our Merry Way*	Leslie Fenton, etc.
1948	*Here Comes Trouble*	Fred Guiol
1948	*The Fuller Brush Man*	S. Sylvan Simon
1948	*I, Jane Doe*	John H. Auer
1948	*Station West*	Sidney Lanfield
1948	*The Girl from Manhattan*	Alfred E. Green
1948	*My Dear Secretary*	Charles Martin
1949	*The Lucky Stiff*	Lewis R. Foster
1949	*Mr. Soft Touch*	Gordon Douglas, Henry Levin
1949	*Miss Grant Takes Richmond*	Lloyd Bacon

Year	Film	Director
1950	*The Good Humor Man*	Lloyd Bacon
1950	*Kill the Umpire*	Lloyd Bacon
1950	*Rogues of Sherwood Forest*	Gordon Douglas
1950	*The Fuller Brush Girl*	Lloyd Bacon
1950	*Union Station*	Rudolph Maté
1951	*Chicago Calling*	John Reinhardt
1951	*Valentino*	Lewis Allen
1952	*The Big Trees*	Felix E. Feist
1952	*Jack and the Beanstalk*	Jean Yarbrough
1952	*Loan Shark*	Seymour Friedman
1952	*Three for Bedroom C*	Milton H. Bren
1952	*Ruby Gentry*	King Vidor
1953	*The Moonlighter*	Roy Rowland
1955	*Captain Lightfoot*	Douglas Sirk
1955	*The Looters*	Abner Biberman
1955	*The Purple Mask*	H. Bruce Humberstone
1955	*Female on the Beach*	Joseph Pevney
1955	*Kiss of Fire*	Joseph M. Newman
1955	*Hell's Horizon*	Tom Gries
1955	*The Square Jungle*	Jerry Hopper
1956	*There's Always Tomorrow*	Douglas Sirk
1956	*World in My Corner*	Jesse Hibbs
1956	*The Price of Fear*	Abner Biberman
1956	*The Creature Walks among Us*	John Sherwood
1956	*Away All Boats*	Joseph Pevney
1956	*Pillars of the Sky*	George Marshall
1957	*Istanbul*	Joseph Pevney
1957	*The Tall T*	Budd Boetticher
1957	*The Night Runner*	Abner Biberman
1957	*The Monster That Challenged the World*	Arnold Laven
1957	*The Land Unknown*	Virgil W. Vogel
1957	*Decision at Sundown*	Budd Boetticher
1958	*This Is Russia!*	Sid Feder
1958	*Ride Lonesome*	Budd Boetticher
1962	*Lad: A Dog*	Aram Avakian, Leslie H. Martinson

ROSE, David (1910–1990) A popular British-born American songwriter, arranger, conductor, composer, and music publisher, he wrote some memorable themes for television and scored twenty Hollywood movies.

Born in London, England, David Rose grew up in Chicago, where he studied piano as a boy and began playing professionally when he was sixteen years old. Working with such bandleaders as Ted Fio Rito, Frank Trumbauer, and Louis Prima, he arranged and composed music for the bands, coming up with some early swings hits such as "Plantation Moods" and "Jigsaw Rhythm." Rose first found recognition on Chicago radio station WGN and was wooed to Hollywood where he formed his own band and was featured on the radio show *California Melodies.* Rose's catchy instrumental piece "Holiday for Strings"

was an immediate hit and was played across the country and in Europe. When World War II broke out, Rose enlisted and continued his music activities. He also met comic actor Red Skelton and later the two would collaborate on films, radio, and television programs. Also during the war, Rose scored his first movie, the government-sponsored propaganda film *Resisting Enemy Interrogation,* followed by another patriotic movie, *Winged Victory,* which was based on the 1943 Broadway hit that Rose had composed and arranged. For his first Hollywood score, the Bob Hope comedy *The Princess and the Pirate,* Rose was nominated for an Academy Award. His song "So in Love" (lyric by Leo Robin) from *Wonder Man* (1945) was also nominated. After the war he returned to conducting his orchestra, writing instrumental pieces, and scoring movie musicals and comedies. Rose wrote some of his biggest song hits in the 1950s, including "Calypso Melody," "Ebb Tide," and the now-cliché piece "The Stripper." This last composition has been heard in countless films, television shows, and stage routines.

In 1959 Rose wrote his most famous TV theme song, the vigorous musical opening for the western series *Bonanza*. Among the other television series he wrote music for are *It's a Great Life*, *The High Chaparral*, *Highway Patrol*, *Bracken's World*, *Banacek*, *Little House on the Prairie*, *Father Murphy*, *Highway to Heaven*, and *The Red Skelton Hour*, which used Rose's "Holiday for Strings" as its theme song. He also scored twenty TV movies, including *Along Came a Spider* (1970), *The Birdmen* (1971), *The Loneliest Runner* (1976), *Killing Stone* (1978), and *Suddenly, Love* (1978). He formed his own publishing company and produced hundreds of records of his own music and of others. Rose was a conductor familiar to concert and television audiences, partially because he was music director for Red Skelton's various TV programs and other specials. His three wives include performers Martha Raye and Judy Garland, which also added to his celebrity status. Rose was active in show business up until the day he died at the age of eighty.

Known as the King of Strings, Rose defined a particular sound that mixed classical with swing and jazz. This sound was best interpreted by a large orchestra with a strong string section as opposed to a small jazz combo or solo instrument. His compositions often feature a particular instrument, such as the leering trombone in "The Stripper." His limited number of film scores have plenty of variety, featuring musical vehicles for Esther Williams, Doris Day, and other stars; a western (*Hombre*); broad comedies, such as *Operation Petticoat*, *Please Don't Eat the Daisies*, and *Never Two Late*; and a few dramas, as with *This Rebel Breed* and *Sam's Son*. The scores are also diverse. Rose's music for the musicals *Texas Carnival*, *Jupiter's Darling*, and *Everything I Have Is Yours* is incidental at best, the songs by others being used for much of the scoring. The music in the comedy *Please Don't Eat the Daisies* is dominated by Joe Lubin's popular title song. The military comedy *Operation Petticoat* has a jazzy score with a playful tone. There is even a hint of some "The Stripper"-like vamping for the movie's many double entendres when a group of women are forced to reside with sailors on a U.S. Navy sub. The sentimental Skelton vehicle *The Clown* has a warm and conventional score using a full orchestra to tug at the heartstrings. The main theme is a waltzing lullaby that conveniently moves from the comic to the melodramatic. The documentary-like drama *This Rebel Breed* has a very bluesy score befitting its urban setting and interracial theme. A solo saxophone plays the mournful theme that wails cautiously up and down the scale. *Sam's Son*, a father-son melodrama, has a graceful theme played on piano. It too is cautious in its tempo but the music is more nostalgic and accessible. For Rose's only western, the Paul Newman vehicle *Hombre*, he wrote a gliding, lush theme that at first seems very far from the Old West, but the use of flutes, a tribal underscore, and ethnic-sounding instruments convey that this is indeed a western but not a typical example of the genre. Newman plays a white man raised by Apaches who is trying to fit in to a new world. The music has a melancholy sound that turns the lyrical melody into something weary and regretful. Rose's scoring for the action scenes and the muted romance is also quite effective, making *Hombre* perhaps his finest screen score. The fact that *Hombre* was one of the few first-class Hollywood projects that Rose got to compose music for should not be forgotten. As with his television scoring, Rose's movie career might seem like little more than slumming, his heart being in the Big Band world, which he fought to keep alive into the 1970s. Certainly his best work was done outside of Hollywood. Official website: www.davidrosepublishing.com.

Credits

(all films USA)

Year	Film	Director
1944	*Resisting Enemy Interrogation*	Bernard Vorhaus
1944	*The Princess and the Pirate* (AAN)	David Butler, Sidney Lanfield
1944	*Winged Victory*	George Cukor
1950	*The Underworld Story*	Cy Endfield

Year	Film	Director
1951	*Texas Carnival*	Charles Walters
1952	*Just This Once*	Don Weis
1952	*Young Man with Ideas*	Mitchell Leisen
1952	*Everything I Have Is Yours*	Robert Z. Leonard
1953	*The Clown*	Robert Z. Leonard
1953	*Confidentially Connie*	Edward Buzzell
1953	*Bright Road*	Gerald Mayer
1955	*Jupiter's Darling*	George Sidney
1957	*Public Pigeon No. One*	Norman Z. McLeod
1959	*Operation Petticoat*	Blake Edwards
1960	*This Rebel Breed* (aka *Lola's Mistake*)	Richard L. Bare, William Rowland
1960	*Please Don't Eat the Daisies*	Charles Walters
1964	*Quick Before It Melts*	Delbert Mann
1965	*Never Too Late*	Bud Yorkin
1967	*Hombre*	Martin Ritt
1984	*Sam's Son*	Michael Landon

ROSENMAN, Leonard (1924–2008) An innovative concert composer and respected conductor, he occasionally worked in Hollywood and in television and has some superb scores to his credit.

Leonard Rosenman was born in the New York City borough of Brooklyn and from a young age had aspirations to become a painter, but after serving in the air force in the Pacific during World War II, Rosenman became more interested in music. He studied theory at the University of California at Berkeley and composition with Arnold Schoenberg and other distinguished teachers. Rosenman was fascinated with the musical avant-garde then getting recognition in America, including Schoenberg's twelve-tone row. He wrote music for New York theatre productions and operas, and conducted at Tanglewood for several summers but still needed to give piano lessons to make ends meet. One of his pupils was the young actor James Dean who was about to make his first movie, *East of Eden*. Dean introduced Rosenman to the director-producer Elia Kazan who hired the composer even though he had never scored a film before. Unfamiliar with the way movies were made, Rosenman was present every day of the filming of *East of Eden* and nurtured musical ideas for the score over the shooting period. The result was a superior score and a dazzling screen debut for the young composer. Two other notable films followed, *The Cobweb* and *Rebel without a Cause*, and again Rosenman was roundly applauded. But he did not want to give up his concert career, so over the next forty years he would average only one movie per year.

Although he scored a variety of genres, Rosenman had some of his greatest successes with science fiction movies, including *Fantastic Voyage*, *Beneath the Planet of the Apes*, *Battle for the Planet of the Apes*, *Star Trek IV: The Voyage Home*, *RoboCop 2*, and the animated version of *The Lord of the Rings*. Other notable composing credits are *Pork Chop Hill*, *Hell Is for Heroes*, *The Outsider*, *Countdown*, *An Enemy of the People*, and *A Man Called Horse*. Rosenman also scored several television series, such as *Combat!*, *Garrison's Gorillas*, *Law of the Plainsman*, *The Virginian*, and *Marcus Welby, M.D.*, as well as over thirty TV movies, including *Alexander the Great* (1968), *The Savage Land* (1969), *Vanished* (1971), *In Broad Daylight* (1971), *The Phantom of Hollywood* (1974), *Sybil* (1976), *Friendly Fire* (1979), *Murder in Texas* (1981), and *Keeper of the City* (1991). He was nominated for an Oscar four times and won for his adaptation of existing music in *Barry Lyndon* (1975) and *Bound for Glory* (1976). Rosenman's concert music includes piano and violin concertos, chamber pieces, art songs, and symphonies, as well as instrumental suites based on some of his film scores.

One can hear the influence of the avant-gardist composers in Rosenman's screen work although such sounds are sometimes so subtly used that the scores appear to be conventional to the average moviegoer. *East of Eden* is filled with dissonance and unexpected harmonic progressions yet audiences had no trouble with it. The theme for Cal (Dean), the wayward son in this biblical-like story taken from John Steinbeck's novel, is a sparse, restless piece played by two bassoons and a pair of clarinets. Contrasting all this is a lyrical main theme headed by a six-note phrase that is pleasing to the ear. This theme recurs throughout the movie much like a leitmotif in an opera, such as during the blossoming love between Cal and his brother's sweetheart Abra (Julie Harris). It returns for the final scenes, an uninterrupted ten-minute musical piece under the bedside reconciliation between Cal and his father (Raymond Massey). Because Rosenman was still learning about film scoring, there is a freshness and even some audacity in this marvelous score. When asked to score *The Cobweb*, a drama set in a mental institution, Rosenman asked producer John Houseman if he could write an atonal score and not worry about a pretty love theme. Houseman and director Vincente Minneli agreed and the result was Hollywood's first score to use a twelve-tone row. The music in *The Cobweb* is more severe and, appropriate for its setting, unrelenting. The main motif that represents the hospital itself is a series of glissandos on kettledrums as the strings restlessly scratch out notes in a furious manner. The disturbing film was not a hit, considered by many to be too abrasive. Certainly much of that came from the very offbeat score.

Another James Dean film, *Rebel without a Cause*, has much in common with *East of Eden* but the story this time is contemporary and Rosenman came up with a score filled with jazz. The main theme uses blues and even a bit of swing to set up the small-town locale and the attitude of the teenagers. There is also a more melodic theme played on strings that is used for the romance between the "rebel" and his girlfriend (Natalie Wood). Rosenman uses some dissonance throughout, climaxing with the movie's big confrontation between two rival teens. Like the two antiheroes that Dean played in *East of Eden* and *Rebel without a Cause*, the central figure in *The Outsider* is a restless youth. The Native American Ira Hamilton Hayes (Tony Curtis) is a U.S. Marine in the Pacific during World War II and feels ostracized even within the band of comrades who fight on Imo Jima. The score begins with the expected trumpets and crashing cymbals in a military mode but as the movie progresses the music moves away from patriotism and grows more dissonant, particularly in a surreal dream that turns into Hayes's death scene. Two other war movies scored by Rosenman deserve mention. For the Korean War drama *Pork Chop Hill*, Rosenman used an ancient Chinese folk

lullaby and set it to a march tempo, suggesting both the military and the personal conflicts in the story. Asian sounds permeate the film even though most of the characters are Americans. It is also piquant that the military fanfares heard in the main theme take on a weary, minor-key flavor by the bittersweet ending. The World War II movie *Hell Is for Heroes* is about a small band of American soldiers trying to convince the encroaching Germans that they are more plentiful and powerful than they really are. Shrill brass instruments play the main theme, quickly and piercingly firing notes as if gunshots. There is more tension than action in the film and Rosenman seems to understand the significance of this. Musically, this is war as a suspense thriller.

Perhaps Rosenman's experimental use of atonal music in screen soundtracks makes most sense in his science fiction films. For *Fantastic Voyage*, about scientists shrinking themselves to microscopic size and entering a human body, the studio requested a jazz score. Rosenman convinced director Richard Fleischer that no music should be used until the medical team was safely inside the body. Only typewriter keys, ticking clocks, heartbeats, electric sounds, and discordant noise are heard during the first section of the movie. Once inside the body, the sounds are eerie and fragmented but definitely musical. Sections are patterned with descending glides or creepy fanfares creating a very unique suspense score. A different kind of noise is used for the sci-fi sequel *Beneath the Planet of the Apes*. Deep bass notes and high-pitched strings battle in a chaotic score in which a melody could actually be detected within all the strange noise. A choir of mutant humans sings a pseudoliturgical hymn as they worship an atomic missile. At one point Rosenman takes the hymn "All Things Bright and Beautiful" and turns it into a bizarre ape army march, musically satirizing both man and beast. *Star Trek IV: The Voyage Home* is considered one of the most entertaining of the series with a surprising amount of humor in the adventure. Because this episode was set in present-day California, Rosenman suggested to director Leonard Nimoy that a jazzier score be used rather than the expected sci-fi music. The main theme starts with the trumpet fanfare viewers anticipate but quickly the music becomes classical and animated, suggesting a comic adventure to follow. Rosenman includes some interesting space-age vibrations and electronic waves when the crew are deep in space but once on planet Earth he takes his cue from the singing whales and writes an echoing kind of music. *Star Trek IV* is one of those movies where it is difficult to tell where sound effects end and music begins. The futuristic sequel *RoboCop 2* was deemed an unsatisfying mess by the public and the press, so little attention was paid to Rosenman's compelling score. The main theme simulates a mechanical temperament by having the brass instruments rapidly repeat a six-note phrase as if grinding away at work. A choir of voices and lovely flutes and violins are used at times to suggest the humanity that lies beneath a high-tech world. This is an exciting score but what was seen on the screen was so banal that even the music must have grated on moviegoers after a while. Also oddly unsatisfying is Ralph Bakshi's part-animated, part-live-shadow-action version of *The Lord of the Rings* released in 1978, two dozen years before the acclaimed three-film version. Again the score ought to have gotten more attention. The main theme is a regal march with a touch of mysticism. The battle scenes are scored with a tinny horn that suggests miniature armies while the magical sequences are supported by lonely oboes and twinkling bells that recall drops of water hitting the surface of a pond.

In the opinion of some, Rosenman's finest score is the one he wrote for the antiwestern *A Man Called Horse*. An English aristocrat (Richard Harris) is captured by the Sioux tribe and, after some torturous ordeals, learns to become one of them. Rosenman wrote the first movie score to totally embrace Native American instruments and sounds without romanticizing it for a mainstream audience. Tribal chants, rattles and whistles, rhythmic drums, and even an authentic Sioux choir are used brilliantly to re-create the primitive sounds of the prairie even as they are given an avant-garde twist. At one point the deep brass sound just like the chanting of bass voices. One passage uses simple native flutes against a high clarinet, the two sounds mingling poignantly. This is movie music at its most daring. Along with Alex North, Rosenman is credited with bringing avant-garde music to Hollywood. Such experimentation rarely leads to commercial success, but both men managed to reach an audience even as they challenged them.

Credits

(all films USA unless stated otherwise)

Year	Film	Director
1955	East of Eden	Elia Kazan
1955	The Cobweb	Vincente Minnelli
1955	Rebel without a Cause	Nicholas Ray
1957	Edge of the City	Martin Ritt
1957	The Young Stranger	John Frankenheimer
1957	Bombers B-52	Gordon Douglas
1958	Lafayette Escadrille	William A. Wellman
1959	Pork Chop Hill	Lewis Milestone
1960	The Rise and Fall of Legs Diamond	Budd Boetticher
1960	The Bramble Bush	Daniel Petrie
1960	The Savage Eye	Ben Maddow, etc.
1960	The Crowded Sky	Joseph Pevney
1960	The Plunderers	Joseph Pevney
1961	The Outsider	Delbert Mann
1962	Hell Is for Heroes	Don Siegel
1962	Convicts 4	Millard Kaufman
1962	The Chapman Report	George Cukor
1966	Fantastic Voyage	Richard Fleischer
1967	A Covenant with Death	Lamont Johnson
1967	Countdown	Robert Altman
1968	Hellfighters	Andrew V. McLaglen
1970	A Man Called Horse	Elliot Silverstein
1970	Beneath the Planet of the Apes	Ted Post
1971	The Todd Killings	Barry Shear

Year	Film	Director
1972	Irish Whiskey Rebellion	Chester Erskine
1973	Battle for the Planet of the Apes	J. Lee Thompson
1977	The Car	Elliot Silverstein
1977	September 30, 1955	James Bridges
1978	An Enemy of the People	George Schaefer
1978	The Lord of the Rings (GGN)	Ralph Bakshi
1979	Prophecy	John Frankenheimer
1979	Promises in the Dark	Jerome Hellman
1980	Hide in Plain Sight	James Caan
1980	The Jazz Singer	Richard Fleischer
1982	Making Love	Arthur Hiller
1983	Cross Creek (AAN)	Martin Ritt
1984	Heart of the Stag	Michael Firth (New Zealand)
1985	Sylvia	Michael Firth (New Zealand)
1986	Star Trek IV: The Voyage Home (AA)	Leonard Nimoy
1989	Circles in a Forest	Regardt van den Bergh (So. Africa)
1990	RoboCop 2	Irvin Kershner
1991	Ambition	Scott D. Goldstein
1994	The Color of Evening	Steve Stafford
1995	Mrs. Munck	Diane Ladd
1997	Levitation	Scott D. Goldstein
2001	Jurij	Stefano Gabrini (Italy)

ROSENTHAL, Laurence (b. 1926) A very busy and popular composer, conductor, and arranger for television, he wrote some memorable screen scores in the 1960s and 1970s.

He was born in Detroit and took piano lessons as a child, later studying piano and composition at the Eastman School of Music and in Paris with Nadia Boulanger. After further study in Salzburg, Rosenthal served in the U.S. Air Force where he composed music for the Air Force Documentary Film Squadron. When Rosenthal was discharged, he settled in New York City where he wrote incidental music for Broadway plays and musicals and composed for the ballet and concert hall. Because of his experience scoring documentary films, he was hired to score two movies in the 1950s, and by 1960 he was working in television. Rosenthal's screen score for the landmark drama *A Raisin in the Sun* was well received and he was hired to score other dramatic films, including *Requiem for a Heavyweight*, *Becket*, and *The Miracle Worker*. In all, he has written scores for twenty-five feature films over a forty-year period, among the notable being *Hotel Paradiso*, *The Comedians*, *Rooster Cogburn*, *The Return of a Man Called Horse*, *The Island of Dr. Moreau*, *Clash of the Titans*, *Meteor*, *Who'll Stop the Rain*, *Meetings with Remarkable Men*, and *Heart Like a Wheel*. Rosenthal also arranged and conducted music for other movies, getting an Oscar nomination for his work on *Man of La Mancha*.

Rosenthal was kept busier in television where he scored several series and over seventy TV movies and miniseries. Nearly half of these were biographical dramas that were highly acclaimed, receiving twelve Emmy nominations and winning six times. His television series include *Coronet Blue*, *Logan's Run*, *Fantasy Island*, and *The Young Indiana Jones Chronicles*, and among his TV movies and miniseries are *Rashomon* (1961), *The Power and the Glory* (1961), *Sweet, Sweet Rachel* (1971), *Pueblo* (1973), *The Missiles of October* (1974), *The Amazing Howard Hughes* (1977), *The Day Christ Died* (1980), *The Patricia Neal Story* (1981), *George Washington* (1984), *Mussolini: The Untold Story* (1985), *Peter the Great* (1986), *Anastasia: The Mystery of Anna* (1986), *The Bourne Identity* (1988), *Billy the Kid* (1989), *Blind Faith* (1990), *Mark Twain and Me* (1991), *The Member of the Wedding* (1997), *Inherit the Wind* (1999), *Master Spy: The Robert Hanssen Story* (2002), and ten installments of *Young Indiana Jones* features for video and television. In addition to his incidental music for some New York plays, he contributed to the Broadway musicals *Sherry!*, *The Music Man*, *Goldilocks*, *Take Me Along*, *George M!*, and *Donnybrook!* Rosenthal has also written chamber pieces, symphonies, art songs, choral works, and instrumental suites based on his film music, many of them performed by renowned orchestras.

The American theatre classics *A Raisin in the Sun* and *The Miracle Worker* were filmed with most of the stage casts reprising their roles and the plays were opened up effectively for the screen. *A Raisin in the Sun*, about a struggling African American family in 1950s inner-city Chicago, has two major musical themes, each relating to a major character. A flowing, minor-key melody that climbs the scale hopefully is for the family matriarch Lena (Claudia McNeil) who wants to use her late husband's life insurance check to find a decent house for her family. A jazzy, flippant theme relates to her son Walter (Sidney Poitier) who wants to get into big money by investing in a liquor store. The music for *The Miracle Worker* is more dissonant and disjointed, suggesting the blind and silent world of the young Helen Keller (Patty Duke). The determination of her teacher Annie Sullivan (Anne Bancroft) is heard in some strident passages with low rumbling woodwinds. When the two women finally connect, the music is delicate and quiet, barely breaking the silence. The film of *Requiem for a Heavyweight* was not based on a play but on Rod Serling's acclaimed television drama and it too was turned into a first-class screen drama. This tale of a washed-up boxer (Anthony Quinn) is scored with a restless blues-jazz theme that seems to plod along as violins waver and trumpets play a monotonous fanfare. Music is used sparingly in all three of these dramas, something Rosenthal had learned from writing for the theatre. Yet in all three films the score is rich in mood and powerful in evoking character.

Probably the biggest production Rosenthal was asked to score for the movies was *Becket*, a lavish period piece about the friendship and rivalry between King Henry II (Peter O'Toole) and Thomas Becket (Richard Burton). The main theme is a masterful combination of Gregorian chant, medieval fanfares, and a modern section with violins and woodwinds moving into dissonance and sardonic sounds. A three-note theme for Becket is used in various ways throughout the film, from a hedonistic frolic for his misspent youth to a solemn interpretation with a male choir for his martyrdom. Rosenthal's exceptional score for *Becket* received a lot of attention, so it is surprising that he was not offered other big productions. The closest he came to such a piece was the mythological adventure *Clash of the Titans* about the hero Perseus (Harry Hamlin). This no-holds-barred tale allowed Rosenthal to write his most vigorous screen score. The main theme is a series of splashing crescendos played by gleeful brass and slaphappy violins. There is plenty of rousing music for the many action sequences but the most exhilarating theme is heard when Perseus tames and flies on the winged horse Pegasus. The music not only soars but seems to be celebrating the glory of flying itself.

Although he scored fewer movies than most screen composers, there is plenty of variety in Rosenthal's credits. For the sequel *The Return of a Man Called Horse*, the music concentrates on the majesty of the land that the Sioux tribe is trying to defend. The main theme is a luscious piece of bucolic harmony with French horns and strings held together by a subtle harp. Rosenthal ingeniously takes this same theme and gives it a driving rhythm for a scene in which the Sioux hunt buffalo. Another sequel, and Rosenthal's other major western, is *Rooster Cogburn*, which features the character and actor (John Wayne) from *True Grit*. The Northwest scenery prompts a more aggressive musical theme as trumpets seem to announce the arrival of the pioneer spirit. For the macabre thriller *The Island of Dr. Moreau*, the music echoes the demented doctor (Burt Lancaster) who turns human captives into animals. Much of the music is painfully dissonant and harsh but there is a very lyrical love theme that seems angelic amid all the horror. On the other hand, few scores are as frolicsome as Rosenthal's pseudo-French music for the farce *Hotel Paradiso*. A clarinet and oboe compete in a silly manner during the opening theme for this Belle Epoque farce. As the plotting gets more complicated, the music grows more frivolous. The humor in *Hotel Paradiso* may be an acquired taste, but the music is easily savored. Although *The Comedians* may sound like another comedy, it is in fact a political thriller set in Haiti. This is made clear in Rosenthal's opening music in which lazy strings and lively percussion hint not only of the Caribbean locale but at sinister doings as well. A rhythmic children's chorus is used effectively in some passages, a chaotic piano in others, and creepy chimes to convey the secrecy everywhere. Even the love theme has a disquieting mystery to it, as if afraid to resolve itself in a final musical line. Perhaps Rosenthal's most exotic score is the one he wrote for *Meetings with Remarkable Men* by avant-gardist Peter Brook. As a cult leader (Dragan Maksimovic) journeys across Asia searching for the meaning of life, the score moves from enchanting folk music to atonal chanting, most of it played on ethnic instruments. It is the kind of score one would have trouble selling on television, to say the least. By 1983, Rosenthal left movies and concentrated on television. Yet it is remarkable how much territory Rosenthal covered in only two dozen movies. He is a composer who thoroughly understands the medium and has left us the music to prove it. Official website: www.laurencerosenthal.com.

Credits

(all films USA unless stated otherwise)

Year	Film	Director
1955	Yellowneck	R. John Hugh
1957	Naked in the Sun	R. John Hugh
1961	A Raisin in the Sun	Daniel Petrie
1961	Dark Odyssey	William Kyriakis, Radley Metzger
1962	The Miracle Worker	Arthur Penn
1962	Requiem for a Heavyweight	Ralph Nelson
1964	Becket (AAN; GGN)	Peter Glenville (UK/USA)
1966	Hotel Paradiso	Peter Glenville (UK)
1967	The Comedians	Peter Glenville (USA/France)
1969	Three	James Salter (UK)
1971	A Gunfight	Lamont Johnson
1972	Lapin 360	Robert Michael Lewis
1975	Rooster Cogburn	Stuart Millar
1976	The Return of a Man Called Horse	Irvin Kershner
1977	The Island of Dr. Moreau	Don Taylor
1978	Who'll Stop the Rain	Karel Reisz
1978	Brass Target	John Hough
1979	Meetings with Remarkable Men	Peter Brook (UK)
1979	Portrait of a Hitman	Allan A. Buckhantz
1979	Meteor	Ronald Neame
1981	Clash of the Titans	Desmond Davis
1983	Heart Like a Wheel	Jonathan Kaplan
1983	Easy Money	James Sigorelli
2002	A Time for Dancing	Peter Gilbert
2008	Stealing America: Vote by Vote	Dorothy Fadiman

ROTA, Nino (1911–1979) A prolific Italian composer of opera, ballet, and concert works, he is arguably the most important figure in the history of music in the Italian cinema. Rota's work with director Federico Fellini is one of the most prodigious collaborations of the movies, but he is perhaps most known for his scores for *The Godfather* films.

Born Giovanni Rota Rinaldi in Milan, Italy, into a musical family, his composition talents were recognized at an early age. Rota was a celebrated child prodigy, writing his first oratorio when he was eleven years old and the next year it was performed in Milan and in Paris. When he was older he studied composition at the Milan Conservatory, the Santa Cecilia Academy in Rome, and the Curtis Institute of Philadelphia before pursuing a degree in music literature at the University of Milan. Rota began teaching after graduation and would continue to do so even as his composing career flourished. In 1950 he was named director of the Liceo Musicale in Bari, Italy, a post he held until one year before his death twenty-nine years later. Rota wrote ten operas, five ballets, and numerous concertos, oratorios, chamber pieces, choral works, and orchestra compositions, as well as over 150 film scores. Most of these were for Italian movies, but by the 1950s he was internationally known and was asked to write for many American, British, and French films as well.

Rota contributed music to a few short films while still a student, and in 1933, when he was only twenty-two years

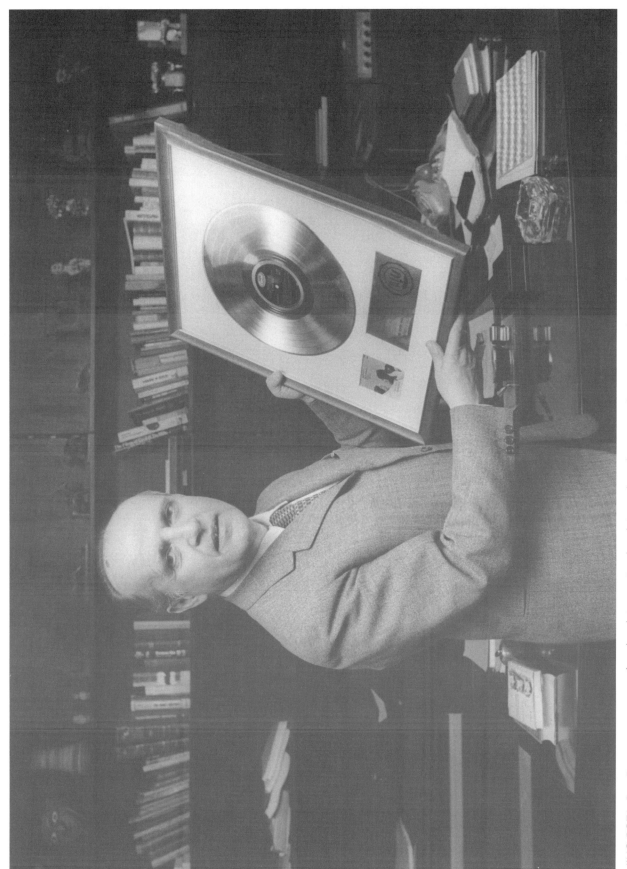

NINO ROTA. Few European composers found such international acclaim as the Italian Rota, whose music spoke every language. Here he proudly holds up a plaque honoring his best-selling soundtrack album from *Romeo and Juliet* (1968). *Photofest*

old, he wrote his first feature score. He did not return to the movies until a decade later with his score for *Zaza*, which was very well received. Rota's screen projects increased after World War II and in 1952 he worked with Fellini for the first time. The comedy *The White Sheik* was not an international success, but by the mid-1950s Fellini's movies started getting worldwide attention and Rota's music was noticed and praised. Among the outstanding Fellini-Rota collaborations are *I vitelloni*, *La strada*, *Nights of Cabiria*, *La dolce vita*, *8 1/2*, *Juliet of the Spirits*, *The Clowns*, and *Amarcord*. Rota composed music for just about every notable Italian director in the postwar years, including Vittorio De Sica, Renato Castellani, Luchino Visconti, Mario Soldati, and Franco Zeffirelli. His famous movies with these and other Italian directors include *Rocco and His Brothers*, *The Best of Enemies*, *Love and Anarchy*, *Boccaccio '70*, *The Condemned of Altona*, *Romeo and Juliet*, *Phantom Lovers*, *The Taming of the Shrew*, and *The Leopard*. Rota's international movies to find wide recognition include *War and Peace*, *Mambo*, *The Glass Mountain*, *The Assassin*, *Purple Noon*, *Waterloo*, and *Death on the Nile*, but by far his biggest successes were the first two *Godfather* films. He was an acclaimed conductor and served in that capacity on many of his films. Rota also made many recordings of his screen and concert music. He continued to work as a composer, conductor, and teacher until his death at the age of sixty-seven. In 1995 the Nino Rota Foundation was established in Venice to promote the work of Italian composers.

Rota's music is characterized by strong melody, inventive harmony, a willingness to experiment with new forms, an acknowledgment of jazz and other popular music, and remarkable variety. Although he was impressed with and often used Arnold Schoenberg's twelve-tone technique, Rota let each project dictate its own technique. Because of his extensive knowledge of classical and popular music, Rota was able to draw on many styles and philosophies when he wrote for the movies, resulting in everything from cool jazz to circus music. Fellini's movies were sometimes the most demanding, so many feel he did his finest work in those films. Some have pointed out a satirical tone in many of his screen scores, as if the music is wryly commenting on the characters or the situations. This is best seen in Fellini's more sarcastic or ironic works. *La dolce vita* is a good example. This modern epic about empty lives parading as joie de vivre icons is satire with a melancholy subtext. Rota composed individual music for each of the film's episodes but it is all united by a central theme. It sounds like the fanfares for an ancient Roman epic yet the insistent interruptions by various instruments makes the theme modern, especially as jazzy muted trumpets and an electric piano come in. One passage is a delightful jazz piece with clarinet and electric guitar, another is a sexy cha-cha that is as sleek as it is nonchalant. The blues theme is played by various solo instruments, each having its individual commentary. The score ends with a lively theme that is a carefree dance, suggesting that the sweet life continues even as the characters on-screen are standing in the light of a somber dawn. *La dolce vita* may be an allegory but it is rather realistic (for Fellini) and Rota's music always seems to be coming from a nearby nightclub or some other probable place. For the surreal *8 1/2*, the music is as inexplicable as the movie itself. A famous movie director (Marcello Mastroianni) struggles to come up with the subject of his next film and is haunted by memories of the different women in his life. The main theme is a daffy circus march even though much of the action takes place in a sanitarium. Young boys pursue a grotesque prostitute on a beach while the music is a jazzy foxtrot. An imaginary harem is scored with an accordion playing breezy cafe music. There is a silly march featuring a klezmer-like clarinet, passages that are morose and tuneless, and sections with organ and strings that are furiously frantic. When a movie is as expressionistic as *8 1/2*, anything goes and Rota's music goes everywhere.

One expects circus music in Fellini's quasi-documentary *The Clowns* and one is not disappointed. The main circus march theme is robust and colorful and there is a funeral for a famous clown with music that is painfully cheerful, yet there are some disarmingly tender passages in the film as well. *Nights of Cabiria* has a lush and fully orchestrated theme with a jaunty beat. This bittersweet tale of an ever-hopeful streetwalker (Giulietta Masina) is scored without satire. Most passages have long musical lines; there is a restrained rumba, and a sunny ending with carefree voices supporting the optimistic music. *La strada* is much darker but musically even richer. The principal theme is a lonely and delicate blues played by a solo trumpet then picked up by the strings and the rhythm changes beautifully. Because the story follows a traveling sideshow there are passages of circus music but Rota's score concentrates on the characters and the complicated relationship between a carnival strong man (Anthony Quinn) and the waif (Masina) who loves him. Neither character is much of a talker so music is needed in *La strata* as in few other Fellini films. The main theme for *Juliet of the Spirits* is a casual jazz piece played on electronic instruments. The whole score has a very detached feeling as we stand back and watch the heroine (Masina again) without totally understanding her. There are plenty of dreams and fantasy sequences in *Juliet of the Spirits* and Rota uses singing voices, waltzing passages, sound effects, and even some pseudo-Asian music to bring them to life. But this is not one of Fellini's best efforts, and one is tempted to say the music is often better than the film. One can say the same thing about *Casanova*, a period film with a gracefully ingratiating score. Rota mixes romance and mystery in the minor-key main theme, a languid waltz that has a delicacy not found in the movie itself. Finally, one cannot fail to mention *Amarcord*, probably Fellini's most personal movie. This funny, nostalgic look at his own youth is scored with a warm and lively set of themes that manage to be slightly satiric and loving at the same time. The main theme is an entrancing foxtrot played on woodwinds, sentimental but knowing, with a steady tempo. Rota uses different variations of this catchy theme throughout the movie and it is flexible enough to fit many different moods. There is wonderful festival music with laughing trombones, a romantic tango heard on the accordion, a rapid Aram Khachaturian–like passage with exotic flourishes, a heartfelt guitar ballad, and a cool jazz theme that glides back and forth comfortably as if to say the past is simply a remembered melody. Just as many rank *Amarcord* among Fellini's finest movies, so too is Rota's score deserving of superlatives.

Of course there is much more to Rota than Fellini. Working with directors with a much different sensibility than Fellini, he was still able to create many exceptional scores. What can be further from Fellini's quirky world than *War and Peace*? King Vidor's rather Hollywoodized version of Tolstoy's great Russian novel may be a bit uneven, but Rota's ambitious symphonic score is masterful. The main theme moves from forceful waves of music to a delicate, tinkling lullaby to robust Russian folk dance passages. There is a sprightly waltz for Natasha (Audrey Hepburn) at the ball, a gliding promenade for the regal class and passionate gypsy music for the seamier side of Russian society, a rousing military theme for the battle of Borodino which quotes from both the French and Russian anthems,

and a memorably mournful passage on muted brass for the aftermath of war. This might be considered a very conventional and unsurprising score for Rota but it is nevertheless excellent. Arguably Rota's best non-Fellini Italian movie is Luchino Visconti's *The Leopard*. This melancholy period piece, about the waning of a Sicilian aristocrat (Burt Lancaster) and his world, is scored with a classical flavor but there is enough dissonance and minor keys to indicate a modern cynicism. Again there is a sparkling waltz for a ball sequence, but much of the rest of the score is darker and reflective, in particular a Gustav Mahler–like passage that seems to hesitate before letting the melody surface on occasion. *The Leopard* took many years to be acknowledged as Visconti's masterpiece; Rota's score is still generally overlooked. Two Shakespeare films directed by Franco Zeffirelli reveal Rota in a different mode. *The Taming of the Shrew* has a felicitous Renaissance tone that soon gives way to vigorous music that tries to keep up with all the brawling on the screen. A lovely passage played on strings and woodwinds is captivating as a satisfying respite from the series of fanfares, dances, pomp and banquet music, chase themes, and drinking songs. The full orchestral sound of *The Taming of the Shrew* is reduced to a smaller period ensemble for Zeffirelli's popular *Romeo and Juliet*. Emphasizing the power of teenage love, the movie quickly became the most romantic of its era with both its score and featured song "What Is a Youth" (later more popularly known as "A Time for Us" with a lyric by Eddie Snyder and Larry Kusik) getting on the charts. The film was accepted by younger generations as hip and timely, yet it is a very traditional movie with historically accurate costumes, locales, and music. Rota's theme for Romeo (Leonard Whiting) is a languid piece in a minor key and played by strings and a solo English horn. This theme is manipulated quite masterfully into the love theme for the couple with instrument and key changes. (It is also the melody for the popular song.) The rest of the score is equally entrancing. There is a lilting dance passage for the Capulet ball where Romeo and Juliet (Olivia Hussey) meet, a festive piece for the revelers, and an ominous passage that returns several times to foreshadow the fateful ending. It is no exaggeration to say that the surprising success of this *Romeo and Juliet* owes a great deal to its music.

Equally popular around the world was *The Godfather* which boasted an equally famous score by Rota. Director Francis Ford Coppola at first wanted his father Carmine, an expert flautist and sometime composer, to write the music for the film. But he soon realized that a born and bred Italian composer was needed and Rota was brought in on the project. (Some of Carmine Coppola's music is heard during the dancing at the opening wedding scene.) While this familiar score has been heard at weddings and other events, it is not a very ingratiating one. Almost all of the music is in a minor key, the instrumentation is often chilling and distant, and there is a sense of menace throughout that should leave the listener uncomfortable. The main theme is an eerie waltz first heard on a solo trumpet. As woodwinds are added it takes on different moods and unites the movie musically. The love theme is not introduced until the young gangster Michael (Al Pacino) is in Sicily and falls in love with a local girl. The mandolin plucks out this simple but intoxicating Italianate melody, which is as sad as it is romantic. This music was later turned into an instrumental love song retitled "Speak Softly Love." The violence in the movie is scored with a slow but determined funeral march that has its own appeal. The descending notes wryly comment on the destruction taking place yet by the final credits the same melody is given a lush orchestration and has quite a different mood. These three distinct themes are used ingeniously throughout the film, illustrating Rota's talent for uniting a score even when pop songs from the period were heard in various scenes. As praised as the score was, the Academy withdrew its nomination for Best Score when it was learned that Rota had taken a few of the passages from his forgotten 1958 Italian film *Fortunella* and reused them in *The Godfather*. It mattered little, for the score had already become one of the most recognized and renowned in movie history.

Ironically, much of *The Godfather* music was heard again in the acclaimed sequel two years later but this time the Academy gave Rota the Oscar. (He shared the award with Carmine Coppola who again contributed to the score.) *The Godfather Part II* is that rare instance in which the sequel equals or surpasses the original. The canvas is even greater this time, with scenes in Sicily and Little Italy that take place years before the events of the first movie, as well as a story that continues where *The Godfather* ended. The score reflects this and has even more musical variety. The theme for the immigrant boy Don Corleone (Oreste Baldini) is flowing and optimistic in a way that none of the music in the first score was. Again the mandolin returns to revive the memories of Sicily. The scenes in Manhattan's Little Italy have deliciously festive music, the jaunty folk instruments actually taking on a comic flavor. The music for the modern scenes is very melancholy, such as the sad foxtrot theme for the disintegrating marriage of Michael and Kay (Diane Keaton). The violence in the sequel is, in many ways, more disturbing and the music for those scenes is often harsher than what was heard in *The Godfather*. These two superb film scores must really be thought of as one and, as such, they are arguably Rota's masterpiece in a career filled with superior scores. Biography: *Nino Rota: Music, Film and Feeling*, Richard Dyer (2010). Official website: www.ninorota.com.

Credits

(all films Italy unless stated otherwise)

Year	Film	Director
1933	Treno popolare	Raffaello Matarazzo
1942	Giorno di nozze	Raffaello Matarazzo
1943	Il birichino di papà	Raffaello Matarazzo
1944	Zaza	Renato Castellani
1944	Mountain Woman	Renato Castellani
1945	La freccia nel fianco	Alberto Lattuduada, Mario Costa
1945	My Widow and I	Carlo Ludovico Bragaglia
1945	Le miserie del Signor Travet	Mario Soldati
1946	Un Americano in vacanza	Luigi Zampa
1946	Professor, My Son	Renato Castellani
1946	Roma, citta libera (La notte porta consiglio)	Marcello Pagliero
1946	Albergo Luna, camera 34	Carlo Ludovico Bragaglia
1947	To Live in Peace	Luigi Zampa

Year	Film	Director
1947	*Vanita*	Giorgio Pastina
1947	*Flesh Will Surrender*	Alberto Lattuada
1947	*Daniele Cortis*	Mario Soldati
1948	*Toto al giro d'Italia*	Mario Mattoli
1948	*Amanti senza amore*	Gianni Franciolini
1948	*Senza pieta*	Alberto Lattuada
1948	*Fuga in Francia*	Mario Soldati
1948	*Anni difficili*	Luigi Zampa
1948	*Guagilo*	Luigi Comencini
1948	*L'eroe della strada*	Carlo Borghesio
1948	*Sotto il sole di Roma*	Renato Castellani
1948	*Woman in Trouble*	Mario Camerini
1948	*How I Lost the War*	Carlo Borghesio
1948	*Be Seeing You, Father*	Camillo Mastrocinque
1949	*The Glass Mountain*	Henry Cass (Italy/UK)
1949	*The Hidden Room* (aka *Obsession*)	Edward Dmytryk (UK)
1949	*Campane a martello*	Luigi Zampa
1949	*Children of Chance*	Luigi Zampa (UK)
1949	*The Masked Pirate*	Edgar G. Ulmer, Giuseppe Maria Scotese (Italy/USA)
1949	*Come scopersi l'America*	Carlo Borghesio
1950	*It's Forever Springtime*	Renato Castellani
1950	*Side Street Story*	Eduardo De Filippo
1950	*Vita da cani*	Mario Monicelli, Steno
1950	*The Taming of Dorothy* (aka *Her Favorite Husband*)	Mario Soldati (Italy/UK)
1950	*His Last Twelve Hours*	Luigi Zampa (Italy/France)
1950	*The King's Guerillas*	Mario Soldati (Italy/France)
1950	*Il monello della strada*	Carlo Borghesio
1950	*Honeymoon Deferred*	Mario Camerini (Italy/UK)
1950	*E arrivato il cavaliere*	Marion Monicelli, Steno
1951	*Valley of the Eagles*	Terence Young (UK)
1951	*Era lui, si, si!*	Marino Girolami, etc.
1951	*Never Take No for an Answer*	Maurice Cloche, Ralph Smart (UK/Italy)
1951	*Anna*	Alberto Lattuda (Italy/France)
1951	*Toto and the King of Rome*	Mario Monicelli, Steno
1951	*Napoleone*	Carlo Borghesio
1951	*Filumena Marturano*	Eduardo De Filippo
1952	*Un ladro in paradiso*	Domenico Paolella
1952	*Wonderful Adventures of Guerrin Mescino*	Pietro Francisci
1952	*Something Money Can't Buy*	Pat Jackson (UK)
1952	*The White Sheik*	Federico Fellini
1952	*The Assassin* (aka *Venetian Bird*)	Ralph Thomas (UK)
1952	*The Three Pirates*	Mario Soldati
1952	*Gli angeli del quartiere*	Carlo Borghesio
1952	*The Queen of Sheba*	Pietro Francisci
1952	*Ragazze da marito*	Eduardo De Filippo
1952	*Marito e moglie*	Eduardo De Filippo
1953	*Hell Raiders of the Deep*	Duilio Coletti (France/Italy)
1953	*Finishing School*	Bernard Vorhaus (France/Italy)
1953	*Jolanda, the Daughter of the Black Corsair*	Mario Soldati
1953	*The Wild Oat*	Henri Verneuil (France/Italy)
1953	*Riscatto*	Marino Girolami
1953	*I vitelloni*	Federico Fellini (Italy/France)
1953	*Easy Years*	Luigi Zampa
1953	*The Ship of Condemned Women*	Raffaello Matarazzo
1953	*The Most Wanted Man*	Henri Verneuil (France/Italy)
1953	*Musoduro*	Giuseppe Bennati (Italy/France)
1953	*What Rascals Men Are*	Glauco Pellegrini
1953	*Scampolo 53*	Giorgio Bianchi

Year	Film	Director
1953	*La domenica della buona gente*	Anton Giulio Majano
1954	*The Stranger's Hand*	Mario Soldati (Italy/UK)
1954	*Star of India*	Arthur Lubin (Italy/UK)
1954	*100 Years of Love*	Lionello De Felice
1954	*Appassionatamente*	Giacomo Gentilomo
1954	*La strada*	Federico Fellini
1954	*Mambo*	Robert Rossen (Italy/USA)
1954	*Modern Virgin*	Marcello Pagliero
1954	*The Two Orphans*	Giacomo Gentilomo (Italy/France)
1954	*Loves of Three Queens*	Marc Allégret, Edgar G. Ulmer
1954	*Forbidden*	Mario Monicelli (Italy/France)
1954	*Via Padova 46*	Giorgio Bianchi
1955	*Bella non piangere!*	David Carbonari
1955	*We Two Alone*	Marcello Marchesi, etc.
1955	*Torpedo Zone* (aka *Submarine Attack*)	Duilio Coletti
1955	*Melodie immortali—mascagni*	Giacomo Gentilomo (Italy/France)
1955	*Il bidone* (aka *The Swindle*)	Federico Fellini (Italy/France)
1955	*The Woman in the Painting*	Franco Rossi (France/Italy/Spain)
1955	*The Belle of Rome*	Luigi Comencini
1955	*Accadde al penitenziario*	Giorgio Bianchi
1955	*Folgore Division*	Duilio Coletti
1955	*Io piaccio*	Giorgio Bianchi
1956	*War and Peace*	King Vidor (USA/Italy)
1956	*The House of Intrigue*	Duilio Coletti
1956	*Ragazze al mare*	Giuliano Biagetti
1957	*Il Momento Piu Bello*	Luciano Emmer (Italy/France)
1957	*Nights of Cabiria*	Federico Fellini (Italy/France)
1957	*A Hero of Our Times*	Mario Monicelli
1957	*Le notti bianche*	Luchino Visconti (Italy/France)
1957	*This Angry Age*	René Clément (Italy/USA/France)
1957	*Doctor and the Healer*	Mario Monicelli (Italy/France)
1957	*Italia piccola*	Mario Soldati
1958	*Citta di notte*	Leopoldo Trieste
1958	*Giovani mariti*	Mauro Bolognini (Italy/France)
1958	*Fortunella*	Eduardo De Filippo (Italy/France)
1958	*The Italians They Are Crazy*	Duilio Coletti, Luis María Delgado (Italy/Spain)
1958	*Piece of the Sky*	Aglauco Casadio (Italy/France)
1958	*The Law Is the Law*	Christian-Jaque (Italy/France)
1958	*El Alamein*	Guido Malatesta
1959	*The Great War*	Mario Monicelli (Italy/France)
1960	*La dolce vita*	Federico Fellini (Italy/France)
1960	*Purple Noon*	René Clément (France/Italy)
1960	*Under Ten Flags*	Duilio Coletti (Italy/USA)
1960	*Rocco and His Brothers*	Luchino Visconti (Italy/France)
1961	*Phantom Lovers* (aka *Ghosts of Rome*)	Antonio Pietrangeli
1961	*The Best of Enemies*	Guy Hamilton
1961	*The Brigand*	Renato Castellani
1962	*Boccaccio '70*	Luchino Visconti, Federico Fellini, Vittorio De Sica, Mario Monicelli (Italy/France)
1962	*The Condemned of Altona*	Vittorio De Sica (Italy/France)
1962	*The Reluctant Saint*	Edward Dmytryk (USA)
1962	*Arturo's Island*	Damiano Damiani
1963	*8½*	Federico Fellini (Italy/France)
1963	*The Leopard*	Luchino Visconti (Italy/France)
1963	*The Teacher from Vigevano*	Elio Petri
1965	*Juliet of the Spirits*	Federico Fellini (Italy/France)
1965	*Kiss the Other Sheik*	Eduardo De Filippo, etc. (Italy/France)
1966	*Shout Louder, Louder . . . I Don't Understand*	Eduardo De Filippo

Year	Film	Director
1967	La tormenta	Raúl Araiza (Mexico)
1967	The Taming of the Shrew	Franco Zeffirelli (Italy/USA)
1968	Romeo and Juliet (GGN; BAFTA-N)	Franco Zeffirelli (UK/Italy)
1968	Spirits of the Dead	Federico Fellini, etc. (Italy/France)
1969	Fellini Satyricon	Federico Fellini
1970	A Quiet Place to Kill (aka Paranoia)	Umberto Lenzi (Italy/France/Spain)
1970	The Clowns	Federico Fellini (Italy/France/W. Germany)
1970	Waterloo	Sergey Bondarchuk (Italy/USSR)
1972	Fellini's Roma	Federico Fellini (Italy/France)
1972	The Godfather(AAN; GG; BAFTA)	Francis Ford Coppola (USA)
1973	Love and Anarchy	Lina Wertmüller
1973	Amarcord	Federico Fellini (Italy/France)
1973	Sunset, Sunrise	Koreyoshi Kurahara (Japan)
1974	The Abdication	Anthony Harvey (UK)
1974	The Godfather: Part II (AA; GGN; BAFTA-N)	Francis Ford Coppola
1976	Caro Michele	Mario Monicelli
1976	Fellini's Casanova	Federico Fellini (Italy/USA)
1976	Ragazzo di Borgata	Giulio Paradisi
1978	Death on the Nile	John Guillermin (UK)
1978	Orchestra Rehearsal	Federico Fellini (Italy/W. Germany)
1979	Hurricane	Jan Troell (USA)

RÓZSA, Miklós (1907–1995) Equally lauded for his music for the concert stage and the movies, the Hungarian-born composer had a long and distinguished career in both venues. Because of his symphonic and chamber music, Rózsa was well established before he scored his first films in England. He then went on to become one of Hollywood's most respected and successful composers.

He was born in Budapest, Hungary, the son of an engineer and a pianist mother who loved music and encouraged her son, providing violin and piano lessons. Rózsa showed a remarkable talent at a young age and later enrolled at the University of Leipzig to study music and (to please his father) chemistry. It was soon clear that music was his field, and he transferred to Leipzig's Conservatory of Music. By the time he graduated in 1929, Rózsa had several of his compositions published, and two years later he was settled in Paris, where his music was performed and praised. His 1933 orchestral work *Theme, Variations, and Finale* was roundly applauded, and over the years it has been performed around the world. Although he made Paris his home and associated with the artists there, it was an English film producer, Alexander Korda, who convinced Rózsa to write for the movies. He scored a handful of movies for Korda before finding international recognition in 1940 with his magical music for the fantasy *The Thief of Bagdad*, a score that earned the young composer

his first Academy Award nomination. By 1941 Rózsa was in Hollywood and working with various directors, most memorably writer-director Billy Wilder. In the 1940s the two men collaborated on such outstanding movies as *Five Graves to Cairo*, *Double Indemnity*, and *The Lost Weekend*. Other notable movies that Rózsa scored in the 1940s include *Jungle Book*, *Sahara*, *Spellbound*, *A Double Life*, *Madame Bovary*, and *The Killers*. This last was an early and influential film noir work and its dynamic score was so powerful that for a while Rózsa was pegged as a composer of dark, brooding, urban melodramas. Some of his best examples in that genre include *The Asphalt Jungle*, *The Naked City*, *Criss Cross*, and *East Side, West Side*. After Rózsa began working for MGM in 1949, he was given a wider variety of movies to score, ranging from comedies like *Adam's Rib* to period pieces such as *Ivanhoe*.

His score for the Roman epic *Quo Vadis* in 1951 was so admired that Rózsa soon found himself singled out for other historic spectaculars. Over the next ten years he scored such big-budget giants as *Plymouth Adventure*, *Knights of the Round Table*, *Julius Caesar*, *El Cid*, *Sodom and Gomorrah*, *King of Kings*, and *Ben-Hur*. By the mid-1960s Rózsa wrote fewer film scores as he concentrated on his concert music but still managed to write some noteworthy screen music up through 1982. His final film, *Dead Men Don't Wear Plaid*, was a spoof of the kind of

MIKLÓS RÓZSA. Hollywood's favorite composer of spectacular epics in the 1950s, Rózsa liked to add exotic instruments to his scores. Here he demonstrates the ancient horn called the buccina during the filming of *Quo Vadis* (1951). *MGM / Photofest © MGM*

classic noir movies Rózsa had scored during Hollywood's golden age. Because he never abandoned the concert hall even while scoring nearly one hundred movies, Rózsa's classical output is impressive. His dozens of symphonies, concertos, chamber pieces, choral works, art songs, and other compositions were performed by the finest musicians and usually recorded as well. He even took eleven of his film scores and turned each one into a suite for the concert hall. Although Rózsa suffered a stroke in 1982 and retired from movies, he continued to compose for the concert hall until his death thirteen years later at the age of eighty-eight. His life's work is preserved and perpetuated by the Miklós Rózsa Society and his manuscripts are maintained by Syracuse University.

The quality of Rózsa's screen music for his first films with Korda in England is quite high, probably because the thirty-year-old composer was already very experienced before writing his first movie score. His early effort, the 1937 sultry thriller *Knight without Armor*, was set in Russia during the revolution and Rózsa incorporated Russian folk songs that surrounded a lush love theme for the sparks between Robert Donat and Marlene Dietrich. His colorful score for *The Thief of Bagdad* three years later boasted several different themes ranging from comic sea chanteys to exotic Arabian Nights lullabies. The main theme is a delightful mixture of brass fanfares and furious harps, while the love theme is so delicate it seems to float on the air like one of the film's flying carpets. It is easy to understand how this score quickly put Rózsa in the forefront of movie composers. His score for *Jungle Book* is also composed of several distinct themes, most of them for specific animals in the story. The opening music is an exotic theme on horns and percussion that conjures up mystery and adventure in its gushing section but then is romantic and beguiling in its slower and more soothing passages. The music for the different animals is clever and distinct, including such tracks as a low string bass playing a plodding passage, a graceful theme with swirling strings with harp accents, sinister music on low brass at first then higher brass are added, a funny oboe and strings piece with a dizzy feeling, and a delicate and intoxicating theme on various reeds with string support. Like Prokofiev's *Peter and the Wolf*, the piece later found popularity in concert halls and on record with a narrator describing the different animal-musical motifs. Before parting ways with producer Korda, Rózsa scored a handful of romantic mov-

ies for him in England. For *That Hamilton Woman*, he wrote an entrancing love theme. This time the music flows with hesitant stops that give the theme a tentative quality. The same kind of quality can be found in the echoing love theme for *Lydia*, a melodrama whose score includes a gliding waltz and a piano lesson about music that is performed for a group of children.

With *Five Graves to Cairo*, Rózsa became a bona fide Hollywood composer, and his career took a turn for more eclectic music. This interesting war thriller is about an undercover British agent (Franchot Tone) who sniffs out where the Nazis have buried supplies in the Egyptian desert. Rózsa's opening music for this Wilder film is an exotic theme with an explosive series of crescendos that transitions into a quick-time march on brass that then grows more lyrical with strings added. There is also a dissonant march in a minor key in which the brass compete with the strings even as they echo each other. The lovely romantic theme on strings and woodwinds shimmers with emotion, building and ascending with grace and passion. The Hollywood executives disliked the odd, dissonant score for *Five Graves to Cairo*, but Wilder defended Rózsa and the two went on to collaborate on the crime drama classic *Double Indemnity*. Again the score was dissonant and the harsh, pounding music was ideal for the tough-as-nails story and its steamy-chilly romance. An insurance salesman (Fred MacMurray) and his lover (Barbara Stanwyck) kill her husband (Tom Powers) and make it look like an accident, but complications set in when an insurance analyst (Edward G. Robinson) suspects foul play. The opening music consists of a pounding kettle drum that sets the pace as strings and brass repeat a nervous musical phrase with menacing determination. The theme for the femme fatale played by Stanwyck is a languid blues piece with descending musical lines, a lot of smooth sensuality, and a hint of danger. The score also includes a passage on low and grumbling woodwinds, and a track with swirling and confused strings that are too fast to be romantic. One of the best film noir works of the 1940s, *Double Indemnity* was a triumph for director Wilder and it pushed Rózsa to the top ranks of Hollywood composers. Hitchcock was among the famous directors to come calling, asking Rózsa to come up with a new sound for his psychological thriller *Spellbound*. The composer obliged with an outstanding score that used the early electronic instrument known as the theremin, a high-pitched, quivering sound that was very otherworldly.

He balanced this unusual effect with a beautiful love theme that has a touch of the manic, appropriate for this tale of a psychiatrist (Ingrid Bergman) and the patient (Gregory Peck) she loves. Hollywood loved the unique sound of the theremin and often Rózsa was requested to use it in his scores. The composer wisely showed restraint and used it on only three other occasions: *The Lost Weekend*, *The Red House*, and *Dead Men Don't Wear Plaid*. One of the first and still most powerful movies about alcoholism, *The Lost Weekend* follows a reformed alcoholic (Ray Milland) who falls off the wagon and goes on a four-day bender. The weird sound of the theremin is used effectively to go inside the mind-set of the alcoholic writer who is tormented by his addiction. There is a dreamlike theme in which the theremin and strings rise and fall in a dazed manner that conveys a sense of being lost and confused. There is also a slow and steady passage that climbs the scale with determination, but it is still minor keyed and haunted. The theremin was used effectively in the film noir mystery *The Red House* but Rózsa then abandoned the instrument for twenty-five years. In his last film, *Dead Men Don't Wear Plaid*, the theremin is heard on occasion throughout the movie but instead of creating an eerie effect it is comic. This spoof on the private eye genre features Steve Martin as the tough-as-nails detective who pursues a murder case and encounters Humphrey Bogart, Burt Lancaster, Bette Davis, and other Old Hollywood stars in some cleverly used archival footage. Rózsa composed a delightful pastiche score that echoed the sound of his noir films yet with a silly undercurrent in the music that is delicious.

The Killers is the 1946 film that demonstrated that Rózsa was a master of the film noir genre. When some professional killers murder a gas station attendant (Burt Lancaster), an insurance investigator (Edmond O'Brien) looks into the victim's past and discovers a whole network of crime and betrayal. The theme for the hit men is an abrasive four-note phrase played on brass that is rushed and even frantic as strings and other instruments join in and push forward as if obsessed. This stark four-note motif is familiar to modern audiences because it is so close to the later *Dragnet* theme by Walter Schumann; so close that a plagiarism suit by Rózsa's music publisher led to an out-of-court settlement. But there is so much more to *The Killers'* score than those four foreboding notes. The score also features a weird march in which different parts of the orchestra push ahead with the melody and then are overtaken by other instruments. There is an urgency in Rózsa's music that has been copied so often it almost seems like cliché. Although Rózsa did only a few sections of the score for *Naked City*, the musical and dramatic highlight of the movie is the final chase scene followed by a heartfelt urban tone poem of sorts. This Aaron Copland–like section features gentle woodwinds and moves so delicately that is takes time before the melody surfaces. Another arresting passage in *Naked City* consists of different string instruments rapidly overtaking each other as the piece climbs the scale and speeds up and then horns are added and the music get more chaotic but just as driven. In a different kind of noir piece, *A Double Life*, the score suggests classical music at times. This movie, about an actor (Ronald Colman) who is playing Othello onstage and starts to take on the jealousy of the character, includes theatre scenes from the Venice-set *Othello*. Rózsa scores them with music inspired by the Venetian composer Giovanni Gabrieli. The way Rózsa carries parts of this period music into the modern setting is masterful. The film opens with a celebratory theme that is like a fast parade and different instruments bounce up and down the scale to trumpet fanfares; it is all so rushed that it has a manic tone rather than a festive one. There is also a moody passage with descending horns and questioning strings; a smooth and lyrical adagio on strings that is comforting despite its minor key and dissonant touches in the lower register; and a furious theme with complaining brass, grumbling woodwinds, and nervous strings—all punctuated by flittering piccolos that sound like panicking birds. At MGM, Rózsa was able to branch out beyond his film noir label and turn to more romantic scores. For *Madame Bovary*, Gustav Flaubert's classic tale about a bored French housewife (Jennifer Jones) and her tragic fate, Rózsa created a swirling waltz featuring strings that is elegant and maintains a moderate tempo for a while. When the waltz grows to a swifter and more sensuous piece, it seems harsh and even dangerous. The central theme for the film is a minor-key passage in which strings and horns slowly climb the scale to reach a level in which the swift and passionate melody is fully realized. Another effective romantic score is that for *The Story of Three Loves*, in which a flute keeps returning to simplify the gliding love theme. There is an obsessive quality to the score for *The Strange Love of Martha Ivers*, a melodrama that softens a noir kind of tale. Music is used sparingly in the Van Gogh biopic *Lust for Life*, much of the score understated until it explodes in moments that illustrate the tormented artist's madness.

The Roman spectacular *Quo Vadis* launched another fertile aspect of Rózsa's career: the sweeping sounds of historical epics. He did a great deal of research on Roman music and instruments of the time. (Nero could not have fiddled while Rome burned because anything resembling a violin had not been invented yet.) Sometimes using the lyre and other period instruments, Rózsa aimed for a sound that was regal and ancient. But he also employed Gregorian chant and other later forms to give the movie the emotional push it needed. For Nero (Peter Ustinov) there is a semicomic theme on woodwinds and for the central lovers (Robert Taylor and Deborah Kerr) the music flirts with nineteenth-century romanticism. This love theme is stately and formal yet there is some warmth in the way different musical phrases overlap without becoming competitive. The title theme for *Quo Vadis* begins with a complex brass fanfare then a chorale sings a rousing and complicated hymn as the percussion and horns march ahead with a grim purpose. There is a hymn to Apollo played on woodwinds that is slow and meandering as it slides up and down the scale, and robust dance music for the Vestal Virgins, with a female choir singing a rhythmic chant that uses march time as different instruments explode in crescendos all around. A chariot chase is scored with a propulsive theme with anxious horn fanfares and angry percussion. Ironically, the music for the burning of Rome includes a gentle song played on a lute. This is such an exciting score that it served as the basis for countless epics of the ancient world, including Rózsa's own masterpiece *Ben-Hur*. The 1959 version of this action-packed story of the friendship and then rivalry between a Roman (Stephan Boyd) and a Jew (Charlton Heston) has over two hours' worth of music, so the composer was able to demonstrate a variety of themes. The central motif involves overlapping trumpet fanfares and some full orchestral crescendos that lead into a rhythmic sweeping piece with a traveling tempo that takes time to move into more flowing sections with an exotic flavor. The love theme has fluttering woodwinds and soothing strings that cautiously etch out a simple melody with slight flourishes at the end of each musical line. Early scenes, such as the journey of the Magi and the Nativity, are simple, almost primitive with flute and strings. The Christ theme is an inventive piece that uses a four-note motif in a variety of ways. The music for action scenes

matches the spectacle on the screen without slipping into cliché. The march of the chariots begins with a sparkling series of fanfares that break into a rigorous processional in which different brass instruments echo each other's phrase. The whole piece builds into a grandiose march that repeats its musical ideas each time in a higher register. The rhythmic music for galley slaves rowing into battle uses low strings that ascend and descend a few notes to create a pattern of dread and pain. When the piece speeds up, horns and strings are added that play variations of a simple tune without escaping from the oppressive pattern of the drums. Oddly enough, the movie's most famous scene, the chariot race to the death, has no music once the race begins. One hears only the sounds of horses and the crowd. *Ben-Hur* may be the pinnacle of Rózsa's career, but in reality it is just one aspect of his versatility.

Each of Rózsa's historical movies offers something of interest outside the "epic" sound. *Plymouth Adventure* uses early American folk songs, Elizabethan airs are heard throughout *Young Bess*, a five-note motif involving strings and drums highlight *Knights of the Round Table*, a rhythmic Spanish quality propels the music in *El Cid*, and there is a sparkling six-note motif on strings in *The Golden Voyage of Sinbad*. Even Rózsa's other Roman-biblical film scores have distinctive moments. *Julius Caesar* has two contrasting themes, one fluid for Caesar (Louis Calhern) and the other melancholy for Brutus (James Mason). *King of Kings* may use the soaring voices a bit too often but it does not repeat the *Ben-Hur* score, featuring instead strings over brass and using melodies that often resemble folk songs. Hollywood made less epics in the 1960s and Rózsa again got to concentrate on smaller films that were either romantic or suspenseful. For *The V.I.P.s*, which was basically a contemporary melodrama mostly set in an airport, Rózsa came up with a tender theme for the love triangle and a comic one (featuring harpsichord, no less) for the comic character played by Margaret Rutherford. The haunting main theme in *Providence* is something of a funeral ode so it is surprising when it develops into a sublime waltz. The 1940s noir sound can be heard in the thriller *Last Embrace*. Both the film and the score recall a Hitchcock movie at times, not only in its suspense sequences but in Rózsa's fiery romantic theme. This is also true of the time-traveling movie *Time after Time* in which popular songs from the past are woven within a score that has many contrasting themes, from a modern chase sequence to an elegant Victorian waltz. It would seem that by the 1980s Hollywood would not be interested in Rózsa and his golden age sound. Yet the music in these last films is as commanding and as accessible as his work in the 1940s and 1950s. The grand master of Hollywood pomp and spectacle seemed at home in the new Hollywood.

Like movie composers Franz Waxman, Bronislau Kaper, and Dimitri Tiomkin, who also came from Mittel-Europe, Rózsa brought to Hollywood a strong classical musical education and experience in the concert hall.

These four important screen composers found ways to continue what Richard Wagner began on the opera stage: the blending of music and drama into a new and different music-theatre experience. Rózsa was adept at scores that required a rich European sound but was equally successful in incorporating genuinely American music, especially in his film noir scores. Autobiography: *Double Life* (1989); memoir: *A Composer's Notes: Remembering Miklós Rózsa*, Jeffrey Dane (2006); biography: *Miklós Rózsa: A Sketch of His Life and Work*, Christopher Palmer (1975). Official website: www.miklosrozsa.org.

Credits

(all films USA unless stated otherwise; * for Best Song; ** for Music Adaptation)

Year	Film	Director
1937	*Thunder in the City*	Marion Gering (UK)
1937	*Knight without Armor*	Jacques Feyder (UK)
1937	*Murder on Diamond Row* (aka *The Squeaker*)	William K. Howard (UK)
1937	*The Green Cockatoo*	William Cameron Menzies (UK)
1938	*The Divorce of Lady X*	Tim Whelan (UK)
1939	*The Spy in Black*	Michael Powell (UK)
1939	*The Four Feathers*	Zoltan Korda (UK)
1939	*The Fugitive* (aka *On the Night of the Fire*)	Brian Desmond Hurst (UK)
1940	*Ten Days in Paris*	Tim Whelan (UK)
1940	*The Thief of Bagdad* (AAN)	Michael Powell, Ludwig Berger, etc. (UK)
1941	*That Hamilton Woman*	Alexander Korda (UK)
1941	*New Wine*	Reinhold Schünzel
1941	*Lydia* (AAN)	Julien Duvivier
1941	*Sundown* (AAN)	Henry Hathaway
1942	*Jungle Book* (AAN)	Zoltan Korda
1942	*Jacaré*	Charles E. Ford
1943	*Five Graves to Cairo*	Billy Wilder
1943	*Sahara*	Zoltan Korda
1943	*So Proudly We Hail!*	Mark Sandrich
1943	*The Woman of the Town* (AAN)	George Archainbaud
1944	*Double Indemnity* (AAN)	Billy Wilder
1944	*The Hour before Dawn*	Frank Tuttle
1944	*Dark Waters*	André De Toth
1945	*A Song to Remember* (AAN**)	Charles Vidor
1945	*The Man in Half Moon Street*	Ralph Murphy
1945	*Blood on the Sun*	Frank Lloyd
1945	*Lady on a Train*	Charles David
1945	*Spellbound* (AA)	Alfred Hitchcock
1945	*The Lost Weekend* (AAN)	Billy Wilder
1946	*Because of Him*	Richard Wallace
1946	*The Strange Love of Martha Ivers*	Lewis Milestone
1946	*The Killers* (AAN)	Robert Siodmak
1947	*Song of Scheherazade*	Walter Reisch
1947	*The Red House*	Delmer Daves
1947	*Time out of Mind*	Robert Siodmak
1947	*The Macomber Affair*	Zoltan Korda
1947	*The Other Love*	André De Toth

Year	Film	Director
1947	*Brute Force*	Jules Dassin
1947	*Desert Fury*	Lewis Allen
1947	*A Double Life*(AA)	George Cukor
1947	*Secret beyond the Door*	Fritz Lang
1948	*A Woman's Vengeance*	Zoltan Korda
1948	*The Naked City*	Jules Dassin
1948	*Kiss the Blood off My Hands*	Norman Foster
1948	*Command Decision*	Sam Wood
1949	*The Bribe*	Robert Z. Leonard
1949	*Criss Cross*	Robert Siodmak
1949	*Madame Bovary*	Vincente Minnelli
1949	*The Red Danube*	George Sidney
1949	*Adam's Rib*	George Cukor
1949	*East Side, West Side*	Mervyn LeRoy
1950	*The Asphalt Jungle*	John Huston
1950	*Crisis*	Richard Brooks
1950	*The Miniver Story*	H. C. Potter
1951	*Quo Vadis* (AAN)	Mervyn LeRoy
1952	*The Light Touch*	Richard Brooks
1952	*Ivanhoe* (AAN; GGN)	Richard Thorpe
1952	*Plymouth Adventure*	Clarence Brown
1953	*The Story of Three Loves*	Vincente Minnelli, Gottfried Reinhardt
1953	*Young Bess*	George Sidney
1953	*Julius Caesar* (AAN)	Joseph L. Mankiewicz
1953	*All the Brothers Were Valiant*	Richard Thorpe
1953	*Knights of the Round Table*	Richard Thorpe
1954	*Men of the Fighting Lady*	Andrew Marton
1954	*Crest of the Wave* (aka *Seagulls over Sorrento*)	John and Ray Boulting (UK)
1954	*Valley of the Kings*	Robert Pirosh
1954	*Green Fire*	Andrew Marton
1955	*Moonfleet*	Fritz Lang
1955	*The King's Thief*	Robert Z. Leonard
1956	*Diane*	David Miller
1956	*Tribute to a Bad Man*	Robert Wise
1956	*Bhowani Junction*	George Cukor (USA/UK)
1956	*Lust for Life*	Vincente Minnelli
1957	*Something of Value*	Richard Brooks
1957	*The Seventh Sin*	Ronald Neame
1957	*Tip on a Dead Jockey*	Richard Thorpe
1958	*A Time to Love and a Time to Die*	Douglas Sirk
1959	*The World, the Flesh and the Devil*	Ranald MacDougall
1959	*Ben-Hur* (AA)	William Wyler
1961	*King of Kings*(GGN)	Nicholas Ray
1961	*El Cid* (AAN, AAN*; GGN)	Anthony Mann (Italy/USA)
1962	*Sodom and Gomorrah*	Robert Aldrich (USA/Italy/France)
1963	*The V.I.P.s*	Anthony Asquith (UK)
1968	*The Power*	Byron Haskin
1968	*The Green Berets*	Ray Kellogg, John Wayne
1970	*The Private Life of Sherlock Holmes*	Billy Wilder (UK)
1973	*The Golden Voyage of Sinbad*	Gordon Hessler
1977	*Providence*	Alain Renais (France/Switzerland/UK)
1977	*The Private Files of J. Edgar Hoover*	Larry Cohen
1978	*Fedora*	Billy Wilder (France/W. Germany)
1979	*Last Embrace*	Jonathan Demme
1979	*Time after Time*	Nicholas Meyer
1981	*Eye of the Needle*	Richard Marquand (UK)
1982	*Dead Men Don't Wear Plaid*	Carl Reiner

S

SAKAMOTO, Ryûichi (b. 1952) An experimental Japanese arranger, performer, composer, and record producer with an international reputation, he has scored thirty-five feature films and documentaries on three continents.

Ryûichi Sakamoto was born in Tokyo and began playing piano at the age of three. In high school Sakamoto performed in jazz bands then studied music at the Tokyo National University of Fine Arts and Music. After graduating with a BA in composition and an MA in electronic and ethnic music, he cofounded the techno-pop trio Yellow Magic Orchestra, a "fusion" group that combined Asian and Western music in a cutting-edge manner. YMO became popular in Japan then their 1980 single "Computer Game" became an international success. Although he continued to perform with YMO for years and the trio has reunited on occasion, Sakamoto has also pursued a solo career singing, recording, and composing. His first film score was for the Japanese movie *It's All Right, My Friend* in 1983 but it was his music and acting performance in the British-Japanese World War II movie *Merry Christmas Mr. Lawrence* that same year that launched his screen career. Sakamoto collaborated with David Sylvian on the score, which included the popular song "Forbidden Colors" (lyric by Sylvian). Throughout his screen career, Sakamoto would often work with other composers. The international success of *Merry Christmas Mr. Lawrence* brought Sakamoto to the attention of European and American directors with whom he later collaborated, such as Bernardo Bertolucci, Pedro Almodóvar, and Brian De Palma. His greatest international triumph was scoring Bertolucci's *The Last Emperor* with David Byrne and Cong Su, a film in which he also acted. Other notable movies with music by Sakamoto include *The Handmaid's Tale, The Sheltering Sky, Wuthering Heights, Women without Men, Snake Eyes, The Adventures of Milo and Otis, Little Buddha, Femme Fatale,* and *High Heels.* An activist on the antinuclear front, he scored such related documentaries as *Nuclear Nation, Alexei and the Spring,* and *Metamorphosis,* as well as organizing the international concert *No Nukes 2012.* His other documentary features include *Love Is the Devil, Derrida, Ana Ana,* and *Light Up Nippon.* Sakamoto has composed music for Japanese television, video games, anime shorts and features, and special events, such as the Barcelona Olympics in 1992.

Just as Sakamoto is an international talent, his music embraces many cultures, combining them in unique ways. His movies have various locations, from Manhattan to China, but the scores rarely stick to one local style. The music for *Merry Christmas Mr. Lawrence,* set in a Japanese prison camp, has a New Age sound combined with Asian percussion and repetitive melody. The instrumentation includes electronic keyboard, restless strings, and exotic chimes. Such music seems an unlikely basis for a song but "Forbidden Colors" succeeds because Sylvian's lyric is made up of short haiku-like phrases that flow with the very Asian music. North Africa is the setting for *The Sheltering Sky,* but the main theme is rather European with its intoxicating five-note phrase played on Western strings. Other passages, such as a halting piece in which various strings have a series of intrusive rests, is similarly graceful. Sakamoto adds some Islamic chanting in the background to denote the locale, but this score mostly follows the mind-set of an American couple (John Malkovich and Debra Winger) searching for fulfillment in an exotic land. The stylish thriller *Femme Fatale* has a bolero-like main theme played on woodwinds and percussion, its slowly building repetition suggesting another exotic locale. Sections of the score are atonal and very electronic, with sound effects and music resulting in an eerie background for its suspense plot. The Spanish film *High Heels,* about the rivalry between a mother (Marisa Paredes) and a daughter (Victoria Abril) over the same man (Miguel Bosé), has rhythmic music that is an odd cross between flamenco and disco. Vocal accents recall the pop sound of 1960s bossa nova hits with their electric organ and rapid percussion. The main theme is a rather sad lament with a lovely subdued passion, moving from tentative phrases to a flowing melody.

Set in a futuristic world, *The Handmaid's Tale* is scored with brooding yet engaging music, such as the main theme in which a wordless chorus, sustained organ chords, and the sound of water dripping create a reflective yet disturbing effect. This is a chilly movie and Sakamoto's throbbing, insistent music adds to the sterile atmosphere. Even the more lyrical passages, such as a delicate nocturne played on Asian strings or a melancholy dirge, have a forbidding aspect to them. The 1992 remake of *Wuthering Heights*, set firmly in the past, also has some melancholy passages, such as the main theme, in which a solo primitive flute is heard against a felicitous symphonic piece that conveys the desolate beauty and loneliness of the Yorkshire moors. Although modernist David Byrne wrote the capti-

vating opening music for *The Last Emperor* and Chinese composer Cong Su provided the ethnic Chinese passages, most of the score was by Sakamoto, who used choral and electronic touches against a traditional orchestra. The music for the coronation is both lyrical and ponderous with a world-weary subtext. Another passage uses various Asian percussion and pipe instruments to capture the sound of the wind whereas rain is scored with gliding strings and howling horns. In many ways this is Sakamoto's most Asian score but even it has a Western flavor as the epic tale enfolds on a large canvas. Official website: www.sitesaka moto.com.

Credits

(all films Japan unless stated otherwise)

Year	Film	Director
1983	It's All Right, My Friend	Ryû Murakami
1983	Merry Christmas Mr. Lawrence (BAFTA)	Nagisa Ôshima (UK/Japan)
1984	YMO Propaganda	Makoto Satô, Saito Shin
1986	The Adventures of Milo and Otis	Masanori Hata
1987	Wings of Honneamise	Hiroyuki Yamaga
1987	The Last Emperor (AA; GG; BAFTA-N)	Bernardo Bertolucci (China/Italy/UK)
1990	The Handmaid's Tale	Volker Schlöndorff (USA/Germany)
1990	The Sheltering Sky (GG)	Bernardo Bertolucci (UK/Italy)
1991	High Heels	Pedro Almodóvar (Spain/France)
1992	Tokyo Decadence	Ryû Murakami
1992	Wuthering Heights	Peter Kosminsky (UK/USA)
1993	Little Buddha	Bernardo Bertolucci (Italy/France/UK)
1995	Wild Side	Donald Cammell (UK/USA)
1999	Snake Eyes	Brian De Palma (USA/Canada)
1998	Love Is the Devil: Study for a Portrait of Francis Bacon	John Maybury (UK/France/Japan)
1999	Gohatto (aka Taboo)	Nagisa Ôshima (Japan/France/UK)
2002	Derrida	Kirby Dick, Amy Ziering (USA)
2002	Alexei and the Spring	Seilchi Motohashi
2002	Femme Fatale	Brian De Palma (France/Switzerland)
2003	Life Is Journey	Seilchi Tanabe
2004	Tony Takitani	Jun Ichikawa
2005	Shining Boy and Little Randy	Shunsaku Kawake
2007	Silk	François Girard (Canada/France/Italy/Japan)
2009	Women without Men	Shirin Neshat, Shoja Azari (Germany/Austria/France/Italy/Morocco/Ukraine)
2011	Hara-Kiri: Death of a Samurai	Takashi Miike (Japan/UK)
2012	Nuclear Nation	Atsushi Funahashi
2012	Light Up Nippon	Kensaku Kakimoto
2012	I Have to Buy New Shoes	Eriko Kitagawa
2013	Ana Ana	Petr Lom, etc. (Norway/Netherlands/Egypt/Canada)
2013	Metamorphosis	Jun Hori

SALTER, Hans J. (1896–1994) A prodigious film composer, arranger, and conductor at Universal for three decades, he is most known for his scores for the studio's horror movies.

Born Hans Julius Salter in Vienna, when it was the center of Austria-Hungary, he studied at the Vienna Academy of Music. Salter's musical education also included instruction from such famous Austrian composers as Franz Schreker and Alban Berg. He rose to become assistant music director at the Vienna Volksopera and then director for the State Opera in Berlin by the early 1930s when he also started writing scores for German and Austrian movies. Salter left Germany in 1937 to escape the Nazis and went to Hollywood where his vast musical experience was quickly recognized. At Universal he was hired to conduct, orchestrate, and compose a variety of films, mostly westerns and horror features. Among the classic and camp-classic horror movies he scored are *Black Friday*, *The Wolf Man*, *The Mummy's Hand*, *The Mole People*, *Creature from the Black Lagoon*, *The Ghost of Frankenstein*, *Abbott and Costello Meet the Mummy*, *Hold That Ghost*, *Frankenstein Meets the Wolf Man*, *The Black Cat*, *Son of Dracula*, and *The Incredible Shrinking Man*. Salter's other memorable movies include *Scarlet Street*, *Pittsburgh*, *The Web*, *The 5,000 Fingers of Dr. T.*, *If a Man Answers*, *Beau Geste*, *Walk the Proud Land*, *The Spoilers*, *Autumn Leaves*, and *Return of the Gunfighter*. He received Academy Award nominations for his scoring for *It Started with Eve*, *The Amazing Mrs. Holliday*, *The Merry Monahans*, *Christmas Holiday*, *This Love of Ours*, and *Can't Help Singing*. In all, Salter contributed music to about two hundred features, rarely getting screen credit. A great deal of his work became stock music that Universal reused in another one hundred movies. In the late 1950s he started composing for television as well, writing themes and/or soundtrack music for western series such as *Wagon Train*, *The Virginian*, *Wichita Town*, and *Laramie*. Salter became a U.S. citizen in 1942, retired from Hollywood in 1967, and twenty-seven years later died at the age of ninety-eight.

Because Salter was a consummate musical director, arranger, and conductor, his composing talents were often mixed together with the work of others so that identifying his particular musical style is difficult. Also, Universal was notorious for adding stock music from one composer into the score by another artist. Yet Salter wrote so much music

during his Hollywood career that there are enough solo examples of his work to draw some conclusions. While he was far from an innovative composer, Salter was adept at coming up with the right kind of music for each genre. One might dismiss his scores as routine but they are nevertheless often quite effective. The Fritz Lang melodrama *Scarlet Street*, for example, has a superb film noir score. The story is about a middle-aged artist (Edward G. Robinson) who is being fleeced by the woman (Joan Bennett) he loves and her boyfriend (Dan Duryea). Salter uses the song standard "My Melancholy Baby" throughout, turning the ballad into a menacing theme as the plot darkens. The main original theme is a robust and lushly orchestrated flourish with a sense of urgency. The romantic theme uses the expected violins but the tone is chilly and menacing. There is some life and optimism in the scoring for the art gallery opening, but more often than not music puts one on the edge in this movie. In a memorable scene in which Robinson hallucinates, the music begins with simple piano chords that lead into dark underscoring, nervous violins, and haunting speaking voices that echo and reverberate in time to the music. This is not routine scoring. The main theme for the western *Return of the Gunfighter* is a driving march with a trumpet solo and a featured harmonica that manages to avoid the genre's musical clichés. Even finer is the expert score for *The Last of the Fast Guns*. The lyrical main theme is a Mexican serenade, the action scenes use a series of fanfares and descending notes, and there is a merry fiesta theme plucked on a guitar with horns celebrating in the higher register. Salter scored seven Deanna Durbin vehicles and, while the songs were by various tunesmiths, the soundtrack music is often a creative blending of original music and quotations from the musical numbers. Perhaps the best of them is *Can't Help Singing*, a musical set mostly out West with songs by Jerome Kern and E. Y. Harburg. Salter arranged and conducted the score, also composing some vibrant patriotic passages, rustic and atmospheric sections, some masculine marches, and a comic motif for the two con men (Akim Tamiroff and Leonid Kinsky). The romantic melodrama *This Love of Ours* has a flowing title theme that alternates between the dreamy and bucolic and the harsh and dramatic. It is a sentimental score for a sentimental movie but done with sincerity and care. Perhaps the most bizarre movie Salter got to score was the fantasy *The 5,000 Fingers of Dr. T.*, a comical yet disturbing nightmare told from a child's point of view.

The Dr. Seuss story was told with imaginative sets unlike those seen in any Hollywood movie in the 1950s. There are some deliciously offbeat songs by Frederick Hollander and Seuss but the nightmarish soundtrack is scored by Salter and Hollander. The simple piano exercises that the youth Bartholomew (Tommy Rettig) practices are, in his imagination, extrapolated into frenzied and even avant-garde piano pieces. For some passages Salter employs the theremin in a mock salute to sci-fi movie scores. In one gloriously eccentric scene, two twin men with connected beards roller skate to a wacky circus march.

Whatever Salter's accomplishments in the fields of westerns, musicals, melodramas, or fantasy, his reputation rests on his horror film scores. Universal excelled at these in the 1930s but by the time Salter came on board in 1939 the studio had somewhat exhausted the genre and was more concerned with making sequels and spoofs featuring Frankenstein, Dracula, the Invisible Man, and other ghastly characters that had raised the studio into the major league. All the same, Salter provided outstanding horror scores even when the movies themselves were lacking. When he was given a first-rate horror film, he often outdid himself. The original *The Wolf Man*, for instance, is a marvel of such scoring. The low and minor-key music heard first is in the romantic vein, brooding but felicitous. There is even the suggestion of chirping birds in the woodwinds. The aggressive passages are abrasive but do not lose their musicality. Salter never surrenders to sound effects but maintains melody in the most explosive sections. The quiet moments between the furious passages are disarmingly tranquil with a solo trumpet or even a harp sometimes offering a graceful theme before danger strikes again. Less lyrical and more blunt is the score for *Creature from the Black Lagoon*. This early schlock classic looks cheap and artificial and one feels the music adds to this with garish passages that scream with obviousness. Shrill trumpets, growling percussion, and blaring woodwinds leave little to the imagination. Yet even this campy movie has some delicate music for the breathing periods. If the music in *The Wolf Man* gave that film class, the score for the lagoon creature seems right in line with the tawdry but undoubtedly effective nature of the movie. *The Incredible Shrinking Man* is perhaps one of the more cerebral works of this genre and Salter responded with a very unusual score. The main theme is a weird trumpet solo with honky-tonk piano and some eerie vocals, a kind of horror jazz piece. Another passage has muted brass alternating with raspy horns as the strings wearily play a repetitive counter-melody. The effect is almost sexy, surely not expected in a horror movie. *The Incredible Shrinking Man* has little dialogue, even for a creature feature, so the score is needed not just for atmosphere and suspense but also to convey the emotional changes going through the shrinking man (Grant Williams) as he struggles to survive. This is arguably Salter's best score, one in which he serves the horror genre and, at the same time experiments with the possibilities for screen music.

Credits

(all films USA unless stated otherwise)

Year	Film	Director
1931	*L'homme qui assassina*	Curtis Bernhardt, Jean Tarride (France/Germany)
1931	*The Man Who Committed the Murder*	Curtis Bernhardt (Germany)
1931	*True Jacob*	Hans Steinhoff (Germany)
1931	*Gloria*	Hans Behrendt (Germany/France)
1931	*The Office Manager*	Hans Behrendt (Germany)
1932	*El hombre que asesinó*	Dimitri Buchowetzki, Fernando Gomis (UK)
1932	*Holzapfel Knows Everything*	Victor Janson (Germany)
1932	*My Friend the Millionaire*	Hans Behrendt (Germany)
1934	*Carnival of Love*	Carl Lamac (Austria)
1935	*De vier mullers*	Rudolf Meinert (Austria/Netherlands)
1935	*Alles für die Firma*	Rudolf Meinert (Austria)
1936	*Catherine the Last*	Henry Koster (Austria)
1936	*An Orphan Boy of Vienna*	Max Neufeid (Austria)

Year	Film	Director
1939	*Ex-Champ*	Phil Rosen
1939	*The Great Commandment*	Irving Pichel
1939	*Call a Messenger*	Arthur Lubin
1939	*Miracle on Main Street*	Steve Sekely
1939	*The Big Guy*	Arthur Lubin
1940	*The Invisible Man Returns*	Joe May
1940	*West of Carson City*	Ray Taylor
1940	*Honeymoon Deferred*	Lew Landers
1940	*Black Friday* (aka *Friday the Thirteenth*)	Arthur Lubin
1940	*Zanzibar*	Harold D. Schuster
1940	*The Mummy's Hand*	Christy Cabanne
1940	*Spring Parade*	Henry Koster
1940	*Seven Sinners*	Tay Garnett
1940	*Dark Streets of Cairo*	László Kardos
1940	*Trail of the Vigilantes*	Allan Dwan
1940	*San Francisco Docks*	Arthur Lubin
1941	*Meet the Chump*	Edward F. Cline
1941	*The Man Who Lost Himself*	Edward Ludwig
1941	*Man Made Monster* (aka *Atomic Monster*)	George Waggner
1941	*Model Wife*	Leigh Jason
1941	*The Black Cat*	Albert S. Rogell
1941	*Bachelor Daddy*	Harold Young
1941	*Raiders of the Desert*	John Rawlins
1941	*Hold That Ghost*	Arthur Lubin
1941	*Badlands of Dakota*	Alfred E. Green
1941	*The Kid from Kansas*	William Nigh
1941	*It Started with Eve* (AAN)	Henry Koster
1941	*Burma Convoy* (aka *Halfway to Shanghai*)	Noel M. Smith
1941	*Arizona Cyclone*	Joseph H. Lewis
1941	*The Wolf Man*	George Waggner
1942	*The Ghost of Frankenstein*	Erie C. Kenton
1942	*The Strange Case of Doctor Rx*	William Nigh
1942	*The Spoilers*	Ray Enright
1942	*Top Sergeant*	Christy Cabanne
1942	*Invisible Agent*	Edwin L. Marin
1942	*The Silver Bullet*	Joseph H. Lewis
1942	*Sin Town*	Ray Enright
1942	*Pittsburgh*	Lewis Seiler
1943	*The Amazing Mrs. Holliday* (AAN)	Bruce Manning, Jean Renoir
1943	*Keep 'Em Slugging*	Christy Cabanne
1943	*Frankenstein Meets the Wolf Man*	Roy William Neill
1943	*Get Going*	Jean Yarbrough
1943	*The Strange Death of Adolf Hitler*	James P. Hogan
1943	*Son of Dracula*	Robert Siodmak
1943	*Never a Dull Moment*	Edward C. Lilley
1943	*His Butler's Sister*	Frank Borzage
1944	*The Invisible Man's Revenge*	Ford Beebe
1944	*Christmas Holiday* (AAN)	Robert Siodmak
1944	*The Merry Monahans* (AAN)	Charles Lamont
1944	*San Diego I Love You*	Reginald Le Borg
1944	*House of Frankenstein* (aka *Chamber of Horrors*)	Erie C. Kenton
1944	*Can't Help Singing* (AAN)	Frank Ryan
1944	*The Spider Woman* (aka *Sherlock Holmes and the Spider Woman*)	Roy William Neill
1945	*Patrick the Great*	Frank Ryan
1945	*That's the Spirit*	Charles Lamont
1945	*The Strange Affair of Uncle Harry*	Robert Siodmak
1945	*River Gang*	Charles David

Year	Film	Director
1945	*That Night with You*	William A. Seiter
1945	*This Love of Ours* (AAN)	William Dieterle
1945	*Scarlet Street*	Fritz Lang
1946	*So Goes My Love*	Frank Ryan
1946	*Lover Come Back* (aka *When Lovers Meet*)	William A. Seiter
1946	*The Dark Horse*	Will Jason
1946	*Little Miss Big* (aka *Baxter's Millions*)	Erie C. Kenton
1946	*Magnificent Doll*	Frank Borzage
1947	*The Michigan Kid*	Ray Taylor
1947	*The Web* (aka *Black Velvet*)	Michael Gordon
1947	*That's My Man* (aka *Gallant Man*)	Frank Borzage
1947	*Love from a Stranger*	Richard Whorf
1948	*The Sign of the Ram*	John Sturges
1948	*Black Bart*	George Sherman
1948	*Man-Eater of Kumaon*	Byron Haskin
1948	*An Innocent Affair*	Lloyd Bacon
1949	*Cover Up*	Alfred E. Green
1949	*The Reckless Moment* (aka *The Blank Wall*)	Max Ophüls
1950	*Borderline*	William A. Seiter
1950	*Please Believe Me*	Norman Taurog
1950	*The Killer Who Stalked New York*	Earl McEvoy
1950	*Frenchie*	Louis King
1951	*Tomahawk*	George Sherman
1951	*Apache Drums*	Hugo Fregonese
1951	*The Fat Man*	William Castle
1951	*The Prince Who Was a Thief*	Rudolph Maté
1951	*Thunder on the Hill*	Douglas Sirk
1951	*You Never Can Tell*	Lou Breslow
1951	*The Golden Horde*	George Sherman
1952	*Finders Keepers*	Frederick De Cordova
1952	*Bend of the River*	Anthony Mann
1952	*The Battle at Apache Pass*	George Sherman
1952	*Flesh and Fury* (aka *Hear No Evil*)	Joseph Pevney
1952	*Untamed Frontier*	Hugo Fregonese
1952	*Against All Flags*	George Sherman
1953	*The 5,000 Fingers of Dr. T.*	Roy Rowland
1954	*Creature from the Black Lagoon*	Jack Arnold
1954	*O'Rourke of the Royal Mounted*	Raoul Walsh (Canada/USA)
1954	*Yankee Pasha*	Joseph Pevney
1954	*Black Horse Canyon*	Jesse Hibbs
1954	*Tanganyika*	André De Toth
1954	*Johnny Dark*	George Sherman
1954	*The Far Country*	Anthony Mann
1954	*The Black Shield of Falworth*	Rudolph Maté
1954	*The Human Jungle*	Joseph M. Newman
1954	*Naked Alibi*	Jerry Hopper
1954	*Four Guns to the Border*	Richard Carlson
1954	*Bengal Brigade*	Laslo Benedek
1954	*Sign of the Pagan*	Douglas Sirk
1955	*Man without a Star*	King Vidor
1955	*The Far Horizons* (aka *Blue Horizons*)	Rudolph Maté
1955	*This Island Earth*	Joseph M. Newman, Jack Arnold
1955	*The Purple Mask*	H. Bruce Humberstone
1955	*Abbott and Costello Meet the Mummy*	Charles Lamont
1955	*Wichita*	Jacques Tourneur
1955	*Kiss of Fire*	Joseph M. Newman
1955	*Lady Godiva of Coventry*	Arthur Lubin
1955	*The Rawhide Years*	Rudolph Maté

Year	Film	Director
1955	*The Spoilers*	Jesse Hibbs
1956	*Red Sundown*	Jack Arnold
1956	*Raw Edge*	John Sherwood
1956	*Navy Wife*	Edward Bernds
1956	*Autumn Leaves* (aka *The Way We Are*)	Robert Aldrich
1956	*Hold Back the Night*	Allan Dwan
1956	*Walk the Proud Land* (aka *Apache Agent*)	Jesse Hibbs
1956	*Three Brave Men*	Philip Dunne
1956	*The Mole People*	Virgil W. Vogel
1957	*The Incredible Shrinking Man*	Jack Arnold
1957	*The Oklahoman*	Francis D. Lyon
1957	*The Midnight Story*	Joseph Pevney
1957	*The Land Unknown*	Virgil W. Vogel
1957	*Joe Dakota*	Richard Bartlett
1957	*Appointment with a Shadow*	Richard Carlson
1957	*Man in the Shadow*	Jack Arnold
1957	*The Tall Stranger*	Thomas Carr
1957	*Love Slaves of the Amazons*	Curt Siodmak
1958	*The Female Animal*	Harry Keller
1958	*Day of the Badman*	Harry Keller
1958	*The Last of the Fast Guns*	George Sherman
1958	*Wild Heritage*	Charles F. Haas
1958	*Raw Wind in Eden*	Richard Wilson
1959	*The Gunfight at Dodge City*	Joseph M. Newman
1959	*The Wild and the Innocent* (aka *The Buckskin Kid and the Calico Gal*)	Jack Sher
1959	*The Man in the Net*	Michael Curtiz
1960	*The Leech Woman*	Edward Dein
1961	*Come September*	Robert Mulligan
1962	*Hitler*	Stuart Heisler
1962	*Follow That Dream*	Gordon Douglas
1962	*If a Man Answers*	Henry Levin
1963	*Showdown*	R. G. Springsteen
1964	*Bedtime Story*	Ralph Levy
1965	*The War Lord*	Franklin J. Schaffner
1966	*Incident at Phantom Hill*	Earl Bellamy
1966	*Gunpoint*	Earl Bellamy
1966	*Beau Geste*	Douglas Heyes
1967	*Return of the Gunfighter* (aka *As I Rode Down to Laredo*)	James Neilson

SARDE, Philippe (b. 1945?) A prolific French composer who has been active in European and American movies for over four decades, he has scored nearly two hundred feature films since 1970.

Born in Neuilly-sur-Seine, France (some sources say in 1948), Philippe Sarde is the son of singer Andrée Gabriel, who sang at the Paris Opera and who encouraged his son to explore music at a young age. Sarde loved movies and music as a child and made amateur films that he also scored. While studying composition at the Paris Conservatory, he made a low-budget short movie and scored it himself. In 1970 film director Claude Sautet asked the eighteen-year-old composer to score his feature film *The Things of Life* which was a surprise hit at the Cannes Film Festival and then across Europe. Sarde and Sautet have since collaborated on nine movies, most memorably *Max and the Junkmen*, *César and Rosalie*, *A Bad Son*, *A Few Days with Me*, *Nelly and Monsieur Arnaud*, and *Vincent, François, Paul and the Others*. Sarde has worked with most of the top French and Italian directors of the past four decades, as well as with Roman Polanski, in particular the international successes *Tess* and *The Tenant*, and a handful of Americans. His many other noteworthy movies include *Quest for Fire, La grande bouffe, Lancelot of the Lake, The Bear, Ponette, The Matchmaker, Beau Pere, The Manhattan Project, Madame Rosa, Cop or Hood, Drummer-Crab, I Sent a Letter to My Love, La fille des collines, On Guard, The Innocents, Reunion, My Favorite Season, Coup de torchon, Music Box, Lovesick, The Princess of Montpensier, Joshua Then and Now,* and *A Less Bad World.* Since the year 2000, Sarde has done fewer films each year but has scored some documentaries, miniseries, and movies for television.

Because Sarde worked on so many films (and on such different genres) with a wide range of directors, it is his variety that first impresses one. He moves from jazz to classical forms, from intimate solos to full symphonic sounds, and from the solemn to the joyous in his screen scores. Both his early movies and his most recent works are full of new ideas and musical surprises. Even when Sarde was saddled with a series of uninspired screen projects in the 1980s, his music did not suffer. It is little wonder that he has been in such demand in Europe since his first effort in 1970. That first movie, *Les choses de la vie* but widely released as *The Things of Life,* is about an engineer (Michel Piccoli) who, seriously hurt in a traffic accident, recalls moments from his past life. Sarde's main theme is a flowing piano and string piece that is full of life even as the tempo is restrained and the melody remains within a narrow range; the result is romantic yet casual. When slowed down to a hesitant pace, the same theme is poignant and heartbreaking. When played on demanding strings and a nervous piano, the piece becomes anxious and worried. This is a characteristic of Sarde's work. His scores repeat a favorite theme but in many guises. *La grande bouffe,* which has been translated as *The Big Feast* and *The Great Feed,* is a hedonistic dark comedy about four successful men of the world (Marcello Mastroianni, Ugo Tognazzi, Michel Piccoli, and Philippe Noiret) who rent a villa to go and gorge themselves on food and prostitutes. The film opens with a flute solo that flutters through a jazzy piece with a primitive folk sensibility. Only later does Sarde introduce the main theme, a jazz passage featuring a saxophone, piano, xylophone, and bongo drums that is rhythmic yet listless and languid as it suggests a sultry tango. This catchy theme, which became quite popular when the movie did, is heard throughout the rest of the film, sometimes played on a piano in a bar, other times as

a dance tune on the radio, and even as underscoring for an ultimately sad conclusion.

Although there are several themes in *Quest for Fire,* Sarde again got multiple uses out of his primary piece of music. This engrossing prehistoric tale, with the original French title *La guerre du feu* (*The War of Fire*), is about three tribesmen who must travel far and endure great obstacles in their search for a flame to rekindle their tribal fire. With so little dialogue, *Quest for Fire* tells its story through visuals and almost every moment of the film's one hundred minutes are musicalized. Just as Anthony Burgess created an original primitive language for the movie, Sarde experimented with unique musical sounds. He utilized the pan flute for the upper register and a bass flute for the lower, mixing them with a large traditional orchestra and a choir that sometimes accompanied the music, other times sang a cappella. The central recurring theme, played on the two kinds of flute with strings and woodwinds, is a simple melody that keeps returning to a five-note phrase as the tribal percussion keeps time. A slower, calmer version of this passage serves as the love theme; a rumbling version on xylophone and tribal drums is used to create suspense. The score also includes a brass and drum passage that foreshadows something wondrous and possibly dangerous; a chase theme on agitated strings, blaring brass, and pounding drums; and some tribal chanting, echoed by strings and reeds, that climbs the scale carefully but with force. *Quest for Fire* was Sarde's first movie to become an international hit and the soundtrack album showed up on the music charts.

Jean-Jacques Annaud, who had directed *Quest for Fire,* had another global success with *The Bear,* about an orphaned cub who survives the wilds of British Columbia by befriending a giant grizzly. Again there is little dialogue and Sarde's music is nearly nonstop. The sweeping symphonic main theme captures the grandeur of the vast natural setting and it returns in different forms throughout the movie. There is also a fluid orchestral passage that keeps returning to an ascending musical phrase filled with wonder, a deep dissonant theme on low brass and woodwinds that is awkward and foreboding, and a frolicking track with French horns leading the way up and down the scale with a sense of abandon and delight. Classical in temperament but not symphonic is Sarde's score for *Le chat* (*The Cat*). As an old and unhappy married couple (Jean Gabin and Simone Signoret) wait for the wrecking ball to destroy their pathetic house, the husband relies on the pet cat for companionship and meaning in his life. This grim little drama has a tentative solo piano theme that slowly breaks away from a sonorous four-note phrase to explore a bit, then returns to it with resignation. The classical sound of the piece is a cruel contrast to the mundane setting and weary tone of the story. Perhaps no other musical theme illustrates Sarde's dexterity with the modern and the classical as that in the comic crime movie *Flic ou voyou*, better known outside of France as *Cop or Hood*. A police detective (Jean-Paul Belmondo) is sent to clean up the police corruption in Nice but one is not sure which side of the law he is on. Sarde's leitmotif is a kind of double theme. A classical string quartet plays a stimulating fast waltz with all kinds of baroque flourishes. Then a cool jazz theme, featuring a solo trumpet and restless percussion, takes over and conjures up a slick and jaded atmosphere. Then Sarde fuses the two sounds together into a totally captivating piece of music that mirrors the film's title and the dual quality of the main character. Perhaps this one track is the essence of Sarde the screen composer.

Two films by Roman Polanski that Sarde scored deserve some attention, the two works being good examples of the two sides to his music. *Tess* is an expert screen adaptation of Thomas Hardy's novel *Tess of the D'Ubervilles*, the quietly tragic story of a pretty young peasant (Nastassja Kinski) who is loved by an idealistic minister's son (Peter Firth) and a so-called cousin (Leigh Lawson) and how both contribute to her destruction. Sarde's score is true to the Victorian period and the rural sounds of Wessex County but the music is usually in a minor key and employs a dissonance that conveys the tragic tone of the film. The main theme is a melancholy waltz with high woodwinds providing birdlike accents. There is a somber passage on strings that maintains a brisk pace without losing its woeful attitude; a surging folk theme played on fiddles and horns; and a dissonant, angry track on strident strings and squealing woodwinds. A lively dance on folk instruments is contrasted with a restless piece with pipes and horns playing over agitated strings, and a heavyhearted folk theme that repeats a dour musical phrase on different instruments. Polanksi's *The Tenant* is a contemporary tale about a bureaucrat (Polanski) who rents an apartment in Paris and is slowly but effectively tormented by his neighbors into paranoia and possible suicide. This fascinating psycho-drama is scored with modern music filled with avant-garde touches. The mysterious and unsettling main theme features a solo clarinet that is both enticing and grim; when slowed down and heard later, it is reflective and sad. There is a suspenseful passage on electric keyboard, balalaika, and deep woodwinds, as well as a nervous track with jittery strings repeating the same phrase with frustration. Also memorable is an odd dance piece on high and low horns with a sprightly solo violin, and a solo oboe and bassoon are featured in a morose theme that seems to grumble and complain as it moves along at a steady but worried pace. No matter what kind of movie Sarde scores, there is usually something intriguing in the music. And to think that he has been intriguing listeners for over forty years is nothing short of remarkable.

Credits

(all films France unless stated otherwise; * nominated for a César Award)

Year	Film	Director
1970	The Things of Life	Claude Sautet (France/Italy/Switzerland)
1970	Sortie de secours	Roger Kahane
1970	La liberté en croupe	Édouard Molinaro
1971	Max and the Junkmen	Claude Sautet (France/Italy)
1971	The Cat	Pierre Granier-Deferre (France/Italy)
1971	The Widow Couderc	Pierre Granier-Deferre (France/Italy)
1972	Love to Eternity (aka Seclusion)	Marco Ferreri (Italy/France)
1972	Hellé	Roger Vadim
1972	The Right to Love (aka Brainwashed)	Eric Le Hung (France/Italy)
1972	César and Rosalie	Claude Sautet (France/Italy/W. Germany)
1973	The Son	Pierre Granier-Deferre (Italy/France)
1973	Le grande bouffe	Marco Ferreri (France/Italy)

Year	Film	Director
1973	*The Heavenly Bodies*	Gilles Carle (Canada/France)
1973	*Man in the Trunk*	Georges Lautner
1973	*Two Men in Town*	José Giovanni (France/Italy)
1973	*The Last Train*	Pierre Granier-Deferre (France/Italy)
1973	*Charlie and His Two Checks*	Joël Séria
1974	*The Clockmaker of St. Paul*	Bertrand Tavernier
1974	*Don't Touch the White Woman!*	Marco Ferreri (France/Italy)
1974	*Dorothea's Revenge*	Peter Fleischmann (W. Germany/France)
1974	*Creezy (aka Jet Set)*	Pierre Granier-Deferre (France/Italy)
1974	*Someone Is Bleeding*	Georges Lautner (Italy/France)
1974	*Lancelot of the Lake*	Robert Bresson (France/Italy)
1974	*Vincent, François, Paul and the Others*	Claude Sautet (France/Italy)
1975	*A Happy Divorce*	Henning Carlsen (France/Denmark)
1975	*The Cage*	Pierre Granier-Deferre
1975	*No Problem!*	Georges Lautner
1975	*Mad Enough to Kill*	Yves Boisset (France/Italy)
1975	*Cookies*	Joël Séria
1975	*French Provincial*	André Téchiné
1975	*7 Deaths by Prescription*	Jacques Rouffio (France/W. Germany/Spain)
1975	*The French Detective*	Pierre Granier-Deferre
1975	*A Bag of Marbles*	Jacques Doillon
1976	*The Judge and the Assassin**	Bertrand Tavernier
1976	*The Last Woman*	Marco Ferreri (Italy/France)
1976	*The Tenant*	Roman Polanski
1976	*The Bottom Line*	Georges Lautner
1976	*Marie, the Doll*	Joël Séria
1976	*Mado*	Claude Sautet (France/Italy/W. Germany)
1976	*Barocco**	André Téchiné
1977	*Le sheriff*	Yves Boisset
1977	*Violette & François*	Jacques Rouffio
1977	*The Purple Taxi*	Yves Boisset (France/Ireland/Italy)
1977	*The Devil, Probably*	Robert Bresson
1977	*As the Moon*	Joël Séria
1977	*Spoiled Children*	Bertrand Tavernier
1977	*Madame Rosa*	Moshé Mizrahi
1977	*Drummer-Crab**	Pierre Schoendoerffer
1977	*Death of a Corrupt Man (aka Twisted Detective)*	Georges Lautner
1978	*Bye Bye Monkey*	Marco Ferreri (Italy/France)
1978	*These Sorcerers Are Mad*	George Lautner
1978	*Le Sucre*	Jacques Rouffio
1978	*A Simple Story**	Claude Sautet (France/W. Germany)
1978	*The Key Is in the Door*	Yves Boisset
1979	*The Adolescent*	Jeanne Moreau (France/W. Germany)
1979	*Cop or Hood*	Georges Lautner
1979	*Seeking Asylum*	Marco Ferreri (Italy/France)
1979	*Tess* (AAN)*	Roman Polanski (France/UK)
1979	*The Medic*	Pierre Granier-Deferre
1979	*Cold Cuts*	Bertrand Tavernier
1980	*The Woman Cop*	Yves Boisset
1980	*Le Guignolo*	Georges Lautner (France/Italy)
1980	*I Sent a Letter to My Love*	Moshé Mizrahi
1980	*A Bad Son*	Claude Sautet
1981	*Allons z'enfants*	Yves Boisset
1981	*Est-ce bien raisonnable?*	Georges Lautner
1981	*The Wings of the Dove*	Benoît Jacquot
1981	*Choice of Arms*	Alain Corneau
1981	*Birgit Haas Must Be Killed*	Laurent Heynemann (France/W. Germany)
1981	*Tales of Ordinary Madness*	Marco Ferreri (Italy/France)

Year	Film	Director
1981	*Beau Pere*	Bertrand Blier
1981	*Coup de torchon*	Bertrand Tavernier
1981	*Hotel America*	André Téchiné
1981	*Ghost Story*	John Irvin (USA)
1981	*Quest for Fire**	Jean-Jacques Annaud (Canada/France/USA)
1981	*Strange Affair*	Pierre Granier-Deferre
1982	*A Thousand Billion Dollars*	Henri Verneuil
1982	*The North Star*	Pierre Granier-Deferre
1982	*Contract in Blood*	Robin Davis, Alain Delon
1982	*Que les gros salaires levent le doigt!*	Denys Granier-Deferre
1982	*A Captain's Honor*	Pierre Schoendoerffer
1983	*The Story of Piera*	Marco Ferreri (Italy/France/W. Germany)
1983	*I Married a Dead Man*	Robin Davis
1983	*Lovesick*	Marshall Brickman (USA)
1983	*Une jeunesse*	Moshé Mizrahi
1983	*Stella*	Laurent Heynemann
1983	*My Other Husband*	Georges Lautner
1983	*A Friend of Vincent*	Pierre Granier-Deferre
1983	*Waiter!*	Claude Sautet
1984	*First Desires*	David Hamilton (France/W. Germany)
1984	*Fort Saganne*	Alain Corneau
1984	*The Pirate*	Jacques Doillon
1984	*La Garce*	Christine Pascal
1984	*Happy Easter*	Georges Lautner
1985	*Next Summer*	Nadine Trintignant
1985	*Sincerely Charlotte*	Caroline Huppert
1985	*The Cowboy*	Georges Lautner
1985	*Outlaws*	Robin Davis
1985	*Rendez-vous*	André Téchiné
1985	*Joshua Then and Now*	Ted Kotcheff (Canada)
1985	*The Temptation of Isabelle*	Jacques Doillon (France/Switzerland)
1985	*L'Homme aux yeux d'argent*	Pierre Granier-Deferre
1985	*Harem*	Arthur Joffé
1985	*Ça n'arrive qu'á moi*	Francis Perrin
1986	*My Brother-in-Law Killed My Sister*	Jacques Rouffio
1986	*Pirates*	Roman Polanski (France/Tunisia)
1986	*Scene of the Crime*	André Téchiné
1986	*The Manhattan Project (aka Deadly Game)*	Marshall Brickman (USA)
1986	*Private Tuition*	Pierre Granier-Deferre (Israel/USA)
1986	*Every Time We Say Goodbye*	Moshé Mizrahi
1986	*State of Grace*	Jacques Rouffio
1987	*Les mois d'avril sont meurtriers*	Lautent Heynemann
1987	*Poker*	Catherine Corsini
1987	*Funny Boy*	Christian Le Hémonet
1987	*Comédie!*	Jacques Doillon
1987	*The Two Crocodiles*	Joël Séria
1987	*Widow's Walk*	Pierre Granier-Deferre (France/Italy)
1987	*Ennemis intimes*	Denis Amar
1987	*Engagements of the Heart*	Robert Enrico
1987	*The Innocents**	André Téchiné
1988	*The Murdered House*	Georges Lautner
1988	*A Few Days with Me*	Claude Sautet
1988	*The Bear*	Jean-Jacques Annaud (France/USA)
1988	*The House of Jade*	Nadine Trintignant
1988	*La couleur du vent*	Pierre Granier-Deferre
1988	*Mangeclous*	Moshé Mizrahi
1989	*Beyond Innocence*	Scott Murray (Australia)
1989	*Lost Angels*	Hugh Hudson (USA)

Year	Film	Director
1989	*Reunion*	Jerry Schatzberg (France/W. Germany/UK)
1989	*L'invité surprise*	Georges Lautner
1989	*Winter of 54: Father Pierre*	Denis Amar
1989	*Separate Bedrooms*	Jacky Cukier
1989	*Music Box*	Costa-Gavras (USA)
1990	*C'est la vie*	Diane Kurys
1990	*La fille des collines*	Robin Davis
1990	*Lord of the Flies*	Harry Hook (USA)
1990	*Forgery and the Use of Forgeries*	Laurent Heynemann
1990	*The Little Gangster*	Jacques Doillon
1991	*Eve of Destruction*	Duncan Gibbins (USA)
1991	*The Tribe*	Yves Boisset
1991	*For Sasha*	Alexandre Arcady
1991	*Jealousy*	Kathleen Fonmarty (France/Italy)
1991	*The Old Lady Who Walked in the Sea*	Laurent Heynemann (France/Italy)
1991	*I Don't Kiss*	André Téchiné (France/Italy)
1992	*The Voice*	Pierre Granier-Deferre
1992	*Room Service*	Georges Lautner
1992	*L.627*	Bertrand Tavernier
1992	*Max & Jeremie*	Claire Devers (Italy/France)
1993	*The Little Apocalypse*	Costa-Gavras (France/Italy/Poland)
1993	*Young Werther*	Jacques Doillon
1993	*My Favorite Season*	André Téchiné
1993	*Sunfish*	Bertrand Van Effenterre
1993	*Night Taxi*	Serge Leroy
1993	*Revenge of the Musketeers**	Bertrand Tavernier, Riccardo Freda
1994	*The Favorite Son*	Nicole Garcia
1994	*Uncovered*	Jim McBride (UK/Spain/France)
1995	*The Little Boy*	Pierre Granier-Deferre
1995	*Dis-moi oui . . .*	Alexandre Arcady
1995	*Nelly and Monsieur Arnaud**	Claude Sautet (France/Italy/Germany)
1996	*Thieves*	André Téchiné
1996	*Ponette*	Jacques Doillon
1997	*Lucie Aubrac*	Claude Berri
1997	*K*	Alexandre Arcady
1997	*Brother*	Sylvie Verheyde
1997	*On Guard**	Philippe de Broca (France/Italy/Germany)
1998	*Alice and Martin*	André Téchiné (France/Spain)
1998	*I'm Alive and I Love You*	Roger Kahane (France/Belgium)
2000	*Return to Algiers*	Alexandre Arcady
2000	*Princesses*	Sylvie Verheyde (France/Belgium)
2001	*Mademoiselle*	Philippe Lioret
2002	*Break of Dawn*	Alexandre Arcady (France/USA)
2003	*The Mystery of the Yellow Room*	Bruno Podalydes (Belgium/France)
2003	*Strayed*	André Téchiné (France/UK)
2003	*Raja*	Jacques Doillon (France/Morocco)
2004	*A Less Bad World*	Alejandro Agresti (Argentina)
2004	*Me and My Sister*	Alexandra Leclere
2005	*The Perfume of the Lady in Black*	Bruno Podalydes
2006	*Le grand Meaulnes*	Jean-Daniel Verhaeghe
2006	*Call Me Elisabeth*	Jean-Pierre Améris
2007	*The Witnesses*	André Téchiné
2009	*The Girl on the Train*	André Téchiné
2010	*The Three-Way Wedding*	Jacques Doillon
2010	*The Princess of Montpensier**	Bertrand Tavernier (France/Germany)
2010	*The Matchmaker (aka Once I Was)*	Avi Nesher (Israel)
2010	*Streamfield, les carnets noirs*	Jean-Luc Miesch
2012	*And They Call It Summer*	Paolo Franchi (Italy)
2013	*The French Minister*	Bertrand Tavernier

SCHARF, Walter (1910–2003) A highly respected composer, arranger, and conductor in Hollywood for four decades, he scored over one hundred movies and worked on the music for twice that number.

Walter Scharf was born in New York City into a theatrical family of Polish Jewish immigrants. His mother was Bessie Zwerling, a comic actress in the flourishing Yiddish theatre in New York. Scharf began playing the piano at a young age and worked with his uncle providing live music for silent movies. By the time he was seventeen, he was arranging and orchestrating the music for Broadway shows and worked as a sessions musician for recording studios. With his earnings, Scharf studied music at New York University and then spent time doing further study in Berlin. During the 1930s he served as accompanist for torch singer Helen Morgan and performed as part of Rudy Vallee's orchestra. When Vallee and the ensemble went to Hollywood to appear in the film *Sweet Music* in 1935, Scharf remained in California and soon was in demand for his arrangements and orchestrations. He was the principal arranger for Alice Faye and other singing stars and the orchestrator behind numerous musicals and nonmusical movies. Between 1942 and 1946 he was in charge of all the music for Republic Pictures and from 1948 to 1954 he was arranger and conductor for a popular radio show starring Faye and Phil Harris. Although Scharf was mostly thought of as an expert orchestrator and arranger, he contributed music to dozens of films, at first usually with other composers but after World War II, he usually was sole composer for his movies. He wrote incidental music for musicals and full scores for westerns and melodramas, but particularly for comedies.

He received Oscar nominations for his work on the musicals *Hit Parade of 1943*, *Hans Christian Andersen*, *Funny Girl*, and *Willy Wonka & the Chocolate Factory*, but these were for his outstanding arrangements of other composers' songs into screen soundtracks. He also got Oscar nods for his dramatic scores for *Mercy Island*, *Johnny Doughboy*, *In Old Oklahoma*, *Brazil*, and *The Fighting Seabees*. Among the many other dramas he scored are *The Glass Key*, *The Joker Is Wild*, *Sierra*, *Spy Hunt*, *Time Table*, *Ben*, and *Walking Tall* and its two sequels. But Scharf was most often hired to write music for comedies and was the chosen composer for screen clowns Judy Canova, Abbott and Costello, Jerry Lewis, Danny Kaye, and even silent star Harold Lloyd, who asked Scharf to write the music for two popular anthology movies of his early comedies. He scored a handful of vehicles for Lewis and Dean Martin then, when the team split up, he worked with Lewis on ten other films, most memorably *Sad Sack*, *Cinderfella*, *The Errand Boy*, and *The Nutty Professor*. Scharf's other comedy credits include *Francis the Talking Mule*, *Mexican Hayride*, *The Court Jester*, *Pocketful of Miracles*, *The Cheyenne Social Club*, and *If It's Tuesday, This Must Be Belgium*. Scharf got involved with television early on. He won an Emmy Award for his musical direction of the variety show *Texaco Star Theatre* in 1948 and later scored such popular TV series as *Ben Casey*, *The Travels of Jamie McPheeters*, *Bonanza*, *The Man from U.N.C.L.E.*, *That Girl*, *Mission: Impossible*, and *The Love Boat*, as well as some TV movies. He also scored award-winning documentaries by the National Geographic Society and TV specials about Jacques Cousteau's marine explorations. His music for the last was later turned into the symphonic work *The Legend of the Living Seas*. Despite his busy screen and TV career, Scharf occasionally found time to write for the concert hall, and when he retired from movies and television in the late 1970s he concentrated on orchestral work. Among his best-known works are *The Palestine Suite*, *The Tree Stands Still*, and *Israeli Suite*. Scharf continued to write music until close to his death in 2003 at the age of ninety-two.

Like many of Hollywood's top music arrangers, Scharf was not thought of as a composer and spent most of his career making other composers sound good. Not until the 1960s was he consistently hired to write screen music and that was mostly for light comedies. Listening to his original music over the decades, one finds some laudable work. The John Wayne western *In Old Oklahoma* is an intelligent film about early oilmen and their efforts to drill on the land inhabited by Native Americans. The opening music is highly dramatic with wailing brass, stirring strings, and rapid harp glissandos with the touch of a western folk tune hidden in the music. A train theme is regal and inspiring as if announcing something momentous; there is a pleasant waltz on strings and a sprightly comic passage with dancing strings and piping woodwinds. The romantic theme, with weeping strings, uses a slow version of a music hall song heard earlier in the score. The action scenes are scored with furious orchestral racing filled with fanfares and crescendos. This may not be an inspired score but it has a dramatic sense that was strong enough to get the attention of the Academy, which was hesitant to nominate movies from a second-class studio like Republic. Dramatic in another way is Scharf's score for *Time Table*, a contemporary crime film about a fake doctor (Wesley Addy) who steals the payroll from a night train crossing the Arizona desert and the insurance investigator (Mark Stevens) who pursues him. The opening music is unusual. A guitar folk tune is punctuated by orchestral explosions then screaming strings and growling low brass take over. When the noise settles, one can finally hear the main melody, a restless passage heard on solo guitar and strings. Scharf wrote the music for a romantic Spanish ballad titled "Salud, Felicidad y Amor" (lyrics by Jack Brooks) which is heard in a Mexican border nightclub. The suspense scenes are scored with rumbling drums and chaotic piano phrases echoed by low strings, and the climax of the movie features dramatic descending phrases by the orchestra as the brass instruments reach for high notes.

Near the end of his career Scharf wrote a notable score for the crude but effective *Walking Tall*. The sheriff (Joe Don Baker) of a small Tennessee town uses unorthodox methods to clean up the corruption in his community, even when it puts his life and that of his family in danger. Based on a real sheriff, the movie struck a nerve and was a sleeper hit followed by two sequels. For such a blunt film, the opening music is a lovely string and horn piece that moves like a travel song as it echoes its main phrase back and forth. This same music is later slowed down and becomes the domestic theme for the sheriff's family. There is a rowdy country music theme on fiddles and horns, as well as some harsh passages on blasting brass used for the action scenes. Scharf also wrote the music for the lilting title song (lyric by Don Black) which Johnny Mathis sings on the soundtrack. Scharf and Black also wrote the title song for the horror movie *Ben*, and this time the song was so catchy it was nominated for an Oscar and became a big hit for several singers, most memorably Michael Jackson who sang it on the soundtrack. An odd but potent movie,

Ben is about a lonely youth (Lee Montgomery) who has a pet rat, Ben, that has a powerful control over the aggressive rats in town. The main theme (and also the music for the song) is a surprisingly lyrical piece with a steady pop beat as it jumps up and down the scale in an arresting manner. Variations of this melody are used throughout the film, the notes even becoming nasty for some of the unpleasant scenes.

Scharf's music for comedies in the 1960s and 1970s is just as accomplished as his so-called serious scores. Perhaps the best comedy (and score) is the Jerry Lewis vehicle *The Nutty Professor*, a clever takeoff on the Jekyll and Hyde legend. A nerdy chemistry professor (Lewis) has no luck with the ladies, so he concocts a formula that turns him temporarily into a suave heartbreaker called Buddy Love, sometimes with hilarious complications. Buddy sings a few romantic standards in the film (often coming across as more funny than sexy) but it is the rest of the score that is so delightful. The main theme is a jazzy march with a wild xylophone and other percussion instruments and giddy strings and brass that hop along at an energetic tempo. There is also a silly theme with brass and frantic percussion jumping all over the scale as pizzicato strings complain loudly, a jazzy piece with piano and woodwinds bebopping along with a breezy and confident air, and an easy jazz passage on flute, muted trumpet, and piano that is so casual and sophisticated it is laughable. When the professor is transformed into Buddy, the music consists of low strings and high brass that are playfully menacing. Also enjoyable is the very retro romantic theme, an old-fashioned slow foxtrot on muted trumpet and strings that must have seemed ancient even in 1963. Listening to the music in *The Nutty Professor*, it is easy to see why Scharf was the composer requested by Lewis and other comics. It is interesting that Scharf distinguished himself as a composer late in his career but he is still remembered as one of the leading music arrangers of his era.

Credits

(all films USA unless stated otherwise; * for Best Song)

Year	Film	Director
1937	*You Can't Have Everything*	Norman Taurog
1938	*Josette*	Allan Dwan

Year	Film	Director
1940	Hit Parade of 1941 (aka Romance and Rhythm)	John H. Auer
1941	Las Vegas Nights	Ralph Murphy
1941	Sis Hopkins	Joseph Santley
1941	Puddin' Head (aka Judy Goes to Town)	Joseph Santley
1941	Mercy Island (AAN)	William Morgan
1941	Henry Aldrich for President	Hugh Bennett
1942	The Glass Key	Stuart Heisler
1942	Johnny Doughboy (AAN)	John H. Auer
1943	Hit Parade of 1943 (aka Change of Heart) (AAN)	Albert S. Rogell
1943	Shantytown	Joseph Santley
1943	Thumbs Up	Joseph Santley
1943	Someone to Remember (aka Gallant Thoroughbred)	Robert Siodmak
1943	Nobody's Darling	Anthony Mann
1943	In Old Oklahoma (aka War of the Wildcats)(AAN)	Albert S. Rogell
1944	The Fighting Seabees(aka Donovan's Army) (AAN)	Edward Ludwig
1944	The Lady and the Monster	George Sherman
1944	Atlantic City	Ray McCarey
1944	Brazil (aka Stars and Guitars) (AAN)	Joseph Santley
1945	Earl Carroll Vanities (aka Moonstruck Melody)	Joseph Santley
1945	The Cheaters (aka The Castaways)	Joseph Kane
1945	Dakota	Joseph Kane
1946	I've Always Loved You (aka Concerto)	Frank Borzage
1948	Are You With It?	Jack Hively
1948	Casbah	John Berry
1948	The Saxon Charm	Claude Binyon
1948	The Countess of Monte Cristo	Frederick De Cordova
1948	Mexican Hayride	Charles Barton
1949	City across the River	Maxwell Shane
1949	Red Canyon	George Sherman
1949	Take One False Step	Chester Erskine
1949	Yes Sir, That's My Baby	George Sherman
1950	Francis the Talking Mule	Arthur Lubin
1950	Buccaneer's Girl	Frederick De Cordova
1950	Curtain Call at Cactus Creek	Charles Lamont
1950	Sierra	Alfred E. Green
1950	Spy Hunt (aka Spy Ring)	George Sherman
1950	Peggy (aka Rose Bowl Queen)	Frederick De Cordova
1950	Deported	Robert Siodmak
1950	South Sea Sinner	H. Bruce Humberstone
1951	Two Tickets to Broadway	James V. Kern
1952	Hans Christian Andersen (AAN)	Charles Vidor
1954	The French Line	Lloyd Bacon
1954	Living It Up	Norman Taurog
1954	3 Ring Circus (aka Big Top)	Joseph Pevney
1955	You're Never Too Young	Norman Taurog
1955	Artists and Models	Frank Tashlin
1955	The Court Jester	Melvin Frank, Norman Panama
1956	Time Table	Mark Stevens
1956	The Birds and the Bees	Norman Taurog
1956	Three for Jamie Dawn	Thomas Carr
1956	Three Violent People	Rudolph Maté
1956	Hollywood or Bust (aka Beginner's Luck)	Frank Tashlin
1957	Loving You (aka Running Wild)	Hal Kanter
1957	The Joker Is Wild (aka All the Way)	Charles Vidor
1957	The Sad Sack	George Marshall
1958	King Creole	Michael Curtiz
1958	Rock-a-Bye Baby	Frank Tashlin
1958	The Geisha Boy	Frank Tashlin

Year	Film	Director
1959	Don't Give Up the Ship	Norman Taurog
1960	The Bellboy	Jerry Lewis
1960	Cinderfella	Frank Tashlin
1961	The Ladies Man	Jerry Lewis
1961	The Errand Boy	Jerry Lewis
1961	Pocketful of Miracles	Frank Capra
1962	Harold Lloyd's World of Comedy	Harold Lloyd
1962	It's Only Money	Frank Tashlin
1963	My Six Loves	Gower Champion
1963	The Nutty Professor	Jerry Lewis
1963	The Funny Side of Life	Harry Kerwin
1964	Honeymoon Hotel	Henry Levin
1964	Where Love Has Gone	Edward Dmytryk
1965	Tickle Me (aka Isle of Paradise)	Norman Taurog
1968	Funny Girl (AAN)	William Wyler
1969	Pendulum	George Schaefer
1969	If It's Tuesday, This Must Be Belgium	Mel Stuart
1970	The Cheyenne Social Club	Gene Kelly
1971	Willy Wonka & the Chocolate Factory (AAN)	Mel Stuart
1972	Ben (AAN*; GG*)	Phil Karlson
1973	Walking Tall	Phil Karlson
1974	Journey Back to Oz	Hal Sutherland
1975	Walking Tall Part II	Earl Bellamy
1975	Backbone	Vlatko Gilic (Yugoslavia)
1977	Final Chapter: Walking Tall	Jack Starrett
1981	This Is Elvis	Malcolm Leo, Andrew Solt
1982	Twilight Time	Goran Paskaljevic (USA/Yugoslavia)

SCHIFRIN, Lalo (b. 1932) A South American–born pianist, composer, and conductor, he has scored over two hundred films and television shows, often providing memorable scores for action movies. Schifrin has found fame everywhere from renowned concert halls to small jazz clubs but he is probably best known for his movie and TV music.

He was born Boris Claudio Schifrin in Buenos Aires, Argentina, the son of the concertmaster of the Philharmonic Orchestra of Buenos Aires. Schifrin studied music and law in his native country then furthered his music education at the Paris Conservatory of Music. Although he received a classical music education, he was greatly interested in jazz and in the 1950s performed with jazz bands in Argentina. Dizzy Gillespie, visiting South America on a State Department tour in 1957, was impressed with Schifrin's talent and hired him to arrange and play piano for his band's concerts and recordings. At the same time Schifrin wrote arrangements for Xavier Cugat, Count Basie, Stan Getz, and other bandleaders. Before moving to the States permanently in 1960, Schifrin wrote music for Argentine

theatre, television, short movies, and the feature film *The Boss* in 1958. Living in New York City, he wrote for the concert stage and continued to perform in jazz clubs, but by 1963 he was in Hollywood where he scored the feature *Rhino!* and rearranged the theme music for the TV series *The Man from U.N.C.L.E.* Both were well received and Schifrin was soon in demand for both media. Over the next five decades he would bring his classical and jazz background to the big and small screen, writing innovative soundtracks that often became popular themes used in other works. His memorable jazz theme for the television series *Mission: Impossible*, with its unusual 5/8 time signature and distinctive bass line, is arguably Schifrin's most recognized piece of music as it continues to be heard on TV and in movies.

Although he has scored a wide variety of genres, from comedies to horror movies, Schifrin seems to have found his greatest success with tough action films. Among the most popular in this genre are *Bullitt, Charley Varrick, Enter the Dragon, The Eagle Has Landed, Rush Hour, Rollercoaster, The Osterman Weekend,* and *Dirty*

Harry and its sequels. In other genres, Schifrin scored such noteworthy movies as *The Exorcist, Once a Thief, Coogan's Bluff, The Fox, Kelly's Heroes, Murderers' Row, Voyage of the Damned, Brubaker, Cool Hand Luke, THX 1138, The Cincinnati Kid, The Amityville Horror, Tango, Money Talks, The Sting II, The Neptune Factor, The Four Musketeers, The Brotherhood, Hell in the Pacific*, and *The Competition*. Schifrin has enjoyed an equally successful career in television, having written scores for dozens of series, miniseries, and TV movies. Among his notable series are *Blue Light, T.H.E. Cat, Glitter, Bronk, The Big Valley, Mannix, Planet of the Apes*, and *Starsky and Hutch*. In 1964, Schifrin scored *See How They Run*, one of the first TV movies made in America. His subsequent television films and miniseries include *The Doomsday Flight* (1966), *Sullivan's Empire* (1967), *Escape* (1971), *Hunter* (1973), *Brenda Starr* (1976), *The Nativity* (1978), *Falcon's Gold* (1982), *Rita Hayworth: The Love Goddess* (1983), *Princess Daisy* (1983), *Beverly Hills Madam* (1986), *Earth Star Voyager* (1988), *Original Sin* (1989), *A Woman Named Jackie* (1991), and *The Neon Empire* (1991). Throughout his career, Schifrin has remained active in composing, performing, and conducting for the concert stage and the recording studio. His instrumental works range from piano sonatas to tangos to jazz pieces and he has recorded over forty albums that cover several genres of music. Schifrin has also written a theory book titled *Music Composition for Film and Television* (2011).

The quirky prison movie *Cool Hand Luke* has what many consider to be Schifrin's finest score. This off-beat comedy-drama concerns an unconventional renegade (Paul Newman) and his adventures (and misadventures) when sentenced to work on a chain gang. The bluegrass theme for the title character is remote, quiet, and detached, much like the man himself. This free-and-easy piece is played by various instruments throughout the movie. For the opening credits, one guitar plays the melody then another plays the harmony, the two not combining until the end of the sequence. Later the theme is played by a solo trumpet, then a banjo, then a flute. The music heard while the convicts pave a road in the hot Southern sun is scored with a banjo riff, restless violins, and a strong bass line. For a chase scene, a furious banjo is joined by a harmonica and strings. There is no romance in *Cool Hand Luke*, but there is a soft theme titled "Arletta's Blues" that is quite engaging. Too rarely would Schifrin be given such a superior

and complex film to score. Consider the popular action movies that left little room for subtlety. The score for the Steve McQueen vehicle *Bullitt* is filled with jazz, blues, and even a little rock. The movie is an action-packed thriller about a San Francisco cop (McQueen) hunting down an organized crime mobster. There is little melody in the title music but a lot of attitude as musical phrases repeat, percussion instruments riff, and the brass explodes. A blues theme on the flute feels free and improvised, while the famous chase up and down the hills of San Francisco is scored with a furious theme with piano, drums, and trumpets racing each other. *Dirty Harry*, about another cop (Clint Eastwood) but one with more unorthodox methods, has a score that is even more jazz oriented and again melody takes a backseat to riffs and percussive variations. Schifrin brings violins in at the least expected moments, their sound just flat enough to make the listener a little slaphappy. The theme for the villain Scorpio (Andrew Robinson) moves from jazz to abstract music in an effort to convey his psychopathic nature. It is very abrasive music yet thrilling in a disconcerting way. The movie ends with a mournful cool jazz passage using electric piano and slurred violins. The scores for *Bullitt* and *Dirty Harry* were fresh and thrilling and Schifrin for a time was saddled mostly with action films. Because he was such an expert on jazz and blues he was able to oblige without repeating himself.

Schifrin's more lyrical side can be heard in *The Fox*, a quiet yet seething drama about a romantic triangle. Two women (Sandy Dennis and Anne Heywood) trying to run a chicken farm in Canada find their world turned upside down by the arrival of a stranger (Keir Dullea). A solo flute plays the main theme, a morose and lonely piece that is nevertheless enchanting. The six-note phrase does not grow monotonous, particularly when a muted piano and a gentle harp are added. The characters in this D. H. Lawrence tale live in a remote place and the music seems to take the audience there with every chord. A ship full of German Jewish refugees in *Voyage of the Damned* are equally remote as they search for a port that will accept them. Schifrin's music is fully orchestrated this time but still feels lonely and removed. There are some dramatic flourishes, but much of the score is subdued, even the waltzing song "Wein Wein" and the ship's dance band music. There is a lovely theme in *The Competition*, a romance about competing pianists (Amy Irving and Richard Dreyfus) who fall in love. A simple four-note phrase is delicately repeated in different keys then expands into a flowing contemporary ballad. With a lyric by Will Jenning, the piece became the very pleasing song "People Alone." Also melodic, but in a jazz and blues mode, is the score for *The Cincinnati Kid*. Set among poker players in New Orleans, the movie is filled with wonderfully atmospheric music. There is a soulful funeral procession theme in which piano and trumpet alternate in an improvised manner. A cool jazz theme sounds classic and contemporary at the same time. The main theme has a western flavor when sung as a song (lyric by Dorcas Cochran) by Ray Charles but as used later it is closer to hot jazz. A delightfully atypical score by Schifrin is heard in *The Four Musketeers*. His education in classical music must have come in handy in writing this sprightly score that drew on French court music, Italian tarantella, and English pomp and circumstance.

For the early George Lucas futuristic sci-fi film *THX 1138*, Schifrin experimented with electronic music. This futuristic tale centers on two drugged, robotic humans (Robert Duvall and Maggie McOmie) who rebel against the highly controlled system. For the main title a choir singing a creepy Gregorian chant is heard over a lot of vibrating sounds and echoing reverberations. Other sections of the score have traditional music (tango, calypso, etc.) played on electric instruments so there is an icy tone to everything in this nightmare world of the future. Schifrin did not get to score many more science fiction movies but he certainly got his fair share of horror flicks. Perhaps his best score in that genre is the one from *The Amityville Horror*. A pair of newlyweds (Margot Kidder and James Brolin) moves into a house where a murder has occurred and face a series of horrors. There is little exceptional about this haunted house shocker except the music, which is endlessly creative. The opening title is a gentle lullaby in which children's innocent voices are accompanied by subdued piano arpeggios and high-strung violin cries. It is a remarkably subtle theme for such an obvious movie. As the tension builds and the music moves into suspense, Schifrin uses unlikely French horns with the expected violins. He also played with electronic instruments and a synthesizer for some of the more ghastly scenes. All in all, it is a superior hor-

ror film score. Schifrin went even further in his score for *The Exorcist*. This very popular book about a young girl (Linda Blair) possessed by the devil was turned into an equally popular movie. The electronic sounds in this score are harsher, the chords more oppressive, and the echoing reverberations more unnerving. The surprising use of a synthesized harp tends to put the listener at false ease only to be jarringly assaulted by violent violins cascading down the scale as if going over a cliff. It is all very overpowering, perhaps too overpowering. When *The Exorcist* trailer was shown to preview audiences with Schifrin's music, moviegoers were so upset with the shocking visuals and audio that the studio instructed director William Friedkin to have the composer soften some of the music. Instead, Friedkin disposed of the entire score and substituted it with different pieces of existing music by different composers. But today one can hear Schifrin's original music on CD and it is dazzling.

Of Schifrin's more recent screen scores, perhaps the most satisfying are two that draw on his own understanding of South American music. *The Bridge of San Luis Rey*, based on Thornton Wilder's novel, is set in eighteenth-century Peru and explores the lives of a handful of people who died when a famous rope bridge collapsed. Both European Spanish and native music can be heard in this rich and embracing score. Simple flute and guitar tunes alternate with lush orchestral passages, just as liturgical organ music gives way to Spanish flamenco. The Argentine-Spanish film *Tango* is about a choreographer (Mario Suarez) staging a dance performance in which the tango is used to illustrate Argentina's history. For this highly stylized movie, Schifrin explores the many facets of the tango, from a military interpretation to a sensual one. Voices fill the soundtrack score, a discordant accordion plays wearily, violins angrily protest, a piano repeats a minor phrase over and over, and guitars romance each other lazily. It is an oddly fascinating movie and Schifrin's music is a good part of its mesmerizing effect. Perhaps all of Schifrin's music can be described as mesmerizing. It certainly cannot be missed or ignored. Autobiography: *Mission Impossible: My Life in Music* (2008). Official website: www.schifrin.com.

Credits

(all films USA unless stated otherwise; * for Best Song)

Year	Film	Director
1958	*The Boss*	Fernando Ayala (Argentina)
1964	*Rhino!*	Ivan Tors
1964	*Joy House*	René Clément (France)
1965	*Once a Thief*	Ralph Nelson (France/USA)
1965	*Dark Intruder*	Harvey Hart
1965	*The Cincinnati Kid*	Norman Jewison
1965	*The Liquidator*	Jack Cardiff (UK)
1965	*Blindfold*	Philip Dunne
1966	*Way . . . Way Out*	Gordon Douglas
1966	*I Deal in Danger*	Walter Grauman
1966	*Murderers' Row*	Henry Levin
1967	*The Venetian Affair*	Jerry Thorpe
1967	*Who's Minding the Mint?*	Howard Morris
1967	*Cool Hand Luke* (AAN)	Stuart Rosenberg
1967	*The Fox* (AAN)	Mark Rydell (Canada)
1967	*The President's Analyst*	Theodore J. Flicker
1968	*Sol Madrid*	Brian G. Hutton
1968	*Coogan's Bluff*	Don Siegel
1968	*Bullitt*	Peter Yates
1968	*The Brotherhood*	Martin Ritt
1968	*Hell in the Pacific*	John Boorman
1969	*Che!*	Richard Fleischer
1969	*Eye of the Cat*	David Lowell Rich
1969	*Mission Impossible versus the Mob*	Paul Stanley
1970	*Pussycat, Pussycat, I Love You*	Rod Amateau
1970	*Kelly's Heroes*	Brian G. Hutton (Yugoslavia/USA)
1970	*WUSA*	Stuart Rosenberg
1970	*Imago*	Ned Bosnick
1970	*I Love My Wife*	Mel Stuart
1971	*THX 1138*	George Lucas
1971	*Mrs. Pollifax—Spy*	Leslie H. Martinson
1971	*The Beguiled*	Don Siegel
1971	*Pretty Maids All in a Row*	Roger Vadim
1971	*The Christian Licorice Store*	James Frawley
1971	*Dirty Harry*	Don Siegel
1972	*Prime Cut*	Michael Ritchie
1972	*The Wrath of God*	Ralph Nelson
1972	*Joe Kid*	John Sturges
1972	*Rage*	George C. Scott
1973	*The Neptune Factor*	Daniel Petrie (Canada)
1973	*Enter the Dragon*	Robert Clouse (Hong Kong/USA)
1973	*Hit!*	Sidney J. Furie
1973	*Charley Varrick*	Don Siegel
1973	*Harry in Your Pocket*	Bruce Geller
1973	*Magnum Force*	Ted Post
1974	*Man on a Swing*	Frank Perry
1974	*Golden Needles*	Robert Clouse
1974	*The Four Musketeers: Milady's Revenge*	Richard Lester (Spain/Panama/UK)
1975	*The Master Gunfighter*	Frank Laughlin
1976	*Sky Riders*	Douglas Hickox
1976	*Special Delivery*	Paul Wendkos
1976	*St. Ives*	J. Lee Thompson
1976	*Voyage of the Damned* (AAN; GGN)	Stuart Rosenberg (UK)
1976	*The Eagle Has Landed*	John Sturges (UK)

Year	Film	Director
1977	Day of the Animals	William Girdler
1977	Rollercoaster	James Goldstone
1977	Telefon	Don Siegel
1978	Return from Witch Mountain	John Hough
1978	The Manitou	William Girdler (Canada/USA)
1978	Nunzio	Paul Williams
1978	The Cat from Outer Space	Norman Tokar
1979	Love and Bullets	Stuart Rosenberg, John Huston (UK)
1979	Escape to Athena	George P. Cosmatos (UK)
1979	Boulevard Nights	Michael Pressman
1979	The Amityville Horror (AAN; GGN)	Stuart Rosenberg
1979	The Concorde . . . Airport 79	David Lowell Rich
1980	When Time Ran Out . . .	James Goldstone (Canada/USA)
1980	Serial	Bill Persky
1980	The Nude Bomb	Clive Donner
1980	Brubaker	Stuart Rosenberg
1980	The Big Brawl	Robert Clouse (USA/Hong Kong)
1980	The Competition (AAN*; GGN)	Joel Oliansky
1981	Loophole	John Quested (UK)
1981	Caveman	Carl Gottlieb
1981	The Fridays of Eternity	Héctor Olivera (Argentina)
1981	La Pelle	Liliana Cavani (Italy/France)
1981	Buddy Buddy	Billy Wilder
1982	The Seduction	David Schmoeller
1982	A Stranger Is Watching	Sean S. Cunningham
1982	Fast-Walking	James B. Harris
1982	The Class of 1984	Mark L. Lester (Canada)
1982	Amityville II: The Possession	Damiano Damiani (Mexico/USA/Italy)
1983	The Sting II (AAN)	Jeremy Kagan
1983	Doctor Detroit	Michael Pressman
1983	The Osterman Weekend	Sam Peckinpah
1983	Sudden Impact	Clint Eastwood
1984	Tank	Marvin J. Chomsky
1985	The New Kids	Sean S. Cunningham
1985	The Mean Season	Phillip Borsos
1985	Bad Medicine	Harvey Miller
1986	Black Moon Rising	Harley Cokeliss
1986	The Ladies Club	Janet Greek
1987	The Fourth Protocol	John Mackenzie (UK)
1988	The Dead Pool	Buddy Van Horn
1988	Berlin Blues	Ricardo Franco (Spain)
1989	Return from the River Kwai	Andrew V. McLaglen (UK)
1993	The Beverly Hillbillies	Penelope Spheeris
1995	Manhattan Merengue!	Joseph B. Vasquez
1996	Scorpion Spring	Brian Cox
1997	Money Talks	Brett Ratner
1998	Something to Believe In	John Hough (UK/Germany)
1998	Tango	Carlos Saura (Spain/Argentina)
1998	Rush Hour	Brett Ratner
2001	Rush Hour 2	Brett Ratner (USA/Hong Kong)
2001	Longshot	Lionel C. Martin
2003	Bringing Down the House	Adam Shankman
2004	After the Sunset	Brett Ratner
2004	The Bridge of San Luis Rey	Mary McGuckian (UK/Spain/France)
2006	Abominable	Ryan Schifrin
2007	Rush Hour 3	Brett Ratner (USA/Germany)
2012	Love Story	Florian Habicht (New Zealand)
2014	Sweetwater	Martin Guigui

SCHUMANN, Walter (1913–1958) A busy music arranger and conductor for radio and movies, he only composed a handful of pieces in his too-short life but they include a famous television theme and a unique film score.

Born in New York City, Walter Schumann took piano lessons as a child, although he had no interest in music until he was a student at the University of Southern California. While he was studying for a law degree, Schumann started his own college band and was so successful he quit school and went professional. He arranged and conducted the music for Eddie Cantor's radio show and worked on several Andre Kostelanetz recordings before becoming the musical director of the Armed Forces Radio Service during World War II. After the war he went to Los Angeles where he found work arranging, conducting, and occasionally composing for films and early television. Schumann wrote the screen scores for four Abbott and Costello comedies in the late 1940s, but his Hollywood career was not flourishing so he concentrated on radio and television. When asked to come up with a theme song for a new police radio show called *Dragnet*, Schumann wrote the famous four-note opening, a musical phrase that is now one of the most recognized around the world. The theme was used in the 1951 television show *Dragnet*, the 1954 screen version, and later TV series in the 1960s and in 2003. Schumann won an Emmy Award for his *Dragnet* theme, the first awarded in television to a composer. Celebrated movie composer Miklós Rózsa sued Schumann, claiming he himself had used the same four notes in his score for the 1946 movie *The Killers*. The suit and Schumann's countersuit received a lot of publicity, and musicologists pointed out that the same four notes can be found in several pieces of classical music. The suit was settled out of court with both parties getting royalties from the *Dragnet* theme. In the mid-1950s, Schumann formed his own choral group, the Voices of Walter Schumann, which recorded several easy-listening albums, including an innovative musical piece titled *Exploring the Unknown*, for which Schumann composed some ahead-of-its-time space age music. He also composed the music for the opera *John Brown's Body* (1953) and wrote the music for and appeared in the Broadway revue *3 for Tonight* (1955). Schumann continued to arrange and conduct for television and composed the theme music for the popular series *Steve Canyon*.

His last movie credit was his most acclaimed: the score for the highly stylized movie *The Night of the Hunter*. In 1958 Schumann was admitted to the Mayo Clinic and underwent open-heart surgery, one of the first such operations performed in Minnesota. He survived the operation, but complications set in and he died at the age of forty-four. The Voices of Walter Schumann, who were being featured on Tennessee Ernie Ford's television show, continued on after their founder's death, some of their records still on the charts five years later.

Considering Schumann's traditional musical background, it is surprising that actor Charles Laughton chose him to score his very unconventional film *The Night of the Hunter*. (It was Laughton's first and only directing credit.) The movie is a dark drama about a psychotic preacher (Robert Mitchum) who murders a young widow then torments her two children (Sally Jane Bruce and Billy Chapin) in order to find where a cache of stolen money is hidden. The story is an allegory for good and evil, innocence and madness, and Laughton films it like a bizarre nightmare. Everything in the movie, from the acting to the lighting, is stylized to the point of artificiality and Schumann's score is no exception. The film opens with menacing deep chords that lead to a children's chorus singing the traditional "Dream, Little One, Dream." This lullaby returns throughout the movie, sometimes in a comforting manner, other times as a pathetic commentary on innocence. An original children's song by Schumann, "(Once Upon a Time There Was a) Pretty Fly" (lyric by Davis Grubb), is sung by echoing distorted children's voices as the two kids travel downriver to escape their demented tormentor. An old woman (Kitty White) is heard singing another Schumann lullaby (lyric by Grubb) as the children seek shelter in a barn, the strangeness of the music not providing the comfort or safety they need. The instrumental music in between these songs is sometimes bucolic, other times disturbing. Crickets and other sounds of nature are magnified in some scenes, overpowering the music. Like the movie itself, Schumann's music is odd and wondrous; a truly unique score for its or any other time. *The Night of the Hunter* was not a box office hit in 1955 but over the years has become a cult favorite. Appreciation for Schumann's music was too late in coming. But he will always be known as the man who wrote those four famous notes for *Dragnet*.

Credits

(all films USA)

Year	Film	Director
1947	*Buck Privates Come Home*	Charles Barton
1947	*The Wistful Widow of Wagon Gap*	Charles Barton
1948	*The Noose Hangs High*	Charles Barton
1949	*Africa Screams*	Charles Barton
1954	*Dragnet*	Jack Webb
1955	*The Night of the Hunter*	Charles Laughton, Robert Mitchum, Terry Sanders

SCOTT, John (b. 1930) A lesser-known but highly respected British musician, arranger, and composer who first found success with pop and jazz, he has scored many films and TV movies in both England and the States.

He was born Patrick John O'Hara Scott in Bristol, England, the son of a musician in the group Police Band, and studied violin and clarinet as a child. By the time he was fourteen, Scott was a boy musician in the Royal Artillery Band in Woolwich and was also performing on the saxophone and harp. He began his adult music career as a musician and arranger for the popular Ted Heath Orchestra, soon becoming an arranger and conductor for EMI Records where he worked with many recording stars, including the Beatles. (He was the featured flute soloist on the 1965 single "You've Got to Hide Your Love Away.") Scott also had two successful jazz groups of his own in the 1960s: the Johnny Scott Trio and the Johnny Scott Quintet. His first experience with the movies was as a musician for London recording sessions, and he was encouraged to pursue screen arranging and composing by Henry Mancini. After scoring some documentary shorts, Scott was hired in 1965 to write the music for the British Sherlock Holmes film *A Study in Terror*. He gained little recognition scoring some forgettable English films in the late 1960s, including two schlock thrillers, *Berserk* and *Trog*, starring a desperate Joan Crawford. Scott's new score for the 1920 silent *Dr. Jekyll and Mr. Hyde* received some compliments, but he was not roundly applauded until his music for the Australian movie *Wake in Fright*, which was released in the States as *Outback*.

Few composers have experienced such an up-and-down movie career as Scott. Just as he started building a reputation as an A-list composer, he was saddled with a series of movies that were critical and box office bombs.

Yet his European successes, such as *England Made Me* and *Antony and Cleopatra*, caught the attention of Hollywood and by the 1970s he was working on both sides of the Atlantic. Again his career was plagued with many dreadful misfires, so rarely was Scott offered first-class projects. All the same, he was able to be linked with a well-received movie on occasion, works as varied as *North Dallas Forty*, *The Shooting Party*, *The Final Countdown*, *Winter People*, and *Greystoke: The Legend of Tarzan, Lord of the Apes*. Scott has been luckier scoring many feature documentaries (including some memorable ones by Jacques Cousteau), TV movies and programs, and miniseries both in Great Britain and in the States. Although Scott has scored over one hundred film and television features, much of his career has been outside of the media. In addition to composing two symphonies, a ballet, an opera, and small instrumental pieces, he has enjoyed a busy career as a conductor. Scott has conducted his own work and music by others with leading symphonies around the world. He founded the Hollywood Symphony Orchestra in 2006 and has run his own record company, JOS Records, since 1989.

If Scott has too few hits to his credit, it is not because the scores are lacking. He has written so much commendable music for the screen that it is easy to see why he is so respected by the film community. While a superior score cannot save a weak movie, it is possible for audiences and critics to respond to fine music during an unsatisfactory moviegoing experience. The more one looks at Scott's films, hits and misses, the more one appreciates his talent. His first score, for the Sherlock Holmes thriller *A Study in Terror*, sounds like the work of a veteran. A solo violin overrides the orchestra to suggest not only Holmes's love of the instrument but to express the chilly and aloof aspect of his personality. Another early score, that for the Shakespeare adaptation *Antony and Cleopatra*, surprises one by avoiding the Roman bombast and instead takes its cue from the exotic Egyptian setting and the central romance. Sometimes a full orchestra is used, other times a solo string instrument suffices. There is a quixotic quality to the sonorous main theme in *England Made Me*, a drama about English citizens in Germany between the two world wars. The waltz seems to doubt itself, giving the listener an unsettling feeling. The European thriller *Man on Fire* has some resplendent sections that recall the romantic soundtracks of the 1940s. The movie itself may be about kidnapping and revenge but the music is often restlessly passionate and frequently crescendos appear unapologetically. Similarly, the action picture *Lionheart* has a soundtrack that throbs rhythmically but usually retains a flowing romantic theme. The lyrical score for the IRA drama *Hennessy* has some melodious passages despite its tale about a plot to assassinate the Queen. Scott got to score too few comedies. Perhaps his most popular was the football flick *North Dallas Forty*, which boasts a jazzy main theme that borders on the funky.

The majestic score for the fantasy-war film *The Final Countdown* has an epic quality to it. There are stirring marches, expansive passages denoting valor and excitement, and a furious theme for battle that recalls a flight of angry bees. A similar majesty can be found in Scott's score for the adventure film *The Boy from Wolf Mountain*, also titled *The Time of the Wolf*. The main theme suggests the vastness of the wilderness even as it denotes loneliness and a morose acceptance of nature. The Edwardian period piece *The Shooting Party* is a quiet film about the passing of an era, and Scott's score contains all the elegance and melancholy of the tale. Often the music under the scenes seems to be coming from the next room, as if this was an era in which there was always music around you. Perhaps Scott's finest screen score is that for *Greystoke*. Unlike most Tarzan films, much of this version takes place in England, so the soundtrack has its bucolic sections for the jungle and lovely Victorian melodies for civilization. There are no African tribal drums in this version but instead a lilting theme for the innocence of nature and a sweeping waltz for the fussy England of Queen Victoria. The lush and lyrical passages in *Greystoke* make one wonder what Scott might have done for movie music if he had been handed more high-quality projects such as this one. Official site: www.josrecords.com.

Credits

(all films UK unless stated otherwise)

Year	Film	Director
1965	*A Study in Terror*	James Hill
1966	*Carnaby, M.D.* (aka *Doctor in Clover*)	Ralph Thomas
1967	*The Hunch*	Sarah Erulkar
1967	*Those Fantastic Flying Fools* (aka *Rocket to the Moon*)	Don Sharp
1967	*The Violent Enemy*	Don Sharp
1967	*The Million Eyes of Su-Muru*	Lindsay Shonteff
1967	*Cop-Out*	Pierre Rouve
1967	*The Long Duel*	Ken Annakin
1967	*Berserk*	Jim O'Connolly
1968	*Her Private Hell*	Norman J. Warren
1968	*Loving Feeling*	Norman J. Warren
1969	*Sophie's Place* (aka *Crooks & Coronets*)	Jim O'Connolly
1970	*Lola* (aka *Twinky*)	Richard Donner (Italy/UK)
1970	*Amsterdam Affair*	Gerry O'Hara
1970	*Trog*	Freddie Francis
1970	*Lisa's Folly*	John Alderman (USA)
1971	*Dr. Jekyll and Mr. Hyde* (1920)	Robert S. Robertson (USA)
1971	*Girl Stroke Boy*	Bob Kellett
1971	*Wake in Fright* (aka *Outback*)	Ted Kotcheff (Australia/USA)
1972	*The Jerusalem File*	John Flynn (Israel/USA)

Year	Film	Director
1972	Doomwatch	Peter Sasdy
1972	Antony and Cleopatra	Charlton Heston (UK/Spain)
1973	Hexen Geschändet und zu Tode gequält	Adrian Hoven (W. Germany/UK)
1973	England Made Me	Peter Duffell (Yugoslavia/UK)
1974	Billy Two Hats	Ted Kotcheff (USA)
1974	Craze	Freddie Francis
1974	Symptoms	José Ramón Larraz (UK/Belgium)
1974	S*P*Y*S	Irvin Kershner (USA)
1974	Penny Gold	Jack Cardiff
1975	Hennessy	Don Sharp
1975	That Lucky Touch	Christopher Miles (UK/W. Germany)
1976	Evil Heritage (aka Satan's Slave)	Norman J. Warren
1977	The People That Time Forgot	Kevin Connor
1978	Bloody Ivory	Simon Trevor
1979	North Dallas Forty	Ted Kotcheff (USA)
1980	The Final Countdown	Don Taylor (USA)
1981	Clipperton: The Island Time Forgot	Jacques-Yves Cousteau (France/USA)
1981	Horror Planet	Norman J. Warren
1982	Du grand large aux Grands Lacs	Jacques-Yves Cousteau (Canada/France)
1983	To the Ends of the Earth	William Kronick
1983	Yor, the Hunter from the Future	Antonio Margheriti (Italy/Turkey)
1984	Greystoke: The Legend of Tarzan, Lord of the Apes	Hugh Hudson (UK/USA)
1985	The Shooting Party	Alan Bridges
1986	Jacques Cousteau: The First 75 Years	John Soh (USA)
1986	The Whistle Blower	Simon Langton
1986	King Kong Lives	John Guillermin (USA)
1987	Man on Fire	Élie Chouraqui (France/Italy)
1988	Shoot to Kill	Roger Spottiswoode (USA)
1988	Dog Tags	Romano Scavolini (USA)
1988	The Deceivers	Nicholas Meyer (India/UK)
1989	Winter People	Ted Kotcheff (USA)
1989	Black Rainbow	Mike Hodges
1990	Lionheart	Sheldon Lettich (USA)
1990	King of the Wind	Peter Duffell
1991	Journey of Honor	Gordon Hessler (Japan/USA/UK)
1991	Becoming Colette	Danny Huston (Germany/UK/France)
1992	Homeboys	Lindsay Norgard (USA)
1992	Ruby	John Mackenzie (UK/USA/Japan)
1993	Der Fall Lucona	Jack Gold (Germany)
1995	Far from Home: The Adventures of Yellow Dog	Phillip Boros (USA)
1996	The North Star	Nils Gaup (France/UK/Norway)
1997	Walking Thunder	Craig Clyde (USA)
1997	The Second Jungle Book	Dee McLachlan (USA)
1997	Robin Hood (1922)	Allan Dwan (USA)
1998	The Scarlet Tunic	Stuart St. Paul
1998	The New Swiss Family Robinson	Stewart Raffill (USA)
1999	The Long Road Home	Craig Clyde (USA)
1999	Shergar	Dennis C. Lewiston (UK/USA)
2000	Married 2 Malcolm	James Cellan Jones (UK/Germany)
2002	The Boy from Wolf Mountain (aka Time of the Wolf)	Rod Pridy (Germany/Canada)
2003	Whales of Atlantis: In Search of Moby Dick	Jean-Chrisophe Jeauffre (France)
2003	Expédition Jules Verne	Jean-Christophe Jeauffre (France)
2003	Small Cuts (aka Petites Coupures)	Pascal Bonitzer (France/UK)
2011	The Wicker Tree	Robin Hardy

SHAIMAN, Marc (b. 1959) A major multihyphenate in movies, television, theatre, and the record business, the songwriter-arranger-performer-composer has scored forty feature films and worked behind the scenes on dozens of others.

Born in Scotch Plains, New Jersey, Marc Shaiman played the piano as a child, and was interested in all kinds of popular music. Shaiman began his career as a pianist and arranger for cabaret acts and then teamed up with singer Bette Midler, acting as her vocal coach, arranger, and sometime producer for her recordings, concerts, and 1980 Broadway show. He also served as musical director or vocal arranger for the Broadway musicals *Up in One* (1979), *Haarlem Nocturne* (1984), and *Leader of the Pack* (1985). Shaiman was soon in demand for supervising the music for television shows and specials, concerts, special events, nightclubs and cabarets, and recordings. In 1979 Shaiman and lyricist Scott Wittman met while working on an Off-Broadway show and became life and professional partners. The two artists wrote songs for television and various artists before finding Broadway success with their musical *Hairspray* in 2002. Shaiman appeared in and wrote songs for the satirical Broadway revue *Martin Short: Fame Becomes Me* (2006), then he and Wittman scored the Broadway musical *Catch Me If You Can* (2011) and the London musical *Charlie and the Chocolate Factory* (2013). Shaiman's movie career began when he arranged the music for the Bette Midler comedy *Big Business* in 1988. Two years later he scored his first feature film, the thriller *Misery*. Director Rob Reiner knew Shaiman from his recurring role as pianist Skip St. Thomas on TV's *Saturday Night Live* and was impressed enough to hire him for such a serious movie when most of Shaiman's work had been in satirical comedy. Reiner and Shaiman have since collaborated on eleven other films, most memorably *A Few Good Men*, *The American President*, *Ghosts of Mississippi*, *The Bucket List*, *Flipped*, and *The Magic of Belle Isle*. Shaiman has also worked with actor-director-writer Billy Crystal on many projects, including the movies *City Slickers*, *Mr. Saturday Night*, *Forget Paris*, and *My Giant*. Among the other notable films scored by Shaiman are *The Addams Family* and its sequel, *Sleepless in Seattle*, *Mother*, *The First Wives Club*, *In and Out*, *Simon Birch*, *Patch Adams*, *South Park: Big-*

ger, Longer & Uncut, and *Hairspray*. Shaiman has also written for television, most memorably the songs he and Wittman wrote for the series *Smash*.

Because Shaiman's theatre work is mostly musical comedy, one is not surprised to find his screen scores for comedies so delightful. What is surprising is the depth and rich nature of his music for so-called serious films. There is a daffy, sarcastic tone to the comedy scores. The others are in the style of Aaron Copland with full-bodied pieces of Americana. The comedy *City Slickers* actually has a touch of both. This somewhat predictable but still enjoyable romp is about some middle-aged Manhattan office workers who join a cattle drive in the Southwest. The main musical theme is a bucolic piece with piano, strings, and woodwinds tripping along with a tranquil and contented tone. There is also a graceful passage on guitar and woodwinds that is warm and comfortable. More mocking is a robust cowboy theme, with blaring trumpets and vigorous percussion, that moves at a gallop as it pastiches the virile western music from the past. (The score also includes passages from the TV theme songs for *Bonanza* and *Rawhide*.) The comedy in the movie is supported by a silly theme with giggling clarinets, eccentric piano, farcical harmonica, and slaphappy percussion. Also funny is a raucous hoedown passage with a gospel-rock-soul orchestration and ridiculous chanting. The highly stylized comedy *The Addams Family*, inspired by the popular television sitcom and Charles Addams's bizarre cartoons, opens with Vic Mizzy's famous finger-snapping theme from the small screen then Shaiman takes over and provides a deliciously satiric score. The recurring waltz theme, played first on strings and gentle percussion that has a few comic flourishes on the harpsichord, is heard in different formats throughout the movie, from a sleek violin solo to a frenzied tango played on klezmer instruments. There is another cock-eyed waltz with a heavy beat that seems more oppressive than joyous and Shaiman wrote the tune for an incongruous Cossack song and dance titled "Mamushka" (lyric by Betty Comden and Adolph Green). *The First Wives Club*, a comedy with an edge to it, concerns three divorcees (Goldie Hawn, Diane Keaton, and Bette Midler) who take revenge on their ex-husbands, who all left them for younger women. Shaiman's main theme is a comic tour de force. It is cartoonish chase music on swirling strings, cockeyed brass, and bouncing woodwinds that rushes ahead like a speeded-up parade to a symphonic climax. *George of the Jungle*, a live-action farce based on a children's television cartoon show, is broad and obvious, but the score is sly and wild. Shaiman uses some Spike Jonze techniques in his music, tossing in all kinds of crashing and buffoonish sound effects, and scores the oafish George (Brendan Fraser) and his jungle misadventures with vaudeville-like tunes and merry swing band music.

Shaiman takes a very different approach to scoring his comedy-dramas, musicalizing the sincere and emotional elements in the story rather than the humorous ones. *The American President* is about the difficult romance between a widower, who happens to be the president of the United States (Michael Douglas), and an environmental activist (Annette Bening). This is perhaps Shaiman's most Coplandesque score with a mixture of symphonic celebration and intimate, rural folk music. The stately main theme has a full orchestra overflowing with warmth rather than pomp. Woodwinds are featured in a slow and elegant passage that rolls along with dignity, and there is a vivacious theme with furious strings against slow sustained woodwinds. The love theme is a delicate passage on piano that is tentative at first, but when strings are added it comes to life. *The American President* may be an uneven movie and not quite the piece of Americana it aims for but the music certainly is. *Patch Adams*, a sentimental comedy-drama about a med student (Robin Williams) who upsets the status quo by using humor in his treatment of patients, is not for all tastes, but Shaiman's score is first rate and, even better, far from saccharine. The main theme is a fragile piano solo that has a classical tone until strings and oboe are added and it gets more emotional and contemporary sounding. There is also a lullaby-like passage on piano and orchestra that is simple and childlike but enticing; a poignant theme on restrained instruments that is so cautious that it seems to stop and then find the will to continue on; and a sprightly track that moves ahead happily but in control as strings provide the energy and woodwinds the melody. Equally as accomplished is the score Shaiman wrote for a better comedy-drama *The Bucket List*. This bittersweet tale, about two very different men (Morgan Freeman and Jack

Nicholson) dying of cancer who set out together on a road trip to do those "before-you-die" things on their list, has a similarly bittersweet score. The main theme is a piano and solo trumpet passage with subdued strings that moves forward steadily but never departs from its major musical phrase. There is also a tentative piano lament that is filled with remorse until a solo trumpet is added and it finds a melody that gives it life. Shaiman was also the pianist on the soundtrack of this lovely, subtle score.

Of the dramas-without-comedy that Shaiman scored, two stand out. The disturbing thriller *Misery*, one of the best of the many adaptations of Stephen King books, was Shaiman's first feature score but it has none of the signs of the beginner. A celebrated novelist (James Caan) is rescued from a car crash by an obsessed fan (Kathy Bates) who proceeds to imprison and then torture him. This King story has no supernatural elements and director Reiner creates a realistic setting that is all the more creepy for being so. Shaiman's main theme is disarmingly dulcet, featuring a harmonious oboe and piano. The piece is surprisingly soothing even though it is in a minor key and filled with dissonance. As the tension in the movie builds, the score utilizes bass strings against high violins crying out as they ascend the scale. Also suspenseful is a forceful theme with racing strings and heavy percussion, and a passage with pizzicato strings and floating woodwinds that is spirited but frightened all the same. Reiner also directed *A Few Good Men*, a solid adaptation of Aaron Sorkin's stage drama. A young military lawyer (Tom Cruise) doesn't take his job very seriously until he investigates the murder of a young Hispanic Marine and the unspoken system that killed him. The recurring musical theme is a quietly disturbing concerto with questioning reeds, a wailing trumpet solo, and sustained strings. Also effective is a piano and woodwinds passage that overrides an undercurrent of danger in the strings and percussion. When the suspense becomes unbearable, Shaiman uses strident notes on an electric keyboard while bass instruments growl and the percussion delivers gunshot-like blasts. Written only two years after *Misery*, the score for *A Few Good Men* was Shaiman's first for a realistic drama. Yet it has the confidence and maturity of a veteran. One might say that about all of his screen scores.

Credits

(all films USA unless stated otherwise; * for Best Song)

Year	Film	Director
1990	*Misery*	Rob Reiner
1991	*Scenes from a Mall*	Paul Mazursky
1991	*City Slickers*	Ron Underwood
1991	*The Addams Family*	Barry Sonnenfeld
1992	*Sister Act*	Emile Ardolino
1992	*Mr. Saturday Night*	Billy Crystal
1992	*A Few Good Men*	Rob Reiner
1993	*Sleepless in Seattle* (AAN*)	Nora Ephron
1993	*Heart and Souls*	Ron Underwood
1993	*Addams Family Values*	Barry Sonnenfeld
1994	*City Slickers II: The Legend of Curly's Gold*	Paul Weiland
1994	*North*	Rob Reiner
1994	*Speechless*	Ron Underwood
1995	*Stuart Saves His Family*	Harold Ramis
1995	*Forget Paris*	Billy Crystal
1995	*The American President* (AAN)	Rob Reiner
1996	*Bogus*	Norman Jewison
1996	*Mother*	Albert Brooks
1996	*The First Wives Club* (AAN)	Hugh Wilson
1996	*Ghosts of Mississippi*	Rob Reiner
1997	*George of the Jungle*	Sam Weisman
1997	*In & Out*	Frank Oz
1998	*My Giant*	Michael Lehmann
1998	*Simon Birch* (aka *A Prayer for Owen Meany*)	Mark Steven Johnson
1998	*Patch Adams* (AAN)	Tom Shadyac
1999	*The Out-of-Towners*	Sam Weisman
1999	*South Park: Bigger, Longer & Uncut* (AAN*)	Trey Parker
1999	*The Story of Us*	Rob Reiner
2000	*The Kid*	Jon Turteltaub
2001	*One Night at McCool's*	Harald Zwart
2003	*Down with Love*	Peyton Reed (USA/Germany)
2003	*Alex & Emma*	Rob Reiner
2005	*Rumor Has It . . .* (aka *Otherwise Engaged*)	Rob Reiner (USA/Germany)
2007	*Hairspray*	Adam Shankman (USA/UK)
2007	*The Bucket List*	Rob Reiner
2010	*Flipped*	Rob Reiner
2012	*The Magic of Belle Isle*	Rob Reiner
2012	*Parental Guidance* (aka *Us & Them*)	Andy Fickman
2014	*And So It Goes*	Rob Reiner

SHIRE, David (b. 1937) A prolific composer and arranger for television, he has also scored stage musicals and forty-two feature films. Because he has had few hits in all three media, he is far from a household name but in the business Shire is widely respected and admired.

Born David Lee Shire in Buffalo, New York, the son of a local bandleader who also gave piano lessons, he studied English and music at Yale, where he met and teamed up with writer-director Richard Maltby jr. They wrote some school musicals together, beginning a collaboration that would last over forty-five years. While still a student, Shire played piano in a jazz band then attended Brandeis University briefly before serving in the National Guard. In 1960 he and Maltby went to New York City together to write musicals and their revue *The Sap of Life* was presented Off-Broadway the next year. To earn a living, Shire worked as a rehearsal and pit band pianist in the theatre, but he found better jobs in television, where he started composing theme songs and background music for different series. In 1971 he scored his first TV movie, *Harpy*, and his first feature film, *Summertree*. Recognition didn't come until three years later with his haunting score for *The Conversation* directed by Francis Ford Coppola. (At the time Shire was married to Coppola's sister, Talia Shire.)

Shire's film career has been filled with forgettable movies, but he did score such successful pictures as *The Taking of Pelham One Two Three*, *Saturday Night Fever*, *All the President's Men*, *Norma Rae*, *The Promise*, and *Zodiac*. Yet there is much to admire in his scores for such box office failures as *The Hindenburg*, *The Big Bus*, *Return to Oz*, and *Farewell, My Lovely*. Shire's few awards have been for songs rather than scores. "I'll Never Say Goodbye" (lyric by Marilyn and Alan Bergman) from *The Promise* was nominated for an Academy Award and "It Goes Like It Goes" (lyric by Norman Gimbel) from *Norma Rae* won the Oscar. He has also had a handful of nonmovie song hits over the years, most memorably "With You I'm Born Again," "Washington Square," "What about Today," and "Starting Here, Starting Now." Shire is also known as an expert arranger and conductor. The disco songs in *Saturday Night Fever* were by the Bee Gees but it was Shire's original music and his disco arrangements such as "Night on Disco Mountain" and "Manhattan Skyline" that helped propel that popular movie. Most of Shire's career has been in television. He has scored seventy-six TV movies and miniseries, among them *Killer Bees* (1974), *Amelia Earhart* (1976), *Raid on Entebbe* (1976), *Mayflower Madam* (1987), *The Women of Brewster Place* (1989), *The Kennedys of Massachusetts* (1990), *Sarah, Plain and Tall* (1991), *The Heidi Chronicles* (1995), *Streets of Laredo* (1995), and *Rear Window* (1998). Shire has also scored several television series, including *The Virginian*, *McCloud*, *Tales of the Unexpected*, *Alice*, *Sarge*, *Shining Time Station*, and *Amazing Stories*. His stage credits are few but highly respected, never having found a runaway hit in the theatre. The Off-Broadway revues *Starting Here, Starting Now* (1977) and *Closer Than Ever* (1989) were well received, but his Broadway efforts *Baby* (1983) and *Big* (1996) failed to run very long despite superior scores. All were written with librettist-director Maltby. The team's most recent stage effort is the provocative *Take Flight* (2007).

Shire's music can be described as more subtle than most film composers' work. He avoids musical clichés or predictable musical phrases. In many cases his music is best appreciated on second and subsequent hearings. For this reason, his movie scores are not as well known to the public as they should be. Yet even the most casual moviegoer was struck by the mournful solo piano in *The Conversation*, even if one did not notice how the piano recordings were sometimes distorted or electronically altered to give the movie a paranoia flavor. His score for *The Taking of Pelham One Two Three* uses both jazz and rock to illustrate the pulse and temperament of New York City. More subtle is the score for *All the President's Men* with music that suggests mystery and an urban ennui. *Farewell, My Lovely* has a bluesy noir feeling to it while the gleeful clarinet in *Max Dugan Returns* is both comic and frantic. For *One Night Stand*, he used a female chorus with an arrangement of synthesizers, cello, flute, oboe, and guitar to achieve a unique chamber ensemble-like sound. Shire's most overlooked score is that for the poorly received *Return to Oz*. He composed various themes for the different fantasy characters, each one an evocative piece that stands on its own yet seems a part of the whole. Shire's busy career includes conducting his and other composers' work in concert halls and in recording studios and he is a favorite arranger for pop singers, such as Barbra Streisand, Melissa Manchester, and John Pizzarelli. Without becoming a well-known name, Shire's music has been heard and enjoyed by millions in different media. Official website: www.davidshiremusic.com.

Credits

(all films USA unless stated otherwise; * for Best Song)

Year	Film	Director
1971	*Summertree*	Anthony Newley
1971	*Drive, He Said*	Jack Nicholson
1971	*Skin Game*	Paul Bogart

Year	Film	Director
1972	To Find a Man	Buzz Kulik
1973	Steelyard Blues	Alan Myerson
1973	Two People	Robert Wise
1973	Class of '44	Paul Bogart
1973	Showdown	George Seaton
1974	The Conversation	Francis Ford Coppola
1974	The Taking of Pelham One Two Three (BAFTA-N)	Joseph Sargent
1975	The Fortune	Mike Nichols
1975	Farewell, My Lovely	Dick Richards
1975	The Hindenburg	Robert Wise
1976	All the President's Men	Alan J. Pakula
1976	Harry and Walter Go to New York	Mark Rydell
1976	The Big Bus	James Frawley
1978	Straight Time	Ulu Grosbard
1979	Fast Break	Jack Smight
1979	Norma Rae (AA*)	Martin Ritt
1979	The Promise (AAN*)	Gilbert Cates
1979	Old Boyfriends	Joan Tewkesbury
1981	The Night the Lights Went Out in Georgia	Ronald F. Maxwell
1981	Only When I Laugh	Glenn Jordan
1981	Paternity	David Steinberg
1982	The World according to Garp	George Roy Hill
1983	Max Dugan Returns	Herbert Ross
1984	Oh, God! You Devil!	Paul Bogart
1984	2010	Peter Hyams
1985	Return to Oz	Walter Murch (UK/USA)
1986	Short Circuit	John Badham
1986	'Night, Mother	Tom Moore
1988	Vice Versa	Brian Gilbert
1988	Backfire	Gilbert Cates (USA/Canada)
1988	Monkey Shines	George A. Romano
1991	Paris Trout	Stephen Gyllenhaal
1991	Bed & Breakfast	Robert Ellis Miller
1994	The Journey Inside	Barnaby Jackson
1995	One Night Stand	Talia Shire
2002	Ash Wednesday	Edward Burns
2004	The Tollbooth	Debra Kirschner
2007	Zodiac	David Fincher
2009	Beyond a Reasonable Doubt	Peter Hyams

SHORE, Howard (b. 1946) A much-in-demand Canadian composer, conductor, and orchestrator, he has scored a variety of movies and television programs but is most known for his unconventional films with director David Cronenberg and for Peter Jackson's *Lord of the Rings* movies.

He was born Howard Leslie Shore in Toronto and took saxophone lessons as a child. Attending summer camp as a teenager, he befriended Lorne Michaels and the two wrote and presented musical productions and improv sketches. Shore was educated at the Berklee School of Music in Boston and then began his career playing saxophone for the rock group Lighthouse which toured extensively for four years. He moved away from performing and turned to arranging and composing when he was hired by the Canadian Broadcasting Company (CBC) to score various programs. Shore's screen career began when he wrote music for nature documentaries shown at national parks centers across Canada. He left Canada in 1975 when Michaels hired him to arrange, compose, and conduct the music for his new NBC-TV show *Saturday Night Live*. Shore remained with the popular program for six years, during which time he began scoring Canadian movies. He worked with director Cronenberg for the first time on

The Brood in 1979 but it was the success of their *Scanners* two years later that brought wide recognition to both director and composer. The two have gone on to work together on thirteen subsequent movies to date, among them *The Fly*, *Dead Ringers*, *M. Butterfly*, *A History of Violence*, *Eastern Promises*, *Crash*, *A Dangerous Method*, and *Cosmopolis*. By the mid-1980s, Shore was a major composer in Hollywood, working with a variety of directors and scoring such notable movies as *Big*, *The Silence of the Lambs*, *Prelude to a Kiss*, *Philadelphia*, *Mrs. Doubtfire*, *Ed Wood*, *Nobody's Fool*, *The Truth About Cats and Dogs*, *That Thing You Do!*, *Doubt*, *The Twilight Saga: Eclipse*, *Gangs of New York*, *The Departed*, *The Aviator*, and *Hugo* (the last four with director Martin Scorsese). All of these were somewhat eclipsed when Shore was hired by New Zealand director Peter Jackson to score his acclaimed *The Lord of the Rings* trilogy, followed by *The Hobbit* trilogy. Shore has also composed for the concert hall. His opera *The Fly*, with a new score divorced from his screen music, premiered in Paris in 2008, and other orchestral works have been presented around the world. Shore has also contributed music to television shows, video games, and radio documentaries. He is a well-respected conductor who has presented concerts of his own music as well as others' with leading orchestras in the States and Europe.

Because of his background in rock music, it is not surprising that his early screen scores have a very contemporary sound. *Scanners* opens with ominous chords in the Gothic horror tradition, then the synthesizer takes over and the tone is very modern and high tech. Yet even this slick approach has its warm side, as when the theme becomes a waltz played on electronic strings. Another theme mixes synthesizer music with a clarinet solo while one passage employs electric static, various percussion instruments, and high-frequency sound effects. For its variety and its innovative use of the synthesizer, *Scanners* boldly introduces a new major screen composer. *The Fly*, another early Shore score, has a full orchestral sound. The opening theme is robust and lush, strings and woodwinds alternating in presenting both fanfares and reflective sections. One passage is a series of crescendos to heighten suspense while a later theme is rather lyrical and in the romantic style. Shore's first major Hollywood project was the comedy-fantasy *Big* and he provided a conventional but pleasing score. The opening theme is breezy with a touch of jazz as piano and guitar are featured. The myste-

rious music heard when the young Josh (David Moscow) becomes grown-up Josh (Tom Hanks) is charming and playful rather than oppressive. With its carnival-like feeling, this sci-fi music might be considered the diametrical opposite of the sounds of *Scanners*. Shore's love of classic rock and roll can be heard in other parts of *Big* but mostly this is a traditional romantic comedy score and a very accomplished one at that. The same can be said for his music for *Silence of the Lambs* which is a superb example of a thriller score. There is nothing supernatural about this disturbing tale of a brilliant, cannibalistic criminal (Anthony Hopkins) so Shore uses a conventional orchestra with wavering strings and a repetitive bass line heard in the brass section. The main theme is a flowing piece of romanticism with an ominous tone. The music for the female agent (Jodie Foster) who hopes to use the demented criminal is more graceful, yet it too is unsettling as horns repeat a questioning musical phrase. Only in the climactic scene in the cellar does Shore rely on some electronic sounds, with reverberating notes and rumbling chords. All the same this is a long way from the explosive sounds of *Scanners*, just as Jonathan Demme's movie is so different from Cronenberg's.

Tim Burton's biopic *Ed Wood* has a peculiar tone: affectionate and satiric. Shore's score for this salute to the master of bad movies (played by Johnny Depp) pastiches the music from such low-budget camp classics. He uses the theremin on occasion, mocking the sci-fi sound of the 1950s. There is also jazz played on bongos and muted brass, a mock march for Wood's unflagging optimism, and a European-style gypsy theme for Bela Lugosi (Martin Landau). There is even a warm and engaging theme, "This Is the One," that slowly builds as strings climb the scale and horns follow. Another biopic about a film director is Martin Scorsese's *Hugo* about the silent screen innovator Georges Méliès (Ben Kingsley). The story is told from the point of view of a young urchin (Asa Butterfield) who lives in a somewhat surreal train station in France, and often the score sounds like we are in some kind of time-warp circus. The main theme is mysterious but friendly. The magic in this movie is ingratiating and the fable enfolds with warm and intoxicating music. There is some French café music in the score, the accordion playing against strident strings, while other passages are minimalist in the flavor of Philip Glass, as with some musical phrases that are repeated until they take on a mantra. These two highly stylized films are contrasted by two very down-to-earth, realistic movies, *Philadelphia* and *Nobody's Fool*. The first is a social drama about a lawyer (Tom Hanks) suffering from AIDS and looking for justice as well as hope. Bruce Springsteen's popular song "Streets of Philadelphia" is among the half dozen songs heard on the soundtrack but Shore's moving incidental music between these numbers conveys the true heart of the story. A melancholy but not morose theme with strings and a solo trumpet is quite moving, particularly in the way it avoids sentiment. Lighter but just as incisive is Robert Benton's *Nobody's Fool* about an aging construction worker (Paul Newman) and his seriocomic relationships with others in his small upstate New York town during one winter. The main theme is a delectable piece involving wooden flute, guitar, and clarinet. It is a reflective piece with a brisk tempo and a sense of casual freedom. Another passage is a tentative passage that seems to wander yet moves ahead with some delicious musical surprises. Shore's entire score is filled with warmth, as contrasted with the chilly locale. *Nobody's Fool* is not gritty realism like *Philadelphia* and its truthful but playful tone is established by this superior score.

Just as putting J. R. R. Tolkien's trilogy *The Lord of the Rings* on-screen was a daunting enterprise, scoring the three movies was Shore's biggest challenge. Since director Peter Jackson saw the project as a grand mythological epic, Shore saw his job akin to Richard Wagner's scoring his Ring Cycle. As with the opera, Shore decided to use several motifs in order to characterize certain people and places but also to tie the long epic together musically. The main theme, used behind the explanation of the ring's history and at other points in the long story, is a minor-key piece built around nine notes that is solemn and forbidding, aided by a choir and some evocative horns. The motif for the Shire where the Hobbits live is a major-key folk song played on pipes, conveying domestic happiness in the form of a merry dance. This motif returns at different points to remind the adventurers and the audience of the kind of life they are trying to preserve. The motif for the wizard Gandalf (Ian McKellan) is in a minor key as it suggests the destruction that must be stopped. The theme for the evil Lord Sauron (Sala Baker) is related to Gandalf's but with subtle differences that attempt to show how closely good and evil are linked in this tale. The theme for the Orcs is an oppressive march that also serves for their leader Saruman (Christopher Lee). As new characters and places are introduced over the course of the trilogy, Shore composes new motifs. Even more impressive is the way he uses these motifs, sometimes combining two in one passage, other time inverting the notes from one motif to create a different but related theme. It is estimated that the three *The Lord of the Rings* movies have around fifty motifs employing a wide range of orchestration. Such diverse instruments as the double-reed rhaita, dulcimer, pan flute, and Hardanger fiddle were played alongside the one-hundred-piece London Philharmonic Orchestra and large mixed and boys' choirs. The result is an exhilarating cinema music classic. Shore won three Oscars for the trilogy and solidified his reputation as one of the top composers of his era. Critical study: *The Music of The Lord of the Rings: A Comprehensive Account of Howard Shore's Scores*, Doug Adams (2010). Official website: www.howardshore.com.

Credits

(all films USA unless stated otherwise; * for Best Song)

Year	Film	Director
1978	*Drop Dead, Dearest* (aka *I Miss You, Hugs and Kisses*)	Murray Markowitz (Canada)
1979	*The Brood*	David Cronenberg (Canada)
1981	*Scanners*	David Cronenberg (Canada)
1983	*Videodrome*	David Cronenberg (Canada)
1984	*Nothing Lasts Forever*	Tom Schiller
1985	*After Hours* (aka *A Night in Soho*)	Martin Scorsese
1986	*Fire with Fire*	Duncan Gibbins
1986	*The Fly*	David Cronenberg (USA/UK/Canada)
1987	*Heaven*	Diane Keaton
1987	*Nadine*	Robert Benton

Year	Film	Director
1988	*Moving*	Alan Metter
1988	*Big*	Penny Marshall
1988	*Dead Ringers*	David Cronenberg (Canada/USA)
1989	*Signs of Life*	John David Coles
1989	*An Innocent Man*	Peter Yates
1989	*The Lemon Sisters*	Joyce Chopra
1989	*She-Devil*	Susan Seidelman
1990	*The Local Stigmatic*	David F. Wheeler
1991	*The Silence of the Lambs* (BAFTA-N)	Jonathan Demme
1991	*A Kiss before Dying*	James Dearden (UK/USA)
1991	*Naked Lunch*	David Cronenberg (Canada/UK/Japan)
1992	*Prelude to a Kiss*	Norman René
1992	*Single White Female*	Barbet Schroeder
1993	*Silver*	Phillip Noyce
1993	*Guilty as Sin*	Sidney Lumet
1993	*M. Butterfly*	David Cronenberg
1993	*Mrs. Doubtfire*	Chris Columbus
1993	*Philadelphia*	Jonathan Demme
1994	*The Client*	Joel Schumacher
1994	*Ed Wood*	Tim Burton
1994	*Nobody's Fool*	Robert Benton
1995	*Seven*	David Fincher
1995	*Moonlight and Valentino*	David Anspaugh (UK/USA)
1995	*White Man's Burden*	Desmond Nakano (France/USA)
1996	*Looking for Richard*	Al Pacino
1996	*Before and After*	Barbet Schroeder
1996	*The Truth about Cats and Dogs*	Michael Lehmann
1996	*Crash*	David Cronenberg (Canada/UK)
1996	*Striptease*	Andrew Bergman
1996	*That Thing You Do!*	Tom Hanks
1997	*Cop Land*	James Mangold
1997	*The Game*	David Fincher
1999	*Gloria*	Sidney Lumet
1999	*eXistenZ*	David Cronenberg (Canada/UK)
1999	*Analyze This*	Harold Ramis (USA/Australia)
1999	*Dogma* (aka *Bearclaw*)	Kevin Smith
2000	*High Fidelity*	Stephen Frears (UK/USA)
2000	*The Yards*	James Gray
2000	*Esther Kahn*	Arnaud Desplechin (France/UK)
2000	*The Cell*	Tarsem Singh (USA/Germany)
2001	*The Score*	Frank Oz (USA/Germany)
2001	*The Lord of the Rings: The Fellowship of the Ring* (AA; GGN; BAFTA-N)	Peter Jackson (N. Zealand/USA)
2002	*Panic Room* (aka *Safe Room*)	David Fincher
2002	*Spider*	David Cronenberg (Canada/UK)
2002	*The Lord of the Rings: The Two Towers*	Peter Jackson (USA/N. Zealand)
2002	*Gangs of New York* (BAFTA-N)	Martin Scorsese (USA/Italy)
2003	*The Lord of the Rings: The Return of the King* (AA; AA*; GG; GG*; BAFTA-N)	Peter Jackson (USA/N. Zealand)
2004	*The Aviator* (GG; BAFTA-N)	Martin Scorsese (USA/Germany)
2005	*A History of Violence*	David Cronenberg (USA/Germany)
2006	*The Departed*	Martin Scorsese (USA/Hong Kong)
2007	*The Last Mimzy*	Robert Shaye
2007	*Eastern Promises* (GGN)	David Cronenberg (USA/UK/Canada)
2008	*The Betrayal—Nerakhoon*	Ellen Kuras, Thavisouk Phrasavath
2008	*Doubt*	John Patrick Shanley
2010	*Edge of Darkness*	Martin Campbell (UK/USA)
2010	*The Twilight Saga: Eclipse*	David Slade

Year	Film	Director
2011	*A Dangerous Method*	David Cronenberg (UK/Germany/Canada/ Switzerland)
2011	*Hugo* (AAN; GGN; BAFTA-N)	Martin Scorsese
2012	*Cosmopolis*	David Cronenberg (Canada)
2012	*The Hobbit: An Unexpected Journey*	Peter Jackson (USA/N. Zealand)
2013	*Jimmy P.*	Arnaud Desplechin (France/USA)
2013	*The Hobbit: The Desolation of Smaug*	Peter Jackson (USA/N. Zealand)
2014	*The Hobbit: There and Back Again*	Peter Jackson (N. Zealand/USA)

SHOSTAKOVICH, Dmitri (1906–1975) The distinguished Russian pianist and composer of symphonies, sonatas, string quartets, opera, and ballet, he was directly involved with cinema perhaps more than any other "classical" composer of the twentieth century.

Dmitri Dmitrivevich Shostakovich was born in St. Petersburg, the son of a chemical engineer and a pianist mother who taught him music as a young child. Shostakovich studied at the St. Petersburg Conservatory, where he began composing, going on to write the controversial opera *Katerina Izmailova* (aka *Lady Makbeth of Mtsensk*) in 1934. Although the opera was a great success, it roused the displeasure of Stalin, and for the rest of his career Shostakovich had to balance his creative ambitions with a strict Soviet manifesto. During his prodigious career, he composed fifteen symphonies, many other instrumental pieces, ballets, and theatre music. Shostakovich's association with film began in his student days, when he earned money playing the piano in the silent movies houses in St. Petersburg. He was only twenty-two years old when he contributed to the music for the Sergei Eisenstein classic *October, or Ten Days That Shook the World*. Working with various Soviet directors, Shostakovich composed scores for over thirty Russian movies. His concert music can be heard in over sixty other international films as diverse as *Ice-Capades* (1941), *Rollerball* (1975), *Eyes Wide Shut* (1999), *Fantasia/2000*, and *Junebug* (2005).

Shostakovich's concert pieces are a bold mixture of classical forms and dissonant innovations. In many ways he was restricted by the Communist Party from experimenting with radical new music forms and his work is considered more conservative than many of his contemporaries. Yet he was a master of exciting orchestral compositions and vivid pieces for smaller ensembles. His film scores range from the grandiose, as in the passionate

The Defense of Volotchayevka, to the gentle, as with *The Young Guard*, to the disturbing, as with *Hamlet* and *King Lear*. Shostakovich even wrote the music for the lighthearted Russian musical curiosity *Cherry Town*. Because of Shostakovich's stature as a classical composer, most of his film music has been recorded by symphonies around the world. Yet as effective as the music is in the concert hall, it is in the context of the films that they were written for that the scores are best appreciated. For example, the music for the 1964 screen version of *Hamlet* is thrilling as an orchestral suite but as a movie score it is outstanding. The festive theme for the arrival of the traveling players is so spirited it seems to convey all the excitement of live theatre. It is a percussive piece that marches along, repeats some forceful phrases, and then continues on with panache. A ball at the palace is scored with an allegro passage on various strings that races along with a fury that is exhilarating and more than a little frenzied. The poisoning of the king and other quietly sinister scenes are scored with plucked strings and cautious horns that seem to tiptoe along. The climactic duel is accompanied by furious strings and horn fanfares in a minor key, both rising in intensity as they climb the scale. The music for the death of Hamlet (Innokently Smoktunovskiy) is not solemn or morose but instead a series of descending crescendos by full orchestra. The score for *King Lear* has less variety (as dictated by the play itself) but is nearly as accomplished as *Hamlet*. The opening music sets the tone for this bleakest of all tragedies: wailing woodwinds and abrupt brass lead into a flowing string passage with rumbling percussion. A solo piccolo is featured in a disarmingly minor-key lament that aches with sorrow, and there is a melancholy theme on strings and brass that seems confused and even dizzy as it grows in volume and intensity. The fierce storm that represents Lear (Jüri Järvet) losing his reason is scored with furious modern music with the strings screaming in one tempo but the brass and percussion pounding away in another. These two superb Shakespeare adaptations, both directed by Grigori Kozintsev, reveal Shostakovich at his most theatrical.

The first film scored by Shostakovich, Eisenstein's *October*, is a landmark in Russian cinema and some of its power can be attributed to the compelling score. The fall of the monarchy and the birth of the revolution in October of 1917 is told in a somewhat documentary style, but the music surges with emotion. The tone of World War I dragging on is set with a weary passage in which a march dwindles down to a string and reed passage that plods along with weight and remorse. There is a flighty waltz theme with lighthearted accents by strings and woodwinds that accelerates until it is frenzied and triumphant, a kind of dance of death for the aristocracy. This is contrasted by a delicate theme on woodwinds that has the flavor of a folk tune but the cadence of a march. The revolution breaks out with an anxious and optimistic passage that speeds up and gains weight until it turns into a victorious anthem. *The Fall of Berlin* is an actual documentary but again the music is far from dispassionate or objective. This powerful propaganda film, made from actual footage and released soon after the Russian army captured Berlin, features some of Shostakovich's most rousing music. The central theme consists of mighty brass fanfares, triumphant choral singing, and a stately but not too formal march as it climbs the scale for a bombastic climax. In contrast is a serene theme on woodwinds and strings with chime accents that seems to float along in total peace, especially during a lyrical clarinet solo. Similarly, there is a flowing string and reed track with female chanting that is hymnlike yet not so solemn. The actual attack is scored with a robust march that seems more joyous than aggressive.

Two lesser-known Soviet movies scored by Shostakovich deserve some attention. *Golden Mountains* can be described as a "proletarian" film, but its characters are as interesting as its politics. A naive youth (Boris Poslavsky) from the countryside goes to St. Petersburg in 1914 and gets hired as a scab during a strike at a metallurgy factory. The boy is used by the bosses to try to assassinate the Bolshevik strike leader (Ivan Shtraukh) but he eventually realizes that the strikers are in the right. Shostakovich's ardent main theme involves a full orchestra featuring vivid brass fanfares, the whole piece moving like a grandiose procession. The score also has a fugue on pipe organ that is lively and even playful as it bounces about like a fanciful baroque piece, and a funeral march on low woodwinds and plucked strings that creeps along in a disturbing way. The symphonic finale has a full orchestra marching up the scale with pomp, then tumbling down so it can build again to an explosive climax. *The Gadfly* has more variety in its score and one can see why this music has found popularity in concert halls around the world. The film is again political but the characters come across as more than symbols. In 1840s Italy, which is occupied by the Austrians, a romantic young man (Oleg Strizhenov) joins a youth movement, gets involved in a revolutionary crowd, experiences a tragic love affair, and matures into a socially aware citizen. The brilliant score's most famous theme is a romantic one: a poignant waltz on piano and violin that flows so seamlessly that it seems to be one long musical line. This passage became popular on its own and has been used in many movies and television programs, most memorably as the theme for the series *Reilly, Ace of Spies* (1983). Also smooth and engaging is an intermezzo track on strings and horns that moves reverently yet with a warmth that is enticing. On the livelier side are: a festival dance that is so exuberant that it seems out of control, a barrel organ waltz played on high woodwinds and merry strings that is elegant rather than earthy, and a galop (a merry dance with leaps at the end of each musical phrase) with slaphappy woodwinds, boastful brass, and vivacious strings all racing about with contagious glee. The score also includes a tender but doleful nocturne in which a solo violin is echoed by other strings. The march finale, featuring percussion and brass with high woodwind accents, is very determined, yet the piece takes a break at times and offers some slower and quieter passages before it continues on.

Shostakovich was fully involved in filmmaking and wrote about his belief that music was an essential part of the cinematic experience. His legacy was carried on by his son Maxim (b. 1938), a celebrated conductor, and his grandson Dmitri Maximovich Shostakovich Jr. (b. 1961?), a respected pianist. Memoir: *Testimony*, with Solomon Volkov (1979); biographies: *Shostakovich: A Life Remembered*, Elizabeth Wilson (revised 2006); *Shostakovich and His World*, Laurel Fay (2004).

Credits

(all films USSR)

Year	Film	Director
1928	October (Ten Days That Shook the World)	G. Aleksandrov, S. Eisenstein
1929	The New Babylon	G. Kozintsev, L. Trauberg
1931	Alone	G. Kozintsev, L. Trauberg
1931	Golden Mountains	Sergei Yutevich
1932	Shame	F. Ermler, S. Yutevich
1935	Love and Hate	A. Gendelshtein, P. Kolomytsev
1935	The Youth of Maxim	G. Kozintsev, L. Trauberg
1936	Three Women	Lev Arnshtam
1937	The Defense of Volotchayevka	G. Vasilyev, S. Vasilyev
1937	The Return of Maxim	G. Kozintsev, L. Trauberg
1938	Great Citizen	Fridrikh Ermler
1939	Friends	Lev Arnshtam
1939	The Man with the Gun	Sergei Yutkevich
1939	New Horizons	G. Kozintsev, L. Trauberg
1945	Simple People	G. Kozintsev, L. Trauberg
1945	Zoya	Lev Arnshtam
1945	The Fall of Berlin	Y. Raizman, Y. Svilova
1947	Pirogov (aka Professor Pirogov)	Grigori Kozintsev
1949	The Young Guard	Sergei Gerasimov
1949	Life in Bloom	Aleksandr Dovzhenko
1949	Meeting on the Elbe	G. Aleksandrov, A. Utkin
1950	The Fall of Berlin	Mikheil Chiaureli
1951	The Unforgettable Year 1919	Mikheil Chiaureli
1953	Belinskiy	Grigori Kozintsev
1956	The Gadfly	Aleksandr Faintsimmer
1957	The First Echelon	Mikhail Kalatozov
1960	Khovanschina (AAN)	Vera Stroyeva
1963	Cherry Town (aka Song Over Moscow)	Gerbert Rappaport
1964	Hamlet	Grigori Kozintsev
1967	Sofiya Perovskaya	Lev Arnshtam
1971	King Lear	G. Kozintsev, I. Shapiro

SILVESTRI, Alan (b. 1950) A much-in-demand composer, arranger, and conductor for television and movies, he has scored over one hundred films, including several hits for director Robert Zemeckis.

Born Alan Anthony Silvestri in New York City, he was raised in Teaneck, New Jersey, and as a youth learned to play drums, bassoon, clarinet, saxophone, and guitar. With dreams of becoming a bebop jazz musician, Silvestri formed his own band during his teen years and began writing his own music. He studied composition at the Berklee College of Music in Boston for two years and then began his career as arranger and performer for touring bands, most memorably Wayne Cochran and the CC Riders. By the time he was twenty-two years old, Silvestri was in Hollywood where he cowrote with Bradford Craig the 1972

score for the action movie *The Doberman Gang*. Three years later he was sole composer for *Las Vegas Lady* and other low-budget films. Wide recognition did not come until 1978 when Silvestri took over the scoring of the TV cop series *CHiPs* and his exciting, percussive music attracted the attention of Hollywood. Director Robert Zemeckis liked the *CHiPs* music and in 1984 hired Silvestri to score the adventure movie *Romancing the Stone*. The two artists have since collaborated on twelve more movies together, including such notable works as *Back to the Future* and its two sequels, *Who Framed Roger Rabbit*, *Forrest Gump*, *Contact*, *Cast Away*, *Beowulf*, and *Flight*, as well as the animated/computerized features *The Polar Express* and *A Christmas Carol*. With other directors, Silvestri has written music for a wide variety of films. He has been fortunate that so many of his movies were popular enough to spawn one or more sequels that he also scored, including *Predator, Father of the Bride, Grumpy Old Men, Stuart Little,* and *Night at the Museum.* His trumpet solo theme for the romantic drama *The Bodyguard* became very popular, and the soundtrack album, featuring several songs sung by the star Whitney Houston, remains one of the top-selling movie albums. Among Silvestri's other noteworthy films are *Cat's Eye, The Delta Force, Flight of the Navigator, Outrageous Fortune, Overboard, The Abyss, Soapdish, The Long Kiss Goodnight, The Parent Trap, Serendipity, Identity, Van Helsing, The A Team, Captain America: The First Avenger,* and *The Avengers,* as well as the animated features *FernGully: The Last Rainforest, Lilo & Stitch, The Wild,* and *The Croods.* In addition to *CHiPs,* Silvestri has scored such TV series as *Starsky and Hutch, Manimal, Tales from the Crypt,* and *Cosmos: A SpaceTime Odyssey.* He often conducts the recordings of his scores. Silvestri is also an active vintner and he and his family run the Silvestri Vineyards on California's central coast.

While some of the Silvestri scores may be labeled quiet or subtle, the most noticeable characteristic of his screen music is its propulsive and rhythmic nature. This is expected in action films, but he often writes piercing, penetrating music for his comedies as well. Silvestri's first important film, the high-flying adventure *Romancing the Stone,* is both an action movie and a comedy. A romance novelist (Kathleen Turner) and a wily soldier of fortune (Michael Douglas) find danger, thrills, and love while cavorting through the Colombian jungle and being chased by criminals trying to steal their treasure map. The main theme, breezy cool jazz music played on saxophone and synthesized instruments that moves along with confidence, is not at all typical of an adventure score but supports the comic and romantic tone of the movie. Once the action takes over, Silvestri provides exhilarating chase music performed by a rock band with blasting trumpets, nimble-fingered guitar, and furious percussion. The score also includes a funky passage on guitar, flute, and various kinds of percussion that bubbles with rhythmic delight, and a slow-paced love theme on synthesized keyboard and strings that is graceful and enticing. Even more exuberant is Silvestri's score for the fantasy-comedy *Back to the Future.* When a teenager (Michael J. Fox) travels back to the 1950s in a time machine in the form of a DeLorean car, he meets his parents as teenagers and almost changes his

family history. The soundtrack has plenty of period pop songs but the real energy of the film comes from Silvestri's rousing orchestral score played by ninety-eight musicians. The score opens with a symphonic fanfare that leads into a racing theme with shouting brass, piercing strings, and dynamic percussion that all gradually combine into a bombastic march interrupted by explosive crescendos. This theme, based on a nine-note musical phrase, is used frequently throughout the movie but in different variations. There is also an oddball allegro passage with sour notes, chaotic noise, rumbling piano, and pizzicato strings, and a mysterious theme with muted brass, twinkling strings, and high-pitched electronic notes giving the impression of falling through time and space. Also effective is a quieter section on solo flute and electronic keyboard that is magical, and a silly theme with laughing woodwinds, repetitive piano chords, and hyperactive strings.

Perhaps the best of Silvestri's vigorous action scores is the one he wrote for the ingenious comedy *Who Framed Roger Rabbit.* A brilliant fusion of live actors and animated characters, the 1940s detective spoof centers on a private eye (Bob Hoskins) who gets caught up in a murder for which the animated Roger is blamed. Because the plot involved music in nightclubs and bars, and since the on-screen musicians were animated, much of the score was written before filming began. The music ranges from stylish jazz to dark film noir themes to wacky cartoon tunes. The main theme is a cool jazz piece featuring piano, solo trumpet, and saxophone in a bluesy melody that is casual and moody. Later, a speeded-up version is used for some of the movie's many chase scenes. At other times the theme is slowed down for a sexy and languid tone. The Acme factory, where all kinds of crazy devices are manufactured, is scored with oppressive music on low strings broken up by bells and high-pitched woodwinds. For the fight scenes, nervous strings, brass pounding up and down the scale, and screaming woodwinds are used effectively. Then there are passages that are just funny, as with a comic track played on laughing woodwinds and dizzy strings. Silvestri's ability to write such brash and high-voltage music made him a prime candidate for comedies, melodramas, and serious action films.

The other side of Silvestri's music, the gentle and lyrical side, has been equally successful. The score for the very popular *Forrest Gump* is arguably the best example. The slow-witted but bighearted title hero (Tom Hanks) stumbles through decades of American history, protected by his simple philosophy and unabashed innocence. The main theme is a simple piano piece that has a childlike quality even when strings and woodwinds are added and the sound becomes fuller. This is contrasted by the movie's running theme, a vivacious orchestral track with trumpet fanfares, vigorous strings, and rousing percussion that races ahead with victorious confidence. The more inspiring scenes are scored with a sweeping orchestral passage that keeps repeating an ascending phrase effectively until it finally breaks into a flowing melody. Also memorable are a classical piano piece with woodwinds accompanying the elegant melody, and a chanted theme that is stirring even though the voices and the orchestra are muted and take their time to reach the finale. Hanks played a very different hero in *Cast Away*, a drama about an urban executive (Tom Hanks) stranded on a deserted island who is forced to use untapped resources to survive. Director Zemeckis wanted the soundtrack to feature the sounds of nature rather than music so the scoring is minimal. Once the hero sets off in his man-made boat, music finally enters and then returns for key scenes. This recurring theme consists of a solo clarinet that slowly plays a simple musical phrase that is picked up by strings that develop the idea without losing the sustained notes and gentle harmony. Also minimal is Silvestri's score for the sci-fi drama *The Abyss*. The plot concerns a crew of Navy SEALs who investigate a sunken submarine only to discover an alien life form deep in the ocean. The score includes subtle electronic noises and high-frequency notes to suggest the underwater setting where sound travels differently. The main theme features a celestial mixed chorus singing a hymnlike passage that is picked up by a full orchestra as it climbs the scale with majesty. This unusual but thrilling score also includes percussive chase music with furious strings, shouting brass, and pounding percussion; echoing synthesized sounds that call out like a siren or accelerate into a loud scream; and a lament on synthesized sustained strings that barely moves up and down the scale as they weep. Then pounding percussion enters and the piece gains weight and gloom. There is an optimistic piece on piano and muted woodwinds and brass that cautiously rises up from its sorrow to embrace a higher plane. Another sci-fi movie with an equally pleasing score is *Contact* about an astronomer (Jodie Foster) who has spent her career trying to get a response from life forms in another galaxy. Silvestri again uses electronic sounds in his score but *Contact* is more poetic and lilting than *The Abyss*, especially when the celesta is used to convey the twinkling mystery of distant stars. The main theme is a four-note leitmotif played on piano and strings that is fragile and lighter than air as it carefully repeats its main idea at different pitches. There is also a busy passage with confused piano and restless strings under slow brass fanfares, and a serene section on piano and restrained strings and woodwinds that flows smoothly and seems to defy gravity. This kind of scoring is the antithesis of the music in *Back to the Future* and *Romancing the Stone*. The way Silvestri handles both sides of the coin is part of his exceptional talent. Official website: www.alansilvestri.com.

Credits

(all films USA unless stated otherwise; * for Best Song)

Year	Film	Director
1972	The Doberman Gang	Byron Chudnow
1975	Las Vegas Lady	Noel Nosseck
1976	The Amazing Dobermans	Byron Chudnow
1978	The Fifth Floor	Howard Avedis
1983	Tiger Man (aka Fist of Don Won)	Matt Cimber
1984	Romancing the Stone	Robert Zemeckis (Mexico/USA)
1984	How Did You Get In? We Didn't See You Leave	Philippe Clair (France)
1985	Fandango (aka Breaking Loose)	Kevin Reynolds
1985	Cat's Eye	Lewis Teague
1985	Back to the Future	Robert Zemeckis
1985	Summer Rental	Carl Reiner
1986	The Clan of the Cave Bear	Michael Chapman

Year	Film	Director
1986	The Delta Force	Menahem Golan (USA/Israel)
1986	American Anthem	Albert Magnoli
1986	Flight of the Navigator	Randal Kleiser (USA/Norway)
1986	No Mercy	Richard Pearce
1987	Critical Condition	Michael Apted
1987	Outrageous Fortune	Arthur Hiller
1987	Predator (aka Alien Hunter)	John McTiernan
1987	Overboard	Garry Marshall
1988	Who Framed Roger Rabbit	Robert Zemeckis
1988	Mac and Me	Stewart Raffill
1988	My Stepmother Is an Alien	Richard Benjamin
1989	She's Out of Control (aka Daddy's Little Girl)	Stan Dragoti
1989	The Abyss	James Cameron
1989	Back to the Future Part II	Robert Zemeckis
1990	Downtown	Richard Benjamin
1990	Back to the Future Part III	Robert Zemeckis
1990	Young Guns II	Geoff Murphy
1990	Predator 2	Stephen Hopkins
1991	Shattered	Wolfgang Petersen
1991	Soapdish	Michael Hoffman
1991	Dutch (aka Driving Me Crazy)	Peter Faiman
1991	Ricochet	Russell Mulcahy
1991	Father of the Bride	Charles Shyer
1992	Stop! Or My Mom Will Shoot	Roger Spottiswoode
1992	FernGully: The Last Rainforest	Bill Kroyer (Australia/USA)
1992	Death Becomes Her	Robert Zemeckis
1992	The Bodyguard	Mick Jackson
1992	Sidekicks	Aaron Norris
1993	Cop and ½ (aka Cop and a Half)	Henry Winkler
1993	Super Mario Bros.	Annabel Jankel, Rocky Morton (UK/USA)
1993	Judgment Night	Stephen Hopkins (USA/Japan)
1993	Grumpy Old Men	Donald Petrie
1994	Clean Slate	Mick Jackson
1994	Forrest Gump (AAN; GGN)	Robert Zemeckis
1994	Blown Away	Stephen Hopkins
1994	Richie Rich	Donald Petrie
1995	The Quick and the Dead	Sam Raimi (USA/Japan)
1995	The Perez Family	Mira Nair
1995	Judge Dredd	Danny Cannon
1995	Father of the Bride Part II	Charles Shyer
1995	Grumpier Old Men	Howard Deutch
1996	Sgt. Bilko	Jonathan Lynn
1996	Eraser	Chuck Russell
1996	The Long Kiss Goodnight	Renny Harlin
1997	Fools Rush In	Andy Tennant
1997	Volcano	Mick Jackson
1997	Contact	Robert Zemeckis
1997	Mousehunt (aka Mouse Trap)	Gore Verbinski
1998	The Odd Couple II	Howard Deutch
1998	The Parent Trap	Nancy Meyers
1998	Holy Man	Stephen Herek
1998	Practical Magic	Griffin Dunne (USA/Australia)
1999	Stuart Little	Rob Minkoff (Germany/USA)
2000	Reindeer Games (aka Deception)	John Frankenheimer
2000	What Lies Beneath	Robert Zemeckis
2000	Cast Away	Robert Zemeckis
2000	What Women Want	Nancy Meyers
2001	The Mexican	Gore Verbinski

Year	Film	Director
2001	*The Mummy Returns*	Stephen Sommers
2001	*Serendipity*	Peter Chelsom
2002	*Showtime*	Tom Dey (USA/Australia)
2002	*Lilo & Stitch*	Dean DeBlois, Chris Sanders
2002	*Stuart Little 2*	Rob Minkoff
2002	*Maid in Manhattan*	Wayne Wang
2003	*Identity*	James Mangold
2003	*Lara Croft Tomb Raider: The Cradle of Life*	Jan de Bont (USA/Germany/Japan/UK)
2004	*Van Helsing*	Stephen Sommers (USA/Czech Republic)
2004	*The Polar Express* (AAN*; GGN*)	Robert Zemeckis
2006	*The Wild*	Steve "Spaz" Williams (Canada/USA)
2006	*Night at the Museum*	Shawn Levy (USA/UK)
2007	*Beowulf*	Robert Zemeckis
2009	*Night at the Museum: Battle of the Smithsonian*	Shawn Levy (USA/Canada)
2009	*G.I. Joe: The Rise of Cobra*	Stephen Sommers (USA/Czech Republic)
2009	*A Christmas Carol*	Robert Zemeckis
2010	*The A Team*	Joe Carnahan
2011	*Captain America: The First Avenger*	Joe Johnston
2012	*The Avengers*	Joss Whedon
2012	*Flight*	Robert Zemeckis
2013	*The Croods*	Kirk De Micco, Chris Sanders
2013	*RED 2*	Dean Parisot (USA/France/Canada)
2014	*Night at the Museum: Secret of the Tomb*	Shawn Levy (USA/UK)
2015	*Run All Night* (aka *The All Nighter*)	Jaume Collet-Serra
2015	*To Reach the Clouds* (aka *To Walk the Clouds*)	Robert Zemeckis

SIMON, Carly (b. 1945) A popular singer-songwriter in the pop-rock-folk genres, her songs have been heard in several movies and she has scored a few feature films as well.

Carly Elizabeth Simon was born in the Bronx borough of New York City into a musical family. Her father was a prominent publisher (cofounder of Simon & Schuster) who was a classical pianist, her mother was an activist and singer, and three of her uncles were, respectively, a music director for a classical radio station, a musicologist-author, and an authority on jazz. Her older sister Lucy has written scores for stage musicals, most memorably the Broadway success *The Secret Garden* (1991). Simon taught herself to play the guitar as a youth and, with Lucy, later formed a duet act, the Simon Sisters. She attended Sarah Lawrence College briefly, leaving to pursue a professional singing career with Lucy. The siblings made a few records and enjoyed a modest hit with "Winkin', Blinkin', and Nod" in 1964. The act broke up when Lucy married and Simon pursued her songwriting-singing career on her own. Her first solo album in 1971 provided her first song hit, "That's the Way I've Always Heard It Should Be." Other successes quickly followed, making her a top recording star by 1972 with her million-copy-seller "You're So Vain." Two dozen albums and many other hits have followed, as well as several television and concert appearances over the decades. Simon has composed many children's songs and written five notable children's books. She also has a career singing songs by others, in particular standards from the golden age of Tin Pan Alley.

The first Simon song heard in a film was "Long Term Physical Effects" which she sang on camera in *Taking Off* (1971). But it was her singing "Nobody Does It Better" on the soundtrack of the James Bond film *The Spy Who Loved Me* (1977) that became a hit and launched Simon's Hollywood career. Her songs have been heard in over fifty movies, including full musical scores for the animated features *Piglet's Big Movie* (2003) and *Pooh's Heffalump Movie* (2005). Her most successful film song is the Oscar-winning "Let the River Run" from the comedy *Working Girl*. Although Simon was not listed as composer of the score, the song's music was used very effectively throughout the film. *Working Girl* was directed by Mike Nichols, who hired Simon to score two of his other movies, *Heart-*

burn and *Postcards from the Edge*. She also scored Nora Ephron's family drama *This Is My Life*. Although Simon is considered a songwriter rather than a movie composer, her handful of soundtrack scores is quite accomplished. She sings her slightly rocking song "Coming Around Again" on the soundtrack for *Heartburn*, and the tune returns as a recurring motif throughout the movie. At one point it is heard in counterpoint to the children's ditty "Itsy Bitsy Spider," the contrapuntal number working beautifully in the film. *Postcards from the Edge* uses the country-flavored "You Don't Know Me" as its theme. Meryl Streep sings it in a nightclub and the music returns as a motif in this comedy-drama about the backstage world of Hollywood. Simon wrote four songs for the drama *This Is My Life* and sang them all on the soundtrack. The film lacks a theme, but each song provides the mood and tone for certain scenes. Simon's "Let the River Run" remains her most effective song/score. This thrilling number that mixes gospel, pop, and rock captures the New York City of the ambitious characters in *Working Girl*. A rhythmic chorus backs Simon on some of the tracks in the score and for some scenes the choir provides a soft background accompaniment that can be either sexy or reverent. This is superb screen scoring and it is unfortunate that Simon has not returned to film music for over two decades. Biography: *More Room in a Broken Heart: The True Adventures of Carly Simon*, Stephen Davis (2012). Official website: www.carlysimon.com.

Credits

(all films USA; * for Best Song)

Year	Film	Director
1986	*Heartburn*	Mike Nichols
1988	*Working Girl* (AA*; GG*; BAFTA-N)	Mike Nichols
1990	*Postcards from the Edge* (BAFTA-N)	Mike Nichols
1992	*This Is My Life*	Nora Ephron

SKINNER, Frank (1897–1968) A prolific orchestrator and composer for dance bands, music publishers, and movies, he scored over 250 feature films between 1937 and his death in 1968.

Born in Meredosia, Illinois, Frank Skinner took up the piano at a young age. As a teenager Skinner toured the vaudeville and riverboat circuit with his brother-drummer Carl, billed as the Skinner Brothers Dance Band. After studying at the Chicago Musical College (today the Chicago Conservatory of Music), he found work arranging music for dance orchestras regionally. In 1925 Skinner went to New York City where he was employed by Robbins Publishing, arranging over two thousand songs over the next ten years. In 1934 he wrote the textbook *F. Skinner's Simplified Method for Modern Arranging*. Skinner arrived in Hollywood in 1935 and worked as an arranger for MGM, orchestrating *The Great Ziegfeld* (1936). The next year he moved to Universal where he spent the next three decades arranging and composing music for a wide variety of films. Skinner's first original score was for the musical comedy *Top of the Town* which he scored alone. He worked with other composers on many of his screen scores, most often with Hans J. Salter. With Charles Previn he scored the Deanna Durbin vehicle *Mad about Music* and received his first Oscar nomination. (His other four nominations were for *The House of the Seven Gables*, *Back Street*, *Arabian Nights*, and *The Amazing Mrs. Holliday*.) While Skinner worked with such diverse directors as Raoul Walsh and Alfred Hitchcock, he is perhaps most remembered for his movies with director Douglas Sirk, including *The Lady Pays Off*, *Magnificent Obsession*, *Interlude*, *Written on the Wind*, *All That Heaven Allows*, *The Tarnished Angels*, and *Imitation of Life*. He wrote scores for several comedies featuring W. C. Fields, such as *You Can't Cheat an Honest Man*, *The Bank Dick*, and *My Little Chickadee*, and for Abbott and Costello, as with *One Night in the Tropics*, *It Ain't Hay*, *Keep 'Em Flying*, *Pardon My Sarong*, and *Abbott and Costello Meet Frankenstein*, as well as such Universal series as the Basil Rathbone *Sherlock Holmes*, *Francis the Talking Mule*, *Bedtime for Bonzo*, and

Tammy and the Bachelor. Many feel that Skinner's scores for the studio's horror films are among his best, including *Son of Frankenstein*, *The Black Cat*, and *The Wolf Man*. Among his many other notable movies are *One Hundred Men and a Girl*, *That Certain Age*, *I Stole a Million*, *Tower of London*, *Destry Rides Again*, *Zanzibar*, *Seven Sinners*, *Mississippi Gambler*, *Saboteur*, *Hellzapoppin'*, *Eagle Squadron*, *Two Tickets to London*, *The Suspect*, *Dark Angel*, *The Dark Mirror*, *The Egg and I*, *Ride the Pink Horse*, *The Exile*, *The Naked City*, *Harvey*, *Bright Victory*, *Six Bridges to Cross*, *The Shrike*, *Man of a Thousand Faces*, *Midnight Lace*, *The Ugly American*, *Madame X*, *Shenandoah*, and *Captain Newman, M.D.* Skinner arranged or orchestrated most of his films as well as over 150 movies scored by others. In 1950, he wrote one of the first books about film music, *Underscore*, which is still considered a classic in the field. Skinner was active composing and arranging up to his death at the age of seventy.

About two hundred of Skinner's screen scores were solo efforts, so there are plenty of opportunities to study and evaluate his composing skills. At the same time, such a multitude of movies and scores make it difficult to pin down any particular musical style. Skinner the composer is usually heard through Skinner the arranger, and his music is influenced by his early years as a dance band orchestrator. His music, be it for a Sherlock Holmes adventure or an Abbott and Costello comedy, really moves. One might say that all his music has a dance sensibility. The lush scores for the Douglas Sirk melodramas, for example, are sometimes as overheated as the characters. Skinner's music is unabashedly dramatic yet it rarely wallows in mood, preferring to move forward with passion. *Written on the Wind*, for example, is a high-strung drama about a rich and troubled family and is scored with forceful music that seems like one long nightmarish tango. The movie opens with a furious explosion of brass instruments that transition into a frantic, seething theme much in the film noir style. This surging music then relaxes and gets soft and romantic when turned into the title song by Victor Young (music) and Sammy Cahn (lyric) and sung by the Four Aces over the credits. Sirk's 1959 remake of *Imitation of Life* has a somewhat softer score. The oft-told tale of parental and racial conflicts between two mothers and two daughters has a flowing, reflective theme featuring strings and woodwinds with twinkling accents on harp and flute. The drama is still terse but the music has a feminine touch.

Less overwrought is Sirk's quiet romantic drama *All That Heaven Allows* about a rich widow (Jane Wyman) who falls in love with a much younger nursery owner (Rock Hudson). The setting is the verdant suburbs and Skinner's bucolic music matches the rural setting. The romantic theme is a subdued piece on piano which is tentative and tender yet keeps a steady tempo. Even when events get dramatic, the strings are restrained and the piano chords remain subtle. Wyman and Hudson are again the troubled lovers in Sirk's *Magnificent Obsession* in which a spoiled playboy learns to eat humble pie in order to win the love of a widow. There is not much subtlety in Skinner's euphonic score. The main theme is restless and sensual as a female chorus chants over piano and orchestra. When the strings are highlighted, the piece gets less contemporary and takes on a classical tone. Another theme is a minor-key passage with descending strings that is not ashamed to be downright morose. There is also a dramatic track with rushing brass and weeping strings that eventually slows down into a lament featuring a solo oboe. Sirk's *Interlude* (later rereleased as *Forbidden Interlude*) has a good deal of music, including an entrancing title song (lyric by Paul Francis Webster) sung by the Maguire Sisters on the soundtrack. The story of the difficult romance in Munich between an American (June Allyson) and a temperamental conductor (Rossano Brazzi) is mostly melodramatic claptrap but the score soars. There is a passionate rhapsody featuring piano and orchestra that jumps all over the scale as it discovers new crescendos; a solemn passage on strings and woodwinds that is melancholy but not slow nor sluggish; a romantic theme that carefully ascends the scale, sweeps along for a few measures, then continues to climb; and a cautious minuet on harpsichord and strings that is delicate but has a somber subtext as it refuses to slow down. This is all Skinner and Sirk at their most passionate.

Skinner's music for all kinds of non-Sirk dramas is also sometimes compelling. The 1941 remake of *Back Street* has a memorable score. The often-filmed tale concerns a good woman (Margaret Sullavan) who, due to unfortunate circumstances, becomes the mistress of the man she loves (Charles Boyer) rather than his wife. Skinner's love theme for *Back Street* is a glittering string and harp passage that is lush and passionate yet keeps a brisk pace. There is also a classical-sounding theme with nervous strings and woodwinds against a casual piano melody. The suspense in the story is scored with a dramatic track with various strings at various tempos all swirling out of control. Of the many westerns that Skinner scored, *Shenandoah* is one of the best and it has the most memorable music. A pacifist Virginia farmer (James Stewart) tries to keep out of the Civil War but his sons are soon swept up in the national tragedy. The haunting score is more a result of Skinner the arranger than composer. The traditional folk song "Oh Shenandoah" is the main theme and Skinner's skillful variations turn the simple melody into practically a whole soundtrack. The theme is heard as everything from a lonesome ballad played on a solo harmonica to a rousing war march given the fife and drums treatment. There are sections of original music in *Shenandoah* but it is that emotive little tune that one remembers.

The playful side of Skinner's music, as heard in his many comedies, is just as commendable as his serious compositions. The W. C. Fields vehicle *You Can't Cheat an Honest Man* opens with a series of fanfares, some exotic sideshow music, a circus march, and even a swinging Big Band theme. Such chaotic zaniness can also be found in the Francis the Talking Mule comedies and the Abbott and Costello farces. The more romantic *Tammy and the Bachelor* uses a lot of jaunty folk music played on the banjo as the backwoods title teenager (Debbie Reynolds) romances a Southern gent (Leslie Nielsen). But moviegoers most remember the pop ballad "Tammy" by Jay Livingston and Ray Evans which was heard twice in the film and on the charts with Reynolds's hit recording. A better example of Skinner's comic scoring is *Harvey*, about the pleasantly inebriated Elwood P. Dowd (James Stewart) and his invisible friend Harvey, a six-foot rabbit. The opening musical theme is a sprightly waltz with a touch of frivolity as strings and woodwinds dance up and down the scale. The musical theme for Elwood is a lighthearted classical piece with cheerful strings and woodwinds that maintain an aristocratic air without getting stuffy. The unseen Harvey has his own theme, a bluesy passage with dissonant descending chords that is mysterious but not oppressive. When *Harvey* turns from comedy to farce, Skinner uses rambunctious pizzicato strings that seem to laugh at the characters. It is an outstanding screen score for a comedy, but it does its job so well the music is hardly noticed.

Since Universal was the home to the great horror films of the 1930s and 1940s, it is not surprising that Skinner worked on so many. Yet his major contribution to the genre was his orchestrations, giving horror movies a distinctive sound that would be copied for decades. Hans Salter actually composed more of these thrillers than Skinner did and the two worked on several together. They were joined by Charles Previn for the score for the classic favorite *The Wolf Man*, yet it is felt the music is mostly the work of Skinner. The score opens with a mellow passage on low, moody woodwinds that slowly come to life as they reach up the scale and the brass and strings are added to creating a foreboding theme. There is a delicate passage on reeds that gains speed and tension until it explodes, and a lovely violin theme that is woeful and tender as it carefully descends the scale and is echoed by a solo trumpet. Suspense is created with heavy brass chords and strings that race up the scale, fall somewhat, then rise again. Skinner was the sole composer for *Son of Frankenstein* and many consider it his best horror music, if not his finest score of all. The most memorable track is that for the death of Ygor (Bela Lugosi), a symphonic piece in which descending brass notes are contrasted with ascending woodwinds so it is at once mysterious and thrilling. There is also a quiet passage that resembles a hymn with its organ accents and solemn strings until the brass instruments introduce a more sinister element to the piece. Also notable is a seductive but ominous theme with chaotic chords and a driving force that is quite exciting, and the climax which is scored with furious strings, pounding drums, and oppressive brass. Such marvelous music makes one realize how underrated Skinner is as a screen composer and how unfortunate that he is still too little known.

Credits

(all films USA unless stated otherwise)

Year	Film	Director
1937	*Top of the Town*	Ralph Murphy, etc.
1937	*When Love Is Young*	Hal Mohr

Year	Film	Director
1937	*As Good as Married*	Edward Buzzell
1937	*One Hundred Men and a Girl*	Henry Koster
1938	*Mad about Music* (AAN)	Norman Taurog
1938	*Letter of Introduction*	John M. Stahl
1938	*Freshman Year*	Frank McDonald
1938	*Personal Secretary*	Otis Garrett
1938	*That Certain Age*	Edward Ludwig
1938	*The Storm*	Harold Young
1938	*Little Tough Guys in Society*	Erie C. Kenton
1938	*Exposed* (aka *Candid Camera Girl*)	Harold D. Schuster
1938	*Strange Faces*	Errol Taggart
1938	*Secrets of a Nurse*	Arthur Lubin
1938	*Swing, Sister, Swing*	Joseph Santley
1938	*Newsboys' Home*	Harold Young, Arthur Lubin
1939	*Son of Frankenstein*	Rowland V. Lee
1939	*You Can't Cheat an Honest Man*	George Marshall, Edward F. Cline
1939	*The Spirit of Culver*	Joseph Santley
1939	*Three Smart Girls Grow Up*	Henry Koster
1939	*East Side of Heaven*	David Butler
1939	*Code of the Streets*	Harold Young
1939	*Big Town Czar* (aka *Fighting the Racketeers*)	Arthur Lubin
1939	*Ex-Champ*	Phil Rosen
1939	*They Asked for It*	Frank McDonald
1939	*The Sun Never Sets*	Rowland V. Lee
1939	*Unexpected Father* (aka *Sandy Takes a Bow*)	Charles Lamont
1939	*The Forgotten Woman* (aka *Convicted Women*)	Harold Young
1939	*I Stole a Million*	Frank Tuttle
1939	*When Tomorrow Comes* (aka *Modern Cinderella*)	John M. Stahl
1939	*The Under-Pup*	Richard Wallace
1939	*Two Bright Boys*	Joseph Santley
1939	*Rio*	John Brahm
1939	*Little Accident*	Charles Lamont
1939	*Tower of London*	Rowland V. Lee
1939	*Destry Rides Again*	George Marshall
1939	*The Big Guy* (aka *Warden of the Big House*)	Arthur Lubin
1939	*Charlie McCarthy, Detective*	Frank Tuttle
1940	*The Invisible Man Returns*	Joe May
1940	*Green Hell*	James Whale
1940	*My Little Chickadee* (aka *The Lady and the Bandit*)	Edward F. Cline
1940	*Framed*	Harold D. Schuster
1940	*The House of the Seven Gables* (AAN)	Joe May
1940	*Black Friday* (aka *Friday the Thirteenth*)	Arthur Lubin
1940	*Double Alibi*	Phil Rosen
1940	*Zanzibar*	Harold D. Schuster
1940	*Ski Patrol*	Lew Landers
1940	*La Conga Nights*	Lew Landers
1940	*Black Diamonds*	Christy Cabanne
1940	*When the Daltons Rode*	George Marshall
1940	*The Boys from Syracuse*	A. Edward Sutherland
1940	*Argentine Nights*	Albert S. Rogell
1940	*Hired Wife*	William A. Seiter
1940	*The Mummy's Hand*	Christy Cabanne
1940	*A Little Bit of Heaven*	Andrew Marton
1940	*Seven Sinners*	Tay Garnett
1940	*One Night in the Tropics*	A. Edward Sutherland
1940	*The Bank Dick*	Edward F. Cline
1940	*The Invisible Woman*	A. Edward Sutherland
1941	*Back Street* (AAN)	Robert Stevenson

Year	Film	Director
1941	*Meet the Chump*	Edward F. Cline
1941	*Nice Girl?* (aka *Love at Last*)	William A. Seiter
1941	*The Lady from Cheyenne*	Frank Lloyd
1941	*The Flame of New Orleans*	René Clair
1941	*The Black Cat*	Albert S. Rogell
1941	*Too Many Blondes*	Thornton Freeland
1941	*In the Navy* (aka *Hello, Sailor*)	Arthur Lubin
1941	*Hello, Sucker* (aka *Partners Wanted*)	Edward F. Cline
1941	*Bachelor Daddy* (aka *Sandy Steps Out*)	Harold Young
1941	*Badlands of Dakota*	Alfred E. Green
1941	*Moonlight in Hawaii*	Charles Lamont
1941	*Never Give a Sucker an Even Break*	Edward F. Cline
1941	*South of Tahiti* (aka *White Savage*)	George Waggner
1941	*Appointment for Love*	William A. Seiter
1941	*Keep 'Em Flying*	Arthur Lubin, Ralph Ceder
1941	*The Wolf Man*	George Waggner
1941	*Melody Lane*	Charles Lamont
1941	*Hellzapoppin'*	H. C. Potter
1942	*Don't Get Personal*	Charles Lamont
1942	*North to the Klondike*	Erle C. Kenton
1942	*Jail House Blues*	Albert S. Rogell
1942	*Ride 'Em Cowboy*	Arthur Lubin
1942	*Butch Minds the Baby*	Albert S. Rogell
1942	*The Strange Case of Dr. Rx*	William Nigh
1942	*Mississippi Gambler*	John Rawlins
1942	*Saboteur*	Alfred Hitchcock
1942	*Broadway*	William A. Seiter
1942	*Eagle Squadron*	Arthur Lubin
1942	*Lady in a Jam* (aka *The Sheltered Lady*)	Gregory La Cava
1942	*There's One Born Every Minute*	Harold Young
1942	*Pardon My Sarong*	Erle C. Kenton
1942	*Between Us Girls*	Henry Koster
1942	*Sherlock Holmes and the Voice of Terror*	John Rawlins
1942	*Who Done It?*	Erle C. Kenton
1942	*Nightmare*	Tim Whelan
1942	*Pittsburgh*	Lewis Seiler
1942	*Sherlock Holmes and the Secret Weapon*	Roy William Neill
1942	*Arabian Nights* (AAN)	John Rawlins
1943	*It Comes Up Love* (aka *On the Beam*)	Charles Lamont
1943	*The Amazing Mrs. Holliday* (AAN)	Bruce Manning, Jean Renoir
1943	*Keep 'Em Slugging*	Christy Cabanne
1943	*It Ain't Hay*	Erle C. Kenton
1943	*Sherlock Holmes in Washington*	Roy William Neill
1943	*White Savage*	Arthur Lubin
1943	*Two Tickets to London*	Edwin L. Marin
1943	*Hers to Hold*	Frank Ryan
1943	*Honeymoon Lodge*	Edward C. Lilley
1943	*We've Never Been Licked*	John Rawlins
1943	*Fired Wife*	Charles Lamont
1943	*Top Man*	Charles Lamont
1943	*Gung Ho! The Story of Carlson's Makin Island Raiders*	Ray Enright
1944	*Sing a Jingle* (aka *Lucky Days*)	Edward C. Lilley
1944	*Weekend Pass*	Jean Yarbrough
1944	*Hat Check Honey* (aka *Cross Your Fingers*)	Edward F. Cline
1944	*This Is the Life*	Felix E. Feist
1944	*Twilight on the Prairie*	Jean Yarbrough
1944	*South of Dixie*	Jean Yarbrough

Year	Film	Director
1944	The Mummy's Ghost	Reginald Le Borg
1944	Allergic to Love	Edward C. Lilley
1944	Reckless Age	Felix E. Feist
1944	In Society	Jean Yarbrough, Erie C. Kenton
1944	Hi, Beautiful (aka Be It Ever So Humble)	Leslie Goodwins
1944	The Suspect	Robert Siodmak
1944	Destiny	Reginald Le Borg, Julien Duvivier
1945	Night Club Girl	Edward F. Cline
1945	She Gets Her Man	Erie C. Kenton
1945	I'll Remember April	Harold Young
1945	Blonde Ransom	William Beaudine
1945	Honeymoon Ahead	Reginald Le Borg
1945	Easy to Look At	Ford Beebe
1945	Strange Confession	John Hoffman
1945	The Daltons Ride Again	Ray Taylor
1945	Pillow of Death	Wallace Fox
1945	Frontier Gal	Charles Lamont
1946	Idea Girl	Will Jason
1946	Night in Paradise	Arthur Lubin
1946	The Runaround	Charles Lamont
1946	Inside Job	Jean Yarbrough
1946	Canyon Passage	Jacques Tourneur
1946	Black Angel	Roy William Neill
1946	Wild Beauty	Wallace Fox
1946	The Dark Mirror	Robert Siodmak
1946	Swell Guy	Frank Tuttle
1947	I'll Be Yours	William A. Seiter
1947	Smash-Up: The Story of a Woman	Stuart Heisler
1947	The Egg and I	Chester Erskine
1947	The Vigilantes Return	Ray Taylor
1947	Ride the Pink Horse	Robert Montgomery
1947	The Exile	Max Ophüls
1948	The Naked City	Jules Dassin
1948	Hazard	George Marshall
1948	Abbott and Costello Meet Frankenstein	Charles Barton
1948	Tap Roots	George Marshall
1948	For the Love of Mary	Frederick De Cordova
1948	Family Honeymoon	Claude Binyon
1949	The Fighting O'Flynn	Arthur Pierson
1949	Tulsa	Stuart Heisler
1949	The Life of Riley	Irving Brecher
1949	The Lady Gambles	Michael Gordon
1949	Sword in the Desert	George Sherman
1949	The Gal Who Took the West	Frederick De Cordova
1949	Free for All	Charles Barton
1949	Bagdad	Charles Lamont
1950	Francis the Talking Mule	Arthur Lubin
1950	One Way Street	Hugo Fregonese
1950	Comanche Territory	George Sherman
1950	Louisa	Alexander Hall
1950	Peggy (aka Rose Bowl Queen)	Frederick De Cordova
1950	The Desert Hawk	Frederick De Cordova
1950	The Sleeping City	George Sherman
1950	Harvey	Henry Koster
1951	Double Crossbones	Charles Barton
1951	Katie Did It	Frederick De Cordova
1951	Bedtime for Bonzo	Frederick De Cordova
1951	Francis Goes to the Races	Arthur Lubin

Year	Film	Director
1951	*The Fat Man*	William Castle
1951	*Hollywood Story*	William Castle
1951	*Bright Victory*	Mark Robson
1951	*The Mark of the Renegade*	Hugo Fregonese
1951	*The Lady Pays Off*	Douglas Sirk
1951	*The Raging Tide*	George Sherman
1951	*Week-End with Father*	Douglas Sirk
1952	*The Treasure of Lost Canyon*	Ted Tetzlaff
1952	*Red Ball Express*	Budd Boetticher
1952	*No Room for the Groom*	Douglas Sirk
1952	*The World in His Arms*	Raoul Walsh
1952	*Sally and Saint Anne*	Rudolph Maté
1952	*Bonzo Goes to College*	Frederick De Cordova
1952	*It Grows on Trees*	Arthur Lubin
1952	*Because of You*	Joseph Pevney
1953	*The Mississippi Gambler*	Rudolph Maté
1953	*Desert Legion*	Joseph Pevney
1953	*Thunder Bay*	Anthony Mann
1953	*Francis Covers the Big Town*	Arthur Lubin
1953	*The Man from the Alamo*	Budd Boetticher
1953	*Wings of the Hawk*	Budd Boetticher
1953	*The Stand at Apache River*	Lee Sholem
1953	*Back to God's Country*	Joseph Pevney
1953	*Forbidden*	Rudolph Maté
1954	*Taza, Son of Cochise*	Douglas Sirk
1954	*Playgirl*	Joseph Pevney
1954	*Magnificent Obsession*	Douglas Sirk
1954	*Dawn at Socorro*	George Sherman
1954	*Naked Alibi*	Jerry Hopper
1954	*Sign of the Pagan*	Douglas Sirk
1955	*Six Bridges to Cross*	Joseph Pevney
1955	*Chief Crazy Horse*	George Sherman
1955	*The Shrike*	José Ferrer
1955	*Foxfire*	Joseph Pevney
1955	*One Desire*	Jerry Hopper
1955	*All That Heaven Allows*	Douglas Sirk
1955	*Lady Godiva of Coventry*	Arthur Lubin
1955	*The Rawhide Years*	Rudolph Maté
1956	*Never Say Goodbye*	Jerry Hopper, Douglas Sirk
1956	*Star in the Dust* (aka *Law Man*)	Charles F. Haas
1956	*Away All Boats*	Joseph Pevney
1956	*Written on the Wind*	Douglas Sirk
1956	*The Snow Queen*	Lev Atamanov (USSR)
1957	*Battle Hymn*	Douglas Sirk
1957	*The Tattered Dress*	Jack Arnold
1957	*Tammy and the Bachelor*	Joseph Pevney
1957	*Man of a Thousand Faces*	Joseph Pevney
1957	*Interlude* (aka *Forbidden Interlude*)	Douglas Sirk
1957	*My Man Godfrey*	Henry Koster
1957	*The Tarnished Angels*	Douglas Sirk
1958	*This Happy Feeling*	Blake Edwards
1958	*Once Upon a Horse . . .* (aka *Hot Horse*)	Hal Kanter
1958	*Kathy O'*	Jack Sher
1958	*The Perfect Furlough*	Blake Edwards
1958	*The Restless Years*	Helmut Käuter
1959	*Imitation of Life*	Douglas Sirk
1960	*Portrait in Black*	Michael Gordon
1960	*Midnight Lace*	David Miller

Year	Film	Director
1961	*Back Street*	David Miller
1963	*The Ugly American*	George Englund
1963	*Tammy and the Doctor*	Harry Keller
1963	*Captain Newman, M.D.*	David Miller
1964	*Bullet for a Badman* (aka *Renegade Posse*)	R. G. Springsteen
1965	*Shenandoah*	Andrew V. McLaglen
1966	*Madame X*	David Lowell Rich
1966	*The Appaloosa*	Sifney J. Furie
1967	*Ride to Hangman's Tree*	Alan Rafkin

SMALL, Michael (1939–2003) An esteemed conductor, arranger, and composer who scored nearly fifty feature films, he is most known for his music for thrillers directed by Alan J. Pakula.

The son of actor and later Shubert theatre manager Jack Small, Michael Small was born in New York City and grew up in Maplewood, New Jersey, where he took piano lessons as a child. While a music student at Williams College in Williamstown, Massachusetts, Small wrote original stage musical comedies and planned on a career in the theatre. After studying English literature briefly at Harvard, he moved to New York City in 1962, where he took private lessons in composition with Meyer Kupferman and attended the BMI Lehman Engel Theatre Workshop. He began his professional career writing background music for plays in Manhattan, most memorably the choral music for the 1973 Broadway revival of *Medea*. Small first got involved with movies when he scored the documentary short *Cities in Crisis: What's Happening?* in 1967. Two years later he wrote music for his first feature film, the low-budget comedy-drama *Out of It*. Although he wrote exceptional scores for *Puzzle of a Downfall Child* and *The Sporting Club*, recognition did not come until the 1971 mystery-thriller *Klute* directed by Alan J. Pakula. The two men collaborated on eight subsequent movies, including such significant works as *Love and Pain and the Whole Damn Thing*, *The Parallax View*, *Comes a Horseman*, *Orphans*, and *Consenting Adults*. With such distinguished directors as John Scheslinger, Arthur Penn, Bob Rafelson, Michael Apted, and Robert Wise, Small scored several memorable films, including *The Stepford Wives*, *The Drowning Pool*, *Marathon Man*, *Night Moves*, *The Driver*, *Going in Style*, *Brighton Beach Memoirs*, *Mountains of the Moon*, and the 1981 remake of *The Postman Always Rings Twice*. He also wrote music for three acclaimed documentaries: *American Dream*, *The Endurance*, and *Pumping Iron*, which introduced Arnold Schwarzenegger to moviegoers. His score for the disturbing 1979 drama *The China Syndrome* was rejected by director James Bridges, and the studio and the film was released without an original soundtrack, the only music heard coming from a radio and other sources. Small's score was finally released thirty years later and was highly praised. His television credits include the series *A Nero Wolfe Mystery* and a handful of TV movies and miniseries. He often conducted the recordings of his scores and was active in the movies up to his death at the age of sixty-four from prostate cancer. Small is not to be confused with the British composer Michael Small (b. 1988) who scored the Canadian documentary *Ages and Stages: The Story of the Meligrove Band* (2012).

Although he was thoroughly trained in classical music and orchestra arrangements, Small avoided the full orchestral sound and preferred chamber-sized ensembles for most of his screen scores. He often used jazz, blues, synthesized music, and even minimalism in his movie work. This is particularly evident in the thrillers. *Marathon Man*, probably his most famous movie, has a riveting score that contributes greatly to the suspense. A young New Yorker (Dustin Hoffman) unwittingly gets involved with stolen diamonds, murdered government agents, and a notorious Nazi war criminal (Laurence Olivier). Small's creepy and disconcerting main theme consists of high-frequency sounds heard over synthesized chords as a piano tentatively etches out a simple melody picked up by the strings. This recurring passage beautifully conveys the confusion of the young hero who finds himself surrounded by evil. In another suspenseful passage, a solo trumpet and strings echo each other in a threatening way. The score also includes a slow-motion march played on muted brass, electronic bells, and percussion; a fluid bluesy track on piano, trumpet, and oboe with descending strings that is filled with sorrow; and an ominous theme on synthesized keyboard and woodwinds with electronic accents. Less popular than *Marathon Man* but just as exciting is *The Parallax View*, which has an even more modern and minimalist score. When a reporter (Warren Beatty) investigates the assassination of a U.S. senator, he uncovers a worldwide conspiracy organization that seems to control international events. The score's main theme is a slow-motion trumpet call with dissonant notes and noises by other conventional and synthesized instruments. Also impressive is a foreboding theme with rumbling sustained notes and high-pitched accents on piano and reeds. In another passage echoing synthesized notes on keyboard and woodwinds avoid melody and suggest danger around every corner, while in a very abstract track dissonant sustained strings and muted brass create a sour and confused sound. In *The Driver*, about a crook (Ryan O'Neal) who drives the getaway car for robbers, Small gets even more minimal, as in a theme in which echoing electronic trumpet riffs suggests a car honking and a muted saxophone cries out like a wounded animal.

More melodic but just as effective is the music for *Klute*, Small's first successful film. A small-town detective (Donald Sutherland) comes to Manhattan looking for a missing man and finds that a high-class prostitute (Jane Fonda) is his primary lead. *Klute* is less a chase than a search through squalid New York City, and the score has a less frantic but still suspenseful tone. The main theme is a mournful waltz played on violins and piano with a synthesized dulcimer-like sound plucking out a swirling melody that has a dark subtext. The piece has a European flavor but also a bluesy jazz feeling. In one passage, a synthesized keyboard plays a metronome-like theme as a theremin wails, a solo female voice chants, and electronic noises create a chaos that climaxes in confusion. More conventional is an arresting slow-jazz passage, played on solo guitar and trumpet, that is weary and jaded, much like the character of the prostitute. Critics disparaged the 1981 remake of *The Postman Always Rings Twice*, but the torrid sex scenes between a drifter (Jack Nicholson) and a bored housewife (Jessica Lange) helped the movie to find an audience. Few noticed Small's superior score featuring a solo oboe rather than the traditional sexy saxophone. The main theme is both seductive and dangerous as the oboe interacts with a flute while menacing string phrases suggest discontent and sexual frustration. There is also a woeful oboe pas-

sage with descending strings that weep as they seem to dissolve in the lower register. The sensual theme for those infamous sex scenes again features an oboe, this time set against sustained electronic notes and wavering strings. The melodic and the minimalist sound are both found in *The Stepford Wives*, a thriller with a touch of sci-fi and a laconic commentary about the sexes. An idealistic suburb of New York City maintains its utopian demeanor by replacing all the local wives with perfectly behaved robots. The plot follows a photographer (Katharine Ross) who moves to Stepford with her family and gradually discovers the town's secret. Small's score begins with a dreamy and sprightly theme on guitar, trumpet, and orchestra that is optimistic if a bit artificial in its cheerfulness. As the heroine starts to suspect something is wrong with the wives in town, the music turns to a bluesy theme that is soothing in its tempo but disconcerting in its subtext. When the town's facade starts to crumble, the music takes on an eerie, mysterious quality with sustained strings and indecisive piano phrases. By the climax of the movie, the jazzy electronic music is abstract and out of control.

Mountains of the Moon is unusual for Small's repertoire in that it is a period piece and has a traditional symphonic score. The engrossing true story is about how Captain Richard Francis Burton (Patrick Bergin) and Lieutenant John Hanning Specke (Iain Glen) went into the African jungle to discover the source of the Nile in the name of Queen Victoria. This is not a film that calls for jazz or modern music. Instead Small provides a sweeping score with a Victorian sentiment even as it is set against the tribal sounds of the Dark Continent. The stirring main theme is a symphonic anthem with soaring trumpets, expansive strings, and forceful woodwinds; all of it cries of British Empire. As the explorers make their way through a desert, ethnic percussion instruments are heard under a slow and solemn theme played on sustained woodwinds and wavering strings. There is a stately adagio passage played by full orchestra that slowly builds in strength and tension as brass and chanting are added. The film ends with a joyous track with tribal drums, celebratory trumpets, and robust strings and woodwinds that use short musical phrases to climb the scale and, once there, find a free-flowing melody that is filled with life. Small was rarely given the opportunity to write this kind of music; though, judging by the high quality of his modern music, it is not difficult to understand why he was most in demand for contemporary films.

Credits

(all films USA unless stated otherwise)

Year	Film	Director
1969	*Out of It*	Paul Williams
1970	*Jenny* (aka *And Jenny Makes Three*)	George Bloomfield
1970	*The Revolutionary*	Paul Williams
1970	*Puzzle of a Downfall Child*	Jerry Schatzberg
1971	*The Sporting Club*	Larry Peerce
1971	*Klute*	Alan J. Pakula
1972	*Dealing, or The Berkeley-to-Boston Forty-Brick Lost-Bag Blues*	Paul Williams
1972	*Child's Play*	Sidney Lumet
1973	*Love and Pain and the Whole Damn Thing*	Alan J. Pakula
1974	*The Parallax View*	Alan J. Pakula
1975	*The Stepford Wives*	Bryan Forbes
1975	*Night Moves* (aka *The Dark Tower*)	Arthur Penn
1975	*The Drowning Pool*	Stuart Rosenberg
1976	*Marathon Man*	John Schlesinger
1977	*Pumping Iron*	George Butler, Robert Fiore
1977	*Audrey Rose*	Robert Wise
1978	*The Driver*	Walter Hill (USA/UK)
1978	*Girlfriends*	Claudia Weill
1978	*Comes a Horseman*	Alan J. Pakula
1979	*Going in Style*	Martin Brest
1980	*Those Lips, Those Eyes*	Michael Pressman
1981	*The Postman Always Rings Twice*	Bob Rafelson (USA/W. Germany)
1981	*Continental Divide*	Michael Apted
1981	*Rollover*	Alan J. Pakula
1982	*Miss Right*	Paul Williams
1983	*The Star Chamber*	Peter Hyams
1984	*Kidco*	Ronald F. Maxwell
1984	*Firstborn* (aka *Moving In*)	Michael Apted
1985	*Target*	Arthur Penn
1986	*Dream Lover*	Alan J. Pakula
1986	*Brighton Beach Memoirs*	Gene Saks
1987	*Black Widow*	Bob Rafelson
1987	*Jaws: The Revenge* (aka *Jaws 4*)	Joseph Sargent
1987	*Orphans*	Alan J. Pakula
1987	*Heat and Sunlight*	Rob Nilsson
1988	*1969*	Ernest Thompson
1989	*See You in the Morning*	Alan J. Pakula
1990	*Mountains of the Moon*	Bob Rafelson
1990	*American Dream*	Barbara Kopple, etc. (USA/UK)
1991	*Mobsters* (aka *Gangsters*)	Michael Karbelnikoff
1992	*Consenting Adults*	Alan J. Pakula
1994	*Wagons East*	Peter Markle
1998	*Into My Heart* (aka *Elements*)	Sean Smith, Anthony Stark
2000	*The Endurance*	George Butler (USA/Germany/UK/Sweden)

SMITH, Paul J. (1906–1985) A busy Disney composer, orchestrator, and musical director for over three decades, he scored cartoons, animated features, documentaries, and live-action movies for the studio.

Paul Joseph Smith was born in Calumet, Michigan, the son of a clerk who played the violin and introduced his four sons to different musical instruments. When Smith was ten years old, the family moved to Caldwell City,

Idaho, where the father worked as a bank accountant. As a youth, Smith quickly learned various instruments and in high school he conducted the school band. When his father was named a professor of music at the College of Idaho in Caldwell, Smith took classes there and then transferred to the Bush Conservatory of Music in Chicago. After graduation he taught brass instruments at Elmhurst College and music at Elmhurst High School before moving to Los Angeles, where he studied English at UCLA. While still a student, Smith formed his own dance band, which he conducted and wrote original arrangements for. Fellow student Larry Morey got Smith his first job with Walt Disney, writing background music for early cartoon shorts. His first solo score was for the cartoon favorite *Barnyard Concert* in 1930, in which Mickey conducts an eight-piece ensemble of animal musicians. Smith's musicianship was widely noticed, and he went on to score sixty-eight subsequent shorts; most of these after 1936 were solo efforts. Among the classic cartoons Smith scored are *Mickey's Circus* (1936), *Clock Cleaners* (1937), *Bone Trouble* (1940), *Donald Gets Drafted* (1942), *Donald's Day Off* (1944), *Pecos Bill* (1948), *Dude Duck* (1951), *Father's Day Off* (1953), and the series of Goofy *How To . . .* shorts such as *How to Play Baseball* (1942), *How to Swim* (1942), *How to Be a Sailor* (1944), and so on. When Disney embarked on his first feature-length animated movie, *Snow White and the Seven Dwarfs* in 1937, Smith joined Frank Churchill and Leigh Harline in composing the extensive soundtrack score, winning an Oscar nomination for their efforts. Smith also contributed to the scores for the Disney animated features *Pinocchio* (winning the Oscar this time), *The Three Caballeros*, the documentary *Victory through Air Power*, *Song of the South*, and *Cinderella*, getting Oscar nominations for them all. He also contributed to the animated musical anthology movies *Saludos Amigos*, *Fun and Fancy Free*, and *Melody Time*. While all of these were written with other Disney composers, Smith was sole composer for the nostalgic *So Dear to My Heart*, which was a live-action feature with animated sections. After writing a sparkling score for the Disney nature documentary *The Vanishing Prairie* in 1954, Smith did not return to animated movies and spent the rest of his career as the sole composer for nature documentaries, live-action features, and television. His groundbreaking wildlife documentaries were *The African Lion*, *Secrets of Life*, and *Perri*, the last affording Smith his seventh Oscar

nomination. Among his outstanding live-action Disney movies are *20,000 Leagues under the Sea*, *Pollyanna*, *The Parent Trap*, *The Shaggy Dog*, and *The Three Lives of Thomasina*. Smith scored dozens of episodes of the television series *Walt Disney's Wonderful World of Color*, as well as many episodes of the non-Disney sitcom *Leave It to Beaver* in the early 1960s. Often Smith arranged and conducted his solo scores and, usually working with lyricist Hazel George (who used the pen name Gil George), he wrote several songs heard in Disney movies and on *The Mickey Mouse Club* television series. Smith retired in 1982 and died three years later at the age of seventy-eight.

The landmark scores for *Snow White and the Seven Dwarfs* and *Pinocchio* defined the sound of animated features by the Disney studio and the soundtracks are masterworks of screen music. But Smith's actual contribution to these and other animated feature scores is unclear because other staff composers worked on them as well. Looking at Smith's solo efforts is more useful, in particular his nature documentaries and live-action comedies and dramas. In many ways, Disney popularized the wildlife documentary and made it accessible to wide audiences. Painstakingly and beautifully filmed, these feature films were composed through with narration over the continuous music. Today there is a wide difference of opinion about these nature scores. Many feel that the narration and music try to humanize the animals, turning the footage into a live-action cartoon of sorts. Others appreciate these challenging scores that seek to musicalize nature, providing a variety of emotions through the different musical themes. *The Vanishing Prairie*, one of the first Disney documentaries, has a rich symphonic score by Smith. The vast landscape is matched with expansive music that captures the grandeur of nature. Some passages have a simple folk song theme with a traveling tempo and a banjo and harmonica are used to convey the arrival of settlers to the prairie. Just about every second of the movie's seventy-one minutes is set to music, constituting a major effort on the part of Smith. *The African Lion*, on the other hand, has a more narrow range as it follows one lion over the course of three years. This documentary is filled with the humanizing effects that bother certain moviegoers. There is a languid theme on woodwinds the accompanies the sleeping lions, complete with bass strings to accompany the lions' yawns. There is a zippy theme for the lion cubs played on muted trumpet and reeds that changes from a frolic to a march as the young lions play then fight. The hard life of the lions in times of hunger is scored with a ponderous passage with repetitive string phrases and low woodwind chords. This is expert screen scoring even if one disagrees with the whole concept.

Smith's scores for the Disney live-action comedies are mostly delightful romps and often resemble the risible music he wrote for the studio's cartoon shorts. His first effort, *The Shaggy Dog*, is Disney's first live-action comedy and remains one of the studio's best. A teenager (Tommy Kirk) comes across a mysterious amulet that changes him into a sheepdog at the most inopportune times. Smith's main theme features a piccolo frolicking about the scale much as an anxious puppy playing with a toy. There is a mysterious theme for the curse of the amulet with eerie harp strings and odd-sounding phrases on the reeds yet the effect is still more comic than sinister. The teen's first transformation into a dog is scored with echoing percussion, high woodwinds, and descending strings; once again, the effect is still comic rather than menacing.

The quaint piece of Americana, *Pollyanna*, has a warmer and more enticing score. This oft-told tale, about an optimistic teenager (Hayley Mills) whose relentless good spirits affect everyone in her small town, avoids mawkishness through Mills's spunk and Smith's music. The opening theme is a merry march with chipper brass, silly horns, and slaphappy percussion. There is a similarly cheerful domestic theme on strings and brass that bounces along happily with a polka beat. The score also includes a fun waltz with strings and horns making comic comments as they bounce along, and a heartwarming theme on strings with a sentimental touch even as it keeps a brisk pace.

Perhaps the finest of the era's Disney action dramas is *20,000 Leagues under the Sea* which takes liberties with Jules Verne's prophetic story about submarine travel. The movie has long been lauded for its special effects (which are still impressive), but it also boasts a superior score. Smith often returns to a lyrical theme whose rising and falling musical phrases on strings and percussion suggest the crashing of waves. Also very nautical is an undulating passage with harp and horns, conveying the feeling of sailing across the sea. The score features a lighthearted allegro with giggling woodwinds and brass that move trippingly across the scale, and a sinister theme with descending glissandos on strings and brass. The attack by the natives is scored with vigorous tribal music on drums, high reeds, and low brass, and the submarine's famous encounter with a giant sea squid is accompanied by a fearsome march with squawking brass, military drums, and furious strings. Because he spent just about his entire career at the Disney studio, Smith may have missed opportunities to score more high-quality dramas. Yet he managed to come up with some splendid music working within the confines of a studio most acclaimed for animation.

Credits

(all films USA)

Year	Film	Director
1937	*Snow White and the Seven Dwarfs* (AAN)	William Cottrell, etc.
1940	*Pinocchio* (AA)	Norman Ferguson, etc.
1942	*Saludos Amigos* (AAN)	Wilfred Jackson, etc.
1943	*Victory through Air Power* (AAN)	James Algar, etc.
1944	*The Three Caballeros* (AAN)	Norman Ferguson, etc.
1946	*Song of the South* (AAN)	Wilfred Jackson, Harve Foster
1947	*Fun and Fancy Free*	Jack Kinney, etc.
1948	*Melody Time*	Clyde Geronimi, etc.
1948	*So Dear to My Heart*	Harold D. Schuster, etc.
1950	*Cinderella* (AAN)	Clyde Geronimi, etc.
1954	*The Vanishing Prairie*	James Algar
1954	*20,000 Leagues under the Sea*	Richard Fleischer
1955	*The African Lion*	James Algar
1956	*The Great Locomotive Chase*	Francis D. Lyon
1956	*Secrets of Life*	James Algar
1957	*Perri* (AAN)	Paul Kenworthy, Ralph Wright

Year	Film	Director
1959	The Shaggy Dog	Charles Barton
1960	Pollyanna	David Swift
1961	The Parent Trap	David Swift
1962	Moon Pilot	James Neilson
1962	Bon Voyage!	James Neilson
1963	Miracle of the White Stallions	Arthur Hiller
1963	Yellowstone Cubs	Charles L. Draper
1963	The Three Lives of Thomasina	Don Chaffey

SNELL, David (1897–1967) A prolific composer, conductor, and musical director at MGM for twenty-one years, he scored more than one hundred feature films and over seventy musical, dramatic, comedic, and documentary shorts for the studio.

Born in Milwaukee, Wisconsin, David Snell showed a proficiency at the piano as a youth. He studied music at Wisconsin College and the Meyer Conservatory of Music before beginning his career as a musical director for theatre productions. He formed his own orchestra in the late 1920s and wrote original music and songs, some of which found some popularity for a time. By 1929 Snell was working for MGM as musical arranger and conductor, and three years later some of his original music was interpolated into feature films. In 1935 he scored his first short for the studio, the comic western *Windy*, followed by dozens of others over the next dozen years. Snell usually composed, arranged, and conducted these diverse shorts, sometimes writing original songs as well. The first feature film he scored was the comedy *Dangerous Number* in 1937, although he had contributed music to many MGM movies before that. Several of Snell's films were part of popular series, such as those featuring Andy Hardy (Mickey Rooney), Maisie (Ann Sothern), Dr. Kildare (Lew Ayres), Tarzan (Johnny Weissmuller), and Nick (William Powell) and Nora Charles (Myrna Loy) in *The Thin Man* comic-thrillers. Among the many notable movies Snell scored are *Madame X*, *Love Finds Andy Hardy*, *The Thirteenth Chair*, *Young Dr. Kildare*, *The Women*, *Blackmail*, *Andy Hardy Meets Debutante*, *Gold Rush Maisie*, *Love Crazy*, *Shadow of the Thin Man*, *Tarzan's New York Adventure*, *The Cockeyed Miracle*, *Andy Hardy's Blonde Trouble*, *Tarzan's Secret Treasure*, *Lady in the Lake*, *Song of the Thin Man*, *Killer McCoy*, and *A Southern Yankee*. It is estimated Snell also contributed some music to over fifty films scored by others. He continued to conduct and arrange music for MGM until the mid-1950s when he retired; Snell died in 1967 at the age of sixty-nine. He is not to be confused with the British conductor and harpist David Snell (b. 1936).

Because he was musical director for so many MGM films, Snell worked with many of the staff composers and often cowrote his scores with them, in particular Edward Ward, Daniele Amfitheatrof, and Lennie Hayton. All the same, he is listed as the sole composer for sixty feature films and for most of the shorts. It does not detract from Snell's reputation that many of the best scores were written with others. The acerbic comedy *The Women*, for example, was scored with Ward and is as clever as it is entertaining. The screen version of the popular Clare Boothe Luce play, about high-society women taking pleasure over their best friends' marital woes, has an all-star cast, which is introduced as part of the credits. The score opens with a series of crashing crescendos and teasing glissandos on harp and horns before settling into a rolling melody that has the pace and temperament of urban social life. Then each of the major actress/characters is introduced with the image of an animal that transposes into the face of the star. Snell and Ward add to the fun by providing a musical theme for each woman. (The cast consists entirely of women.) The gentle, innocent Norma Shearer is presented as a doe with a bucolic harp and woodwind theme that drips with sentimental schmaltz. The gossipmonger Rosalind Russell is seen as a self-satisfied house cat as busy woodwinds spring up and down the scale. The predatory gold digger Joan Crawford is a jaguar, and her motif is a sultry jazz passage on trumpet and reeds. The rustic Marjorie Main is seen as a horse while a hoedown theme is played on fiddles. And so the animal similes are continued for all nine principal roles. These different motifs return later in *The Women* as the characters show up in the plot. Because Shearer gets the most screen time, the score has more than enough sentimental music, but this is relieved by the sharp, biting themes for most of the other characters. Snell worked with MGM composer Maurice Goldman on the film noir mystery *Lady in the Lake*, based on a Raymond Chandler book. The thriller is unique in that the whole movie is filmed from the point of view of the antihero, private eye Philip Marlowe (Robert Montgomery, who also directed). The subjective camerawork gets annoying at times (one only gets glimpses of Montgomery when there is a mirror conveniently nearby) and the film is more a curiosity than a classic. Again the opening credits are clever. A series of title cards are lifted before the camera and under the last card sits a gun. The plot takes place at Christmastime, and the music for the credits is a montage of different holiday carols sung a cappella by a choir, creating an unembellished sound that is not quite as festive as one expects. The same unaccompanied choir is heard singing other carols on the soundtrack and the only original music is some noirish underscoring for the suspense scenes.

Snell was solo composer on most of the MGM series he scored. His background with dance bands is evident in much of this music which moves along in a contemporary way using swing, tango, foxtrot, rumba, and other forms as orchestrated by a Big Band or smaller swing ensemble. In the Maisie movies, Ann Sothern plays a spirited showgirl with less luck at gold digging than getting herself into mischief. Snell's theme for the character in the various films is a mocking striptease in the sultry blues style but the effect is more comic than sexy. Often the blaring trumpet and raspy saxophone seem to be laughing at Maisie, dryly commenting on her amusing sex appeal. More serious is the music Snell wrote for the Dr. Kildare movies. Melodrama and romance went hand in hand in this series about a young, idealistic, and sometimes radical doctor (Lew Ayres). The recurring theme is a waltz that keeps getting interrupted by repeated notes on brass but still manages to get through to the end of its musical idea. The romantic themes differed from film to film but usually emphasized fluid strings and facile reeds as opposed to the dramatic scoring, which favored the low brass and agitated strings. The series that has become even more popular over time is the *Thin Man* films. Although Snell didn't score the first entry in the series, he wrote music for the sequels and provided some swanky music for the penthouse world and suspense passages for the mystery aspects of the plots. There is a recurring theme in *Shadow of the Thin Man* and *Song of the Thin Man* that captures the cockeyed sophistication of the sleuthing couple. It is a rhythmic foxtrot with a touch of swing that conveys much about Manhattan in the 1940s. The Andy Hardy films were the most successful series Snell scored; they were probably MGM's most popular series of all. The everyday humor and heartbreak of a teenager (Mickey Rooney) in a small all-American town was just what moviegoers wanted to see before, during, and after World War II. The character was introduced in 1937 in *A Family Affair*. Snell was sole composer for the domestic comedy-drama as he was for most of the eighteen sequels. The second entry, *You're Only Young Once*, gave Snell the opportunity to write lively swing music for a dance scene. With *Love Finds Andy Hardy*, one of the most popular entries in the series, a jaunty theme song played by a Big Band was added and repeated in many of the later films. Each movie has a healthy dose of domestic sentiment, and Snell scored such scenes with warm and soothing music that was (and still is) very effective. Snell was never listed among the top MGM composers, yet his work was heard by millions and, with such series as these, became part of the American consciousness.

Credits

(all films USA)

Year	Film	Director
1937	*Dangerous Number*	Richard Thorpe
1937	*A Family Affair*	George B. Seitz
1937	*The Thirteenth Chair*	George B. Seitz
1937	*Married before Breakfast* (aka *Married by Noon*)	Edwin L. Marin
1937	*My Dear Miss Aldrich*	George B. Seitz
1937	*Madame X*	Sam Wood, Gustav Machaty
1937	*You're Only Young Once*	George B. Seitz
1938	*Judge Hardy's Children*	George B. Seitz
1938	*Love Finds Andy Hardy*	George B. Seitz

Year	Film	Director
1938	*Young Dr. Kildare*	Harold S. Bucquet
1938	*Out West with the Hardys*	George B. Seitz
1939	*Burn 'Em Up O'Connor*	Edward Sedgwick
1939	*The Hardys Ride High*	George B. Seitz
1939	*Calling Dr. Kildare*	Harold S. Bucquet
1939	*Stronger Than Desire*	Leslie Fenton
1939	*They All Come Out*	Jacques Tourneur
1939	*Andy Hardy Gets Spring Fever*	W. S. Van Dyke
1939	*These Glamour Girls*	S. Sylvan Simon
1939	*The Women*	George Cukor
1939	*Blackmail*	H. C. Potter
1939	*Thunder Afloat*	George B. Seitz
1939	*Dancing Co-Ed*	S. Sylvan Simon
1939	*The Secret of Dr. Kildare*	Harold S. Bucquet
1939	*Joe and Ethel Turp Call on the President*	Robert B. Sinclair
1939	*Henry Goes Arizona*	Edwin L. Marin
1939	*Judge Hardy and Son*	George B. Seitz
1940	*The Ghost Comes Home*	Wilhelm Thiele
1940	*Dr. Kildare's Strange Case*	Harold S. Bucquet
1940	*20 Mule Team*	Richard Thorpe
1940	*Phantom Raiders*	Jacques Tourneur
1940	*Andy Hardy Meets Debutante*	George B. Seitz
1940	*Gold Rush Maisie*	Edwin L. Marin, etc.
1940	*The Golden Fleecing*	Leslie Fenton
1940	*Dr. Kildare Goes Home*	Harold S. Bucquet
1940	*Wyoming*	Richard Thorpe
1940	*Sky Murder*	George B. Seitz
1940	*Dr. Kildare's Crisis*	Harold S. Bucquet
1941	*Maisie Was a Lady*	Edwin L. Marin
1941	*The Wild Man of Borneo*	Robert B. Sinclair
1941	*The Penalty*	Harold S. Bucquet
1941	*Washington Melodrama*	S. Sylvan Simon
1941	*The People vs. Dr. Kildare*	Harold S. Bucquet
1941	*Love Crazy*	Jack Conway
1941	*Billy the Kid*	David Miller, Frank Borzage
1941	*Ringside Maisie*	Edwin L. Marin
1941	*Unholy Partners*	Mervyn LeRoy
1941	*Shadow of the Thin Man*	W. S. Van Dyke
1941	*Tarzan's Secret Treasure*	Richard Thorpe
1942	*The Vanishing Virginian*	Frank Borzage
1942	*Born to Sing*	Edward Ludwig
1942	*The Courtship of Andy Hardy*	George B. Seitz
1942	*Tarzan's New York Adventure*	Richard Thorpe
1942	*Sunday Punch*	David Miller
1942	*Pacific Rendezvous*	George Sidney
1942	*Grand Central Murder*	S. Sylvan Simon
1942	*Jackass Mail*	Norman Z. McLeod
1942	*The Omaha Trail*	Edward Buzzell, Edward L. Cahn
1942	*Tish*	S. Sylvan Simon
1942	*The War against Mrs. Hadley*	Harold S. Bucquet
1942	*Northwest Rangers*	Joseph M. Newman
1943	*The Youngest Profession*	Edward Buzzell
1943	*The Man from Down Under*	Robert Z. Leonard
1944	*See Here, Private Hargrove*	Wesley Ruggles
1944	*Andy Hardy's Blonde Trouble*	George B. Seitz
1944	*Gentle Annie*	Andrew Marton
1945	*Keep Your Powder Dry* (aka *There Were Three of Us*)	Edward Buzzell
1945	*Between Two Women*	Willis Goldbeck

Year	Film	Director
1945	*Twice Blessed*	Harry Beaumont
1945	*Dangerous Partners*	Edward L. Cahn
1945	*The Hidden Eye*	Richard Whorf
1945	*What Next, Corporal Hargrove?*	Richard Thorpe
1946	*Up Goes Maisie*	Harry Beaumont
1946	*Bad Bascomb*	S. Sylvan Simon
1946	*The Cockeyed Miracle* (aka *The Return of Mr. Griggs*)	S. Sylvan Simon
1946	*The Show-Off*	Harry Beaumont
1946	*Love Laughs at Andy Hardy*	Willis Goldbeck
1947	*The Mighty McGurk*	John Waters
1947	*Lady in the Lake*	Robert Montgomery
1947	*Undercover Maisie*	Harry Beaumont
1947	*Song of the Thin Man*	Edward Buzzell
1947	*Merton of the Movies*	Robert Alton
1947	*Killer McCoy*	Roy Rowland
1948	*Alias a Gentleman*	Harry Beaumont
1948	*A Southern Yankee*	Edward Sedgwick

STALLING, Carl. W. (1891–1972) A pioneer in scoring animated shorts for Walt Disney and Warner Brothers, he wrote music for over seven hundred cartoons and laid the foundations for composing and adapting music for animation.

He was born in Lexington, Missouri, the son of German immigrants, and began piano lessons at the age of six. By the time he was a teenager, Stalling earned money as the piano accompanist for the local silent movie theatre. After graduating from high school, he moved to St. Louis, where for a time he was organist at the city's movie palace. He then relocated to Kansas City where he conducted the orchestra for the Isis Movie Theatre. Stalling often improvised original tunes on the theatre organ, catching the attention of Walt Disney, who was beginning to make animated shorts in Kansas City. The novice composer scored some of these and, when Disney moved his operations to California, Stalling went with him and wrote the music for such early musical cartoons as *Plane Crazy* (1928), *The Barn Dance* (1929), *The Opry House* (1929), and *Mickey's Follies* (1929). It was Stalling who came up with the idea of a series of musical shorts called *Silly Symphonies*. The first of the series was *The Skeleton Dance* in 1929, followed by dozens of others over the next ten years. These cartoons had little or no dialogue but continuous music, either original or adapted from classical themes. Stalling developed a system of bar sheets in which the musical notation was written out on the storyboard. The music was then recorded and given to the animators who used the bar sheets to coordinate music and action. The *Silly Symphonies* were creative and popular hits and the young Disney Studio flourished. But Stallings left the company after two years and in 1936 ended up at Warner Brothers where he stayed for twenty-two years, scoring hundreds of cartoons under various directors. Because the studio owned the rights to a huge library of music, Stallings was able to draw from a wide variety of music to score his shorts. He particularly liked to use stock music that Raymond Scott (1908–1994) had written for Warners in the late 1930s and 1940. Stalling was responsible for giving the *Looney Tunes* and the *Merrie Melodies* series their distinctive sound. Among the legendary Warners animators Stalling worked with were Fritz Freleng, Tex Avery, and Bob Clampett, but his most memorable collaborations were with Chuck Jones. Stalling's musical ideas and Jones's antic sense of humor were in harmony and resulted in the Road Runner, Bugs Bunny, Porky Pig, and other beloved cartoons. Stalling retired from Warners in 1958 and died fourteen years later at the age of eighty-one.

Stalling had a very definite approach to scoring animated shorts. He used stock Warner music, public domain classical music, popular songs of the day, and his own compositions to create one or two new cartoon scores each week for decades running. As prolific as he was, Stalling was far from a musical hack. His musical notations were complex and carefully written out. Familiar music was rearranged to suit the animated action, and original scoring was used to tie it all together. Stalling also developed the use of musical puns in cartoons. He would add a few bars of familiar music under the action, commenting on the character or situation in a comic way. Some cartoons spoofed opera and classical orchestral works, while others changed musical styles as rapidly as the situation on-screen called for it. Stalling also promoted the idea of adding sound effects into the musical notation, thereby coordinating visuals, music, and sound to make a new kind of film style. Stalling never scored a feature film (though his earlier scores were reused later for Warner animated features) and he cannot be evaluated on his composition skills alone, but he remains an important influence in the history of movie music.

STEINER, Max (1888–1971) The first and arguably the most important of the three "Godfathers of movie music," the Austrian-born composer and conductor brought years of operetta experience to Hollywood and quickly raised the level of movie music. The prolific Steiner was among the first to think of screen scores not as a series of mood pieces but as a musical whole with different themes and motifs for different characters and scenes.

Born Maximilian Raoul Walter Steiner in Vienna, he was the grandson of operetta impresario Maximilian Steiner, who encouraged Franz von Suppe and Johann Strauss Jr. to write for the theatre. His parents were Gabor Steiner, a theatre manager and entertainment producer, and Maria, a former actress who inherited three Viennese restaurants. The young Steiner was a child prodigy at the piano and other instruments and was taught by the best teachers available, including Robert Fuchs and Gustav Mahler. As a teenager he began to compose, and when he attended the Imperial Academy of Music, he completed the four-year program of study in one year. In his twenties he composed and conducted operettas in Vienna and was soon in demand throughout Europe. Steiner spent eight years in London conducting his works and others but when World War I broke out, his fellow Austrians and Germans were being interned and he was lucky enough to flee to America. For fifteen years Steiner arranged, orchestrated, and conducted Broadway shows ranging from European-like operettas by Victor Herbert to jazz-flavored musical comedies by George Gershwin. As conductor for the hit musical *Rio Rita*, Steiner was brought to Hollywood when the film version was made. Although he had scored the silent movie *The Bondman* in 1916, his screen

composing debut was in 1929, and his work was noticed two years later for his score for *Cimarron*. Steiner was one of the few classically trained composers in Hollywood at the time, so he was kept very busy, writing music for thirty-two features films in 1931 and 1932. When he scored *Symphony for Six Million* for beginner producer David O. Selznick, Steiner made an effort to change the way movies were being scored. While most films had an opening and closing theme then atmosphere music for certain scenes, Steiner looked at the characters and wrote music that was appropriate for them and their important scenes. He also used music sparingly, making an impact by having a long period of music-free footage punctuated by the entrance of music at an important moment. The effect was not subtle but revolutionary, and Steiner quickly became the most sought after composer in the business. He also developed the click-track, a mechanism that allowed one to match up the music cues to the film stock itself, resulting in a fully synchronized soundtrack. A variation of this technique is still in use today.

Highlights from his 1930s scores include *Bill of Divorcement*, *King Kong*, *Little Women*, *Lost Patrol*, *Little Lord Fauntleroy*, *The Informer*, *Garden of Allah*, *Charge of the Light Brigade*, *Dark Victory*, and *Gone with the Wind*. Unlike many Hollywood composers, Steiner was not pegged for certain kinds of moves and got to score a variety of genres, coming up with superb music for westerns, melodramas, historical pieces, comedies, romances, and even musicals. (He did not write the songs for this last category but provided the soundtrack that surrounded songs by Cole Porter, Jerome Kern, Sigmund Romberg, and others.) Usually working for Warner Brothers or RKO, Steiner continued to score a half dozen movies each year throughout the 1940s and 1950s. Memorable Steiner films from these decades include *The Letter*, *The Treasure of the Sierra Madre*, *The Big Sleep*, *The Adventures of Don Juan*, *Johnny Belinda*, *Casablanca*, *A Summer Place*, *The Searchers*, *Battle Cry*, *The Caine Mutiny*, and *Now, Voyager*. Steiner's pace slowed down in the 1960s, and he retired in 1965, dying six years later at the age of eighty-three. In all, he scored 242 movies and assisted or supervised the music for dozens of others. Although he scored only one television show, the series *Hawaiian Eye*, his music from other sources has been heard in dozens of TV shows and many movies, particularly westerns. Tinseltown cruelly neglected Steiner in his last years,

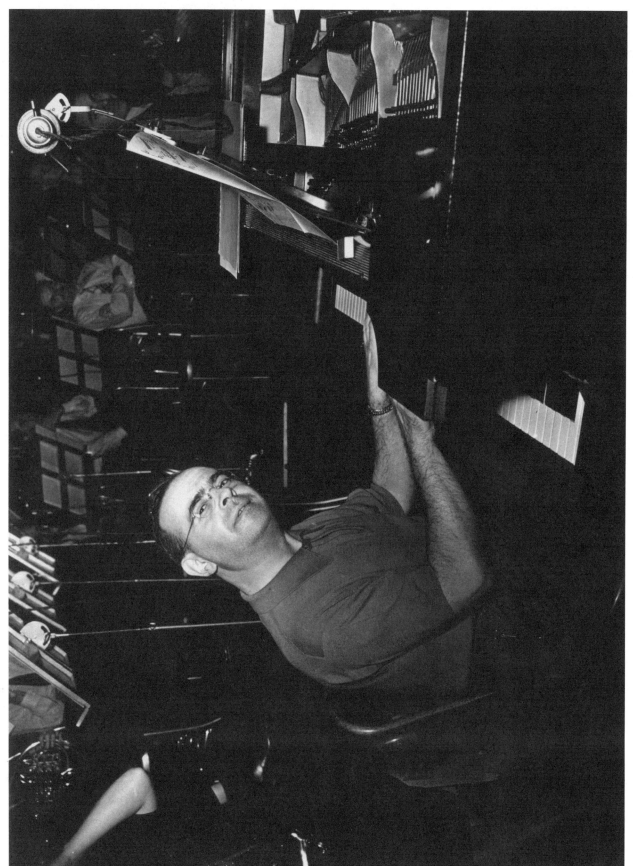

MAX STEINER. The prolific composer may appear to be relaxed here as he poses during a break in writing the score for *Gone with the Wind* (1939) but the ordeal was far from relaxing. It was a furious race to musicalize the four-hour movie classic by opening night in Atlanta. *MGM / Photofest © MGM*

and he ended his screen career with some bitterness. But for decades he had been Hollywood's top composer and influenced movie music more than any other individual.

Just as important as the way in which Steiner used music on film is the music itself. With such a huge and eclectic body of work, it is not easy to categorize his musical style. His Viennese background can be found in many scores, yet his music for westerns is clearly in an American folk tradition. Steiner is a romantic in many ways, even his action sequences having a touch of lyricism about them. Yet he is also fond of the more modern composers and homages to Richard Wagner can be heard in some Steiner scores. When he started composing for the screen, RKO gave him only a ten-piece orchestra to work with, and he was clever in the ways he made the ensemble sound much grander. Steiner eventually convinced the studio that a full orchestra would give even the cheapest of pictures a quality of richness and support the emotions and action in the movie. The full symphonic sound was not new to Hollywood (many silent films had been accompanied by seventy-piece orchestras in the big movie palaces), but Steiner was interested in more than just a big sound. He was a master at knowing when a simple accompaniment or even silence worked best and when a fuller sound should take over. Steiner's versatility can only begin to be understood by looking at his various screen credits. He has provided music for locales around the globe, for many different historic periods, and for a multitude of genres. He appears to have had an endless imagination and an unlimited capacity for musical ideas. Since he did not write for the concert stage or pursue other media once he went to Hollywood, Steiner put all his energies into screen music. It is a remarkable body of work.

The prairie movie *Cimarron*, about a restless newspaperman (Richard Dix) who helps establish an Oklahoma Territory boomtown, has Steiner's first notable score and it displays some of the qualities that could be found throughout his career. There is not a great deal of music in the movie: an opening montage of drums and fanfares that leads into two more melodic themes, some music leading up to the land rush, and a slow march for the final scene. *Symphony of Six Million* has music under roughly 40 percent of the film, and by the time he scored *Bird of Paradise* Steiner had music under most of the movie. For this tropical island melodrama he included some traditional Hawaiian melodies in his original score, uniting the whole by using ukuleles, marimbas, vibraphones, and a steel guitar. These are considered the cliché instruments for island movies today but in 1932 it was a bold decision to move away from a traditional Western orchestra. Steiner had to argue with Selznick and other producers of these early movies that underscoring should be determined by content. For the thriller *The Most Dangerous Game*, there is plenty of music during the first part of the film, mostly a waltz theme that the villain (Leslie Banks) actually plays on his piano to show off his cultured personality. Yet when the famous manhunt begins, Steiner dispenses with music and relies only on a drumbeat to accent the action. The heart-tugging melodrama *Bill of Divorcement* has very little music until the climactic ending when the estranged daughter (Katharine Hepburn) sits at the piano and plays the unfinished sonata that her father (John Barrymore) began many years earlier. This lovely theme (later published as "Unfinished Sonata") is picked up by the orchestra for the movie's touching ending.

A landmark score for Steiner and Hollywood is that for *King Kong* in 1933. The producers were not pleased with the rough cut of the overly expensive ape thriller and hoped some stock music would turn the picture into a hit. Steiner instead managed to get permission to use a forty-five member orchestra (the largest ensemble RKO had yet allowed) to play his symphonic score. The film's main theme—three dark and foreboding chords descending with power—created a sense of awe that prepared the audience for the ape, giving him a mythic majesty not found in the music-less footage. Throughout the score Steiner uses some impressionist dissonance, tribal rhythms, and an expansive love theme. Not only is the music thrilling, the way it is used is equally impressive. Music matches the action, the heights of the composition echo the heights of the action, and the music even stops abruptly when the action does. The *King Kong* score is an early masterpiece of screen music, and it has been imitated to the point of cliché. The technique of having the music repeat the action on-screen would become a favorite in early sound cartoons, and so the effect was later given the derogatory term "Mickey Mousing." Having music copy movement on-screen can easily become redundant and trying when overdone or done poorly. But that unfortunate side effect does not diminish the importance and the power of the *King Kong* score. Steiner's early use of matching music and action can be found in the quieter but equally intense melodrama *The Informer* two years later. The antihero (Victor McLaglen) marches uncertainly to the police station to inform on a colleague, and each footstep is accompanied by a deep, disturbing chord. When water drips on the prisoner in the jail cell, the tempo of the drips and the music are the same. *The Informer* is also one of Steiner's earliest attempts to create specific themes for individual characters. This technique was later adopted by Hollywood and, when overused or ill used, became another movie soundtrack cliché.

Perhaps a reasonable way to look at Steiner's massive body of work is to examine some genres in which he excelled. His scores for westerns, for example, sound American even though they are usually constructed like European romantic music. *They Died with Their Boots On* glorifies Custer (Errol Flynn) and his final battle and the music is understandably heroic. The Irish march ditty "Garryowen" is used in different ways throughout the movie, and the love theme for the lovers (Olivia de Havilland and Flynn) is a flowing and poignant piece that would not be out of place in a European operetta. The main theme is a propulsive march that has both tribal and military aspects to it, particularly the way the percussion changes from one style to the other. There is also a raucous march that is playful and even a bit silly, as if used for circus clowns. *Dodge City*, another western featuring Flynn and de Havilland, has vigorous music that parallels the racing trains and galloping stagecoaches as they conquer the West. Steiner suggests Americana in his arrangement of the music but the notes sweeping up and down the scale suggest an opera aria at times. There is also traveling music that moves along with confidence and a boastful march that is very masculine and a bit cocky. The main march theme in *Cheyenne* is perhaps more all-American by using a galloping theme. This tale of hunting down the mysterious "poet" who is robbing Wells Fargo stagecoaches is given a fast pace by director Raoul Walsh, and Steiner matches it with one of his most invigorating scores. The cult western favorite *The Searchers* is about the hunt for a girl (Natalie Wood) who has been kidnapped by the Comanches. The search takes on a more complex meaning as character revelations cloud the simple code of the West. Steiner's score tends to concentrate on the Native American sound, though purists have pointed out that the music of the tribesmen is more Navajo than Comanche. The opening music is very tribal and vigorous.

This is contrasted by a lovely wandering theme played on strings and solo guitar that is both romantic and melancholy. The travel music for *The Searchers* is sometimes brisk and adventurous, as in a passage with bouncy brass and excited strings. But other parts of the searching are scored with a dissonant and lonely sound, especially when a solo clarinet rises above the strings. Steiner scored over thirty westerns, most of them sounding authentic without being totally accurate. In fact, many of his musical ideas for scoring Native Americans have been so copied that today they are Hollywood clichés.

While some of Steiner's work in the genre of period or contemporary melodrama may have dated with the stories themselves, he managed to write some superior music. For the 1937 version of *A Star Is Born*, he came up with a spirited waltz that echoed the optimism of the small-town heroine (Janet Gaynor) when she arrives in Hollywood. He even included phrases from the popular song "California, Here I Come" to suggest her naiveté. The opening music is a romantic piece with plenty of crescendos and lots of glamour. This is contrasted with the warm domestic theme for the town she hails from. For the antebellum melodrama *Jezebel*, a sweeping waltz is used ingeniously throughout the score. A spoiled, selfish Southern belle (Bette Davis) cannot seem to win the love of a New Orleans banker (Henry Fonda) until a yellow fever epidemic humbles her. To establish the aristocratic world of the 1852 South, the waltz is heard over the opening credits and at the famous ball when Jezebel arrives wearing a scandalously red dress. This same waltz turns harsh as the cruel reality of the story moves from lighthearted ballroom dancing to a morose lament during the fever outbreak. This is one of Steiner's most contagious waltz melodies, seeming to leap into the air with every new musical phrase. Another Bette Davis film (Steiner scored eighteen of her movies), *Now, Voyager*, is a contemporary melodrama with a long convoluted story about a spinster (Davis) who suffers a nervous breakdown, the doctor (Claude Rains) who cures her, and the married man (Paul Henreid) whom she falls in love with. Steiner's love theme for the movie is justly famous. It is an entrancing, rhapsodic piece that wavers in the air uncertainly then releases into a flowing, melodic line. It is not surprising that the music was later turned into the best-selling song "It Can't Be Wrong." The opening music is a fanfare that transitions into a robust passage in which the strength comes from the brass as the violins fill out the sound. The dramatic scenes in *Now, Voyager* are scored with a restless passage that effectively quotes the love theme in sections. Steiner must have been somewhat obsessed with this romantic theme, since he used it again three years later in *Mildred Pierce*, a melodrama vehicle for Joan Crawford. She plays a single mother who sacrifices everything for her spoiled daughter (Ann Blyth) only to be betrayed and become embittered. This is a much tougher melodrama than *Now, Voyager* and the score is less gentle, even its romantic themes having a harsher edge. The opening music is furious and agitated as brass competes with strings in carrying the ascending musical phrases up the scale. Some of the most melodramatic scenes are scored with descending phrases on harp and horns as a piano frantically runs up and down the scale. For the seething discontent of the heroine, there is a passage with grumbling drums and low piano chords. This is contrasted with a lively, optimistic theme that moves freely and happily. Then there is the return of that love theme from *Now, Voyager*, yet this time around it seems a little sour. Such uplifting love seems out of place in the madcap melodramatics of *Mildred Pierce*.

The wartime domestic drama *Since You Went Away* has a great deal of music. In fact, only *Gone with the Wind* has more Steiner music. While a soldier is away fighting in World War II, his wife (Claudette Colbert) and daughters (Jennifer Jones and Shirley Temple) deal with money problems, an eccentric boarder (Monty Woolley), and romantic complications. Steiner's main theme is a rolling, passionate piece that is romantic with its chimes and crescendos and quotes from "Home Sweet Home" and "You're in the Army Now" as well as the wedding march, "Here Comes the Bride." The score includes separate themes for the major characters and even the family maid (Hattie McDaniel), who is accompanied by a languid and easygoing passage on muted trumpet that is contagiously contented. There is a waltz at a dance for soldiers that is not too fast but moves steadily as it hints at heartbreak; a sprightly theme for the romance between the elder daughter (Jones) and a corporal (Robert Walker) that is more playful than passionate; and a tentative love theme for the wife and a family friend (Joseph Cotton), which is based on the waltz from *A Star Is Born*. It is a romantic and heart-tugging score, climaxing when the young lovers must part at the station and the music speeding up as the train gains velocity. Although such a musical trick is a cliché today,

it was quite effective on first use. The melodrama *Johnny Belinda* is set in Nova Scotia, so Steiner introduces some Scottish themes in his music. This daring film concerns a deaf-mute (Jane Wyman) who is raped and is the center of a scandal when found to be pregnant. Ironically, the central theme is a bucolic piece on woodwinds and solo violin that seems at peace with nature as it skips along in a carefree manner. There is also a simple folk melody played on the flute with an oboe answering each musical phrase. The love theme, for the girl and the doctor (Lew Ayers) who teaches her sign language, has long and lingering musical lines on strings while woodwinds and brass add effective accents. The most effective (and disturbing) use of music in the movies is the painful out-of-tune violins playing when the title character is raped. But the birth of her baby is the cue for a lovely lullaby that is quite memorable.

Jane Wyman plays a less handicapped but still damaged girl in the 1950 screen version of Tennessee Williams's play *The Glass Menagerie*. This classic story of a domineering mother (Gertrude Lawrence), her rebellious son (Kirk Douglas), and her fragile daughter (Wyman) has some superb character themes. The shy, reclusive daughter is presented musically with the tinkling of piano, glockenspiel, and celesta, all of it as fragile as her collection of glass figurines. Her bitter brother is scored with a bluesy saxophone that cautiously turns nostalgic. The main theme for this family drama is a tentative piece on strings and solo harp that moves in a carefree manner yet it is in a minor key and there are enough blue notes to suggest discontent. By the 1960s, melodrama had a different sound, as displayed by Steiner's very contemporary score for *A Summer Place*. When two former lovers (Dorothy McGuire and Richard Egan), unhappily married to others, rekindle their romance one summer, their teenage offspring (Sandra Dee and Troy Donahue) fall into an equally disastrous affair. The theme for the young lovers is almost pop in its catchy melody and rhythmic bass line. The music climbs the scale with dramatic steps, sometimes on strings, sometimes on woodwinds, often with the help of harp glissandos. The catchy theme was successful as a song (lyric by Mack Discant), but it was an orchestra version recorded by Percy Faith that became a best seller. The score for *A Summer Place* also has a skipping theme that is so innocent and carefree it is almost idiotic, a blues passage on solo clarinet and piano that is very 1960s, and a lyrical track with quivering strings and soothing horns that is quite beguiling. Probably the most beloved Steiner movie in the romantic melodrama genre is *Casablanca*. This classic tale of love and intrigue in the North African city during World War II has a score built around the song "As Time Goes By," written by Herman Hupfeld some years before. This decision was made by the studio, and Steiner was not happy with it, arguing that he could come up with an original love theme that was just as effective. But the movie had been shot with references to the song and with Dooley Wilson singing it at the piano, so Steiner was forced to use it. He turned Hupfeld's music into the romantic theme and the world fell in love with it. Actually, there is quite a bit of other music in *Casablanca*, ranging from nightclub songs to the dramatic underscoring for the intrigue aspects of the story. The movie's opening music is exotic as it suggests the mystery and danger of the city. The music then takes on the tone of a film noir score as the theme turns harsh and moves rapidly forward as if chased by someone. The flashback, which shows Rick (Humphrey Bogart) and Ilsa (Ingrid Bergman) in Paris, is scored with a sprightly theme that has a cosmopolitan flavor at the same time that is slows down for some very romantic and engaging sections. Steiner also works national songs into the score to illustrate the international goings-on in the city. Sections of the French "La Marseillaise" and the German "Deutschland über Alles" and "Die Wacht am Rhein" are heard and sometimes even sung. All the music seems so unified in *Casablanca* that most assume "As Time Goes By" was written for the film. Never has such a haphazardly created movie turned into cinema perfection.

Tough guy films, most featuring Humphrey Bogart, offered Steiner the opportunity to create suspenseful scores removed from any sentiment. For the iconoclastic private eye film *The Big Sleep*, the music sometimes has a romantic weariness, other times a heavy, foreboding flavor. Private eye Philip Marlowe (Bogart) gets involved with a rich but dysfunctional family, and soon he is deep in murder, blackmail, drugs, and some offbeat romance. The opening music is an angry piece with furious brass and strident strings that keep clashing in bitter crescendos. Under the suspense scenes plucked strings and echoing kettle drums are heard. Even the love theme is tentative and a bit chilly, suggesting that even romance in Marlowe's world is dangerous. Less stylish and more gritty is *Key Largo* in which a gangster (Edward G. Robinson) and his mob take over a small hotel in the Florida Keys and no one will stand up to

them except an ex-G.I. (Bogart). Steiner's score is rather maritime in places, the restless music sometimes matching the crashing waves in the Keys. For the opening theme, the music is dissonant and restless as it rises and falls like an unsteady sea. Later in the talky film is a quieter passage on solo trumpet that is resigned and reflective as it meanders through the lower parts of the scale. More hopeful is a track with a solo violin that seems to rise and glow with the dawn. James Cagney is the tough guy in *White Heat* about a psychopathic crook and a payroll robbery that goes wrong. The most interesting aspect of the score is Steiner's decision to create the propulsive musical sounds of a speeding train, as if the antihero's furious and downward path is like a runaway locomotive.

Steiner scored two Bogart movies—*The Caine Mutiny* and *The Treasure of the Sierra Madre*—in which the actor gives outstanding performances in very unlikable roles. His paranoid Captain Queeg in the former is in charge of a supply ship during World War II and he behaves so erratically during a typhoon that his crew relieves him of his command. Steiner wrote one of his most spirited marches for the film. It is filled with blaring brass parading over the percussion, capturing the majesty of naval ships plowing through the seas. Yet the march has a different tone when the *Caine* returns to San Francisco under the shadow of a mutiny. There is also a bluesy foxtrot for a nightclub scene in which the band sounds weary and a bit jaded, but there is not much more music in the movie. The typhoon and the court-martial in which Queeg breaks down are both presented without music. *The Treasure of the Sierra Madre* is about an old prospector (Walter Huston) leading two Americans (Bogart and Tim Holt) into the Mexican mountains to find gold. Greed and hysteria set in, the men turn on each other, and all their gold dust is blown away by the wind. It is a classic character study and, with its superb acting and direction (by John Huston), the movie improves with age. Steiner sets up the locale in the opening music, which consists of a feverous anxious call on brass with a Mexican flavor as the percussion and strings race ahead in a kind of frenzy. The search for gold begins with a lighthearted passage in which the woodwinds bounce along optimistically. As weariness sets in, their futile search for gold is accented by a plodding, weighty theme. The music of celebration when they think they have found gold is lively and hopeful, made more fervent by the use of harps, celesta bells, vibraphones, and cymbals. As the gold dust blows away in the wind, these same instruments return with a sour flavor.

Finally, one cannot neglect the historic spectacle genre for which Steiner wrote some of his most famous scores. *The Charge of the Light Brigade*, written early in his career, uses a central march theme inventively throughout the movie. This thrilling adventure film about the 27th Lancers in 1856 India has some superior battle scenes but just as many tender or romantic ones as well. The march theme takes on different moods throughout the movie. Sometimes it is plodding and tedious as the soldiers tramp along, other times it is a sparkling processional with boastful pomp. For the famous charge, the tempo is not only increased but Steiner brings in the patriotic British "Rule Britannia" and the Russian "God Save the Czar," creating a truly rousing piece of screen scoring. Errol Flynn, who led the troops in *The Charge of the Light Brigade*, was also the Spanish lover and swordsman in *The Adventures of Don Juan*. While helping his queen (Viveca Lindfors) through some political intrigues, the Don finds time for amorous pursuits and plenty of dueling. Steiner scores this merry escapade as the grand opera piece it is with a variety of tuneful themes. The recurring one is a vibrant march with repeating phrases that allow it to build dramatically into an exuberant climax. There is also a lyrical serenade on solo flute, high strings, and low woodwinds that underscores the romance between all the derring-do. As expected, there is a Spanish flavor running through much of the score, including a furious flamenco, an exotic tango, and a haunting habanera. In a similar vein is the medieval adventure *The Flame and the Arrow*, which is more comic than romantic. A bandit-hero (Burt Lancaster) leads a band of rebels against a German overlord (Frank Allenby) in twelfth-century Lombardy. Steiner uses a rapid mandolin for the film's merry main theme, an Italianate march. The troupe of circus-like ruffians is scored with some bombastic fanfares and even the love theme is rambunctious and sunny. Interestingly, there is no music during the climactic sword fight. The main theme for *Helen of Troy* is lush and flowing, pure Hollywood rather than anything suggesting ancient Greece. The love theme is a hesitating waltz that suggests a bucolic cruise down a river rather than on the plains of Ilium. Yet the whole score is so regal that it captures the mythic quality of the tale.

For the granddaddy of this genre, *Gone with the Wind*, Steiner composed his longest and most famous score. Pro-

ducer David Selznick originally wanted him to use famous classical pieces to give the movie grandeur and cultural status. Steiner argued that familiar music would not involve the audience emotionally in the story and characters as an original score would. With only three months to write the score of the longest movie yet made, Steiner came up with nearly three hours of music consisting of sixteen separate musical themes. (It took five top Hollywood orchestrators to prepare Steiner's music for recording.) There are separate themes for the four major characters. The determined Scarlett (Vivien Leigh) has a lyrical but strongly melodic theme based on the Irish ditty "Katie Belle." (Scarlett's father always calls her Katie in the film.) This is contrasted by a soothing, lyrical motif for sweet-natured Melanie (Olivia de Havilland). The dashing rogue Rhett Butler (Clark Gable) is scored with a strutting march theme, while the genteel gentleman Ashley (Leslie Howard) has a fanciful yet formal theme with an Old World aristocratic air. There are also leitmotifs for the secondary characters, most memorably the sentimental Irish ballad for Scarlett's father Gerald (Thomas Mitchell) and a plodding but lighthearted ragtime tune for the servant Mammy (Hattie McDaniel). Even the whorehouse madam Belle Watling (Ona Munson) gets a distinctive musical motif—a lazy and languid lullaby—though she is only in a few scenes. There are two separate love themes: a warm and sentimental one for the romance of Ashley and Melanie and another, less sweet one, for Scarlett and Ashley. Significantly, there is no love theme for Rhett and Scarlett. Each retains his or her own music in their many scenes together, underlying the difficulty in their relationship. Of course the most memorable theme of all is the "Tara" theme, central to the score just as the house is to the story. One of the most effective pieces ever written for the screen, the surging music, reaches a crest, pulls back, and then surges again. Although it found popularity in the 1940s as the song "My Own True Love" (lyric by Mack David), Steiner's indelible music is most remembered today as a wordless theme for perhaps the most famous movie of all time. During the course of the long score for *Gone with the Wind*, Steiner brought in some familiar music ranging from Stephen Foster slave songs to "Dixie" but they were only accents. The thrust of the complicated score was Steiner's European-sounding romanticism that tied the many loose threads together. The result is not just a movie score but an all-encompassing piece of American music. It is difficult to imagine *Gone with the*

Wind with other music, but it would certainly have been much less a film.

Steiner once stated that in the movies "music should be felt rather than heard." It is a tall order but one that he often rose to. A meticulous craftsman who created his own system of determining and notating the tempo of a movie, he knew that much of screen scoring is grinding work. Once he had determined what kind of music, what tempo was needed, and the length of each passage, Steiner felt he was ready to compose. In this way he changed the sound of movie music and made the young art form more exciting than ever. Reference: *The Max Steiner Collection*, James D'Arc, John W. Gillespie (1996); critical study: *Max Steiner: Composing, Casablanca and the Golden Age of Film Music*, Peter Wegele (2014).

Credits

(all films USA unless stated otherwise)

Year	Film	Director
1916	The Bondman	Edgar Lewis
1929	Side Street	Malcolm St. Clair
1929	The Delightful Rogue	Lynn Shores, Leslie Pearce
1930	Dixiana	Luther Reed
1931	Beau Ideal	Herbert Brenon
1931	Cimarron	Wesley Ruggles
1931	Kept Husbands	Lloyd Bacon
1931	Cracked Nuts	Edward F. Cline
1931	Bachelor Apartment	Lowell Sherman
1931	Transgression	Herbert Brenon
1931	The Public Defender	J. Walter Ruben
1931	High Stakes	Lowell Sherman
1931	The Runaround	William James Craft
1931	The Gay Diplomat	Richard Boleslawski
1931	Friends and Lovers	Victor Schertzinger
1931	Fanny Foley Herself	Melville W. Brown
1931	Consolation Marriage	Paul Sloane
1931	Are These Our Children	Wesley Ruggles
1931	Way Back Home	William A. Seiter
1931	Secret Service	J. Walter Ruben
1931	Peach-O-Reno	William A. Seiter
1931	Men of Chance	George Archainbaud
1932	Girl of the Rio	Herbert Brenon
1932	The Lost Squadron	George Archainbaud
1932	Symphony of Six Million	Gregory La Cava
1932	State's Attorney	George Archainbaud
1932	Is My Face Red?	William A. Seiter
1932	What Price Hollywood?	George Cukor
1932	Roar of the Dragon	Wesley Ruggles
1932	Bird of Paradise	King Vidor
1932	The Most Dangerous Game	Irving Pichel, Earnest B. Schoedsack
1932	Thirteen Women	George Archainbaud
1932	A Bill of Divorcement	George Cukor
1932	The Conquerors	William A. Wellman
1932	The Half Naked Truth	Gregory La Cava
1932	The Animal Kingdom	Edward H. Griffith
1933	The Monkey's Paw	Wesley Ruggles, Ernest B. Schoedsack
1933	The Cheyenne Kid	Robert F. Hill
1933	Lucky Devils	Ralph Ince
1933	King Kong	Merian C. Cooper, Ernest B. Schoedsack
1933	Christopher Strong	Dorothy Arzner

Year	Film	Director
1933	*Sweepings*	John Cromwell
1933	*Diplomaniacs*	William A. Seiter
1933	*The Silver Cord*	John Cromwell
1933	*Melody Cruise*	Mark Sandrich
1933	*Morning Glory*	Lowell Sherman
1933	*Little Women*	George Cukor
1933	*The Right to Romance*	Alfred Santell
1933	*The Son of Kong*	Ernest B. Schoedsack
1934	*The Lost Patrol* (AAN)	John Ford
1934	*Stingaree*	William A. Wellman
1934	*The Life or Vergie Winters*	Alfred Santell
1934	*Murder on the Blackboard*	George Archainbaud
1934	*Of Human Bondage*	John Cromwell
1934	*The Fountain*	John Cromwell
1934	*The Age of Innocence*	Philip Moeller
1934	*The Gay Divorcee* (AAN)	Mark Sandrich
1934	*The Little Minister*	Richard Wallace
1935	*Star of Midnight*	Stephen Roberts
1935	*The Informer* (AA)	John Ford
1935	*Break of Hearts*	Philip Moeller
1935	*She*	Lansing C. Holden, Irving Pichel
1935	*The Three Musketeers*	Rowland V. Lee
1935	*I Dream Too Much*	John Cromwell
1936	*Follow the Fleet*	Mark Sandrich
1936	*Little Lord Fauntleroy*	John Cromwell
1936	*The Garden of Allah* (AAN)	Richard Boleslawski
1936	*The Charge of the Light Brigade*	Michael Curtiz
1937	*God's Country and the Woman*	William Keighley
1937	*Green Light*	Frank Borzage
1937	*A Star Is Born*	William A. Wellman
1937	*Kid Galahad*	Michael Curtiz
1937	*Slim*	Ray Enright
1937	*The Life of Emile Zola*	William Dieterle
1937	*That Certain Woman*	Edmund Goulding
1937	*Submarine D-1*	Lloyd Bacon
1937	*First Lady*	Stanley Logan
1937	*Tovarich*	Anatole Litvak
1938	*White Banners*	Edmund Goulding
1938	*The Adventures of Tom Sawyer*	Norman Taurog
1938	*Gold Is Where You Find It*	Michael Curtiz
1938	*Jezebel* (AAN)	William Wyler
1938	*Crime School*	Lewis Seiler
1938	*The Amazing Dr. Clitterhouse*	Anatole Litvak
1938	*Four Daughters*	Michael Curtiz
1938	*The Sisters*	Anatole Litvak
1938	*Angels with Dirty Faces*	Michael Curtiz
1938	*The Dawn Patrol*	Edmund Goulding
1939	*They Made Me a Criminal*	Busby Berkeley
1939	*The Oklahoma Kid*	Lloyd Bacon
1939	*Dodge City*	Michael Curtiz
1939	*Dark Victory* (AAN)	Edmund Goulding
1939	*Confessions of a Nazi Spy*	Anatole Litvak
1939	*Daughters Courageous*	Michael Curtiz
1939	*Each Dawn I Die*	William Keighley
1939	*The Old Maid*	Edmund Goulding
1939	*Dust Be My Destiny*	Lewis Seiler
1939	*Intermezzo: A Love Story*	Gregory Ratoff
1939	*We Are Not Alone*	Edmund Goulding

Year	Film	Director
1939	Gone with the Wind (AAN)	Victor Fleming
1939	Four Wives	Michael Curtiz
1940	Dr. Ehrlich's Magic Bullet	William Dieterle
1940	Virginia City	Michael Curtiz
1940	All This, and Heaven Too	Anatole Litvak
1940	City for Conquest	Anatole Litvak
1940	A Dispatch from Reuter's	William Dieterle
1940	The Letter (AAN)	William Wyler
1940	Santa Fe Trail	Michael Curtiz
1941	The Great Lie	Edmund Goulding
1941	Shining Victory	Irving Rapper
1941	Sergeant York (AAN)	Howard Hawks
1941	The Bride Came C.O.D.	William Keighley
1941	Dive Bomber	Michael Curtiz
1941	One Foot in Heaven	Irving Rapper
1941	They Died with Their Boots On	Raoul Walsh
1942	Captains of the Clouds	Michael Curtiz
1942	In This Our Life	John Huston
1942	The Gay Sisters	Irving Rapper
1942	Desperate Journey	Raoul Walsh
1942	Now, Voyager(AA)	Irving Rapper
1942	Casablanca (AAN)	Michael Curtiz
1943	Mission to Moscow	Michael Curtiz
1943	Watch on the Rhine	Herman Shumlin
1944	Passage to Marseille	Michael Curtiz
1944	Up in Arms	Elliott Nugent
1944	The Adventures of Mark Twain (AAN)	Irving Rapper
1944	Since You Went Away (AA)	John Cromwell
1944	Arsenic and Old Lace	Frank Capra
1944	The Conspirators	Jean Negulesco
1945	Roughly Speaking	Michael Curtiz
1945	The Corn Is Green	Irving Rapper
1945	Mildred Pierce	Michael Curtiz
1945	Saratoga Trunk	Sam Wood
1945	San Antonio	David Butler
1946	Tomorrow Is Forever	Irving Pichel
1946	My Reputation	Curtis Bernhardt
1946	One More Tomorrow	Peter Godfrey
1946	A Stolen Life	Curtis Bernhardt
1946	The Big Sleep	Howard Hawks
1946	Cloak and Dagger	Fritz Lang
1946	The Beast with Five Fingers	Robert Florey
1947	Pursued	Raoul Walsh
1947	Love and Learn	Frederick De Cordova
1947	The Unfaithful	Vincent Sherman
1947	Cheyenne	Raoul Walsh
1947	My Wild Irish Rose (AAN)	David Butler
1947	Night and Day (AAN)	Michael Curtiz
1947	Deep Valley	Jean Negulesco
1947	Life with Father (AAN)	Michael Curtiz
1947	The Voice of the Turtle	Irving Rapper
1948	The Treasure of the Sierra Madre	John Huston
1948	My Girl Tisa	Elliott Nugent
1948	April Showers	James V. Kern
1948	Winter Meeting	Bretaigne Windust
1948	The Woman in White	Peter Godfrey
1948	Silver River	Raoul Walsh
1948	Key Largo	John Huston

Year	Film	Director
1948	*Johnny Belinda* (AAN)	Jean Negulesco
1948	*Fighter Squadron*	Raoul Walsh
1948	*Adventures of Don Juan*	Vincent Sherman
1948	*The Decision of Christopher Blake*	Peter Godfrey
1949	*South of St. Louis*	Ray Enright
1949	*A Kiss in the Dark*	Delmer Daves
1949	*Flamingo Road*	Michael Curtiz
1949	*The Fountainhead*	King Vidor
1949	*White Heat*	Raoul Walsh
1949	*Beyond the Forest* (AAN)	King Vidor
1949	*Without Honor*	Irving Pichel
1949	*The Lady Takes a Sailor*	Michael Curtiz
1949	*Mrs. Mike*	Louis King
1950	*Caged*	John Cromwell
1950	*The Flame and the Arrow* (AAN)	Jacques Tourneur
1950	*The Glass Menagerie*	Irving Rapper
1950	*The Breaking Point*	Michael Curtiz
1950	*Rocky Mountain*	William Keighley
1950	*Dallas*	Stuart Heisler
1951	*Close to My Heart*	William Keighley
1951	*Operation Pacific*	George Waggner
1951	*Sugarfoot*	Edwin L. Marin
1951	*Raton Pass*	Edwin L. Marin
1951	*Lightning Strikes Twice*	King Vidor
1951	*I Was a Communist for the FBI*	Gordon Douglas
1951	*On Moonlight Bay*	Roy Del Ruth
1951	*Force of Arms*	Michael Curtiz
1951	*Jim Thorpe—All American*	Michael Curtiz
1951	*Distant Drums*	Raoul Walsh
1952	*Room for One More*	Norman Taurog
1952	*Mara Maru*	Gordon Douglas
1952	*The Lion and the Horse*	Louis King
1952	*The Miracle of Our Lady of Fatima* (AAN)	John Brahm
1952	*This Is Cinerama*	Merian C. Cooper, Gunther von Fritsch
1952	*Springfield Rifle*	André de Toth
1952	*The Iron Mistress*	Gordon Douglas
1952	*The Jazz Singer* (AAN)	Michael Curtiz
1953	*Trouble Along the Way*	Michael Curtiz
1953	*The Desert Song*	H. Bruce Humberstone
1953	*The Charge at Feather River*	Gordon Douglas
1953	*So This Is Love*	Gordon Douglas
1953	*So Big*	Robert Wise
1954	*The Boy from Oklahoma*	Michael Curtiz
1954	*The Caine Mutiny* (AAN)	Edward Dmytryk
1954	*King Richard and the Crusaders*	David Butler
1955	*The Violent Men*	Rudolph Maté
1955	*Battle Cry* (AAN)	Raoul Walsh
1955	*The Last Command*	Frank Lloyd
1955	*The McConnell Story*	Gordon Douglas
1955	*Illegal*	Lewis Allen
1955	*Hell on Frisco Bay*	Frank Tuttle
1956	*Helen of Troy*	Robert Wise (USA/Italy)
1956	*Come Next Spring*	R. G. Springsteen
1956	*The Searchers*	John Ford
1956	*Bandido*	Richard Fleischer (USA/Mexico)
1956	*Death of a Scoundrel*	Charles Martin
1957	*All Mine to Give*	Allen Reisner
1957	*China Gate*	Samuel Fuller

Year	Film	Director
1957	Band of Angels	Raoul Walsh
1957	Escapade in Japan	Arthur Lubin
1958	Darby's Rangers	William A. Wellman
1958	Fort Dobbs	Gordon Douglas
1958	Marjorie Morningstar	Irving Rapper
1959	The Hanging Tree	Delmer Daves
1959	John Paul Jones	John Farrow
1959	A Summer Place	Delmer Daves
1959	The FBI Story	Mervyn LeRoy
1960	Ice Palace	Vincent Sherman
1960	Cash McCall	Joseph Pevney
1960	The Dark at the Top of the Stairs	Delbert Mann
1961	The Sins of Rachel Cade	Gordon Douglas
1961	Portrait of a Mobster	Joseph Pevney
1961	Parrish	Delmer Daves
1961	Susan Slade	Delmer Daves
1961	A Majority of One	Mervyn LeRoy
1962	Rome Adventure	Delmer Daves
1963	FBI Code 98	Leslie H. Martinson
1963	Spencer's Mountain	Delmer Daves
1964	A Distant Trumpet	Raoul Walsh
1964	Youngblood Hawke	Delmer Daves
1965	Two on a Guillotine	William Conrad
1965	Those Callaways	Norman Tokar

STEVENS, Leith (1909–1970) A versatile arranger, conductor, and composer for radio, movies, and television, he scored fifty-seven very diverse feature films and is most known for his use of jazz in various kinds of movies.

Leith Stevens was born in Mount Moriah, Missouri, and grew up in Kansas City, where he showed a high proficiency at the piano at a young age. Stevens was still quite young when he was selected to accompany the international opera contralto Madame Schumann-Heink in concert. After graduating from high school, he earned money accompanying voice students at the Horner Institute of Music and conducting local bands. In the late 1920s Stevens moved to New York City where he studied at Juilliard and then worked as a vocal arranger for CBS Radio. By 1933 he was staff conductor at the studio, arranging and conducting music for shows such as *Saturday Night Swing Club*, *The Ford Summer Hour*, and *The Columbia Workshop*. Stevens went to California in 1939 and continued to work in radio, composing, arranging and conducting the music for the popular series *Big Town*. Three years later he began his movie career when he was hired as musical director and soundtrack composer for the musical *Syncopation* in 1942. His instrumental piece

"American Rhapsodie" was played in the film and found life in the concert hall, and Stevens was suddenly in great demand in Hollywood. But he left California, and for the rest of World War II served as radio director for the Office of War Information covering the Southwest Pacific. He also was musical director for the government-sponsored weekly radio program *Three Thirds of a Nation*. Stevens returned to movies after the war, scoring the romantic drama *Night Song* in 1947. The soundtrack included Stevens's Rachmaninoff-like "Piano Concerto in C Minor" played by Arthur Rubinstein and the Philadelphia Orchestra which reestablished Stevens in Hollywood and the concert hall. Even as he returned to movies, Stevens continued to work in radio, arranging and conducting music for such popular series as *Escape*, *The Abbott and Costello Show*, *Yours Truly, Suspense*, *The Burns and Allen Show*, and *Academy Award Theatre*.

In 1953, he was again the talk of Hollywood for his score for the Marlon Brando motorcycle rebel drama *The Wild One*, which featured an all-jazz soundtrack. Although it was not the first jazz score in American cinema, *The Wild One* was quite innovative and strongly influenced later composers who utilized jazz in their screen music. Other

Stevens scores that were heavily jazz oriented include *Private Hell 36*, *Crashout*, *World without End*, *The James Dean Story*, and *Violent Road*. Yet jazz was only one aspect of his film music. Steven brought a unique sound to three sci-fi favorites: *Destination Moon*, *The War of the Worlds*, and *When Worlds Collide*. He also wrote commendable scores for westerns, melodramas, musical biographies, and even vehicles for Dean Martin and Jerry Lewis, Danny Kaye, and Elvis Presley. Among the other outstanding films scored by Stevens are *All My Sons*, *Larceny*, *The Glass Wall*, *Eight Iron Men*, *Crazy Legs*, *The Scarlet Hour*, *The Green-Eyed Blonde*, *The Five Pennies*, *Scared Stiff*, *The Gene Krupa Story*, *Hell to Eternity*, *A New Kind of Love*, and four movies directed by actress Ida Lupino: *Not Wanted*, *Never Fear*, *The Hitch-Hiker*, and *The Bigamist*. In the 1960s, Stevens worked less in films and more in television, arranging, composing, and/or conducting such series as *Cheyenne*, *Dante*, *Michael Shayne*, *Gunsmoke*, *Mr. Novak*, *Burke's Law*, *Custer*, *Daniel Boone*, *Voyage to the Bottom of the Sea*, *Land of the Giants*, and *Lancer*. He was a founder of the Composers and Lyricists Guild of America and served as its president for eight years. Stevens continued to work in television until 1970 when, on hearing that his wife had died in an auto accident, he suffered a heart attack and died at the age of sixty.

Stevens's particular kind of jazz has been labeled West Coast jazz with rhythms and Hispanic touches that distinguish it from New York jazz. For his two finest jazz film scores—*The Wild One* and *Private Hell 36*—Stevens was able to assemble some of the finest West Coast jazz musicians, including Shorty Rogers (who also orchestrated), Bud Shank, Russ Freeman, Shelly Manne, Bob Cooper, Jimmy Giuffre, and Maynard Ferguson. The tale of two rival motorcycle gangs, the Black Rebels and the Beetles, who hunt each other and terrorize a small town was considered so inflammatory in 1953 that *The Wild One* was denounced by the righteous and banned in Great Britain for fifteen years. The harsh black-and-white photography had a distinctive look and Stevens gave the movie a unique sound. The opening music is a frantic jazz theme on piano and brass that races along in tempo to the motorcycles. This is dangerous jazz with a cocky confidence that captures the belligerent nature of the characters and the story. The score also has a smooth jazz passage, with sprightly solo trumpet sections, that moves quickly yet still seems casual and detached. The film noir caper *Private Hell 36*

is much less known today yet its score is even more exhilarating. Two detectives (Howard Duff and Steve Cochran) find $80,000 cash on a dead crook and are tempted to use it to change their lives, the plan complicated by the allure of a demanding woman (Ida Lupino). The West Coast jazz score is even richer than that for *The Wild One* as Cuban sounds are mixed with blues and dance music. There is a salsa-flavored jazz theme on horns and percussion that zips along carelessly, as opposed to a breezy passage on solo trumpet, muted brass, and percussion with xylophone accents that repeats a confident musical phrase at different pitches and tempos. The score also includes a bluesy cool jazz theme on piano and trumpet with bass and percussion that moves from a casual attitude to a dramatic crescendo; a vibrant jazz track that swings like a dance as various brass instruments are featured and a saxophone and trumpet do a dueling riff; and a slow jazzy foxtrot featuring solo trumpet and piano and some dreamy sections on reeds. Even less known than *Private Hell 36* is *The Story of James Dean*, which many cite as Stevens's finest jazz score. It is an unusual documentary film in that directors Robert Altman and George W. George present a montage of still photographs of Dean, his movies, fellow actors, and offscreen life as Martin Gabel narrates and the voices of people who knew Dean are heard. This works because of Stevens's jazz score, which is, in essence, a long symphonic biography. The music conveys Dean's youth and carefree days with smooth jazz that bounces along to a jaunty dance tempo. The score also captures Dean's volatile side, his fascination with danger, and his obsession with speed. Little seen today, *The Story of James Dean* is perhaps not high tech enough for modern moviegoers, but Stevens's extensive and thrilling score survives on record.

Even before Stevens's jazz scores were first heard in a movie, he caused a stir among screen music enthusiasts in 1950 with a different sound. *Destination Moon* is considered the first sci-fi movie to have a sci-fi score. What makes it different from the music heard in previous sci-fi films is Stevens's subtle use of polytonality, creating an eerie effect by letting the ear hear music played in more than one key at the same time. He also uses unusual harmonies which adds to the unworldly sound. *Destination Moon* is a rather realistic treatment of a mission to the moon with a matter-of-fact attitude about procedure and a good deal of scientific accuracy. It is probably too tame by today's sci-fi standards, but the movie still is engrossing and the surprisingly subtle score is quite effective. Over the *Star Wars*–like rolling credits is heard a moody lament played on strings and woodwinds that is punctuated by brass explosions. The piece starts out calmly but slowly gains strength as it sets up the tension for a launch that tragically fails. The plot then centers on the preparation and execution of another attempt at a moon landing. Unexpected but logical complications set in, and the drama heightens. Stevens uses mechanical and electronic sounds in place of music during some scenes, such as the crucial launch, which is terrorizing in its own way. The astronauts' space walk is scored with gentle woodwinds that, because of the polytonal music, convey a sense of awe and danger. The first moon walk is scored with harp glissandos and flowing flutes and bassoons, this time tranquility and harmony overriding the danger. The final return to Earth gets a symphonic treatment with swirling strings and proud brass fanfares. *The War of the Worlds* is probably Stevens's most famous film and remains one of the best of all sci-fi movies. This updating of the H. G. Wells story to the nuclear age is most known for George Pal's special visual effects, although the sound effects are equally impressive. For example, recordings of electric guitars played in reverse provided the unforgettable sound of the Martians' heat ray. Stevens's job was to incorporate some of these sci-fi sounds into his score. The opening music is rather conventional, a propulsive march with brass fanfares, pounding drums, and vibrant strings that climb the scale with force. Once the Martians start landing, the score turns more ominous but still remains earthbound, with a chilling theme on low brass and reeds that is suspenseful without getting too fast or too loud. The Martians themselves are scored with electronic vibrations and high-pitched whistles, straddling the fine line between music and noise. The efforts by the armed forces to ward off the Martian attacks are accompanied by a military march on drums with explosive brass and vibrant strings. Another memorable passage is during the evacuation of Los Angeles with a resigned theme on piano and orchestra that moves in a plodding manner yet slowly climbs the scale and gains in intensity. Amid all the action is a quiet and lyrical track with low woodwinds, cautious strings, and sustained electronic chords to remind us that the Martian danger is not far away. *The War of the Worlds* is one of those happy circumstances when all the elements work together so well, the music being no small part of the powerful result. Perhaps the day will come when Stevens is known and appreciated by more than jazz and sci-fi music enthusiasts.

Credits

(all films USA; * for Best Song)

Year	Film	Director
1942	Syncopation	William Dieterle
1947	Night Song	John Cromwell
1948	All My Sons	Irving Reis
1948	Feudin', Fussin' and A-Fightin'	George Sherman
1948	Larceny	George Sherman
1949	Not Wanted (aka The Wrong Rut)	Elmer Clifton, Ida Lupino
1949	Never Fear (aka The Young Lovers)	Ida Lupino
1950	The Great Rupert (aka A Christmas Wish)	Irving Pichel
1950	Destination Moon (GGN)	Irving Pichel
1950	The Sun Sets at Dawn	Paul Siloane
1951	No Questions Asked	Harold F. Kress
1951	When Worlds Collide	Rudolph Maté
1952	Navajo	Norman Foster
1952	The Atomic City	Jerry Hopper
1952	Storm over Tibet (aka Mask of the Himalayas)	Andrew Marton
1952	Beware, My Lovely (aka Day without End)	Harry Horner
1952	Eight Iron Men	Edward Dmytryk
1953	The Glass Wall	Maxwell Shane
1953	The Hitch-Hiker	Ida Lupino
1953	Scared Stiff	George Marshall

Year	Film	Director
1953	The War of the Worlds	Byron Haskin
1953	Crazylegs	Francis D. Lyon
1953	The Bigamist	Ida Lupino
1953	The Wild One	Laslo Benedek
1954	Private Hell 36 (aka Baby Face Killers)	Don Siegel
1954	The Bob Mathias Story (aka The Flaming Torch)	Francis D. Lyon
1955	Crashout	Lewis R. Foster
1955	Mad at the World	Harry Essex
1955	The Treasure of Pancho Villa	George Sherman
1956	World without End	Edward Bernds
1956	The Scarlet Hour	Michael Curtiz
1956	Great Day in the Morning	Jacques Tourneur
1956	Julie (AAN*)	Andrew L. Stone
1957	Lizzie	Hugo Haas
1957	The Garment Jungle (aka Garment Center)	Vincent Sherman, Robert Aldrich
1957	The James Dean Story	Robert Altman, George W. George
1957	The Careless Years	Arthur Hiller
1957	Ride Out for Revenge	Bernard Girard
1957	Eighteen and Anxious	Joe Parker
1957	The Green-Eyed Blonde	Bernard Girard
1958	Seven Guns to Mesa (aka Terror in Mesa City)	Edward Dein
1958	Violent Road (aka Hell's Highway)	Howard W. Koch
1958	Bullwhip	Harmon Jones
1958	The Gun Runners	Don Siegel
1959	The Five Pennies (AAN)	Melville Shavelson
1959	But Not for Me	Walter Lang
1959	The Gene Krupa Story	Don Weis
1960	Hell to Eternity (aka Beyond the Call)	Phil Karlson
1961	On the Double	Melville Shavelson
1961	Man-Trap (aka Deadlock)	Edmond O'Brien
1962	The Interns	David Swift
1963	It Happened at the World's Fair	Norman Taurog
1963	A New Kind of Love (AAN)	Melville Shavelson
1966	The Night of the Grizzly	Joseph Pevney
1966	Smoky	George Sherman
1967	Chuka	Gordon Douglas
1968	The Legend of Custer	Norman Foster, Sam Wanamaker

STOLL, George (1902–1985) A busy composer, musical director, arranger, and conductor for movie musicals at MGM during the heyday of the genre, he was also an acclaimed jazz violinist and an in-demand conductor in the recording business.

Born George Martin Stoll in Minneapolis, Minnesota, he was a child prodigy on the violin, touring the country with various vaudeville acts and appearing in the early talkie *The Jazzmania Quintet* (1928). Later Stoll turned to conducting and performing with his own trio called the Rhythm Aces; he was heard on various radio shows and performed in the film short *Old Songs for New* (1932). In 1934 he was made musical director at CBS Radio and with his own orchestra started to work in the movies. Stoll ar-

ranged and conducted some films beginning in 1936 and even appeared with his band in the short *Swing Banditry* that same year. His fruitful association with MGM began the next year when he was musical director for *Broadway Melody of 1940*. Stoll went on to write arrangements and incidental music, conducted dozens of MGM musicals, and was nominated for Oscars for his work on *Babes in Arms* (1939), *For Me and My Gal* (1942), *Meet Me in St. Louis* (1944), and *Love Me or Leave Me* (1955), winning for *Anchors Aweigh*, which he also co-composed. Usually working with others, Stoll composed and conducted and/ or arranged the music for such MGM favorites as *The Wizard of Oz*, *Strike Up the Band*, *Girl Crazy*, *A Date with Judy*, *Neptune's Daughter*, and *In the Good Old*

Summertime. He not only worked with Judy Garland on eight films, but he guided and conducted her through her first albums, the two having a chart hit with "The Trolley Song." Stoll also worked on seven movies starring Esther Williams. In the late 1950s, as the number and quality of musicals waned, Stoll found himself working on four Elvis Presley musicals, as well as the occasional comedy, such as *The Courtship of Eddie's Father*, *A Ticklish Affair*, and *Made in Paris*. He retired from films in 1966 and continued to do recordings for another decade before giving up music altogether. He remained in Southern California until his death at the age of eighty-two.

Because he was a card-playing friend of Louis B. Mayer, Stoll was treated well by MGM, earning enough money to acquire many valuable antiques and to live in palatial luxury. Yet he rarely was the sole composer on a musical or a comedy and often was not accurately credited for all that he did on a movie musical. Oddly, this is the way Stoll wanted it. In fact, he kept such a low profile that today it is difficult to even find a photograph of him. Stoll was a studio man through and through. He left his mark on dozens of movies yet it is impossible to identify or characterize that mark. He was sole composer on only a handful of movies and those featured songs by others, offering little original scoring by Stoll. Yet he was considered tops in his field. If Stoll the composer is hidden under a bushel, his supervision of music was noticed and enjoyed by many.

Credits

(all films USA)

Year	Film	Director
1936	Go West Young Man	Henry Hathaway
1939	Babes in Arms (AAN)	Busby Berkeley
1940	Broadway Melody of 1940	Norman Taurog
1940	Strike Up the Band (AAN)	Busby Berkeley
1940	Little Nellie Kelly	Norman Taurog
1940	Go West	Edward Buzzell
1941	Road Show	Hal Roach
1941	Lady Be Good	Norman Z. McLeod, Busby Berkeley
1942	Ship Ahoy	Edward Buzzell
1942	Panama Hattie	Norman Z. McLeod
1943	Presenting Lily Mars	Norman Taurog
1943	Swing Fever	Tim Whelan
1943	Girl Crazy	Norman Taurog
1944	Two Girls and a Sailor	Richard Thorpe
1945	Thrill of a Romance	Richard Thorpe
1945	Anchors Aweigh (AA)	George Sidney
1945	Her Highness and the Bellboy	Richard Thorpe
1946	Holiday in Mexico	George Sidney
1946	No Leave, No Love	Charles Martin
1947	This Time for Keeps	Richard Thorpe
1948	On an Island with You	Richard Thorpe
1948	A Date with Judy	Richard Thorpe
1948	The Kissing Bandit	Laslo Benedek
1949	Neptune's Daughter	Edward Buzzell
1949	In the Good Old Summertime	Robert Z. Leonard
1950	Nancy Goes to Rio	Robert Z. Leonard
1950	Duchess of Idaho	Robert Z. Leonard
1950	The Toast of New Orleans	Norman Taurog
1950	Two Weeks with Love	Roy Rowland
1950	Watch the Birdie	Jack Donohue
1951	Excuse My Dust	Roy Rowland
1951	The Strip	László Kardos
1953	I Love Melvin	Don Weis

Year	Film	Director
1953	*Dangerous When Wet*	Charles Walters
1953	*Latin Lovers*	Mervyn LeRoy
1953	*Easy to Love*	Charles Walters
1956	*The Opposite Sex*	David Miller
1957	*Ten Thousand Bedrooms*	Richard Thorpe
1957	*This Could Be the Night*	Robert Wise
1960	*Where the Boys Are*	Henry Levin
1962	*The Horizontal Lieutenant*	Richard Thorpe
1963	*The Courtship of Eddie's Father*	Vincente Minnelli
1963	*A Ticklish Affair*	George Sidney
1964	*Viva Las Vegas*	George Sidney
1964	*Looking for Love*	Don Weis
1965	*The Man from Button Willow*	David Detiege
1965	*Girl Happy*	Boris Sagal
1966	*Made in Paris*	Boris Sagal
1966	*Spinout*	Norman Taurog

STOTHART, Herbert (1885–1949) A significant composer, conductor, and arranger who left a successful career in the theatre to score films, he was MGM's chief soundtrack composer and musical director in the 1930s and 1940s.

Herbert Stothart was born in Milwaukee, Wisconsin, and pursued a career in history at the University of Wisconsin with the idea of teaching. But when Stothart got involved in college theatricals, composing and conducting the music, he changed his plans and went to Europe to study music. Once back in America, Stothart wrote songs for vaudeville, getting the attention of lyricist-librettist Oscar Hammerstein II, who hired him as musical director for the Broadway operetta *High Jinks* in 1914. For several years he conducted and arranged music for shows in New York and on the road, finally getting to compose a score with the 1917 musical *Furs and Frills*. Stothart contributed to the scores for eight more Broadway musicals until finding wide recognition for *Rose-Marie* (1924), which he cowrote with composer Rudolf Friml. He worked with George Gershwin on *Song of the Flame* the next year, followed by the hits *Golden Dawn* (1927) and *Good Boy* (1928). Among his famous songs from the stage and his movies are "Bambalina," "Cuban Love Song," "I Wanna Be Loved by You," "The Rogue Song," "When I'm Looking at You," "Dark Night," and "The Donkey Serenade."

With the advent of the talkies, Louis B. Mayer was building up a music department at MGM and hired Stothart as a conductor, arranger, and composer. For the next twenty years he practically ran the music department at the studio, composing soundtracks for 105 films and arranging and conducting dozens of others. His first original score was for the Russian film *The End of St. Petersburg*, a 1928 silent movie that MGM released in the States with Stothart's music soundtrack. Stothart scored a wide variety of movies, ranging from literary adaptations, such as *Pride and Prejudice* and *David Copperfield*, to history pieces, like *Queen Christina* and *Northwest Passage*, to wartime dramas, such as *Mrs. Miniver* and *Thirty Seconds over Tokyo*. Although he never scored the songs for an MGM musical, he was musical director for many popular ones, such as all the Jeanette MacDonald–Nelson Eddy vehicles. Arguably Stothart's greatest musical achievement is the soundtrack music for *The Wizard of Oz*, filled with memorable themes outside of the Harold Arlen–E. Y. Harburg songs.

Stothart scored so many different kinds of movies that a particular style is not obvious. His work is more restrained than most of the composers at MGM. While Max Steiner's often-grandiose scores were more popular, Stothart's subtle musical themes were effective without being noticed. He utilized the lush sound of violins that were required by the studio yet his scores never seem to drip with sentiment. Because he had an education in classical music, Stothart often borrowed musical phrases from classical composers and slipped them into the scores for *A Tale of Two Cities*, *The Picture of Dorian Gray*, *Conquest*, and other period films. He was also quite accomplished at pastiching the music of different countries while still maintaining a traditional Hollywood sound. He evokes Russian

HERBERT STOTHART. Perhaps the most overlooked artist involved with the beloved classic *The Wizard of Oz* (1939) is Stothard, who composed, conducted, and arranged most of the soundtrack music. Here he conducts a recording session for the practically nonstop music in the film. *MGM / Photofest* © MGM music in such movies as *The End of St. Petersburg*, *Queen Christina*, and *Rasputin and the Empress*; a Chinese style in *The Good Earth* and *Dragon Seed*; an exotic Middle Eastern tone in *Kismet*; a Spanish flavor in *Sevilla de mis amores* and *The Cuban Love Song*; and a French manner in *La chanteur de Séville* and *Marie Antoinette*. His music added excitement to such adventure movies as *Treasure Island* and *Northwest Passage*; gave a melancholy air to *Camille*, *Waterloo Bridge*, and other dramas; and provided a heartwarming atmosphere for such all-American melodramas as *Ah, Wilderness!*, *The Human Comedy*, and *The Yearling*. Stothart scored many Hollywood films set in the British Isles, and he was very adept in capturing both the urban sounds of *The Picture of Dorian Gray* and *David Copperfield* and the rural sounds of *What Every Woman Knows* and *Mrs. Miniver*. Yet his efforts usually went unnoticed by the public. (He was nominated for an Oscar ten times, winning only once—for *The Wizard of Oz*.) Stothart is a gleaming example of a soundtrack composer whose work disappears within the world of the film.

Many of Stothart's finest scores were for classic movies based on renowned novels. MGM seemed to raid the shelves of the world's best books in the 1930s and 1940s, and often it was Stothart who provided the musical voice of these literary adaptations. For the 1935 adaptation of *Mutiny on the Bounty*, Stothart matched the authentic-looking location shooting with some pseudo-Polynesian music for the natives on Tahiti. For good measure, he also included Bronislau Kaper and Walter Jurmann's "Love Song of Tahiti" to add to the exotic atmosphere. Of course most of the movie takes place on the British ship captained by the infamous Bligh (Charles Laughton) so much of the score is in a British naval vein. Military marches mix with sea chanteys and Stothart includes a majestic version of "Rule Britannia" when the *Bounty* pulls out of the harbor and heads to sea. The sailors' discontent with Bligh is scored with low woodwinds and subdued brass chords while the captain himself is accompanied by a seething dissonant theme that is so low it seems to be grumbling. A storm at sea has some vigorous music with dizzying brass and spiraling violins. Another British classic, *Pride and Prejudice*, has a very different tone. The 1940 version of Jane Austen's tale of matchmaking and romance in nineteenth-century rural England is greatly abridged but is still a very pleasing adaptation. There is a somewhat melancholy yet romantic love theme for the stuffy Darcy (Lau-

rence Olivier) and the critical Elizabeth (Greer Garson) in which the music wavers back and forth, much as the lovers do in their feelings for each other. The film captures Austen's whimsical air at times and so does Stothart's music. For the foolish relative Mr. Collins (Melville Cooper), there is a bouncy funny theme on woodwinds that suggests the waddling of a duck. Greer Garson starred in a more modern British movie based on a lesser-known book, *Mrs. Miniver*. This patriotic yet very human tale of a family struggling to get through World War II has some hymns and patriotic songs but also some delectable original music. The opening theme includes the chiming of church bells then a lilting melody that sounds like an anthem for domestic happiness. Another recurring motif is a simple, childlike folk theme that might even be a school alma mater with its fervent sincerity. The bustle of London is scored with busy strings and brass that echo taxi and bus horns while the quiet of the English countryside is conveyed with serene and bucolic music.

Pearl S. Buck's best-selling novel *The Good Earth* was turned into a surprisingly effective film in 1937. The difficult everyday life of a Chinese peasant (Paul Muni) who lives and suffers by the land is far from typical Hollywood fare, but it is a beautifully directed and filmed movie that still impresses. The one complaint by modern audiences is the use of Caucasian actors for the Chinese characters, although in the case of Luise Rainer as the faithful, steadfast wife, it is difficult to imagine a better performance. Stothart studied Asian music and utilized some authentic Eastern instruments in his score. He based his melodies on the pentatonic scale instead of the Western one and, using a traditional Hollywood orchestra, managed to suggest the Orient without slipping into Charlie Chan movie clichés. The theme for the wife is a simple folklike piece with plucked strings and a few high notes on a wooden flute. The peasant hero's theme is a series of notes that seem to trickle down the scale. The precious land has its own theme, much as Tara does in *Gone with the Wind*, but this music is calm and reflective, conveying the patience and suffering it takes to conquer it. There is a passage with repeated notes that is very oppressive to Western ears and ideal for some of the more chaotic or violent scenes in the film. A tale of Americans struggling with the land is told in Marjorie Kinnan Rawlings's *The Yearling*, which was filmed with taste in 1946. As his family toils to make a go of their Florida farm after the Civil War, a young boy (Claude

Jarman Jr.) is given a baby deer, a yearling, to care for and the tragicomic events that follow bring on a brutal maturity. Stothart wrote one of his best nature scores for the movie. The main theme is a fluid passage that rolls along with help from harp glissandos and a chanting choir, the result giving the feeling of discovery of something beautiful. The theme for the yearling is a simple piece played on woodwinds filled with innocence. There is a melancholy passage on low horns and a playful march that stops for some quieter sections. Even finer is an optimistic piece on flutes and other woodwinds that seems to rise up with the light of dawn.

The most famous of the many famous movies Stothart scored is obviously *The Wizard of Oz* although it is known that George Stoll, Murray Cutter, Paul Marquardt, Leo Arnaud, Bob Stringer, Conrad Salinger, and George Bassman all worked on the music, not to mention Harold Arlen (music) and E. Y. Harburg (lyrics) who wrote the songs. It is generally believed that Stothart composed the bulk of the soundtrack, and he is the only one listed in the screen credits. As with most musical movies, the soundtrack composer takes the completed songs and uses them in the underscoring. Stothart must have known "Over the Rainbow" was a winner and used it throughout the movie, though it must be said he showed restraint and did not bombard the moviegoer with the music. Other songs were also used for underscoring, but a majority of the nonsinging soundtrack is original and most of it was written by Stothart. He opens the movie with a chaotic and threatening section from his tornado music then transitions into a flowing version of "Over the Rainbow" on strings. This melody then turns into a march that introduces the Munchkin theme sung by a celestial choir then played by a symphonic orchestra. All this occurs during the credits as a kind of overture of sorts. Throughout the rest of the movie there are a dozen or so different themes, some taken from established music, such as Robert Schumann's "The Happy Farmer" as a motif for the dog Toto, Modeste Mussorgsky's "Night on Bald Mountain" during some scenes in the castle of the Wicked Witch (Margaret Hamilton), and strains of "Home Sweet Home" for the final scene back in Kansas. The other themes are original, most memorably the funny, terrifying travel music for Miss Gulch (Hamilton).

This insistent string theme that suggests the peddling of her bicycle is just as effective when it turns into the Witch's music for flying on her broomstick. The music is so simple and indelible that it is perhaps as well known as any of the songs in *The Wizard of Oz*. Stothart provides a goofy music motif for three farmhands (Ray Bolger, Jack Haley, and Bert Lahr) which is heard briefly when they show up in Oz as the Scarecrow, Tin Man, and Cowardly Lion. The good witch Glinda (Billie Burke) is introduced each time with magical music punctuated with twinkling chimes, a rush of voices, and then a calm section on sustained notes. The chases in and about the Witch's castle are scored with restless, agitated chords and rapid glissandos. Also memorable is the theme for the Witch's guards or Winkies. They chant a bass march theme that is silly and still rather frightening. Two sequences in *The Wizard of Oz* stand out musically. When Dorothy (Judy Garland) steps out of her crashed farmhouse and enters Munchkinland for the first time, one hears a few measures of "Over the Rainbow" (which is literally where she is). Then an enticing, mysterious piece of music is heard before the dialogue begins. After the arrival of Glinda, her theme music turns into the film's most complex song sequence, in which Glinda, Dorothy, and the Munchkins sing eight different songs. Another exceptional musical sequence is the tornado scene, which incorporated several different themes. Stothart reprises Gulch's theme with a nastier tone as it becomes the Witch's motif, the slapstick music for the farmhands is heard when they are seen rowing through the storm in a bathtub, then a furious section with harp glissandos, blaring brass, and music spiraling down the scale is heard as the house falls to earth. It lands with a loud thud and then silence. This is screen scoring at its best.

Stothart's personal life was far from smooth (his wife committed suicide in front of him), so he buried himself in work. It was not unusual for him to score a half dozen movies each year. While visiting Scotland in 1947, Stothart suffered a near-fatal heart attack. He recovered and wrote the instrumental work "Heart Attack: A Symphonic Poem" about the experience. Two years later he died from spinal cancer. His passing was felt strongly by MGM, but the general public took little notice. Stothart did his job so well that his work went practically undetected.

Credits

(all films USA unless stated otherwise; * Oscar for Musical Direction)

Year	Film	Director
1928	The End of St. Petersburg	V. Pudovkin, M. Doller (USSR)
1929	Devil-May-Care	Sidney Franklin
1930	The Florodora Girl	Harry Beaumont
1930	Sevilla de mis amores (aka Call of the Flesh)	Ramon Navarro
1931	The Prodigal	Harry A. Pollard
1931	La chanteur de Séville	Ramon Novarro
1931	The Squaw Man	Cecil B. DeMille
1931	The Cuban Love Song	W. S. Van Dyke
1932	The Son-Daughter	Clarence Brown
1932	Rasputin and the Empress	Richard Boleslawski
1933	The White Sister	Victor Fleming
1933	The Barbarian	Sam Wood
1933	Peg o' My Heart	Robert Z. Leonard
1933	Turn Back the Clock	Edgar Selwyn
1933	Night Flight	Clarence Brown
1933	Christopher Bean	Sam Wood
1933	Going Hollywood	Raoul Walsh
1933	Queen Christina	Rouben Mamoulian
1934	The Cat and the Fiddle	William K. Howard
1934	Riptide	Edmund Goulding
1934	Viva Villa!	Jack Conway
1934	Laughing Boy	W. S. Van Dyke
1934	Treasure Island	Victor Fleming
1934	Chained	Clarence Brown
1934	The Barretts of Wimpole Street	Sidney Franklin
1934	What Every Woman Knows	Gregory La Cava
1934	The Painted Veil	Richard Boleslawski
1935	Biography of a Bachelor Girl	Edward H. Griffith
1935	The Night Is Young	Dudley Murphy
1935	Sequoia	Chester M. Franklin
1935	David Copperfield	George Cukor
1935	The Winning Ticket	Charles Reisner
1935	Vanessa: Her Love Story	William K. Howard
1935	Pursuit	Edwin L. Marin
1935	China Seas	Tay Garnett
1935	Anna Karenina	Clarence Brown
1935	Mutiny on the Bounty	Frank Lloyd
1935	A Night at the Opera	Sam Wood
1935	Ah, Wilderness!	Clarence Brown
1935	A Tale of Two Cities	Jack Conway
1936	Rose-Marie	W. S. Van Dyke
1936	Wife vs. Secretary	Clarence Brown
1936	Robin Hood of El Dorado	William A. Wellman
1936	Moonlight Murder	Edwin L. Marin
1936	Small Town Girl	William A. Wellman
1936	San Francisco	W. S. Van Dyke
1936	Romeo and Juliet	George Cukor
1936	The Gorgeous Hussy	Clarence Brown
1936	The Devil Is a Sissy	W. S. Van Dyke
1936	Camille	George Cukor
1936	After the Thin Man	W. S. Van Dyke
1936	The Good Earth	Sidney Franklin
1937	Conquest	Clarence Brown
1938	Of Human Hearts	Clarence Brown

Year	Film	Director
1938	*The Girl of the Golden West*	Robert Z. Leonard
1938	*Sweethearts (AAN)*	W. S. Van Dyke
1938	*Marie Antoinette (AAN)*	W. S. Van Dyke
1939	*Idiot's Delight*	Clarence Brown
1939	*The Wizard of Oz (AA)*	Victor Fleming
1939	*Broadway Serenade*	Robert Z. Leonard
1939	*Balalaika*	Reinhold Schünzel
1940	*Northwest Passage*	King Vidor
1940	*Edison, the Man*	Clarence Brown
1940	*Waterloo Bridge (AAN)*	Mervyn LeRoy
1940	*Susan and God*	George Cukor
1940	*New Moon*	Robert Z. Leonard
1940	*Pride and Prejudice*	Robert Z. Leonard
1941	*Come Live with Me*	Clarence Brown
1941	*Men of Boys Town*	Norman Taurog
1941	*Ziegfeld Girl*	Robert Z. Leonard, Busby Berkeley
1941	*Blossoms in the Dust*	Mervyn LeRoy
1941	*They Met in Bombay*	Clarence Brown
1941	*Smilin' Through*	Frank Borzage
1941	*The Chocolate Soldier (AAN*)*	Roy Del Ruth
1942	*Rio Rita*	S. Sylvan Simon
1942	*Mrs. Miniver*	William Wyler
1942	*I Married an Angel*	W. S. Van Dyke
1942	*Cairo*	W. S. Van Dyke
1942	*Random Harvest (AAN)*	Mervyn LeRoy
1942	*Tennessee Johnson*	William Dieterle
1943	*The Human Comedy*	Clarence Brown
1943	*Three Hearts for Julia*	Richard Thorpe
1943	*Thousands Cheer (AAN)*	George Sidney
1943	*Madame Curie (AAN)*	Mervyn LeRoy
1943	*A Guy Named Joe*	Victor Fleming
1944	*The White Cliffs of Dover*	Clarence Brown
1944	*Dragon Seed*	Harold S. Bucquet, Jack Conway
1944	*Kismet(AAN)*	William Dieterle
1944	*Thirty Seconds Over Tokyo*	Mervyn LeRoy
1944	*National Velvet*	Clarence Brown
1945	*The Picture of Dorian Gray*	Albert Lewin
1945	*Son of Lassie*	S. Sylvan Simon
1945	*The Valley of Decision (AAN)*	Tay Garnett
1945	*They Were Expendable*	John Ford
1945	*Adventure*	Victor Fleming
1945	*The Green Years*	Victor Saville
1946	*Undercurrent*	Vincente Minnelli
1946	*The Yearling*	Clarence Brown
1947	*The Sea of Grass*	Elia Kazan
1947	*High Barbaree*	Jack Conway
1947	*The Unfinished Dance*	Henry Koster
1947	*Desire Me*	Jack Conway, etc.
1947	*If Winter Comes*	Victor Saville
1948	*Three Daring Daughters*	Fred M. Wilcox
1948	*The Three Musketeers*	George Sidney
1948	*Hills of Home*	Fred M. Wilcox
1949	*Big Jack*	Richard Thorpe

STOTT, Wally See MORLEY, Angela.

TAKEMITSU, Tôru (1930–1996) An internationally acclaimed Japanese composer for the concert hall, movies, and television, the avant-garde artist and writer was very active in films in the 1960s and 1970s and scored some of the most important works in Japan's New Wave cinema.

Tôru Takemitsu was born in Tokyo, lived in the Chinese province in Manchuria for the first five years of his life, and then returned to Japan for elementary school. At the age of fourteen he was conscripted into the army for the last year of World War II. Because Western music was banned in Japan during the war, Takemitsu did not get to hear much classical or popular music from the West until the American occupation after the war, when he listened to the U.S. Armed Forces Radio Network. A self-taught composer, Takemitsu at first rejected traditional Japanese music and relied on Western music for his inspiration. But as he matured, the young composer learned to incorporate his native musical forms into his experimental work with electronic and abstract music. During the 1950s Takemitsu created unique piano and other instrumental works that used electronics and multimedia, such as recording part of a composition and altering it as it was heard against live music. Takemitsu first gained an international reputation when composer Igor Stravinsky visited Japan in 1958 and was so impressed with the young artist's music that he arranged for commissions in the West. Although he was labeled an avant-garde artist, Takemitsu embraced many different forms of music, and his numerous works show influences of everyone from John Cage to Claude Debussy. His concert hall repertoire includes many chamber works, piano solos, guitar works, and orchestral pieces with and without featured solo instruments.

Part of the little formal music training Takemitsu received was in the early 1950s when he studied privately with the celebrated film composer Fumio Hayasaka. The young Takemitsu was fascinated with the possibilities in screen music and in 1955 he scored his first movie, a short documentary titled *Bicycle in Dream*. The next year he scored the feature drama *Crazed Fruit*, which was not only a success in Japan but, because of the urging of French director François Truffaut, was widely shown in the West. By the 1960s, Takemitsu was scoring several Japanese films each year, working with such distinguished directors as Masahiro Shinooda, Hiroshi Teshigahara, Noboru Nakamura, Masaki Kobayashi, and Akira Kurosawa. Among his many movies that found international recognition are *The Inheritance, Harakiri, Woman in the Dunes, Ghost Stories, Double Suicide, Dodes'ka-den, The Ceremony, Ran, Wuthering Heights, Black Rain,* and *Sharaku.* His only American film was the crime drama *Rising Sun*; it was not a fruitful experience for the composer and he refused all subsequent offers from Hollywood. By the 1980s Takemitsu concentrated on his concert work and was less involved in movies, yet he still scored several short and feature-length documentaries for the big screen and for television. He also wrote twenty books about music theory and practice. Two years before Takemitsu died at the age of sixty-five, he was the subject of the American film documentary *Music for the Movies: Tôru Takemitsu* (1994). The Tôru Takemitsu Composition Award is an international competition for young composers of orchestral works.

Takemitsu was an evolving composer who took on many different kinds of music during his fifty-year career, always experimenting with new forms, different philosophies of music, and recent technological innovations. This eclectic quality can be heard in his eighty-two movie scores because they were written over a period of four decades. Takemitsu claimed that the inspiration for his film music was the director's vision, each project becoming a new experiment. He was fortunate to work with some outstanding directors who trusted him enough to let him fill his scores with abstract music, manufactured noise, and, at times, pure silence. One of his earliest works, Kobayashi's *Seppuku* (known in the West as *Harakiri*), is very revealing. When an aging samurai (Tatsuya Kakadai) prepares to commit ritual suicide in a feudal lord's house, his past comes back to haunt him. Although the tale is set in seventeenth-century Japan, the soundtrack is abstract and dramatic, a kind of film noir score played on unconventional instruments, making the dark tone even more oppressive. In one passage, vibrating chords are punctuated with metal clanging that creates uncomfortable suspense. Various forms of unconventional percussion with low brass accompaniment push another theme forward with a strange hypnotic power. There is also a furious passage played on metal strings that seem to growl with anger even as the music slips into some familiar Asian folk phrases on reverberating strings. At several points in the movie, crashing sounds echo and vibrate with icy silence in between each explosion. Teshigahara's *Woman in the Dunes* is a masterwork of Japanese New Wave cinema and boasts one of Takemitsu's finest scores. The plot is a bizarre but intriguing tale of an entomologist (Eiji Okada) who travels to a remote village to study the seaside insects and is kidnapped by a strange and beautiful woman (Kyôko Kioshida). The music is very modern with barely a traditional melody to be heard as sounds of nature (wind, waves, thunder, etc.) are mixed with echoing musical chords, again with potent silence in between. The movie opens with a montage of urban sounds that lead into the credits scored with wooden knocking, harsh chords, high-frequency electronic notes, and agitated horns and strings. A later passage consists of distorted electronic sounds that accompany a bass violin and some atonal phrases played on strings and reeds. Two other memorable themes are a low grumbling track on low strings and high-pitched synthesized sounds that creates a sense of internal chaos, and a percussion passage played on various metal objects and wire strings as an echoing high note suggests the cry of a seagull.

Takemitsu's less abstract, more melodic side can be heard in Kurosawa's slice-of-life drama *Dodes'ka-den*. (The title is an onomatopoeic phrase for the sound of a train as it goes "clickety-clack" over the rails.) The episodic plot covers various inhabitants of an urban slum in Tokyo, each resident dealing with poverty in different ways. Despite the squalid setting and grim reality of the filming, Takemitsu's music is shockingly cheerful. A solo guitar with xylophone accompaniment transitions into a poetic and free-flowing melody featuring a harmonica and then a muted trumpet and then a recorder. Also lighthearted is a bouncy waltz on reeds and strings with recorder and harp accents; an oddly catchy dance theme played by a small ensemble and featuring solos by trumpet, recorder, harmonica, and clarinet; and a sweeping passage in which a harmonica and vibraphone contribute to the merry piece. Despite the frivolous tone, the dire circumstances of the residents are suggested in a restful and flowing theme with distorted accompaniment so that it is both soothing and disturbing. Perhaps the most memorable track is a repetitive but engaging piece on oboe and pipes that plods along happily, gaining richness as new instruments are added. A Takemitsu score that embraces both the modern and the traditional is the sterling one he wrote for Kurosawa's *Ran*, a highlight of Japanese filmmaking. This version of the King Lear legend set in feudal Japan involves a Great Lord (Tatsuya Nakadai) who divides his kingdom into sections and gives them to his sons only to be betrayed by them. The movie is a visual treat with startling images and compelling action scenes. Many consider Takemitsu's music in *Ran* to be the best he wrote for the screen. It is certainly used in a brilliant way. Sometimes a furious battle is scored with serene musical sounds and at other times a casual conversation is accompanied by agitated music on the soundtrack. The main theme consists of whistling Asian flutes and pipes, electronic sustained notes, ethnic percussion, and low string glissandos. There is a disturbing passage with various percussion instruments heard against repeating pipe phrases, as well as a theme on Asian and Western strings that moves from a tentative melody to atonal phrases then back again. Also effective in the score is a track with dissonant phrases played on brass and strings that suggest a wind that kicks up then subsides; echoing electronic and conventional horns and strings in a weary passage that seems to tumble up and down the scale with resignation; an Asian flute solo that explores different musical ideas with no accompaniment, giving the passage a forlorn tone; and a theme in which growling brass and angry percussion are undercut by swirling strings and wailing pipes. Many of Takemitsu's ideas about music, both lyrical and abstract, can be found in the score for *Ran*. How fortunate that one of the twentieth century's giants of modern music devoted so much of his career to the cinema. Critical study: *The Music of Tôru Takemitsu*, Peter Burt (2001).

Credits

(all films Japan unless stated otherwise)

Year	Film	Director
1956	*Crazed Fruit*	Kô Nakahira
1957	*Doshaburi*	Noboru Nakamura
1960	*Dry Lake* (aka *Youth in Fury*)	Masahiro Shinoda
1960	*Mozu*	Minoru Shibuya
1961	*Bad Boys*	Susumu Hani
1962	*The Inheritance*	Masaki Kobayashi
1962	*Pitfall*	Hiroshi Teshigahara
1962	*Harakiri*	Masaki Kobayahi
1962	*Tears on the Lion's Mane* (aka *A Flame at the Pier*)	Masahiro Shinoda
1963	*Koto* (aka *Twin Sisters of Kyoto*)	Noboru Nakamura
1963	*Wonderful Bad Woman*	Hideo Onchi
1963	*Pressure of Guilt*	Hiromichi Horikawa
1963	*She and He*	Susumu Hani
1963	*Alone Across the Pacific*	Kon Ichikawa
1963	*Children Hand in Hand*	Susumu Hani
1964	*Woman in the Dunes*	Hiroshi Techigahara
1964	*The Body*	Masashige Narusawa
1964	*Pale Flower*	Masahiro Shinoda
1964	*Escape from Japan*	Yoshishige Yoshida
1964	*Car Thieves*	Yoshinori Wada
1964	*Assassination*	Masahiro Shinoda
1964	*Ghost Stories*	Masaki Kobayashi
1965	*With Beauty and Sorrow*	Masahiro Shinoda
1965	*Illusion of Blood*	Shirô Toyoda
1965	*Beast Alley*	Eizo Sugawa
1965	*Samurai Spy*	Masahiro Shinoda
1966	*Saigô no shinpan*	Hiromichi Horikawa
1966	*The River Kino*	Noboru Nakamura
1966	*Captive's Island*	Masahiro Shinoda
1966	*The Face of Another*	Hiroshi Teshigahara
1966	*The Call of Flesh*	Hideo Onchi
1966	*Once a Rainy Day*	Hideo Onchi
1967	*The Izu Dancer*	Hideo Onchi
1967	*Samurai Rebellion*	Masaki Kobayashi
1967	*The Song of Bwana Tosji*	Susumu Hani
1967	*Two in the Shadow*	Mikio Naruse
1967	*Clouds at Sunset*	Masahiro Shinoda
1968	*Two Hearts in the Rain*	Hideo Onchi
1968	*Nanami: The Inferno of First Love*	Susumu Hani
1968	*A Man without a Map*	Hiroshi Teshigahara
1968	*Hymn to a Tired Man*	Masaki Kobayashi
1969	*Double Suicide*	Masahiro Shinoda
1969	*Bullet Wound*	Shirô Moritani
1970	*The Man Who Put His Will on Film*	Nagisa Ôshima
1970	*Dodes'ka-den*	Akira Kurosawa
1971	*Yomigaeru daichi*	Noboru Nakamura
1971	*The Ceremony*	Nagisa Ôshima
1971	*At the Risk of My Life*	Masaki Kobayashi
1971	*Silence*	Masahiro Shinoda
1972	*Dear Summer Sister*	Nagisa Ôshima
1972	*Summer Soldiers*	Hiroshi Teshigahara
1973	*Seigen-Ki*	Tôichirô Narushima
1973	*The Petrified Forest*	Masahiro Shinoda
1974	*Himiko*	Masahiro Shinoda

Year	Film	Director
1974	*Shiawase*	Hideo Onchi
1975	*The Fossil*	Masaki Kobayashi
1975	*Under the Blossoming Cherry Trees*	Masahiro Shinoda
1977	*Sabita honoo*	Masahiro Sadanaga
1977	*Ballad of Orin*	Masahiro Shinoda
1978	*Empire of Passion*	Nagisa Ôshima
1979	*Glowing Autumn*	Masaki Kobayashi
1980	*Ocean to Cross*	Kei Kumai
1981	*Rennyo and His Mother*	Kihachiro Kawamoto
1985	*Ran* (aka *Revolt*)	Akira Kurosawa (Japan/France)
1985	*Family without a Dinner Table*	Masaki Kobayashi
1985	*Fire Festival*	Mitsuo Yanagimachi
1986	*Gonza the Spearman*	Masahiro Shinoda
1988	*Wuthering Heights*	Yoshishige Yoshida
1989	*Black Rain*	Shôhei Imamura
1989	*Rikyu*	Hiroshi Teshigahara
1992	*Basara—The Princess Goh*	Hiroshi Teshigahara
1993	*Rising Sun*	Philip Kaufman (USA)
1995	*Sharaku*	Masahiro Shinoda

THEODORAKIS, Mikis (b. 1925) A popular Greek composer and songwriter with an international reputation, he has scored over forty movies on four continents, many of them with strong political subject matter. Because of the worldwide popularity of his scores for *Zorba the Greek*, *Z*, *State of Siege*, and other films, he is arguably the most famous Greek composer of the twentieth century.

Born Mihail Theodorakis on the Greek island of Chios, the son of a lawyer, he grew up in different rural towns across Greece, learning the folk music of the people and the traditional music of the Greek Orthodox Church. Theodorakis was fascinated by music from an early age but had no access to musical instruments, so he composed tunes in his head. As a teenager he got to study music in schools in Pyrgos and Patras, formed his own choir, and gave performances for the public. When World War II broke out, Theodorakis joined the Resistance movement and was caught and tortured by the occupying Nazis. After the war he was active during the Greek Civil War in the late 1940s, was again arrested and tortured, and wrote his first symphony while in prison. Released in 1948, Theodorakis studied music at the Athens Conservatory and the Paris Conservatory. It was in Paris that he began composing for the concert stage. His first symphonies, concertos, ballets, oratorios, song cycles, and other works were performed across Europe and the United States in the 1950s, and in the early 1960s he returned to Greece, where he founded the Little Orchestra of Athens and other ensembles. Because of his contribution in the war and his strong political beliefs, Theodorakis was named to the Greek Parliament in 1964. When the junta came to power in Greece in 1967, he was critical of the new Fascist government, was arrested, and was sent to a concentration camp in Oropos. An international group of artists petitioned the government to have Theodorakis released and in 1970 his sentence was changed to exile. When the junta collapsed in the late 1970s, he returned to Greece where he served again in Parliament and was active in many musical and political organizations. Although Theodorakis scored a handful of movies in the 1950s, he did not actively pursue a screen career until the 1960s. It was his popular score for *Zorba the Greek* in 1964 that made him an international celebrity and such politically charged movies as *The Roundup*, *State of Siege*, *A Member of the Firing Squad*, *Biribi*, and *Z* confirmed his reputation as an international political activist. Theodorakis remains a visible figure in Greek politics. In 2010, he founded Spitha: The People's Independent Movement to combat Greece's economic situation and oppose the standing government.

Theodorakis's screen work is an eclectic collection of movies made by such disparate nations as France, Australia, Hungary, Great Britain, Yugoslavia, Turkey, Germany, and the United States. While many of his movies have a strong political theme, they are all very different in location, story, characters, and time period. Half of these films were made in Greece, and Greek culture and music are prevalent throughout his scores. He has written music for screen versions of Greek classical drama, such as *Electra*, *The Trojan Women*, *Iphigenia*, and the modern version of *Phaedra*. Of his American films, the police drama *Serpico* is perhaps his most known. In addition to feature films, Theodorakis has written music for many television and movie documentaries on potent political subjects. His screen career has not hindered his musical achievements elsewhere. Throughout his life, Theodorakis has often returned to his love of Greek folk songs and he has written over one thousand songs of his own, many of them now part of the Greek consciousness. He has often worked in the theatre, writing music for dozens of productions of classic and new plays. Theodorakis has also written poetry, some of which has been translated into English, and he has often written about his art, as in the 1983 book *Music and Theatre*.

Zorba the Greek was not the first film to dazzle the world with Greek music. Four years earlier Jules Dassin's popular *Never on Sunday* had a riveting score by Mano Hadjidakis which sold many records and won an Oscar. But the music in *Zorba the Greek* was the first to illustrate the many shades of Greek music because this film has very dark as well as joyous moments. The famous main theme, "Zorba's Dance," is a rapid, exuberant piece played on a solo bouzouki with other strings doing the bass line. This same theme slowed down can become very sexy or, with minor chords, mournful. For the end of the movie, when the staid Englishman (Alan Bates) asks Zorba (Anthony Quinn) to teach him how to dance, the rhythmic piece begins carefully then is filled out with busier harmony as the tempo picks up, eventually returning to the rapid-fire version heard at the top of the film. This is the theme that audiences embraced (and danced to) around the world. But the movie is filled with other wonderful passages. "Catastrophe" is a melancholy lament played on the violin while "Questions without Answers" is an eccentric mix of swift bouzouki notes and long echoing chords that gradually speed up into an unhappy frenzy. There is also a lazy waltz performed on accordion and strings as it descends the scale in a delectable manner. This is a movie overflowing with music and one cannot imagine *Zorba the Greek* without Theodorakis's score. When the film was turned into the Broadway musical *Zorbá* in 1968 with a fine score by John Kander (music) and Fred Ebb (lyrics), the major

complaint by the critics was how unnecessary it all was. This tale had already been beautifully musicalized.

French director Costa-Gavras's controversial *State of Siege* is set in Uruguay, and the score uses native flutes and guitars to capture the locale. While one recognizes the ingenious use of various strings for melody and harmony, there is a very un-Greek sound to the score. The selections are both modern and traditionally Spanish, rhythmic and percussive yet not festive. The music may be melodic, but there is an oppressive undertone to it all that is more than appropriate for a film about political assassination. The American cop drama *Serpico* may seem to be out of place in Theodorakis's credits until one realizes the thrust of the story is about an honest police officer (Al Pacino) who goes against the establishment. The main musical theme may sound a bit too Mediterranean for the Manhattan setting, but the echoing electronic instruments certainly convey an urban ambiance. Other selections use jazz and funk in a restless and overheated manner and Theodorakis firmly places us in the underside of New York City. The modern retelling of *Phaedra* has a similar restlessness. The main theme moves along at a feverish pace, much like the ill-fated passion between a woman (Melina Mercouri) and her stepson (Anthony Perkins). The love theme is slower and fully orchestrated at first but soon a solo guitar overrides all the other instruments and an overheated tone takes over. For those traditionally told Greek legends brought to the screen, Theodorakis's music is a lovely blending of ancient Greek and contemporary instruments. The theme for *Iphigenia* has high flutes and low strings that move at a steady pace as they forebode the tragedy to come. *Electra* opens with a very ancient tribal theme with various drums and the roar of a crowd all part of the music. The murder of Aegisthus is scored with a chaotic fusion of deep brass, electronic sounds, and piercing woodwinds, and the climactic ending uses the bouzouki in a furious display of passion. Perhaps the finest of these Greek classic screen versions is *The Trojan Women*. While there is less action in this film, the grief portrayed is overwhelming in a way the other stories are not. There is no opening theme but rather eerie electronic sounds as the women of Troy are rounded up from the burning city. The rest of the film is also scored with restraint, often just low drums heard in the distance, other times chanting voices, even electronic chords at moments. There is silence during some of the most horrendous scenes, such as the murder of Hector's little boy, but the burning of Troy at the end is scored with chaotic drums, rumbling thunder, and finally a solo horn.

The Battle of Sutjeska, a Yugoslav film about a landmark battle during World War II, is one of the biggest productions Theodorakis ever scored. Yet he opens the huge film with a simple lullaby played by solo oboe with an orchestral background. There are other quiet, if chilling, passages in the score, which often sounds more like a suspense film than an action one. Even the scoring for the battle scenes, played by a full orchestra, has understated music that points out the sadness of the events rather than the action itself. *The Day the Fish Came Out* is a quirky film about the threat of an atomic explosion in Spain. Theodorakis opens the film with a solo castanet playing under the narration then launches into a mock-bullfight march. The flamenco strings throughout the movie are often electronic as is the organ and other instruments. It is a delightfully odd score for a sly offbeat, if unsuccessful, movie.

Theodorakis's interest in Greek music and politics reaches its height in Costa-Gavras's celebrated 1969 film *Z*. The story of a political assassination and the government cover-up that follows intrigued the world, particularly Americans when a few years later the Watergate cover-up was revealed. Theodorakis's score is very Greek, yet this is not the dancing folk tunes of *Zorba the Greek*. The main theme is a riveting piece of musical commentary. Traditional Greek instruments play the propulsive rhythm section while horns play the marchlike melody. This is later repeated with electronic instruments for a chase scene and other action moments. There is a casual foxtrot with various strings that has a weary tone. Suspense is generated by pounding drums and other percussion instruments, and reconstructions of the assassination are scored with distorted music and a wood block providing a clocklike ticking. The mock march played while all the corrupt officials are in turn questioned and arrested is a marvelous use of music to wryly comment on the visuals. But *Z* does not have a happy ending, and the final music is mournful, not only for the innocent victims in the affair but for Greece itself. Theodorakis has been able to use music as both an artistic and political expression as few composers have. Most remarkably, he has done so and remained popular. Along with fellow composer Mano Hadjidakis, he is responsible for making Greek music popular around the world and establishing the bouzouki as a distinctive musical sound. Biographies: *Mikis Theodorakis: Music and Social Change*, George Giannaris (1972); *Mikis Theodorakis, the Greek Soul*, George Logothetis (2004); *Mikis Theodorakis: Finding Greece in His Music*, Angelique Mouyis (2010). Official website: www.mikis-theodorakis.net.

Credits

(all films Greece unless stated otherwise)

Year	Film	Director
1953	The Barefoot Battalion	Gregg C. Tallas (Greece/USA)
1953	Eva	Maria Plyta
1954	O golgothas mias orfanis	Dimis Dadiras, Spyros Nikolaidis
1957	Night Ambush	Michael Powell, Emeric Pressburger (UK)
1960	Faces in the Dark	David Eady (UK)
1961	The Shadow of the Cat	John Gilling (UK)
1961	Synoikia to Oneiro	Alekos Alexandrakis
1962	Electra	Mihalis Kakogiannis
1962	Les amants de Teruel	Raymond Pouleau (France)
1962	Phaedra	Jules Dassin (France/Greece/USA)
1962	Five Miles to Midnight	Anatole Litvak (France/Italy)
1962	Betrayed Love	Errikos Thalassinos
1964	Zorba the Greek (GGN)	Mihalis Kakogiannis (USA/Greece)
1965	The Roundup	Adonis Kyrou
1965	Kataigida	Kostas Andritsos
1965	Angels without Wings	Kostas Yeorgoutsos
1966	Devil at My Heels	Jean-Daniel Pollet (France/Greece)
1967	The Day the Fish Came Out	Mihalis Kakogiannis (Greece/UK/USA)
1968	The Lost Generation	András Kovács (Hungary)

Year	Film	Director
1968	A Member of the Firing Squad	Manos Zacharias (Soviet Union)
1969	Z (BAFTA)	Costa-Gavras (France/Algeria)
1971	Biribi	Daniel Moosmann (France/Tunisia)
1971	The Trojan Women	Mihalis Kakogiannis (UK/USA/Greece)
1972	State of Siege	Costa-Gavras (France/Italy/W. Germany)
1973	The Battle of Sutjeska	Stipe Delic (Yugoslavia)
1973	Serpico (BAFTA-N)	Sidney Lumet (USA/Italy)
1974	Tactical Guerilla	Stole Jankovic (USA/Yugoslavia)
1974	The Rehearsal	Jules Dassin (UK/Greece)
1975	Order: Kill Makarios	Kostas Dimitriou, Pavlos Filippou
1975	Der Geheimnisträger	Franz Josef Gottlieb (W. Germany)
1976	Actas de Marusia (aka Letters from Marusia)	Miguel Littin (Mexico)
1976	O thanasis sti hora tis sfaliaras	Panos Glykofrydis, Dinos Katsouridis
1977	Iphigenia	Mihalis Kakogiannis
1979	Easy Road	Andreas Thomopoulos
1979	Kostas	Paul Cox (Australia)
1980	The Man with the Carnation	Nikos Tzimas
1986	Les clowns de Dieu	Jean Schmidt (France)
1988	Mist	Zülfü Livanelli (Sweden/W. Germany/Turkey)
1988	Misioni përtej detit	Lisenko Malaj (Albania)
2000	Beware of Greeks Bearing Guns	John Tatoulis (Australia/Greece)
2001	The Seventh Sun of Love	Vangelis Serdaris (Greece/Bulgaria/Turkey)

THIRIET, Maurice (1906–1972) A distinguished French composer for the concert hall and movies, he scored fifty-two feature films between 1933 and 1961, most memorably three French masterworks with director Marcel Carné.

Born in Meulan-en-Yvelines, France, Maurice Thiriet studied composition and orchestration at the Paris Conservatory of Music. After graduating in 1931, Thiriet began writing orchestral pieces for the concert hall. His friend and fellow composer Maurice Jaubert got him interested in screen scoring and in 1933 he cowrote with Marcel Delannoy the score for the drama *Once Upon a Time*. The next year Thiriet composed his first solo score, for Maurice Tourneur's *Le voleur*, followed by other dramatic features in the prewar 1930s, including the Hollywood romance *The Woman I Love* in 1937 (his only American film). During the Nazi occupation, Thiriet continued to compose for the struggling French movie industry. In 1942 he worked with director Carné on the fantasy drama *Les visiteurs du soir* which has become one of the most applauded French films of that period. Even more accomplished was Carné's *Children of Paradise* in 1945, considered by many to be the greatest of all French movies. Thiriet and Carné worked together again in 1953 on the acclaimed crime romance *The Adultress* based on the Émile Zola novel *Therese Raquin*. Collaborating with renowned French and other European directors,

Thiriet scored such notable films as *Southern Carrier*, *Fantastic Night*, *Queen's Necklace*, *La figure de proue*, *Riptide*, *Portrait of an Assassin*, *Fan-Fan the Tulip*, *King on Horseback*, *The Possessors*, and two movies based on Dostoyevsky novels, *L'idiot* and *Crime and Punishment*. Approximately one-fifth of Thiriet's movies were scored with someone else. Thiriet often returned to classical music throughout his career, and his output is considerable, including two operas, ten ballets, many concertos, chamber pieces, and full orchestral works, as well as numerous art songs. He continued to compose up until his death at the age of sixty-six in 1972, the year he scored the French TV movie *Figaro-ci, Figaro-là*.

There is a lyrical quality to all of Thiriet's music, often in the form of French romantic impressionism. Yet the movie scores can also be very dramatic and theatrical. One can find the influence of music by Maurice Jaubert, the mentor and source of inspiration for the younger composer. Thiriet's scores for three Carné films illustrate the range and temperament of his screen music. *Les visiteurs du soir*, sometimes listed as *The Devil's Envoys*, is a fanciful romantic drama about two fifteenth-century minstrels (Alain Cuny and Arletty) who arrive at the castle of a Baron (Fernand Ledoux) to do the devil's work but end up discovering love. The score is a sparkling set of themes that suggest a medieval world yet remain quite modern. The score opens with a robust theme with blaring trumpet phrases that are echoed by other instruments in a full orchestra, all of it climaxing with some splashing crescendos. This is contrasted by a lyrical passage featuring strings and woodwinds that slows down to a pause then finds the power to continue on. The court of the Baron is scored with a majestic processional with quieter string and reed sections. Also memorable is a serene theme on oboe and strings that has a melancholy air as it hesitates before moving forward, a lovely flute and violin duet that seems to float in the air, and a sad waltz with chiming accents that is tentative yet keeps moving with a mournful tone. It must be pointed out that the Hungarian-born Joseph Kosma is listed as the co-composer for *Les visiteurs du soir*, but the score is considered to be mostly by Thiriet. Carné's *The Adultress* has a very different tone and both the movie and Thiriet's score (a solo effort) might be described as romantic film noir. This updated version of Zola's *Therese Raquin* concerns a wife (Simone Signoret) and her lover (Raf Vallone) who murder her boring husband (Jacques Duby) then find themselves the victims of blackmail. The film is dark and passionate, as conveyed in the opening music, which is a restless passage with different instruments each on their own track as the melody is etched out piece by piece. This same theme later serves as the sensual and dissonant love theme, with violins wandering up and down the scale until they break into a full-fledged passionate melody. Thiriet also composed a sprightly song for the soundtrack, "Sur un air de Limonaire," which has a doleful subtext.

Thiriet's expansive score for the epic *Children of Paradise* might be considered his screen masterwork. Made under the watchful eyes of the German occupiers, the enthralling film utilized many Resistance members behind the scenes and on-screen, some of whom were arrested before filming was completed. The expensive movie was partially financed by Italian companies, but when Italy fell to the Allies, the funding was lost. All the same, the production values of the movie are still impressive today, particularly the re-creation of Paris's Boulevard du Crime of the 1830s, the huge cast of characters and extras, and the scenes inside various theatres. Jacques Prévert's Dickens-like script centers on the love a mime performer (Jean-Louis Barrault) has for an actress (Arletty) and how it perseveres over time even when he marries another woman (María Casares) and his beloved falls under the protection of a powerful aristocrat (Louis Salou). *Children of Paradise* (the title refers to spectators who sit up high in the theatre balcony) is also about theatre, illusion vs. reality, and other fascinating ideas. There is so much music in the long (163 minutes) movie that Thiriet's friend Kosma contributed by providing the scoring for some of the mime sequences. Thiriet's main theme is a festive passage filled with eager strings and happy brass and the percussion celebrates with marchlike flourishes. The many crowd scenes are scored with rambunctious carnival music. At one point an early form of cancan is played on woodwinds and a leaden drum, and rapid circus music is heard during a fight scene in the theatre. Thiriet uses the waltz form at different points in the story. There is a swirling waltz with a Viennese air played for an upper-class ball and a clumsy waltz on strident strings for a street dance. Also memorable is a melancholy waltz with minor-key flourishes that returns for some of the potent scenes of unrequited love. Thiriet's talent for capturing the romantic and the dramatic reaches its height in *Children of Paradise* and the legendary movie is a testament to his place in cinema music.

Credits

(all films France unless stated otherwise)

Year	Film	Director
1933	Once Upon a Time	Léonce Perret
1933	Le voleur	Maurice Tourneur
1936	The Terrible Lovers	Marc Allégret
1937	Southern Carrier	Pierre Billon
1937	The Woman I Love	Anatole Litvak (USA)
1938	Adrienne Lecouvreur	Marcel L'Herbier (France/Germany)
1942	Fantastic Night	Marcel L'Herbier
1942	L'homme qui joue avec le feu	Jean de Limur
1942	Les visiteurs du soir	Marcel Carné

Year	Film	Director
1943	*A Star to the Sun*	André Zwoboda
1943	*The Wolf of the Malveneurs*	Guillaume Radot
1943	*The Roquevillards*	Jean Dréville
1943	*The Secret of Madame Clapain*	André Berthomieu
1943	*Vautrin the Thief*	Pierre Billon
1944	*Angel of the Night*	André Berthomieu
1944	*Le Bal des Passants*	Guillaume Radot
1945	*Children of Paradise*	Marcel Carné
1945	*Paméla*	Pierre de Hérain
1946	*L'idiot*	Georges Lampin
1946	*The Eternal Husband*	Pierre Billon
1946	*Queen's Necklace*	Marcel L'Herbier
1947	*They Are Not Angels*	Alexander Esway
1947	*The Scarlet Bazaar*	Paul Mesnier
1947	*Chemins sans loi*	Guillaume Radot
1948	*Éternel conflit*	Georges Lampin
1948	*La figure de proue*	Christian Stengel
1948	*Three Boys, One Girl*	Maurice Labro
1948	*Le destin exécrable de Guillemette Babin*	Guillaume Radot
1949	*Riptide*	Yves Allégret (France/Netherlands)
1949	*La louve*	Guillaume Radot
1949	*Portrait of an Assassin*	Bernard-Roland
1950	*Cartouche, roi de Paris*	Guillaume Radot
1950	*Mystere a Shanghai*	Roger Blanc
1951	*Passion*	Georges Lampin
1952	*The House on the Dune*	Georges Lampin
1952	*Fan-Fan the Tulip*	Christian-Jaque (Italy/France)
1953	*Follow That Man*	Georges Lampin
1953	*Fatal Affair*	Henri Calef
1953	*Lucrece Borgia*	Christian-Jaque (Italy/France)
1953	*The Adultress (aka Therese Raquin)*	Marcel Carné (France/Italy)
1954	*Flesh and the Woman*	Robert Siodmak (Italy/France)
1954	*Air of Paris*	Marcel Carné (France/Italy)
1956	*Crime and Punishment*	Georges Lampin
1957	*There's Always a Price Tag*	Denys de la Patelliere (Italy/France)
1958	*Therese Étienne*	Denys de la Patelliere (Italy/France)
1958	*King on Horseback*	Georges Lampin (France/Yugoslavia/Italy)
1958	*The Possessors*	Denys de la Patelliere
1959	*Eyes of Love*	Denys de la Patelliere (Italy/France)
1961	*Bernadette of Lourdes*	Robert Darene (Italy/France)

THOMSON, Virgil (1896–1989) An eminent American composer and music critic, he scored only two feature films and two full-length documentaries, but his screen music ranks with the finest written for the medium.

Born Virgil Garnett Thomson in Kansas City, Missouri, he began playing the piano at the age of five without instruction. Thomson later took piano and organ lessons, becoming the organist for his local church and others in the Kansas City area. After serving in the army during World War I, he went to Harvard, where he began composing and sang in the university glee club. It was while singing with that group that Thomson first toured Europe, and he was so taken with the artistic climate in Paris in 1925 that he remained there for fifteen years. Thomson not only met and befriended American and European artists, he also collaborated with some of them, most famously with Gertrude Stein on the modern opera *Four Saints in Three Acts* (1928). Returning to the States in 1940, Thomson pursued careers as an organist and composer even as he became music critic for the *New*

York Herald-Tribune. His blunt and controversial criticism made him some enemies but also established Thomson as a singular and unique mind in modern American music. Thomson worked in theatre on occasion, most memorably as the composer of incidental music for Orson Welles's production of *Macbeth*, and scored his first film in 1936 when he was commissioned to write music for the documentary short *The Plow That Broke the Plains*. The score was widely praised, and two years later Thomson was again applauded for his music for the short documentary *The River*. Not until 1948 did he score a feature-length movie, the semidocumentary *Louisiana Story*. The score was highly acclaimed and won the Pulitzer Prize for Music, the only occasion in which a movie soundtrack was so honored. Thomson was so busy composing and writing music criticism that he did not score another movie until a decade later, the Hollywood melodrama *The Goddess*. His final two film projects were the British documentary *Power among Men* and the American documentary *Journey to America*. The last was first shown at the American pavilion at the New York World's Fair in 1964 and its music was later turned into an orchestral suite titled *Pilgrims and Pioneers*. Thomson's later years were spent as mentor to young American composers who experimented with new forms of music.

Although Thomson's concert and opera music has been described as everything from atonal to minimalist, his film music is clearly in an American folk tradition. The captivating score for *The Plow That Broke the Plains* is filled with rousing rural music, bucolic passages celebrating nature, patriotic sections, jazz interludes, and finally somber music with a modern flavor to illustrate the desertion of the Dust Bowl as families moved west. The score for *The River* is also a piece of Americana with varying tones. Sometimes woodwind fanfares illustrate the Mississippi River and rustic melodies wax sentimental over the Old South. Vigorous musical passages accompany the industrial expansion of the river valley, then melancholy themes with a folk flavor tell of the soil erosion and the flooding of the area. The movie ends with a bold passage that gives the Mississippi majesty and power. These two short films, totaling only fifty-six minutes, have music throughout and

can be considered as two orchestral suites with separate movements. They have often been performed in concert halls, but the music is best appreciated as soundtracks to exceptionally fine documentaries. *Louisiana Story* has documentary elements but is really a feature film with a story. A young boy (Joseph Boudreaux) living in the Louisiana bayou watches his homeland change when oil companies come and start drilling. Thomson's score uses touches of French folk songs to suggest the Creole background of the characters and local Acadian dance tunes are incorporated as well. Yet most of the music in *Louisiana Story* is a beautiful blending of different instruments to depict the sounds of nature. Again the music is almost continuous; so much so that the score was later turned into two lengthy orchestra pieces: *The Louisiana Story Suite* and *Acadian Songs and Dances*. Thomson's music for *The Goddess* also embraces Americana in the first reels when the heroine (Patty Duke) is in rural Maryland. Jazz and other urban music take over once she is older (played by Kim Stanley) and in Hollywood. It is a strong and capable score but not up to the quality and richness of Thomson's earlier screen work.

It is difficult to determine where to place Thomson in movie music. Like Aaron Copland, he helped raise the bar for screen music because he was a renowned composer outside of the movies and proved that his screen work would not feel out of place in the concert hall. On the other hand, Thomson's movie credits are not varied enough to know just how versatile he might have been in Hollywood over a long period of time. Because Thomson was a leading light in modern American music and because he did write a handful of exceptional scores for the screen, his contribution to the art should not be ignored. In addition to his music, Thomson's written criticism of music has been collected and published. The Virgil Thomson Foundation continues to give grants to promising composers and organizations that present American music. Autobiography: *Virgil Thomson* (1985); biographies: *Virgil Thomson: Composer on the Aisle*, Anthony Tommasini (1998); *Virgil Thomson: His Life and Music*, Kathleen Hoover, John Cage (1959). Website: www.virgilthomson.org.

Credits

(all films USA unless stated otherwise)

Year	Film	Director
1948	*Louisiana Story*	Robert J. Flaherty
1958	*The Goddess*	John Cromwell
1959	*Power among Men*	Alexander Hammid, Gian Luigi Polidoro, V. R. Sama (UK)
1964	*Journey to America*	Benjamin Jackson

TIOMKIN, Dimitri (1894–1979) A Russian-born pianist, composer, and songwriter who is considered one of the most influential of Hollywood composers, he wrote memorable scores that often produced memorable songs. Tiomkin worked with a wide selection of directors, from Fred Zinnemann and John Huston to Howard Hawks and Alfred Hitchcock, but he made his most successful films with Frank Capra.

Dimitri Zinovievich Tiomkin was born in Kremenchuk in present-day Ukraine, the son of a physician and a music teacher, and grew up in St. Petersburg, where he studied piano as a youth. He attended St. Petersburg Conservatory and honed his piano skills under Felix Blumenfeld while playing piano for silent films in the local cinemas to help pay his tuition. While still in Russia, Tiomkin became aware of and was fascinated by American ragtime, jazz, and blues, which he heard in a few clubs in St. Petersburg. After the revolution broke out, he relocated to Berlin, where his reputation as a classical pianist grew. With fellow pianist Michael Kariton, Tiomkin toured Europe and first came to America in 1925 when the duo was invited to appear on first-class vaudeville circuits. While touring he met the Austrian ballerina and choreographer Albertina Rasch and the two married, Tiomkin remaining in the States to compose and arrange the music for her dance company. Rasch was a respected and in-demand choreographer on Broadway by the end of the decade, but work dried up after the stock market crash in 1929, so the couple relocated to Hollywood. She quickly found work choreographing spectacular dance sequences for the early musical films, Tiomkin often composing the music for her screen ballets. His first credit for a nonmusical movie was the score for the 1931 screen version of Tolstoy's *Resurrection*. Tiomkin then returned to Broadway as a composer but found little success, so he returned to Hollywood for good in 1933, getting some recognition for his score for the all-star *Alice in Wonderland*.

His career took an important turn in 1937 when he became an American citizen and he first worked with director Frank Capra, the two having a major hit with *Lost Horizon*. Over the next ten years they worked on seven more movies, including such popular favorites as *You Can't Take It with You*, *Mr. Smith Goes to Washington*, *Meet John Doe*, and *It's a Wonderful Life*, as well as several short and feature-length patriotic documentaries during the 1940s. It was during this decade that Tiomkin started to get a reputation for his evocative scores for westerns. Throughout his career he would write the music for some of the most popular movies in the genre, including *Red River*, *Duel in the Sun*, *High Noon*, *The Big Sky*, *Rio Bravo*, *The Westerner*, *Gunfight at the O.K. Corral*, and *The Alamo*. Yet Tiomkin was fortunate not to be labeled in Hollywood, and a wide variety of movies were offered to him. He scored suspense films (including four for Hitchcock), action adventures, gangster flicks, romantic melodramas, historic epics, domestic dramas, and comedies. Tiomkin was often honored (he was nominated for the Oscar sixteen times, winning four times), so he was in great demand and was approached for every sort of project. Tiomkin was unique in that he refused to sign with one studio so was approachable by all moviemakers. Consequently, his body of work is more eclectic than many Hollywood composers. Such variety can be seen in a list of his major scores. In addition to the above mentioned, he wrote the music for such notable films as *Only Angels Have Wings*, *Giant*, *Friendly Persuasion*, *Shadow of a Doubt*, *The Corsican Brothers*, *Portrait of Jennie*, *Champion*, *D.O.A.*, *Cyrano de Bergerac*, *Strangers on a Train*, *Dial M for Murder*, *The Fall of the Roman Empire*, *The High and the Mighty*, and *The Old Man and the Sea*.

DIMITRI TIOMKIN. How ironic that some of the best music written for westerns and other forms of Americana on-screen was by the Russian-born Tiomkin. Here he is standing over star Gary Cooper as he plucks out some of the score from *Friendly Persuasion* (1956). *Allied Artists Pictures / Photofest © Allied Artists Pictures*

Tiomkin was also a very successful songwriter, many of his hits coming from his film scores. On several occasions a musical theme from the score was put to lyrics and the song that resulted was put into the movie. Among the popular songs created this way are "Do Not Forsake Me, Oh My Darlin'" from *High Noon*, "The Green Leaves of Summer" from *The Alamo*, "Strange Are the Ways of Love" from *The Young Land*, "Thee I Love" from *Friendly Persuasion*, "A Duel of Two Hearts" from *Duel in the Sun*, "The Need for Love" from *The Unforgiven*, "This Then Is Texas" from *Giant*, "So Little Time" from *55 Days at Peking*, and the title songs from *Town without Pity*, *Wild Is the Wind*, *The War Wagon*, *The Sundowners*, *The Old Man and the Sea*, and *The High and the Mighty*. This trend of the studios hoping for hit songs from nonmusical movies began with *High Noon* in 1952 and was the fashion for over a decade, yet Tiomkin was one of the few screen composers to come up with a series of popular songs. He often conducted his own recording sessions and gained renown as a conductor of symphony orchestras. He wrote little for television but his theme for the series *Rawhide* is one of the most familiar of all small-screen songs. When his wife died in 1967, Tiomkin decided to retire from Hollywood and lived out his last twelve years in England and France. His only return to movies was arranging the music for the Russian biopic *Tchaikovsky* in 1971. Although he had had a remarkable forty-year career in Hollywood, Tiomkin never felt that his screen music was taken seriously. It was not until the late 1970s that interest in Hollywood composers from the golden age were rediscovered, their music once again performed and recorded. Tiomkin's music has also been used in other movies and television shows, ranging from *Hairspray* and *Beverly Hills, 90210* to *Inglourious Basterds* and *The Sopranos*.

The only characteristic of Tiomkin's music that is easy to pinpoint is his felicitous talent for melody. No wonder the scores often lent themselves to songs. There is little evidence of Tiomkin's Russian roots in his music, something that even the best European composers had difficulty in hiding at times. His first Hollywood score, *Resurrection*, and his last screen credit, arranging the music for *Tchaikovsky*, are obviously very Russian but few of the 120 movies in between rely on such a foreign sound. Tiomkin has too often been categorized as a composer for westerns, which is inaccurate but understandable. His western scores are superb, starting with his first effort *The*

Westerner in 1940. Perhaps his finest work in the genre is the music for *High Noon*, arguably the quintessential Hollywood western. The movie is minimalist in its look and story so Tiomkin's music is simple and direct. Strings are used sparingly as low woodwinds predominate. The main theme "Do Not Forsake Me," which is sung by Tex Ritter over the opening credits, returns in various forms throughout the movie. As tension builds and all eyes are on the clocks in town as noon approaches, Tiomkin adds some disturbing chords and subtly lets the music count the minutes. There is not a full burst of music until after the famous gunfight and the sheriff rides out of town with his bride. *High Noon* is a brilliant movie on many levels, and Tiomkin's arresting score is no small part of its success.

Of Tiomkin's many other westerns, a handful deserve special mention. *Gunfight at the O.K. Corral* also centers on a famous gunfight, but this time the music is more vivacious with whistling, a choir of heavenly voices, and the bombastic singing of Frankie Laine. Also far from minimalist are the epics *Duel in the Sun* and *The Alamo*. The former is an overblown western that is the butt of many jokes (wags call it "lust in the dust") but Tiomkin's music is romantic and uncomplicated without being ridiculous. Producer David Selznick wanted a sumptuous score to match the visuals. Tiomkin obliged without making a fool of himself. *The Alamo* has a lovely folk song, lyrical Latin-flavored guitars, and lone trumpet or accordion airs. For the extensive battle scenes the music gets vigorous and patriotic yet there is a melancholy undertone appropriate for the story of a lost cause. *Rio Bravo* also has a graceful Mexican-flavored folk song played by a solo trumpet that turns dissonant and forebodes trouble. The main theme, mixing harmonica with plucking guitar strings, is lazy and idyllic. With two singers in the cast, Dean Martin and Ricky Nelson, *Rio Bravo* has its fair share of singing, giving it almost the tone of a musical. The tone in the *Red River* score is uplifting and even spiritual. The feeling of the open prairie and the determination of the characters is echoed in the robust main theme. There is also an inspiring anthem, some comic passages, a fervent choir, and a solemn section that manages to be both melancholy and heartwarming. Tiomkin's last Hollywood assignment was the western *The War Wagon*, and his talent for scoring westerns is in top form. The main theme song is a jaunty number that suggests the rhythm of a wagon and the dreams its gold contents inspire.

Tiomkin worked well with director Capra, and their collaboration resulted in some major hits and superior scores. Their first movie together, *Lost Horizon*, offered the opportunity for very unique music. Set in the fictional kingdom of Shangri-La high in the Himalayas, the film has a Westerner's point of view of the exotic East. The opening theme suggests wonderment and romance, using a traditional orchestra to convey a mysterious place. Yet soon Asian instruments, such as metal gongs and high-pitched bells, are added and the music seems to leave the West behind. Tiomkin doesn't try to imitate or re-create the musical sounds from that part of the world, but he uses the pentatonic scale instead of the Western one to create a strangeness that is beguiling and still accessible. The use of a celestial choir may not correspond to the ensemble singing of Asia, but it certainly propels the listener to a faraway place. The *Lost Horizon* score is rich with memorable themes, including a gentle love theme, an absorbing funeral march, and even a children's ditty. Many argue that it is Tiomkin's finest score. Quite a contrast is provided by two Capra urban movies: *Mr. Smith Goes to Washington* and *Meet John Doe*. In both cases an honest, humble, and naive hero from a small town goes to the big city and barely survives having his ideals shattered by the corruption he meets there. The story of Mr. Smith (James Stewart) is musicalized with a variety of American folk songs, ranging from "Yankee Doodle" to "Taps," and Tiomkin adds his own patriotic themes. The marches and anthems in *Mr. Smith Goes to Washington* are perhaps the most American Tiomkin ever wrote, unabashedly patriotic as is the movie. *Meet John Doe* is a much more cynical film but ends up almost as optimistic as Mr. Smith's story. Again Tiomkin uses various American songs in his score and much of the original music is nimble and sarcastic. For the so-called John Doe (Gary Cooper), a country rube, the music turns rural and suggests a hayseed in the big city. A similarly wry sense of humor shows up in Tiomkin's score for *You Can't Take It with You*, Capra's take on bucking the establishment. The most popular of these Capra collaborations has turned out to be *It's a Wonderful Life*. Although the film is set in a small city, the score is rather classical with several nods to Beethoven. In fact, there originally was a very flowing main theme that evoked dancing and holiday spirit. Capra didn't like it and turned the old chestnut "Buffalo Gals" into the main theme. Several other liberties were taken

with Tiomkin's music, which so angered the composer he never worked with Capra again.

For Hitchcock he wrote a superb score for *Shadow of a Doubt*. The "Merry Widow Waltz" is an important clue in the story and Tiomkin uses the catchy waltz effectively throughout the score, sometime making it harsh and threatening, other times cockeyed and comic. Other famous waltz themes pop up in this masterful score where humor and suspense flow side by side. Hitchcock was pleased with Tiomkin's work and hired him for three other films. For the brilliant *Strangers on a Train*, the main theme is symphonic with crashing cymbals and ominous chords. A carousel is important to the plot and Tiomkin uses a menacing merry-go-round theme at times, including the climactic final scene with a runaway carousel. The main theme for *I Confess* is dreamy and even a bit weary as the strings waver uncertainly until they seem to collapse in confusion. The story concerns a priest (Montgomery Clift) who learns of a murder in confession so Tiomkin brings in Gregorian chant in sections, the religious music taking on an oppressive tone. A fine example of a suspense score is Tiomkin's music for Hitchcock's talky but enthralling *Dial M for Murder*. There is a bluesy love theme but more memorable is the striking percussion and string theme during the film's one action scene, the arranged murder that goes wrong.

Because he was not under contract with one studio, Tiomkin worked with a variety of top directors, usually more than once. The composer was known for being affable and willing to try different genres. When he experimented with the science fiction field, he came up with an estimable score for *The Thing from Another World* for director Howard Hawks. Virtually abandoning melody, Tiomkin wrote a series of chords and percussive phrases using an odd assortment of instruments. The result is a score that is certainly otherworldly, an intergalactic version of *Lost Horizon*. For another very different Hawks project, *The Land of the Pharaohs*, Tiomkin mixed melody with a throbbing set of chords, suggesting not only the Egyptian setting but also a passionate love affair. In contrast to this is the rich yet subdued music in *Friendly Persuasion*, the story of a Quaker family during the Civil War. The main theme is so captivating it is not surprising it became the best-selling song "Thee I Love." The rest of the score is equally splendid, from a lighthearted polka to the domestic theme that glows with affection. For the

French period piece *Cyrano de Bergerac*, a baroque orchestra plays the vigorous score, the harpsichords and strings competing like racehorses. Cyrano's nose gets its own dissonant horn theme and the battle scenes are scored with glittering panache. A score that is considered by some to be ahead of its time is *Champion* in 1949. This hard-driving boxing movie has no string instruments in the scoring, relying instead on brass punctuated by cymbals. This often has a jazz feeling, which would not become commonplace in films until the mid-1950s. The theme from the airplane drama *The High and the Mighty* is indeed soaring, using the harp and strings to convey a sense of flight. It is a film filled with music, unlike the quiet character drama *Old Man and the Sea* in which Tiomkin only brings in his delicate, ebb-and-flow music sporadically. The most music he wrote for one movie was his score for the epic melodrama *Giant*. The main theme is a rousing march sung by a male chorus and suggesting an emotion as expansive as Texas itself. It recurs in the long film, usually when the characters fight against losing their way of life. The love theme for the central couple (Elizabeth Taylor and Rock Hudson)

is passionate and demanding. The theme for the antihero played by James Dean is a listless harmonica tune that alters in different directions; it turns lyrical with his love for Taylor and vicious in his rivalry with Hudson. The score has references to popular favorites "The Eyes of Texas Are upon You" and "The Yellow Rose of Texas," some catchy folk dance music, Latin-flavored tunes, and many other themes. *Giant* may not be Tiomkin's best score, but it is certainly his most ambitious.

Fellow composers Max Steiner and Alfred Newman made their Hollywood debuts with Tiomkin in 1931, and the three men are considered the founding fathers of the American movie score. Tiomkin's influence on movie music is considerable, particularly in the western genre. How ironic that a Russian-born composer would help define the musical sound of the American West. Yet there is much more to Tiomkin's screen music than westerns and much more to his craftsmanship than was widely understood during his lifetime. Autobiography: *Please Don't Hate Me*, with Prosper Buranelli (1959); biography: *Dimitri Tiomkin: A Portrait*, Christopher Palmer, Warren M. Sherk (2012). Official website: www.dimitritiomkin.com.

Credits

(all films USA unless stated otherwise; * for Best Song)

Year	Film	Director
1931	*Resurrection*	Edwin Carewe
1933	*Alice in Wonderland*	Norman Z. McLeod
1935	*The Casino Murder Case*	Edwin L. Marin
1935	*Mad Love*	Karl Freund
1935	*I Live My Life*	W. S. Van Dyke
1937	*Lost Horizon*	Frank Capra
1937	*The Road Back*	James Whale
1938	*You Can't Take It with You*	Frank Capra
1938	*Spawn of the North*	Henry Hathaway
1939	*Only Angels Have Wings*	Howard Hawks
1939	*Mr. Smith Goes to Washington* (AAN)	Frank Capra
1940	*Lucky Partners*	Lewis Milestone
1940	*The Westerner*	William Wyler
1941	*Meet John Doe*	Frank Capra
1941	*Forced Landing*	Gordon Wiles
1941	*Scattergood Meets Broadway*	Christy Cabanne
1941	*Flying Blind*	Frank McDonald
1941	*The Corsican Brothers* (AAN)	Gregory Ratoff
1942	*A Gentleman after Dark*	Edwin L. Marin
1942	*Twin Beds*	Tim Whelan
1942	*The Moon and Sixpence* (AAN)	Albert Lewin
1943	*Shadow of a Doubt*	Alfred Hitchcock
1943	*Report from the Aleutians*	John Huston

Year	Film	Director
1943	The Unknown Guest	Kurt Neumann
1943	The Battle of Russia	Frank Capra, Anatole Litvak
1944	Ladies Courageous	John Rawlins
1944	Strange Confession (aka The Impostor)	Julien Duvivier
1944	The Bridge of San Luis Rey (AAN)	Rowland V. Lee
1944	Attack! Battle of New Britain	Robert Presnell Sr.
1944	When Strangers Marry	William Castle
1944	Here Is Germany	Frank Capra
1945	Forever Yours	William Nigh
1945	Dillinger	Max Nosseck
1945	China's Little Devils	Monta Bell
1945	War Comes to America	Frank Capra, Anatole Litvak
1945	Know Your Enemy—Japan	Frank Capra, Joris Ivens
1945	Pardon My Past	Leslie Fenton
1946	Whistle Stop	Léonide Moguy
1946	Black Beauty	Max Nosseck
1946	Angel on My Shoulder	Archie Mayo
1946	The Dark Mirror	Robert Siodmak
1946	It's a Wonderful Life	Frank Capra
1946	Duel in the Sun	King Vidor, Otto Bower, etc.
1947	The Long Night	Anatole Litvak
1948	Tarzan and the Mermaids	Robert Florey
1948	The Dude Goes West	Kurt Neumann
1948	So This Is New York	Richard Fleischer
1948	Red River	Howard Hawks, Arthur Rosson
1948	Portrait of Jennie	William Dieterle
1949	Champion (AAN)	Mark Robson
1949	Home of the Brave	Mark Robson
1949	Canadian Pacific	Edwin L. Marin
1949	Red Light	Roy Del Ruth
1950	Dakota Lil	Lesley Selander
1950	Guilty Bystander	Joseph Lerner
1950	D.O.A.	Rudolph Maté
1950	Champagne for Caesar	Richard Whorf
1950	The Men	Fred Zinnemann
1950	Cyrano de Bergerac	Michael Gordon
1951	Mister Universe	Joseph Lerner
1951	The Thing from Another World	Christian Nyby, Howard Hawks
1951	Strangers on a Train	Alfred Hitchcock
1951	Peking Express	William Dieterle
1951	Drums in the Deep South	William Cameron Menzies
1951	The Well (GGN)	Leo C. Popkin, Russell Rouse
1952	Bugles in the Afternoon	Roy Rowland
1952	Mutiny	Edward Dmytryk
1952	My Six Convicts	Hugo Fregonese
1952	The Lady in the Iron Mask	Ralph Murphy
1952	High Noon (AA; AA*; GG)	Fred Zinnemann
1952	The Big Sky	Howard Hawks
1952	The Four Poster	Irving Reis
1952	The Happy Time	Richard Fleischer
1952	The Steel Trap	Andrew L. Stone
1952	Angel Face	Otto Preminger
1953	I Confess	Alfred Hitchcock
1953	Jeopardy	John Sturges
1953	Return to Paradise	Mark Robson
1953	Blowing Wild	Hugo Fregonese
1953	Take the High Ground!	Richard Brooks
1953	Cease Fire!	Owen Crump

Year	Film	Director
1954	*The Command*	David Butler
1954	*His Majesty O'Keefe*	Byron Haskin, Burt Lancaster
1954	*The High and the Mighty* (AA; AAN*)	William A. Wellman
1954	*Dial M for Murder*	Alfred Hitchcock
1954	*A Bullet Is Waiting*	John Farrow
1954	*The Adventures of Hajji Baba*	Don Weis
1955	*Strange Lady in Town*	Mervyn LeRoy
1955	*Land of the Pharaohs*	Howard Hawks
1955	*The Court-Martial of Billy Mitchell*	Otto Preminger
1956	*Tension at Table Rock*	Charles Marquis Warren
1956	*Giant* (AAN)	George Stevens
1956	*Friendly Persuasion* (AAN*)	William Wyler
1957	*Gunfight at the O.K. Corral*	John Sturges
1957	*Night Passage*	James Neilson
1957	*Search for Paradise*	Otto Lang
1958	*Wild Is the Wind* (AAN*)	George Cukor
1959	*The Old Man and the Sea* (AA)	John Sturges, Henry King, Fred Zinnemann
1959	*Rio Bravo*	Howard Hawks
1959	*The Young Land* (AAN*)	Ted Tetzlaff
1960	*Last Train from Gun Hill*	John Sturges
1960	*The Unforgiven*	John Huston
1960	*The Alamo* (AAN; AAN*; GG)	John Wayne
1961	*The Sundowners*	Fred Zinnemann (UK)
1961	*Town without Pity* (AAN*; GG*)	Gottfried Reinhardt (USA/W. Germany)
1962	*The Guns of Navarone* (AAN; GG)	J. Lee Thompson (UK/USA)
1963	*Without Each Other* (aka *Pity Me Not*)	Saul Swimmer
1964	*55 Days at Peking* (AAN; AAN*)	Nicholas Ray, Guy Green
1964	*The Fall of the Roman Empire* (AAN; GG)	Anthony Mann
1964	*Circus World* (GG*)	Henry Hathaway (USA/Spain)
1965	*36 Hours*	George Seaton
1967	*The War Wagon*	Burt Kennedy
1968	*Great Catherine*	Gordon Flemyng (UK)

TYLER, Brian (b. 1972?) A busy arranger, conductor, musician, and composer for movies and television since the turn of the new century, he has scored over sixty feature films, many of them big-budget action movies and sci-fi thrillers that have been box office hits.

Brian Tyler was born and raised in Orange County, California, the grandson of Oscar-winning Hollywood art director Walter H. Tyler. As a child he taught himself how to play various instruments that were in his home, starting with drums and piano. By adulthood he was playing over twenty different instruments. Tyler grew up listening to Motown music but received an informal education on classical music as well. He was educated at UCLA and Harvard but did not concentrate on music until he began playing with different bands in the Los Angeles area and composing his own music. Tyler's first work in movies was scoring the independent film *Bartender* in 1997, fol-lowed by a handful of small films before getting noticed for his score for the crime thriller *Frailty* in 2001. The music brought him to the attention of director William Friedkin, who hired Tyler to score his action drama *The Hunted* in 2003. Soon Tyler was assigned bigger projects and he has since become an in-demand composer for sci-fi and action movies. Among his many notable films are *Bubba Ho-Tep*, *Constantine*, *The Greatest Game Ever Played*, *Partition*, *Rambo*, *Law Abiding Citizen*, *Timeline*, *Standing Up*, *Now You See Me*, *Thor: The Dark World*, and *Teenage Mutant Ninja Turtles*. Perhaps his biggest screen hits are installments in popular screen series such as *The Expendables*, *Fast & Furious*, *Final Destination*, and *Iron Man*. Tyler has been very active in television since the late 1990s, scoring TV movies and miniseries, as with *Final Justice* (1998), *Sirens* (1999), *Trapped in a Purple Haze* (2000), *Jane Doe* (2001), *Fitzgerald* (2002), *Children of*

Dune (2003), and *Painkiller Jane* (2005), as well as some series and several TV documentaries. He is a songwriter for Sony Music and other organizations and has also composed the music for many video games, some of them based on his film scores. Tyler frequently orchestrates and conducts his own scores, often using the London Symphony Orchestra or the Hollywood Studio Symphony.

Tyler's fascination with both traditional and electronic instruments in his screen scores is in evidence from the beginning of his career. By the time he scored *The Hunted* for Friedkin, the young composer had already developed a style for aggressive music that was as unrelenting as the stories being told. *The Hunted* is about a former Special Forces gunman (Benicio Del Toro) now killing off humans in the woods of Oregon and the retired FBI agent (Tommy Lee Jones) who sets out to stop him. This high-tension tale is scored with an angry recurring theme in which furious strings repeat themselves as pounding percussion and synthesized descending chords add to the fury. One of the chase scenes is accompanied by a feverish passage that consists of repetitive, insisting strings and unpredictable percussion. The score has a few quieter moments, as with a slow lament with a sense of weariness, yet there is something soothing about it. Also memorable is a solo trumpet featured in a melancholy track with strings and electronics echoing the same musical phrase as a solo piano adds some intriguing accents. The same year he did *The Hunted*, Tyler had to quickly write a full score for the sci-fi adventure *Timeline* based on a popular Michael Crichton novel. The circumstances were not pleasant. Veteran screen composer Jerry Goldsmith had completed and recorded his score for *Timeline*, then director Richard Donner and the studio made some changes in the final cut and asked for score changes. Goldsmith, dying of cancer and proud of what he suspected would be his last movie score, refused. So Tyler was hired to create a completely new score for *Timeline*. Because the Goldsmith score was already recorded, it is possible today to compare his and Tyler's scores. The movie is about some archeology students who travel back through time to fourteenth-century France to rescue their professor (Billy Connolly) who is trapped there. Goldsmith's score stresses the human elements in the story and his music is often lyrical and full of wonder. Tyler, taking his cue from what Donner wanted, saw *Timeline* as an action film and gives it a much more strident sound. The main theme is a brass and reeds march with echoing percussion that is forceful and confident as it gallops forward with excitement. The battle scenes are scored with a persistent percussion beat, but the chanting voices give the piece an inspiring tone as the strings join in with a triumphal procession of sorts. Often in the movie one hears reverberating electronic sounds against repeating musical phrases on strings. The film's love theme is a serene piece played on high woodwinds with string accents as it flows cautiously up the scale. (In fact, this passage is not unlike the romantic theme Goldsmith had written.) Comparisons of the two very different scores are unsatisfying. The seasoned composer Goldsmith provides a richer musical experience, but Tyler's brash score served Donner's ideas better.

So many of Tyler's movies are in the high-tech, high-action vein that it is understandable that the scores have similarities. Two of his more recent action scores will serve to illustrate his use of modern and classical forms. *Thor: The Dark World*, a sci-fi adventure in the Marvel Comics style, has a plot and characters loosely based on Scandinavian legend. Tyler's main theme is a pounding march played on percussion and trumpets with a male chorus chanting in a determined manner as female voices float above. The many action scenes are scored with propulsive electronic and conventional percussion passages as dissonant strings and blaring trumpets race ahead. The softer and more lyrical parts of the score include a reflective passage on woodwinds, strings, and questioning vocals, and an enticing theme with delicate strings playing a tentative melody as they climb the scale with the help of some celebratory horns. Another Marvel Comic to find major success on the screen is the *Iron Man* series. Tyler scored the third installment with propulsive music and high-tech effects. The main theme for *Iron Man 3* is a seething passage featuring agitated percussion, repetitive trumpet phrases, and a chanting chorus. There is also a foreboding passage with nervous strings, subdued brass, and sinister electronic accents. The score has a rousing section with wavering strings as a forceful melody is played on various electronic and conventional instruments. Even more modern is a rhythmic section on electronic percussion with descending strings working against all the furor. At times Tyler limits himself to conventional orchestration, as with a passage played on sustained strings and low brass that create an uneasy feeling and a quiet sense of danger.

There may not be many Tyler films that fall outside the action genre but those that exist often have very commendable (and different) scores. The period sports drama *The Greatest Game Ever Played* is about the 1913 competition between the British golfing champ Harry Vardon (Stephen Dillane) and young American rookie Francis Ouimet (Shia LaBeouf). Tyler's score is far from harsh or strident, yet it still has power. The main theme is an inspiring passage with strings and horns floating casually until they transition into a sprightly folk tune with a lively tempo and robust crescendos. Also sparkling is a lively theme in which woodwinds play a fluid folk melody with string support and some piano accents. The score also includes an allegro string passage punctuated by pounding percussive accents, unaware that the strings are increasing in tempo and tension, and a lovely, reflective piano solo that keeps moving even as it seems tentative and uncertain. Even richer is the score for *Partition*, in which Tyler mixes Hindu and Western musical forms. The movie is about the unlikely romance between a Sikh ex-soldier (Jimi Mistri) and a displaced Muslim woman (Kristin

Keruk) set against the tumultuous partition of India and Pakistan by the British in 1941. The score opens with Asian instruments playing a simple folk melody as subdued Western instruments growl underneath and electronic vibrations subtly undercut any sense of serenity. There is a sorrowful theme with wailing strings, subdued horns, and resigned percussion that reaches up the scale then flows back down. Among the many potent tracks in this score are a slow but steady Hindu dance theme on ethnic instruments that has a sense of majesty; a disquieting theme on Asian strings that is gentle but still oppressive; and a reflective passage with sustained notes on Western strings and horns, to which Asian instruments are added to fill out the musical line, which takes the form of a slow-motion dance. The score (and movie) concludes with an inspiring theme played by a Western orchestra that gracefully builds from an adagio to a stirring anthem. Because Tyler is in such demand for action movies, he too rarely gets to write this kind of music. Yet how reassuring it is to know that he can. Official website: www.briantyler.com.

Credits

(all films USA unless stated otherwise)

Year	Film	Director
1997	Bartender	Gabe Torres
1998	Six-String Samurai (aka The Blade)	Lance Mungia
1999	The Settlement	Mark Steilen
1999	The 4th Floor	Josh Klausner
1999	Simon Sez	Kevin Elders (Germany/Belgium/USA)
2000	Shadow Hours	Isaac H. Eaton
2000	Panic	Henry Bromell
2000	Four Dogs Playing Poker	Paul Rachman
2000	Terror Tract (aka Bobo)	Lance W. Dreesen, Clint Hutchison
2001	Strings	Jill Tanner
2001	Plan B	Greg Yaitanes (USA/Denmark)
2001	Frailty	Bill Paxton (USA/Germany)
2002	Bubba Ho-Tep	Don Coscarelli
2002	Vampires: Los Muertos	Tommy Lee Wallace
2003	Darkness Falls (aka Don't Peek)	Jonathan Liebesman
2003	The Hunted	William Friedkin
2003	The Big Empty	Steve Anderson
2003	Timeline	Richard Donner
2003	Thoughtcrimes (aka Clairvoyance)	Breck Eisner
2004	Perfect Opposites (aka A Piece of My Heart)	Matt Cooper
2004	The Final Cut	Omar Naim (USA/Canada/Germany)
2004	Godsend	Nick Hamm (USA/Canada)
2004	Paparazzi	Paul Abascal
2005	Constantine (aka Hellblazer)	Francis Lawrence (USA/Germany)
2005	The Greatest Game Ever Played	Bill Paxton (USA/Canada)

Year	Film	Director
2006	*Annapolis*	Justin Lin
2006	*Bug*	William Friedkin (USA/Germany)
2006	*The Fast and the Furious: Tokyo Drift*	Justin Lin (USA/Germany)
2006	*Finishing the Game: The Search for a New Bruce Lee*	Justin Lin
2006	*Partition* (aka *Destiny's Bride*)	Vic Sarin (Canada/So. Africa/UK)
2007	*War* (aka *Rogue*)	Philip G. Atwell (USA/Canada)
2007	*Aliens vs. Predator: Requiem*	Colin and Greg Strause
2008	*Rambo*	Sylvester Stallone (USA/Germany)
2008	*Bangkok Dangerous* (aka *Time to Kill*)	Oxide Pang Chun, Danny Pang
2008	*Eagle Eye*	D. J. Caruso (USA/Germany)
2008	*The Lazarus Project* (aka *The Heaven Project*)	John Glenn (USA/Canada/UK)
2009	*The Killing Room* (aka *Manbreak*)	Jonathan Liebesman
2009	*Dragonball: Evolution*	James Wong (USA/Hong Kong/UK)
2009	*Fast & Furious 4*	Justin Lin (USA/Japan)
2009	*Middle Men*	George Gallo
2009	*Final Destination 4*	David R. Ellis
2009	*Law Abiding Citizen*	F. Gary Gray
2010	*The Expendables*	Sylvester Stallone
2011	*Battle Los Angeles* (aka *World Invasion*)	Jonathan Liebesman
2011	*Fast Five*	Justin Lin
2011	*Final Destination 5*	Steven Quale (USA/Canada)
2012	*John Dies at the End* (aka *Dave's Story*)	Don Coscarelli
2012	*Columbus Circle*	George Gallo
2012	*Break*	Gabe Torres
2012	*The Expendables 2*	Simon West (USA/Bulgaria)
2013	*Standing Up* (aka *Goat Island*)	D. J. Caruso
2013	*Iron Man 3*	Shane Black (USA/China)
2013	*Now You See Me*	Louis Leterrier (France/USA)
2013	*Thor: The Dark World*	Alan Taylor
2014	*Into the Storm*	Steven Quale
2014	*The Expendables 3*	Patrick Hughes
2014	*Teenage Mutant Ninja Turtles*	Jonathan Liebesman
2015	*Fast & Furious 7*	James Wan
2015	*Avengers: Age of Ultron*	Joss Whedon

VAN PARYS, Georges (1902–1971) A prolific French songwriter and composer for the stage, radio, movies, and television, he scored over two hundred feature films from the first French talkies to international movies in the 1960s.

Georges Van Parys was born in Paris, where he studied piano as a youth and began composing as a teenager, greatly influenced by Claude Debussy, Maurice Ravel, and the modern composers known as Les Six. Van Parys began his career as an accompanist for Yvonne George, Gaby Montbreuse, and other popular singers. In 1927 he had his first stage success with *Chez Fyscher* and went on to write the music for several operettas, musical comedies, and opera bouffes, including *La Tour Eiffel qui tue, Virginie Déjazet, Minnie Moustache*, and *Une femme per jour*. Van Parys also wrote many popular songs for cabarets, radio, and the stage, some of which are still considered French standards. He first got involved in movies in 1929 when he and Philippe Pares scored the early talkie *Paris Girls*. After contributing some music to the musical *The Road Is Fine* the next year, Van Parys scored the Luis Buñuel surreal masterwork *L'age d'or* (1930) which was one of the most controversial films in early French cinema. He first worked with director René Clair in 1931 when he was one of three composers to score the comic masterpiece *Le million*. Clair and Van Parys later collaborated on *Beauties of the Night, Man About Town, The Lace Wars*, and *The Grand Maneuver*. He most frequently scored movies by directors André Berthomieu, Henri Decoin, and Jean Boyer, yet his three most famous films were by others: Jacques Becker's *Casque d'or*, Max Ophüls's *The Earrings of Madame de . . .* , and Henri-Georges Clouzot's *Diabolique*. Among Van Parys's many other notable movies are *Jim la houlette, Café de Paris, Nightclub Hostess, Pour le maillot jaune, Cheque au porteur, Le prince charmant, The Benefactor, Marie-Martine, The London Man, The Loves of Colette, Fan-Fan the Tulip, Before The Deluge, The Sheep Has Five Legs, Les misérables, The Man in the Raincoat*, and *Signed, Arsene Lupin*. He also scored a handful of American and British films, as with *The Million-aires, The Happy Road*, and *I Like Money*. Approximately one-fifth of Van Parys' scores were written with others, and he contributed to many other movies uncredited. In the 1960s he scored some television series and TV movies and remained active in film until his death in 1971 at the age of sixty-eight.

The infamous *L'age d'or*, written by Salvador Dali and director Buñuel, caused so much commotion when it premiered in 1930 that in many countries it was not shown for fifty years. The nearly plotless surreal movie makes fun of the bourgeois, the law, and religion. It is filled with bizarre scenes and startling images. Van Parys's music is not surreal or even all that modern but the way the music is used in the movie adds to the unorthodoxy of this cockeyed classic. *L'age d'or* (sometimes billed as *The Golden Age*) is filled with eccentric moments made all the more surreal by Van Parys's musical commentary. There is no music during the opening credits, then a classical chamber piece with vigorous strings and vivacious woodwinds is heard over a narrated documentary in which scorpions are crawling, mating, and fighting. In a later scene a restful violin solo is heard as a man kicks a violin down the sidewalk, while in another sequence buildings collapse as a lighthearted passage on woodwinds is played. There is a bucolic nature theme with harp accents that has an oppressive subtext as thieves struggle over a rocky terrain. The same rocks are the setting for a religious ceremony in which a serene piece on woodwinds accompanies dissonant Gregorian chanting and the sound of waves. A sprightly waltz is played as a man is led to prison, a photograph of a woman comes alive as strings play unfinished melodic phrases, a furious string allegro accompanies a court procedure, a dog barking punctuates a low string theme with rattling percussion, and a military percussion track is heard as feathers tumble forward and a nobleman (who looks like Jesus) comforts a woman after an orgy in his castle. Perhaps the most infamous scene is when a woman meditates on her unrequited love and a gentle lullaby is heard. Then the camera cuts to a toilet and the sound of the flushing temporarily drowns out the music. The movie ends with slaphappy music heard as female scalps are seen hanging from a crucifix and blowing in the wind.

After *L'age d'or*, the rest of Van Parys's movies seem very tame. Some are also very accomplished. The wry romantic drama *The Earrings of Madame de . . .* is one of the best. This movie about a pair of expensive earrings that pass through the hands of various people in nineteenth-century Paris is both enchanting and beguiling. Van Parys's period music is also charming. The main theme is an entrancing waltz with a brisk but not frivolous tempo. There is also a slow passage on strings that is stately but warm rather than stuffy. Also memorable is a serene theme played by a full orchestra that turns sour as a minor key, dissonant notes, and other elements combine to create an uneasiness that is not unpleasant. Much darker but even better known is the thriller *Diabolique*. The wife (Véra Clouzot) and mistress (Simone Signoret) of a vicious school headmaster (Paul Meurisse) murder him and dump the body in a swimming pool. Yet the next day the body is not there and the two murderesses are slowly driven to distraction by subsequent events. Van Parys's main theme is both exciting and dangerous. It is a foreboding passage on low strings as higher brass seem to shout out in pain and strings screech oppressively. All this is made more bizarre when a strident children's choir chants and a pipe organ adds some sinister chords. The mental state of the two women is scored with a seesaw-like theme with strings and organ sliding back and forth, the music losing its grip just as the characters do. Another dramatic but more conventional score is the one Van Parys wrote for Jean-Paul Le Chanois's 1958 version of *Les misérables*. This accurate adaptation of Victor Hugo's novel, with Jean Gabin as the hero Jean Valjean and Bernard Blier as his nemesis Javert, is perhaps the best screen version of the epic tale. The score is filled with stirring music that captures the period and the tone of the story. Vibrant strings are featured in a fervent theme that is lyrical but also forceful as boastful trumpets are added and a mandolin rattles underneath with fiery energy. There is a robust processional that announces itself with pride, as well as a dramatic track with mandolins racing and violins and brass sweeping over them with long melodic lines. A particularly effective theme is one in which horns and strings echo each other in a competitive manner.

Van Parys also scored many comedies and his lighter touch can be enjoyed in the music for the comic mystery *Signed, Arsene Lupin*. The title character of the gentleman thief (Robert Lamoureaux) is taken from a series of mystery stories by Maurice Leblanc and in this tale, set in a chateau in 1919, the mystery takes a backseat to the charming whimsy. The opening theme is a merry march on trumpets and other brass as strings dance along with the catchy tune. There is a waltz played on a xylophone, with help from strings and reeds, that has a weary tone even though the pace is maintained. Similarly, a piano solo in one track has a steady tempo and a carefree attitude. Another theme is a slow but lively foxtrot featuring low xylophone notes; the music picks up speed as other instruments join in and the whole thing turns into a bouncy dance. Even more playful are the oboe and piccolo featured in a comic theme in which a trumpet and a high-pitched xylophone copy each other. *La bella Otero* is a musical biography of the notorious Spanish courtesan, dancer, and actress Carolina Otero (Maria Félix). Van Parys wrote two sprightly songs and plenty of dance music for the movie. The opening theme is a zesty waltz in quick time that is almost overpowering in its energy. Another waltz is similarly vivacious but the tempo varies and there are some slower and more romantic sections in the track. There is also a glittering passage in which spirited strings are answered by equally lively woodwinds. If all this seems a world away from the sardonic use of music in *L'age d'or*, it is a good illustration of Van Parys's eclectic musical talents.

Credits

(all films France unless stated otherwise)

Year	Film	Director
1929	*Paris Girls*	Henry Roussel
1930	*L'age d'or*	Luis Buñuel
1931	*Je serai seule après minuit*	Jacques de Baroncelli
1931	*Black and White*	Marc Allégret, Robert Florey
1931	*Dragnet Night*	Carmine Gallone

Year	Film	Director
1931	*Mitternachtsliebe*	Carl Froelich, Augusto Genina (France/Germany)
1932	*Sailor's Song*	Carmine Gallone
1932	*A Son from America*	Carmine Gallone (France/Hungary)
1933	*Le crime du Bouif*	André Berthomieu
1933	*Jeunesse*	Georges Lacombe
1933	*Mademoiselle Josette, ma femme*	André Berthomieu
1933	*I Will Love You Always*	Mario Camerini, Henri Decoin (Italy)
1933	*The Old Devil*	Anatole Litvak
1933	*The Blue Ones of the Sky*	Henri Decoin
1933	*Feu Toupinel*	Roger Capellani
1934	*An Ideal Woman*	André Berthomieu
1934	*Les filles de la concierge*	Jacques Tourneur
1934	*The House on the Dune*	Pierre Billon
1934	*L'aristo*	André Berthomieu
1935	*Quelle drôle de gosse!*	Léo Joannon
1935	*Happy Days*	Marc Allégret
1935	*Jim la houlette*	André Berthomieu
1936	*The Happy Road*	Georges Lacombe
1936	*Counsel for Romance*	Jean Boyer
1936	*Prends la route*	Jean Boyer
1937	*Franco de port*	Dimitri Kirsanoff
1937	*Mademoiselle, ma mere*	Henri Decoin
1937	*Abused Confidence*	Henri Decoin
1938	*My Foster Sister*	Jean Boyer (Germany/France)
1938	*Escadrille of Chance*	Max de Vaucorbeil
1938	*Riviera Express*	Pierre Caron
1938	*The Train for Venice*	André Berthomieu
1938	*Cafe de Paris*	Yves Mirande, Georges Lacombe
1938	*Mother Love*	Jean Boyer
1938	*Mon curé chez les riches*	Jean Boyer
1939	*Cocoanut*	Jean Boyer (France/Germany)
1939	*Nightclub Hostess*	Albert Valentin (France/Germany)
1939	*Extenuating Circumstances*	Jean Boyer
1939	*Le chemin de l'honneur*	Jean-Paul Paulin
1940	*The Mondesir Heir*	Albert Valentin (France/Germany)
1940	*Marseille mes amours*	Jacques Daniel-Norman
1940	*Miquette*	Jean Boyer
1940	*Sixieme étage*	Maurice Cloche
1940	*Pour le maillot jaune*	Jean Stelli
1941	*L'acrobate*	Jean Boyer
1941	*First Ball*	Christian-Jaque
1941	*Le club des soupirants*	Maurice Gleize
1941	*Romance de Paris*	Jean Boyer
1941	*Ce n'est pas moi*	Jacques de Baroncelli
1941	*Cheque au porteur*	Jean Boyer
1942	*La maison des sept jeunes filles*	Albert Valentin
1942	*Caprices*	Léo Joannon
1942	*Bolero*	Jean Boyer
1942	*Le prince charmant*	Jean Boyer
1942	*Sideral Cruises*	André Zwoboda
1942	*Cap au large*	Jean-Paul Paulin
1942	*A vos ordres, madame*	Jean Boyer
1942	*Frédérica*	Jean Boyer
1942	*The Benefactor*	Henri Decoin
1942	*The Big Fight*	Bernard-Roland
1943	*Marie-Martine*	Albert Valentin
1943	*Mademoiselle Béatrice*	Max de Vaucorbeil
1943	*Le soleil de minuit*	Bernard-Roland

Year	Film	Director
1943	The London Man	Henri Decoin
1944	The White Blackbird	Jacques Houssin
1945	Échec au roy	Jean-Paul Paulin
1945	Ils éraient cinq Permissionaires	Pierre Caron
1946	La troisieme dalle	Michel Dulud
1947	Histoire de chanter	Gilles Grangier
1947	Man About Town	René Clair (France/USA)
1947	Le château de la derniere chance	Jean-Paul Paulin
1947	Carré de valets	André Berthomieu
1947	Tierce a cour	Jacques de Casembroot
1948	Par la fenêtre	Gilles Grangier
1948	The Loves of Colette	Jean Faurez
1948	Blanc comme neige	André Berthomieu
1948	The Cupboard Was Bare	Carlo Rim
1948	Scandale	René Le Hénaff
1948	Le cour sur la main	André Berthomieu
1949	Jean de la Lune	Marcel Archard
1949	Une femme par jour	Jean Boyer
1949	La voix du rêve	Jean-Paul Paulin
1949	L'inconnue No. 13	Jean-Paul Paulin
1949	Unusual Tales	Jean Faurez (France/Belgium)
1949	Drame au vel'd'hiv'	Maurice Cam
1950	Rome Express	Christian Stengel
1950	Le 84 prend des vacances	Léo Joannon
1950	Voyage a trois	Jean-Paul Paulin
1950	A Certain Mister	Yves Ciampi
1950	Lady Paname	Henri Jeanson
1950	Tuesday's Guest	Jacques Deval
1950	Les anciens de Saint-Loup	Georges Lampin
1950	Mademoiselle Josette, ma femme	André Berthomieu
1950	Banco de Prince	Michel Dulud
1951	The Red Rose	Marcello Pagliero
1951	Mr. Peek-a-Boo	Jean Boyer (France/Italy)
1951	Ils étaient cinq	Jacques Pinoteau
1951	Two Pennies Worth of Violets	Jean Anouilh
1951	La maison Bonnadieu	Carlo Rim
1952	Allô . . . je t'aime	André Berthomieu
1952	Love, Madame	Gilles Grangier
1952	Casque d'or (aka Golden Marie)	Jacques Becker (Italy/France)
1952	Fan-Fan the Tulip	Christian-Jaque
1952	This Age without Pity	Marcel Blistene
1952	Jupiter	Gilles Grangier
1952	Beauties of the Night	René Clair (France/Italy)
1952	Adorable Creatures	Christian-Jaque (France/Italy)
1952	Drôle de noce	Léo Joannon
1952	Three Women	André Michel
1953	Caroline, Cherie	Jean-Devaivre
1953	Wonderful Mentality	André Berthomieu
1953	Françoise Steps Out	Jacques Becker
1953	Midnight . . . Quai de Bercy	Christian Stengel
1953	Le chemin de la drogue	Louis S. Licot
1953	Inside a Girls' Dormitory	Henri Decoin
1953	The Earrings of Madame de . . .	Max Ophüls (France/Italy)
1953	Virgile	Carlo Rim
1954	Before the Deluge	André Cayatte (France/Italy)
1954	Les révoltés de Lomanach	Richard Pottier (France/Italy)
1954	The Plotters	Henri Decoin
1954	Flesh and the Woman	Robert Siodmak (Italy/France)

Year	Film	Director
1954	*J'y suis . . . j'y reste*	Maurice Labro
1954	*Oh No, Mam'zelle*	Yves Allégret (France/Italy)
1954	*The Secret of Helene Marimon*	Henri Calef (France/Italy)
1954	*The Bed*	Henri Decoin, etc. (France/Italy)
1954	*Men Think Only of That*	Yves Robert
1954	*The Sheep Has Five Legs*	Henri Verneuil
1954	*Service Entrance*	Carlo Rim
1954	*La patrouille des sables*	René Chanas
1954	*Scenes de ménage*	André Berthomieu
1954	*Madame du Barry*	Christian-Jaque (France/Italy)
1954	*La bella Otero*	Richard Pottier (France/Italy)
1954	*Human Cargo*	Pierre Chevalier
1954	*Papa, Mama, the Maid and I*	Jean-Paul Le Chanois
1954	*French Cancan*	Jean Renoir (France/Italy)
1955	*Diabolique*	Henri-Georges Clouzot
1955	*Caroline and the Rebels*	Jean-Devaivre
1955	*Papa, Mama, My Wife and Me*	Jean-Paul Le Chanois
1955	*Nana*	Christian-Jaque (France/Italy)
1955	*Girl on the Third Floor*	Pierre Gaspard-Huit
1955	*The Grand Maneuver*	René Clair (France/Italy)
1955	*The French, They Are a Funny Race*	Preston Sturges
1955	*Maid in Paris*	Pierre Gaspard-Huit
1956	*If All the Guys in the World . . .*	Christian-Jaque
1956	*Meeting in Paris*	Georges Lampin
1956	*It Happened in Aden*	Michel Boisrond
1956	*Club of Women*	Ralph Habib (Italy/France)
1956	*Mitsou ou comment l'esprit vient aux filles . . .*	Jacqueline Audry
1957	*The Man in the Raincoat*	Julien Duvivier (France/Italy)
1957	*Et par ici la sortie*	Willy Rozier
1957	*Action immédiate (aka To Catch a Spy)*	Maurice Labro
1957	*Until the Last One*	Pierre Billon (Italy/France)
1957	*The Happy Road*	Gene Kelly (France/USA)
1957	*Crazy in the Noodle*	Maurice Régamey
1957	*This Pretty World*	Carlo Rim
1957	*Give Me My Chance*	Léonide Moguy
1957	*Filous et compagnie*	Tony Saytor
1957	*The Foxiest Girl in Paris*	Christian-Jaque (Italy/France)
1957	*Charming Boys*	Henri Decoin
1957	*Lock Up Your Spoons*	Carlo Rim
1958	*King on Horseback*	Georges Lampin (France/Yugoslavia/Italy)
1958	*Les misérables*	Jean-Paul Chanois
1958	*School for Coquettes*	Jacqueline Audry
1958	*My Darned Father*	Georges Lacombe (France/Italy)
1958	*The Mask of the Gorilla*	Bernard Borderie
1958	*Clara et les méchants*	Raoul André
1959	*Nina*	Jean Boyer
1959	*The Tiger Attacks*	Maurice Labro
1959	*Guinguette*	Jean Delannoy (Italy/France)
1959	*Les affreux*	Marc Allégret
1959	*Rue de Paris*	Denys de La Patelliere (Italy/France)
1959	*Atomic Agent*	Henri Decoin (France/Italy)
1959	*Signed, Arsene Lupin*	Yves Robert (France/Italy)
1959	*Work and Freedom*	Louis Grospierre
1960	*Marie of the Isles*	Georges Combret (France/Italy)
1960	*Premeditated*	André Berthomieu
1960	*Port of Point-du-Jour*	Jean Faurez
1960	*Passionate Affair*	Henri Decoin

Year	Film	Director
1960	*The Millionairess*	Anthony Asquith (UK)
1960	*Double Deception*	Serge Friedman
1961	*I Like Money*	Peter Sellers (UK)
1961	*Captain Fracasse*	Pierre Gaspard-Huit (France/Spain/Italy)
1961	*All the Gold in the World*	René Clair (Italy/France)
1961	*The Busybody*	Alex Joffé
1962	*Hitch-Hike*	Jacqueline Audry
1962	*Arsene Lupin vs. Arsene Lupin*	Édouard Molinaro (France/Italy)
1962	*The Iron Mask*	Henri Decoin (Italy/France)
1962	*Mandrin*	Jean-Paul Le Chanois (Italy/France)
1963	*The Trip to Biarritz*	Gilles Grangier (France/Italy)
1963	*Cadavres en vacances*	Jacqueline Audry
1964	*Monsieur*	Jean-Paul Le Chanois
1964	*The Spy I Love*	Maurice Labro (France/Italy/Belgium)
1965	*The Lace Wars*	René Clair (France/Romania)
1968	*Leontine*	Michel Audiard
1969	*L'auvergnant et l'autobus*	Guy Lefranc
1970	*She Does Not Drink, Smoke or Flirt But . . . She Talks*	Michel Audiard

VANGELIS (b. 1943) The Greek-born internationally known composer who has utilized rock, pop, jazz, orchestral, and synthesized music in his albums and screen scores, he brought a refreshing and new synthesized sound to the movies in the 1980s.

He was born Evangelos Odysseus Papathanassiou in Volos, Greece, and began playing the piano and composing music at the age of four without any musical training. Two years later he studied at a music school in Athens but later pursued painting at the Academy of Fine Arts. In the 1960s Vangelis formed and played in the pop band the Formynx, which made several recordings of his compositions. He cofounded the progressive rock band Aphrodite's Child in 1968 and they had some top-selling records, the most popular being the psychedelic double album *666* in 1972. After the group disbanded in the 1970s, Vangelis did solo songs and albums then teamed up with Jon Anderson from the band Yes, the two recording some duo albums that found success. In 1975 Vangelis relocated to London, where he set up his own record studio, Nemo Studios, and produced albums for RCA Records. The most famous, *Heaven and Hell*, became an international hit and established Vangelis's synthesized sound in which the classical and the electronic coexisted in a thrilling new way. (One movement from the album was later used as the theme for the Carl Sagan documentary series *Cosmos* on PBS-TV.) His film career began in 1963 when he scored the Greek comedy *My Brother, the Traffic Policeman*, followed by some other features and a series of French documentaries, whose scores got the attention of American and British film studios. Vangelis's hypnotic synthesized score for the popular British film *Chariots of Fire* brought him an Oscar and a best-selling soundtrack album. The main theme from the score was a top-selling single as well. The sci-fi action movie *Blade Runner* was also a hit and its score was highly praised. Vangelis's other significant scores include those for *Missing*, *The Bounty*, *Antarctica*, *Bitter Moon*, and *1492: The Conquest of Paradise*, as well as the biographical films *Alexander*, *Kavafis*, and *El Greco*. He has scored several television and film documentaries and the music from his albums and movies has been heard at the Olympic Games and other sporting events, on TV commercials and series, and in other films, ranging from *The Year of Living Dangerously* (1982) to *Madagascar* (2005). Because of his busy recording and producing career, Vangelis has found time to score only two dozen feature films but he has had a huge impact on screen music, particularly in the 1980s when he inspired a new generation of synthesizer composers.

The way Vangelis uses the synthesizer in creating an orchestral sound has been labeled "symphonic electronica" by some musicologists. Yet there are other elements of music that are evident in his screen scores, such as Greek folk music, religious choral arrangements, and the use of ethnic instruments such as the Hindustani sitar, the Turkish finger cymbal, and the Armenian double-reeded duduk. Vangelis often conducts his soundtrack recordings and is involved in the electronic mixing of the different tracks so he has almost total control over the sound of his scores. Listeners have embraced the sound so fully that such music can be used in the most unlikely circumstances. Consider how effective the synthesized music is in *Chariots of Fire*, which is set during the Paris Summer Olympics of 1924. Electronic music for a period movie was not as common in 1981 as it is today and the juxtaposition of synthesizer and costume drama should have been startling. Yet this is a sports movie at heart and Vangelis's music stirs up strong emotions about the glory of victory. The famous main theme has synthesized keyboard chords and trumpet calls that provide the energy behind a conventional piano melody. For a racing theme it is not very fast yet has a propulsive power that makes it seem to be rushing forward. The score also has a stately theme with gentle brass playing the melodic line as sustained synthesized notes support it, as well as a reflective passage on high keyboard notes as strings waver underneath. There is also a delicate piano duet with a synthesized solo horn that has a melancholy air that is quite captivating. This kind of movie requires a victory theme and Vangelis provides a triumphal track that is again in slow motion as brass and keyboard move majestically up the scale.

Synthesized music seems a more likely choice for *Blade Runner*, a dark sci-fi movie set in a nightmarish Los Angeles of the future. A cop (Harrison Ford) combs the city looking for four escaped human clones which he must destroy before they become destructive. Vangelis's synthesized score promotes optimism in *Chariots of Fire* but captures an urban pessimism in *Blade Runner*. In the main title, seething electronic sounds slowly build in tension and volume until a vibrating fanfare is heard on synthesized horns with harp and twinkling accents. Eventually the piece transitions into a series of descending glissandos on various electronic instruments that conveys a sense of fatalistic gloom. The score is filled with different musical forms. There is a jazzy passage on synthesized keyboard with a rhythmic beat, a blues theme with an echoing synthesized harmonica playing a tentative melody that barely finds the will to continue, and a love theme that is a slow-jazz piece played on solo synthesized saxophone with chiming accents. The sci-fi elements in the score can

be heard in a track in which a female vocal chants a lovely but unsettling melody as electronic notes fall like raindrops and in the chase music consisting of vibrant percussive chords, echoing horns, and rapid string glissandos, all set against reverberating electronic sounds. Also nightmarish but contemporary and very real is *Missing*, a disturbing drama about a father (Jack Lemmon) and his daughter-in-law (Sissy Spacek) who go to Chile to find the son/husband who has disappeared during a military coup. Vangelis's opening theme has a fragile melody played on a piano that slowly gains in power when it gets string and electronic horn support. The South American locale is suggested in some of the musical tracks, most memorably in a slow bolero-like theme heard on electronic instruments during a nightclub scene.

The five-hundredth anniversary of Christopher Columbus's arrival in the New World was celebrated in the French-Spanish epic *1492: Conquest of Paradise*. Instead of glorifying Columbus (Gérard Depardieu), the movie concentrates on the explorer's tragic attempts to civilize the indigenous people. Vangelis's score is again very electronic for a costume drama but by 1992 moviegoers were used to the idea and there were less critical complaints about a modern score for a period piece. There is a great deal of choral work in the score, so often the synthesized music actually feels historically appropriate. The opening music captures the film's cultural clash. Native flutes and percussion quietly play against electronic glissandos and echoes; then a military-like passage with choral chanting enters softly but firmly singing a hymn that becomes almost threatening as it builds into an electronic march on piano and synthesized orchestra. There is a ponderous hymn sung in Latin that starts reverently but soon becomes oppressive in its weight and power, and a flowing passage with sustained electronic notes and mandolins providing the beat. Also effective is an eerie theme with echoing electronic sounds and tribal percussion playing against native chanting, and a slow Spanish folk tune on guitar is heard under doleful native wailing. This is an uneven movie, but the score is often compelling. Vangelis has been dismissed by some as a pop music figure who was in vogue for a time. To others he is the renowned granddad of synthesized screen music. Whichever is true, he has had a considerable influence on movie scoring. Independent Vangelis website: www.elsew.com.

Credits

Year	Film	Director
1963	*My Brother, the Traffic Policeman*	Filippos Fylaktos (Greece)
1966	*Five Thousand Lies*	Giorgos Konstadinou (Greece)
1967	*Vortex*	Nikos Koundouros (USA/Greece)
1970	*Sex-Power*	Henry Chapier (France)
1971	*Frenitis*	Giannis Hristodoulou (Greece)
1972	*Hello Jerusalem*	Henry Chapier (France)
1974	*Love*	Henry Chapier (France)
1975	*Do You Hear the Barking?*	François Reichenbach (France/Mexico)
1976	*Crime and Passion* (aka *Ace Up My Sleeve*)	Ivan Passer (UK/W. Germany)
1978	*De mantel der Liefde*	Adriaan Ditvoorst (Netherlands)
1980	*Mother Dearly Beloved*	José Antonio Saigot (Spain)
1981	*Chariots of Fire* (AA)	Hugh Hudson (UK)
1982	*Missing* (BAFTA-N)	Costa-Gavras (USA)
1982	*Blade Runner* (GGN; BAFTA-N)	Ridley Scott (USA/Hong Kong/UK)
1983	*Antarctica*	Koreyoshi Kurahara (Japan)
1984	*The Bounty*	Roger Donaldson (UK/USA)
1985	*Wonders of Life*	Ed Kong (USA/Hong Kong)
1988	*Vampire in Venice*	Augusto Caminito, etc. (Italy)
1989	*Francesco* (aka *St. Francis of Assisi*)	Liliana Cavani (Italy/W. Germany)
1992	*Bitter Moon*	Roman Polanski (France/UK/USA)
1992	*1492: Conquest of Paradise* (GGN)	Ridley Scott (France/Spain)
1996	*Kavafis*	Yannis Smaragdis (Greece)
2004	*Alexander*	Oliver Stone (Germany/USA/UK/ Netherlands/France/ Italy)
2007	*El Greco*	Yannis Smaragdis (Greece/Spain/Hungary)

VAUGHAN WILLIAMS, Ralph (1872–1958) One of the most acclaimed of twentieth-century British composers, he scored only six feature films but his music has been heard in dozens of other movies and television programs.

Ralph Vaughan Williams was born in Down Ampney in Gloucestershire, England, the son of a vicar, and began piano lessons and composing songs as a young boy. Vaughan Williams was educated at Charterhouse School, the Royal College of Music, and Trinity College at Cambridge University, where he studied not only music theory but music history, giving him a lifelong fascination with and devotion to English folk songs. He pursued all aspects of music, including arranging choral groups, conducting, lecturing on music, editing musical publications, and composing. His first art song was published in 1902 and five years later he went to Paris to study under Maurice Ravel who prompted Vaughan Williams to pursue composition more fully. His first major success as a composer was his *Fantasia on a Theme by Thomas Tallis* in 1910, followed soon after by such acclaimed works as *A Sea Symphony* and *A London Symphony*. Over the next fifty years he composed five operas, five ballets, nine symphonies,

dozens of concertos, choral works, art songs and hymns, chamber pieces, organ works, and arrangements of Christian hymns. Vaughan Williams is equally important for his work in locating, transcribing, and printing nearly one hundred English folk and Tudor songs and carols which had never been written down and risked extinction. In addition to conducting the Leith Hill Music Festival orchestra for nearly fifty years, Vaughan Williams conducted and recorded with the finest orchestras and artists of his era. Few composers of his century have had such long, prodigious, and diverse careers in so many areas of music.

Although Vaughan Williams served in the Royal Army Medical Corps during World War I, he felt guilty that he was too old and in poor health to contribute directly to the World War II effort. Fellow composer Muir Mathieson, who had served as music director for several British films, urged Williams to work on movies that would help morale. He scored the documentary shorts *Welfare of the Workers* (1940), *The People's Land* (1943), and *The Stricken Peninsula* (1945) as well as the full-length documentary *Coastal Command* in 1943. Vaughan Williams also wrote music soundtracks for the British feature films *49th Parallel, The*

Flemish Farm, *The Loves of Joanna Godden*, and *Bitter Springs*, but his most popular movie was the adventure *Scott of the Antarctic*. He returned to movies and television a few times after the war, scoring documentary shorts about art and history. Since his death, Vaughan Williams's music has been heard in many films and TV movies, both documentaries and fictional works. His choral and instrumental music can be heard in such very different movies as *Women without Men* (1956), *The Year My Voice Broke* (1987), *Eat Drink Man Woman* (1994), *Ed Wood* (1994), *Enigma* (2001), and, most memorably, *Master and Commander: The Far Side of the World* (2003).

Vaughan Williams's lifelong interest in music from Britain's past influenced his concert and cinema work. There is a sense of patriotism and awe for the natural beauty of England in much of his music, particularly in the documentaries he scored. There is also a timelessness in his music because of his love for medieval, Tudor, and dateless folk songs. His music can sound very old and historic even as it uses some modern techniques and contemporary idioms. Vaughan Williams was nearly seventy when he wrote his first feature score for the wartime adventure *49th Parallel*. The main theme is beautifully restrained, a flowing orchestral piece that avoids bombast even as it inspires the listener. This stirring hymnlike music was later turned into the popular choral piece "The New Commonwealth." Although *49th Parallel* was released in the States before America was involved in the war, this engrossing drama, about Canadian civilians pursuing Nazi soldiers trying to reach the States, was very popular and remains one of the finest wartime films to come from England. The score for

the documentary *Coastal Command* is more aggressive and stirring in a different way. The vigorous main theme is a rapid march that uses strings as much as it relies on brass. The music for the section of the film about Scotland suggests an ancient folk song even as the arrangement of strings is mysterious and very modern.

A lovely passage set at dawn is a moving hymn while the aerial action sequence is scored with a bold march. Of the handful of nonwar movies Vaughan Williams scored, the standout is the drama *Scott of the Antarctic*, an accurate re-creation of the doomed expedition of 1912 led by Robert Falcon Scott (John Mills). Vaughan Williams uses various solo instruments, a wind machine, and a female choir to convey the brutally sparse landscape. Yet much of the score is uplifting and majestic rather than grim and defeatist. There is even a delightful sequence in which penguins frolic on the icy terrain and Vaughan Williams scores the scene with lighthearted glee. The woodwinds cleverly echo the penguins' waddling and sliding, resulting in a delectable comic ballet. The quality of the music in *Scott of the Antarctic* is so consistently superior that it is no wonder Vaughan Williams later turned it into a concert piece, the popular *Sinfonia Antarctica*. Most of Vaughan Williams's cinema music is concert worthy and much of his screen score music has shown up in concert halls around the world. Vaughan Williams's sojourn into the movies may have been brief but the music that resulted from it is often remarkable. Biography: *R. V. W.: A Biography of Ralph Vaughan Williams*, Ursula Vaughan Williams (his wife), (1993). Website: www.rvwsociety.com.

Credits

(all films UK unless stated otherwise)

Year	Film	Director
1941	*49th Parallel* (aka *The Invaders*)	Michael Powell
1943	*Coastal Command*	J. B. Holmes
1943	*The Flemish Farm*	Jeffrey Dell
1947	*The Loves of Joanna Godden*	Charles Frend, Robert Hamer
1948	*Scott of the Antarctic*	Charles Frend
1950	*Bitter Springs*	Ralph Smart (UK/Australia)

WALKER, Shirley (1945–2006) A busy composer, conductor, orchestrator, and arranger for television and movies, she scored some popular action and horror films before her premature death. Walker was one of the first notable female composers in Hollywood and the first woman to receive solo composing credit on a major American movie.

Born Shirley Rogers in Napa, California, where her parents were amateur musicians, she was a virtuoso on the piano as a young girl. While she was still in high school, Walker was a featured piano soloist with the San Francisco Symphony and performed in local jazz clubs. She attended San Francisco State University on a scholarship and studied both composition and the piano. After graduation she started her composing career writing jingles for radio and television and scoring industrial films, even as she continued to perform with the Oakland Symphony and other orchestras. She changed her name in 1967 when she married Donald Walker (not to be confused with the theatre-film orchestrator Don Walker). Her screen career began in 1979 when she was hired as the synthesizer soloist for the soundtrack recording of Carmine Coppola's music for *Apocalypse Now*. Walker was soon kept busy in television and movies as an arranger, musician, and conductor. Her first composing credit was for two episodes of the TV series *Lou Grant* in 1980 and two years later she was solo composer for the small independent film drama *The End of August*. Some other composing projects followed, but her first major-studio production did not come until 1990 with *Chicago Joe and the Show Girl*. Hans Zimmer was contracted to write the score but Walker ended up doing it (with Zimmer's name still credited because of legal reasons) and the music was noticed in Hollywood. Sometimes solo, sometimes as co-composer, Walker went on to score such action or horror films as *Escape from L.A.*, *Memoirs of an Invisible Man*, *Turbulence*, *Willard*, and *Final Destination* and two of its sequels.

Walker remained in demand as an arranger and/or conductor and supervised the music in such movies as *Children of a Lesser God* (1986), *Scrooged* (1988), *Batman* (1989), *Teenage Mutant Ninja Turtles* (1990), *Dick Tracy* (1990), *Edward Sissorhands* (1990), *Gladiator* (1992), *A League of Their Own* (1992), *True Lies* (1994), and *Batman Forever* (1995). Walker did similar work in television where she was given more composing jobs than in the movies. In addition to scoring such live-action and animated series as *Falcon Crest*, *China Beach*, *The Flash*, *Batman*, *Space: Above and Beyond*, *The New Batman Adventures*, *Superman*, and *The Others*, Walker also wrote scores for twelve TV movies, including *Majority Rule* (1992), *The Haunting of Seacliff Inn* (1994), *It Came from Outer Space II* (1996), *The Crying Child* (1996), *Asteroid* (1997), and *Disappearance* (2002). As one of a very small group of women screen composers, Walker was very active in entertainment organizations, such as the American Society of Composers, Authors and Publishers (ASCAP), the Recording Musicians Association, and the Academy of Motion Picture Arts & Sciences. Soon after completing the score for the feature thriller *Black Christmas*, Walker died at the age of sixty-one of complications from a stroke.

Because of her expert musical proficiency, Walker was often hired as a "score doctor" who fixed up, rearranged, or even composed music for existing scores. She also provided music for many movies without getting credit because of contractual agreements. For example, she co-composed the score for *The Black Stallion* (1997) with Carmine Coppola but received no screen credit. Yet there are plenty of her solo compositions so that one can evaluate Walker's musical skills. She wrote mostly in the classical mode with straightforward harmonies and strong melody lines. Walker particularly excelled at scoring horror, science fiction, or fantasy movies, although she was hired for all genres. Her strongest impact was felt in television where she established a new and exciting sound for animated action series, particularly the *Batman* cartoons. Although she was never nominated for an Oscar, she was honored with several television awards. Of her seventeen feature films, her finest work can be found in *Final Destination* and its sequels. The first installment concerns a teenager (Devon Sawa) who foresees death coming and is consequently suspected by the FBI of causing the destruction he has avoided. Walker worked with Adam Hamilton on the score, whose main theme is very menacing, as a simple but hypnotic motif is played by various instruments. While no technical tricks are used, this theme has a very eerie and otherworldly flavor, high strings and low brass contrasting each other effectively. Other parts of the score are more suspenseful with a pulsating bass line and screaming strings abruptly entering and exiting. The most horrific scenes are punctuated with electronic sounds that explode like thunder as kettle drums and other rhythmic pounding turn the music into a frantic chase. More electronics are used in the scores for the *Final Destination* sequels, some passages moving completely away from a traditional orchestra. Yet sections of *Final Destination 2* are very lyrical with strings used classically. These three scores taken together are a good illustration of Walker's talent for dramatic music.

Others scores reveal offbeat aspects of her music. The horror film *Willard* has an insistent main theme played by an odd assortment of instruments, ranging from a sour accordion to fluttering flutes. The effect is not quite comic but quirky all the same. *Black Christmas*, another horror entry, has a conventional suspense score but the use of brass fanfares at unexpected moments is quite original. The animated feature *Batman: Mask of the Phantasm* uses some of the musical ideas Walker introduced on television. The main theme has a choir that gives the tale a mythic opening. Later sections use chimes and other twinkling instruments to create a fantastical and dreamy tone. The action scenes sometimes include celestial voices competing with the bold symphonic sound. *Chicago Joe and the Show Girl*, a more realistic kind of thriller that is set in England during World War II, has a dramatic score that has its feet on the ground and in traditional screen scoring. There is a touch of jazz at times, the blues enters into the mix, and the romantic theme has a habit of turning sinister at times. Walker was a pioneer in Hollywood, the first woman to gain acceptance as a screen composer in a very male-dominated field. At the time of her death, she had scored more major-studio movies than any woman previously and she had opened the doors for other female composers to follow. Official website: www.walker.cinemusic.net.

Credits

(all films USA unless stated otherwise)

Year	Film	Director
1982	The End of August	Bob Graham
1983	Touched	John Flynn
1984	Ragewar	David Allen, etc.
1985	Ghoulies	Luca Bercovici
1990	Strike It Rich	James Scott (UK)
1990	Chicago Joe and the Show Girl	Bernard Rose (UK)
1991	Born to Ride	Graham Baker
1992	Memoirs of an Invisible Man	John Carpenter (USA/France)
1993	Batman: Mask of the Phantasm	Alan Burnett, etc.
1996	Escape from L.A.	John Carpenter
1997	Turbulence	Robert Butler
2000	Final Destination	James Wong (USA/Canada)
2002	Ritual	Avi Nesher
2003	Final Destination 2	David R. Ellis (USA/Canada)
2003	Willard	Glen Morgan (Canada/USA)
2006	Final Destination 3	James Wong (Germany/USA/Canada)
2006	Black Christmas	Glen Morgan (USA/Canada)

WALLACE, Oliver (1887–1963) A successful British-born conductor, songwriter, musician, and composer who scored 139 Disney cartoon shorts, he also wrote scores for many of that studio's features and documentaries.

He was born Oliver George Wallace in London where he studied piano at the local Music Conservatory. At the age of seventeen Wallace immigrated to Canada then moved on to the States where he continued to study music in Chicago, Seattle, Los Angeles, and San Francisco as he worked as a pianist in vaudeville. In the last city he was house organist for the Granada Theatre, the famous silent movie palace, then moved to Los Angeles where he was organist for Sid Grauman's Rialto Theatre. Legend has it that Wallace was the first to use a pipe organ to accompany a silent film when he worked at a cinema in Seattle in 1910. Wallace became a U.S. citizen in 1914 and four years later had a hit song with "Hindustan." He also contributed songs to the Broadway revue *Silks and Satins* (1920). By 1933 Wallace was working in Hollywood, writing music for B westerns and other low-budget Universal and Columbia films and working behind the scenes as a musician, arranger, and conductor. In 1935 he provided the organ playing on the soundtrack for *The Bride of Frankenstein*. Wallace was kept busy for four years but was looking for new challenges. They came in 1936 when he was hired by the Disney studio to score cartoons featuring Mickey Mouse and other beloved characters, beginning with *Mickey's Amateurs* (1937). Wallace wrote both the music soundtracks and often songs as well, most memorably the satirical Nazi propaganda song "Der Fuehrer's Face" for the 1942 Donald Duck short of the same name. Other outstanding shorts that Wallace scored include *Boat Builders* (1938), *The Autograph Hound* (1939), *Window Cleaners* (1940), *The Clock Watcher* (1945), *A Knight for a Day* (1946), *Donald's Double Trouble* (1946), *Bootle Beetle* (1947), *Pluto's Surprise Package* (1949), *Ben and Me* (1953), and *Toot Whistle Plunk and Boom* (1953), the first Cinemascope cartoon.

Wallace's first animated feature for Disney was *Dumbo*. He cowrote the soundtrack score with Frank Churchill (winning an Academy Award) and three of the songs (lyric by Ned Washington) including "Pink Elephants on Parade" and "When I See an Elephant Fly." He was among the Disney composers to contribute to the animated anthologies *Make Mine Music* and *Fun and Fancy Free* then worked solo on the soundtrack scores for the beloved classics *The Adventures of Ichabod and Mr. Toad*, *Alice in Wonderland*, *Peter Pan*, and *Lady and the Tramp*. In 1954 Disney moved into television and Wallace was a frequent contributor for the music in *Disneyland*. The 1950s also saw the first Disney live-action films and feature nature documentaries. Among these scored or coscored by Wallace are *Old Yeller*, *Tonka*, *Big Red*, *Darby O'Gill and the Little People*, *White Wilderness*, *Ten Who Dared*,

and *The Incredible Journey*. Wallace has the distinction of being one of the few composers ever nominated for Oscars for documentaries, which he did with *Victory through Air Power* and *White Wilderness*. Soon after completing the score for a 1963 episode of *Disneyland* he died at the age of seventy-six.

Because the songs in *Dumbo*, *Peter Pan*, *Alice in Wonderland*, and the other animated Disney features are so memorable, less attention is paid to the soundtrack scoring. Yet animated films call for much more music than most live-action features, and often whole sections of the score are not based on the melodies of those songs. The opening titles for *Dumbo*, for example, are scored with an original circus theme that is not based on any of the musical numbers that follow. It is a raucous, rapid piece of music played by horns and percussion, then a section is played on the calliope, then the brass make squawking sounds like clowns laughing. This theme returns throughout the film, turning into a nightmarish theme for the scene when Dumbo's mother goes berserk trying to protect her baby. The famous surreal sequence called "Pink Elephants on Parade" is a visual masterpiece, yet the use of trumpet fanfares, cockeyed xylophone, and pipe organ certainly add to the unique quality of the scene. *Peter Pan* has a delicious theme for the crocodile, played on a bassoon with percussive ticking and pizzicato strings. Originally written by Wallace as the song "Never Smile at a Crocodile," the number was cut but the music remains and is as memorable as any of the songs. Since Tinker Bell never speaks, all of her scenes are musicalized, making it clear what she means and feels, using everything from a piccolo to a harpsichord. Peter's theme is a series of boastful fanfares punctuated by a pan flute motif, while Captain Hook is scored with quivering strings and low chords. *The Legend of Sleepy Hollow* section of *The Adventures of Ichabod and Mr. Toad* has a very playful score. While the nineteenth-century story is narrated (and sung) by Bing Crosby, the background music is a marvelous blend of 1940s swing and 1930s horror film pastiche. *Alice in Wonderland* has more songs than any other Disney feature yet in between these short musical vignettes is a soundtrack score that draws on a variety of musical styles and quite a cornucopia of instruments. Alice's falling down the rabbit hole alone has a multitude of musical ideas expressed by everything from a harp to a theremin.

While Disney's live-action films of the 1950s rarely can compare to the animated ones, some have expert scores. Wallace's score for *Darby O'Gill and the Little People* is both romantic and silly, the Irish flavor in full force with a pixie-like theme for the Little People. The fiddle theme during the fox chase is furious and contagious and Wallace also wrote a charming folk pastiche called "Pretty Irish Girl" that is very pleasing. The adventure movie *Ten Who Dared*, about an expedition to chart the Colorado River through the Grand Canyon, has a vigorous score with a full symphonic sound for the action scenes and somber, wistful music for the character scenes. A similarly robust score can be found in *Tonka* about the lone Union horse to survive Custer's Last Stand and the Native American (Sal Mineo) who tames him. The horse has his own theme, a mixture of military fanfare and tribal rhythms. *Big Red* also has a boy (Gilles Payant) befriending an animal, the Irish setter of the title. But this tale is set in rural Quebec and has a French flavor in its nostalgic score. Wallace also scored what is perhaps the quintessential boy-dog movie, *Old Yeller*. The film begins with a cheerful title song in the western folk tradition, complete with banjo and whistling. The music remains light and frolicsome for the dog's misadventures, then dramatic for the more serious encounters. For the tragic demise of the canine hero, a scene that has traumatized millions of children, the music is restrained but builds steadily to the fatal gunshot and then silence. This is all a far cry from Wallace's cartoon music from the 1930s but another aspect of his considerable talent. Had he worked with studios other than Disney, Wallace's career might have been much different and he would have had the opportunity to score some superior live-action films. Yet within the range of his animated shorts and features and his nine live-action movies he did amazingly well.

Credits

(all films USA)

Year	Film	Director
1934	Sixteen Fathoms Deep	Armand Schaefer
1934	City Limits	William Nigh
1935	Life Returns	Eugene Frenke, James P. Hogan
1935	It Happened in New York	Alan Crosland
1935	Straight from the Heart	Scott R. Beal
1935	Alias Mary Dow	Kurt Neuman
1935	Girl in the Case	Eugene Frenke
1935	Outlawed Guns	Ray Taylor
1935	The Throwback	Ray Taylor
1935	Murder by Television	Clifford Sanforth
1935	Bulldog Courage	Sam Newfield
1936	Black Gold	Russell Hopton
1936	Roarin' Guns	Sam Newfield
1937	High Hat	Clifford Sanforth
1938	Sinners in Paradise	James Whale
1939	Straight Shooter	Sam Newfield
1941	Dumbo (AA)	Samuel Armstrong, etc.
1943	Victory through Air Power (AAN)	James Algar, etc.
1946	Make Mine Music	Robert Cormack, etc.
1947	Fun and Fancy Free	Ben Sharpsteen
1949	The Adventures of Ichabod and Mr. Toad	James Algar, etc.
1951	Alice in Wonderland (AAN)	Clyde Geronimi, etc.
1953	Peter Pan	Cylde Geronimi, etc.
1955	Lady and the Tramp	Wilfred Jackson, etc.
1957	Old Yeller	Robert Stevenson
1958	White Wilderness (AAN)	James Algar
1958	Tonka	Lewis R. Foster
1959	Darby O'Gill and the Little People	Robert Stevenson
1959	Jungle Cat	James Algar

Year	Film	Director
1960	Ten Who Dared	William Beaudine
1961	Nikki, Wild Dog of the North	Jack Couffer, Don Haldane
1962	Big Red	Norman Tokar
1962	The Legend of Lobo	James Algar
1963	Savage Sam	Norman Tokar
1963	The Incredible Journey	Fletcher Markle

WALTON, William (1902–1983) A distinguished and prolific British composer who wrote for the concert hall and the stage, his forays into film were limited but often extraordinary. In the movies, he is most associated with actor-director Laurence Olivier.

William Turner Walton was born in Oldham, England, the son of a voice teacher and church organist, and studied piano and violin at an early age but was more proficient as a singer. As a youth, Walton was accepted by the Christ Church Cathedral School in Oxford, where he sang for six years, then at the age of sixteen began a university education at Christ Church. He was so busy learning about the new European composers and writing his own music that he never completed his studies at Oxford. Instead he spent his time writing music in the modernist style and befriending many of the literary figures of the 1920s, in particular the Sitwell family, with whom he lived for fifteen years. Because of his bold and nontraditional musical style, Walton's work was more criticized by the press than encouraged, but he struggled on. Not until the late 1930s did he receive widespread recognition for such works as his Viola Concerto, the cantata *Belshazzar's Feast*, and his First Symphony. Walton was a slow and meticulous composer but he managed to produce a variable and substantial body of work. His music was often labeled avant-garde but he could also be very traditional, as with his *Crown Imperial*, a march written for the coronation of King George VI, and his opera *Troilus and Cressida* (1954). He also wrote for the ballet, theatre productions, radio, and television.

Although Walton was dismissive of film music, he wrote screen scores on occasion, usually as a favor to the director. For the Hungarian immigrant Paul Czinner, he scored four movies in the 1930s. The most memorable of the quartet is *As You Like It*, an early sound adaptation of the comedy featuring a young Olivier in his first filmed Shakespeare movie. Walton scored a series of pro-British movies during World War II but he did not rate this music very highly. For another Hungarian émigré, Gabriel

Pascal, he scored the screen version of George Bernard Shaw's *Major Barbara*. After the war, Walton only returned to movies when requested by Olivier, resulting in three of the finest Shakespeare films ever made: *Henry V*, *Hamlet*, and *Richard III*. Near the end of both his and Olivier's careers, the two men teamed up one more time in 1970 for *Three Sisters*, a screen version of an earlier London stage production of the Anton Chekhov classic. Walton's screen career ended on a sour note. He wrote a full score for the big-budget action film *Battle of Britain* (1969) but two weeks before the movie premiered, Walton's score was replaced by a new one by Ron Goodwin. Olivier, who was in the film, protested and threatened to have his name removed from the credits, so one air battle sequence from the Walton score was retained.

While Walton's concert and stage works range from romanticism to modernism, his screen scores are mostly in the traditional vein. His music in *As You Like It* is symphonic with a very rural flavor, the flutes chiming in like birds in the Forest of Arden. Conversely, the music in *Major Barbara* is urban pomp and circumstance with a march tempo. Walton provided rousing patriotic music for *Spitfire* and the other war-era propaganda films. With *Henry V*, in many ways another propaganda piece, Walton wrote his first great score. Director Olivier opens the movie with Elizabethan spectators gathering at the Globe Theatre where the performance soon transitions to a more medieval and filmic look. Walton's opening theme, filled with soaring voices, transports the moviegoer to the past as it segues into a pseudomadrigal. Subsequent scenes use fanfares, regal marches, courtly dances, and military airs. The most thrilling scene in *Henry V*, both cinematically and musically, is the stirring battle at Agincourt. Walton uses brass against furious violins to accompany the flying arrows and charging horses. The effect may strike contemporary viewers as a glorification of war but in 1944 the sequence must have been rousing to say the least. Even Walton must have thought this score was above usual screen music standards and in 1963 he arranged the music into a concert suite and conducted it himself. The fanfares and regal music in *Hamlet* take on a very different tone from those in *Henry V*. Walton's music suggests a corrupt kingdom and the melancholy underscoring is more mournful than dramatic. Hamlet's encounter with the ghost, his argument with Ophelia (Jean Simmons), and other crucial scenes are played without music. The court scenes are accompanied by a few madrigal instruments and even the climactic duel with Laertes (Terence Morgan) and the multiple deaths is scored with harsh but muted music. *Richard III* has a fuller sound, the fanfares more vigorous and the action scenes more symphonic. The opening theme suggests power and progress as the music seems to plow ahead with royal confidence. The battle on Bosworth Field may not be as fine as the Agincourt sequence but its music is equally vibrant. Even when it is clear that Richard (Olivier) is doomed, the music continues in a vivacious manner as if celebrating his defeat. Like the score from

Henry V, the music from *Hamlet* and *Richard III* has also been heard in the concert hall and on recordings. Walton may have dismissed his screen work but the music lives on in and outside of the cinema.

Walton is considered one of the outstanding British composers of the twentieth century, yet during his lifetime he was frequently criticized. Traditionalists scoffed at his modern sounds and avant-gardists complained when his music was too conventional. In his later years he was roundly honored: the Royal Philharmonic Society's Gold Medal, the Order of Merit, and a knighthood in 1951. His music continues to be admired and performed, and his name is also kept alive through the William Walton Trust. As for his screen scores, the best of them are so expert that one wishes he spent more time in film. Biographies: *William Walton: The Romantic Loner*, Humphrey Burton and Maureen Murray (2002); *William Walton: Muse of Fire*, Stephen Lloyd (2002); *Portrait of Walton*, Michael Kennedy (1989).

Credits

(all films UK)

Year	Film	Director
1935	*Escape Me Never*	Paul Czinner
1936	*As You Like It*	Paul Czinner
1937	*Dreaming Lips*	Paul Czinner
1939	*Stolen Life*	Paul Czinner
1941	*Major Barbara*	Gabriel Pascal
1942	*The Next of Kin*	Thorold Dickinson
1942	*The Foreman Went to France*	Charles Frend
1942	*Spitfire*	Leslie Howard
1942	*Went the Day Well?*	Alberto Cavalcanti
1944	*Henry V* (AAN)	Laurence Olivier
1948	*Hamlet* (AAN)	Laurence Olivier
1955	*Richard III*	Laurence Olivier
1970	*Three Sisters*	Laurence Olivier, John Sichel

WARBECK, Stephen (b. 1953) A versatile British performer and composer for theatre, television, and movies, he has scored films produced by over a dozen different countries.

Born in Southampton, England, by the age of five Stephen Warbeck was not only playing piano but composing songs as well. Warbeck later studied the violin, then, as a teenager, he embraced rock music and formed his own

band. At this time he also became interested in the theatre, so when he attended Bristol University he studied drama and French rather than music. After graduation, Warbeck worked as an actor and musical director in some small London theatres and in 1991 wrote music for an episode of the British TV series *4 Play*. That same year he scored the miniseries *Prime Suspect* which became internationally popular, returning for new episodes six times. Warbeck's feature film debut as a composer was the thriller *Sister My Sister* in 1994, but recognition for his screen work did not come until the Queen Victoria biopic *Mrs. Brown* three years later. That movie was directed by John Madden, who hired Warbeck the next year to score his romantic period piece *Shakespeare in Love*, which won Oscars for Best Picture and Score. The wide success of *Shakespeare in Love* led to international assignments in Europe and North America and a screen career as diverse as it is busy. Among Warbeck's seventy films are such notable credits as *Billy Elliot*, *Quills*, *Captain Corelli's Mandolin*, *Mystery Men*, *Charlotte Gray*, *Proof*, *The Other Man*, *Mystics*, *Winter Butterfly*, *Angels Crest*, *Jadoo*, and *Gallowwalkers*. He has scored several television series, miniseries, and TV movies (including the 1999 version of *A Christmas Carol* with Patrick Stewart), and over sixty theatre productions for such distinguished organizations as the Royal Court, National Theatre, Almeida, and the Royal Shakespeare Company, where he is an associate artist. Warbeck founded and performs with the singing group The hKippers (pronounced "Kippers").

Warbeck is often associated with period films, when in fact most of his movies are contemporary dramas and comedies. Perhaps the best known of these is *Billy Elliot* about a working-class youth (Jamie Bell) who discovers the beauty of ballet during a time of labor turmoil in England. There is only one piece of traditional ballet music in the film (Tchaikovsky's *Swan Lake*) for Billy dances mostly to bebop, jazz, and rock, some of which Warbeck composed. The nondance scenes are scored with folk-like themes that are both rustic and elegant. One lovely theme played on flute and strings captures the reflective yet restless nature of Billy while there is a daffy, merry jig heard under some of the movie's lighter moments. The drama *Proof*, in which a brilliant mathematician (Gwyneth Paltrow) fears for her sanity, has a probing, insistent main theme in which a metric pattern is offset by a slowly building melody. The effect is a bit disturbing until the pattern breaks and a warm melodic sequence takes over. *Proof* is a quiet drama and the score is restrained to the point of being tentative in manner. Even the romantic theme starts off so shy that one is not surprised that it fails to blossom musically. Another contemporary drama with a fine score is *Oyster Farmer*, in which an Australian youth (Alex O'Loughlin) flees the big city and finds himself when he lives among the poor oyster fishermen in a small village. A

lone fiddle with backup strings, a Jew's harp, and percussion play the main theme, a rhythmic folk piece that is a series of repetitive crescendos. The rest of the score uses the same instruments to create atmosphere and underscore the episodes, sometimes with cockeyed humor.

Two very different films set during World War II afforded Warbeck the opportunity to write exceptional scores. *Charlotte Gray*, in which a Scottish woman (Cate Blanchett) becomes involved in the French underground, grows in intensity as the story progresses and so does the score. The main theme is a flowing but somber lament played on accordion and guitar, suggesting both a Scottish and a Gallic flavor. Once Charlotte is ensconced in France, the music has a pounding and ominous beat that puts a dark cloud over the romantic strings. By the end of the movie, when Charlotte returns to France years later, the music finally flows freely with a resigned but triumphant air. *Captain Corelli's Mandolin* is set on a Greek island where Italian troops land and find more romance than warfare. The love theme, titled "Pelagia's Song," is sung on the soundtrack by Russell Watson and heard throughout; it is played, as expected, with some intricate finger work on a mandolin. Most of the score is more Italian than Greek and even incorporates some traditional Italianate themes. Warbeck wrote a gliding waltz for one passage, a hymnlike piece for guitar and mandolin for another, and a mellow march for the arrival of the Italians. Also romantic in a darker if not perverse way is the music for *Quills* about the imprisoned Marquis de Sade (Geoffrey Rush) and the laundress (Kate Winslet) he uses for sex and for sneaking out his manuscripts. Pipes and choral voices are used effectively in the period score, which also has touches of modern dissonance to convey the insanity that surrounds de Sade in the asylum. Although *Quills* eventually turns nasty and sour, the music remains glowing throughout. A very different period piece, *The Winter Butterfly*, concerns a samurai (Tomas Trinidad) in 1899 Japan who moves from idealistic hero to a corrupt bully. Warbeck uses Western instruments in creating the pseudo-Asian music, the violin taking on the sound of the high strings and the piano playing the lower strings. What is lost in authenticity is gained in its classical romanticism.

Warbeck's two most popular movies are the period pieces *Mrs. Brown* and *Shakespeare in Love*. The former, about the widowed Queen Victoria (Judi Dench) and how a Scottish Highlander (Billy Connolly) helps her break out of her mourning, is scored in a Scottish manner with flutes, fiddles, and the low sustained sound of bagpipes, but the music never slips into cliché and provides the right tone for this quiet but penetrating relationship. The main theme is a melancholy lament with spirit. Other passages are evocative of the Highland setting yet never sound like a background score for a travelogue. *Shakespeare in Love* uses Tudor lute, pipes, and tabor for a few festive scenes but most of the score avoids period authenticity and offers instead passionate contemporary music. This is more than appropriate, for, regardless of its Elizabethan look, *Shakespeare in Love* is very modern in attitude. The main title

consists of restless violins and anxious woodwinds moving forward like a feverish lover. There is a delicate love theme that is all the more touching because it is so tentative and fragile. The more serious scenes are scored with wavering strings that seem to be caught in a funeral dirge. The music throughout the score rarely resolves itself but pushes on fervently, heading for a climax that never comes. This is not unlike the doomed romance between Shakespeare (Joseph Fiennes) and his aristocratic lover (Gwyneth Paltrow), not to mention its parallels to *Romeo and Juliet*. This may not be Warbeck's best score, but it is his most popular and is filled with wonderful moments.

Credits

(all films UK unless stated otherwise)

Year	Film	Director
1994	Sister My Sister	Nancy Meckler
1995	Brothers in Trouble	Udayan Prasad
1995	Nervous Energy	Jean Stewart
1996	Different for Girls	Richard Spence (UK/France)
1996	Element of Doubt	Christopher Morahan
1997	Mrs. Brown	John Madden (UK/Ireland/USA)
1997	My Son the Fanatic	Udayan Prasad (UK/France)
1998	Shakespeare in Love (AA; BAFTA-N)	John Madden (USA)
1999	Heart	Charles McDougall
1999	Mystery Men	Kinka Usher (USA)
1999	Fanny and Elvis	Kay Mellor
2000	Billy Elliot (BAFTA-N)	Stephen Daldry (UK/France)
2000	Quills	Philip Kaufman (USA/UK/Germany)
2001	Captain Corelli's Mandolin	John Madden (UK/France/USA)
2001	Very Annie Mary	Sara Sugarman (UK/France)
2001	Gabriel & Me	Udayan Prasad
2001	Birthday Girl	Jez Butterworth (UK/USA)
2001	Charlotte Gray	Gillian Armstrong (UK/Australia/Germany)
2002	Desire	Gerardo Vera (Spain/Argentina)
2003	Mystics	David Blair (Ireland/UK)
2003	Blackball	Mel Smith
2003	The Memory of a Killer	Erik Van Looy (Belgium/Netherlands)
2004	Love's Brother	Jan Sardi (Australia/UK)
2004	Two Brothers	Jean-Jacques Annaud (France/UK)
2004	Everybody Is a Killer	Dominique Deruddere (France/Belgium/UK)
2004	Secret Passage	Ademir Kenovic (Italy/Portugal/Luxembourg)
2004	Mickybo and Me	Terry Loane
2004	Oyster Farmer	Anna Reeves (Australia/UK)
2005	On a Clear Day	Gaby Dellal
2005	Housewarming	Brigitte Roüan (France/UK)
2005	Proof	John Madden (USA)
2005	Opa!	Udayan Prasad (UK/Greece)
2006	Cargo	Clive Gordon (Spain/UK/Sweden)
2006	Alpha Male	Dan Wilde (USA/UK)
2007	Miguel and William	Inés Paris (Spain)
2007	Goal II: Living the Dream	Jaume Collet-Serra (UK/Spain/Germany)

Year	Film	Director
2007	*Flawless*	Michael Radford (UK/Luxembourg)
2008	*Love at First Kill*	John Daly (Canada/Belgium)
2008	*Freakdog* (aka *Red Mist*)	Paddy Breathnach
2008	*Machan*	Uberto Pasolini (Sri Lanka/Italy/Germany)
2008	*The Other Man*	Richard Eyre (USA/UK)
2008	*French Film*	Jackie Oudney
2009	*The Hessen Conspiracy*	Paul Breuls (Belgium/Canada)
2009	*Princess Kaiulani* (aka *After Heaven*)	Marc Forby (USA/UK)
2010	*A View of Love*	Nicole Garcia (France)
2010	*The Winter Butterfly*	Marcus Tozini
2011	*There Be Dragons*	Roland Joffé (Spain/USA)
2011	*Angels Crest*	Gaby Dellal (Canada/UK)
2011	*Polisse*	Maïwenn (France)
2012	*Papadopoulos & Sons*	Marcus Markou
2012	*Much Ado About Nothing*	Jeremy Herrin
2012	*Gallowwalkers*	Andrew Goth (USA/UK)
2012	*City of Lights* (aka *City of Angels*)	Daniele Thompson (France/Belgium)
2013	*Jadoo*	Amit Gupta
2013	*Day of the Flowers*	John Roberts (UK/Cuba)
2013	*Down to Earth*	Renata Heinen, Rolf Winters
2014	*Je te survivrai*	Sylvestre Sbille (Belgium)
2014	*Keeping Rosy*	Steve Reeves (USA/UK)
2014	*Seve*	John-Paul Davidson (UK/Spain)

WARD, Edward (1900–1971) A busy Hollywood conductor, songwriter, arranger, and composer in the 1930s and 1940s, he is credited with scoring over one hundred movies and his music was heard in another one hundred features.

Edward Ward was born in St. Louis, Missouri, and studied at the local Beethoven Conservatory before beginning his career as a songwriter on Tin Pan Alley. Ward went to Hollywood when sound movies began and wrote songs for musical shorts and features beginning in 1928. Over the next two decades he contributed dozens of songs (working with different lyricists) for a variety of comedies and musicals, most memorably "Always and Always," "For Ev'ry Lonely Heart," "West Wind Whistlin'," "Pennies for Peppino," "Beloved," and "Lullaby of the Bells." Ward's first full soundtrack score was written with Leon Rosebrook for the exotic adventure *Kismet* in 1930. Two years later he was solo composer for the comedy *A Fool's Advice*, followed over the years by music for such notable films as *The Sweetheart of Sigma Chi*, *The Countess of Monte Cristo*, *Affairs of a Gentleman*, *Great Expectations*, *Mystery of Edwin Drood*, *The Murder Man*, *The Bishop Misbehaves*, *Kind Lady*, *Wife vs. Secretary*, *San Francisco*, *After the Thin Man*, *Night Must Fall*, *The Last Gangster*, *A Yank at Oxford*, *The Shopworn Angel*, *Boys Town*, *It's a Wonderful World*, *The Women*, *Another Thin Man*, *Young Tom Edison*, *Maisie*, *Bad Little Angel*, *Ali Baba and the Forty Thieves*, *It Happened on Fifth Avenue*, *Bowery to Broadway*, and *Ah, Wilderness!* He received Oscar nominations for his scores for *All-American Co-Ed*, *Tanks a Million*, *Flying with Music*, *Cheers for Miss Bishop*, and *Phantom of the Opera*, also getting nominated for Best Song for "Always and Always" from *Mannequin* and "Pennies for Peppino" from *Flying with Music* (lyrics for both songs by Chet Forrest and Bob Wright). Ward served as conductor or musical director for many movies for Universal, MGM, and United Artists, where he was under contract at different times. He also worked in theatre on occasion, such as composing the music for the Broadway revue *Tattle Tales* (1933) and conducting the popular 1947 Broadway revival of *The Red Mill*. Although Ward retired from his musical chores for the movies in 1950, he remained active in Hollywood in different administrative positions until his death in 1971 at the age of seventy-one.

About two dozen of Ward's scores were co-composed with David Snell, Herbert Stothart, and others, and he often contributed music to movies with three or more composers credited. So it is most fruitful to look only at the movies he scored alone. Of the many musicals that Ward scored, the songs themselves were usually written by others and were often the source for the soundtrack music. Yet, even after eliminating all of these, there are plenty of first-class movies and scores by Ward left to examine. He was assigned all kinds of movies and the western seems to be the only genre not well represented in his credits. The many comedies range from sophisticated comedies of manners to broad farce. Two films that are somewhere in between are *Maisie* and *It's a Wonderful World*. The former features Ann Sothern as the title character, a sassy showgirl who is stranded in a Wyoming town when the show she has contracted to appear in closes prematurely. The spunky Maisie gets a job in a carnival, chases a ranchman (Robert Young), gets involved in a murder case, and has other misadventures. Audiences were so taken with Sothern and Maisie that nine *Maisie* comedies followed. This was the only one Ward scored but his theme for the heroine was used in the subsequent installments. It is a bouncy theme with a bit of sass as strings and brass instruments jump all over the scale. The score also has a silly march on high, giggling woodwinds, a swing number with a vivacious beat and robust musical phrases, and a catchy, smooth foxtrot theme with brass and woodwinds moving at a comfortable pace so that it can be used as the movie's romantic theme. Comedy and crime are also mixed in *It's a Wonderful World*, a delightful lark about a detective (James Stewart) who is wrongly accused of murder and is on the run, matters become complicated further when he is joined by a poet (Claudette Colbert) who unwittingly keeps getting him in deeper trouble. Ward's score keeps the story from getting too serious. The opening credits begin with a gliding string theme that transitions into a jazzy Big Band piece. There is also a sprightly foxtrot track on woodwinds and brass that is equally danceable. The soothing romantic theme on strings, woodwinds, and harp is so restrained it seems shy. The score also includes a merry comic theme with slaphappy woodwinds and silly strings, a very noticeable ditty that is heard at different points in the movie.

A good example of Ward's more dramatic music is his Oscar-nominated score for *Cheers for Miss Bishop*. This sentimental melodrama is about the midwestern teacher of the title (Martha Scott) who loses her fiancé to her manipulating cousin (Mary Anderson). When the cousin dies in childbirth, Miss Bishop raises the baby girl and continues her life dedicated to teaching. This distaff version of *Goodbye, Mr. Chips* uses the college and school songs to unify the story. The stately opening theme is a weighty alma mater–like anthem with chiming bells and a portentous air; it is sung as the school song later in the film. The school itself is scored with a domestic theme on woodwinds and strings, and the more heart-tugging scenes are given a solemn lullaby passage with a hymnlike flavor. The love theme is romantic but restrained, the solo violin heard over the crooning woodwinds stopping just short of sappy. All this melodrama is relieved by a clodhopping comic theme with frivolous strings and dancing reeds. Despite its title, *The Last Gangster* is a complex character drama and not an action film. When a mobster (Edward G. Robinson) is sent to prison for ten years, his wife (Rose Stradner) divorces him and marries a newspaper reporter (James Stewart), making for a very difficult situation when the hood is released from jail. Ward's main theme for the drama is a heavy march with drum rolls like machine guns, ponderous chords on brass, and strings that descend the scale so quickly they sound like they are dying. The anti-hero's bitterness is conveyed in some suspense passages that include a series of deep disturbing chords. One of the best dramas Ward got to score was *Night Must Fall*, a potent screen version of the popular stage thriller. When a cranky old dowager (Dame May Whitty) is taken with her new handyman (Robert Montgomery), her niece (Rosalind Russell) is also fascinated by the youth even though she suspects he is a murderer. Because the moviegoer is not quite sure if the charming fellow is a murderer or not, the score balances the tone between romantic and suspicious. The main theme is a sunny and wholesome piece on strings and reeds but quickly the music shifts into a minor-key passage that is unsettling without being too obvious. The niece's suspicions are scored with a series of strings ascending the scale then slowly tumbling down again. *Night Must Fall* is a superior thriller and the ambiguous use of music adds to its potency.

The 1943 screen version of *Phantom of the Opera*, with Claude Rains as the title villain, is generally thought of as the best of the many sound films and TV movies based on the famous tale. The movie also is Ward at his best as a composer and arranger. Only the scene from the opera *Martha* is performed as originally composed by Friedrich von Florow. Ward created the other opera sequences by adapting music by Chopin and Tchaikovsky into duets and arias. All of the music in the film not heard from the stage is original compositions by Ward. The opening credits are scored with a bombastic series of crescendos and fanfares on different instruments with parts of a lullaby heard briefly. This lullaby returns throughout the film as a leitmotif. It is sometimes heard as a lush passage with piano glissandos and sweeping strings. Other times its simple melody floats through the air, and once it becomes a violin solo that sounds lonely and forlorn. Yet the lullaby can easily become sinister as the tone changes, the piano becomes frantic, and the brass gets agitated. It is also sung as the duet "Lullaby of the Bells" (lyric by George Wag-

gner) sung by Susanna Foster and Nelson Eddy. The song was later picked up and performed by various artists, both as a vocal and an instrumental. *Phantom of the Opera* is filled with music by Ward. The phantom's piano concerto is a feverish piece that bridges romanticism and dissonant obsession. There is also robust gypsy dance music, a vigorous processional in an opera with chorus in full force, suspense music that uses irritated strings and sustained notes on woodwinds, and a chase theme with a full orchestra racing ahead with accents on a pipe organ. Rarely was Ward given such a musical feast to compose and arrange and he turned the opportunity into his finest moment.

Credits

(all films USA unless stated otherwise; * for Best Song)

Year	Film	Director
1930	Kismet	John Francis Dillon
1932	A Fool's Advice (aka Meet the Mayor)	Ralph Ceder
1932	Hypnotized (aka Little Gypsy)	Mack Sennett
1933	The Sweetheart of Sigma Chi	Edwin L. Marin
1934	The Countess of Monte Cristo	Karl Freund
1934	I Like It That Way	Harry Lachman
1934	Uncertain Lady	Karl Freund
1934	The Vanishing Shadow	Lew Landers
1934	Let's Be Ritzy	Edward Ludwig
1934	Affairs of a Gentleman	Edwin L. Marin
1934	Romance in the Rain	Stuart Walkert
1934	Million Dollar Ransom	Murray Roth
1934	Gift of Gab	Karl Freund
1934	Embarrassing Moments	Edward Laemmle
1934	Great Expectations	Stuart Walker
1934	Cheating Cheaters	Richard Thorpe
1934	Girl o' My Dreams (aka Love Race)	Ray McCarey
1934	Strange Wives	Richard Thorpe
1935	Mystery of Edwin Drood	Stuart Walker
1935	I've Been Around	Philip Cahn
1935	Times Square Lady	George B. Seitz
1935	Public Hero #1	J. Walter Ruben
1935	No More Ladies	Edward H. Griffith, George Cukor
1935	The Murder Man	Tim Whelan
1935	Here Comes the Band	Paul Sloane
1935	The Bishop Misbehaves	Ewald André Dupont
1935	Whipsaw (aka Unexpected Bride)	Sam Wood
1935	Kind Lady (aka House of Menace)	George B. Seitz
1935	Ah, Wilderness!	Clarence Brown
1936	Riffraff	J. Walter Ruben
1936	Exclusive Story	George B. Seitz
1936	Wife vs. Secretary	Clarence Brown
1936	Moonlight Murder	Edwin L. Marin
1936	Small Town Girl (aka One Horse Town)	William A. Wellman, Robert Z. Leonard
1936	Speed	Edwin L. Marin
1936	San Francisco	W. S. Van Dyke

Year	Film	Director
1936	*Women Are Trouble*	Errol Taggart
1936	*Sworn Enemy*	Edwin L. Marin
1936	*The Longest Night*	Errol Taggart
1936	*Sinner Take All*	Errol Taggart
1936	*After the Thin Man*	W. S. Van Dyke
1937	*Man of the People*	Edwin L. Marin
1937	*Mama Steps Out* (aka *Burnt Fingers*)	George B. Seitz
1937	*The Good Old Soak*	J. Walter Ruben
1937	*Night Must Fall*	Richard Thorpe
1937	*Saratoga*	Jack Conway
1937	*Bad Guy* (aka *Black Lightning*)	Edward L. Cahn
1937	*The Women Men Marry*	Errol Taggart
1937	*Double Wedding*	Richard Thorpe
1937	*Live, Love and Learn*	George Fitzmaurice
1937	*The Last Gangster*	Edward Ludwig
1937	*Navy Blue and Gold*	Sam Wood
1937	*Mannequin* (aka *Class*) (AAN*)	Frank Borzage
1938	*Love Is a Headache*	Richard Thorpe
1938	*Paradise for Three*	Edward Buzzell
1938	*A Yank at Oxford*	Jack Conway (UK)
1938	*Hold That Kiss*	Edwin L. Marin
1938	*The Toy Wife*	Richard Thorpe
1938	*Lord Jeff*	Sam Wood
1938	*The Shopworn Angel*	H. C. Potter
1938	*The Chaser*	Edwin L. Marin
1938	*The Crowd Roars*	Richard Thorpe
1938	*Boys Town*	Norman Taurog
1938	*Stablemates*	Sam Wood
1939	*Society Lawyer* (aka *Penthouse*)	Edwin L. Marin
1939	*Broadway Serenade*	Robert Z. Leonard
1939	*It's a Wonderful World*	W. S. Van Dyke
1939	*6,000 Enemies*	George B. Seitz
1939	*Maisie*	Edwin L. Marin
1939	*Stronger Than Desire*	Leslie Fenton
1939	*They All Come Out*	Jacques Tourneur
1939	*Andy Hardy Gets Spring Fever*	W. S. Van Dyke
1939	*These Glamour Girls*	S. Sylvan Simon
1939	*The Women*	George Cukor
1939	*Blackmail*	H. C. Potter
1939	*Thunder Afloat*	George B. Seitz
1939	*Dancing Co-Ed*	S. Sylvan Simon
1939	*Bad Little Angel*	Wilhelm Thiele
1939	*Another Thin Man*	W. S. Van Dyke
1939	*Joe and Ethel Turp Call on the President*	Robert B. Sinclair
1939	*Nick Cater, Master Detective*	Jacques Tourneur
1939	*Remember?*	Norman Z. McLeod
1940	*Congo Maisie*	H. C. Potter
1940	*Young Tom Edison*	Norman Taurog
1940	*My Son, My Son!*	Charles Vidor
1940	*Kit Carson*	George B. Seitz
1940	*The Son of Monte Cristo*	Rowland V. Lee
1941	*Mr. and Mrs. Smith*	Alfred Hitchcock
1941	*Cheers for Miss Bishop* (AAN)	Tay Garnett
1941	*Tanks a Million* (AAN)	Fred Guiol
1941	*All-American Co-Ed* (AAN)	LeRoy Prinz
1941	*Miss Polly*	Fred Guiol
1941	*Fiesta*	LeRoy Prinz
1941	*Hay Foot*	Fred Guiol

Year	Film	Director
1942	*Brooklyn Orchid*	Kurt Neumann
1942	*Flying with Music* (AAN; AAN*)	George Archainbaud
1942	*Men of Texas*	Ray Enright
1942	*Fall In*	Kurt Neumann
1943	*Taxi, Mister*	Kurt Neumann
1943	*Prairie*	Hal Roach Jr.
1943	*Yanks Ahoy*	Kurt Neumann
1943	*Phantom of the Opera* (AAN)	Arthur Lubin
1944	*Ali Baba and the Forty Thieves*	Arthur Lubin
1944	*Cobra Woman*	Robert Siodmak
1944	*The Climax*	George Waggner
1944	*Bowery to Broadway*	Charles Lamont
1945	*Song of the Sarong*	Harold Young
1945	*Salome Where She Danced*	Charles Lamont
1945	*It Happened on Fifth Avenue*	Roy Del Ruth
1947	*Copacabana*	Alfred E. Green
1948	*The Babe Ruth Story*	Roy Del Ruth
1949	*Two Knights from Brooklyn*	Kurt Neumann

WAXMAN, Franz (1906–1967) A dedicated and prolific composer and conductor from Eastern Europe, he contributed to some 150 movies and is most known for his scores for melodramas by Billy Wilder, Alfred Hitchcock, Victor Fleming, and other A-list directors.

Born Franz Wachsmann in Konigshutte, Germany (today Poland), he was the youngest of six children of an industrialist who allowed the boy to take music lessons but discouraged his son from trying to make a living in music. At the age of sixteen, Waxman began work as a teller in a bank, using his wages to continue his music lessons. In 1926 he quit his bank job and moved to Dresden where he worked as a pianist in cabarets and performed with the Weintraub Syncopaters, a popular jazz group. Much of that band's music was written and/or arranged by Friedrich Hollaender who took an interest in the young and talented Waxman. When the Syncopaters were hired by producer Erich Pommer to score Josef von Sternberg's *The Blue Angel* in 1930, Hollaender wrote the score but had Waxman arrange and conduct it. This led to other German films scored by Waxman, often with Hollaender as co-composer.

Waxman, who was still using the name Wachsmann, received his first wide recognition for his solo score for *Liliom*, Fritz Lang's film made in France in 1933. After the Jewish Wachsmann was roughed up by some pro-Nazis in Berlin, he moved to Paris where he worked on a handful of movies and scored Billy Wilder's first film. Hollaender and

Wachsmann were both invited to Hollywood in 1934 to work on *Music in the Air*. Both accepted and changed their names to Frederick Hollander and Franz Waxman, respectively. The latter was quickly noticed for his first original score there, *The Bride of Frankenstein*. Universal put the twenty-eight-year-old Waxman in charge of their music department and during the next two years he composed, arranged, and/or conducted nearly fifty movies. Waxman was then hired by MGM, where he wrote such memorable scores as *Captains Courageous*, *A Day at the Races*, *Dr. Jekyll and Mr. Hyde*, *A Christmas Carol*, *On Borrowed Time*, *The Philadelphia Story*, and *The Adventures of Huckleberry Finn*. When he was loaned out to David Selznick, Waxman received his first Oscar nominations for *The Young in Heart* and *Rebecca*. Much of the rest of Waxman's career was spent at Warner Brothers, where he scored many melodramas, comedies, and war films. Among the many renowned movies composed by Waxman over the decades are *Sunset Blvd.*, *Woman of the Year*, *Suspicion*, *Air Force*, *Old Acquaintance*, *To Have and Have Not*, *The Two Mrs. Carrolls*, *A Place in the Sun*, *The Spirit of St. Louis*, *Peyton Place*, *Stalag 17*, *Rear Window*, *Sayonara*, *The Nun's Story*, and *Come Back, Little Sheba*. He continued working into the 1960s, still receiving plaudits for such movies as *Sunrise at Campobello*, *Lost Command*, and *Taras Bulba*. He also took up writing music for television in the 1960s, scoring such shows as *Gunsmoke*, *Kraft Suspense Theatre*, *The Fugitive*, and *The Virginian*.

Waxman had studied composition and conducting at the Berlin Music Conservatory while he composed his German films, and he never abandoned his love for conducting the classics. In 1947 he founded the Los Angeles Music Festival, where for twenty years he premiered major works by Shostakovich, Stravinsky, Schoenberg, and others. Waxman also wrote for the concert hall, composing such oft-revived works as *Overture for Trumpet and Orchestra*, *Sinfonietta for String Orchestra and Timpani*, the violin and orchestra works *Carmen Fantasie* and *Tristan and Isolde Fantasy*, the song cycle *The Song of Terezin*, and the oratorio *Joshua*, as well as symphonic pieces based on some of his movie scores. In addition to his film awards, he received the Cross of Merit from West Germany and honorary degrees from American and European universities. Waxman was only sixty years old when he died of cancer in Los Angeles in 1967, still in top form as a composer and conductor.

Because he revered classical music and took music composition very seriously, Waxman thought of movie scores as a second-class art form. He loved the subtlety of great music and was convinced such subtlety was not effective on the screen where audiences had to grasp the music quickly. So he composed dramatic and catchy musical themes for Hollywood, knowing what worked best. Ironically, Waxman's film music is among the most understated and complex of all the great screen composers. He may have been aiming for the obvious but often his musical craftsmanship reveals amazing subtlety and can only be fully appreciated after careful study. Consider what is arguably his most famous score, that for Wilder's *Sunset Blvd.* The major theme in the movie is swift and suspenseful with a violin vigorously matching the opening chase scene. The way the strings alternate with low-pitched instruments makes for a complex kind of tension much more sophisticated than the expected Hollywood scoring. The theme for the deluded silent screen star Norma (Gloria Swanson) often suggests Richard Strauss's opera *Salome*, the same story that Norma hopes to use to make her screen comeback. It is an exotic theme suggesting desert sands and a Valentino silent movie as it wavers and builds alluringly. For the famous finale, when Norma has lost her reason and faces the newsreel cameras, the music moves from a subtle woodwind section into the exotic theme then into furious chords that flow with Norma's final close-up. *Sunset Blvd.* is so well written, acted, and filmed that it

might have been a success with an inferior score. But Waxman's music raised the picture from clever melodrama to high art. Waxman wrote another superior, if very different, score for Wilder's *The Spirit of St. Louis*, the biopic about Charles Lindbergh (James Stewart). There are long sections of the movie, particularly during Lindbergh's famous flight across the Atlantic, with no dialogue so music is very important in the movie. The aviator's loneliness and his exhilaration in flying are each expressed with contrasting musical themes. Waxman uses a good deal of dissonance to illustrate the aviator's self-doubts and this is heard from the opening credits until the triumphant landing in Paris. (Producer Jack Warner disliked the unmelodic nature of the score and brought in studio composers Ray Heindorf and Roy Webb to rewrite the opening music.)

Three of Waxman's scores for Hitchcock stand out in a career filled with outstanding work. The soundtrack for *Rebecca* is an entrancing mixture of romance and mystery. It is Waxman's music that provides the emotional pull of the movie. The final scene, in which the mansion Manderley burns and the camera moves into a close-up of Rebecca's embroidered pillow, is a beautifully sustained piece of music drama, the weighty chords climbing the scale with a vengeance. Waxman pulls off similar magic in *Suspicion*, a film that seems casual and matter of fact on the surface but grows in intensity as a wife (Joan Fontaine) suspects her husband is a murderer and she is his next victim. Since Cary Grant plays the husband the audience tends to consider him innocent so the music has to illustrate the doubt in the wife's mind. The romantic theme is captivating but there is an unsettling aspect to it as well. Waxman experimented with the instrumentation in *Suspicion*, using an electric violin, clarinet, and vibraphone to create an odd sensation in the ear. Throughout the film the underscoring is not overpowering but the final scene with a car speeding down a dangerously winding road is a series of full-throttle crescendos. The classic Hitchcock film *Rear Window* has little suspense music, making one question whether or not there is really a murder or just the imagination of the bedridden hero (James Stewart). The opening theme is an urban jazz piece that picks up the tempo of the city which we can barely see through an alley. The tympani and woodwinds suggest traffic and hustle and bustle, and there is even a cat's meow worked into the music. The theme accompanying the hero's observation of his neighbors is light, jaunty, and even comic at times and there is a sexy yet cool theme for his fashionable girlfriend (Grace Kelly). Surprisingly, the climactic encounter between the hero and the murderer (Raymond Burr) has no musical underscoring at all. It is just one of the many unusual aspects of this brilliant and unique film.

Another director Waxman worked well with was James Whale. Of their handful of movie collaborations, the most unforgettable is *The Bride of Frankenstein*. This cult favorite may not be the best horror film to come out of Hollywood but it arguably has the best score ever written for the genre. The theme for the bride (Elsa Lanchester) is a three-note phrase that manages to be romantic as well as eerie. (Thirteen years later Richard Rodgers used the same three notes for the song "Bali Hai.") The theme for the monster (Boris Karloff) is a five-note phrase and the two pieces of dissonant music are intertwined during the dramatic scene when the bride is created through electricity. The score also has some elegant sections, such as a lighthearted minuet played on chimes, some somber funeral-march themes heard on an organ, and exciting chase music with ominous chords. Waxman's score for *The Bride of Frankenstein* opened doors for better horror film music. Parts of the score itself were reused by Universal for many years for other horror flicks. What is so surprising is that not only was this Waxman's first Hollywood movie but he had no previous experience or familiarity with the horror genre. Six years later Waxman wrote another superior horror score, this time for the Spencer Tracy version of *Dr. Jekyll and Mr. Hyde*. Impressed by the moral tone under the surface of the story, Waxman used some religious music in his score. The old music hall song "See Me Dance the Polka" (by George Grossmith) is used several times in the score, the pleasant little ditty turning dark and foreboding as Waxman rearranges it to fit into the score thematically. Two contemporary suspense movies scored by Waxman also deserve mention. *Sorry, Wrong Number* uses music sparingly while *The Two Mrs. Carrolls* has a fully orchestrated score with a flowing main theme that turns sinister as the truth about Mr. Carroll (Humphrey Bogart) is revealed.

Waxman had a talent, like so many other refugee composers from Europe, for picking up the American musical vernacular. His scores for such pieces of Americana as *The Adventures of Huckleberry Finn*, *Cimarron*, and many World War II movies have little European romanticism. Perhaps the best of his war film scores is *Objective,*

Burma! The main theme suggests the exotic sounds of the Asian jungle but the thrust is very American with a rousing march. The music during the paratroopers' landing and their trek through the jungle is a masterwork of conveying danger and weariness. The final climb up the hill is accompanied by a simple musical passage that stops abruptly when they reach the top and silence takes over. It was a sobering ending for a movie that did not trade in glorious heroics. The same can be said for *The Edge of Darkness*, a war film with an exceptional score by Waxman. It is set in a small Norwegian fishing village occupied by the Nazis and the score quotes some traditional Norwegian folk tunes. More interesting is the way Waxman takes the Lutheran hymn "A Mighty Fortress Is Our God" and uses it in different ways, the music sometimes becoming harsh and forbidding. *Mister Roberts* is a very different wartime story, being more a comedy about the drudgery of war and serving on a supply ship in the Pacific. The Waxman score has its expansive moments but much of the music is intimate with touches of minor keys to express the tedium aboard the vessel. Another version of Waxman's Americana can be seen in the films about small-town life. *Come Back, Little Sheba* has a flowing waltz for its main theme but the loneliness and despair of the central characters is hinted at throughout. Waxman uses a smoldering blues for the main theme for *A Place in the Sun* about the haves and have-nots in a town. The award-winning score has a very romantic theme as well, the lone saxophone suggesting glamour and lust during the scenes between Elizabeth Taylor and Montgomery Clift. For the encounters between the hero and his lower-class girlfriend (Shelley Winters), the music is tentative and awkward. Perhaps Waxman's best depiction of a small town is his score for *Peyton Place*, a melodrama based on a best-selling potboiler about the various love affairs in a small New England village. The main theme suggests a Puritan hymn before moving into gliding waltz music that is used in ingenious ways throughout the movie. Because the catchy theme was also used in *Return to Peyton Place* and in the popular television series, it is perhaps the most familiar of all of Waxman's music.

Romantic melodramas and "women's pictures" seemed to be a Waxman specialty and often he was able to turn a weepie into palatable drama. He scored several Bette Davis movies that match this description, the best being *Old Acquaintance* and *Mr. Skeffington*. For the former, Waxman quotes from "Auld Lang Syne" then launches into a pastiche of a late nineteenth-century parlor piano ballad. The music in *Mr. Skeffington* suggests its early twentieth-century setting (several period tunes are heard on the soundtrack) but often feels more like the 1940s melodrama that it is. It is worth noting that Waxman put a great amount of labor and inspiration into such pictures. When he was handed a first-class drama, such as *The Nun's Story*, the script was worthy of his music. Church bells may set the tone for this rich score that is structured after Gregorian chants but it has so much variety in it that the score can hardly be labeled religious. The European romanticism is appropriate for a story set in Belgium and the Belgian Congo. It is often a quiet score with delicate passages that reflect the trials and self-doubts of the heroine (Audrey Hepburn). Yet the music can quickly become harsh, as in the memorable scene in the insane asylum in which Waxman uses a twelve-tone scale, something he said he never used elsewhere on-screen. Another quality script that Waxman got to score was *Sayonara*, a tragicomedy set in postwar Japan. The mixture of Asian musical phrases and lush Western melodies parallels the movie's plot about two GIs (Marlon Brando and Red Buttons) falling in love with Japanese women (Miiko Taka and Miyoshi Umeki). The movie may open with a solo female voice chanting a pseudo-Japanese hymn, but soon the music stretches out and encompasses a full Hollywood sound. Also, Waxman uses both Oriental instruments and a full Western orchestra, sometimes in inventive ways. The Asian strings and percussion, for example, are sometimes used in the dramatic underscoring of Western themes.

Two genres which Waxman was too infrequently hired for were comedies and historical pieces. His music for the Marx Brothers' vehicles *A Day at the Races* and *At the Circus* are delightful even though one tends to remember the songs more than the score. There is also sportive music by Waxman in two Katharine Hepburn classics: *The Philadelphia Story* and *Woman of the Year*. In both cases there is not too much music, both movies involving so much talk (and delicious dialogue it is!). Yet Waxman underscores the various relationships with quiet but insinuating romantic music that never draws attention to itself. Hollywood made so many historic and biblical epics in the 1950s that even the small-melodrama expert Waxman was handed big-budget projects such as *Prince Valiant*, *The Silver Chalice*, *Demetrius and the Gladiators*, *The Story of Ruth*, and *Taras Bulba*. These scores have some of Waxman's most vigorous screen music, such as the bold and exciting main theme for *Prince Valiant* in which the horns seem to be racing each other. In the Roman parable *Demetrius and the Gladiators*, a male chorus sings a "Gloria" march, female voices chant a hymn, and the orchestra moves at full throttle. There is a stirring Russian flavor to the Cossack epic *Taras Bulba*, in which the strings climb up and down the scale in a manic manner. These colorful and dazzling scores may not be typical of Waxman but they are nonetheless superbly crafted.

Whatever Waxman thought of film music as an art form, he took movie music seriously and was known for his integrity when it came to his scores. He was stubborn about changing music at the whim of producers, refused to tamper with other composers' scores, and was so upset when Alfred Newman's score for *The Robe* was not even nominated for an Oscar that he resigned from the Academy. Highly respected by his fellow composers, Waxman set high standards for movie music and others were challenged to meet them. His screen music continues to be studied, performed, and recorded. It seems the man who took music so seriously is finally being taken seriously by others. Official site: www.franzwaxman.com.

Credits

(all films USA unless stated otherwise)

Year	Film	Director
1930	Das Kabinett des Dr. Larifari	Robert Wohlmuth (Germany)
1930	Murder for Sale (aka Einbrecher)	Hanns Schwarz (Germany)
1931	Der mann, der seinen Mörder sucht	Robert Siodmak (Germany)
1931	Flagrant délit	Hanns Schwarz, Georges Tréville (Germany)
1931	Das Lied vom Leben	Alexis Granowsky (Germany)

Year	Film	Director
1931	*Un peu d'amour*	Hans Steinhoff (Germany)
1932	*Montparnasse Girl*	Hanns Schwarz (Germany/France)
1932	*Das erste Recht des Kindes*	Fritz Wendhausen (Germany)
1932	*Ein Mädel der Strasse*	Hans Steinhoff (Germany)
1932	*Paprika*	Carl Boese (Germany)
1933	*Ich und die Kaiserin*	Friedrich Hollaender (Germany)
1933	*Gruss und Kuss—Veronika*	Carl Boese (Germany)
1934	*Liliom*	Fritz Lang (France)
1934	*The Only Girl*	Friedrich Hollaender (Germany/USA/UK)
1935	*La crise est finie*	Robert Siodmak (France)
1934	*Mauvaise graine*	Alexander Esway, Billy Wilder (France)
1935	*The Bride of Frankenstein*	James Whale
1935	*The Affair of Susan*	Kurt Neumann
1935	*Diamond Jim*	A. Edward Sutherland
1935	*Three Kids and a Queen*	Edward Ludwig
1935	*Remember Last Night?*	James Whale
1935	*East of Java*	George Melford
1935	*Magnificent Obsession*	John M. Stahl
1936	*The Invisible Ray*	Lambert Hillyer
1936	*Next Time We Love*	Edward H. Griffith
1936	*Dangerous Waters*	Lambert Hillyer
1936	*Don't Get Personal*	Charles Lamont, William Nigh
1936	*The First Offence*	Herbert Mason (UK)
1936	*Sutter's Gold*	James Cruze
1936	*Love before Breakfast*	Walter Lang
1936	*Absolute Quiet*	George B. Seitz
1936	*Trouble for Two*	J. Walter Ruben
1936	*Fury*	Fritz Lang
1936	*The Devil-Doll*	Tod Browning
1936	*His Brother's Wife*	W. S. Van Dyke
1936	*Love on the Run*	W. S. Van Dyke
1937	*Personal Property*	W. S. Van Dyke
1937	*Captains Courageous*	Victor Fleming
1937	*A Day at the Races*	Sam Wood
1937	*The Emperor's Candlesticks*	George Fitzmaurice
1937	*The Bride Wore Red*	Dorothy Arzner
1938	*Man-Proof*	Richard Thorpe
1938	*Arséne Lupin Returns*	George Fitzmaurice
1938	*Test Pilot*	Victor Fleming
1938	*Three Comrades*	Frank Borzage
1938	*Port of Seven Seas*	James Whale
1938	*Too Hot to Handle*	Jack Conway
1938	*The Young in Heart (AAN)*	Richard Wallace
1938	*The Shining Hour*	Frank Borzage
1938	*Dramatic School*	Robert B. Sinclair
1938	*A Christmas Carol*	Edwin L. Marin
1939	*The Adventures of Huckleberry Finn*	Richard Thorpe
1939	*The Ice Follies of 1939*	Reinhold Schünzel
1939	*On Borrowed Time*	Harold S. Bucquet
1939	*Lady of the Tropics*	Jack Conway
1939	*At the Circus*	Edward Buzzell
1940	*Strange Cargo*	Frank Borzage
1940	*Rebecca (AAN)*	Alfred Hitchcock
1940	*Florian*	Edwin L. Marin
1940	*Sporting Blood*	S. Sylvan Simon
1940	*I Love You Again*	W. S. Van Dyke
1940	*Boom Town*	Jack Conway
1940	*Escape*	Mervyn LeRoy

Year	Film	Director
1940	Flight Command	Frank Borzage
1940	The Philadelphia Story	George Cukor
1941	The Bad Man	Richard Thorpe
1941	Dr. Jekyll and Mr. Hyde (AAN)	Victor Fleming
1941	Unfinished Business	Gregory La Cava
1941	The Feminine Touch	W. S. Van Dyke
1941	Honky Tonk	Jack Conway
1941	Suspicion (AAN)	Alfred Hitchcock
1941	Design for Scandal	Norman Taurog
1941	Kathleen	Harold S. Bucquet
1942	Woman of the Year	George Stevens
1942	Tortilla Flat	Victor Fleming
1942	Her Cardboard Lover	George Cukor
1942	Seven Sweethearts	Frank Borzage
1942	Journey for Margaret	W. S. Van Dyke
1942	Reunion in France	Jules Dassin
1943	Air Force	Howard Hawks
1943	Edge of Darkness	Lewis Milestone
1943	Old Acquaintance	Vincent Sherman
1943	Destination Tokyo	Delmer Daves
1944	In Our Time	Vincent Sherman
1944	Mr. Skeffington	Vincent Sherman
1944	To Have and Have Not	Howard Hawks
1944	The Very Thought of You	Delmer Daves
1945	Objective, Burma! (AAN)	Raoul Walsh
1945	Hotel Berlin	Peter Godfrey
1945	God Is My Co-Pilot	Robert Florey
1945	The Horn Blows at Midnight	Raoul Walsh
1945	Pride of the Marines	Delmer Daves
1945	Confidential Agent	Herman Shumlin
1946	Her Kind of Man	Frederick De Cordova
1946	Humoresque (AAN)	Jean Negulesco (USA)
1947	Nora Prentiss	Vincent Sherman
1947	The Two Mrs. Carrolls	Peter Godfrey
1947	Cry Wolf	Peter Godfrey
1947	Possessed	Curtis Baernhardt
1947	Dark Passage	Delmer Daves
1947	The Unsuspected	Michael Curtiz
1947	That Hagen Girl	Peter Godfrey
1947	The Paradine Case	Alfred Hitchcock
1948	Sorry, Wrong Number	Anatole Litvak
1948	No Minor Vices	Lewis Milestone
1948	Whiplash	Lewis Seiler
1949	Alias Nick Beal	John Farrow
1949	Night Unto Night	Don Siegel
1949	Rope of Sand	William Dieterle
1949	Task Force	Delmer Daves
1949	Johnny Holiday	Willis Goldbeck
1950	Night and the City	Jules Dassin (UK)
1950	The Furies	Anthony Mann
1950	Sunset Blvd. (AA; GG)	Billy Wilder
1950	Dark City	William Dieterle
1951	Only the Valiant	Gordon Douglas
1951	He Ran All the Way	John Berry
1951	A Place in the Sun (AA)	George Stevens
1951	Anne of the Indies	Jacques Tourneur
1951	The Blue Veil	Curtis Bernhardt
1951	Red Mountain	William Dieterle

Year	Film	Director
1951	*Decision before Dawn*	Anatole Litvak
1952	*Phone Call from a Stranger*	Jean Negulesco
1952	*Lure of the Wilderness*	Jean Negulesco
1952	*Come Back, Little Sheba*	Daniel Mann
1952	*My Cousin Rachel*	Henry Koster
1953	*Man on a Tightrope*	Elia Kazan
1953	*Botany Bay*	John Farrow
1953	*Stalag 17*	Billy Wilder
1953	*I, the Jury*	Harry Essex
1953	*A Lion Is in the Streets*	Raoul Walsh
1954	*Prince Valiant*	Henry Hathaway
1954	*Elephant Walk*	William Dieterle
1954	*Demetrius and the Gladiators*	Delmer Daves
1954	*Rear Window*	Alfred Hitchcock
1954	*This Is My Love*	Stuart Heisler
1954	*The Silver Chalice* (AAN)	Victor Saville
1955	*Untamed*	Henry King
1955	*Mister Roberts*	John Ford, Mervyn LeRoy
1955	*The Virgin Queen*	Henry Koster
1955	*The Indian Fighter*	André De Toth
1956	*Miracle in the Rain*	Rudolph Maté
1956	*Crime in the Streets*	Don Siegel
1956	*Back from Eternity*	John Farrow
1957	*The Spirit of St. Louis*	Billy Wilder
1957	*Sayonara*	Joshua Logan
1957	*Peyton Place*	Mark Robson
1958	*Run Silent Run Deep*	Robert Wise
1959	*Count Your Blessings*	Jean Negulesco
1959	*The Nun's Story* (AAN)	Fred Zinnemann
1959	*Career*	Joseph Anthony
1959	*Beloved Infidel*	Henry King
1960	*The Story of Ruth*	Henry Koster
1960	*Sunrise at Campobello*	Vincent J. Donehue
1960	*Cimarron*	Anthony Mann
1961	*Return to Peyton Place*	José Ferrer
1961	*King of the Roaring 20's: The Story of Arnold Rothstein*	Joseph M. Newman
1962	*My Geisha*	Jack Cardiff
1962	*Hemingway's Adventures of a Young Man*	Martin Ritt
1962	*Taras Bulba* (AAN; GGN)	J. Lee Thompson (Yugoslavia/USA)
1966	*Lost Command*	Mark Robson
1967	*The Longest Hundred Miles*	Don Weis

WEBB, Roy (1888–1982) A prodigious composer, arranger, conductor, and songwriter who also worked on Tin Pan Alley, Broadway, television, and movies, he scored over 250 feature films and his music was used by the studios in many other movies as well.

Born in New York City, Roy Webb showed a talent for art as a youth, so in his teens he enrolled at the Art Students League. Webb later studied classical music at Columbia University, where he wrote the school fight song and worked on student theatricals. After graduat-

ing in 1910, Webb teamed up with his younger brother, Kenneth S. Webb (1892–1966), and wrote songs for music publishers on Tin Pan Alley. By 1913 he was orchestrating, conducting, and writing incidental music for Broadway, most memorably a series of musicals by Richard Rodgers (music) and Lorenz Hart (lyrics), such as *Peggy-Ann* (1927), *A Connecticut Yankee* (1927), *Present Arms* (1928), and *Chee-Chee* (1928). By 1929 Kenneth Webb was directing shorts and features in Hollywood, so he hired his brother to arrange music and serve as musical director for some early talkies. The first two features Webb composed original music for, *Side Street* and *The Delightful Rogue*, were written with fellow composer Max Steiner in 1929. Later that same year he scored his first solo effort, the melodrama *Night Parade*, and for the next three decades Webb was kept busy as musical director and composer for an average of fifteen feature films a year. He worked on every genre, from musicals and westerns to comedies and horror movies. About fifty of his films were written with others, but over two hundred were solo works. Webb was nominated for an Oscar seven times but never won. His nominated scores were for *Quality Street*, *My Favorite Wife*, *Joan of Paris*, *I Married a Witch*, *The Fallen Sparrow*, *The Fighting Seabees*, and *The Enchanted Cottage*. Yet his most famous films and lauded scores were outside of these seven movies. Among the many significant movies scored by Webb are *Becky Sharp*, *Alice Adams*, *The Last of the Mohicans*, *Stage Door*, *The Last Days of Pompeii*, *The Mad Miss Manton*, *Bringing Up Baby*, *The Great Man Votes*, *Love Affair*, *Trouble in Sundown*, *Five Came Back*, *Bachelor Mother*, *Abe Lincoln in Illinois*, *Kitty Foyle*, *Cat People*, *Journey into Fear*, *Mr. Lucky*, *The Seventh Victim*, *The Curse of the Cat People*, *The Body Snatcher*, *The Spiral Staircase*, *Notorious*, *Crossfire*, *The Locket*, *I Remember Mama*, *Out of the Past*, *Mighty Joe Young*, *The Window*, *Clash by Night*, *Split Second*, *Houdini*, *The Raid*, *Marty*, *Teacher's Pet*, and *Murder, My Sweet*, as well as several Bert Wheeler–Robert Woolsey comedies and installments in the series of movies featuring the Falcon and the Saint (both starring George Sanders). His music was often picked up by the studios and placed in subsequent films. Some of his music can even be heard in Orson Welles's first two films, *Citizen Kane* (1941) and *The Magnificent Ambersons* (1942). Webb retired from movies in 1958, scored seven episodes of the television series *Wagon Train*, then in 1960 retired from show business to work on concert compositions. He kept copies of the sheet music from many of his scores but they, and his unpublished concert work, were all lost in a 1961 house fire. Webb was despondent over the loss and stopped writing music. He died of a heart attack in 1982 at the age of ninety-four. Today some of his studio scores are in a collection at Syracuse University but most of Webb's music exists only on the film stock soundtracks and too few of them have been released as recordings.

Despite the wide variety of movies Webb scored, it is his horror and mystery films that seem to be most appreciated for their music. The 1942 cult favorite *Cat People* has a rather lame premise—a Serbian immigrant (Simone Simon) fears that intimacy with her husband (Kent Smith) will turn her into a panther—yet the movie is so bizarre and stylish that it works despite the low budget and short shooting schedule producer Val Lewton had to work with. The panther is very effective because it is kept in the shadows and Webb's music does the rest. The opening music is a surprisingly romantic theme with the hint of a children's singsong ditty amid the ominous horn fanfares and swirling strings. The later suspense music is not so subtle. A theme on woodwinds and brass gets more and more agitated until it reaches a climax and only a solo oboe remains. The panther is scored with screeching strings and electronic echoes that blend in with the sound of the cat's growl and screech. *Cat People* was a surprise hit and Lewton came back with *The Curse of the Cat People* and other horror offerings. One of the best is *The Body Snatcher*, based on a story by Robert Louis Stevenson, in which a medical student (Russell Wade) realizes that his mentor and teacher (Henry Daniell) has been getting his supply of corpses from a cabbie (Boris Karloff) who threatens to expose the doctor-professor. The main theme is a fearsome march with drum rolls and strings weaving back and forth in a melodic but chilling manner. A solo oboe is used effectively while other woodwinds descend the scale and seem to surround the haunting tune. Again there is not much subtlety in the scoring but neither is there in the filmmaking. For a more delicate touch, one must turn to Webb's music for *The Spiral Staircase* which is more a thriller than a horror film. A wealthy old invalid (Ethel Barrymore) has a premonition that her mute servant (Dorothy McGuire) will be the next victim of a serial killer who goes after women with physical afflictions. Despite the old woman's efforts, the girl ends up playing cat and mouse with the murderer in a dark mansion during a thunderstorm. This classic thriller gets much of its potency from Webb's music. He utilizes the theremin throughout the score, creating sounds that quietly but potently send chills up the spine. This weird-sounding instrument is first heard during the opening credits when the electronic humming has a slightly sinister tone. Before one of the murders, the theremin accompanies the close-up shot of the killer's eye in the shadows. Another memorable use of music during the film is during the servant girl's dream in which a lilting waltz is heard as she dances with a handsome doctor (Kent Smith) at a dance. When the dream shifts to their wedding ceremony, she is unable to speak the wedding vows and Webb lets the music turn sour with dissonance and a menacing change of tone.

Alfred Hitchcock's *Notorious* gave Webb the opportunity to score another classic thriller and he came up with a very passionate main theme that manages to be sensual, dangerous, and still romantic. An American secret agent (Cary Grant) convinces the daughter (Ingrid Bergman) of a convicted Nazi to spy on a group of Nazis in South America. Matters get complicated when she and the agent fall in love but she has to marry a key Nazi (Claude Rains) as part of the assignment. Perhaps Hitchcock's most sensual film, *Notorious* has very little music but Webb's restless, desperate love theme is so powerful that it seems like the movie is through-scored. There is a Latin-flavored theme for Rio de Janeiro that is more frantic than festive, suspense music that is often more lyrical than abrupt or strident, and some distorted horns and out-of-tune strings for a sequence in which the female spy is drugged by her captors. Perhaps the most famous scene in the film takes place during a party at the mansion while the two lovers-agents search the wine cellar for clues and discover uranium in the wine bottles. The background music is a gentle rumba heard from the party and serves as an effective contrast to the tension in the basement. *Notorious* can be included with the many film noir movies that Webb scored. One of the best is the Raymond Chandler tale *Murder, My Sweet* in 1944 in which Dick Powell plays the iconic private detective Philip Marlowe. Based on Chandler's *Farewell, My Lovely*, it is a complicated yarn with plenty of villains and beautiful women who can't seem to tell the truth. The main theme is a dark but melodic passage with strings sawing away as brass and percussion try to undercut them. This music is actually from Webb's score for the noir thriller *The Stranger on the Third Floor* four years earlier. He must have felt it did not get the attention it deserved so he rearranged it for this more famous noir movie. The suspense passages include brass notes that rush up the scale while strings descend just as quickly. Another memorable track is the music and

sound effects during a nightmare scene. The beaten and drugged Marlowe dreams in surreal fashion and the music is an odd march with brass and reeds, echoing notes on the theremin, fluttering clarinets, and repeated chords on various instruments that go nowhere. Some musicologists feel that Webb invented (or at least developed) the musical sound of film noir in *The Stranger on the Third Floor* and *Murder, My Sweet*.

Two romance movies about unlikely lovers have expert scores by Webb. *The Enchanted Cottage* brings together a homely woman (Dorothy McGuire) and a scarred ex-soldier (Robert Young) who fall in love more out of loneliness than passion. Yet because of true love they both appear to be beautiful to each other. This 1945 romantic fantasy works thanks to the strong performances and Webb's intoxicating main theme. It is a mystical and somewhat exotic passage with a disquieting undercurrent that is eventually overridden by the melody on strings that returns to a catchy four-note phrase as it flows along briskly and with a purpose. Webb must have been quite taken with this theme but instead of using it again in another movie, he turned it into a piano and orchestra concerto which was performed at the Hollywood Bowl later in 1945. A decade later the drama *Marty* concerned a tentative romance between an overweight, unattractive Bronx butcher (Ernest Borgnine) and a plain schoolteacher (Betsy Blair). His friends and family find her unacceptable but the butcher overcomes everyone's doubts and marries her for love. The main theme for the low-budget, black-and-white sleeper hit is a sparkling waltz played on strings, woodwinds, and harp that never gets too fancy or grandiose for this ordinary couple. The melody actually comes from the title song by Harry Warren (music) and Paddy Chayefsky (lyric) sung over the opening credits. It is a bouncy and playful song but only when Webb adapted it and arranged it for the soundtrack score does it become an entrancing love theme. Although he scored so many movies, was nominated by the Academy, and was a well-respected artist in Hollywood for thirty years, Webb was never much known to the public during his lifetime and he has nearly slipped into obscurity because so little of his music exists on CDs or even records. It is hoped that he does not disappear from sight or, more importantly, from sound.

Credits

(all films USA)

Year	Film	Director
1929	Side Street (aka Forty-Ninth Street)	Malcolm St. Clair
1929	The Delightful Rogue	Lynn Shores, Leslie Pearce
1929	Night Parade	Malcolm St. Clair
1930	Girl of the Port (aka The Fire Walker)	Bert Glennon
1930	Alias French Gertie	George Archainbaud
1930	Inside the Lines	Roy Pomeroy
1930	Shooting Straight (aka Dead Game)	George Archainbaud
1930	Conspiracy	Christy Cabanne
1933	Topaze	Harry d'Abbadie d'Arrast
1933	Our Betters	George Cukor
1933	Diplomaniacs	William A. Seiter
1933	Emergency Call	Edward L. Cahn
1933	Blind Adventure (aka Fog Bound)	Ernest B. Schoedsack
1933	Ann Vickers	John Cromwell
1933	Aggie Appleby Maker of Men	Mark Sandrich
1933	The Right to Romance	Alfred Santell
1933	If I Were Free (aka Behold We Live)	Elliott Nugent
1934	Hips, Hips, Hooray!	Mark Sandrich
1934	This Man Is Mine	John Cromwell
1934	Strictly Dynamite	Elliott Nugent
1934	Let's Try Again (aka Sour Grapes)	Worthington Miner
1934	Cockeyed Cavaliers	Mark Sandrich
1934	Down to Their Last Yacht (aka Hawaiian Nights)	Paul Sloane
1934	Kentucky Kernels	George Stevens
1934	By Your Leave	Lloyd Corrigan
1935	The Nitwits	George Stevens
1935	Becky Sharp (aka Lady of Fortune)	Rouben Mamoulian, Lowell Sherman
1935	The Arizonian (aka Boom Days)	Charles Vidor
1935	Alice Adams	George Stevens
1935	The Last Days of Pompeii	Ernest B. Schoedsack
1935	The Rainmakers	Fred Guiol
1935	In Person	William A. Seiter
1935	Sylvia Scarlett	George Cukor
1935	We're Only Human	James Flood
1936	Two in the Dark	Benjamin Stoloff
1936	Silly Billies	Fred Guiol
1936	The Last of the Mohicans	George B. Seitz
1936	Mummy's Boys	Fred Guiol
1936	A Woman Rebels	Mark Sandrich
1936	Make Way for a Lady	David Burton
1936	Wanted: Jane Turner (aka Federal Offense)	Edward Killy
1936	Night Waitress	Lew Landers
1936	The Plough and the Stars	John Ford
1937	Racing Lady (aka All Scarlet)	Wallace Fox
1937	They Wanted to Marry	Lew Landers
1937	We're on the Jury (aka We, the Jury)	Ben Holmes
1937	Quality Street (AAN)	George Stevens
1937	The Outcasts of Poker Flat	Christy Cabanne
1937	You Can't Buy Luck (aka Borrowed Time)	Lew Landers
1937	Meet the Missus	Joseph Santley
1937	New Faces of 1937 (aka Young People)	Leigh Jason
1937	On Again—Off Again	Edward F. Cline
1937	Four Naughty Girls	Edward F. Cline
1937	The Life of the Party	William A. Seiter

Year	Film	Director
1937	Stage Door	Gregory La Cava
1937	Saturday's Heroes	Edward Killy
1937	High Flyers	Edward F. Cline
1937	Wise Girl	Leigh Jason
1937	She's Got Everything	Joseph Santley
1938	Lawless Valley	David Howard
1938	Bringing Up Baby	Howard Hawks
1938	Condemned Women	Lew Landers
1938	This Marriage Business	Christy Cabanne
1938	Go Chase Yourself	Edward F. Cline
1938	Gun Law	David Howard
1938	The Saint in New York	Ben Holmes
1938	Having Wonderful Time	Alfred Santell
1938	Sky Giant	Lew Landers
1938	Mother Carey's Chickens	Rowland V. Lee
1938	I'm from the City	Ben Holmes
1938	Fugitives for a Night (aka Birthday of a Stooge)	Leslie Goodwins
1938	The Mad Miss Manton	Leigh Jason
1938	A Man to Remember	Garson Kanin
1938	The Law West of Tombstone	Glenn Tryon
1938	Next Time I Marry (aka Trailer Romance)	Garson Kanin
1939	The Great Man Votes	Garson Kanin
1939	Arizona Legion	David Howard
1939	Boy Slaves (aka Saints without Wings)	P. J. Wolfson
1939	Beauty for the Asking	Glenn Tryon
1939	The Saint Strikes Back	John Farrow
1939	Love Affair	Leo McCarey
1939	Trouble in Sundown	David Howard
1939	They Made Her a Spy	Jack Hively
1939	The Flying Irishman	Leigh Jason
1939	Fixer Dugan (aka Double Daring)	Lew Landers
1939	The Rookie Cop	David Howard
1939	Sorority House	John Farrow
1939	Panama Lady	Jack Hively
1939	Five Came Back	John Farrow
1939	Timber Stampede	David Howard
1939	Bachelor Mother	Garson Kanin
1939	Career	Leigh Jason
1939	In Name Only (aka The Kind Men Marry)	John Cromwell
1939	Bad Lands	Lew Landers
1939	Full Confession	John Farrow
1939	Three Sons	Jack Hively
1939	Sued for Libel	Leslie Goodwins
1939	That's Right—You're Wrong	David Butler
1939	Reno	John Farrow
1939	Two Thoroughbreds	Jack Hively
1940	Laddie	Jack Hively
1940	Abe Lincoln in Illinois	John Cromwell
1940	The Saint's Double Trouble	Jack Hively
1940	Curtain Call	Frank Woodruff
1940	Irene	Herbert Wilcox
1940	My Favorite Wife (AAN)	Garson Kanin
1940	You Can't Fool Your Wife	Ray McCarey
1940	A Bill of Divorcement	John Farrow
1940	Millionaires in Prison	Ray McCarey
1940	Stranger on the Third Floor	Boris Ingster
1940	Wildcat Bus	Frank Woodruff
1940	Men against the Sky	Leslie Goodwins

Year	Film	Director
1940	I'm Still Alive	Irving Reis
1940	Mexican Spitfire out West	Leslie Goodwins
1940	You'll Find Out (aka The Old Professor)	David Butler
1940	Little Men	Norman Z. McLeod
1940	Kitty Foyle	Sam Wood
1941	The Saint in Palm Springs	Jack Hively
1941	A Girl, a Guy, and a Gob	Richard Wallace
1941	Tom Dick and Harry	Garson Kanin
1941	Parachute Battalion	Leslie Goodwins
1941	Father Takes a Wife	Jack Hively
1941	Weekend for Three	Irving Reis
1941	Look Who's Laughing	Allan Dwan
1941	Playmates	David Butler
1942	Joan of Paris (AAN)	Robert Stevenson
1942	Obliging Young Lady	Richard Wallace
1942	The Tuttles of Tahiti	Charles Vidor
1942	My Favorite Spy	Tay Garnett
1942	The Big Street	Irving Reis
1942	The Falcon's Brother	Stanley Logan
1942	Highways by Night	Peter Godfrey
1942	Here We Go Again	Allan Dwan
1942	Army Surgeon	A. Edward Sutherland
1942	The Navy Comes Through	A. Edward Sutherland
1942	I Married a Witch (AAN)	René Clair
1942	Seven Days' Leave	Tim Whelan
1942	Cat People	Jacques Tourneur
1943	Hitler's Children	Edward Dmytryk, Irving Reis
1943	Journey into Fear	Norman Foster, Orson Welles
1943	Flight for Freedom (aka Stand to Die)	Lothar Mendes
1943	Ladies' Day	Leslie Goodwins
1943	The Falcon Strikes Back	Edward Dmytryk
1943	I Walked with a Zombie	Jacques Tourneur
1943	The Leopard Man	Jacques Tourneur
1943	Bombardier	Richard Wallace, Lambert Hillyer
1943	Mr. Lucky	H. C. Potter
1943	The Falcon in Danger	William Clemens
1943	Petticoat Larceny	Ben Holmes
1943	The Adventures of a Rookie	Leslie Goodwins
1943	Behind the Rising Sun	Edward Dmytryk
1943	The Fallen Sparrow (AAN)	Richard Wallace
1943	The Lady Takes a Chance (aka Cheyenne)	William A. Seiter
1943	The Seventh Victim	Mark Robson
1943	The Iron Major	Ray Enright
1943	Gangway for Tomorrow	John H. Auer
1943	The Ghost Ship	Mark Robson
1944	Passport to Destiny (aka Magnificent Adventure)	Ray McCarey
1944	Action in Arabia (aka Danger in Damascus)	Léonide Moguy
1944	The Curse of the Cat People	Gunther von Fritsch, Robert Wise
1944	The Falcon out West	William Clemens
1944	Marine Raiders	Harold D. Schuster
1944	The Seventh Cross	Fred Zinnemann
1944	Bride by Mistake	Richard Wallace
1944	Rainbow Island	Ralph Murphy
1944	The Master Race	Herbert J. Biberman
1944	Tall in the Saddle	Edwin L. Marin
1944	The Fighting Seabees (AAN)	Edward Ludwig
1944	Murder, My Sweet	Edward Dmytryk
1944	Experiment Perilous	Jacques Tourneur

Year	Film	Director
1945	*The Enchanted Cottage* (AAN)	John Cromwell
1945	*Betrayal from the East*	William Berke
1945	*Two O'Clock Courage*	Anthony Mann
1945	*Zombies on Broadway* (aka *Loonies on Broadway*)	Gordon Douglas
1945	*Those Endearing Young Charms*	Lewis Allen
1945	*The Body Snatcher*	Robert Wise
1945	*Back to Bataan* (aka *The Invisible Army*)	Edward Dmytryk
1945	*Radio Stars on Parade*	Leslie Goodwins
1945	*Love, Honor and Goodbye*	Albert S. Rogell
1945	*George White's Scandals*	Felix E. Feist
1945	*Sing Your Way Home*	Anthony Mann
1945	*The Spiral Staircase*	Robert Siodmak
1945	*Dick Tracy*	William Berke
1945	*Cornered*	Edward Dmytryk
1946	*Riverboat Rhythm*	Leslie Goodwins
1946	*Badman's Territory*	Tim Whelan
1946	*Bedlam* (aka *Chamber of Horrors*)	Mark Robson
1946	*The Well-Groomed Bride*	Sidney Lanfield
1946	*Without Reservations*	Mervyn LeRoy
1946	*Notorious*	Alfred Hitchcock
1946	*Genius at Work* (aka *Genius, Inc.*)	Leslie Goodwins
1946	*The Locket* (aka *What Nancy Wanted*)	John Brahm
1947	*Sinbad, the Sailor*	Richard Wallace
1947	*The Perfect Marriage*	Lewis Allen
1947	*Easy Come, Easy Go*	John Farrow
1947	*The Devil Thumbs a Ride*	Felix E. Feist
1947	*Riffraff*	Ted Tetzlaff
1947	*They Won't Believe Me*	Irving Pichel
1947	*Crossfire* (aka *Cradle of Fear*)	Edward Dmytryk
1947	*Magic Town*	William A. Wellman
1948	*I Remember Mama*	George Stevens
1948	*Fighting Father Dunne*	Ted Tetzlaff
1948	*Race Street*	Edwin L. Marin
1948	*Rachel and the Stranger*	Norman Foster
1948	*Blood on the Moon*	Robert Wise
1948	*Bad Men of Tombstone*	Kurt Neumann
1949	*Roughshod*	Mark Robson
1949	*The Window*	Ted Tetzlaff
1949	*Mighty Joe Young*	Ernest B. Schoedsack
1949	*Make Mine Laughs*	Richard Fleischer, Hal Yates
1949	*My Friend Irma*	George Marshall
1949	*Easy Living* (aka *Interference*)	Jacques Tourneur
1949	*Holiday Affair*	Don Hartman
1950	*The Secret Fury*	Mel Ferrer
1950	*The White Tower*	Ted Tetzlaff
1950	*Where Danger Lives* (aka *White Rose for Julie*)	John Farrow
1950	*Branded*	Rudolph Maté
1950	*Vendetta*	Mel Ferrer, etc.
1950	*Gambling House* (aka *Alias Mike Fury*)	Ted Tetzlaff
1951	*Sealed Cargo*	Alfred L. Werker
1951	*Hard, Fast and Beautiful* (aka *Mother of a Champion*)	Ida Lupino
1951	*Flying Leathernecks* (aka *Devil Dogs of the Air*)	Nicholas Ray
1951	*Fixed Bayonets!*	Samuel Fuller
1952	*At Sword's Point*	Lewis Allen
1952	*A Girl in Every Port*	Chester Erskine
1952	*Clash by Night*	Fritz Lang
1952	*The Lusty Men* (aka *Cowpoke*)	Nicholas Ray, Robert Parrish
1952	*Operation Secret*	Lewis Seiler

Year	Film	Director
1953	*Split Second*	Dick Powell
1953	*Affair with a Stranger*	Roy Rowland
1953	*Houdini*	George Marshall
1953	*Second Chance*	Rudolph Maté
1953	*Alaska Seas*	Jerry Hopper
1954	*She Couldn't Say No* (aka *She Had to Say Yes*)	Lloyd Bacon
1954	*Dangerous Mission* (aka *Rangers of the North*)	Louis King
1954	*The Raid*	Hugo Fregonese
1954	*Track of the Cat*	William A. Wellman
1955	*The Americano*	William Castle
1955	*Underwater!* (aka *The Big Rainbow*)	John Sturges
1955	*Marty*	Delbert Mann
1955	*The Sea Chase*	John Farrow
1955	*The Kentuckian* (aka *The Gabriel Horn*)	Burt Lancaster
1955	*Bengazi*	John Brahm
1955	*Blood Alley*	William A. Wellman, John Wayne
1956	*The River Changes*	Owen Crump
1956	*Our Miss Brooks*	Al Lewis
1956	*The First Texan*	Byron Haskin
1956	*The Search for Bridey Murphy*	Noel Langley
1956	*The Girl He Left Behind*	David Butler
1957	*Top Secret Affair* (aka *Melville Goodwin, USA*)	H. C. Potter
1957	*Shoot-Out at Medicine Bend*	Richard L. Bare
1958	*Teacher's Pet*	George Seaton

WILLIAMS, John (b. 1932) Arguably the most successful movie composer in the history of the medium, he has scored more megahit movies, been honored with more awards, and enjoyed more financial gains than anyone else in his field. Williams is also one of the most prodigious of American composers, writing for the concert stage, special events, and television, as well as the movies, even as he maintained for many years a busy conducting career. Often associated with director Steven Spielberg (he scored all but two of the director's feature films), Williams gained equal notoriety working with George Lucas, Mark Rydell, Oliver Stone, Chris Columbus, and other directors. He composed some of the most recognized movie themes from the 1970s into the new century but his body of work is much more than a series of hit tunes.

He was born John Towner Williams in Floral Park on Long Island, New York, the son of a jazz percussionist who had a successful career playing in the Raymond Scott Quintet. When Williams was sixteen, the family moved to Los Angeles, where he started composing serious concert pieces, finishing his first sonata by the time he was nineteen. He attended UCLA where he polished his piano skills and studied conducting as well as composition.

During his stint in the military, Williams played piano in the U. S. Air Force Band, eventually arranging music and conducting that famous ensemble. Back in civilian life, he studied at Juilliard and the Eastman School of Music as he earned his living playing piano in jazz clubs. These jobs led to arranging and playing for television (he was the pianist for the famous "*Peter Gunn* Theme") then, after moving back to Los Angeles, in the movies. Williams was a musician for several movie scores, including *South Pacific* (1958), *Days of Wine and Roses* (1962), and *Charade* (1963). His first composing credits were not for the big screen but for television, scoring such shows as *Gilligan's Island*, *Bachelor Father*, and *Lost in Space*.

Williams's first feature film credit as a composer was the low-budget *Daddy-O* in 1958, followed by ten years of mostly forgettable movies that brought him little recognition. Within the business, he was gaining a reputation as an inventive arranger, conductor, and composer of lightweight scores. In 1967 his score for *The Valley of the Dolls* was noticed and earned him his first Academy Award nomination. Other noteworthy assignments and nominations followed (he won his first Oscar for scoring *Fiddler on the Roof*) but Williams did not get wide recognition until

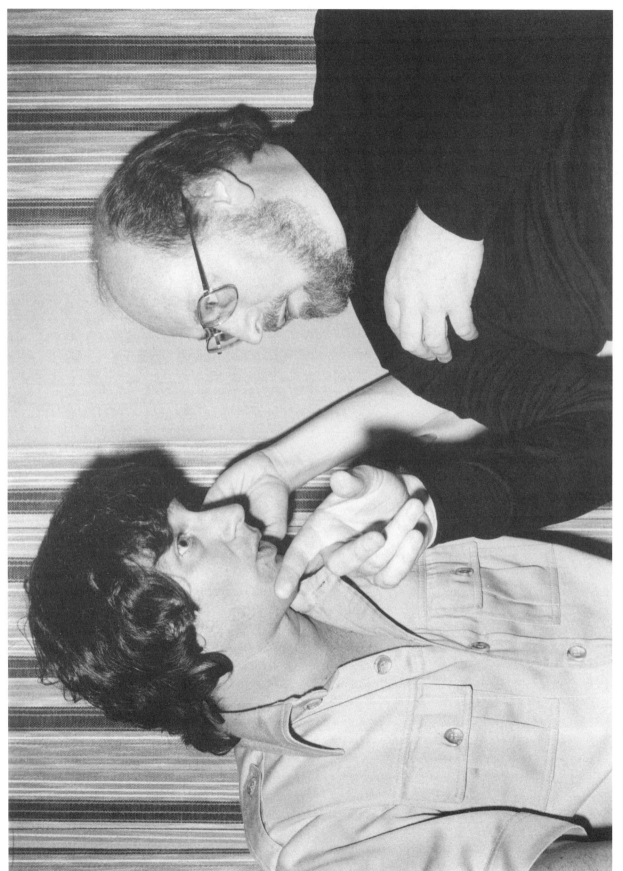

JOHN WILLIAMS. Director Steven Spielberg (left) and Williams worked out the central musical idea for *Close Encounters of the Third Kind* (1977) long before filming began. It was their third film together and has been followed by many more, one of the most fruitful collaborations in the history of the movies. *Columbia Pictures / Photofest © Columbia Pictures*

his bombastic scores for a series of disaster films, including the *Poseidon Adventure*, *Earthquake*, and *The Towering Inferno*. Greater renown came in 1975 with his tense and chilling score for another kind of disaster movie, *Jaws*. It was his second film with Spielberg (Williams had scored the director's first feature, *The Sugarland Express*, the year before) and the first of a long line of hits over the next four decades. Highlights in their fruitful collaboration include *Close Encounters of the Third Kind*, *Raiders of the Lost Ark*, *E.T.*, *Empire of the Sun*, *Jurassic Park*, *Schindler's List*, *Saving Private Ryan*, *Catch Me If You Can*, *War Horse*, and *Lincoln*. A shorter but equally lucrative collaboration with director-producer George Lucas resulted in the *Star Wars* films, perhaps Williams's most famous scores. By the 1980s he was the most in-demand composer in Hollywood which afforded him the opportunity to score small intimate films, such as *The Reivers*, *The Accidental Tourist*, *The River*, *Sabrina*, *Stanley and Iris*, and *Angela's Ashes*, as well as big-budget pictures like *Superman*, *JFK*, *Far and Away*, *The Patriot*, and *War of the Worlds*. Even when he wrote the music for a slight comedy such as *Home Alone* for director Chris Columbus, the picture turned out to be a surprise hit. Columbus worked with Williams on a string of other movies, most memorably *Harry Potter and the Sorcerer's Stone*.

Such an active Hollywood career did not keep Williams from composing for the concert hall. Even as he scored an average of three movies a year, he has written fifteen concertos, five chamber works, and over a dozen orchestral pieces. These compositions were presented by eminent conductors and performed by celebrated musicians and orchestras. He composed the theme song for four Olympic Games and wrote music for other special occasions, such as the rededication of the Statue of Liberty. Williams was equally active in conducting, from concerts of his movie music to the Boston Pops Orchestra, which he was maestro of for thirteen years. Recordings by the Pops, his movie soundtracks, and his concert pieces have brought Williams over twenty gold and platinum records and a record fifty-one Grammy nominations (winning twenty-one times). Only Walt Disney accumulated more Oscar nominations than Williams but the composer's forty-one nominations have resulted in only five Academy Awards. He holds over fifteen honorary degrees from colleges and universities and has received another dozen special awards and citations.

Yet Williams's career is more than impressive numbers and popular achievements. His film music is far richer and more eclectic than an armful of popular themes might suggest. Williams's music is often in the tradition of nineteenth-century romanticism. Like some of the masters of that century, he uses recurring themes (or leitmotif) within a score to bring unity to the soundtrack. He prefers a large orchestral sound, but that is because so many of his movies are large scale and grandiose. Even his large-scale compositions often rely on a simple three or four-note motif which he varies with finesse to create a classical flavor. In the case of *Jaws*, only two notes were used and repeated and speeded up to characterize the unseen but fully sensed killer shark. This groundbreaking movie, about a great white shark that terrorizes the residents and vacationers of a small seaside community, ushered in a new kind of thriller: nature as predator. The main theme is played on low woodwinds and strings as a deadly kind of march is propelled forward with a vengeance. The unrelenting beat and the way the different instruments get more and more tense makes this one of the great suspense compositions of modern movies. Other notable tracks in the *Jaws* score include a passage with furious strings and piano rushing up and down the scale, an oddly merry little march on horns with restless strings underneath, a frivolous theme with dancing strings and giddy woodwinds, a dizzying section with screaming violins and crazed harp glissandos, and a serene passage that conveys the peace of calm seas.

While some of the most famous Williams themes are in a vigorous march tempo, such as the opening credits for *Star Wars*, *Raiders of the Lost Ark*, and *Superman*, these are not true representations of the full scores. The first *Star Wars* installment, for example, is filled with variety. What is remarkable about the *Star Wars* music is that it has no sci-fi musical techniques, no synthesized or computerized orchestrations, and no electronic sound effects to convey a futuristic world. Instead Williams scores *Star Wars* like a swashbuckler from Hollywood's golden age with full orchestra exploding in passionate rather than electronic ways. The composer has cited Erich Wolfgang Korngold as his inspiration in scoring the *Star Wars* series and the famous opening march does have some similarities to Korngold's opening music for *Kings Row*. This march is a series of fanfares that might serve for a Roman army as much as intergalactic space travel. Because director George Lucas pastiches the cinema techniques of the old

Flash Gordon and other space serials, such old-fashioned music is more than appropriate. Yet audiences did not find the *Star Wars* music old fashioned. It struck them as exciting and new and it still does. Returning to that first installment, one can recall much more music than the opening march. There is the tender and poetic theme for the binary sunset that is surprisingly quiet and reflective for an action film. Sustained strings and featured woodwind solos move cautiously in this dreamlike passage which hints at the deeper aspects the movie will eventually explore. The indelible theme for Darth Vader is a minor-key march with a menacing tone and a chilling sense of evil. This march is also used sometimes for the imperial forces and is very effective with its Fascist-like way of parading forward mechanically. The motif for Princess Leia (Carrie Fisher) is a delicate piece of music on horns and is used, in an altered way, as the music for Ben Kenobi (Alec Guinness) who is linked thematically with Leia in the story. As for the scoring of the action scenes, the most memorable music is the throbbing, tense composition for the final Death Star attack. In contrast is the silly music played by a cantina band in the bar, a jazzy piece with a cockeyed circus flavor. The fact that all these themes seem consistent and even futuristic is part of Williams's masterful craftsmanship. He scored all six of the *Star Wars* adventures and in each one adds splendid new themes, many of them in a more dissonant and melancholy mode as the story line grows darker and more complex.

Williams's score for *E.T.* is deceptively simple, using subtle musical themes that grow more elegant as the friendship between the boy Elliott (Henry Thomas) and the extraterrestrial grows, climaxing in a spirited flight of fancy by the end of the film. The opening music is slightly synthesized as sound effects blend into a seven-note motif for the extraterrestrial creature with music that is eerie without being frightening. There is a dreamy theme on harp for Elliott that conveys wonder and mystery. When the youth is intoxicated by E.T.'s beer drinking, the music is dizzy and wavering with some playful phrases on woodwinds. Perhaps the most exhilarating music in the movie is the vivacious flying theme heard when the boys' bicycles defy gravity and take flight. Various instruments climb the scale in different ways until the whole piece seems to be airborne. Another sci-fi film that is more about character than action is *Close Encounters of the Third Kind*. The score is unique in that the music (the five-note phrase used

to communicate with the aliens) is an essential part of the plot. Williams worked on the score with Spielberg as the director was plotting out the movie on paper. Spielberg did not want the phrase to have a melody, fearing it would not sound alien enough. Williams came up with dozens of seven-note phrases but all were rejected because that many notes tended to be too musical. They then experimented with five-note arrangements and eventually came up with the simple but mesmerizing combination in the final film. Williams then built his score around this important musical phrase but was careful to keep the pattern tentative until the climactic scene when it is used as a communication device. The score also features a beguiling two-note phrase with sustained strings underneath as the theme for Devil's Tower, the rock formation that draws various characters to the place where the aliens will arrive. Williams's music pastiches the Gregorian *Mass for the Dead* in his theme for the dangerous aspects of the encounters. The movie concludes with a series of musical tracks as the five-note phrase is expanded into a fully musical form and the final measures in the score quote from the Disney classic "When You Wish Upon a Star" (music by Leigh Harline).

Another way to explore the musical talents of Williams is to study his lesser-known movie scores. *The Reivers*, composed in 1969 when Williams was just starting to find fame in Hollywood, is a delightful domestic score. The story concerns a young boy (Mitch Vogel) in 1905 Mississippi who has an amusing and maturing adventure when he sets off with two of his grandfather's employees (Steve McQueen and Rupert Crosse) for Memphis when his parents are away. The score captures a nostalgic Southern charm without becoming sentimental. The use of guitar and harmonica not only creates a rural sound but adds to the comic tone that pervades most of the film. There is a freewheeling theme played on rapid strings that overflows with excitement, as well as a more lyrical passage on harmonica that is filled with lazy contentment. The Winton Flyer automobile they travel in has its own theme, a raucous piece played on banjo, Jew's harp, and piano. The rousing horse race at the climax of *The Reivers* is scored with a full orchestra that gets fuller and more romantic as the race builds, matching the poetic narration (by Burgess Meredith) in its expansive sense of childlike joy. *The Sugarland Express* score also uses the harmonica but in a mournful and melancholy way. Toots Thielemans is the soloist on the soundtrack and he captures a variety of moods on the harmonica, which this comedy-tragedy requires. When her baby is taken from her by Social Services, a young mother (Goldie Hawn) and her escaped-convict husband (William Atherton) take a cop (Michael Sacks) as hostage to try and get the child back. Alternately funny and quirky, the movie ends tragically. The main theme in the score is a bluesy harmonica solo with cautious string accompaniment. Once the chase is on, the score takes on a traveling mode which is sometimes rustic and carefree, other times nervous and frantic. Quite different is the Eastern European music Williams wrote for the film version of *Fiddler on the Roof*. The songs from the Broadway production are by Jerry Bock (music) and Sheldon Harnick (lyrics) but as rearranged for the screen and with Williams's original scoring the story takes on a rich Russian flavor that is closer to Tchaikovsky than the stage work. The lonesome clarinet solo in the *Stepmom* soundtrack, the authentic-sounding gospel chanting in *Rosewood*, and the fiery Irish fiddling in *Far and Away* are other examples of Williams's less bombastic musical skills. Perhaps Williams's most unique score is the avant-garde one he wrote for director Robert Altman's hallucination drama *Images*, in which percussionist Stomu Yamashta produced hypnotic sounds on steel wire sculptures creating a discordant effect paralleling the movie's psychological frenzy.

Although it was not a small movie, *Schindler's List* has a quietly poignant score that does not draw attention to itself. This grim yet inspiring movie, about Oskar Schindler (Liam Neeson) and his efforts to save thousands of Jews during the Holocaust, is so emotional that Spielberg and Williams thought that passionate or dramatic music would be numbing. Instead Williams composed a slow and dignified score that underscored the events with great restraint. The main theme, played so beautifully on the soundtrack by violinist Itzhak Perlman, is a flowing reverie that is not morose yet has a tender and doleful tone. The score also includes a sad waltz that seems to be resigned to death, a slow-motion folk dance filled with pathetic hope, and a piano solo that tentatively etches out a lyrical melody. Also filled with restraint is Williams's score for *Lincoln*, a low-key but enthralling look at the president (Daniel Day-Lewis) and his efforts to get his Emancipation Proclamation passed by Congress. A solo clarinet is featured in the main theme which is a hymnlike piece of Americana as it mixes a folk sound with a symphonic one. Also in the

Copland-like score is a lilting passage that moves like a country dance, a brisk and rustic polka on various instruments, a military march on fife and drum that leads into a "Battle Cry of Freedom" chorale, dissonant and disturbing passages to convey Lincoln's nightmares and fears, a sparkling hoedown musical section, and an elegant and heartfelt elegy played on weeping strings. There is also a moving elegy in the score for *Saving Private Ryan*. Titled "Hymn to the Fallen," it is a slow march on trumpets and percussion featuring a solo clarinet and a wordless choir. The theme is used at different points in this World War II film about the efforts of a captain (Tom Hanks) to find and return a private (Matt Damon) to his home that has already lost three men to the war. In perhaps the movie's most powerful scene, the D-Day landing on Omaha Beach, there is little music as the sounds of battle predominate. Then Williams quietly brings in a gentle anthem that is serene and hopeful. For the World War I movie *War Horse*, Williams provides a more romantic score in a poetic frame of mind. The story concerns a farm horse conscripted into the military and the struggles his young owner (Jeremy Irvine) endures to find him in the battlefields of France. It is a British tale and the music is often very European. The sounds of the English countryside are heard in parts of the film, including some folk themes and rural music. But the rest of the score is symphonic and grand with vigorous music during the battles, graceful passages for the character scenes, and inspiring sections for the noble aspects of the movie.

Because Williams has been so popular for so long, there has often been disgruntled criticisms of his movie music, arguing that much of it is a variation of the same flamboyant march theme. It is true that the *Superman* march and *The Raiders of the Lost Ark* theme are relatives to the *Star Wars* galactic march and that they share a similar kind of energy of composition. But that is like complaining that too much of George Gershwin's music is so jazz infiltrated that it all sounds alike. Williams often works within the romantic style (one might say neo-romantic) and, given the movies he usually scores, goes for a big sound. The fact that he does this and still manages to come up with musical phrases or full melodies that appeal to a modern audience is no little accomplishment. His scores are popular not just because the films are big hits but because he connects with contemporary moviegoers in a way few Hollywood composers have. Perhaps his greatest accomplishment is the way he turned the direction of movie music. In the 1960s, pop songs on the soundtrack were starting to replace full orchestral movie scores. Studios liked the new trend because it was less costly than large orchestras and sometimes a movie produced a hit single. Williams made the orchestrated movie score fashionable again with *Star Wars* and other popular films. That, perhaps, is his greatest legacy. Biography: *Strings Attached: The Life and Music of John Williams*, William Starling (2013). Critical study: *John Williams' Film Music*, Emilio Audissino, 2014. Official website: www.johnwilliams.org.

Credits

(all films USA unless stated otherwise; * for Best Song)

Year	Film	Director
1958	Daddy-O	Lou Place
1960	I Passed for White	Fred M. Wilcox
1960	Because They're Young	Paul Wendkos
1961	The Secret Ways	Phil Karlson
1962	Bachelor Flat	Frank Tashlin
1963	Diamond Head	Guy Green
1963	Gidget Goes to Rome	Paul Wendkos
1964	The Killers	Don Siegel
1965	None but the Brave	Frank Sinatra (USA/Japan)
1965	John Goldfarb, Please Come Home!	J. Lee Thompson
1966	The Rare Breed	Andrew V. McLaglen
1966	How to Steal a Million	William Wyler
1966	The Plainsman	David Lowell Rich
1966	Not with My Wife, You Don't!	Norman Panama
1966	Penelope	Arthur Hiller
1967	A Guide for the Married Man	Gene Kelly
1967	Fitzwilly	Delbert Mann
1967	Valley of the Dolls (AAN)	Mark Robson
1968	Sergeant Ryker	Buzz Kulik
1969	Daddy's Gone A-Hunting	Mark Robson
1969	Goodbye, Mr. Chips (AAN)	Herbert Ross
1969	The Reivers (AAN)	Mark Rydell
1970	Story of a Woman	Leonardo Bercovici (Italy/USA)
1971	Fiddler on the Roof (AA)	Norman Jewison
1972	The Cowboys	Mark Rydell
1972	Images (AAN)	Robert Altman (UK/USA)
1972	The Poseidon Adventure (AAN; GGN)	Ronald Neame
1972	Pete 'n' Tillie	Martin Ritt
1973	The Man Who Loved Cat Dancing	Richard C. Sarafian
1973	The Paper Chase	James Bridges
1973	Cinderella Liberty (AAN*; GGN)	Mark Rydell
1973	Conrack	Martin Ritt
1973	The Sugarland Express	Steven Spielberg
1974	Earthquake (GGN)	Mark Robson
1974	The Towering Inferno	John Gullermin
1974	The Eiger Sanction	Clint Eastwood
1974	Jaws (AA; GG; BAFTA)	Steven Spielberg
1975	Family Plot	Alfred Hitchcock
1975	The Missouri Breaks	Arthur Penn
1976	Midway	Jack Smight
1976	Black Sunday	John Frankenheimer
1976	Star Wars (AA; GG; BAFTA)	George Lucas
1977	Close Encounters of the Third Kind (AAN; GGN; BAFTA-N)	Steven Spielberg
1978	The Fury	Brian De Palma

Year	Film	Director
1978	*Jaws 2*	Jeannot Szwarc
1978	*Superman* (AAN; GGN)	Richard Donner (UK)
1979	*Dracula*	John Badham (USA/UK)
1979	*1941*	Steven Spielberg
1980	*Star Wars V: The Empire Strikes Back* (AAN; GGN; BAFTA)	Irvin Kershner
1981	*Raiders of the Lost Ark* (AAN; BAFTA-N)	Steven Spielberg
1981	*Heartbeeps*	Allan Arkush
1982	*E.T. the Extra-Terrestrial* (AA; GG; BAFTA)	Steven Spielberg
1982	*Yes, Giorgio* (AAN*; GGN*)	Franklin J. Schaffner
1982	*Monsignor*	Frank Perry
1983	*Star Wars VI: Return of the Jedi* (AAN)	Richard Marquand
1984	*Indiana Jones and the Temple of Doom* (AAN)	Steven Spielberg
1984	*The River* (AAN; GGN)	Mark Rydell
1986	*SpaceCamp*	Harry Winer
1987	*The Witches of Eastwick* (AAN)	George Miller
1987	*Empire of the Sun* (AAN; GGN; BAFTA)	Steven Spielberg
1988	*The Accidental Tourist* (AAN; GGN)	Lawrence Kasdan
1989	*Stanley & Iris*	Martin Ritt
1989	*Indiana Jones and the Last Crusade*	Steven Spielberg
1989	*Born on the Fourth of July* (AAN; GGN)	Oliver Stone
1989	*Always*	Steven Spielberg
1990	*Presumed Innocent*	Alan J. Pakula
1990	*Home Alone* (AAN*)	Chris Columbus
1991	*Hook* (AAN*)	Steven Spielberg
1991	*JFK* (AAN)	Oliver Stone (USA/France)
1992	*Far and Away*	Ron Howard
1992	*Home Alone 2: Lost in New York*	Chris Columbus
1993	*Jurassic Park*	Steven Spielberg
1993	*Schindler's List* (AA; GGN; BAFTA)	Steven Spielberg
1995	*Sabrina* (AAN*; GGN*)	Sydney Pollack (Germany/USA)
1995	*Nixon* (AAN)	Oliver Stone
1996	*Sleepers* (AAN)	Barry Levinson
1997	*Rosewood*	John Singleton
1997	*The Lost World: Jurassic Park*	Steven Spielberg
1997	*Seven Years in Tibet* (GGN)	Jean-Jacques Annaud (USA/UK)
1997	*Amistad* (AAN)	Steven Spielberg
1998	*Saving Private Ryan* (AAN; GGN; BAFTA-N)	Steven Spielberg
1998	*Stepmom*	Chris Columbus
1999	*Star Wars I: The Phantom Menace*	George Lucas
1999	*Angela's Ashes* (AAN; GGN)	Alan Parker (USA/Ireland)
2000	*The Patriot* (AAN)	Roland Emmerich (Germany/USA)
2001	*A. I. Artificial Intelligence* (AAN; GGN)	Steven Spielberg
2001	*Harry Potter and the Sorcerer's Stone* (AAN)	Chris Columbus (USA/UK)
2002	*Star Wars II: Attack of the Clones*	George Lucas
2002	*Minority Report*	Steven Spielberg
2002	*Harry Potter and the Chamber of Secrets*	Chris Columbus (USA/UK/Germany)
2002	*Catch Me If You Can* (AAN; BAFTA-N)	Steven Spielberg (USA/Canada)
2004	*Harry Potter and the Prisoner of Azkaban* (AAN)	Alfonso Cuarón (UK/USA)
2004	*The Terminal*	Steven Spielberg
2005	*Star Wars III: Revenge of the Sith*	George Lucas
2005	*War of the Worlds*	Steven Spielberg
2005	*Memoirs of a Geisha* (AAN; GG; BAFTA)	Rob Marshall
2005	*Munich* (AAN)	Steven Spielberg (USA/Canada/France)
2008	*Indiana Jones and the Kingdom of the Crystal Skull*	Steven Spielberg
2011	*The Adventures of Tintin* (AAN)	Steven Spielberg (USA/New Zealand)
2011	*War Horse* (AAN; GGN; BAFTA-N)	Steven Spielberg
2012	*Lincoln* (AAN; GGN; BAFTA-N)	Steven Spielberg
2013	*The Book Thief* (AAN; GGN)	Brian Percival (USA/Germany)

WILLIAMS, Paul (b. 1940) A popular actor and singer-songwriter who has contributed songs to nearly one hundred movies, he scored six feature films, most memorably the first *The Muppet Movie*, which introduced his hit song "Rainbow Connection."

Paul Williams was born in Bennington near Omaha, Nebraska, the son of an electrical engineer who died when his son was thirteen years old. Williams grew up in his aunt's home in Long Beach, California, and participated in music and theatre activities in high school. Because of his height (5 feet 2 inches), Williams pursued a career as a professional jockey, but soon turned to acting, getting some roles on the stage and bit parts in movies. Frustrated with the way his career was going, he turned to songwriting and was more successful. He wrote the Tiny Tim hit song "Fill Your Heart" (with Biff Rose), got a contract to write songs for Warner Brothers, and formed the rock band Holy Mackerel. Williams also recorded his own solo album but did not find major success in the music business until he wrote hit songs for Three Dog Night, the Carpenters, the Monkees, Anne Murray, Bobby Sherman, and others. Among the many hit songs he has penned over the years are "Rainy Days and Mondays," "You and Me against the World," "We've Only Just Begun," "Cried Like a Baby," "I Won't Last a Day without You," "Talk It Over in the Morning," "Old Fashioned Love Song," and "Family of Man." Just as he found fame as a songwriter, Williams's acting career took off with featured and leading roles in over seventy-five movies and television appearances.

Williams's screen scoring career began in 1972 when he and his brother Mentor wrote the soundtrack music for the motorcycle documentary *On the Line*, the two brothers also appearing in the film. Two years later he received wide recognition for his ten songs and soundtrack score for the horror spoof *Phantom of the Paradise*, also playing a leading role in the Brian De Palma takeoff on *Phantom of the Opera*. In 1976 he wrote songs and score for another spoof, the all-kids gangster musical *Bugsy Malone*. Both musicals were nominated for an Oscar, as was his score and song "The Rainbow Connection" (with Ken Ascher) from *The Muppet Movie*. Williams's only other screen scores to date are the comedy *The End* and the documentary *Lucky Ducks*. Yet his songs have been heard in many movies scored by others. He was nominated for the Oscar for Best Song "Nice to Be Around" (with John Williams) from *Cinderella Liberty* (1973) and won for the song "Ev-

ergreen" (with Barbra Streisand) and the score for *A Star Is Born* (1976). Among the many other films he has written songs for are *Thunderbolt and Lightfoot* (1974), *Day of the Locust* (1975), *Lifeguard* (1976), *One on One* (1977), *Agatha* (1979), *The Secret of NIMH* (1982), *Rocky IV* (1985), *Ishtar* (1987), and *The Muppet Christmas Carol* (1992), as well as many television series, including *The Love Boat* and *The Muppet Show*, and TV movies, as with *Go Ask Alice* (1973) and *The Boy in the Plastic Bubble* (1976).

Primarily a songwriter, Williams is not thought of as a composer in Hollywood yet the music in the few films he has scored is quite accomplished. *Phantom of the Paradise* is a musical that utilizes rock, both the songs and the score gently mocking various rock-pop styles. Much of it is rather silly but the Phantom's theme is a bittersweet pop ballad that also works nicely as background music and the horror aspects of the movie are scored with heavy metal arrangements. A very different kind of pastiche is *Bugsy Malone*, a Depression-era musical cast entirely with kids playing adult roles. The odd but engaging movie by Alan Parker contains one of Williams's best scores, both the songs and the soundtrack capturing the period and the temperament of 1930s gangster melodramas and those gritty Warner Brothers musicals. The title theme is a bluesy rag with a casual but slick tone. The movie also has delectable Charleston tunes for nightclubs, a minor-key march for the breadlines, and a merry Depression chaser for the finale. Sometimes the music in *Bugsy Malone* goes beyond parody and offers something totally satisfying in itself, as in the blues number "Tomorrow," a heartfelt lament sung and danced by two overlooked, overworked African American characters. *The Muppet Movie* has seven songs by various songwriters but it is Williams and Ascher's "The Rainbow Connection" that unifies the scattered plot both as a song and as scoring. The music is a very old-fashioned slow waltz yet its music is very accessible to modern listeners. It has justifiably become the theme music for Kermit the Frog and the whole Muppet empire. The comedy *The End* is not a musical but has a theme song that is breezy and engaging. Much of the rest of the score is equally pleasing, a lightweight but melodic series of themes that have the right tone for this seriocomic tale about suicide. Williams will always be recognized as a songwriter-singer-actor but one wishes he would score more films because the results have been highly enjoyable. Official website: www.paulwilliamsofficial.com.

WILLSON, MEREDITH

Credits

(all films USA unless stated otherwise; * for Best Song)

Year	Film	Director
1971	*On the Line*	Lee Stanley
1974	*Phantom of the Paradise* (AAN; GGN)	Brian De Palma
1976	*Bugsy Malone*	Alan Parker (UK)
1978	*The End*	Burt Reynolds
1979	*The Muppet Movie* (AAN, AAN*; GGN)	James Frawley (UK/USA)
2009	*Lucky Ducks*	Tracey Jackson

WILLIAMS, Ralph Vaughan See VAUGHAN WILLIAMS, RALPH.

WILLSON, Meredith (1902–1984) A successful stage, radio, and television songwriter and conductor, he worked briefly in the movies and scored three exceptional feature films.

Born Robert Reiniger Meredith Willson in Mason City, Iowa, the son of a piano teacher, he took piccolo and flute lessons as a boy and played in the civic band. After studying music at Juilliard, he played flute in John Philip Sousa's band, and by 1924 was a member of the New York Philharmonic under Toscanini. Willson later became music director at ABC and conducted the music on several popular radio and television shows, writing songs for some of them, such as the popular "You and I" and "May the Lord Bless and Keep You." Among his other song hits are "Seventy-Six Trombones," "I See the Moon," "Till There Was You," "Dolce Far Niente," and "It's Beginning to Look (a Lot) Like Christmas." His boyhood in Iowa served as the background for his first Broadway musical, the smash hit *The Music Man*, which he scripted with Franklin Lacy and for which he wrote both music and lyrics; it was turned into a very successful film in 1962. His two other Broadway musicals were not runaway hits but had admirable scores: *The Unsinkable Molly Brown* (1960), which was filmed in 1964, and *Here's Love* (1963), a musicalization of the film *The Miracle on 34th Street* (1947). Willson also composed for the concert hall, writing symphonies, chamber music, and tone poems, as well as songs for various causes, such as the collegiate "Iowa Fight Song" and "Chicken Fat" for JFK's physical fitness program.

Willson first worked in movies in 1929 when he scored the early talkie *The Lost Zeppelin*, an adventure based on a true story. He did not return to Hollywood until 1940 when he cowrote with director-actor Charles Chaplin the soundtrack score for *The Great Dictator*. For the acclaimed drama *The Little Foxes*, Willson wrote the hymn "Never Too Weary to Pray," heard at the beginning and end of the film, as well as the background music in between. These three movies each have significant scores. *The Lost Zeppelin*, about a doomed airship expedition to Antarctica, has a dramatic opening with a triumphal march in the Sousa tradition. There is a gentle love theme, but little music during the actual expedition, the sounds of whistling winds providing the only music. The early sound process is primitive and the music is not well presented, but the sets and special effects in the movie are impressive and *The Lost Zeppelin* was fairly popular. It is curious that Willson was not hired for other talkies, although the emergence of radio is probably the reason he did work not in films again for another eleven years. When Chaplin decided to write the score for his first all-talking movie, he knew he lacked the composition skills needed, so he hired the reliable Willson to take his musical ideas and turn them into a fully notated score. The original music and the use of classic pieces by Johannes Brahms and Richard Wagner combine to create a superior score, but it cannot accurately be called a Willson score. *The Little Foxes*, on the other hand, is all Willson, and it is masterful. The gospel hymn passage sets up the post–Civil War Southern setting, then music is used sparingly during the talky but riveting melodrama about the power struggle within a wealthy family. There is atmospheric rural music as needed and a graceful theme for Alexandra (Teresa Wright), one of the few characters not grasping for money. The movie's most gripping scene is when the scheming Regina (Bette Davis) allows her husband (Herbert Marshall) to collapse from a heart attack without getting him his medicine. The scene is scored with restraint, only a few sustained chords heard during his struggle to crawl up the steps, the music finally exploding when he falls. Again it is curious that Willson never returned to Hollywood after *The Little Foxes* (the scores for both this film and *The Great Dictator* were nominated for Oscars), but by then television was gaining popularity and he was in great demand in the new medium. Broadway and television's gain was Hollywood's loss. Autobiographies: *And There I Stood with My Piccolo* (1948); *Eggs I Have Laid* (1955); *But He Doesn't Know the Territory* (1959); biographies: *Meredith Willson: The Unsinkable Music Man*, John C. Skipper (2000); *Meredith Willson: America's Music Man*, Bill Oates (2010).

Credits

(all films USA)

Year	Film	Director
1929	*The Lost Zeppelin*	Edward Sloman
1940	*The Great Dictator* (AAN)	Charles Chaplin
1941	*The Little Foxes* (AAN)	William Wyler

WISEMAN, Debbie (b. 1963) A versatile British television and film conductor and composer who has been very busy since the early 1980s, she has scored two dozen very different feature films.

Debbie Wiseman was born in London and took piano lessons as a child, from the start composing short pieces for the keyboard. Wiseman took classes and gave Saturday recitals at a program for gifted children at Trinity College of Music. In her late teens she studied music at the college and at the Guildhall School of Music and Drama. After graduation, Wiseman played in bands for social occasions and sent samples of her compositions to television studios. After writing some commercial jingles, she began composing theme music for television in 1982 with the series *A Week in Politics* followed by some TV documentaries and other series. Her first movie credit, the biographical *Tom & Viv* about poet T. S. Eliot and his wife, was an international success in 1994. Wiseman's score for *Haunted* the next year solidified her reputation, and she has remained an in-demand composer ever since. Among her notable feature films are *Wilde, Lighthouse, The Guilty, Before You Go, The Face at the Window, Freeze Frame, Adventures of Arsene Lupin, Middletown, Flood*, and *Vampire Killers*. Wiseman has been even busier in television, where she scored many British series, including *The Upper Hand, All Along the Watch Tower, Brotherly Love, P.O.W., The Inspector Lynley Mysteries, Jekyll, Father Brown*, and *Land Girls*. Wiseman has written scores for over forty TV movies and miniseries, including literary classics, biographies, historical tales, and documentaries. Among her notable ones are *A Strike Out of Time* (1990), *Chappaquiddick* (1994), *The Death of Yugoslavia* (1995), *The Churchills* (1996), *The Office* (1996), *Dear Nobody* (1997), *The Flint Street Nativity* (1999), *Rebel Heart* (2001), *Endgame in Ireland* (2001), *Othello* (2001), *Hans Christian Andersen: My Life as a Fairy Tale* (2003), *The Private Life of Samuel Pepys* (2003), *Catherine the Great* (2005), *Random Quest* (2006), *Sherlock Holmes and the Baker Street Irregulars* (2007), *Walter's War* (2008), and *The Whale* (2013). Wiseman is an acclaimed conductor and a recognized presenter of musical events on television, such as the annual *BBC Proms*. She is also an educator, being a visiting professor at the Royal College of Music and the composer of *Different Voices* (2008), an orchestral piece used in schools to teach young people about music.

Wiseman's study of classical music and music history has been helpful in scoring her many period pieces and biographical films and TV movies. Regardless of the genre, Wiseman seems to be a classicist. Her music may change from film to film but her devotion to classical forms is steady. The moving Oscar Wilde story, *Wilde*, uses a solo oboe over a restless orchestra to introduce the turmoil that befalls the Irish writer (Stephen Fry) of the title. Wiseman's music suggests a Victorian-era symphony yet there are minor chords and a dissonance on occasion that keep the score surprisingly modern. This is very emotional music that rises above sentimentality, which is more than appropriate for Oscar Wilde himself. *Tom & Viv*, about the troubled marriage between T. S. Eliot (Willem Dafoe) and his wife Vivienne Haigh-Wood (Miranda Richardson) in the 1920s, has a felicitous main theme heard on the piano with string accompaniment. It has a classical structure, as the main musical phrase is varied and developed into a pleasing finale. There is also a bittersweet romantic theme featuring woodwinds that glides along, gaining a fuller sound and a deeper resonance as it goes. A solo trumpet introduces the luscious main theme of *Adventures of Arsene Lupin* set in fin de siècle France. There is also a sweeping waltz, French cafe music, a dreamy fantasia with enticing flutes, and a robust but hesitant passage that conveys a playful sense of adventure. Wiseman even manages intoxicatingly romantic music in disaster movies, as in *Flood*, about a giant wave submerging Britain underwater. The solo female voice in the main theme is bewitching and soothing at the same time. The full orchestra moves from ponderous to triumphant in one passage and the actual disaster is scored with rapid brass fanfares and rhythmic percussive chords. An atypical project for Wiseman, the comic horror film *Lesbian Vampire Killers* (released as *Vampire Killers* in most places), has an eerie suspense score yet even here there are passages that are classically romantic. Wiseman uses the expected genre orchestra (demanding kettle drums, frantic strings, shouting brass, etc.) yet the music seems closer to Tchaikovsky than Hans J. Salter. Is there any contemporary movie composer with such an affinity for classical music as Wiseman? Official website: www.debbie wiseman.co.uk.

Credits

(all films UK unless stated otherwise)

Year	Film	Director
1994	Tom & Viv	Brian Gilbert (UK/USA)
1995	Haunted	Lewis Gilbert (UK/USA)
1996	Female Perversions	Susan Streitfeld (Germany/USA)
1997	Wilde	Brian Gilbert (UK/Germany/Japan)
1999	Tom's Midnight Garden	Willard Carroll (UK/USA/Japan)
1999	Lighthouse (aka Dead of Night)	Simon Hunter
2000	The Guilty	Anthony Waller (UK/USA/Canada)
2001	Randall's Flat	Chris Atkins
2001	The Island of the Mapmaker's Wife	Michie Gleason (UK/Netherlands)
2002	Deserter	Martin Huberty
2002	Before You Go	Lewis Gilbert
2004	The Face at the Window	Graeme Harper
2004	Freeze Frame	John Simpson (UK/Ireland)
2004	Adventures of Arsene Lupin	Jean-Paul Salomé (France/Italy/Spain/UK)
2005	The Truth about Love	John Hay
2006	Middletown	Brian Kirk (UK/Ireland)
2007	Flood	Tony Mitchell (UK/S. Africa/Canada)
2008	The Hide	Marek Losey
2009	Vampire Killers (aka Lesbian Vampire Killers)	Phil Claydon
2011	Lost Christmas	John Hay
2013	Rubicon	Pail Kimball (Canada/UK)
2014	The Other Side of Love	Ian Armer
2014	A Poet in New York	Aisling Walsh

YARED, Gabriel (b. 1949) An internationally acclaimed composer for the concert hall, ballet, and film, he is perhaps best known for his movie scores for British director Anthony Minghella.

Born in Beirut, Lebanon, Gabriel Yared began taking music lessons at the age of nine, first the accordion and then the piano. Four years later he was named organist for the local Jesuit school Saint Joseph University and wrote his first piano composition. Yared later studied law at the school, but his heart was in music theory and composing. At the age of eighteen he left Beirut and spent a year in Brazil, where he studied the local musical styles and formed a small ensemble that performed his original compositions. In Paris, Yared continued to study music and got work arranging music for concerts and recordings. He had no interest in writing for the movies until he was hired to score a Belgian film in 1974. It was his collaboration with French director Jean-Luc Godard five years later on *Sauve qui peut (La vie)* (titled *Every Man for Himself* in the States and *Slow Motion* in Britain) that was a turning point for Yared, and from then on he concentrated on movie scores. The international success of such European films as *Hanna K.*, *Betty Blue*, and *Camille Claudel* opened doors for Yared, who went on to score such American and British films as *Beyond Therapy*, *Clean and Sober*, *Vincent & Theo*, *Romero*, *The King's Whore*, *Message in a Bottle*, *Autumn in New York*, *Possession*, *Shall We Dance*, and *Amelia*. He has found his greatest success scoring a series of popular movies by Anthony Minghella, getting Oscar nominations for *The Talented Mr. Ripley* and *Cold Mountain* and winning for *The English Patient*. Some Hollywood insiders claim that Yared's finest score has not been heard. In a controversial decision, the producers of the epic movie *Troy* (2004) removed Yared's score after a test screening and hired James Horner to write a new one. Warner Brothers owns the original Yared score and it has not been released, nor is it allowed to be recorded by others. Yared has also written four ballets that premiered in Europe and his chamber and orchestral pieces have been performed around the world.

Yared's year in Brazil had a profound effect on his musical style, just as he incorporates European and Asian forms in his work as well. Yet his film scores do not come across as ethnic or localized. His interest in classical forms seems to override all these, and his music often conveys a timelessness that creates mood rather than place. The Costa-Gavras film *Hanna K.*, for example, has a piano and string theme that is mysterious and romantic, sounding classical and modern at the same time. For Godard's *Every Man for Himself* there is also a cautious piano theme that is reluctant to resolve itself, while *The Lover* (*L'amant*) has a bewitching main theme heard on harp, woodwinds, and piano, a slow-motion waltz that teases and still satisfies. *Betty Blue* has a piano theme that mixes classical with blues, sort of a lazy concerto in which a simple phrase is repeated effectively. The main theme in the Sylvia Plath biopic *Sylvia* is morose and tentative and, as played on a lonely piano, is filled with painful nostalgia. The horror film *1408* uses distorted choral chanting while the biopic *Camille Claudel* has a fully orchestrated sweeping waltz with dissonant touches that make it distinctive. There is a more Hollywood sound in *Message in a Bottle*, which boasts a lush romantic theme in which an enticing musical phrase is repeated and varied in a lyrical manner. Also highly romantic is the theme for the contemporary love story *Autumn in New York*, in which strings and piano seem to dance on air. The animated *Azur & Asmar: The Princes' Quest* has a magical theme that draws from Yared's Asian heritage, as does the released fragments of his score for *Troy*, such as the rousing vocals and a pounding, thundering theme with strong brass that suggest both ancient times and Igor Stravinsky.

The scores for the Minghella films are Yared's most known screen music and perhaps his finest. The World War II drama *The English Patient* has an evocative main theme played by a solo clarinet with a stately elegance. The love theme is fully orchestrated, with emphasis on strings, and has a tragic undertone. For the Hungarian count (Ralph Fiennes) mistaken for a wounded Englishman,

Yared wrote a motif drawn from Hungarian folk songs and sung on the soundtrack in a mesmerizing manner by Marta Sebestyén. For the French nurse (Juliette Binoche) who cares for the count, the music uses J. S. Bach's *Goldberg Variations*. Another period movie but this time set in the Roaring Twenties, *The Talented Mr. Ripley* has a score that utilizes jazz, in particular a passage using a vibraphone and cool-jazz percussion. Yet the main theme is again classical, in which oboe and strings restlessly and feverishly race side by side creating suspense and suggesting exotic danger. The Civil War drama *Cold Mountain* has an American folk score that uses fiddle and banjo at times but not in a lively or playful way. The bleak tale is scored with somber but not depressing music, as in the main theme, which has a rustic flavor even as it is classically restrained. There is also a melancholy passage on clarinet with strings that echoes with a haunting and painful refrain. Has there ever been a movie about the Civil War that was scored in such a non-Hollywood manner? Yared's extensive knowledge of music history and theory is mostly self-taught, and the classical tradition is the backbone of his music. The movies he scores are often unconventional or even oddball, yet the music is fully entrenched in the traditional. He consistently succeeds in merging the modern with the established foundation of classical music. Official website: www.gabrielyared.com.

Credits

(all films France unless stated otherwise)

Year	Film	Director
1974	*Miss O'Gynie et les hommes fleurs*	Samy Pavel (Belgium)
1980	*Every Man for Himself* (aka *Slow Motion*)	Jean-Luc Godard
1981	*Malevil*	Christian de Chalonge (France/W. Germany)
1982	*Invitation au voyage*	Peter Del Monte (France/Italy/W. Germany)
1982	*Lucie sur Seine*	Jean-Louis Bertuccelli
1982	*Les petites guerres*	Maroun Bagdadi (France/Lebanon)
1983	*Sarah*	Maurice Dugowson
1983	*The Moon in the Gutter*	Jean-Jacques Beineix (France/Italy)
1983	*La Java des ombres*	Romain Goupil
1983	*Hanna K.*	Costa-Gavras (Israel/France)
1983	*Scarlet Fever*	Gabriel Aghion
1984	*Dangerous Moves*	Richard Dembo
1984	*Tir à vue*	Marc Angelo
1984	*Nemo* (aka *Dream One*)	Arnaud Sélignac (France/UK/USA)
1985	*The Telephone Always Rings Twice*	Jean-Pierre Vergne
1985	*Adieu Bonaparte*	Youssef Chahine (Egypt/France)
1985	*Scout toujours . . .*	Gérard Jugnot
1986	*Zone Red*	Robert Enrico
1986	*Betty Blue*	Jean-Jacques Beineix
1986	*Flagrant désir* (aka *Trade Secrets*)	Claude Faraldo (France/USA)
1986	*Disorder*	Olivier Assayas
1987	*Last Song*	Dennis Berry (France/Switzerland)
1987	*Beyond Therapy*	Robert Altman (USA)
1987	*Agent Trouble*	Jean-Pierre Mocky
1987	*L'homme voilé*	Maroun Bagdadi (France/Lebanon)
1988	*Gandahar* (aka *Light Years*)	René Laloux
1988	*Les saisons du plaisir*	Jean-Pierre Mocky
1988	*Le testament d'un poète juif assassiné*	Frank Cassenti (Israel/France)
1988	*Une nuit a l'Assemblée Nationale*	Jean-Pierre Mocky
1988	*Clean and Sober*	Glenn Gordon Caron (USA)
1988	*Camille Claudel*	Bruno Nuytten
1989	*Tennessee Waltz* (aka *Tennessee Nights*)	Nicolas Gessner (Switzerland/W. Germany)
1989	*Romero*	John Duigan (USA)
1990	*Tatie Danielle*	Étienne Chatillez

Year	Film	Director
1990	Les 1001 nuits	Philippe de Broca (France/Italy/Germany)
1990	Vincent & Theo	Robert Altman (Netherlands/UK/France)
1990	The King's Whore	Axel Corti (UK/Austria/France/Italy)
1992	The Lover	Jean-Jacques Annaud (France/UK/Vietnam)
1992	Map of the Human Heart	Vincent Ward (Australia/UK/Canada/France)
1992	IP5: L'île aux pachydermes	Jean-Jacques Beineix
1992	La fille de l'air	Maroun Bagdadi
1992	Angel's Wings	Richard Dembo (France/Belgium/Switzerland)
1993	Les marmottes	Élie Chouraqui
1993	Low Profile	Claude Zidi
1994	Des feux mal éteints	Serge Moati
1995	Black for Remembrance	Jean-Pierre Mocky
1996	The English Patient (AA; GG; BAFTA)	Anthony Minghella (USA/UK)
1996	Hercule & Sherlock (aka Mutts)	Jeannot Szwarc
1997	Tonka	Jean-Hugues Anglade (Italy/France)
1998	City of Angels	Brad Silberling (Germany/USA)
1999	Message in a Bottle	Luis Mandoki (USA)
1999	The Talented Mr. Ripley (aka The Strange Mr. Ripley) (AAN; GGN; BAFTA-N)	Anthony Minghella (USA)
2000	Autumn in New York	Joan Chen (USA)
2001	Lisa	Pierre Grimblat (France/Switzerland)
2001	Not Afraid, Not Afraid	
2002	The Idol	Samantha Lang (France/Germany/Japan)
2002	Possession	Neil LaBute (USA/UK)
2002	The One and Only	Simon Cellan Jones (UK/France)
2003	Bon Voyage	Jean-Paul Rappeneau
2003	Les marins perdus	Claire Devers
2003	Sylvia (aka Ted and Sylvia)	Christine Jeffs (UK)
2003	Cold Mountain (AAN; GGN; BAFTA)	Anthony Minghella (USA/UK/ Romania/Italy)
2004	Shall We Dance	Peter Chelsom (USA)
2005	L'avion	Cédric Kahn (France/Germany)
2005	Underexposure	Oday Rasheed (Germany/Iraq)
2006	The Lives of Others	Florian Henckel von Donnersmarck (Germany)
2006	Azur & Asmar: The Princes' Quest	Michel Ocelot (France/Belgium/Spain/Italy)
2006	Breaking and Entering	Anthony Minghella (UK/USA)
2007	1408	Mikael Håfstrom (USA)
2008	Adam Resurrected	Paul Schrader (Germany/USA/Israel)
2008	A Matador's Mistress	Menno Meyjes (Spain/UK/France/USA)
2008	Food Beware: The French Organic Revolution	Jean-Paul Jaud
2009	All about Actresses	Maïwenn
2009	Coco Chanel & Igor Stravinsky	Jan Kounen (France/Japan/Switzerland)
2009	The Hedgehog	Mona Achache (France/Italy)
2009	Amelia	Mira Nair (USA/Canada)
2011	In the Land of Blood and Honey	Angelina Jolie (USA)
2012	A Royal Affair	Nikolaj Arcel (Denmark/Sweden/Czech Rep)
2012	Haute Cuisine	Christian Vincent
2012	Tous cobayes?	Jean-Paul Jaud
2012	Belle du Seigneur	Glenio Bonder (France/Luxembourg/ Germany/ Belgium/Switzerland/UK)
2013	Tom at the Farm	Xavier Dolan (Canada/France)
2013	A Promise	Patrice Leconte (France/Belgium)
2013	In Secret (aka Therese)	Charlie Stratton (USA)

YOUNG, Christopher (b. 1957) A successful film and television composer who has written the music for over one hundred movies ranging from violent action thrillers to tender character dramas, he is known mostly for his scores for horror films.

Born Robert Gilchrist Ilsley Young in Red Bank, New Jersey, as a youth he wanted to be a jazz drummer. When he discovered the music of Bernard Herrmann, Young shifted his concentration to screen scoring. He studied music at Hampshire College in Massachusetts and North Texas State University before going to Los Angeles in 1980. He continued his studies at the UCLA Film School where he worked on student films and scored his first Hollywood movie, *The Dorm That Dripped Blood*. It was a horror film, a genre that Young would specialize in over the next thirty years. Among his many horror scores are those for *Hellraiser*, *Urban Legend*, *Sinister*, *Drag Me to Hell*, *A Nightmare on Elm Street 2: Freddy's Revenge*, *Tales from the Hood*, *The Grudge*, *The Exorcism of Emily Rose*, and *Deliver Us from Evil*. In contrast, Young has scored such realistic dramas as *The Shipping News*, *Sweet November*, *Lucky You*, *The Rum Diary*, *Love Happens*, *Murder in the First*, *Rounders*, *The Informers*, *Wonder Boys*, and *The Black Tulip*. Among his credits are two intriguing biopics, *The Hurricane* about boxer Hurricane Carter and *Creation* about Charles Darwin, and such thrillers and action movies as *Spider-Man 3*, *Murder at 1600*, *Invaders from Mars*, *The Baytown Outlaws*, *Untraceable*, *Runaway Jury*, *Shade*, and *Killing Season*. Young has also scored the TV movies *American Harvest* (1987), *Max and Helen* (1990), *Last Flight Out* (1990), *Norma Jean and Marilyn* (1996), *The Warden* (2001), and *Something the Lord Made* (2004). He has taught screen scoring at the Thornton School of Music and the University of Southern California.

Young believes that scores for horror movies have been traditionally dismissed by Hollywood as inferior screen music. (His only Oscar nomination has been for his non-horror drama *The Shipping News*.) Yet it is still his favorite genre and he has shown remarkable variety in scoring so many over the years. In his first feature film, *The Dorm That Dripped Blood*, Young seems to be offering an homage to Bernard Hermann's *Psycho* score, with its screaming violins, but other passages are very much his own, such as a trickling theme with a distorted, moaning bass line, a rumbling passage in which stretched strings climb up the scale ominously, and a hesitant piano theme that seems to

be frightened of its own sound. *Hellraiser* has a thundering yet regal theme in which the brass and percussion both impress even as they threaten.

In *The Exorcism of Emily Rose*, a solo female voice chants a wordless hymn that is both enticing and fearsome. Similarly, the main theme in *Bless the Child* uses a Latin chant by a mixed choir that seems to be screaming rather than praying. *The Grudge* uses gentle chimes and bells against ominous deep chords making for a poetic kind of suspense. A solo French horn plays against sustained strings in one of the more fascinating themes in *A Nightmare on Elm Street 2: Freddy's Revenge*. Another is a frightened flute solo with wavering strings interrupted by startling percussion and low piano chords. A children's chorus is the distinctive aspect of Young's score for *Drag Me to Hell*. There are some disarmingly gentle and soothing passages in this eclectic score that includes a furious violin solo, a full Carl Orff–like choir with pipe organ, electronically created chaos, a reflective piano piece, and a macabre march of brass instruments and voices. Despite its title, this score might almost be described as heavenly.

There is even more variety to be found in Young's non-horror scores. *The Hurricane* is filled with blues and jazz with scat singing that slips into gospel, yet with a heavy downbeat to suggest the boxing world. The use of electric organ in some passages, a solo cello in others, are highly evocative as are the score's many lyrical moments. *Creation*, Young's other biography score, avoids a Victorian sound and portrays the passion Darwin (Paul Bettany) has for scientific exploration with heartfelt strings and piano. The main theme is melancholy yet determined: other passages are more lilting as with a lovely hesitation waltz. *The Shipping News*, set in a remote village in Newfoundland, is scored with a Celtic flavor. Young employs an Irish fiddle, a penny whistle, a Celtic tabor, uilleann pipes, and other ethnic instruments in his gentle, atmospheric music for this quiet character drama. The main rhythmic theme moves briskly yet has a reflective tone to it. There is a lively folk passage that still manages to have a touch of sorrow to it and a delicate harp theme that conjures up all those sorrowful tales told by people who live near the sea. A very different ethnic sound can be found in *The Black Tulip* set in contemporary Afghanistan. The folk music here is exotic, involving, and very accessible. Sung in Afghan and English, one passage has a restrained kind of power as it slowly builds from a morose solo to a robust chorale.

Strings and flutes dominate the score, which suggests authenticity without being slavish to it. The nightmare that descends on the family in *The Black Tulip* makes Young's artificial horror movies pale in comparison. How correct he was to keep the music secondary, for no soundtrack could match the horrors in this story.

The scores for Young's thrillers, science fiction, and action movies are often as different as they are exciting. *Copycat* has a furious passage also reminiscent of Hermann's Hitchcock scores. The strings seem to be screaming and the percussion is spitting bullets. The main theme is more melodic, a full orchestra supporting a piano solo that seems not to notice the menacing countermelody. A similar kind of combination can be detected in the restless main theme for *Spider-Man 3*. By the new century, comic book heroes had become darker and the music more grandiose. Young's score is no exception, with its pulsating brass, hyperactive strings, choral voices, and thumping percussion complete with sound effects. A better sci-fi score is Young's music for the remake *Invaders from Mars*. (His earlier avant-garde score was vetoed by the studio so instead he supplied a very conventional but highly pleasing new score.) A solo flute is hardly the way to start an alien invasion movie but Young does so here, adding other delicate instruments to create a flowing theme that conveys harmony and idealized America. Of course the music changes as planet Earth is threatened. Militaristic marches, jazzy passages filled with teasing anticipation, brassy fanfares, and symphonic explosions all arrive on cue and it is all so much more fun than the movie itself.

Untraceable, one of Young's many serial killer thrillers, has a beguiling score. In the main theme, the music seems to fade and disappear and hide for a few rests then reluctantly return. In another passage, strings and piano seem so nervous that the melody is lost amid the glissandos. In the action-packed *Killing Season*, the main theme is a surprisingly tender piece, a lonely, lazy fiddle sawing away languidly as the folklike melody slowly emerges. This is contrasted with much of the rest of the score, such as a rapid, pounding passage when the two war veterans (Robert De Niro and John Travolta) with an old vengeance hunt each other down. Even more invigorating is Young's score for the sci-fi disaster film *The Core*. This is perhaps Young at his most gloriously symphonic. A full chorus echoes the fervent crescendos of the orchestra, musically announcing itself with giddy pride. There is a rousing anthem-like passage that would not be out of place in a *Star Wars* movie and a boastful march that inspires six scientists to travel to the earth's core in order to restore the planet's electromagnetic field. When they succeed, the music is a gigantic hymn for symphony and voices. Perhaps *The Core* is another Young horror score raised to intergalactic levels. One never knows with his music where it will lead next. Official website: www.officialchristopher young.com.

Credits

(all films USA unless stated otherwise)

Year	Film	Director
1982	*The Dorm That Dripped Blood* (aka *Pranks*)	Stephen Carpenter, Jeffrey Obrow
1982	*Highpoint*	Peter Carter (Canada)
1984	*The Power*	Stephen Carpenter, Jeffrey Obrow
1984	*The Oasis*	Sparky Greene
1985	*Avenging Angel*	Robert Vincent O'Neill
1985	*Def-Con 4*	Paul Donovan, etc. (Canada)
1985	*Wheels of Fire*	Cirio H. Santiago (USA/Philippines)
1985	*Wizards of the Lost Kingdom* (aka *Wizard Wars*)	Héctor Olivera (Argentina/USA)
1985	*A Nightmare on Elm Street 2: Freddy's Revenge*	Jack Sholder
1985	*Barbarian Queen*	Héctor Olivera (USA/Argentina)
1986	*Getting Even*	Dwight H. Little
1986	*Torment*	Samson Aslanian, John Hopkins
1986	*Invaders from Mars*	Tobe Hooper
1986	*Trick or Treat*	Charles Martin Smith

Year	Film	Director
1987	Hellraiser (aka Sadomasochists from Beyond the Grave)	Clive Barker (UK)
1987	Flowers in the Attic	Jeffrey Bloom
1988	The Telephone	Rip Torn
1988	Haunted Summer	Ivan Passer
1988	Hellbound: Hellraiser II	Tony Randel (UK/USA)
1988	Bat*21	Peter Markle
1989	The Fly II	Chris Walas
1989	Hider in the House	Matthew Patrick
1989	Vietnam War Story: The Last Days	David Burton Morris, etc.
1990	Bright Angel	Michael Fields
1992	The Vagrant (aka Scream 911)	Chris Walas (France/USA)
1992	Rapid Fire	Dwight H. Little
1992	Jennifer Eight	Bruce Robinson
1993	The Dark Half	George A. Romero
1993	Dream Lover	Nicholas Kazan
1994	Judicial Consent	William Bindley
1995	Murder in the First	Marc Rocco (USA/France)
1995	Tales from the Hood (aka Boys Do Get Bruised)	Rusty Cundieff
1995	Species	Roger Donaldson
1995	Virtuosity	Brett Leonard
1995	Copycat	Jon Amiel
1996	Unforgettable	John Dahl
1996	Set It Off	F. Gary Gray
1996	Head above Water	Jim Wilson
1997	Murder at 1600	Dwight H. Little
1997	The Man Who Knew Too Little (aka Watch That Man)	Jon Amiel (USA/Germany)
1998	Hard Rain (aka The Flood)	Mikael Salomon (USA/UK/Denmark/ France/Japan/N. Zealand/Germany)
1998	Hush (aka Bloodline)	Jonathan Darby
1998	Rounders	John Dahl
1998	Judas Kiss	Sebastian Gutierrez
1998	Urban Legend	Jamie Blanks (USA/France)
1999	Entrapment	Jon Amiel (USA/UK/Germany)
1999	In Too Deep	Michael Rymer
1999	The Big Kahuna (aka Hospitality Suite)	John Swanbeck
1999	The Hurricane (aka Lazarus and the Hurricane)	Norman Jewison
2000	Wonder Boys	Curtis Hanson (USA/Germany/UK/Japan)
2000	Bless the Child	Chuck Russell (USA/Germany)
2000	The Gift	Sam Raimi
2001	Sweet November	Pat O'Connor
2001	Swordfish	Dominic Sena (USA/Australia)
2001	Scenes of the Crime	Dominique Forma (Germany/USA)
2001	The Glass House	Daniel Sackheim
2001	Bandits (aka Outlaws)	Barry Levinson
2001	The Shipping News (GGN)	Lasse Hallström
2002	The Tower	E. Gedney Webb, Jim Elliott
2002	The Country Bears	Peter Hastings
2003	The Core	Jon Amiel (USA/Germany/Canada)
2003	Shade	Damian Nieman
2003	Runaway Jury	Gary Fleder
2003	Shortcut to Happiness (aka The Devil and Daniel Webster)	Harry Kirkpatrick (aka Alec Baldwin)
2004	The Grudge	Takashi Shimizu (USA/Japan)
2005	Beauty Shop	Bille Woodruff
2005	The Exorcism of Emily Rose	Scott Derrickson
2006	The Grudge 2	Takashi Shimizu (USA/Japan)
2007	Ghost Rider	Mark Steven Johnson (USA/Australia)

Year	Film	Director
2007	Spider-Man 3	Sam Raimi
2007	Lucky You	Curtis Hanson (USA/Germany/Australia)
2008	Untraceable (aka Streaming Evil)	Gregory Hoblit
2008	Sleepwalking (aka Ferris Wheel)	Bill Maher (Canada/USA)
2008	The Informers	Gregor Jordan (USA/Germany)
2009	The Uninvited	Charles and Thomas Guard (USA/Canada)
2009	Drag Me to Hell	Sam Raimi
2009	Creation (aka Origin)	Jon Amiel (UK)
2009	Love Happens	Brandon Camp (USA/Canada/UK)
2010	When in Rome	Mark Steven Johnson
2010	Gone with the Pope (aka Kiss the Ring)	Duke Mitchell
2010	The Black Tulip	Sonia Nassery Cole (Afghanistan/USA)
2011	Priest	Scott Stewart
2011	The Ghostmaker	Mauro Borrelli
2011	The Rum Diary	Bruce Robinson
2012	Sinister (aka Found Footage)	Scott Derrickson (USA/UK)
2012	The Baytown Outlaws	Barry Battles
2012	Scary or Die (aka The Crossing)	Michael Emanuel, etc.
2013	Killing Season (aka Shrapnel)	Mark Steven Johnson (Belgium)
2013	A Madea Christmas	Tyler Perry
2014	The Monkey King	Pou-Soi Cheang (China/Hong Kong/USA)
2014	The Single Mom's Club	Tyler Perry
2014	Deliver Us from Evil	Scott Derrickson

YOUNG, Victor (1900–1956) A prolific composer, conductor, arranger, bandleader, and songwriter who worked on over 350 movies during a career that lasted only twenty years, he also had an extensive career in radio and records. He scored dozens of movie musicals in which the songs were by others but several of Young's own movie themes became popular songs.

Victor Young was born in the slums of Chicago, the son of Polish parents who loved music and saw that the boy received violin lessons. When he was ten, Young's mother died, so he and his sister were sent to live with their grandparents in Warsaw, Poland. There he studied at the Warsaw Imperial Conservatory and after graduation made his concert debut as a violinist with the Warsaw Philharmonic Orchestra. The young musician quickly gained a lauded reputation in Europe, and in 1917 he was performing in St. Petersburg for Czar Nicholas II when the Russian Revolution broke out. Young was arrested by the Bolsheviks and sentenced to die, but a revolutionary who admired Young's musical skills helped him escape. Back in Poland, he was arrested by the Germans and sentenced to die, but again was saved by his musical gifts. He survived the rest of the war and didn't return to the United States until 1920 when he picked up his violinist career and performed for top orchestras in Chicago. Young soon realized that there was more money to be made in silent movies when he was hired by the movie house chain Balaban and Katz to write, arrange, and conduct music for their many cinemas. By the end of the 1920s, Young began his recording career, arranging and conducting music for Brunswick Records. When he took Hoagy Carmichael's piano piece "Stardust" and rearranged it featuring a solo violin, the song found new life. Later a lyric was added by Mitchell Parish and the song, using Young's arrangement, went on to become one of the most recorded ballads of the century.

When Young began scoring movies in Hollywood in 1935, he was already a well-known figure in the music business, his Victor Young Orchestra heard on dozens of records and on the radio. Paramount hired him to compose, arrange, and conduct screen scores, but not until he had composed over thirty films did he start to get screen credit. He was often given the thankless job of writing and arranging the background music for musicals, all the attention going to songs by someone else. In fact, his first screen assignment at Paramount was the Cole Porter musical *Anything Goes*. Over the next twenty years he would "fill in" for over fifty movie musicals, including the vehicles for boy soprano Bobby Breen, most of Bing Crosby's musicals, all-star musicals like *The Big Broadcast of 1937* and its sequels and spin-offs, and the Hope-Crosby "road" pictures. Young often arranged and conducted Paramount films with scores and/or songs by others, making him the most influential musician at the studio and one of Hollywood's top musical directors. As for the approximately 175 movies that he did score, they range from Cecil B. DeMille epics and lush melodramas to Hope comedies and westerns. Young was a fast and efficient worker who never seemed to run out of energy or musical ideas. He continued to write and conduct for radio throughout his career, contributed some songs to Broadway shows, and worked in television during his last years. Although Young seemed to be overlooked by the public, the movie industry was aware of his astounding contribution. He was nominated for an Oscar twenty-two times but didn't win until 1956 for his score for *Around the World in Eighty* Days. Ironically, a few months before Young had died of a heart attack at the age of fifty-six.

Young's musical output is vast, but critics dismiss much of it as mediocre or just serviceable. Young himself admitted that he worked quickly on a project then moved on to the next, often having no emotional or inspirational attachment to his work. Yet on occasion he got excited about a film and the result was resplendent. Among the movies that illustrate his talent for original and compelling scores are *For Whom the Bell Tolls*, *The Uninvited*, *Samson and Delilah*, *Scaramouche*, *The Greatest Show on Earth*, *The Quiet Man*, *One Minute to Zero*, *Shane*, *Love Letters*, *Johnny Guitar*, *My Foolish Heart*, *The Glass Key*, *Reap the Wild Wind*, *Palm Beach Story*, *Arizona*, *September Affair*, *Rio Grande*, *Golden Boy*, and the already-mentioned *Around the World in Eighty Days*. From the themes from these and other scores came such beloved songs as "Stella by Starlight," "My Foolish Heart," "Golden Earrings," "Around the World in Eighty Days," "Sweet Sue," "Johnny Guitar," "Love Letters," "Street of Dreams," "A Ghost of a Chance," and "When I Fall in Love." Music came easily to Young, perhaps too easily. He loved composing and conducting but enjoyed life more, his drinking, eating, and party existence leading to his early death. Yet what he accomplished during his twenty years in Hollywood is astounding by any measure.

One project that excited Young was the screen version of Hemingway's *For Whom the Bell Tolls*. The combination of action, romance, and noble ideas give the movie its impetus.

The score alternates between a thrilling Spanish motif (the story is set during the Spanish Civil War) and a sweeping love theme. Sometimes the two overlap, giving the film more life than its long and meandering footage. The chemistry between Gary Cooper and Ingrid Bergman survives the dull stretches in the film and, with Young's music behind them, the two stars save the movie. A very different kind of chemistry can be found between John Wayne and Maureen O'Hara in the Irish rough-and-tumble film *The Quiet Man*. The main title quotes passages from Irish favorites "I'll Take You Home Again, Kathleen" and "The Isle of Innisfree" and variations of the two songs pop up throughout the score. But for the robust fight between Wayne and Victor McLaglen, Young composed his own Irish jig theme that is fast and furious even as it has a wry sense of comedy. *The Quiet Man*, as beautifully directed by John Ford, is a lovely balance of comedy, romance, and Irish pluck and Young's score hits the right tone all the time. *The Uninvited* is another project that must have captivated Young. A romantic ghost story, it calls for a British composer (Ray Milland) to write a piano serenade for Stella (Gail Russell), the daughter of the ghost who inhabits the house. The theme that the composer character (and Young) comes up with is highly romantic and dreamy with a classical touch. Given a lyric by Ned Washington, the music found wide popularity as the song "Stella by Starlight." Another entrancing love song came from the Susan Hayward melodrama *My Foolish Heart*, the title song also boasting lush and intoxicating music and again a dreamy lyric by Washington. The western *Johnny Guitar* may only be a camp favorite for Joan Crawford fans, but it boasts a fine score that includes some highly dramatic movements and a weepy love theme that became the title song with a lyric by Peggy Lee, who sang it on the soundtrack. The Jennifer Jones–Joseph Cotton melodrama *Love Letters* may not have been very memorable either, but the title song (lyric by Edward Heyman) has enjoyed a long life. It is a stubbornly old-fashioned kind of love song that flows easily yet dramatically up and down the scale. The war romance movie *One Minute to Zero* produced what is arguably Young's most famous song, the enduring ballad "When I Fall in Love." With another lyric by Heyman, the song is a simple testament to love, the music rising and falling with romantic determination. Not only did it receive dozens of recordings, it later showed up in other movies, including *Sleepless in Seattle* (1993) in which it became a hit all over again.

Hit songs aside, Young's scores for a handful of dramatic classics impress on their own. The landmark yet atypical western *Shane* has a superb score that covers several moods effectively. The open prairie has rarely been musicalized as well as Young's theme "The Call of the Faraway Hills." Simple yet enthralling, the music never grows too grandiose but remains solidly confident. The vigorous music under the routine cutting of a tree stump turns the pioneer scene into something majestic. The music for the action scenes uses brass and pounding percussion in a call-and-response pattern that is masterful. The bittersweet ending, with the departure of Shane (Alan Ladd), is scored with unabashed affection, the music rolling over the echoing shouts of the boy (Brandon De Wilde). An urban melodrama with a similarly potent score is *Golden Boy*, the boxing movie in which the young hero (William Holden) is torn between the ring and the violin. Young works violin solos into the soundtrack, as one would expect, but the way he moves from a gliding classical sound into a harsh, grinding theme for the boxing scenes is laudable. Of the handful of film noir movies Young scored, perhaps the two best are the Alan Ladd–Veronica Lake dramas *The Blue Dahlia* and *The Glass Key*. There was considerable chemistry between the two, as cool and detached as Lake may be on-screen. Young scores both movies with little music, bringing in a violin rather than the expected noir saxophone. The action scenes rely on low, rumbling horns but even then the violins perform a kind of tense riff. Young might have been a master of melody but he also knew when to avoid the melodic line for dramatic effect.

Three big-budget epics directed by Cecil B. DeMille and scored by Young deserve mention. Such spectaculars were usually given to Miklós Rózsa or Franz Waxman to score, but at Paramount Young was assigned everything, so he got to write some big symphonic music for the wide screen. *Reap the Wild Wind* is a robust period adventure set in the Florida Keys that climaxes with an undersea encounter with a giant squid. Young's music is pretty robust itself with sustained violins seesawing and bursts of waves of brass for the action sequences. The romantic theme is not terribly convincing but then neither is the romantic triangle with Paulette Goddard, John Wayne, and Ray Milland. For the biblical melodrama *Samson and Delilah*, Young found much more variety. The main theme has the expected crashing cymbals to indicate the Bible setting but the melody itself is very engaging in a modern way. The score also includes some sultry pagan dancing, a mournful lament for the oppressed Hebrews, a lovely theme for Miriam (Olive Deering) and a worldly one for Delilah (Hedy Lamarr). Young manages to include some Hebraic sounds in this very romantic score. The destruction of the palace and the somber conclusion are so splendidly scored that DeMille's old-fashioned melodramatics become palatable. For DeMille's contemporary spectacular, *The Greatest Show on Earth*, Young utilized a variety of familiar circus themes in his score. His original music was equally sprightly with two songs sung by Betty Hutton, "Be a Jumping Jack" and the title number. Surprisingly, no music was used under the colossal train wreck or its tragic aftermath, one of the few pieces of restraint in the overdone movie. Although not directed by DeMille and not at Paramount, the swashbuckler *Scaramouche* inspired Young to write his best big-budget score. This tale set in pre-revolution France has the hero (Stewart Granger) disguised as a member of a theatrical troupe as he plots revenge for his friend's death. The main title explodes with symphonic glee as trumpets and strings seem to be fighting a duel. There is a sublime waltz that serves as the love theme and some felicitously frolicsome music for the theatre sequences. As with *The Greatest Show on Earth*, there is no music under the climactic duel between Granger and Mel Ferrer which has been clocked as the longest in a Hollywood film.

Young's last outstanding score was for the Mike Todd travelogue-comedy-drama *Around the World in Eighty Days*, a movie with so many locations, scenes, stars, and cameo appearances that scoring it was akin to writing music for an Academy Awards ceremony. To solve the problem, Young quotes many familiar international songs in the long score. As Phileas Fogg (David Niven) travels the world, so does the score. Sometimes these recognized tunes are used for comic effect, such as the Mexican ditty "La Cucaracha" used for Fogg's Hispanic sidekick Passepartout (Cantinflas). Inspector Fix (Robert Newton), who chases Fogg around the globe, is scored with familiar musical clichés from the silent movies. Fogg himself is identified with "Rule Britannia" while the scenes in America are scored with dashes of everything from "Yankee Doodle" to "The Lone Ranger" from Rossini's *William Tell*. There is plenty of original music by Young and it holds its own with the established tunes. The train journey in India has a bewitching theme with strings tumbling down the scale like a musical waterfall. A train trip across the American desert has an expansive western theme that turns comic when Fogg and Passepartout transform their sidecar into a sailing vehicle. The most memorable piece of music in *Around the World in Eighty Days* is the entrancing title theme heard as Fogg and Passepartout soar over the French countryside in a hot-air balloon. This scintillating waltz not only suggests flight but also a sparkling spirit. Young repeats the theme in other parts of the film, such as background for the tentative romance between Fogg and the Indian princess Aouda (Shirley MacLaine). With a lyric by Harold Adamson, the theme became a popular song, but in this case the words added little; the music is so radiant that it needs no embellishment. How satisfying that one of Young's last scores was so highly applauded. His legacy today lies in his many songs but his reputation is secured by his best soundtrack scores. Unofficial website: www.victoryoung.czechian.net.

Credits

(all films USA unless stated otherwise; * for Best Song)

Year	Film	Director
1936	Anything Goes	Lewis Milestone
1936	Klondike Annie	Raoul Walsh
1936	Frankie and Johnnie	Chester Erskine, John H. Auer
1936	Fatal Lady	Edward Ludwig
1936	My American Wife	Harold Young
1936	The Big Broadcast of 1937	Mitchell Leisen
1937	Maid of Salem	Frank Lloyd
1937	Swing High, Swing Low	Mitchell Leisen
1937	Make Way for Tomorrow	Leo McCarey
1937	Mountain Music	Robert Florey
1937	Easy Living	Mitchell Leisen
1937	Vogues of 1938	Irving Cummings
1937	Double or Nothing	Theodore Reed
1937	Ebb Tide	James P. Hogan
1937	Wells Fargo	Frank Lloyd
1938	The Big Broadcast of 1938	Mitchell Leisen
1938	Romance in the Dark	H. C. Potter
1938	The Gladiator	Edward Sedgwick
1938	Army Girl (AAN)	George Nichols Jr.
1938	Breaking the Ice (AAN)	Edward F. Cline
1938	Peck's Bad Boy with the Circus	Edward F. Cline
1938	Flirting with Fate	Frank McDonald
1939	Fisherman's Wharf	Bernard Vorhaus
1939	Union Pacific	Cecil B. DeMille
1939	Man of Conquest (AAN)	George Nichols Jr.
1939	Undercover Doctor	Louis King
1939	Heritage of the Desert	Lesley Selander
1939	Grand Jury Secrets	James P. Hogan
1939	Way Down South (AAN)	Leslie Goodwins, Bernard Vorhaus
1939	Island of Lost Men	Kurt Neumann
1939	Death of a Champion	Robert Florey
1939	Range War	Lesley Selander
1939	Golden Boy (AAN)	Rouben Mamoulian
1939	Honeymoon in Bali	Edward H. Griffith
1939	Law of the Pampas	Nate Watt
1939	Raffles	Sam Wood
1939	Our Neighbors—The Carters	Ralph Murphy
1939	The Night of Nights	Lewis Milestone
1939	The Llano Kid	Edward D. Venturini
1939	All Women Have Secrets	Kurt Neumann

Year	Film	Director
1939	Gulliver's Travels (AAN)	Dave Fleischer
1939	Escape to Paradise	Erie C. Kenton
1939	The Light That Failed	William A. Wellman
1940	Santa Fe Marshal	Lesley Selander
1940	The Farmer's Daughter	James P. Hogan
1940	Road to Singapore	Victor Schertzinger
1940	Dark Command (AAN)	Raoul Walsh
1940	The Light of Western Stars	Lesley Selander
1940	Buck Benny Rides Again	Mark Sandrich
1940	The Way of All Flesh	Louis King
1940	The Ghost Breakers	George Marshall
1940	Three Faces West	Bernard Vorhaus
1940	Those Were the Days!	Theodore Reed
1940	Untamed	George Archainbaud
1940	Mystery Sea Raider	Edward Dmytryk
1940	Knights of the Range	Lesley Selander
1940	Rhythm on the River	Victor Schertzinger
1940	I Want a Divorce	Ralph Murphy
1940	Arise, My Love (AAN)	Mitchell Leisen
1940	North West Mounted Police (AAN)	Cecil B. DeMille
1940	Dancing on a Dime	Joseph Santley
1940	Three Men from Texas	Lesley Selander
1940	Arizona (AAN)	Wesley Ruggles
1940	A Night at Earl Carroll's	Kurt Neumann
1940	Moon Over Burma	Louis King
1940	Love Thy Neighbor	Mark Sandrich
1941	Virginia	Edward H. Griffith
1941	The Mad Doctor	Tim Whelan
1941	The Roundup	Lesley Selander
1941	I Wanted Wings	Mitchell Leisen
1941	Road to Zanzibar	Victor Schertzinger
1941	Reaching for the Sun	William A. Wellman
1941	One Night in Lisbon	Edward H. Griffith
1941	Caught in the Draft	David Butler
1941	Kiss the Boys Goodbye	Victor Schertzinger
1941	World Premiere	Ted Tetzlaff, Otis Garrett
1941	Aloma of the South Seas	Alfred Santell
1941	Hold Back the Dawn (AAN)	Mitchell Leisen
1941	Buy Me That Town	Eugene Forde
1941	Nothing but the Truth	Elliott Nugent
1941	Skylark	Mark Sandrich
1941	Glamour Boy	Ralph Murphy, Ted Tetzlaff
1942	The Fleet's In	Victor Schertzinger
1942	The Remarkable Andrew	Stuart Heisler
1942	Reap the Wild Wind	Cecil B. DeMille
1942	The Great Man's Lady	William A. Wellman
1942	Take a Letter, Darling (AAN)	Mitchell Leisen
1942	Beyond the Blue Horizon	Alfred Santell
1942	Sweater Girl	William Clemens
1942	Priorities on Parade	Albert S. Rogell
1942	Mrs. Wiggs of the Cabbage Patch	Ralph Murphy
1942	Flying Tigers (AAN)	David Miller
1942	The Glass Key	Stuart Heisler
1942	The Forest Rangers	George Marshall
1942	The Palm Beach Story	Preston Sturges
1942	My Heart Belongs to Daddy	Robert Siodmak, Cullen Tate
1942	Road to Morocco	David Butler
1942	Silver Queen (AAN)	Lloyd Bacon

Year	Film	Director
1943	No Time for Love	Mitchell Leisen
1943	The Crystal Ball	Elliott Nugent
1943	Young and Willing	Edward H. Griffith
1943	The Outlaw	Howard Hughes, Howard Hawks
1943	Salute for Three	Ralph Murphy
1943	China	John Farrow
1943	Buckskin Empire	Lesley Selander
1943	For Whom the Bell Tolls (AAN)	Sam Wood
1943	Hostages	Frank Tuttle
1943	Riding High	George Marshall
1943	True to Life	George Marshall
1944	The Uninvited	Lewis Allen
1944	And the Angels Sing	George Marshall
1944	The Story of Dr. Wassell	Cecil B. DeMille
1944	The Great Moment	Preston Sturges
1944	Frenchman's Creek	Mitchell Leisen
1944	Ministry of Fear	Fritz Lang
1944	And Now Tomorrow	Irving Pichel
1944	Practically Yours	Mitchell Leisen
1945	A Medal for Benny	Irving Pichel
1945	The Great John L.	Frank Tuttle
1945	You Came Along	John Farrow
1945	Love Letters (AAN; AAN*)	William Dieterle
1945	Kitty	Mitchell Leisen
1945	Masquerade in Mexico	Mitchell Leisen
1946	Two Years before the Mast	John Farrow
1946	To Each His Own	Mitchell Leisen
1946	The Blue Dahlia	George Marshall
1946	Our Hearts Were Growing Up	William D. Russell
1946	The Searching Wind	William Dieterle
1947	California	John Farrow
1947	Suddenly It's Spring	Mitchell Leisen
1947	Calcutta	John Farrow
1947	The Imperfect Lady	Lewis Allen
1947	The Trouble with Women	Sidney Lanfield
1947	Golden Earrings	Mitchell Leisen
1947	Unconquered	Cecil B. DeMille
1947	Where There's Life	Sidney Lanfield
1948	I Walk Alone	Byron Haskin
1948	So Evil My Love	Lewis Allen
1948	The Big Clock	John Farrow
1948	The Emperor Waltz (AAN)	Billy Wilder
1948	State of the Union	Frank Capra
1948	Dream Girl	Mitchell Leisen
1948	Beyond Glory	John Farrow
1948	Night Has a Thousand Eyes	John Farrow
1948	Miss Tatlock's Millions	Richard Haydn
1948	The Paleface	Norman Z. McLeod
1949	The Accused	William Dieterle
1949	A Connecticut Yankee in King Arthur's Court	Tay Garnett
1949	Streets of Laredo	Leslie Fenton
1949	Chicago Deadline	Lewis Allen
1949	Song of Surrender	Mitchell Leisen
1949	Sands of Imo Jima	Allan Dwan
1949	Samson and Delilah (AAN)	Cecil B. DeMille
1949	My Foolish Heart (AAN*)	Mark Robson
1950	The File on Thelma Jordan	Robert Siodmak
1950	Gun Crazy (aka Deadly Is the Female)	Joseph H. Lewis

Year	Film	Director
1950	*Paid in Full*	William Dieterle
1950	*Riding High*	Frank Capra
1950	*Bright Leaf*	Michael Curtiz
1950	*Our Very Own*	David Miller
1950	*September Affair* (GG)	William Dieterle
1950	*The Fireball*	Tay Garnett
1950	*Rio Grande*	John Ford
1951	*Belle Le Grand*	Allan Dwan
1951	*Payment on Demand*	Curtis Bernhardt
1951	*The Lemon Drop Kid*	Sidney Lanfield, Frank Tashlin
1951	*Bullfighter and the Lady*	Budd Boetticher
1951	*Appointment with Danger*	Lewis Allen
1951	*This Is Korea!*	John Ford
1951	*A Millionaire for Christy*	George Marshall
1951	*Honeychile*	R. G. Springsteen
1951	*The Wild Blue Yonder*	Allan Dwan
1951	*My Favorite Spy*	Norman Z. McLeod
1952	*The Greatest Show on Earth*	Cecil B. DeMille
1952	*Something to Live For*	George Stevens
1952	*Anything Can Happen*	George Seaton
1952	*Scaramouche*	George Sidney
1952	*The Quiet Man* (GGN)	John Ford
1952	*The Story of Will Rogers*	Michael Curtiz
1952	*One Minute to Zero*	Tay Garnett
1952	*Thunderbirds*	John H. Auer
1952	*The Star*	Stuart Heisler
1952	*Blackbeard, the Pirate*	Raoul Walsh
1953	*The Stars Are Singing*	Norman Taurog
1953	*The Sun Shines Bright*	John Ford
1953	*A Perilous Journey*	R. G. Springsteen
1953	*Shane*	George Stevens
1953	*Fair Wind to Java*	Joseph Kane
1953	*Little Boy Lost*	George Seaton
1953	*Flight Nurse*	Allan Dwan
1953	*Forever Female*	Irving Rapper
1954	*Jubilee Trail*	Joseph Kane
1954	*Knock on Wood*	Melvin Frank, Norman Panama
1954	*Three Coins in the Fountain*	Jean Negulesco
1954	*Johnny Guitar*	Nicholas Ray
1954	*Trouble in the Glen*	Herbert Wilcox (UK)
1954	*About Mrs. Leslie*	Daniel Mann
1954	*Drum Beat*	Delmer Daves
1954	*The Country Girl*	George Seaton
1955	*Timberjack*	Joseph Kane
1955	*Strategic Air Command*	Anthony Mann
1955	*Son of Sinbad*	Ted Tetzlaff
1955	*The Left Hand of God*	Edward Dmytryk
1955	*The Tall Men*	Raoul Walsh
1955	*A Man Alone*	Ray Milland
1956	*The Conqueror*	Dick Powell
1956	*The Maverick Queen*	Joseph Kane
1956	*The Proud and Profane*	George Seaton
1956	*The Vagabond King*	Michael Curtiz
1956	*Around the World in Eighty Days* (AA)	Michael Anderson
1956	*The Brave One*	Irving Rapper
1956	*Written on the Wind* (AAN*)	Douglas Sirk
1957	*The Buster Keaton Story*	Sidney Sheldon
1957	*China Gate*	Samuel Fuller
1957	*Run of the Arrow*	Samuel Fuller
1957	*Omar Khayyam*	William Dieterle

Z

ZIMMER, Hans (b. 1957) An extremely popular movie and pop composer-producer with best-selling albums in both fields, he was one of the first artists to combine electronic music with conventional orchestral instruments in his movie scores.

Hans Florian Zimmer was born in Frankfurt am Main, Germany, the son of an engineer-inventor, and as a child he experimented with the family piano by attaching electronic appliances and other machines to the keyboard. Zimmer lived in London as a teenager and began his music career playing keyboard and synthesizer for various bands, most famously the New Wave group the Buggles. That pop band was one of the first to find fame through MTV rather than just by album sales. As a record producer, Zimmer experimented with mixing electronic music with traditional instruments for his recordings. He became interested in movies when he assisted composer Stanley Myers on a handful of films, cowriting the music for some and eventually serving as solo composer on some European movies. Zimmer found recognition in the States with his score for *Rain Man*, followed by acclaim for such movies as *Driving Miss Daisy*, *Thelma and Louise*, *A League of Their Own*, and other 1990s hits. For the movie *The Power of One* in 1992, Zimmer researched African music and added tribal chanting and drums to the soundtrack. This score got the attention of the Disney studio, which was preparing the animated feature *The Lion King*. Elton John (music) and Tim Rice (lyrics) wrote the songs but it was Zimmer's African-sounding soundtrack that was roundly applauded, winning an Oscar and putting him on the A-list of Hollywood composers. Among Zimmer's other impressive screen credits are his scores for *Crimson Tide*, *Gladiator*, *The Last Samurai*, *Pearl Harbor*, *The Dark Knight*, *The Da Vinci Code*, *Inception*, *Frost/Nixon*, and *Pirates of the Caribbean* and its sequels, as well as such animated features as *The Prince of Egypt*, *Road to El Dorado*, *Spirit: Stallion of the Cimarron*, *Kung Fu Panda*, *The Simpsons Movie*, *Rango*, and *Madagascar* and its sequels. For television, he has scored the series *Space Rangers* and his TV movies and miniseries include *First Born*

(1988), *The Pacific* (2010), and *The Bible* (2013). Even as Zimmer has scored a handful of movies each year, he is active in experimenting with music at his Remote Control Productions, has mentored many young composers, and has conducted his screen music in concert and on record.

While one can sometimes identify Zimmer's music by his use of the synthesizer, choral and solo voices, and ethnic instruments, his scores are eclectic enough that many of them have no distinguishing characteristics. For example, the music in the character comedy-drama *Driving Miss Daisy* is played on a jazzy clarinet and moves into a Southern folk theme, the tone changing as the movie progresses along with the relationship of the two main characters. A wilder and more unsettling theme is used for a very different pair of characters in *Thelma and Louise*. Again there is a Southern flavor but the electronic instruments glide and modulate to suggest restlessness and discontent. The score for *A League of Their Own* is more romantic, mixing nostalgia with a quietly fervent sense of entitlement. Percussion takes over for most of the score for *Crimson Tide*, building suspense by having lyrical passages broken up with rapid pounding.

The main theme for his early success, *Rain Man*, is a minor-key piece that blends flutes and electric instruments and moves from an eerie tone to a more rhythmic one as percussion is added. A solo clarinet, the voice of Bobby McFerrin, and some synthesized sounds are used effectively in *Regarding Henry*. For the violent melodrama *True Romance*, Zimmer utilized nine marimbas to create a Caribbean sound that undercuts the bloodletting. A similar Jamaican sound was heard in *Cool Runnings* about Olympic contenders from the islands. For the period movie *Gladiator*, Zimmer made no effort to create a Roman sound but scored the movie like a modern suspense drama. There are grandiose sections but just as many guitar sequences, mournful vocals, optimistic crescendos, and rhythmic chanting. The soundtrack for *Gladiator* went on to sell three million copies, audiences liking the very modern sound for a very old subject. In the same way, the historical romance *Pearl Harbor* rarely echoed

HANS ZIMMER. The internationally popular screen composer is pictured here with some of his high-tech paraphernalia. This is appropriate; no one brought the synthesized sound to the movies as successfully as Zimmer did in the 1980s. *Photofest*

the 1940s sound. The music is lush and dreamy for the love stories, rousing for the action scenes, and solemn for the aftermath.

One expects a synthesized score for a science fiction movie about mental adventures, and the music for *Inception* is perhaps Zimmer's most electrical. Rarely using melody or lyricism, the score is a dazzling series of sounds that often seem to be instrumentless. A pulsing heartbeat with various tempos is the unifying force, often with a furious violin underscoring the action. There is more variety in *The Dark Knight*, a similarly sinister action movie. Often hyper violins are heard under the propulsive musical theme but there is a majesty to this score that frequently gives the somber urban thriller a mythic quality. When Zimmer scored a true myth, *King Arthur*, he opted for a primitive folk sound complete with sorrowful chanting, tribal-like percussion, and some full orchestral bombast. With *The Last Samurai*, the music echoes Japanese sounds at times, even using some traditional Nippon instruments. Yet much of the score is subdued and aims for a mysterious tone more often than it does for action or romance. There is very little Victorian music in the 2009 *Sherlock Holmes*. Zimmer's score is modern, the main theme suggesting a chase through a factory of mechanical sounds. For *The Lone Ranger*, a painfully lonely violin gives way to lively synthesized strings as the main theme bounces along in an almost satiric vein. In the action scenes, Zimmer spoofs Rossini's *William Tell Overture*, the theme for the popular television series. *The Lone Ranger* is surely one of Zimmer's oddest scores. Also playful but more satisfying is his music for the *Pirates of the Caribbean* films. The scores for these adventure-comedies are rousing without being pretentious. Even the choral passages and symphonic explosions manage to be thrilling as they accompany what is often a fun cartoon. Perhaps Zimmer's most enthralling sound is found in two "African" pictures. The chanting vocals, pulsating drums, and rhythmic crescendos in *The Power of One* and *The Lion King* proved that a very foreign sound could be very accessible to Western audiences. There is just enough melody to please the ear, but enough strangeness to make the music unique. In fact, some of the musical sections from *The Lion King* were easily turned into songs when that film was rethought for the Broadway stage in 1997. Despite all the synthesized music and quirky mixing of sounds, Zimmer is essentially a traditional screen composer in the way that he romanticizes his subject matter and gives movies that big Hollywood sound. He may give even the most period score a modern twist, but his hundred-plus movies are a testament to music as an embellishment of what is happening on the screen. Official website: www.hans-zimmer. com.

Credits

(all films USA unless stated otherwise; * for Best Song)

Year	Film	Director
1984	*Success Is the Best Revenge*	Jerzy Skolimowski (France/UK)
1984	*Histoire d'O: Chapitre 2*	Eric Rochat (France/Spain/Panama)
1985	*Insignificance*	Nicolas Roeg (UK)
1986	*Separate Vacations*	Michael Anderson (Canada/USA)
1986	*The Zero Boys*	Nico Mastorakis
1987	*Terminal Exposure*	Nico Mastorakis
1988	*The Nature of the Beast*	Franco Rosso (UK)
1988	*Taffin*	Francis Megahy (UK/Ireland/USA)
1988	*The Fruit Machine*	Philip Saville (UK)
1988	*A World Apart*	Chris Menges (UK/Zimbabwe)
1988	*Death Street USA* (aka *Nightmare-at Noon*)	Nico Mastorakis (UK/USA)
1988	*Paperhouse*	Bernard Rose (UK)
1988	*Burning Secret*	Andrew Birkin (UK/W. Germany)
1988	*Rain Man* (AAN)	Barry Levinson
1989	*Twister*	Michael Almereyda
1989	*Black Rain*	Ridley Scott
1989	*Dark Obsession*	Nick Broomfield (UK)
1989	*Driving Miss Daisy*	Bruce Beresford

Year	Film	Director
1990	*Chicago Joe and the Showgirl*	Bernard Rose (UK)
1990	*Bird on a Wire*	John Badham
1990	*Fools of Fortune*	Pat O'Connor (UK)
1990	*Days of Thunder*	Tony Scott
1990	*Pacific Heights*	John Schlesinger
1990	*Green Card*	Peter Weir (France/Australia/USA)
1991	*Backdraft*	Ron Howard
1991	*Thelma and Louise* (BAFTA-N)	Ridley Scott (USA/France)
1991	*Regarding Henry*	Mike Nichols
1991	*Where Sleeping Dogs Lie*	Charles Finch
1991	*K2*	Franc Roddam (UK/Japan/USA)
1992	*Radio Flyer*	Richard Donner
1992	*The Power of One*	John G. Avildsen (Australia/France/USA)
1992	*A League of Their Own*	Penny Marshall
1992	*Spies Inc.*	Antony Thomas
1992	*Toys*	Barry Levinson
1993	*Point of No Return*	John Badham
1993	*Younger and Younger*	Percy Adlon (Germany/USA)
1993	*Calendar Girl*	John Whitesell
1993	*True Romance*	Tony Scott (USA/France)
1993	*Cool Runnings*	Jon Turteltaub
1993	*The House of the Spirits*	Bille August (Portugal/Germany/Denmark/USA)
1994	*I'll Do Anything*	James L. Brooks
1994	*Renaissance Man*	Penny Marshall
1994	*The Lion King*	Roger Allers, Rob Minkoff
1994	*Drop Zone*	John Badham
1995	*Crimson Tide*	Tony Scott
1995	*Beyond Rangoon*	John Boorman (UK/USA)
1995	*Nine Months*	Chris Columbus
1995	*Something to Talk About*	Lasse Hallström
1995	*Two Deaths*	Nicolas Roeg (UK)
1996	*Broken Arrow*	John Woo
1996	*Muppet Treasure Island*	Brian Henson
1996	*The Rock*	Michael Bay
1996	*The Fan*	Tony Scott
1996	*The Preacher's Wife* (AAN)	Penny Marshall
1997	*Smilla's Feeling for Snow* (aka *Smilla's Sense of Snow*)	Bille August (Denmark/Germany/Sweden)
1997	*The Peacemaker*	Mimi Leder
1997	*As Good as It Gets* (AAN)	James L. Brooks
1998	*The Last Days*	James Moll
1998	*The Prince of Egypt* (AAN; GGN)	Brenda Chapman, Steve Hickner, Simon Wells
1998	*The Thin Red Line* (AAN)	Terrence Malick
1999	*Chill Factor*	Hugh Johnson
2000	*The Road to El Dorado*	Bibo Bergeron, Will Finn, Don Paul, David Silverman, Jeffrey Katzenberg
2000	*Gladiator* (AAN; GG; BAFTA-N)	Ridley Scott (USA/UK)
2000	*Mission: Impossible II*	John Woo (USA/Germany)
2000	*An Everlasting Piece*	Barry Levinson
2001	*The Pledge*	Sean Penn
2001	*Hannibal*	Ridley Scott (UK/USA)
2001	*Pearl Harbor* (GGN)	Michael Bay
2001	*Invincible*	Werner Herzog (UK/Germany/Ireland/USA)
2001	*Riding in Cars with Boys*	Penny Marshall
2001	*Black Hawk Down*	Ridley Scott (USA/UK)
2002	*Spirit: Stallion of the Cimarron* (GGN*)	Kelly Asbury, Lorna Cook
2002	*The Ring*	Gore Verbinski (USA/Japan)
2003	*Tears of the Sun*	Antoine Fuqua
2003	*Matchstick Men*	Ridley Scott

Year	Film	Director
2003	*The Last Samurai* (GGN)	Edward Zwick
2003	*Something's Gotta Give*	Nancy Meyers
2004	*King Arthur*	Antoine Fuqua
2004	*Thunderbirds*	Jonathan Frakes (UK/France)
2004	*Shark Tale*	Bibo Bergeron, Vicky Jenson, Rob Letterman
2004	*Laura's Star*	Piet De Rycker, Thilo Rothkirch (Germany)
2004	*Spanglish* (GGN)	James L. Brooks
2005	*Madagascar*	Eric Darnell, Tom McGrath
2005	*Batman Begins*	Christopher Nolan (USA/UK)
2005	*The Little Polar Bear 2: The Mysterious Island*	Piet De Rycker, Thilo Rothkirch (Germany)
2005	*The Weather Man*	Gore Verbinski (USA/Germany)
2006	*The Da Vinci Code* (GGN)	Ron Howard (USA/Malta/UK/ France)
2006	*Pirates of the Caribbean: Dead Man's Chest*	Gore Verbinski
2006	*The Holiday*	Nancy Meyers
2007	*Pirates of the Caribbean: At World's End*	Gore Verbinski
2007	*The Simpsons Movie*	David Silverman
2008	*Casi divas*	Issa López (Mexico)
2008	*Kung Fu Panda*	Mark Osborne, John Stevenson
2008	*The Dark Knight* (BAFTA-N)	Christopher Nolan (USA/UK)
2008	*The Burning Plain*	Guillermo Arriaga (USA/Argentina)
2008	*Frost/Nixon* (GGN)	Ron Howard (USA/UK/France)
2008	*Madagascar: Escape 2 Africa*	Eric Darnell, Tom McGrath
2009	*Henri 4 (aka Henry Navarre)*	Jo Baier (Germany/France/Austria/Spain)
2009	*Pirate Radio*	Richard Curtis
2009	*Angels & Demons*	Ron Howard (USA/Italy)
2009	*It's Complicated*	Nancy Meyers
2009	*Sherlock Holmes* (AAN)	Guy Ritchie (USA/Germany)
2010	*Inception* (AAN; GGN; BAFTA-N)	Christopher Nolan (USA/UK)
2010	*Megamind*	Tom McGrath
2010	*How Do You Know*	James L. Brooks
2011	*The Dilemma*	Ron Howard
2011	*Rango*	Gore Verbinski
2011	*Pirates of the Caribbean: On Stranger Tides*	Rob Marshall
2011	*Kung Fu Panda 2*	Jennifer Yuh
2011	*Jealous of the Birds*	Jordan Bahat (USA/Germany/Poland)
2011	*Sherlock Holmes: A Game of Shadows*	Guy Ritchie
2013	*Madagascar 3: Europe's Most Wanted*	Eric Darnell, Tom McGrath, Conrad Vernon
2013	*The Dark Knight Rises*	Christopher Nolan (USA/UK)
2013	*Rise of the Undead*	Nick Woltersdorf
2013	*Man of Steel*	Zack Snyder (USA/Canada/UK)
2013	*The Lone Ranger*	Gore Verbinski
2013	*Mr. Morgan's Last Love*	Sandra Nettelbeck (Germany/Belgium/ USA/France)
2013	*Rush*	Ron Howard (USA/Germany/UK)
2013	*12 Years a Slave* (GGN)	Steve McQueen
2014	*Winter's Tale*	Akiva Goldsman
2014	*The Amazing Spider-Man 2*	Marc Webb
2014	*Interstellar* (GGN)	Christopher Nolan (USA/UK)

BIBLIOGRAPHY

I. BOOKS

(Biographies and autobiographies are listed in the individual composer's entry.)

Anderson, Gillian B. *Music for Silent Films, 1894–1925*. Washington, DC: Library of Congress, 1988.

Bazelon, Irwin. *Knowing the Score: Notes on Film Music*. New York: Van Nostrand Reinhold, 1975.

Bellis, Richard. *The Emerging Film Composer: An Introduction to the People, Problems and Psychology of the Film Music Business*. Amazon Digital, 2006.

Bernstein, Charles H. *Film Music and Everything Else*. Beverly Hills, CA: Turnstyle Music, 2000.

Biesen, Sheri Chinen. *Music in the Shadows*. Baltimore: Johns Hopkins University Press, 2014.

Brown, Royal S. *Overtones and Undertones: Reading Film Music*. Berkeley: University of California Press, 1994.

Buhler, James, Caryl Flinn, and David Neumeyer (eds.). *Music and Cinema*. Hanover, NH: Wesleyan University Press, 2000.

Buhler, James, David Neumeyer, and Rob Deemer. *Hearing the Movies: Music and Sound in Film History*. New York: Oxford University Press, 2009.

Burlingame, Jon. *The Music of James Bond*. New York: Oxford University Press, 2012.

——. *Sound and Vision: 60 Years of Motion Picture Soundtracks*. New York: Watson-Guptill Publications, 2000.

Burt, George. *The Art of Film Music*. Boston: Northeastern University Press, 1995.

Callaway, Kutter. *Scoring Transcendence: Contemporary Film Music as Religious Experience*. Waco, TX: Baylor University Press, 2013.

Conrich, Ian, and Estella Trincknell (eds.). *Film's Musical Moments*. Edinburgh, UK: Edinburgh University Press, 2006.

Cooke, Mervyn. *A History of Film Music*. New York: Cambridge University Press, 2008.

——. *The Hollywood Film Music Reader*. New York: Oxford University Press, 2010.

Darby, William, and Jack Du Bois. *American Film Music: Major Composers, Techniques, Trends, 1915–1990*. Jefferson, NC: McFarland, 1999.

Davis, Richard. *The Complete Guide to Film Scoring: The Art and Business of Writing Music for Movies and TV*. Boston: Berklee Press, 2000.

Deutsch, Didier C. *Musichound Soundtracks: The Essential Album Guide to Film, Television, and Stage Music*. Detroit, MI: Visible Ink Press, 2000.

Donnelly, Kevin J. *Film Music: Critical Approaches*. Edinburgh, UK: Edinburgh University Press, 2001.

Evans, Mark. *Soundtrack: The Music of the Movies*. New York: Da Capo Press, 1979.

Fleeger, Jennifer. *Sounding American: Hollywood, Opera, and Jazz*. New York: Oxford University Press, 2014.

Francillon, Vincent J. (ed.). *Film Composers Guide*. Los Angeles: Lone Eagle Press, 1997.

Gengaro, Christine Lee. *Listening to Stanley Kubrick: The Music in His Films*. Lanham, MD: Scarecrow Press, 2013.

Heldt, Guido. *Music and Levels of Narration in Film: Steps across the Border*. Bristol, UK: Intellect, 2013.

Hickman, Roger. *Reel Music: Exploring 100 Years of Film Music*. New York: W. W. Norton & Co., 2005.

Hubai, Gergely. *Torn Music: Rejected Film Scores*. Los Angeles: Silman-James Press, 2012.

Hubbert, Julie. *Celluloid Symphonies*. Berkeley, CA: University of California Press, 2011.

Kalinak, Kathryn. *Film Music: A Very Short Introduction*. New York: Oxford University Press, 2010.

——. *How the West Was Sung: Music in the Westerns of John Ford*. Berkeley: University of California Press, 2007.

——. *Settling the Score: Music and the Classical Hollywood Film.* Madison: University of Wisconsin Press, 1992.

Karlin, Fred. *Listening to Movies: The Film Lover's Guide to Film Music.* New York: Schirmer Books, 1994.

Karlin, Fred, and Rayburn Wright. *On the Track: A Guide to Contemporary Film Scoring.* New York: Routledge Press, 2004.

Kassabian, Anahid. *Hearing Film: Tracking Identifications in Contemporary Hollywood Film Music.* New York: Routledge Press, 2000.

Kompanek, Sonny. *From Score to Screen: Sequencers, Scores, and Second Thoughts on the New Film Scoring Process.* Indianapolis, IN: Schirmer Press, 2011.

Larsen, Peter. *Film Music.* Translated by John Irons. London: Reaktion Books, 2008.

Larson, Randall D. *Film Music around the World: Interviews, Reports, and Examinations.* San Bernardino, CA: Borgo Press, 1987.

——. *Music from the House of Hammer.* Lanham, MD: Scarecrow Press, 1996.

——. *Musique Fantastique: A Survey of Film Music in the Fantastic Cinema.* Metuchen, NJ: Scarecrow Press, 1985.

Limbacher, James L. (ed.) *Film Music: From Violins to Video.* Metuchen, NJ: Scarecrow Press, 1974.

MacDonald, Laurence E. *The Invisible Art of Film Music: A Comprehensive History.* 2nd ed. Lanham, MD: Scarecrow Press, 2013.

Marks, Martin Miller. *Music and the Silent Film.* New York: Oxford University Press, 1997.

Marmorstein, Gary. *Hollywood Rhapsody: Movie Music and Its Makers, 1900–1975.* New York: Schirmer Books, 1997.

McCarty, Clifford. *Film Composers in America: A Filmography, 1911–1970.* 2nd ed. New York: Oxford University Press, 2000.

McMahon, Orlene Denice. *Listening to the French New Wave: The Film Music and Composers of Postwar French Art Cinema.* New York: Peter Lang, 2014.

McQuiston, Kate. *We'll Meet Again: Musical Design in the Films of Stanley Kubrick.* New York: Oxford University Press, 2013.

Meyer, Stephen C. *Epic Sound: Music in Postwar Hollywood Biblical Films.* Bloomington: Indiana University Press, 2014.

Morgan, David. *Knowing the Score: Film Composers Talk about the Art, Craft, Blood, Sweat, and Tears of Writing for Cinema.* New York: HarperCollins Publishers, 2000.

Morricone, Ennio, and Gillian B. Anderson. *Composing for the Cinema: The Theory and Praxis of Music in Film.* Lanham, MD: Scarecrow Press, 2013.

Neumeyer, David (ed.). *The Oxford Handbook of Film Music Studies.* New York: Oxford University Press, 2013.

O'Brien, Wesley J. *Music in American Combat Films: A Critical Study.* Jefferson, NC: McFarland, 2012.

Palmer, Christopher. *The Composer in Hollywood.* London: Marion Boyers, 1990.

Pendergast, Roy M. *Film Music: A Neglected Art.* 2nd ed. New York: W. W. Norton & Co., 1992.

Reay, Pauline. *Music in Film: Soundtracks and Synergy.* London: Wallflower Press, 2004.

Rogers, Holly. *Music and Sound in Documentary Film.* New York: Routledge Press, 2014.

Rothbart, Peter. *Synergy of Film and Music: Sight and Sound in Five Hollywood Films.* Lanham, MD: Scarecrow Press, 2012.

Russell, Mark, and James Young. *Film Music.* Boston: Focal Press, 2000.

Schelle, Michael. *The Score: Interviews with Film Composers.* Los Angeles: Silman-James Press, 1998.

Scheurer, Timothy E. *Music and Mythmaking in Film: Genre and the Role of the Composer.* Jefferson, NC: McFarland, 2007.

Strong, Martin C. *Lights, Camera, Soundtracks: The Ultimate Guide to Popular Music in the Movies.* New York: Canongate U.S., 2008.

Thomas, Tony. *Film Score: The Art and Craft of Movie Music.* Burbank, CA: Riverwood, 1991.

——. *Music for the Movies.* 2nd ed. Los Angeles: Silman-James Press, 1997.

Tietyen, David. *The Musical World of Disney.* Milwaukee, WI: Hal Leonard Publishing Corp., 1990.

Timm, Larry M. *The Soul of Cinema: An Appreciation of Film Music.* London: Pearson Publishing Co., 2013.

Tonks, Paul. *Film Music.* Harpenden, UK: Oldcastle Books, 2001.

Wierzbicki, James. *Film Music: A History.* New York: Routledge Press, 2008.

——. (ed.). *Music, Sound and Filmmakers: Sonic Style in Cinema.* New York: Routledge Press, 2012.

Wierzbicki, James, Nathan Platte, and Colin Roust. *The Routledge Film Music Sourcebook.* New York: Routledge Press, 2011.

Wojcik, Pamela Robertson, and Arthur Knight (eds.). *Soundtrack Available: Essays on Film and Popular Music.* Durham, NC: Duke University Press, 2001.

Wright, Rayburn. *On the Track: A Guide to Contemporary Film Scoring.* New York: Routledge Press, 2004.

II. JOURNALS AND WEBSITES

Official and unofficial websites for individual composers are listed in the composer's entry.

American Cinematheque (USA) www.americancinematheque calendar.com

The American Society of Composers, Authors and Publishers (ASCAP) (USA) www.ascap.com

Audiophilia (USA) www.audiophilia.com

British Academy of Film and Television Arts (UK) www.bafta. org

British Academy of Songwriters, Composers and Authors (BASCA) (UK) www.basca.org.uk

Broadcast Music, Inc. (BMI) (USA) www.bmi.com

The Cue Sheet: Journal of the Film Music Society (USA) www. filmmusicsociety.org

Film Music Magazine (USA) www.filmmusicmag.com

Film Music Media (USA) www.filmmusicmedia.com

Film Music Network (USA) www.filmmusic.net

FilmScore ClickTrack (USA) www.filmscoreclicktrack.com

Film Score Monthly (USA) www.filmscoremonthly.com

Film Sound (USA) www.filmsound.org

Filmtracks: Modern Soundtrack Reviews (USA) www.filmtracks. com

The International Film Music Critics Association (USA) www. filmmusiccritics.org

Internet Movie Database (USA) ww.imdb.com

The Journal of Film Music (USA) www.equinoxpub.com

Music Academy (USA) www.musicacademyonline.com

Music and Film Industry Association of America (MAFIAA) (USA) www.mafiaa.org

Music and the Moving Image (USA) www.press.uillinois.edu

Music Connection (USA) www.musicconnection.com

M(usic) Files (UK) www.mfiles.co.uk

Music, Sound, and the Moving Image (USA) www.muse.jhu.edu

Naxos (USA) www.naxos.com

ScreenRant (USA) www.screenrant.com

The Society of Composers and Lyricists (USA) www.thescl.com

The Soundtrack (UK) www.intellectbooks.co.uk

Soundtrack Collector (USA) www.soundtrackcollector.com

TITLE INDEX

NAME INDEX

Note: Numbers in bold refer to the composer's entry in the encyclopedia.

Abbott and Costello, 596, 604, 623–25

Abril, Victoria, 584

Adams, Brooke, 465

Adams, Bryan, 385

Adams, Richard, 458

Adams, Robert, 92

Adamson, Harold, 244, 357, 388, 735

Addams, Charles, 608

Addinsell, Richard, **1–2**

Addison, John, **3–5**

Addy, Wesley, 597

Adler, Larry, **5–6**

Ahrens, Lynn, 493

Aiello, Danny, 349

Aimée, Anouk, 416

Akira, Ifukube, 307

Albee, Edward, 510

Albright, Lola, 242

Aldrich, Robert, 181, 242

Alexander, Jeff, **6–8**

Alexander, Van, **8–10**

Alford, Kenneth, 24

Allan, Richard, 393

Allen, Rex, 107

Allen, Woody, 256, 296, 298, 349–50, 375, 539

Allenby, Frank, 645

Allred, Julie, 182

Allyson, Jane, 624

Alpert, Herb, 133, 298

Altman, Mike, 439

Altman, Robert, 190, 651, 719

Alwyn, William, **10–12**, 70

Amalric, Mathieu, 117

Almodóvar, Pedro, 584

Ames Brothers, 39

Amfitheatrof, Aleksander, 13

Amfitheatrof, Daniele, **13–16**, 635

Andersen, Hans Christian, 205

Anderson, Jon, 460, 686

Anderson, Mary, 699

Andrews, Dana, 545

Andrews Sisters, 128

Anka, Paul, 463

Annakin, Ken, 240

Annaud, Jean-Jacques, 591

Ant, Adam, 459

Antheil, George, **16–18**

Antonioni, Michelangelo, 187, 250–51, 300

Anwar, Gabrielle, 157

Apted, Michael, 21, 630

Arkin, Alan, 3

Arlen, Harold, 375, 655, 658

Arletty, 667–68

Arliss, George, 69

Armstrong, Craig, **18–20**

Armstrong, Louis, 218

Arnaud, Leo, 658

Arnold, David, **20–23**

Arnold, Malcolm, **23–26**

Arnoul, Françoise, 412

Aronofsky, Darren, 440–41

Arthur, Jean, 17

Arzner, Dorothy, 294

Ascher, Ken, 722

Ashman, Howard, 450

Asner, Ed, 253

Church, Thomas Haden, 396

Churchill, Frank, **128–29**, 301, 633

Cicognini, Alessandro, **129–33**

Clair, René, 26, 124, 369–70, 681

Clampett, Bob, 638

Clapton, Eric, 142, 384–85

Clark, Petula, 133, 208, 280

Clarke, Robert, 113

Claudel, Paul, 335, 451

Clayburgh, Jill, 137

Clayton, Jack, 167

Clayton, Justin, 385

Clément, René, 362, 417

Clift, Montgomery, 197, 245, 275, 674, 704

Clooney, George, 397

Clooney, Rosemary, 110, 458, 549

Clouzot, Henri-Georges, 27, 681

Clouzot, Véra, 682

Coates, Phyllis, 108

Cobb, Lee J., 42

Cochran, Dorcas, 601

Cochran, Steve, 651

Cochran, Wayne, 618

Cocteau, Jean, 16, 26–27, 451

Coen, Ethan, 99–100

Coen, Joel, 99–100

Cohan, George M., 557

Colbert, Claudette, 643, 699

Cole, George, 225

Cole, Nat "King," 59, 112, 181–82, 283–84, 357, 549

Cole, Natalie, 329

Colin, Sid, 85

Collette, Toni, 383

Collins, Judy, 500

Collins, Phil, 134, 194, 261, 430–31

Colman, Ronald, 292, 580

Colombier, Michel, **133–36**

Columbus, Chris, 715, 717

Comden, Betty, 535, 608

Comingore, Dorothy, 319

Compton, Fay, 85

Condon, Bill, 100–101

Connelly, Jennifer, 379

Connelly, Reginald, 372

Connery, Sean, 275–75, 525

Connolly, Billy, 678, 696

Connors, Carol, 136

Conrad, Joseph, 206

Conried, Hans, 333

Constant, Marius, 318

Conti, Bill, **136–39**, 458

Convertino, Michael, **139–41**

Cooder, Ry, **141–43**

Cooper, Bob, 651

Cooper, Gary, 17, 294, 486, 672, 674, 733

Cooper, James Fenimore, 380

Cooper, Melville, 657

Copeland, Stewart, **143–46**

Copland, Aaron, 76, 78–79, **146–48**, 274, 462, 509, 608, 670

Coppola, Carmine, **149–50**, 159, 335, 574, 690

Coppola, Francis Ford, 144, 149–50, 401, 574, 611

Coppola, Sofia, 149

Cord, Alex, 94

Cordell, Frank, **150–52**

Corigliano, John, **152–53**

Corigliano, John, Sr., 152

Corman, Roger, 59–60, 340

Coslow, Sam, 119, 305

Costa-Gavras, 167, 250, 665–66, 726

Costner, Kevin, 51, 341, 346, 385, 506, 541

Cotton, Joseph, 393, 643, 733

Coulthard, Jean, 451

Courage, Alexander, 254

Courtenay, Tom, 365

Courtney, Jeni, 157

Cousteau, Jacques, 605

Craig, Bradford, 618

Craig, Daniel, 345

Craven, Wes, 65–66, 340

Crawford, Joan, 9, 182, 605, 635, 643, 733

Crewe, Bob, 237

Crichton, Michael, 678

Croce, Jim, 384

Cromwell, John, 294

Cronenberg, David, 612–13

Crosby, Bing, 208, 225, 311, 732–33

Crosby, Bob, 8, 44

Croisille, Nicole, 416

Crosse, Rupert, 718

Crow, Sheryl, 21

Crowe, Russell, 441

Cruise, Tom, 224, 270, 609

Crystal, Billy, 608

Cugat, Xavier, 599

Cukor, George, 167

Cuny, Alain, 667

Curb, Mike, 364

Curtin, Hoyt, 163

Curtis, Jamie Lee, 123

Curtis, Tony, 480, 566

ABOUT THE AUTHOR

Thomas S. Hischak is an internationally recognized author and teacher in the performing arts and the author of twenty-four nonfiction books about film, popular music, and theatre, including *The Oxford Companion to the American Musical*, *Through the Screen Door*, *Disney Voice Actors*, *American Plays and Musicals on Screen*, *The Tin Pan Alley Encyclopedia*, *Film It with Music*, *The Disney Song Encyclopedia*, *American Literature on Stage and Screen*, and *The Oxford Companion to American Theatre*. He is also the author of thirty-three published plays, which are performed in the United States, Canada, Great Britain, and Australia. Hischak is professor of theatre at the State University of New York at Cortland and a Fulbright scholar who has taught and directed in Greece, Lithuania, and Turkey.